D1560328

SALES MANAGEMENT

STRATEGY • TECHNOLOGY • SKILLS

SALES
MANAGEMENT

STRATEGY • TECHNOLOGY • SKILLS

William C. Moncrief
TEXAS CHRISTIAN UNIVERSITY

Shannon H. Shipp
TEXAS CHRISTIAN UNIVERSITY

ADDISON-WESLEY

An imprint of Addison Wesley Longman, Inc.

Reading, Massachusetts • Menlo Park, California • New York • Harlow, England
Dan Mills, Ontario • Sydney • Mexico City • Madrid • Amsterdam

Acquisitions Editor: Mike Roche
Developmental Editor: Liz McDonnell
Project Editor: Elizabeth LaManna
Senior Design Manager: John Callahan
Text Design: Dorothy Bungert/*EriBen Graphics*
Art Studio: Vantage Art, Inc.
Electronic Production Manager: Su Levine
Desktop Administrator: Laura Leever
Senior Manufacturing Manager: Willie Lane
Electronic Page Makeup: Dorothy Bungert/*EriBen Graphics*
Printer and Binder: R. R. Donnelley & Sons Company
Cover Printer: The Lehigh Press, Inc.

ISBN 067-346903-4

Library of Congress Cataloging-in-Publication Data

Moncrief, William C., 1953–
    Sales managment / William Moncrief, Shannon Shipp.
       p. cm.
    Includes bibliographical references and indexes.
    ISBN 0-673-46903-4
    1. Sales management.   I. Shipp, Shannon. II. Title.
  HF5438.4.M658 1996
  658.8′1--DC20   96-24657
                                           CIP

999897–DOC–12345678910

BRIEF CONTENTS

END-OF-PART CASES

CONTENTS

Part II

MANAGING YOUR PRIMARY SALES RESOURCES: SALES INDIVIDUALS 151

CHAPTER 6

Sales Managers and Leadership 185

Part III

MANAGING YOUR ACCOUNTS IN A COMPETITIVE WORLD: THE CUSTOMER 237

Part IV

MANAGING YOUR SALES RESOURCES: ORGANIZATIONAL TACTICS *371*

Part V

**MANAGING YOUR SALES RESOURCES:
CORPORATE STRATEGY 579**

CHAPTER 16

Sales Strategy: Planning and Implementation 613

CHAPTER 17

Sales Strategy: Controlling 643

PREFACE

Sales Management has several unique characteristics: its approach to what sales management is and will become in the future; its discussion of global, ethical, environmental, and technological issues; and the organization of the book around a sales framework.

In the past, the fundamental question for sales managers was "How do we improve the productivity and efficiency of the *field salesforce?*" This led previous sales management books to focus on topics such as motivation, territory management, training, and recruiting. All of these topics are aimed at improving the effectiveness and efficiency of the field salesforce. We contend, however, that the new fundamental question driving sales management is "How do we improve the productivity and efficiency of the *selling approach?*" We can see this new reality in salesforce downsizings, replacement of high-cost personal selling with lower-cost telemarketing, catalogs, and electronic sales over the Internet. Our book recognizes this new reality by reducing the focus on field salespeople and increasing coverage of other selling approaches, such as telemarketing, national account management, independent sales reps, technology, electronic data interchange, and team selling. These new methods allow sales managers to reduce costs and improve productivity. Throughout each chapter we have tried to incorporate the management of nontraditional salesforces to reinforce our argument that the sales managers of today and tomorrow must be aware of all the selling methods at their disposal.

Sales Management also recognizes major structural changes occurring in sales and marketing. In many firms, sales is being merged with marketing, and the sales function is being incorporated in jobs with titles such as *marketing representative, customer representative,* and *account manager.* The result of this has been an increase in relationship selling, a concept that is highlighted throughout the text. In addition, rather than featuring technology, ethics, the sales environment, and globalization in separate boxes as many texts do, we have developed chapters or major sections for those topics and integrated the issues throughout the text. Our experience has been that students react to boxes as interesting side material unrelated to the major topics of the chapter and text. We feel that by incorporating these topics in the text, students will see that they are a fundamental part of managing today's selling effort.

Another unique feature of the book is the sales management model we use as a foundation for the organization of the text. This model shows the relationships among the different topics covered in the book and how they contribute to the overall mission of managing the salesforce.

THE MODEL

The model is comprised of five interrelated dimensions: (1) environment, (2) sales individual, (3) customer, (4) sales management tactics, and (5) sales strategy. The sales individual, the customer, sales management, and sales strategy are all directly or indirectly related and work within an ongoing and evolving environment. This text consists of multiple chapters tied to each dimension.

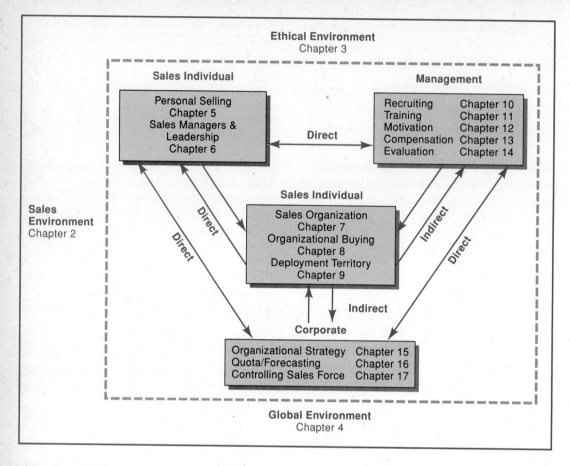

The Environment

The **environment** consists of those elements that we cannot control but that we must react to. Some elements of the environment include the economy, foreign competition, the legal and regulatory environment, and changing market characteristics.

Chapter 2, The Sales Environment, presents a general discussion of sales history, tracing its evolution from ancient times to present-day professional and relationship sellers. The sales environment also examines how the salesperson and sales management have changed in the past decade. Many of these changes have occurred because of shifts in the selling environment, such as increasing use of technology, growing sophistication of buyers, and an influx of global competition. Sales management has had to respond to a changing environment, and Chapter 2 looks at specific new sales strategies that have evolved in response to those changes. Last, this chapter examines the daily activities of a salesperson and how the sales job differs by level of activity.

Chapter 3, The Legal and Ethical Environment, describes the legal and ethical issues facing today's salespeople and sales managers. Sales managers must be aware of laws affecting the relationships between sellers and other members of a market, such as buyers, competitors, and distributors. They must also be aware of laws that affect working conditions for salespeople. Recent surveys show critical gaps in salespeople's knowledge in these areas, and a thorough grounding in these principles is necessary to ensure that the firm operates within legal guidelines.

In addition to meeting legal requirements, many firms seek to establish high ethical standards for their salespeople and sales managers. High ethical standards are critical for establishing trust between buyers and sellers, an important ingredient in relationship selling. High ethical standards also make it easier to recruit and retain a high-quality salesforce.

Chapter 4, The Global Environment, describes issues related to sales management in international settings. American corporations sell to global markets with global salesforces. Selling abroad requires sales managers to rethink salesforce compensation, salesforce organization, and a host of other issues. It also requires firms to be sensitive to cultural, religious, and ethnic diversity. Many countries also have unique legal requirements. The chapter provides an overview of sales management issues in selling abroad, such as the external and internal reasons for selling globally; selecting a selling method on entering a foreign market; coping with differences in language, culture, religion, and business practices; and careers in international sales. This chapter does not cover all possible issues in global sales management. Global issues in compensation, recruiting, and evaluation are covered in their respective chapters.

The Sales Individual

While this text is designed to teach students how to manage a salesforce rather than to teach students how to sell, it is necessary for a potential sales manager to understand the salesperson's perspective, which involves knowing what the salesperson does on a daily basis.

Chapter 5, Personal Selling, takes the student through the basics of the seven steps of selling, beginning with the prospecting and qualifying step. The chapter describes each step in the process and discusses the key issues that salespeople must face. The chapter also focuses on linking the steps of the selling process to developing customer relationships and managing account relationships.

Chapter 6, Sales Managers and Leadership, examines the organization from the perspective of the district sales manager, which is the first level of sales management. A district sales manager is responsible for meeting revenue targets and controlling expenses for a district that is typically composed of six to eight salespeople. Many sales management decisions are made at the district level, and the effectiveness of these decisions can greatly determine the success of the organization. However, there is more to being a successful district manager than just making decisions and being an administrator. What separates an average manager from a great one is leadership. The chapter examines the components of leadership and differing management and leadership styles; it concludes with a discussion of the three common places an organization looks to find new sales managers.

The Customer

The third section of the text contains three chapters dealing with customers. Much of what we must do as sales managers and salespeople is dictated by the type and size of the customer, and more specifically by the needs of the customer. One primary goal of a sales organization (and thus the salesperson) is to develop relationships with a set of customers and potential customers. Relationship strategy entails making decisions on developing, maintaining, and expanding relationships with accounts and customers.

Chapter 7, Purchasing and Organizational Buying, examines how industrial customers buy. It describes the differences between organizational buying and consumer purchasing, the types of industrial customers, the organizational buying process, and buying centers. It also discusses issues in negotiating and dealing with difficult customers.

Chapter 8, Sales Organization, specifically examines how the organization will serve the complex service needs of a diverse set of customers. Fifteen years ago most accounts were handled by a field salesperson.

Each salesperson was responsible for a set number of accounts in a given territory and was given a great deal of independence in determining how to serve and build the customer base. Today, the methods of managing the customer base are diverse. Salespeople can be organized by product, market, geography, stage in the selling process, customer size, or by a combination of methods. Salesforce types range from electronic links between buyers and sellers to telemarketing, field salesforces, and national account management. Salesforces can be composed of employees of the selling firm or independent agents. The key to success for sales organizations is to find the best "organizational structure" that matches the seller's capabilities with customers' needs.

Chapter 9, Salesforce Deployment, addresses three interrelated issues: classifying customers, determining salesforce size, and designing sales territories.

Management

There are a number of important sales management functions, including recruiting, selecting, training, compensating, motivating, and evaluating. These sales management activities can be performed at several managerial levels. Recruiting and selecting, for example, are the direct responsibility of the district managers in many companies. However, after the first round of interviewing, the successful recruit may be sent to the regional or corporate headquarters for subsequent interviews and selection processes. As a result, multiple levels of managers become responsible for the recruiting and selecting.

Chapter 10, Selecting and Recruiting the Salesforce, examines the process of recruiting and selecting new salespeople for the organization. The chapter begins with a description of the process sales managers follow in planning for their selection needs. This process includes a discussion of turnover, which occurs when salespeople leave their positions in a firm. The second part of the chapter discusses methods of locating prospective recruits and

how these methods have changed in the past decade. Currently, there is a strong emphasis on internal recruiting of sales personnel through lateral promotions or through the hiring of interns. External hiring occurs by many methods but networking has grown in importance to the organization, as well as to the person seeking to be hired. The third part of the chapter is the actual selection process, which includes evaluating the prospective recruit. Throughout the chapter, diversity and its impact on the recruiting and selection process are discussed, and tips are provided for prospective salespeople who are undergoing or planning to undergo the recruiting process.

Chapter 11, Training the Salesforce, examines a variety of methods of training new employees and retraining or continually training existing employees. This chapter examines training techniques and training content in detail. Rapidly changing technology has led to the emergence of several innovative training techniques. Sales managers use new tools such as computer-based training, interactive television, teleconferencing, and other technological innovations to provide state-of-the-art training. These tools are described in depth with numerous examples. Relationship development, team building, account management, and a number of developmental skills are now featured prominently in training programs, and they are covered in this chapter.

Motivating the salesforce, examined in Chapter 12, remains an important topic for sales managers as sales resources become more diverse, more independent from the local office, and more important in an overall sales team concept. The ability to motivate the salesperson has always been an important skill for the sales manager. Although motivational theories have remained similar over time, the implementation of the techniques has changed as the selling world has also changed. The chapter begins with a basic discussion of the motivational processes. Needs of the salesperson are discussed based on various career stages, and a number of motivational theories are presented and discussed.

Chapter 13, Compensating the Salesforce, explores the financial and nonfinancial rewards for the sales team. Financial compensation has traditionally been based on commissions, salary, or some combination of the two. Although the traditional methods of paying a salesforce have not changed much, the reasons using the various strategies have changed. For example, the move to long-term relationship selling has prompted many firms to reward the salesperson through more emphasis on salary. Other issues such as team pay and differences in global pay have also changed financial strategies. This chapter examines some traditional strategies but from current viewpoints.

In addition, there are other financial compensation incentives that must be considered, such as the use of a car, benefits, stock options, profit sharing, expense accounts, and others. Nonfinancial incentives are also discussed, including promotion, recognition programs, perks, contests, and educational programs.

The last chapter in the management section is titled Evaluating the Salesforce (Chapter 14). All managers, regardless of their level, must evaluate the personnel under their authority. This chapter describes the purpose of performance appraisal and whether it should focus on behavior or outcomes. Various methods of salesforce performance appraisal are presented, and the means to select the most appropriate method for a given situation are shown. Various other issues of performance appraisal, such as legal and ethical issues, are also discussed.

Sales Strategy

The final section of the text includes chapters on the relationship of sales to marketing and business strategy, on forecasting and quotas, and on controlling the salesforce. These decisions are made with input from district managers, but often involve higher-level sales managers or perhaps even general management.

Chapter 15 has two major topics, forecasting and quotas. Sales forecasting, most typically performed by sales managers, is a function with pervasive effects throughout the organization. Sales forecasts are used by production, human resources, accounting, finance, and purchasing, among other areas in the firm. The chapter explains different types of forecasts, including market potential, market forecast, sales potential, sales forecast, and sales quota. It describes qualitative and quantitative forecasting techniques, and identifies criteria that can be used to select the proper forecasting technique for a given situation. Sales quotas are financial or activity goals that are set for all levels of sales, from salespeople to regional sales managers. The chapter discusses how the quotas are set as part of the overall process of forecasting.

Chapter 16, Sales Strategy: Planning and Implementation, examines the development of corporate, business unit, marketing, and sales strategies for the sales organization. It also discusses how these processes are implemented. Different decision-making processes are examined, with a discussion of the advantages and disadvantages of each.

Chapter 17, Sales Strategy: Control, centers on evaluating the effectiveness and productivity of the selling approach. It provides details on several methods to evaluate and assess the costs, sales, profitability, and productivity of the sales organization. One important means of control is through the budgeting process. The chapter explains what types of budgets exist and how they are derived. Perhaps the most exhaustive means of evaluating the sales structure is the sales audit. The process of conducting a sales audit is explored, and the advantages and disadvantages of sales audits are explained.

CHAPTER FEATURES

Each chapter contains the following features to enhance students' learning and understanding of the material and to provide multiple perspectives on important issues in sales management.

Chapter Objectives

Each chapter opens with a series of questions that the student should be able to answer after reading the chapter. The opening questions serve as chapter objectives and indicate major subject areas that should be learned.

Opening Vignettes

Each chapter opens with a real-world example from an organization that reflects some aspect of the material in the chapter. The opening vignette is designed to draw student interest in the topic area.

Chapter Summaries

Each chapter concludes with a summary of the important information found in each chapter. The summary serves as a brief synopsis of the chapter.

Key Terms

Key terms found throughout the chapter are highlighted and then listed at the end of the chapter and defined in the Glossary. These highlighted terms are important concepts the student should know and understand.

Discussion Questions

Ten discussion questions are provided at the end of each chapter allowing students to test their knowledge of the information found in the chapter.

Problems

Each chapter contains three or four problems that are designed to summon the student's ability to discuss issues. Each problem draws on specific information from the chapter, combined with the student's views on an issue.

Short Cases

Beginning with Chapter 2, a short case is presented at the end of each chapter. The short cases are designed to tie chapter information to real-world sales management problems. Based on material in the chapter and material presented in the short case, students should be able to examine the issue and provide a solution to the problem.

Role Plays

Fourteen of the 17 chapters have a role play that is designed to discuss information found in the chapter. The purpose of the role plays is to provide the student with a practical approach to exploring concepts in sales management. Each role play has a different set of characters that a team of students are to become. For each role play, the student is provided with a description of the characters in the role play, the description of the sales management situation, and key dialogue to be presented. Each role play is divided into three or four scenes. The final scene is the resolution of the problem. Role plays can either be videotaped or performed live in front of the class. The presenting role-play team must examine the issue/problem, create workable alternatives, pick a solution, and be prepared to defend it.

The sales management role plays are designed to be fun, entertaining, and a good learning experience. Further, sales management role plays help students in at least three areas: development of important sales management skills, career preparation, and classroom learning of important sales management concepts.

Long (End-of-Part) Cases

At the conclusion of each of the five sections of the book, long cases are presented. These cases are designed to teach students how to analyze information, prepare alternatives, and seek solutions to one or more sales management problems. The long cases provide information in much more depth than do the role plays or the short cases. In addition, the long cases can be assigned as individual or team projects in written or oral presentations.

SUPPORT MATERIALS

Sales Management comes with an excellent ancillary package designed to further the education of the student and to aid the instructor in teaching sales management. The ancillary package includes an Instructor's Manual with Test Bank and Transparency Masters (Instructor's Resource Book), Computerized Test Bank, Grades, Computer Simulations, and Videos.

Instructor's Resource Book. Prepared by William Strahle of Rider College, the text authors, Brett Boyle of DePaul University, and Dan Weilbaker of Northern Illinois University, this extensive manual includes suggested course syllabi, audiovisual references, a synopsis of the chapter objectives, chapter outline and lecture notes, supplemental lecture material, and answers to all of the text questions and cases. The manual also includes over 150 transparency masters that are keyed to the lecture outlines, teaching notes, and case solutions. In addition, material for using the role plays and a comprehensive set of suggestions for leading class discussion for each role play are provided. These teaching notes include questions to ask, key points to raise, and typical responses, which provide instructors with a wealth of information that will facilitate using this pedagogical device. The Instructor's Resource Book also provides a sample script for each role play and alternative solutions, with discussion of strengths and weaknesses of each solution. Also there is a test item bank that includes over 800 questions, including a mix of factual and application questions. Multiple-choice, true-false, and short-answer formats are included.

TestMaster. This computer program allows instructors to assemble their own customized tests from the items included in the test bank. If desired, the test items can be viewed on screen, edited, saved, and printed. In addition, you can add questions to any test or item bank. A real time-saver, the TestMaster is available for IBM-PC and compatible personal computers.

Videos. A series of videos that complement the role plays is available to qualified adopters of *Sales Management*.

Electronic Transparencies. All 150 transparency masters are available in electronic form for use with an IBM-PC and compatible projection systems.

Grades. Free to qualified adopters, this computerized grade-keeping and classroom management package for use on the IBM-PC or compatible systems maintains data for up to 200 students.

Computer Simulations. The book is supported by two dynamic computer simulations. Sales force territory mapping software is available to complement Case 11, The May Chemical Company. The software works with IBM-PC and compatible computers. Also available is *The Manager's Workshop: Motivation,* authored by Randy Dunham of the University of Wisconsin–Madison, which is a multimedia CD-ROM for both IBM and Macintosh PCs that has been widely acclaimed as the ideal supplement to a course using *Sales Management*. This simulation provides your students with a multimedia approach to sales management where they are placed in the role of a sales manager who must manage five underachieving salespeople. The simulation complements Case 12, Motivation, in this book. Contact your local Addison-Wesley sales representative for more information regarding pricing and packaging options.

ACKNOWLEDGMENTS

Writing this text has been an enjoyable experience, but also an enormous amount of work. Certainly, the successful completion of the project could not have occurred without the valuable help of numerous people.

We have had a number of colleagues throughout the United States who have provided valuable input. We deeply appreciate their insights, suggestions, and the time they devoted to the project. The reviews throughout the various stages of the creation of this text were instrumental in providing us with direction and feedback. We wish gratefully to thank the following individuals:

Zafar U. Ahmed, Minot State University

Ramon A. Avila, Ball State University

David Bejou, University of North Carolina–Wilmington

Joseph A. Bellizzi, Arizona State University West

James Boles, Georgia State University

Robert Collins, University of Nevada–Las Vegas

Martha Devaney, SUNY at Albany

Jim Dupree, Grove City College

Robert C. Erffmeyer, University of Wisconsin–Eau Claire

Joyce L. Grahn, University of Minnesota

James I. Gray, Florida Atlantic University

Joel Greene, Hofstra University

John M. Gwin, University of Virginia

Jon Hawes, University of Akron

Earl D. Honeycutt, University of North Carolina–Wilmington

Mark W. Johnson, Louisiana State University

Richard C. Leventhal, Metropolitan State College

Ronald E. Michaels, Indiana University

Elaine Notarantonio, Bryant College

Bradley S. O'Hara, Southeastern Louisiana University

Donald Outland, The University of Texas at Austin

Dennis A. Pitta, University of Baltimore

Robert G. Roe, University of Wyoming

Bob E. Smiley, Indiana State University

Brock Smith, The University of Victoria

Fred Smith, University of Oklahoma

William Strahle, Rider University

Harish Sujan, Pennsylvania State University

Shelley R. Tapp, St. Louis University

We would also like to thank the sales management individuals and organizations who provided stories, exhibits, charts, and interviews to help us provide the latest information possible about the changing sales environment. Without the cooperation of these people and organizations, this book would not have been possible.

Certainly, we could not have begun or completed this project without the help of the people at Addison-Wesley Publishers. Specifically, Anne Smith was with us from the beginning and she was a great help and supporter. Susan Katz, Mimi Melek, and Mike Roche have all been especially supportive of our efforts. We also would like to thank Elizabeth MacDonell for her tireless work editing the manuscript. Her suggestions, motivation, and cooperation were instrumental in bringing the project to a close. Project editor Elizabeth LaManna skillfully shepherded the text through production.

We gratefully acknowledge the support we have received from the M. J. Neeley School of Business at TCU. Dean Kirk Downey has provided us with an excellent working environment. Luis Andrade, Cheri Bailey, Monique Breidenstein, Fran Eller, Rachel Ford, Yvette Gonzalez, Byron Simpson, Jinger Lord, and Sarah Tempel have all made major contributions to this project. Truly, we could not have accomplished the final results without these outstanding people.

Last, we wish to thank our families for their understanding and love over the past three years. Sheila, Will, Caitlin, and Cherie have been inspirations and we gratefully acknowledge their support.

William Moncrief
Shannon Shipp

INTRODUCTION TO SALES MANAGEMENT

Marketing is very closely related to the art of selling. In fact, that's the reason for its existence. So I think it would be very useful for you to work in sales—of any kind.

ANDREW S. GROVE, CEO, INTEL CORPORATION

Everyone is in sales: accountants, engineers—everyone has to sell their ideas to other people. All of these people have two jobs, their profession and selling. Salespeople are the ones who said, "Why work two jobs?"

CHUCK REAVES, PRESIDENT, XXI ASSOCIATES, ATLANTA

LEARNING OBJECTIVES

After studying this chapter, you should be able to answer the following questions:

- What are *personal selling* and *sales management,* and how are they related?
- What role does sales management play in marketing, and how might that role change in the future?
- Why is it important to study sales management?
- In what categories can selling be classified?
- What activities do sales personnel perform?
- What are the trends in sales management for the next decade?

Seiichi Takikawa, chairman and chief executive of Canon Sales Company, returned to Tokyo in 1977 to wake up a dormant Canon sales division. In the decade that followed, he employed some unusual sales strategies and increased Japanese market share of Canon from 10 percent to 30 percent. Today Takikawa feels that Canon and Japanese selling have entered a crucial third wave in post–World War II business.

The dominant philosophy in wave 1 was that Japanese companies could sell virtually anything they produced. Wave 2, which began in the mid-1960s, forced Canon and other Japanese manufacturers to *push* their products (hard sell) onto both retailers and consumers. The third and current wave has been defined by Japan's sharp trade frictions with the United States and Europe, beginning in the mid-1980s. According to Takikawa, this is an era of **two-way global marketing,** when relationships and markets must be built globally as well as domestically. For example, Canon produces and sells copiers in the United States, Germany, and France. However, to compete in Japan, the Japanese customer expects added value to its copiers, which means importing products into Japan. In other words, to sell a copier in Japan, Canon offers the copier plus an Apple Macintosh computer and U.S. software.

Not only is this an era of two-way global marketing, but salespeople today must be expert consultants to their customers. Sales organizations must be aware of global changes and emphasize quality consultative selling to customers. Takikawa maintains, "Real sales activity begins *after* you sell." Certainly, the methods of Takikawa and Canon are indicative of changing selling philosophies, and throughout this text we will examine these changing strategies.[1]

In the past the fundamental question for sales managers has been, "How do we improve the productivity and efficiency of the traditional *field salesforce?*" Today, however, the fundamental question driving sales management is, "How do we improve the productivity and efficiency of the *selling approach.*" Now and in the foreseeable future selling will focus less on field salespeople and more on alternative selling methods such as teleselling (telemarketing), national accounts management, the use of independent sales representatives, technology, electronic data interchange, and team selling.

Sales management is one of the most exciting and fastest moving fields in business. Sales managers must manage a diverse workforce and perform duties such as recruiting, training, selecting, motivating, forecasting, controlling, and administering salespeople—while facing the primary responsibility of generating revenue for their firms. Sales managers must satisfy multiple constituencies—customers, suppliers, salespeople, and top management—while seeking to achieve sales and profitability goals. Becoming a sales manager is one of the best ways to learn the products and customers of an organization. In addition, being a sales manager is an excellent opportunity to prepare for higher-level corporate positions or to take lateral positions in the organization (such as training, marketing, or product development).

Chapter 1 is divided into six sections. The first section examines the relationship between personal selling and sales management. The evolving role that sales management is playing in marketing is discussed in section two. Section three explores the importance of studying sales and sales management. The fourth section identifies the categories into which sales are usually classified, while section five examines the daily activities of salespeople and sales managers. Finally, section six discusses sales management trends that will take us into the twenty-first century.

PERSONAL SELLING AND SALES MANAGEMENT

Sales managers are active in selling and managing others who sell. To understand sales management we must first understand personal selling. **Personal selling** is personal communication between the seller and the buyer for the purpose of determining and satisfying customer needs. Personal selling typically involves an individual or a team building a relationship with customers over time. In the course of building a relationship, the salesperson must determine the customer's needs and eventually influence or persuade the customer to purchase the selling organization's product.

Sales management involves the planning, organizing, direction, and control of the selling activities of a business unit. When managing a salesforce, it is important to consider the changes that have come about during the past decade. One of the most important changes has been the shifting composition of the salesforce due to

| | EXHIBIT 1.1 | | |
| | WHO'S SELLING | | |
	Number of Salespeople	% of Total	Growth in Number 1980–1990 (%)
Sales Occupations[a]	14.4 million	100.0	40.7
Male	7.3 million	50.8	39.4
Female	7.1 million	49.2	42.1
White	12.1 million	83.5	28.1
Black	1.1 million	7.0	89.1
Hispanic	887,426	6.1	110.5
Asian	409,899	2.8	190.5

[a]Includes commodity sales reps, financial and business services sales reps, salaried supervisors and proprietors, sales workers in retail and personal services, and sales-related occupations.

SOURCE: Based on "What's Selling? Sales Jobs," *Sales and Marketing Management* (September 1993): 11, and Census Bureau, *1990 Census of Population Supplementary Reports Detailed Occupation and Other Characteristics from the EEO File for the U.S.* (1990) CP-S-1-1.

the influx of women and minorities into sales organizations. As illustrated in Exhibit 1.1, there are over 7 million women in the U.S. salesforce (including retail), comprising about 49 percent of all salespeople. This represents a 42 percent increase since 1980. Minorities now comprise 15.9 percent of the total salesforce, but

| EXHIBIT 1.2 | |
SALESPERSON PROFILE	
Average age	37
Percent who are female	26%
Education	62% have college degree
Average time with company	6.9 years
Average number of calls per day	3.6
Number of calls to close a sale	4.2
Average cost of training	$6,225
Average annual salary	
Senior rep	$53,300
Intermediate rep	$40,000
Entry-level	$30,000
Average benefits	$6,838
Average annual sales volume	$1,097,260
Average hours a week	
Hours spent selling	45.5
Face-to-face	14

SOURCE: Dartnell Corporation, *27th Survey of Sales Force Compensation* (1992).

the percentage of increase since 1980 has been significant, and the trend should continue.[2] Indeed, diversity in the sales environment has been recognized by management as an important goal if an organization is to compete successfuly in today's global environment.

Exhibit 1.2 provides a snapshot of the average industrial salesperson in the United States. That average salesperson is about 37 years old, has a college education (an increasing trend), has been with his or her current employer for 6.9 years. The average salesperson makes 3.6 calls per day, with 4.2 calls necessary to close a single sale.[3] The statistics provided in Exhibits 1.1 and 1.2 are averages. Industries and the type of selling conducted may increase or decrease percentages in any one category. For example, in Exhibit 1.1 the number of women in sales, including retail (which has a traditionally heavy female composition) and services, is listed as 49 percent, whereas Exhibit 1.2 indicates that women comprise 26 percent of the salesforce in the industrial sales world. The difference is the inclusion or exclusion of retail salespeople. The industrial sales world has not traditionally been heavily populated by women and minorities.

Sales management occurs at multiple organizational levels. A typical sales organization chart is shown in Exhibit 1.3. A person at the first level of sales management is commonly called a sales manager, district manager, sales supervisor, or area

---

EXHIBIT 1.3

SAMPLE SALES ORGANIZATION STRUCTURES

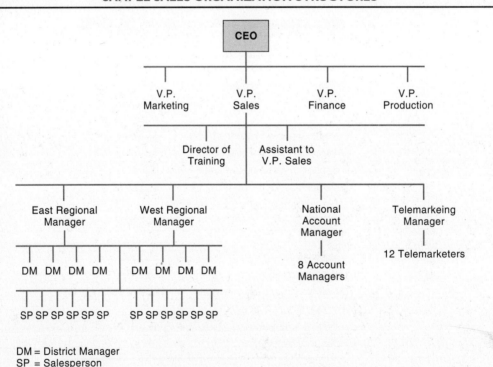

DM = District Manager
SP = Salesperson

---

manager. The district sales manager's primary responsibility is to manage 5 to 15 salespeople and to administer the district. The district sales manager typically reports to a regional sales manager, although this title may vary too. The regional sales manager may supervise three to six district sales managers and have indirect responsibility for as many as 90 salespeople. Depending upon the company there may be zero, one, or two more levels of management above the regional manager, usually culminating with a vice-president of sales. National accounts and telemarketing units may have a similar hierarchical format, or the two units may be much more shallow than the field salesforce hierarchy. One trend that will be discussed throughout the text is the elimination of many managerial levels in organizations— that is, a *flattening,* or decrease in the number of levels, of the "typical" sales structure pictured in Exhibit 1.3.

Sales management functions happen at every level. In general, salespeople and district sales managers are responsible for tactical decision making such as planning calls and setting short-term quotas. Higher-level sales managers are responsible for strategic decisions such as how to organize the salesforce, determine sales compensation, forecast long-term sales, and control the sales organization.

THE ROLE OF SALES MANAGEMENT IN MARKETING

When you hear the term *marketing,* do you automatically think of selling? Are *marketing* and *selling* synonymous? The answers to these questions are important considerations in how we approach the study of sales management. Many people perceive marketing and selling as synonymous, but as we will see, the two are in fact separate but complementary.

Marketing is foremost a philosophy that stresses the importance of satisfying customer needs and wants through exchange processes. More precisely, the American Marketing Association defines **marketing** as "the process of planning and executing the conception, pricing, promotion, and distribution of ideas, goods, and services to create exchanges that satisfy individual and organizational objectives."[4]

Marketing occurs in virtually every aspect of life. As consumers of goods and services, we all participate in the marketing process many times each day. Even if a purchase is not planned, on any given day individuals are exposed to over 1,500 marketing-related messages, ranging from television advertising to point-of-purchase displays. Every time you make a purchase or consider making a purchase you become a part of the marketing process, and a part of the sales process. In fact, approximately 50 cents of every consumer dollar is spent on some marketing activity (which includes sales). Businesspeople likewise make marketing decisions on the job every day. Regardless of specialization or function within an organization, it is essential that a businessperson be conversant in marketing principles and fundamentals.

As you may remember from your first marketing management class, marketing managers "control" many marketing functions that center around the product, the price to be set, the methods of distribution, and the methods of communication and promotion. All of these controllable elements must be considered along with all of the uncontrollable environmental elements when creating sales strategy. (This topic will be discussed in greater detail in Chapter 2, 15, 16, and 17.)

EXHIBIT 1.4

THE SELLING MIX AND ITS RELATIONSHIP TO MARKETING

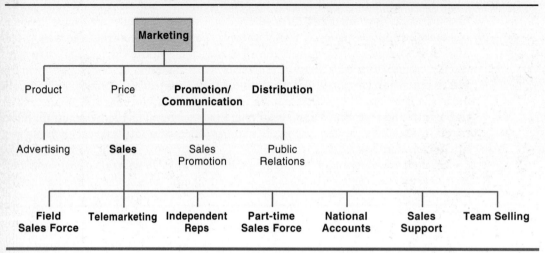

Are marketing and selling synonymous? As Exhibit 1.4 diagrams, sales is actually one dimension of promotion, which in turn is a component of the marketing process. In most consumer goods firms, sales and product marketing have historically been managed as separate but equal departments, with the result being unnecessary competition. Traditionally, the primary goal of the marketing department has been to position and differentiate a product enough to *pull* customers to the firm. The sales department, on the other hand, has traditionally attempted to sell and *push* the product through the channels and make them available to consumers.

Many times these opposing strategies of pulling versus pushing put marketing and sales at odds. For example, in 1910 an executive at Shredded Wheat Company stated, "If the advertising department does what it should, the salesmen will be merely distributors. It is their job to keep in touch with the trade. They don't need to sell goods. The goods are already sold.[5]"

Today, however, a new philosophy concerning the relationship between marketing and sales may be emerging, with both functions being done by the same person. Many scholars characterize today's trendsetting salespeople in this way:

- They work in teams.
- The computer is their primary sales tool.
- They do not sell to customers; rather they *partner* with them.
- The term *salesperson* is out, *relationship manager* is in.
- Commission selling is out because of undue pressure on the customer.
- Marketing managers and sales managers may become the same person.[6]

According to this theory, marketing and sales may soon be done by the same person. However, some scholars argue that salesforces should be taken out of the marketing strategy completely, returning to a version of the previously mentioned 1910 philosophy. In this scenario, the organization installs a computer-based video server that provides 24-hour service to the customer base and allows customers and suppliers to interface at any time. Thus marketing becomes the dominant player because the communication and promotion lines are the critical feature of the process. The argument for this type of marketing system also assumes lower costs for the customer; companies save money by not maintaining a salesforce and pass that savings onto their customers. Some companies that have already implemented this type of program include Lotus Development Corporation, Federal Express, Johnson and Higgins, and Charles Schwab.[7]

Another argument for eliminating the salesforce can be seen in the growing popularity of television home-shopping networks. For example, Quay Hays, head of General Publishing Group (GPG), had one of GPG's books sold on QVC one Sunday afternoon. Hays was dubious about using the QVC outlet, but after 17 minutes the entire available inventory had been sold and Hays had $240,000 in revenue. GPG is now considering using home-shopping networks to sell most of its products.[8] Some small organizations that cannot afford a salesforce may profit from this growing sales trend.

Let's return to the original question, "Are marketing and selling synonymous?" Companies seem to be moving closer to a single marketing entity, but regardless of philosophy or organizational structure, marketing and sales functions must be closely in tune with the organizational mission and work closely to accomplish the objectives based on that mission.

Not only are the role of sales within an organization changing, but the types of sales methods are also changing. Look again at Exhibit 1.4 and notice that *field selling*—traditional face-to-face calls on buyers—is but one of several forms of selling options. Relatively recently personal selling has come to include telemarketing (sales by telephone), national accounts management (selling to the largest and most profitable accounts only), team selling, independent reps, part-time salesforces, and electronic selling. The combination of all these selling methods to create an overall selling strategy is referred to as an organization's **selling mix.**[9]

The personal selling component of the selling mix has been changing rapidly in the last 10 to 15 years, with significant consequences for sales management. One of the main reasons for the changes is that the fundamental question of sales management is changing. As we mentioned earlier, in the past firms have taken for granted the need for a face-to-face salesforce. Therefore, the driving question for sales management has been, "How can we make our salesforces more efficient?" This question has led business to focus on how to train, recruit, motivate, and compensate salesforces to a higher level of efficiency.

While these are still important issues, the cornerstone question has begun to change. Now the sales world is beginning to concentrate more on the processes of selling rather than the salesforce. The variety of methods of covering the sales accounts we mentioned above are becoming more common. A decade ago business-to-business telemarketing was in its infancy; now it is a major strategic sales tool. Large accounts are covered by national accounts managers who concentrate their efforts on only the most profitable accounts. Independent reps are used to cover some accounts and become brokers for the company. Part-time sales reps, particularly in the pharmaceutical industry, are covering accounts at a fraction of the cost. Many simple reorders are handled computer-to-computer without any human interaction. Today and in the future the sales manager's job is more than making the salesforce as efficient as possible; the sales manager must also make the selling function as efficient as possible.

THE IMPORTANCE OF STUDYING SALES AND SALES MANAGEMENT

In the 1950s the Pierson and Howell Report indicated that selling should not be taught in America's universities. Instead, the report said the teaching of sales should be relegated to trade schools. As a result, U.S. universities began dropping selling and sales management courses from their curriculum. By the late 1960s, however, personal selling courses began to reemerge in the marketing curriculum as academicians and economists began realizing the importance of the sales field to the economy of the United States. By the 1970s marketing and business were becoming very popular majors. As such, selling and sales management courses became more commonplace. By the mid-1980s one or both courses were requirements of many marketing majors, and almost all universities offered one or both courses continuing to the present.

The change of focus on sales from the neglect of the 1950s to its importance in the 1980s and 1990s can be explained by a number of reasons, including: (1) personal selling is the most important promotion method in business-to-business marketing, (2) personal selling is the primary point of contact with the customer, (3) sales ability is important throughout one's career, (4) sales offers high career potential, and (5) studying sales offers students the opportunity to correct misperceptions about sales and sales management. Let's look at each of these reasons in detail.

Importance of Sales in Business-to-Business Marketing

Personal selling is the most commonly used promotion method in business-to-business situations. It is used more frequently than advertising, public relations, or sales promotion because it offers the seller the ability to match product offerings directly to customer needs. When Procter & Gamble sells bath soap to individual consumers, the small size of the purchase does not allow the firm to talk to each customer individually and customize its soap to fit the needs of each. Therefore, advertising becomes the primary means of promotion.

On the other hand, if an organization is selling industrial painting systems to Ford Motor Company for use in its manufacturing plants, the highly technical nature of the product, the need to customize it to the customer's needs, and the high revenues to be generated if the sale is made require the seller to use personal selling. Another way to look at the importance of sales is in terms of allocation of the promotional budget. In most industrial firms, personal selling comprises the majority of the promotional budget and is a significant part of the overall budget. In one of Ecolab's divisions, for instance, personal selling costs equal 30 percent of its total sales.

Sales as the Primary Point of Customer Contact

An advantage of personal selling is that customers often perceive salespeople as the firm. If the salesperson is well-prepared, organized, knowledgeable, and helpful, the customer will develop a favorable impression of the firm. Unfortunately, salespeople who do not have these qualities can leave negative impressions of the firm with customers. Sales management must therefore play a key role in selecting salespeople with positive qualities. Sales managers must also provide their salesforces with appropriate training and territory management skills.

In addition, personal selling is one of very few methods of marketing communication that allows the organization (that is, the organization's representative) to foster a personalized and interactive dialogue with the customer. Unlike advertising, feedback is immediate and the salesperson can respond to the customer's needs. This person-to-person contact provides the organization with the best opportunity to practice the marketing concept.

Career Importance of Sales

Many college students believe that obtaining sales skills and knowledge is unnecessary unless they want a career in sales. This is a misperception for several reasons. First, in a longitudinal study of management success, sales ability has been found to be a leading indicator of success for all managerial jobs, not just those in sales.[10] Salespeople have first-hand experience with the product, the market, the competition, and customer needs. This valuable experience gives salespeople unique perspectives as they rise through the ranks of management. As a result, they are better able to plan strategies based on what they have observed in the field. A sales career can also provide a multitude of skills—selling, communication, problem solving, self-dependence, competitiveness, and the ability to think on one's feet—all of which will be important throughout an individual's career. Can you imagine a rising executive who didn't have these skills?

Second, sales is a fundamental component of many jobs that do not have "sales" in the job title. For example, people who go into banking will probably be required to sell loans or other financial products. People who become retail buyers or purchasers certainly must understand salesforce management.

Third, almost every businessperson—at least indirectly—comes into contact with salespeople on a routine basis. To maintain a career in any type of business function requires at least a working knowledge of what role the salesforce plays in the overall operation of the organization.

High Career Potential Within Sales

A 1990 census showed that there were approximately 14.4 million people employed in some type of sales position in the United States, an increase of 40 percent since the 1980 census.[11] As you can see in Exhibit 1.5, a beginning job in sales can lead to a number of different career paths. First, there is a career in sales itself. Career salespeople can obtain promotions to titled positions such as senior sales rep or national account representative.

A second career path is sales management. This path may culminate with a promotion to vice-president of sales or CEO of an organization. One research firm reported that sales and marketing are the most traveled routes to the CEO position and have increased their lead over other functions since 1979.[12] The number of different sales management promotions depends on the size of the organization and the number of hierarchical levels (as mentioned previously, the current trend is for flatter organizations).

EXHIBIT 1.5

SALES AND MARKETING CAREER PATHS

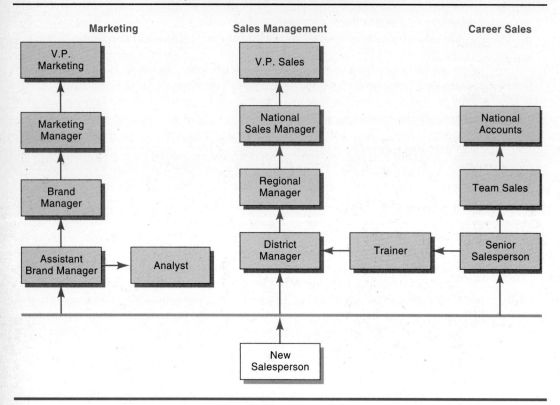

A third career path is to move into marketing. After accumulating some field experience, a salesperson may have an opportunity to move into product management or take a marketing staff position. Upward advancement can take a number of routes ending in a vice-president's job of marketing or the ultimate CEO position. Most organizations of any size require people seeking marketing careers to begin in the field as a salesperson. The reason for this is quite logical: By spending time as a salesperson responsible for a territory (profit center), an individual learns the market, the products, the competition, the customer base, and marketing strategies. It is exceedingly difficult to hire someone into a marketing role and expect that person to create marketing strategy and perform these marketing activities without having experience in the actual market.

Lastly, sales can also lead to a number of staff jobs such as trainer or analyst. The route to these staffing positions will vary, but, again, sales experience gives the individual a better chance of landing the job.

Placement in Sales Positions.   Two issues are dramatically affecting placement of students into first-time sales jobs. The first is restructuring among large firms in the United States, and the second is the change in the way that many firms have orga-

---

EXHIBIT 1.6

CURRENT FINANCIAL COMPARISONS FOR MARKETING CAREERS

Sales	Marketing Research	Advertising	Public Relations	Retail
Vice-President Sales or Marketing $100,000–$500,000+				
National Sales Manager $65,000–$100,000+				Store Vice-President $50,000–$100,000+
Regional Sales Manager $50,000–$70,000+				Store Manager $25,000–$50,000
	Director Market Research $35,000–$55,000	Director Advertising $35,000–$50,000	Director, Public Relations $35,000–$65,000+	Merchandise Manager $25,000–$45,000
District Sales Manager $35,000–$60,000	Market Analyst $22,000–$35,000	Media/Product Manager $20,000–$35,000		Buyer $18,000–$34,000
Sales Representative $14,000–$65,000+	Research Trainee $17,000–$24,000	Copywriter/Artist $18,000–$33,000	Public Relations Specialist $18,000–$35,000	Management Trainee $17,000–$28,000
		Media Traffic $12,000–$19,000	Public Relations Trainee $10,000–$17,000	Retail Sales $15,000–$30,000

---

nized the sales and marketing departments. Beginning in the early 1980s many *Fortune 500* companies such as IBM and General Motors began reducing their personnel, known as *downsizing* or *rightsizing,* while others such as Alberto Culver eliminated their entire salesforces in favor of independent reps. In order to achieve these reductions and eliminations, large companies offered many salespeople and other employees early retirements and left empty positions unfilled. Territories were merged and covered through other methods such as telemarketing. The net effect of corporate rightsizing was a dramatic slowdown in hiring new college graduates. As a result, the best opportunities for hiring today may be among smaller and medium-sized firms. Graduating students are finding that these companies offer some unique advantages over larger companies and are now attracting some of our universities' best students. (Chapter 10 will examine this trend in more depth.)

Financial Status of Sales Positions.   How does a sales career compare financially to other marketing careers? Exhibit 1.6 indicates that sales can be more financially rewarding than other marketing careers. Sales jobs can lead to high salaries and a variety of benefits and perquisites or ("perks,") including the use of a car or a car allowance. It also should be noted that sales compensation can vary widely depending

EXHIBIT 1.7				
SELECTED EMPIRICAL STUDIES OF STUDENTS' PERCEPTIONS OF SALES CAREERS				
Researcher(s)	Research Objective	Respondents	Analytical Technique	Findings
The American Salesman (1958)	Determine the attitudes of students toward selling.	3,000 students in 31 colleges/ universities	Word association	The public's poor image of salespeople keeps good talent out of selling careers.
Sales Management (1962a, 1962b, 1962c)	Examine the selling function among males and the underlying attitudes.	919 male students in 123 colleges/ universities	Crosstabs, frequencies	Students consider salespeople to be forceful, deceitful, holding positions with low status and prestige, with little security.
Paul and Worthing (1970)	Examine students' attitudes toward a sales career by college major and by personal values.	200 students	Multiple regression, pairwise comparison	Students across college majors have low opinions of sales careers.
Bellenger et al. (1974)	Investigate students' attitudes toward selling as a career.	332 students	Chi-square, ANOVA	Selling as a career is perceived much lower than professional-type positions.
Dubinsky (1980)	Compare students' perceptions of sales careers with vocational needs.	219 students	T-tests	A majority of students have a favorable image of sales positions.
Dubinsky (1981)	Compare students' perceptions and salespeople's perception of selling.	219 students and 121 industrial salespeople	T-tests	Students have misconceptions about sales positions when compared with industrial salespeople.
Swinyard (1981)	Examine students'. preferences for marketing-related careers.	1,203 students from 13 colleges/ universities	Ranking procedures	An industrial sales position is preferred least among marketing-related careers.

on industry, compensation package, performance, and type of compensation, such as commission versus salary (see Chapter 13). For example, salespeople paid by commission may earn considerably more than a salaried individual.

Correcting Misperceptions

For over three decades studies have been conducted to determine the perceptions of students regarding the field of sales (see Exhibit 1.7). Students, like many other people, have viewed the sales field negatively.[13] These negative impressions are fueled by television and movie characterizations of salespeople as fast-talking, slick, sell-at-all-cost, unprofessional hucksters. One recent study found that students still view a salesperson as a stereotypical "door-to-door" salesperson infringing upon others.[14] Let's look at some typical misperceptions and give a brief rebuttal for each.

EXHIBIT 1.7 (continued)				
SELECTED EMPIRICAL STUDIES OF STUDENTS' PERCEPTIONS OF SALES CAREERS				
Researcher(s)	Research Objective	Respondents	Analytical Technique	Findings
Dubinsky and O'Connor (1983)	Conduct a multi-dimensional analysis of among seven types of sales jobs.	203 students	Paired comparison MDS	Students' preferences differ for seven sales jobs.
Cook and Hartman (1986)	Examine female interest in sales careers.	296 students from three universities	MANOVA ANOVA	Females are significantly more reluctant to enter sales-related fields than are their male counterparts.
Weeks and Muehling (1987)	Determine salient thoughts students have with regard to personal selling.	300 students	Frequencies	The stereotypical view of selling as a "door-to-door" profession remains quite prevalent in the minds of college students.
Muehling and Weeks (1988)	Investigate women's perceptions of personal selling.	300 students	MANOVA ANOVA	College females are more favorably predisposed to per-.sonal selling than college males.
Lagace and Longfellow (1989)	Investigate the impact of classroom style on student attitude toward sales careers.	153 students	MANOVA	A participative-style sales class may be beneficial in changing and improving students' attitudes toward sales positions.

SOURCE: Michael J. Swenson, William R. Swinyard, Frederick W. Langrehr, and Scott M. Smith, "The Appeal of Personal Selling as a Career: A Decade Later," *The Journal of Personal Selling and Sales Management,* 13(1) (Winter 1993): 51–64.

Myth 1   Salespeople are going to sell products that customers really need.

Rebuttal   Salespeople who do not put the best interest of their customers first will not be in business very long. Companies are looking for long-term profits and focusing on short-term sales will not build relationships with customers for long-term profits.

Myth 2   All sales jobs consist of nothing more than door-to-door selling.

Rebuttal   Most sales calls today are set up by appointment and consist of calling on and servicing a set customer base with some prospecting for new customers.

Myth 3   Salespeople are aggressive and self-serving.

Rebuttal   Most salespeople today are highly educated and have strong communication skills, a strong sense of empathy, and a confidence and desire to serve and succeed.

BOX 1.1
SHOULD SALESPEOPLE BE CERTIFIED?

There's a certification process for accountants, trainers, meeting planners, financial planners, and any number of other professions and semiprofessions. Why shouldn't there be one for salespeople as well?

That's the question that some 65 sales executives from companies like Avon Products, Digital Equipment, Sony, and Upjohn recently addressed. The First National Congress of Sales Professionals, sponsored by the Sales & Marketing Executives of Greater New York (SME/GNY), was the first step toward the creation of a set of competency requirements that would form the basis of a testing and certification program for sales professionals.

And just what comprises a "sales professional"? According to the definition hammered out by the session's Education, Training, and Testing Subcommittee, a sales professional "is someone who sells with integrity; treats customers with respect and enthusiasm; is committed to ongoing professional development; and applies professional selling skills to achieve the highest levels of customer satisfaction." While that might leave out some of the folks you often meet at car dealerships (who happen to be involved in developing a "Salesperson Certification Program" of their own through the National Automobile Dealers Association), it still opens the door to a wide range of professionals who have for years labored against the perception that there was something less-than-professional about a career in sales.

SOURCE: "Should Salespeople Be Certified?" *Sales and Marketing Management* (September 1992): 37.

Myth 4　Salespeople push unwanted products on people.

Rebuttal　Salespeople are trained to follow the marketing concept which, briefly stated, is to "determine the needs and wants of their customers" and then sell them a product that will satisfy their needs.

Myth 5　All a salesperson does is sell, sell, sell.

Rebuttal　Only about 30 percent of a salesperson's time is spent selling. The other 70 percent is spent performing numerous activities, which will be explained later in the chapter.

Contrary to what many people believe, sales is a job that requires a great deal of professionalism. In fact, one movement that is gaining momentum is to certify salespeople in the same way as other professionals, such as accountants, architects, and lawyers (see Box 1.1). For example, upon successfully completing the CPA exam and meeting certain experience requirements, accountants are licensed to practice public accounting. Salespeople in real estate, insurance, and retail stock brokerage have been able to pursue certification for many years. Recently other industries, such as the automotive industry, have begun to explore certifying their salespeople as well.[15] Certification of salespeople would help advance the professionalism of today's salesperson.

CLASSIFICATION OF SELLING

Selling and sales management can be classified into three broad categories: industrial, retail, and services. Each of these categories has major differences, along with some similarities. Although this book is concerned mainly with the industrial and

EXHIBIT 1.8
INDUSTRIAL SELLING: SIC CODES 20–39

2-Digit SIC Code	SIC Label
20	Food and kindred products
21	Tobacco
22	Textile mill products
23	Apparel and other finished fabric products
24	Lumber and Wood
25	Furniture
26	Paper
27	Printing, publishing, and allied industries
28	Chemicals and allied products
29	Petroleum
30	Rubber and miscellaneous plastics
31	Leather and leather products
32	Stone, clay, glass, and concrete products
33	Primary metal industries
34	Fabricated metal products except machinery and transportation equipment
35	Machinery except electrical
36	Electrical and electronic machinery equipment
37	Transportation equipment
38	Measuring, analyzing, and controlling instruments
39	Miscellaneous manufacturing industries

SOURCE: *Standard Industrial Classification Manual* (1987): 69–263.

services sector, many of the same sales management principles and strategies are appropriate in the retailing as well.

Industrial Selling

The industrial sector is comprised of codes 20–39, "manufacturing," in the **Standard Industrial Classification (SIC) Code**. The SIC code is a classification system which puts all organizations into very broad categories such as "manufacturing," then into very specific subcategories such as "salty snack manufacturers." SIC codes 20–39 are listed in Exhibit 1.8. The manufacturing segment is very diverse, ranging from medical sales to food products to heavy equipment. Industrial selling can be subdivided into four groups according to the type of customer base.

1. *Selling to resellers.* A **reseller** is a wholesaler or a retailer or some type of agent/broker that buy finished goods in bulk and resell them. In this situation the salesperson sells to the reseller who in turn sells to the ultimate consumer. Frito-Lay, NAPA auto parts, General Mills, and Mattel Toys are examples of companies that sell to resellers. In very simple terms, the salesperson attempts to acquire prominent shelf space, point-of-purchase displays, and other advantages so that the product can reach the ultimate consumer.

2. *Selling to business users.* Business users need the salesperson's product to help produce their own product. For example, Excel, a maker of mining equip-

ment, sells to mining operations who in turn use Excel's products to produce coal (their product). Other examples of organizations that sell to business users include producers of heavy machinery, ball bearings, fork lifts, and electrical cable. Salespeople sell in this category to the ultimate consumer.

3. *Selling to institutions.* Institutions use the salesperson's products in their day-to-day operations. For example, a hospital purchases needles, sterile gloves, operating equipment, copiers, and computers as well as thousands of other products that are used in its daily running. Salespeople from companies such as Hewlett Packard, Baxter Hospital Supply, and Xenos Computers might all call on the hospital to sell their goods. In this category of selling, the salesperson sells to the ultimate consumer but the product is used in support of the buyer's business, rather than in producing the buyer's products.

3. *Selling to governments.* Government purchasing includes all Federal, State, county, and city governments. An example would be Wallace Computer Services selling computerized forms to the city of Chicago. The salesperson's ultimate customer is the governmental entity.

Retail Selling

Retailing includes all activities directly related to the sale of goods and services to the ultimate consumer for personal, nonbusiness use or consumption. The primary difference between retailing sales and industrial sales is the actual location of the sale. In a retailing environment the customer typically goes to the seller; in an industrial environment the seller typically goes to the customer. A retailer usually sells directly to the ultimate home consumer. (This text does not discuss retail sales in any depth. Retailing is a separate subdiscipline of marketing; most universities offer separate retailing courses.)

Services Selling

The service sector is as diverse in products as is the industrial sector. **Services** are activities or benefits provided to consumers. Four unique characteristics distinguish services from goods:

1. *Intangibility.* The product cannot be touched, seen, tasted, heard, or felt like a physical good. For example, if you buy a ticket to a concert you are employing a service to entertain you. There is no physical good. The good in this case is entertainment, which is an intangible. You hear the music but you cannot physically grasp the concept of entertainment, unlike buying a physical good such as a guitar.

2. *Inseparability.* Unlike goods, services are often sold, produced, and consumed at the same time. When you get a haircut, you consume (a new haircut) what the stylist produces at the same time.

3. *Heterogeneity.* Services are less standardized and uniform than physical goods. Physical goods generally look alike as they roll off an assembly line. If you buy a car you can get different colors and options but the car itself is somewhat standardized. Services can be very individualized because the good is not tangible.

4. *Perishability.* Services cannot be stored, warehoused, or inventoried. If a hotel room is not filled for the night, the sale of that product is lost for the day. You cannot hope to sell double the amount the next day as you can with physical goods.

Some services are very much like retail selling in that you have to go to the servicer for the product—like a haircut or a hotel room. Other services, such as insurance, financial sales, and real estate are more similar to industrial sales. These types of services tend to be commission oriented and directed by sales managers, and business is usually away from their office.

SALES ACTIVITIES

A sales job today includes a lot more marketing, research, and other activities than it did just a few years ago. Exhibit 1.9 indicates, only about one-third of a salesperson's time is spent "selling" face-to-face, and this percentage may continue to decrease in the future as salespeople do more marketing functions (territory analysis, research, planning, promotion, etc.) and as the selling task increases in complexity. Salespeople spend more and more time on the phone selling, setting up appointments, checking on orders, and so on. They also spend a great deal of time (16 percent) servicing current accounts (this should continue to increase in the future). One-fifth of a salesperson's time is spent traveling, out-of-town as well as in-town. Administration and internal meetings take up the remaining 15 percent.

The information in Exhibit 1.9 is designed to draw a picture of the "average" salesperson across industries. It is important to remember that sales and sales activities continue to evolve and change. The evolution of Gerber is a good example. In October of 1994 Gerber made a major commitment to remain the dominant producer of baby food. As a part of this effort Gerber fully automated its 600 sales

---

EXHIBIT 1.9

HOW SALESPEOPLE SPEND THEIR TIME

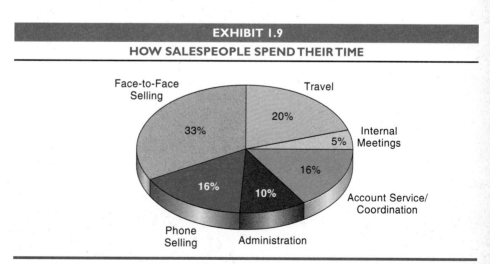

Source: "How Salespeople Spend Their Time," *Sales and Marketing Management* (January 1990):39.

EXHIBIT 1.10	
ACTIVITIES OF SALESPEOPLE	
Activity Name	**Selected Activities**
Conferences/meetings	Attend sales conferences; set up exhibitions, trade shows.
Training/recruiting	Look for new sales representatives; train new sales representatives.
Entertaining	Take clients to lunch, golf, etc.
Out-of-town traveling	Spend the night on the road; travel out of town.
Working with distributors	Establishing relations with distributors; extend credit; collect past due accounts.
Selling function	Search out leads; prepare sales presentations; make sales calls; overcome objections.
Working with orders	Correct orders; expedite orders; handle shipping problems.
Servicing the product	Test equipment; teach safety instructions; supervise installation.
Information management	Provide feedback to superiors; receive feedback from clients.
Servicing the account	Inventory; set up point-of-purchase displays; stock shelves.

SOURCE: William C. Moncrief, "Ten Key Activities of Industrial Salespeople," *Industrial Marketing Management,* 15 (1986): 309–318.

reps, key account managers, and sales managers, which resulted in major changes in the reps' daily activities and a drop in administrative tasks from 12 percent to 5 percent. Senior vice-president of sales Lewis Ammirati says, "Automation has saved field reps eight hours a week and division managers up to sixteen hours a week." Gerber sales information and presentations are now more time efficient too. As a result, Gerber now sells brands and products in addition to its own, while providing data to aid retailers in their marketing.[16]

Depending on the selling environment, individual salespeople will perform different selling activities at different frequencies. For example, a salesperson for Baxter Hospital Supply will not sell the same way as a person who sells for Kraft Foods. The day-to-day activities will be different, as will the amount of time spent on each activity. A study of 1,393 salespeople indicated that there are broad differences in what activities salespeople perform.[17] Exhibit 1.10 divides these selling activities into ten general categories. Most salespeople are involved with all ten categories in performing their sales jobs, but the level of frequency may vary extensively by industry.

Also the daily activities vary according to the country in which the selling takes place. A later extension of the previously mentioned study compared the daily activities of U.S. salespeople to German and Danish salespeople. The results indicate that sales activities differ among the three countries, with the activities of German salesforces more like those of U.S. salesforces than their Danish counterparts.[18] It is quite possible that a similar study conducted today might indicate some new activities (possibly based around new technological advances) with both U.S. and non–U.S. salespeople or at least new levels of frequency of performance of the activity. The point is that the daily activities of the sales job are not stagnant; they continue to evolve and change, and they are different for each salesperson.

CURRENT TRENDS IN SALES MANAGEMENT

Like individual sales jobs, the sales world is rapidly changing. Of the numerous important developments occurring in the field, here are seven specific trends and issues that we think will be the focus of sales management through the year 2000 and beyond. In no particular order of importance they are: (1) new selling methods, (2) relationship selling, (3) continued evolution of technology, (4) global issues, (5) ethics in the sales world, (6) diversity in the sales world, and (7) an increased emphasis in customer orientation and quality (see Exhibit 1.11). These are not the only issues confronting sales managers today and tomorrow, but they have particular importance and should be emphasized. We will introduce each trend briefly in the following section, then discuss them in greater detail throughout the text.

New Selling Methods

The traditional individual salesperson calling on an individual buyer is rapidly disappearing in many industries. The late 1980s and early 1990s saw a dramatic up-

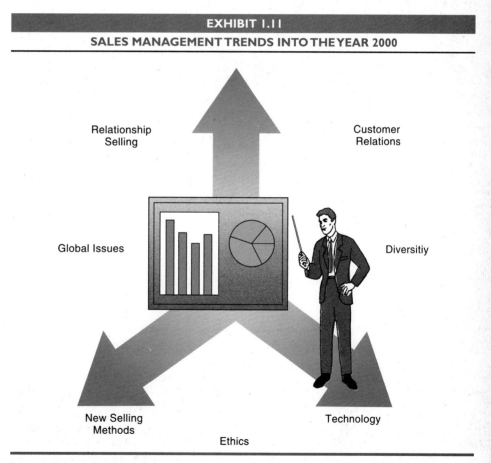

EXHIBIT 1.11

SALES MANAGEMENT TRENDS INTO THE YEAR 2000

Relationship Selling

Customer Relations

Global Issues

Diversitiy

New Selling Methods

Technology

Ethics

SOURCE: *Sales and Marketing Management* (December 1994): 9. "Sales Trends for 2000"

surge in sales organizations' use of nontraditional methods of selling such as tele-marketing, national accounts management, part-time selling, team selling, and electronic sales offices. For example, Electronic Label Technology, an Oklahoma-based company that sells bar code printing systems, has turned to cross-function selling. In **cross-function selling** the salesperson teams up with experts in various departments to provide higher-level service to the customer at all levels. Tim Wright, CEO of Electronic Label Technology, wants technical support people at most presentations made by his salespeople. After the sale is made, a different software specialist team takes over.[19]

Relationship Selling

No sales concept has received as much publicity, study, and discussion in the past decade as relationship selling. *Relationship selling* implies that the selling–buying process is a continuous stream of transactions rather than a single business exchange. The long-term association between buyer and seller becomes the focus of business with the customer. Part of the impetus for relationship selling is business realizing that it is much easier (and cheaper) to keep a customer than to find a new one. Some companies have gone so far as to dismiss their salesforces and concentrate all their selling efforts on serving their existing customers.

G&F, a small plastics manufacturer, assigns a full-time employee to each of its large customers. The employees work at the customer's facility. According to G&F's president, the change has been extremely successful. G&F has grown at an annual rate of 25 percent to 40 percent per year, whereas the plastics industry as a whole is depressed. The secret is that G&F spends little time trying to get new accounts. Instead, it concentrates all its efforts on developing relationships with existing customers and looking for opportunities to expand business with them.[20] This strategy will not work for everyone, but it is growing in popularity. Clearly, to be successful like G&F, sellers must develop long-term relationships with their customers. These relationships should cover a broad range of individuals within the buying organization. This allows sellers to seek new opportunities to sell their products and help buyers become more efficient.

Technology

Probably no single variable has made such an immediate impact on the sales world as has the changing world of technology. Technology is having an impact in two ways: (1) in terms of the selling function as a whole and (2) in terms of the performance of the selling function by individual salespeople (see Box 1.2).

Technology is allowing many companies to streamline their selling function through salesforce automation.[21] For example, sellers who have direct electronic links with large customers do not have to send salespeople to take routine reorders. The information from the link (often tied to cash registers) is used to generate reorders without need for human intervention. This directly reduces costs since salespeople no longer have to call on customers for these rebuy orders. It also reduces costs indirectly because buyers will get fresh shipments more rapidly and will be less likely to run out of needed items. Hallmark uses data derived from bar codes scanned at the checkout counters of retailers to supply information to Hallmark

BOX 1.2

SALES TRENDS FOR 2000

Sales automation is driving some powerful trends, says Timothy McMahon, manager of management consulting for Sales Technologies, Inc., and author of *Selling 2000: The Vision and the Promise of Sales Automation.* The following are the top five automation-related trends (in no particular order) McMahon has seen materializing in the 150 companies he has consulted with over the past two years:

- Salespeople and managers are moving from tactics to strategies. Salespeople and managers have always known how to make calls and manage territories, but because automation provides better sources of information, they're taking a more strategic look at the business opportunities in those territories.
- Companies are starting to look at each salesperson as a micro-businessperson who is funded, supported, and nourished by the corporation. By the same token, salespeople are expected to show the return on that investment, which is easier for them to do with automation.
- A corporate information highway is emerging that links corporate functions, field management, and field sales reps. Sales automation systems are becoming the company's real-time sensors—they tell management what's really going on out in the field. This gives the corporation the ability to change course quickly.
- Automation is helping to redefine the sales manager's role. Managers don't have to spend all their time gathering information about salespeople's activities anymore, so their role is changing from police officer to mentor. With automation, they'll already know what's going on, and they can devote themselves to helping salespeople create strategies and providing them with the resources they need.
- It will be easier to create added-value programs. To provide customers with real value, you need to know what constitutes value in their eyes. That requires better customer information and better coordination of everybody who touches the customer, both of which can come from automation.

SOURCE: Nancy Arrott, "Sales Trends For 2000, Part 2" *Sales and Marketing Management,* (December 1994): 9.

salespeople. This information allows Hallmark to supply the retailer with tailored displays and promotions designed for the retailers' customers based on their buying preferences.[22] Unisys, Pfizer, and Hewlett Packard have also integrated their information, sales, and marketing divisions, allowing them to gather consumer information which is then used by their salesforces.[23]

Technology is also having major effects on individual salespeople's jobs. For example, in the fall of 1989 the fastest notebook computer modem transmitted data at 2,400 bytes per second. Just six years later that speed had increased to 28,800 bytes per second—a dramatic increase in performance.[24] This performance increase has allowed salespeople much faster access to customer order information, price data, and bid specifications.

One effect of improving technology is that more salespeople can work from their homes. Salespeople are already heavy users of home computers, faxes, home copiers, voice mail, and cellular phones. New palm-size computers make it even easier for salespeople to bring information to the customer's place of business, or to link with other computers at home or in the office. Salespeople can use the Internet or various network services such as CompuServe or Prodigy to make plane reservations, send electronic mail to customers or home offices, and access breaking information about new products or competitors. As technology continues to improve, the world of sales and sales management will have to adapt and keep up. (Chapter 2 will discuss more of these advances and sales changes based on technology. Special boxes and sections throughout the text will also provide examples of technology advances and the effect on sales management.)

Global and Ethical Issues

Global and ethical issues are important singularly and together. Global issues are increasingly becoming important because of the level of global competition and the passage of legislation, such as the North American Free Trade Agreement (NAFTA), the General Agreement on Trades and Tariffs (GATT), and the Treaty of Rome, which encourages economic development within regions of the world. From Shekou, China, to Warsaw, Poland, a migration of millions of people into the ranks of the middle class is creating more and more markets.[25] These markets will require international salesforces that will change the structure, training, and sales approach for conducting business. Executives and salespeople alike will likely increase their level of international business travel (although teleconferencing will help considerably). However, expanding markets also mean expanding competition—both domestically and internationally. As organizations begin competing globally and in larger numbers, the issue of ethics will also increase in importance.

Ethics is an issue that has a moving standard. In other words, what is unethical to some people or some cultures may be perfectly acceptable to others. Sales approaches and techniques cannot be considered universal, and adjustments have to be made to confront the changing global and ethical environments. Robert D. Haas, CEO of Levi Strauss, is a believer of **responsible commercial success**. In other words, Haas believes that an organization is capable of reaping profits and making the world a better place to live. Levi's has a strict standard regarding the environment, business practices, and diversity issues. Haas will not tolerate suppliers or Levi personnel who violate the corporate aspirations. In fact, one-third of every employee's annual evaluation is based on his or her ability to meet these aspirations. Ignoring issues such as empowerment and diversity can keep an employee from getting a raise or a promotion.[26] More and more companies are moving to an ethically based corporate philosophy. Chapters 3 and 4 will examine these issues in more depth, as will each of the remaining chapters.

Diversity

Sales organizations are looking for diversity in experiences, background, culture, and frames of reference for their sales personnel, particularly as the entire U.S. workforce becomes more diverse.[27] Organizations must approach diversity much in the same way that Levi Strauss has approached the issue: by not tolerating any less. Unfortunately, many companies do only what is necessary to stay within federal guidelines, and as a result they do not espouse and practice a corporate diversity philosophy.[28] In fact, human resource experts estimate that only 3 percent to 5 percent of U.S. organizations are effectively diversifying their workforce. Organizations must incorporate counseling programs that include cultural sensitivity, gender awareness, and disability awareness training, as well as promote a harassment-free workplace.[29] Diversity issues, as well as harassment and discrimination, will be covered in Chapter 3 as well as in several places throughout the text.)

Businesses are also becoming more and more international. Even small organizations are competing globally and working with international suppliers. The influx of women and minorities into salesforces along with an increasingly global setting, has mandated a need for creating new approaches to conducting business. Although employees anywhere in the world might benefit from U.S. strategies for valuing diversity, U.S.-based organizations must be particularly aware of cultural sensitivities in international arenas because other countries may not share U.S. views on diversity. Management must be willing to work with international salesforces to smooth initial prejudices that women and minorities may encounter with international customers.[30]

Customer Orientation and Total Quality

Many organizations have traditionally espoused that the customer should be the focal point of the business, but a large number of them have failed to practice what they preach. During the 1970s and into the 1980s brand loyalty among customers was almost a given, even if the supplying organization made mistakes. However, a tightening economy in the mid-1980s caused companies to begin watching the bottom line. Service, quality, and low cost became customer expectations. Now buyers change suppliers if they are dissatisfied with the quality level of support and service provided. Brand loyalty is no longer assumed, and businesses must work hard to keep their customer base. If an organization wants to remain in business for the long term, it must do more than espouse a customer orientation; it must practice it while providing high quality. A **customer orientation** is an organizational philosophy that places the customer as the primary focus of the business strategy. A customer orientation requires a higher commitment of sales resources to ensure that customer needs and wants are being met. This added commitment means that resources must be stretched or new methods of sales effort and service must be found. In later chapters we will explore concepts such as total quality management and reengineering and their resulting effects on salesforces.

SUMMARY

Personal selling is personal communication between the seller and the buyer for the purpose of making or influencing a sale. Sales management is defined as the management of those who are engaged in personal selling or who directly support the salesforce.

Sales management plays an important role in marketing, especially for firms in business-to-business markets. Personal selling is the most used promotional technique in the business markets, and management of the salesforce is an important component of the quality of the selling effort.

There are a number of reasons why we study sales management. Personal selling is the most important promotion method in business-to-business marketing, and personal selling is the primary point of contact with the customer. Sales ability is important throughout one's career regardless of the profession. A career in sales offers high potential. Finally, studying sales offers students the opportunity to correct misperceptions about sales and sales management.

Technological advances are having a profound effect on the way salespeople perform their jobs and on how the selling function is accomplished. The selling function in many industries requires highly trained, professional salespeople. Some industries are considering adopting certification standards for their salesforce. Changes in hiring patterns at large firms, and the consolidation of marketing and sales functions in many firms, are changing the job opportunities for new graduates.

Lastly new selling methods, relationship selling, technology, global changes, ethical considerations, and a growing emphasis on diversity and customer orientation are our picks as the issues and trends for sales organizations in the twenty-first century. These trends will be prominently featured throughout the remainder of the text.

KEY TERMS

two-way global marketing

personal selling

sales management

marketing

selling mix

Standard Industrial Classification (SIC) code

reseller

retailing

services

cross-function selling

responsible commercial success

customer orientation

DISCUSSION QUESTIONS

1. What is the difference between personal selling and sales management?
2. What role does sales management play in the marketing function?
3. What is meant by an organization's sales mix?
4. Why did sales and sales management courses reemerge in university curriculum beginning in the 1970s to its current prominence?
5. What are some typical myths about selling, and why are those myths untrue?
6. What are the three broad categories of selling and sales management?
7. In general terms, what activities does a salesperson perform in an average day?
8. What are some current sales management trends that are expected to continue in the twenty-first century?
9. What does the term *relationship selling* imply, and why has it become such an important concept?
10. Why is diversity of the workplace so important, and how will the workplace change as business becomes more and more global?

PROBLEMS

1. Marcy Rodriguez is a second-generation Mexican American who has been advised by her father to stay away from industrial sales because it isn't a field for women or minorities. Is Marcy's father correct? Why or why not?

2. Beth Walton is a recent college graduate who wants a job in the marketing department of a large manufacturer of consumer products. However, each company she interviews for tells her that she has to start in sales before she can join the marketing department. This is not what she wants to hear. Why would organizations want Beth to start her marketing career in sales?

3. Both of Ralph Lorza's parents work for *Fortune* 500 companies, and Ralph's goal is to join a large corporation immediately after graduation. However, Ralph's marketing professors have been advising him to consider working for a smaller company. Why would Ralph's professors make such a recommendation?

4. Ed Hough has been a successful salesperson for over 25 years. His college-age son has informed Ed that he will be majoring in marketing and looking for a marketing career. Ed replies, "Marketing people don't do anything but get in the way of good salespeople, son. Go into sales and get a meaningful job." Why would Ed perceive marketing and sales to be competitors rather than allies?

NOTES

1. Louis Kraar and Seiichi Takikawa, *Japanese Maverick: Success Secrets of Canon's "God of Sales"* (New York: Wiley, 1994), 15–17.
2. "What's Selling? Sales Jobs," *Sales and Marketing Management* (September 1993), 11.
3. Dartnell's 27th Salesforce Compensation Survey (1992), 8.
4. Peter D. Band, *Dictionary of Marketing Terms* (Chicago: American Marketing Association, 1988), 115.
5. T. A. DeWeese, "The Advertising Manager," *Printers' Ink,* 14 (July 1910): 141, as quoted in Frank V. Cespedes "Coordinating Sales and Marketing in Consumer Goods Firms," *Journal of Consumer Research,* 10(2) (Spring 1993): 37–56.
6. Jaclyn Fierman, "The Death and Rebirth of the Salesman," *Fortune* (July 25, 1994), 80–91.
7. Andy Kessler, "Fire Your Salesforce—The Sequel," *Forbes* (April 11, 1994): 23.
8. David Whitford "TV or Not TV," *Inc* (June 1994): 63–65. See also Chick Harrity, "Purchasing Power: QVC, Television's Home-Shopping Giant," *US News and World Report* (January 31, 1994): 56–59.
9. Richard N. Cardozo and Shannon H. Shipp, "New Selling Methods Are Changing Industrial Sales Management," *Business Horizons* (September–October 1987): 23–28, and Rowland T. Moriarty and Ursula Moran, "Managing Hybrid Marketing Systems," *Harvard Business Review* (November–December 1990): 146–155.
10. This was drawn from W. A. Owens and L. F. Schoenfeldt, "Toward a Classification of Persons," *Journal of Applied Psychology,* 64, 329–332 and L. F. Schoenfeldt, "Utilization of Manpower: Development and Evaluation of an Assessment-Classification Model for Matching Individuals With Jobs," *Journal of Applied Psychology* 59 (1974): 583–594.

11. *Sales and Marketing Management* (September 1993): 11.
12. "Marketing Newsletter," *Sales and Marketing Management* (February 1987): 27.
13. Michael J. Swenson, William R. Swinyard, Frederick W. Langrehr, and Scott M. Smith, "The Appeal of Personal Selling as a Career: A Decade Later," *Journal of Personal Selling and Sales Management,* 13(1) (Winter 1993): 51–64.
14. William A. Weeks and Darrel D. Muehling, "Students' Perceptions of Personal Selling," *Industrial Marketing Management,* 16 (May 1987): 145–151.
15. "Should Salespeople Be Certified?" *Sales and Marketing Management* (October 1993): 47, and "Sales Reps Cram for Exams," *Sales and Marketing Management* (June 1993): 10.
16. Thayer C. Taylor, "It's Child's Play," *Sales and Marketing Management,* (December 1994): 38–39.
17. William C. Moncrief, "Selling Activity and Sales Position Taxonomies for Industrial Salesforces," *Journal of Marketing Research,* 23 (August 1986): 261–270. See also William C. Moncrief and David W. Finn, "Industrial Sales Jobs: A Replication of the Moncrief Taxonomy" (AMA Educators Proceedings, 1989), and Alan J. Dubinsky and P. J. O'Connor, "A Multidimensional Analysis of Preferences for Sales Positions," *Journal of Personal Selling and Sales Management* 3(2) (November 1983): 31–40.
18. William C. Moncrief, "A Comparison of Sales Activities in an International Setting," *Journal of International Consumer Marketing,* 1(1) (1988): 45–62.
19. Cathy Hyatt Hills, "Everybody Sells," *Small Business Reports,* 17(10) (October 1992): 31–40.
20. Susan Greco, "The Art of Selling," *Inc.,* 15(6) (1993): 72–80.
21. Stephen Gondert, "The 10 Biggest Mistakes of SFA (and How to Avoid Them)," *Sales and Marketing Management* (February 1993): 52–57, and Melissa Campanelli and Thayer C. Taylor, "Meeting of the Minds," *Sales and Marketing Management* (December 1993): 80–85.
22. Ani Hadijian, "Death and Rebirth of the Salesman," *Fortune* (July 25, 1994): 80–91.
23. Kate Bertrand, "Culture Clash: Unisys, HP, Pfizer Bridge Gap Between Techies and Reps," *Business Marketing,* 77(9) (September 1992): 96–98.
24. Todd C. Scofield and Donald R. Shaw, "Avoiding Future Shock," *Sales and Marketing Management* (January 1993): 16–21.
25. Rahul Jacob, "The Big Rise: Middle Class Explodes Around the Globe, Bringing New Markets and New Prosperity," *Fortune* (May 30, 1994): 74–80.
26. Russell Mitchell and Michael Oneal, "Managing By Values: Is Levi Strauss' Approach Visionary or Flaky?" *Business Week* (August 1, 1994): 46–52, and Ronald R. Sims, "The Challenge of Ethical Behavior in Organizations," *Journal of Business Ethics,* 11(7) (July 1992): 505.
27. Laurie Ashmore Epting, Saundra H. Glover, and Susan D. Boyd, "Managing Diversity," *Health Care Supervisor,* 12(4) (June 1994): 73–78.
28. Faye Rice, "How to Make Diversity Pay," *Fortune,* 130(3) (August 8, 1994): 44–49.
29. Richard F. Federico, "Multiculturalism Makes Good Business Sense," *Compensation and Benefits Management,* 10(2) (Spring 1994): 32–37.
30. Charlene Marmer Solomon, "Global Operations Demand That HR Rethink Diversity," *Personnel Journal,* 73(7) (July 1994): 40–50.

PART I

MANAGING
THE CHANGING
SALES WORLD:
THE ENVIRONMENT

2

THE SALES ENVIRONMENT

In this interactive, wired world, we may be connected to information and lose our connection to humans.

EDWARD ESBER, JR., PRESIDENT AND COO OF CREATIVE LABS, INC.

LEARNING OBJECTIVES

After reading this chapter, you will be able to answer the following questions:

- What variables comprise the sales environment?
- How have the customers changed in the last decade?
- What effect has the expanding global market had on competition and markets?
- What strategic sales management changes have occurred as a result of changing technology?
- How has the technological revolution changed the way salespeople perform their daily jobs?

In the early 1990s Colgate-Palmolive began developing strategies for introducing a variety of products into the global marketplace. Speed Stick deodorant, acquired with the purchase of Mennen, would be introduced in the newly opened Eastern European markets. Protex soap would be introduced to South Americans and Asians, Palmolive Optims shampoo-conditioner to Africans, and Colgate Total to virtually the entire world.[1] With all this activity occurring simultaneously, the potential for marketing and sales mistakes was high. Suddenly Colgate-Palmolive had an entirely new customer base, and along with it came new competitors, new suppliers, new legal and political environments, and a new diversity of economies. However, with all these new challenges also came new solutions. The rapid development of innovative technology has allowed global markets to become reachable. Colgate-Palmolive found that its worldwide customer base has access to cable or satellite television. Customer homes, suppliers, and salesforces are all linked by the Internet and other computer networks. Moreover, the fax, cellular phones, and portable computers have made conducting global sales a more realistic enterprise.

Like most people, when you hear the word *sales* or *selling* you probably do not perceive an ever-evolving and changing discipline. Selling has been in existence virtually forever, but as a studied discipline it has gone through a lot of changes over the centuries, particularly over the past couple of decades. In this chapter we will examine the world of sales, explore the evolution of sales and sales management, and examine where the future may be taking us. Specifically, we will look at the factors that play a part in creating change in the sales field.

Factors such as changing competition, increases in technology, legal and political influences, fluctuations in the economy, and a constantly evolving customer base keep the sales world from being stagnant. A sales organization that fails to prepare for rapid change probably will not be in business very long. The environment plays a fundamental role in the day-to-day activities of a salesperson and a sales manager. High-performing sales individuals know they cannot control the environment, but they better plan for, and be able to adapt to, changes brought about by the ever-changing environment.

MARKETING AND SALES EVOLUTION

For centuries the sales world has continued to evolve and change, although many people might argue that selling—the basic function—has always been the same.[2] Regardless, sales has been and remains the lifeblood of any product or service organization. Without the sales dimension or function, an organization cannot continue to exist. A company with a great product but no way to sell it will invariably see a great product go to waste.

Many companies house sales and marketing in the same department under one executive, while others consider the two areas to be separate departments and, in some cases, even internally competitive. The fact is, sales and marketing are not synonymous, nor should they be considered as competitive. As we saw in Chapter 1, sales is a part of the promotion function which in turn is a part of marketing. How did marketing and sales get to where they are today? The answer may be found in an examination of the beginnings of marketing.

Selling has been in existence since the first cave people tried to barter fire, and it has continued to evolve over time. For example, in the twelfth and thirteenth centuries Muslim traders were held in high regard. Islam was a society that emphasized trade over industry or art. Much of this trading (selling) philosophy carried over into Europe, where the life of one salesman was chronicled by monk Reginald of Durham.

> Godric of Finchal quit farming in favor of peddling low priced trinkets in rural England in the twelfth century. These were bought in larger towns, then sold door-to-door. Godric's initial territory was the manorial estates dotting the countryside. His contacts with sophisticated urban brokers led to further associations. Moving up the sales ladder, he abandoned home selling for calls on forts, castles, strongholds and cities. He traveled widely, to Scotland, Rome, and Flanders. In a few years Godric went from a shepherd to a respected man of substance.[3]

Starting in the mid-1700s European political ideology and economic statuses were changing. Colonization and mercantilism were ending, and a system of retail was being developed in Europe and the United States. Josiah Wedgwood, an early marketing and sales leader, exemplifies this period. Wedgwood, an Englishman, was an early contributor to some of the marketing and sales practices that are still used today. His contributions include one of the first recorded uses of hiring a sales manager to oversee a traveling salesforce, the development of warehousing, the creation

EXHIBIT 2.1			
NEW PERIODIZATION OF MARKETING			
Era 1	Era 2	Era 3	Era 4
Antecedents	Origins	Institutional Development	Refinement Formalization
Time			
1500s in Europe 1600s in North America	Britain 1750 US and Germany 1830	Britain 1856 US and Germany 1870	1930→
Characteristics			
• Commerce Basic • Production-Transportation • Primitive	• Mass migration to urban areas • Onset of Industrial Revolution	• Mass stimulation of demand • Markets geographically separated	• Redefining of basic institutions • Redefining market functions
Advances			
• Beginning of financial institutions • Capitalism	• Production/transportation improved • Market targeting • Competition	• Physical distribution • Consumerism • Advertising	• Containerization • Air freight • Market analysis
Effects on Sales			
• Yankee peddler—pulled merchandise in wagon • Drummers—fast-talking salespeople	• Selling in urban areas • Retailing	• Regulatory constraints • Growing salesforces	• Large body of knowledge • Professionalism

SOURCE: Based on Ronald Fullerton, "How Modern Is Modern Marketing? Marketing's Evolution and the Myth of the 'Production Era,'" *Journal of Marketing*, 52 (January 1988): 108–125.

of showrooms, the first major historical use of multiple promotions, and the entry and development of new markets.

A few decades after Wedgwood's death the world experienced an incredible acceleration of technological inventions that forever changed the face of selling. The advent of railroads, telegraphs, and postal services in the 1800s again moved the world of selling to another level. Now, goods could be sold, promoted, and easily shipped to other markets. As a result, the need for salespeople began to grow.[4]

In the United States, primarily in the New England area from the late 1700s to the mid-1800s, the *Yankee peddler* was developing a reputation in rural areas as a respectable merchant. The Yankee peddler sold his goods from his wagon and traveled town to town. As the United States began pushing west, the Yankee peddler evolved into the *drummer,* the slick-talking peddler immortalized in movies as selling elixir from the back of his wagon. The reputation of the salesperson began to suffer—and justifiably so. Many salespeople today are still perceived by much of the public as the 1800s' drummer, but as we will see the field of sales has evolved considerably since that time.

Exhibit 2.1 provides a synopsis of the four eras of the European and U.S. marketing evolution and its resulting effects on selling and sales management.[5] Notice that until relatively recently the United States has trailed European nations in the evolution of common business practices. Exhibit 2.1 also directly contradicts some "traditional" views which indicated that sales and marketing evolved through three periods: (1) production (early 1900s), (2) selling (1920s to World War II), and (3) the marketing era (World War II to present). As you can see some sophisticated business and marketing procedures were actually put into practice long before the beginning of the traditional production era.

Regardless of the historical perspective, the sales discipline will continue to evolve. Sales management is an ongoing and expanding discipline of knowledge. Managing and directing a sales organization is and will remain a complex and multifaceted procedure whose outcome, to a large degree, is dependent on the sales environment.

THE SALES ENVIRONMENT

Sales managers need keen insight into the **sales environment**, which can be defined as those forces over which a sales organization has no control. Although sales management cannot control the environment, good sales managers are aware of how the environment can affect the day-to-day operations of a sales unit. Managers who do not plan or forecast based on environmental information and change are doomed to failure.[6] A company cannot control what the competition does or how the market will respond to a changing economy, but managers must anticipate and react to the environmental threats and opportunities.

Exhibit 2.2 displays the environmental variables that have a direct and immediate effect on sales management, all of which reside in a global and ethical framework. Like marketing history, the environment also continues to change and have direct ef-

---

EXHIBIT 2.2
THE SALES ENVIRONMENT

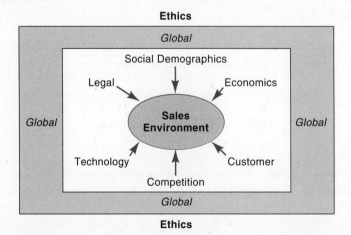

fects on the field of sales management. The past two decades have seen substantial change as a result of the evolving environment. As a result sales managers have encountered new challenges as well as new opportunities. The remainder of this chapter will examine the environmental variables that are shown in Exhibit 2.2. Specifically, we will look at how these variables have changed over the past 15 years, how they are continuing to evolve, and what the changes mean for sales managers in the future.

CUSTOMER

The customer is considered an environmental variable because an organization has no *direct* control over whether a buyer remains a customer. Certainly there are influence strategies that every good sales organization employs to obtain and maintain a customer base. However, as we will see throughout this text, a customer is unpredictable and may change vendors frequently.

By necessity organizations have become both customer oriented and customer conscious in the 1990s, which have even become known as the "Decade of the Customer." This focus should continue well into the twenty-first century. Much of this renewed focus on the customer can be explained by a broadening base of competition in the international arena. The repercussion of expanded competition for customers is that the customer must be an organizational priority—even for the smallest business—or the organization will cease to exist.

The customer has also changed in a variety of ways. Historically, the "traditional" sales organization had a customer base that was typically loyal to the seller over a long period of time. The buying process was somewhat routinized, and the customer base was likely to be the same. In the 1980s, however, the business environment went through changes, and naturally, so did the customer. The following are some ways that customers have changed in the past 10 to 15 years.

Higher Expectations

Customers of the 1990s have higher expectations of their suppliers. Japan has changed the way that U.S. companies and foreign companies competing in the United States (and indeed worldwide) approach the customer base. Because of Japan's success with U.S. customers, the Japanese concepts of quality and value became the key words of the late 1980s and have continued into the 1990s. Harvard Business School professor Robert Hayes has stated, "Fifteen years ago companies competed on price. Today it is *quality*. Tomorrow it will be product design." The Japanese brought a high-quality product with a reasonable price.[7] In many industries, U.S. companies were forced to reduce prices to compete with the Japanese price/quality ratio when these same U.S. companies had always espoused high price/high quality. Companies that had dominated an industry, such as Xerox, experienced high-quality competition from the Japanese resulting in a lower market share. As Professor Hayes has stated, the trend now is quality, but the evolution will continue and soon customers will not only expect high quality, but also state of the art product design.

Customers have also become less tolerant of poor service and mistakes. Today if a company fails to deliver on some dimension, the customer may simply seek out another supplier that will deliver the needed service. In the past customers would remain with the supplier even if the service was not as good as it should have been.

Although brand loyalty is still a primary goal of every selling company, it is becoming much more difficult to maintain. The general rule of thumb today is that a customer *may* stay with you as long as you can maintain a high-quality product with excellent service. Brand loyalty used to be the dominant factor in business, and mistakes could be forgiven. Long-term relationships based on brand loyalty are still very much in vogue, but the concept has become more complex. The salesperson of the pre-1980s tended to have working relationships with one or two key buyers (people). Today, the term *relationship selling* implies that the selling-buying process is a continuous stream of transactions rather than single, discrete business exchanges. Decisions are based on developing, maintaining, and expanding relationships with accounts. Specifically, **relationship selling** is defined as the process whereby a sales organization builds long-term alliances with both prospective and current customers so that seller and buyer work toward a common set of specified goals. By necessity, it has become the dominant philosophy for most marketing and sales organizations.

Relationship selling argues that the seller must build and maintain a relationship with the *entire* buying organization, not just individuals within the organization.[8] Customer organizations change personnel, positions, and duties. Therefore, the seller must build relationships with as many people in the buying organization as possible. We will continue to examine relationship selling and customer orientation throughout this text.

Needs Analysis

Today's seller must have a thorough understanding of the problems of each customer. This understanding begins with a needs analysis. A **needs analysis** dictates that the seller spend time in the customer environment examining the needs and wants of the customer. This examination typically means making several sales calls on the customer and spending substantial time in the customer's environment before an actual sales presentation is even attempted. In the global market the needs analysis becomes even more critical, since many cultures (i.e., Mexico, Japan, much of Europe) require that substantial time be spent "getting to know" one another before it is even possible to determine needs. After a potential customer's needs are assessed, the resulting presentation is directly tailored to match those predetermined customer needs.

The most basic step in a needs analysis is *listening*. One principle subscribed to by most sales managers is that a successful salesperson on a typical sales call should spend more time listening than speaking. Exhibit 2.3 depicts a process in which a salesperson uses cognitive and behavioral listening skills as part of a listening process ultimately leading to higher salesperson performance.

Listening also allows the salesperson to improve overall organizational performance by becoming a fundamental market research tool for the selling organization. The information obtained by the salesperson is relayed to the home office (usually by reports) and becomes a data point for strategic decisions. The salesperson has become a critical link in the sales organization's acquisition of market research. No one knows the territorial market as well as the salesperson assigned to that territory. Indeed, much formalized training is now designed to teach the salesperson how to provide quality market research to the home office.

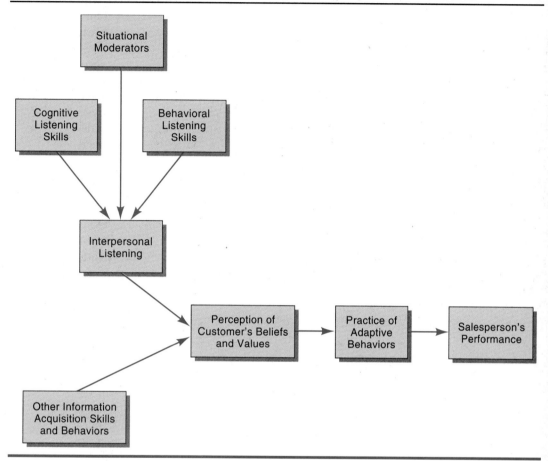

SOURCE: Stephen B. Castleberry and David C. Sheperd, "Effective Interpersonal Listening and Personal Selling," *Journal of Personal Selling and Sales Management,* 13(1) (Winter 1993): 35–49.

The idea for a salesperson to double as a market researcher may seem obvious, but the concept is not as widely employed as it might be. Management has been reluctant to use the salesforce in a research capacity because it takes away from selling time. There have also been doubts about the salesperson's desire and abilities to provide pertinent information.[9] However, the sales job is changing and the salesperson, the sales manager, and the sales organization will have to adapt to the changing business world of the twenty-first century. For example, salespeople are used to gathering competitive intelligence as discussed in Chapter 16.

The Buyer

The physical buyer is another aspect of the customer variable that has changed over the past few years. The buyer is responsible for purchasing for the buying company.

One characteristic of the buyer that has changed recently is that the buyer may now be represented or supported by multiple people who have input into the buying decisions. The resulting **buying centers**, as they are known, would include all the customer personnel who directly or indirectly influence the choice of product or supplier.[10] Many selling organizations are, in turn, beginning to create **selling centers**, which would include anyone active in the selling process to a given set of customers or potential customers. The net effect is that multiple people are now responsible for selling to a customer organization who, in turn, may also be represented by multiple people.

In the past, tradition dictated that the salesperson be the only person to have contact with the buyer or customer. Now, however, multiple contact points are becoming mandatory. For example, suppose Texas Instruments (TI) is attempting to sell a very expensive information system to a retail chain. While the salesperson concentrates on the physical buyer and coordinating selling center contacts, TI would also send technical people to talk with the retailer's technical experts and perhaps even a finance officer to talk with the retailer's vice-president of finance.[11] (Chapter 7 will explore buying and selling centers in more depth.)

Regardless, the personnel in the buyer positions have become much more knowledgeable and well educated. Several years ago it was not uncommon for buyers to have a high school degree only. Now most buyers have a college degree and some are acquiring their masters. Buyers have become very facts oriented and, because of the added time pressures, many buyers do not want a salesperson to come in and "waste" time with small chit-chat before getting down to business. With tough economic times, companies have mandated that their buyers cut costs and be very conscious of the balance sheet's bottom line. Therefore, buyers are not afraid to change suppliers when a better deal can be arranged. The pressure on buyers has become more intense; high-level professionalism has emerged. A salesperson's sales call must reflect this emerging professionalism and be empathetic to a buyer's job pressures.

COMPETITION

A second environmental factor centers around the competition. Like our customer base, we cannot control the competition. Many worldwide industries have or are experiencing mergers, buyouts, downsizing, and business failures. The globalization of business has also brought on new competitors, and even small companies are beginning to sell internationally. Changes brought on by competitors' decisions require a response from sales management. Management must be proactive rather than reactive in evaluating the competition and the market. For example, in 1994 IBM was forced to undergo a total metamorphosis. The worldwide head count for IBM dropped from a peak of 150,000 to about 70,000. Driven by market and competitive forces, and under the leadership of senior Vice President of North American sales and marketing Robert J. LaBant, IBM stripped away layers of management and significantly reduced the number of sales staff members. To remain a major player IBM felt that the costs of sales must be reduced by one-third and sales personnel must increase revenue. The result has been that much of IBM's products are now sold through dealers and distributors, termed **value-added resellers (VAR)**. VARs are retailers or other channel personnel who can provide more service for the ultimate customer than the manufacturer is able to deliver. All of these changes were brought about because of changes in global competitors.[12]

Marion Merrell Dow is another example of how competition can radically change the way that sales strategy and tactics are implemented. In the late 1980s Marion Laboratories merged with Merrell Dow. As a result, products that Marion sales reps had previously sold against were now products that they were themselves selling. The merger eliminated a competitor, but it also brought on the merging of salesforces and sales policies, as well as a realignment of territories. Salespeople were laid off or retired early, and hiring was frozen for a 2- to 3-year period. Interestingly, one of the reasons for the merger was increased competition from international pharmaceutical firms.

Many of the competitive changes that have occurred recently are a direct result of global competitors (particularly Japanese and European firms). As we saw at the beginning of this chapter with Colgate-Palmolive, new markets are opening around the world, and in turn an organization may now compete against a new set of firms. Sales procedures and strategies must continue to change to allow for an ever-expanding and changing competitive force.

Global competition has increased for European firms with European customers due to lowered trade barriers among European countries. In addition, NAFTA has created new markets for many U.S. companies in Mexico and Canada and in return has brought in new competition from these countries. For example, American International Industries (AII), a Mexican firm originally developed to be a subcontractor for General Dynamics, has become a full manufacturer competing in the United States as a supplier of industrial wiring. Other treaties have opened up new Central and South American markets. These treaties have created new potential and new competitors. In a business sense, the world keeps getting smaller, and more and more countries are becoming players in the international sales arena. Besides the United States, Canada, Europe, and Japan, countries and regions that have potential to be major players in sales in the early twenty-first century include South Korea, China, other countries in the Pacific Rim, India, countries that once comprised the former Eastern bloc, and many countries in Central and South America.

ECONOMICS

The U.S. economy of the late 1980s and most of the 1990s has dictated substantial changes in sales strategies. Obviously sales managers must understand and react to this changing economy. Some companies have had to abandon unpromising territories and districts. Other companies (and sometimes whole industries) have suddenly gone from being very profitable to being virtually nonexistent as a result of downward trends—and they will continue to do so. For example, with the end of the cold war, the U.S. defense industry—once strong and vibrant—has been forced to make large- scale cuts. Now its major players, which include General Dynamics and Bell Helicopter, are experiencing large drops in sales. This in turn affects not only the hundreds of smaller companies that have traditionally supplied the defense industry. Suddenly their forecasts for the future have been shattered and they have been forced to make radical changes just to survive. Many small businesses have closed; others have adjusted and shifted manufacturing interests.

When a large-scale industry downturn like this happens, the sales of other companies can be affected in whole regions and/or specific territories. For instance, when Carswell Air Force Base in Fort Worth, Texas, was greatly reduced in 1993, sales of local merchants in the surrounding area of west Fort Worth dropped and sales quotas of Carswell suppliers were not met. The lesson for sales managers is that it is exceedingly difficult to predict what the economy is going to do next year, much less 5 or 10 years from now. However, a good sales manager has contingency plans for direct and indirect economic challenges, such as the ones just illustrated.

SOCIAL DEMOGRAPHICS

One of the biggest changes in the social-demographic structure of sales over the past 10 to 15 years has been the increased number of women in the salesforce and the concomitant decrease in the *good ol' boy network*.[13] Typically, white males who resisted the admittance of anyone who was not a white male to their profession characterized the good ol' boy network. Although there are certainly still industries that are considered white male dominated (see Exhibit 2.4), women and minorities are making great strides in numerous industries.

A significant result of the declining good ol' boy network has been a higher degree of professionalism that continues to grow more and more pervasive in sales.[14] The large influx of women in purchase decision making and in the salesforce has helped bring about a new level of professionalism. A study by Penton Publishing shows that women and minorities account for significant numbers of purchasing decision making. Specifically, 42 percent of all managers, engineers, and purchasing agents are now women or minorities, up 11 percent in the past 10 years.[15] The dirty-joke telling, slap-on-the back, loud-talking salesperson, for the most part, is becoming a thing of the past.[16] It has not been an easy change to be sure because many salespeople and buyers were initially (and possibly still are) very uncomfortable working with women and minorities. Although many of the good ol' boy salesmen have made the transition to the professionalism needed into today's world, the sellers and buyers who have not been able to make the adjustment are being phased out and replaced with personnel who are more comfortable working in a diverse atmosphere.

LEGAL

A number of legal, ethical, and political issues affect a sales organization and the salesperson in the field. Laws and regulations are continually being created, debated, and modified. A firm cannot control legal and political systems, although special interest groups and lobbyists can and do influence the political process. There are three basic types of laws and regulations. Each will be discussed in detail in Chapter 3, They are:

- **Common law**—precedent used to decide future cases. An example would be *caveat emptor,* or "let the buyer beware."
- **Statutory law**—law created by federal, state, and local governments. An example would be the *Green River Ordinance,* which regulated door-to-door solicitation.
- **Administrative law**—law that is created by regulations. An example would be a regulation created by the Food and Drug Administration to prohibit the sale of red dye.

EXHIBIT 2.4		
WOMEN IN SALES: PERCENTAGE BY INDUSTRY		
Industry Group*a*	% of Women Sales Reps	% of Women Sales Managers
Agriculture	7.3	0.0
Amusement/recreation services	63.2	25.0
Apparel/other textile products	44.4	17.0
Business services	34.9	26.2
Chemicals	4.3	0.0
Communications	12.3	2.3
Electronic components	6.2	4.8
Electronics	2.4	10.7
Fabricated metals	3.6	2.6
Food products	29.7	9.5
Instruments	27.8	21.1
Insurance	14.7	6.6
Lumber/wood products	15.4	0.0
Machinery	5.3	0.0
Manufacturing	15.8	2.0
Office Equipment	30.3	24.8
Paper/allied products	28.9	11.0
Primary metal products	18.9	6.7
Printing/publishing	39.7	11.1
Rubber/plastics	12.3	4.8
Wholesale (consumer)	26.2	9.0
Wholesale (industrial)	29.5	12.3
Average	22.3%	9.9%

*a*Categories were selected and reported by Dartnell Corporation. The overall average has been calculated by *Sales and Marketing Management* based on data from these 22 industries.

SOURCE: Dartnell Corporation, *26th Survey of Sales Force Compensation* (1990).

Some of the most important laws affecting the sales world are those commonly referred to as antitrust laws. These laws were created specifically to ensure that organizations compete fairly with one another, and each is designed to regulate a different aspect of competition. (These laws will be discussed in detail in Chapter 3.)

- The *Sherman Act of 1890* prohibits business practices that cause restraint of trade; specifically outlaws illegal contracts.
- The *Clayton Act of 1914* prohibits exclusive deals and tie-in agreements.
- The *Robinson-Patman Act of 1936* prohibits price discrimination. In simple terms, **price discrimination** occurs when a company offers two competing companies the same product amount at different prices. The act does allow quantity discounts. A company can also offer different prices to companies that are not competing against one another.
- The *FTC Act of 1914* prohibits any form of deception or unfair business methods.

In addition to following legal guidelines, today's sales managers have a social responsibility to look beyond restrictions set up by laws. Ethics is a very important consideration in managerial decisions. We will explore ethics and the legal and political system in more detail in Chapter 3.

Like ethics, green marketing is becoming a very important topic worldwide. **Green marketing** are laws and corporate responsibilities that are designed to protect the global environment. Many countries, particularly those in Europe, have become very environmentally conscious. As a result more and more laws are being passed that restrict or regulate marketing efforts that could harm the environment, such as excess packaging or packaging that is not biodegradable. Sales managers in this rapidly evolving global world must be aware of the need for green marketing.

TECHNOLOGY

The single greatest environmental change in the world of sales in the past decade has been the dramatic change in technology. Not only have products themselves become more technical and complex, but so has the way we sell them. Today salesforces sell more than a single product; they emphasize systems. Technology is allowing companies to sell products worldwide and in a timely manner. Products and systems are becoming so complex that we use teams, or centers, of sellers and buyers to negotiate and complete complicated business deals. As a result, the traditional single salesperson may be extinct in some technical industries.

Technology has had an effect on sales organizations at both the macro and micro level. At the macro level, technology has allowed management to improve strategic decision making through a number of methods, which will be discussed in the next section. At the micro level, technology has changed the way salespeople perform their daily jobs. Although it has resulted in vast improvements, technological automation is not cheap. Eastman Kodak's Office Imaging Division has calculated that automating its salesforce costs an average of $14,000 initially and an additional $5,000 a year in maintenance. Pfizer reports a different problem: younger sales reps spend too much time using the technological tools, while older sales reps tend to let the high tech tools go unused because they are resistant to new methods.[17] Let's examine the changing environment brought on by technology.

Macro Improvements: Strategic Decision Making

One of the most dramatic trends in technology has been the improvement in information and communication available through a channel that has been dubbed the Information Superhighway. What is it, and how can it affect business? Simply put, the **Information Superhighway** is a loosely configured, rapidly growing network of 25,000 corporate, institutional, educational, and research computer systems around the world. It began as a creation of the Defense Department in the late 1960s because the U.S. government was interested in an information network that would survive a nuclear attack. After nearly 20 years of being used primarily by research and educational institutions via the Internet, in the last 5 years it has become accessible to a much larger group of people, including individuals in their homes and offices as well as organizations.

How can the Superhighway be strategically useful? In short, it is a tool that is rapidly increasing in popularity in the business world, joining the telephone, fax, and telex as daily means of organizational communication.[18] IBM, for example, does developmental work with other companies and engineers, and strategic leaders communicate with their counterparts using a system such as the Internet. Rather than travel from lab to lab or office to office, the management team logs in on shared workstations among the collaborating institutions.[19] The results have been improved efficiency, improved communication, decreasing expenses, and better relations with new shared partners.

The Information Superhighway is not just for large *Fortune 500* organizations. In a survey commissioned by IBM, small business executives predict that the Information Superhighway will have powerful applications for them as well. Order transmittals, preparation of manufacturing specifications for suppliers or customers, market price checker, video conferencing, tax filing, review of jobs up for bid, and forecasting are just some of the tasks for which the Information Superhighway is used. The Superhighway has a great impact on organizations that want to increase their global business because it allows small businesses to compete globally by shrinking the difference in time and place.[20]

It has become much more cost efficient to compete in markets where much of the business can now be handled through the Superhighway. In fact, many of the business leaders surveyed by IBM feel that the Information Superhighway has leveled the playing field with their larger, more powerful competitors. For example, Larry Grant, owner of Grant's Flowers and Greenhouses, is in the vanguard of this new cyberspace. As a result of using the Internet his 1993 sales matched all his other, more traditional methods of sales.[21]

The rapidly increasing use of the Information Superhighway promises some staggering effects on sales today and tomorrow (see Exhibit 2.5). Don E. Schultz, a marketing communications professor at Northwestern University, indicates that most of the marketing and sales concepts we currently know are becoming obsolete. He shocked an audience at a recent Direct Marketing Day in New York with the

EXHIBIT 2.5		
THE NET EFFECT OF THE INFORMATION SUPERHIGHWAY ON SALES MANAGEMENT		
Item	Possible Upside	Possible Downside
1. Communication	• More immediate communication with customers and suppliers	• Less face-to-face interaction—superficial relationship
2. Sales team	• Organizations can more easily implement team concept; physical distance not a problem	• None
3. Sales calls	• More calls possible in shorter time frame	• Fewer field salespeople needed
4. Sales office	• More offices at home	• Less face-to-face customer contact
5. Management	• More empowerment for salesperson	• Fewer organizational interactions
6. Sales service	• Faster customer information	• Less face-to-face interaction
7. International business	• Less international travel	• None
	• More global interaction	• None

BOX 2.1
THE ELECTRONIC SECRETARY OF THE NEAR FUTURE

It's 7:30 A.M., and you're getting ready to leave your hotel room. You turn to your computer and say, "System on."

"Good morning," the machine responds. "Are you ready to review your appointment calendar?"

"Sure. First summarize e-mail traffic. I didn't have a chance to scan last night because I got in so late."

"You have received 37 messages in the past 24 hours. Twenty are low priority and have been filed in your home machine for review when your trip is over. Ten are medium priority and are stored in my memory for review at your convenience today. I suggest you scan the seven high-priority messages before you begin the day's activities."

"First let's go over my day's schedule. I remember I had six appointments. Are they still on?"

"One was canceled. During the newswire scan you requested, I picked up serious traffic problems that should be resolved by late afternoon, so I contacted the electronic agents of two of your appointments and rescheduled. They have confirmed the new times. I interfaced with your car's mapping system yesterday and the preferred routes are available in memory."

"Any hot points I should remember?"

"Two of your appointments have had birthdays within the past two weeks. Winston of United Products sent a letter of complaint about a delayed shipment four months ago. My records state the issue was resolved to their satisfaction. A special promotion we began last week for American International appears to have already had a positive impact."

"Good. Let's sit down and go over the trends and analysis for each meeting. Sound off. I'll remember better if I just read the text."

SOURCE: Tony Seideman, "Way Cool!" *Sales and Marketing Management* (June 1994): 10–11.

following quote: "Your experience is worthless if you've been in the business five years."[22]

The ability to instantaneously communicate with virtually anyone in the world will undoubtedly change the way we sell. First, it will make global selling much more viable for many sales organizations, although, as Dr. Schultz has stated, they may have to entirely relearn how to conduct business. Sales organizations can also create selling teams that are located at different sites (even multiple countries) but connected by the Internet. Soon we will be able to view individuals on the Information Superhighway, which may mean less need for a mobile salesforce, which in turn may cause territory assignments to be a concept of the past. There may be a downside to no longer needing face-to-face interaction, however. As information becomes more decentralized, there is a danger that users of the Superhighway will become more and more isolated from one another, causing selling relationships to be more difficult to maintain.[23]

The increased use of the Information Superhighway as a sales tool may also help eliminate the need for local or even regional sales offices because salespeople will work from their home offices on-line (virtual office will be considered later in this chapter). Changes brought about by the Information Superhighway are just now beginning to manifest themselves. However, it is clear that the overall increase in computer technology is as important to the environment of sales in this decade as the railroad was to sales in the 1700s and 1800s.

Micro Improvements: Salesforce Automation

The electronic revolution of the past decade has probably transformed day-to-day selling more than any other single change.[24] Tomorrow's field salespeople will start each day by gathering their sales tools: a sub-notebook PC, pen-based computer, palmtop digital assistant (PDA), personal communication assistant (PCA) (see Box 2.1), wireless phone, portable video, and pager.[25] Think of the electronic devices that are routinely used by salespeople today and how they have changed the face of selling. Laptop computers, home-office faxes, cellular phones, and portable copiers have become such an integral part of the daily job that a salesperson who retired 10 or more years ago might not recognize the job today.

Advances in technology have also created a new term, **mobile-oriented selling**, which is defined as advances in technology that allow a salesperson to have all the necessities of a physical office in a nonoffice setting. Mobile-oriented selling allows the salesperson to spend more time with the customer and less time traveling to the business office for account information, copying, or secretarial support.

Virtual Office.   Another trend that is rapidly emerging is the virtual office. A **virtual office** is best described as an office that consists of a portable computer and other technological tools, whether they reside in a home office or are portable. (See Box 2.2 for an example of a hotel virtual office.) Virtual offices allow salespeople to perform many of the duties traditionally provided by a branch office, including storage file, communications, and a place to work. Virtual offices are dependent on (1) the establishment of "anytime, anywhere" communication links between the salesperson and a district office and (2) the sales reps having access to high-quality information.[26]

The instant access created by a virtual office has changed the way salespeople perform their jobs, but it has also created new processes for management. For instance, virtual offices have lessened the need for local sales branch offices. Management is now supervising, leading, motivating, and coaching in absentia rather than in person. The result may be that sales managers will be assigned larger sales units as computer networks play the communication and information roles. Management expert Gil Gordon estimates that by the year 2000 more than one-third of the workforce will maintain nontraditional work schedules and will work at least in part from their virtual home office. GHK Company, an Oklahoma-based natural gas company, has revamped its entire workforce such that its salespeople work out of their homes in smaller, project-oriented teams. Many of the sales personnel are part-timers who meet in "virtual meetings" conducted via video screens.[27]

Lotus Development Corporation has also adopted the virtual office format, with salespeople working from their home computers. Now Lotus sales managers must stay in the field daily to work with their salespeople.[28] In this case, the result of the virtual office is greater responsibility for the salesperson, with more decision making occurring further out in the field.

Virtual offices also have societal advantages. Most two-income families with children at home long to have the ability to have a parent work from home. The virtual office allows one or both working parents to spend time at home, eliminating

---

BOX 2.2
NO MORE DARK AGE HOTELS

Gone are the days when the most high-tech item in a business traveler's hotel room was a telephone. Today there are fax machines and dataport-equipped telephones in nearly every room. Some hotels even offer travelers the option of renting a cellular phone.

Hotel technology is constantly changing. Larry Chervenak, president of Chervenak, Keane & Company, Inc., a New York–based international hotel technology consultant and editor of the *CKC Report: The Hotel Technology Newsletter,* offers some trends to watch for:

- The Philadelphia Marriott has recently become the pilot site for the initial version of the "Room That Works," a joint effort between Marriott International, AT&T, and Steelcase Inc. The mission? To recreate a guest room as a work-friendly environment, which features a large console table and mobile writing desk, a movable task light, an adjustable chair, two power outlets, and a PC modem jack mounted in the console top. This room will be rolled out in 4,000 Marriott rooms in 15 top markets this year.
- In January the Michaelangelo, a 178-room midtown Manhattan hotel that caters to business travelers, added SmartDesks to ten of its larger rooms. The SmartDesk project—a joint effort with Aegis, a Boston-based hotel business services company—lets visitors have a workstation in their rooms for an extra $30–$35 per day. The rooms with workstations, which must be reserved at least one or two weeks ahead of time, are complete with a full-size desk, a Hewlett Packard 486 computer with 14-inch screen and built-in high-speed data modem, and a fax/printer.
- In April Fourth Communications Network, Inc., a San Jose–based interactive television and technology company, began deploying the world's first voice mail-on-television/fax-on-television system in 9,000 rooms in major business hotels across the country. A business traveler gives anyone who might be sending a fax either a special Fourth Communication number or the hotel fax number. The person can see whether or not any faxes have arrived by either checking the room phone for a blinking light or by pressing "fax mailbox" from a television menu of options that appears when the TV set is on. The faxes can then be read from the television screen.

SOURCE: Melissa Campanelli, "No More Dark Age Hotels," *Sales and Marketing Management,* Part 2 (June 1995): 9.

some need for child care programs. A second societal advantage is the reduction of daily commuting, thus saving energy costs and reducing air pollution.[29] In cities such as Mexico City, where individuals can only drive their cars on specified days, the virtual office is becoming an answer to a growing worldwide environmental threat.

For those who must travel, the virtual office concept has gone one step further: the mobile virtual office. Zeeland, Michigan–based MO-V has created a fully equipped office inside a Chevrolet Astro EXT. Chuck Lippert, president of MO-V, states that the mobile office is the perfect solution for the salesperson who needs office technology but who also needs to be in the field daily. The mobile office, which includes a 486 notebook computer, desk ink-jet printer, fax, cellular phone, and desk, can be leased for $600 a month. Jeff Brown of U.S. Cellular makes use of the mobile office while waiting to see a customer. If he must wait for a customer at the customer's place of business, Brown simply goes to the parking lot and works in his mobile office. He is paged when the customer is ready.[30]

The virtual and home office concepts are further enhanced through a number of technological tools. Some of these advances in selling technology include the laptop and portable computers.

Laptop/Notebook Computers. The personal computer has been used by salespeople since the early 1980s, although originally its use was restricted to typing correspondence. By the end of the 1980s, however, laptop-style computers were being used more extensively by salespeople and for multiple purposes. Better technology rapidly improved the laptop as the weight and size continued to diminish (Exhibit 2.6). The five-to-seven-pound notebook computer made great strides in the early 1990s, followed by the four-to-five pound pen-based computer and the one-pound palmtop computer.

The uses for laptop computers have also changed. Originally they were used mainly for developing proposals, writing letters, building databases, and communicating by mail.[31] Now laptops are used for making sales calls in which presentations are tailored to the customer using multimedia computerized graphics, animation, video, and slide shows. **Multimedia** is a broad category that encompasses applications far beyond the simple text and graphic limitations of traditional computing systems and allows access to wider spectrums of technology including full motion video, high-fidelity audio, graphic animation, still photographs, and other developing techniques.[32] The appeal of multimedia has grown because it allows salespeople to take the power and emotion of television and tailor it to the decision maker. Interactive presentations allow customers to decide what they would like to see next in the presentation. Luda Tovey, president of Oberon Productions, a Toronto-based company that creates interactive multimedia CD disks, believes that multimedia presentations are much superior to overheads or flip charts because of the required active participation of the customer.[33] Salespeople at AT&T use multimedia in their sales calls; the company updates the salesforce by mailing CDs with current information.[34] 3M Corporation has found that the use of multimedia will not help an unprepared salesperson, but a good salesperson can use multimedia presentations to boost customer retention of the information being presented.

Laptops have also increased the levels of communication and information sharing between salesperson and headquarters. Sales reps can download account information to their headquarters on a daily basis and thus provide extensive market research information for upper management. Yellow Freight, one of the country's

EXHIBIT 2.6			
LAPTOP, NOTEBOOK, AND POCKET COMPUTER SALES			
U.S. Market	1989	1990	1994
Laptop	976,000	1,100,000	1,900,000
Notebook	69,000	311,000	3,900,000
Hand-held	34,000	159,000	3,200,000

SOURCE: Dataquest and the Gartner Group as quoted in Thayer C. Taylor, "The PC Evolution: Desktop . . . Laptop . . . Palmtop . . . ?" *Sales and Marketing Management* (February 1991): 50–58.

largest trucking companies, has used laptops and the Information Superhighway to greatly improve customer service and has transformed the traditional Yellow Freight salesperson into a customer consultant.[35] Having instantaneous customer information has been critical to Carl Zeiss, Inc, too. Carl Zeiss is a producer of 54 different kinds of microscopes, each of which has 30 to 40 components that must be individually described in catalogs. Before they had laptops, Zeis salespeople had to return to the office to prepare diagrams and bids by researching the spec sheets by hand. The diagrams were then sent to headquarters for confirmation. All tolled, it took 2 to 3 days to get back to the customer. Now the Zeiss salesforce carries laptops, and the entire process is performed in front of the customer in a matter of minutes. On-the-spot preparation has increased the number of orders and reduced the number of errors.[36]

In spite of all the advantages, there are downsides to laptops. Merck Frost, a Canadian subsidiary of Merck Pharmaceuticals, found the laptop reports so useful that they began requiring more and more reports. Sales reps were spending their evenings preparing reports. "We had created a technical monster," says Rod Dranfield, director of sales in the Western region.[37] Fortunately, a companywide task force reduced or redirected the need for the reports. The occasional negatives will not slow the laptop computer from continuing to evolve and play a more important role in daily activities across more industries.

Voice mail/E-mail.   Most companies now have some version of voice mail. **Voice mail** is like a home telephone answering machine without the machine. It allows a caller to leave a detailed message for the salesperson and for the salesperson to retrieve messages from the voice mail system while away from the office. Voice mail has become a major advantage because salespeople can be out of the office for the majority of the day and still be able to call into the office to receive phone messages. Voice mail allows the salesperson to remain in contact with the customer base, management, suppliers, and peers. However, one traditional complaint from many customers is the lack of service received when the salesperson is out of the office, particularly when that salesperson is on the road. Generally speaking, though, voice mail is an important communication technology, and any improvement in communication for an organization means increased selling efficiency and productivity. (See Box 2.3 for a discussion on voice mail.)

Electronic mail, or **e-mail**, as it is more commonly known, has become an even more flexible method of communicating. E-mail allows the salesperson to stay in contact with the customer base through an on-line computer network interface such as the Internet. It also encourages more communication and information sharing among salespeople and their managers, suppliers, and peers, which in turn helps build more team camaraderie.[38]

E-mail is not without its problems, however. The simplicity of the communication process can be problematic because people are sometimes startlingly blunt with their messages. Also, receivers of messages are not able to "read" voice tone, as they might in phone or personal conversations. As a result, e-mail language and symbols have emerged, as shown in Exhibit 2.7. Moreover, the sheer volume of e-mail messages can be overwhelming.

BOX 2.3

GETTING VALUE FROM VOICE MAIL

Voice mail is a technology many salespeople love, but others love to hate. Used effectively, it can eliminate phone tag and speed the transfer of information, a boon to improving customer service.

There's no real magic to voice mail; preparation and a positive attitude are all a salesperson needs to use it effectively. We suggest the following techniques to get the most out of voice mail:

- Be prepared to leave a message on a cold call without a strong referral. Instead, contact the client's secretary to find out when the client will return. If you do have a referral, leave a message stating your name and company, your referral's name and company, and a brief benefit statement.
- If you're calling a client who needs specific information, leave a clear, detailed message with that information. If you need information from a client, leave a concise message asking for the information you need. The request for information can be handled before a call back is necessary.
- Always say your phone number slowly, and repeat it and your name at the end of the message. Your client will appreciate not having to listen to the message twice.
- Smile. It will leave an upbeat-sounding message that will stand out from all the other "Please call me" messages.
- Always ask for a call back day and time. It may not guarantee a call back at that time, but it can help.
- Don't leave bad news on voice mail. Bad news should be delivered directly to the client. Instead, leave a message stating that there's a problem that needs to be handled by such and such a date or time. This should elicit a quick call back.

SOURCE: "Getting Value From Voice Mail," *Sales and Marketing Management* (May 1994): 81.

Sending e-mail messages is so much easier than printing and addressing envelopes—even easier than phoning someone. Now, through the Internet you can receive e-mail messages from virtually anyone in the world. As a result, if you don't check your mail for a couple of days, the number of messages can be overpowering. One sales manager indicated that he gets as many as 100 to 150 e-mail messages a day. To cut down on unnecessary e-mails, many organizations have created **e-mail protocols**, or rules, as to how the e-mail system can be used within the organization.[39]

E-mail technology has improved to the level that, if properly equipped, a salesperson can check e-mail messages anywhere, anytime by wireless transmissions. Joe Davis, CEO of Open Systems Technology, a systems engineering firm that consults with companies about networking through wireless technologies, has become known as the "King of e-mail." Davis and many others use the RadioMail service, which receives Davis's e-mail messages and immediately transmits them to RAM Mobile Data service, which in turn transmits them to his laptop computer and GE Ericsson Mobidem. By using RadioMail in combination with a pager, Davis always knows when a message has come in. Because Davis does much of his sales work from the back seats of cabs, in restaurants, or virtually anywhere else, the e-mail system has replaced his need for cellular phone service.

EXHIBIT 2.7
E-MAIL LANGUAGE

<G>	=	grinning
<L>	=	laughing
LOL	=	laughing out loud
FOCL	=	falling out of chair laughing
:-}	=	smirk
;-?	=	licking lips
:-J	=	tongue in cheek
PTMM	=	Please, tell me more.
OMG	=	Oh My God!
:X	=	Ooops!
:p	=	pppth? (sticking tongue out)
YSWUS	=	Yeah, sure, whatever you say.
SGAL	=	Sheesh, get a life.
-)	=	dumb question or person
PITA	=	pain in the ass
:-(	=	unhappy
:-	=	disgusted
IMO	=	in my opinion
{}	=	hug
****	=	kisses
BRB	=	be right back
YIU	=	Yes, I understand.
:::POOF:::	=	out of here, signing off now
C U L8R	=	See you later.

SOURCE: Ross Weiland, "The Message is the Medium," *Performance* (September 1995): 37.

Video Conferencing.   In an age of economic woes, video conferencing capabilities can do a lot to reduce expenses and provide time-saving productivity. **Video conferencing,** the most popular form of multimedia in the world today, allows people in separate geographic locations to see each other and work together over phone lines. At present, most video conferencing systems connect two or more parties by using rooms equipped with video capability. New technology, such as Intel Corporation's ProShare™, allows PC-based video and data conferencing. As the two parties communicate by computer, their respective live pictures are displayed in one corner of the computer monitor. At the same time, data files can be displayed and worked with on the remainder of the screen.

Video conferencing has reduced the cost levels of many organizations by reducing travel costs. For example, Pier 1 Imports uses video conferencing when buying products from Pacific Rim sellers. Obviously some trips are necessary, but when a new Pier 1 product is being purchased, a video conference session can show the product without either party leaving the office.

Video conferencing is also saving a lot of time and work productivity by allowing long-distance meetings without leaving the office. United Postal Service (UPS) finds that video conferencing allows UPS personnel around the world to meet their peers and some customers whom they had never before seen. Putting a face to a name has been an important outcome for UPS.[40]

As video conferencing capabilities become less expensive and more commonplace, a lot of routine sales business may be conducted by video conference hookup. A 1994 study indicated that 42 percent of *Fortune 500* companies have implemented video conferences as a routine part of business. It is estimated that the video conferencing market will grow from the 1994 amount of $663 million to $10 billion by the year 2000.[41]

Mobile Equipment.   Perhaps the most popular piece of mobile equipment is the cellular telephone. We have all seen people talking as they drive down the interstate or around the city. Although the safety of driving and talking is questionable, there is no doubt about the advantage of cellular phones for salespeople. Cellular phones are great for making appointments while stuck in traffic or for a quick check-in at the office. They allow salespeople to stay in touch with their offices or provide customer service even when traveling. They can also enable a salesperson to close deals without actually meeting with the customer. For example, one employee of Above Software, Inc., had a doctor's appointment that she had already postponed three times, but she also had a customer who wanted to close a deal at the same time. Instead of having to choose one over the other, she accomplished both! First she read the proposal and used her cellular telephone to call the customer and discuss the details. When she arrived at her doctor's office, she used the doctor's fax to send the contract proposal to the customer. The customer reviewed the document, signed it, and faxed the document back to the doctor's office and the sales individual. The Above Software rep closed the order and kept the doctor's appointment simultaneously.[42]

As cellular costs continue to decrease, more and more companies will begin investing in cellular phones for their salesforces.[43] Cellular phones are also becoming more technically advanced. Chrysler was one of the first automobile companies to produce the visorphone, a dealer-installed cellular telephone with automatic redial, 100-number memory and a 5-year warranty. Just flip your driver visor down to dial and then flip it back up to talk—leaving your hands free.[44]

Pagers are another form of mobile equipment that have been an integral part of many salespeople's lives for some time because they allow the salespeople to leave their offices yet remain in constant contact. Pager' capabilities range from indicating a phone number to transmitting short messages.

Dictaphones have also become popular with salespeople who spend a lot of time in their cars and who also may have significant correspondence. The messages can later by typed on the salesperson's laptop or taken to the office (if there is one!) for keyboarding.

Faxes.   Although facsimile, or fax, technology has existed since the early 1970s, faxes did not become standard business tools until the late 1980s. Faxes allow letters and documents to be sent over a phone line so they can be received and acted upon immediately. If a salesperson needs a customer to see a bid or product specification, the customer can have it in moments—quite an improvement over alternatives such as overnight delivery by companies such as Federal Express.

In a recent study of purchasing managers, the fax machine was listed as the most essential machine in conducting business.[45] Faxes may soon become a secondary communication device, however, as computer-generated video conferencing and e-mail systems become more universally accepted. With video conferencing and e-mail, information can be sent computer-to-computer without any retyping. In addition, lengthy documents can be transmitted easily and instantaneously, which is a big advantage over the fax system. Computer will also have the advantage of having multiple parties communicating simultaneously. Nonetheless, the fax currently remains an important daily sales tool and has clearly increased the efficiency of conducting business.

Videotape.   Videotapes are used in most training programs, especially for taping and reviewing role plays. Salespeople should view themselves on tape to help improve their communication skills and critique their own presentation abilities. Many companies also send videotapes as an infomercial prior to a sales call or even in place of a sales call.

One form of videotape is **interactive video**, which is being used in salesforce training (see Chapter 11 for more detail). Interactive video is a merger of computer, laser disc, and video technology that allows the participant to conduct trial sales presentations on computer-generated customers, who then react to the decisions and approaches made by the salesperson.

Electronic Sales Offices.   The **electronic sales office** is the process of taking orders from the customer's computer to the seller's computer. It is used primarily for simple reorder and rebuy situations. The process begins with the buyer's computer calling the seller's computer and ordering a quantity of the seller's product. Human interaction does not occur until the product is actually picked up and delivered. The electronic sales office can reduce expenses by taking the salesperson out of the routinized, simple rebuy order. The field salesperson stays involved with the account by periodically calling on the account to maintain relationships, upgrade the product being sold, and determine if there are problems with the account. However, by eliminating the salesperson from routine calls, a great deal of the salesperson's time and effort are saved, thereby resulting in an enormous reduction of expenses for an organization. Understandably, some salespeople are concerned that the electronic sales office will eventually eliminate their jobs. In reality, however, the electronic sales office is a low threat to the field salesperson because of its very limited and specific capabilities. Human interactions will always remain important because the human element is a large part of any business decision.

Telemarketing.   Telemarketing is a technological advance that has played an important role in sales strategy, particularly in the past 15 years. **Telemarketing** is defined as a systematic and continuous program of communicating with customers and prospects via telephone and/or other person-to-person electronic media. Telemarketing began as a means of facilitating customer service. Traditionally, telemarketing departments staffed the 1-800 numbers that were used for complaints, prod-

| | | Company | |
| | What Caller | Representative's | Caller's Time |
Company	Receives	Phone Manner	on Hold
SmithKline	Refund	Cheerful	None
Duracell	Coupon	Sympathetic	None
Kraft General Foods	Coupon	Professional	None
Mars Inc.	Refund[a]	Efficient	None
Nestle SA	Coupon	Efficient	None
Warner-Lambert	Refund[a]	Efficient	None
Gerber	Coupon	Earnest	30 seconds
Frito-Lay	Refund	Cheerful	1 minute
Mattel	Refund	Professional	3 minutes
Colgate-Palmolive	Coupon	Cheerful	3 minutes, 46 seconds
Binney & Smith	Coupon	Cheerful	5 minutes
Dow	Refund	Professional	5 minutes

EXHIBIT 2.8

CALLING THE HOTLINES: WHAT WE FOUND

[a] *Consumer gets the refund after the product is returned.*

SOURCE: Carl Quintanilla and Richard Gibson, "Do Call Us: More Companies Install 1-800 Phone Lines," *The Wall Street Journal* (April 20, 1994): B1.

uct inquiries, and other forms of information. Customer service people today typically work with incoming and outgoing calls and remain an important strategy in keeping customers satisfied (see Exhibit 2.8).

Telemarketing is sometimes negatively perceived by the public because of home consumer telemarketing (which many companies now refer to as *teleselling* because of the negative image of the term *telemarketing*). Unfortunately, many people still perceive telemarketing as the phone call that arrives during dinner attempting to sell you something you really don't want. In a business setting, however, telemarketing is time and cost efficient for both parties. Many sales organizations use telemarketing as a part of their sales strategy (see Chapter 8 for more detail). A business telemarketing program has a much more favorable image and has become a necessity to buyers and sellers in many industries.

Telemarketing has cut costs in a number of companies because it is a much less expensive sales tool than a field salesperson. Organizations needed a way to cut some of their sales call expenses and at the same time maintain or even improve customer satisfaction. While telemarketing is an efficient alternative for many companies, it is not designed to be a replacement for the field salesforce; rather it serves as a support unit for the salesforce. Telemarketing can perform certain activities in a more financially expedient manner. For example, in some industries making calls on rural accounts proves to be very costly for field salespersons. Sales executives at Procter & Gamble have found that telemarketing is an excellent tool for allowing them to call on many of their rural accounts for a fraction of the cost. In turn, P&G field salespeople are free to concentrate on the larger, more profitable accounts.[46]

SUMMARY

Selling is an ever-evolving discipline that has a long and varied history. Selling and marketing have evolved through four eras, as illustrated in Exhibit 2.1. The sales environment can be defined as those variables that have an immediate effect on sales and sales management and which are beyond the control of the organization. Variables included in the sales environment are the customer; competitors; economics; social-demographics, legal, and political forces; and technology. In the past two decades the customer has begun to have higher expectations based on quality and value. Relationship selling has become a key concept in the 1990s. Salespeople must conduct needs analyses with the customer account and develop relationships throughout the buying organization.

Competition has increased domestically in the United States and from international sources. Economics have dictated different sales strategies for different customers depending upon the economic stability and growth in a region. The demographics of the salesforce is changing dramatically with an increase in women, minorities, and international employees. Diversity has become a necessity in the sales organization. Last, the political and legal environment dictates sales activities that are regulated by antitrust laws, including the Sherman Act, the Clayton Act, the Robinson-Patman Act, and the FTC Act.

Finally, technology has evolved such that the electronic revolution has produced technological innovations for both strategic management (macro) and the day-to-day tactical operations (micro). The macro innovation revolves around the new and developing Information Superhighway which has allowed global and domestic selling to expand. Micro innovation revolves around technological sales tools such as the virtual office, laptop computer, voice mail, e-mail, video conferencing, mobile equipment, fax machines, videotape, electronic field offices, and telemarketing. These technologies have become a vital part of the daily activities of today's salespeople.

KEY TERMS

sales environment	Information Superhighway
relationship selling	mobile-oriented selling
needs analysis	virtual office
buying center	multimedia
selling center	voice mail
value-added reseller	electronic mail
common law	e-mail
caveat emptor	e-mail protocols
statutory law	video conferencing
administrative law	interactive video
price discrimination	electronic sales office
green marketing	telemarketing

DISCUSSION QUESTIONS

1. How did marketing and sales evolve prior to the 1900s?
2. What is the sales environment, and what are the variables that comprise the environment?
3. How has the customer changed over the past two decades?
4. Who is the physical buyer, and how has that definition changed with the advent of buying and selling centers?
5. How can laws and politics affect the sales organization?
6. How has technology changed the way salespeople and sales managers do their daily jobs?
7. What is mobile-oriented selling, and why has it had an effect on the sales organization?
8. How has technology improved communication within the sales organization?
9. Is the electronic sales office a threat to future sales jobs? Why or why not?
10. What are some arguments for and against the use of telemarketing?

PROBLEMS

1. Jennifer Jackson is talking with one of her best customers, who has just informed her that he will be changing suppliers after eight years of doing business with her. "You screwed up my delivery and it cost me money! I'm going with the Mitsubishi line." What can Jennifer do to salvage the situation?

2. Stan Wickowski is a sales representative for a pharmaceutical company. He has just learned that his company has merged with a former competitor and now he will be selling his product as well as the former competitor's. How will this affect Stan and his job?

3. Lee Martin is a 54-year-old salesperson who is not used to working with businesswomen. He likes to party with his customers, tell an off-color joke or two, and do things the way they have always been done. What does the future hold for Lee?

4. Barbara Lopez has just been issued a new laptop computer to go with her home-office fax, cellular phone, and portable copier. She thinks about how times have changed since she began selling 8 years ago. How has technology changed the way salespeople work, and what effect has technology had on Barbara?

5. Pat Davis spends half of his day talking on the phone to customers, tracking orders, and looking for new business. Recently, one of his colleagues implied that he was becoming a telemarketer. Pat did not like the inference. Why was Pat unhappy with the inference? How have telemarketing activities become a part of the sales job?

SHORT CASE
WHAT TO DO ABOUT THE ENVIRONMENT?

BACKGROUND

John Jankowski has been selling in the chemical industry for the past 15 years. John majored in chemistry and minored in business at a well-respected California University. He accepted a sales job for Alton Chemicals and was pleased to be in the chemical industry. He began selling immediately after his graduation from college. In 1985 John was promoted to sales manager for the northwest territory, which included Washington, Oregon, Idaho, and Northern California. In 1994 John became regional manager for the western United States with managerial responsibility over seven districts. Alton Chemical is a very conservative sales organization that has chosen not to invest in a lot of technological sales tools because of salesforce resistance to new selling methods. During the past 15 years the chemical industry has had its ups and downs, but John is basically happy that he chose the chemical industry for his career.

SITUATION

Alton Chemical has 82 salespeople, 93 percent of whom are Caucasian and male. The average age of the salesforce is 42, and the average tenure of the salesperson with Alton is 9.3 years. Sales have decreased 18 percent companywide over the past 5 years, primarily because of new global competition. Customers have become more demanding and price competitive. Alton Chemical was recently sued for misrepresentation of product attributes even though the mistaken claim

seems to have been an honest misunderstanding. The productivity and efficiency of the salesforce is not what it should be. Jim Jarrod, vice-president of sales, has called in John and his eastern counterpart, Charlie Parentin, to discuss some of these environmental problems. Jim says, "Gentlemen, it is time for us to reexamine our sales organization. Sales are not as high as they should be, and our market share has slipped. We seem to be beset with sales problems. I'm not convinced our salesforce is as efficient as it should or could be."

PROBLEM

John and Charlie have been told to do a complete analysis of the sales environment and how that environment might affect Alton. The two managers have 2 weeks to finish the analysis. Jim has told them to concentrate on examining the needs of the customers and how the Alton salesforce can satisfy those needs. John thinks, "Great, where do we start?"

QUESTIONS

1. What sales environment variables should be examined by John and Charlie, and why?
2. What problems does the current composition of the Alton Chemical salesforce possess?
3. Why might Alton's customer needs and wants have changed over time and, in general, what could account for decreasing sales and market share?
4. Could technology improve sales efficiency? If so, which technological tools would you recommend for Alton?

PHARMICEAUX, INC.—ETHICAL DRUG DIVISION

The role play exercises which appear at the end of Chapters 3–17 are based on sales management situations that occur at a large fictional pharmaceutical company named

Pharmiceaux. Please read the following case carefully and refer back to it as necessary as you complete the role play exercises throughout the book.

PHARMICEAUX HISTORY

Pharmiceaux, Inc. (pronounced *far-ma-co*) was established in 1939 by William M. Russell, an established general practitioner and weekend gourmet cook, in the garage of his home in Lafayette, Louisiana. Russell's mission for Pharmiceaux was "to contribute to the betterment of society through quality research and development of pharmaceutical products." In the years since, Pharmiceaux has enjoyed constant growth, interrupted only by a tragic laboratory fire in 1944 that halted operations for a 10-month period. Although the company went public in 1951, the Russell family continues to hold majority ownership. Pharmiceaux's involvement in all aspects of the pharmaceutical business—from

EXHIBIT I				
PHARMICEAUX BALANCE SHEETS				
December 31, 1996 and 1995				
	1996 (000s)		1995 (000s)	
Assets				
Current Assets				
Cash and Cash Equivalents	$ 300,772	12.4%	$ 177,417	9.6%
Receivables	450,719	18.6	364,216	19.8
Inventories	258,681	10.7	210,682	11.4
Other Current Assets	555,068	22.9	400,894	21.8
Total Current Assets	1,565,240	64.6	1,153,209	62.6
Property and Equipment	413,890	17.1	356,539	19.4
Goodwill	175,377	7.2	104,915	5.6
Other Assets	267,450	11.1	227,742	12.4
	$2,421,957	100.0%	$1,842,405	100.0%
Liabilities and Stockholders' Equity				
Current Liabilities				
Accounts Payable	$328,832	13.6%	$247,360	13.5%
Income Taxes Payable	51,736	2.1	23,030	1.2
Current Portion of Long-Term Debt	80,000	3.3	100,000	5.4
Other Current Liabilities	339,151	14.0	193,420	10.5
Total Current Liabilities	799,719	33.0	563,810	30.6
Deferred Income Taxes	5,262	0.2	23,883	1.3
Long-Term Debt, less current portion	189,407	7.8	129,651	7.0
Other Liabilities	37,706	1.6	56,296	3.1
	1,032,094	42.6	773,640	42.0
Stockholders' Equity				
Common Stock	27,638	1.1	27,638	1.5
Additional Paid-in Capital	450,000	18.6	450,000	24.4
Retained Earnings[a]	912,225	37.7	591,127	32.1
	1,389,863	57.4	1,068,765	58.0
	$2,421,957	100.0%	$1,842,405	100.0%

[a]Dividends of $191,880 were paid in 1996.

EXHIBIT 2				
PHARMICEAUX STATEMENTS OF INCOME				
Years Ended December 31, 1996 and 1995				
	1996 (000s)		1995 (000s)	
Net Sales	$2,500,000	100.0%	$2,100,000	100.0%
Cost of Sales	578,744	23.1	535,662	25.5
Gross Profit	1,921,256	76.9	1,564,338	74.5
Selling, General, and Administrative Expenses	832,164	33.3	655,930	31.2
Research and Development	344,616	13.8	305,361	14.5
Income from Operations	744,476	29.8	603,047	28.7
Other Income	54,366	2.2	49,472	2.4
Interest Expense	(13,153)	0.5	(11,942)	0.6
Income Before Income Taxes	785,689	31.4	640,577	30.5
Income Taxes	272,711	10.9	225,183	10.7
Net Income	$512,978	20.5%	$415,394	19.8%
Earnings per Share	$1.86		$1.50	

research and discovery to development, marketing, and delivery—has allowed the company to build global brand identity.

Operational performance was superb in 1996 as Pharmiceaux attained its twentieth consecutive year of increased sales and earnings (see Exhibit 1). Pharmiceaux continued to move forward strategically and to increase its investments in advanced technology and new customer-service capabilities. Rapid change within the global health-care market continues to create enormous opportunity, and Pharmiceaux continues to rise to the challenges presented. Operating income increased to over $744 million (see Exhibit 2). Pharmiceaux also made significant progress on its strategic priorities of concentrating resources more intensively on selected high-potential growth opportunities, and of shifting its mix of business toward areas that will prosper in the type of health-care environment that it will face in the next decade.

Pharmiceaux is composed of several major divisions. The largest and oldest organizational unit is the Ethical Drugs Division (EDD). This division develops, manufactures, and distributes prescription drugs to pharmacies and hospitals. Pharmiceaux's other divisions include Medical Equipment, International, and National Accounts and Telemarketing. (See Exhibits 3 and 4 for organizational charts of the two Pharmiceaux regions.)

EDD OBJECTIVE

EDD's objective for the 1990s is to be the worldwide best-cost producer in its core pharmaceutical business. EDD considers "best-cost" to mean having low costs relative to competitors while attaining levels of quality and value that set the standards for the industry. EDD believes that in health care, where lives depend on drugs, high quality and value standards are mandatory. It is this conviction that motivates EDD in all aspects of its operation.

EDD ENVIRONMENT

EDD faces challenges in many aspects of its environment, including competition, government regulation, and changes in political and consumer preferences.

Competition

The world ethical drug market increased 13 percent from 1995 to $180 billion in 1996.

EXHIBIT 3

PHARMACEUTICAL DIVISION, EAST REGION

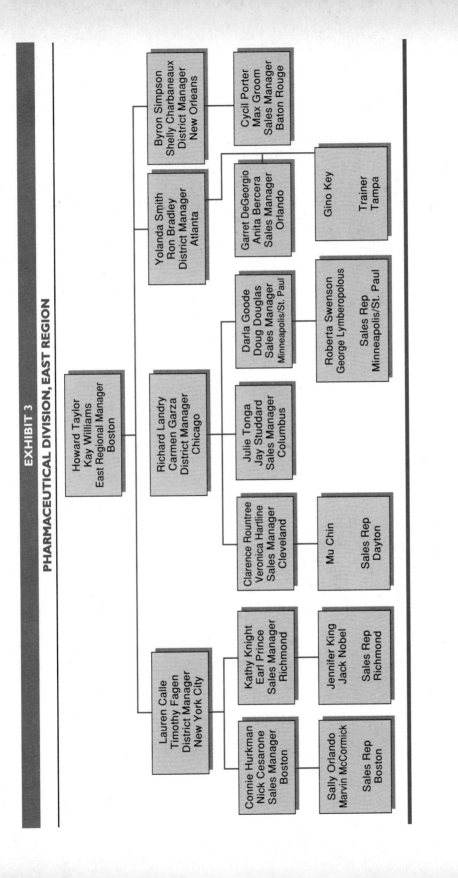

EXHIBIT 4

PHARMACEUTICAL DIVISION, WEST REGION

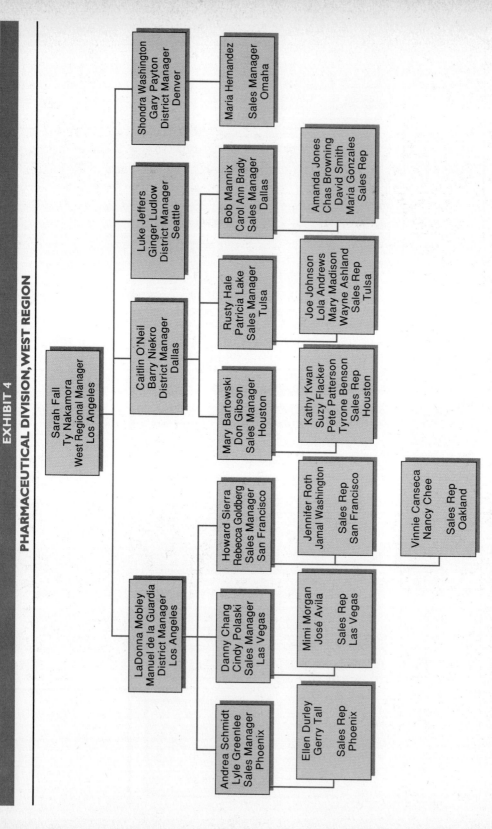

*If only one sales manager is used in the leadership role play, have Johnson, Andrews, Madison, and Ashland report to Houston.

The industry is somewhat fragmented with the top ten companies in the world taking only 28 percent market share among them. There have been few changes in the world ranking of pharmaceutical companies in 1996, with the top six occupying the same positions as in 1995. The principal reason for the stability in ranking is that all these companies are devoting significant resources to developing new products that will allow them to retain market share.

There is little doubt that the pharmaceutical industry has entered into a considerably tougher competitive global environment in the 1990s than in the 1980s. Two major reasons account for this: the large number of top-selling drugs expected to lose patent protection in the coming decade and the increasingly multinational nature of the market for drugs. Pharmiceaux EDD and other industry leaders are looking into market consolidation in order to counteract rising costs. Thus far, however, there have been few recent significant takeovers or mergers in the sector.

Government Regulation

EDD's major interaction with the government is with the drug approval process through the Food and Drug Administration (FDA). While this process has grown steadily more complex and time-consuming for most drugs, recent legislation speeds the process for drugs targeted for use by people with fatal or very rare diseases. EDD has maintained an excellent record with the FDA regarding drug approval.

Another regulatory issue is disposal of toxic waste. EDD was recently named by the Environmental Protection Agency as a potentially responsible party for cleanup costs at several hazardous waste sites. While EDD followed all the regulations in effect at the time the dumps were made, recent scientific findings point out the possible dangers to animal life posed by some of the chemical EDD dumped. Investigation of some of these sites is in a very preliminary stage. Although liability

for cleanup costs of such sites may legally be imposed without regard to the quantity of waste contributed, the company believes, based on all information available, it unlikely that it will incur any material costs in connection with these sites. EDD will also incur minimal costs in public relations, employee briefings on the situation, and corrective actions to prevent a recurring situation.

Consumer and Political Preferences

Political tension and public demand are making cost-effective treatment a financial imperative. The growing elderly population will create large potential new markets for treatment of disease with high medical need among patients over 65. However, since most of these patients are on some form of government insurance to pay for drugs, the drug industry must be extremely sensitive to changes in governmental policy on payment for drugs.

EDD'S MARKETING STRATEGY
Product

Five of the leading domestic drugs are currently manufactured by EDD.

- *Hydrazene* is the number one vaccine for hepatitis B and contributes 18 percent of Pharmiceaux's annual sales.
- *Beatbetter xlt*, a heart medication prescribed for patients with congenital heart disease, produces approximately 12 percent of Pharmiceaux's annual sales.
- *Pharmizeez*, a muscle relaxer, is one of EDD's oldest and most widely known medications. Despite competition from over-the-counter substitutes, sales of Pharmizees have been stable in the past nine quarters, varying from $197 to $198 million (approximately 7.9 percent of Pharmiceaux's annual sales).
- *Ulsir EX*, which is used in the short-term treatment of duodenal ulcers and other gastrointestinal disorders, is one of EDD's two fastest growing new products on the market. More than 3 million prescriptions

have been filled in the United States since its introduction in October 1989, and more than 500 clinical trials have been conducted involving more than 25,000 patients. Competitive analysis has shown that in its first three years on the market, Ulsir EX healed more patients in less time than its nearest competitor, resulting in a greater cost efficiency for the patient. One potential problem with this drug exists following questionable results in tests on laboratory mice. While available endoscopic evaluations and histologic examinations of biopsy specimens from humans have not detected a risk from short-term exposure to Ulsir, EDD has allocated an unusually large portion of Ulsir's budget to continued research as a precautionary measure.

- *Pharmipro,* the other new entry into the market, is an antibacterial agent which works through the inhibition of DNA synthesis. Pharmipro's release has been truly exciting to the pharmaceutical industry, as it demonstrates activity against organisms resistant to some other antibacterial agents on the market. The market potential for Pharmipro is substantial as it can be prescribed for all patients one year and older.

Despite these market leaders, however, EDD faces a problem common to all drug manufacturers: rapidly escalating drug development costs. The most recent estimate stands at $230 million per drug brought to the market. Key factors in escalating development costs include increasing regulatory requirements and lengthening regulatory delays, on top of increasing technology and skilled labor costs in the actual research and development process. A long-term trend that is having a significant effect on research and development costs is the change in underlying technology used to produce pharmaceuticals. Biotechnology, rather than inorganic chemistry, is the new frontier for drug development. At the present, however, these technologies are not well understood and are extremely expensive, even

by drug company standards. EDD hopes that increases in the efficiency of new drugs based on biotechnology may warrant premium prices and justify the high costs.

Price

The issue of drug pricing gives industry leaders great concern. Pricing pressures are coming from both government and private buying organizations. This pressure is supported by an ever-increasing number of satisfactory drugs on the market for various disorders, which makes the task of innovation that much more complicated. It is increasingly difficult to obtain price increases that match the rate of inflation, or to introduce new drugs at prices that yield a satisfactory return on investment. EDD must also be sensitive to the increasing number of generic drugs entering the market. Generic drugs available until now have often been unsatisfactory compared to alternatives. In the 1990s, however, increasing availability and quality of generic drugs will lead to their increased use. This will have a downward effect on drug pricing. EDD must also be sensitive to pricing issues related to the unification of Europe. It is currently thought that free flow of drugs across national borders in Western Europe will bring lower average prices since packaging and licensing regulations will become standardized.

Distribution

EDD distributes its products directly to hospitals, clinics, and pharmacies. It is recognized as an industry leader in this area, constantly seeking new means of distributing products more effectively and efficiently. One method EDD uses to serve customers with maximum cost efficiency is a new program within the Ethical Drugs Division called LinkPlus™, which provides "stockless" inventory management for hospitals and medical centers. The program streamlines the distribution of pharmaceuticals, significantly reducing costs in terms of time, storage, and handling. To interface with customers, all telephone lines are toll free. Twenty-two major medical centers are currently using the program, and EDD expects participation by many more within the next 2 years.

Promotion

EDD's promotional program includes advertising in medical journals, sponsoring trade shows and guest lecturers for local medical societies, and participating in public relations efforts aimed at regulators and legislators. Consistent with the rest of the industry, however, the bulk of EDD's promotional budget is spent on personal selling.

Sales Organization. EDD's salesforce is comprised of approximately 300 people (the organizational charts indicate those that appear in a role play). EDD's sales organization is flat and decentralized, allowing managers wide latitude in making decisions in their markets without first obtaining corporate approval. The country is divided into two geographic regions, each with four districts. Each regional manager (East and West) has responsibility for activities within the four districts within the region. These responsibilities include setting and communicating quotas, coordinating monthly and quarterly reports, filing monthly progress reports, conducting performance evaluations, preparing territorial budgets, and conducting division meetings. Each district manager oversees six sales managers and has authority for day-to-day operations within the district. The sales managers oversee six to eight sales representatives within the district and are also responsible for day-to-day operations.

The Salesforce. EDD's companywide emphasis on total quality management and employee empowerment has resulted in the development of a salesforce whose commitment to the company is unmatched in the industry. This is evidenced by the fact that turnover among EDD's sales representatives is half that of its two closest competitors. EDD is renowned for its emphasis on employee development (both personal and professional).

EDD's reputation within the industry is one of quality salesmanship. Representatives, for the most part, are known to be very professional and ethical in their business dealings. Whereas some of their competitors are known for playing dirty by making deals "under the table" or by buying doctors' business with lavish gifts or perks. EDD's policy strictly prohibits this type of conduct, which in some cases could result in termination.

EXHIBIT 5
A TYPICAL EDD SALES REPRESENTATIVE'S DAY

6:45–7:30	Rise and shine! Dress for the day.
7:30–8:00	Review all correspondence by checking voice mail, reading mail, and reviewing e-mail.
8:00–8:30	Print list of physicians in daily routing—review what was discussed last visit and what will be discussed today
9:00–11:30	Aim: To see 4–5 physicians. Review predetermined goal for discussion before each visit. Review names of office personnel. After each call, record details of discussion and goals for next visit. May schedule a lunch appointment.
11:30–12:00	Pick up food for lunch at physician's office. Drive to physician's office and prepare for lunch.
12:00–1:30	Doctor(s) and nurses have finished with patients and are ready for discussion over lunch. After lunch, record each discussion for future detail.
1:30–2:30	2–3 pharmacy calls.
2:30–5:00	Aim: To see 4–5 more physicians.
5:00–5:30	Clean car; reload samples for the next day.
5:30–6:00	Enter daily calls into computer and send via the phone line.

Much of EDD's success is due to its companywide dedication to customer involvement. EDD sales representatives are trained to be keenly aware of their customers to ensure their satisfaction with the service they receive. This trade servicing approach is characterized by emphasizing creative selling, providing detailed and accurate information, and servicing the customer whenever possible.

EDD's representatives must be efficient with their time. A typical sales representative's schedule begins early in the morning and involves meeting with several appointments throughout the day. Exhibit 5 details a typical day.

Recruiting. With a 300-person salesforce, given EDD's historically high retention, EDD must hire approximately 30 new sales persons annually. The 30 new salespeople replace those who resign, retire, or are promoted. It is quite common for a salesperson to be promoted to a sales management or to a marketing or general management position (EDD has made a practice of promoting from within whenever possible). Promoting from within mandates a particular emphasis on recruiting at the entry level. The majority of this entry-level recruiting is done through the top colleges and universities nationwide. In addition to campus recruiting, EDD works with private employment agencies, primarily in filling sales management positions. Owing to the competitive nature of the pharmaceutical industry, the high cost of training, and EDD's emphasis on developing relationships with customers, EDD places great emphasis on recruiting individuals that show strong potential based on leadership capabilities, intelligence, personal characteristics, and experience.

EDD's typical hire follows a five-step process:

Step 1: Introductory Interview. Interviews are first held by sales managers, who are responsible for a preliminary evaluation of applicants, their résumés, and their applications. It is important to screen the applicant's knowledge of the company and to assess the fit between the prospective employee's goals and personality with those of the company.

Step 2: Management Interview. The second interview is typically held in the district manager's office. The prospective employee is given the opportunity to meet with several employees, including the regional manager, whenever schedules permit.

Step 3: Aptitude Testing. EDD relies on a nationally known standardized aptitude test in order to compare various candidates on equal data. The series of tests requires about two hours of the applicant's time and is usually administered as a part of the second round of interviews.

Step 4: Background Check and Analysis of the Aptitude Test. The screening process continues with a background check. This inquiry includes talking with references provided by the applicant, researching the applicant's creditworthiness and driving record, and checking for prior records of illegal drug use. Additionally, each candidate is given a numerical rating based on the previously administered aptitude test.

Step 5: Placement. Once a candidate has successfully completed the interviews and has met set standards on the aptitude test, an offer is extended by the recruiter.

Compensation. Salespeople are compensated through a combination of salary and bonus. Entry-level salaries for newly hired sales representatives are comparable to EDD's number one competitor, as well as to entry-level sales positions with similar companies in other industries. It has been EDD's policy to give annual salary increases. These increases are commensurate with cost of living increases and an individual's merit achievements. In addition to an annual salary increase, all employees are eligible for a year-end bonus, which is determined by the rating earned in the evaluation process. EDD employees receive a comprehensive compensation package with full health and dental benefits. They are also eligible to participate in a companywide 401(k) plan as regulated by the Internal Revenue Service (IRS).

All employees in the salesforce are given a company car upon beginning their territory sales. As an employee moves into management, car upgrades are added as a potential bonus/reward. Sales representatives and managers who are required to travel are reimbursed for miles at the rate set by the IRS.

In 1995 EDD announced a new employee incentive by offering employees a variety of stock options that are payable after only five years of service with the company.

Motivation. Motivation and recognition have always been considered as cornerstones in EDD's human resources policies. This emphasis permeates every level of employee development and management—from recruitment through retirement. Employees are selected not only on the basis of their perceived capability, but also on the degree to which their goals, traits, needs, and wants are consistent with those of the organization. In addition, a great deal of time and resources are expended to maintain employee morale through various programs related to training, job review, and personal development.

To facilitate internal communication, managers are encouraged to operate under an "open door policy." In addition, written surveys are distributed to all employees, asking them to comment on product issues, corporate culture, and personal concerns.

Training. Each year EDD devotes a great deal of money in training to ensure that its employees are professional and well educated on issues affecting its customers, the end users, and the industry as a whole. All of EDD's newly hired sales representatives are required to attend a four-week training institute in New Orleans as Phase I of a three-phase training program. During Phase I training, employees are paid salary plus all expenses. After one year in the field, sales representatives are eligible for Phase II, a two-

week training course held at the corporate headquarters in Fort Worth, Texas. At a time deemed appropriate by the regional manager, the sales representatives will be invited to participate in Phase III. This is a three-week course that prepares sales representatives for the position of sales manager.

Quotas. Sales quotas for each district are set by upper management during the third quarter of each fiscal year for the next year. A national percentage increase in sales revenues is set in accordance with budgeted national sales projections. This percentage then becomes the average percentage quota for individual sales representatives.

Evaluation Process. All EDD employees are given annual performance reviews by their superiors. Evaluations are based on five critical issues: achievement of goals, professional conduct/work habits, territory management, product knowledge, and communication skills. Employees receive a rating (unsatisfactory, satisfactory, exceptional) in each area. Occasionally, sales managers and district managers are able to spend a day on calls with sales representatives. This on-the-job review gives both managers and representatives a unique opportunity to strengthen sales techniques and relationships.

EDD USE OF TECHNOLOGY

EDD has historically positioned itself to be on the cutting edge of technology, both in the development of new products and in the marketing of those products to the industry. The company has recently invested in information technology that will provide long-term growth opportunities in order to strategically allocate its selling effort to current and future customers. Salespeople use notebook-sized personal computers in their daily selling and account management activities. These PCs are used to input order information, to generate invoices, and to detail customer profile information. The notebooks also have software that enables the salesforce to maximize territory coverage through the use of a graphical display of customers within a city, county, or other geographical segment. Detailed time scheduling as well as prospecting and servicing accounts are all possible through this software.

Information from the salesforce is linked with the central computers via modem and compiled with the other customer specific information. This database includes historic demand information and inventory counts. This process is performed in order to maintain detailed customer profiles that are aggregated and fed into models utilizing and revising market forecasts, as well as other internal and external market information. This information is shared with the Strategic Planning Department and other entities throughout the organization in order to analyze current and future opportunities.

NOTES

1. Sharen Kindel, "Selling By the Book," *Sales and Marketing Management,* (October 1994): 101–109.
2. Thomas L. Powers, Warren S. Martin, Hugh Rushing, and Scott Daniels, "Selling Before 1900: A Historical Perspective," *Journal of Personal Selling and Sales Management,* 7 (November 1987): 1–7, and D. G. Brian Jones and David D. Monieson, "Early Development of the Philosophy of Marketing Thought," *Journal of Marketing,* 54 (January 1990): 102–113.
3. Powers, Martin, Rushing, and Daniels (1987), op. cit.
4. R. J. Keith, "The Marketing Revolution," *Journal of Marketing,* 24 (January 1960): 35–38.
5. Ronald A. Fullerton, "How Modern is Modern Marketing? Marketing's Evolution and the Myth of the 'Production Era'" *Journal of Marketing,* 52 (January 1988): 108–125.
6. P. Rajan Varadarajan, Terry Clark, and William M. Pride, "Controlling the Uncontrollable: Managing Your Market Environment," *Sloan Management Review* (Winter 1992): 39–47.
7. "Marketing By Design," *Sales and Marketing Management* (March 1992): 26, and David W. Cravens, Charles W. Holland, Charles W. Lamb, and William C. Moncrief, "Marketing's Role in Product and Service Quality," *Industrial Marketing Management,* 17 (1988): 285–304.
8. Joshua L. Wiener, Raymond W. LaForge, and Jerry R. Goolsby, "Personal Communication in Marketing: An Examination of Self-Interest Contingency Relationships," *Journal of Marketing Research,* 27 (May 1990): 227–231; Charles R. O'Neal, "JIT Procurement and Relationship Marketing," *Industrial Marketing Management,* 18 (1989): 55–63; and Daniel C. Smith and Jan P. Owens, "Knowledge of Customers as a Basis of Sales Force Differentiation," *Journal of Personal Selling and Sales Management,* 15(3) (Summer 1995): 1–15.
9. Douglas M. Lambert, Howard Marmorstein, and Arun Sharma, "Industrial Salespeople as a Source of Market Information," *Industrial Marketing Management,* 19 (1990): 141–148.
10. Robert Erickson and Andrew C. Gross, "Generalizing Industrial Buying: A Longitudinal Study," *Industrial Marketing Management,* 9 (July 1980): 256.
11. Minda Zetlin, "It's All the Same To Me," *Sales and Marketing Management* (February 1994): 71–75.

12. Ira Sager, "The Few, the True, the Blue: IBM Is Remaking Its Sales Force Into a Whole New Machine," *Business Week* (May 30, 1994): 124–127. See also Craig Stedman, "Users Wary of Delays in IBM Sales Transition," *Computerworld,* 28 (August 8, 1994): 12.

13. Patrick L. Schul and Brent M. Wren, "The Emerging Role of Women in Industrial Selling: A Decade of Change," *Journal of Marketing,* 56 (July 1992): 38–54.

14. Robert T. Adkins and John E. Swan, "Improving the Public Acceptance of Sales People Through Professionalism," *Journal of Personal Selling and Sales Management* (Fall–Winter 1981): 32–38.

15. Weld F. Royal, "Goodbye Good Ol' Boys," *Sales and Marketing Management* (December 1994): 12.

16. Darrel D. Muehling and William A. Weeks, "Women's Perceptions of Personal Selling: Some Positive Results," *Journal of Personal Selling and Sales Management,* 21 (1988): 5–14; Ellen J. Kennedy and Leigh Lawton, "Men and Women in Industrial Sales: Satisfaction and Outcomes," *Industrial Marketing Management,* 21 (1992): 5–14; Frederick A. Russ and Kevin M. McNeilly, "Has Sex Stereotyping Disappeared? A Study of Perceptions of Women and Men in Sales," *Journal of Personal Selling and Sales Management,* 8 (November 1988): 43–54; Douglas L. Fugate, Philip J. Decker, and Joyce J. Brewer, "Women in Professional Selling: A Human Resource Management Perspective," *Journal of Personal Selling and Sales Management,* 8 (November 1988): 33–41; and Marvin A. Jolson and Lucette B. Comer, "Predicting the Effectiveness of Industrial Saleswomen," *Industrial Marketing Management,* 21 (1992): 69–75.

17. "High-Tech Selling Eliminates Some Sales Offices," *The New York Times* (March 29, 1994): 1.

18. David A. Andelman, "Betting on the 'Net," *Sales and Marketing Management* (June 1995): 47–59. See also Thayer C. Taylor, "Marketing: The Next Generation," *Sales and Marketing Management* (February 1995): 43–44.

19. Rick Tetzeli, "The Internet and Your Business," *Fortune* (March 7, 1994): 86–104.

20. Peter H. Lewis, "Getting Down to Business on the Net," *The New York Times* (June 19, 1994): sec. 3, p. 1.

21. Nick Tortorello, "Small Companies Embrace Info Highway," *Sales and Marketing Management* (April 1994): 20. See also "On-Ramps to the Info SuperHighway," *Business Week* (February 7, 1994): 108–110.

22. Martin Everett, "Calling Who?" *Sales and Marketing Management* (August, 1993): 26–27.

23. Peter Wright, "Life on the Internet," *Utne Reader* (January/February, 1994): 101–109.

24. Dan T. Dunn and Claude A. Thomas, "High Tech Organizes for the Future," *Journal of Personal Selling and Sales Management,* 10 (Spring 1990): 43–55.

25. Thayer C. Taylor, "Plugging Into the Future," *Sales and Marketing Management* (June 1993): 20–21.

26. Thayer C. Taylor, "A Handy Invention," *Sales and Marketing Management* (January 1994): 77–78.

27. Dottie Enrico, "Logging on Instead of Slogging In to the Office," *Newsday* (October 31, 1993): 126.

28. Thayer C. Taylor, "Going Mobile," *Sales and Marketing Management* (May 1994): 94–102.

29. Dan Piller, "Cottage Technology," *Ft. Worth Star Telegram* (August 7, 1994): sec. D, p. 1.

30. Andy Cohen, "Going Mobile," *Sales and Marketing Management,* Part II (June 1994): 5.

31. William C. Moncrief, Jane Mackay, and Charles W. Lamb, Jr., "Laptop Computers in Industrial Sales," *Industrial Marketing Management,* 20 (1988): 279–285.

32. Jeff Andersen, "Mastering Multimedia," *Sales and Marketing Management* (January 1993): 55–56.

33. Robert E. Calem, "New! Improved! Laptops Change the Art of the Pitch," *The New York Times* (March 13, 1994): 9.

34. Thayer C. Taylor, "It's Better to Show Than Tell," *Sales and Marketing Management* (April 1994): 47–48.

35. Mike Fillon, "Keep on Trucking," *Sales and Marketing Management* (June 1995): 17–19.

36. Thayer C. Taylor, "Making More Time to Sell," *Sales and Marketing Management* (May 1994): 40–41.

37. William Keenan, Jr., "Automation Age Caveat: Communicate!" *Sales and Marketing Management* (June 1995): 33–34.

38. Steven J. Vaughan-Nichols, "E-Mail From Anywhere," *Mobile Office* (July 1995): 42–48.

39. Ginger Trumfio, "Liberty, Equality, E-Mail," Sales and Marketing Management (March 1994): 38.

40. Ross Weiland, "Staying in Touch," *Performance* (June 1995): 40–44.

41. Tim Clark, "Multimedia Growing as a Business Tool," *Advertising Age* (February 28, 1994): 20, and Charles T. Clark, "Get the Picture and the Thousand Words," *Sales and Marketing Management* (January 1994): 38.

42. Dan Gutman and Dennis James, "Quantum Leaps: How to Achieve Radical Increases in Personal Productivity," *Success,* Special Advertising Section (1994).

43. Michael J. Swenson and Adilson Parrella, "Cellular Telephones and the National Sales Force," *Journal of Personal Selling and Sales Management* 12(4) (Fall 1992): 67–74.

44. "On the Road Again," *Sales and Marketing Management* (1994): 37.

45. "Just Fax It," *Sales and Marketing Management* Part II (June 1995).

46. William C. Moncrief, Charles W. Lamb, Jr., Shannon H. Shipp, and David W. Cravens, "Examining the Roles of Telemarketing in Selling Strategy," *Journal of Personal Selling and Sales Management,* 6(2) (August 1989): 43–51; J. Marshall and H. Vrendenburg, "Successfully Using Telemarketing in Industrial Sales," *Industrial Marketing Management* 17 (1988): 15–22; and John I. Coppett and Roy Dale Voorhees, "Telemarketing: Supplement to Field Sales," *Industrial Marketing Management* 14 (1985): 213–216.

3

LEGAL AND ETHICAL ENVIRONMENT

At Carthage, nothing which results in profit is regarded as disgraceful.
POLYBIUS, A GREEK HISTORIAN, EXPLAINING WHY CARTHAGE FELL

Don't govern your life by what is legal and illegal, govern it by what's right or wrong.

H. ROSS PEROT

LEARNING OBJECTIVES

After reading this chapter, you should be able to answer the following questions:

- Why is it so important for sellers to follow legal and ethical guidelines?
- What laws govern the seller's behavior in the marketplace, including its relationships with customers and competitors?
- What laws govern the seller's behavior toward its employees and agents?
- What is the attitude of the general public toward the level of ethical behavior in sales?
- What factors affect the likelihood that a salesperson will act in an ethical manner?
- How can a firm ensure that its salespeople act in an ethical manner?

Several years ago Chrysler Corporation committed fraud when it disconnected the odometers of new cars that were being driven by its executives. When the executives traded their old cars in and received new cars, the odometers on the old cars were reconnected. Therefore, despite possibly having been driven several thousand miles, the old cars showed little if any mileage. These cars were sold to consumers through Chrysler dealerships as new. When the deception was discovered the president and CEO of Chrysler, Lee Iacocca, held a national press conference, discussed the unethical behavior at length, and unveiled a compensation program aimed at reimbursing purchasers of the used "new" cars.[1] He also apologized at the conference and in national advertising.[2]

In the course of everyday business, sellers are required to meet certain legal guidelines. In addition, many sellers see it as their duty to meet additional responsibilities, such as to "do no harm" or to "do good." These additional responsibilities go beyond legal guidelines. They may include commitment to ethical behavior, acceptance of social responsibility, expression of social responsiveness, and establishment of corporate social policy.[3] Firms can be ranked on a pyramid in terms of their

---

EXHIBIT 3.1

MODEL OF CORPORATE MORAL DEVELOPMENT

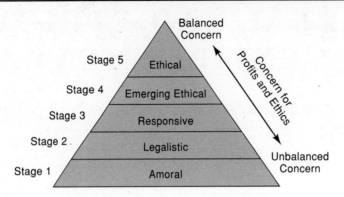

Stage 1   **Amoral Organizations.** *"Win at any cost" attitude; only concern for legal and ethical issues is that they don't get caught.*

Stage 2   **Legalistic Organizations.** *Organization is preoccupied with meeting the letter of the law rather than the spirit. Ethics are usually not considered.*

Stage 3   **Responsive Organizations.** *Organization moves beyond legal compliance. Social pressures force these companies to a greater social role, such as considering the effects of their actions on the community.*

Stage 4   **Emergent Ethical Organizations.** *There is an overt effort to manage the ethical culture of the organization. Management explicitly incorporates ethical concerns in everyday business decision making.*

Stage 5   **Ethical Organizations.** *A common set of ethical values is diffused throughout the organization. The principal differences between stage 4 and stage 5 is that stage 4 organizations still use mechanical means, such as formal planning systems, to guide ethical behavior. Stage 5 organizations have such a strong ethical emphasis that unethical behavior is very unlikely to occur.*

SOURCE: R. Eric Reidenbach and Donald P. Robin, "A Conceptual Model of Corporate Moral Development," *Journal of Business Ethics,* 10 (1991): 273–284.

---

stage of moral development, which encompasses the firm's awareness and concern for ethical issues.[4] Firms at the top of the pyramid place a higher value on social responsibility and have stronger ethical standards than those at the bottom. Exhibit 3.1 shows the stages of moral development for firms.

In this chapter, we will discuss both the legal and ethical aspects of sales management. The first half of the chapter considers legal issues pertinent to sales managers. These issues include relationships with customers, suppliers, and competitors, as well as relationships between sales manager and salespeople. The second half of the chapter explores influences on ethical decision making in sales and provides several means for improving the level of ethical decision making in sales management.

WHY STUDY LEGAL ISSUES IN SALES MANAGEMENT?

The study of legal issues is becoming increasingly important to sales managers for two primary reasons: increasing legalization and the need to practice preventive law. *Increasing legalization* means that there is an ever-increasing number of laws that affect sales managers. These laws, which will be discussed in detail in the next section, govern relationships with sales representatives, transactions with customers, and relationships with competitors and distributors. For example, the Americans With Disabilities Act (1990) is having a major impact on the way organizations select, recruit, and hire employees. In addition, the increased number of women in sales jobs means that managers must be sensitive to issues of equal pay, family leave, and sexual harassment. Since sexual harassment, in particular, is an evolving area of law, sales managers must pay close attention to changing legal standards regarding this issue.

Sales managers must also be aware of legal and ethical issues with customers, particularly with those abroad. With many firms establishing a global sales presence for the first time, sales managers may be unaware of the legal and ethical standards that affect international commercial transactions. For example, bribes are an accepted part of business in many parts of the world, but a U.S. firm that pays a bribe to obtain a foreign contract may violate the Foreign Corrupt Practices Act, which carries stiff penalties for violators.

Knowledge of the law allows sales managers to avoid violating a law that could have serious consequences for the firm. Many salespeople are unaware of laws that control their activities. One study of over 250 industrial goods salespeople showed that the salespeople were unable to correctly classify 9 of 20 commonly encountered sales practices as legal or illegal (see Exhibit 3.2).[5] Many of these practices, such as tying agreements, price discrimination among similar buyers, and dividing the market with rivals, violate federal antitrust statutes. These statutes, which will be discussed later in the chapter, carry significant civil and criminal penalties for violation.

Practicing preventive law means that sellers must understand two important categories of laws. The first category regulates the seller's behavior in the marketplace and includes laws concerning the seller's relationship with competitors, customers, and dealers in domestic and international settings. The second category regulates the seller's behavior toward its employees and includes laws on discrimination, harassment, termination, and other workplace issues.

LAWS CONCERNING THE SELLER'S BEHAVIOR IN THE MARKETPLACE

There are numerous laws at the federal and state levels that regulate the seller's behavior in the marketplace. These laws are important to sales managers and salespeople alike. For sales managers, knowledge of federal antitrust statutes, fraud, treaties governing international commercial transactions, and awareness of ordinances related to the use of a specific selling method such as telemarketing are an integral part of leading the salesforce. For salespeople, awareness of the legal issues

EXHIBIT 3.2
ARE THESE ACTIVITIES LEGAL OR ILLEGAL?

Activity	How Sales-people View This Activity	Actual Legal Status
Price collusion with competitors	Illegal	Illegal
Charging higher prices than rivals	Legal	Legal
Basing sales forecasts on personal opinion rather than objective methods	Legal	Legal
Predatory pricing	Legal[a]	Illegal
Price discrimination to similar buyers	Legal[a]	Illegal
Turning in incomplete reports to higher management	Legal	Legal
Suggesting that prospects buy now, as prices may rise (but this is actually unlikely)	Legal	Legal
Agreeing to divide market with rivals	Legal[a]	Illegal
Stealing trade secrets	Illegal	Illegal
Telling customers they are getting a price break when this is untrue	Legal[a]	Illegal
Selling a low-quality product	Legal	Legal
Aiming the marketing effort at only large customers	Illegal	Legal
Selling products in throw-away, nondegradable containers	Illegal	Legal
Preempting potential competition with prices below costs	Legal[a]	Illegal
Using tying contracts	Legal[a]	Illegal
Selling unsafe products	Illegal	Illegal
Agreeing with rivals to assess identical delivery charges	Legal[a]	Illegal
Selling children's cereal with very high levels of sugar	Legal	Legal
Providing a gift worth $20 to a customer	Legal	Legal
Giving price discounts to low-cost customers who buy in quantity	Legal	Legal

[a]This is a violation that could cost the firm significant civil and criminal penalties.

SOURCE: Based on Robin T. Peterson, "An Examination of Industrial Sales Representative Accuracy in Discriminating Selected Legal and Illegal Actions," *Journal of Personal Selling and Sales Management*, 14 (Spring 1994): 67–72

in areas such as telemarketing and verbal communication with customers regarding the competition can help the firm avoid costly legal battles.

The laws regulating the seller's behavior in the marketplace (to be discussed in this chapter) include antitrust legislation, the Uniform Commercial Code (which governs commercial transactions in all states except Louisiana), and various state and local ordinances regulating the activities of sellers. In addition, firms involved in international commerce must understand international laws and treaties. These firms must also understand contractual issues such as choice of forum for settling grievances and determination of which country's laws will govern the resolution of disputes.

Antitrust Legislation

Antitrust broadly defined means any business practice that reduces competition or involves the misuse of economic power. Key antitrust legislation for sales managers

---

EXHIBIT 3.3

KEY PROVISIONS OF MAJOR ANTITRUST LEGISLATION

The Sherman Act (1890)

Section 1: forbids every contract, organizational combination, or conspiracy to restrain trade.
Section 2: forbids firms to monopolize any part of trade singly or in combination with other firms.

Penalties: Violations of the Sherman Act carry criminal and civil penalties

The Clayton Act (1914)

Section 2: deals with price discrimination—later amended by Section 2 of the Robinson-Patman Act.
Section 3: makes it illegal for firms to make exclusive dealing contracts, tying agreements, or requirements contracts where the effect is to reduce competition or create a monopoly.
Section 4: Sets out civil remedies available for persons injured by reason of anything forbidden by antitrust statute.

Penalties: Besides the penalties already available under Sherman, the person or firm injured may recover three times the amount of the injury (treble damages). These remedies also apply to the Sherman Act and to the Robinson-Patman Act.

The Robinson-Patman Act (1936)

It is illegal for firms to sell the same product in the same quantity to different customers for different prices, where the effect of such price discrimination is to substantially lessen competition or create a monopoly.

---

to be aware of includes the Sherman Act, the Clayton Act, and the Robinson-Patman Act. Some of the key wording in each act is reproduced in Exhibit 3.3. These acts affect issues such as whether a seller can refuse to sell to a given customer, the prices a seller can charge for items, and the terms of a sale.

Sherman Act (1890). The **Sherman Act** was the first major piece of federal antitrust legislation. Most subsequent federal antitrust legislation modified or clarified Sherman, particularly in the areas of price discrimination and restraint of trade, while others, such as the FTC Act, specified the agency that would enforce Sherman's provisions. Exhibit 3.4 shows the relationships between Sherman and selected subsequent federal antitrust legislation.

The Sherman Act regulates several business practices that reduce competition. These practices include agreements by competitors to allocate markets, price fixing, the boycotting of certain resellers, and tying contracts. These practices constitute what are known as *per se* **violations,** meaning that if a company is found guilty of the act, no defense or justification is allowed. Each *per se* violation is described below.

Agreements by competitors to allocate markets are those in which a group of sellers agree that one will have the exclusive right to sell in one market, while another has the exclusive right to sell in another market. For example, if two soft drink companies agree to divide Texas in two, such that one firm sells only in south Texas and the other sells only in north Texas, a *per se* violation of the Sherman Act would occur.

EXHIBIT 3.4		
THE SHERMAN ACT: CLARIFICATIONS AND REVISIONS		
Price Discrimination	Restraint of Trade	Enforcement
Clayton Act (1914)	Clayton Act (1914)	FTC Act (1914)
Robinson-Patman Act (1936)		Wheeler-Lea Act (1938)
Miller-Tydings Act (1937)		
Consumer Goods Pricing Act (1975)		

Price fixing is also a *per se* violation of the Sherman Act. There are two types of price fixing: horizontal and vertical. **Horizontal price fixing** occurs when competitors at the same level (manufacturers, wholesalers, or retailers) collude to set a price for a certain commodity. For example, if three steel manufacturers agree to charge a certain price for a ton of steel, they have committed horizontal price fixing. Horizontal price fixing can also occur if prices are set by mechanisms such as trade associations. One practice which is considered a violation of the Sherman Act is the setting of commission rates by many local real estate organizations. It is a *per se* violation for a local board of real estate agents to set a commission rate that its members must charge to all customers. Individual real estate agencies and real estate agents must be allowed to set their own commission rates.

Vertical price fixing occurs when a manufacturer refuses to sell to a distributor or a retailer unless the buyer agrees to charge a minimum price for the commodity. For example, a perfume manufacturer might refuse to sell to a department store unless it agrees to charge a price set by the manufacturer. This process is also known as **resale price maintenance**. The courts use a three-part test to determine whether resale price maintenance exists. If the answers to all three questions are yes, the company has committed vertical price fixing and is in violation of federal antitrust statutes. The test consists of the following questions:

1. Was there a conspiracy to set prices?
2. Was there a written agreement confirming the conditions of this conspiracy or agreement?
3. Was coercion used to enforce the agreement?

Sales managers can become involved in vertical price fixing while trying to be responsive to customer demands. Assume that a software manufacturer's sales manager sells a software package for $60 per unit to three distributors, A, B, and C. Distributors A and B resell the package for $100 per unit while distributor C charges $90. Suppose distributors A and B write letters to the manufacturer's sales manager urging the manufacturer to force distributor C to raise its prices. Based on these letters, the sales manager writes distributor C a letter demanding it raise its prices or be terminated as a distributor. Has a violation of Sherman occurred? Use the three-part test to decide. There is a conspiracy between the manufacturer and distributors A and B to set prices. There was a written agreement (as evidenced by the letters) to confirm the conditions of the agreement. Coercion was present because the sales manager threatened to terminate distributor C if it did not charge a higher price for the software package. As a result, the three-part test has been met and the manufacturer is in violation of Sherman.

Vertical price fixing is one of the most problematic of the antitrust provisions, and it has gone through numerous changes throughout the twentieth century.[6] Originally, refusal to sell to a buyer who would not charge a minimum price was a *per se* violation of the Sherman Act. In 1937, however, the Miller-Tydings Act was passed, allowing individual states to set their own resale price maintenance statutes. In 1975 the Consumer Goods Pricing (CGP) Act was passed; it overturned the Miller-Tydings Act and once again made resale price maintenance a *per se* violation of the Sherman Act. The CGP Act remains in force today.

Boycotting certain purchasers is another *per se* violation of Sherman. Sellers have a generally respected right to sell to whom they choose. For example, it is legal for a manufacturer to refuse to sell to a distributor who has bad credit or inadequate storage facilities. However, a manufacturer cannot agree with certain distributors not to sell to another distributor. In other words, a manufacturer cannot require its other distributors to refuse to sell to a discounter, nor can it agree with other manufacturers to refuse to sell to a discounter. Agreements between sellers or between sellers and distributors to refuse to sell are *per se* violations of Sherman.

The last of the *per se* violations of the Sherman Act is tying agreements. **Tying agreements** occur when, as a condition of the sale of the initial product a buyer wishes to purchase, the seller requires the buyer to purchase not only that item but also another product, referred to as the "tied product." For example, suppose that a software company has a broad line of relatively slow-moving software games. This year, however, the company introduced a hot-selling video game. Under the Sherman Act (and further clarified by the Clayton Act), it is illegal for the software company's salespeople to require buyers to purchase the slow-moving software games as a condition for the purchase of the hot-selling game.

The provisions of the Sherman Act were originally enforceable by the Justice Department. However, owing to the specialized nature of the investigations required to pursue a Sherman violation, Congress passed the **FTC Act** in 1914, which created the Federal Trade Commission (FTC). The FTC is charged with enforcing laws pertaining to unfair methods of competition. It is also empowered to issue regulations relating to competition. For example, the FTC has issued regulations concerning the amount of time consumers have to reconsider major purchases. The regulation requires door-to-door salespeople to furnish the buyer with a contract which states that the buyer has the right to rescind the contract (i.e., revoke his or her offer) any time prior to the third business day after the date of the transaction.[7] Door-to-door sellers who do not provide such a contract are liable for court-imposed fines of up to $10,000. The FTC Act was strengthened by the Wheeler-Lea Act of 1938, which extended the FTC's enforcement to include deceptive advertising.

The Clayton Act (1914).   Section 3 of the **Clayton Act** clarifies Sherman on several issues, the most important of which to sales managers is exclusive dealing. **Exclusive dealing** occurs when the seller agrees to sell to a buyer only if the buyer agrees not to purchase the same items from any other seller. A violation of Clayton occurs when the intent or effect of the exclusive dealing arrangement is to create a monopoly or to substantially reduce competition. For example, if a clothing manufacturer requires that retailers carry its line of clothing and no other, a violation of the Clayton Act has occurred. If, however, the dealer decides on its own to purchase all of its clothing from a single manufacturer, no Clayton violation exists.

The Robinson-Patman Act (1936). The **Robinson-Patman Act** was enacted to clarify some of the language in the second section of the Clayton Act, which refers to price discrimination. **Price discrimination** differs from price fixing in that it refers to instances where sellers charge two customers different prices for the same product amount. The Robinson-Patman Act is of particular importance to sales managers who have some leeway in setting prices for the goods they sell. Robinson-Patman makes it illegal to charge two customers different prices for commodities of like grade and quality.

For a Robinson-Patman violation to exist, the following six conditions must hold:

1. A sale must take place.
2. The sale must be of goods rather than services or other intangibles.
3. The goods must be of like grade and quality.
4. The goods must be sold at different prices—this includes promotional allowances, favorable credit terms, and other price adjustments that may have the effect of creating different prices for different purchasers of commodities of like grade and quality
5. The sale must injure competition—not just a single competitor (although the Supreme Court's definition of this has varied over the years).
6. The act only applies to goods in *interstate* commerce. Sales occurring entirely within one state do not fall under the provisions of the act.

Consequences of Violating Federal Antitrust Statutes

Violators of antitrust laws are liable for severe penalties. Violations of the Sherman Act are felonies, and the criminal penalties for individuals involved in violating the Sherman Act can be up to 3 years in prison. The Sherman Act also allows for civil suits to encourage enforcement by individuals. Parties who can show injury under the Sherman Act can collect up to three times the amount of actual damages they sustain (called *treble damages*). In addition, when the harmed parties are small and cannot mount their own suit, the attorneys general of individual states are allowed to sue business violators of the Sherman Act (under the Hart-Scott-Rodino Antitrust Improvements Act of 1976) for treble damages. For violators of the Clayton Act and the Robinson-Patman Act, injured parties may recover treble damages, plus the amount of attorneys' fees and other costs of the suit. In short, sales managers must know the major federal antitrust statutes since violations are extremely costly to the firm.

Manufacturers can follow some straightforward rules to avoid problems with federal antitrust legislation. First, firms should avoid coercion with established dealers. They should not use annual contracts for their distributors that are dependent on the distributor charging a certain price for its products. Firms should also take pains to act unilaterally, that is, without agreeing with other manufacturers or distributors to engage in a group boycott of a distributor. Manufacturers should also be careful not to reference complaints by other dealers as a justification for action regarding another dealer, since this will be interpreted as indicative of an agreement to fix prices and limit competition.

The Uniform Commercial Code and Common Law

The **Uniform Commercial Code (UCC)** consists of a body of statutes, or regulations, defined by legislators. It was adopted by 49 states (all but Louisiana) in the 1960s as a means of establishing uniform rules across the United States for commercial transactions. Since that time, many of its provisions have been clarified through decisions by judges made when ruling on a case for which no prior or superseding precedent or rule exists. Judges' decisions in these cases become **common law**, which are precedents used to decide future cases.

The UCC statutes and common law that are of particular interest to sales managers and salespeople include (1) fraud statutes, (2) warranties, (3) dilution of warning effectiveness, (4) false representations of competing products, and (5) interference with a competitor's right to conduct business.[8] Exhibit 3.5 shows instances where salespeople's statements in each of the five areas created legal liability for their firms. Thus, sales managers and salespeople need to understand the potential legal consequences of certain statements or acts.

Fraud Statutes.   Sellers commit **fraud** when they knowingly misrepresent material facts on which buyers rely, which cause damage. As described in the opening scenario of this chapter, Chrysler committed fraud when it sold used cars as new. In making the purchases, the buyers relied on dealer representations that the cars were new and the buyers suffered damage because the used cars were not worth as much as new cars. This case also has ethical consequences, which will be discussed more fully in the second half of this chapter.

Fraud also occurs when salespeople make statements about competitors that are false or that misrepresents some aspect of the selling situation. False statements about competitors include unsubstantiated disparaging remarks. If a salesperson for one firm tells a customer that a competitor's product has had significant service problems and is not durable, and the salesperson has no evidence for the charges, the salesperson has committed fraud.

Misrepresenting the selling situation occurs when a salesperson knowingly provides false information to a buyer. For example, if a salesperson tries to pressure a customer into purchasing a house by stating that another buyer is about to make an offer—but if no other buyer actually exists—the salesperson is misrepresenting the selling situation. Misrepresentation can also occur when a salesperson tells a prospective customer that a product can perform a certain task, when in fact the product is not designed to perform that task.

If misrepresentation occurs, the seller has committed fraud and is liable for actual and punitive damages. The courts are particularly strict on misrepresentation when the salesperson is required by law to have certain expertise, such as a real estate agent, or when an accrediting body for salespeople exists in the industry, such as in insurance or securities.

EXHIBIT 3.5
SALESPERSON STATEMENTS THAT CAN CREATE LEGAL OBLIGATIONS FOR THE FIRM

Legal Issues[a]	Illustrative Cases	Salesperson Indiscretions	Consequences
Creation of unintended warranties	*Lindemann v. Eli Lilly* (1987)	Salesperson inadvertently overstated chemical product's technical capabilities	$6,000 (total price of product) awarded to plaintiff
	Carpetland v. Payne (1989)	Salesperson promised a 1-year warranty for carpet, though sales agreement expressly denied any warranties	$2,388 (total price of product) awarded to plaintiff
Dilution of warning effectiveness	*In re First Commodity* (1987)	Salesperson told clients that warnings in securities prospectus were unimportant	Plaintiffs certified for class action litigation (prior cases settled for $260,000–$3 million)
	Stevens v. Parke, Davis (1973)	Salespeople vigorously promised drug product without mentioning warnings	$400,000 awarded to plaintiff in wrongful death claim
Disparagement of competitive offerings	*Systems v. Scientific* (1976)	Salespeople claimed that rival's game tickets could be "read" without tampering	Defendant's sales staff prohibited from making such claims
	Testing v. Magnaflux (1987)	Salespeople made unverified negative statements about rival's chemical products	Plaintiff's claims ruled actionable —trial delayed until proper forms filed with court
Misrepresentation of own offerings	*Dunn v. Honeywell* (1982)	Salesperson intentionally over-stated the capabilities of computer software	$61,573 actual + $30,768 punitive damages + legal fees ($24,628) awarded to plaintiff
	Scott v. Mid Carolina (1988)	Salesperson lied to buyer about the condition of mobile home	$3,600 actual + $6,400 punitive damages awarded to plaintiff
Tortious interference with business relationships	*Leigh v. Isom* (1982)	Sales agent made false accusations about franchisee before franchisee's customers	$65,000 actual + $35,000 puni-tive damages awarded to plaintiff

[a]These five categories are the legal causes of action where salesperson behavior has been a prominent factor. They are based on a 3/1/90 review of the Lexis (1985) legal database for all reported federal and state cases since 1940 involving salespeople. The search phrase included: "salesperson, salesman, saleswoman, salespeople, sales agent, manufacturer's representative, and manufacturer's agent."

SOURCE: Karl A. Boedecker, Fred W. Morgan, and Jeffrey J. Stoltman, "Legal Dimensions of Sales-persons' Statements: A Review and Managerial Suggestions," *Journal of Marketing*, 55 (January 1991): 70–80.

Warranties.   **Warranties** are promises by sellers that the product is fit for use in a certain way. Warranties can be either express or implied. **Express warranties** occur when the seller publishes the warranty, when promotional brochures or advertising make certain promises, or when the salesperson states that the product can be used for a certain purpose. Salespeople must be very careful when making statements about their products. The courts have found that a salesperson's statements about a particular product—even if they contradict the promotional literature published by the company—result in an express warranty and are therefore enforceable by the customer. The loophole that many sellers have relied on as a defense is "puffery." **Puffery** occurs when the salesperson overstates the product's performance during the sales presentation. While sellers have often relied on the puffery defense in the past, the courts are taking an increasingly dim view of it, especially when the seller is knowledgeable and the buyer is not. In one case, a car salesperson assured a customer that a used car was "in A-1 shape" and "mechanically perfect." Unfortunately, the car was neither. The buyer sued and the court found that the salesperson's statements constituted an express warranty for the car. The used car company, therefore, was liable for damages.

A salesperson's statements can also create implied warranties. **Implied warranties** occur when the seller knows how the buyer plans to use the product and the buyer relies on the salesperson's knowledge in making the purchase. In one case, a buyer needed a heater for his chinchilla house (chinchillas are small animals raised for their fur). After conferring with a heating equipment salesperson, the buyer purchased a space heater. Unfortunately, the space heater used up all the oxygen in the room, leading to the death of the animals. The buyer sued the salesperson for having an implied warranty of fitness for the job of heating the chinchilla pen and won damages equal to the cost of the animals.

Dilution of Warning Effectiveness. Firms generally follow the spirit and the letter of the law when providing warnings to customers regarding a purchase that can be dangerous or otherwise cause damage (examples include pharmaceutical labeling and warnings provided in prospectuses for stock sales for new firms). Salespeople can, however, in the course of their conversations and letters to clients, effectively dilute the warning that is provided to prospective customers. In one case, a pharmaceutical firm was found guilty of failing to provide adequate warning of the hazards of using a product, despite the presence of a warning label on the product itself, because salespeople encouraged use of the product for a broader set of conditions than was appropriate and failed to highlight the possible dangers of the drug. In another case, salespeople for a securities firm told clients to ignore warnings in a prospectus. When the company went bankrupt and clients lost substantial amounts of money, the clients successfully sued the firm on the grounds that the salespeople had diluted the effectiveness of the warning in the prospectus.

False Representation of Competing Products. It is legal for a salesperson to explain the advantages of his or her firm's products to a prospective buyer as long as they are accurate. However, it is not legal to make false representations about another firm or its products. For example, it is legal to say "Our product is the best," or "Our product is better than others on the market." These are statements of opinion and do not disparage specific competitors. However, if the salesperson for a compact disc manufacturing machine says, "Our product produces 20 percent fewer bad discs than our competitor's," the salesperson needs to have proof to support that assertion. It appears that the courts are beginning to compare the verbal product comparisons of salespeople to the rules governing product comparisons in comparative advertising.[9] This means that the courts expect specific statements (e.g., "20 percent fewer bad discs") to be backed by specific research.

Interfering With Competitor's Right to Do Business.   Salespeople are not allowed to interfere with a competitor's right to do business. Salespeople who commit an act which interferes with that right have committed a crime known as **tortious interference with business relationships**. One common way that salespeople run afoul of the competitor's right to do business is by committing "dirty tricks"—actions that divert and take business from a competitor. For example, in the packaged goods industry, grocery store sales are closely related to the amount of display space that a product has. If the salesperson from one firm rearranges a competitor's products to reduce the amount of shelf space the competitor has, the salesperson has interfered with the competitor's right to do business. The question becomes, Which practices by the salesperson are illegal, and which are part of the normal competitive behavior in the marketplace? Unfortunately, the courts have not made a specific determination of the line separating the two. As a result, salespeople who commit dirty tricks may find themselves guilty of tortious interference.

Guidelines for ensuring that sales management practices comply with UCC statutes and common law are provided in Exhibit 3.6.

State and Local Ordinances

There are numerous state and local ordinances that control the activities of salespeople in the marketplace, particularly those who are selling to customers in their homes. Many states have laws mandating **cooling-off periods**; customers who purchase an item in their home have a certain period of time (usually 72 hours) to change their minds. Some cities have **Green River ordinances**, which require nonresident door-to-door salespeople to pay a fee, put up a bond (in many cases), and obtain a city license. Green River ordinances are so named because the first such legislation was passed in Green River, Wyoming, in 1933.

Laws and Regulations Pertaining to Telemarketing

Telemarketing has become an extremely important part of many firms' sales efforts. In some cases, it has even replaced the firm's field salesforce. We have discussed many laws that apply equally to telemarketing as to other types of selling, such as those pertaining to fraud and disparaging competitors. Because telemarketing involves in-home selling, it is also subject to numerous state and local ordinances and common law. For example, telemarketers are subject to the same cooling-off periods and other laws already affecting in-home sellers.

In addition, telemarketing is subject to two sets of laws not applicable to other forms of selling. First, since telemarketing requires the use of the telephone, it is regulated by the Communications Act (1934). This act forbids the use of the phone for obscene or illegal purposes. Second, many states have established regulations regarding issues unique to telemarketing, such as asterisk bills, automated dialing ma-

---

EXHIBIT 3.6

GUIDELINES FOR ENSURING SALES MANAGEMENT PRACTICES COMPLY WITH UCC STATUTES AND COMMON LAW

1. Be sure all specific product claims (technical characteristics, useful life, and performance capabilities) can be accomplished or are provable.
2. Be certain that all specific positive statements about product offerings can be verified. Any strong positive statement that cannot be demonstrated should be very general (high quality, great value).
3. Customers should be reminded to read warnings, particularly if they seem to be paying little attention to them or if the customers are not sophisticated. Never suggest to customers that warnings can be ignored or taken lightly.
4. Immediately caution customers who appear to be contemplating improper use of the product. Cautionary statements should be very specific and related to each customer's product usage situation.
5. Assess each customer's level of sophistication—the more inexperienced the customer, the greater the salesperson's obligation to deal cautiously with the customer.
6. Be able to verify all negative statements about competitor's products, business conduct, and financial status. Salespeople should avoid saying anything negative about competitors, particularly on topics that could be construed as rumors.

SOURCE: Karl A. Boedecker, Fred W. Morgan, and Jeffrey J. Stoltman, "Legal Dimensions of Salespersons' Statements: A Review and Managerial Suggestions," *Journal of Marketing*, 55 (January 1991): 70–80.

---

chine legislation, registration, disclosures, and solicitation hours.[10] A brief discussion of each of these issues and its related laws follows.

Asterisk Bills.   **Asterisk bills** have been passed or are being considered in many legislatures. These bills require publishers of telephone directories or firms that sell prospect lists to include asterisks by the names of consumers or firms that do not wish to be solicited over the telephone. To attempt to head off this legislation, the Direct Marketing Association, a trade group for telemarketers, maintains a list of individuals and firms that do not wish to be solicited by telephone and distributes this list to its members. The use of this list by telemarketers is voluntary, however, and failure to use it carries no penalty.

Automated Dialing Machine Legislation.   Some telemarketers use automated dialing machines to contact prospective customers. These machines call, play a pre-recorded message, and usually offer the customer the chance to respond to the offer with a live operator. These machines are regulated in many states, and the number of states adopting regulation concerning their use is growing. In Texas, for example, a telemarketer may not use an automated dialing machine for outbound calls unless the customer has already given permission to be contacted in that way. The penalties for violating the law vary from state to state and range from fines to revocation of the telemarketer's license to conduct telemarketing in the state.

Registration.   In many states, telemarketers are required to register with the state government. In California, for example, telemarketing firms must register with the

---

EXHIBIT 3.7
LEGAL AND ETHICAL RULES IN TELEMARKETING

1. Never use deceptive trade names or words.
2. Always state your name, the name of your company, and the reason for your call.
3. Never misstate the source or manufacturer of the products you are selling.
4. Never make disparaging remarks about competitors or their products.
5. Never misrepresent the value of free gifts or represent an item as "free" if there is actually a charge.
6. Never use testimonials, endorsements, or factual statements in a misleading way.
7. Never exaggerate claims about any product.

Source: Robert J. McHatton, *Total Telemarketing* (New York: Wiley, 1988).

---

state and submit any scripts they plan to use to the California State Attorney General's Office.

Disclosures. Some telemarketing firms have been accused of failing to disclose that "free gifts" actually have a cost, or that a "survey" is actually a sales pitch. To overcome these failures to disclose, the FTC adopted new disclosure rules in 1995. According to these rules, telemarketers must announce at the outset of their call that they are making a sales call. They must also disclose the nature and cost of the products and services they are offering. If the call is for a sweepstakes or a prize drawing, they must disclose the odds of winning prizes and make it clear that consumers can win without buying anything.[11]

Many nonprofit organizations use telemarketing to solicit funds. Often, the telemarketers are independent firms working under contract with the nonprofit organization. There have been numerous consumer complaints about the high overhead charged by these firms, and the failure of the firms to disclose the percentage of the funds raised that actually go to the nonprofit organization. In response, some states have established limits for profits that can be made by telemarketing firms raising money. For example, telemarketing fund-raisers in Maine cannot take more than 30 percent of the revenues raised (after phone charges) for their overhead.

Solicitation Hours. Telemarketing is very convenient to the seller, since the seller can choose the time to make the call. But as anyone knows, the telephone always rings at the most inopportune time—generally while the customer is showering or eating. Although legislation may not be able to address this problem, some state legislatures have restricted solicitation hours. In New York, for example, state law forbids telemarketers from calling before 10:00 A.M., after 8:00 P.M., and during the dinner hour (5:00–7:00 P.M.).

Telemarketing solicitation is a complex area that requires understanding laws pertaining to selling and also to communication. There are federal, state, and local laws that regulate telemarketing. Exhibit 3.7 provides some general guidelines to ensure that a firm's telemarketing operation is legal. Specific rules should be obtained for each state and locale in which telemarketing occurs.

Laws Concerning International Commerce

With the recent increase in the number of firms pursuing global markets, laws concerning transactions among firms headquartered in different countries have become an important issue for many sales managers. Some of the most significant legal issues in international commercial transactions include relevant treaties and legislation in the United States that controls the behavior of U.S. firms in foreign countries.

Relevant Treaties.   All firms with operations in Western Europe come under the jurisdiction of the **Treaty of Rome** (1957). This treaty, along with its amendments (Single European Act [1986] and the Treaty of Maastricht [1993]), includes many of the same regulations governing commercial transactions in the United States. For example, Article 85 of the Treaty of Rome forbids certain agreements and practices between businesses that have the effect of restricting competition. Practices such as price fixing, price discrimination, and tying agreements are expressly forbidden. In this way, it is similar to Section 1 of the Sherman Act. The treaty is administered by the Commission of European Community, whose decisions have the force of law. For U.S. firms operating in Western Europe, the commission has specifically defined the types of agreements that will be acceptable under Article 85.

Under NAFTA (North American Free Trade Act), the member states (Mexico, the United States, and Canada) have agreed to pursue antitrust violators vigorously under the laws of their own country. NAFTA does not have a single tribunal, such as the Commission of European Community, to adjudicate conflicts.

For U.S. firms operating outside Western Europe and North America, the rules are not as clear. In the Far East and elsewhere, rules of commerce are established by treaties between countries and through contractual agreements among parties. There is no single treaty or agreement that is universally recognized.

Specific U.S. Legislation to Control Foreign Transactions.   In the United States, certain federal laws regulate sales in foreign markets. For example, the **Foreign Corrupt Practices Act (FCPA)** (1976, amended in 1988) restricts the giving of bribes by U.S. companies to foreign nationals to obtain contracts.[12] If a salesperson pays a bribe, the salesperson and the selling firm are in violation of this statute. Violators of the FCPA can be severely punished, as illustrated in Box 3.1.

Other administrative rules affect the types of products that can be sold to different countries. For example, the **Export Administration Act** (1979) forbids U.S. firms from selling to certain countries computer technology that could be used in developing weapons. Moreover, gun control legislation makes it illegal to sell guns to foreign nationals.

LAWS GOVERNING THE SELLER'S BEHAVIOR TOWARD ITS EMPLOYEES

Sales managers need to understand the laws relating to the relationship between the employer and the employee. Laws that are particularly important to managers include those relating to (1) employee termination, (2) discrimination in hiring, selec-

---

BOX 3.1

CONSEQUENCES OF VIOLATING THE FOREIGN CORRUPT PRACTICES ACT

Napco International, Inc., and its parent company, Venturian Corporation of Hopkins, Minnesota, pleaded guilty to paying more than $130,000 in bribes to officials in the Republic of Niger. The purpose of the bribes was to obtain and keep an aircraft service contract funded by the U.S. government's foreign military sales program. The companies pleaded guilty to conspiracy, tax violations, and violation of the 1977 Foreign Corrupt Practices Act, which prohibits U.S. companies from paying bribes to foreign officials.

The company paid bribes to Tahirou Barke Doka, then the First Counselor at Niger's embassy in Washington, D.C., and Captain Ali Tiemogo, then the Chief of Maintenance of the nation's air force, to use their influence to provide spare parts and maintenance service for C-130 cargo aircraft. The contract was worth more than $3 million.

From 1983 to 1987, the company engaged in an elaborate effort to set up and conceal the bribery scheme. The firm opened a Minnesota bank account in the name of a fictitious commission agent named "E. Dave" and listed two relatives of Tiemogo as Napco's agents in Niger, when in fact they served as intermediaries for the bribe payments. The fraud was uncovered when the name of one of the agents was checked by U.S. officials with the government of Niger.

Under the terms of the plea agreement, the company paid $685,000 for violating the FCPA, $100,000 for filing a false tax return, and $75,000 to the IRS to settle its civil tax liabilities. It also paid $140,000 in civil penalties to be credited to the Republic of Niger's Foreign Military Sales Account.

SOURCE: Ruth Marcus, "Minnesota Defense Contractor Fined for Bribing Two Niger Officials," *The Washington Post* (May 3, 1989): F1.

---

tion, promotion, and compensation practices, and (3) working conditions. The following is an overview of the legislation that exists in those areas.

Employee Termination

Most managerial employees in the United States work under what is known as the "employment at will" doctrine. **Employment at will** means that either the employer or the employee can end the relationship at any time for virtually any reason. If the employee provides cause for firing, such as theft, false invoices, appropriation of company property, or some other generally recognized unacceptable act, the employer has a legal right to dismiss the employee. Employees can sue, however, if they feel their dismissal was wrongful. **Wrongful dismissal** occurs when the employer shows bad faith or is malicious in dismissing the employee. For example, if a salesperson had just earned a significant bonus, and the employer fired the salesperson to avoid having to pay the bonus, the salesperson might have a cause of action for wrongful dismissal. Wrongful dismissal suits can be very expensive for employers. Two studies showed that ex-employees win between 90 percent and 95 percent of cases that go to jury, and that the average damage award ranges from $450,000 to $548,000.[13]

Another area of law related to employee termination pertains to firing employees who are "whistleblowers." **Whistleblowers** are employees who detect company wrongdoing and make their charges public or go over the heads of their immediate supervisors. A sales manager might become involved if one of his or her salespeople found out that a key product performance claim was based on false data and "blew the whistle" to the press. If the sales manager fired the salesperson for talking to the press, the salesperson would have cause for a wrongful dismissal suit if the state in which the firing occurred had a whistleblowing statute. Whistleblowing statutes currently exist in only three states; however, this is an emerging area of law and several more states are considering similar statutes.[14]

Discrimination

It is legal to discriminate among employees based on performance. For example, employers may discriminate in pay among commission-based salespeople based on level of sales. This means that higher-performing salespeople can be paid more than lower-performing salespeople. Unlawful discrimination occurs when companies use non-performance-related criteria in making decisions in areas such as recruiting, selecting, compensating, and terminating. Non-performance-related criteria include race, gender, national origin, age, disability, and religion. Employers cannot discriminate among employees based on non-performance-related criteria. If they do, they violate the Civil Rights Act of 1964, which is perhaps the most significant piece of legislation prohibiting discrimination on non-performance-related criteria.

Civil Rights Act (1964).   The **Civil Rights Act** is a sweeping piece of legislation that covers all firms with more than 15 employees engaged in interstate commerce. The act makes it unlawful for an employer to discriminate on the basis of race, color, religion, gender, or national origin with respect to the following specific issues: (1) classified advertising, (2) testing for the purpose of hiring or promoting, (3) hiring or terminating employees, (4) pay, job classification, or job assignment, (5) transfers and promotions, (6) use of company facilities, (7) fringe benefits, such as insurance and vacations, (8) pensions, (9) training, (10) disability leave and pay, and (11) any other terms and conditions of employment.

Subsequent legislation has added to the number of bases on which discrimination is not allowed. The **Age Discrimination in Employment Act** (1967) extended Title VII of the Civil Rights Act to include individuals 40 years of age and older. All the same provisions already stated are now applicable to older workers. The **Vocational Rehabilitation Act** (1973) extends Title VII protection to the disabled. However, the organizations affected by the act are limited to state, federal, and local governments, their agencies, and certain federal contractors. The **Pregnancy Discrimination Act** (1978) amended Title VII to include discrimination based on pregnancy, childbirth, or associated medical conditions. With the steady increase of women in selling (see Chapter 2), this has become a significant issue for many firms.

One of the more recent legislative acts is the **Americans With Disabilities Act** (**ADA**) (1990), which extends Title VII of the Civil Rights Act and the Vocational Rehabilitation Act to include disabled workers in the private sector. Managers are required not to discriminate against a disabled individual who is otherwise capable of performing the essential functions of the job. Managers are also responsible for making reasonable accommodations in the workplace for the disabled worker. For example, if a blind worker is qualified for a position as a telemarketer, the firm must make reasonable accommodation in terms of the work environment, such as making documents and equipment accessible, so that the disabled worker can perform the job effectively.

Working Conditions

Sales managers are also responsible for maintaining proper control of the work environment. Two important emerging areas for sales managers to be aware of include sexual harassment and stress-related disability. Telemarketing sales managers must also be aware of legislation regarding call monitoring, which is a popular means of controlling telemarketing employees.

Sexual Harassment.   According to the Equal Employment Opportunity Commission (EEOC), **sexual harassment** exists when unwelcome sexual advances, requests for sexual favors, and physical contact of a sexual nature occur in the workplace *and* if (1) submission to such treatment is made a condition of employment, (2) employment decisions are based on the individual's submission or rejection of such treatment, or (3) such conduct has the purpose of unreasonably interfering with an individual's work performance and creates a hostile work environment.[15] The characteristics of sales jobs make salespeople particularly vulnerable to sexual harassment, which means that sales managers must be sensitive to this issue. Some of the characteristics of sales jobs that create conditions under which sexual harassment can occur include nonsupervision, social interaction with customers and colleagues, relationship building with customers, sales for multinationals, and third-party sexual harassment.[16] The last two characteristics are particularly noteworthy. Sales for multinationals is an evolving area for sexual harassment claims because Title VII of the Civil Rights Act was only extended to U.S. citizens working for U.S. firms abroad by the Civil Rights Act of 1991.

Third-party sexual harassment is of particular relevance for sales managers who manage outside salespeople. If a customer sexually harasses a salesperson, the salesperson may have a cause for action against his or her employer for failing to maintain a work environment that is free of sexual harassment.[17] There have only been a few suits brought under this theory, but it is an emerging area that has many sales managers considering what they can do to affect the behavior of their purchasers.

Sales managers must respond to all charges of sexual harassment because of the sensitivity of the issue, the possible effect of salesforce morale, and the financial consequences to the firm if the complaint is mishandled.[18] In confronting or resolving a sexual harassment complaint a sales manager should use the procedures outlined in Exhibit 3.8.

Stress[19].   Employees in highly stressful jobs are increasingly holding their employers liable for the effects that stress has on their health. Given that sales jobs are traditionally stressful, sales managers must be particularly vigilant in monitoring their employees' level of stress and make efforts to keep stress at tolerable levels. Employees' suits for stress are brought in state court, typically as part of a claim for worker's compensation. Since the suits are brought in state court, there is little consistency across states in terms of the extent to which the court will hold companies liable. However, the trend seems to be that employers must shoulder a heavier portion of the responsibility for their employees' psychological health.

In order to reduce a firm's exposure to suits for stress, managers should take the following steps:

EXHIBIT 3.8
SEXUAL HARASSMENT

How to Respond to a Sexual Harassment Occurrence
1. Look the harasser in the eye.
2. State, "When you [*whatever the act is*], I feel [*describe how you feel*].
3. Ask the person to please stop the behavior.
4. Do not attack the individual directly, only the behavior.
5. If it happens again, write the individual a letter stating again how you feel and ask the person to stop. Send the letter by registered mail and keep a copy.
6. If the individual persists, complain to your supervisor.

How to Deal With a Sexual Harassment Complaint (as a Supervisor)
1. Determine the answers to the following questions from the victim:
   a. What was the offensive behavior?
   b. Who did it?
   c. When did it occur?
   d. Did it happen more than once?
   e. Where did it occur?
   f. What did the victim do in response?
   g. Were there any witnesses?
   h. What does the victim want done?
2. Interview the alleged harasser.
3. Interview any witnesses, remembering that confidentiality is to be maintained.
4. Follow company procedures for further steps.

How to Avoid Unwelcome Sexual Harassment Behaviors (Particularly in a Sales Position)
1. Do not get too friendly with co-workers of the opposite gender.
2. Do not tell off-color stories.
3. Do not drink alcoholic beverages.
4. Arrange for your own transportation.
5. Communicate with co-workers when you experience or observe behavior that can be considered harassment.
6. Handle it with humor.

How to Avoid Being Accused of Sexual Harassment
1. If a behavior is unwelcome, stop the behavior.
2. When in doubt, do not say it or do it.
3. If in doubt, ask if the behavior is appropriate.
4. Do not assume friendliness means sexual interest.

SOURCE: Cathy Owens Swift and Luther (Trey) Denton, "Teaching About Sexual Harassment Issues: A Sales Management Approach," *Marketing Education Review* (Fall 1994): 37.

1. Understand the legal risks that could apply to the jobs in question.
2. Develop a system to diagnose levels of stress on the job. Issues such as the reward system, work load, organizational structure, performance appraisal system, and job security can increase stress. The nature of selling probably precludes eliminating stress entirely, but a system that monitors stress can help keep it within tolerable limits.

3. Have the firm take active steps to reduce stress, such as providing physical fitness facilities (which have been shown to reduce levels of stress).

4. Evaluate current programs that monitor and reduce stress to ensure they are functioning properly.

5. Document what is done. Some courts have gone so far as to require companies to take responsibility for their employees' health, and to demonstrate the steps taken to ensure a healthy working environment.

Call Monitoring.   Telemarketing supervisors often monitor the calls made by telemarketing representatives for a variety of reasons, including to ensure that the script is followed and that appropriate questions are asked, as well as to ascertain the need for additional training. Many states require the consent of at least one party before call monitoring can take place. This is typically handled by having telemarketing representatives sign a document stating that they are aware their conversations will be monitored periodically. In several states, however, call monitoring requires the consent of all parties to the call. In at least one state (Wyoming), however, it is illegal to monitor any telephone line regardless of whether prior consent has been obtained.

In summary, meeting legal requirements is not a simple matter, but it is of crucial importance to the sales manager. Federal and state legislatures frequently create new laws and amend old ones. The enforcement of laws may be stricter or laxer under different administrations, particularly in the area of antitrust law. The courts have leeway in interpreting various statutes and common legal precedents, and over time the interpretations can amend, clarify, strengthen, or weaken the original statute.

Sales executives should be aware of the basic laws that govern all commercial transactions in the United States. In addition, sales managers should be aware of the specific laws that apply to their method of selling (such as telemarketing or door-to-door sales), to the place where the transactions take place (e.g., in the European Community), and to the specific industry in which the sales take place (e.g., laws pertaining to securities and real estate sales). In terms of managing salespeople, sales managers must be aware of laws pertaining to termination and discrimination, and those related to the work environment.

ETHICAL ISSUES IN SALES MANAGEMENT

Salespeople are not generally perceived as having the highest ethical standards. Popular films and plays, such as *The Music Man, Glengarry Glen Ross, Tin Men, Cadillac Man,* and *Death of a Salesman* all depict salespeople as chasing the fast buck and being willing to engage in questionable practices to ensure making quotas or meeting sales objectives.

Are these portrayals in the media and the perceptions by the public completely accurate? Probably not. One study found that marketing managers were less likely than finance or product managers to use unethical procedures or to set aside personal values in making decisions with ethical overtones.[20] In addition, sales professionals have the same standards as other members of the marketing profession with respect to ethical beliefs and perceptions.[21]

No doubt there are some salespeople who cut corners, use questionable business practices, or mislead clients in pursuit of a sale. Patrick Murphy and Gene Laczniak, two marketing professors who have studied sales ethics extensively, summed it up this way: "[Since] almost every consumer has been pressured to buy something that she/he did not intend to buy, sales representatives are often categorically labeled as being unethical."[22] Salespeople have gained this reputation in large part because they are uniquely vulnerable to being placed in situations where unethical behavior can occur. Members of a salesforce generally work with little supervision; experience little daily contact with supervisors, subordinates, or peers; and make most of their decisions with little direct input from others in the company. They also often have high performance standards with a great deal of freedom of action in terms of how to meet those standards, and frequently experience ethical conflict because of differing demands by supervisors, customers, peers, and family.[23] Also, the process of negotiating sales lends itself to dishonesty and exaggeration, such as the practice of puffery described previously.[24] Sales managers are also faced with making numerous decisions with ethical consequences, including decisions regarding hiring, territories, house accounts, gifts, quota setting, and performance evaluation.

WHY SHOULD SALESPEOPLE AND SALES MANAGERS ACT ETHICALLY?

There are numerous reasons for salespeople and sales managers to act ethically. First and foremost, it is the right thing to do and should be its own reward. Also, marketers who are not ethical will incur significant personal and organizational losses.[25] From a personal standpoint, unethical actions can lead to loss of trust from customers and the destruction of business relationships. For example, one buyer for a large retail chain told a seller that she liked his products and would order them when inventory levels warranted. The seller offered to "make it worthwhile for her personally" if she would make the order now. Not only did the buyer not place the order, she saw to it that the salesperson was permanently prohibited from calling on her chain.[26]

There are also substantial organizational costs that can arise from unethical selling practices. A recent instance where an unethical selling practice led to substantial organizational cost occurred when salespeople at Sears service centers in California were found guilty of selling unneeded services to customers. Not only did Sears suffer significant dollar fines, it also lost an incalculable amount of trust, prestige, and brand equity.[27]

INFLUENCES ON ETHICAL DECISION MAKING IN SALES MANAGEMENT

There are many influences on ethical decision making in sales management (see Exhibit 3.9), including the industry, the company, the sales manager, the salesperson, and the customer.[28] Each of these influences, and its observed relationship on ethical practice in sales management, will be discussed below.

Industry

The characteristics of the industry can have a great deal to do with the general level of ethical behavior encountered in the industry. Industries where buyers and sellers tend

EXHIBIT 3.9

INFLUENCES ON ETHICAL DECISION MAKING IN SALES

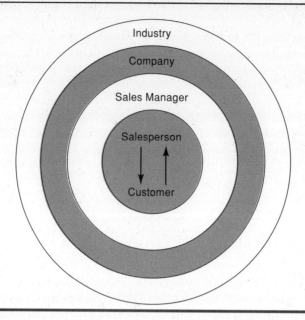

to have long-standing relationships, where products are complex or order sizes are quite large, or where the product is an abstract service (such as pension fund management or insurance), tend to have higher levels of ethics because sales agents must build a long-term relationship based on trust with their clients to ensure mutual benefits.[29] In these industries, unethical behavior can lead to a refusal by buyers to enter a relationship, and without buyers, it is difficult for the seller to continue to grow and prosper.

In addition, many industries have codes of ethics intended to govern the behavior of their members. A profession's **code of ethics** "embodies the collective conscience of a profession and is testimony to the group's recognition of its moral dimension."[30] The American Marketing Association, the National Association of Securities Dealers, the Association of Certified Life Underwriters, and the National Board of Realtors are examples of organizations that, through the dissemination of a code of ethics, attempt to regulate the ethical behavior of their members in selling situations. Penalties for violating the codes of ethics can range from losing one's membership in the organization to losing one's license to practice. Criteria for developing a code of ethics are discussed later in this chapter.

Company

Companies have ethical values that are a composite of the ethical values of their managers and employees as well as the firm's formal and informal policies.[31] Formal and informal policies that have an influence on ethical values include (1) setting corporate standards for ethical practice, (2) requiring corporate personnel to undergo ethics awareness training, and (3) visible actions on the part of top management.

Corporate Standards for Ethical Practice.   Some firms use their corporate mission statement to formalize their commitment to ethical principles, whereas others rely on codes of ethics statements. Codes of ethics statements are attempts by firms to articulate the expected levels of ethics that should exist in company dealings. One report indicated that 75 percent to 80 percent of all major corporations have formal, written codes of ethics.[32]

Ethics Training.   After firms establish a code of ethics, they often look for additional ways to encourage their employees to act ethically. One popular means is through ethics training, which can range from messages from the CEO to corporate classes on ethics. Recent estimates indicate that over 40 percent of large firms have ethics training programs.[33] The content of the training programs typically includes (1) messages from the CEO, (2) discussion of codes of ethics, and (3) procedures for discussing or reporting unethical behavior.

Actions of Top Management.   Top managers can forestall unethical behavior by setting an example for their employees, including acting ethically during a crisis and reducing employees' incentives to commit unethical behavior. The behavior of top managers during a crisis affects not only those who have suffered directly from the company's actions, but also the attitude and morale of other members of the organization, including salespeople and sales managers. In the Chrysler case discussed previously, some Chrysler managers obviously felt that it was acceptable to sell used cars as new; however, it is clear from Iacocca's actions that top management did not feel the same way. Since this episode, no similar incidents have occurred.

Top management can also set ethical examples by reducing the incentive to act in an unethical way. Three conditions that can lead to unethical behavior are (1) unusually high rewards for good performance, (2) unusually severe punishment for poor performance, and (3) implicit sanctioning of explicitly forbidden acts.[34]

Unusually high rewards can occur when a firm offers a very high bonus for exceeding a quota. To illustrate, if a salesperson has been diligently pursuing new leads and has completely exhausted all avenues to find new customers but still needs a few new customers to exceed the quota, the salesperson might be tempted to fabricate a few names. In this case, management needs to take steps to ensure the high potential bonus does not blind the salesperson to the need for maintaining ethical standards. The firm might also consider not offering a high bonus for exceeding a quota, but pay on a percent on quota achieved instead.

Unusually stiff punishments lead to similar problems. If salespeople are told they will be fired unless they obtain certain business, management is sending a loud signal: Results are more important than sales activities. Thus, salespeople are encouraged to do whatever is necessary, even if it is unethical, to get results. While a seller might achieve short-term gains with this approach, unethical behavior leads to long-term loss of customer trust, which will result in erosion of sales over time. As a consequence, top management must make sure that unusually stiff punishments are not the norm.

Last, if management says they explicitly forbid a practice but overlooks or perhaps even rewards offenders as long as their performance is high, employees can become cynical about the real values of the organization. Top managers who outwardly project an image of high ethics while tolerating unethical acts from their subordinates are setting the firm up for a major ethics crisis.

Sales Manager

Managers have a unique responsibility for creating an atmosphere in which ethical decision making becomes the norm. One observer at GTE says:

> While education can highlight the importance of ethics and clarify ways in which rational business decisions can include ethical considerations, behavior change can only come about when the organization as a whole provides both the environment and the mechanisms for supporting ethical practices. It is incumbent on all managers, from the most senior levels to the first-line supervisors, to set clear standards and expectations for ethical conduct and to model, by their own behavior, the highest ethical practices.[35]

Sales managers set standards through their own behavior and through their control of the salespeople who report to them. Based on their behavior regarding ethical issues, we can categorize four types of managers: (1) crooks, (2) Good Samaritans, (3) seekers, and (4) rationalizers.[36] On one end of the spectrum are **crooks,** who know that taking a certain action is morally wrong, but they take it anyway using the justification of personal gain or temporary organizational gain. Most firms do their best to weed out such individuals. On the other end are the **Good Samaritans,** who generally arrive at moral and just decisions based on careful analysis of relevant moral principles.

The middle ground is occupied by seekers and rationalizers. **Seekers** are those who want to do the right thing, but who do not have the tools to make the appropriate decisions or to recognize that a given situation has ethical overtones. These individuals are typically younger and have less experience with the company and the industry. **Rationalizers** recognize that certain decisions have ethical consequences, but they look for ways to justify the solution that yields the highest economic payoff, regardless of its ethicality. The salesperson's job activities will no doubt be influenced by which type of manager he or she has. Having a crook for a boss might encourage the salesperson to seek the easy way out in difficult ethical situations, while having a Good Samaritan will encourage the salesperson to maintain a high level of ethical behavior.

Another way in which sales managers affect the ethical behavior of their salespeople is through their response to unethical actions. It is important for sales managers to provide consistent, visible discipline for salespeople who are caught behaving unethically. Unfortunately, sales managers do not always apply punishment objectively. Several studies have shown that sales managers are more likely to provide harsh sanctions against a salesperson when the salesperson is a poor performer, when the salesperson's actions lead to negative consequences for the firm, when the salesperson is overweight, and when the salesperson tries to provide a justification for his or her action based on unethical behavior on the part of the buyer.[37]

Sales managers, regardless of type, experience dilemmas with ethical overtones regarding their salespeople in at least three areas: territory design, performance evaluation, and designation of house accounts. In *territory design,* sales managers must often split territories that have grown too large for a single salesperson to cover adequately. The dilemma arises in terms of how to compensate the representative who was responsible for building the territory to its current size. Should that salesperson continue to receive credit for the customers he or she developed, particularly if the purchases made by the customer today are a consequence of previous actions taken by the salesperson?

In *performance evaluation,* one dilemma is how much emphasis to place on results, such as sales versus behaviors, such as number of calls made or number of training sessions held. Performance evaluations that are completely result-based should be more likely to encourage unethical behavior. Performance evaluations that take behavior of the salesperson into account are more likely to encourage ethical behavior.

A third dilemma is designation of house accounts. **House accounts** are typically large customers in a salesperson's territory for which the salesperson does not receive compensation. A seller might designate a customer as a house account if the level of service required to maintain the account exceeds that which can be provided by the salesperson. For example, suppose a territory has a corporate headquarters for a manufacturing firm, but the firm's purchasing is handled at local plants. If the firm decides to centralize purchasing (i.e., make all purchasing decisions at the corporate headquarters), the salesperson may not be able to handle the number of inquiries and service requests for all plants. Therefore, the seller may designate the corporate headquarters as a house account to be served directly by the sales manager. Sales managers must be very careful in designating a customer as a house account, however, especially if the salesperson has spent significant time developing the relationship with the customer or if the salesperson is responsible for providing service to that account.

Salesperson

The personal characteristics of salespeople and their effects on ethical decision making are a constant source of study. It has been found that demographic variables such as age and education; behavioral variables such as empathy and stage of moral development; and positional variables such as status in the corporate hierarchy and functional area of responsibility are all related to ethical decision making. Individuals who are older, better-educated, more empathic, at a higher stage of moral development, at higher levels of the organization, and in marketing positions are more likely to perceive ethical issues in decisions and more likely to act in ethical ways when making decisions.[38]

One of the most studied salesperson variables is the stage in moral development. Philosophers argue that individuals progress through an irreversible sequence of six moral judgment stages (see Exhibit 3.10). As salespeople enter higher levels of moral reasoning, they become increasingly concerned about right and wrong and about what is fair or just. A person's stage of moral development has been shown to affect managerial behavior. One experiment found that MBA students who would pad an expense account operated at the first three stages of moral reasoning, while those who would refuse operated at the three higher stages.[39]

EXHIBIT 3.10
STAGES OF MORAL DEVELOPMENT

Stage 1:	Obedience and punishment orientation
Stage 2:	Instrumental purpose and exchange
Stage 3:	Interpersonal accord, conformity, mutual expectations
Stage 4:	Social accord and system maintenance
Stage 5:	Social contract and individual rights
Stage 6:	Universal ethical principles

SOURCE: J. Rest, E. Turiel, and L. Kohlberg, "Level of Moral Development as a Determinant of Preference and Comprehension of Moral Judgments Made by Others," *Journal of Personality*, 37 (1969): 225.

Customer

The actions of the purchaser also have an effect on the salesperson's level of ethical behavior. For instance, if a purchaser offers to buy only if the salesperson does something unethical, such as split a commission or pay a bribe, the salesperson may calculate the value of the commission less the payoff and conclude that it is a lucrative (but not ethical) decision to make the payoff. A decision like this can be dangerous for several reasons. Not only is paying bribes to purchasing agents unethical and expressly forbidden by most corporate codes of ethics, in the case of government purchasing agents the salesperson paying the bribe is breaking the law and can go to jail. Also, the more unethical a purchasing agent considers a selling practice, the less likely he or she is to select that source as a supplier.[40] Purchasing agents are also more likely to take a hard line with unethical practices—actions that a salesperson may see as a sharp business practice but which are viewed by the purchasing agent as being unethical.[41] Unethical practices regarding purchasing agents, therefore, not only affect the immediate sale but also the long-term relationship with the customer.

One important area where unethical practices occur with purchasing agents is in giving gifts. One recent estimate puts the annual value of gifts in business at over $1.5 billion. Ninety-seven percent of all organizational buyers accept gifts or favors from their vendors. The gifts range from liquor and food, lunches, and tickets to sporting or entertainment events, to faster delivery times and inventory control assistance.[42] The extent of gift giving concerns purchasers and sellers alike, to the extent that most firms with codes of ethics specify acceptable gift giving and receiving practices.

RESPONDING TO ETHICAL CONCERNS

Companies respond to ethical concerns by a variety of means. One of the most overarching approaches is to develop an ethical corporate culture (see Exhibit 3.11). Firms with an ethical corporate culture must be vigilant in maintaining that culture, which may involve updating the corporate mission statement or code of ethics, providing managers with a set of rules or guidelines for ethical thinking, and developing pertinent training seminars and courses.

EXHIBIT 3.11

AN AGENDA FOR DEVELOPING AN ETHICAL CORPORATE CULTURE

1. Ensure that a code of ethics is in place and followed.
2. Ensure that a procedure for whistleblowing and/or ethical concerns is established for internal problem solving.
3. Involve line and staff employees in the identification of ethical issues in order to gain understanding and resolve issues.
4. Determine the link between departments and the issues affecting the company, then make them known to employees in the departments.
5. Integrate ethical decision making into the performance appraisal process.
6. Publicize, in employee communications and elsewhere, executive priorities and efforts related to ethical issues and decision making.

SOURCE: Susan J. Harrington, "What Corporate America Is Teaching About Ethics," *Academy of Management Executive,* 5(1) (1991): 21–30.

Company Mission Statements and Codes of Ethics

The codes of ethics of many firms have been criticized for being too vague or for having a limited applicability to actual business practices of the firm. Unfortunately, many corporate codes of ethics do not have a great impact on the types of decisions that are made in the company.[43] To ensure that their codes will have some impact on behavior, firms need to ensure that their codes are (1) communicated, (2) specific, (3) pertinent, (4) enforced, and (5) revised.[44]

To *communicate* their codes of ethics, employers often require new employees to sign a statement that they have read and understand the firm's code of ethics. However, the code is often not referred to again, and employees can forget the provisions in the press of everyday business. To avoid this, some firms require their employees to read and reaffirm their knowledge and commitment to the code of ethics annually.

The code should offer *specific* guidance to sales managers. For example, the Donnelly Mirror's code gives specific guidance on gifts from salespeople to clients: "If you can't eat it, drink it, or use it up in one day, don't give it or anything else of greater value." There is not much room for ambiguity here!

The code should be *pertinent* to the industry. In other words, the code should address the key ethical dilemmas that employees of the firm are likely to encounter in their work. For example, the code of ethics for an insurance firm should discuss treatment of elderly clients. A telemarketing firm's code should contain specific prohibitions against the use of high-pressure sales tactics.

Codes of ethics should be visibly *enforced*. If a salesperson for Donnelly Mirror gives a gift of greater than the specified value, the salesperson will be reprimanded. If the behavior continues, termination could result.

Last, codes of ethics should be *revised* periodically to ensure they remain current. If not, with changes in markets, customers, and accepted business practices, the code runs the risk of not reflecting actual business conditions. If that occurs, employees are unlikely to pay much attention to it.

EXHIBIT 3.12
GENERAL ETHICAL CHECKLIST

1. Does my decision treat me or my company as an exception to a convention that I must trust others to follow?
2. Would I repel customers by telling them?
3. Would I repel qualified job applicants by telling them?
4. Have I been cliquish? (If yes, answer questions (4a) thru (4c); if no, skip to question 5)
   a. Is my decision partial?
   b. Does it divide the constituencies of the company?
   c. Will I have to pull rank (use coercion) to enact it?
5. Would I prefer to avoid the consequences of this decision?
6. Did I avoid any of the questions by telling myself that I could get away with it?

Scoring: (1)   Respond to each question with a "Yes" or "No."
             (2)   Count the number of each response. A decision with any "Yes" responses should be changed or discarded.

SOURCE: Michael R. Hyman, Robert Skipper, and Richard Tansey (1990), "Ethical Codes Are Not Enough," *Business Horizons,* 33 (March–April): 15–22.

Rules or Guidelines for Ethical Thinking

Some firms provide their managers with simple lists of rules to be used when making decisions. Those lists include questions such as, Would you like for this decision to appear on *60 Minutes* [an investigative news television show]? Other firms have proposed a set of such questions as guidelines or rules for making ethical decisions. One such list of rules appears in Exhibit 3.12. The questions may help managers make better decisions by reducing the ethical variables involved to a simple list of rules. The simplicity of the rules, however, can also cause problems. Some have argued that the lack of specificity to a particular industry or firm renders them ineffective. Making the rules relevant to the industry is more likely to yield employee acceptance.

Seminars and Courses

Seminars and courses are a popular means of addressing companies' desires to heighten ethical awareness among their employees.

SUMMARY

Knowledge of legal issues by sales managers is important because (1) laws and regulations change frequently, thereby requiring sales managers to study and monitor relevant regulations, and (2) awareness of the relevant regulations by sales managers allows them to practice preventive law. Knowledge of ethical issues is important if firms seek to act in a more socially responsible manner than that required by law.

Legal issues are divided into laws concerning the seller's behavior in the marketplace and the seller's behavior toward its employees. Important laws concerning the seller's behavior in the marketplace include antitrust, UCC and common law, state and local ordinances, telemarketing regulations, and laws concerning international commerce. These laws regulate domestic and international commercial transactions. Important laws concerning the seller's behavior toward its employees include regulations pertaining to unlawful discrimination and laws pertaining to working conditions, such as sexual harassment, stress, and call monitoring.

Following the letter of the law, however, represents only the minimal acceptable behavior by firms. Many firms have sought to pursue a more ethical approach to business. Several key factors influence ethical decision making in sales management, including the industry, the company, top management, sales management, the salesperson, and the purchaser. Firms can respond to ethical concerns by creating an ethical corporate culture, developing and communicating a code of ethics, providing guidelines for ethical thinking, and sending managers to seminars and courses on ethics.

KEY TERMS

antitrust	cooling-off periods
Sherman Act	Green River ordinances
per se violations	asterisk bills
price fixing	Treaty of Rome
horizontal price fixing	Foreign Corrupt Practices Act
vertical price fixing	Export Administration Act
resale price maintenance	employment at will
tying agreements	wrongful dismissal
FTC Act	whistleblowers
Clayton Act	Civil Rights Act
exclusive dealing	Age Discrimination in Employment Act
Robinson-Patman Act	Vocational Rehabilitation Act
price discrimination	Pregnancy Discrimination Act
Uniform Commercial Code (UCC)	Americans With Disabilities Act
common law	sexual harassment
fraud	code of ethics
warranties	crooks
express warranties	Good Samaritans
puffery	seekers
implied warranties	rationalizers
tortious interference with business	house accounts
relationships	

DISCUSSION QUESTIONS

1. Why is it important for sellers to follow legal and ethical guidelines?
2. What is preventive law? When practicing preventive law, what two broad categories of law are important to the seller?
3. What laws govern the seller's behavior in the marketplace, including its relationships with customers and competitors?
4. What laws govern the seller's behavior toward its employees and agents?

5. What legal issues are most significant when a firm has international dealings?
6. What is the attitude of the general public toward the level of ethical behavior in sales? What has fueled these perceptions?
7. Why is it in a firm's best interest for salespeople and sales managers to act ethically?
8. What factors influence a salesperson's ethical/nonethical behavior? Which influences are under the control of the firm?
9. How can a firm ensure that its salespeople act in an ethical manner?
10. How should a firm respond to unethical behavior?

PROBLEMS

1. Chuck Walters, a sales rep for a large copier firm, is in the final stages of closing a major sale. The client asks Chuck about the speed of the copier. Chuck tells her that his copier is 20 percent faster than the major competitor's. Chuck knows, however, that this is not true. The two copiers actually operate at about the same speed. When Chuck closes the deal, he brags to his manager that all it took was a little bending of the facts to get the sale. Did Chuck's actions create a legal or ethical problem for the firm? What should the manager say to Chuck?

2. John Lewis, a sales rep for a major heavy equipment manufacturer, closes an important overseas sale for several million dollars worth of equipment for road building. One week after closing the deal, a minor official in the transportation department of the national government contacts John to request a $1 million payment to the minister of the department to ensure that future transactions run smoothly. John immediately reports the request to his manager. What should the manager do?

3. Daniel Spencer, a new sales rep for an industrial chemicals firm, attended a training session on the company's newest chemical product. Before attending the training session, however, Daniel researched the product. His research revealed that although the product was very useful for cleaning equipment, it was difficult to dispose of and very dangerous to the environment. During the session, the trainer recommended this product to be sold to firms operating in fragile environments, such as national parks and bird sanctuaries. Should Daniel approach top management with his concerns about the product?

SHORT CASE
GDI CHEMICAL

BACKGROUND

GDI Chemical sells a variety of industrial chemicals used to maintain equipment in production lines. The company has three primary customers that account for 74 percent of GDI's sales. Although GDI has traditionally only had male sales representatives, Maria Ignacio-Lopez was hired two years ago as a sales rep and she has consistently exceeded her sales quota. Because of her accomplishments, Maria was granted one of the company's major clients, Performa Corporation, a top manufacturer of high-tech electronic equipment. Soon after she was given the Performa account, Maria's manager, Bill Edwards, noticed that Maria's performance was deteriorating and she appeared to be less focused and motivated.

SITUATION

Bill calls Maria into his office and begins by saying, "Maria, you have impressed us all by your accomplishments here at GDI Chemical. However, since you received the Performa account, you have fallen short of our expectations. What seems to be the problem?"

After a short pause, Maria says, "Bill, I have been very fortunate to have been granted the Performa account, but in order to properly service the client I am afraid that I need your help."

"How could *I* help?" asks Bill hesitantly.

"I feel that I am being sexually harassed by the contact person at Performa. At every meeting he insists that we discuss the deal over dinner and drinks. When I refuse, he makes degrading sexual comments. He is also calling me at the office, asking me to go out with him. This whole situation has really affected my performance on all my accounts, and I'm not sure what else I can do except to refuse his offers."

"Well, Maria," Bill says, "I can't believe this is happening. I never imagined we would have this sort of problem at GDI. As you know, you're the first female sales representative that we've had, and frankly I don't know how to handle this situation. Do you have any suggestions?"

"I have tried everything I can think of to distract the client, such as ignoring his behavior and not returning his calls. I've been trying to avoid him for five weeks now, and I don't know what else to do. It's starting to affect my other work, and I am beginning to dread all contact I must make with the Performa account."

PROBLEM

Bill understands the pressures Maria is under but is unclear about the solution. One thing, however, is certain: saving the Performa account is crucial to the profitability of GDI. Bill doesn't think he can help Maria because the client is not an employee, but if Maria's performance doesn't improve, Bill will be forced to give her a less important account.

QUESTIONS

1. What should Bill do to help remedy the situation? What should Maria do?
2. What could Maria have done to perhaps prevent the situation from occurring?
3. Is Bill right in thinking that he cannot discipline the client because the employee is not a GDI employee?

ETHICS ROLE PLAY

CHARACTERS

Salesperson: George Lymberopolous or Roberta Swenson
Customer: Dr. Mel Patterson or Dr. Myra Lolitch
Sales Manager: Doug Douglas or Darla Goode

SCENARIO

Salesperson Roberta Swenson is talking with Dr. Mel Patterson at a Ulsir EX seminar being sponsored by EDD. The seminar was arranged by Swenson with a noted national scholar speaking on gastrointestinal disorders. Swenson has invited fifteen specialists to the seminar. She is particularly pleased that Dr. Patterson has attended. Swenson has worked hard maintaining Dr. Patterson's business and, in fact, Dr. Patterson has prescribed Ulsir EX regularly for the past three years.

SCENE 1

Swenson approaches Dr. Patterson, greets him warmly, and thanks him for attending the seminar. (The discussion should contain the information in the beginning scenario.) Swenson asks Dr. Patterson what he thinks of the speaker. After a positive response, Swenson kiddingly says, "I told you that Ulsir EX was the best drug on the market for ulcers. I really have appreciated your business over the past few years, and I look forward to more of the same in the future." Dr. Patterson responds by implying that he may be changing drugs for the future. "What?" replies Swenson. "Why?" Dr. Patterson states, "I need a new VCR for my waiting area and the rep for Myopic drugs has promised me one if I strongly consider his drug. You know it is a pretty good drug." Swenson says that she does not want to lose Patterson's business. "Well, get me my VCR and maybe we can maintain the status quo." Swenson replies that EDD has a strict policy on this type of "gift." "We can't give this kind of incentive. My boss, Doug Douglas, won't allow it." Patterson responds, "Roberta, you're a bright young woman. You figure it out."

SCENE 2

Swenson has a meeting with her manager, Doug Douglas. Swenson tells Douglas that she has a problem and reviews the situation. Douglas becomes enraged that a doctor is trying to extort a VCR from EDD. Douglas reaches for the phone, "I'm going to call that quack and tell him what I think of his values" Swenson tries to calm Douglas by stating that it would guarantee EDD's losing the business. Swenson explains how important the account is because of the amount of business that Patterson has given in the past. Swenson tells Douglas, "This account probably is my fourth or fifth most productive account." The two then discuss various alternatives to keep the business and long-term consequences of each alternative. Finally, Douglas says, "I'll do my best to back you. Roberta, play it smart, but whatever you do, *don't lose* the account."

SCENE 3

The third scene is yours and can include any of the characters and be in any location. Remember there is no correct answer. Consider the alternatives and consequences and resolve Swenson's dilemma.

CHARACTER DESCRIPTIONS

Name: Darla Goode
Gender: F
Age: 45
Marital Status: Married
Education: BBA—Northeast Louisiana State
Title: Sales Manager
Office Location: Minneapolis
Reports to: District Manager—Chicago
Employment history: Started as Sales Rep; moved up to Training, has been in management for 9 years
Personality: Likeable; stern but fair; easy-going; prefers to avoid controversy
Notes: Sensitive to the policies and rules of the company; has 2 children and 3 dogs
Grapevine: Possible candidate for District Manager

Name: Doug Douglas
Gender: M
Age: 54
Marital Status: Married
Education: BBA—Boise State University
Title: Sales Manager
Office Location: Minneapolis
Reports to: District Manager—Chicago
Employment history: With Pharmiceaux for 22 years, 15 years as a manager
Personality: Likeable; stern but fair; prefers to avoid controversy
Notes: 4 children (2 in college); loyal to company; has plateaued with Pharmiceaux; avid golfer
Grapevine: Possible early retirement candidate

Name: Roberta Swenson
Gender: F
Age: 33
Marital Status: Single
Education: BBA—St. Thomas, MBA—University of Minnesota
Title: Senior Sales Rep
Office Location: Minneapolis
Reports to: Sales Manager—Minneapolis/St. Paul
Employment history: With Pharmiceaux for 6 years
Personality: Motivated; self-starter; leadership qualities; aggressive; straightforward, no-nonsense; follows the rules
Notes: Top performer for 1991; avid skier; likes outdoor activities

Grapevine: May be moving to marketing department

Name: George Lymberopolous
Gender: M
Age: 34
Marital Status: Married
Education: BBA—James Madison MBA—University of Virginia
Title: Senior Sales Rep
Office Location: Minneapolis
Reports to: Sales Manager—Minneapolis/St. Paul
Employment history: With Pharmiceaux for 10 years
Personality: Motivated; goal-oriented; leader; puts company goals ahead of personal goals
Notes: Active in community; avid golfer; consistently in top third in sales
Grapevine: In line for National Accounts position

Name: Dr. Mel Patterson
Gender: M
Age: 48
Marital Status: Married
Education: M.D.—State Medical University
Title:
Office Location:
Reports to:
Employment history: Family practitioner
Personality: Abrasive; greedy; competent; dedicated
Notes: Senior partner in a large practice

Grapevine: Opinion leader in the medical community; will use his influence

Name: Dr. Myra Lolitch
Gender: F
Age: 42
Marital Status: Married
Education: M.D.—State Medical University
Title:
Office Location:
Reports to:
Employment history: Family practitioner
Personality: Abrasive; greedy; competent; dedicated
Notes: Senior partner in a large practice
Grapevine: Opinion leader in the medical community; will use her influence

QUESTIONS

1. Is providing a VCR to a customer in order to receive their business ethical? Why or why not?
2. According to the guidelines discussed in this chapter, what incentives should Swenson provide?
3. List at least four realistic alternatives in this case. What are the long-term consequences of each alternative?
4. Which of the alternatives in question 3 should Swenson select? Defend your answer fully.

NOTES

1. "Chrysler to Pay 40,000 Customers; Each Will Get at Least $500 in Odometer Suit Settlement," *The New York Times* (August 24, 1988): A12.
2. O. C. Ferrell and John Fraedrich, "Understanding Pressures that Cause Unethical Behavior in Business," *Business Insights,* 9 (Spring/Summer 1990): 1–4
3. Edwin M. Epstein, "The Corporate Social Policy Process: Beyond Business Ethics, Corporate Social Responsibility, and Corporate Social Responsiveness," *California Management Review,* 29 (Spring 1987): 99–109.
4. R. Eric Reidenbach and Donald P. Robin, "A Conceptual Model of Corporate Moral Development," *Journal of Business Ethics,* 10 (1991): 273–284.
5. Robin T. Peterson, "An Examination of Industrial Sales Representative Accuracy in Discriminating Selected Legal and Illegal Actions," *Journal of Personal Selling and Sales Management,* 14 (Spring 1994): 67–72.
6. Mary Jane Sheffet and Bebra L. Scammon, "Resale Price Maintenance: Is It Safe to Suggest Retail Prices?" *Journal of Marketing,* 49 (Fall 1985): 82–91.
7. Federal Trade Commission, "Trade Regulation Rule: Cooling-Off Period for Door-to-Door Sales," 16 C.F.R. Part 429 (1982).
8. This discussion is drawn from Karl A. Boedecker, Fred W. Morgan, and Jeffrey J. Stoltman, "Legal Dimensions of Salespersons' Statements: A Review and Managerial Suggestions," *Journal of Marketing,* 55 (January 1991): 70–80, and from

Richard G. Shell, "When Is It Legal to Lie in Negotiations?" *Sloan Management Review,* 32 (Spring 1991): 93–101.

9. Paul E. Pompeo, "To Tell the Truth: Comparative Advertising and the Lanham Act Section 43(A)," *Catholic University Law Review,* 36 (Winter 1987): 565–583.

10. Robert J. McHatton, *Total Telemarketing* (New York: Wiley, 1988).

11. "Telemarketing Rules Ok'd," *Marketing News,* 29 (September 11, 1995): 1.

12. Jack G. Kaikati and Wayne A. Label, "American Bribery Legislation: An Obstacle to International Marketing," *Journal of Marketing,* 44 (Fall 1980): 38–43.

13. See M. Blackburn, "Restricted Employer Discharge Rights: A Changing Concept of Employment at Will," *American Business Law Journal* (1979): 114, and J. Lopatka "The Emerging Law of Wrongful Dismissal," *Business Lawyer* (1984): 1.

14. R. Malin, "Protecting the Whistleblower From Retaliatory Discharge," *Michigan Journal of Law Reform* (1983): 227.

15. 29 C.F.R. 1604.11 (1984).

16. Cathy Owens Swift and Russell L. Kent, "Sexual Harassment: Ramifications for Sales Managers," *Journal of Personal Selling and Sales Management,* 14(1) (1994): 77–87.

17. L. A. Winokur, "Harassment of Workers by 'Third Parties' Can Lead Into a Maze of Legal, Moral Issues," *The Wall Street Journal* (October 26, 1992): B1.

18. The steps in dealing with sexual harassment complaints are dealt with in more detail in Swift and Kent (1994), op. cit.

19. This discussion is drawn from John M. Ivancevich, Michael T. Matteson, and Edward P. Richards III, "Who's Liable for Stress on the Job?" *Harvard Business Review,* 63 (March–April 1985): 60–72.

20. D. J. Lincoln, M. M. Pressley, and T. Little, "Ethical Beliefs and Personal Values of Top-Level Executives," *Journal of Business Research,* 10 (1982): 475–487.

21. Anusorn Singhapakdi and Scott J. Vitell, "Marketing Ethics: Sales Professionals Versus Other Marketing Professionals," *Journal of Personal Selling and Sales Management,* XII (Spring 1992): 27–38.

22. Patrick E. Murphy and Gene R. Laczniak, "Marketing Ethics: A Review With Implications for Marketers, Educators, and Researchers," in *Review of Marketing 1981,* eds. Ben M. Enis and Kenneth J. Roering (Chicago: American Marketing Association, 1981), 257.

23. These reasons why salespeople act unethically are based on Alan J. Dubinsky, Roy D. Howell, Thomas N. Ingram, and Danny N. Bellenger, "Salesforce Socialization," *Journal of Marketing,* 50 (October 1986): 192–207, and Thomas R. Wotruba,, "A Comprehensive Framework for the Analysis of Ethical Behavior, With a Focus on Sales Organizations," *Journal of Personal Selling and Sales Management,* 10 (Spring 1990): 29–42.

24. Joseph A. Bellizzi and Robert E. Hite, "Supervising Unethical Salesforce Behavior," *Journal of Marketing,* 53 (April 1989): 36–47.

25. Gene R. Laczniak and Patrick E. Murphy, "Fostering Ethical Marketing Decisions," *Journal of Business Ethics,* 10 (1991): 259–271.

26. Raymond Dreyfack, "Bad Guys Finish Last," *American Salesman* (February 1990): 25–28.

27. Lawrence M. Fisher, "Accusation of Fraud at Sears; Auto Repair Shops Cited by California," *The New York Times* (June 12, 1992): C1.

28. The model of influences on ethical decision making in sales is based on O. C. Ferrell and Larry G. Gresham, "A Contingency Framework for Understanding Ethical Decision Making in Marketing," *Journal of Marketing,* 49 (Summer 1985): 87–96, and Thomas R. Wotruba, "A Comprehensive Framework for the Analysis of Ethical Behavior, With a Focus on Sales Organizations," *Journal of Personal Selling and Sales Management,* 10 (Spring 1990): 29–42.

29. Lawrence A. Crosby, Kenneth R. Evans, and Deborah Cowles, "Relationship Quality in Services Selling: An Interpersonal Influence Perspective," *Journal of Marketing,* 54 (July 1990): 68–81.

30. Mark S. Frankel, "Professional Codes: Why, How, and With What Impact," *Journal of Business Ethics,* 8 (1980): 109.

31. Shelby D. Hunt, Van R. Wood, and Lawrence B. Chonko, "Corporate Ethical Values and Organizational Commitment in Marketing," *Journal of Marketing,* 53 (July 1989): 79–90.

32. W. Matthews, "Codes of Ethics: Organizational Behavior and Misbehavior," in *Research in Corporate Social Performance and Policy,* eds. Frederick, et al. (Greenwich, Conn.: JAI Press, 1987).

33. Susan J. Harrington, "What Corporate America Is Teaching About Ethics," *Academy of Management Executive,* 5(1) (1991), 21–30.

34. Saul W. Gellerman, "Managing Ethics From the Top Down," *Sloan Management Review,* 30 (Winter 1989): 73–79.

35. Kenneth R. Andrews, "Ethics in Policy and Practice at GTE Corporation," in *Corporate Ethics: A Prime Business Asset—A Report on Policy and Practice in Company Conduct,* ed., James Keogh, (New York: The Business Roundtable, 1988), 61.

36. T. R. Martin, "Ethics in Marketing: Problems and Prospects," in *Marketing Ethics: Guidelines for Managers,* eds., Gene R. Laczniak and Patrick E. Murphy (Lexington, Mass: D.C. Heath, 1986).

37. Joseph A. Bellizzi and Robert E. Hite, "Supervising Unethical Salesforce Behavior," *Journal of Marketing,* 53 (April 1989): 36–47, and Joseph A. Bellizzi and D. Wayne Norvell, "Personal Characteristics and Salesperson's Justifications as Moderators of Supervisory Discipline in Cases Involving Unethical Salesforce Behavior," *Journal of the Academy of Marketing Science,* 19(1) (1991): 11–16. Bellizzi and Hite's finding of gender bias in sales manager control was challenged in Shay Sayre, Mary L. Joyce, and David R. Lambert, "Gender and Sales Ethics: Are Women Penalized Less Severely Than Their Male Counterparts?" *Journal of Personal Selling and Sales Management,* 11 (Fall 1991): 49–54.

38. For a review of these studies, see Thomas R. Wotruba, "A Comprehensive Framework for the Analysis of Ethical Behavior, With a Focus on Sales Organizations," *Journal of Personal Selling and Sales Management,* 10 (Spring 1990): 29–42.

39. William E. Stratton, W. Randolph Flynn, and George A. Johnson, "Moral Development and Decision-Making: A Study of Student Ethics," *Journal of Enterprise Management,* 3(1) (1981): 35–41.

40. Fred I. Trawick, John E. Swan, Gail W. McGee, and David R. Rink, "Influence of Buyer Ethics and Salesperson Behavior on Intention to Choose a Supplier," *Journal of the Academy of Marketing Science,* 19 (Winter 1991): 17–23.

41. Alan J. Dubinsky and John M. Gwin, "Business Ethics: Buyers and Sellers," *Journal of Purchasing and Materials Management,* 17 (Winter 1981): 9–15.

42. Joanne Levine, "Even Santa Had Helpers," *Sales and Marketing Management* (August 1989): 56–62; Gary L. Frazier, Robert E. Spekman, and Charles R. O'Neil, "Just-in-Time Relationships in Industrial Markets," *Journal of Marketing,* 52 (October 1988): 52–67; and Robert L. Janson, *Purchasing Ethical Practices,* (National Association of Purchasing Management, 1988).

43. Lawrence B. Chonko and Shelby D. Hunt, "Ethics and Marketing Management: An Empirical Analysis," *Journal of Business Research,* 13 (August 1985): 356, and Donald R. Cressey and Charles A. Moore, "Managerial Values and Corporate Codes of Ethics," *California Management Review,* 25 (Summer 1983), 73–4.

44. Laczniak and Murphy (1991), op. cit.

GLOBAL ENVIRONMENT

World trade means competition from anywhere.

MARY ANN ALLISON, VICE-PRESIDENT, CITICORP

LEARNING OBJECTIVES

After reading this chapter, you should be able to answer the following questions:

- Why is selling in the global marketplace so important?
- How are the different modes of entry into foreign markets unique?
- What are the sales management implications of different market entry modes?
- What is the impact of cultural differences in language, business practices, and religion on sales management?
- What are the career implications of an overseas assignment?

Dell Computer uses telemarketing to sell directly from its telemarketing and manufacturing facility in Austin, Texas, to customers throughout Europe. To persuade European customers to purchase its products, Dell has had to develop a global service capacity, which it provides through a third-party service firm. Dell's sales in Europe went from zero in 1987 to over $300 million in 1991, which was about one-third of Dell's total sales.[1]

Like Dell, firms around the world are continually seeking to expand their markets beyond their national borders. The reasons for this range from increased opportunities with foreign market to saturation of home markets. Whatever the reasons, success in international markets is heavily dependent on sales management. Good sales management practices drive the development of relationships with key customers abroad, whereas poor sales management practices prohibit the development of these customer relationships.

International sales management has all of the problems of sales management within the United States, with the added issues of cultural differences in language, business practices, and religion. Exhibit 4.1 shows the problems U.S. firms face when operating in Saudi Arabia; some relate directly to sales management. Item 2, for example, involves the process of negotiation, which is typically the responsibility of the salesforce. Items 3 and 7 relate to how firms respond to customers' questions, while items 5, 6, and 11 point to problems with agent representatives of U.S. firms. Although some of these issues no doubt occur with domestic customers as well, the added distance and cultural differences can magnify the problems.

EXHIBIT 4.1
ISSUES CONTRIBUTING TO POOR U.S. EXPORT PERFORMANCE IN SAUDI ARABIA

1. U.S. spare parts inventories are often in short supply.
2. U.S. agreements made locally, even by senior negotiators, can be overturned by their boards or lawyers in the United States.
3. U.S. firms are slow to comment on quotations.
4. U.S. businesspeople do not mingle with the general population. They stick to three market centers (Jeddah, Riyadh, and Dharan) and never travel to secondary towns.
5. Many U.S. firms use export management companies that bring little except higher margins.
6. Many U.S. companies appoint two or more agents who compete against each other.
7. Many U.S. firms do not answer fax inquiries.
8. Few U.S. firms adapt the product to the local market.
9. The reputation of all U.S. firms has been tarnished by exporters who substitute second-rate products for those originally offered.

SOURCE: Secil Tuncalp, "U.S. Needs More Marketing in the Saudi Arabian Market," *Marketing News* (June 19, 1987): 10.

In general, sales managers find it difficult to take a sales approach developed in one country and successfully apply it in another. This is because the cultural differences in language, business practices, and religion can make sales practices that are acceptable in one country unacceptable in another. As a result, sales management in a global environment must be sensitive to local customs and practices while trying to meet the parent company's objectives. As will be discussed throughout this chapter, this can be a delicate balancing act, and one that requires highly skilled sales managers.

This chapter explains the global context in which sales management decisions must be made. Today's sales managers need to be aware of the rapid changes in the global economy, as well as the changes in legal and political systems around the world. Changes to these environmental variables affect not only the global markets that firms choose to pursue but also the home markets in which they will compete. Specific issues in international sales management, such as training, motivation, compensation, and recruiting, will be discussed later in this text.

This chapter is organized into four major sections. The first section is a rationale for a global marketing presence. To answer the question "Why go global?", we discuss the external and internal issues driving the need for a global marketing effort. The second section outlines the choices firms must consider when entering foreign markets. These choices range from decisions about exporting to making direct investments in foreign countries. The way a firm enters a foreign market has a major impact on the sales management issues the firm will encounter on a global basis. The third section outlines some of the cultural issues in global markets. Sales managers must be aware of issues such as language, business practices, and religion, which affect sales management practices in each country or culture. The fourth section deals with career and personal issues sales managers and salespeople face when accepting a foreign assignment.

WHY GO GLOBAL?

There are several reasons for firms to pursue global markets. These can be categorized as either external or internal. External reasons include economic, competitive, political, and legal factors beyond the control of the firm. Internal reasons are those based on company goals or management preferences.

External Reasons for Going Global

Firms consider entering foreign markets for external reasons such as foreign market opportunities (global and regional), foreign trade opportunities, foreign direct investment, levels of exports, unsolicited orders, response to customer requests, small or saturated home markets, and high levels of foreign competition in the home market. Let's look at each reason in detail.

Foreign Market Opportunities. One noted marketing authority has stated that technology has standardized global markets; therefore, companies should try to introduce standardized products to consumers in markets throughout the world at the same time.[2] One standardized product, disposable diapers, illustrates this concept. Procter & Gamble has been slow to introduce Pampers disposable diapers to foreign markets. As a result, despite their commanding market share lead in the United States, Pampers lag behind competing products in market acceptance abroad.

Foreign Trade Opportunities. Increased foreign trade is being encouraged by the lessening of trade barriers around the world and the growth of regional markets. One of the most important influences on lessening global trade barriers is the **General Agreement on Tariffs and Trade (GATT)**. GATT's rules govern trade among more than 90 countries. GATT offers its members a chance to negotiate trade differences and has the goal of reducing trade barriers around the world.

Another influence on the growth of global trading opportunities is the development of free market reforms throughout the world. For example, Eastern Europe, Russia, Southeast Asia, and Latin America are pushing their economies toward a free market system. This means that companies may be allowed to sell products in these countries that were formerly closed to outside competition. Products ranging from those offered by McDonald's, Pepsi, and Coca-Cola to heavy oil field equipment and telecommunications satellites are now being sold by Western companies to Eastern Europe and Russia—markets that opened in the 1980s.

The growth of **regional markets,** which are geographic areas with common sets of regulations and economic policies, has also accelerated the globalization process in marketing. Exhibit 4.2 shows a list of some of the regional markets in the world. While these markets vary in terms of the degree to which they share regulations and economic policy, the trend is clear: Countries are joining regional markets to facilitate trade. The North American Free Trade Association (NAFTA), whose members are Canada, Mexico, and the United States, is the largest of the newly developed regional market. These three countries have a combined population of 363 million people and a combined Gross Domestic Product (GDP) of $6.2 trillion, placing it well ahead of the European Union, which has 326 million inhabitants and a $4.4 trillion GDP. Within NAFTA, there are agreements among the countries to eliminate trade barriers

	EXHIBIT 4.2	
	REGIONAL TRADE ASSOCIATIONS	
Name	Members	1994 Total Population (1,000)
Association of Southeast Asian National (ASEAN)	Brunei, Indonesia, Malaysia, the Philippines, Singapore, Thailand	352,156
Andean Common Market	Bolivia, Colombia, Ecuador, Peru, Venezuela	98,187
Benelux	Belgium, Luxembourg, the Netherlands	25,833
European Union (EU)	Belgium, Denmark, France, Germany, Greece, Ireland, Italy, Luxembourg, the Netherlands, Portugal, Spain, the United Kingdom	350,153
European Free Trade Association (EFTA)	Austria, Finland, Iceland, Norway, Sweden, Switzerland	33,421
Latin American Integration Association	Argentina, Bolivia, Brazil, Chile, Colombia, Ecuador, Mexico, Paraguay, Peru, Uruguay, Venezuela	405,405
North American Free Trade Association (NAFTA)	Canada, Mexico, the United States	381,030

SOURCE: *Statistical Abstract of the United States 1994: The National Data Book*, U.S. Department of Commerce.

so as to facilitate trade.[3] Another example is the Treaty of Asuncion (1991), in which the presidents of Argentina, Brazil, Paraguay, and Uruguay created a free trade zone that eliminated all trade barriers among their countries by the end of 1994.

The growth of regional markets, which are also known as economic unions, affects exporters in at least two ways. First, there is a **preference effect,** which means businesses located within a regional market are favored by others within that regional market, resulting in the potential exclusion of businesses outside the regional market. To combat the preference effect, firms located outside the regional market may have to make an investment in plant and equipment in the regional market to ensure continued access to the market. Second, there is the **growth effect,** which means that the existence of reduced trade barriers within the regional market should increase overall trade opportunities. Increased trade opportunities should, in turn, offer increased sales opportunities to all firms within the regional market.[4]

The existence of regional markets does not eliminate differences among the various nations that comprise the market. Consumer preferences differ substantially among trading partners. Differences in language, customs, religion, and culture do not vanish simply because of political changes. The main effect of regional markets is the development of a common set of regulations that have an impact on the movement of goods within the market and between market members and nonmembers.

Level of Foreign Direct Investment.   **Foreign direct investment (FDI)** is the book value (total cost less depreciation) of the investment in a country by firms headquartered in another. Exhibit 4.3 shows FDI in the United States by foreign firms and by U.S. firms in countries abroad for the years 1989–1992. The level of FDI by all na-

EXHIBIT 4.3

FOREIGN DIRECT INVESTMENT (FDI)/ U.S. DIRECT INVESTMENT (USDI)

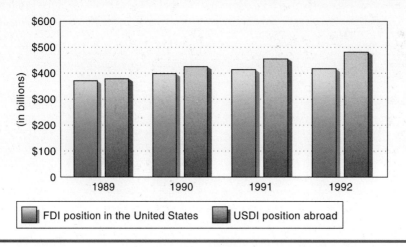

Source: *Statistical Abstract of the United States 1994: The National Data Book*, U.S. Department of Commerce.

EXHIBIT 4.5

1993 TOP TEN U.S. EXPORTERS

Company	Industry	Sales (in $ billions)	Exports (in $billions)	Export (%)
General Motors	Motor vehicles and parts	133.6	14.9	11.2
Boeing	Commercial aircraft	25.3	14.6	57.8
Ford Motor	Motor vehicles and parts	108.5	9.5	8.7
General Electric	Jet engines, turbines, plastics, medical systems, locomotives	60.8	8.5	14.0
Chrysler	Motor vehicles and parts	43.6	8.4	19.3
International Business Machines	Computers and related equipment	62.7	7.3	11.6
Motorola	Communications equipment, semiconductors	17.0	5.0	29.4
Hewlett Packard	Measurement and computation products and systems	20.3	4.7	23.3
Philip Morris	Tobacco, beer, food products	50.6	4.1	8.1
Caterpillar	Heavy equipment, engines, turbines	11.6	3.7	32.2

SOURCE: Rob Norton, "Strategies for the New Export Boom," *Fortune*, 130 (August 22, 1994): 124–132.

EXHIBIT 4.4

1984–1992 U.S. EXPORTS OF GOODS AND SERVICES VERSUS GDP

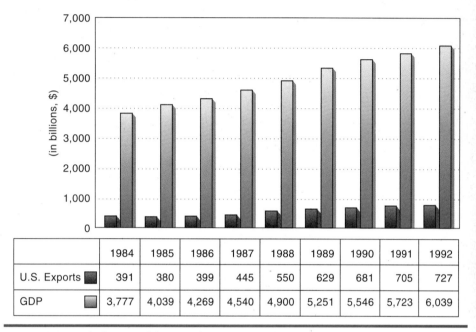

		1984	1985	1986	1987	1988	1989	1990	1991	1992
U.S. Exports	▪	391	380	399	445	550	629	681	705	727
GDP	▪	3,777	4,039	4,269	4,540	4,900	5,251	5,546	5,723	6,039

SOURCE: *Statistical Abstract of the United States 1994: The National Data Book*, U.S. Department of Commerce.

tions has been increasing, indicating that firms are becoming aware of the need to invest in facilities that will serve customers in other markets. The impact of FDI on sales management is that the increases in FDI show that more and more firms are willing to invest abroad and are therefore required to develop global sales operations.

Level of Exports. In 1994 the United States exported over $700 billion in goods and services. This amounted to about 10 percent of the U.S. GDP (see Exhibit 4.4), which means that exports play an important role in the U.S. economy. Since 1986 total U.S. exports have risen at a rate four times that of the increase in GDP.[5] The United States sells about 20 percent of its industrial production and about 33 percent of its agricultural production abroad. Most U.S. exports are made by a relatively few large firms (a list of some key U.S. exporters is shown in Exhibit 4.5). About 250 companies account for over 85 percent of all exports of manufactured goods. Most of the remainder of the exports are accounted for by approximately 25,000 manufacturing firms (10 percent of the 250,000 manufacturing firms in the United States) who export their goods on a regular basis. From a sales management perspective, most of the large exporters have well-developed global sales operations. Opportunities in global sales exist for the firms that are in the process of developing a global market presence.

Unsolicited Orders. **Unsolicited orders** come from buyers in countries where no organized effort to generate sales has taken place. For example, suppose a clothing manufacturer sells only through independent representatives in the United States. If the manufacturer received an order from a U.K. firm, it would be an unsolicited order because no sales effort was aimed at the U.K. market. If enough orders are received, the clothing manufacturer might contemplate developing a global sales operation.

Response to Customer Request. Firms may also enter foreign markets as a result of response to customer requests. For example, Caterpillar has a commitment to provide high levels of service for its customers anywhere in the world. In order to meet its service commitment, Caterpillar must receive rapid service from its suppliers. Therefore, Caterpillar's suppliers often establish sales outlets in countries where it has a major presence so as to provide the rapid response Caterpillar requires.

Small Home Market. Another reason for pursuing foreign markets is small home markets. For companies headquartered in countries with small populations, such as Norway, Sweden, and Taiwan, exports are the major way to achieve economies of scale. In countries with large populations and high levels of consumer demand, such as the United States and China, exporting has traditionally been a less important means of increasing sales, thereby creating opportunities for global sales operations.

Saturated Home Markets. For companies in countries with saturated markets (i.e., markets with limited growth potential), foreign sales represent attractive new markets. For example, beer sales in the United States are expanding at about 2 percent per year, while Korean beer sales are expanding at 15 percent per year. As a result, Coors is establishing a joint venture with Jinro, Korea's largest producer of alcoholic beverages.[6] Coors has chosen to focus on high-growth markets outside the United States, specifically Mexico and eastern Europe.[7]

High Levels of Foreign Competition. Finally, firms that experience high levels of foreign competition often export for defensive reasons. For example, Kodak launched a major campaign to increase film sales in Japan after Fuji entered the U.S. film market, but Kodak failed to prevent Fuji from establishing a solid presence here. If firms can keep their competitors engaged in their home markets, the competitors will have fewer resources to attack new markets.

Internal Reasons for Going Global

While external reasons highlight potential new markets for a firm to sell its products abroad, the firm must be motivated to seek out those markets. Those motivations are the internal reasons for going global. They include managerial urge, marketing advantages, economies of scale, risk diversification, extending sales of a seasonal product, and excess capacity.

Managerial Urge. Managerial urge is the extent to which the managers of a firm have a global outlook. These managers, called **globetrotters,** are trained to think in global, not domestic, terms.[8] In the United States there has traditionally been a low number of these individuals. However, as we will discuss later in this chapter, many firms are now beginning to train personnel for assignments around the world.

Marketing Advantages.   Marketing advantages exist for a company when it has a particular competence in an area of marketing. For example, firms can have a marketing advantage of strong customer support on a global basis. Boeing and Caterpillar, two large U.S. exporters, are well known throughout the world for high quality of customer service regardless of location.

Economies of Scale.   Economies of scale occur when the costs of production can be spread over more units. For industries with high fixed costs, such as automobiles, sales in foreign markets allow the firm to spread the costs of developing new products and constructing new plants and equipment over more units.

Risk Diversification.   **Risk diversification** occurs when a company tries to spread its risk over a large number of markets. Risk takes several forms, including currency fluctuations, economic downturns, political turmoil, competitor encroachment, and changes in regulations. By operating in several markets, companies can shield themselves from problems in any single market.

Extending Sales of Seasonal Products.   Companies that manufacture seasonal items, such as clothing and sporting goods, can stretch their season by selling products throughout the world. It may be winter in January in the United States, but in Australia it is summer. Therefore, swimwear designers and suntan lotion companies can extend their seasons by operating in both countries.

Excess Capacity.   Excess capacity occurs when a company has greater production capacity than its current markets can absorb. Firms in high fixed-cost industries, such as automobiles and semiconductors, must operate at a high percent of capacity to generate adequate revenues. If the firm operates in a market that cannot absorb enough product to allow the firm to generate adequate revenue to cover fixed costs, additional markets must be sought.

FOREIGN ENTRY MODES

If a firm weighs the internal and external reasons for entering foreign markets and finds there are sufficient reasons to pursue those markets, it must then make several decisions regarding which markets to enter, how to enter those markets, and how to manage the firm's selling effort. Determining which markets to enter requires detailed analysis of such factors as the country's economic, political, and cultural milieu. Box 4.1 summarizes the results of the analysis Matsushita performed before entering 38 countries. (Further information on foreign market analysis can be found in any text on international marketing or international management that deals with issues such as economic and political risk assessment prior to market entry.)

Firms have several options when entering a foreign country: exporting, licensing, joint ventures, and foreign direct investment (FDI). These options vary in terms

---

BOX 4.1
MATSUSHITA'S LESSONS FOR GOING GLOBAL

- Be a good corporate citizen in every country, respecting cultures, customs, and languages.
- Give overseas operations your best manufacturing technology.
- Keep expatriate headcount down and groom local managers to take over.
- Let plants set their own rules, fine-tuning manufacturing processes to match the skills of workers.
- Develop local research and development to tailor products to markets.
- Encourage competition among overseas outposts and with plants back home.

SOURCE: Cindy Kano, "Matsushita Shows How to Go Global," *Fortune* (July 11, 1994): 159–166

---

of the type of risk and level of resources committed by the parent firm. For example, a firm may elect to enter an overseas market by simply shipping in response to unsolicited orders. This strategy, known as direct exporting, requires very little planning or commitment of resources from the parent firm. On the downside, a firm can possibly incur opportunity cost by failing to pursue the market in a more orderly way. FDI, by contrast, involves a great deal of planning and commitment of resources. Exhibit 4.6 lists the options firms have in entering foreign markets, organized by level of risk and return.

The choice of market entry mode is very important in terms of sales management requirements. Some modes require very little sales management expertise and support, while others require highly skilled sales managers. Exhibit 4.7 shows the selling methods used and common sales management decisions for each market entry method. The following section describes each method of entering foreign markets and discusses some of the sales management issues that are faced by firms following each method.

EXHIBIT 4.6
RISK/RETURN OF VARIOUS ENTRY METHODS

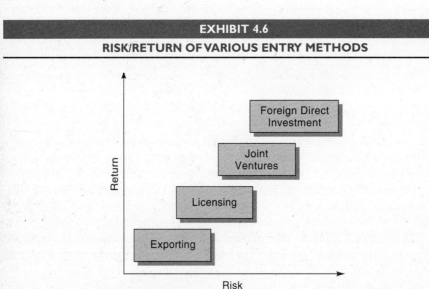

EXHIBIT 4.7		
SALES MANAGEMENT IMPLICATIONS OF MARKET ENTRY MODES		
Market Entry Mode	Selling Methods	Sample Sales Management Decisions
Exporting	• Shipping • Telemarketing • Sales offices • Commercial agents • Distributors	• Selecting, training, motivating, and compensating agents or distributors • Terminating agents or distributors • Managing telemarketing operations
Licensing	• Selling handled by the local partner	• Must make sure agreement with local partner covers sales management practices
Joint ventures	• Selling often handled by local partner	• Selection of partners; assurance that partners share benefits
Foreign direct investment	• Whatever firm chooses	• Depends on selling method chosen • Personnel decision is particularly important —whether to use expatriates, third-country nationals, or local hires

Exporting

Exporting is one of the most frequently used methods of entering foreign markets. Exporters ship from manufacturing or distribution facilities in one country to customers in another. It is often cited as the lowest-cost method of entering a foreign market because it does not require the exporter to build manufacturing facilities or commit large fixed resources to a market until market potential is established. Exporting also becomes necessary when the source of the product is fixed. Many raw materials, such as diamonds, rubber, lumber, and other commodities must be exported because the raw materials are found in a limited number of locations. For example, Perrier mineral water is exported from its only source located in France.

Firms export in several ways: order fulfillment, sales offices, agents, and distributors. The methods vary in terms of the level of marketing resources required.

Filling Orders.   Some firms export by simply filling orders from other countries. They don't necessarily solicit the orders, nor do they have a network of customer support facilities available in the market. This is particularly common when a firm first enters a market.

Sales Offices.   Sales offices are branches of the manufacturer that sell to customers in a given market. Establishing a sales office offers a manufacturer several advantages, including control of pricing and other marketing efforts. It can be problematic, however, if the salesforce is not familiar with host country business practices or if sales in the country are based on long-term relationships between buyers and sellers. In that case, firms often use commercial agents or independent distributors.

Commercial Agents.   **Commercial agents** solicit orders for a manufacturer but they do not take title to the goods. In the specialty chemical industry, for example, commercial agents are quite common. They are very familiar with the needs of customers in a certain industry, and they solicit orders for one or more chemical manufacturers.

Independent Distributors.   **Independent distributors** are local firms with an in-depth knowledge of the market that purchase products from manufacturers (i.e., take title to the goods) and resell them. When Japan opened its razor market to foreign firms in 1962, Schick distributed its products through Seiko, which has a large distribution network in Japan. Seiko still imports Schick razors from the United States and sells them to 150,000 wholesalers in Japan. Gillette, on the other hand, tried to establish its own salesforce in Japan. Unfortunately, its salesforce did not have the level of access to the Japanese market enjoyed by Seiko. As a result, although Gillette dominates the razor market in the United States, Schick is the market leader in Japan.[9]

It is estimated that more than one-half of the world's trade is handled by commercial agents or distributors.[10] Commercial agents and independent distributors can be extremely valuable in establishing the contacts necessary to sell a product in a given country. They also allow the firm to forego the expense of setting up an office in a new market and to enjoy rapid access to markets where a newcomer may have to spend a long period of time developing relationships.

The primary disadvantages for firms using independent distributors are lack of control over the distributor's actions and lower margins due to sharing the margin with the distributor. Because of these disadvantages, many firms use commercial agents or independent distributors to enter a market and then switch to sales branches as volume allows. For example, Guiness, a U.K.–based firm that sells Johnnie Walker scotch and Guiness beer, used independent distributors to enter the Japanese market. Several years ago, because of problems with marketing practices of the Japanese distributors, Guiness purchased the distributors and established its own sales offices.[11] Similarly, Nissan used an independent distributor to enter the U.K. market. After a dispute with the distributor, Nissan terminated the distributor and established its own sales subsidiary in the United Kingdom.[12] The economics of switching from commercial agents or independent distributors to company sales offices will be discussed in Chapter 8.

Firms must be aware of legal issues surrounding their use of commercial agents and distributors.[13] For example, when considering terminating a commercial agent, laws and regulations vary widely from country to country in terms of the conditions under which agents can be terminated, and the rights and remedies available to agents who are terminated. The European Union has established a directive (Directive 86/653/EEC) on commercial agents covering issues such as termination and exclusive territories.[14] All members of the EU had to implement this directive in law by January 1, 1994. This single directive has replaced national laws of the member states. In the past, if a manufacturer terminated an agent or distributor in Belgium, for example, the agent or distributor was able to claim the value of any increase in goodwill, expenses for developing the business, plus full reimbursement for all compensation claimed by discharged employees who worked on the account.[15] In France national law allowed terminated agents to claim one year's commission from the principal. The EU directive is much less punitive to manufacturers who terminate agents.

The EU directive on terminating commercial agents does not apply to independent distributors. Therefore, across the EU, regulations concerning the relationships between commercial agents and manufacturers are uniform. The laws that apply to the relationships between independent distributors and manufacturers are those of the country to which the contract is subject.

Latin American countries are even harsher in their treatment of firms who terminate agents. In Puerto Rico agents who are terminated without just cause can claim an amount equal to profits for the last 5 years. In Mexico terminated agents are given the same protections as dismissed employees.

The sales management implications of the maze of different national laws for the termination of agents is that the choice of an agent should be made very carefully. If the decision is made without due care and termination becomes necessary, the firm may encounter significant costs and loss of goodwill. On the other hand, if it is necessary to enter a market quickly, an agent or distributor may be the only option, especially in countries where sales are a function of long-term relationships between buyers and sellers.

Licensing

Licensing occurs when one firm allows another to use its patents, trademarks, technology, or something else of value. Licensing can also be very useful because it can be very low risk. Licensors can write into the licensing agreement that the licensee has to pay a set fee, or that the fee is a percentage of total sales or total profits. This allows the licensor to enjoy the fruits of its property without committing any resources. Licensing can be the only means of market entry in countries where nondomestic companies are not allowed, although the number of countries where this is the case is very low.

Licensing makes sales management the problem of the licensee. However, the licensor must monitor the licensee to ensure it uses proper selling techniques. The licensor must also be careful to include a clause in the licensing agreement to allow for termination if the licensee does not execute its sales responsibilities properly.

Joint Ventures

Under a **joint venture,** two or more companies share stock ownership of a new entity. Joint ventures are particularly common in countries such as China where foreign investors are only allowed to have minority ownership positions. By 1991 over 10,000 joint ventures had been formed in China.[16] Joint ventures are also commonly used to enter markets restricted on some other basis. For example, Corning Glass Works, a U.S.–based company, uses joint ventures to gain access to local telephone companies who favor local suppliers. As of 1989 Corning had participated in over 23 foreign joint ventures, which accounted for more than half of Corning's operating profits. As another example, General Foods tried to establish a market presence in Japan for Maxwell House coffee in the 1970s, but found that maintaining a significant market position on its own was extremely difficult. As a result, in 1975 General Foods established a joint venture with Ajinomoto, a Japanese food manufacturer, to gain access to the Japanese distribution system and to form relationships with retailers. Within two years the market position of Maxwell House began to improve, and by 1982 the company had 25 percent of the Japanese instant coffee market. This was an increase of almost 100 percent over what General Foods had been able to capture on its own.[17]

From these examples it is clear that joint ventures offer great advantages in terms of access to markets. The local partner builds relationships with local customers that would be difficult if not impossible for the foreign partner to develop on its own. However, problems can arise between local and foreign partners. The partners may feel that benefits are not evenly shared, or problems with regard to time frames, business practices, or culture and political differences can occur.

One important problem that can arise is when one partner feels it cannot control the actions of the other. This may be particularly relevant in terms of controlling the behavior of the salesforce. If personal selling is the primary means of communicating with customers, and the local partner is not communicating with customers properly, the local partner can harm the reputation of the foreign partner even though the local partner is at fault. As a result, the sales management practices of the local partner must be closely monitored and the contract governing the joint venture must include forbidden sales management practices as a cause for termination.

Direct Investment

With **direct investment** the firm has 100 percent ownership of its foreign subsidiaries. In this case, the firm has the greatest exposure to risk with foreign markets and local business practices, but it eliminates the possibility of disagreements with local partners. Firms often choose direct investment after they have gained experience in a market through exporting. For example, as previously discussed, Nissan made a direct investment in the United Kingdom after it had gained experience selling through an independent distributor.

Sales management issues in foreign wholly owned subsidiaries can range from hiring, selecting, compensating, and motivating to training. In essence, firms with foreign subsidiaries face all the sales management issues they do at home, but with the added problems of differences in language and in business practices, as well as management of expatriates and foreign nationals.

PROBLEMS AND ISSUES UNIQUE TO GLOBAL SALES MANAGEMENT

The overriding problem in international sales management is the differences in cultures between the local market and the foreign seller. Understanding differences in cultures is an absolute prerequisite for a sales manager to be successful across different markets. **Culture** is defined as "a learned, shared, compelling, interrelated set of symbols whose meanings provide a set of orientations for members of a society."[18]

Sales managers must recognize several important elements about culture in this definition.

- Culture is learned; it is not innate. People learn it as members of a given society. As a result, practices which are perfectly permissible in one society may be forbidden in another.

- Culture is shared by all members of a society. It is a means of distinguishing between members and nonmembers of the society.
- Members of a society are bound by the dictates of their culture. One of the important functions of culture is to provide a code of behavior that delineates acceptable actions by members of the society. These codes can be laws, or they can be less formal rules for behavior, such as closing your mouth while chewing and putting your hand in your lap while eating.
- Culture provides a yardstick against which to measure relative terms. Consider views toward time. In some cultures, people are expected to be quite punctual, while in others a more relaxed attitude prevails. Knowing how a particular culture views time can be important for salespeople in setting appointments or promising delivery dates.
- Culture provides a context in which communication occurs. The message can be communicated by content as well as the background of the communicators.

In **low-context cultures** the message is communicated primarily by the content of the message. For example, the United States and Germany are considered to be low-context cultures. In these countries, legal documents spell out all rights and obligations of both parties to a contract. If an item is not covered in the contract, it is not considered to be part of the deal. By contrast, in **high-context cultures** the message is communicated as much by the background and relationships between the communicators as by the actual content of the message. For example, in Japan and Saudi Arabia, which are high-context cultures, legal documents are less prevalent as a means of governing relationships between parties. The relationships between the parties, their social standing, families, company affiliations, and the like are much more important as a means of controlling the behavior of both parties.[19] Sales managers from a high-context culture dealing with a buyer from a low-context culture—or vice-versa—must be careful to ensure contracts cover all pertinent issues.

Sales managers who want to understand a new culture must be aware of three important cultural elements. These elements include language, business practices, and religion. Each of these elements will be discussed in the following sections.

Language

Sales managers must be familiar with verbal and nonverbal means of communication when operating in a foreign culture. In spoken language, meanings must be extremely clear. Unfortunately, certain spoken communication is prone to misinterpretation. Humor, for example, rarely translates well, and social chit-chat has numerous potential pitfalls. For example, while Americans are used to providing a short verbal résumé to new acquaintances, certain European countries consider it uncouth in a social setting to ask someone what they do for a living. In Arab countries, it is important to engage in social chit-chat because coming to the point of the sales call immediately is considered rude. However, the chit-chat should not include questions about the family, as that is also considered quite rude.

Nonverbal communication can be even more hazardous. In Arab countries it is extremely rude to hand something to someone with the left hand. The left hand is considered unclean. It is also rude to show the soles of one's feet to others in the room. Conversational space also varies in different cultures. In Brazil personal space is small. Businesspeople think very little of speaking while standing only inches apart. In the United States such close conversation implies intimacy and can be very uncomfortable. However, if an American salesperson were to back away because of discomfort due to the closeness of the other person, the action might be interpreted as standoffish. Touching is also a major part of many cultures. In Italy and Latin America it is quite common for members of both sexes to touch each other frequently during conversation. In Turkey it is not uncommon for male friends to hold hands while walking down the street.

Gestures can also have many different meanings. An American salesperson may indicate closure of a deal by creating an "O" with the forefinger and thumb. While this means "okay" in the United States, in Southern France the manager has indicated that the sale is worthless, in Japan that a bribe is expected, and in Brazil a gross insult has been made.

In written communication, it is to the advantage of sellers and buyers to have the sales documents translated, and then translated back by a different interpreter to ensure that the meaning of the original agreement is maintained. This process is known as *back-translation*. Certain languages do not lend themselves to precise meanings. For example, Japanese is inherently vague. As a result, very precise contractual obligations are often difficult to specify. Japanese businesspeople often prefer their contracts to be in English, which has a very rich vocabulary of business terms that can be used to specify contract terms in a precise way.[20]

Business Practices

Several business practices are culturally determined. These practices include the attitudes of local businesspeople toward time, gift giving, and relationships with prospective foreign customers and business partners.

Time.   Attitudes toward time are quite different across cultures. Foreign businesspeople can unintentionally offend their local partners if they do not understand the rules. For example, Japanese and German businesspeople are very punctual, but in Latin America attitudes toward time are much more relaxed. When conducting business in Lagos, Nigeria, appointments are often made "for the morning" or "for the afternoon," because of the city's notorious traffic jams. This is also true for Hong Kong. As a result, foreign businesspeople in these countries must be prepared for events not to occur with split-second timing.

Not only is the attitude toward time different, but the designated times for events such as the start and close of business and lunch breaks can be quite different throughout the world as well. Box 4.2 shows the problems that a globe-trotting salesperson or sales manager operating in different countries might have in something as simple as setting a luncheon appointment.

Gift Giving.   Giving gifts is considered normal business practice in many parts of the world. In the United States, for example, gifts are often given to important customers at Christmas. However, the gifts are not usually expensive because giving

---

BOX 4.2

HOW CAN EUROPE HAVE A SINGLE MARKET IF IT CAN'T AGREE ON LUNCHTIME?

Europe's determination to have lunch at 3:00 (Spain) or 12:00 (Germany) or 1:00 (the United Kingdom) means that catching a European business contact may be challenging. In Greece, no one makes telephone calls between 2 and 5 in the afternoon. Greeks doing business with Germans have to get to their German counterparts in the morning hours because Germans start going home at 4:00.

The British tend to arrive at their desks at 9:30 A.M., but they do not like to be rung on the phone at that hour. They do paperwork and drink their morning beverage while collecting themselves. They can rarely be reached after 5:30 P.M. even if they are at their desks; switchboards have closed by then. The French, like the Germans, tend to start early, occasionally attending working breakfasts. Civil servants in Italy work from 8:00 to 2:00 and then go home (although they work six days a week).

Stereotyping about national hours and character are risky. The levantine Turkish business community keeps hours similar to the British. The Irish (who used to say that when God created time he made plenty of it) have produced a new breed of businesspeople who pride themselves on taking phone calls from Hong Kong at 4 A.M.

The challenges are as great in European countries outside the EU. Norwegians get to the office at 8:00, leave for lunch at 11:00, and may have dinner as early as 5:00. Visitors are often mystified at finding restaurants getting ready to close at 9 P.M. Zurich bankers have been known to make appointments for 7 A.M. with visitors expected to arrive 5 minutes early.

SOURCE: "Europe Sans Horaires," *The Economist* (May 21, 1988): 60.

---

lavish gifts to customers is normally frowned upon in the United States. Indeed, many firms have established ethics codes which govern giving and accepting gifts (as discussed in Chapter 3).

Local customs of colors and numbers should be considered before gifts are presented. Colors have different meanings across cultures. White, for example, is the color of mourning in some Asian countries. Thus, giving a white present is inappropriate. In Japan giving presents in sets of four is considered unlucky, since the number four in Japanese is similar to the word for death. Some gift giving practices in different countries are discussed in Box 4.3.

Relationships With Prospective Foreign Customers and Business Partners.   As it is in the U.S., relationship selling is a dominant business practice in many countries. Many purchasers wish to deal with suppliers on a long-term basis; therefore, they expect suppliers to make a long-term commitment to serving their needs.

Motorola, after deciding to enter the Japanese pager market, hired a former U.S. government trade representative to guide its campaign. Motorola determined that it needed to focus on the public communications monopoly, Nippon Telephone and Telegraph. To demonstrate its commitment to the Japanese market, Motorola built a special assembly line to manufacture pagers to Nippon's specifications. Motorola also sought certification for mobile telephone equipment, which was a tedious, 18-month process. Building the manufacturing facility and seeking certification demonstrated Motorola's commitment to the market, and was instrumental in their market entry.[21]

BOX 4.3

GIFT-GIVING PRACTICES AROUND THE WORLD

Customs concerning gift giving are extremely important to understand. In some cultures gifts are expected, and failure to present them is an insult. In other countries, however, offering a gift is considered offensive. Business executives need to know when to present gifts (on the initial visit or afterward, in public or private), what type of gift to present, what color it should be, and how many to present.

Gift giving is an important part of doing business in Japan. Exchanging gifts symbolizes the depth and strength of a business relationship to the Japanese. Gifts are usually exchanged in the first meeting. When presented with a gift, companies are expected to respond by giving a gift. In sharp contrast, gifts are rarely exchanged in Germany and are usually not appropriate. Small gifts are fine, but expensive items are not a general practice.

Gift giving is not a normal custom in Belgium or the United Kingdom either, although in both countries flowers are a suitable gift if one is invited to someone's home. Even that is not as easy as it sounds. International executives must use caution to choose appropriate flowers. For example, avoid sending chrysanthemums (especially white ones) in Belgium and elsewhere in Europe since they are mainly used for funerals. In Europe, it is also considered bad luck to present an even number of flowers. Beware of white flowers in Japan and purple flowers in Mexico and Brazil because they are associated with death.

SOURCE: "Gifts That People Prefer," *Business America*, 112(2) (1991): 26–27.

Religion

Religion has a pervasive impact on society's values. These values are reflected in the business environment. Exhibit 4.8 shows the impact of Islam on business practices in Islamic countries. It should be clear from Exhibit 4.8 that doing business in Islamic countries is extremely difficult without a clear appreciation and understanding of the Islamic faith and its associated culture.

Religion also has a direct impact on specific issues such as hours of operation, holidays, and terms of sale. In southern Germany, for example, where the population is equally divided between Catholics and Protestants, workers receive both sets of religious holidays off, for a total of more than 20 religious holidays a year. This can cause problems with worker productivity and the ability for salespeople to meet with clients.

CAREER ISSUES IN INTERNATIONAL SALES

Importance of Global Sales Experience

The increasing globalization of business can have a tremendous effect on a salesperson's career. As more firms move into selling their products in international markets, the importance of understanding foreign markets makes overseas assignments a necessity for those seeking upper management positions. For example, international experience is a requirement for promotion to senior management at Colgate. One senior Colgate manager said, "The career track to the top—and I'm talking about the CEO and key executives—requires global experience . . . Not everyone in the company has to be a global manager, but certainly anyone who is developing strategy does."[22]

EXHIBIT 4.8	
PERSONAL SELLING IN ISLAMIC COUNTRIES	
Element of Islam	Implication for Sales Management
Unity	Strong brand loyalty
Legitimacy (fair dealing, reasonable level of profits)	Less formal product warranties, switch from profit maximizing to profit satisficing
Zakaat (2.5% annual compulsory tax on all people not classified as "poor")	Corporate donations for charity, use of excess profits for charitable actions
Usury (cannot charge interest)	Avoid direct use of credit as a marketing tool; offer discounts for cash and raise prices for products sold on installment; consider using banks from non-Islamic countries
Abstinence (Muslims must fast during Ramadan)	Take care in scheduling appointments with clients
Worship (Muslims must pray to Allah five times a day)	Take worship into account in planning sales calls, salesperson schedules, and customer service hours
Obligation to family	Customer referrals are critical
Obligation to extend hospitality to insiders and outsiders	Always partake in proffered hospitality; be sure to offer it yourself if acting as host
Strict codes of sexual conduct	Female salespeople must dress modestly to avoid offense; women are often not allowed to drive themselves— they must have a chauffeur

SOURCE: Adapted from Muchtaq Luqmani, Zahir A. Quraeshi, and Linda Delene, "Marketing in Islamic Countries: A Viewpoint," *MSU Business Topics* (Summer 1980): 20–21.

To obtain global experience, some companies have established formal programs to ensure a steady supply of executives with global experience. For example, Colgate has established a "Global Marketing Training Program" that provides it with a steady source of top-notch marketers who are capable of operating virtually anywhere in the world. The program is two years in length, and entry is highly selective. Applicants must have excellent academic credentials, fluency in at least one other language besides English, and some experience with working, studying, or living abroad for a year or more. Most of the graduates of the program are sent to markets in developing countries. Because non–U.S. markets are so important to Colgate, it does not automatically return the managers to the United States at the end of their assignment, but instead may send them to another post in another country.

The EU is also working diligently to create such a managerial corps. The European (High) School in Brussels has 15,000 students from 12 nations. Each year the students take fewer courses in their mother tongue, until they are taking courses in as many as four languages in their eleventh year.[23] These students also take classes in history, politics, and music from the perspective of all European countries. They are therefore prepared to live in any European country from the perspective of language and cultural awareness.

EXHIBIT 4.9
MIXED SIGNALS ABOUT THE IMPORTANCE OF INTERNATIONAL EXPERIENCE

OF THE PERSONNEL MANAGERS SURVEYED AT 56 MULTINATIONAL FIRMS:

- 56 percent say a foreign assignment is either detrimental or immaterial in one's career.
- 47 percent say their returning expatriates aren't guaranteed jobs with the company upon completion of their foreign assignments.
- 65 percent say their expatriates' foreign assignments are not integrated into their overall career planning.
- 45 percent view returning expatriates as a problem because they are so hard to fit back into the company.
- 20 percent consider their company's repatriation policies adequate to meet the needs of their returning expatriates.

SOURCE: Thomas F. O'Boyle, "Little Benefit to Careers Seen in Foreign Stints," *Wall Street Journal* (December 11, 1989): B1.

Not all firms have a global outlook. A survey of personnel managers at 56 multinational firms showed mixed support for international experience (see Exhibit 4.9). Despite the lukewarm reception to international experience shown in this survey, firms continue to seek international market opportunities, so the importance of international experience in a sales career will only increase.

Personnel Choices in International Sales

When firms move into foreign markets, they have three choices of personnel: local hires, expatriates, and third-country foreign nationals. Each has significant advantages and disadvantages.

Local Hires.   **Local hires** are host-country nationals who are hired by the foreign firm. In some countries, the number of host-country nationals who must be hired is a matter of law. Some firms have policies aimed at increasing the representation of host-country nationals. For example, Unilever and IBM depend primarily on host-country nationals for sales jobs.[24] Local hiring can represent enlightened self-interest on the part of the hiring firm. It is much more difficult for a country to nationalize a firm if the majority of the employees are local. Moreover, local hiring establishes the firm's reputation as a good corporate citizen.

The major advantages of a local salesforce are control and familiarity with the territory. Control is achieved through the ownership of the sales effort. Companies with local salesforces can coordinate the sales and promotional efforts. Local sales forces also represent important bridges to the local business community. They speak the language, have established contacts within the community, and are familiar with local business practices.

There are also disadvantages to local hiring of the salesforce. There may be difficulties with differences in business practices between the host country nationals and the foreign firm's employees. For example, it is quite common in Europe and Africa for mid-level executives to be provided with a company car. Conflict can result if this is not the case with the home country. Conflict can also result if socializ-

---
BOX 4.4

WESTINGHOUSE CORP. INTERNATIONAL EMPLOYEE POLICIES

International assignments can be a valuable supplement to the normal training and development programs for the high-potential employee.

GUIDELINES

1. *Pre-assignment*—A pre-assignment orientation program should be planned and implemented on a timely basis to assure that candidates and their dependents are fully prepared to undertake international assignments. Organization units assigning personnel internationally will define in writing all known conditions of assignment, including but not limited to the employee's salary, allowances, duration of assignment, etc. The employee should be provided copies of all applicable policies and procedures.
2. *Repatriation and reassignment*—Organization units should periodically review the status of their international assignees and develop specific repatriation plans for each employee. Where performance continues to be satisfactory, it is the responsibility of these units to assure that personnel selected for international assignments will have upon return a position at least equivalent to the level held by the employee prior to accepting the international assignment. For coordination reasons, it is also the responsibility of these units to keep Key Personnel Services advised of their repatriation plans or problems.
3. *Application*—This procedure applies to all organization units assigning personnel internationally, as well as to all management and professional personnel who accept an international assignment, with the exception of those engaged in service and other activities which normally require international travel or who are assigned for a limited time to specific international customer contracts abroad.

SOURCE: Westinghouse internal documents.

ing is much more important in the host country than in the home country. In Japan, for example, socializing is expected, and business entertaining is given favorable tax law treatment. In the United States, by contrast, business entertaining is expected under many circumstances, but businesses may only deduct 50 percent of the cost of meals and entertainment. As a result, entertaining is often more lavish in Japan than in the United States. However, if the Japanese office is held to the same entertainment rules as the U.S. office, customers may be offended.

Expatriates.   **Expatriates** are home-country nationals on assignment in the host country. For example, if IBM has a U.S. citizen on assignment in China, the U.S. citizen is considered an expatriate. The advantages of using expatriates are that the firm has an easier time communicating with the employee, and the employee receives important foreign experience that may be used in the future by the firm. Expatriate employees can be evaluated and compensated in a manner similar to home-country employees. Recruiting and training of expatriates are also significantly easier. Box 4.4 details how one company, Westinghouse, manages the selection, assignment, and repatriation of home-country nationals who desire overseas assignments.

The disadvantages of using expatriates include expense, role conflict, family problems, and levels of commitment by the expatriate to the home firm. Expatriates can be quite expensive, costing as much as 2.5 times their annual salary in income tax adjustments, education and housing allowances, and annual home leaves. Firms

BOX 4.5

SPOUSES MUST PASS THE TEST BEFORE GLOBAL TRANSFERS

Employees' families are playing a bigger role in international transfers. The inability of spouses or children to adapt to their new surroundings is the number one cause of failure in overseas transfers, including premature returns, and job-performance slumps. With overseas postings costing an average of $225,000 to $250,000 a year, companies are trying to smooth the way.

Many companies include spouses in the screening process for overseas assignments, including a formal assessment of such qualities as flexibility, patience, and adaptability. Ford Motor Company interviews spouses before the move. Exxon also meets with spouses and children. Minnesota Mining and Manufacturing offers spouses educational benefits and uses electronic mail to introduce employees' children to peers in the target country. 3M recently found new housing for one Japanese executive in the United States so his dog could rejoin the family.

The programs are largely a response to pressure from employees. As many as 75 percent of international transfers end in family problems such as marital discord or adjustment problems in children. Companies are finding that it's difficult to get someone to go unless they address these issues.

SOURCE: Sue Shellenbrger, "Spouses Must Pass Test Before Global Transfers," *The Wall Street Journal* (September 6, 1991): B1.

must often make salary adjustments upon repatriation, either to recognize the increased potential offered by an employee with international experience or to compensate for differences in pay scales across countries.

Expatriates often experience work problems related to adjustment difficulties encountered by their families. To overcome these problems, firms with extensive foreign operations, such as 3M, encourage the spouses and children of employees to undergo training and counseling to prepare them for living in another country. The importance of family concerns as addressed by some firms is described in Box 4.5.

Expatriates can also experience significant role conflict primarily in terms of different demands by the home and host country. Suppose that an U.S. expatriate in Australia is given the task by the home office of making a certain number of sales calls in the upcoming week. If that week included Derby Day (a national holiday in Australia), the expatriate would have a difficult time meeting the sales call requirement since few clients would be available.

One study found that expatriates can be classified by their levels of commitment to the local operation and to the parent firm (see Exhibit 4.10). For example, "free agents" have little loyalty to either the parent or the local operation. Expatriates who "go native" identify more closely with the office in the country where they are stationed than the home office. Free agents and "go native" expatriates cause the home firm to lose the primary advantage of using expatriates, which is the level of commitment by the expatriate to the home country's goals.

Expatriates who "leave their hearts at home" remain loyal to the home office but never identify with the host country. While these managers may carry out instructions well, they will not be sensitive to the needs of the host country. "Dual citizens" are expatriates who see themselves as equally accountable to the parent and the local operation. Ideally, firms would send only dual citizens overseas because

---

EXHIBIT 4.10

FORMS OF EXPATRIATE ALLEGIANCE

		Allegiance to the Local Operation	
		Low	High
Allegiance to the Parent Firm	Low	Expatriates who see themselves as free agents	Expatriates who "go native"
	High	Expatriates who leave their hearts at home	Expatriates who see themselves as dual citizens

SOURCE: J. Stewart Black and Hal B. Gregersen, "Serving Two Masters: Managing the Dual Allegiance of Expatriate Employees," *Sloan Management Review,* 33 (Summer, 1992): 61–71

those employees have the greatest likelihood of successfully completing the assignment and repatriating. The guidelines listed in Exhibit 4.11 are intended to help sales managers create true dual citizens of the employees they send abroad.

Third-Country Nationals. **Third-country nationals (TCNs)** are employees who are transferred from one host country to another, but who are citizens of neither the host country nor the home country of the firm.[25] TCNs often speak several languages and are quite adaptable to living in different cultures. The graduates of the European High School discussed earlier in this chapter are a good example of individuals preparing to become TCNs.

EXHIBIT 4.11

GUIDELINES FOR DEVELOPING DUAL CITIZENS

1. *Limit time away from the corporate office.* This reinforces the link between the manager and the parent firm.
2. *Send managers with strong ties to the corporation.* Send managers with a strong sense of identity with the firm. One way to measure this is through the amount of time the employee has been with the firm. However, with international assignments being increasingly used to develop high-potential managers, this may not be possible.
3. *Establish corporate sponsor programs.* Corporate sponsors are senior managers in the home country who act as a career mentor with expatriates. Having a mentor ensures that the expatriate is not "out of sight, out of mind" when it comes to promotions and other recognition.
4. *Provide pre-departure and post-arrival cross-cultural training.* It is preferable to provide this for the expatriate and his or her family.
5. *Facilitate cross-cultural adjustment.* Encourage the family to participate in the native culture rather than remaining isolated. This helps with adjustment for the family as a whole.
6. *Encourage host sponsorship programs.* These are programs where managers in the host country help expatriates become familiar with the new culture.

SOURCE: J. Stewart Black and Hal B. Gregersen, "Serving Two Masters: Managing the Dual Allegiance of Expatriate Employees," *Sloan Management Review,* 33 (Summer, 1992): 61–71.

Firms are increasingly relying on TCNs. Pioneer HiBred International, a supplier of hybrid seeds for increased agricultural yields, employs TCNs in increasing numbers abroad because they are willing to accept difficult living conditions in developing countries. Scott Paper, whose TCNs increased from two in 1987 to thirteen in 1990, is actively recruiting TCNs willing to relocate frequently throughout Europe or around the Pacific.

As with using local hires and expatriates, firms also face advantages and disadvantages in using TCNs. Advantages include a willingness to accept difficult living conditions and rapid adaptation to a new environment. The disadvantages include the difficulty of developing loyalty to the parent firm if frequent relocations occur without repatriation, and the possible problems of adapting management styles and techniques based on business practices in one culture to another. TCNs also encounter problems such as blocked promotions, anxiety over their next relocation, gaps in income between their salaries and those of host-country or home-country nationals, adaptation difficulties (especially if transfers have been frequent), avoidance of long-term projects if transfers are imminent, and insufficient authority in industrial relations.[26]

SUMMARY

The global conditions that affect sales management are changing rapidly. Going global is an increasingly common way of doing business. There are numerous external and internal reasons for entering global markets. External reasons include global and regional foreign market opportunities, foreign trade opportunities, foreign direct investment, levels of exports, unsolicited orders, response to customer requests, small or saturated home markets, and high levels of foreign competition. Internal reasons include managerial urge, marketing advantages, economies of scale, risk diversification, extending sales of seasonal products, and excess capacity.

If a firm chooses to enter a foreign market, it has several means to do so. Those means include exporting, joint ventures, licensing, and direct investment. Each means of foreign market entry carries different sales management requirements.

As a firm enters markets in other countries, one of the biggest challenges it faces is adapting to the culture of the host country. An important characteristic of culture is the level of context. Host countries with high-context cultures are those in which the relationships among parties are based on a complex web of business and social relationships. Low-context cultures are those in which relationships among parties are based on contract language. Other important cultural issues for sales managers include language, business practices, and religion.

Firms that enter foreign markets must make certain personnel choices and address career issues for their salespeople and sales managers. It seems inevitable that as the importance of international trade continues, and more firms enter international markets, the level of international experience desired by firms will increase. As a result, salespeople and sales managers may need to seek opportunities to obtain foreign experience.

When firms enter foreign markets, they have three choices for staffing those sales operations. They can use host-country nationals, expatriates, or third-country nationals (TCNs). There are several advantages and disadvantages for each staffing choice. Firms who use expatriates must be careful to have an organized process by which high-potential managers are identified, trained, and repatriated.

KEY TERMS

General Agreement on Tariffs and Trade (GATT)	independent distributors
	licensing
regional markets	joint ventures
preference effect	direct investment
growth effect	culture
foreign direct investment (FDI)	low-context cultures
unsolicited orders	high-context cultures
globetrotters	local hires
risk diversification	expatriates
exporting	third-country foreign nationals (TCNs)
commercial agents	

DISCUSSION QUESTIONS

1. Why is selling in the global marketplace so important?
2. Why would a company want to become globally focused? What are the external and internal motivations?
3. In your opinion, how can sales managers determine whether or not there is sufficient reason to pursue global markets?
4. How can firms enter a foreign market? What are the advantages and disadvantages of each mode of entry?
5. Rate each mode of entry on its risks and capital requirements.
6. What are the sales management implications of different market entry modes?
7. How does culture, as it is defined in this text, play a role in the success of international sales?
8. What are the three broad cultural elements discussed in this chapter? How could a sales manager specifically prepare to deal with these elements?
9. What are the career implications of an overseas assignment?
10. What personnel choices does a firm have when entering a foreign market? What makes each choice unique?

PROBLEMS

1. Lars Johnasson, a sales manager for a firm that sells construction equipment, is talking with Jack Smires, a salesperson who has recently returned from Saudi Arabia. Jack says, "The sales call went well until the final meeting. When I arrived for the meeting, I made brief small talk by asking about their families. Since I was in a hurry to cover all the last minute details of the pur-

chase, I tried to keep the conversation on course, which meant that I turned down their offers of coffee and tried to cut short their discussion of a recent horse race. When they refused to be hurried, I just sat back and propped my feet on the coffee table, since the meeting was quite informal, and waited until they finished their conversation. Finally, I was able to make my sales pitch. Now they tell me I didn't get the order. I just don't understand. Our product's performance is the best in the industry and the price is right. We also have the service capability they need." What errors did Jack make in his presentation? What suggestions should Lars have for Jack, and for training programs at the construction firm?

2. As a sales manager at a U.S. firm that sells personal computers, you realize that the growth in Europe is much greater than the growth in the United States. Your firm, however, has always used telemarketing as its primary selling method in the United States, and you have heard that the only way to sell personal computers in Europe is through a field salesforce. A field salesforce is an expense that your firm is not willing to bear. What options do you have for expanding to Europe?

3. As the vice-president of sales for a large securities firm in the United States, you must approve all monthly expense reports from the district offices. Two years ago your firm established a sales branch in Japan. Their entertainment expenses have been consistently above the norm, despite repeated notices to keep entertainment costs at a reasonable level. The situation is now threatening to cause problems elsewhere in the firm. District managers from the United States have heard of the high levels of entertainment expenses in Japan and are complaining that they are not allowed as much leeway as the Japan office receives. Worse yet, the Japanese office, despite the high expenses, is one of the lowest performers in terms of number of new accounts established and total assets managed. What should you do? Is it time to put stringent rules for entertainment expenses into place? Should all district offices be subject to the same guidelines for expenses? Should you press the Japanese office for higher levels of new accounts and assets?

SHORT CASE

COMPSELECT, INC.

BACKGROUND

CompSelect Inc. sells personal computers in the United States. Over the past 7 years, CompSelect has focused marketing efforts on domestic market awareness and education. As a direct result of its efforts, the company has established high brand recognition and is ranked by a major computer publication as one of the highest in quality.

Over the last few years, while CompSelect focused on the growth of its domestic sales, its competitors began entering the European market. The growth of personal computer usage in Europe is much greater than the growth in domestic markets because in the past computers were not seen as a household item. Europeans used to perceive computers only as a tool for powerful individuals in organizations. The foreign market was essentially untapped, and CompSelect failed to notice its growing attractiveness because it was too narrowly focused on important issues in the domestic market.

SITUATION

Sam Bush, a sales manager for CompSelect, is concerned about the company's lack of involvement in the market overseas. Understanding that operations in a foreign market are distinctly different than those in the domestic market, Sam begins to research various European countries to compare advantages and disadvantages of CompSelect expanding into each. Although several countries seem very attractive, he has narrowed the list to France and Turkey.

France appears to be a logical fit for CompSelect expansion because of the country's high level of education in the field of personal computers. The U.S. companies that have already entered this market have spent a large amount of money educating the public and stimulating demand. The market is not yet saturated and, therefore, is inviting to the company. The primary disadvantage to this country is that the communication network is very unstable. Because CompSelect primarily does its selling through telemarketing, expanding to France will involve a drastic change in selling methods.

The other country that is appealing is Turkey. Contrary to France, Turkey has an excellent communications network, but personal computers are very new to the market. This market believes that the only use for computers is in processing and storing vast amounts of data at large firms. Entering into this market would involve an intense education campaign.

The markets in France and Turkey have two similarities. First, the customers expect high quality. It is essential for CompSelect to maintain its high standards of quality and position itself as the quality leader in order to be successful in the foreign marketplace. Second, in either country computer repairs will need to be made quickly if necessary.

PROBLEM

After researching the issue, Sam is even more puzzled about CompSelect's best option. CompSelect has used telemarketing as its primary domestic selling strategy in the past. This approach has been very successful in reaching and educating prospective customers, but Sam has heard that the only way to sell personal computers in Europe is through a field salesforce. A field salesforce is very expensive and will not reasonably fit within Sam's sales budget. Sam, however, can petition for a larger budget if he has significant reason for incurring the added expense.

QUESTIONS

1. What are Sam's sales strategy options? What are the advantages and disadvantages of each when considering expansion into foreign markets?
2. Which country is the best fit for CompSelect? Why? Which sales strategy would best complement that country?

GLOBAL ROLE PLAY

CHARACTERS

Salesperson: Karen White
District Manager: Byron Simpson
Customer: Ali Tobruk, Minister of Health

SCENARIO

Karen White has been a sales rep for Pharmiceaux for the past 6 years selling from the Richmond office. Recently White was promoted and transferred to the international division of Pharmiceaux, where she will be selling hospital supplies in Africa and the Middle East. She is being assigned to the Cairo, Egypt, office although she will travel extensively. The first scene opens with White meeting her boss, Byron Simpson, who is also new to the Cairo office after having worked in Denmark for 5 years. Simpson is describing a potentially highly profitable account in Cairo. Scene 2 has White calling on Ali Tobruk, the Minister of Health for Egypt. Tobruk is polite but not very communicative. Scene 3 has White and Simpson discussing the failed meeting.

SCENE 1

White enters Simpson's office and introduces herself to him. Simpson replies, "Welcome to Cairo. I've heard a lot of good things about you. I've examined your sales records and they are very impressive." "Thank you," Karen responds, "I look forward to the challenge of working in international sales." Simpson laughs and says, "You may change your mind after a few weeks of selling in the international arena." "I don't think so," Karen replies.

Simpson tells White about a potentially very large and lucrative account in Cairo. He has set up a meeting with the Minister of Health. "Ali Tobruk is the Minister of Health for Egypt, and he has a great deal of power in determining what company will distribute hospital supplies. He has an MBA from the University of Chicago and is very influential in the Cairo community. We need to impress him. I've set up an appointment between you and him for Friday. Do your homework."

SCENE 2

White enters Tobruk's office. She smiles, offers her hand, and tells Tobruk that it is a pleasure to meet him. She asks him about his Chicago experience. Tobruk is very polite but not overly responsive. Finally White begins talking about Pharmiceaux and how Pharmiceaux wants his business. She shows him a notebook full of products and says that Pharmiceaux guarantees that they can deliver the products at a better price than any of the competitors. Tobruk seems unimpressed and

looks at his watch. "You will have to excuse me, I have an appointment. Thank you for coming by. It was a pleasure to meet you." The scene ends with White being very surprised at the quick end to the meeting.

SCENE 3

White again meets with Simpson and explains what happened at her meeting with Tobruk. "I don't understand" she says. "He was charming but didn't seem to care about our products at all. I guess I blew it." The scene continues with Simpson and White talking about what went wrong and how to get Tobruk interested in the product. The role players should plan another meeting and how the meeting will be approached. The role play may include a fourth scene with a new meeting.

CHARACTER DESCRIPTIONS

Name: Karen White
Gender: F
Age: 31
Marital status: Single
Education: B.A., University of West Virginia
Title: Sales Rep
Office location: Richmond
Reports to: Sales Manager, Richmond
Employment history: 6 years with Pharmiceaux
Personality: Personable; born to sell; problem solver
Notes: Active in the community; sorority officer; part-time salesperson in college
Grapevine: Career sales, but leaving Pharmiceaux

Name: Byron Simpson
Gender: M
Age: 40
Marital status: Married
Education: B.A., McGill University; MBA, University of Western Ontario
Title: District Manager
Office location: Denmark
Reports to: European Manager
Employment history: Began with Pharmiceaux at 24; was a manager at 29
Personality: Warm, sympathetic, sincere, friendly
Notes: Two of his recent salespeople are now sales managers; championship pistol shooter, home defense expert

Grapevine: Good mentor and trainer

Name: Ali Tobruk
Gender: M
Age: 59
Marital status: Married
Education: MBA, University of Chicago
Title: Minister of Health
Office location: Cairo, Egypt
Reports to:
Employment history:
Personality: Polite, but not very communicative; a
  leader
Notes: Influential in the Cairo community; pow-
  erful decision maker
Grapevine:

QUESTIONS

1. What are the career implications of Karen's being transferred to the international division?
2. What are some of the problems women face when selling in Islamic cultures?
3. What goals should a salesperson have for an initial contact with a customer in Cairo? How is that different than the goals for an initial contact in the United States?
4. List at least four realistic alternatives Karen has for her next meeting with Tobruk. What are the long-term consequences of each alternative?
5. Which of the alternatives in question 4 should Karen select? Defend your answer fully.

NOTES

1. Dell Computer Patrick Oster "Breaking into European Markets by Breaking the Rules," *Business Week* (January 20, 1992): 88–89.
2. Theodore Levitt, "The Globalization of Markets," *Harvard Business Review,* 61 (May–June 1983): 92–102.
3. The discussion of regional trade in Latin America is based on Jon I. Martinez, John A. Quelch, and Joseph Ganitsky "Don't Forget Latin America," *Sloan Management Review,* 33 (Winter 1992): 78–92.
4. The discussion of preference and growth effects is drawn from Gerald Albaum, Jesper Strandskov, Edwin Duerr, and Laurence Dowd, *International Marketing and Export Management,* (Reading, Mass.: Addison-Wesley, 1989).
5. Rob Norton, "Strategies for the New Export Boom," *Fortune,* 130 (August 22, 1994): 124–132.
6. "Coors Brews Big Plans for Korea," *Business Week* (December 9, 1991): 44.
7. "Coors: In Global Beer Parlance 'We're Learning More Every Day'," *Beverage World,* vol. 113, Issue 1578 (October 31, 1994): 10–12.
8. Hans Thorelli and Helmut Becker, *International Marketing Strategy,* 2nd ed. (New York: Pergamon Press, 1980).
9. "Schick Versus Gillette in Japan," *The Wall Street Journal* (February 4, 1991): B1.
10. Thomas F. Clasen, "An Exporter's Guide to Selecting Foreign Sales Agents and Distributors," *Journal of European Business,* vol. 3, Issue 2 (November/December 1991): 28–32.
11. "Guiness in Japan: A Combination of Luck with Some Judgment," *Financial Times* (July 13, 1989): 13.
12. "Nissan Gets Back in the Driving Seat," *Financial Times* (December 31, 1990): 10.
13. Susanne Meier Robinson, "Drafting High-Performance Agency and Distribution Agreements," *Journal of European Business,* vol. 4, Issue 2 (November/December 1992): 36–39.
14. Shannon H. Shipp, Robert T. Rhodes, and Andrea Harbusch, "Commercial Agents and Distributors in the European Union," working paper (Texas Christian University M. J. Neeley School of Business, 1994).
15. Warren J. Keegan, *Global Marketing Management,* 4th ed. (Englewood Cliffs, N.J.: Prentice-Hall, 1989).

16. "Foreigners Find China Ventures Difficult to Quit," *The Wall Street Journal* (March 12, 1991): A15.
17. Kenichi Ohmae, *Triad Power* (New York: The Free Press, 1985).
18. Vern Terpstra and Kenneth David, *The Cultural Environment of International Business,* 3rd ed. (Cinncinnati, Ohio: South-Western, 1991).
19. Edward T. Hall, *Beyond Culture* (Garden City, N.Y.: Anchor Press/Doubleday, 1976).
20. Eric J. Adams, "Scaling the Tower of Babel," *World Trade* (April 1991): 42–45.
21. "Motorola Leaps a Japanese Barrier," *Business Week* (June 7, 1982): 33.
22. "Colgate's Global Marketing Training," *Business International* (September 10, 1990): 306.
23. Glynn Mapes, "Polyglot Students Are Weaned Early Off Mother Tongue," *The Wall Street Journal* (March 6, 1990): A1.
24. W. Chan Kim and R. A. Manborgue "Cross-Cultural Strategies," *Journal of Business Strategy* (Spring, 1987): 29.
25. The discussion of TCNs is based on "Wooing Third Country Nationals," *The Wall Street Journal* (September 16, 1990): B1.
26. Problems encountered by TCNs are found in Yoram Zeira and Ehud Harari, "Managing Third Country Nationals in Multinational Corporations," *Business Horizons,* 20, (5) (1977): 83–88.

RETZEL PHARMACEUTICALS (B)

This case was prepared by David G. Burgoyne for the sole purpose of providing material for class discussion at the Western Business School. Certain names and other identifying information may have been disguised to protect confidentiality. It is not intended to illustrate either effective or ineffective handling of a managerial situation.

Mr. Rajh Gawrytuloui had been hired as a salesperson to cover the Kubaman (a fictitious country) market by Retzel Pharmaceuticals in October, 1989. His supervisor Mr. C. Schmidt, Assistant International Sales Manager based in Cologne, Germany considered Mr. Gawrytuloui's efforts and accomplishments over the ensuing ten months as barely adequate. In Mr. Schmidt's view Mr. Gawrytuloui was capable and made effective calls on Doctors and Pharmacists. He also had developed a good relationship with Mr. Ahmed Djibril an agent for Retzel who was responsible for obtaining product listings with the government and all aspects of physical distribution. Unfortunately, Mr. Gawrytuloui's work habits and overall effort were lacking and therefore the number of calls being made were not what Mr. Schmidt would have liked.

In July, these issues paled in comparison with the situation that developed in Kubaman. The country had been invaded and all contact with Mr. Gawrytuloui had been cut off. Just this morning (August 25th) Mr. Schmidt had received a telephone call from the Retzel agent in an adjoining country to Kubaman to say that Mr. Gawrytuloui and his two children had contacted the agent to say that they had escaped from Kubaman and were being held as refugees at the local airport. The agent had located the family, cleared them through immigration control as tourists with the local agent assuming responsibility for them, given them funds, had them checked by a Doctor and registered them in a hotel. Although Mr. Gawrytuloui and the children were suffering from fatigue, stress and malnutrition they were otherwise fine physically. They had escaped by Mr. Gawrytuloui trading his car, furniture and personal possessions plus his local savings of some $10,000 U.S. for passage out.

Mr. Schmidt was preparing to brief senior management on this situation. He fully expected that they would want to know what he would recommend to do with, and for, the Gawrytuloui's both now and in the future.

DATA GENERAL AND NEW YORK'S DIVISION OF SUBSTANCE ABUSE SERVICES (A)

By Andrew D. Dyer, Georgetown University, under the supervision of Professor N. Craig Smith. The assistance of Edward T. Dominelli of the New York Office of State Inspector General and funding from the John F. Connelly Program in Business Ethics at Georgetown University School of Business are gratefully acknowledged. This case was written from public sources, solely for the purpose of stimulating student discussion.

On June 28, 1991, Data General Corporation was informed that it had been successful in winning a major contract with New York State's Division of Substance Abuse Services (DSAS).

For sales representative Daniel Snell it was no doubt a satisfying win. Both he and his manager, Kenneth Canastar, had worked hard over recent months to build a close relationship with DSAS and to put together a proposal for its computer requirements. Canastar and Snell had managed to win over both the state agency's staff and consultants at Diversified Business Enterprises of America, Inc., a third-party consulting firm hired to assist with vendor selection.

But celebrations were short-lived. On September 6, 1991, before the computer equipment had been installed, Snell received an appearance subpoena from New York's Office of the State Inspector General for an investigation of events surrounding the Data General order. Data General management had to determine quickly whether there was a problem with this particular transaction, how it should respond to the Inspector General's request, and whether to proceed with the equipment installation, scheduled for late September.

DATA GENERAL

In 1990, Data General's business was the design, manufacture, and sale of multiuser computer systems and associated products and services. Based in Westboro, Massachusetts, the corporation did business in over 70 countries around the world, through 26 subsidiaries and 300 sales and service offices. Total sales were $1.22 billion, on which the firm incurred a loss of $140 million. It employed 10,600 people, down from 15,400 in 1988, and operated manufacturing plants in the United States, Canada, Mexico, and the Philippines. Exhibit 1 provides a 5-year summary of Data General's financial performance.

The modern computer had its origins in the late 1940s, meeting the needs of the military, large corporations, and university research laboratories. At that time, computers were used for repetitive applications such as bookkeeping and solving mathematical problems. They were large and required controlled environments for their operation. As a result, computers were expensive to buy and operate, and most organizations opted for a single large machine (a mainframe) to serve their needs. Over time, it became clear that individual user needs were not being met by this centralized approach. Difficulties arose for two major reasons: (1) users resented the monopoly-like control exercised by computer departments and (2) mainframe computer technology had severe limitations in the area of user-defined applications. Users, especially scientists and engineers, called for a relatively inexpensive computer that they could operate themselves. Their demands led to the birth of the minicomputer and, with it, manufacturers such as Digital Equipment Corporation (DEC), Hewlett Packard, and Data General.

Data General was founded in 1968 by a small team of engineers led by Edson de Castro. De Castro had been part of the design team for the DEC PDP-8, a highly successful minicomputer. After leaving DEC, de Castro and his team incorporated Data General and began producing their own minicomputers. Data General's first product, the NOVA, was unveiled at the 1969 National Computer Conference and was an immediate success in the fast-growing minicomputer marketplace. Over the next 10 years, Data General grew at a phenomenal rate. By 1978, it was ranked third in sales of minicomputers; in the same year it made the Fortune 500 list for the first time.

Changes in Strategy

Minicomputer vendors such as Data General, Digital Equipment Corporation (DEC), and Hewlett Packard originally produced products that used proprietary architectures. That meant that the operating system software (the software that directs all the computer's functions) was unique to the manufacturer, and therefore all applications had to be specifically designed to run on the manufacturer's equipment under the manufacturer's operating system. Thus, for example, an application running on a DEC computer could not run on a Data General computer without extensive modification (or "rewrite"). Hence, when an organization selected a particular computer vendor, they were locked in to that vendor for future equipment purchases unless they decided to modify their applications, or implement new applications, which would run on

a machine from a different vendor. Within organizations, individual departments using different vendors were often unable to communicate via computer or share data, and each department would set up its own computer support group to manage and administer its own system.

Toward the end of the 1980s, the growing popularity of UNIX (an operating system developed by AT&T and the University of California at Berkeley) changed the minicomputer market dramatically. UNIX was an "open" system, defined by a set of public domain standards; all interested manufacturers could design their computers to operate under UNIX. Applications then became portable between the different computers that supported UNIX, allowing a customer to be totally vendor-independent. Data General, DEC, Hewlett Packard, and a number of other major vendors began introducing UNIX products to meet this new demand. Price competition increased on minicomputers as vendors positioned themselves to maintain or acquire market share in this new environment.

As a result, Data General's strategy changed from being a supplier of proprietary systems, developing long-term customers with a stable installed base, to being a supplier of low-cost, generic computers that could be sold to virtually any organization (regardless of the incumbent computer vendor) as well as to other equipment manufacturers, including its traditional competitors, such as IBM and Unisys. Key to Data General's success in the 1990s was to aggressively pursue the fast-growing open systems marketplace while profitably providing support and solutions to its extensive base of proprietary systems customers.

In 1991, Data General offered to the marketplace a mix of open and proprietary solutions: AViiON and Eclipse MV.

Introduced in 1989, the AViiON open system product line comprised 17 models of servers and 7 workstations, designed using RISC (reduced instruction set computing) processors. AViiON operated under Data General's UNIX operating system software, and over 3000 soft-

EXHIBIT I

DATA GENERAL CORPORATION:
FIVE YEAR-SUMMARY OF SELECTED FINANCIAL DATA
(DOLLAR AMOUNTS IN THOUSANDS)

	Year Ended Sept. 29, 1991	Sept. 29, 1990	Sept. 30, 1989	Sept. 24, 1988	Sept. 26, 1987
Total revenues	$1,228,854	$1,216,401	$1,314,395	$1,364,734	$1,274,348
Total cost of revenues	659,559	692,015	722,084	694,869	685,778
Research and development	101,986	140,743	149,023	156,421	157,499
Selling, general, and administrative	384,317	444,583	490,653	470,616	437,675
Restructuring charge		71,700	80,000	48,700	53,800
Total costs and expenses	1,145,862	1,349,041	1,441,760	1,370,606	1,334,752
Income (loss) from operations	82,992	(132,640)	(127,365)	(5,872)	(60,404)
Gain on sale of subsidiary and facilities	13,000	—	14,857	5,889	
Interest expense, net	4,451	3,905	1,422	6,754	9,545
Income (loss) before income taxes, net loss from unconsolidated affiliate, and extraordinary items	91,541	(136,545)	(113,930)	(6,737)	(69,949)
Income tax provision (benefit)	5,900	3,230	5,800	8,800	(10,400)
Income (loss) before net loss from unconsolidated affiliate and extraordinary items	85,641	(139,775)	(119,730)	(15,537)	(59,549)
Net loss from unconsolidated affiliate					19,958
Income (loss) before extraordinary items	85,641	(139,775)	(119,730)	(15,537)	(79,507)
Extraordinary losses					44,158
Net income (loss)	$85,641	($139,775)	($119,730)	($15,537)	($123,665)
Primary net income (loss) per share					
Before extraordinary items	$2.62	$(4.65)	$(4.10)	$(.55)	$(2.95)
Including extraordinary items	$2.62	$(4.65)	$(4.10)	$(.55)	$(4.59)
Net income (loss) per share assuming full dilution					
Before extraordinary items	$2.45	$(4.65)	$(4.10)	$(.55)	$(2.95)
Including extraordinary items	$2.45	$(4.65)	$(4.10)	$(.55)	$(4.59)

ware programs were available from suppliers of database products, languages, compilers, and word processing and other applications packages. (A *server* is a computer shared by one or

EXHIBIT I (continued)				
DATA GENERAL CORPORATION:				
FIVE YEAR-SUMMARY OF SELECTED FINANCIAL DATA				
(DOLLAR AMOUNTS IN THOUSANDS)				

	As Of				
	Sept. 29, 1991	Sept. 29, 1990	Sept. 30, 1989	Sept. 24, 1988	Sept. 26, 1987
Current assets	$ 690,537	$ 595,602	$ 709,988	$ 669,803	$ 641,609
Current liabilities	284,694	447,027	442,491	390,417	383,287
Working capital	405,843	148,575	267,497	279,386	258,322
Total assets	$ 944,046	$ 909,437	$1,040,165	$1,077,713	$1,068,311
Annual expenditures for property, plant, and equipment	$ 82,766	$ 85,066	$ 91,467	$ 96,592	$ 142,918
Long-term debt	$ 164,911	$ 56,918	$ 70,748	$ 65,945	$ 79,990
Stockholders' equity	$ 494,441	$ 405,492	$ 522,126	$ 611,921	$ 591,656
Cumulative computers shipped	326,200	297,600	276,800	253,600	226,400
Employees	8,500	10,600	13,700	15,400	15,700

NOTES: Results of operations are for 52-week periods except for 1989 which is a 53-week period. The company has not declared or paid cash dividends since inception.

SOURCE: Data General *Annual Report*, 1991.

more users through a local area network. The server can provide sharing of data and applications among local users as well as acting as a communications gateway to other computers or networks. The term *workstation* generally refers to a high-powered desktop computer that can be used for processor-intensive applications, such as computer-aided design and drawing, mapping, and complex problem solving, as well as general commercial applications.)

The Eclipse MV was a proprietary system product line that had been introduced in 1980. The MV product ranged from desktop models to models with mainframe power. Over 45,000 systems had been installed, and users had access to a range of industry-specific applications.

Data General also provided systems integration and professional, education, and maintenance services to complement its products and meet customer needs.

Data General products and services were sold through a variety of distribution channels. Direct sales were handled by over 700 salespeo-

ple, supported by approximately 600 sales engineers. The sales force was located around the world and marketed the full Data General product line to large organizations. Data General also used third-party distribution channels including original equipment manufacturers, value-added resellers, system suppliers, and independent hardware and software vendors. Data General's international sales were conducted through foreign subsidiaries, independent representatives, and distributors, with the majority of its international revenues coming from Western Europe, Canada, Japan, and Australia.

Data General customers represented a diverse range of industries, including health care, manufacturing, finance, business administration, retail, telecommunications, utilities, and government. With its AViiON products, Data General was also penetrating new growth markets such as geographic information systems and financial services. Data General's customer base was diverse. No single customer represented more than 8 percent of the firm's revenues, and total sales made directly to various agencies of the United States federal government represented only 2 percent of Data General's revenues.

THE COMPUTER INDUSTRY IN 1991

The Buying Process

The computer industry in 1991 consisted of thousands of organizations worldwide that provided equipment, software, facilities installation and management, and a wide variety of professional and advice services. There were many different types of vendors in the industry, as well as many types of buyers and buying criteria. Computer buyers ranged from technical staff, making purchase decisions based on the equipment's price and capabilities, to executives, making purchase decisions based on application requirements and/or strategic issues, with equipment as a secondary consideration. Equipment vendors like Data General tended to focus on the technical decision maker, often the actual end user. Service providers, such as consultants and system integrators, tended to focus on executives and marketed top-down to the customer organization.

Equipment vendors generally concentrated their direct sales force on large customers, where there were opportunities for high revenues and multiple sales. A sales representative was assigned a territory on either an industry or geographic basis and was responsible for generating sales from that territory as well as maintaining overall customer satisfaction. The representative would be part of a sales unit or branch, located within or close to the territory. The sales unit could also contain product or technical specialists who would assist the sales representative.

Computer equipment sales representatives were generally compensated through revenue commissions and product bonuses. A representative would be allocated a quota (which could be a monthly, quarterly, or annual target) of sales to make, and paid a base salary plus commission (in proportion to his or her achievement against quota). Quota targets were based on a number of measurements, but the most common were revenue, profit, or points. (*Points,* a measure used by some companies, including IBM until 1990, were a numerical value placed on a product that reflected a combination of the revenue, profit, and strategic significance of the product. The point score was fixed and did not take into account any discount offered on the product.) In addition to quota achievement compensation, sales representatives could receive bonuses for strategic product sales, displacing a competitor's system, or selling multiple units of a particular product to a single customer. In 1991, computer industry sales representatives could earn from as little as $25,000 to over $250,000 per annum.

Although computer systems and services were bought by organizations, quite often the purchase decision or recommendation came down to a single individual within an organization. A competent sales representative would normally determine who that individual was and then attempt to build a strong relationship with the customer. The nature of these relationships varied widely. Some were strictly business, where the sales representative developed a strong relationship by providing excellent service and support. Others involved more personal elements, where the sales representative developed a strong relationship through hosting external activities for the customer, including lunches, dinners, attendance at sporting activities, and other events. Some customers expected the latter type of relationship, just as some sales representatives expected customers to be more likely to buy if they had been appropriately entertained. As the value of computer contracts was significant (typically ranging from $1 million to $40 million), the relative expense of such entertainment was small. A sales representative would typically have an expense budget of $2000 to $10,000 for a sales quota of around $5 million (i.e., 0.04 to 0.20 percent of sales). Government agencies, however, often limited the amount of entertainment that could be received from vendors by its employees, requiring both sales representatives and customer employees to be cautious in their activities. For example, New York State officers and employees were required to abide by the guidelines set forth in the state publication *A Guide to the Ethics Law.* An extract from the Guide is provided in Exhibit 2.

To assist organizations with these complex and significant purchase decisions, external consultants were often called in to provide an independent assessment. The consultants would either manage the entire procurement process under contract or provide specialist advice to the customer, usually on technical matters. Consultants were used to assist with buying equipment, software, and services and, depending on their contract and relationship with the client, could have a significant influence on a purchase decision. Competent sales representatives were aware of the involvement of external consultants and tailored their marketing plans accordingly.

Sometimes, individual departments in an organization used the proprietary nature of different computer brands to "protect" the department's role. For example, if Department A used Brand X computer and Department B used Brand Y, the incompatibility of the two brands meant that Department A could not use B's computer or applications. As long as the two departments continued to run different types of systems, they could not be easily merged and neither department could "take over" the other department's computer operations. Sales representatives were aware that the political advantage of having a unique system would often be a factor in a computer purchase decision.

Declining Profitability

The computer industry was intensely competitive in 1991, particularly for equipment sellers. IBM-compatible personal computers and UNIX-based minicomputers had become "commodity" products, with less and less differentiation available to vendors (such as value-added support and services) that would be valued by buyers. The industry's overall profitability had fallen sharply, with return on sales dropping from around 9.5 percent in 1984 to −1.0 percent in 1991 (profits as a percent of sales for 92 computer companies, accord-

ing to McKinsey and Company). New competitors were entering all sectors of the industry, and unprecedented numbers of new products were introduced in 1991. Purchase decisions were being driven more by price and machine performance. With the large number of suppliers competing in the marketplace, sales representatives such as Data General's Kenneth Canastar and Daniel Snell worked under enormous pressure to continually win business and meet sales targets.

PROCUREMENT POLICIES IN THE PUBLIC SECTOR

Public sector organizations such as DSAS required formal procedures to be followed for the procurement of goods and services. These procedures were to ensure that the department or agency was getting the lowest price possible and that there was clear accountability and an audit traii for the spending of public funds.

Typically, purchases over a prescribed value—say $50,000—required the agency to go out to the marketplace with a formal quotation request, often referred to as a request for proposal (RFP). Vendors then had a fixed time period to respond with a written quotation and proposal, usually agreeing to the buyer's terms. The agency then evaluated the proposals against a set of criteria (such as price, functionality, service, support, etc.) and made a recommendation to management. The level of expenditure dictated how high within the organization a recommendation needed to go for approval.

Certain types of purchases also required the approval of departments other than the department originating the order. For example, it might be mandatory for a computer purchase to be approved by a central information systems group with companywide responsibility for systems applications. If a central or statewide computer procurement contract was in place, a financial group might have to sign off on a purchase. Although there were advantages in involving these groups, and usually their involvement was mandatory, the procurement process could become more complex and take longer to complete.

EXHIBIT 2
THE NEW YORK STATE ETHICS CODE

New York State has an official Code of Ethics that was created by Section 74 of the Public Officers Law. It is contained in the *Public Officers Law* booklet that all State employees receive when they join state service.

While many private companies and professional associations have their own codes of ethics, there is a major difference between their codes and the state's code: The state code is also the law. The following material summarizes some of the applicable provisions of the *Public Officers Law*.

GENERAL SUMMARY

You are prohibited from engaging in any activity that is in substantial conflict with the proper discharge of your duties in the public interest, accepting other employment that would impair your judgment in the exercise of your official duties, and disclosing confidential information which you gain from your State position.

You cannot use your official position to secure unwarranted privileges for yourself or others. If you have a financial interest in a business entity, you should not engage in any transaction between the State and that entity which might be in conflict with the proper discharge of your official duties. You also must avoid making personal investments in enterprises that you might reasonably believe may be directly involved in decisions you make or that might create a conflict of interest.

You cannot, by your conduct, leave the impression that anyone can influence you based on their family relationship, rank, position or influence. Nor should you act in a way that raises a suspicion among the public that you are likely to be engaged in acts that are in violation of your public trust.

If you are a full-time employee, neither you nor any firm or association of which you are a member—or a corporation which you own or control—can sell goods or services to any person, firm or association which either is licensed or has its rates set by the State agency in which you are employed.

*Extract from the **Public Officers Law**—Section 74(3)*

f. An officer or employee of a state agency, member of the legislature or legislative employee should not by his conduct give reasonable basis for the impression that any person can improperly influence him or unduly enjoy his favor in the performance of his official duties, or that he is affected by the kinship, rank, position or influence of any party or person.

h. An officer or employee of a state agency, member of the legislature or legislative employee should endeavor to pursue a course of conduct which will not raise suspicion among the public that he is likely to be engaged in acts that are in violation of his trust.

GIFTS

The following is from *New York Ethics: A Guide to the Ethics Law*. The New York State Ethics Commission, New York, 1991.

Gifts may come in many forms and from many people: a keychain from the company that delivers overnight mail; tickets to the ballgame from a vendor who deals with your agency; even flowers from a satisfied taxpayer. Some companies consider the distribution of such "freebies" to be part of an effective marketing plan, while others consider it good public relations.

Under the law, covered individuals may not accept any gifts valued at more than $75, in whatever form, under circumstances in which it could be inferred that the gift was intended to influence or reward the recipient in performing official duties, or was offered in anticipation of some action. Gifts under $75 may also be suspect, under Section 74 of the law, if they were intended to influence or reward the recipient.

Example: A complaint has been filed with the Department of Health regarding the facilities at a local health club. Rita, a State investigator, screens the complaint and decides that no action should be taken. The grateful club owner offers Rita a club membership valued at $300. She cannot accept the membership.

Example: Denyce, an auditor for the Department of Taxation and Finance, audits the returns of a local automobile dealership. She may not accept money for a favorable report and may not take delivery on a car from the dealership at a special discount—normally unavailable to the public—during or after the audit.

Despite the controls and accountability guidelines, there was generally enough flexibility for the buyer to ensure that his or her choice would be the successful tenderer. For example, the specifications issued could be based upon a particular vendor's product or solution, or the evaluation criteria could deliberately emphasize a particular vendor's (or product's) strengths. The individual buyer thus had substantial influence on the outcome of the procurement process and was a logical target of vendors' marketing plans.

DIVISION OF SUBSTANCE ABUSE SERVICES

DSAS was one of a number of divisions of the state of New York that managed substance abuse programs. New York's programs were aimed at both prevention of drug trafficking and related criminal activities and at treatment of the growing number of substance abuse victims in the state. DSAS administered funds for pro-grams to support the prevention of drug abuse and the treatment of drug abusers. The division did not actually operate any of the programs directly; instead it used a variety of external organizations to administer or operate each program. These programs included school- and community-based prevention efforts; expanding drug-free treatment by making more beds and ambulatory service slots available; maintaining a statewide registry of eligible methadone recipients; and doing substance abuse research, focusing on the culture of drug use and how and where drugs were obtained. All program operators (i.e., contractors) were monitored by the division through its Quality Assurance department. DSAS also played a regulatory role in ensuring that the quality of service given by treatment providers met state standards. The DSAS budget in 1990–1991 was $400 million. (The total budget for New York State at the time was $55 billion.) The organization of the division is shown in Exhibit 3.

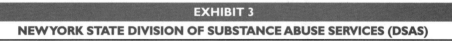

EXHIBIT 3
NEW YORK STATE DIVISION OF SUBSTANCE ABUSE SERVICES (DSAS)

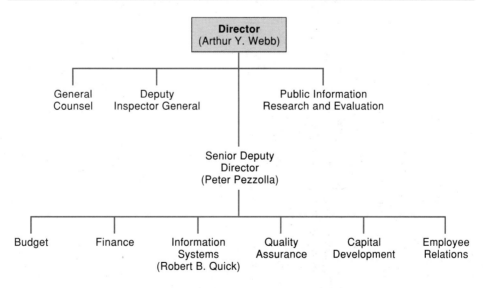

* The Deputy Inspector General reports to the State's Inspector General and is assigned to DSAS to audit its activities, with a dotted-line reporting to Webb.

Discussions had been under way for a number of years regarding merging DSAS with the Division of Alcoholism and Alcohol Abuse, an agency that performed a similar function in the area of alcohol abuse. The merger could eliminate duplication of functions and expenditure incurred by the two separate divisions. Merger discussions had intensified during 1991 and were expected to be completed within 12 months.

In 1990, in an effort to streamline the management of some of its programs, DSAS decided to upgrade its computer facilities and implement new applications. Management commissioned an Information Resource Management (IRM) Plan as a starting point for the project. In February 1991, Peter Pezzolla, a senior DSAS director, hired Robert Quick to develop the IRM Plan. Quick was appointed to the position of Assistant Director of Management Information and Analysis. Prior to joining the division, Quick had worked for another New York State department, the Office of Mental Retardation and Developmental Disabilities, where he worked on computer-related contracting matters as an Assistant Director in the office's Information Services Group. Pezzolla, who joined DSAS in February 1990, had previously been Assistant Deputy Commissioner at the Office of Mental Retardation and Developmental Disabilities, where he was Quick's second line manager. Quick had limited information systems education. He had been hired primarily for his administrative skills.

The purpose of the IRM Plan was to document current DSAS information systems and hardware components, define systems requirements for future computer applications, and define the requirements for future hardware and software. The plan would form the basis for selecting a new computer system for the division, to be implemented later that year. DSAS had engaged a consultant, Diversified Business Enterprises of America, to assist with producing the plan and selecting a computer vendor. Diversified, headed by Glenn Mazula, quoted the division a fixed price fee of $169,500 for these services. The primary application for the new system was an upgraded Client Tracking System to better match clients with available services. The system was being funded under the Target Cities Program, a federal program designed to assist certain United States cities with economic and social difficulties. DSAS had a large office in New York City, one of the cities targeted under this program.

Working with three computer vendors that had been selected by Robert Quick and Diversified Business Enterprises, a generic set of computer specifications was developed for the new computer system, which was to replace the department's antiquated system. The three vendors were Data General, DEC, and Hewlett Packard. After completing the IRM Plan and the system specification, DSAS invited all three vendors to submit design and cost proposals for the new system. Data General proposed one of its AViiON products (i.e., an open system), together with a Database Manager to be supplied directly by ORACLE (a database software vendor).

Dan Snell had been assigned by Data General to win the DSAS contract. An experienced sales representative with over 10 years in the computer industry, Snell worked closely with Ken Canastar, his manager, on the sale. He dealt primarily with the technical people, while Canastar worked more with Mazula and Quick. Canastar was the firm's senior salesperson at Albany. He reported to a regional manager, located in Pittsburgh. Canastar was also a seasoned sales representative and understood the significance of winning this deal and the potential future business for his sales territory. He also understood that losing the sale could jeopardize the future of the firm's Albany office.

After receiving the vendor bids, Diversified and the division's staff analyzed the proposals and determined that Hewlett Packard had the lowest bid. After reviewing the bid results, Quick informed his staff that the bids were too high and there were insufficient funds to cover costs. As a result, the vendors were asked to resubmit their bids and propose a less costly system. During the interim period, Quick advised Canastar and Snell that he was looking favorably on awarding the contract to Data General. Diversified reviewed and analyzed the second vendor proposals and submitted the results to Quick, who, along with his staff, found Data General was the lowest bidder. Peter Pezzolla approved Quick's selection and on June 28, 1991, Data General was notified in writing of its success. The initial DSAS order was for computer equipment at a cost of $536,000.

The sale by Canastar and Snell was a significant achievement for Data General, especially as sister departments to DSAS (such as the Division of Alcoholism and Alcohol Abuse and the Office of Mental Retardation and Developmental Disabilities) were strong DEC users and there was substantial pressure on DSAS by the Division of Alcoholism and Alcohol Abuse to implement a DEC-based solution. Because Data General's annual sales to New York State were currently only $2 million, this particular sale had the attention and involvement of Data General's president and CEO, Ronald Skates. Skates, who had viewed DSAS as a strategic opportunity, met with Quick in Albany during the selling phase and subsequently called Quick to demonstrate his support for the deal.

ROBERT QUICK AND VENDOR RELATIONSHIPS

During his time at the Office of Mental Retardation and Developmental Disabilities, Quick had dealt regularly with computer vendors. The vendors, keen to maintain their relationships and business with the department, had made regular donations to events and funds that Quick was associated with. These included the Information Systems Group Christmas parties and summer picnics, and the Kevin Quick Memorial Scholarship Fund. The Fund was established in January 1990 by friends of Robert Quick in honor of his deceased son. It was designed to award a $1000 scholarship to a graduating senior of Amsterdam High School in Albany. Quick's friends were designated as trustees of the fund.

It was in April 1990, when Quick was still at the Office of Mental Retardation and Devel-

opmental Disabilities, that Pezzolla had asked him for suggestions for the request for proposal to select consultants for the DSAS IRM Plan development. Quick had nominated CMA, General Electric Consulting Services, and Diversified Business Enterprises. (Diversified Business Enterprises at the time was co-owned by Glenn Mazula. Mazula sold his interest in this firm in early 1991 and formed Diversified Business Enterprises of America; the latter firm was hired by DSAS to assist with implementing its IRM Plan. Mazula was the sole proprietor of the new firm.) All three companies had made donations to the Information Systems Group functions and/or the scholarship fund. Typical donations ranged between $500 and $1000 per vendor, per event. Quick chose not to disclose information about these donations to Pezzolla. However, they were apparently common knowledge within the computer industry.

Quick and Mazula had first met in the late 1970s when both were employed at the New York State Department of Social Services. Quick had a passion for sports, and Mazula had the potential to assist Quick with financing and with access to sporting venues. In April 1990, Quick approached Mazula, by then a well-known sports entrepreneur in the Albany area, about financial sponsorship of a softball team that Quick managed on his own time. Mazula agreed to Quick's suggestions and provided over $60,000 between June 1990 and August 1991 for the softball team's salaries and expenses. Meanwhile, Pezzolla, using the information supplied by Quick, chose Diversified Business Enterprises to produce the request for proposal to select the IRM consultants.

Glenn Mazula, then head of Diversified Business Enterprises, had worked at the Department of Social Services for 3 years and the state Medicaid payment unit for another year before becoming a data administrator back at Social Services. Using his acquired knowledge in the administration of nursing homes and acute health care, Mazula then started a consulting business in 1980, specializing in the health and human services field. Mazula was also co-owner of the Albany Patroons (basketball) and Albany Firebirds (arena football) teams.

Diversified Business Enterprises, Mazula's original consulting firm, completed the request for proposal for the Information Resource Management consultants in August 1990, billing DSAS for $19,500 in fees. However, in its haste to expedite the project's start date, the division had never signed a formal contract for the work, so payment of the $19,500 was delayed until a contract was finally issued, in June 1991.

The 1990 RFP was never used to select a consultant, however. Instead, Quick, arriving at his new $70,000 a year job at DSAS in February 1991, hired Mazula's new firm, Diversified Business Enterprises of America, to produce the IRM Plan without soliciting competitive bids. To establish a contract directly between the division and Diversified would have required a number of approvals and a competitive bidding process. Instead, Quick used NDRI-State, a nonprofit corporation largely supported by DSAS funding, as the vehicle to establish a contract with Diversified, bypassing the normal state contracting procedures. The division's funding to NDRI-State was approximately $7.4 million in 1991.

Diversified was given an initial payment of $20,000 in April 1991 for IRM Plan services. Later that month, some $17,000 was transferred from Diversified's corporate bank account to the Albany Professional Baseball Inc. account, which had been opened by Mazula. These funds were then used to cover expenses incurred by Quick's team.

Quick also hired Diversified for a related project—assisting the division with the takeover of the methadone registry from Creative Socio-Medics, another DSAS vendor. The registry was a database service accessed by methadone providers so that they could ensure recipient eligibility. The database contained a confidential roster of methadone recipients across the state. Creative Socio-Medics was paid $200,000 per year for providing the methadone registry service. Creative Socio-Medics also generated revenues of some $3.5 million per annum for providing related services that used information from the database. Di-versified negotiated a fee of $85,000 with Quick for initial work on the registry takeover. The project would include software development and programming, and also opened up the opportunity for Diversified to sell the software to agencies of other states. Diversified commenced this work without a formal contract, leaving the ownership of software rights in question.

On May 18 and 19, 1991, the second annual memorial softball tournament was held to benefit the Kevin Quick Memorial Scholarship Fund. (The first softball tournament had been held May 19 and 20, 1990. A Kevin Quick Memorial Golf Tournament had taken place in August 1990. Detailed figures were not publicly available for the softball tournament; however, the golf tournament had yielded a net contribution of $127 to the Fund while $1200 worth of prizes had been awarded.) Quick solicited donations to fund the tournament from a number of vendors, including those bidding for the division's computer contract. DEC's sales representative made a $500 donation on May third, and Canastar and Snell made a $1000 personal donation at a breakfast meeting with Quick on May 10. Canastar and Snell planned to claim back the $1000 from Data General by submitting, under the guise of legitimate expenses, receipts for personal expenditures, such as restaurant meals unrelated to business.

Prior to the breakfast meeting, Canastar and Snell had held discussions with Mazula to explore the possibility of Diversified becoming a Data General subcontractor and software supplier should Data General be successful at DSAS. Mazula had told the Data General representatives during the discussion that the scholarship fund was important to Quick. These discussions between Data General and Diversified did not result in any formal business relationship. In fact, Canastar's proposal to pay Diversified a 5 percent commission bonus if it won the DSAS deal was rejected by Stan Driban, Data General's Director of Contract Negotiations, in late May 1991. He said, "This smacks of a bribe." Mazula continued discussions with Canastar and Snell beyond Data General's initial rejection in the first round of bidding. Mazula also had discussions with Hewlett Packard, and suggested that Hewlett Packard entertain Quick during a trip to New York City. Exhibit 4 provides a chronology of events leading up to the award of the contract to Data General.

THE NEW YORK STATE OFFICE OF STATE INSPECTOR GENERAL

The Office of the New York State Inspector General was established by Governor Mario M. Cuomo in 1986 under an Executive Order. (An extract from the Executive Order establishing

---

EXHIBIT 4
CHRONOLOGY OF EVENTS

1990

January: Kevin Quick Memorial Scholarship Fund was established by friends of Quick. Quick solicited and accepted both Fund donations and contributions to Fund-related activities during the year, in excess of $4000. (Quick is employed at the Office of Mental Retardation and Developmental Disabilities.)

April: Quick asked by Pezzolla to identify a consultant to produce an RFP for soliciting vendors to develop an Information Resources Management (IRM) Plan for DSAS. Quick recommends CMA, GECON, and Diversified Business Enterprises; all three firms have previously made donations to Information Systems Group Christmas parties and/or to the Fund. Quick approaches Mazula (co-owner of Diversified Business Enterprises) regarding the possibility of Mazula becoming the financial sponsor of Quick's softball team.

May: Pezzolla approves Diversified Business Enterprises to begin work on the request for proposal for a fee of $19,500. No contract is put in place.

June 13: Mazula provides $4650 in "seed" money to cover expenses for Quick's softball team. Over the next 12 months, Mazula provides in excess of $60,000 to Quick's softball team for expenses and salaries.

August: Diversified Business Enterprises completes the request for proposal and submits it to DSAS. Payment cannot be made by DSAS due to absence of formal contract. DSAS announces the contract in the NYS Contract Reporter in October, awards the contract to Diversified Business Enterprises in April 1991, and finally disburses payment of $19,500 on June 24, 1991.

1991

January: Quick prepares and submits to Mazula a final 1991 budget for a new softball team Quick is to manage, showing a budget deficit of $18,000. Mazula incorporates Diversified Business Enterprises of America, Inc.

February: Quick transfers to DSAS from the Office of Mental Retardation and Developmental Disabilities, to direct the development of the division's IRM Plan. The request for proposal is not used to select a vendor to develop the plan. Diversified is hired, without competitive bids, to perform the work by Pezzolla based on Quick's recommendation.

April: Diversified signs a contract with NDRI-State for the IRM Plan services. It is paid an initial amount of $20,000 on the $169,500 contract.

April 18: $17,000 transferred from Diversified's corporate bank account to another account, opened by Mazula in the name of Albany Professional Baseball, Inc. These funds are used to pay for Quick's team expenses.

April: Diversified is hired by Quick to assist DSAS in taking over the methadone registry from another DSAS vendor, Creative Socio-Medics. Diversified's fee for initial work is $85,000. Pezzolla is aware of discussions with Diversified but unaware of this verbal agreement between the firm and Quick.

May: Data General, Hewlett Packard, and DEC are presented with an information package prepared by DSAS and Diversified, specifying the proposed computer system resulting from the IRM plan. Quick solicits these firms for donations to a memorial softball tournament to benefit the Fund. DEC's sales representative, Peter Link, makes a $500 donation to the fund in the form of a check.

EXHIBIT 4 (continued)

CHRONOLOGY OF EVENTS

Mazula informs Data General representatives Canastar and Snell that the Fund is important to Quick. The three also discuss establishing a business relationship between Diversified and Data General, including subcontracting to Data General for the forthcoming DSAS contract and becoming a Data General software supplier.

Quick meets with Canastar and Snell and receives a $1000 personal donation to the fund, in the form of a check.

June 4: Data General, Hewlett Packard and DEC submit their proposals to DSAS.

June 5–10: DSAS and Diversified review and evaluate the proposals and deem that Hewlett Packard has the lowest bid.

Quick informs DSAS and Diversified staff that the bids were too high and there are insufficient funds to cover costs. Quick directs the vendors to resubmit proposals for a less costly centralized system.

June 10–11: Quick advises Snell and Canastar that he is looking favorably on awarding the contract to Data General.

June 11: Mazula suggests to Hewlett Packard that a relationship with Quick should include dinners and a trip to New York City.

June 12: Diversified presents its analysis of the revised bids to DSAS. Data General is now the lowest bidder, with Hewlett Packard second and DEC third.

June 28: Quick formally notifies Data General in writing of the award.

September 6: Subpoena issued to Snell.

September 19: Subpoena issued to Canastar.

---

the Office of State Inspector General is provided as Exhibit 5.) As Governor Cuomo explained, "The public has every right to demand integrity in its government. This new mechanism, the Office of the State Inspector General, will ensure that New York State's government remains as free as possible from activities that reduce public confidence." The Office was established primarily to prevent fraud, abuse, and corruption in New York State government and was one of six such offices in the United States. It had a budget of around $1.5 million and a staff of twenty-seven people. Investigations were often initiated by complaints by vendors or members of the public. A complaint by a vendor had prompted the DSAS investigation.

When Dan Snell received the appearance subpoena from the Inspector General, on September 6, 1991, Data General senior management realized it had some important decisions to make.

- How should the company respond to Snell and (shortly after) Canastar's subpoenas by the New York State Inspector General?

- Was there genuine cause for concern over how Data General's representatives had made the sale to DSAS, and, if so, should Data General take internal action?

- Should Data General delay delivery of the equipment, scheduled for September 13?

REFERENCES

"Albany Drug Agency is Accused of Sidestepping Bidding Rules." *The New York Times,* July 30, 1992, p. B4.

"Arenaball Could Be Right for Glory-Seeking Businessmen." Gannet News Service, August 21, 1991.

Data General Annual Reports, 1991 & 1992.

Data General Corporation 1992 Securities and Exchange Commission Form 10k.

Data General Prospectus $110,000,000 7&3/4% Convertible Subordinated Debentures Due 2001. June 13, 1991. Prepared by Morgan Stanley & Co. and Kidder Peabody & Co.

"Foreclosure by Bank Will Pave Way for New Owners at Adult Care Home," *Capital District Business Review,* November 25, 1991, sec. 1, p. 1.

EXHIBIT 5

EXTRACT FROM EXECUTIVE ORDER ESTABLISHING THE OFFICE OF STATE INSPECTOR GENERAL

I. **Authority of the State Inspector General**
 1. Pursuant to section 6 of the Executive Law, the State Inspector General is authorized to examine and investigate the management and affairs of the covered agencies concerning fraud, abuse or corruption and, if there exist reasonable grounds that justify further inquiry, may specifically:
    a. subpoena and enforce the attendance of witnesses;
    b. administer oaths and examine witnesses under oath; and
    c. require the production of any books or papers deemed relevant and material.
 2. The State Inspector General is further authorized to perform any other functions necessary to fulfill the duties and responsibilities of the office.

II. **Duties and Responsibilities of the State Inspector General**
 1. The State Inspector General shall receive complaints of fraud, abuse or corruption in covered agencies and determine whether they warrant investigation.
 2. The State Inspector General shall investigate complaints of fraud, abuse or corruption when appropriate, determine whether disciplinary action, civil or criminal prosecution or further investigation by relevant Federal, State or local agencies is warranted and take further action as appropriate.
 3. The State Inspector General shall report complaints of fraud, abuse or corruption to such Federal, State or local agencies when there is evidence that non-state agency personnel have engaged in what may be criminal activity and when otherwise appropriate, and shall otherwise cooperate with them in any further action.
 4. The State Inspector General shall help prevent fraud, abuse or corruption in covered agencies by periodically reviewing policies and procedures and monitoring day-to-day operations and making recommendations for improvement.
 5. In performing his duties and responsibilities, the State Inspector General shall keep the Director of Criminal Justice informed of allegations and evidence of fraud, abuse or corruption in covered agencies and of the progress of any investigation, and shall keep the appropriate agency commissioner or director so informed unless, in the judgment of the State Inspector General, special circumstances require full confidentiality.
 6. The State Inspector General shall prepare written reports of investigations as appropriate and such reports shall be released to the public, subject to any reductions needed to protect witnesses, unless the Director of Criminal Justice determines that release of all or portions of the report should be deferred so as not to compromise an ongoing investigation.

III. **Responsibilities of Covered Agencies**
 1. All officers and employees in covered agencies shall extend full cooperation and all reasonable assistance to the State Inspector General and his designees. No provision of this order shall be construed to diminish the responsibility of said officers and employees to be vigilant in preventing and reporting fraud, abuse or corruption.
 2. Complaints of fraud, abuse or corruption shall be made to the agency inspector general, agency commissioner or director, Deputy Inspector General or the State Inspector General as appropriate. The agency inspector general and agency commissioner or director shall report all complaints of fraud, abuse or corruption to the State Inspector General.

IV. **Covered Agencies**
   The following agencies shall be subject to the provisions of this order and the authority of the State Inspector General: Department of Environmental Conservation; Office of General Services; Division of Housing and Community Renewal; Insurance Department; State Liquor Authority; New York State Lottery; Department of Transportation; Division for Youth; and such other agencies as may from time to time be determined by the State Inspector General.

"An Introduction to Data General Systems." Data General Brochure, 1990.

Kidder, Tracy. *The Soul of a New Machine.* New York: Avon, 1990.

New York Ethics: A Guide to the Ethics Law. The New York State Ethics Commission, New York, 1991.

"No-Bid Contractor Sponsors Team Run by Agency Manager." *The Times Union,* October 31, 1991, p. B-11.

"Patroons Want Business to Provide Season-Ticket Boost." *Capital District Business Review,* September 28, 1992, sec. 1, p. 1.

Public Officers Law, The New York State Ethics Commission, New York, 1990.

Report of Investigation Concerning Awarding of No-Bid Contracts and Related Contracting Matters, New York State Office of Inspector General, July 28, 1992. File #009-029.

"Survey: The Computer Industry," *The Economist,* February 27, 1993.

The Wall Street Journal, October 8, 1992.

"Washington County Town Becoming Host to Fourth Private Adult Home." *Capital District Business Review,* January 6, 1992, sec. 1, p. 2.

SOME ETHICAL DILEMMAS IN BUSINESS-TO-BUSINESS SALES

The following were actual situations experienced by the case writer during more than 15 years in business-to-business sales and sales management. The names of firms and individuals have been disguised due to the nature of the material in this case.

HALCO MANUFACTURING

Dave MacDonald was excited when he got the unexpected phone call from Nicki Steele, a senior buyer from Halco Manufacturing.

"I know it's a year since we bought that prototype reel from you, but we just got a contract from the government to build ten more "bear traps" and we desperately need to hold our price on these units. Could you possibly sell us 10 new reels at the same price you charged last year?" Nicki inquired.

"I'll see what I can do and call you back today," Dave replied.

Dave immediately retrieved the file from the previous year and saw that they had supplied the reel for $6,990.00 F.O.B. the customer's warehouse. There was a breakdown of the pricing on the file:

Manufacturer's list price	$4,000.00
Special engineering charge (25%)	1,000.00
Total list price	5,000.00
Distributor discount (20%)	1,000.00
Distributor net cost	4,000.00
Estimated Currency Exchange (8%)	320.00
Estimated Duty (22-1/2%)	972.00
Estimated Freight	245.00
Estimated Brokerage	55.00
Estimated distributor cost, F.O.B. destination	5,592.00
Mark-up (25%)	1,398.00
Selling Price, F.O.B. destination	$6,990.00

There were some notes on the file that Dave reviewed. The reel was designed as part of a "bear trap" on Canadian navy ships. These bear traps would hook onto helicopters in rough weather and haul them safely onto landing pads on the ship decks. The reel was really a model SM heavy duty steel mill reel, except some of the exposed parts were to be made of stainless steel to provide longer life in the salt water atmosphere. There was a special engineering charge on the reel as it was a non-standard item that had to be specially engineered. The manufacturer had suggested at the time they quoted that Dave could keep the full 20 percent discount as they thought there was only one other manufacturer capable of building this unit, and their price would likely be much higher.

When Dave got a price from the manufacturer on the 10 new units, he was surprised they quoted a price of only $3,200.00 each, less 40/10 percent. When he asked the price be verified, the orderdesk clarified the pricing. First, there had been a 20 percent reduction in all SM series reels. That made the manufacturer's list price only $3,200.00. Then, because there was a large quantity, the distributor discount was increased to less 40/10 percent instead of the 20 percent that was given on the original reel.

As Dave estimated his cost, things got better. The original reel was imported from the United States at 22-1/2 percent duty as "not otherwise provided for manufacturers of iron or steel, tariff item 44603-1." In the interim, the company Dave worked for got a duty remission on series SM steel mill reels as "machinery of a class or kind not manufactured in Canada, tariff item 42700-1" and the duty was remitted (and the savings supposedly passed on to the end customer). The currency exchange rate also improved in Dave's favour, and the estimated freight and brokerage charges per unit dropped considerably because of the increased shipment size. Dave estimated his new cost as follows:

Manufacturer's list price	$3,200.00
Distributor discount (40/10%)	1,472.00
Distributor net cost	1,728.00
Estimated Currency Exchange (2%)	35.00
Estimated Duty (remitted)	0.00
Estimated Freight	85.00
Estimated Brokerage	14.50
Estimated distributor cost,	
F.O.B. destination	1,862.50

Now that he had all the figures, Dave had to decide what the selling price should be to his customer.

CROWN PULP AND PAPER LTD.

Bill Siddall had been promoted to the position of salesperson, and he was pleased when he received an order for nearly $10,000 for stainless steel fittings from the new pulp mill being built in his territory. Unfortunately, he quoted a price that was 40 percent below his cost.

"We have to honour the price quoted," Bill insisted.

"I know if you let me talk to Rory, he'll let us raise the price," replied Dave MacDonald, the Sales Manager. "Rory used to be the purchasing agent at one of my best accounts before he came to the mill."

"No. You gave me responsibility for this account, and I want to build a good relationship with Rory myself. He gave us the order over two weeks ago. He can't change suppliers now because he needs the material next week, and I don't want to put him on the spot now because it would be unfair. Since this is our first order, I would like to supply it without any problems. We'll get back the money we lost on this order many times if we can get their future business. This material is needed for a small construction job, and they haven't even started to consider their stores inventory yet."

After much discussion, it was agreed that the order would stand, but Dave would call the fitting manufacturer's Sales Manager, Chuck Knowles, as the two men were good friends.

"We need some help on that last order we placed with you. Bill sold it at 40 percent below our cost," said Dave.

"How could that happen?" Chuck seemed amazed.

"Well," replied Dave, "you give us a 25 percent distributor discount and we gave 10 percent to the customer due to the size of the order. What we forgot was to double the list price because the customer wanted schedule 80 wall thickness on the fittings instead of standard schedule 40. This was Bill's first large inquiry and he made an honest mistake. He doesn't want me to get involved with the customer, and I don't want to force the issue with him, so I'm hoping you can help us on this one order. We expect to get a lot of business from this account over the next few years."

"I'll split the difference with you. What you're selling now for $0.90, you're paying $1.50 for, and if I give you an additional 20 percent discount, your cost will come down to $1.20. Can you live with that?" Chuck asked.

"It's a help. We appreciate it. We'll see you on your next trip to our territory, and I'll buy lunch."

"A deal. See you next month." The conversation ended.

When it was over, Dave was feeling reasonably satisfied with himself, but he still felt somewhat uneasy. He promised not to call Rory, and he promised not to interfere with the account, but he still thought something could be done.

On Saturday morning, Dave went to the Brae Shore Golf Club. He was confident Rory would be there. Sure enough, at 8:00 A.M., Rory was scheduled to tee-off. Dave sat on the bench at the first tee and waited for Rory to appear. Promptly, Rory arrived with Bob Arnold, one of his senior buyers. The three men greeted each other pleasantly and Rory asked who Dave was waiting for.

"Just one of my neighbors. He was supposed to be here an hour ago but I guess he won't show."

"Join us. We don't mind. Besides we might need a donation this fall when we have our company golf tournament. We'll invite you of course, and we'll invite Bill if he plays golf."

"He doesn't play often, but he's pretty good. Beat me the last time we played. How is he doing at your mill? Is everything okay?" Dave asked.

"Checking up on him? Sure. He's fine. He made a mistake the other day when he went to see our millwright foreman without clearing it through my office first, but he'll learn. He'll do a lot of business with us because we want to buy locally where possible, and you have a lot of

good product lines. I think he'll get along well with all of us as well. He seems a bit serious, but we'll break him in before long. We just gave him a big order for stainless fittings a few weeks ago, but we told him to visit at ten o'clock next time and to bring the doughnuts."

"I know," replied Dave. "Unfortunately, we lost a lot of money on that order."

"Your price was very low. I couldn't understand it because I knew your material wasn't manufactured offshore. Did you quote the cheaper T304 grade of stainless instead of the T316 we use?"

"No. We quoted schedule 40 prices instead of schedule 80. The wall thickness for schedule 80 is twice as thick, and the price should have been double as well."

"Heck. Double the price. We'll pay it. I'll make a note on the file Monday. I know you're not trying to take us and I can appreciate an honest mistake. At double the price, you might be a bit high, but you know we want to place the order with you anyway because you're local. Eventually we'll want you to carry some inventory for us, so we might just as well make sure we're both happy with this business."

STRAIT STRUCTURAL STEEL LTD.

Dave MacDonald was sitting in the outer office waiting to see Stan Hope, the purchasing agent for Strait Structural Steel, a new account that had just begun operations in a remote, coastal location about forty miles from the nearest city. Stan had telephoned Dave the previous week and had an urgent request for four large exhaust fans that were required to exhaust welding fumes from enclosed spaces where welders were at work. The union had threatened to stop the project unless working conditions were improved quickly, and although Dave didn't sell fans at the time, he found a line of fans and negotiated a discount from the manufacturer, along with an agreement to discuss the further possibility of representing the fan manufacturer on a national basis.

When Stan gave the order to Dave for the fans, the two men discussed other products that Dave sold. Dave sold products for a company that was both a general-line and specialty-line industrial distributor. Included in the general-line products were such items as hand and power tools, cutting tools (drills, taps, dies), safety equipment, wire rope and slings, fasteners (nuts, bolts), and fittings (stainless steel, bronze, and carbon steel flanges, elbows, tees). Included in the specialty-line products were such items as electric motors and generators, motor controls, hydraulic and pneumatic valves and cylinders, rubber dock fenders, and overhead cranes. When the men finally met, they were almost instantly friends, and it was obvious that the opportunities for them to do further business were great. "One item that really interests me," said Stan, "is PTFE tape. We need some and we will be using a lot of it."

"We have the largest stock of PTFE tape in the country," replied Dave. We import it directly from Italy, but it's high quality and is the same standard size as all others on the market; 1/2 wide, 3.9 thick, and 48.9 long. How much are you interested in?"

"Let's start with 400 rolls," Stan suggested.

PTFE tape was a white, non-adhesive tape that was used as a pipe thread sealant. It was wrapped around the threads of pipe or fittings before they were screwed together to make a leak-proof seal. The tape first came on the market in the late 1960s at prices as high as $3.60 per roll, but since then prices had dropped considerably. North American manufacturers were still selling the tape for list prices near $1.80, and were offering dealer discounts between 25 and 50 percent depending on the quantities that dealers bought. Dave was importing the tape from Italy at a landed cost of $0.17 per roll.

"We have a standard price of $1.00 per roll as long as you buy 200 rolls," Dave offered.

"No question. You have an excellent price. How much would you charge M H Sales?"

"I don't know. Who is M H Sales?" asked Dave.

"A small industrial supply company located in my basement. The "H" is for Hope. I share the company with Bruce Malcolm, the "M," and

he's in purchasing at Central Power Corporation. M H Sales is a small company and we are looking for additional products to sell. Between Strait Structural and Central Power, we could sell several thousand rolls of PTFE tape each year."

MCCORMICK GLEASON LIMITED

Dave MacDonald telephoned Clarey Stanley, a Senior Buyer at McCormick Gleason Limited. "Clarey, I'm calling about that quote we made on Lufkin tapes. Can we have your order?"

"Sorry. Your price was high. I gave the order to Ken Stafford. You need a sharper pencil."

"How much sharper?" Dave asked.

"I can't tell you that. But you were close." Clarey replied. "By the way, Kenny called me from the stores department this morning and he has a large shipment of electric relays that was delivered yesterday. They weren't properly marked and he can't identify the ones with normally open contacts from the ones with normally closed contacts. Do you want them returned, or can someone see him and straighten it out here?"

"Tell him I'll see him immediately after lunch. I can tell them apart and I'll see they get properly identified."

When the conversation ended, Dave made a note to see Clarey about the tapes. There was a problem somewhere. Dave knew his cost on Lufkin tapes was the lowest available, and he quoted twelve percent on cost because he really wanted the order. The order was less than $1,500, but it meant that Dave could place a multiple-case order on the manufacturer and get the lowest possible cost for all replacement inventory. That would increase the margin on sales to other customers who bought smaller quantities. There was no possibility that Stafford Industrial, a local, one-person, "out-of-the-basement" operation that bought Lufkin tapes as a jobber, not as a distributor, could match his price.

That afternoon, while waiting to see Ken MacKay, the Stores Manager, Dave noticed a carton from Stafford Industrial Sales being unloaded from a local delivery van. Although he knew that Stafford supplied quite a few maintenance, repair and operating (MRO) supplies to this customer, Dave decided to play ignorant.

"What do you buy from Stafford Industrial?" he asked the young stores clerk who was handling the package.

Opening the carton, the clerk read the packing slip. "It says here we ordered 144 measuring tapes, 3/4 in. 9 wide by 25 ft. long."

"Are those things expensive?" Dave asked.

"Don't know. There's no price on the packing slip. Clarey Stanley in purchasing ordered them. You could talk to him." The clerk continued to unpack the shipment. As he did, Dave noticed the tapes were manufactured offshore and were poor quality compared to the Lufkin tapes that he sold, and that he quoted to Clarey Stanley the previous day.

"Aren't those supposed to be Lufkin tapes?" Dave asked.

"Not that I know. The packing slip just says tapes. Wait and I'll haul our copy of the purchase order." The clerk went to a filing cabinet next to his desk and returned with a carbon copy of the purchase order. "No, it just says tapes. It doesn't specify any brand."

There was something wrong, and Dave was determined to get an answer.

PART II

MANAGING
YOUR PRIMARY SALES
RESOURCES:
SALES INDIVIDUALS

5

PERSONAL SELLING

Selling is as basic to our society as metabolism is to life.

THEODORE LEVITT, *INNOVATIONS IN MARKETING*

LEARNING OBJECTIVES

After reading this chapter, you should be able to answer the following questions:

- What is relationship selling, and why is it important?
- What is the difference between a suspect and a prospect?
- Why will the preapproach stage determine the success or failure of the sales call?
- What part of the approach stage can have the most dramatic effect on the customer? How might this differ in a global selling?
- How do salespeople overcome objections?
- What are some strategies and techniques for closing a sale?
- In this age of relationship selling, why is the follow-up stage considered to be the most important of the selling stages?

"Get Met . . . It Pays" has been MetLife's slogan for several years, and most people recognize the Peanuts gang as the "spokespeople" for the company. Unfortunately, people also are aware of MetLife's $40 million rebate payments for deceptive selling. The problem began in the fall of 1993 when the Tampa, Florida, office sold a group of nurses life insurance policies dubbed "retirement savings." Nowhere in the literature was the word *insurance* mentioned. Now the government is investigating MetLife's sales processes in at least 15 states. MetLife has responded by creating a business standards committee composed of senior executives. It has also centralized and made improvements to its customer service department.

The MetLife problem is not an uncommon problem in insurance organizations or in other industries.[1] Problems arise when salespeople are too aggressive in selling and overstate or understate the attributes of the product. As we discussed in Chapter 3, ethics in selling has become a major focus in business for a variety of reasons. One primary reason is the development of a concept known as *relationship selling*. This chapter focuses on relationship selling, along with the fundamental seven steps of selling. Specifically, this chapter emphasizes some basic selling techniques and introduces selling terminology.

Even if you find that your career takes you to other fields, you should find value in the sales process. Most individuals at some point or another begin the process of searching for employment and then must "sell" themselves and their abilities. Even after beginning the new job, they soon find the need to sell their position on some issue, or their viewpoint to a client. Not only is selling a fundamental part of the everyday business world, but everyone uses sales techniques daily. Studying the seven step process becomes a building block for future business transactions.

Why is personal selling so important if you are studying sales management? Almost exclusively, sales managers are promoted from the sales field. Most marketing managers must also spend some time in the field. However, regardless of career path, good sales managers must maintain their presence in the field since most managers will continue to sell. To understand and effectively manage salespeople, it is also important to examine the sales process that salespeople confront on a daily basis.

RELATIONSHIP SELLING

As discussed in Chapter 2, personal selling is not a static process; rather, it is evolving, dynamic, and interactive. In a successful organization, sales personnel adapt to the communication styles and needs of the buyer or buying center. This long-term adaptation to buying needs—building buyer-seller trust while providing marketing and selling skills—is commonly referred to as relationship marketing or relationship selling. Recall from Chapter 2 that relationship selling is defined as the process whereby a sales organization builds long-term alliances with both prospective and current customers so that seller and buyer work toward a common set of specified goals. A model of relationship selling is presented in Exhibit 5.1. These goals are met by:

1. Understanding customer expectations.
2. Building with customer service partners.
3. Empowering employees to satisfy customer needs, possibly requiring employee initiatives beyond the company norms.
4. Providing customers with the best possible quality relative to individual need.[2]

Three types of selling can create long-term relationships. They are consultative, dyadic, and just-in-time.

Consultative Selling

Eastman Chemical takes relationship selling a step further. It has developed a quality management program (QMP) which begins with an assessment of all customer relations, identifies opportunities for improvement, and reports those improvements back to the customer. One key ingredient in this program is the prominent role played by the salesforce. Eastman strives for its salesforce to make Eastman the preferred supplier with all customers through a variety of internal programs and goals.[3]

In order for Eastman or any other organization to develop quality relations with a customer base, it must be willing and able to perform consultative selling. **Consultative selling** is establishing the end user's particular needs with regard to not only price, but also applications, urgency of service, quality of products, and other factors important to the customer.[4] In conjunction with relationship selling, consultative selling dictates that salespeople are now consultants who come into a customer's place of business to solve problems, not to just sell a product. Successful

EXHIBIT 5.1
EFFECTIVE RELATIONSHIP MARKETING

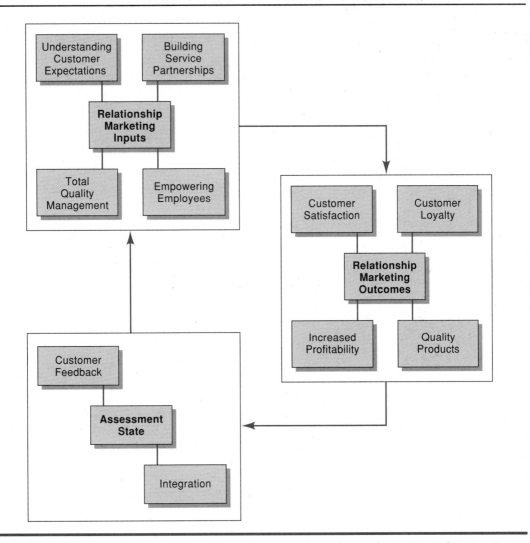

SOURCE: Joel R. Evans and Richard L. Laskin, "Relationship Marketing Can Help a Firm Escape Commodity Like Status," *Industrial Marketing Management*, 23(5) (December 1994): 440–441.

consultative sellers must possess certain skills including: listening, communication, attention to detail, empathy, and follow-through.[5] This has changed the entire philosophy of selling, as we will see throughout this chapter.

Dyadic Selling Relationships

Individual buyers and sellers have traditionally maintained a one-on-one relationship, which is called a **dyadic relationship.** The word *dyad* literally means "two."

Traditionally, a dyad implied a relationship between two *people*.[6] Because of the growing importance of relationship selling, a dyad may now imply a relationship between two *organizations*. Regardless, dyadic relationships imply that both parties are active and participative in the relationship. Dyadic relationships can be further divided into two categories: discrete transactions and relational exchanges.[7]

Discrete Transactions.   **Discrete transactions** are single transactions based on no previous relationships and assume no future relationships. To say it another way, each selling situation is a unique event. Today in business-to-business sales, discrete transactions are the least prevalent form of dyadic relationships.[8] An example of a discrete transaction in today's world is an encyclopedia salesperson who goes door-to-door selling the product. The encyclopedia salesperson probably has never called on the customer previously and most likely will never call on the customer again, regardless of purchase. As discussed in Chapters 1 and 2, this type of transaction is very outdated in terms of current sales practices. A reputable company cannot remain in business today without the prospect of a long-term relationship among a majority of the company's customer base. A company simply cannot afford to conduct only discrete transactions and remain competitive.

Relational Exchanges.   **Relational exchanges** assume that a relationship is ongoing. This is the most common exchange in the existing business-to-business selling environment. The relationship has a moderate to long-term horizon and focuses on more than just price. Both the salesperson and the selling and buying companies must make a substantial investment of time and service to maintain a reoccurring dyadic relationship.

The relational exchange assumes that relationships are being created throughout the organization and that the relationship will continue over time. Many sales calls are made to simply stay in touch and strengthen the long-term relationship. Like any form of relationship, work must be done to maintain the relationship or it will falter. There are no guarantees that the customer will buy every time, but if the relationship is maintained, the selling organization should remain a primary supplier.

Dyadic relationships have assumed a new role in global selling. Organizations such as General Motors, Xerox, and General Dynamics have begun building dyadic relationships with countries. For instance, General Dynamics sold a multi-billion dollar F-16 fighter aircraft deal to Turkey and, in turn, agreed to purchase scores of Turkish products to sell in the United States, as well as invest in some Turkish projects. B. V. Vikberg executive vice-president of Xerox, Brazil, says this countertrade approach has become necessary when engaging in international selling in many developing countries.[9]

Countertrade can be viewed as a modern-day barter system. The two international dyadic partners agree to help one another in the selling or developing of their respective products and needs.

Just-in-Time Exchange Relationships

One method to achieve relational selling that has gained momentum over the past 10 years is conducting business on a just-in-time (JIT) basis. A **just-in-time exchange**

can be defined as the delivery or exchange of the precise amount of needed
with a minimum of waste in the exchange. Waste might include excesses of
tory, labor, and negotiations. The just-in-time exchange assumes that there is a sy
biotic relationship in which both buyer and seller rely on one another to maintain
the business strengths of each, and that both parties have a strong mutual self-interest in maintaining the relationship.[10] Because the relationship is strong, a switch to
another vendor would mean a high cost and possible sacrifice, even if a competitor
has a less expensive product. Additional costs for the customer could come in the
form of quality inspection of the new product, reinspection, handling charges,
warehousing, new inventorying, new administrative expenses, and lost time for new
start-ups. It is vital that sales management emphasizes the importance of high-quality service and support for the customer.

The purest form of JIT relationships are relatively rare in most industries since
most buyers will use, or at least consider, multiple vendors. Just-in-time relationships tend to occur where a seller can provide virtually all needs for the buyer and,
in turn, the buyer does not have to work with multiple vendors.

Even when JIT relationships occur, management of both the selling and buying
organizations must be careful not to rely too heavily on the relationship because
changes in the sales environment might mean eventual changes in the relationship.[11]
Consider the experience of Panel Components, for instance. In 1986 Panel Components, which manufactures power components, lost orders from four major customers comprising 44 percent of its business. The customers had expanded their
businesses globally, set up new suppliers in the world market and stopped ordering
from Panel Components. Based on this experience, Bob Wersen, owner of Panel
Components, no longer allows any of his 4,200 customers to comprise more than 3
percent of his company's sales.[12]

The just-in-time exchange relationship assumes that both parties need and rely
on each other. When one party changes the terms of the relationship, both may suffer. Although the mutual dependency of supplier and buyer can be advantageous in
good times, it can be disastrous when relying too heavily on a small number of customers in a changing business environment.

THE SEVEN STEPS OF SELLING

The 1990s have proven to be the decade of relationship selling. Salespeople who
refuse to "buy into" a relationship approach to selling may find that their selling
future is limited because of a lack of repeat, long-term purchasers. Now that we
have defined and explored relationship selling, we can describe how relationship
selling is incorporated into the seven basic steps of selling. Exhibit 5.2 depicts the
seven steps of selling. They are (1) prospecting and qualifying, (2) preapproach,
(3) approach, (4) presentation, (5) overcoming objections, (6) closing, and (7) follow-up. Each step is highly interrelated with the previous step, and the steps build
on one another. For instance, a salesperson would find it exceedingly difficult to
get to closure if he or she ignored prospecting and preapproach. In reality, the dis-
tinctions between steps are not always clear, but for ease of discussion each step
will be explained separately. Regardless of the order, successful salespeople must

EXHIBIT 5.2

FLOW DIAGRAM OF THE SEVEN STEPS OF SELLING

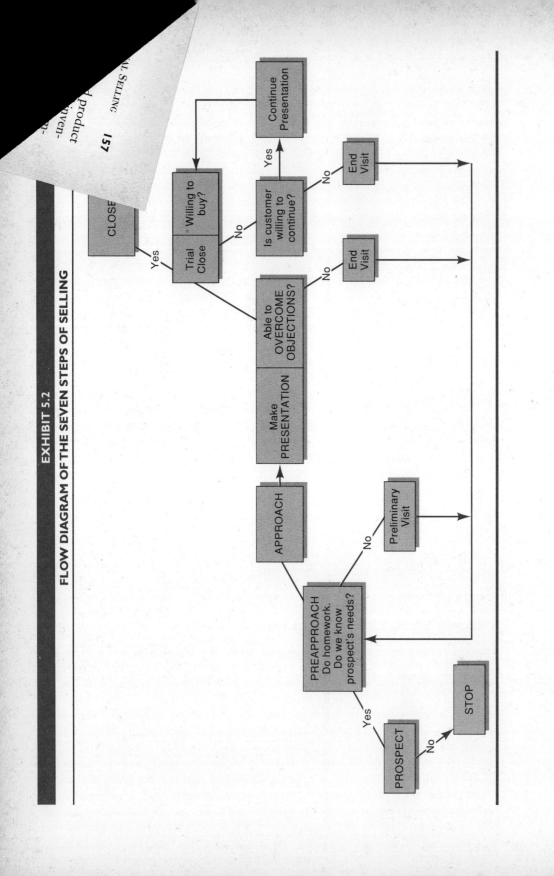

complete each step in the selling process while maintaining long-term customer relationships.[13]

STEP 1: PROSPECTING

While it is certainly important for companies to maintain relationships with customers, every company must also continually look for new customers. The search for potential new customers is called **prospecting**. One obvious reason for prospecting is the expansion of business by increasing sales from new customers. More important, the prospecting process must occur because the average firm suffers attrition of at least 15 to 20 percent of its business each year. Part of the sales manager's job is to ascertain whether the attrition was preventable with better salesperson skills and relations, or if the attrition was unavoidable. A company must replace these lost customers in order to remain in business.

The level and amount of prospecting to which a company must commit resources depends on the type of sales job, the type of industry, the resources of the sales organization, and the sales individual. For instance, Excel, a mining equipment producer, does very little prospecting because the customer base is small and very well known to all producers. In contrast, Xerox must continually prospect for new customers.

In recent years many organizations have begun committing more of their salespeople's sales efforts to continuing to build relationships with existing customers and letting the primary prospecting process and sales support be initiated by telemarketers. Telemarketers can contact a much larger number of prospects at much lower cost than field sales reps (see Chapter 8). Regardless, a salesperson cannot sell a product to a new customer unless the potential customer has first been prospected by the salesperson or someone else in the selling company. Prospecting is by no means an exact science. No two managers will give the same advice about how to specifically conduct the prospecting process. The remainder of this section will focus on the various types and sources of prospects a salesperson may encounter and, at the same time, discuss the ways prospecting can occur.

Prospects Versus Suspects

Is everyone a **prospect**—a potential customer who may have a need for a product? The answer is an emphatic no. Even people who might need the product are not necessarily prospects. There are many more suspects than there are prospects.[14] It is important to recognize the difference.

A **suspect** is a person or organization that may become a customer prospect based on the personal reflections or perceptions of the salesperson. In other words, the salesperson *thinks* a suspect may become a prospect but does not have any factual evidence to support that belief. For example, suppose that you work for Milliken, makers of high-quality industrial carpet. You call on Miller Industrials (MI) and secure the following information:

- MI is in the process of completing a new district office.
- MI is a successful company.
- MI may not have purchased any carpet.

Do you consider MI a prospective customer based on this information? Not necessarily. At this point, MI is a suspect. What would make MI a prospect, (see Exhibit 5.3)? For a suspect to become a prospect he or she must be **qualified**,[15] which can be defined by satisfying the following three conditions:

1. It must have a need or want that can be satisfied by the purchase of the product.
2. It must have the financial means to purchase the product along with the authority to make a purchase decision.
3. It must be receptive to a sales contact by the selling organization.

Notice that this definition of *prospect* relies on factual information on the potential customer, not merely the feelings, prejudices, or hopes of the salesperson.

In the preceding Milliken example, MI may not be a prospect because it may not have the financial ability to purchase the high-quality carpet that Milliken makes, or it may have already purchased carpet. MI also may feel that it does not need carpet and would prefer hardwood, tile, or linoleum flooring instead. Perhaps the buyer already has a relationship with a salesperson from another floor covering company, and therefore is not willing to meet the Milliken rep. The net result is that MI remains a suspect and not a prospect until the salesperson or telemarketer begins the qualifying process on Miller.

Salespeople must qualify all potential accounts because they cannot afford to spend time on suspects or even prospects that cannot or will not buy. This is not to say that the salesperson may make a sale on every call. Well-qualified accounts may not buy on this call or ever, or they may choose to buy from a competitor.

Sources of Prospects

Prospects come from a variety of sources, and there are a number of methods and techniques that can be employed when looking for qualified prospects. For convenience, several sources and methods are compiled into the following four categories: referrals, networking, promotions, and cold canvassing.

Referrals.   A **referral** is a prospect that is provided to the salesperson by someone else. Referrals can come from internal or external sources. Referrals from internal company sources may come from other salespeople, service personnel, managers, or telemarketers. For example, Southern New England Telephone (SNET) pays its nonsales staffers every time they generate leads for the salesforce. Burgess Harrison, program manager for SNET, says, "We want all of our employees to keep their eyes and ears open for possible sales leads, which they can find almost anywhere." If the employee prospect leads to a sale, the employee can win up to $25 in cash or awards. The program generated over $1 million in sales for SNET in 1993.[16]

Referrals from outside sources are also an excellent method of increasing the likelihood of a successful sale. Some referrals may come from satisfied customers. When a salesperson tells a prospective buyer, "Your friend Jane Symanski is using

EXHIBIT 5.3

A MODEL OF PROSPECTING RELATIONSHIPS

Regions: 1, not qualified, not contacted; 2, qualified, but not contacted; 3, identified as qualified, called on; 4, improperly judged as qualified, called on in error; 5, qualified nonsuspect contacted by sales calls; 6, unqualified nonsuspects contacted by sales call.

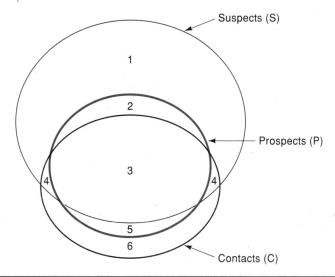

SOURCE: Marvin A. Jolson and Thomas K. Wotruba, "Selling and Sales Management in Action: Prospecting: A New Look at This Old Challenge," *Journal of Personal Selling and Sales Management,* 12(4), (1992): 59–66.

our product and she thought that it might work well for you too," the chances of making a presentation are enhanced. The salesperson has now progressed from stranger to acquaintance because of the commonality of knowing Jane Symanski. In some cultures, a referral is a necessity in beginning a business relationship. Mexico and Japan have cultures in which a third-party referral can be critical to the success of an initial sales call.

Another type of referral is known as a bird dog. A **bird dog** is an individual who is paid to provide a referral. The referral may be produced by an inside or outside company source. For example, many apartment complexes will pay tenants a fee if they bring in a new renter for the complex. Car dealers will also frequently pay a bird-dog fee to customers who bring in other customers.

Teleprospecting is also being conducted by outside agencies. Fisons Instruments has hired an external agency, Contact Software International, for lead fulfillment, lead qualification, and all associated recordkeeping. Contact Software uses ACT!, a software package that is a full-featured prospect tracking contact and management package. Fison receives detailed scripts of the conversations with prospects, assessment of the prospect, and other related information. All of this information is downloaded onto the field salesperson's personal computer for the salesperson to use when preparing a sales presentation.[17] Fison is a good example of a company using technology and taking advantage of new selling methods.

The last type of referral is called snowballing. **Snowballing** begins by asking a customer for two or more names of people who might be interested in the product. Those names are contacted and after a sales presentation is made, the new prospect is asked for two or more names until a prospecting list develops. Over a short period of time, salespeople can develop extensive lists of prospects by snowballing.

Networking.   **Networking** is defined as the method of using friends, business contacts, co-workers, and acquaintances as a means of making new contacts. Many business people and salespeople join professional and civic organizations in part to meet a wide variety of people. Organizations might include country clubs; health clubs; professional organizations such as Sales and Marketing Executives Association; civic organizations such as Rotary, Kiwanis, and Lions clubs; churches and synagogues; and many others. The wider the circle of friends and acquaintances, the better the odds for developing some leads on qualified prospects.

Networking is particularly important because people prefer to do business with people they like. It can also lead to other job prospects and opportunities, and has become an important aspect of a businessperson's daily routine. As a student, you should already be creating a network of past employers, faculty, peers, parental friends, and business leaders who can help as you begin looking for a job or for new opportunities.

Promotions.   Many types of promotions are designed in part to help the salesforce develop leads for their prospecting. The most common forms of promotion leading to prospects is an advertisement with a 1-800 number for the reader or television viewer to call for more information, or a mail-in inquiry asking for more information. By adding a phone number or coupon to a promotional piece, a database can be created of people who have expressed an interest in the advertised product.[18] The real advantage to this form of prospecting is that the suspect/prospect comes to the seller. At a minimum, one can assume from this action that the prospect has a strong interest in the product or desires more information on the product or company. With the increased attention being paid to cable TV, infomercials, and home shopping, the 1-800 number will continue to play a dominant role for prospective customers as we enter the twenty-first century.

Trade shows are another excellent promotional method for obtaining a list of probable, highly qualified prospects. People who typically attend trade shows have a particular interest in the product category being sold. People (buyers) who stop by an exhibit will typically sign up for a drawing or some other promotional items and an instant list of prospects is created. For example, the FMI (Food Market Institute) is an annual trade show that allows national food manufacturers such as General Mills, Breyers, and others to display their company products. Representatives from the grocery industry attend to build relations and talk with the various manufacturers. People who come by the booth become instant prospects if they are not already current customers.

Cold Canvassing.   Perhaps the most mentally painful method of prospecting is **cold canvassing**, which is synonymous with door-to-door selling. This method can be very time consuming and expensive for an organization. The rejection rate is extraordinarily high. However, there are certain types of companies that must rely on the cold canvas—at least in part—to produce leads. For example, Xerox might assign a salesperson a downtown territory with a number of large office buildings. Since the likelihood is high that all the businesses in the building use copiers, the salesperson must visit each office looking for leads who might be interested in a new one.

Many industries, such as office supplies, fax equipment, telecommunications equipment, insurance, financial services, and delivery services, can sell to virtually anyone and the cold canvas is an important prospecting tool for them. Other industries with a very specific customer base, such as heavy machinery, pharmaceuticals, and publishing houses, obtain prospects by other methods and may find that the cold canvas approach is very inefficient.

A purchased broker's list is a common source of names that have been partially screened. These names are typically suspects and not prospects and are a good source for cold canvassing. If you subscribed to a magazine and then received solicitations from other magazines wanting you to subscribe, your name was sold to a broker who resold your name to other companies seeking prospective lists of possible purchasers. The next time you purchase a magazine or some other subscription, you might use a nickname just to track how many different companies will buy access to your name. There are also a number of quality directories that can be good prospect sources. These include the *Yellow Pages,* Cole's directory, Standard Industrial Classification Code (SIC Code), government directories, databases,[19] and others.

Teleprospecting.   As mentioned earlier in this chapter, the use of telemarketing has become widely accepted as a method of prospecting and has led to the term *teleprospecting.* **Teleprospecting** is defined as qualifying new organizational customers through telephone surveys.[20] Ron Sturgeon, CEO of AAA Small Auto World, uses a minicomputer system with teleprospecting. Sturgeon has a prospect list of 350,000 people. A monthly report from the computer database tracks successful teleprospect sales by state, city, and ZIP code. Sturgeon then diverts resources to concentrate on areas with higher closing ratios. The results have been a decrease in expenses of 40 percent and an increase in sales of 10 percent.[21]

Teleprospecting is conducted by field salespeople or by telemarketers. Teleprospecting in a business setting has a much more favorable image than does consumer home prospecting. Field salespeople are spending more time on the phone prospecting than ever before in order to save time and expenses. Specific advice for successful teleprospecting is featured in Box 5.1.

STEP 2: PREAPPROACH

The **preapproach** step can best be described as being prepared before walking into a customer's office. Sellers must do their research about the customer organization, the individual buyer(s), and relevant others who might affect the purchase decision. A lack of proper preapproach work greatly diminishes the likelihood of a successful sale.

The preapproach step can be divided into five stages (see Exhibit 5.4). These stages are critical when calling on a new prospective customer, but they are equally

---

BOX 5.1

TOP TEN METHODS OF PROSPECTING

Paul Goldner, co-founder and executive vice-president of the Sales Performance Group in Tarrytown, New York, tells how to prospect in the 1990s.

- *Set aside an hour each day to prospect.* Effective prospecting requires discipline. It's too easy to say that the time isn't right.
- *Work without interruption.* Spend your hour uninterrupted by calls, questions, or meetings.
- *Be prepared with a list of names before you call.* Have at least one month's worth of leads, so you'll always have enough during your prospecting hour.
- *Make as many calls as possible.* If you are only calling the most qualified prospects, then the more calls, the better.
- *Make your call brief.* The purpose of a prospecting call is to get an appointment, so introduce yourself and the product and, of course, make an appointment.
- *Prospect during off-peak times.* Catch prospects when they are not guarded by secretaries and your competitors think they're out: 8 A.M. to 9 A.M., noon to 1 P.M., and 5 P.M. to 6 P.M.
- *Vary your call times.* By prospecting at various times, you'll be able to reach more prospects.
- *Be organized.* Use a contact management system, preferably computerized, that makes it as easy to remember to call back in six months as the next day.
- *Begin with the end in mind.* Picturing a successful result before you pick up the phone will instill confidence and enthusiasm that can only help when you do make the call.
- *Don't stop.* Remember, most sales take place after the fifth call, but most salespeople stop after the first, so be persistent. Don't stop short of the gold.

SOURCE: Ginger Trumfio, "Panning for Gold," *Sales and Marketing Management* (December 1993): 54.

---

important when calling on existing customers. Relationship selling requires commitment, and the preapproach step is an important preparation for any sales call. Gary Slavin, president of Multimedia Marketing, says, "They [salespeople] really have to learn as much as possible about the client *beforehand*. They need to get annual reports, 10(k) reports, the works."

Preparation does not end after the completion of a sale, either.[22] Salespeople who desire to maintain good customer relations must begin preparing for the next call on the customer as soon as the existing call is completed.

Research the Company

The most important step in the preapproach stage involves doing research on the company and industry on which you plan to call. Kenneth Ranucci, senior account executive with Contempo Design, feels that in-depth research on the customer combined with creativity can set the salesperson apart.[23] Michael Friedman, sales account manager for Pepperidge Farm, feels that a failure to do sales research leads not only to lost sales but to a poor reputation for the salesperson and the company.[24]

Doing preapproach research for an existing account involves reviewing the files on the customer company, including discussions from previous sales calls. The files may also include updated information on the customer, such as sales figures, records of correspondence, problems that have arisen since the last call, or articles on the company that have appeared in the business press. An extensive and continually updated database is important in maintaining a selling relationship. Therefore,

EXHIBIT 5.4

STEPS IN THE PREAPPROACH STAGE

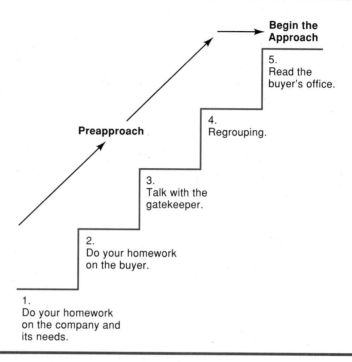

after each sales call the salesperson should update the files with new information obtained from the completed sales call. The salesperson should also make phone calls to predetermine what new needs may have arisen since the last sales call was made.

For a new customer or prospect, the salesperson may find little information available on file. In this case, the salesperson must seek out information about the customer. This information can be acquired from trade magazines, directories, government documents, the Internet, or other library sources. Suppliers, current customers, peers, or "friendly" personnel inside the customer's operation can also provide key knowledge. Friendly personnel can include acquaintances of the salesperson or other selling personnel.

The lack of available information on prospective customers can make a salesperson's call difficult. The first call thus becomes part of the research stage; the seller is not attempting to sell the product as much as he or she is attempting to build relations with the prospect and get to know the prospective customer.

Know the Buyer

As we defined in Chapter 2, the buyer is the specific person(s) responsible for purchasing for the buying company. The buyer is the target of the sales call. The salesperson who has called on the firm before may already know the primary buyer. In this case, the preapproach step consists of reviewing previous sales conversations for ideas about appropriate presentation information. On the other hand, the salesperson who is calling on an organization for the first time, or calling on other individuals in the buying center (as should be the case in relationship selling), has more work to do.

First and foremost salespeople are better prepared for sales calls when they can predetermine the name of the individual buyer. It is also helpful to know the buyer's background, current business pressures, personality, and any other relevant information pertaining to the upcoming sales presentation. As with prospecting, other people are valuable sources for this information. For example, a salesperson who is waiting for an appointment with a prospect has a good opportunity to talk with the secretary about the buyer. The salesperson can obtain valuable information such as the correct pronunciation of the buyer's name or something as simple as the mood of the buyer. One sales rep of BGR Enterprise, seller of industrial windows, was waiting to call on a buyer. In conversation with the secretary, he learned that the buyer was in a poor mood because of a BGR competitor's lack of delivery of a promised product. The sales rep was able to determine the needs of the buyer and the buyer's mental frame of mind and planned his presentation accordingly.

Talk With the Gatekeeper

A **gatekeeper** is an individual who, by design or by chance, controls the flow of information among the members of the buying center and between the buying centers and the sellers. In a selling scenario, a gatekeeper is typically a secretary, a receptionist, or a junior executive. (Chapter 7 looks at the gatekeeper from the purchasing side.) Gatekeepers wield substantial power because they can determine access to the buyer. To be successful in relationship selling, the salesperson must not underestimate the power of gatekeepers. For example, pharmaceutical sales representatives typically keep detailed files on doctors' receptionists. The salesperson must attempt to build friendly relationships with the receptionists (gatekeeper) because it is the receptionist who usually determines when and if the salesperson is allowed to call on the doctor.

Regroup

Regardless of whether a salesperson has made one sales call that day or ten, he or she must appear to be enthusiastic and professional. Salespeople do not have the luxury of showing their fatigue or emotions. If they have had a bad day and it shows, the bad day will probably continue. To regroup, the salesperson should sit for a couple of moments, take a deep breath, review customer notes, mentally organize the sales presentation, and gear up for the next sales call. Many salespeople regroup in the waiting room prior to seeing the buyer while others regroup in the car prior to walking into the customer's place of business, and still others regroup over a cup of coffee in a nearby coffee shop.

Read the Office

The last stage of the preapproach step (or some might say the first in the approach step) is to read the customer's office. Briefly examining the customer's office will tell the salesperson a lot about the individual buyer and can be beneficial in the small talk that often precedes the real sales presentation. Finding some common interests with the buyer is an important tactic for successful salespeople. For example, a seller walks into a buyer's office and sees a diploma from the University of Michigan. The seller was also graduated from the University of Michigan. The two now have something in common to discuss to overcome the initial awkwardness in the sales encounter.

There are a number of signs that salespeople can look for, such as pictures of the buyer's family, service awards, sporting paraphernalia, plaques, and desk mementos. Again, the salesperson's goal in this stage is to initiate friendly pre-sales conversation. After viewing a family picture, the salesperson might ask, "How old is your daughter?" Golf clubs in the corner may lead to "So you're a golfer?"

Reading the office also may indicate some of the personality traits of the buyer, which may in turn translate into a different type of approach. A very neat office with everything in place may indicate a person who is very organized or compulsive. A desk between the buyer and seller may indicate the need for a more formal relationship.

Even if the seller already knows the buyer, a quick read of the office can provide new information, such as updated pictures of the family, which may lead to social conversation about the buyer's family. Reading the office should only take a couple of seconds and may occur peripherally, but it can give important information that will help the seller determine the approach and presentation strategies to be implemented.

STEP 3: APPROACH

The **approach** can be defined as the strategies and tactics employed by salespeople when gaining an audience and establishing rapport with prospects. This stage starts as the salesperson enters the customer's office and continues until the beginning of the sales presentation. If a strong relationship has already been established with the buyer, then the approach becomes less important. In this case, listening to updated information from the customer about changing needs becomes the focus. Carol Samuel, senior vice-president of Communispond, says, "Listening is the most powerful tool salespeople have. Salespeople can't build client relationships without listening."[25]

Preset appointments will ensure that the customer is expecting you and has thought about what is needed from you. This, in turn, allows the seller to have a higher probability of learning new information about the customer. Relationship selling dictates that the buyer and seller build a level of trust that begins with a high level of continual service. The approach step is designed to reinforce the service and trust levels.

If the sales call is on a prospective customer, the approach becomes particularly important. Typically the first 30 seconds of the approach dictate the overall tone of the sales call. Although a positive beginning does not guarantee a successful sales call, an initial negative impression by the salesperson may prove to be fatal for that sales call.

Favorable First Impressions

Initial impressions made by the buyer and seller will dramatically affect the nature, character, and direction of the buyer/seller dyad.[26] Most first impressions are garnered through the handshake, appearance, and level of eye contact made by the salesperson (see Box 5.2 for a Code of Business Conduct).

BOX 5.2

CODE OF BUSINESS CONDUCT

- Don't promise what you can't deliver.
- Don't be late for meetings. If you are late, don't make it a big deal, just apologize.
- Get out of the office as much as you can—especially if you're with clients or customers.
- Learn to remember people's names. If your memory is poor, develop a system.
- Always have an agenda.
- Learn how to give first-rate presentations so that the message you're trying to deliver is the same one the audience receives.
- The true test of whether you (and your company) are customer-driven is how you set priorities. If the question "How will this affect customers?" is always the first one asked, the chances are good the organization is customer-driven.
- Be known as someone who enhances customer service.
- If you don't know the answer, say so.
- Never go into a meeting without knowing what you want the outcome(s) to be.
- Act like the customer is royalty, even if no one else in your organization does.
- Don't be internally focused. Learn what's important to customers and clients.
- The best training is provided by your customers.

SOURCE: Ginger Trumfio, "I Knew That," *Sales and Marketing Management* (February 1994): 60.

Handshake. The handshake is the initial greeting procedure in most Western cultures and typically occurs within the crucial first 30 seconds. In the United States the handshake will dictate the perceptions of the other businessperson. The handshake should be a firm grip regardless of whether the businessperson is male or female. A weak handshake is generally perceived as representative of a weak personality. Remember, perceptions are not necessarily fair or right, but they do partially dictate the way business will or will not be conducted. If you perceive the other person as weak, you may tend to be more aggressive and confident. The tone of the entire selling experience may subconsciously change. Because the first 30 seconds are so crucial, it becomes very important to make a favorable first impression, beginning with the handshake.

In other cultures, the handshake may be radically different. In Latin American cultures, for instance, the handshake is soft and less obtrusive. In some European countries, the handshake is also soft. A firm handshake is perceived as a sign of an aggressive personality, which is considered a negative trait. It should be noted, however, that a firm handshake is becoming more common worldwide.

Appearance. A salesperson's appearance is also judged in the first 30 seconds. Salespeople need to be professionally attired when dealing with a professional customer. One general rule is to dress at the same level that the customer dresses. If the customer typically wears a suit, so should the seller. On the other hand, if the salesperson is selling parts in an oil field to a buyer who is in jeans, it may be appropriate for the seller to also be in jeans. People tend to buy from people they like. The commonality of the buyer and seller can positively affect the likability of the other individual, and the seller's appearance will play a large part of the perceived commonality.

Eye Contact. Eye contact is another key to making a favorable first impression. One lesson that many students have to learn is that in Western cultures, particularly in the United States, eye contact should always be maintained in a business scenario. People perceive that salespeople have something to hide or lack confidence when they are unable to look the buyer in the eye and maintain contact. In Japan, however, eye contact is perceived as an overly aggressive personality and thus discouraged in negotiations.

Good Impressions in Culturally Diverse Settings

Initial favorable impressions in an international setting may become even more important than in domestic settings. Sellers must be concerned with how **cultural universals**—the unique aspects of a particular society such as etiquette and manners, courtship, socialization, gestures, status, customs, values, and materialism—affect potential markets and the negotiation of products for that market. The more complex the marketing involvement or the more unique the product, the greater the need for the study of cultural universals.

In a culturally diverse atmosphere, the seller must take special care that local cultural universals are not violated. For example, triangular shapes have negative connotations in Hong Kong and Korea and should not be used in presentations; the number seven is bad luck in Kenya; white is the symbol of death in some Asian cultures; in Bulgaria a nod means "no" but shaking the head from side to side means "yes"; arriving late for a meeting in Germany is unacceptable, whereas arriving late in Mexico is the cultural norm.[27] Salespeople in any non–home country must be aware of the cultural universals or risk damaging the developing relationships. Many of the cultural issues affecting sales management were discussed in Chapter 4.

STEP 4: SALES PRESENTATION

Not every sales call results in a presentation. In fact, ideally a formal presentation should not occur until after the salesperson has determined the needs of the customer. It may take as many as three or four sales calls, or multiple calls over years to understand customers, their business, and their needs before a sales presentation is finally made. The first few sales calls are designed to get to know the customer and develop the selling relationship.

After determining the needs of the customer, the salesperson begins building a presentation tailored to the specific needs of the customer. The objective of a **sales presentation** is to convince the prospect or customer that the seller's product and product attributes can satisfy the customer's needs better than can those of the competition.

Sales presentations will vary in their goals. For first-time buyers, the presentation may have to be extensive to provide adequate product and company information. For repeat customers, the presentation may be less formal and designed to move the customer into the next level of product or ensure a repurchase of the product. Sales presentations are typically constructed around the product features and the benefits that they provide, or specific customer needs.

	EXHIBIT 5.5	
	PRESENTATION APPROACHES	
Scenario Title	Description	Keys to Success
1. Buyer in a hurry	Buyer has no time available—seller has only 5 minutes	• Adapt presentation
2. Angry	Seller's company made error in previous delivery; buyer is *very* angry	• Reassure buyer • Correct previous problems • Listen
3. Chauvinist	Buyer is sexist, flirtatious, and obnoxious	• Remain professional
4. The talker	Buyer impressed with self, frequently sidetracks scenario to talk about his or her experiences in life and business	• Control the flow of the presentation
5. The procrastinator	Refuses to make commitment; wants to put off decision	• Handle delaying objections • Beat the objections
6. Brand loyal	Buyer content with existing product	• Determine needs • Address price and service
7. Low-knowledge buyer	Buyer is a rookie; lacks information	• Provide basic information • Reassure buyer
8. Arrogance	Buyer is someone you dislike; hostile and conceited; noncooperative	• Remain professional
9. Fatigue	Buyer has had a bad day; doesn't want to be in a sales situation	• Reschedule and come back
10. Ready to buy	Buyer needs and wants the product	• Immediately ask for the order • Avoid verbal overkill

SOURCE: William C. Moncrief and Shannon H. Shipp, "Making Role Plays More Realistic," *Marketing Education Review,* (1)4 (Spring 1994): 45–50.

A salesperson may make multiple presentations in a day, each differing according to the specific needs of customers, or perhaps even depending on the moods of the buyers. As you can see from Exhibit 5.5, salespeople should be ready to adapt their presentations at a moment's notice to the need of the buyer.

Preparation

The preparation of the presentation actually begins in the preapproach stage or in previous calls when the salesperson is attempting to determine the needs of the customer. After reviewing previous notes and research, the salesperson prepares a call agenda and a written proposal for the sales presentation.

Call Agenda. A **call agenda** is an outline of the purpose of the call and what the salesperson hopes to present on this particular sales call. Call agendas can be short or elaborate. For example, a Baxter Health Care representative could have a short agenda designed to introduce a new Baxter product to a hospital purchaser. The call

---

EXHIBIT 5.6

SAMPLE CALL AGENDA

KIEBLIFT PALLET TRUCKS

Account: Franklin Supplies (FS)
Key Contact: James Smith
Phone: 345-4555

PREVIOUS CALL

Date: 6/18/97
Discussion: Determined FS needs for the new warehouse on South Freeway
Specifically: Discussed JP Series Models A&C
          J Series Model A
Needs: Narrow Aisle Forklift

NEXT CALL

Date: 8/12/97
Time: 2:30

To Discuss: 1. Comparative presentation of J-Series, Model A to competition
                2. Financial arrangements
                3. Repair parts
                4. Delivery date

I expect the call to last about 1 to 1½ hours.

---

agenda might include a brief introduction of the new product and a short presentation guide about two key points on the product. An elaborate agenda may be for a new long-term stocking program for the hospital pharmacy. In this case, the call agenda would contain a detailed statement of purpose, and the presentation guide would contain presentation points for each member of the buying center. An example of a short call agenda appears in Exhibit 5.6.

In many cases the call agenda is sent to the prospective customer ahead of time so that both parties know exactly what is to occur on this specific sales call. Call agendas allow the salesperson to be more organized and prepared for a sales call. It keeps the salesperson focused on the particular customer's needs and tends to be very time effective. Buyers appreciate the professionalism a pre-sent agenda shows. When a call agenda is mailed to the buyer prior to the sales call, the buyer has an opportunity to think his or her companies needs.

Sales Proposal. A **sales proposal** is a written document that specifies why the buyer should buy from the selling company. The first part of the proposal typically reviews in detail the salesperson's perceptions of the buyer's needs and explains how those needs can be satisfied. The second section typically outlines the specifications of the seller's product and equipment, concentrating on the attributes. The sales proposal will also address the timing of delivery, service and maintenance issues, warranties, installation and training, and price.

Sales proposals can be concise, two-page briefs or detailed, lengthy documents complete with drawings and other appendixes. The sales proposal has the advantage of providing pertinent information in writing—which is particularly important if there are multiple people involved in the buying process. Many buyers require a sales proposal prior to allowing a sales presentation. Proposals are also the norm in sales to government entities and institutional buyers. Sales proposals are discussed in greater detail in Chapter 7.

Presentation Methods

Traditionally, presentations have been a one-on-one, in-person process. As we have seen in this text, more organizations are now using nontraditional methods to either replace or support traditional selling methods. Teleselling, team selling, teleconferencing, computer networks, and multimedia computer presentations are changing the way the sales world delivers sales presentations.

The uses for teleselling go beyond merely prospecting or customer service responsibilities. DuPont uses teleselling to streamline its selling process. Jerry Hale, the manager for DuPont teleselling, sees the sales process as a circle of events beginning with need recognition and ending with sales service. The steps between gaining general interest and closing the sale involve multiple contacts, many of which can be done by tellsellers. DuPont tellsellers often make small informational presentations and close deals by phone.[28]

Because many products sold today are highly technical, it has become difficult to hire good salespeople who are also technically competent in complex products. Electronic Label Technology has found the answer to be team presentations. Sales presentations to customers are made by a team of sales personnel, technical experts, and management, with each member of the team providing useful and specific attributes for the presentation.[29] For Electronic Label Technology, team sales presentations have led to an increase in sales and customer satisfaction.

Teleconferencing provides one very important advantage over teleselling in that the customer can see the product. Presentations are now made to buyers who are thousands of miles away, and the product can be demonstrated via a teleconference.

Computer networks have also helped in long-distance presentations. The Information Superhighway allows large amounts of information to be instantly transmitted to a buyer in another location. Also, multimedia presentations that have been designed for laptop computers allow a salesperson to provide high-quality, detailed information through a highly visual medium.

Diversity Issues in Presentations

Although the number of women in industrial sales has increased significantly since the 1980s, women still face more challenges than men in customer presentations. Female sales reps must quickly "present" their competence in the field. Their initial presentations, therefore, may be somewhat different from those of their male peers. For example, Krissann Kosesky is a sales rep with the industrial products division of Goodyear Tire and Rubber. She is one of five female reps for the Goodyear division, and her customers are overwhelmingly male. Being female has advantages and disadvantages, according to Kosesky. The uniqueness of a female rep allows her to see a new customer more often than her male peers, but she must instantly establish her credibility. "In most cases, product knowledge and a willingness to get involved in the business are enough to break down the gender barriers," she says. Successful sales closures may require multiple visits with very organized and specially tailored presentations designed to present the female rep's knowledge and abilities. However, once the initial resistance is overcome, Kosesky feels that long-term relationships may be easier to maintain because of the uniqueness.

Sherri Sorrensen is another female rep in a male-dominated industrial sales job. She works for James Clem Corp (JGC), makers of industrial liners. Sorrensen sells internationally, with Europe being her primary market. She finds that first meetings and presentations can be very awkward. "A lot of European businessmen are less tolerant of women in business than Americans are." The key to presentations, according to Sorrensen, is to maintain a high level of professionalism and expertise.[30]

STEP 5: ENCOUNTERING OBJECTIONS

Objections are customer questions and hesitancies about the product or company. Objections are a normal part of any sales discussion and relationship. Many new salespeople perceive a customer objection as a negative. However, experienced sales reps argue that, in reality, objections provide a clearer picture of customer needs and are an expected step in the selling process.[31] Objections are a sign that either there is a lack of information and understanding or the buyer has reservations about the seller's presentation. Our discussion of step 5 explores the reasons for objections and then outlines ways of countering them successfully.

Reasons for Objections

There are five common reasons why a customer makes objections during sales presentations and discussions. These include poor qualifying, as a negotiation tool, brand loyalty to a competitor's product, a lack of information, and procrastination. There are also times when a customer simply does not want to talk to a salesperson. Other commitments, fatigue, a lack of time, a bad day, or a lack of desire to talk to any salesperson are all reasons why a customer may not want to entertain a sales call. In the past, salespeople have tried to force the sales call anyway. In most of these cases, however, the buyer did not end up buying and may in fact have become alienated by the seller. The end result: a lack of sale now and maybe in the near future. The salesperson is better off setting up an appointment for another, more convenient time.

Poor Qualifying.   The first reason for objections is a poor job of qualifying the suspect. If the salesperson did not research the account, the presentation will most likely be a waste of time. When this occurs, the salesperson should stop the presentation and concentrate on determining needs and building a relationship for the future, or if the product is inappropriate for the account, the salesperson should cease trying to sell the product. If this objection scenario is frequently repeated with other customers, the salesperson or sales organization needs to reevaluate the qualifying process they use.

Negotiation Tool.   Many objections are made through a sense of habit. Buyers may not want to immediately agree to the purchase because they feel that the buying process requires objections or the seller will perceive them as weak negotiators. Thus, many objections take the form of pseudo objections. **Pseudo objections** are based on a stalling approach; the buyer hopes to improve its negotiation position by not immediately showing a desire or need for the product. Many pseudo objections occur because the buyer is hoping to gain concessions in the negotiation process.

Think of times when you have gone to purchase a relatively expensive item, such as a car or a new stereo system. The tendency is to keep asking questions about the product even if you already know the answer. Eventually, you agree to buy the product even though you knew you were probably going to buy when you first entered the store.

Pseudo objections are easily handled if they are quickly recognized. The buyer is seeking assurances that it is purchasing the right and best product, and that it has negotiated the best possible deal.

Brand Loyalty.   Customers who raise objections because they are brand-loyal to the competition are much tougher to sell, but they can be sold. The typical buyer's response to the seller is, "Why should I buy your product when I am happy with the product that I've been using?" The seller may attempt to convince the buyer of the superior attributes of the product, but usually the way to break brand loyalty is a cheaper price or other price incentive (i.e., discounts, better financing of the purchase). An equivalent or better product at a lower price may be enough to break brand loyalty, but a similar price will probably not be persuasive enough for the buyer to change vendors.

Lack of Information.   The most common reason for objecting during a presentation—and perhaps the easiest to deal with—is an objection based on a lack of information. The buyer is interested in the product but does not possess enough information to make a decision. The salesperson should be able to recognize this objection and provide specific answers to the buyer's questions. If the seller can provide enough information to adequately satisfy the needs of the buyer, the chances of a successful completion of the sale are dramatically increased.

Procrastination.   This objection occurs when the buyer does not want to commit for fear of making an incorrect decision. Procrastinators will stall and make objection after objection, even though they need the product and are satisfied with the product's capabilities. They will offer excuses such as, "I need to talk with my boss," or, "I need to think about it." Either response may be truthful or it may simply be a stalling technique. The key is not to let the buyers off the hook. If they need to talk to their boss, attempt to set up an appointment with both parties. If they need a day to think about it, the salesperson should set up an appointment for the next day to come back and see them again. When dealing with a procrastinator, the seller must aggressively seek a closure and overcome all objections.

Confronting Objections

Important attributes for a salesperson in overcoming objections are an empathetic attitude toward the buyer and the ability to discern the real objections from pseudo objections. Buyers will often make numerous objections to a product when they really have only one primary objection, such as price. The salesperson's job is to determine which objections are real and which are pseudo objections.

	EXHIBIT 5.7	
	METHODS FOR ANSWERING OBJECTIONS	
Method	Description	Most Useful When ...
Direct answer	Provide a direct response to the exact question raised by the prospect.	... the prospect is experiencing strong feelings of risk or when the prospect raises an invalid objection.
Comparison with rival products	Compare the company products or services to those of competitors to point out the advantages and benefits.	... the prospect is negative toward the company or representative, the prospect is not familiar with the company or when the prospect is experiencing strong feelings of risk.
Compensation	The rep admits the prospect's objection, but points out advantages that compensate for the objection.	... the prospect is very sensitive (thin-skinned) or the prospect has a big ego.
Comparison or contrast	The rep minimizes the prospect's objection by comparing it with something quite acceptable.	... the prospect is negative toward or unfamiliar with the company or representative.
Answer an objection with a question	The sales rep tries to overcome the customer's objection by asking a question related to the objection.	... the prospect will not reveal its feelings about the product.

SOURCE: Robin T. Peterson, "How Do You Answer Objections?" *The American Salesman* (February 1993): 9–11.

Whenever there is an objection—stated or unstated—it should be dealt with immediately. Postponing the answer until later in the presentation can alienate the customer who is concerned about the objection *now*. Many times getting the buyer out of his or her environment, such as going to lunch or a sporting event, can lessen the buyer's defensive nature.[32] Exhibit 5.7 offers some common responses to counter a buyer's objections.

STEP 6: CLOSING

Closing is defined as the successful completion of the sales presentation culminating in the acceptance of a product or service order. Closing for many people is the hardest part of the sales process. Once objections have been conquered, the time approaches in which the salesperson must attempt to close the sale and obtain the order. Buyer closures are rarely voluntary. Instead, the salesperson must be proactive in the process and ask for the order.

Probably the most common complaint by sales managers who spend time in the field with their sales personnel is that the salesperson does not read the scenario correctly and go for the closure. Closing too early is rarely a disaster if performed correctly. In fact, it can help the seller determine true objections and deal with them. About the worst that can happen is the buyer says he or she is not ready to buy. The seller simply goes back into the sales presentation. These **trial closes,** or early closure attempts, help salespeople determine the status of the presentation and on what information or objection they need to concentrate.

EXHIBIT 5.8
TOP TEN CLOSING STRATEGIES

Silent close	SP stops selling and hopes the silence brings about a closure
Assumptive close	Seller assumes buyer is ready based on his/her inuition
Alternative decision	Offer the prospect alternative choice- "Cash or Credit"
Summary * affirmative	Summarize attributes and get confirmation before closing
Balance sheet	Summarize pros and cons of all products under consideration
Kicker	Throw in added value if close now
Standing room only	If don't purchase now, same offer will not be available later
Warranty	Guarantee Satisfaction
Ask for order	Simply ask if ready to buy
Stimulus response	Use leading questions that have "yes" answers so that they become used to saying yes

It is very common for salespeople to make multiple close attempts prior to success. Gil Cargill, president of IDK Group, a business-to-business consulting firm, says, "Ninety percent of reps quit selling before the prospect is ready to buy, despite the fact that 80 percent of sales are made after the fifth contact." If the prospect is not ready to close on this sales call, Cargill recommends maintaining "low-cost, nonconfrontational contacts" including teleselling contacts, correspondence, promotional materials, and additional low-pressure sales calls.[33] Although it is important to close the deal, remember that relationship selling is concerned with the long-term needs of the customer. There are times when closing the sale may not be in the best interest of the customer, and the sale should not be made. For example, one salesperson had the opportunity to sell a product to a long-standing customer but instead recommended a competitor's product because it would better serve the customer's need. The result of the lost sale is a customer that trusts the salesperson and will continue to buy other products over time.

Every salesperson is going to have different strategies regarding how to close a sale. There are a number of different methods and approaches to closing a sale and the given scenario may somewhat determine which method is best. Closing is a skill that improves with experience. Exhibit 5.8 presents a number of closing techniques.

STEP 7: FOLLOW-UP AND AFTERMARKETING

The last step in the sales process may actually be the most important. The **follow-up** occurs after a sale has been completed and is designed to ensure that the customer remains happy with its purchase decision and that the relationship, which has been developed throughout the selling process, continues to fluorish.

Most sales depend on some type of postsale service such as delivery, maintenance, product training, or product installation. In addition, many times new products don't work as they should (see Box 5.3 for some staggering examples). It is up to the sales organization to continually check on the status of the product, particu-

BOX 5.3
EXAMPLES OF QUALITY CONTROL PROBLEMS

In this era of Total Quality Management, plenty of bad products and services still slip through the cracks. In the next year companies will ship:

- 5,517,200 cases of flat soft drinks
- 2,488,200 books with the wrong cover
- 811,000 faulty rolls of 35mm film
- 268,500 defective tires
- 114,500 mismatched pairs of shoes
- 14,208 defective personal computers
- 55 malfunctioning automated teller machines
- $761,900 worth of tapes and compact discs that won't play

SOURCE: Weld F. Royal, "It's No Wonder We Need the Baldrige," *Sales and Marketing Management* (August 1994): 16.

larly if the salesperson is relying on someone else to physically deliver or install the product. Quality service is expected of the selling organization regardless of the circumstances. Consider the following example.

Miller Business Systems is one of the largest office supply dealers in the country. One day the warehouse manager went to James Miller, the CEO of the organization, and said, "We have a very large order that the customer wants filled today, but we have no trucks or personnel available." Miller's solution was simple and rather unusual for a CEO. He rented a truck and then went with the warehouse foreman to deliver the order. Miller's motto is, "If you promise a customer, deliver."[34] Quality service means being able to maintain the trust of the customer.

All too often as an organization seeks new customers, it unintentionally ignores existing customers, and the customers defect to the competition for the support and service that was promised by the selling organization. Therefore, sales organizations must conduct selling and marketing activities after the product or service has been sold. **Aftermarketing** is a strategic program designed to maintain the business of existing customers. Basically, aftermarketing changes the focus from competing for and completing a sale to beginning and maintaining a relationship.[35]

A satisfied customer will likely repurchase from the same vendor. If the customer has a bad experience with the product, the salesperson may find future sales with this customer to be very difficult, if not impossible, to obtain. No one wants to feel that buying the product was a mistake. This feeling of uneasiness or regret about a purchase or decision is referred to as **cognitive dissonance.** If it is strong enough, cognitive dissonance can ensure that the customer will not make the same purchase again in order to avoid experiencing similar mental anguish. The more important the purchase decision is to a buyer, the greater the likelihood of cognitive dissonance. It is the seller's responsibility to continually reassure the buyer of the appropriateness of the purchase decision and to be there to correct any problems that may arise.

Good salespeople will do everything in their power to make sure the buyer does not have a bad experience with the product, because bad results can mean a failure to purchase again in the future.

Follow-up after a successful sale may be something as simple as a thank-you letter to the customer or a follow-up visit to make sure everything is working well. Follow-up after a nonsale should include a written statement of what was learned from the call and what information should be stressed the next time the customer is called upon. Productive salespeople will spend at least as much time working with the customer after the sales call as they did prior to and during the sales presentation.

SUMMARY

Relationship selling must be a fundamental part of every progressive sales organization. Consultative selling, a part of relationship selling, says that the salesperson must become an active part of the customer's environment, solving problems and providing quality service. Dyadic selling can take the form of discrete transactions or relational exchanges. Just-in-time relationships provide delivery of precise amounts of needed product with a minimum of waste.

There are seven basic steps in selling. The process begins with prospecting and qualifying a suspect. To become a qualified prospect, the individual must have a need for the product, have financial means to purchase the product, and be receptive to a sales call. Prospects can be found through a wide variety of techniques and methods.

The second step in the selling process consists of the preapproach stage, which includes doing background work on the customer, the buyer, and the gatekeeper. The approach follows the preapproach and contains the first few minutes of a sales presentation. Particularly important are the first 30 seconds. Included in the approach are the initial handshake, eye contact, and the seller's physical appearance.

The presentation is designed to convince the prospect or customer that the seller's product and product attributes can satisfy the customer's needs. Preparation may begin with a call agenda and a sales proposal. The presentation itself may be one-on-one in person, or it may be nontraditional, such as teleselling, team selling, teleconferencing, or multimedia computer presentations.

Objections are common to any sales presentation and can be real and meaningful. They can also be pseudo objections based on habit or procrastination. There are a number of reasons for objections and a variety of methods for dealing with them.

After all objections have been overcome, the salesperson must attempt to close the sale. Many new salespeople have difficulty in closing because of fear or simply a failure to ask for the order. There are a multiplicity of closing methods and procedures.

The last step in the sales process is follow-up. The follow-up includes all postsales activities.

KEY TERMS

consultative selling	just-in-time exchange
dyadic relationship	prospecting
discrete transactions	prospect
relational exchanges	suspect
countertrade	qualified

referral	sales presentation
bird dog	call agenda
snowballing	sales proposal
networking	objections
cold canvasing	pseudo objections
teleprospecting	closing
preapproach	trial close
gatekeeper	follow-up
approach	aftermarketing
cultural universals	cognitive dissonance

DISCUSSION QUESTIONS

1. What is the difference between relationship selling and consultative selling?
2. Why is prospecting an important activity to any sales organization, and what are some typical methods of prospecting?
3. What is the difference between a suspect, a prospect, and a qualified prospect?
4. What are the five stages in the preapproach selling step?
5. How can a salesperson make a favorable first impression in the approach step?
6. How do cultural universals affect the approach step?
7. What is meant by a nontraditional presentation method, and how can they support a more "traditional" presentation?
8. How can a salesperson confront an objection in a sales presentation?
9. What are some sales closing techniques?
10. Why do many sales managers argue that the follow-up step may be the most important in the selling process?

PROBLEMS

1. Melissa Rodriguez is a salesperson for a large office supply company. She calls on a favorite customer only to find that the buyer for the company has left her position and a new buyer is in place. Now Melissa doesn't know the buyer or anyone else in the company. Because companywide relationships had not been established, Melissa must begin the sales process over. What was Melissa's greatest mistake? What can Melissa do to ensure that this mistake doesn't occur again?

2. Through ordinary attrition Scott Sanderson, a salesperson for Harris Electrical, has lost 20 percent of his customer base from the previous year. How can Scott find new customers to replace the ones he lost?

3. Bill Atwater sells plumbing fixtures and is planning to call on an architect at Kimball and Associates because they are planning a new high-rise building. One problem is that Bill has never met the architect. He recalls that an old college friend works for Kimball and Associates. He calls the friend and

some of his other architect customers to obtain information on his prospective customer, including hobbies, personality type, and other general information. Why would Bill be searching for this type of information?

4. Jane Joyce has spent the past 30 minutes attempting to sell a new communication system to a small business. The office manager says to Jane, "I need to think about this. I'm not ready to buy right now. I should probably talk to the owner." Jane is now at a crucial point of the sale. What should she do?

5. Juan Gutierrez has just closed a huge sale that should allow him to reach quota for the year. Juan thinks about relaxing now that the sale has been completed. Ginger, his boss, tells him that he's not through with the sale yet. He still has some work to do. What work does Juan still have to do?

SHORT CASE

THE PRESENTATION BLUES

BACKGROUND

Stanley Ross was graduated from the University of Mississippi in 1990. After graduation, Stan contemplated attending pharmacy school, but instead decided to pursue a sales career in the medical industry. Although he wanted a job with a pharmaceutical firm, he accepted a job with a small medical supply company and moved to Memphis, Tennessee. After two years of experience with the medical supply firm, where most of his sales business was conducted over the phone, Stan finally landed the job of his dreams with a leading pharmaceutical company. Stan went through the training process, studied hard, and vowed to be the most prepared sales rep in the company. He began preparing detailed reports, color graphics, and testimonials so that he could be completely ready for each doctor visit.

SITUATION

After two weeks of attempting to obtain an appointment with Dr. John Martin, a leading surgeon at the city's largest hospital, Stan has finally met with success and is scheduled to see the doctor from 3:00 until 3:20 this afternoon. Stan's company has a new drug that recently received FDA approval. If Dr. Martin agrees to prescribe the drug, Stan's quota and reputation might be well on the way to being made. Unfortunately, Dr. Martin is known to be very de-

manding and a tough individual to sell. The thought of meeting with such a demanding doctor, combined with the anxiety of promoting a newly approved drug, has led Stanley to once again feverishly prepare for a presentation with "the works." Getting off to a good start with Dr. Martin is extremely important to Stan.

PROBLEM

Entering the hospital, Stan is prepared, complete with color charts and detailed reports concerning the drug. His nerves begin to settle as he sees Dr. Martin smiling in the distance. As Stan approaches, Dr. Martin waves and says, "I'm on my way to surgery. Walk with me and give me the highlights." Stan is mortified. Not only are his reports and charts virtually useless, but Stan is completely caught off guard.

QUESTIONS

1. What mistakes did Stan make concerning the sales call and the presentation?
2. What should have been the focus of the sales call?
3. Given the problem, how should Stan make the presentation?
4. Given the importance of this potential account, how would you have approached Dr. Martin, and what would you have done to prepare for the presentation?

PERSONAL SELLING ROLE PLAY

CHARACTERS

Sales Manager: Anita Bercera or Garrett Degeorgio

Salesperson: Courtney Knipper or Roger Lamb

Customers: Dr. Shannon Greer and Dr. Cris Matulich or Dr. Pat Peters

SCENARIO

Courtney Knipper, a new sales rep for Pharmiceaux, has been in her territory for only two weeks. Although Knipper has very little previous selling experience, she is enthusiastic and excited about her new job. She has been calling on her customers with some mixture of success and problems. On one particular day Knipper calls on three customers, and the sales calls were ineffective for differing reasons. The first customer was unhappy with some previous Pharmiceaux service and took it out on Knipper. The second customer seemed to be in a hurry and didn't have time to listen to her. Customer 3 seemed to be more interested in her personally than the products she represents. Knipper was discouraged by the end of the day but fortunately she had a prearranged meeting with her manager, Garrett Degeorgio. In scene 2, Knipper and Degeorgio discuss her approaches to each of the problem customers. Scene 3 should be a remake of scene 1, except Courtney successfully deals with the problems.

SCENE 1A

Courtney Knipper enters the office of Dr. Shannon Greer and notices immediately that this may not be a pleasant call. A very angry Greer says, "I wondered when I would see somebody from your company. Are you going to be as incompetent as your predecessor?" A flustered Knipper stammers out, "What do you mean?" Greer responds, "I was promised support for a seminar I was giving. Where were you? You were going to provide some samples and be at the seminar!" Knipper has no idea about what Greer is talking. This is the first time she has heard anything about a seminar, plus she has only been on the job for two weeks. She does a poor job of responding and eventually is asked to leave.

SCENE 1B

Knipper, still reeling from her run-in with Greer, calls on Dr. Cris Matulich. Matulich has been a long-time user of Pharmiceaux products but indications are that she may be thinking about switching to one of the competitors. Knipper has prepared a lengthy presentation with visuals and is providing lunch for Matulich and her staff. She approaches Matulich with a smile and is told, "Hi, Courtney, I have about three minutes for you. I'm behind and I need to see several patients. Unfortunately, I do not have time for lunch but I'm sure my staff will enjoy what you've brought. So what's new with hydrazene?" Again Courtney seems flustered. She thinks to herself that all this hard work has been lost.

SCENE 1C

After leaving Matulich's office she calls on Dr. Pat Peters, who seems to be very glad to see her. Peters says, "My you are much easier on the eyes than your predecessor George was." It becomes painfully evident that Peters is a chauvinist and his mind is not on work. Peters says, "Courtney, let's go to lunch and we can talk further, or maybe dinner would be a better time." Knipper says she has another appointment and leaves.

SCENE 2

Knipper goes to see her manager, Garrett Degeorgio, and replays her day for him. Degeorgio attempts to boost her sagging morale and then talk about what she might have done with each of her problem customers. After some lengthy discussion, Knipper thanks Degeorgio and leaves the office feeling better about the job and knowing next time how she will handle each of the people.

SCENE 3 (OPTIONAL)

Replay scene 1, except Knipper is able to use the advise given by Degeorgio. In each scene she does a better job of dealing with the problem at hand.

QUESTIONS:

1. How should Knipper have handled an angry and unhappy customer?
2. What mistakes did Knipper make with the presentation plans to Dr. Matulich? What could she have done when the lengthy presentation was not going to be allowed?
3. What options does a salesperson have when a customer is displaying inappropriate behavior regarding sexual advances, harassment, or unprofessionalism?
4. What help should the sales manager give the salesperson in the three customer scenarios? Should the manager be more involved in one or more of the scenarios versus others?

Name: Anita Bercera
Gender: F **Age:** 39 **Marital status:** Single
Education: B.B.A., University of Colorado
Title: Sales Manager **Office location:** Orlando
Reports to: District Manager, Atlanta
Employment history: 3 years with the company; 5 years experience in pharmaceutical sales; restaurant manager before that
Personality: Stern but fair; office cutup; everyone's favorite manager
Notes: Likes hiking and cooking; makes doll houses
Grapevine: Good sixth sense

Name: Garrett Degeorgio
Gender: M **Age:** 43 **Marital status:** Married
Education: B.S. (management), University of California at Davis
Title: Sales Manager **Office location:** Orlando
Reports to: District Manager, Atlanta
Employment history: 7 years with the company; 4 years previous experience in pharmaceutical sales
Personality: Family man; mild mannered
Notes: National champion skeet shooter; flies ultralight aircraft
Grapevine: Pushes his people hard, but very supportive

Name: Courtney Knipper
Gender: F: **Age:** 23 **Marital status:** Single
Education: B.A., Sonoma State
Title: Sales Representative **Office location:** Tampa
Reports to: Sales Manager, Orlando
Employment history: First full-time job
Personality: Enthusiastic and vivacious; wants to succeed
Notes: Still very nervous about the new job
Grapevine: Management feels that she has high potential

Name: Roger Lamb
Gender: M **Age:** 24 **Marital status:** Single
Education: B.A., Austin College
Title: Sales Representative **Office location:** Tampa
Reports to: District Manager, Orlando
Employment history: Worked one year for family business; has been with Pharmaceaux for 3 months
Personality: Independent and competitive; goal-oriented
Notes: Avid baseball fan; likes scuba diving
Grapevine: Probable fast-tracker; should be in present position only 2 years

Name: Dr. Shannon Greer
Gender: M[a] **Age:** 42 **Marital status:** Married, no children
Education: B.S., Appalachian State; MD, University of North Carolina
Title: Physician **Office location:** Tampa
Reports to:
Employment history: Physician for 14 years
Personality: Lives and breathes medicine; perfectionist
Notes: Expects high service levels from pharmaceutical reps
Grapevine: Concerned about changing medical world; wants satisfied patients

Name: Dr. Cris Matulich
Gender: F[b] **Age:** 38 **Marital status:** Married, one child
Education: B.S., Central Florida; MD, John Hopkins
Title: Physician **Office location:** Tampa
Reports to:
Employment history: Physician for 8 years
Personality: Caring, very bright, empathetic
Notes: Puts patient needs above all else
Grapevine: Will change suppliers if it's in the best interest of patients

---

[a]Can be female if role group needs a female character.

[b]Can be male if role group needs a male character.

Name: Dr. Pat Peters	**Reports to:**
Gender: M **Age:** 52 **Marital status:** Divorced	**Employment history:** Physician for 24 years
Education: B.A., Central State; MD, South Central Medical	**Personality:** Aggressive, cocky
	Notes: Twice divorced, heavy partier
Title: Physician **Office location:** Orlando	**Grapevine:** Being sued for sexual harassment

NOTES

1. Nancy Arnott, "Can MetLife Insure Honest Selling?" *Sales and Marketing Management* (March 1994): 13.
2. Joel R. Evans and Richard L. Laskin, "The Relationship Marketing Process: Conceptualization and Application," *Industrial Marketing Management*, 23 (1994): 439–452.
3. William Keenan, Jr., "What's Sales Got to Do With It?" *Sales and Marketing Management* (March 1994): 66–73.
4. *Industrial Distribution* 83(8), (August 1994): 47.
5. Nancy Arnott, "A Women's World," *Sales and Marketing Management* (March 1995): 55–59.
6. John J. Cronin, "Analysis of the Buyer-Seller Dyad: The Social Relations Model," *Journal of Personal Selling and Sales Management*, 14(3) (Summer 1994): 69–78.
7. Robert F. Dwyer, Paul H. Schurr, and Sejo Oh, "Developing Buyer-Seller Relationships," *Journal of Marketing*, 51 (April 1987): 11–27, and Morgan P. Miles, Danny R. Arnold, and Henry W. Nash, "Adaptive Communication: The Adaptation of the Seller's Interpersonal Style to the Stage of the Dyad's Relationship and the Buyer's Communication Style," *Journal of Personal Selling and Sales Management*, 10 (February 1990): 21–27.
8. Ian R. MacNeil, "Contracts: Adjustments of Long-Term Economic Relations Under Classical, Neoclassical, and Relational Contract Law," *Northwestern Law Review*, 72 (1978): 854–902.
9. Sam C. Okoroafo, "Implementing International Countertrade: A Dyadic Approach," *Industrial Marketing Management*, 23 (1994): 229–234.
10. Gary L. Frazier, Robert E. Spekman, and Charles R. O'Neal, "Just-in-Time Exchange Relationships in Industrial Markets," *Journal of Marketing*, 52 (October 1988): 52–67.
11. Johan Arndt, "Toward a Concept of Domesticated Markets," *Journal of Marketing*, 43 (Fall 1979): 69–75.
12. Mark Henricks, "Too Big, Too Few, Too Risky?" *Small Business Reports*, 18(10) (October 1993): 49–58.
13. Alan J. Dubinsky, "A Factor Analytic Study of the Personal Selling Process," *Journal of Personal Selling and Sales Management* (Fall/Winter 1980–1981): 26–33; see also Thomas H. Ingram, "Improving Salesforce Productivity: A Critical Examination of the Personal Selling Process," *Review of Business* (Summer 1990): 7–12.
14. Marvin A. Jolson and Thomas R. Wotruba, "Prospecting: A New Look at This Old Challenge," *Journal of Personal Selling and Sales Management*, 12(4) (Fall 1992): 59–66.
15. Marvin A. Jolson, "Qualifying Sales Leads: The Tight and Loose Approaches," *Industrial Marketing Management*, 17 (1988): 189–196; see also Donald L. Brady, "Determining the Value of an Industrial Prospect: A Prospect Preference Index Model," *Journal of Personal Selling & Sales Management*, 7 (August 1989): 27–32, and Tracy Emerick, "The Trouble With Leads," *Sales and Marketing Management*, (December 1992): 57–59.

16. Geoffrey Brewer, "Let Employees Take the Lead," *Sales and Marketing Management* (January 1994): 37.

17. Paul Gillyon, "How Fisons Instruments Measures Sales Opportunities," *Business Marketing Digest,* 18(3) (Third Quarter 1993): 18–28.

18. Edward Nash, "Prospecting for Leads," *Sales and Marketing Management* (February 1994): 33–34, also "Advertising Scores High in Lead Generation," *Sales and Marketing Management* (April 1994): 25.

19. Doris C. Van Voren and Thomas A. Stickney, "How to Develop a Database for Sales Leads," *Industrial Marketing Management,* 19 (1990): 201–208.

20. J. David Lichtenthal, Sameer Sikri, and Karl Fold, "Teleprospecting: An Approach for Qualifying Accounts," *Industrial Marketing Management,* 18 (1989): 11–17; see also Herbert E. Brown and Roger W. Brucker, "Telephone Qualification of Sales Leads," *Industrial Marketing Management,* 16 (1987): 185–190, and Marvin A. Jolson, "Prospecting by Telephone Prenotification: An Application of the Foot-in-the-Door Technique," *Journal of Personal Selling and Sales Management,* 6 (August 1986): 39–42.

21. Phaedra Hise, "The Do-It-Yourself Marketing Effort Analysis," *Inc.* (June 1994): 81–82.

22. "What Common Mistakes Do Your Salespeople Make?" *Sales and Marketing Management* (May 1993): 28–29.

23. Ginger Trumfio, "Opening Doors," *Sales and Marketing Management* (May 1994): 81.

24. "What Common Mistakes Do Your Salespeople Make?" *Sales and Marketing Management* (May 1993): 28–30.

25. "Shut Up and Sell," *Sales and Marketing Management* (February 1994): 60; see also Stephen B. Castleberry and David C. Shepherd, "Effective Interpersonal Listening and Personal Selling," *Journal of Personal Selling and Sales Management,* 13(1) (Winter 1993): 35–49, and Raymond Dreyfack, "Deformalize Buyer-Seller Relationships," *American Salesman,* 39(2) (February 1994): 26–30.

26. Tony L. Henthorne, Michael S. LaTour, and Alvin J. Williams, "Initial Impressions in the Organizational Buyer-Seller Dyad: Sales Management Implications," *Journal of Personal Selling and Sales Management,* 12 (Summer 1992): 57–65.

27. Lemore Skenazy, "How Does Slogan Translate?," *Advertising Age* (October 12, 1987): 84.

28. Martin Everett, "It's Jerry Hale on the Line," *Sales and Marketing Management* (December 1993): 75–79.

29. Cathy Hyatt Hills, "Everybody Sells," *Small Business Reports,* 17(10) (October 1992): 31–40.

30. Bill Kelley, "Selling in a Man's World," *Sales and Marketing Management* (January 1991): 28–35.

31. Paul H. Schurr, Louis H. Stone, and Lee Ann Beller, "Effective Selling Approaches to Buyers' Objections," *Industrial Marketing Management,* 14 (1985): 195–202.

32. David W. Finn and William C. Moncrief, "Salesforce Entertainment Activities," *Industrial Marketing Management,* 14 (1985): 227–234.

33. Nancy Arnott, "Hang in There, Baby," *Sales and Marketing Management* (December 1993): 17.

34. James B. Miller, "Bailing Out Customers," *Sales and Marketing Management* (January 1994): 29.

35. Tery G. Vavra, "Selling After the Sale: The Advantages of Aftermarketing," *Marketing Review* (1994): 10–12.

6

SALES MANAGERS AND LEADERSHIP

To be a good leader, first you have to be a good servant.

DAVID GLASS, WAL-MART

LEARNING OBJECTIVES

After reading this chapter, you should be able to answer the following questions:

- What are the daily activities and responsibilities of a sales manager?
- What is the difference between management, leadership, and supervision?
- How is the management role changing as we approach the twenty-first century?
- What are the various power and management styles a leader can use?
- What skills do effective leaders and managers need?
- How do organizations find new sales managers?

Xerox has had a long and sometimes controversial history. In the 1960s when it introduced its first copier, Xerox was the dominant producer of photocopiers in the world. By the mid- to late-1970s, however, the Japanese had entered the market with a less expensive copier and were suddenly making life tough for the market leader. In addition to contending with Japanese competition, Xerox also had lost an antitrust lawsuit and was forced to open 1,700 patents to its competitors. In less than 5 years, Xerox's market share had dropped from 85 percent to 40 percent.

In 1983 the top 25 executives at Xerox made a commitment to implement a total quality program they called "Leadership Through Quality." As a result of the new program Xerox began to turn around its declining market share through aggressive customer service. The turnaround was not without controversy, however. In his book *The Force*, David Dorsey profiles a team of Cleveland Xerox salespeople who risk health and happiness for team Xerox. The Cleveland office was led by district manager Frank Pacetta, who had a reputation for his insatiable appetite to win. His attitude: "Sales is like war, you have to beat the other guy to the sale before he beats you."[1] Pacetta led by putting fear into his employees but also through a level of emotion in which employees desperately wanted to please the "godfather" of sales.

Fred Thomas, a 20-year employee of Xerox, was one of Pacetta's sales managers who desperately wanted to meet the expectations set by Pacetta. Late in the sales year, as his ability to meet quota was in doubt, Thomas began pressuring sales reps to close their deals no matter what the method or cost. The results were sales closed but through methods that were ethically and strategically questionable.[2] Pacetta's and Thomas's managerial styles led to highly productive sales reps, but at what cost? Do managers have an ethical responsibility to their sales personnel as well to their customers?

How one answers these questions helps determine what makes a good manager. While few would argue that Pacetta was not effective in producing sales, the question of whether he treated his employees ethically could be debated. Many people at Xerox feel Pacetta was very successful, but others question his methods.

In this chapter we will examine these ethical issues and many more as we look at sales management and leadership. Although sales managers can be anyone from the vice-president of sales to the first-line sales manager, this chapter revolves primarily around the responsibilities, power, management style, and needed skills of the first-line sales manager, who is critical to the daily sales success of the organization.

Section one examines the sales manager's role, including his or her daily activities, responsibilities, and future directions. The next section explores styles of power and management, while the third section discusses the types of skills found in successful sales managers, which encompass communicating, empowering, coaching, and praising. The last section examines the new sales manager, concentrating on finding and hiring the new manager, and the steps the new manager must take to become successful in the organization.

THE SALES MANAGER'S ROLE

Before we begin our discussion about the sales manager's activities and responsibilities we need to clearly define three words which many people erroneously believe are synonymous: *management, leadership,* and *supervision.*

Management involves rationally analyzing situations, setting goals, and then organizing, coordinating, and directing employees to achieve those goals. Good managers are critical for the success of any organization. Sales managers manage the selling *process,* not just salespeople. According to Jack Falvey, speaker and author on sales management, "If you manage the sales process, sales will be the inevitable result. If you think the process will manage itself you are living in a fool's paradise."[3]

Although managers keep sales organizations moving forward, they may not be as capable as strong leaders of getting peak performances out of people or providing vision for future organizational growth. **Leadership** involves the use of influence with other people through communication processes to obtain specific goals and objectives (see Exhibit 6.1).

A leader goes beyond basic management and gets the best out of people and the organization. A leader is a special individual who, through experience and training, has become a unique form of manager. Many of an individual's leadership skills are developed early in life, beginning with leadership roles in high school and college. Every organization will have numerous managers but only a few leaders.

Warren Bennis, professor, former university president, and author of two dozen books says, "All the leaders I know have a strongly defined sense of purpose. And when you have an organization where the people are aligned behind a clearly defined vision or purpose, you get a powerful organization." Michael Eisner, CEO of

EXHIBIT 6.1	
DEFINITION OF LEADERSHIP BEHAVIOR	

Leadership Behavior	Definition
Trust and support	The extent to which an individual has feelings of trust and confidence in a supervisor, and to which the supervisor is aware of and responsive to the needs of subordinates
Goal emphasis and work facilitation	The leader's emphasis on high standards of performance and his or her behavior, which helps goals attainment
Interaction facilitation	The leader's behavior, which encourages the development of close, mutually satisfying relationship within the group
Psychological influence	The extent to which subordinates feel that their ideas and opinions are sought by the supervisor and taken into consideration when designing jobs and evaluating their performance
Hierarchical influence	The degree to which subordinates feel that their supervisor is successful in getting management to recognize their problems and successes

SOURCE: Pradeep K. Tyagi, "Relative Importance of Key Job Dimensions and Leadership Behaviors in Motivating Salesperson Work Performance," *Journal of Marketing,* 49 (Spring 1985): 76–86.

Disney, feels a leader also needs strong points of view. "What amazes me is that it's always the person with the strong point of view that influences the group, who wins the day."[4]

Supervision is a single function of a manager's job; it is the day-to-day control of the salesforce under routine operating conditions.[5] How important is first-line supervision? A study conducted in a manufacturing environment found that teams who were left to run their own work lacked direction. Team members also did not have skills to solve many of the daily problems.[6] Salespeople, on the other hand, operate to one degree or another as separate profit centers and, therefore, must be able to conduct activities without daily supervision. Daily supervision is certainly important in any organization, but good supervision skills are not as hard to develop as good management or leadership skills.

Sales Manager: Salesforce or Management?

Is a sales manager part of the salesforce world or part of management? The answer is both. The sales manager is a seller *and* an administrator or manager. This dual role creates some unusual challenges. The sales manager becomes the person in the middle, a role that is known as a **boundary spanner**.[7] Boundaries represent invisible barriers that the sales manager must successfully negotiate to keep the selling process running smoothly. The sales manager must span the boundary between management and the salesforce. Unfortunately, the first-line sales manager belongs to both groups, which can create internal conflict because the manager must serve these two often conflicting factions. The manager may more closely identify with the salesforce, but the organization recognizes sales managers as a part of the management team.

Exhibit 6.2 presents the **vertical dyad linkage (VDL) model,** which is an extension of the boundary spanning concept. The VDL model argues that the manager spans or links two levels and that the organization is only as strong as its weakest link. Notice that the links occur at every level throughout the sales organization.

EXHIBIT 6.2

VERTICAL DYAD LINKAGE MODEL

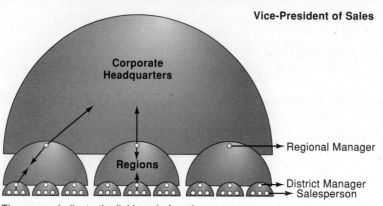

The arrows indicate the linking pin function

SOURCE: Stephen B. Castleberry and John F. Tanner, Jr., "The Manager Salesperson Relationship: An Exploratory Examination of the Vertical Dyad Linkage Model," *Journal of Personal Selling and Sales Management,* 6(3) (November 1986): 29–38.

link. Notice that the links occur at every level throughout the sales organization. For example, a district manager links the salesperson with a regional manager. The regional manager, in turn, links the district managers with corporate headquarters.[8] If the manager at any level is unable to provide solid leadership and managerial skills, the organization suffers. If too many of the links fail, the sales organization becomes untenable and eventually will falter. A sales organization must maintain strong sales management at all links in the organization to ensure the opportunity to thrive and grow.

Sales Manager Activities

Good sales managers are invaluable to a sales organization. The sales manager must be able to perform a variety of activities, ranging from sales to detailed administration. Exhibit 6.3 compares the daily activities of a sales manager with the daily activities of a salesperson (discussed in Chapter 2). Although there are a number of similarities in the activities, notice that the percentages of time spent on these activities differ. For example, sales managers spend about half as much time in the field selling as do sales reps. Typically, the number of accounts will be much smaller, but the sales value of those accounts will be much higher. Although sales managers continue to sell their administrative duties dramatically increase in terms of time. Simply stated, the sales manager spends substantial time managing, which includes meetings and administrative activities. One interesting observation from Exhibit 6.3 is that time spent on account service and coordination remains virtually the same as that of the salesperson even though selling time has decreased—a result of the size and importance of the sales manager's accounts. In this era of relationship selling, a large and important customer account requires much more

EXHIBIT 6.3

DAILY ACTIVITIES OF THE SALES MANAGER COMPARED TO THE SALESPERSON

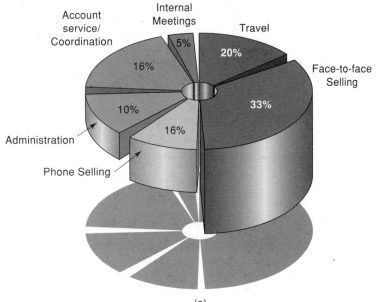

(a)
How salespeople spend their time.

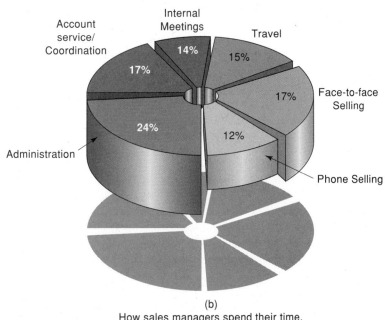

(b)
How sales managers spend their time.

SOURCE: "The Shape of Things to Come," *Sales and Marketing Management* (January 1990): 39.

Sales Manager Responsibilities

Specific sales management responsibilities can be divided into two broad categories: (1) managing the salesforce and (2) managing the district (see Exhibit 6.4).[9] The responsibilities of the sales manger are diverse and, in part, are what make the job exciting and challenging. Let's examine some specifics of the sales manager's job and how that role is changing.

Managing the Salesforce.   The single largest segment of a typical field sales manager's time consists of managing three to eight salespeople in the district. Sales managers are responsible for interviewing and selecting, training, developing, motivating, and evaluating their sales reps. We will discuss each of these responsibilities in detail in Part IV, "Managing Your Sales Resources." Sales managers are evaluated by their superiors based in large part on the overall performance of the district salespeople. A sales manager's time commitments depend partially on the experience levels of the salespeople reporting to the manager, as well as the amount of individual attention the salespeople require.

Many people go into sales to have a high degree of job autonomy and freedom, and thus feel constrained by close supervision. No two organizations exhibit the same levels of need and desire for supervision among their salesforce. Exhibit 6.5 depicts two companies with different levels of need and desire for close supervision. The vertical axis (*want*) represents a desire by the salesperson for close supervision. The horizontal axis (*need*) is management's perspective of the need for close supervision.

Individuals in cell 1 require a lot of close supervision from both a need and want dimension. In other words, these salespeople feel they need help, and management concurs with the feeling. New salespeople who lack experience and are possibly encountering job stress and uncertainty might represent cell 1. A salesperson in Cell 1 may not remain there over time. As the person gains experience and confidence, he or she may neither want nor need close supervision.

Salespeople in cell 2 want a lot of individual attention but don't really need it to perform well. The people represented in this cell are very demanding for a manager because they want the sales manager to spend time with them even though arguably they do not need it. The manager in company A of Exhibit 6.5 will spend much more time supervising than will the manager in company B based on cell 2.

Cells 3 and 4 represent the salespeople who do not desire supervision. Salespeople in cell 3 may actually need some supervision but do not want it. These individuals are less likely to follow company rules and regulations, and most are not as productive as they could be. Cell 4, however, contains people who are very self-sufficient and, as a result, do not want or require close supervision. Obviously, the more salespeople in cell 4, the easier the job for the sales manager.

Most of the management functions require the sales manager to commit time to the salespeople even as they are being hired. Although time with any individual salesperson is a matter of need and desire, a number of managerial functions require at least minimum time with the salesperson.

Managing the District.   In addition to the day-to-day management of the salesforce, sales managers must also manage the affairs of the district. The sales manager must conduct administrative duties that represent organizational requirements.

EXHIBIT 6.4

THE SALES MANAGER ROLE

Managing the Sales Force	**Managing the District**
Interviewing/Selecting	**Administration**
Training	Sales Office
Development	Enforcing Company Policies
Performance Standards	Communication
Motivation	Reports and Meetings
Evaluation	
	Marketing
	Developing New Business
	Forecasting
	Market, Competitive
	Information
	Personal Selling
	Account Development
	Relationship Selling
	Fieldwork with reps
	Finance
	Budgets
	Expense Reduction

Many revolve around administering the office and enforcing organizational policies. As we saw earlier in this chapter, the sales manager is the link between the salesforce and upper management. Thus, sales manager must provide quality communication links.

Most strategic marketing decisions are made at corporate headquarters, but the local sales manager must be able to implement tactical (day-to-day) marketing decisions, as well as provide competitive intelligence. Salespeople provide the manager with important information on their specific territories, the competition, and the

---

EXHIBIT 6.5

NEED-WANT CHART SUPERVISOR GRID

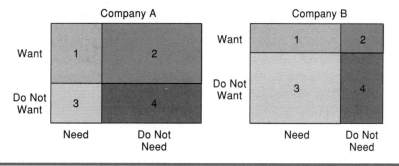

SOURCE: Frank E. Moriya and John C. Gockley, "Grid Analysis for Sales Supervision," *Industrial Marketing Management*, 14 (1985): 235–238.

marketplace. The manager must compile this information, analyze it, and provide concise marketing reports to the corporate headquarters.

As we saw in Exhibit 6.2, most sales managers also maintain account responsibilities. Although the amount of time spent selling may have decreased, the importance of the accounts typically does not. Sales managers are most likely to have been excellent salespeople. As such, the accounts that sales managers maintain are typically strong and important regional accounts. In managing them, sales managers perform the same duties as salespeople. This is one reason why sales managers sometimes consider themselves a salesperson first and a manager second.

Sales managers must also spend time in the field with each of their salespeople. This is called a **ride-with**. The amount of time spent with each salesperson varies according to performance levels, experience, and need. New salespeople usually require extensive time commitments from the sales manager. There are also times when salespeople need their sales manager to ride with them to help close a particularly tough or important account. With the growth and reliance on relationship selling, the presence of a manager may be essential in the selling process to indicate the importance of the customer to the selling firm.

Lastly, sales managers are responsible for financial information and administration. Each manager has some type of budget that must be administered and adhered to. The late 1980s and the 1990s brought substantial changes to organizational budgets, mostly resulting in a need to decrease organizational costs. As a result, sales managers have been asked to decrease expenses in each of their districts. In general, managers have responded by reducing salesperson expense accounts.

The Changing Managerial Role

With the advent of the virtual office, teleconferencing, part-time salesforces, flex-time, and global salesforces, sales managers may find managing in the twenty-first century a bit different from past decades (see Exhibit 6.6). In addition, downsizing, mergers, and global expansion often mean that fewer people must do more work. Sales managers must give their salespeople the flexibility to do this expanding work with less supervision and yet maintain control over a widely dispersed salesforce. Let's examine some of these issues.

As discussed in Chapter 2, the virtual office has become a reality. More and more salespeople and managers work from their homes with personal computers as their links to the organizational office. Teleconferencing allows "virtual meetings" to be conducted across video screens all around the world. For example, AT&T has developed technology that will allow individuals to see one another as they talk on the phone. Inexpensive video cameras attached to computer monitors allow people to see one another as they communicate over the Internet. AT&T is also developing computer technology that will instantly print translations of someone who is speaking in another language. The result of these technological advances is that managers no longer must be located in the same district, region, or even country as their salespeople. The concept of managing a geographical territory may disappear. In addition, the number of people a sales manager manages may increase. Seiichi Takikawa, CEO of Canon, believes that managers have different abilities. Some can successfully lead and manage 10 people, others 100 people, and still others 1,000 people.[10] In this era of shrinking numbers of middle managers, an organization must find those who can manage larger numbers of personnel.

Sales managers are also managing a different type of workforce. According to experts, by the year 2000 many businesses will be streamlined units made of two tiers consisting of permanent full-time and temporary part-time salesforces linked by computers, modems, video screens, and faxes. Flex-time (working flexible hours) and part-time work have grown in companies like American Express, NYNEX, Time Warner, Avon, and Hewlett Packard. According to Hewitt and Associates, 60 percent of over 1,000 organizations surveyed offer some form of flexible work, which include flex-time, compressed work time (40 hours in 4 days), job sharing, and part-time employment.[11]

These changes are beneficial in many regards, but they may also cause new managerial problems. Barney Olmsted, co-director of a consulting firm, says, "Many managers say their biggest concern about flex-time and telecommuting is how to monitor employee productivity." Other managerial concerns include un-availability of key employees at needed times, evaluation of performance, customer acceptance, and daily monitoring of work.[12]

EXHIBIT 6.6

A DAY IN THE LIFE OF A SALES MANAGER, YEAR 2010

By 2010 sales will be characterized by world territories, continual technological advances, and cultural diversity. Consider the following daily schedule of Teresa O'Brien, Sales Manager:

6:00	Gently awakened by her talking computer; coffee brewing.
6:15	Computer reads e-mail to Teresa.
6:30	Computer phones Teresa's salesperson in Brussels, Belgium (13:30 local time).
7:15	Leaves for the office (her home office in the back bedroom of the house), which contains a wide variety of technological products: computers with videoconference lines, worldwide e-mail, miniature copier, multiple monitors.
8:30	Accompanies her salesperson on a key presentation to a multinational customer in Prague. The salesperson arrives in person, Teresa by videoconference.
9:30	Contracts are signed by *all* parties in the Prague sales calls and transmitted by computer to the New York headquarters.
10:00	Attends her Spanish class at the local university from the comfort of her den (two-way videoconference links executives to the instructor). Teresa is already fluent in German.
11:00–14:00	Takes her daily "personal time" to attend school functions with her daughter.
14:00	Mediates dispute between her Egyptian customer and French supplier. Her cultural skills seem to be used daily.
14:30	Designs a computerized multimedia presentation to be used the following week by two of her salespeople.
16:30	Videoconference with her boss, Fritz Rohring, in New York.
17:00–20:00	Family time.
20:00	Videoconference using four monitors with company people in Los Angeles, Honolulu, Manilla, and Tokyo.
21:00	Reads computerized trade reports and checks e-mail.
22:00	Bedtime.

However, it is not just salespeople who are adopting flex-roles. Laura Palumbo Meier and Loriann Meagher, both 13-year employees of Xerox, are now sharing a sales management job in which they oversee eight sales employees. Their proposal to management to job-share was over 30 pages long and detailed the day-to-day tasks and how they would manage the sales team. Evaluation of the team management concept has been very favorable in the short duration of its existence.[13]

The result of all these changes is that sales managers must adapt to a changing environment and managerial role. Face-to-face interactions may be replaced by long-distance management, and managers in the twenty-first century will be managing a changing flex-oriented salesforce.

POWER AND MANAGEMENT STYLES

Every organization needs high-quality management and strong leadership. The effectiveness of managers is determined in part by their own skills and abilities, and also on the perceptions of the people they lead. All effective managers and leaders have different approaches to the use of power and management in obtaining desired performance levels from their subordinates. The following sections examine the concepts of power and management style.

Power

Sales managers generally hold some type of power over their subordinates, but the use of that power is instrumental in determining whether a manager is also a leader. Other sales relationships, with customers, suppliers, and support personnel, can also be influenced by power.

Power can be defined as a position of controlling influence over others. Problems occurring because of perceptions or misperceptions related to power arise daily in the workplace. Usually the problems arise not because of an intentional insensitivity of one party, but because people fail to understand how strongly hierarchical positions affect others in the organization. Workplace conflicts can be attributed to personalities, or more commonly, to the unevenness of power between individuals. This unevenness of power subtly influences how managers and subordinates relate to each other. As you read Box 6.1, think about how the unevenness in power affected the relationship between the people involved.[14]

The power held by an individual can be one or more of the following five types: (1) legitimate, (2) expert, (3) referent, (4) reward, and (5) coercive.[15]

Legitimate Power. **Legitimate power** is based on the manager's hierarchical position in the organization. Legitimate power is exhibited, for example, when a sales manager asks her salespeople to be at a meeting Friday morning. Because of the superior/subordinate relationship, the salespeople will most likely be at the meeting. Sales managers have the right to ask their salespeople to perform some act (attend a meeting), and because it is a reasonable request most subordinates will respond. All managers have legitimate power because of the nature of the job, but legitimate power alone will not make a leader.

Expert Power. **Expert power** is based on a manager's specialized or perceived specialized knowledge and skills. If a sales manager has had a distinguished career

BOX 6.1

POWER PROBLEMS

Let's look at two typical problems where an uneveness of power and a lack of communication caused internal problems:

- Brian Dolan and John Miller, both salespeople in an electronics company, worked well as colleagues in their company's salesforce. Their relationship was friendly and informal. Each felt free to drop in on the other unannounced to discuss technical problems or swap company gossip.

  Then Brian was promoted to area manager, and shortly thereafter he called John and asked him to come to his office to discuss installation plans for an important account. The call puzzled and angered John. Brian was only two doors away. Why didn't he just drop by? After all, they were good friends. Why did he have to play the boss? When John went to Brain's office, it was all he could do to hide his irritation. Brain greeted him warmly, but John was reserved during their discussion.

  Why, Brian wondered on the trip home that evening, had John acted so oddly? Was it because he and not John had been promoted? That had to be it. John was jealous. John, on the other hand, didn't understand how Brian's new position could make him insensitive to how John might react.

- Dick Rapp, vice-president of sales for a household appliance manufacturer, told his subordinates that his priority was increased sales and cost containment. He wanted expenses brought down, but he emphasized that the division should be results driven, not rule driven. "If you have to bend a rule to get the job done, do it," Rapp would say.

  At first his employees took him at his word and assumed that any improvements in efficiency would be welcome. But they quickly learned otherwise. Dick Rapp cared as much about style and form as he did about substance. How memos were worded and typed, for example, seemed to concern him as much as what they said. He also chewed out several salespeople for approving price changes and not going through the chain of command. Understandably, this behavior frustrated Dick's salespeople. They faced conflicting expectations, and they had to take time away from important tasks to meet what they considered frivolous demands. No one tried to understand, though, why bosses prefer to have things done their way and how this may be their means of heightening their feelings of being in control and reducing uncertainty. And nobody dared to explore these issues with Dick, nor could Dick see that he was sending mixed messages and burying people in the very red tape he wanted them to cut through.

  How did these situations develop? Why did Brian Dolan subconsciously need to pull rank on subordinates? Why did Dick Rapp enjoy tripping up his people? How did the subordinates feel about accepting authority and taking direction?

SOURCE: Fernando Bartolome and André Laurent, "The Manager: Master and Servant of Power,"

in sales prior to being promoted to sales manager, a request or suggestion about how to approach a type of customer might be followed—not because the manager is the boss but because of the manager's previous successes. The source of power becomes the expertise that the manager possesses or is perceived to possess.

Referent Power.   A manager's influence on others, based on a sense of friendship and respect, is known as **referent power**. Typically individuals who have recently been promoted to sales manager are suddenly managing some of their friends and peers. Many will respond to the new manager because of this level of friendship or

EXHIBIT 6.7
THE MANAGER'S USE OF POWER

Bob replies "sure," but depending on the work relationship between Bob and Jane, he may be thinking of one of the following:

Power Mode	Bob thinks:
1. Legitimate Power	She's the boss.
2. Expert Power	Those reports must be important. I better get them done.
3. Referent Power	If Jane needs the reports, I'll be happy to get them in.
Reward Power	Maybe if I do a good job I'll get that promotion.
4. Coercive Power	If I don't get those reports finished, I'll be in trouble.

respect. Those who have been managers for some time may have developed a strong sense of respect from their subordinates. There are a number of managers who are so well respected that subordinates will follow them virtually anywhere. Referent power is not easily acquired, nor is it really trainable. Referent power comes from a manager's personality and natural abilities, and from a high level of earned respect. Managers who command a strong base of referent power are likely to be more of a leader than just a manager.

Reward Power.   **Reward power** is based on a manager's ability to reward subordinates for acquiescence and performance. For example, a sales manager wants new accounts opened, and management is willing to pay a year-end bonus for new account performance. Salespeople who open new accounts are responding, in part, to the reward power. Reward power can be a prime motivator and allow managers to accomplish their goals. The power to reward is certainly part of a manager's abilities, but it will not necessarily differentiate a leader from a manager.

Coercive Power.   **Coercive power** refers to the ability to sanction subordinates for lack of compliance. Although coercive power is a negative approach, it is useful in many situations—particularly as a last resort. In coercive power situations the salesperson responds to a request by the sales manager because the salesperson could be terminated for lack of compliance. Coercive power is not the ideal way to gain acquiescence to set goals but there are times when it is necessary for managing people.

As this discussion shows, managers acquire power by virtue of their being managers and based on the perceptions of their subordinates. Exhibit 6.7 offers a summary on the manager/subordinant power relationship.

Management Styles

You have probably had a manager whom you could classify into one of the cells shown in Exhibit 6.8. The four quadrants are not all encompassing, but they provide good, general examinations of managerial personalities and approaches. Most managers will not fall directly into any one quadrant but will display characteristics that can be a mixture of quadrants.

The vertical dimension of Exhibit 6.8 is anchored by hostility/warmth, while the horizontal dimension is anchored by submissive/dominance. Warmth implies a high regard for others, such as sensitivity to others needs. Hostility is a lack of regard for others, or a "me first" mentality. Dominance is the drive to take control in face-to-face situations. It implies leadership in personal encounters, control, and independence. Submission is an unassertive attitude where the individual prefers to avoid confrontation and is passive in making decisions.

The Dominator (Q1).   The **dominator** is a manager who believes that people must be pushed and prodded to do their work. These managers have power and use it to gain compliance. They are the boss and want everybody to know it. There is only one correct way to do things and that's the manager's way. If performance occurs according to the manager's method, the salesperson will be rewarded. Dominators are quick to blame and slow to praise. They are results-driven, sometimes called go-getters. They usually produce high results but often at the expense of their subordinates. The concept of mentoring is typically foreign. Subordinates under this type of manager will have difficulty being promoted out from under the manager and, therefore, learn to live within the system, or quit and move on.

The Pipeline Manager (Q2).   Managers found in quadrant 2 are concerned that no one draws attention to them. These managers are basically weak but don't want to advertise that fact. Turmoil is heavily discouraged. It's everyone for themselves and the company be damned. One strongly held belief by this type of manager is that "flashy managers come and go, but those who know how to fade into the background stay around a long time."

These managers can be described as **pipeline managers** because they convey decisions from above to those below but add no value to the process. Pipeline managers do not like to make decisions and will delay them as long as possible. Salespeople under a Q2 manager receive very little reinforcement, positive or negative.

The Humanist (Q3).   Managers in quadrant 3 can be considered **humanists,** which implies that they believe the human element is the organization's most prized possession. Subordinates should be treated with respect and warmth. "Salespeople do good work only when they are content." Sanctions and punishments have limited value and are usually avoided.

Humanists are nonconfrontational, feeling that confrontation only leads to discomfort. The Q3 manager may be poorly structured or organized. Policies and procedures have limited value. Very few demands are made on employees. A poor performing salesperson has the best chance to hide in this type of environment.

EXHIBIT 6.8		
SALES MANAGEMENT STYLES		
	Dominant	Submissive
	Quadrant 1: "The Dominator"	**Quadrant 2: "The Pipeline Manager"**
Hostile	*Planning:* Rarely involves subordinate	*Planning:* Relies heavily on own boss; leans on tradition
	Organizing: Tight, very close supervision	*Organizing:* Relationships vague
	Leading: Pushy, demanding, driven	*Controlling:* Caretaker; does only what is required
		Leading: Passive; downplays own power
	Quadrant 4: "The Leader"	**Quadrant 3: "The Humanist"**
Warm	*Planning:* Consults others when planning	*Planning:* Generalities rather than details; gives subordinates plenty of room
	Organizing: Stimulates collaboration and interdependence	*Organizing:* Loosely structured sociability; makes sure everyone is happy
	Controlling: Develops subordinates who control themselves; provides structure for those who can't	*Controlling:* Relies on high morale
	Leading: Develops people	*Leading:* A cheerleader

SOURCE: V. R. Buzzota and R. E. Lefton, "Is There a Preferred Style of Sales Management?" *Journal of Personal Selling and Sales Management* (November 1982): 2.

Humanist managers want to be liked and have difficulty making controversial and unpopular decisions. A big happy family is the format that this manager sells, and socializing is an important element.

It is quite possible that Q3 managers can inspire productive work if the sales environment is stable and requires low levels of leadership. If tough decisions must be made by their managers, particularly involving the salesforce, the district may suffer.

The Leader (Q4).   **Leaders** believe that their job is to get the best out of the salesforce and to provide outstanding results. They give their salespeople a great degree of autonomy to do their jobs, and they also look at the individual needs of salespeople in terms of required levels of supervision. Those who can perform with minimum interference will be allowed to do so; those who need and want supervision will be given it.

Typically, Q4 managers involve their subordinates in decision making, seek out their advice, and willingly delegate responsibilities. They believe in individuality. These managers tend to serve as mentors or at least see to it that their people are developed to their maximum.

The Q1 manager may be very demanding and may get high performances but subordinates will probably not be mentored or developed. A company can be productive with a lot of Q1s but possibly only for the short-run. The Q2 manager pro-

---

EXHIBIT 6.9

SWEET SIXTEEN OF LEADERSHIP

1. Lead by example.
2. Develop vision: dare to dream.
3. Trust your subordinates.
4. Keep your people informed; communicate.
5. Encourage risk taking.
6. Give credit where credit is due.
7. Maintain your composure.
8. Praise in public and criticize in private.
9. Criticize constructively.
10. Give people a sense of direction.
11. Support people.
12. Avoid giving orders.
13. Be innovative.
14. Invite dissent; welcome new ideas.
15. Maintain high expectations.
16. Dare to be different.

---

vides very little worth to an organization and should be ferreted out and replaced. This type of manager limits talented subordinates and hinders productivity. Unfortunately, every company has Q2s who do manage to stay hidden and stay employed. If they would take more of a decisive role, Q3s could be very good managers. The warmth (humanistic) approach can be very motivating and productive for many people, but the tendency to avoid confrontations can also result in long-term sales problems. The Q4 manager is generally the most productive manager and is the closest to being a true leader. He or she works closely with subordinates and encourages input and initiative. The Q4 wants to develop subordinates and work together to perform excellence. Exhibit 6.9 depicts 16 ways to be the typical leader found in quadrant 4.

DEVELOPING OF MANAGERIAL SKILLS

Certain skills identify potential leaders. Exhibit 6.10 identifies the skills that individuals must possess to become good leaders. These include the ability to anticipate, diagnostic abilities, empowerment, communication skills, mentoring, a willingness to praise, cultural awareness and the incorporation of diversity, and a sense of vision.

Anticipation

A good leader must be proactive and not merely reactive to problems and potential problems. Being proactive means *anticipating* potential problems. Managers do not have to be psychic to be good leaders; no one can anticipate every future problem. By continually being cognizant of the internal and external environment, however, potential problems may not grow to have devastating consequences. With a good sense of anticipation, leaders are better able to respond to a crisis when it occurs.

One way of developing a sense of anticipation is to continually seek feedback from the salesforce, suppliers, customers, and upper management. A concept that has become popular in the last decade is called **management by walking around (MBWA)**. MBWA ensures that managers are continually talking with their salespeople and other publics. The result is that sales managers are better prepared to deal with problems as they arise. MBWA may include more days in the field with the salesforce, more spontaneous visits with customers, visits to a buyer's corporate headquarters, and close monitoring of reports and salesperson inputs. Anticipation requires work and is not something that just "happens." A good leader must always strive to gather more and more relevant data.

Another concept that has recently become associated with anticipation is that of the learning organization. The **learning organization** focuses on continual learning rather than controlling. We are born with the insatiable desire to learn and expand, but for many people and organizations this learning ceases to be the driving force, and maintenance of the status quo becomes the dominant drive. Organizations whose personnel focus on performing for a manager's approval rather than organizational results probably predestines them for mediocrity. Superior performance depends on superior learning. If leaders are in a learning mode they are much more likely to be anticipatory.[16]

Diagnostic Abilities

Problems rarely are what they first appear, and solutions too quickly implemented may cause a rippling effect that in turn may create problems elsewhere. Effective leaders must first identify the true underlying source of the problem rather than identify mere symptoms. This is not as easy as it might seem. Managers who attempt to take the path of least resistance may miss the underlying problem all together and react to a symptom. Experience has shown that dispensing solutions based on symptoms is a very short-term solution. Managers with strong leadership skills look beyond the initial, most evident symptom and examine the underlying problems.

The role plays included at the end of each chapter in this book are designed to help develop **diagnostic skills,** which is defined as the ability to recognize a problem, develop alternatives, and formulate a solution. The initial problem in each role play seems to generate a couple of immediate solutions, but these solutions will typically cause other problems.

Courses in MBA programs are also designed, in part, to provide students with strong diagnostic, analytical, and problem-solving skills. Many businesses are sending their managers back to executive education programs to help in the further development of the diagnostic skills. Likewise, many training programs are designed to provide a basis for either training on diagnostic abilities, or identifying future managers that have strong analytical skills. For example, the U.K. division of British Transportation attempts to identify junior managers who have the abilities to move into sales management. Specifically, the company looks for competence in analytical and strategic thinking as well as the ability to plan and organize work.[17]

Communication

Communication abilities are skills that on the surface may seem easy to master but in practice are very difficult. Have you ever had the experience of reading a book when you suddenly realized you were thinking about an event scheduled for later that day and that you had no idea what you just read? Has the author successfully communicated to you? No! There must be two active participants for communication to occur. The same is true in the workplace. As was true in personal selling (Chapter 5), listening is a vital component of good communication. Managers have to listen to what is being conveyed by their salespeople (either orally or in a written format). Managers who listen to their subordinates are more likely to earn the sales reps' respect and are much more likely to be or become good leaders. Managers must also listen to their sales rep's responses. Managers who issue orders but do not attempt to determine if the recipient understands them are probably not communicating well.

Communication also means informing your subordinates of your decisions and the decisions from above. Managers who leave their people "in the dark" regarding helpful information are never going to have as productive an organization as the leader who continually communicates. When there is a lack of information being communicated rumors take over. As anyone who has been in an organization can testify, the grapevine can be deadly accurate or totally off base. By not communicat-

---

EXHIBIT 6.10

LEADERSHIP SKILLS

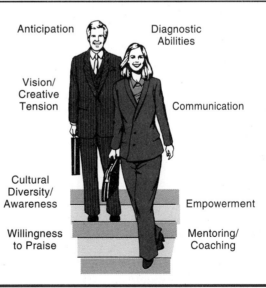

Anticipation

Diagnostic Abilities

Vision/ Creative Tension

Communication

Cultural Diversity/ Awareness

Empowerment

Willingness to Praise

Mentoring/ Coaching

ing to subordinates, chances are good that information being circulated will be misleading or wrong. Either way, it is the manager who loses in terms of respect and following.

Empowerment

Empowerment, which is defined as the process of involving the salesforce in their work through the concept of inclusion, has become very popular in the last few years. Empowerment implies that leaders are willing to share power with their followers by involving them in setting objectives and planning. For example, George Martin, executive vice-president of sales for Dunn & Bradstreet, says, "The change taking place is about empowerment, encouraging our people to take risks, and supporting them 200 percent when they make mistakes." Martin believes that if you let salespeople use their own style they will achieve or exceed all expectations.[18]

Owens-Corning has combined empowerment with salesforce automation. Bob Boylard, vice-president of sales, says, "We have less than half the management that we did in 1986." The reason has been empowerment of the salesforce and the use of Field Automation Sales Team (FAST), which allows salespeople to concentrate on the accounts and less on detail work. Prior to FAST, management was forced to deal with customer complaints, watch for problem orders, and resolve disputed issues. Now, the salesforce is responsible for all aspects of the account, allowing management time to spend on their own accounts. FAST has also allowed managers to keep track of things as they happen and thus change strategies at a moment's notice. The salesforce is responsible for all tactical decisions. As a result, management is responsible for more salespeople and salespeople are responsible for more of the day-to-day business. As management expands the span of control, the salesforce becomes more empowered.[19]

The results of empowerment are ultimately evaluated by bottom-line performance. Trusting salespeople to be responsible for critical decisions and involving them in planning can lead to a greater performance by individuals and the group as a whole. It is important for leaders to spend time with the salespeople and make them feel involved and a part of the team. Obviously, it is easier to empower more experienced personnel and those who are traditionally top performers. Empowerment does not imply that all salespeople are given the same latitude of power. Leaders must decide how much to empower each of their subordinates.

Mentoring

Good leaders continually attempt to provide guidance for their subordinates. **Mentoring,** or coaching, is either a formal or informal program in which sales executives take junior sales employees under their wings and make a concerted effort to help them develop and learn the job and organizational system. Mentoring needs to be a one-on-one activity so that a trust develops between the manager and subordinate. Mentoring activities can happen formally on the job, on the golf course, in a social setting, or in any other dimension of the job. As a mistake, misjudgment, or other event occurs the sales manager should immediately provide some feedback in a constructive atmosphere. Mentors are also important in providing long-term career guidance. They can guide the subordinates as they make career decisions. Mentors can also be "behind the scenes," voicing support for individuals. A person's career can be greatly enhanced if there is a mentor providing support.[20]

Mentoring should continue throughout a subordinate's tenure under the manager. In order for subordinates to become good salespeople or future managers, they must learn the nuances of the job. For many managers, learning to be a manager came through watching and relating to their own field managers.

Minorities and women comprise 54 percent of the workforce, and that percentage is growing. Many organizations have implemented mentoring programs to provide an effective method to bring the most qualified individuals, regardless of race or gender, into the managerial fold. The greatest accomplishment of a formal mentoring program is to attract and retain a diverse group of potential managers.[21]

One form of mentoring is typically referred to as a **curbstone conference**, which can be defined as an in-person observation and critique by the manager following a joint call on one of the salesperson's customers. The old-style curbstone conference typically had the sales manager observe and make some comments after the sales call was complete. Now, curbstone coaching teaches a new way of thinking about selling and managing. The manager needs to ask, "How was the relationship with the customer advanced?"

Syntex Laboratories in Palo Alto, California, uses district sales managers to begin coaching new personnel on relationship selling prior to entering the sales field.[22] Since people have a greater latitude of freedom in sales than other types of jobs, it becomes important for a good manager to coach the salesperson on how to develop good work habits. Similarly, because salespeople are usually somewhat isolated it may take considerable effort on the manager's part to become a good coach, but the importance of the coaching function cannot be underestimated.

One aspect of mentoring that has increased in importance in the 1990s is the need for employee counseling. **Counseling** refers to the ability of the organization to provide professional help for employees with personal problems. Even though personal problems may not be caused in the workplace, they tend to affect the salesperson on the job. Personal problems can include alcohol or drug dependency,[23] marital woes, depression, harassment, or personal financial problems. Some managers are now being trained to deal with their personnel's personal problems. Other organizations have programs available for troubled employees. For example, AT&T's Employee Assistance Program (EAP) includes a professional staff responsible for offering counseling and referral services. AT&T believes that the EAP is there to help employees as well as managers. David Tiffin, district manager for the EAP, says, "We encourage the manager to focus on job performance issues and leave the personal problems for us to handle."[24] Unfortunately, most managers may not have the good fortune of having a program such as the EAP available to them and must have some counseling ability themselves.

Providing Praise

"I can live for two weeks on a good compliment," Mark Twain once said. Maybe Twain could live on such sporadic compliments but most of us would probably like to have compliments more frequently. A compliment, particularly in public, and especially when it comes directly from a leader or manager, can work wonders for the self-esteem of an individual. Providing continual praise to subordinates is known as *oilcan management.* The oilcan (i.e., a compliment) works much better than a wrench or hammer (i.e., criticisms) when you want someone to perform. Put praise in writing and send it to the individual while also sending a copy up the organizational channels. One manager has stated that after a day in the field with one of his salespeople he writes up only the good things that the person did and sends it upward. This can build terrific loyalty to the manager.[25]

Jack Falvey, sales management consultant and author, says, "Identifying weaknesses is not the sales manager's job; anyone can do that. The challenge is determining what is being done correctly, thus encouraging more of it."[26] Falvey feels that because sales professionals are somewhat isolated they need more encouragement than do people in other professional fields. The concept of providing encouragement is not an easy one for many people, but it is important for leaders who want more productivity from their salesforce.

Cultural and Diversity Awareness

Developing a cultural sensitivity is becoming more and more important for today's manager. As the world becomes more interdependent in a business sense, managers will be forced to work in a variety of culturally diverse settings. One aspect of some firms' education programs has been to provide training in social skills so that salespeople and managers can be in control under certain social scenarios. The same is needed for cultural differences so that managers are comfortable when placed in unfamiliar international settings (see Exhibit 6.11 for a comparison of Japanese and U.S. cultures). Cultural skills allow individuals to convey interest and respect for people of differing cultures and tolerate the frustrations that may occur because of cultural dissimilarities. A nonjudgmental attitude based on the contrasts in business customs and traditions among various cultures is a necessity if a manager is to become effective as a leader.[27]

Sales managers must also have insight into the importance of diversity in the salesforce of today and tomorrow. Diversity has become a priority at many organizations. At U.S. West diversity is one of the six priority business issues. President and CEO Richard D. McCormick says, "There is some self-interest here; [diversity] it's the right thing to do and it's also good for business."[28] Every level of management is expected to be cognizant of the diverse needs of the organization. Most large organizations, such as Digital Equipment Corporation, Procter & Gamble, and Eastman Kodak, have implemented programs to deal with the multicultural, diverse workforce. These programs encompass employee recruitment, management, and retention.[29]

Diversity also includes flexibility in meeting the needs of "diverse lifestyles," including single parents, unmarried employees with spousal equivalents, gay couples, job-sharers, two-income families, and the physically challenged. Managing a diverse workplace can also include flex-hours, part-time workers, and subsidized day care. Electronics companies have been the vanguard of the diversity movement. Greg Doherty, vice-president of human resources for the Santa Cruz Organization (SCO), says, "Most corporations grow around conformity, not diversity, but if you manage talents effectively, you can use the differences as strengths."[30]

Perhaps one of the greatest issues to arise from the diversity issue is that of sexual harassment. Victims of sexual harassment can suffer from anger, withdrawal, and humiliation, as well as emotional duress. The cost to an average Fortune 500 firm is estimated to be $6.7 million a year due to turnover, absenteeism, and reduced productivity. The $6.7 million does not include costs for defending legal actions.[31] As discussed in Chapter 3, employees, particularly managers, need to understand that sexual harassment affects everyone in the organization. Sales managers must understand sexual harassment so that they can communicate the issues to their subordinates. Salespeople have some unique susceptibilities to sexual harassment because most of their business is conducted away from the organizational office in a nonsupervisory role and often in social settings. The problem is compounded when salespeople are involved in international selling.

Vision/Creative Tension

Creative tension comes from "seeing where we want to be, our 'vision,' and telling the truth about where we are, our 'current reality.' The gap in the two generates a natural tension."[32] Exhibit 6.12 displays the principle of creative tension. Basically, creative tension can be diminished by raising the current reality toward the vision or by lowering the vision toward the current reality. Creative tension is a positive because without vision there can be no creative tension.

A quality leader must have both vision and the strength to direct the organization through the creative tension toward the vision. Many managers fail because they try to substitute analysis for vision. Many managers are viewed as nice people, but they lack leadership because they lack vision. What does this mean? It may mean that the person is a great manager, and thus an important asset for the organization, but lacks the ability to be a good leader. What "might be" has always been a powerful tool to motivate people to accomplish feats that they thought unreachable. However, vision must have a basis in current reality. If we do not understand where we are, it will be exceedingly difficult to get to where we want to be.

THE NEW SALES MANAGER

Where do new managers come from? Where do we find the organization's leaders of tomorrow? What can sales personnel expect when a new manager (at any level) enters the organization? These three questions are important for the future of a sales organization, and the answers affect the daily working activities of all sales personnel. In this section we provide some answers concerning the development of new managers and leaders. Specifically, we discuss how an organization hires new managers and what happens when a new manager comes on board.

Hiring a New Sales Manager

Where does an organization find new sales managers? There are three common alternatives. Traditionally, new sales managers are promoted from the ranks of the salesforce, with the highest producers becoming the next sales managers. The second most popular method is to hire from other organizations. Third, firms are also beginning to hire from within the salesforce, but not necessarily the top sales producers. The following sections examine each of these alternatives.

EXHIBIT 6.11

COMPETITIVE ISSUES IN CORPORATE MANAGEMENT—
JAPAN AND THE UNITED STATES

Social Issues	Japan	United States
1. National Identity	Japanese or not, assimilation vs. replication, oneness	All can be American, bring your baggage with you, freedom
2. Family Roles	Dad, Mom, defined roles, extended families, social duty	Dual-income/career families, breakdown, materialism vs. social duty
3. Education	Strict, intense, high expectation, standardized, "hard" courses	Nonstandardized, cater to individual, emphasis on "soft" courses
4. Groupism and Society	Identity from group, self-sacrifice, social pressure, harmony	Individual Identity, pioneer spirit, "me against the world," maverick
5. Work Ethic	Be the best of whatever you are, your lot in life = religion	Success measured by title, pay grade, possessions, power
6. Economy	Few natural resources	World's largest economy within own borders, export excess
7. Crime	Low, social nonacceptance, conformity, low/no drugs	High, family breakdown, gangs, drugs and underworld
8. Justice System	Commit the crime = do the time, social ostracism10	Lawyers, over-sophistication, parole, "rights," propensity to sue

How They Manifest in the Workplace

1. Employment	One joins/belongs to a company (gains identity)	One gets a job (pay, perks, title)
2. Worker Quality	Essentially the same (education, etc.), police self	Varied background, education, social, ethnic, economic
3. Basic Thinking	Think virtually on the same basis, homogenous	Multiple backgrounds (education, social, economic, ethnic)
4. Trust	Employee/employer relationship begins with trust	Trust must be proven, earned, not automatic
5. Decision Making	Consensus (horizontal) and bottom up	Single decision maker (vertical, pyramid), top down
6. Individuality	Identity derived from corporation (groupism)	Individualism, make name for self, "make our mark"
7. Departmentalism	Concerned for welfare of whole process	"It's not my department," self-preservation, job-description
8. Living Philosophy	Relative—situational, society makes the rules	Black and White, Right and Wrong, Judeo-Christian morality and ethics
9. Class Consciousness	Large middle class (92%), vertical (association) dependent	Lifestyle (economic) dependent—high, middle, low class, racial element
10. Status of Employee	Companies most important resource, part of the family	Human capital (equipment), layoffs common, "temp" labor

EXHIBIT 6.11 (continued)

COMPETITIVE ISSUES IN CORPORATE MANAGEMENT—
JAPAN AND THE UNITED STATES

Social Issues	Japan	United States
11. Job Skill Improvement	Seniority system, promotions/pay, rotations, broad background	Fast-track, make self marketable, better skill = higher pay, specialists
12. Job Mobility	Low—lifetime employment, company switching taboo	High—shop the market place, resume builders
13. Technical Continuity	Relatively easy, same people for long time	Difficult due to personnel turnover, retraining, discontinuity
14. Company Education	Large effect, investment with long-term payback	Seen as bonus, employee turnover, short term
15. Job Responsibility	Not clear, inefficiency due to overlap	Clearly defined, job descriptions, compartmentalized, efficient
16. Influence in Private Life	"Live-to-work," facilities, paternalistic view, karoshi, hours	"Work-to-live," weekends/vacation time important for mental health
17. Management and Labor	Strong ties, we sink or swim together, common goals	Adversarial, mistrust, strikes/lock-outs, collective bargaining, Us vs. Them
18. Job Security	Very little worry, lifetime employment	Emphasis on performance, yearly review, MBO, layoffs, temps
19. Sense of Time	Long haul, invest in long term, gaman	Short-term oriented, profits now, perform now
20. Corporate Family	Zaibatsu = > keiretsu, security, corporate shareholders	Vertical sub-contracting, must answer to stockholders, perform or reorganize
21. Corporate Life	Belief in perpetual existence, in it for the long haul	Entity is a commodity, bought/sold, stock price, M&A
22. Creativity	Stifled, too homogenous, development of existing ideas	Varied backgrounds breeds ideas and creativity, initiate ideas, individualism
23. Government Influence	Strong connections, semimanaged economy	Government should stay out of business, true free-market and capitalism
24. Competition	Ichiryuu, market share at all cost, high quality and service	Friendly competition, compete within reason
25. Military	Prohibited from offensive, military, actions	World's police officer, take firm stances in favor of democracy, open economy
26. R&D	Invest in future, improve on ideas in "public domain," long-term	Initiate products, sometimes sell out, minimize to increase today's bottom line
27. Market Research	Adapt concept to local conditions, customer is #1	What's good enough for us is good enough for them
28. Industrial Base	New since WWII, robotics and technology	Some industries now having to retool, strong labor movements

SOURCE: Published with permission from Richard Scott of Alcon Laboratories.

EXHIBIT 6.12

THE PRINCIPLE OF CREATIVE TENSION

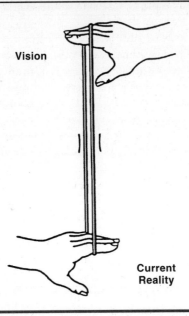

SOURCE: Peter M. Segne, "The Leader's New Work: Building Learning Organizations," *Sloan Management Review* (Fall 1990): 7–23.

Promoting Top Performing Salespeople. Sales managers have traditionally been promoted from the organization's salesforce. Top performing salespeople are "rewarded" by becoming managers. The advantage to the organization is that new managers are familiar with the market, the company, the customer base, and the competition. The high-quality field performance should qualify the new managers as experts in selling and, in theory, since they are hard working and high performers, they should be quality managers. This promotion and hiring procedure may seem to be logical because the new managers have routinely performed above their peer average. However, there are a number of problems with hiring only top salespeople as managers.

First, organizations spend substantial amounts of time and money resources recruiting and training salespeople but very little time or money recruiting and training sales managers—yet solid sales managers are arguably more important than individual salespeople. Very few organizations train new sales managers in how to be effective managers. As a result, promoting the top salesperson is no guarantee of effective managerial skills.

Second, does an organization really want their top salespeople promoted out of the field? If they prove to be mediocre managers or worse, the organization loses on two fronts. For many organizations, salespeople who are promoted to managers remain in management even if they are mediocre. Now the organization has mediocre management leading the salesforce, and the salesforce has been weakened because the top producers are in management. Certainly many top sellers do make great managers, but there is little rationale as to why this should always be so. Good salespeople learn to be independent, but for sales managers independence is not necessarily a favorable trait.

Third, not every salesperson wants to become a manager or will accept the promotion. Some people enter sales intending to remain in sales and never moving into a managerial position. The perception—and probably the reality—is that management robs individuals of their freedom and changes the entire focus of their job.

Fourth, sales managers of the twenty-first century must be able to manage a broader diversity of salespeople and customers. The growing impact of global marketing and selling, the increasing numbers of minorities and women in the salesforce, new technological advances, and the broadening scope of the management job will mean the new managers need a much broader skill base than just being an expert seller (refer back to Exhibit 6.10).

Hiring From Outside the Salesforce.   Another common approach to hiring a new sales manager is to bring in someone with previous managerial experience from outside the organization. The advantages to this method are that the new manager does not have preexisting biases toward organizational salespeople and the "outside" person brings a different insight into managing the sales resources. In addition, the new manager typically has existing managerial experience, unlike someone promoted from inside the salesforce. The downside is a possible resentment from the salesforce that an outsider has been hired for management when there are a number of capable "inside" personnel.

Promoting Top Internal Management Prospect.   The third approach is to examine the aptitude levels of existing salespeople and promote the ones that seem to have the ability to be good managers, even if they are only mediocre producers of sales. As mentioned previously, organizations are beginning to emphasize necessary managerial skills that go beyond typical sales-related skills. The advantage of this approach are twofold: you may find some excellent managers with multiple skills and your leading salespeople remain salespeople.

Unfortunately, the disadvantages make this approach a difficult procedure to follow. First, organizations may be passing over people who are high producers and who out-performed the person who is being "rewarded" with a promotion. If the high performers do not want to move into management then minimum conflict may exist. However, if management passed over the high performers based on the judgment that they would not necessarily make good managers, then discontent may exist, producing resentment from some of the organization's top sales producers. In turn, ripple effects of "injustice" may affect the morale of the rest of the selling organization.

A second reaction may be a lack of respect for the promoted individuals because they were not top producers. It may be easier to follow directions from someone who was a high producer and therefore considered to be "expert" in selling, as opposed to someone who was is considered to be a mediocre salesperson.

Making the Transition to New Manager

What happens when a new manager comes on board at any level? Obviously, the higher the level of the new manager the more intense the transition will be for the organization. A new manager usually has a sense of trepidation and excitement about the new job. Similarly subordinates also wonder what the new manager will be like and what type of relationship will be built between the new manager and each subordinate. Subordinates must prove themselves anew to the entering manager, and this can produce some real anxiety on the part of the subordinates. The new manager should be aware of their subordinates' feelings, as they are a normal outcome of change.

As new managers attempt to take charge they typically go through five stages: (1) taking hold, (2) immersion, (3) reshaping, (4) consolidation, and (5) refinement.[33] Each of these stages are discussed in the following sections.

Taking Hold.   The first stage in the process, called *taking hold,* typically lasts three to six months and often sets the tone for the remainder of the transition period. If the new assignment is a major or first promotion, the newcomer may initially feel overwhelmed. During this first period, a new manager is wrestling with the nature of the new job, its tasks and its people. Evaluation and orientation are important, even if the new manager is moving up within the same organization. Imagine the first day as a manager. You will probably feel pride, energy, anticipation, nervousness, and maybe some indecision about what you should do first. Even experienced managers experience these same feelings on new jobs.

The salesforce, experiencing similar emotions, waits to see what new directions the manager will take. The taking hold stage is characterized by anticipation and freshness.

Immersion.   Compared to the taking-hold stage, the *immersion* period is quiet because the new manager is in less of a learning stage. Now the new manager is revising his or her initial viewpoints of the job based on the learning that has occurred over the past few months. Other problems that were initially masked by larger problems begin to emerge. The new manager is also beginning to get a feel for the salesforce, the district, opportunities, and where problems may exist. The new manager is now fully enveloped in the job and is attacking the issues.

In this stage salespeople are forced to make adjustments to their own lives and ways of doing things as the manager begins setting new directions. The salesforce is also beginning to understand the ways of the new manager.

Reshaping.   In the *reshaping* period, learning becomes more diminished and routine. The new manager is now directing attention to making changes in the organization—people, procedures, or processes. This can be a very busy period, particularly if the job requires substantial changes because of previously low productivity or the strongly different personality of the previous manager. Reshaping ends when a manager has implemented as much of the new program as circumstances allow.

It is important to note here that people fear or resent change for the most part. Therefore, as new managers begin implementing changes, communication becomes essential to alleviate fears and misperceptions. New managers may succeed or fail in their jobs depending on the approach they take in incorporating changes that effect the salesforce.

Consolidation.   The *consolidation* stage begins with a continuation of steps taken in the reshaping period, but now the emphasis is on more evaluative dimensions. Problems that have arisen because of changes made in the reshaping stage must be addressed. The challenge of management is that for every decision made there will be a ripple effect. In other words, the manager's decisions may solve the immediate problem while creating problems elsewhere. The consolidation period may mean backing off from decisions made in the reshaping period, or minimally making adjustments to some initial decisions.

Refinement.   The *refinement* stage is characterized by little change and is thus a calm period. By this point the new manager is very comfortable with the job and has mastered the daily tasks and duties. Indeed, the manager is no longer being perceived as "new." The manager has now taken charge and his or her methods are in place and are accepted as the way of life for the district or organization. This does not imply that the methods are approved of or liked by the salesforce, but everyone understands the methods of daily interaction.

SUMMARY

Management involves rationally analyzing situations, setting goals, and then organizing, coordinating, and directing employees to achieve these goals. Leadership involves influencing other people through communication processes to obtain specific goals and objectives. A good manager is not always a good leader too.

Sales managers perform many of the same activities that salespeople do but in differing levels of frequencies. These activities include field selling, service accounts, travel, attend meetings, and administrative tasks.

Sales managers are boundary spanners linking the salesforce to corporate management. As such, they serve as a vital communication link between the two. The sales manager job consists primarily of managing the salesforce, administration, marketing, personal selling, and financial duties.

Managers lead through the power and influence they yield. There are different types of power: legitimate, expert, referent, reward, and coercive. Management styles can generally be divided into dominant or submissive and warm or hostile roles. These four types create a four-celled grid representing various management styles and problems.

Unfortunately, most managers are not necessarily good leaders. A good leader must have a set of skills which includes a sense of anticipation, diagnostic skills, a sense of empowerment, communication skills, mentoring (coaching) abilities, a willingness to praise, cultural and diversity awareness, and a sense of vision.

New sales managers tend to be promoted from among top-performing sales personnel, but this may not be the best approach. Other approaches are to bring in a manager from outside the organization or train internal salespeople who display managerial potential. As new managers come on board they must make adjustments to the new personnel, company policies, and the requirements of the job. There are five basic steps that new managers go through as they attempt to take charge: taking hold, immersion, reshaping, consolidation, and refinement.

KEY TERMS

management	dominator
leadership	pipeline manager
supervision	humanist
boundary spanners	leader
vertical dyad linkage (VDL) model	management by walking around (MBWA)
ride-with	learning organization
power	diagnostic skills
legitimate power	empowerment
expert power	mentoring
referent power	curbstone conferencing
reward power	counseling
coercive power	

DISCUSSION QUESTIONS

1. What are the differences between management, supervision, and leadership?
2. What are the typical activities of a sales manager?
3. How can the changing role of management in the twenty-first century be characterized?
4. How do the concepts of power and management style affect a manager's daily job?
5. What are the various types of power? Give an example of each.
6. What skills does a manager need to possess to become a leader?
7. What is meant by the term *empowerment?*
8. Why is cultural and diversity awareness becoming such an important skill for today's manager?
9. Where does a sales organization typically find new sales managers?
10. What are the five stages that new managers go through as they take on management responsibilities?

PROBLEMS

1. Maria Suarez has just been promoted to sales manager, and she is excited and a little apprehensive. She still has selling responsibilities and must now manage people who were once her peers. Someone asks her, "Are you sales or management?" She hesitates before answering. How should she answer?

2. A group of salespeople are talking about their manager, Bob Thomas. They agree that he is a very nice guy but has absolutely no vision. What do they mean?

3. John Jones has resigned as district manager of the west region. He is being replaced by an outsider. The salesforce is apprehensive about a new upper-level boss. They are somewhat concerned about what the change might mean to them personally. How can a new manager affect the life of a salesperson?

4. Edith Cranston is a manager who demands perfection and does not tolerate poor performance. She rules with absolute authority, and her district routinely makes quota. Her superiors appreciate the quality performance, but her subordinates dislike her intensely. Is Edith an effective manager? If so, how can she be more effective? If not, why is she ineffective?

5. Pete Lawson has been hired as the new sales manager for the Southwestern region. This is Pete's first managerial assignment, and he eagerly awaits his new responsibilities. He talks with his mentor Jan Hooper and asks her what steps he should take as the new manager. If you were Jan, what advice would you give Pete?

SHORT CASE

MANAGEMENT UNCERTAINTY

BACKGROUND

Carl Clancy is regional sales manager for Wesley Electronics with ultimate responsibility for four district managers and 32 salespeople. Recently Joe Jackson, sales manager for district 3, has decided to retire. Joe has been district 3's sales manager for 12 years and his district has consistently been above average, although there has been a slip in sales in the last 3 years. Joe has eight salespeople reporting to him, five of whom have been with the company 5 years or longer.

SITUATION

Carl has been told to refill Joe's job as quickly as possible. Upper management has gone through some changes recently, and they are beginning to modify some of the sales policies and methods and want all management on board immediately. Carl has also been told that Wesley is implementing a computer system in which all salespeople will be issued a laptop. Although this is good news, it also means that the salesforce's responsibilities will be expanded. Specifically, sales personnel will

have to acquire more market and competitive information and pass it on to headquarters through the computer system. Even though the new computer system will give salespeople instant account information, there is expected to be some resistance to the new way of selling, especially by some of the older salespeople. Finally, management has begun a diversity program and is strongly encouraging the hiring of minority and female applicants. Carl looks at the district 3's personnel and makes the following notes.

NAME	YEARS WITH COMPANY	AGE	EVALUATION (1–10, 10 HIGH)	1995 % OF QUOTA
1. James Hart	14	43	7	1.20
2. Gene Alpert	8	48	5	.95
3. Chance Majeski	6	34	8.5	1.30
4. Roger Byers	6	45	4	.85
5. Mary Johansson	3	26	7	1.00
6. Bill Weathers	5	33	7	1.05
7. Sean Caprice	3	26	5	.95
8. Junior Nottingham	1	24	4	.75

Carl knows there will be resistance by some of district 3 to change. He also knows that this district has a lot of potential. There are some very effective experienced personnel and some high-potential young personnel. He has heard the gossip about who is going to replace Joe and that the "team" is very concerned about who their new manager will be.

PROBLEM

Carl is concerned about the diversity mandate as well as the development of the district. He knows the district can perform better than it has in the past 3 years. After much interviewing, Carl has narrowed the manager choices to the following four candidates; two internal and two external:

1. *James Hart.* James is the most senior of district 3's sales personnel. He is well liked by everyone and might very well be a quiet leader. He had consistently produced high results but has never been promoted to management. He will be much like Joe Jackson and may be deserving of the promotion.
2. *Chance Majeski.* If anyone deserves to be promoted based on productivity it is Chance. His sales have been in the top 10

percent of the salesforce his entire career with Wesley. He is very competitive and wants to win at all costs. He gets the job done but is not as well liked as James Hart.

3. *Byron Jackson.* Byron, an African-American, is 27 with 3 years sales management experience with a leading competitor. He is personable and team-oriented; he had a very good interview.
4. *Sharon Martin.* Sharon has been a sales manager for 6 years in another industry. Her district finished third of ten in sales. She had a good interview and seems to be a no-nonsense individual. The organization that she is currently working for has been using laptops for 5 years.

QUESTIONS

1. What are the critical components that must be considered when making the hiring decision?
2. What leadership styles and traits do each of the candidates possess?
3. What are the pros and cons of hiring each of the candidates?
4. Which candidate would you hire and why?

LEADERSHIP ROLE PLAY

CHARACTERS

Good Leader Sales Manager: Mary Bartkowski or Don Gibson
Poor Leader Sales Manager: Bob "Rusty" Nale or Patricia (Patty) Kake
Salesperson #1: Joe "Maverick" Johnson or Lola Standards
Salesperson #2: Mauri "Juice" Madison or W. C. Lushman
Salesperson #3: Pete "Goofball" Patterson or Suzy Slacker
Salesperson #4: Kathy Kwan or Tyrone Benson

SCENARIO

Mary Bartkowski is a first-level manager of eight salespeople. She has to manage a variety of difficult personalities. She often thinks to

herself, "Why me? Why do I get stuck with the pain-in-the-butt types?" Mary starts to think about her current "headaches" and begins to wonder what to do with these people. She has four salespeople who follow directions and are at least moderately successful. These are the easy ones. However, the other four present an assortment of problems. She decides to have a meeting with each of the four problem salespeople to discuss ways they can improve their performance.

SCENE 1

Joe "Maverick" Johnson enters Bartkowski's office and asks, "You wanna see me?" Johnson is a top seller and has won a number of selling awards for the company. He is extremely cocky and self-assured. He's good and he knows it. He has been selling for 10 years, 6 for this company.

Bartkowski tells Maverick that his selling performance has been good as usual. Johnson replies, "Good? You mean great, don't you?" Bartkowski says, "Yes, but you've missed the last two sales meetings, and you never get your reports in on time. I need some cooperation from you." Johnson returns, "I'm a salesman, I sell, I don't have time for this other crap! I bring in a lot of business for this company. I can do it for EDD or I can do it for the competition."

Johnson is good and good salespeople are hard to find. What can Bartkowski do with Johnson? What are her options? How will this affect the other salespeople? Finish the scene with your solution.

SCENE 2

Mauri "Juice" Madison has been selling for EDD for 6 years. She performed well for the first 3 or 4 years, but lately her performance has been down dramatically. There have been complaints from customers about Madison, and there are insinuations that she may have a drinking problem. Bartkowski calls Madison into her office to confront her about her poor performance and the rumors. After initial irritated denials, Madison admits that she may be drinking a little more than she should but also that she and her husband have been separated for the past 6 months and he wants a divorce.

Should personal problems and alcohol/drug problems be treated differently from a managerial problem? How should Bartkowski handle Madison? Finish the scene with your solution.

SCENE 3

Pete "Goofball" Patterson has always been a low performer. He seems to do just enough to get by. He is always below the district average. Bartkowski has about had it with Patter-

son. She has warned him on several occasions that his performance needs to improve. This morning she must confront him with evidence that customer satisfaction is low in his territory, and that potential is being missed.

Nothing Bartkowski has done so far has seemed to help. What should Bartkowski do with Patterson? Finish the scene with your solution.

SCENE 4

Kathy Kwan has been with the company less than a year. She was just graduated from the University of Hawaii and has completed the standard training. She is still attempting to learn the system. She has good potential and the ability, but currently she is not doing well and is getting discouraged with the job. Management perceives that with a little more experience she can become a good rep. Bartkowski must make sure that Kwan does not quit or let her initial problems affect her future performances.

What should Bartkowski do to manage Kwan? Finish the scene with your solution.

Carefully think about alternatives in each of the four scenarios! Each solution may cause other problems. Think about leadership styles and what will happen to the individual salesperson in each scenario, as well as the other salespeople in the district.

OPTIONAL

Bob "Rusty" Nale has the same job as Mary Bartkowski. Bob is much less tolerant of mistakes and doesn't want anyone challenging his authority or causing him problems. The grapevine on Nale has never been very positive. If you can get the job done he will reward you; if you have problems, tough! The same scenes can be run but with a poor leader (Nale) dealing with the four salespeople. The class discussion should focus on the differences between leadership styles between Nale and Bartkowski.

CHARACTER DESCRIPTIONS

Name: Don Gibson
Gender: M
Age: 35
Marital status: Married
Education: B.B.A., University of Texas at Austin
Title: Sales Manager
Office location: Houston
Reports to: District Manager, Dallas
Employment history: Has been with the company since graduation; worked as a sales rep for 7 years
Personality: Sensitive to employees' needs; puts company goals ahead of personal ones; strong leader
Notes: Youth group leader; active in the community; coaches basketball at area Boy's Club
Grapevine: Being considered for district manager

Name: Mary Bartkowski
Gender: F
Age: 34
Marital status: Single
Education: B.B.A., University of Florida
Title: Sales Manager
Office location: Houston
Reports to: District Manager, Dallas
Employment history: Started with company straight out of school; was a sales rep for 7 years; worked her way up
Personality: Success-driven; compassionate, sensitive to subordinates' needs; places company needs ahead of her personal goals
Notes: Very active in the community; involved in environmental issues; teaches Sunday school
Grapevine: Being considered for district manager

Name: Bob "Rusty" Nale
Gender: M
Age: 33
Marital status: Married
Education: B.S., Northern Tech
Title: Sales Manager
Office location: Tulsa
Reports to: District Manager, Dallas
Employment history: Recruited from competitor; has been with Pharmiceaux for 4 years
Personality: Cocky; chip on his shoulder; confrontational; defensive; negative person; intolerant of mistakes
Notes: A loner, always looking out for himself; resistant to change; passed over twice for a promotion
Grapevine: Future with company is uncertain

Name: Patricia "Patty" Kake
Gender: F

Age: 35
Marital status: Divorced
Education: B.A., Southwest Central State University
Title: Sales Manager
Office location: Tulsa
Reports to: District Manager, Dallas
Employment history: Recruited from the competition; has been with Pharmiceaux for 6 years
Personality: Power-hungry; territorial; defensive; confrontational
Notes: Passed over twice for promotion; recently divorced
Grapevine: Future with company is uncertain

Name: Tyrone Benson
Gender: M
Age: 22
Marital status: Single
Education: B.A., Howard University
Title: Sales Rep
Office location: Houston
Reports to: Sales Manager, Houston
Employment history: Recent graduate; just finished training
Personality: Lacks maturity; intelligent; out-going, friendly, likeable
Notes: Class leader; tops in his training class; graduated college with honors; lacks experience; is having trouble making the adjustment to the industry
Grapevine: High potential; needs a good mentor

Name: Kathy Kwan
Gender: F
Age: 22
Marital status: Single
Education: B.B.A., University of Hawaii
Title: Sales Rep
Office location: Houston
Reports to: Sales Manager, Houston
Employment history: Recent graduate; just finished training
Personality: Lacks maturity; lacks confidence, intelligent; out-going; class leader
Notes: Tops in training class, but lacks experience; graduated college with honors
Grapevine: High potential; needs a good mentor

Name: Suzy Slacker
Gender: F
Age: 26
Marital status: Single
Education: B.B.A., Central State University
Title: Sales Rep **Office location:** Houston
Reports to: Sales Manager, Houston
Employment history: Two years with Pharmiceaux; previous experience as department store clerk and telemarketing

Personality: Lacks ambition; no career goals; weak work ethic
Grapevine: Possible termination candidate

Name: Pete "Goofball" Patterson
Gender: M
Age: 27
Marital status: Single
Education: B.A., South Central Tech
Title: Sales Rep
Office location: Houston
Reports to: Sales Manager, Houston
Employment history: Two years with Pharmiceaux; previous experience in sales and telemarketing at two other companies
Personality: Lacks ambition; class clown—lacks seriousness; is not respected
Notes: Graduated with a 2.2 GPA; weak work ethic; lives on the golf course
Grapevine: Possible termination candidate

Name: Joe "Maverick" Johnson
Gender: M
Age: 37
Marital status: Single
Education: Associates Degree, Lake Junior College
Title: Sales Rep **Office location:** Tulsa
Reports to: Sales Manager, Tulsa
Employment history: A sales rep with several companies; sold everything from cars to office supplies; with Pharmiceaux for 6 years
Personality: High ego; cocky, aggressive, demanding, fearless; competitive; borderline unethical
Notes: Has no close friends; respected for his level of sales but not his methods; has been reprimanded on several occasions but has led the district in sales several times
Grapevine: Will never leave sales, but may leave Pharmiceaux

Name: Lola Standards
Gender: F
Age: 38
Marital status: Single
Education: B.S., Western State University
Title: Sales Rep
Office location: Tulsa
Reports to: Sales Manager, Tulsa
Employment history: Sales rep for 12 years with various companies; with Pharmiceaux for 6 years
Personality: Cocky, confident, aggressive, demanding, competitive
Notes: Plays by the "good ol' boy" rules; can drink with the best of them
Grapevine: Will never leave sales, but may leave Pharmiceaux

Name: Mary "Juice" Madison
Gender: F
Age: 29
Marital status: Separated
Education: B.S., Southwest Tech
Title: Sales Rep
Office location: Tulsa
Reports to: Sales Manager, Tulsa
Employment history: Selling for Pharmiceaux for 6 years
Personality: Perfectionist; suffers under high stress; easily discouraged; driven
Notes: Recently separated from her husband; has had good sales levels; won the top trainee award in her training class
Grapevine: Divorce is imminent; rumors of heavy drinking, possibly on the job

Name: W. C. Lushman
Gender: M
Age: 40
Marital status: Married
Education: B.S., Southwest Tech
Title: Sales Rep
Office location: Tulsa
Reports to: Sales Manager, Tulsa
Employment history: With Pharmiceaux for 6 years; 10 years of previous selling experience
Personality: Good-natured, everybody's friend; very dedicated; ambitious
Notes: Steady producer over the years; sales have slipped over the past 2 years; uncertain future; did not reach his dreams
Grapevine: Rumors of mid-life crisis and drinking on the job; depressed

QUESTIONS

1. What options do you have in managing "Maverick"? Can Pharmiceaux afford to let him quit?
2. Alcohol and drug problems clearly can affect productivity, but what responsibilities does the company have to an alcoholic or drug abuser? Should employees with such problems be terminated? Why or why not?
3. If a manager decides to terminate an employee, what procedures should be followed?
4. What ways can you lead people who are not producing what is expected of them? Does it matter if the person is a rookie and just lacking confidence?
5. What traits were demonstrated by the leader/manager in each scene? How do these traits tie into what you've read/know about leadership?

NOTES

1. Ginger Trumfio, "Managing From the Trenches," *Sales and Marketing Management* (February 1994): 39.

2. Brian Silverman, "Copying the Best," *Sales and Marketing Management* (May 1994): 134–135. See also David Dorsey, *The Force* (New York: Random House, 1994).

3. Jack Falvey, "The Progress of the Process," *Sales and Marketing Management* (September 1992): 12–13.

4. Joyce E. Davis, "Where Leaders Come From," *Fortune* (September 19, 1994): 241–242.

5. Ajay K. Kohli, "Some Unexplored Supervisory Behaviors and Their Influence on Salespeople's Role Clarity, Specific Self-Esteem, Job Satisfaction, and Motivation," *Journal of Marketing Research,* 12 (November 1985): 424–433.

6. Janice A. Klein and Pamela A. Posey, "Good Supervisors Are Good Supervisors—Anywhere," *Harvard Business Review* (November–December 1986), 125–128.

7. Steven J. Lysonski and Eugene M. Johnson, "The Sales Manager as a Boundary Spanner: A Role Theory Analysis," *Journal of Personal Selling and Sales Management* (November 1983): 8–21.

8. Stephen B. Castleberry and John F. Tanner, Jr., "The Manager Salesperson Relationship: An Exploratory Examination of the Vertical Dyad Linkage Model," *Journal of Personal Selling and Sales Management* (November 1986): 29–37.

9. Rodney E. Evans, "Field Sales Executives Through Their Own Eyes," *Oklahoma Business Bulletin* (September 1971): 31–37.

10. Louis Kraar and Seiichi Takikawa, *Japanese Maverick* (New York: Wiley, 1994), 111.

11. Dottie Enrico, "Logging on Instead of Slogging In to the Office," *Newsday* (October 31, 1993).

12. *Ibid.*

13. "Teaming Up to Manage," *Working Women,* 18(9) (September 9, 1993): 31–32.

14. Fernando Bartolome and Andre Laurant, "The Manager: Master and Servant of Power," *Harvard Business Review* (November–December 1986): 77–81.

15. Based on John French, Jr., and Bertram Raven, "The Bases of Social Power," in *Studies in Social Power,* D. Cartwright (ed.) (Ann Arbor, Mich.: The University of Michigan Press, 1959). See also Paul Busch, "The Sales Manager's Bases of Social Power and Influence Upon the Salesforce," *Journal of Marketing,* 44 (Summer 1980): 95.

16. Peter M. Segne, "The Leader's New Work: Building Learning Organizations," *Sloan Management Review* (Fall 1990): 7–23.

17. Keith Coaley, R. K. Knightley, and David Beard, "The Identification of Management Potential," *Executive Development,* 6(2) (1993): 7–8.

18. Joseph Conlin, "The Preacher," *Sales and Marketing Management* (April 1994): 74.

19. Tom Eideman, "Who Needs Managers?" *Sales and Marketing Management* (June 1994, part 2): 14–17.

20. "Is Mentoring a Useful Training Tool?" *Sales and Marketing Management* (January 1994): 14–15.

21. William Heery, "Corporate Mentoring Can Break the Corporate Ceiling," *HR Focus* 71(5) (May 1994): 17–18.

22. Stephen X. Doyle and George Thomas Roth, "Selling and Sales Management in Action: The Use of Insight Coaching to Improve Relationship Selling," *Journal of Personal Selling and Sales Management,* 12(1) (Winter 1992): 59–64.
23. Betsy Wiesendanger, "Last Call!" *Sales and Marketing Management* (December 1993): 62–67.
24. "A Program for Troubled Salespeople," *Sales and Marketing Management* (November 1993): 32.
25. Jack Falvey, "'Oil Can' Management," *Sales and Marketing Management* (October 1992): 14–15.
26. Jack Falvey, "Encouragement's the Word," *Sales and Marketing Management* (April 1991): 8–9.
27. Jean McEnery and Gaston DesHarnais, "Culture Shock," *Training and Development Journal* (April 1990): 43–47.
28. Patricia A. Galagan, "Navigating the Differences: A Special Report on Diversity," *Training and Development,* 47(4) (April 1993): 28–30.
29. Jaideep Motwani, Earl Harper, Ram Subraminian, and Ceasar Douglas, "Managing the Diversified Workforce: Current Efforts and Future Directions," *SAM Advanced Management Journal,* 58(3) (June 22, 1993): 16–21.
30. Barbara Jorgensen, "Diversity: Managing a Multicultural Work Force," *Electronic Business Buyer,* 19(9) (September 1993): 70.
31. Cathy Owens Swift and Russell L. Kent, "Sexual Harassment: Ramifications for Sales Managers," *Journal of Personal Selling and Sales Management,* 14(1) (Winter 1994): 77–87.
32. Peter M. Segne, "The Leader's New Work: Building Learning Organizations," *Sloan Management Review* (Fall 1990): 7–23.
33. John J. Gabarro, "When a New Manager Takes Charge," *Harvard Business Review* (May–June 1985): 110–123.

A WEEK IN THE LIFE OF JIM ROBERTS, INDUSTRIAL SALES REP

Case contributed by W. E. Patton III and the late Ronald H. King, Professors of Marketing, Appalachian State University.

INTRODUCTION

Jim Roberts went to work with Appalachian Equipment Company right after receiving his bachelor's degree in marketing from the University of Colorado. He completed Appalachian's entry-level management training program in eight months after working in the warehouse in Denver, in manufacturing in Spruce Pine, North Carolina, and Atlanta, Georgia, in marketing in the headquarters office in Asheville, North Carolina, and in customer relations in the Spartanburg, South Carolina, plant. At the end of eight months, Jim thought he knew Appalachian's business. Then he was assigned to the sales department.

Appalachian Equipment Company is a marketer of a wide range of processing equipment, components and parts, packaging materials, and operating supplies used by the food processing industry (major SIC Group 20). The product lines range from food cookers to jar finishing machines to materials-handling equipment to replacement valves to lubricants. The firm distributes most of its lines through its thirty-five sales branches in the major food processing markets. Each sales branch is run by a branch manager and includes a complete warehouse operation, an outside sales force, inside counter sales, clerical staff, and so on.

Jim's first job in sales was as a counter sales rep in the Columbia, South Carolina, branch. There he spent much of his time on the telephone answering questions and taking orders. The rest of his time was usually taken up by customers at the counter, many of whom needed help in identifying parts, applications, or in finding items in the catalogs on the counter. After several months on the counter, Jim was allowed to travel with Morris Alexander, the senior outside rep in the Carolinas for 3 weeks. Then Jim was assigned a small territory in North Carolina as his own.

During the next several months, Jim spent most of his time trying to figure out what to do next. By the end of six months he had met all of his customers and got to know their businesses and their problems. By the end of the first year, Jim knew the food processing business even better than he knew the equipment business. By the end of the second year, Jim was recognized at award ceremonies in Asheville as the most improved sales rep in the Southeast. The next day, Jim was rewarded by being transferred to the company's top sales territory out of the sales branch in Orlando, Florida.

Jim's first week in the territory was really a busy one. He spent most of the time contacting prospects he had located through both primary and secondary information sources. He ended up spending much of his time with one particular company, Hialeah Marmalade, Inc., which has been a regular customer of Appalachian's for years. Hialeah Marmalade is one of Florida's largest orange marmalade producers and buys over 1 percent of Florida's fresh orange crop and 15 percent of the state's processed orange rind.

MONDAY

Although Jim visited several of the food processing establishments in the Orlando and Dade County areas during his first week in Florida, he

R.W. Haas Business Marketing, 6th ed., Cincinnati: Southwestern Publishing Company, 1995. Reprinted with permission.

spent most of his time with Hialeah Marmalade personnel since they were a long-established account for Appalachian. Jim visited the purchasing agent's office at Hialeah's headquarters bright and early on Monday morning and met Alice Smith (the purchasing agent's secretary) in the outer office of the purchasing division. He introduced himself, explained that he was Appalachian Equipment's new sales representative for Florida, and asked to speak to Mrs. Brown, the corporate purchasing agent. Alice informed Jim that Mrs. Brown was busy but could see him later in the day. She suggested, however, that Jim might want to visit with Ralph Owens, the equipment buyer.

Jim spent 30 minutes with Mr. Owens discussing food processing equipment and providing Mr. Owens with Appalachian's up-dated catalogs and brochures. Mr. Owens seemed to like Jim and suggested that they take a tour of plant #3, which adjoined the corporate offices. They spent the next hour walking through the plant, examining equipment, and meeting people. On the tour, Jim had a chance to visit for a few minutes with the plant engineer (Joe Smaltz), three or four processing equipment operators, the quality control people, and the head of maintenance and repair (Arlen Edwards). They finished the tour with a meeting with Butch Vanderfoefen, the plant manager.

During the tour, Jim spent a few moments with Gus Moretz, the operator of the jar finishing equipment. He noted that Gus had to operate *two* very old pieces of equipment to put the tops on the #16 jars and then to put on the labels. He gave Gus a brochure on Appalachian's new GF 6803 jar finishing machine and pointed out that the GF 6803 would do everything the two old machines would do—with less effort and less time. Gus seemed impressed and told Ralph Owens that Hialeah ought to buy one of the GF 6803s. Ralph laughed and told Gus to take the idea to his boss.

After the meeting with the Plant Manager, Jim returned to the purchasing office. Alice immediately took Jim in to see Mrs. Brown in her large, handsome office. Mrs. Brown was somewhat aloof, but welcomed Jim to Florida and offered him some orange juice. She told Jim that she delegated most buying decisions to her division and product buyers, but she herself would be involved in making decisions regarding major purchases along with the managers who had operating and budget authority concerning the purchase. She explained the basics of the general order routine and the firm's payment policy, and she spent quite a bit of time discussing the firm's automated reorder process, which she had designed.

After leaving Mrs. Brown, Jim stopped by Alice's desk to thank her for her help in getting him an appointment with Mrs. Brown. Alice was pleased and told Jim that Ralph Owens had invited him to come have lunch with Ralph and Joe Smaltz in the company cafeteria. Jim joined the two men for lunch, then spent the rest of the day visiting three other food processors in the area.

TUESDAY

On Tuesday, it was evident that Jim's visit to Hialeah had paid off. He got an early call from Ralph Owens requesting Jim's help in doing a value analysis on the steam by-pass valves used in the firm's marmalade cookers. Hialeah regularly bought Appalachian R20 valves, but Ralph was wondering if perhaps they wouldn't be better off buying the less expensive R10 valves.

Jim said he would be happy to help. He immediately drove out to the plant and met with Joe Smaltz and Arlen Edwards to get information on usage at Hialeah, and then returned to his office so he could go through his own information in order to complete the valve analysis. All of the information available to Jim is shown in Exhibit 1.

WEDNESDAY

On Wednesday there was great turmoil at Hialeah. Arlen Edwards discovered that they had run out of silicon lubricant, and they needed to lubricate the throw-jig idler arms on several jar finishing machines. He called the purchasing office, but everyone except Alice was in a very important meeting with Mrs. Brown. Arlen told Alice that he was desperate and had to have the lubricant *now* and asked Alice to please help him.

EXHIBIT I

INFORMATION FOR STEAM BY-PASS VALVE VALUE ANALYSIS

Hileah processes 50,000 gallons of fancy grade marmalade per year through five Appalachian Super Cook steam cookers. The steam cookers are steam-heated, with live steam entering through two steam by-pass valves on each cooker. These valves are subject to a great deal of pressure and heat and must be replaced at fairly regular intervals to avoid breakdowns and ensure safety.

Hialeah currently uses Appalachian's R20 steam by-pass valves and is considering going to the Appalachian R10 valve instead. Whichever valve they go with, they will do so at the first of November when they will replace all the valves on all five cookers. They also plan to replace all steam inlet pipes at that time, so there should be no "problem" installations on the initial installation of the valve they go with.

THE R20 VALVE

The R20 valve will cost Hialeah $80 each for the valves they purchase, and the initial installation in November will involve no direct cost for labor or materials since it is part of a planned retrofit. Studies indicate that the R20s will have to be replaced twice a year to ensure safety and avoid breakdowns. Replacement is normally quite easy because of the R20's advanced design, and normal replacement of one R20 valve costs only $8.00 for labor and $4.00 for materials.

Sometimes, however, the replacement job gets tricky and becomes a real problem. Sometimes the knurl nut jams on the fiddle threads, and the old valve has to be removed with a torch and cutting tools. This may be a relatively simple matter and involve only $16.00 in labor and $4.00 for materials for replacing one valve. At other times, the inlet pipe breaks in the attempt to remove the jammed nut, the labor costs go up to $32.00 per replacement, and the materials costs jump to $8.00.

A review of past maintenance and repair records indicates that replacement of R20 valves can be accomplished without jamming a knurl nut nine out of ten times a valve is replaced. If the knurl nut jams, the probability of the inlet pipe breaking (thus causing a "tough fix") is only 40 percent. Otherwise, it would be a relatively easy repair even if the nut jams.

THE R10 VALVE

The R10 valve will cost Hialeah $30.00 each for the valves they purchase, and the initial installation will involve no direct costs for labor or materials since this would be part of a planned retrofit. Studies indicate that each R10 will have to be replaced five times per year. Normal replacement of an R10 valve involves $16.00 for labor and $8.00 for materials, which is somewhat higher than the costs for an R20 because the R10 does not have the advanced features of the R20.

If the knurl nut on the R10 jams and the inlet pipe breaks while attempting to remove the jammed nut, the cost of replacement soars to $48.00 for labor and $22.00 for materials per valve. If the nut jams and the pipe does not break, the relatively simple repair and replacement will cost only $32.00 for labor and $18.00 for materials.

Conversations with customers who currently use the R10 valve in applications similar to Hialeah's indicate that the knurl nut jams 60 percent of the time a valve is replaced, and when the nut jams, the pipe breaks 70 percent of the time. However, thirty percent of the replacements involving nut jams are relatively easy to repair.

OTHER INFORMATION

It appears that the actual costs of the valves themselves ($80 for the R20 and $30 for the R10) are charged to the general operating budget of the plant, which is the responsibility of the plant manager. The costs of labor and materials for replacing the valves are charged to the maintenance and repair (M&R) budget, for which the head of the M&R section (Arlen Edwards) is held responsible.

There are no costs of lost production time involved in replacing the valves since time M&R work on the cookers is planned in advance.

Alice pulled out the files and discovered that Hialeah had bought the silicon lubricant from Appalachian the last seven times it was purchased, so she took it on her own initiative to call Jim Roberts and ask him to please send out two cases of lubricant. Jim was happy to comply. He had noticed that the sales branch at Appalachian had just received a replenishment order for 10,000 #8 jar tops from Hialeah under Hialeah's automated reorder system standing blanket purchase order to Appalachian, so he helped the warehouse people load the jar tops on a truck, threw in two cases of silicon lubricant (properly invoiced, of course), and rode with the truck driver out to Hialeah to make the delivery.

Arlen was delighted to get the lubricant so quickly and said so to Butch Vanderfoefen, the plant manager, who was there when Jim made the delivery. Butch called Jim aside and told Jim that Gus Moretz had visited with him and had initiated a request that the firm buy a new GF 6803 jar finishing machine to replace the two old pieces of equipment Gus operated. Butch had instructed Joe Smaltz to investigate the engineering requirements for such a machine, and Joe had indicated that Jim might be a big help in drawing up the specs.

Jim met for several hours with Joe to help work up the specs. They had to redesign some of the wiring in the plant, and Joe had to call a structural engineering firm to see if the floor would hold the new machine. By four in the afternoon, they had worked out the details and took them up to Butch Vanderfoefen's office. Butch asked them what the entire setup would cost and was shocked to hear that it would run over $100,000, but he told them to go ahead and start a procurement request.

Butch also told Jim Roberts that this whole thing would take some time since it was an extremely important piece of equipment. He indicated that Jim should submit a formal, written proposal to Ralph Owens, who would be responsible for issuing the purchase order, but he also asked Jim to make a personal presentation to himself and Mrs. Brown. They would evalu-ate the proposal, and if they decided to go ahead and buy the GF 6803, they would instruct Owens to buy it.

THURSDAY

On Thursday, Jim received a bid request from Ralph Owens. Hialeah had been buying #40 jars from two of Appalachian's major competitors, but was now ready to make a sole-source procurement for #40 jars for the next year. The bid request asked for a firm bid on 100,000 jars to be delivered by the successful bidder as needed under Hialeah's automatic reorder system. Jim knew that Ralph Owens used the same vendor analysis system used by Carolina Jam and Jelly Company (see the cases *Carolina Jam and Jelly (A) and (B)* for details on the vendor analysis system) and would buy from the vendor with the lowest adjusted bid.

Jim was certain that the only two bidders for the contract would be Baker Glass Co., Inc., and Florida Supply Company, both of whom have been supplying Hialeah with jars in the past. Jim called Ralph Owens to get some more information on the bid, but Ralph was out in the plant. Alice offered to help, and Jim was surprised to find that she was willing to give him quite a bit of information on the performance of Baker Glass and Florida Supply over the past year. With the information Alice supplied, along with information he gathered by calling a few other customers and information in the Appalachian branch office files, Jim was able to develop an estimate of the "points" Appalachian and the competitors might earn under the vendor cost ratio rating system used by Hialeah. (See Exhibit 2 for Jim's estimates.)

The next step for Jim was to review the past bids of the two competitors. Jim's predecessor had attended every bid opening possible and had kept thorough records. Jim, after an hour or so wading through the data on bids to Hialeah and to other customers, was able to get a good feel for what the competitors might bid. His best guess was that Baker would bid $9.00 per hundred jars and Florida Glass would bid $8.80 per hundred. By 5 P.M. Jim was ready to develop his bid.

EXHIBIT 2
ESTIMATED COST RATIO RATING POINTS FOR POTENTIAL JAR VENDORS

Attribute	Company		
	Appalachian	Baker Glass	Florida Supply
Quality	1.05	1.00	1.40
Delivery	−0.01	−0.01	0.07
Expediting	−0.02	−0.02	0.03
Order Routine	−0.005	−0.005	0.01
Technical Cooperation	−0.005	0	0
Facilities	0	−0.005	0
Financial Status	0	−0.01	0.02
Value of Sales Calls	−0.01	0	0.01
Proportion of Vendors' Business	0.01	0	0.05

FRIDAY

On Friday, Jim's boss (the Southeastern sales manager) called Jim for some help. He wanted Jim to develop a sales forecast for Florida for silicon lubricants. The sales manager indicated that he had developed a solid forecast for the Georgia market (which he thought was similar to that of Florida in many respects) of 15,000 cases per year. He gave Jim a basic market profile of the Georgia market and told Jim to use whatever methods he could to develop a forecast. Jim went to work digging out internal information, and even called several of his customers to get a feel for what they expected to buy in the next year.

Jim was quite surprised at the consistency of response from the customers he called. All were willing to make an estimate of the *total* amount of silicon lubricants they would buy for next year, and based on Jim's calculations, the average establishment in SIC 20 in Florida would buy 405 cases of the lubricant in 1992, with a 95 percent confidence interval of plus or minus 10 cases. None of the customers would say exactly how much they would buy from Appalachian, but Jim got the feeling that he could expect Appalachian's market share to remain fairly stable for 1992.

By the end of the day, Jim had developed the figures shown in Exhibit 3 and was ready to develop his forecast for Appalachian Equipment's silicon lubricant's sales in Florida for 1992.

SATURDAY

On Saturday, Jim met Ralph Owens at Jim's country club for tennis and lunch. They both enjoyed a morning of fun without the pressures of business. Ralph pointed out that one of the things he liked about purchasing and buying is that he didn't have to fool with the nitwits in the plants but instead could work with people like Jim who were out in the real world. Jim and Ralph agreed to make the Saturday morning tennis a regular event and planned to invite their wives along for dinner that evening.

SUNDAY

Jim slept in until 7:00 Sunday morning. He spent the morning in the typical Sunday morning way with his family. He devoted Sunday afternoon to paperwork and planning the next week. He left home at 8:00 P.M. to drive to Jacksonville so he could call on a customer early Monday morning.

DISCUSSION QUESTIONS

1. In Jim Roberts' first week as an Appalachian Equipment sales rep in Florida he was involved in several transactions (or potential transactions) with Hialeah Marmalade, Inc.

EXHIBIT 3
(I) DATA AVAILABLE FOR FORECASTING LUBRICANT SALES FOR 1994

Measures in SIC 20	Florida	Georgia
Number of establishments	60	45
Average number of employees	90	100
Total number of employees	5,400	4,500
Shipments ($ millions)	1,610	1,350
Materials purchased ($ millions)	950	800
Value added ($ millions)	660	550
Number of competitors[a]	4	5

[a]Competitors in Florida are about the same size and strength as those in Georgia

(2) PAST FIVE YEARS' SALES OF SILICON LUBRICANTS IN FLORIDA AND MARKET SHARE FOR APPALACHIAN'S SILICON LUBRICANT

Year	Industry Sales	Appalachian Market Share
1989	55,950	25.02%
1990	61,300	24.96%
1991	67,775	25.01%
1992	74,450	24.98%
1993[a]	82,000	25.00%

NOTE: Sales shown in number of cases.

[a]Estimated.

These included: (1) the GF6803 finishing machine, (2) the steam by-pass valves, (3) the silicon lubricant, (4) the #40 jars, and (5) the #8 jar tops.

a. What is the classification of industrial products involved in each transaction situation?

b. What is the "buy class" involved in each transaction situation?

c. For each of the transaction situations, give the names of the people who filled the following roles: (1) initiator, (2) gatekeeper, (3) influencer, (4) decider, (5) purchaser, and (6) user.

d. For each situation, which people will probably be the key buying influences?

2. a. Put yourself in Jim Roberts' shoes on Tuesday and develop a complete value analysis for the steam by-pass valves. Write a memo (with attachments) to Ralph Owens giving the results of your analysis.

b. Which valve do you think the plant manager will want to buy? Which will Arlen Edwards want to buy? Which valve do you think Hialeah will buy? Explain.

3. Put yourself in Jim Roberts' shoes on Thursday and analyze the bid proposal situation for the #40 jars.

a. What is the highest price Jim can bid and expect to get the bid?

b. If Jim were to get word that Florida Glass was going to bid $7.00 per hundred, what should Jim do if he wants to get the bid?

4. Put yourself in Jim Roberts' shoes on Friday and analyze the data available for developing Appalachian's sales forecast for silicon lubricants for Florida.

a. Write a memo to Jim's boss giving the forecast and the justification for the forecast. Include tables, graphs, or whatever else is necessary so Jim's boss will know *exactly* how you came up with the figures.

b. What *other* information would you have liked to have in developing the forecast? How would you use this information?

c. How would you get the information given in part 1 of Exhibit 3? Be specific in naming the exact source that you would use for each item.

ROYAL CORPORATION

Case contributed by Hubert C. Hennessey. Associate Professor, Babson College and Barbara Kalunian.

As Mary Jones, a third-year sales representative for the Royal Corporation, reviewed her call plans for tomorrow, she thought about her sales strategy. It was only July 1983 but Jones was already well on her way toward completing her best year financially with the company. In 1982, she had sold the largest dollar volume of copies of any sales representative in the northeast and was the tenth most successful rep in the country.

But Jones was not looking forward to her scheduled activities for the next day. In spite of her excellent sales ability, she had not been able to sell the Royal Corporate Copy Center (CCC). This innovative program was highly touted by Royal upper management. Jones was one of the few sales reps in her office who had not sold a CCC in 1982. Although Jones had an excellent working relationship with her sales manager, Tom Stein, she was experiencing a lot of pressure from him of late because he could not understand her inability to sell CCCs. Jones had therefore promised herself to concentrate her efforts on selling the CCC even if it meant sacrificing sales of other products.

Jones had five appointments for the day—9 A.M., Acme Computers; 9:45 A.M., Bickford Publishing; 11:45 A.M., ABC Electronics; 12:30 P.M., CG Advertising and 2:00 P.M., General Hospital. At Acme, Bickford, and ABC, Jones would de-velop CCC prospects. She was in various states of information gathering and proposal preparation for each of the accounts. At CG, Jones planned to present examples of work performed by a model 750 color copier. At General Hospital, she would present her final proposal for CCC adoption. Although the focus of her day would be on CCCs, she still needed to call and visit other accounts that she was developing.

ROYAL INTRODUCES THE CCC CONCEPT

In 1980, Royal had introduced its Corporate Copy Center facilities management program (CCC). Under this concept, Royal offered to equip, staff, operate, and manage a reproduction operation for its clients on the clients' premises. After analyzing the needs of the client, Royal selected and installed the appropriate equipment and provided fully trained, Royal-employed operators. The CCC equipment also permits microfilming, sorting, collating, binding, covering, and color copying, in addition to high-volume copying. The major benefits of the program include reproduction contracted for at a specified price, guaranteed output, tailor-made capabilities, and qualified operators.

As she pulled into the Acme Computers parking lot, she noticed that an unexpected traffic jam had made her ten minutes late for the 9:00 A.M. appointment. This made her uncomfortable, as she valued her time and assumed that her clients appreciated promptness. Jones had acquired the Acme Computers account the previous summer and had dealt personally with Betty White, director of printing services, ever since. She had approached White six months earlier with the idea of purchasing a CCC, but had not pursued the matter further until now because Betty had seemed very unreceptive. For today's call, Jones had worked several hours preparing a detailed study of Acme's present reproduction costs. She was determined to make her efforts pay off.

Jones gave her card to the new receptionist, who buzzed White's office and told her that Jones was waiting. A few minutes later, Betty appeared and led Jones to a corner of the lobby. They always met in the lobby, a situation that Jones found frustrating but it was apparently company policy.

"Good morning, Betty, it's good to see you again. Since I saw you last, I've put together the complete analysis on the CCC that I promised. I know you'll be excited by what you see. As you are aware, the concept of a CCC is not that unusual anymore. You may recall from the first presentation that I prepared for you, the CCC can be a tremendous time and money saver. Could you take a few moments to review the calculations that I have prepared exclusively for Acme Computers?" Betty flipped through the various pages of exhibits that Jones had prepared, but it was obvious that she had little interest in the proposal. "As you can see," Jones continued, "the savings are really significant after the first two years."

"Yes, but the program is more expensive the first two years. But what's worse is that there will be an outsider here doing our printing. I can't say that's an idea I could ever be comfortable with."

Jones realized that she had completely lost the possibility of White's support, but she continued.

"Betty, let me highlight some of the other features and benefits that might interest Acme."

"I'm sorry, Mary, but I have a 10 o'clock meeting that I really must prepare for. I can't discuss this matter further today."

"Betty, will you be able to go over these figures in more depth a little later?"

"Why don't you leave them with me. I'll look at them when I get the chance," White replied.

Jones left the proposal with White hoping that she would give it serious consideration, but as she pulled out of the driveway she could not help but feel that the day had gotten off to a poor start.

The Royal Corporation established the Royal Reproduction Center (RRC) division in 1956. With fifty-one offices located in twenty-four states in the United States, the RRC specializes in high-quality quick-turnaround copying, duplicating, and printing on a service basis. In addition to routine reproduction jobs, the RRC is capable of filling various specialized requests including duplicating engineering documents and computer reports, microfilming, color copying, and producing overhead transparencies. In addition, the RRC sales representatives sell the Royal 750 color copier (the only piece of hardware sold through the RRC) and the Royal Corporate Copy Center program (CCC). Although the RRC accepts orders from "walk-ins," the majority of the orders are generated by the field representatives who handle certain named accounts that are broken down by geographic territory.

At 9:45 A.M., Jones stopped at Bickford Publishing for her second sales call of the day. She waited in the lobby while Joe Smith, director of corporate services, was paged. Bickford Publishing was one of Jones's best accounts. Last year her commission from sales to Bickford totaled 10 percent of her pay. But her relationship with Joe Smith always seemed to be on unstable ground. She was not sure why, but she had always felt that Smith harbored resentment toward her. However, she decided not to dwell on the matter as long as a steady stream of large orders kept coming in. Jones had been calling on Bickford ever since Tim McCarthy, the sales representative before her, had been transferred.

Competition among the RRC sales reps for the Bickford account had been keen, but Stein had decided that Jones's performance warranted a crack at the account, and she had proven that she deserved it by increasing sales 40 percent within six months.

"Good morning, Miss Jones, how are you today?" Smith greeted her. He always referred to her formally as Miss Jones.

"I'm fine, Mr. Smith," Jones replied. "Thank you for seeing me today. I needed to drop by and give you some additional information on the CCC idea that I reviewed with you earlier."

"Miss Jones, to be perfectly honest with you, I reviewed the information that you left with me, and although I think that your CCC is a very nice idea, I really don't believe it is something that Bickford would be interested in at this particular point in time."

"But Mr. Smith, I didn't even give you any of the particulars. I have a whole set of calculations here indicating that the CCC could save Bickford a considerable amount of time, effort, and money over the next few years."

"I don't mean to be rude, Miss Jones, but I am in a hurry, I really don't care to continue this conversation."

"Before you go, do you think that it might be possible to arrange to present this proposal to Mr. Perry (Tony Perry, V.P. corporate facilities, Joe Smith's immediate supervisor) in the near future? I'm sure that he would be interested in seeing it. We had discussed this idea in passing earlier, and he seemed to feel that it warranted serious consideration."

"Maybe we can talk about that the next time you are here. I'll call you if I need to have something printed. Now I really must go."

As Jones returned to her car, she decided that, in spite of what Smith had told her about waiting until next time, she should move ahead to contact Perry directly. He had seemed genuinely interested in hearing more about the CCC when she had spoken to him earlier, even though she had mentioned it only briefly. She decided that she would return to the office and send Perry a letter requesting an appointment to speak with him.

Although Jones was not yet aware of it, Joe Smith had returned to his desk and immediately began drafting the following memo to be sent to Tony Perry:

To: Tony Perry, V.P. Corporate Facilities
From: Joe Smith, Corporate Services
Re: Royal CCC

Tony:

I spoke at length with Mary Jones of Royal this morning. She presented me with her proposal for the adoption of the CCC program at Bickford Publishing. After reviewing the proposal in detail, I have determined that the program: a) is not cost effective, b) has many problem areas that need ironing out, c) is inappropriate for our company at this time.

Therefore, in light of the above, my opinion is that this matter does not warrant any serious consideration or further discussion at this point in time.

ROYAL 750 COLOR COPIER

The Royal 750 color copier made its debut in 1973 and was originally sold by color copier specialists in the equipment division of Royal. But sales representatives did not want to sell the color copier exclusively and sales managers did not want to manage the color copier specialists. Therefore, the 750 was not a particularly successful product. In 1979, the sales responsibility for the color copier was transferred to the RRC division. Since the RRC sales representatives were already taking orders from customers needing the services of a color copier, it was felt that the reps would be in an advantageous position to determine when current customer requirements would justify the purchase of a 750.

Jones arrived back at her office at 10:45. She checked her mailbox for messages, grabbed a cup of coffee, and returned to her desk to draft the letter to Tony Perry. After making several phone calls setting up appointments for the next week and checking on client satisfaction with some jobs that had been delivered today, she gathered up the materials she needed for her afternoon sales calls. Finishing her coffee, she noticed the poster announcing a trip for members of the "President's Club." To become a member, a sales representative had to meet 100 percent of his or her sales budget, sell a 750 color copier, sell a CCC program, and sell a short-term rental. Jones believed that making budget would be difficult but attainable, even though her superior performance in 1982 led to a budget increase of 20 percent for 1983. She had already sold a color copier and a short-term rental. Therefore, the main thing standing in her way of making the President's Club was the sale of a CCC. Not selling a CCC this year would have even more serious ramifications, she thought. Until recently, Jones had considered herself the prime candidate for the expected opening for a senior sales representative in her office. But Michael Gould, a sales rep who also had three years' experience, was enjoying an excellent year. He had sold two color copiers and had just closed a deal on a CCC to a large semiconductor manufacturing firm. Normally everyone in the office celebrated the sale of a CCC. As a fellow sales rep was often heard saying, "it takes the heat off of all of us for a while." Jones, however, found it difficult to celebrate Gould's sale, for not only was he the office "golden boy" but now, in her opinion, he was also the prime candidate for the senior sales rep position. Gould's sale also left Jones as one of the few reps in the office without the sale of a CCC to his or her credit. "It is pretty difficult to get a viable CCC lead," Jones thought, "but I've had one or two this year that should have been closed." Neither the long discussions with her sales manager nor the numerous in-service training sessions and discussions on how to sell the CCC had helped. "I've just got to sell one of these soon," Jones resolved.

On her way out, she glanced at the clock. It was 11:33. She had just enough time to make her 11:45 appointment with Sam Lawless, operations manager at ABC Electronics. This was Jones's first appointment at ABC and she was excited about getting a foot in the door there. A friend of hers was an account assistant at ABC. She had informed Jones that the company spent more than $15,000 a month on printing services and that they might consider a CCC proposal. Jones knew who the competition was, and although their prices were lower on low volume orders, Royal could meet or beat their prices for the kind of volume of work for which ABC was contracting. But Jones wasn't enthusiastic about garnering the account for reproduction work. She believed she could sell ABC a CCC.

Jones's friend had mentioned management dissatisfaction with the subcontracting of so much printing. Also, there had been complaints regarding the quality of work. Investment in an in-house print shop had been discussed. Jones had assessed ABC's situation and had noticed a strong parallel with the situation of Star Electronics, a multidivision electronics manufacturing firm that had been sold CCCs for each of their four locations in the area. That sale, which occurred over a year ago, was vital in legitimatizing the CCC with potential customers in the northeast. Jones hoped to sell ABC on the same premise that Fred Myers had sold Star Electronics. Myers had been extremely helpful in reviewing his sales plan with Jones and had given her ideas on points he felt had been instrumental in closing the Star deal. She felt well prepared for this call.

Jones had waited four months to get an appointment with Lawless. He had a reputation for disliking to speak with salespeople, but Jones's friend had passed along to him some CCC literature and he had seemed interested. Finally, after months of being unable to reach him by telephone or get a response by mail, she had phoned two weeks ago and he had consented to see her. Today she planned to concentrate on how adoption of the CCC program might solve ABC's current reproduction problems. She also planned to ask Lawless to provide her with the necessary information to produce a convincing proposal in favor of CCC. Jones pulled into a visitor parking space and grabbed her briefcase.

"This could end up being the one," she thought as she headed for the reception area.

Jones removed a business card from her wallet and handed it to the receptionist. "Mary Jones to see Sam Lawless. I have an appointment," Jones announced.

"I'm sorry," the receptionist replied, "Mr. Lawless is no longer with the company."

Jones tried not to lose her composure. "But I had an appointment to see him today. When did he leave?"

"Last Friday was Mr. Lawless's last day. Mr. Bates is now operations manager."

"May I see Mr. Bates, please?" Jones inquired, knowing in advance the response.

"Mr. Bates does not see salespeople. He sees no one without an appointment."

"Could you tell him that I had an appointment to see Mr. Lawless? Perhaps he would consider seeing me."

"I can't call him, but I'll leave him a note with your card. Perhaps you can contact him later."

"Thank you, I will." Jones turned and left ABC, obviously shaken. "Back to square one," she thought as she headed back to her car. It was 12:05 P.M.

Jones headed for her next stop, CG Advertising, still upset from the episode at ABC. But she had long since discovered that no successful salesperson can dwell on disappointments. "It interferes with your whole attitude," she reminded herself. Jones arrived at the office park where CG was located. She was on time for her 12:30 appointment.

CG was a large, full-service agency. Jones's color copy orders from CG had been increasing at a rapid rate for the past six months and she had no reason to believe that their needs would decrease in the near future. Therefore she believed the time was ripe to present a case for the purchase of a 750 color copier. Jones had been dealing primarily with Jim Stevens, head of creative services. They had a good working relationship, even though on certain occasions Jones had found him to be unusually demanding

about quality. But she figured that characteristic seemed to be common in many creative people. She had decided to use his obsession with perfection to work to her advantage.

Jones also knew that money was only a secondary consideration as far as Stevens was concerned. He had seemingly gotten his way on purchases in several other instances, so she planned her approach to him. Jones had outlined a proposal that she was now ready to present to Jim.

"Good morning, Jim, how's the advertising business?"

"It's going pretty well for us here, how's things with you?"

"Well, I don't know; our current situation seems to be working out rather well. I really don't see any reason to change it."

"I'm not sure that you're fully aware of all the things that the 750 color copier is capable of doing," Jones pressed on. "One of the technicians and I have been experimenting with the 750. Even I have discovered some new and interesting capabilities to be applied in your field, Jim. Let me show you some of them."

She reached into her art portfolio and produced a wide variety of samples to show Stevens. "You know that the color copier is great for enlarging and reducing as well as straight duplicating. But look at the different effects we got by experimenting with various sizes and colors. Don't you think that this is an interesting effect?"

"Yes, it really is," Stevens said, loosening up slightly.

"But wait," Jones added, "I really have the ultimate to show you." Jones produced a sheet on which she had constructed a collage from various slides that Stevens had given her for enlarging.

"Those are my slides! Hey, that's great."

"Do you think that a potential client might be impressed by something like this? And the best part is you can whip something like this up in a matter of minutes, if the copier is at your disposal."

"Hey, that's a great idea, Mary, I'd love to be able to fool around with one of those machines. I bet I'd be able to do some really inventive proposals with it."

"I'm sure you would, Jim."

"Do you have a few minutes right now? I'd like to bounce this idea off Bill Jackson, head of purchasing, and see how quickly we can get one in here."

Jones and Stevens went down to Jackson's office. Before they even spoke, Jones felt that this deal was closed. Jim Stevens always got his own way. Besides, she believed she knew what approach to use with Bill Jackson. She had dealt with him on several other occasions. Jackson had failed to approve a purchase for her the prior fall on the basis that the purchase could not be justified. He was right on that account. Their present 600 model was handling their reproduction needs sufficiently, but you can't blame a person for trying, she thought. Besides, she hadn't had Stevens in her corner for that one. This was going to be different.

"How's it going, Bill? You've met Mary Jones before haven't you?"

"Yes, I remember Miss Jones. She's been to see me several times, always trying to sell me something we don't need," he said cynically.

"Well, this time I do have something you need and not only will this purchase save time, but it will save money, too. Let me show you some figures I've worked out regarding how much you can save by purchasing the 750 color copier." Jones showed Jackson that, at their current rate of increased orders of color copies, the 750 would pay for itself in three years. She also stressed the efficiency and ease of operation. But she knew that Jackson was really only interested in the bottom line.

"Well, I must admit, Miss Jones, it does appear to be a cost-effective purchase."

Stevens volunteered, "Not only that, but we can now get our artwork immediately, too. This purchase will make everyone happy."

Jones believed she had the order. "I'll begin the paperwork as soon as I return to the office.

May I come by next week to complete the deal?"

"Well, let me see what needs to be done on this end, but I don't foresee a problem," Jackson replied.

"There won't be any problem," Stevens assured Jones.

"Fine, then. I'll call Jim the first of next week to set up an appointment for delivery."

Jones returned to her car at 1:00. She felt much better having closed the sale on the 750. She had planned enough time to stop for lunch.

During lunch, Jones thought about her time at Royal. She enjoyed her job as a whole. If it weren't for the pressure she was feeling to sell the Corporate Copy Center program, everything would be just about perfect. Jones had been a straight "A" student in college where she had majored in marketing. As far back as she could remember, she had always wanted to work in sales. Her father had started out in sales, and enjoyed a very successful and profitable career. He had advanced to sales manager and sales director for a highly successful Fortune 500 company and was proud that his daughter had chosen to pursue a career in sales. Often they would get together, and he would offer suggestions that had proven effective for him when he had worked in the field. When Jones's college placement office had announced that a Royal collegiate recruiter was visiting the campus, Jones had immediately signed up for an interview. She knew several recent graduates who had obtained positions with Royal and were very happy there. They were also doing well financially. She was excited at the idea of working for an industry giant. When she was invited for a second interview, she was ecstatic. Several days later, she received a phone call offering her a position at the regional office and she accepted immediately. Jones attended various pretrial workshops for six weeks at her regional office preparing her for her two-week intensive training period at the Royal Training Headquarters. Her training consisted of product training and sales training. She had excelled there, and graduated from that course at the head of her class and from that point on everything continued smoothly . . . until this problem with selling the CCC.

After a quick sandwich and coffee, Jones left the restaurant at 1:30. She allowed extra time before her 2:00 appointment at General Hospital, located just four blocks from the office, to stop into the office first, check for messages, and check in with her sales manager. She informed Tom Stein that she considered the sale of a 750 to CG almost certain.

"That's great, Mary. I never doubted your ability to sell the color copiers, or repro for that matter. But what are we going to do about our other problem?"

"Tom, I've been following CCC leads all morning. To tell you the truth, I don't feel as though I've made any progress at all. As a matter of fact, I've lost some ground." Jones went on to explain the situation that had developed at ABC Electronics, and how she felt when she learned that Sam Lawless was no longer with the company. "I was pretty excited about that prospect, Tom. The news was a little tough to take."

"That's okay. We'll just concentrate on his replacement, now. It might be a setback, but the company's still there and they still have the same printing needs and problems. Besides, you're going to make your final presentation to General Hospital this afternoon, and you really did your homework for that one." Stein had worked extensively with Jones on the proposal from start to finish. They both knew that it was her best opportunity of the year to sell a CCC.

"I'm leaving right now. Wish me luck."

He did. She filled her briefcase with her personals and CCC demonstration kit that she planned to use for the actual presentation and headed toward the parking lot.

Jones's appointment was with Harry Jameson of General Hospital. As she approached his office, his receptionist announced her. Jameson appeared and led her to the board room for their meeting. Jones was surprised to find three other individuals seated around the table. She was introduced to Bob Goldstein, V.P. of operations, Martha Chambers, director of account-

ing, and Dr. J. P. Dunwitty, chairman of the board. Jameson explained that whenever an expenditure of this magnitude was being considered, the hospital's executive committee had to make a joint recommendation.

Jones set up her demonstration at the head of the table so that it was easily viewed by everyone and began her proposal. She presented charts outlining the merits of the CCC and also the financial calculations that she had generated based on the information supplied to her by Jameson.

Forty minutes later, Jones finished her presentation and began fielding questions. The usual concerns were voiced regarding hiring an "outsider" to work within the hospital. But the major concern seemed to revolve around the loss of employment on the part of two present printing press operators. One, John Brown, had been a faithful employee for more than five years. He was married and had a child. There had never been a complaint about John personally, or with regard to the quality or quantity of his work. The second operator was Peter Dunwitty, a recent graduate of a nearby vocational school and nephew of Dr. Dunwitty. Although he had only been employed by the hospital for three months, there was no question about his ability and performance.

In response to this concern, Jones emphasized that the new equipment was more efficient, but different, and did not require the skills of experienced printers like Brown and Dunwitty. She knew, however, that this was always the one point about the adoption of a CCC program that even she had the most difficulty justifying. She suddenly felt rather ill.

"Well, Miss Jones, if you'll excuse us for a few minutes, we'd like to reach a decision on this matter," said Jameson.

"There's no need to decide right at this point. You all have copies of my proposal. If you'd like to take a few days to review the figures, I'd be happy to come by then," said Jones, in a last-ditch attempt to gain some additional time.

"I think that we'd like to meet in private for a few minutes right now, if you don't mind," interjected Dunwitty.

"No, that's fine," Jones said as she left the room for the lobby. She sat in a waiting room and drank a cup of coffee. She lit a cigarette, a habit she seldom engaged in. Five minutes later, the board members called her back in.

"This CCC idea is really sound, Miss Jones," Jameson began. "However here at General Hospital, we have a very strong commitment to our employees. There really seems to be no good reason to put two fine young men out of work. Yes, I realize that from the figures that you've presented to us, you've indicated a savings of approximately $30,000 over three years. But I would have to question some of the calculations. Under the circumstances, we feel that maintaining sound employee relations has more merit than switching to an unproven program right now. Therefore, we've decided against purchasing a CCC."

Jones was disappointed, but she had been in this situation often enough not to show it. "I'm sorry to hear that, Mr. Jameson. I thought that I had presented a very good argument for participation in the CCC program. Do you think that if your current operators decided to leave, you might consider CCC again before you filled their positions?"

"I can't make a commitment to that right now. But feel free to stay in touch," Jameson countered.

"I'll still be coming in on a regular basis to meet all your needs for other work not capable of being performed in your print shop," Jones replied.

"Then you'll be the first to know if that situation arises," said Jameson.

"Thank you all for your time. I hope that I was of assistance even though you decided against purchase. If I may be of help at any point in time, don't hesitate to call," Jones remarked as she headed for the door.

Now, totally disappointed, Jones regretted having scheduled another appointment for that afternoon. She would have liked to call it a day. But she knew she had an opportunity to pick up some repro work and develop a new account. So she knew she couldn't cancel.

Jones stopped by to see Paul Blake, head of staff training at Pierson's, a large department store with locations throughout the state. Jones had made a cold call one afternoon the previous week and had obtained a sizeable printing order. Now she wanted to see whether Blake was satisfied with the job, which had been delivered earlier in the day. She also wanted to speak to him about some of the other services available at the RRC. Jones was about to reach into her briefcase for her card to offer to the receptionist when she was startled by a "Hello, Mary" coming from behind her.

"Hello, Paul," Jones responded, surprised and pleased that he had remembered her name. "How are you today?"

"Great! I have to tell you, that report that you printed for us is far superior to the work that we have been receiving from some of our other suppliers. I've got another piece that will be ready to go out in about an hour. Can you have someone come by and pick it up then?"

"I'll do better than that. I'll pick it up myself," Jones replied.

"See you then," he responded as he turned and headed back toward his office.

"I'm glad I decided to stop by after all," Jones thought as she pressed the elevator button. She wondered how she could best use the next hour to help salvage the day. When the elevator door opened, out stepped Kevin Fitzgerald, operations manager for Pierson's. Jones had met him several weeks earlier when she had spoken with Ann Leibman, a sales rep for Royal Equipment Division. Leibman had been very close to closing a deal that would involve selling Pierson several "casual" copying machines that they were planning to locate in various offices to use for quick copying. Leibman informed Jones that Tom Stein had presented a CCC proposal to Pierson's six months earlier but the plan was flatly refused. Fitzgerald, she explained, had been sincerely interested in the idea, but the plan involved a larger initial expenditure than Pierson's was willing to make. Now, Leibman explained, there would be a much larger savings involved, since the "casual" machines would not be needed if a CCC were involved. Jones had suggested to Fitzgerald that the CCC proposal be reworked to include the new machines so that a current assessment could be made. He had once again appeared genuinely interested and suggested that Jones retrieve the necessary figures from Jerry Query, head of purchasing. Jones had not yet done so. She had phoned Query several times, but he had never responded to her messages.

"Nice to see you again, Mr. Fitzgerald. Ann Leibman introduced us. I'm Mary Jones from Royal."

"Yes, I remember. Have you spoken with Mr. Query yet?"

"I'm on my way to see him right now," Jones said as she thought this would be the perfect way to use the hour.

"Fine, get in touch with me when you have the new calculations."

Jones entered the elevator that Fitzgerald had been holding for her as they spoke. She returned to the first floor and consulted the directory. Purchasing was on the third floor. As she walked off the elevator on the third floor, the first thing that she saw was a sign that said, "Salespeople seen by appointment only. Tuesdays and Thursdays, 10 A.M.–12 Noon."

"I'm really out of luck," Jones thought, "not only do I not have an appointment, but today's Wednesday. But I'll give it my best shot as long as I'm here."

Jones walked over to the receptionist who was talking to herself as she searched through a large pile of papers on her desk. Although Jones knew she was aware of her presence, the receptionist continued to avoid her.

"This could be a hopeless case," Jones thought. Just then the receptionist looked up and acknowledged her.

"Good afternoon. I'm Mary Jones from Royal. I was just speaking to Mr. Fitzgerald who suggested that I see Mr. Query. I'm not selling anything. I just need to get some figures from him."

"Just a minute," the receptionist replied as she walked toward an office with Query's name on the door.

"Maybe this is not going to be so bad after all," Jones thought.

Mr. Query will see you for a minute," the receptionist announced as she returned to her desk.

Jones walked into Query's plushly furnished office. Query was an imposing figure at 6'4", nearly 300 pounds, and bald. Jones extended her hand, which Query grasped firmly. "What brings you here to see me?" Query inquired.

Jones explained her conversations with Ann Leibman and Kevin Fitzgerald. As she was about to ask her initial series of questions, Query interrupted. "Miss Jones, I frankly don't know what the hell you are doing here!" Query exclaimed. "We settled this issue over six months ago, and now you're bringing it up again. I really don't understand. You people came in with a proposal that was going to cost us more money than we were spending. We know what we're doing. No one is going to come in here and tell us our business."

"Mr. Query," Jones began, trying to remain composed, "the calculations that you were presented with were based on the equipment that Pierson's was using six months ago. Now that you are contemplating additional purchases, I mentioned to Mr. Fitzgerald that a new comparison should be made. He instructed me to speak with you in order to obtain the information needed to prepare a thorough proposal," Jones tried to explain.

"Fitzgerald! What on earth does Fitzgerald have to do with this? This is none of his damn business. He sat at the same table as I six months ago when we arrived at a decision. Why doesn't he keep his nose out of affairs that don't concern him. We didn't want this program six months ago, and we don't want it now!" Query shouted.

"I'm only trying to do my job, Mr. Query. I was not part of the team that presented the proposal six months ago. But from all the information that is available now, I still feel that a CCC would save you money here at Pierson's."

"Don't you understand, Miss Jones? We don't want any outsiders here. You have no control over people that don't work for you. Nothing gets approved around here unless it has my signature on it. That's control. Now I really see no need to waste any more of my time or yours."

"I appreciate your frankness," Jones responded, struggling to find something positive to say.

"Well, that's the kind of man I am, direct and to the point."

"You can say that again," Jones thought. She said, "One other thing before I go, Mr. Query. I was noticing the color copies on your desk."

"Yes, I like to send color copies of jobs when getting production estimates. For example, these are of the bogs that we will be using during our fall promotion. I have received several compliments from suppliers who think that by viewing color copies they get a real feel for what I need."

"Well, it just so happens that my division of Royal sells color copiers. At some time it may be more efficient for you to consider purchase. Let me leave you some literature on the 750 copier, which you can review at your leisure."

Jones removed a brochure from her briefcase. She attached one of her business cards to it and handed it to Query. As she shook his hand and left the office Jones noted that she had half an hour before the project of Blake's would be ready for pick-up. She entered the donut shop across the street and as she waited for her cof-

fee, she reviewed her day's activities. She was enthusiastic about the impending color copier sale at CG Advertising, and about the new repro business that she had acquired at Pierson's. But the rest of the day had been discouraging. Not only had she been "shot down" repeatedly, but she'd now have to work extra hard for several days to ensure that she would make 100 percent of budget for the month. "Trying to sell the CCC is even harder than I thought it was," Jones thought.

DISCUSSION QUESTIONS

1. What three products/services are sold by the RRC? Who is the decision maker for each of these products/services?
2. What are the benefits to the user of each of these three products/services?
3. Examine Mary Jones's efforts at Acme Computers, Bickford Publishing, and General Hospital. What are the similarities among these situations?
4. Should Mary Jones directly contact Tom Perry of Bickford Publishing? Why or why not?
5. What could Mary Jones have done differently to sell the CCC to General Hospital?
6. What actions should Tom Stein (Jones's sales manager) take regarding Mary Jones?

PART III

MANAGING YOUR ACCOUNTS IN A COMPETITIVE WORLD: THE CUSTOMER

ORGANIZATIONAL BUYING/PURCHASING

My expectation of salespeople is that they've done their homework, uncovered some of our needs, probed to uncover other needs, and presented a convincing argument of mutual benefits for both organizations.[1]

LYNN DEEGAN, DIRECTOR OF PROCUREMENT, RAYCHEM CORPORATION.

I expect support from service people, from upper management, from shipping, the whole cycle. Everyone [at the supplier] should be trying to make J.C. Penney number one and get more of our business. That needs to come across to us.[2]

TERRY PALMER, SENIOR PROJECT MANAGER, J.C. PENNEY

LEARNING OBJECTIVES

After reading this chapter, you should be able to answer the following questions:

- How do organizations purchase needed goods and services?
- What are the different types of business-to-business buyers?
- What is the organizational purchasing process?
- What is a buying center?
- How do industrial buyers view salespeople?
- How do industrial buyers and sellers negotiate price and terms of purchase?

MedCo, a large distributor of pharmaceuticals, is an example of the changing nature of purchasing in the health-care industry. Traditionally, pharmaceutical distributors offered as many drugs as possible from a variety of sources for each condition so as to allow doctors maximum flexibility in prescribing their choice of drug. MedCo, however, works with a limited number of drug companies to obtain one or two drugs for a given condition. As a result, MedCo has been able to procure significant discounts from drug manufacturers and, in turn, to offer substantially discounted prices to its customers, such as health maintenance organizations (HMOs), clinics, and hospitals.

Since increasing competition in the health-care industry is pressing these organizations to save money wherever possible, MedCo's offer has been well received. Hospitals, clinics, and HMOs require doctors who prescribe drugs that are not on MedCo's list to justify their prescriptions.[3] Drug manufacturers who get their product on MedCo's list are virtually assured of significant sales. Conversely, pharma-

EXHIBIT 7.1

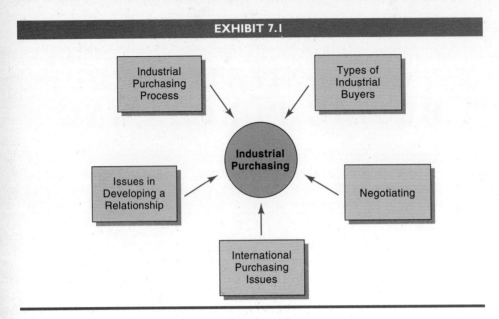

ceutical firms who do not secure a place on MedCo's list of medications face loss of market share in hospitals, clinics, and HMOs that use MedCo.

The purchase of goods by firms for use in making other goods or for eventual resale to other firms, such as distributors (like MedCo) or retailers, is known as **organizational buying** or **purchasing.** This chapter will describe the organizational buying process in a way that will improve the ability of sales managers and salespeople to develop a selling approach tailored to the needs of their customers.

We begin with a discussion of the differences between organizational buying and consumer purchasing. This will orient you to the characteristics of the industrial market (also known as the business-to-business market), which, as discussed in Chapter 2, is the focus of this text. The next section identifies current trends in purchasing. These trends help develop the thesis that knowledge of the purchasing process is a fundamental key to success for salespeople and sales managers. As can be seen from the MedCo example, a pharmaceutical manufacturer that is not aware of the purchasing trends in its market may not achieve wide distribution of its products. Finally, the remainder of the chapter is organized around topics that are unique to industrial purchasing (see Exhibit 7.1), including types of industrial buyers, the industrial purchasing process, types of industrial purchasing situations, industrial buying centers, negotiating, building a relationship, and international issues in purchasing.

DIFFERENCES BETWEEN ORGANIZATIONAL BUYING AND CONSUMER PURCHASING

Organizational, or industrial, buying differs from consumer purchasing in three important ways: characteristics of the buyers, characteristics of the purchasing situation, and demand characteristics. The differences between industrial buying and consumer purchasing are summarized in Exhibit 7.2.

	EXHIBIT 7.2	
DIFFERENCES BETWEEN ORGANIZATIONAL BUYERS AND CONSUMERS		
	Industrial	Consumer
Buyer Characteristics		
Number of customers	Few	Many
Level of expertise	High	Low
Level of negotiation	High	Low
Number of individuals in purchasing process	Many	Few
Characteristics of the Purchasing Situation		
Purchase volume	Large	Small
Purchase process	Complex	Simple
Channels of distribution	Short	Long
Use of reciprocity	Yes	No
Use of leasing	Yes	No
Existence of large buying centers	Yes	No
Demand Characteristics		
	Derived	Direct
	Inelastic	Elastic
	Joint	Not joint
	Fluctuating	Stable

Buyer Characteristics

Compared to consumer purchases, industrial purchasing situations typically involve fewer customers, buyers with high levels of expertise, higher levels of negotiation, and more people involved in the buying process. In purchasing corporate aircraft, for example, there are a limited number of corporate customers who can afford and are willing to purchase their own aircraft. Buyers often plan the purchases far in advance, consult with other users and with many different departments within the firm to ensure the plane being considered meets corporate needs, and negotiate with the manufacturers on price, delivery dates, and optional equipment.

Characteristics of the Purchasing Situation

Industrial purchasing involves greater quantities of goods purchased, shorter channels of distribution, and greater use of leasing and reciprocity than consumer purchasing. It also involves a more lengthy, rational, and complex purchasing process (this topic will be explored in detail later in this chapter).

Large purchase quantities allow buyers to negotiate on price because the cost for sellers to supply large orders is typically smaller on a per-unit basis than the cost to supply small orders. *Shorter channels of distribution* simply means that products generally pass through fewer channel intermediaries, such as wholesalers and distributors, in industrial markets than they do in consumer markets. *Leasing* is a financing arrangement whereby customers rent, rather than buy, equipment. Leasing allows customers to reduce their capital outlays, gain tax advantages, and receive periodic upgrades of equipment. Leasing is particularly common in automobiles and computers. *Reciprocity* occurs when companies purchase from each other. For example, a large manufacturer of automobile headlights may purchase its company cars from an automobile manufacturer that uses its headlights exclusively.

Demand Characteristics

The demand characteristics of industrial markets are also different from consumer markets. In industrial markets, demand is often derived, inelastic, joint, and fluctuating. Organizational purchasing involves **derived demand** because products are purchased to be used in the production of other products that will eventually be resold. For example, computer manufacturers purchase chips, hard drives, and monitors to produce computers for the consumer market. The demand for chips, hard drives, and monitors is directly linked to the anticipated demand for computers by the computer manufacturer's customers.

Organizational purchasing also involves **inelastic demand,** which means that an increase or decrease in the price of the product will not have a material effect on the number of products purchased. In industrial purchasing situations, manufacturers must often buy numerous parts that make up a finished product. An increase or decrease in the price of a part that constitutes only a percentage of the finished price of the product will not materially affect the demand for that part. For example, if a certain computer chip increases in price by 50 percent and the chip constitutes less than 1 percent of the price of a finished computer, the price increase will probably not affect the demand for that part (at least in the short run), assuming that there are no readily available substitutes.

Joint demand occurs when two or more commodities are purchased and used together in a finished product. Items that are used together can be combined by the seller to increase the amount of purchases by a given customer. Light assemblies and light bulbs in automobiles are examples of joint demand. If the light assembly were sold to the car manufacturer with the light bulb already inside, the car manufacturer would not have to purchase the items separately. This reduces the purchasing burden on the car manufacturer and offers the light assembly manufacturer a competitive advantage over other manufacturers that do not package bulbs with their assemblies.

Fluctuating demand means that demand for business products is more unstable than for consumer products. For example, assume that Ford Motor Company in Europe uses 25 stamping machines (used to make car chassis) in its automobile manufacturing plant in Cologne, Germany. Assume also that five of the machines wear out and must be replaced each year. If demand for cars goes down one year, Ford may not replace the stamping machines that wear out because the work can be done by the remaining machines. However, if demand picks up the next year, Ford might have to buy two extra machines to handle additional demand, plus replace the five machines that will wear out this year, plus replace the five machines that wore out last year. As a result, the manufacturer of the stamping machines had no sales to Ford last year, but sells 12 machines this year. This type of fluctuating purchasing pattern exists in many industrial purchasing situations.

Demand characteristics affect the purchasing process. For example, if demand for a buyer's products is derived and fluctuating, the buyer might not be willing to negotiate a long-term contract that specifies quantities to be purchased because the buyer is not able to predict with certainty demand for its products. If a buyer is purchasing a product that is used jointly with another, sellers must continually monitor competitors' product offerings. If a competitor offers the product as part of a larger assembly, the seller may consider offering the same assembly to buyers. These demand characteristics also affect the forecasting process, which will be discussed in greater detail in Chapter 15.

TRENDS IN ORGANIZATIONAL BUYING

Organizational buying is undergoing tremendous change as evidenced by several important trends. These trends include (1) changes in the role of purchasing, (2) shifts in purchasing models, (3) reductions in supplier lists, and (4) closer vendor-supplier relationships.

Changes in the Role of Purchasing

Industrial firms spend more than half of every sales dollar on purchased products and services. A well-organized purchasing function can "easily spell the difference between leadership in an industry and an untenable competitive position."[4] Buyers who save money through well-planned purchasing can contribute to an increase in company profits, or the company can pass those savings along to customers and achieve a stronger market position. As a result, buying is achieving a much higher profile in many companies. It is becoming viewed as a strategic weapon instead of simply as a means to obtain needed products and services.

Purchasing in today's environment requires new skills. Many purchasers are finding that in order to achieve maximum efficiency in their total operations, they must seek supplier input at a much earlier stage in the product design process and share much more information regarding their long-term goals with their suppliers.[5] As a result they must focus on developing strong relationships with a smaller group of suppliers. Purchasing agents at progressive firms are being evaluated less on whether they can obtain discounts from list prices and more on overall return on corporate assets, demonstrable quality improvements, and reductions in total manufacturing costs.

In keeping with the changing role of purchasing, many large firms such as General Motors are elevating the importance of the purchasing function. The chief purchasing officer at GM now reports to the CEO instead of being part of the administrative support function. The reason for the administrative change is that GM has realized the importance of purchasing in maintaining profitability levels.[6]

Shift in Purchasing Models

A second important trend in purchasing is the shift from an "adversarial" model of purchasing to a "cooperative" model.[7] The traditional **adversarial model of purchasing** relies on three major components. First, the buyer maintains a large number of suppliers who can be pitted against one another in a bid for any business. Second, the buyer is careful to allocate purchases among all suppliers. By doing this, the buyer keeps sellers in a state of tension as to whether they will continue to be used as a source of supply. Third, the buyer uses only short-term contracts to be able to shift from one supplier to another as market conditions dictate.

While buyers employing the adversarial approach often obtain low prices, they expose themselves to potential problems if market conditions change. For example, if a computer chip buyer has only short-term contracts with its suppliers and demand for chips increases, thereby putting them in short supply, the suppliers would be under no contractual obligation to make chips available to the buyer. If no substitute for the chips is on the market, the buyer would essentially be out of business until a new source of supply could be found.

The **cooperative model of purchasing,** by contrast, focuses less on price and more on joint buyer-seller efforts to achieve common goals. The cooperative model is characterized by the use of a limited number of suppliers and long-term agreements between the parties. For example, Donaldson Company, Inc. (DCI) discovered that dealers for one of its largest customers (Caterpillar) were having some difficulty selling Caterpillar-brand filter products. The Caterpillar-brand filter products were manufactured by Donaldson. To help Caterpillar (and Donaldson) sell more filters, DCI entered an agreement under which it would train Caterpillar service technicians and service counter personnel so that they could be more effective in selling Caterpillar-brand filters to customers. DCI was willing to invest in this expensive training because Caterpillar was one of its largest customers. Caterpillar also had a long-term contract for DCI to supply all of its filter needs. If the relationship between Caterpillar and DCI had been short-term, it is doubtful that DCI would have been willing to undertake the expensive training.

Reduced Supplier Lists

Many firms are not using as many suppliers as they have in the past. Xerox has reduced the number of suppliers from which it buys by over 50 percent.[8] The MedCo example at the beginning of this chapter demonstrates the move to reduced supplier lists in the health-care industry. Reductions in supplier lists have significant effects on industrial sellers. If the seller does not make it onto the buyer's list of approved suppliers, the seller loses all of its business with that customer. If a seller is on the reduced list, it may be assured of a larger volume of business than it had previously. The buyer's rationale for reducing supplier lists is to increase service and obtain better terms of sale (such as pricing, delivery, and/or technical support). If a buyer reduces the number of suppliers, it increases the purchases from each supplier. This leads to increased volume discounts, and perhaps more important, to increased efforts by the sellers to meet large buyers' service needs.

Closer Vendor-Supplier Relationships

Many customers are developing closer relationships with fewer suppliers. Customers are finding that by developing closer relationships with their suppliers, they can obtain better service, prices, and technical support. One customer persuaded Graco, a Minneapolis-based manufacturer of industrial painting systems, to allow it access to Graco's order-tracking system so the customer could instantly check the status of any order it had made. Graco incurred significant costs in developing specialized order-tracking software and improving the security of its computer systems to prohibit the customer from accessing unauthorized information. Yet owing to the level of business with the account, Graco was willing to honor the customer's request.

TYPES OF INDUSTRIAL BUYERS

Industrial buyers purchase goods or services for resale or for use in making products for resale. Major categories of industrial buyers include producers, institutions, resellers, and governments. Exhibit 7.3 shows selected data by category of industrial buyers.

Producers

Producers are individuals or organizations that purchase goods and services for the purpose of using them to generate sales and profits. Producers purchase several types of goods and services, including capital goods, raw materials, components, and maintenance, repair, and operations items. *Capital goods* such as machine tools

EXHIBIT 7.3		
SELECTED DATA ON ORGANIZATIONAL BUYERS		
	Number of firms (1,000s)	Receipts (billion $)
Producers (1990)		
Agriculture, forestry, fishing	614	108
Mining	213	124
Construction	2,248	653
Manufacturing	710	3,521
Transportation, public utilities	800	938
Finance, insurance, real estate	2,762	2,126
Services	8,631	1,140
Institutions (1987)		
For-profit (health services, selected educational services, social services)	1,276	211,874
Not-for-profit	176	267,490
Resellers (1990)		
Wholesale and retail trade	3,849	3,563
	Number of Units	Gross Expenditures (billions $)
Government (1992)		
Federal	1	1,527
State	50	700
Local	86,692	655

SOURCE: U.S. Department of Commerce, Bureau of the Census, *Statistical Abstract of the United States: 1994* (114th ed.), Washington, D.C.

are used to produce other goods. Ford Motor Company in Europe uses stamping machines (capital goods) capable of pressures of up to 150 tons per square inch to make sheets of steel into car parts. Producers also purchase *raw materials* to use in the production process. For example, Ford must purchase the steel with which to build cars, and Weyerhauser must purchase trees to make boards, plywood, paneling, and other wood products.

Components are products that are used in the construction of other products, or are offered for resale without substantial change in form. For example, Caterpillar purchases air filters from DCI. These air filters are stamped with the Caterpillar brand name and sold through Caterpillar's dealer network. Producers, as well as other business-to-business users, also purchase many *maintenance, repair, and operations items* that are used in day-to-day business, such as stationery, paper clips, memo pads, pens and pencils, computer disks, grease, and hacksaw blades.

Institutions

Institutions are for-profit and not-for-profit service organizations such as hospitals, universities, churches, labor unions, civic clubs, and foundations that purchase goods for their own use. The purchasing processes of these organizations can pose quite a challenge to sellers because they often rely on donations of products, services, and money. Donations of products and services can alter the purchase process and purchase criteria in several ways. Institutions may use donated products or services instead of purchasing those items. If a computer manufacturer donates computers for a university classroom, other manufacturers will not have a chance to sell their products for that use. The overall level of monetary donations also affects purchasing. If donations to a university go down, for example, the school may postpone construction of new buildings or defer maintenance of existing buildings and equipment.

Resellers

Resellers include retail and wholesale firms or some type of agent/broker that buy finished goods in bulk and resell them. Retailers sell primarily to consumers, while wholesalers sell primarily to retailers and businesses. The line between retailers and wholesalers is blurring somewhat with the growth of warehouse clubs and membership retailers, such as Sam's and Costco. Many small businesses purchase items for business use at warehouse clubs because of the low prices, quantity discounts, and convenient locations.

The reseller market is very large (over 3.5 million firms). The level of trade at the wholesale level is about twice what it is at the retail level, meaning that the average product goes through two resellers before it is sold at the retail level.

Governments

Government purchasers include all federal, state, county, and city government units. Their combined purchasing accounts for about 20 percent of the United States gross domestic product. Government purchasing procedures can be arcane and frustrating for the first-time seller. Detailed specifications, cumbersome bidding processes, long delays in decision making, the uncertainty of the budget process, and other considerations can make selling to many governmental units very difficult. For example, in the United States firms working on the construction of the Super-Conducting Super Collider in Texas (a $10 billion federal construction project) had their funding almost cut off by Congress several times, only to have all funding eliminated in 1993. Firms working on the construction project were required to hire workers, buy materials, and plan as if the funding would continue. The cancellation of the project left these firms with excess product and personnel.

Smaller government units, such as cities, school districts, hospital districts, and highway departments, can be easier to sell to owing to less cumbersome purchasing procedures. However, various political pressures that affect the purchasing process can also arise here. One recent example is the Buy American Act. This act, passed in 1988 and revised in 1993, requires the federal government to purchase products produced in the United States whenever possible.[9]

The "Buy American" movement has led to some interesting dilemmas on the part of purchasing agents for firms and state and local governments, as it is not always possible to determine the national origin of an item simply by the brand name. For example, Ford's Crown Victoria, its largest car and one often purchased by police departments, is produced in Canada. Hence, these cars are classified by the U.S. government as imports, despite bearing the name of an American manufacturer. On the other hand, the majority of the Hondas sold in the United States are assembled in the United States, therefore qualifying as domestic cars despite their Japanese parent. One town purchased a John Deere excavator rather than a Komatsu, even though the Komatsu was $15,000 cheaper, due to "Buy American" sentiment. The city was embarrassed to find out later that the Komatsu was produced in the United States through a joint venture between Komatsu and Dresser, which is headquartered in Lincolnshire, Illinois. The John Deere was produced in Japan through a joint venture with Hitachi.[10]

The point of these examples is to show that when selling to governmental units, non-product-related issues can have a significant impact on the consideration of the firm's product offerings. As a result, salespeople must be aware of the political environment surrounding the purchase of their products, as well as the technical specifications.

THE ORGANIZATIONAL BUYING PROCESS

Making a purchase in an organization can be quite complex. Purchasing a sewage disposal system for a city is a different buying process than purchasing paint for a bathroom in your home. While there are numerous descriptions of the organizational purchasing process, the following model captures the important common elements. It includes ten stages: problem recognition, determination of need, devising product specifications, searching for qualified sellers, requesting and obtaining proposals, evaluating proposals, selecting product and seller, negotiating transaction terms, establishing the order routine, and product and vendor evaluation. This model is illustrated in Exhibit 7.4.[11]

Although the stages in the industrial purchasing process appear neat and well defined, actual industrial purchasing rarely follows such a neat stream. Several steps

EXHIBIT 7.4

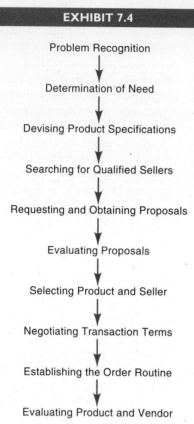

Problem Recognition

↓

Determination of Need

↓

Devising Product Specifications

↓

Searching for Qualified Sellers

↓

Requesting and Obtaining Proposals

↓

Evaluating Proposals

↓

Selecting Product and Seller

↓

Negotiating Transaction Terms

↓

Establishing the Order Routine

↓

Evaluating Product and Vendor

can be performed simultaneously, decisions made at one step may preclude options at other steps, and the purchaser may get to a certain step and find that the situation has changed and earlier decisions need to be reconsidered.

In larger organizations the traditional purchasing process tends to be very formal, with each stage requiring numerous approvals and significant amounts of time. In smaller organizations, the purchasing process tends to be less formal; the stages require fewer approvals and can be performed faster.

Problem Recognition

Problem recognition is the identification of the problem that the product or service is intended to remedy.[12] It is perhaps the most important step in the purchasing process. In a sense, all organizational purchasing is an attempt to solve a problem or keep a problem from occurring. Salespeople who are astute at solving problems or at recognizing problems before they become apparent to the purchaser have a clear advantage over their competitors.

Problems can be identified internally or externally. **Internal problem recognition** occurs when a member of the purchasing organization finds a problem that exists in the organization. This can occur, for example, when a scientist in the R&D

department finds that her current microscope is inadequate to perform certain tests and a new, improved model exists that can perform the tests. It can also occur when a manufacturing manager finds that a certain machine requires replacement, or when a service contract for a machine expires. **External problem recognition** occurs when a consultant, salesperson, or other source outside the purchasing organization identifies or highlights a problem that exists in the organization. An industrial machine salesperson can call on a prospective customer and demonstrate how a new machine can increase efficiency or reduce costs. Likewise, purchasing agents can visit trade shows, read industry magazines, or talk with acquaintances in other companies and get ideas about new products or services that would solve problems.

Determination Need

After the purchaser's problem or potential problem is identified, the problem solver forms a general description of the product or service that would address the problem. This process is called **determination of need.** Defining the problem too narrowly can reduce the likelihood of an innovative solution. For example, if an auto manufacturer is having problems with a particular switch that is attached to the windshield wiper assembly, it can put pressure on the switch supplier to improve quality. If the salesperson for the manufacturer of the windshield wiper assembly is an astute problem solver, however, he could increase sales by offering to produce the windshield wiper assembly including the switch. The manufacturer of the windshield wiper assembly would then be responsible for the quality of the switch, which would have the effect of eliminating the auto manufacturer's quality control problem.

Devising Product Specifications

Based on the determination of need, the organization must specify which products and services are required. The **product specifications** (or specs) are exact statements of requirements. These requirements typically include quantity, desired quality levels, timeliness, and other issues related to the characteristics of the specific product or service. In government procurement and many purchasing departments, product specifications are typically contained in a formal document called a **request for proposal (RFP).** Prospective suppliers make bids based on the information in the RFP.

Salespeople can make or break a sale at this point in the purchasing process. For example, suppose for a major construction project an architect specifies a certain brand of shingle in the RFP. As a sales manager of a competing firm reading the RFP for the project, you know that your firm carries a product with identical performance characteristics at a lower cost. You give the salesperson information that demonstrates the similarity between the products. If your salesperson persuades the architect to rewrite the specification based on product performance characteristics rather than brand name, your firm has an opportunity to obtain business that would not have been possible before.

Searching for Qualified Suppliers

Buyers can find qualified suppliers by searching for them at trade shows or other industry events, by reading industry magazines or promotional literature, or by wait-

EXHIBIT 7.5		
SOURCES OF NAMES FOR APPROVED VENDOR LISTS		
Source of Names	Number of Times Used	Percent
Salesperson call	175	82
Company records	121	57
Trade magazines	99	46
Thomas Register[a]	98	46
Company buyers	9	45
Trade shows	83	39
Company managers	51	24
Company engineers	46	21
Company merchandising people	27	13
MacRae's Blue Book[b]	18	8

[a]*Thomas Register of American Manufactures, 1996.*

[b]*MacRae's Blue Book: Serving the Original Equipment Market.*

SOURCE: Ralph W. Jackson and William M. Pride, "The Use of Approved Vendor Lists," *Industrial Marketing Management*, 15 (1986): 165–169

ing for them to make sales presentations. For products that have been purchased before, many firms maintain **approved vendor lists,** which are rosters of products, services, and sellers that have been qualified by the purchasing firm. Purchasing agents rely on the approved vendor list as a very helpful reference. Purchases often have to be made quickly, and the presence of a seller on the approved vendor list keeps the purchasing agent from having to check the references of the seller. The list is also very helpful to sellers because being on a vendor list ensures the seller that if their product or service is needed, they will have a chance at the business. Given the importance of approved vendor lists to sellers, it is important to know how these lists are devised. Exhibit 7.5 shows the major sources of names for approved vendor lists.[13] Salespeople play a role in identifying the qualifications necessary to be on the approved vendor list and in providing service necessary to stay on the list.

Requesting and Obtaining Proposals

In the next stage, purchasers request proposals from *qualified suppliers* (those on the approved vendor list, if the purchasing firm has one). If the RFP is from a government agency or institutional entity, the outline of the prospective purchase will often appear in a classified advertisement in a local newspaper or in a newsletter published by the agency or institution. This ad will contain information about where the entire RFP can be obtained. Public notification of the RFP ensures that all qualified suppliers have an equal chance to make a proposal.

Once the proposals are obtained, procedures vary as to what occurs next. In highway construction bidding situations, suppliers are asked to submit sealed bids for a certain project. All sealed bids are opened at the same time, and the lowest bidder obtains the job. In other bidding situations, especially when the product is complex or unique (such as supplying the people moving system for a new airport), suppliers may

EXHIBIT 7.6	
ATTRIBUTES OF SELLERS MOST FREQUENTLY MENTIONED BY BUYERS	
Buyer Preference	Percent of Mentions (over a 6-year period)
1. Willingness to fight for the customer	63
2. Thoroughness/follow-through	59
3. Knowledge of the product line	47
4. Market knowledge/willingness to share	45
5. Imagination	36
6. Knowledge of the buyer's needs	34
7. Preparation for sales calls	20
8. Diplomacy in dealing with operating departments	15
9. Technical education	13
10. Regularity of sales calls	6

SOURCE: James Morgan, "Are Your Supplier Reps Proactive, Knowledgeable?" *Purchasing*, 16 (June 2, 1994): 43–45

be asked to provide supporting information for their bid or to make a final presentation once unsuitable bids have been eliminated from further consideration.

Evaluating Proposals and Selecting Product and Seller

There are several important issues to consider when selecting sellers: the relationship between the purchasing agent and the seller, the characteristics of the seller, and the characteristics of the purchasing situation.

Relationship Between the Purchasing Agent and the Salesperson. The relationship between the purchasing agent and the salesperson has a significant influence on purchasing performance. One study found that 32 percent of the variance in overall purchasing performance was a result of the purchasing agent/salesperson relationship.[14] Given this, it is important to understand what purchasing agents are looking for in salespeople. Exhibit 7.6 lists ten items that have been shown to be important to purchasing agents.[15] The most frequently mentioned items are willingness to go to bat for the buyer within the seller's firm, thoroughness and follow-through, and knowledge of product line.

Characteristics of the Seller. Important characteristics of the seller include (1) the ability to meet certain quality standards and (2) small business– or minority-owned status. *Quality* is one of the buzzwords of the 1990s in industrial purchasing. One reason is because buyers that purchase high-quality component can reduce the number of necessary inspections in the production process and reduce the amount of rework necessary to achieve target quality levels. For example, Ford Motor Company has a Preferred Supplier program for sellers that have met certain quality standards. Ford takes products purchased from these suppliers and puts them on the production line with no intervening inspection. Other car companies, such as Toyota and General Motors, have actually gone inside suppliers' plants to help them improve the quality of their products.

The European Union is establishing quality certification standards for a wide range of products. These standards, known collectively as **ISO 9000,** requires certification of the vendor by a third party, which is rapidly becoming a requirement for doing business in Europe. While only about 1,000 U.S. firms are currently ISO 9000–certified, many firms may soon need certification even if they currently do little business in Europe. The reason for this is that if a U.S. company sells to another U.S. company doing business with a European firm, the European customer may require its vendor and its vendor's vendor to have ISO 9000 certification. Box 7.1 gives more details about ISO 9000.

Large manufacturing companies, in particular, are also interested in the suppliers' ability to meet **just-in-time (JIT)** delivery requirements. Under JIT, the supplier keeps and delivers the precise amount of needed product with a minimum of waste. Suppliers must meet tight delivery schedules to make sure manufacturers do not run out of components and therefore have to shut down their production facilities. To meet JIT requirements, some suppliers in the automotive industry have gone so far as to construct new plants close to their largest customers so as to ensure reliable delivery schedules.[16]

Another issue in supplier selection is the ownership status or size of the supplier. Firms under certain types of ownership or of a certain size must, by law, be given a certain amount of the total contracts for various governmental defense and public works projects. These reserved contracts are known as **set-asides.** Businesses qualifying for set-asides include small firms and firms owned by women or minorities. The government's supplier selection process can be so complicated, however, that many firms eligible for participation in contracts through set-aside programs never even bid on potentially large projects reserved for them.

Characteristics of the Purchasing Situation.   Important characteristics of the purchasing situation include (1) the type of relationship between the buying firm and the selling firm, (2) the characteristics of the products to be purchased, and (3) the characteristics of the market and industry. The *type of relationship* refers to whether the buyer and seller have a blanket contract that covers all purchases, or whether they negotiate each purchase separately. Under a blanket contract, the purchasing process is relatively short, consisting of need recognition and order. If the supplier does not have a blanket contract, supplier selection can be much more complex and may involve a different supplier each time a particular item is ordered.

The *characteristics of the product to be purchased* greatly affect the process of selecting a supplier. For products where significant volume discounts can be obtained by combining orders or where the component is a critical one in the production process, the buyer may choose to select a single supplier or a small group of suppliers rather than spreading orders over a large number of suppliers.[17]

The *characteristics of the industry and market* also affect supplier selection. For example, in high-tech markets the most important attributes sellers can have are high levels of technical service, perceived high product reliability, and high levels of after-sales support; price is less important. In the high-tech market it is vitally important for suppliers to integrate their marketing and technical efforts. This can be done through a variety of organizational mechanisms—through team selling or by having the service department report to marketing. Whatever mechanism the seller

---

BOX 7.1

ISO AT A GLANCE

WHAT

International Standards Organization (ISO) was put together in 1979 by European representatives in the quality field. ISO, or ISO 9000, are the quality standards it worked on for eight years and published in 1987.

WHERE

The organization is based in Geneva, Switzerland. The U.S. delegate is the American National Standards Institute in New York City.

WHY

ISO's intent is to create standards for products traded across international borders and within the unified European economic community. Unified standards, the thinking goes, minimize the need for on-site vendor visits.

HOW

Companies seeking ISO certification put to paper the steps in their operations that ensure the quality of goods and services. There are several certification options: ISO 9001 is the broadest set of standards, while ISO 9003 focuses just on final product inspections. Formal outlines detail what's necessary for each. An auditing firm with the authority to grant or deny certification visits the company. Companies must undergo two follow-up audits per year to maintain certification.

WHO

Roughly 40,000 companies worldwide are ISO-certified. In the United States there are slightly more than 1,000 mostly large companies and divisions of major corporations.

SOURCE: "ISO at a Glance," *Inc.* (June 1993): 99.

---

chooses to integrate their marketing and technical efforts, it is important that these efforts be communicated to clients through sales and promotion efforts. In low-tech markets, price is much more important, and technical service and high levels of after-sales support are less important.

Negotiating Transaction Terms

Negotiating transaction terms include the specifics of the sale and delivery. Specifics of the sale include price, quantity, quality standards, discounts, rebates, and payment terms. Delivery encompasses delivery dates, inspections, locations to ship to, and penalties for late or incorrect shipments. The process of determining these issues will be discussed in greater detail in the section "Negotiation," later in this chapter.

Establishing the Order Routine

The **order routine** includes methods by which orders are made, placed, traced, and inspected. Making and placing orders requires identifying when orders should be made and who is allowed to make them. In some firms this is done by outside salespeople. For example, route salespeople in the grocery industry for companies such as Frito-Lay check the status of shelves in each location and restock according to a mutually agreed stocking plan. The stocking plan details the number of shelf facings for each product and the number of items to be placed within each facing.

Evaluating Product and Vendor

Buyers conduct product and vendor evaluations when they evaluate performance. The key performance question is "How well did the (company, product, or service) solve our problem?" At one time, product and vendor performance focused narrowly on price. The lower the price, the higher the performance. However, new methods of performance evaluation also include on-time performance, quality standards, number of incorrect shipments, and quickness of resolving problems with shipments.

One method of rating suppliers is Rockwell International's Supplier Rating and Incentive Program (SRIP), which started in 1986 and has since been adopted by Motorola, Honeywell, Ford, General Dynamics, Hughes Aircraft, Litton Data Systems, and Northrop.[18] SRIP allows companies to calculate the true cost of products or services from a given supplier through the use of a supplier performance index (SPI). The SPI is calculated by identifying events and assigning a cost to each event. Rockwell identifies the "events" as actions by suppliers that create additional costs.

EXHIBIT 7.7

Defense Electronics
Supplier Rating and Incentive Program

Your Supplier Performance Index (SPI) for the period of 06/23/96 to 12/23/96 is 1.083. This compares to an average SPI of 1.126 for our suppliers in your same commodity category.

Your SPI has been computed based upon the following business activity for the period shown and your quality and delivery schedule deficiencies.

Business Activity
Line Items
  Received: 55
  Behind Schedule: 2
Product Value: $42,745

Deficiencies
Quality:
  Source Inspection Rejections: 0
  Material Review Board Action: 0
  Receiving Inspection Rejections: 2
  Material Returned to Supplier: 3
  Corrective Action Request Letters: 0
  STOPS: 0
Schedule:
  Late Deliveries: 0
  Total Days Late: 0

These events include parts inspections, poor paperwork, reworking of certain parts, incorrectly shipped products that require returns to the supplier, early receipt, interim undershipment, and overshipment. Each of these events requires Rockwell personnel to spend time rectifying them. Rockwell multiplies the cost of an average labor hour by the number of labor hours necessary to resolve the problem. The supplier's SPI is the cost of the items purchased plus the nonproductive costs (events) divided by cost. If the supplier doesn't create any nonproductive costs, the SPI equals 1. Anything above 1 indicates some form of nonproductive costs. Exhibit 7.7 shows a sample supplier rating form for a Rockwell supplier.

The supplier's SPI is used in two ways. First, it serves as a multiplier in comparing bids from different suppliers. If Supplier A has an SPI of 1.5 and Supplier B has an SPI of 1.8, and both make the same bid, Supplier A's would be accepted because the estimated true cost would be lower. Second, it is a method for rating suppliers. Those with unacceptably high SPI are not allowed to bid on new contracts until they can show improved performance. When Rockwell began using SRIP in 1986, the highest acceptable SPI was 2.0. In 1990 the highest acceptable SPI was 1.4.

INDUSTRIAL BUYING CENTERS

Recall from Chapter 2 that a *buying center* is composed of all the customer personnel who directly or indirectly influence the choice of product or supplier. In a sense, buying centers are like a family in making decision about consumer purchases. Different family members play different roles in purchasing decisions. If the family is in the market for a new television, the parents may concentrate on price and ease of service whereas the children may focus on ease of use and ability to use different video games.

Buying centers rarely appear as such on an organizational chart because they are not a formal unit within the buying organization. Rather, their size and composition change depending on the product being purchased. The typical buying center ranges from three to five individuals.[19]

From a sales manager's standpoint, the buying center concept is quite useful for several reasons. First, it focuses attention on multiple buying influences within the buying firm. Second, it explicitly recognizes that each member of the buying center may have his or her own motivation for the purchase and may therefore require different information before making the purchase. For example, one seller of corporate aircraft says, "You must sell to the pilot, the controller, and the board, but if you cannot get the chief executive to get excited about the plane, it will never make it through the purchase process."[20]

The important issues for salespeople to understand regarding buying centers include buying center roles, buying center membership, and types of purchasing situations.

Buying Center Roles

Buying centers have members that play different roles. Some define the problem, while others have an effect on the product selected, and still others have the authority to make the actual purchase. The roles are referred to as initiators, gatekeepers, influencers, deciders, purchasers, and users.[21] The following paragraphs show how each role comes into play when a large pharmaceutical company decides to purchase a new electron microscope.

Initiators are those who recognize that a problem can be solved by the purchase of a product or service. An initiator for office supplies could be a clerk whose duties include maintaining the supplies at a certain predetermined level. In the case of a new electron microscope, the initiator could be a scientist who recognizes that the current lab equipment is inadequate for a certain task. **Gatekeepers,** as we discussed in Chapter 5, are those who control the flow of information among the members of the buying center and between the buying center and the sellers. In the case of the electron microscope purchase, the gatekeeper could be a secretary who controls sellers' access to the scientist. The gatekeeper could also be the scientist who collects information from different companies about the performance specification of their equipment and sends that information to others involved in the purchase decision.

Influencers have expertise that will influence the decisions of others in the buying center. Typically the higher the technical complexity of the purchase, the greater the role played by influencers. An electron microscope is highly complex. As a result the scientists who use the instrument will probably have a great impact on which one is eventually selected. Other influencers may be technicians and maintenance personnel who must maintain the equipment.

Deciders are those people in the organization who have the power to actually make the product and vendor decision. Generally the more significant the purchase, the higher the level of the decider. Since the purchase of an electron microscope is quite expensive, the approval for the purchase will probably have to be put on a capital budget request and submitted to the head of the lab to be considered with other requests for capital equipment. If the need for the item is deemed great enough, the head of the lab will approve the request and send it to the purchasing department to handle the paperwork involved with dealing with the vendor.

Purchasers are responsible for contacting the supplier, negotiating terms of the sale, and actually consummating the sale. The purchaser of the electron microscope will probably be a senior buyer who deals with expensive lab equipment. Finally **users** are members of the organization who actually use the product or service purchased. While their input may or may not be sought in the original purchase, their influence often becomes quite significant in subsequent sales. Since an electron microscope is complex, it is highly doubtful that a purchase would be made without seeking input from users. In any case, it is likely that the scientists' experience with the new microscope will have a significant impact on which microscope is purchased in the future.

Buying Center Membership

Buying center membership varies by purchase. In the previous example of an electron microscope purchase, the buying center included scientists, the department secretary, technicians, maintenance personnel, the buyer, and the head of the lab. In the same firm, however, the buying center for a new machine tool may include the production manager, workers, maintenance and service technicians, the purchasing agent, and, depending on expense, the controller of the firm. As you can see, the members of the buying center vary according the type of product, the number of people in the company who may use the product or who are affected by it, and the technical characteristics of the product.

Not only do the members of the buying center vary, but their influence varies as well. Exhibit 7.8 shows the relative influence of different departments in initiating action about products and vendors. Notice that operations and administration are much more likely to initiate action for taking advantage of new price differentials, while design and development are more likely to initiate action for exploiting newly developed materials.

Exhibit 7.8 also shows that the relative influence of purchasing, manufacturing, design, and production is constant for two product types across four countries.[22] In other words, the relative influence of the departments shown in Exhibit 7.8 are similar in countries around the world.

EXHIBIT 7.8

INFLUENCE OF FUNCTIONAL AREAS IN INITIATING PRODUCT PURCHASES

Country	Overall Corporate Policy and Planning	Operations and Administration (%)	Design and Development Engineering (%)	Production Engineering (%)
Who is the most likely to initiate a project leading to the purchase of material to take advantage of new price differentials?				
Australia	10.0	16.0	3.0	6.0
Canada	7.6	17.8	3.2	10.8
United Kingdom	4.9	14.5	2.4	2.4
United States	9.6	15.1	2.7	5.5
Who is the most likely to initiate a project leading to the purchase of material to exploit newly developed materials?				
Australia	11.0	10.0	22.0	13.0
Canada	10.9	16.8	17.9	20.1
United Kingdom	9.8	7.3	9.8	14.6
United States	15.1	13.7	16.4	6.8
Who is the most likely to initiate a project leading to the purchase of material to accommodate changes in the production process?				
Australia	12.0	22.0	19.0	49.0
Canada	8.3	29.3	15.5	57.5
United Kingdom	7.3	17.1	7.3	56.1
United States	9.6	28.8	13.7	43.8
Who is most likely to initiate a project leading to the purchase of material to meet new performance requirements?				
Australia	8.0	21.0	19.0	28.0
Canada	8.8	29.1	18.1	34.1
United Kingdom	4.9	9.8	19.5	39.1
United States	13.7	20.5	21.9	19.2

SOURCE: Peter Banting, David Ford, Andrew Gross, and George Holmes, "Similarities in Industrial Procurement Across Four Countries," *Industrial Marketing Management*, 14 (1985): 133–144.

Types of Purchasing Situations

One of the most useful ways for sales managers and salespeople to think about prospective customers is in terms of the type of selling situation they are likely to encounter. Selling situations can be categorized (1) by the characteristics of the buying situation and (2) by the characteristics of the buyers.

Characteristics of the Buying Situation.   Major characteristics of the purchasing situation include the importance of the purchase, the uncertainty of the task, the extensiveness of the choice set, and the power of the buyer. For an important but uncertain purchasing situation where the number of product choices is extensive and the buyer has a great deal of power, the buying task becomes very complex. It can take a long time and involve a large buying center. The purchase of a new CAT scanner by a hospital fits this description. This type of purchase can take as long as three years and involve several departments within the hospital, as well as the administrative staff and the board of directors. The purchase of cleaning supplies for a small office, by contrast, may involve one person and take only a few minutes over the phone.

Characteristics of the Buyers.   Some of the important characteristics of the buyer include how actively the buyer is seeking information about the product or service, what type of analysis of the purchase is performed, whether the buyer is actively seeking information or passively awaiting salespeople and other promotional vehi-

---

EXHIBIT 7.9
DESCRIPTION OF BUYING DECISION APPROACHES

Buying Situations	Casual	Routine Low Priority	Simple Modified Rebuy	Judgmental New Task	Complex Modified Rebuy	Strategic New Task
Variables						
Purchase importance	Low	Moderate	High	High	High	Very high
Task uncertainty	Low	Moderate	Low	High	Low	Moderate
Extensiveness of choice set	High	High	Low	Low	High	Low
Buyer power	Low	Moderate	Moderate	Moderate	High	High
Buying Activities						
Search for information	None	Low	Moderate	Moderate	High	High
Use of analysis techniques	None	Moderate	Moderate	Moderate	High	High
Proactive focus	None	Low	High	Moderate	High	Very high
Procedural control	Simply transmit order	Standard procedures	Standard procedures	Little reliance on established procedures	Standard procedures	Little reliance on established procedures

SOURCE: Michele D. Bunn, "Taxonomy of Buying Decision Approaches," *Journal of Marketing,* 57 (January 1993): 38–56.

cles to provide information, and whether the purchase procedure is routine or non-routine.

Based on the characteristics of the selling situation and the characteristics of the buyers, six types of buying decisions emerge. They are casual, routine low priority, simple modified rebuy, judgmental new task, complex modified rebuy, and strategic new task.[23] These buying decisions are shown in Exhibit 7.9.

NEGOTIATION

Negotiation is a decision-making process through which a buyer and seller establish the terms of a purchase agreement.[24] Negotiation is particularly important to firms that embark on long-term relationships, because the outcome of the negotiations will govern the seller's and buyer's actions for some period of time.[25] This discussion of negotiation covers the basic methods of negotiation, negotiating with difficult customers, negotiating in international settings, and expert systems approaches to improving negotiating outcomes.

Methods of Negotiation

Purchasing agents have two basic methods of negotiation: aggressive bargaining and problem-solving. *Aggressive bargaining* is characterized by making explicit or implicit threats, making excessive demands, and refusing to compromise. *Problem-solving, or cooperative, approaches,* on the other hand, are characterized by purchasers working with sellers to develop joint approaches for reducing costs, increasing efficiency, and reducing waste.

Although a few purchasing agents use one or the other method exclusively, depending on their personality, most use a combination of approaches. Buyers who are cooperative and who represent firms with unique specifications are more likely to use a problem-solving negotiation style, whereas buyers in situations with high levels of supplier competition are more likely to engage in aggressive bargaining. Of course, during a long negotiation, both styles may be appropriate.

Negotiating With Difficult Customers

One of the toughest problems in sales management is counseling a salesperson who has done everything correctly in meeting the customer's needs and yet finds the customer continuing to make aggressive demands.[26] The situation is even more difficult when the customer represents a significant new market opportunity or has been identified as the target of significant development efforts. From the purchaser's standpoint, the request for the concession has no cost. The purchaser gains if the concession is granted and loses nothing if the concession is denied. The seller, however, can lose significant profits if it grants the concession. On the other hand, if the seller denies the concession, the contract may be lost.

Sellers have several methods for negotiating with difficult customers. They can accommodate a request for a price discount, offer to compromise, or leave the negotiations. Each approach has problems. If the price is already at the limits of acceptable margins, a price concession can lead to unprofitable business and set a bad precedent for future negotiations. Compromises can be equally problematic from a margin standpoint. Leaving the negotiations can keep the seller from being allowed to bid on future business, as well as provide opportunities for competitors to get the purchaser's business.

Given the problems with accommodation, compromise, and leaving, what can a sales manager and salesperson do to keep the customer? Thomas C. Keiser, a trainer in the field of negotiation, offers several methods for preparing for negotiations, and for moving a customer from using aggressive negotiating tactics to a problem-solving approach where the needs of both the buyer and seller are met.

Guideline 1: Prepare by Knowing Your Absolute Minimum Acceptable Offer. Good negotiators always begin a negotiation knowing the absolute minimum combination of price, terms, services, and quantity that will be acceptable. For sellers, this means knowing the margin attached to different prices, quantities, and services, and how to adjust one to reflect a change in another. For instance, if a customer is adamant about not paying more than a certain price, and the seller knows that it cannot make sufficient margins at that price, the seller may shorten the terms of payment or make the buyer pay for delivery. In other words, by knowing the trade-offs among prices, quantities, and services, sellers can give in to the buyer on the important issue (price) while not sacrificing overall margins.

Guideline 2: Increase the Number of Variables to Work With in the Negotiation. In keeping with the first guideline, good negotiators keep introducing new variables when negotiations seem to stall. If price is the stumbling block, good negotiators may include additional services that do not add greatly to cost but which provide a substantial benefit to the customer. For example, as mentioned earlier, Donaldson Company, Inc. (DCI) offers its R&D capability to customers who need assistance with particular filter applications. This allows DCI not only to offer customers substantial added benefits, but also to amortize the R&D costs over a large number of customers.

Guideline 3: When Under Attack, Listen.   When under attack most negotiators' first instinct is to defend themselves or counterattack. This can take the form of arguing with the customer or becoming aggressive in turn. In either case the negotiations may be harmed. Indeed, winning an argument with a customer may be one of the most costly things a seller can do! When faced with a customer who uses very aggressive bargaining tactics, sellers have several possible countertactics. First, they can ask to reschedule the meeting. This gives the buyer a chance to cool down and gives the seller additional time to prepare, if necessary. Another tactic is to listen quietly and not react quickly. If the attack is a ploy by the purchaser and the seller does not react, the buyer may abandon the tactic. If the attack is based on a legitimate issue, listening and being empathetic may calm the buyer down and allow for constructive negotiation. Third, the seller can react with equally aggressive tactics. This is usually an approach of last resort because if it fails there is a chance that the seller may be taken off the list of approved vendors or eliminated from consideration on the contract.

Guideline 4: Keep Track of Issues Requiring Discussion. It is easy during complex, protracted negotiations to lose track of what has been agreed upon. Frequent pauses to recap what has been agreed to can be helpful for both sides. It also helps maintain momentum by forcing attention to issues that have not yet been decided, versus continuing to discuss those that have.

Guideline 5: Commit to a Solution Only After It's Certain to Work for Both Parties. Negotiators should be careful not to make a binding commitment on any part of a deal until the overall deal is analyzed. The seller should not say "We will agree to a $20 unit price" until it knows the delivery terms, quantities, and other terms of sale. If the negotiator agrees on price while there are still unresolved issues on terms, the buyer can negotiate aggressively on terms and make the value of the entire deal fall below the seller's acceptable minimum. Moreover, if the seller has already committed to certain parts of the deal, it is difficult to take back those concessions. Instead, the seller should say, "We will agree to a $20 unit price, assuming you pay delivery, order in quantities of 1,000 or more, and pay for the shipment in full when it is received."

Guideline 6: Save the Hardest Issues for Last. Starting with the easier issues gives negotiators a chance to get comfortable with each other. It also allows the negotiators to have some successes, which will create momentum to bring the entire deal to fruition.

Guideline 7: Start High and Concede Slowly. Depending on the history with the customer, the negotiator may wish to start off with a high bid and be bargained down. This approach has a price: If the customer is not willing to bargain or makes a decision based on the first bid, the seller can lose the contract. If the customer expects to bargain, however, a negotiator who starts out with the best offer leaves little room for maneuvering.

Negotiating in International Settings

Thomas Keiser, the trainer who developed the guidelines in the previous section, argues that sellers should try to use problem solving instead of aggressive bargaining in negotiations. Although this suggestion may be appropriate for U.S. firms operating in the United States, a study of marketing negotiations in France, the United Kingdom, the United States, and Germany shows that the problem-solving approach may not be appropriate in all cultures, in fact, models in those countries vary widely.[27] For French negotiators, status of the negotiators and context of the negotiations are very important. In U.K. negotiations status of the negotiators also appears to be a key influence. Negotiation outcomes in the United States are a function of problem-solving approaches. German negotiators view the process as win–lose; if sellers meet their objectives, buyers will be disappointed and vice versa. These results are based on only one study, but the implications are clear: Negotiating styles that yield very high outcomes in one culture may yield very different outcomes in another culture.

Expert Systems

One intriguing development in international negotiations is the development of an expert system, NEGOTEX, that will allow negotiators to test different strategies before engaging in actual negotiation.[28] Expert systems are computer software that help novices by developing models based on the experience of human experts. Although NEGOTEX has not yet been used extensively in actual bargaining situations, the state of progress in expert systems is such that other programs should be forthcoming soon.

SUMMARY

This chapter introduced concepts and issues related to organizational buying, which is the purchase of goods or services by firms for use in making other goods or for eventual resale to other firms. Organizational buying differs from consumer purchasing in three important ways: characteristics of the buyers, characteristics of the purchasing situation, and demand characteristics. These differences are important to salespeople and sales managers in determining the best way to approach a potential customer.

Sales managers need to be aware of several trends in organizational buying. These trends include a change in the role of purchasing in the organization, a shift in the model that controls how purchasers buy, changes in purchasing methods so that sales managers no longer have complete control over how a particular customer is served, reduced supplier lists, and closer vendor-supplier relationships. Each trend affects the overall relationship between buyers and sellers. Sellers must be particularly alert to the effects of these trends in their markets to ensure they retain existing customers and create new ones.

Organizational buying can be represented by a ten-stage process: problem recognition, determination of need, devising product specifications, searching for qualified sellers, requesting and obtaining proposals, evaluating proposals, selecting product and seller, negotiating transaction terms, establishing the order routine and product and vendor evaluation.

The buying center consists of individuals who make or influence the purchase decision. Different buying center members play essentially five different roles. Some define the problem or need, others influence the solution of product or service, while still others have the authority to make the purchase. Depending on the type of purchase being made, the membership of the buying center may vary.

Finally, negotiation is the decision-making process through which buyers and sellers set the terms of purchase transactions. Negotiating with difficult customers can be tackled using the seven guidelines offered by Thomas C. Keiser. Negotiations in the United States and in international settings differ and should be approached accordingly.

KEY TERMS

organizational buying

purchasing

derived demand

inelastic demand

joint demand

fluctuating demand

adversarial model of purchasing	approved vendor lists
cooperative model of purchasing	ISO 9000
industrial buyers	just-in-time (JIT)
producers	set-asides
institutions	transaction terms
resellers	order routine
government purchasers	initiators
problem recognition	gatekeepers
internal problem recognition	influencers
external problem recognition	deciders
determination of need	purchasers
product specifications	users
request for proposal (RFP)	negotiation

DISCUSSION QUESTIONS

1. What are the three broad differences that distinguish organizational purchasing from consumer purchasing?
2. How are the four types of demand unique? Give examples to illustrate their characteristics.
3. What are four important trends influencing organizational buying?
4. What are industrial buyers? List and describe the four types of industrial buyers.
5. What are the steps in the organizational purchasing process?
6. Which issues are important when evaluating proposals and selecting products and sellers? What tools are available to evaluate supplier performance?
7. What is an industrial buying center? Why is this concept important to a sales manager?
8. What are the different roles of members of a buying center? Give examples of types of individuals who fit in each role.
9. How can purchasing situations be classified? Describe and illustrate each category.
10. What negotiation guidelines should a salesperson follow?

PROBLEMS

1. Monique LaFleur, a sales rep for a medium-size distributor of office products, is making her monthly sales call on one of her largest accounts. Guy Brossard, the purchasing agent, tells Monique that the firm is considering reducing its number of office-product distributors so that it can qualify for more quantity discounts. As Monique's manager, what suggestions would you give her to ensure that your firm remains on the list of approved suppliers?

2. Stephanie Potter, a sales rep for a large supplier of oil field drilling equipment, has been pursuing a sizable sale to a major supplier of oil field services. Her primary contact has been through Abdul Swazhi, the purchasing agent. Stephanie comes to you, her sales manager, and says she is concerned that

she may not have a complete picture of the customer's situation since she has only spoken to the purchasing agent. As Stephanie's sales manager, what would you counsel her to do?

3. Lane Robinson, a sales rep for a school furniture manufacturer, makes a routine sales call on one of his largest school districts. The school district has purchased most of its furniture for the last five years from Lane's company. Lane enjoys a cordial realtionship with Maverne Lipscomb, the school district's purchasing agent. When Lane asks to see Maverne, however, he is told that she is no longer with the district and has been replaced by Phil Andrews. In their first interaction, Phil tells Lane that all vendor relationships are being reviewed, and that he must come to their next meeting prepared to justify why his firm should continue to be the vendor of choice for the school district. As Lane's manager, what suggestions would you make to help guide Lane in developing a new relationship with Phil?

SHORT CASE
KEEP-IT-CLEAN

BACKGROUND

Keep-It-Clean, a large industrial janitorial service, serves office buildings, hospitals, prisons, educational institutions, and light manufacturing operations throughout the United States. Its services are among the best—its employees are bonded, each employee goes through a two-week training period, and employees receive bonuses based on customer satisfaction surveys. Perhaps not surprisingly, Keep-It-Clean enjoys some of the highest employee retention and customer satisfaction rates in the industry.

SITUATION

Keep-It-Clean has been approached by a state university system that has 12 campuses. The contract is currently held by one of Keep-It-Clean's largest competitors, but the industry grapevine is that the contract has been in jeopardy for some time. The system issued an RFP for cleaning services for all 12 campuses. The contract posed some interesting problems. First, the university system is known for skimping on building maintenance spending. Second, the university is also known as a very demanding customer—students, parents, and faculty expect clean facilities and are quite vocal if they are not in top shape. Third, the usage pattern of the buildings poses challenges for scheduled cleaning. Since most of the facilities are in continuous use from 7:30 A.M. until 10:00 P.M., the cleaning crews must be tightly scheduled to complete their work in the time available. Fourth, it is difficult to rotate crews from one site, such as an office building, to the university because the university's cleaning times are so inflexible.

PROBLEM

Out of ten companies that responded to the original RFP, Keep-It-Clean and another competitor won the initial round of bidding. The university has invited both competitors to the main university offices to make their final presentations. These presentations consist of negotiating sessions with the university's purchasing agents. One of the university purchasing agents is famous for his hard-line tactics, especially related to pricing.

Keep-It-Clean knows that its pricing is probably higher than the competitor's, but that the competitor has a reputation for cutting corners.

QUESTIONS

1. What should Keep-It-Clean's negotiating posture be in the final stages of the bidding process?
2. What guidelines should Keep-It-Clean follow in the negotiating process?
3. How should Keep-It-Clean respond if the hard-line agent takes an aggressive approach to pricing?
4. Is the current purchasing process adversarial or cooperative? How might Keep-It-Clean develop a more cooperative relationship?

PURCHASING ROLE PLAY

CHARACTERS

Salesperson: Mimi Morgan or José Avila
Sales Manager: Danny Chang or Cindy Lou Polaski
Purchaser: Dottie Davis or Bart Hanson

SCENARIO

Southwest Methodist Hospital is one of the largest hospitals in the greater Las Vegas area. Mimi Morgan has called on the hospital for the past 4 years and has had steady business each year. The only person that she has ever dealt with was the buyer, Antonio Vargas. Morgan now finds that Vargas has been replaced because of a change in hospital administration. Vargas had been at the hospital "forever" and was very well liked. Morgan really enjoyed calling on Vargas and always knew that she would leave with an order.

The first scene opens with Morgan calling on Dottie Davis, the purchaser who replaced Vargas. Davis is all business and has been ordered by her superiors to cut costs and reorganize the purchasing department. The sales call does not go well. Scene 2 has Morgan talking with her boss Danny Chang about the new management at Southwest.

SCENE 1

Morgan enters Davis's office and introduces herself. She then asks where Vargas is. "You haven't done your homework," Davis replies. "We're under new management and changes have been made." Morgan responds, "I was aware of the new management team but did not know that Antonio was no longer here. He will be missed. I stopped by to check your inventories and see how the supplies were doing." "Southwest will not be repurchasing its usual order," Davis declares. Your costs are too high! We are looking at alternative suppliers." Morgan responds, "You have always bought from us and have never had problems with our product. We provide better service than any of our competitors, and our product is recognized as the best on the market." "That may be true," says Davis, "but your prices are the highest on the market too." The scene fades out.

SCENE 2

Morgan walks into her sales manager's office and asks if he has heard of the changes at Southwest. Chang replies that he has and asks if there are problems. "You better believe it," says Morgan. "They have replaced Vargas with some young hotshot. The immediate bottom line seems to be the only concern." Chang replies, "I can't say that I'm surprised. That hospital has always been a little fat. I've heard that they've laid off 20 people. Looks like they're getting serious about controlling expenses. How are your relationships with other members of the staff?" Morgan replies reluctantly that she always dealt with Vargas and her current contacts are minimal if not nonexistent. Chang then begins a discussion about how to get back into the hospital and how to win back the account. The discussion looks at short-term and long-term strategies to get and keep the account.

SCENE 3

The third scene consists of the presentation of the strategy to the Southwest Methodist Hospital problem. The scene may include one, two, or all three of the characters, and the location is up to you. How can Morgan maintain the account and satisfy the needs of the new purchaser?

CHARACTER DESCRIPTIONS

Name: Danny Chang
Gender: M
Age: 42
Marital status: Married
Education: Portland State University
Title: Sales Manager
Office location: Las Vegas
Reports to: District Manager, Los Angeles
Employment history: Manager for 15 years; sales rep for 7 years
Personality: No-nonsense; competitive; driven
Notes: Supportive of his people; good with experienced salespeople—gives them room to make decisions; not as good at mentoring; has three children
Grapevine: Dependable

Name: Cindy Lou Polaski
Gender: F
Age: 35
Marital status: Divorced
Education: University of Pittsburgh
Title: Sales Manager
Office location: Las Vegas
Reports to: District Manager, Los Angeles
Employment history: Salesperson for 6 years; human resources for 2 years; sales manager for 4 years
Personality: Enthusiastic; goal-driven; friendly; demands full effort
Notes: The job is her life; wants a district manager position; avid skier
Grapevine: Possible promotion

Name: Mimi Morgan
Gender: F
Age: 30
Marital status: Married
Education: B.A., University of New Hampshire
Title: Sales Rep
Office location: Las Vegas
Reports to: Sales Manager, Las Vegas
Employment history: With EDD for 7 years; has had the same territory for 4 years
Personality: Friendly; energetic
Notes: Won honors during training program; enjoys her job; has always made quota; avid sailor; no children
Grapevine: A career salesperson; does not want management position

Name: José Avila
Gender: M
Age: 31
Marital status: Married
Education: University of New Mexico
Title: Sales Rep
Office location: Las Vegas
Reports to: Sales Manager, Las Vegas
Employment history: With EDD 5 years
Personality: Very friendly; has customers that have become close friends; high producer
Notes: Won the last sales contest; avid golfer; parents are from Mexico
Grapevine: Career sales

Name: Bart "Cowboy" Hanson
Gender: M
Age: 33
Marital status: Married
Education: University of Wyoming
Title: Senior Purchaser, Southwest Methodist Hospital
Employment history: Recent hire at Southwest Methodist; previously senior buyer at Kansas City Hospital.
Personality: Tough; well organized; all business
Notes: Well known buyer; an officer in National Purchasers Association; "a tough sell"
Grapevine: Known to take an aggressive line with suppliers, especially on price

Name: Dottie Davis
Gender: F
Age: 42
Marital status: Married
Education: BBA, University of Iowa
Title: Senior Purchaser, Southwest Methodist Hospital
Employment history: Just hired by Southwest Methodist Hospital; previously employed at New York Hospital.
Personality: No-nonsense, serious; takes no grief from anyone
Notes: Hired to cut expenses; tough; gets the job done; bottom-line oriented; skeet shooter
Grapevine: Known to change suppliers to shake things up

QUESTIONS

1. What mistakes did Morgan make in managing the Southwest Methodist Hospital account? What mistakes did the sales manager make in monitoring Morgan's relationships with the account?
2. What approach should Morgan take to maintain business in the long run?
3. List at least four realistic alternatives to the role play. Discuss the long-term consequences of each alternative.
4. Which of the alternatives for question 3 should Morgan select to resolve this role play? Defend your answer fully.
5. As the sales manager, what steps should you take to keep this from occurring with other salespeople and other accounts?

NOTES

1. Derrick C. Schnebelt, "Turning the Tables," *Sales and Marketing Management,* (January 1993): 22–23.
2. Susan Greco, "The Art of Selling," *Inc.,* 15 (June 1993): 72–80.
3. "Merck Agrees to Buy Medco," *Facts on File,* 53 (August 5, 1993): 574.
4. Thomas G. Noordewier, George John, and John R. Nevin, "Performance Outcomes of Purchasing Arrangement in Industrial Buyer-Vendor Relationships," *Journal of Marketing,* (October 1990): 80–93.
5. Robert E. Spekman, "Strategic Supplier Selection: Understanding Long-Term Buyer Relationships," *Business Horizons* (July–August 1988): 75–81.
6. Al Wrigley, "Lopez Held in Awe by Many GM Execs: Called Agent for Change," *American Metal Market,* 101 (March 17, 1993): 1–2, and "GM Gets New Purchasing Line-Up," *Ward's Auto World,* 28 (June 1992): 10.
7. Cathy Owens Swift, "Preferences for Single Sourcing and Supplier Selection Criteria," *Journal of Business Research,* 32, (1995):105–111.
8. "Xerox Preaches the Gospel of Just-In-Time to Suppliers," *Purchasing* (October 24, 1985): 21–22.
9. This discussion is based on David A. Vaughan, "The Buy American Act of 1988: Legislation in Conflict With U.S. International Obligations," *Law and Policy in International Business,* 20 (Summer 1988): 603–618, and William H. Lash, III, "Some 'Buy American' Rules Ease: The 1993 Act Devised to Foster U.S. Industry Keeps Evolving," *Purchasing* 15 (July 15, 1993): 23.
10. Hillary Appelman, "'Buy American' Vow Buys Town Headaches," *Fort Worth Star-Telegram* (January 25, 1992): A15.
11. The purchasing process outlined here is drawn from several sources, including Patrick J. Robinson, Charles W. Faris, and Yoram Wind, *Industrial Buying and Creative Marketing* (Boston: Allyn and Bacon, 1967); Rosann L. Spiro, William D. Perreault, and Fred D. Reynolds, "The Personal Selling Process: A Critical Review and Model," *Industrial Marketing Management,* 6 (December 1977): 351–364; and U. G. Ozanne and Gilbert A. Churchill, "Five Dimensions of the Industrial Adoption Process," *Journal of Marketing Research* (1981): 322–328.
12. Herbert E. Brown and Roger W. Brucker, "Charting the Industrial Buying Stream," *Industrial Marketing Management,* 19 (1990): 55–61.
13. Ralph W. Jackson and William M. Pride, "The Use of Approved Vendor Lists," *Industrial Marketing Management,* 15 (1986): 165–169.
14. P. A. Dion and P. M. Banting, "Effective Buyers: Are They Cunning or Cooperative?" *Journal of Purchasing and Materials Management,* 20.4 (Winter 1987): 26–31.

15. James Morgan, "Are Your Supplier Reps Proactive, Knowledgeable?" *Purchasing,* 16 (June 2, 1994): 43–45.

16. Gary L. Frazier, Robert E. Spekman, and Charles R. O'Neal, "Just-in-Time Exchange Relationships in Industrial Markets," *Journal of Marketing,* 52 (October 1988): 52–67.

17. Robert E. Spekman, "Strategic Supplier Selection: Understanding Long-Term Buyer Relationships," *Business Horizons* (July–August 1988): 75–81.

18. Tom Stundza, "Can Supplier Ratings be Standardized?" *Purchasing,* 109 (November 8, 1990): 60–64.

19. Robert D. McWilliams, Earl Naumann, and Stan Scott, "Determining Buying Center Size," *Industrial Marketing Management,* 21 (1992): 43–49.

20. Thomas Bonoma, "Major Industrial Sales: Who Really Does the Buying?" *Harvard Business Review,* 60 (May–June 1982): 111–119.

21. These categories are based on a typology proposed by Thomas Bonoma (1982), op. cit.

22. Peter Banting, David Ford, Andrew Gross, and George Holmes, "Similarities in Industrial Procurement Across Four Countries," *Industrial Marketing Management,* 14 (1985): 133–144.

23. Michele D. Bunn, "Taxonomy of Buying Decision Approaches," *Journal of Marketing,* 57 (January 1993): 38–56.

24. Barbara C. Perdue and John O. Summers, "Purchasing Agents; Use of Negotiation Strategies," *Journal of Marketing Research,* 28 (May 1991): 175–189.

25. F. Robert Dwyer, Paul H. Schurr, and Sejo Oh, "Developing Buyer-Seller Relationships," *Journal of Marketing,* 51 (April 1987): 11–27.

26. This discussion is drawn largely from Thomas C. Keiser, "Negotiating With a Customer You Can't Afford to Lose," *Harvard Business Review,* 66 (November–December 1988): 30–34.

27. Nigel G. C. Campbell, John L. Graham, Alain Jolibert, and Hans Gunther Meissner, "Marketing Negotiations in France, Germany, the United Kingdom, and the United States," *Journal of Marketing,* 52 (April 1988): 49–62.

28. Arvind Rangaswamy, Jehoshua Eliashberg, Raymond R. Burke, and Jerry Wind, "Developing Marketing Expert Systems: An Application to International Negotiations," *Journal of Marketing,* 53 (October 1989): 24–39.

8

SALES ORGANIZATION

The company with the second best organization ends up second place in the market.

D. WAYNE CALLOWAY, FORMER CEO, PEPSICO

LEARNING OBJECTIVES

After reading this chapter, you should be able to answer the following questions:

- Why is sales organization important?
- How can newer selling methods, such as selling teams, national account management, and telemarketing, be used to replace or supplement field salesforces?
- What are the advantages and disadvantages of geographic, product, market/account, activity/function, and hybrid field sales organizations?
- When should a firm use independent versus integrated salesforces?

Sales organization is the organizational structure through which sales strategy is implemented. IBM illustrates some of the sales organization choices facing sales managers today. In the past most of its sales managers relied on a field salesforce as the company's primary sales organization. Today, however, IBM uses a field salesforce, telemarketing, and field repair technicians—all coordinated through a sophisticated customer information database—to provide necessary levels of customer service. To coordinate the efforts of telemarketing representatives, the field salesforce, and field repair technicians, IBM has begun what it calls "bottom-up" marketing. The heart of this approach is a database that tracks every contact with an IBM customer or potential customer. According to John McFarlane, manager of integrated marketing for IBM's Chicago office, "We're trying to build relationships, so we have to do it with a database. Everything we send out, every response card, every customer response is tracked. We try to infer from that where the customer is in the buying process. It's truly interactive marketing based on the ability to track relations through the computer. If you were a prospect of mine, the content of our conversations would be in the computer, whether it was telemarketing or a face-to-face call."[1]

Sales organization decisions used to be relatively simple. Given that most industrial firms employed a field salesforce, the most pressing question for upper-level sales managers was how the field salesforce should be organized. There were a limited number of organizational choices, including geographic, product, market, and customer. Once the sales organization decision was made, the firm generally did not have to make many adjustments in the basic sales organization structure. Today the situation is quite different. Customers are much more demanding and much less forgiving of mistakes, and salesforce costs continue to skyrocket. As a result sales organization decisions are now much broader in scope. Rather than focusing solely on how to structure the field salesforce, sales management must consider whether to use other selling methods, such as telemarketing or national accounts management, and how to combine all of the firms' selling methods into a cohesive program to serve customers.

This chapter explores the three major decisions sales managers make in developing a sales organization: (1) What type of salesforce should be used? (2) How should that salesforce be structured? and (3) Should the salesforce consist of company employees or be from independent organizations?

To answer the first question, upper-level sales managers can choose from a variety of selling methods, including a traditional field salesforce, national account management, telemarketing, and electronic data interchange. The answer to the second question depends on the type of salesforce selected. For example, a field salesforce can be structured by geography, product, customer/market, or activity/function, or it can be a hybrid. A national account salesforce can be structured as a separate division or integrated within each division. A telemarketing salesforce can be structured as primary, supporting, or combination. The third question essentially asks whether the firm should "own or lease" its salesforce. If the firm "owns" its salesforce, it employs salespeople directly. "Leasing" the salesforce includes such options as distributors and manufacturers' representatives.

In combination the answers to these three questions comprise the building blocks that managers can use in constructing a sales organization that meets the needs of diverse customers in diverse markets. The answers to the three questions, in part, address the important issue posed in Chapter 1: How do we improve the productivity and efficiency of the selling approach?

SALESFORCE TYPES AND STRUCTURES

The first decision managers must make in salesforce organization is which type of salesforce to use. Types include field salesforces, national account management, team selling, telemarketing (also referred to as teleselling), part-time salesforces, and direct electronic links. After deciding on the type of salesforce, managers must then answer the second question, which is how the salesforce should be structured. This section defines each type of salesforce and discusses the corresponding choices of structure.

Field Salesforces

Field salesforces consist of sales representatives who work primarily with customers in person, although they may also use the telephone or rely on computer links to expedite orders and provide customer service. The decision about how a field salesforce gets structured is usually based on some means of specialization, such as geography, market, product, or activity/function, or a hybrid of these types. One exception to specialization might be very small organizations (such as start-up businesses), where the salesforce consists of the owner who personally calls on all actual and potential customers. With this exception noted, specialization is frequent among salesforces because it allows a firm to focus its selling efforts in order to

	EXHIBIT 8.1			
	PERCENT OF MANUFACTURING COMPANIES USING COMPANY SALESFORCES			

	Percentage of Reporting Companies			
Company Salesforce	Number of Companies	Producers of Industrial Products	Producers of Consumer Products	Producers of Both Consumer and Industrial Products
Generalist (Geographic Sales Org)		66%	58%	71%
Specialist (Total)	68	75	55	75
Specialist (Product)	54	63	38	63
Specialist (Industry)	30	37	13	46
Specialist (Channel)	23	16	28	42
Specialist (Account)	21	19	25	17
Specialist (User)	18	23	8	25

SOURCE: Howard Sutton, *Rethinking the Company's Selling and Distribution Channels,* Report #885 (New York: The Conference Board, 1986), 2.

maximize sales productivity. The prevalence of the field salesforce and of the various means of specializing the salesforce are shown in Exhibit 8.1. Each specialization is discussed in the paragraphs that follow.

Geographically-Based Salesforces.   The most common means of specializing the salesforce is by geographic region. In the **geographically-based salesforce,** a salesperson calls on all current and prospective accounts in a given geographic territory. Exhibit 8.2 shows a geographic specialization for the salesforce of a large pharmaceutical manufacturer.

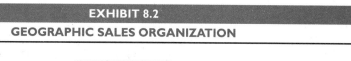

	EXHIBIT 8.2
	GEOGRAPHIC SALES ORGANIZATION

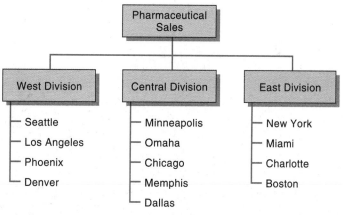

There are three distinct advantages to geographic specialization. First, there is no overlap in account coverage among the company's salespeople, because each salesperson is responsible for all the accounts in his or her territory. This reduces confusion among salespeople in terms of who is responsible for which account. Second, the salespeople can live in the center of the territory, thereby minimizing their travel time (and travel costs) to all the points within the territory. Third, salespeople can become very familiar with local economic and competitive conditions, making them better able to serve local customers.

There are an equal number of disadvantages. For example, if the product line is very complex, it may be difficult for salespeople to become equally proficient in all the lines carried by the seller. The full line might also be too much to cover during the average sales call. Moreover, if account size varies significantly, salespeople may find themselves spending too much time on small accounts that represent a small portion of the territory's potential, while spending too little time on the larger accounts with greatest potential. Conversely, salespeople may devote too much time to the large accounts and ignore the small accounts in their territory.

Finally, geographically-based salespeople may find it difficult to serve large customers with multiple plants located in multiple territories. Salespeople in the different territories may find it difficult to coordinate their selling efforts, and if they have some pricing latitude, there may be discrepancies in prices charged to the same customer at different locations. This problem becomes especially acute if the customer's plants are located in different countries, thereby requiring salespeople in different territories to coordinate their selling efforts while being mindful local customs and currency fluctuations.

Product-Based Salesforces.   Firms that specialize their salesforces according to product line create a **product-based salesforce.** Product-based sales organizations are particularly appropriate for complex products because they allow the salesperson to concentrate on a limited product line during a sales call. A product-based organization also allows the seller to concentrate on training its salespeople on a limited number of products.

Firms that sell both capital equipment and supplies often have a different salesforce to handle each. This is because the purchase cycle is much longer for capital equipment and the sale typically requires more expertise on the part of the salesperson. By contrast, the purchase cycle for supplies can be quite short, and the sale generally requires less expertise on the part of the salesperson. Exhibit 8.3 shows a product-based sales organization for a manufacturer of pharmaceuticals and other medical products and supplies.

The disadvantages of product-based sales organizations include duplication of calls and buyer frustration. *Duplication of calls* occurs when a seller has multiple product lines with multiple salesforces, and a customer needs more than one product line. The result is that, several salespeople from the same sales organization call on the buyer. This duplication of coverage can lead to increased selling costs. It can also lead to buyer frustration because the buyer may not be sure which salesperson to contact for a specific need. Merck Human Health, for example, has multiple divisions, and each has a salesforce representing its products. As a result a single doctor

EXHIBIT 8.3

PRODUCT-BASED SALES ORGANIZATION

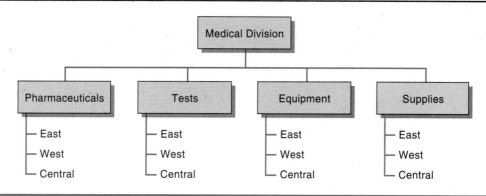

may be called on by a number of salespeople depending on the doctor's specialty. This can lead to problems with scheduling and frustration among doctors who are interrupted multiple times by salespeople from the same company.

Market/Account-Based Salesforces.   **Market or account-based salesforces** are organized by the type of customer market they serve. Donaldson Co., Inc. (DCI), a Minneapolis-based manufacturer of industrial filters and noise reduction equipment, organizes its salesforce by market—such as agricultural, construction, trucking, and stationary applications (see Exhibit 8.4). For DCI, the channels, the characteristics of the products used, and the specific applications of the products in the different markets are sufficiently distinct to justify the organization of the salesforce by market. A market specialization is also appropriate when the buyers for a particular market are geographically concentrated. In the United States, for instance, shoe manufacturers are concentrated in the Northeast. However, shoe repair supplies are purchased by shoe repair shops throughout the country. Therefore, firms selling to the shoe industry concentrate their efforts to sell products related to manufacture of new shoes in the Northeast, while selling shoe repair supplies throughout the United States.

Sales organizations can be structured by account in several ways. First, the firm can divide its accounts by size and assign a different selling method to each group. For example, Ecolab groups its customers by size and uses the selling method that is most cost-effective for each group. Another firm conducted a study which compared its traditional geographically based sales organization to a telemarketing sales organization. The results of the study, which compared two territories of equal size, showed the firm could increase its sales by over 30 percent while reducing its costs by 50 percent by combining the two sales approaches. The combined sales organization targeted large customers to be served by a field salesforce, while mid-sized and small customers were served by a telemarketing operation.[2]

Second, if the customers are sufficiently large, the firm can structure its sales organization by individual customer. This comes about when each customer accounts

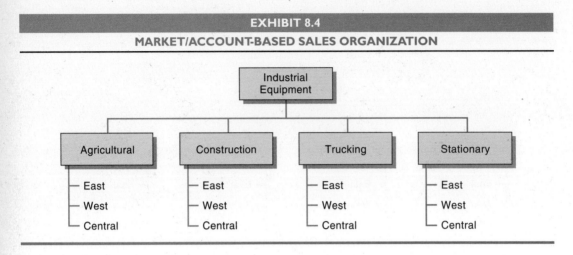

EXHIBIT 8.4

MARKET/ACCOUNT-BASED SALES ORGANIZATION

for high sales volume and has sufficiently unique service needs. Customer-based sales organizations are basically the same as national account organizations, which will be discussed shortly. However, while firms with customer-based organizations serve all their accounts in this fashion, firms with a national account organization typically serve their large accounts with national accounts management, and medium and smaller accounts with another selling method. Customer-based sales-forces are common with firms that serve only large customers, as is the case with corporate aircraft manufacturers.

One advantage of a market/account salesforce organization is that the sales-force becomes familiar with the characteristics of each customer, market, or customer group. This is particularly important when the needs of the different markets are quite distinct. For example, in the coin-counting machine industry, the two largest markets are banks and casinos. As a general rule, banks are much more concerned about speed and reliability, while casinos are more concerned about cost. Banks are also much more widely dispersed across the United States, while casinos are restricted to a limited number of states. Given these characteristics, organizing coin machine salesforces by market is justified.

Customer specialization is also called for when the firm sells a number of different products that are used together by the customer. Xerox has changed its sales-force to a customer-based organization because its customers often use many different Xerox products.

A disadvantage of the market/account salesforce is that, like product-based sales organizations, there may be substantial geographic overlap between salespeo-ple, thereby increasing travel costs. This occurs when a customer has multiple pur-chasing sites that cover a large geographic territory.

A potential disadvantage for customer-based sales organizations is that in fo-cusing so closely on the needs of certain customers, the firm may overlook the changes in the market as a whole. For example, Goodyear Shoe Products exerted so much effort on serving its existing customers that it missed the influx of a new

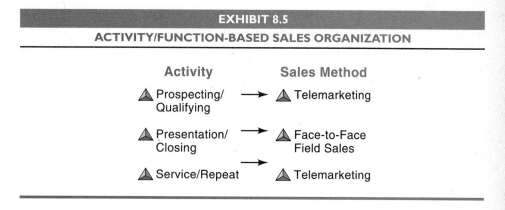

EXHIBIT 8.5

ACTIVITY/FUNCTION-BASED SALES ORGANIZATION

customer group in the Midwest. The firm later established excellent relationships with these new customers, but admitted it had missed some sales by its tardy market entry.[3]

Activity/Function-Based Salesforces. **Activity/function-based salesforces** are organized by sales function, such as prospecting, qualifying, presentation, closing, customer service, or routine reorders (see Exhibit 8.5). Some firms have found that they can substantially reduce costs by using a lower cost method for prospecting and routine reordering, while reserving more costly personal selling for the presentation and closing stages. Honeywell Corporation, for example, uses an activity/function-based sales organization in its Temperature Controls division. Prospects are solicited through trade shows, direct mail, and catalogs. Then the prospects are qualified through a telemarketing group located at the firm's headquarters. Qualified leads are passed to local sales offices, where the lead is contacted by a telemarketing support person. Any literature and quotes the customer desires are sent out prior to contact by a field salesperson. The field salesforce is used for presentation and closing. Service and routine follow-up orders are handled by another telemarketing group at Honeywell headquarters.

An activity/function-based salesforce is able to focus the use of high-cost selling methods, such as face-to-face sales calls, in the stage of the selling process where it is most needed. If the seller has a low rate of conversion of prospects to purchasers, it is more efficient to use a low-cost method such as telemarketing to qualify the leads before using a high-cost method such as face-to-face selling to make presentations and close sales. An activity/function-based salesforce can also be designed to meet the customer service issues that are most important at each stage of the selling process. If a demonstration is necessary for the presentation and closing stage, but frequent contact is most important at the service and reorder stage, the activity/function-based organization can deliver both types of service in a cost-effective manner by using different selling methods.

A disadvantage of using an activity/function-based salesforce is that by using multiple selling approaches to serve a single account, the firm is forced to coordinate the activities of different sales groups, such as national accounts, telemarketing, and face-to-face sales. Coordinating the efforts of different salesforces can be difficult. The salesforces must engage in joint planning or have a top sales executive oversee the coordination of multiple salesforces.

Another disadvantage is the need to continually update the selling approach. For example, if a small account grows, it may become necessary for the firm to change the selling method it uses. Ecolab found that several small accounts served through telemarketing began purchasing more because of the increased frequency of contact. As a result, these accounts were reassigned from the telemarketing group to the distributor that served that territory. Unfortunately, many customers had developed a close relationship with their telemarketing sales representative and did not wish to switch to a different means of service. These situations challenged Ecolab's sales management to continue providing necessary levels of service while keeping the customers satisfied.

Hybrid Salesforces.   **Hybrid salesforces** are sales organizations with two or more organizational types. The firm in Exhibit 8.6 uses a combination of telemarketing, national accounts management, and field sales to serve customers of different sizes at different stages of the selling process.[4] Hybrid salesforces were designed to overcome the problems of the individual sales organization types discussed. Its primary advantage is the ability to offer customers the service they need using the most efficient selling method. Thus, customer satisfaction and cost constraints are simultaneously satisfied.

The primary disadvantage of hybrid salesforces is the difficulty of managing multiple salesforces, whether they are serving the same or different customers. A firm that manages multiple salesforces must change its sales management structure. For example, a firm might have a manager for each type of salesforce (telemarketing, field, and national accounts management) reporting to a vice-president who has overall responsibility for the sales function. Other changes in structure may include changes in planning methods. If multiple salesforces are going to serve the same customers, it is important that they coordinate their efforts. Different types of salesforces can coordinate their efforts several ways, including (1) informal cooperation among salespeople serving the same account, (2) informal coaching by competent supervisors, (3) formal sales training, and (4) formal measurement systems.[5]

EXHIBIT 8.6

HYBRID SALES ORGANIZATION

Activity	Large	Mid-Sized	Small
		Account Size	
Prospecting/qualifying	NAM	TM	TM
Presentation/closing	NAM	FTF	TM
Service/repeat	NAM	TM	TM

NOTE: FTF = face-to-face selling; NAM = national account management; TM = telemarketing

EXHIBIT 8.7
BUYER/NATIONAL ACCOUNT REP SALES INTERACTION

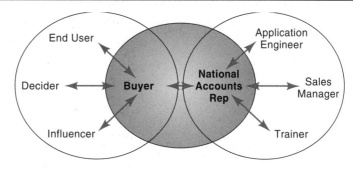

National Account Management

National account management (NAM) is a team approach to selling to a firm's largest customers. National account teams usually combine a national accounts manager, who is responsible for coordinating communication between the customer and the seller, with other members of the selling organization as needed, such as applications engineers, trainers, and service technicians. Exhibit 8.7 shows a range of influences on both the buyer and the salesperson. NAM allows sellers to meet a frequently heard request from major buyers: "Give us one contact who can speak for your entire company."[6]

Why Adopt NAM?   One study shows that the most important reason companies adopt NAM is to increase sales. With NAM sales are expected to increase in three ways: (1) by protecting and retaining large customers, (2) by increasing sales to current customers, and (3) by enhancing working relationships with current customers.[7] NAM programs deliver very high levels of service to major accounts.[8] One firm that uses NAM is Fritz Companies, Inc., a leading provider of logistics services headquartered in San Francisco. The Fritz Companies provides a comprehensive set of transportation services to very large users, including over half of the *Fortune* 1,000. Each user requires a unique set of transportation services, including warehousing at multiple sites, trucking, inland waterway shipping, rail, air, and import and export assistance. Virtually all of Fritz's customers are national accounts, and the salesforce is composed almost solely of national account managers. The national account program was initiated by Lynn Fritz, president and CEO, who saw it as the best means for providing the sophisticated services required by these large customers: "I have been fortunate to accomplish a few things over the course of my career, and one of my most notable accomplishments as far as I am concerned is my activity for the Fritz Companies as National Account Executive Number One."[9]

A Process for Adopting NAM.   Adopting NAM is a six-step process, as shown in Exhibit 8.8.[10]

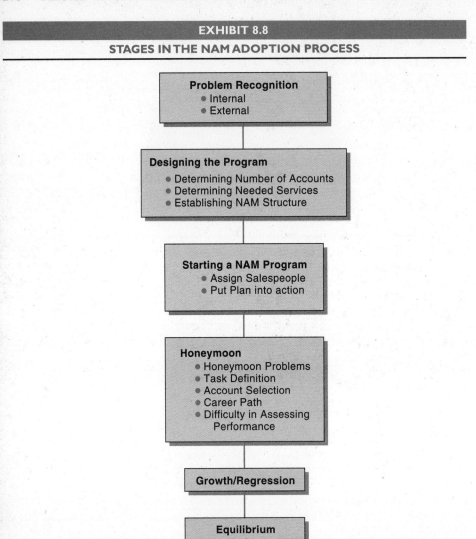

EXHIBIT 8.8

STAGES IN THE NAM ADOPTION PROCESS

Stage 1: Problem Recognition.   The first stage in adopting NAM is to recognize that a problem exists. Usually, there are external and internal signs. *External signs* include customers with special needs, loss of business, and good NAM programs by competitors. These signs usually appear when firms utilize a field salesforce and the salesforce cannot meet customer's special needs.

Internal signs that NAM could be useful include overloaded salespeople and poor internal communication. Salespeople can become overloaded when the needs of customers outstrip their ability to provide service. For example, suppose a large customer makes all copier purchases at headquarters but requires training on the copiers at each location. A single salesperson would be hard-pressed to make the sale and provide service to all the customer's locations. An NAM approach, by contrast, would coordinate training programs at all the customer's locations. Poor internal communication can occur when a customer has multiple locations in different geographic areas served by different salespeople. If one salesperson offers a discount or accelerated delivery, the customer may request similar service from the salespeople in other areas. If the salespeople are not all using the same customer service guidelines, problems with the customer can result.

Stage 2: Designing a Program.   Designing the NAM program consists of three interrelated elements: (1) determining the number of accounts, (2) determining the needed services, and (3) establishing the structure of the NAM organization. *Determining the number of accounts* consists of identifying those accounts that are very large, have very complex purchasing requirements, or have high customer service needs.[11] These issues must be considered in tandem. For instance, it is possible for a small customer to have complex service needs but for its purchases to not justify the expense of NAM.

Determining needed services involves a careful evaluation of the customer's service needs. Often this evaluation may show that the customer has needs that currently are not being served. For example, when J.C. Penney undertook the task of redesigning its work spaces, an office furniture supplier showed Penney's that its interior design group could do the job quicker and cheaper than Penney's could.[12]

In addition, the services provided to national accounts are often the same as those provided to other customers. These services include complaint resolution, prepurchase advising, inventory management, dealer support, post-sale support, and training. The key difference is in the degree of service provided. National accounts receive higher levels of these services than do accounts served by other means.

Establishing the structure of the NAM organization is done by determining whether it is part-time, division, corporate, or a separate division. A part-time structure, staffed by corporate executives or top salespeople, is common when a firm has only a few large customers. The division structure is common when the customer uses only the product made in that division. A corporate structure or a separate division is common when the customer uses products made by different divisions within the selling organization.

Stage 3: Starting an NAM Program.   In starting an NAM program, the firm must assign salespeople to accounts and put the NAM structure into action. NAM salespeople typically have more experience with the company and industry than the salesforce at large. The importance of customers makes it necessary for the seller to ensure that the customer has a high degree of comfort with the salesperson.

In putting the plan into action, the seller can implement NAM gradually or all at once. *Gradual implementation* means that NAM is introduced division by division, market by market, or customer by customer. Gradual implementation is possible in situations where there is no compelling competitive reason to start the program immediately. The advantage of gradual implementation is that it allows the seller to work out any problems without damaging relationships with the seller's large customers. *All-at-once implementation* occurs when there is a compelling competitive reason to do so. The disadvantage of this approach is that any problems with the NAM program will affect all the seller's large customers.

Stage 4: Honeymoon. During the honeymoon period, which is a short period immediately after the NAM program is put into place, both buyers and the seller have great expectations for the rewards that should come from NAM. The potential rewards seem large, and the potential costs seem small.

During this time, however, some of the problems inherent in the NAM approach become apparent. These problems include task definition, account selection, career paths, and measurement criteria. *Task definition* problems generally occur when the responsibilities of the task are not clearly defined. For example, most national account managers become responsible for all communication between the customer and the seller. Although this is fine if the communication is positive, it is often difficult for salespeople to become hard-nosed collectors of past-due payments. Yet, in many cases, since collection is one of the types of communication between buyer and seller, the national account manager becomes responsible for that as well. National account managers must recognize that they are responsible for the entire relationship between the seller and the buyer—including the tasks that may be less palatable.

Account selection problems are of two types. The first occurs when the seller does not include in the national account structure all accounts that require a high level of service. This leads to certain accounts not receiving the level of attention they need and results in lost sales. When the basis of selecting national accounts is current sales levels, this problem is particularly acute. If a major buyer is not currently a large customer, it can be overlooked in selecting accounts for the program. To overcome this, the seller should use actual and potential sales in determining which buyers will become national accounts. A firm that sells parts to the auto industry but does not currently sell to the Chrysler Corporation, for example, should still consider Chrysler a national account because of potential sales.

The other type of account selection problem occurs when the seller identifies too many buyers as national accounts. If this occurs, the seller may be serving accounts whose level of sales cannot justify the expense of a national account effort. To overcome this problem, the seller must gather information on level of sales revenue and cost to serve each account. (See Stage 5: Growth/Regression for more detail.)

Salespeople selected as national account managers can experience some *career path* problems. National account managers can become so important in the relationship between the large customer and the seller that the seller is reluctant to promote the salesperson. As a result, the national account manager has a position with prestige and high pay, but there may be little chance for upward mobility. Further, from the seller's standpoint, if the salesperson leaves the firm the relationship between the seller and the buyer can be jeopardized. Career paths are a continuing question for national account management.

Another problem that occurs during the honeymoon stage is the *difficulty of assessing performance.* The national account manager is in charge of the entire relationship with the major customer but relies on numerous other individuals within the selling firm to provide the high levels of customer service demanded by national accounts. How should the national account manager be compensated and evaluated? Focusing on individual sales may be counterproductive if the goal is to develop a long-term relationship with the customer. (Compensating national account managers is addressed in greater detail in Chapter 13.)

Stage 5: Growth/Regression.   The duration and results of stage 5 are dependent on the resolution of problems in the honeymoon stage. If the honeymoon problems are addressed, the program can grow, adding more accounts and providing additional services to existing accounts. If the honeymoon problems are not addressed, the program can be scaled back significantly or even eliminated.

One of the common issues that occurs in the growth/regression stage is the modification of a seller's information systems. Firms find that in order to manage their NAM program, they need access to information on revenues and costs by account. It is not difficult to get revenue by account, but it can be extremely hard to get cost information by account.[13] Cost information is commonly organized by product, production plant, or market served, but not by customer. Yet without cost information by account, the seller does not know how much it can spend in serving the account and still make profitability targets.

Stage 6: Equilibrium.   In the equilibrium stage, all profitable accounts are under the NAM program. The emphasis shifts from identifying new national accounts to maintaining strong relationships with existing national accounts. One problem that can occur in this stage is that sellers sometimes focus so completely on serving existing accounts that they fail to recognize market changes. For example, in the U.S. agricultural implement industry, the number of major manufacturers has severely dropped in the last 10 years owing to foreign competition and depressed economies in the agricultural states. If a supplier to these manufacturers used national account management, these managers would focus on serving the needs of the agricultural implement manufacturers. National account managers who did not recognize the structural changes occurring in the market as a whole, missed the shift in manufacture of agricultural implements from domestic to foreign producers. If no national account manager was in charge of developing relationships with foreign producers, the supplier would be in the position of having strong relationships with weak domestic producers, and weak relationships with strong foreign producers.

Factors Affecting the Success of NAM.   One of the most important factors affecting the success of NAM is the selling situation. If customers wish to make purchases based on a long-term relationship, then NAM will probably be successful. On the other hand, if customers see sellers as interchangeable, NAM efforts will probably have little success. A variety of other factors affect the success of NAM efforts (see Exhibit 8.9). The most important of these are the integration of NAM into the overall sales effort of the firm and support of NAM from senior management.

Team Selling

A **sales team** is a group of people representing the seller. Sales teams differ from national account teams in several ways. National account teams are assigned to specific customers; they have relatively stable membership and focus on developing long-term customer relationships. Sales teams, however, are assigned to accomplish specific types of transactions; they have fluid membership and focus on transactions.[14] Sales teams include members who have high levels of expertise in different aspects of the product. Metaphor Computer Systems, for example, will put a sales rep, systems engineer, and applications consultant[15] on a sales team to identify a cus-

EXHIBIT 8.9

ISSUES AFFECTING THE SUCCESS OF NAM

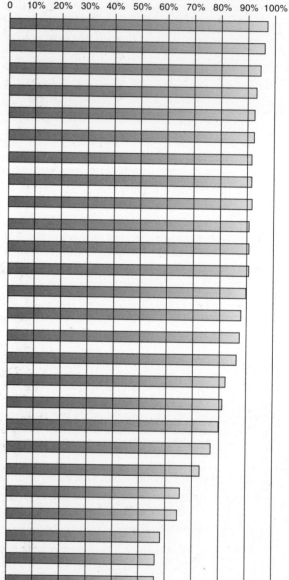

Factors affecting program success

Percent of respondents judging factor to be of "critical" or "considerable" importance to program success*

Integration of national account program into overall sales effort

Senior management's understanding and support of national account unit's role

Clear and practical lines of communication to and from outlying sales and service units

Establishment of national account goals and missions

Compatible working relations with regular sales management and field personnel

Definition and identification of customers for national account status

Full utilization of national account unit's skills and vantage point

National account unit's grasp of company's capabilities for serving national accounts

Organizational structure and position of national account unit(s)

Recognized status for national account unit

Precisely defined responsibilities and authority for national account and personnel

Close monitoring of account activity

Staffing of the national account unit

Development and motivation of national account personnel

Field-level knowledge and support of national account mission

Indoctrination of rest of company on national account aims and program

Overcoming potential resistance by regular sales and service organization to national account missions

Development and maintenance of commercial intelligence on national accounts

Ensuring adherence to agreed-upon sales and service procedures for individual accounts

Specialized backup support for national account personnel

Interfacing and division of labor between regular sales force and national account units

Establishment of national account incentives and rewards for national account units

Equitable resolution of selling credit issues

Appropriate mix of "staff" and "line" roles for national account personnel

Establishment of national account incentives and rewards for regular sales and service units and personnel

Balancing of interests among divisions and between divisions and the corporation as a whole

*Based on information for 122 companies.

SOURCE: Linda Cardillo Platzer, *Managing National Accounts*, Reports #850 (New York: The Conference Board, 1984), 14.

EXHIBIT 8.10

MATCHING SELLING TEAMS AND BUYING CENTERS

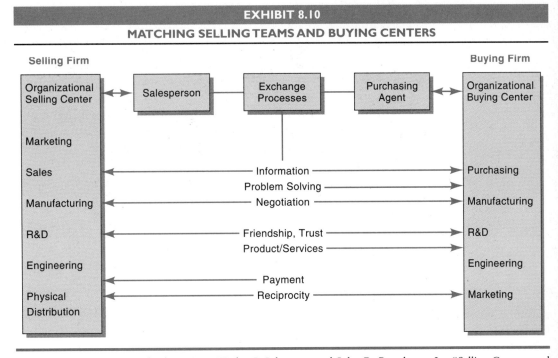

SOURCE: Michael D. Hutt, Wesley J. Johnston, and John R. Ronchetto, Jr., "Selling Centers and Buying Centers: Formulating Strategic Exchange Patterns," *Journal of Personal Selling and Sales Management,* 5 (May 1985): 333.

tomer's needs, design a system to meet those needs, and negotiate the sale. Sales teams are commonly used with customers that have large buying centers (see Chapter 7 for a more detailed discussion of buying centers). Exhibit 8.10 shows how the sales team of the seller matches with the members of the buying center. Notice, for example, that while the salesperson is the contact with the purchasing agent, a manufacturing engineer from the seller may meet with a manufacturing engineer from the buyer to discuss technical issues related to product use.

Telemarketing

Recall from Chapter 2 that telemarketing is a systematic and continuous program of communicating with customers and prospects via telephone and other electronic media. Using the telephone allows sellers to conduct a two-way dialog with their customers that is personal and flexible, although not face-to-face. Telemarketing is one of the fastest growing marketing channels. Over 70 percent of all respondents in a study by the Conference Board (a nonprofit organization that performs research on business issues) report that their firms use telemarketing,[16] and *Business Week* predicts the creation of more than 8 million new jobs in the telemarketing industry by the year 2000.[17] To put that in perspective, in 1994 there were over 2 million people working in the telemarketing industry, and telemarketers generated in excess of $500 billion in sales.[18]

EXHIBIT 8.11

TELEMARKETING JOB CLASSIFICATION SCHEME

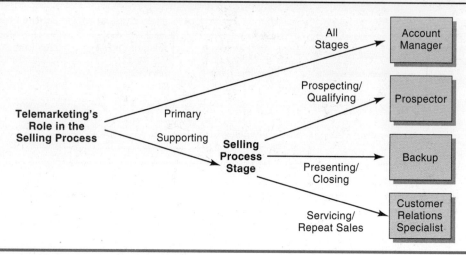

SOURCE: William Moncrief, Shannon Shipp, Charles Lamb, and David Cravens, "Examining the Roles of Telemarketing in Selling Strategies," *Journal of Personal Selling and Sales Management,* 9 (Fall 1989): 1–12.

Telemarketing can be structured in one of three roles: supporting, primary, or combination (see Exhibit 8.11).

Supporting Role.   A **supporting role** is assigned to telemarketing when a field sales-force is required to deliver a high level of face-to-face customer contact. For example, Goodyear's Shoe Products division uses field salespeople to demonstrate the design potential of new shoe sole materials to shoe manufacturers. When shoe manufacturers wish to make a routine reorder, however, they call the telemarketing sales representative. Honeywell's Temperature Controls division also uses telemarketing to support its field salesforce. When a qualified lead is identified, the telemarketing rep contacts the lead and determines if he or she needs any materials, such as samples or product specification sheets, in advance of the field salesperson's visit. By ascertaining the customer's needs in advance, the field salesperson's time can be used more efficiently, and the customer's needs can be addressed more directly during the sales call itself.

Primary Role.   A **primary role** is assigned when a firm uses telemarketing representatives instead of a field salesforce. This is appropriate for firms under the following circumstances: the buying process is routine (such as the straight rebuy discussed in Chapter 7), each purchase has a relatively low dollar value, there is a large and widely dispersed customer base that does not make orders large enough to justify frequent contact by a field salesperson, and the product is standard and nontechnical. Firms using telemarketing as their primary selling method include Dell Computer and Quill Office Products.

Combination Role. A **combination role** is assigned when a firm has large customers that order in sufficient quantity and require high levels of customer service that cannot be satisfied solely through telemarketing, but also small customers who do not order in sufficient quantity to justify field sales calls. In this case, telemarketing acts in a support role with the large customers and in a primary role with the small customers.

Growth in Telemarketing. The growth in telemarketing jobs has occurred for several reasons: cost, territory coverage, ease of expanding or eliminating territories, customer relations, and breadth of account coverage.[19] Each reason is described in greater detail in the following paragraphs.

Cost. Telemarketing can be a significantly less expensive method than field sales representatives for developing and maintaining customer contact. According to a study conducted by McGraw-Hill, the average cost of a face-to-face sales call exceeds $225. The average number of calls to close a single sale is 4.3. A single sale, therefore, can cost close to $1,000. Keep in mind that this is an average, which means the costs to close sales in certain industries can be significantly higher. Moreover, the selling costs can skyrocket if the top managers at a firm become involved in the selling process.

Many smaller accounts do not represent sufficiently high potential to make it profitable for sellers to expend such resources to close the sale. For these smaller customers, sellers look for less expensive means. Since telemarketing sales calls cost, on average, less than $25 each, many sellers have begun to use telemarketing as a means of utilizing their resources more efficiently.

Telemarketers can call on customers locally, within the country, or around the world without incurring travel costs. David Schraffler, the national sales manager of Network Security Systems, Inc. (NSSI), a San Diego–based manufacturer of hardware and software, realized he had a problem when the travel costs for his six-person salesforce exceeded per-sale revenue. He converted his outside salespeople to telemarketers, and reduced costs while increasing sales by 43 percent in 15 months.[20]

Territory Coverage. Firms that use telemarketing can easily expand or eliminate territories. To open a new territory with a field salesforce, a salesperson must be recruited, learn the geography of the territory, and determine the most efficient means to serve the territory. Opening a new territory with a telemarketing representative is much simpler because the telemarketer can focus efforts on learning the customers instead of the territory.

Customer Relations. Telemarketing also allows sellers to create and maintain stronger customer relationships with small accounts than is possible through a field salesforce. One key variable in a strong customer relationship is frequency of contact. Small accounts often do not justify the expense of frequent calls by a field salesperson. Since the cost per contact of a telemarketing call is so much less than that of a field sales call, small accounts can be called upon much more frequently, and their needs can be monitored more closely.

BOX 8.1

TELEMARKETING MYTHS

MYTH 1: TELEMARKETING IS A STAND-ALONE PROGRAM WITHIN THE FIRM

One common use of telemarketing is in the generation and qualification of leads. This is a natural use for telemarketing because its cost per contact is so much less than face-to-face selling. This use must be carefully designed and monitored, however, to ensure that telemarketing representatives and field sales representatives work together. The field salesforce can often feel threatened by their firm's use of telemarketing and concerned that their jobs are at risk. Field salespeople who feel threatened may ignore the telemarketing rep's leads or declare the leads not worth following up, thereby seeking to put the telemarketing efforts in a poor light. To overcome this problem, field salespeople and telemarketing representatives should be jointly trained and managed to ensure their efforts are integrated.

MYTH 2: TO GET STARTED WITH TELEMARKETING, JUST MAKE A FEW CALLS AND SEE HOW IT GOES

Conducting small tests of telemarketing before introducing it to all of the firm's customers or markets is a prudent precaution. However, the small-scale test should be part of a planned strategy to integrate telemarketing into the firm's selling effort. It is not appropriate to simply start telemarketing without carefully considering issues such as the objectives of the telemarketing operation; the relationships with the field salesforce and other elements of the firm's selling effort, and the possible impact of telemarketing sales on manufacturing and delivery schedules with existing customers.

MYTH 3: TELEMARKETING IS EASY; ANYONE CAN DO IT

Too many companies believe that telemarketing is a semiskilled, clerical job. While this may be true with sales jobs that require only order taking, many firms that use telemarketing for more demanding selling tasks find that they need workers with more skills. For example, when Ecolab instituted telemarketing for small accounts in its division that sold dishwashing equipment and supplies, it assumed that the small accounts would purchase only supplies. However, Ecolab found that the small accounts wanted to purchase equipment as well. Since the firm had originally planned for telemarketing reps to handle only routine supply reorders, this customer preference caused Ecolab to upgrade its training of telemarketers so they could also sell equipment.

MYTH 4: ANYONE CAN MANAGE THE TELEMARKETING GROUP; JUST ASSIGN IT TO SOMEONE WHO HAS THE TIME

Telemarketing managers face several unique challenges, including worker issues, difficulties in integrating the telemarketing operation into the overall sales effort, and lack of training. In terms of worker issues, one study found that managers of telemarketers need to pay special attention to

---

Breadth of Account Coverage.   Finally, telemarketers can serve many more accounts than can be covered effectively by a field salesperson. This assumes that the customers are relatively small and need standard products with little technical assistance. Ecolab found that each of its telemarketers could contact 200 customers per week, while few of its field sales representatives could make more than 25 calls per week.

Despite the advantages of telemarketing, many firms are only using it in a limited way. Linda Neff, the president of Marketing Connections, a telemarketing firm with several offices nationwide, suggests several myths that prevent firms from us-

---

Box 8.1 (continued)
TELEMARKETING MYTHS

motivation and job satisfaction issues because many of the intrinsic aspects of the field sales job, such as freedom to set one's hours and travel, are absent from telemarketing.[21] Many telemarketing operations have a combination role: to service small accounts and to help the field salesforce service large customers. As a result, an important part of managing the telemarketing organization is integrating the selling efforts of the telemarketers and the field salesforce.

Unfortunately, despite worker issues and the need to integrate telemarketing with the field salesforce, there are few opportunities for individuals to learn how to manage telemarketers. Few colleges offer courses in telemarketing. Also, only a few managers in most companies have had much experience in telemarketing because it is a relatively new field. To help get telemarketing programs underway, many companies hire consultants to manage such an operation.[22]

MYTH 5: FIELD SALESPEOPLE SHOULD GENERATE THEIR OWN LEADS SO THEY RETAIN CONTROL OF THEIR TERRITORIES

This argument has been used to justify not using telemarketing in a supporting role. However, telemarketing can be a valuable adjunct for field sales. One particularly important area for telemarketing—because of potential cost savings—is in the generation of leads and the qualifying of prospects.

In addition to cost savings, telemarketing can offer significant time advantages. Because a telemarketing representative can contact up to 200 customers or prospects per week, while a field salesperson will average 25 contacts per week, the savings in time using telemarketing can be significant. It would take 5 weeks of a telemarketing rep's time to qualify 1,000 customers, while it would take 50 weeks of a field salesperson's time.

Another reason to use telemarketers to qualify leads is to keep field salespeople from having to make cold calls. Cold-calling is the area of selling that generally yields the highest level of rejection. Not surprisingly, many salespeople avoid cold-calling. Providing pregenerated and prequalified leads is one way to increase the motivation of the field salesforce.

MYTH 6: TELEMARKETING IS CHEAP

Telemarketing calls are certainly less expensive than calls by a field sales representative. However, this does not mean that a company will incur lower selling costs immediately upon implementing telemarketing. First, integrating telemarketing with the field salesforce must be carefully planned. Based on the plan, telemarketers and telemarketing managers must be recruited and trained, and motivation and compensation systems must be implemented. The company will also incur equipment costs for installing telemarketing systems. In the short term, these added costs will probably mask some of the savings that can be accrued through the use of telemarketing.

---

ing telemarketing to its full potential.[21] Those myths and the corresponding realities, are described in Box 8.1.[3]

Part-Time Salespeople

The proportion of **part-time employees,** those who work less than the traditional 40-hour week, has increased considerably over the last 25 years. In 1968, 28.9 percent of all employees worked part-time; in 1990, the proportion had risen to 34.6 percent.[24]

For many companies, part-time salespeople are the answer to two vexing questions in sales management: (1) how to have enough people on hand during the peak seasons without having too many people during the slack seasons, and (2) how to perform additional duties without hiring additional full-time salespeople. The first question is primarily a problem for firms with highly seasonal demand. For example, retail stores in the United States sell a disproportionate amount of merchandise during the Christmas season. As a result, they have a high seasonal demand for salespeople. Retail stores however, do not wish to hire these salespeople on a full-time basis because they are not needed during the rest of the year.

The second question occurs because full-time salespeople are finding that competing demands on their time brought about by a rapid pace of new product introductions increased customer service demands, and increased demands to develop customer relationships keep them from performing all the duties of their job description. Using part-time people to assist full-time salespeople allows the full-timers to concentrate on more complex, challenging selling tasks while redistributing less complicated tasks to part-time sales staff.[25]

Part-time salespeople are used extensively in retailing and by companies who use telemarketing. Lowndes Queensway, a large furniture and retailing company in the United Kingdom, has hired over 1,700 part-time salespeople to staff its stores.[26] Lowndes Queensway has found several advantages in using part-time salespeople. For one, part-time salespeople provide scheduling flexibility. They can be used to staff evenings and weekends, and they can provide peak time staffing during holidays and sale periods. Lowndes Queensway has also found that part-timers are more productive, on an hourly basis, than the full-time salesforce. Another major advantage is that the opportunity to work part-time opens up employment opportunities for those who cannot or do not wish to work full-time, such as students, retirees, and parents with young children. As a result, the workforce has become more diverse and more empathetic to a diverse clientele.

Part-timers are also widely used by telemarketing firms. One national department store chain uses part-time salespeople to call customers who have recently purchased major appliances. These salespeople attempt to sell long-term maintenance agreements that remain in force after the original factory warranty expires. Many magazines and newspapers use part-time telemarketers to sell subscriptions. In the late 1980s, British Airways hired 60 part-time salespeople to make calls on U.S. travel agents. These new salespeople made calls to 10,000 travel agents—up from 4,000 agents the previous year. The result of this effort: British Airways saw a 40 percent increase in leisure travel sales.

Part-time workers pose unique management challenges. Part-time salespeople have different patterns of job satisfaction, feel more role conflict, and are different demographically from the full-time salesforce.[27] They also cost more per sales dollar to train than full-time workers, and they may not be as familiar with their employer's business practices or sales approaches.[28] As a result, traditional sales management practices may not work with part-time salesforces; in fact; they may have a detrimental effect.[29] Exhibit 8.12 shows why full-time and part-time workers quit their jobs. Notice that for full-time salespeople issues such as work surroundings and company assignments are important reasons to leave a job, whereas non-job-

EXHIBIT 8.12	
WHY PART-TIME AND FULL-TIME EMPLOYEES QUIT THEIR JOBS	
Reason for Quitting	More Important To:
Job-related	
Work surroundings/physical conditions	FT
Preference for different company assignments	FT
Reduction in incentive programs	FT
Opportunity for advancement	FT
Friction with supervisor	FT
Compensation/wages	FT
Non-job-related	
Increased responsibility outside of company	PT
Starting/returning to school	PT
Conflict with another job	PT
Transportation problems	PT
Relocation	PT
General scheduling factors	
Time of day scheduled	PT
Too many hours scheduled	PT
Too few hours scheduled	PT

NOTE: FT = full time; PT = part-time.

SOURCE: Ellen F. Jackofsky, James Salter, and Lawrence H. Peters, "Reducing Turnover Among Part-Time Employees," *Personnel* (May 1986): 41–43.

related issues such as increased responsibility outside of the company and starting/returning to school are important for part-time salespeople. This means that to retain part-time salespeople, managers might need to stress scheduling and partial benefits rather than use the more traditional turnover-reducing strategies of realistic job previews, job enrichment, and altering supervisory behavior for full-time salespeople.

Electronic Data Interchange

Electronic data interchange (EDI) is the electronic exchange of information between business partners in a structured format.[30] EDI helps firms increase customer service by shortening order response time, and reduce costs by lowering required inventory levels. The use of EDI is increasing rapidly. Between 1992 and 1994, the usage of EDI approximately doubled, from 21.1 percent of businesses to 40.7 percent.

The role of salespeople in firms that implement EDI changes dramatically because pricing, product availability, and invoicing become mechanized. Because salespeople no longer have to perform these routine clerical tasks, they have the opportunity to be more creative and spend more time identifying and solving customer problems. Some of the possible effects of EDI on the sales function are listed in Exhibit 8.13. In essence, EDI eliminates the need for the routine order taker (see Chapter 1 for a discussion of different types of salespeople).

EXHIBIT 8.13		
POSSIBLE EFFECTS OF EDI ON THE SALES FUNCTION		
Function	Advantage of EDI	Disadvantage of EDI
Sales	• Allows more time for non–order taking functions • Covers more customers • Lowers error rates • Frees salesperson to be more creative, original • Allows better access to diagnostic, trend reports	• Removes salesperson from information loop • All customers may not be able to do EDI—requires dual system
Order processing	• Reduces (eliminates) personnel to receive orders • Allows faster order response • Supplies better accuracy	• May lose some person-to-person contact • Lacks human intervention to find potential errors
Order filling	• Can sort order in warehouse pick sequence	• Needs no original signatures

SOURCE: Ned C. Hill and Michael J. Swenson, "The Impact of Electronic Data Interchange on the Sales Function," *Journal of Personal Selling and Sales Management,* 14(3) (Summer 1994): 82.

INDEPENDENT SALES ORGANIZATIONS

After deciding on the type and structure of the salesforce, managers must decide whether the salespeople should be employees or independent. **Independent sales organizations** are composed of individuals who are not employees of the selling organization. Types of independent sales organizations include manufacturer's representatives, dealers or distributors, brokers, commission merchants, and selling agents. Managers who select an independent sales organization to perform the selling function are relieved of the day-to-day responsibility of management issues such as recruiting, training, compensation, motivation, and performance evaluation.

Manufacturers' Representatives

Manufacturers' representatives, or manufacturer's reps, are independent firms that represent two or more complementary lines of merchandise. They have agreements with the manufacturers they represent (referred to as *principals*) that cover issues such as training, account coverage, pricing, ordering procedures, and other issues related to representing the line. Manufacturers' reps are typically paid on a commission basis only. Exhibit 8.14 shows the rate of usage of manufacturers' reps by company size, product or service, type of buyer, and industry. It also shows the average commission paid by category.

There has been a growing trend over the last few years for firms to increase their use of manufacturers' reps.[31] Some of the advantages of using manufacturers' reps include lower fixed selling costs (since manufacturers' reps are typically paid straight commission), less need for sales management, low cost national coverage (especially important for start-up firms with limited capital or for firms considering entering a new territory or wishing to test a new product), and immediate market coverage (because manufacturers' reps are experienced salespeople who already know their territory, there is little or no "start-up" time).

EXHIBIT 8.14		
USE OF MANUFACTURERS' REPRESENTATIVES		
	Percent Using Manufacturers' Reps	Average Commission (percent of sales)
Company size		
under $5 million	20.2	13.3
$5MM–$25MM	34.9	11.1
$25MM–$100MM	24.5	6.1
$100MM–$250MM	10.0	12.0
over $250MM	14.3	15.3
Product or service		
Consumer products	26.8	11.4
Consumer services	11.3	12.8
Industrial products	33.0	9.1
Industrial services	14.6	13.2
Office products	20.6	15.3
Office services	13.2	15.9
Type of buyer		
Consumers	19.0	14.7
Distributors	25.5	11.0
Industry	23.4	10.5
Retailers	19.5	9.9
Industry		
Business services	12.2	23.8
Chemicals	50.0	13.3
Communications	25.0	8.8
Electronics	50.0	9.4
Fabricated metals	44.4	16.5
Instruments	60.0	10.3
Insurance	7.7	12.0
Machinery	40.0	8.0
Manufacturing	50.0	12.5
Paper and allied products	25.0	9.5
Printing and publishing	28.6	12.5
Retail	25.0	5.0
Wholesale (consumer goods)	9.1	5.0
Wholesale (industrial goods)	15.4	7.5

SOURCE: *A Portrait of Today's Salesforce,* (Dartnell Corp., 1992), 171.

In a study by *Sales and Marketing Management,* however, over 40 percent of the 200 principals surveyed said they were dissatisfied with their reps.[32] Reasons for the dissatisfaction centered around the reps spending too little time on their products, the reps not adequately representing the entire line, limited control by the principal over the types and locations of customer contacts, and the small degree of customer feedback. Additional problems with reps included their unwillingness to undergo training or do anything else that takes away from selling time (since the rep is on a commission basis), and the cost disadvantage of using a commission-only salesforce when sales volumes are high. Along with these specific problems, many managers also felt uncomfortable using a salesforce over which they had little direct control.

EXHIBIT 8.15

INTERNAL SALESFORCE VS. MANUFACTURERS' REPRESENTATIVES

State	Forecasted Sales	Current Sales	Amount Under Forecast	Foregone Margin	Added Fixed Expense	Commission Increase	Gain (Loss)
A	$5,096,000	$2,500,00	$2,596,000	$649,00	$125,000	$230,760	$293,240
B	$4,270,000	$4,00,000	$270,000	$67,500	$125,000	$136,200	($193,700)
C	$1,596,000	$1,300,00	$296,000	$74,000	$125,000	$56,760	($107,760)

Where

Forecasted Sales = Sales forecast for the state

Current Sales = Current sales in the region using manufacturers' representatives

Amount Under Forecast = Forecasted sales minus current sales

Foregone Margin = Amount under forecast times average gross margin, where average gross margin is assumed to equal 25 percent. This assumes that a company salesforce should sell the forecasted amount.

Added Fixed Expenses: Increase in sales management and other fixed costs of keeping a company salesforce in the field. This amount is estimated to be $125,000 for each state.

Commission Increase: Increase in commission expected due to switching to a company salesforce. This figure is based on a manufacturers' representative's commission of 3% on all sales, and a company salesperson's commission on 6% on all sales. To calculate the commission increase, multiply the forecasted sales for the region by 6% (this yields the total commission to be paid to the company salesperson) and subtract 3% times the current sales (this yields the current commission paid to the manufacturers' representatives).

Gain (loss): This is calculated by adding fixed expense and commission increase together and subtracting that total from foregone margin. This is the amount that the company stands to gain or lose by switching to a company salesforce.

Result: From this analysis above, the only territory in which the firm should switch from a manufacturers' representative to an internal salesforce is State A. The firm will lose money by switching to an internal salesforce in States B and C.

It is not surprising, therefore, that some firms have switched from manufacturers' reps to internal salesforces. This decision must not be made lightly, however. Exhibit 8.15 illustrates a method for considering the switch from independent to internal salesforce based on territory potential. Of course, the model should be only one input to the decision. Industry competition, availability of substitute reps, and availability of in-house sales management expertise must also be considered.

Dealers/Distributors

For many firms, dealers are an extremely important route to market.[33] **Dealers** are independent firms that represent a variety of manufacturers. One important type of dealer is the industrial distributor. Industrial distributors buy goods from producers and resell them, along with associated services, to organizational customers such as commercial or government accounts.[34] Industrial distributors that sell plumbing equipment, electrical supplies, lumber, and other products are common in the construction industry. Dealers offer intensive (yet limited) geographic coverage, service capabilities, and (generally) financing terms to creditworthy customers. Dealers can also enhance (or detract from) the image of the product through the quality of the sales support provided. As a result, the recruitment and maintenance of a sound dealer organization is very important for sellers who elect this option.

Unfortunately, from the seller's standpoint, good dealers often have many manufacturers' product lines from which to choose. As a result, sales managers must devote a great deal of time not only to selecting good dealers, but also to persuading them to carry the firm's products as well. Realistically, unless the product line represents a substantial part of the dealer's revenue stream, the seller may not be able to pick and choose among potential dealers. However, if the seller's product line represents a substantial part of the dealer's revenue stream, the seller can be selective in developing a dealer network.

Sales managers should consider the following guidelines in recruiting a dealer network:

- *Develop a profile of preferred dealers.* This profile should be based on the characteristics of successful dealers in the industry and should include information on the dealers' areas of specialization, staffing (number of employees, experience, and training), and business history.
- *Locate dealers who match this profile.* Use trade journal ads, mailing lists, and personal contacts.
- *Contact the dealers who match the profile.* Contact can be made with a telephone call or direct mail solicitation.
- *Qualify the dealers who respond.* This can be a multiple part process involving further telephone contact, a written dealer application, and a credit check. If the number of dealers qualified falls short of the seller's need for market coverage, the seller can recontact those who did not respond to the original solicitation or seek a new mailing list.

Once the dealer network has been recruited, the seller must develop or enhance the dealers' selling skills. To accomplish this, sales managers should follow certain guidelines:

- Provide training on basic product characteristics.
- Perform joint sales calls on important customers using employees of the seller and the salesforce of the dealer. At the beginning of the relationship, the seller's employees may take more of the lead. After some time, the dealer's salesforce should take the lead.
- Conduct weekly telephone briefings and sales analysis.

Continually monitor and upgrade dealers' skills. If a dealer does not meet sales standards, there should be swift action to find out the cause of the problem. If the problem cannot be solved, the dealer should be terminated and the dealer recruitment process should begin anew.

Other Sales Options

Firms can also choose from an array of other methods to sell their merchandise, such as brokers, commission merchants, and selling agents.[35] Many of these methods are specific to a particular type of transaction. For example, a firm that wishes to sell some of its real estate holdings can call a real-estate broker. The main function of a **broker** is to bring together buyers and sellers for the purpose of making a sale. Brokers, unlike dealers, do not take title to goods. Brokers are paid on a straight commission. In addition to real estate, brokers are also common in the insurance and stock brokerage industries. **Commission merchants** sell agricultural commodities from farmers who do not wish to sell their own output and who do not belong to a producers' cooperative. **Selling agents** are independent reps who have contractual authority to sell the entire output of their principals. Selling agents are used to sell textiles, industrial machinery and equipment, coal and coke, bulk chemicals, and bulk metals.

SUMMARY

Sales managers are faced with three decisions when designing a sales organization. The decisions address salesforce type, salesforce structure, and ownership of the salesforce. Types of sales organizations include field salesforce, national account management, team selling, telemarketing, part-time salespeople, and electronic data interchange. Within each type are several structural options for firms to consider. For example, a field salesforce can be organized geographically, by product, by customer, by function or activity, or as a hybrid of these.

Sales managers must also decide the ownership of the salesforce. Should the salesforce be made up of employees from the selling firm or an independent organization? Types of independent sales organizations include manufacturer's representatives, dealers or distributors, brokers, commission merchants, and selling agents. Using independent sales organizations has several advantages for the selling firm, including lower fixed costs, less need for sales management, immediate market coverage, low-cost national coverage, and immediate access to salespeople familiar with the market. The major disadvantage of using independent sales organizations is the lack of the selling firm's control over their activities. Since most independent sales organizations are paid only when a sale is made, they are often reluctant to spend time on nonselling activities that the manufacturer finds important, such as training, customer service, and collections.

KEY TERMS

sales organizations	primary role
field salesforce	combination role
geographically based salesforce	part-time employees
product-based salesforce	electronic data interchange (EDI)
market/account-based salesforce	independent sales organizations
activity/function-based salesforce	manufacturers' representatives
hybrid salesforce	dealers
national account management (NAM)	broker
sales team	commission merchants
supporting role	selling agents

DISCUSSION QUESTIONS

1. Why is sales organization important?
2. What are six salesforce types?
3. How can newer selling methods, such as team selling, national account management, and telemarketing, be used to replace or supplement field salesforces?
4. How can field sales organizations be organized? What are the advantages and disadvantages of each type?
5. Why is national account management (NAM) important to a company?
6. What is the process for adopting NAM?
7. Why has telemarketing become such an important tool in marketing?
8. When should a firm use independent versus integrated salesforces?
9. How should sales managers go about recruiting a dealer network?
10. What are the difference between part-time and full-time salespeople in terms of their reasons for quitting? How might these differences affect sales managers' treatment of the two groups?

PROBLEMS

1. Lamar Burton, a manager for a division of a manufacturer of industrial electrical supplies, is facing a problem in salesforce organization. The firm's largest customers are demanding higher levels of customer service the geographically based field salesforce can provide. Moreover, the cost of using the field salesforce to serve smaller customers is prohibitive. An internal study showed that the firm could add field salespeople to focus on the largest customers, but by focusing on them, the firm may lose the ability to serve smaller customers. What should Burton do?

2. Goltan, Inc., is a medical supplies firm whose main products are lotions for use with surgical gloves. The lotions are well known for reducing chafing and dryness often associated with frequent use of gloves. Goltan uses a telemarketing force to sell its products to clinics, hospitals, pharmacies, and doctor's offices. The telemarketing force is composed of 15 full-time and 40 part-time reps. Recently the firm has noticed higher turnover than usual among its part-time telemarketers. It has tried all its usual remedies, such as changing the incentive program and offering reps a chance for advancement, but to no avail. The high rates of turnover among the part-time reps is continuing. The firm has called you, a consultant specializing in telemarketing, to help solve the turnover problem. What recommendations would you offer?

3. Brad Connors, the manager for national accounts for a large manufacturer of telecommunications equipment, is worried. The firm moved to a national account structure two years ago when it became apparent that the approach was necessary to combat moves by competitors. Connors was on the team that designed the program and was placed in charge of the national accounts division when the program was implemented. Although the program has been successful with some customers, there are signs of strains within Con-

nor's company. The national account managers are complaining that they do not have direct line authority to resolve customer complaints. Further, two account managers have recently left, harming relationships with their customers. The vice-president of sales has sent a memo to Connor asking Connor to define the problems. Connor needs to prepare a memo to the vice-president that explains the problems and his plans to get the program back on track. Prepare Connor's memo.

SHORT CASE
BANK SCORE

BACKGROUND

Justin Tower is the vice-president of sales for BankScore, a computer software developer. The firm's major products are software packages that automate the credit evaluation process. The company sells its products to banks, credit unions, finance companies, and credit card companies throughout the United States using a field salesforce composed of seven salespeople who cover the entire country.

SITUATION

BankScore is facing a severe cost squeeze, and the sales area, long immune to budget cuts, is being eyed by the controller as a fertile area to make significant cost reductions. BankScore's controller has sent a memo to the CEO and to Tower suggesting several possible areas for cutting the sales budget. While Tower feels that several of the controller's suggestions, such as setting a daily ceiling on each salesperson's personal expenditures while on the road and consolidating air travel with a single supplier, are not controversial, one item causes him to take a deep breath. The controller has suggested that Tower replace his field salesforce with a system of independent reps working on straight commission.

The controller makes two key points. First, the independent reps will make a 4 percent commission on each sale, compared to the 7 percent commission earned by the company's salesforce. Second, the seven salespeople each cost the firm an average of $150,000 per year in sales management, travel, and sales support costs. These costs would be eliminated if the firm moved to independent reps.

Tower is appalled. He calls two of his seven salespeople to get their opinion of the proposed change. Both salespeople are shocked by the suggestion. "How will BankScore be able to ensure quality support before and after the sale," one of the salespeople exclaims. "Reps are interested only in making the sale, not in making sure we develop and maintain long-term customer relationships. How can we place a value on that?" The other salesperson is even more emphatic: "If BankScore makes this change, it will go straight into bankruptcy!"

PROBLEM

Tower sympathizes with the salespeople's views, but the controller's case for replacing the field salesforce with independent reps seem convincing. Tower has asked you, a new marketing analyst at the firm, to help him develop a case for retaining the field salesforce. He has the following facts: The current sales of the salesforce is approximately $18 million, and the average margin on sales is approximately 30 percent. Next year's projected sales are $20 million. If the firm switches to independent reps, Tower expects sales to reach only $15 million next year and estimates that it will take 3 years to reach $20 million.

QUESTIONS

1. Are the salespeople being objective in their judgment of the potential impact of independent reps?
2. Who else should get involved in the decision to retain the present salesforce or switch to independent reps? How does this issue relate to overall corporate strategy?
3. What are the pros and cons of using independent reps over a company salesforce? Do the circumstances facing Tower warrant the switch?
4. Based on the current and expected sales for the integreted salesforce and independent reps and the information on average margins, does Tower have a case for retaining the current company salesforce?

SALES ORGANIZATION ROLE PLAY

CHARACTERS

Sales Manager: Howard Sierra or Rebecca Goldberg

LinkPlus Manager: Jane Oliver or Robert Alyesh

Salesperson: Jennifer Roth or Jamal Washington

SCENARIO

The sales organization at Pharmiceaux has begun to undergo significant change over the last 3 years. While the bulk of the selling effort continues to be the responsibility of the field salesforce, electronic data interchange (in the form of LinkPlus, a stockless inventory system for hospitals and medical centers) has begun to assume a larger role in serving customers. Once a salesperson obtains an account, LinkPlus is responsible for handling routine reorders and ensuring that an adequate supply of Pharmiceaux products is in inventory at all times. This frees salespeople to spend their time in developing new customers rather than making routine reorders.

Although LinkPlus is helping the field salesforce become more efficient, individual salespeople are not uniformly in favor of the new arrangement. There have been complaints about poor communication between the field salesforce and LinkPlus, and there are concerns by the field salesforce that their overall commission level is going down.

SCENE I

Salesperson Jamal Washington calls his manager, Rebecca Goldberg, and asks her to lunch. During the meal Washington says, "Rebecca, I'm really concerned about the lack of communication between LinkPlus and me. I have several customers that I see on a monthly basis, and they tell me that they would rather go through me than someone they don't know at LinkPlus. Further, when they go through LinkPlus for a routine order, they don't get the same treatment that they have come to expect from me. Lastly, it was my understanding that LinkPlus was supposed to free up salespeople to make more calls while not reducing our commissions. Well, I'm not getting full credit for all of my sales through LinkPlus. Sometimes the salespeople at LinkPlus say that they make the sales themselves, so I don't get any credit for those sales. You know, Rebecca, I have been behind the LinkPlus program from the start, but I am really starting to get steamed over these problems. Plus, there are a lot of salespeople who always thought this was a bad idea and now they are even more upset."

Goldberg calms him down and promises that she will meet with the LinkPlus manager to see if there is some way to fix the problem.

SCENE 2

Goldberg meets with Jane Oliver of LinkPlus and recounts her conversation with Washington. She asks Oliver what can be done about the problems. Oliver says, "Well, it seems like it is your problem. My salespeople are doing their jobs, no one is complaining, and most customers seem pretty happy with the service they're receiving. It sounds like you just have some salespeople who are unhappy at having to work a little harder than simply taking routine reorders."

Goldberg replies, "Jane, I don't think laziness is the problem. I think Jamal has some legitimate complaints. LinkPlus and field sales need to work together more to avoid these problems." "Rebecca," Jane replies, "if you think we need to work together, we can certainly try, but I'm convinced the problem is on your end. But if it will make you happy, I'm willing to entertain any proposals you may have to ensure closer working relationships."

SCENE 3

Goldberg meets with two salespeople to develop some alternatives to present to Oliver. These alternatives should not only address some of the problems the field salesforce is having, but it should also present some process improvements that can avert similar problems from occurring in the future.

SCENE 4

Goldberg presents her preferred alternative to Oliver. They discuss the pros and cons of the alternative and come to a conclusion about what they should each do in the future to improve communication between the two groups.

CHARACTER DESCRIPTIONS

Name: Howard Sierra
Gender: M
Age: 37
Marital status: Married
Education: B.A., Murray State University
Title: Sales Manager
Office location: San Francisco
Reports to: District Manager, Los Angeles
Employment history: Salesperson for 4 years; manager for 6 years; previously worked for competitor
Personality: Sensitive to employees; company profit takes priority; fair; wants to be liked and respected
Notes: District has always been profitable; spends a lot of time "putting out fires"; owns a Harley
Grapevine: Very loyal to the company

Name: Rebecca Goldberg
Gender: F
Age: 34
Marital status: Married
Education: B.B.A., Lehigh University
Title: Sales Manager
Office location: San Francisco
Reports to: District Manager, Los Angeles
Employment history: Hired as a manager from a competitor
Personality: Sensitive to employees; company profit takes priority; fair; wants to be liked and respected
Notes: District has always been profitable; spends a lot of time "putting out fires"; chess player
Grapevine: Very loyal to the company

Name: Jennifer Roth
Gender: F
Age: 22
Marital status: Single
Education: B.S., Columbia University
Title: Sales Rep
Office location: San Francisco
Reports to: Sales Manager, San Francisco
Employment history: Recent graduate; just finished training
Personality: Leader; very ambitious; self-assured; eager to succeed
Notes: President of student organizations; tops in training class; selected Pharmiceaux over other offers because of greatest job potential; women's rights advocate
Grapevine: Potential fast-track candidate

Name: Jamal Washington
Gender: M
Age: 22
Marital status: Single
Education: B.B.A., Slippery Rock
Title: Sales Rep
Office location: San Francisco
Reports to: Sales Manager, San Francisco

Employment history: Recent graduate; just finished training

Personality: Very ambitious; self-assured; eager to succeed

Notes: Student House of Representatives in college; used to being a leader; model student; likes the nightlife

Grapevine: High potential

Name: Jane Oliver
Gender: F **Age:** 36 **Marital status:** Married
Education: B.B.A., Florida State
Title: LinkPlus Manager **Office location:** San Francisco
Reports to: V-P of marketing
Employment history: Recruited from a major technology company where she was a national accounts salesperson; has been with LinkPlus for 7 years
Personality: Tough, demanding, extremely competitive, very ambitious, fair
Notes: Recently terminated a 10-year veteran for poor performance; has season tickets to the symphony
Grapevine: Wants the V-P job

Name: Robert Alyesha
Gender: M **Age:** 35 **Marital status:** Married
Education: B.B.A., Colorado State
Title: LinkPlus Manager **Office location:** San Francisco
Reports to: V-P of marketing
Employment history: Rapid promotions; started with company at age 18 and has worked his way up
Personality: Very demanding, aggressive, and autocratic; expects perfection
Notes: Youngest sales manager in the last 10 years; handball expert
Grapevine: Probably a future V-P

QUESTIONS

1. How do new technological developments affect the structuring of a salesforce?
2. What compensation issues are involved when there are two different salesforces serving the same customer?
3. What kind of motivational concerns arise out of the current situation with LinkPlus?
4. Discuss at least four alternatives Goldberg and the salespeople should discuss.
5. Which alternative listed in question 4 should Goldberg present to Oliver? Support your answer fully.

NOTES

1. Andrea Rock, "Remarketing IBM," *Business Marketing,* (May 1993): 26, 32
2. Richard N. Cardozo and Shannon H. Shipp, "New Methods of Industrial Distribution," University of Minnesota Graduate School of Business working paper (1985).
3. Personal interview with Goodyear Shoe Products, 1983.
4. This figure is used by permission from Richard N. Cardozo and Shannon H. Shipp, "New Selling Methods Are Changing Industrial Sales Management," *Business Horizons,* 30(5) (1987): 23–28.
5. Frank V. Cespedes, "Sales Coordination: An Exploratory Study," *Journal of Personal Selling and Sales Management,* 12(3) (Summer 1992), 13–29.
6. Linda Cardillo Platzer, *Managing National Accounts,* Report No. 850 (New York: The Conference Board, 1984).
7. Jerome A. Colletti and Gary S. Turbridy, "Effective Major Account Sales Management," *Journal of Personal Selling and Sales Management,* 7 (August 1987): 1–10.
8. Lynn Fritz, "How Fritz Companies Delivers the Goods," *NAMA Journal,* 32(2), (Fall 1990): 13–14.
9. *Ibid.* p. 14.
10. Cardozo and Shipp (1987) op. cit.
11. Thomas H. Stevenson, "Identifying National Accounts," *Industrial Marketing Management,* 8 (1980): 133–136.
12. Susan Greco, "The Art of Selling," *Inc.,* 15 (June 1993), 72–80.

13. Thomas V. Bonoma and Victoria L. Crittenden, "Managing Marketing Implementation" *Sloan Management Review*, 29(2) (Winter 1988): 7–14.
14. Mark A. Moon and Gary M. Armstrong, "Selling Teams: A Conceptual Framework and Research Agenda," *Journal of Personal Selling and Sales Management*, 14 (Winter 1994): 17–30.
15. "Metaphoric High-Cost Sell Pays Off," *Sales and Marketing Management*, (April 1987): 25.
16. Louis A. Wallis, *Computers and the Sales Effort*, (New York: The Conference Board, Inc., New York, 1986).
17. Robert J. McHatton, *Total Telemarketing* (New York: John Wiley, 1988).
18. "Despite Hangups, Telemarketing a Success," *Marketing News*, 29(7) (1995): 19.
19. The following discussion is drawn from G. A. Marken, "High-Tech: How It Maximizes Business Software Customer Contact," *Business Marketing*, 69 (August 1984): 38–42; William C. Moncrief, Charles W. Lamb, Jr., and Terry Dielman, "Developing Telemarketing Support Systems," *Journal of Personal Selling and Sales Management*, 6 (August 1986): 43–49; and William C. Moncrief, Shannon H. Shipp, Charles W. Lamb, Jr., and David W. Cravens, "Examining the Roles of Telemarketing in Selling Strategy," *Journal of Personal Selling and Sales Management*, 9 (Fall 1989): 1–12.
20. "Shifting to Inside Sales," *Sales and Marketing Management*, 146(7) (July 1994): 39.
21. Moncrief, et al. (1986), op. cit.
22. Richard N. Cardozo and Shannon H. Shipp, "New Selling Methods in Industrial Channels," University of Minnesota Graduate School of Business working paper (1985).
23. Linda J. Neff, "Six Myths About Telemarketing," *Sales and Marketing Management* (October 1992): 108–111.
24. Leo G. Rydzewski, William G. Deming, and Philip L. Rones, "Seasonal Employment Falls Over Past Three Decades," *Monthly Labor Review*, 116 (July 1993): 3–14.
25. David G. Burgoyne and Ann Armstrong, "Managing the Part-Time Salesforce," *Business Quarterly*, (Spring 1991): 53–57.
26. "What's In Store for Part-Timers?" *Personnel Management*, 21 (July 1989): 19.
27. William R. Darden, Daryl McKee, and Ronald Hampton, "Salesperson Employment Status as a Moderator in the Job Satisfaction Model: A Frame of Reference Perspective," *Journal of Personal Selling and Sales Management*, 13 (Summer 1993): 1–15.
28. Thomas R. Wotruba, "Full-Time vs. Part-Time Salespeople: A Comparison on Job Satisfaction, Performance, and Turnover in Direct Selling," *International Journal of Research in Marketing*, 7 (August 1990): 97–108.
29. Ellen F. Jackofsky, James Salter, and Lawrence H. Peters, "Reducing Turnover Among Part-Time Employees," *Personnel* (May 1986): 41–43.
30. Ned C. Hill and Michael J. Swenson, "The Impact of Electronic Data Interchange on the Sales Function," *Journal of Personal Selling and Sales Management*, 14(3) (Summer 1994): 79–87.
31. The advantages and disadvantages of using manufacturers' representatives are drawn from Joseph A. Bellizzi and Christine Glacken, "Building a More Successful Rep Organization," *Industrial Marketing Management*, 15 (1986): 207–213, and Thomas L. Powers, "Switching from Reps to Direct Salespeople," *Industrial Marketing Management*, 16 (1987): 169–172.

32. Earl Hitchcock, "What Marketers Love and Hate About Their Manufacturers' Reps," *Sales and Marketing Magazine,* 134 (September 10, 1984): 60–65.

33. The discussion of the dealer option is drawn from Jeffrey Geibel, "Dealer Development," *Sales and Marketing Management* (May 1993): 54–57.

34. Paul Herbig and Bradley S. O'Hara, "Industrial Distributors in the Twenty-First Century," *Industrial Marketing Management,* 23 (1994): 199–203.

35. The examples of industry and transaction-specific sales organizations are drawn from Philip Kotler, *Marketing Management: Analysis, Planning, Implementation, and Control* (Englewood Cliffs, N.J.: Prentice-Hall, 1991).

9

SALESFORCE DEPLOYMENT

Sales force deployment will be a major factor in the survival of some U.S. pharmaceutical companies.

KEVIN LOEHLIN, DIRECTOR OF MARKETING, IMS (A MARKET RESEARCH AND MEDICAL INFOR-
MATION COMPANY BASED IN TOTOWA, N.J.)

LEARNING OBJECTIVES

After reading this chapter, you should be able to answer the following questions:

- What is salesforce deployment, and what decisions does it encompass?

- What methods exist to classify customers in terms of the selling effort they should receive?

- What are the methods to determine the number of salespeople that are needed to achieve sales goals?

- How has the advent of geographic information systems in recent years affected salesforce deployment?

- What process can managers undertake to effectively design territories and allocate salespeople to those territories?

It was time for Jerry Acuff to take action. In early 1993, Acuff, vice-president and general manager of Hoescht Roussel, the pharmaceutical arm of chemical giant Hoescht Celanese, in Somerville, New Jersey, knew that in order to stay competitive in the rapidly changing pharmaceutical industry he had to sit down and take a closer look at who his customers were, where they were, and whether his salesforce was aligned to meet their needs. Market conditions in the pharmaceutical industry were undergoing a tremendous change. Traditionally salespeople sold to as many private-care physicians across the country as they could, but with the ever-increasing influence of managed care on prescription activity, Acuff would first have to find out which managed care companies physicians were subscribing to and consequently what types of drugs they were prescribing. Then he'd have to start reorganizing. "The marketplace has changed. It has become far more sophisticated and complex, with more and more decision makers involved in the purchasing process," says Steve Tarnoff, assistant director of field force development for Hoescht Roussel, who worked with Acuff on this project.

Hoescht Roussel's 5-month long research project helped the company decide to organize its salesforce geographically around three customer segments:(1) primary-care physicians' offices, (2) managed care companies, and (3) hospitals. To serve those customers, Hoescht redeployed, or rearranged, its salesforce. Regions were reduced from nine to six; six regional operations managers (who would be responsible for deploying and training the salesforce at the regional level) were added, and 125 sales representatives were eliminated. The number of salespeople was particularly important. According to Acuff, "When a sales rep is costing your company more than $100,000, [you'd] better know where each salesperson is spending his or her time."

The results of the redeployment have been extremely positive. "We were able to align our salesforce based on high-volume and lower-volume customers within each group," reports Acuff, "and by doing so, reduce our sales costs by about 14 to 15 percent. This should yield us a savings in excess of ten million dollars." The company has also reduced sales calls overall by 200,000, but will do 100,000 more than previously on high subscribers. "We plan to reach our lower-volume customers with direct mail and telemarketing," says Acuff.[1]

In response to changing market conditions, Hoescht Roussel reorganized its salesforce using some of the organizational options discussed in Chapter 8. However, the reorganization went beyond simply selecting an appropriate sales organization. Hoescht Roussel also categorized customers according to how much time would be spent with each, determined how many salespeople would be required, and planned how the salespeople would be strategically arranged around the country to achieve the firm's sales goals. These three decision areas—classifying customers, determining salesforce size, and designing sales territories—are collectively known as **salesforce deployment** (see Exhibit 9.1). This chapter will explore each of these three major decision areas.

EXHIBIT 9.1

SALESFORCE DEPLOYMENT DECISIONS

After completing the chapter, come back and examine the quiz in Box 9.1. The questions cover areas addressed in this chapter and in Chapter 8. They also indicate the complexity and number of decisions that must be made to effectively deploy a salesforce.

CLASSIFYING CUSTOMERS

The first step in salesforce deployment is classifying customers in terms of their likely response to selling efforts. When face-to-face sales calls cost, on average, approximately $225, it is important to concentrate calls on customers where the likely response will cover the cost of the selling effort. To determine which customers should receive which level of sales call coverage, sales managers can classify customers using single-factor models, multiple factor models, and judgment-based or empirically based decision models.[2] Exhibit 9.2 compares the models in terms of the appropriateness of each deployment decision, analytical rigor, data requirements, computer requirements, ease of implementation, expenses, and model output. The following discussions offer examples of each model.

Single-Factor Models

Single-factor models are the simplest way to classify customers. They involve using a single factor, such as sales potential, customer service required, or type of business (e.g., industrial versus government), to determine how many calls will be devoted to a given group of customers. Ecolab's cleaning products division, which sells dishwashing equipment and chemicals to institutions and industrial users, uses a single factor (customer size) to classify its customers as A (large), B (medium), and C (small) (see Exhibit 9.3). Based on the customer classification, Ecolab assigns a selling approach and determines the level of customized service customers will receive. Ecolab uses this classification method because its larger customers are more likely to purchase equipment, whereas its smaller customers primarily purchase chemicals. Selling industrial or institutional dishwashing equipment may require salespeople to make face-to-face contact to ascertain which specific piece of equipment is most likely to serve the customer's needs. By contrast, chemicals are commodities that are sold primarily on the basis of price. Therefore, chemicals require little customer service or direct customer contact and may be serviced through telemarketing.

The primary advantages of single-factor models are that they are easy to calculate, they provide systematic justification for allocating sales calls to different customers based on some important characteristic, and they require little data (in the Ecolab example, the only data necessary was customer sales levels) and little expertise on the part of the sales manager. One important disadvantage of the single-factor models is that they may not take all the relevant characteristics of customers into account. For instance, classifying customers by current size, as in the Ecolab example, does not account for new customers. It also does not recognize for differences among customers in a certain category. Ecolab may find that one of its mid-sized customers is planning to replace a major piece of equipment this year. As a result, its purchases for the year may exceed $50,000, and it may require a higher

BOX 9.1
SALES TERRITORY QUIZ

The following 13 questions were designed by Miller-Heiman, Inc., a sales consulting firm based in Reno, Nevada. The purpose of the quiz is to identify potential problems in a firm's sales territories or its territory design process.

1. Our sales territories are largely composed of:
    a. Companies where we have some indication that there is a possible order.
    b. Every company that has expressed an interest in our company's products/services in the past 20 years.
    c. Good accounts in the territories of the more seasoned reps and poor accounts in the territories of new salespeople.

2. The number of accounts in our sales territories is determined by:
    a. Criteria unknown to me. Our territories were set up years ago, before I took over as manager, and have been virtually the same for years.
    b. Regular territory reviews where territories are adjusted according to sales possibilities and sales representative work loads.
    c. The total number of accounts in my branch, divided by the number of salespeople in the branch.

3. Our salespeople usually find their new selling opportunities by:
    a. Prospecting for new accounts at scheduled events like customer seminars or trade shows.
    b. Following up on leads provided to them by the corporate marketing efforts.
    c. Identifying "ideal" customers within their existing territories and setting an action plan to qualify them.

4. Once a company makes it into one of our sales territories, it is likely to:
    a. Stay in the territory until we determine it is not a viable prospect for a sale.
    b. Stay in the territory forever. If there isn't a sale this year, we'll keep calling and maybe next year there will be one.
    c. Stay in the territory until it closes, when the account is passed along to someone else to service.

5. The best time to evaluate the quantity and quality of selling possibilities in our sales territories is:
    a. When a new representative is hired and a new territory needs to be carved from the territories of other salespeople.
    b. When an open territory is assigned to a new salesperson or transferred from one salesperson to another.
    c. On a regular basis, determined by the amount of time it takes for actions from the last territory review to be completed and by the changes that are taking place in the territory account base.

6. I think our salespeople should call on each account in their territories:
    a. At least three to four times per year.
    b. Only if they are currently pursuing a potential sale at the account.
    c. In different ways depending on whether they are qualifying, covering the bases with those who will make the decision to purchase, or closing.

7. What criteria are used to determine which accounts receive what corporate resources from the seller?
    a. An analysis of the current sales potential, our position in the account, and the resources needed for the payback that we want.
    b. Every salesperson is allowed a certain amount of resources to use as he or she deems necessary.
    c. Our senior salespeople have more resources and more leeway to spend those resources than those who are newer to the company.

8. The status review of all current sales opportunities in each territory takes place:
    a. On a situation-by-situation basis, as needed.
    b. When the weekly call reports are read.
    c. During regularly scheduled meetings.

Box 9.1 (continued)
SALES TERRITORY QUIZ

---

9. The frequency of territory reviews is determined by:
   a. The number of other meetings on a manager's schedule.
   b. The amount of time required to complete the tasks agreed upon in the last review.
   c. Sales forecast requirements from the head office.

10. When there is a problem with one of our accounts or prospects, I learn about it:
    a. So late that I would have to be able to walk on water to solve it and salvage the sale.
    b. Early on, when the problem is brought to my attention by the account representatives.
    c. From the prospect or customer.

11. How many accounts in each sales territory do my salespeople never get around to?
    a. Our company has reorganized and downsized its salesforce so that each territory contains more than twice as many accounts as it is reasonable for a salesperson to pursue.
    b. My salespeople conform to the 80/20 rule—80 percent of their sales come from 20 percent (or less) of their accounts.
    c. Accounts that do not meet our prospect criteria are ultimately dropped from the territory.

12. When my salespeople have more accounts than they can cover, they:
    a. Focus on current accounts that brought in revenue last year.
    b. Try to catch up on the uncovered accounts with a phone blitz.
    c. Systematically look at each account with a manager and determine strategy for prioritizing accounts.

13. Every year, sales quotas are:
    a. Increased a certain percentage over sales from the previous years.
    b. Based upon each manager's knowledge of the accounts within his or her territories.
    c. Determined by someone at corporate with little or no input from the field.

ANSWERS

1. a. Most companies pass territories from salesperson to salesperson with little or no analysis of what is actually in the territory. Often the percentage of viable sales opportunities to "junk" in territories is way out of line. The cure is simple: Clean out the territory so that all that is left are accounts where there is some clear indication of a possible order.

2. b. Branches are traditionally built by taking the target market and dividing it into territories for salespeople to pursue. Unfortunately this means most salespeople are calling on only a small percentage of the total accounts in the territory. A better way to determine how many accounts should be in a territory is to prioritize the opportunities and decide how many tasks will be required to complete the work on those opportunities. Lower priority accounts can be served another way.

3. c. To make prospecting more palatable and more successful at the same time, managers should help salespeople plan a marketing campaign that includes research, letters, and phone calls to prospective companies that the salesperson would like to pursue.

---

level of service than can be accounted for by independent reps. The single-factor model does not account for such annual changes.

Multiple-Factor Models

Multiple-factor models are an extension of single-factor models. They use multiple factors simultaneously to classify customers. For example, Goodyear Shoe Products division classifies its customers on the basis of size and business type, as shown in

BOX 9.1 (continued)
SALES TERRITORY QUIZ

4. a. There are three main reasons accounts find a permanent home in sales territories whether or not they represent selling opportunities. First, territory reviews are not common, so accounts stay on through inertia. Second, salespeople are reluctant to give up on any account where there may be a glimmer of a possibility for a sale. Third, if the salesperson has identified the account as a possibility, if the account does call in, the salesperson gets the credit for the sale.

5. c. Most territory reviews are based on some event, like the transition of the territory from one salesperson to another. Effective management, however, requires that territories be evaluated periodically to ensure that territories are designed to provide adequate customer service to key accounts.

6. c. It is impossible to make a hard and fast rule about how often accounts should be seen without significant understanding of the potential of all accounts in the territory. The correct answer, therefore is "as often as necessary to accomplish account objectives."

7. a. Corporate resources can be defined as any time, money, and effort that is applied toward serving an account or prospect. For a firm to obtain the highest return on its investment in an account, salespeople and their managers should carefully understand the current sales potential of the account, how the seller is positioned with the buying committee members, and how much revenue must be generated to cover those resources devoted to serving the account.

8. c. Managers must review whatever reports are required of salespeople, lest salespeople view the reports as unnecessary. To provide maximum direction to their salespeople, managers should conduct a complete territory review with each salesperson on a regular basis. Salesperson and manager should agree on the next step to be taken with each account.

9. b. In the best of worlds, territory reviews should be conducted on a regular basis. The frequency of the reviews should be determined by their complexity. For instance, if the selling cycle is longer than 2 years, a quarterly review might be all that is necessary. A selling cycle of less than 12 months means actions presented at one review would probably be completed in 4-to-6 weeks, so another review should be scheduled at that time.

10. b. Perhaps the best result of consistent territory planning for sales managers is that it allows for the early identification of problems and other important issues.

11. c. Because most sales territories contain too many accounts for even the best-organized salesperson to cover, accounts should be carefully prioritized so that salespeople spend their time serving only the highest potential accounts. Lower-priority accounts should be served using some other method

12. c. Most salespeople spend their time on accounts that represent the largest amount of current revenue. However, accounts change, new accounts arise, and the competitive situation changes. Therefore, account planning becomes extremely important to achieve a long-term competitive position.

13. b. Managers who regularly conduct territory reviews with their salespeople are more likely to be aware of current market conditions. These managers, as a result, will be able to provide more realistic sales projections than a forecast based on an arbitrary increase over last year's numbers or prepared by an analyst with little "feel" for the market.

SOURCE: Adapted from *Sales and Marketing Management* (1994).

Exhibit 9.4. Goodyear Shoe Products sells heels and sole materials to shoe manufacturers and repair shops throughout the United States. Shoe manufacturers and repair shops have different service needs and represent different levels of potential revenue, hence the classification of customers into these categories. The large shoe manufacturers may have specific needs for a new type of shoe, and they may work closely with Goodyear to develop the appropriate sole or heel material. Shoe repair

EXHIBIT 9.2

COMPARISON OF CUSTOMER CLASSIFICATION APPROACHES

Factor	Single-Factor Model	Multiple-Factor Model	Portfolio Model	Judgment-Based Decision Models	Empirically Based Decision Models
Decision appropriateness	Appropriate for most decisions	Appropriate for most decisions	Deployment	Best suited for within-territory deployment decisions	Best suited for across-territory deployment decisions
Analytical rigor	Low	Fairly low	Moderate	High	High
Data requirements	Minimal	Substantial—multiple factors are evaluated	Substantial—multiple factors are evaluated	Substantial—multiple response estimates are required	Substantial—multiple factors are evaluated
Computer requirements	Minimal—does not require computer analysis	Minimal	Ideally suited for microcomputer applications	Can be substantial, depending upon the size and complexity of the selling situation	Can be substantial, depending upon the size and complexity of the selling situation
Ease of implementation	Relatively easy to implement	Relatively easy to implement	Moderately easy to implement	Somewhat difficult to implement, but incorporation of model user throughout the process aids implementation	Difficult to implement owing to management's lack of understanding the complex nature of analysis
Expenses	Low	Fairly low	Moderate,	Moderate out-of-pocket costs, but substantial time commitment required to obtain response estimates	Can be substantial, but depends upon firm's information system
Model output	Classifications based on analysis of one factor	Classifications based on analysis of multiple factors	Classifications based on multiple factors and recommended effort deployment based on relative attractiveness	The "optimal" deployment of selling effort that will "maximize" the sales or profit objective	The "optimal" deployment of selling effort that will "maximize" the sales or profit objective

SOURCE: Adapted from Raymond W. LaForge, David W. Cravens, and Clifford E. Young, "Using Contingency Analysis to Select Selling Effort Allocation Methods," *Journal of Personal Selling and Sales Management*, 6 (August 1986): 19–28.

EXHIBIT 9.3			
CLASSIFICATION OF ECOLAB CUSTOMERS			
Customer Classification	Annual Purchases by Customer	Selling Approach	Level of Customized Service Provided
A	more than $50,000	National account management	High
B	$10,000–$50,000	Independent reps	Medium
C	less than $10,000	Telemarketing	Low

EXHIBIT 9.4				
GOODYEAR SHOE PRODUCTS DIVISION CUSTOMER CLASSIFICATION				
			Customer Type	
			Manufacturer	Shoe Repair
Customer Size	Large		Face-to-face	Telemarketing
	Small		Telemarketing	Telemarketing

shops, by contrast, purchase materials to replace worn-out soles or heels primarily on the basis of price. As a result, face-to-face selling is not necessary.

One specialized type of multiple-factor model is the portfolio model.[3] **Portfolio models** classify customers on two dimensions: opportunity and competitive strength. The *opportunity* dimension classifies accounts based on the account size and capability to purchase. *Competitive strength* classifies accounts on the basis of any unique advantages the seller has vis-à-vis the buyer. Accounts where both opportunity and the seller's competitive strength are high receive the highest levels of selling effort, whereas those accounts where opportunity and seller's competitive strength are low received relatively little selling effort.

The advantages and disadvantages of multiple-factor models are similar to those of single-factor models. For one, they are easy to calculate. Moreover, while they require more data and expertise on the part of the sales manager, they can be modeled with relative ease on a spreadsheet package.[4] Whereas single-factor models depend on a single characteristic to classify customers, and thereby run the risk of overlooking an important distinguishing characteristic among customers, multiple-factor models attempt to overcome this by using more factors. There is still no guarantee, however, that an important customer characteristic will not be overlooked. As well, the issue of whether there are differences within the categories in terms of customers' response to selling effort is not addressed.

Decision Models

Decision models consist of one or more response functions that relate selling effort to sales response. Exhibit 9.5 shows the relationship between selling effort (measured in terms of number of sales calls) and sales response (measured in terms of marginal revenue) for a single customer. In general, the exhibit shows that as selling effort increases, so does sales response.

EXHIBIT 9.5

MARGINAL REVENUE AND NUMBER OF SALES CALLS

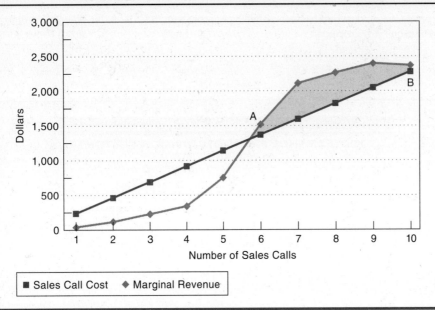

■ Sales Call Cost   ◆ Marginal Revenue

However, the relationship between selling effort and sales response is not linear. While sales call costs is a linear function that reflects a constant cost per sales call, the sales response function is S-shaped, which means that sales response is disproportionately low until a threshold number of sales calls are made. Then it rises until a saturation point is reached; at saturation, sales response to additional sales calls is limited. S-shaped sales response functions could occur because below a certain number of sales calls, the customer may not be aware of the supplier's products. Above a saturation point of sales calls the sales response curve could flatten because the customer has purchased all it needs, or because the customer does not want to purchase any more from the supplier because it wants to keep multiple suppliers for the product (see Chapter 7 for a rationale as to why some customers choose to have multiple suppliers).[5]

The salesperson should make the number of sales calls between point *A* and point *B* on the chart. Point *A* is the point at which marginal revenue from the sales calls exceeds their costs, while point *B* is the point at which the marginal revenue from the sales call is equal to the marginal cost of the sales call.

There are two basic types of decision models: judgment-based and empirically based. The two types differ in the way that the sales response functions are estimated.

Judgment-Based Decision Models.   **Judgment-based decision models** derive the sales response functions by having salespeople or sales managers estimate the likely customer response to given levels of selling effort or numbers of sales calls. For example, a salesperson may be asked to estimate how much sales revenue can be generated from a given customer from five sales calls, ten sales calls, and fifteen sales calls. By plotting the salesperson's responses, the sales manager can generate an estimated sales response function for that customer, similar to the one in Exhibit 9.5. In judgment-based decision models, the only factor explicitly considered for sales response is selling effort, although other factors such as customer size and competitive position are implicitly weighted by the salesperson or sales manager when deriving the customer's response function.

Judgment-based decision models have several advantages. First, they involve salespeople and sales managers in developing sales call guidelines for individual accounts, which increases their acceptance of the guidelines. Of course, this requires experienced salespeople and managers who have the time and expertise to assist salespeople in developing the response functions. In addition, the process of developing response functions for individual customers focuses attention on specific customer needs and can be a valuable means of communication between salespeople and sales managers.

Judgment-based decision models also have several disadvantages. First, they are time-consuming because the salesperson or sales manager must calculate a separate response function for each customer. Also, the salesperson or sales manager must be intimately aware of the customer's likely reaction to different levels of selling effort, which precludes using the technique on a new customer or one that has not been called upon frequently in the past. As a result, this technique is usually reserved for the firm's largest customers.

Empirically Based Decision Models.   **Empirically based decision models,** by contrast, rely not on salesperson judgment but on gathering data on several factors to generate sales response functions. These factors can include, but are not limited to, the customer's previous reactions to different levels of selling effort, previous levels of competition for the account, and the customer's buying patterns (e.g., whether the customer purchases primarily equipment or supplies). The modeler is only limited by the information available in the firm and the cost of collecting additional information.

The primary advantages of empirical modeling approaches are explicit consideration of multiple factors that may relate to sales response and the ability to calculate the customer response function without requiring sales managers or salespeople to have high levels of customer knowledge. As a result, this technique might be quite useful for firms with high levels of sales person or sales manager turnover or those that are entering new territories and wish to estimate the necessary call levels for new accounts.

There are, however, conceptual and mathematical disadvantages of empirical modeling. Conceptually, the process is difficult to explain to nontechnical people, so it may be difficult to persuade salespeople of its worth. Also, the technique may seem mechanical to experienced salespeople who are used to making the determination of appropriate call levels on accounts in their territories. If the model is developed without salesperson input, salespeople may not feel committed to using the results of the analysis.

Mathematically, the method requires a much higher level of expertise to derive and validate customer response functions. It also requires more data than other methods, which may make it more expensive unless the firm's information system has all the data necessary for model construction and validation. Another mathematical problem in using empirical decision models is that it is problematic to predict response outside the observed data range. In other words, if the customer has been called upon between three and five times per year for the last 5 years, predicting what the customer's response would be to eight sales calls is difficult because eight is outside the observed range.

DETERMINING SALESFORCE SIZE

The second major decision in salesforce deployment is the determination of appropriate salesforce size. Through the 1980s and 1990s, firms have experienced relentless pressure to reduce their number of employees. Although the salesforce has traditionally been the last place to experience cuts (owing to the revenue-generation function of the salesforce), it has not been immune from the downsizing that has affected the other functional areas in firms around the world. One of the most notable examples of reduction in salesforce size has been experienced at IBM. Its salesforce, traditionally one of its major market advantages, has been severely reduced in size over the last decade. For example, the IBM sales office in the Greater Silicon Valley trading area had 550 employees in early 1991, 400 employees in 1992, and fewer than 300 in 1993. Some cuts occurred in staff positions, but many sales positions were also cut. The reduction in numbers led the sales manager to reconsider all aspects of the selling approach. Amal Johnson, the head of the Silicon Valley office, says, "If you are focusing on profits, not just revenue, you have to look at how you're selling. You can't just cut 25% to 35% of your people and continue to do the job the same way. It just doesn't work."[6]

The increased emphasis on reducing the number of employees has left sales managers under great pressure to justify salesforce size. As a result, determining appropriate salesforce size is not a decision to be made lightly. This section addresses three primary methods by which salesforce size decisions can be made: breakdown, work load, and incremental. It is important to note that these methods work only within one type of salesforce at a time. In other words, you cannot simultaneously develop an optimal number of salespeople for several types of salesforces using these methods. This problem is partly addressed through the use of *marketing effort analysis,* which is explained in greater detail in Chapter 17. Marketing effort analysis compares the efficiency of different selling approaches and indicates the relative emphasis that should be placed on each selling approach. No approach has yet been developed to determine appropriate salesforce size for several types of salesforces simultaneously. Therefore, the discussion herein focuses on the use of each method to determine the appropriate salesforce size for a single type of salesforce.

Breakdown Method

The **breakdown method** is the simplest means of calculating required salesforce size. It is calculated by dividing the forecasted sales by the average expected sales per salesperson. For instance, if a firm forecasts sales for the coming year of $100 million and the average expected sales per salesperson is $1 million, the number of salespeople required is:

$$\text{Salesforce size} = \frac{\text{sales}}{\text{average expected sales per person}}$$

$$= \frac{\$100,000,000}{1,000,000}$$

$$= 100 \text{ salespeople}$$

The breakdown approach is a very simple, convenient, and widely used method of determining salesforce size. Unfortunately, it suffers from serious flaws. For one, it does not account for turnover, training periods, or changes in the average sales per salesperson. Perhaps its most important flaw is that it reverses cause and effect: it assumes that sales cause the number of salespeople, not the other way around. In reality, adding salespeople should increase the level of sales. Therefore, a method that sets salesforce size on the basis of expected sales, in a sense, limits sales to that expected level.

Work Load Method

The **work load method** sets salesforce size on the basis of the required level of selling effort needed to reach a sales goal. In other words, if a salesforce must make 25,000 sales calls to reach the sales goal, salesforce size is a function of the number of salespeople necessary to make 25,000 calls. If a salesperson can make 500 calls per year, the number of salespeople required for a firm that needs to make 25,000 calls is:

$$\text{Salesforce size} = \frac{\text{number of sales calls to reach sales goals}}{\text{number of sales calls each salesperson can make}}$$

$$= \frac{25,000}{500}$$

$$= 50 \text{ salespeople}$$

GTE Consumer Markets division uses the work load approach to set its required number of telemarketing representatives. GTE calculates the average number of calls coming into its customer service facility on a daily basis and adjusts the number of telemarketing representatives to be able to handle that level of call traffic. One interesting issue GTE deals with is the relationship between call length and number of telemarketing representatives required. If the average length of a call increases by only 10 seconds, GTE must add 60 more representatives to its staff. It should come as no surprise that GTE carefully monitors average call length to ensure calls stay within a target length.[7]

The work load approach is stronger conceptually than the breakdown approach because it is based on the level of sales effort needed to reach a certain goal. Therefore, it assumes the proper cause-effect relationship—that sales effort causes sales. In addition, it is relatively easy to develop, assuming that the firm has historical data on average revenue per sales call. It also implicitly takes into account the level of nonselling activities performed by the salesperson. As discussed in Chapter 2, salespeople do not spend all day every day in customers' offices or on the telephone to customers. They also perform many nonselling activities, ranging from collections to training, which can be readily accounted for in the work load approach. If a salesperson can make six calls per day and works 250 days per year, the salesperson can make 1,500 sales calls per year. If 33 percent of the salesperson's activities are nonselling, however, the salesperson can actually make only 1,000 calls per year. Therefore, when using the work load approach to determine salesforce size, the firm should use the actual number of sales calls the salesperson can make.

One weakness of the work load method is that it lacks sensitivity to changes in the competitive environment and the salesforce. It also forces management to think narrowly about the means by which sales goals can be achieved, in that selling effort is the only variable that is considered to affect sales. This can be inappropriate because as a salesforce is being downsized, managers must think of innovative ways of accomplishing more with less.

Incremental Method

The **incremental method** for determining salesforce size compares the marginal revenue from adding one salesperson to the marginal cost of adding that salesperson. Conceptually this method is rigorous because it requires a salesperson's cost to be supported by the additional revenue that the salesperson can generate. Unfortunately the incremental approach is quite difficult to accomplish in practice, mainly because it is difficult to calculate the incremental revenue derived from an additional salesperson. Training and recruiting costs and the declining marginal utility of additional sales calls have an impact on the incremental revenue generated by an additional salesperson.

The cost-revenue relationship is also affected by the type of compensation the salesperson receives. Assuming the market for the product is finite, having too many commission-only salespeople can lead to serious customer service problems. Since salespeople rely on closing sales to earn commissions, they can become pushy to customers, steal customers from other salespeople, and become prone to turnover owing to an inability to earn a consistent income. In turn, high turnover can lead to higher training and recruiting costs and reduce customer service levels even further as customers are forced to deal with inexperienced sales representatives. Because of these problems, the incremental method should be reserved for use with salary-only or salary-plus-commission salesforces. It should not be used with commission-only salesforces.

DESIGNING SALES TERRITORIES

The final decision in salesforce deployment is how to strategically arrange salespeople in territories that will help the organization achieve its sales and profitability goals. A **territory** is a group of customers and prospects that is the responsibility of a single salesperson or a sales team This section discusses the advantages and disadvantages of territories and then describes the territory design process.

Advantages of Territories

Territories offer firms numerous benefits, including ensuring market coverage, balancing the work load, evaluating sales performance, controlling direct and indirect costs, and maximizing the amount of time salespeople spend in front of customers. Territories are even useful to firms who use national account management.

Perhaps the most compelling reason for territories is *market coverage*. Designating a particular group of accounts as a single salesperson or sales team responsibility ensures that the salesperson or sales team will become familiar with all accounts in the territory and develop small, as well as large, accounts. If no territories are designated, the salesperson or sales team can "skim the cream" by selling only to "easy" accounts. Unfortunately, although sales are made, only the most popular lines are sold and there is no attempt to sell less popular lines. Because new lines often fall into this category, it may be difficult to get market penetration of new products.

Balancing the work load is another important reason for creating territories. Without territories, sales reps would be encouraged to only call on accounts with the highest potential. Unfortunately this would lead to certain accounts receiving multiple calls and others receiving none. As a result important customers can be irritated, and smaller customers can be underserved.

Territories are also useful in *evaluating salesperson performance* because actual and expected territory sales and cost data can be compared within and across districts. Differences in sales potential and travel expenses for different territories can be factored into the quota-setting process. This process will be discussed in greater detail in Chapter 14.

Territories are an important aid in *controlling direct and indirect costs*. Direct costs are reduced by eliminating call duplication and minimizing travel time. Assigning a salesperson to a specific territory eliminates calls by more than one salesperson to a single account. Territory design that takes into account geographic barriers such as rivers and mountains can minimize direct expenses in terms of mileage, overnight travel, and meals. By clarifying the sales task for salespeople, it also reduces indirect expenses such as turnover and employee dissatisfaction.

Proper territory design can also maximize the *amount of time a salesperson spends in front of customers*. This is vital to Diesel Supply Company, an engine and compressor parts supplier. Its accounts are 70 to 80 miles apart, so its salespeople can only make about four calls per day.[8] Maximizing the amount of time a salesperson spends in front of customers allows the firm to enhance customer relationships, because, as discussed in Chapter 1, salespeople can develop relationships with customers through repeated contact. The more familiar the customer is with the salesperson, the stronger the relationship between the customer and the seller.

Territories are useful even to *firms who use national account management*. Chris Lundgren, the director of national accounts for American Business Information (ABI), a firm that supplies business information such as mailing lists and databases to companies for use in database marketing, direct mail, and marketing research, says that assignment of accounts by territory is important, even when the customer is a national account. According to Lundgren, "Most of the major companies want a single point of contact when it comes to data acquisition, but then look for multiple points of contact when it comes to customer service." To provide what national accounts want, ABI has national account reps who act as a single point of contact for customers who wish to purchase or upgrade their lists, and geographically organized salespeople who service local accounts and local branches of national accounts.[9]

Despite the lack of travel restrictions on telemarketers, geographic boundaries, in some instances, may even be appropriate to classify telemarketing accounts. If there are unique laws in a given locale, such as limited times for calling or unique disclosure requirements (see Chapter 3 for a discussion of state and regional laws that regulate telemarketing), geographic territories might be appropriate.

Disadvantages of Territories

Despite the advantages of territories, however, some companies do not organize their sales effort this way. These companies include new firms, firms where sales are based on personal acquaintance, firms with highly specialized and technical products, firms with customers that are sparsely distributed, firms using telemarketing, and firms with customers that need coordinated service across different geographic locations.

New firms often find that small operations can be controlled without spending the effort to define formal territories. When the firm only has one salesperson, it does not make much sense to define formal territories. However, as the firm grows and the number of salespeople increases, the benefits of territories become more apparent.

Some firms sell products on the basis of personal acquaintance. Life insurance and real estate, for example, are typically sold initially to the salesperson's friends and relatives. Restricting that type of salesperson to a specific territory could reduce his or her sales significantly. Moreover, requiring customers to use a salesperson assigned to their territory rather than one they know might encourage them to seek another seller.

Even in life insurance, however, geographic territories can be effectively used and managed. At Erie Insurance Group in Pennsylvania, Mark Squeglia, a market research specialist, has used territory productivity tools to give important market information to independent agents. He examines the characteristics of each market area served, finds the potential, and compares the potential to policies-in-force and independent agents' locations. "Once we've identified areas of opportunity, we work with the branch managers and they take the ball and run with it."[10]

Firms with sophisticated, highly technical products may also choose to forego territories. IBM announced in May 1994 that it was abandoning its geographically aligned salesforce for its worldwide marketing teams. The customer-driven restructuring organized IBM's marketing teams by industry-specific groups. An IBM spokesman said at the time, "After surveying our customers, IBM has realized that what it really wants is salespeople who can speak the language of its customers and understand their industries."[11] As a result, the 30,000-person marketing force was divided into 14 industry segments. Each marketing team became expert in the issues and problems facing a single industry.

Air Products and Chemicals, Inc., went through a similar restructuring in 1994. The company sells industrial gases and chemicals to customers in a broad range of industries. "We surveyed some customers and employees and came up with the conclusion that our sales reps were not experts in any one given product or industry; they basically knew a lot about everything. Our customers didn't want this," says Dave Marek, national sales manager of the performance industries group. As a result, sales reps were assigned specific products to sell to specific customers. Although the reps were still based in certain geographic regions, account assignments were based on the salesperson's product expertise rather than their geographic proximity.

Firms may not wish to use territories if their customers need coordinated customer service across multiple locations. This is quite common with national accounts and is one of the primary benefits of national account management—which provides the customer with a single point of contact between the buyer and the seller. However, while the point of contact for pricing and product configuration may be the national account manager, customer service for national accounts is typically provided at the local level. As noted in Chapter 8, it is not feasible for a customer with 120 locations to have the same account manager to serve each account as well as manage the overall account relationship. Local service is necessary, and this will probably be provided by a geographically based salesforce. IBM (see the restructuring example presented earlier) provides service after the sale via product specialists who are geographically based so that they can offer high levels of service at the local level.

Territory Design

Despite the advantages of territories, the process of territory design used to be so difficult that many firms did not use territories. Territory design was a time-consuming, manual process that required the use of maps, pins, and atlases to determine the location of accounts and the distance between them. At Perdue Frederick Co., a pharmaceutical maker in Norwalk, Connecticut, designing territories was a difficult task. "We used to sit down with our district managers for days and do a ton of manual calculations to put together our territories," says Stephanie Thompson, manager of marketing programs. "Even with the amount of time devoted to the task, it was difficult to design territories. For example, the manual system did not show the existence of physical barriers, such as rivers or mountains, that might increase travel time to certain accounts."[12]

Now sophisticated **geographic information systems (GIS) software** is available to help managers design sales territories. GIS contains detailed maps of specific regions and allows the user to input additional relevant information, such as customer characteristics, to help managers overcome territory design problems. GIS is becoming increasingly popular as prices continue to fall. Some data costs have dropped as much as 90 percent since the mid-1980s owing to an increase in the number of competing data suppliers. According to Dataquest, a research firm that tracks this market, sales of mapping software for business use is expected to increase from $25 million in 1992 to $174 million in 1997.[13] Perdue Frederick now uses new territory design software that generates computer maps to show physical obstacles in sales routes—which helps the managers redesign the routes to minimize those obstacles.

Some firms have found that using mapping software in designing territories has provided them a competitive advantage. General Electric Medical Systems (GEMS) uses mapping software combined with account information to improve territory design. As a manufacturer of diagnostic imaging equipment, GEMS is faced with an important environmental change—hospitals have become more "bottom-line" oriented. Therefore, GEMS has to find an approach that allows it to design territories that targets hospitals which would be most likely to purchase its products, as well as develop a marketing information systems tool that would help it become more attuned to customer needs in the selling process. GEMS adopted a software approach that meets these conditions. Now GEMS can identify a target hospital and determine its trading area. Within the trading area, demographic, disease, and physician databases, as well as spreadsheet projections, are analyzed. The analysis shows the need for medical imaging equipment to the hospital's buying committee. "If reps can come in with valuable information about the market forces driving the need for diagnostic imaging equipment, as well as a profile of the hospital's market, hospital administrators have to be interested," noted David Wells, GEMS program

---

EXHIBIT 9.6

TERRITORY PLANNING MODEL

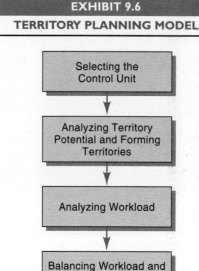

manager for database marketing. "We've essentially moved from taking orders into consultative selling. We get lots of reps telling us the hospital administrators went wild over the maps and information."[14]

Exhibit 9.6 shows the conceptual steps in defining territories: selecting the control unit, analyzing territory potential and forming territories, analyzing work load, balancing work load and territory potential, and assigning salespeople to territories. Each step is further explained in the following section.

Selecting the Control Unit.   The **control unit** is the smallest geographic area used to build sales territories. Control units can be states, counties, trading areas, metropolitan statistical areas (MSAs), or ZIP codes. With the exception of trading areas and ZIP codes, these control units are formed by political boundaries. The major advantages of using areas that are formed by political boundaries is that they are easy to identify for salespeople and there is a significant amount of secondary information available on consumer and business characteristics within political units. The major disadvantage of using political boundaries is that they may not reflect the selling and purchasing patterns of customers within the territory.

In general, firms desire smaller control units because they offer greater convenience in making adjustments in territories. Small control units also allow sales management to assess market potential more accurately. GIS data on smaller control units were extremely expensive and difficult to manipulate a few years ago, but recently the data have become quite reasonable in price and relatively easy to ma-

EXHIBIT 9.7

ADVANTAGES AND DISADVANTAGES OF DIFFERENT CONTROL UNITS

Geographic Control Unit	Defined	Advantages	Disadvantages
States/Countries	Political Boundaries	• Used when a firm wishes to cover a large area with a small salesforce	• States vary tremendously in size and customer concentration • Travel times vary widely • It is difficult to make slight adjustments • It is difficult to determine problem areas in large states • Salespeople may concentrate only on the largest accounts—failing to develop smaller accounts
Trading areas	Includes a principal city and surrounding regions where natural trading occurs	• Recognizes actual shopping and purchasing patterns • Certain trading area maps conform to media coverage, therefore making it easier to coordinate advertising and sales	• It is difficult to find government data • It varies from product to product; if a salesforce represents multiple product lines or a broad range of products, it must contend with overlapping trading areas • Trading area maps vary from vendor to vendor
MSAs	One city with a population of greater than 50,000 or two contiguous cities with a combined population of 50,000; includes the county in which the city is located plus all adjacent counties	• MSAs are concentrated population centers that represent a disproportionate level of the consumer and business population in the United States • Statistical data on characteristics is available from many sources, including the annual "Survey of Buying Power" published by Sales and Marketing Management	• It is a political boundary, not an economic one • MSAs change from census to census
ZIP codes	Postal code designations	• With over 45,000 ZIP codes there is a great deal of flexibility in designing and adjusting territories • Capable of pinpointing areas with high potential	• ZIP codes change—new ones are added and boundaries are redrawn as the population warrants • In general, less information is available by ZIP codes than for other units; this is rapidly changing, however • ZIP codes may not take physical barriers, such as mountains and rivers, into account

nipulate. For instance, in 1994 Craig Heard, president of Gateway Outdoor Advertising, purchased a demographic database management system for under $25,000. The same system, with less information, cost over $750,000 in the early 1980s.[15] Exhibit 9.8 defines each control unit and shows the specific advantages and disadvantages of each.

Analyzing Territory Potential and Forming Territories.   Analyzing territory potential requires the sales manager to understand the customer characteristics, current market share, and competitive position within each control unit. Using this information, managers can forecast levels of sales, costs, and profits. (Methods of forecasting are discussed in greater detail in Chapter 15.) Based on the projected potential in the geographic control units, managers can combine contiguous control units to form territories. Managers should seek to equalize opportunity as much as possible at this stage. This keeps the salesforce from becoming dissatisfied over uneven allocation of major accounts or market potential.

Analyzing Work Load.   Work load analysis consists of determining how much selling effort is required to meet sales objectives for a given region. If more selling effort is required than can be performed by a single salesperson, the boundaries of the territory can be adjusted. Western Sales Co., a California-based independent rep firm that represents ten plumbing supply vendors, uses territory mapping software to adjust territory potential. A territory analysis begins with a selection of an arbitrary region near the salesperson's home. Account and contact information for the region is loaded into the database. The sales manager looks at the quantity and quality of accounts to ensure the salesperson can sell enough to justify the territory's existence. If the territory contains too many accounts for a salesperson to serve, the territory is divided or shared with other reps. Many different potential territories can be constructed and modified in a limited time. Thanks to territory design software, Tom Slankard, Western's marketing vice-president, says, "Now we can try various scenarios in a couple of minutes, whereas before it would have taken ninety days."[16]

Balancing Work Load and Territory Potential.   Managers find it extremely difficult to balance territories so that all offer the same potential for the same level of selling effort. If territories are devised by state, a six-state territory such as Wyoming, Utah, Nevada, Washington, Idaho, and Oregon may constitute the same potential as the state of California, or perhaps even the region of Southern California alone. Yet the travel time required to cover the six states is much greater, and the accounts are much more sparsely distributed than they are in California. Managers must account for this difference when setting quotas and monitoring costs.

Managers have to analyze the potential that exists in different territories to be able to equalize territory potential. Exhibit 9.8 shows two territories that are composed of five trading areas. Although they each contain the same number of trading areas, their levels of potential are quite different. Territory 1 requires .56 salespeople for adequate service. Territory 2, on the other hand, represents more potential—it requires 2.43 salespeople for adequate service. These territories should be adjusted to make the potential more even. If they are not adjusted, significant problems can result. For example, the salesperson in territory 1 may become frus-

	EXHIBIT 9.8		
	TRADING AREA ANALYSIS		
	Trading Area (TA)	Present % of Time Spent Serving the TA	Recommended % of Time to Spend Serving the TA
Territory 1	1	10	4
	2	60	40
	3	15	7
	4	5	2
	5	10	3
Total		100	56
Territory 2	6	18	80
	7	17	30
	8	15	21
	9	35	35
	10	15	77
Total		100	243

SOURCE: Adapted from Raymond W. LaForge, David W. Cravens, and Clifford E. Young, "Improving Salesforce Productivity," *Business Horizons* (September/October 1985): 50–59.

trated at the lack of opportunity. The company is also losing money because too much selling effort is being devoted to territory 1. In territory 2, the salesperson may be able to make his or her quota by calling on a limited number of customers in each trading area. As a result, the company is losing sales, and the salesperson has little incentive to develop smaller customers, search for new customers, or seek out new product applications.

The two territories could be adjusted in several ways. First, when added together, it appears there is enough potential for three salespeople (.56 + 2.43 = 2.99 salespeople). As a result, the manager could divide the trading areas into three territories with roughly equivalent potential. For example, territory 2 might be reduced in size by creating a third territory out of trading areas 6 and 8. Trading area 9 could be given to territory 1. This would leave trading areas 7 and 10 in territory 2. As a result of the realignment, territory 1 would have trading areas 1–5 and 9, for a territory potential of .91; territory 2, with trading areas 7 and 10, would have potential of 1.07; and territory 3, containing trading areas 6 and 8, would have potential of 1.01.

If only two salespeople were available, the trading areas could be reassigned to make more equivalent territories. The salesperson in territory 2 is not devoting nearly enough effort in trading areas 6 and 10 while trading areas 7, 8, and 9 are receiving proportionately more coverage. The first step in adjusting the territories would be to determine whether trading areas 6 or 10 in territory 2 were geographically proximate to territory 1. If so, adding either trading area to territory 1 would help balance the two territories. If the trading areas were not proximate, the territories could be redesigned from scratch.

Another possibility to note is the wide disparity in the level of service needed across the trading areas. Trading areas 1, 3, 4, and 5 together only require .16 sales-

---

EXHIBIT 9.9

ASSIGNING SALESPEOPLE TO TERRITORIES

Table 1:   *Territory Performance Indices by Salesperson*

	Territory Potential	Salesperson A	Salesperson B	Salesperson C
Territory 1	1,000,000	1.2	1.3	1.3
Territory 2	1,250,000	1.1	1.1	1.3
Territory 3	1,350,000	.8	.9	1.0

Table 2:   *Description of Alternative Territory Assignments*

	Alt 1	Alt 2	Alt 3	Alt 4	Alt 5	Alt 6
Territory 1	A	A	B	B	C	C
Territory 2	B	C	A	C	B	A
Territory 3	C	B	C	A	A	B

Table 3:   *Value of Alternative Territory Assignments*

	Alt 1	Alt 2	Alt 3	Alt 4	Alt 5	Alt 6
Territory 1	1,200,000	1,200,000	1,300,000	1,300,000	1,300,000	1,300,000
Territory 2	1,375,000	1,625,000	1,375,000	1,625,000	1,375,000	1,375,000
Territory 3	1,350,000	1,215,000	1,350,000	1,080,000	1,080,000	1,215,000
Total	3,925,000	4,040,000	4,025,000	4,005,000	3,755,000	3,890,000

---

people, while 2, 6, 7, 8, 9, and 10 require 2.83 salespeople. Therefore, the firm could increase its productivity by concentrating its two salespeople in the larger trading areas and using another selling approach to reach the four smaller areas.

Assigning Salespeople to Territories.   The task of assigning salespeople to territories can be extremely difficult because it must take into account several factors, including the match between the salesperson and the territory, the type of selling situation, and the history of the salesforce in that territory. Matching the salesperson and the territory is a function of the ranking of the salesperson and territory potential. Managers can rank salespeople using a 1.0 to represent an average salesperson. Better-than-average salespeople are ranked 1.1, 1.2, or higher. Worse-than-average salespeople are ranked .9, .8, or lower. Salespeople do not always receive the same ranking in each territory. A salesperson might know a particular territory very well or be better at selling to a certain industry that is heavily concentrated in a certain territory. As a result, the rankings must be adjusted to reflect how the salesperson is likely to perform in each territory. Table 1 in Exhibit 9.9 shows how a manager ranks three salespeople in terms of their likely performance in three different territories. Salesperson A, for example, has a performance rating of 1.2 for territory A, 1.1 for territory B, and .8 for territory C.

Managers can use several rules to apply the information in Table 1 to assign salespeople to territories. One simple rule is to assign the salesperson to the territory where he or she has the highest rating. Unfortunately this may not always yield optimal results, as in the additional analyses shown in Tables 2 and 3. Table 2 shows all possible salesperson/territory assignments. Table 3 shows the value of each alternative. The value is derived by multiplying the salesperson's performance index by the territory potential for each alternative. In alternative 1, for example, salesperson A is assigned to territory 1, salesperson B is assigned to territory 2, and salesperson C is assigned to territory 3. By multiplying each salesperson's performance index by the potential sales for the specific territory and summing across the territories, the total value of the alternative is derived. For alternative 1 the total value is $3,925,000.

In Table 3 the alternative that generated the highest revenue was alternative 2. In alternative 2 territory 1 is served by salesperson A, territory 2 is served by salesperson C, and territory 3 is served by salesperson B. This alternative has interesting characteristics. Territory 1 is served by salesperson A, the salesperson with the lowest ranking for that territory. Salesperson B is assigned to territory 3, which is also his lowest ranked territory. These assignments show that the process of matching salespeople to territories is not a simple and straightforward one. Sales managers must consider all salespeople simultaneously when making territory assignments. Further, the use of simple rules such as, "Assign each salesperson to the territory where he or she receives the highest ranking," may result in suboptimal overall territory assignments.

The type of selling situation may also affect assignment of salespeople to territories. For firms that are trying to develop long-term relationships with customers, territory assignments may also be long-term. The rationale for this policy is that salespeople must develop good relationships with customers to ensure a steady stream of orders. Long-term territory assignments are seen as the primary means of developing long-term customer relationships.

Some firms, however, do not think that long-term territory assignments are necessary to foster long-term customer relationships. One company that sells *Yellow Pages* advertising in New England has a ritual at its annual meeting wherein salespeople draw their territory assignments for the upcoming year from a hat. The firm feels it is easier for a new salesperson to ask for a larger ad than the salesperson who asked for the order last year.

Another circumstance under which frequent reassignment of salespeople to new territories might be called for is in industries where the turnover is above average. In those industries, sales managers reason that the image of their company may be harmed if the customer unexpectedly sees a new face or hears a new voice over the telephone. If the firm already follows a policy where accounts are reassigned on a routine basis, customers will not be alarmed when they get a new rep.[17]

Another factor to be considered in the assignment of salespeople to territories is the history of the salesforce in that territory. In the 1980s and 1990s, with consolidation and downsizing occurring in many industries, firms have wound up with multiple salesforces serving given territories. Sales management have been faced with the task of determining how to deploy, and in many cases, how to downsize, these salesforces. One firm, through a series of acquisitions, ended up with three sales organizations covering the same territories. Management kept all salespeople in the field while they worked on other aspects of the acquisitions. Territories were split or divided among three salespeople. When management analyzed the sales results, they found that many of the smaller territories were profitable and continuing to grow. Further investigation showed that the smaller territories allowed salespeople to devote more time to their customers, especially the smaller and mid-sized accounts. Higher sales and profits resulted.[18]

Another firm tried a similar strategy with much less encouraging results. A machine tool company built up its salesforce by hiring from competitors. Each salesperson was allowed to retain his or her best accounts, regardless of location. Sixteen salespeople were hired, and they constantly found themselves crossing paths throughout the United States. Travel expenses skyrocketed, and the salespeople found their customers to be more loyal to their former employers than to their current firm. The consequences were so negative that the salesforce was disbanded and the selling effort was turned over to independent rep firms.[19]

SUMMARY

Based on a broad understanding of customer purchasing patterns, and keeping in mind the alternative selling approaches available, sales management must deploy its salesforce in such a way as to meet sales goals. Salesforce deployment has three major decision areas: classifying customers, determining the size of the salesforce, and designing the territory.

Classifying customers can be done using single-factor, multiple-factor, and judgment-based or empirically based decision models. Single-factor models use a single customer characteristic, such as size, to classify customers into categories. All customers within a given category receive the same level of selling effort. Multiple-factor models, as the name implies, use multiple customer characteristics to place customers into categories that will receive the same level of selling effort. Decision models use salesperson and management judgment (judgment-based) or past data (empirically based) to determine the likely response of customers to different levels of selling effort. Selling resources are allocated according to their most productive use.

Determining salesforce size is the second major decision in salesforce deployment. Sales managers determine salesforce size using breakdown, work load, or incremental methods. The breakdown method divides the sales forecast by the average sales per salesperson. The work load method sets salesforce size on the basis of the required level of selling effort needed to reach a sales goal. In other words, if a salesforce must make 25,000 sales calls to reach the sales goal, salesforce size is a function of the number of salespeople necessary to make 25,000 calls. The incremental method compares the marginal revenue from adding one salesperson to the marginal cost of adding that salesperson. As long as marginal revenue exceeds marginal cost, additional salespeople should be added. The breakdown method is conceptually the weakest, whereas the incremental method is the strongest. In practice, however, the incremental method is extremely difficult to calculate and cannot be used with commission-only salesforces. The breakdown method blends some conceptual rigor with wide applicability.

The third decision area for salesforce deployment is designing territories. Territory design has changed radically in the last 5 to 10 years with the advent of inexpensive geographical information system software that allow sales managers to overlay geographical characteristics, such as street maps, mountains, and rivers, with customer information, such as level of sales, type of products purchased, and other relevant account information. Using GIS, managers can calculate territory designs in minutes or hours instead of weeks or months, as in the past. As a result territory design and realignment has become a more frequently performed task. Conceptually, territory design follows five steps: selecting the control unit, analyzing territory potential and forming territories, analyzing work load, balancing work load and territory potential, and assigning salespeople to territories.

KEY TERMS

salesforce deployment	breakdown method
single-factor model	work load method
multiple-factor models	incremental method
portfolio models	territory
decision models	geographic information systems (GIS) software
judgment-based decision models	control unit
empirically based decision models	

DISCUSSION QUESTIONS

1. What is salesforce deployment, and what decisions does it encompass?
2. What models are available to determine how to classify customers? What are the advantages and disadvantages of each model?
3. Why is determining salesforce size an important decision for a sales manager?
4. What methods are available to determine the appropriate salesforce size?
5. What are territories? Why would sales managers want to strategically arrange salespeople in territories?
6. In what situations would a sales manager not want to define formal salesforce territories?
7. How has the advent of geographic information systems software in recent years affected territory design?
8. What process can managers undertake to effectively design territories and allocate salespeople to those territories?
9. What is a control unit? What are the advantages and disadvantages of using control units to build territories?
10. Why is it difficult for a sales manager to balance work load and territory potential? What options are available to aid the sales manager?

PROBLEMS

1. As a vice-president of sales for a division of a large telecommunications firm, you are in charge of setting the appropriate salesforce size. Traditionally your firm has used the breakdown method. Using an average expected sales per employee of $1 million you have simply taken the forecasted sales for the upcoming year, divided it by $1 million, and adjusted salesforce size as necessary.

In the upcoming year sales for your division are forecast at $400 million. You currently have 350 salespeople. While you would normally suggest increasing salesforce size to 400, you are not sure that this is the best method for setting salesforce size this year. You have recently heard a presentation by a consultant who said that high-performing salesforces often have sales exceeding $6 million per salesperson. You have also heard through the corporate grapevine that a round of downsizing is coming that will probably affect your salesforce. Prepare an estimate for salesforce size for the upcoming year. Support your answer.

2. As the national sales manager for a small but rapidly growing pharmaceuticals firm, you have been drawn into a heated discussion with the director of national accounts and the director of field sales. You feel that the firm's growth justifies the development of territories. The director of national accounts does not see a need for territories because his salesforce is responsible for selling to large customers who have multiple purchasing locations across the country. The director of field sales thinks that territories may be a good idea in concept, but in her experience they are complicated, take a long time to develop, and are difficult to modify. Develop a memo to each manager supporting the idea of developing territories.

3. As the district sales manager for a distributor of car parts and accessories, you are considering reassigning your salespeople to new territories. You have the following information about territory potential and salesperson performance:

	Territory Potential	Salesperson A	Salesperson B	Salesperson C	Salesperson D
Territory 1	1,500,000	.8	1.0	.9	1.0
Territory 2	2,250,000	1.1	1.1	1.2	1.0
Territory 3	2,000,000	1.0	1.1	.8	1.0
Territory 4	1,400,000	.9	1.0	1.3	.8

Which salespeople should be assigned to which territories?

SHORT CASE
INDOCHEM

BACKGROUND

Indochem, a manufacturer and distributor of specialty industrial chemicals, uses a geographically based field salesforce. The salespeople call on industrial purchasing agents and engineers. The company has been growing rapidly, but the salesforce organization has not changed accordingly.

SITUATION

"Bill, we have to rationalize the way we allocate salespeople to territories," is the comment that greeted Bill Weathers, the top district sales manager in the Midwest Region, as he entered his boss's office early one Monday morning. Karen Spratlen, the regional manager, continued, "We have not reevaluated our allocations of salespeople to territories in over 5 years. Our customers have changed a lot in that time. Some of our salespeople have gotten lazy serving easy territories, and others are quitting because the territory potential does not provide them enough to live on."

"Wait a minute," responded Weathers. "Aren't we getting a little ahead of ourselves? My district is ahead of sales quota but I don't know that you would get any of my salespeople to agree that they have easy territories. As far as turnover is concerned, we have experienced our share, but let's not get carried away. Most of the people who left were malcontents who would not have been satisfied under any circumstances."

Spratlen frowned, "Bill, I don't think you realize the magnitude of our problems. We simply can't afford to let salespeople focus only on the high potential accounts. Developing new customers must be done to make sure the company continues to grow. In addition, recruiting and training costs are hitting an all-time high, and we simply can't afford to dismiss turnover as just another cost of doing business."

Weathers started to argue more, but Spratlen cut him off, "I don't want to get into an argument about whether your salespeople are overworked or underworked, or whether turnover happened because of territory assignments or because of poor recruiting practices. What I want to do is start with a look at territory assignments to see if they could be contributing to the problems. I want you to look at a report I had one of our market analysts put together."

Spratlen pulls out a report (see the Appendix) that shows the potential for the territories for which Weathers has overall responsibility. "According to this report, Bill, your salespeople are not allocated by territory potential."

Weathers replies," Well, Karen, I will look the report over, but I am not sure that I want to disrupt the productivity of my territory by making a lot of changes in territory assignments."

"Bill," She says sternly, "I can't emphasize this strongly enough: We must reallocate salespeople into the most productive possible alignment. And your territory is where we are starting."

"OK, Karen, I'll see what I can do."

PROBLEM

Weathers returns to his office with the report and begins to ponder the possible reallocation of his salespeople. He knows there are probably some reallocations that should be performed but is truly concerned about the possible impact of any changes on the salesforce.

QUESTIONS

1. Based on the report, what alignment should Weathers suggest? Defend your approach.
2. How should Weathers sell the approach to the salespeople in his territory?
3. Should Spratlen have done anything differently to convince Weathers of the need for territory realignment?
4. What process might Spratlen consider to avoid problems such as this in the future?

APPENDIX

	Trading Area (TA)	Present % of Time Spent Serving the TA	Recommended % of Time to Spend Serving the TA
Territory 1	1	15	10
	2	50	80
	3	15	25
	4	20	40
Total		100	155
Territory 2	5	25	10
	6	25	10
	7	40	5
	8	10	40
Total		100	65
	9	65	50
	10	15	25
	11	20	50
Total		100	125
	12	65	45
	13	5	30
	14	10	5
	15	15	5
	16	5	25
Total		100	110

TERRITORIES ROLE PLAY

CHARACTERS

Sales Manager: Howard Sierra or Rebecca Goldberg

Veteran Salesperson: Vinnie Canseca or Nancy Chee

Rookie Salesperson: Jamal Washington or Jennifer Roth

SCENARIO

Vinnie Canseca has been a sales representative for EDD for the past 10 years. Oakland has been his territory for 7 of those years. Canseca has been among the top three salespeople in the company for the past 5 years. He is very well respected by his peers and customers.

Canseca's current territory consists of 120 doctors and three large hospitals. Recently EDD has acquired Pharmipro from a Japanese research firm. The sales of this product are expected to be healthy (excuse the pun). He is looking forward to the new potential. He has never been afraid of a challenge.

Howard Sierra has been Canseca's sales manager in the San Francisco district for the past 4 years. There are six salespeople that report to him, with three located in San Francisco and one (Canseca) in Oakland. Because of the recent addition of Pharmipro, analysis indicates that the Oakland territory has more potential than one rep can handle. Sierra is worried about rearranging Canseca's territory. Canseca is a rather emotional person who prefers to be left alone and just do his job. Even though Canseca has trained rookies in the past, he is not thrilled with training new people. The surprising aspect is that Canseca has excellent interpersonal skills with the doctors he calls on and is very well liked; he has a number of long-term customers. Canseca is currently training Jamal Washington, a new recruit straight from college. Sierra plans on using Washington in the new territory if he can figure out how to create it.

SCENE 1

The first scene has Canseca and Sierra meeting. Sierra explains the basic scenario about how the potential has increased and what the new product should do for the company. He compliments Canseca on his development of the territory and his past success. He then informs Canseca that some restructuring is necessary. Sierra says that he is assigning Jamal Washington to part of Canseca's territory. Canseca is very unhappy and expresses his concern about losing customers that he has served for years. "They trust me. They're not going to do business with some beginner. I've worked hard. Don't take my customers away from me!" Sierra replies that he will think about it and do what he can.

SCENE 2

The second scene begins with Canseca, Washington, and Sierra all meeting to discuss the division of the new territory. Sierra tells Canseca that he is going to give Washington West Oakland. Canseca angrily replies that West Oakland contains some of his best customers. He has spent the past 2 years developing the new hospital, which is the largest account in West Oakland. "Give Washington the new accounts and some of my mediocre accounts." Washington responds by saying that he doesn't mind developing new accounts, but he needs some sizable accounts to be fairly compensated. Canseca subtly threatens to quit and take his accounts with him if his territory is changed. The scene continues with various alternatives being suggested and discussed, but at least one of the salespeople rejects each plan.

SCENE 3

Scene 3 is yours to resolve the situation. It may contain any or all of the characters. Be realistic and defend your solution.

CHARACTER DESCRIPTIONS

Name: Rebecca Goldberg
Gender: F
Age: 34
Marital status: Married
Education: B.B.A., Lehigh University
Title: Sales Manager
Office location: San Francisco
Reports to: District Manager, Los Angeles
Employment history: Hired as a manager from a competitor
Personality: Sensitive to employees; company profit takes priority; fair; wants to be liked and respected
Notes: District has always been profitable; spends a lot of time "putting out fires"; chess player
Grapevine: Very loyal to the company

Name: Howard Sierra
Gender: M
Age: 37
Marital status: Married
Education: B.A., Murray State University
Title: Sales Manager
Office location: San Francisco
Reports to: District Manager, Los Angeles
Employment history: Salesperson for 4 years; manager for 6 years; previously worked for competitor
Personality: Sensitive to employees; company profit takes priority; fair; wants to be liked and respected
Notes: District has always been profitable; spends a lot of time "putting out fires"; owns a Harley
Grapevine: Very loyal to the company

Name: Nancy Chee
Gender: F
Age: 43
Marital status: Widowed
Education: B.A. Oklahoma State University
Title: Senior Salesperson
Office location: San Francisco
Reports to: Sales Manager, San Francisco
Employment history: Ten years with Pharmiceaux; same territory for 7 years
Personality: Goal- and task-oriented; very competitive; competent; dependable; very personable

Notes: Among the top three salespeople in Pharmiceaux for the last 5 years; needs little supervision; strong customer advocate; Native American advocate
Grapevine: Likely to produce for a long time

Name: Vinnie Canseca
Gender: M **Age:** 43
Marital status: Married
Education: B.S., Ball State University
Title: Senior Salesperson
Office location: Oakland
Reports to: Sales Manager, San Francisco
Employment history: Ten years with Pharmiceaux; same territory for 7 years
Personality: Emotional; goal- and task- oriented; very competitive; no tolerance for incompetence; very personable with customers; competent; dependable
Notes: Strong customer advocate; among top five salespeople in Pharmiceaux for the last 5 years; needs little supervision; baseball fanatic
Grapevine: Likely to produce for a long time

Name: Jamal Washington
Gender: M
Age: 22
Marital status: Single
Education: B.B.A Slippery Rock
Title: Sales Rep
Office location: San Francisco
Reports to: Sales Manager, San Francisco
Employment history: Recent graduate; just finished training
Personality: Very ambitious; self-assured; eager to succeed
Notes: Student House of Representatives in college; used to being a leader; model student; likes the nightlife
Grapevine: High potential

Name: Jennifer Roth
Gender: F
Age: 22
Marital status: Single
Education: B.S. Columbia University
Title: Sales Rep
Office location: San Francisco
Reports to: Sales Manager, San Francisco
Employment history: Recent graduate; just finished training
Personality: Leader; really ambitious; self-assured; eager to succeed
Notes: President of student organizations; tops in training class; selected Pharmiceaux over other

offers because of greatest job potential; women's rights advocate
Grapevine: Potential fast-track candidate

QUESTIONS

1. How can companies redesign sales territories?
2. What problems occur when territories are redesigned?

3. Is it fair or right to take customers away from Canseca since he is the one who developed the accounts?
4. List at least four alternatives Sierra could use in resolving this role play, and discuss the long-term consequences of each.
5. Which alternative discussed in question 4 should Sierra select to resolve the role play. Defend your answer fully.

NOTES

1. Melissa Campanelli, "Reshuffling the Deck," *Sales and Marketing Management* (June 1994): 83–90.
2. Raymond W. LaForge, David W. Cravens, and Clifford E. Young, "Using Contingency Analysis to Select Selling Effort Allocation Methods," *Journal of Personal Selling and Sales Management,* 6 (August 1986): 19–28.
3. Raymond W. LaForge, David W. Cravens, and Clifford E. Young, "Improving Salesforce Productivity," *Business Horizons* (September/October 1985): 50–59.
4. Clifford E. Young, "Portfolio Analysis Using Lotus 1-2-3," Scott Smith (ed.), *Marketing Applications Using Lotus 1-2-3,* (Palo Alto, CA: Scientific Press, 1988).
5. There is empirical support for the existence of S-shaped sales response curves. William A. Weeks and Lynn R. Kahle, "Salespeople's Time Use and Performance," *Journal of Personal Selling and Sales Management,* 10 (Winter 1990): 29–37.
6. Andrea Rock, "Remarketing IBM," *Business Marketing* (May 1993) 26, 32.
7. Personal communication, James Badders, vice-president, GTE Consumer Markets division, December 5, 1994.
8. Campanelli (1994), op. cit.
9. *Ibid.*
10. Richard Lewis, "Putting Sales on the Map," *Sales and Marketing Management* 149 (9) (August 1992): 76–80.
11. Campanelli (1994), op. cit.
12. Tom Eisenhart, "Drawing a Map to Better Sales," *Business Marketing,* (January 1990): 59–61.
13. David Forrest, "It's Not Just a Pretty Picture," *Computerworld* (March 7, 1994): 87–88.
14. Lewis (1992), op. cit.
15. Forrest (1994), op. cit.
16. Lewis, (1992), op. cit.
17. The discussion of circumstances under which switching salespeople among territories is based on Paul Micali, "If Salespeople Know the Territory Too Well, It's Time to Swap," *Sales and Marketing Management* (January 1990): 77.
18. Jack Falvey, "Getting Organized," *Sales and Marketing Management* (April 1993): 14–16.
19. Micali (1990), op. cit.

YANG TOYLAND PTE. LTD.

This case was prepared by Hellmut Schütte, Affiliate Professor at INSEAD. It is intended to be used as a basis for class discussion rather than to illustrate either effective or ineffective handling of an administrative situation.

For Y.C. Yang the year was practically over at the end of August. He was heading Yang Toyland Pte. Ltd., a small, family owned, toy manufacturer, which he ran together with his older sister and his younger brother in Singapore.

"This year's turnover will reach about S\$7m—an increase of about 20% over the preceeding year", he thought to himself, "and profit will also be good—perhaps even reaching S\$300,000".

He did not expect any more major orders to come in. His customers from the States and Europe had placed their orders, quite a substantial part of which had already been carried out and even shipped to arrive at their destinations in time for Christmas. There would be one or two additional orders within the next weeks, but after that his company would be able to turn their attention again to finding and developing ideas for new products.

DEVELOPMENT OF THE FIRM

When his father died nine years ago, the company had only eight people and had just launched its first toy car with an electrical, battery-driven motor. The chassis and body were made of plastic with some metal used for parts such as axles, fixtures, tirecaps, etc. At that time Yang Toyland's turnover was below half a million dollars, and its profitability was very low. Y.C. and his younger brother had had difficulties convincing their father to add the motor to one of their existing models which they had produced for many years but which had become unattractive. He had finally given in when he saw that competitors were selling battery-driven cars like hot cakes while Yang Toyland's products were not moving.

Since those days they had regularly upgraded up their product range of toy cars by adding features such as lights, sirens, and a steering system using a wire which connected the car to a small wheel fixed to a plastic box. This box the child held in his hand when following the car. Models ranged from fancy racing and luxury cars to jeeps, trucks, pick-ups, police cars and fire engines. Presently, their top-of-the-line product was a remote-controlled, four-wheel driven jeep which could move forwards and backwards, stop and accelerate, turn to the right and the left, and climb steep hills with a gradient of up to 40°. Control was exercised with the help of a telecommander which transmitted the various commands to the car. Both the transmitter and the car were equipped with antennas. Some of their models can be seen in Exhibit 1.

Y.C.'s brother, Paul, was the driving force behind the technological developments in Yang Toyland Pte. Ltd. As an electrical engineer from Singapore's Ngee Ann Polytechnic, he spent twelve to fifteen hours per day in the factory to deliver the goods which his brother had sold and to look for new ideas on how to improve the production process and the products. Some sophisticated equipment and machinery had been introduced but in most cases the batch sizes for the various parts to be manufactured were too small to make automation or even semi-automation feasible, so that the whole process was still fairly labour-intensive. Motors and the control system were purchased from outside. Most of the product ideas were derived from models found abroad or described in catalogues and trade journals. Paul's present dream was to come out with some innovations which would make use of cheap microelectronics and increase the manoeuvrability of the toy cars.

The factory now employed some 40 people. Ten additional employees were involved in administration and sales. Y.C.'s sister, Rosy, was in charge of purchasing, personnel, finance and general administration. Unlike her brother she had initially insisted on making her own career outside the family firm in a bank. Later, when sales were growing rapidly and Y.C. and Paul had difficulties managing the firm, she acceded to the request of her brothers and joined the company. From that day on many administrative problems became easier to handle and the relationship with their bank improved. Rosy also knew how to take advantage of various government programmes set up to assist smaller firms and was able to obtain a long-term loan from the government at a very favourable rate.

SALES ACTIVITIES

Y.C. was responsible for sales. Over the years he had developed valuable contacts with buyers from the US, Europe, and recently also Japan. Many of the buyers he met in Singapore when they came around for shopping trips in the Far East, usually during the spring. Some of his bigger customers had buying offices in Hong Kong, two even in Singapore. The majority of his customers were wholesale importers. Others, especially from the USA, bought directly for their chains of specialised toy shops. So far he had obtained very few orders from department stores and other large retail groups. In terms of geographical spread, 55% of sales were shipped to the United States and 30% to Europe. Exports to Japan amounted to only 3% of total sales. The rest—12%—was sold in the local market. Some of these products found their way from Singapore into Malaysia, Indonesia and other Asian countries.

Since his sister had joined the firm, it had been possible for Y.C. to go abroad twice a year

for about two weeks each time, once to the United States and once to Europe. The trips were scheduled in such a way that he could attend the major international toy fairs and at the same time pay visits to his existing and potential customers. He had participated in a few fairs in which Singapore products were displayed, but considered a stand for Yang Toyland alone too expensive and thus not feasible.

At least twice a year he produced and dispatched a six-page, coloured brochure in English which showed their products and prices. In each brochure it was pointed out that specifications of the various models could be slightly changed according to customers' demand for which prices would be quoted on request. This gave Yang Toyland the flexibility to determine their prices according to the negotiation power of the potential buyer and their own capacity utilisation. Apart from the brochures, Yang Toyland placed some ads in trade journals in Singapore, the United States, the United Kingdom and Germany. Results from these advertisements were mixed.

THE MARKET

Competition in toy cars was very tough and came from multinationals such as Fisher-Price and Mattel as well as from a large number of smaller manufacturers in Asia, particularly in Hong Kong, Taiwan and Korea. The industry was characterised by the sudden creation of bestsellers such as remote-controlled, four-wheel-driven cars which made other models obsolete within a very short time. To keep up with the market and to be quick to adapt to new trends was therefore essential for survival. Singapore's higher wages in comparison with other Asian producers made it necessary to be at the forefront of technology, since older, standard models were sold only on price.

The fact that Yang Toyland had so far been successful in the business was according to Y.C. due to their decision to concentrate on a narrow range of products. At the same time, their specialisation made them vulnerable to market changes. Y.C., however, did not rate this risk

EXHIBIT 2	
Ordervolume in S $ p.a.	Number of Accounts
0–5,000	38
5,000–50,000	63
50,000–100,000	35
100,000–250,000	12
250,000–500,000	1
Total Number of Accounts	149

very high: "Boys want cars, first as kids, later as adults. Toy cars are an essential part of the upbringing of boys—they are basic needs!"

Last year, Yang Toyland had 149 customer accounts. Two thirds of those had placed orders of less than S$50,000 p.a.. Only one customer, a chain store from the US, had bought products for more than S$250,000 during that year (for further details see Exhibit 2). This year the situation would not be very different. From experience Y.C. knew that only 50–60% of his customers would purchase from him again during the following year. This percentage was lower among the smaller purchasers which meant that stability of the business came mainly from the larger purchasers. It was not clear to Y.C. whether the high fluctuation among his customers was a specific problem of his company or the industry in general. His impression was that customer satisfaction had been relatively high in the past and that some of his former customers had returned to him after having bought from his competitors for a limited period.

CONTACTS WITH DIRECT MAIL ORDER HOUSES

Two years ago, Y.C. had started to attract orders from direct mail order houses. He had prepared special samples for them and arranged for various certificates to prove that his goods complied with the requirements and norms of the respective purchasers. He had met several times with their representatives in Singapore and visited three major direct mail order houses in the US and two each in the UK and Germany. He remembered how surprised he was initially by the professionalism and the shrewdness of their buy-

ers and their deep knowledge of the market. When, a year ago, he presented his latest model to a German direct mail order house, the buyer—a certain Herr Clausen—knew immediately from where his brother had adopted the design. It took him only four minutes to point out the weak spots in the construction and another three minutes to convince him that his asking price was indeed too high. But Herr Clausen had also given him some advice on how to improve certain aspects of the car and how to reduce costs. "In fifteen minutes I had learned more than I normally would in one year, but there wasn't even a hint of giving me an order", Y.C. reported to his brother and sister, on his return from Europe. His experience in the UK had not been more encouraging. Both companies there were basically interested in low prices to replace the models of competitors which they considered too expensive.

In the US the buyers seemed to be hooked on Taiwanese and Hong Kong producers with whom they had done business for many years. At Sears, the biggest direct mail order house in the world (see list in Exhibit 3a), he had not been able to see the man in charge of toy purchases. An assistant manager had talked about quantities which were much too big for Yang Toyland to handle.

Y.C. had developed the contacts further, especially with Herr Clausen from Gross-Versand and one of the British houses. Since Gross-Versand had a purchasing office in Singapore, communication with Germany had been relatively easy. But procedures for getting samples accepted were very time consuming and tedious. The remote-control system in particular had created problems due to the strict frequency regulations in Europe. Although Yang Toyland imported the system from Japan where it was certified not to interfere with any radiowaves, Gross-Versand had insisted on special tests in Germany the cost of which had to be shouldered by the Singaporean exporter.

THE OFFER

It was on the 3rd of September that Y.C. was invited to see Mrs. Petra Müller, Gross-Versands'

EXHIBIT 3A	
THE WORLD'S 10 LARGEST MAIL-ORDER COMPANIES	
Name	Mail-Order Sales in DM Million
1. Sears Group, USA	7,330[a]
2. Otto Group, Germany	6,819[b]
3. Quelle Group, Germany	6,343[b]
4. GUS Group, UK	3,296[a]
5. Penney, USA	2,791[a]
6. Littlewoods, UK	2,760[a]
7. La Redoute, France	2,084[a]
8. Montgomery Ward, USA	2,039[a]
9. Neckermann, Germany	1,848[b]
10. Freemans, UK	1,329[b]

[a]1980 figures.

[b]1981 figures.

EXHIBIT 3B	
RELATIVE MARKET SHARE OF THE MAIL-ORDER INDUSTRY IN SELECTED PRODUCT GROUPS	
Product Group	Market Share
Bed linen	30%
Blankets and rugs	30%
Books	20%
Photographic equipment	20%
Men's underwear	18%
Women's underwear	17%
White goods (refrigerators, washing machines)	16%
Vacuum cleaners	12%
Dresses	12%
Corsetry	12%
Skirts and blouses	11%
Colour television sets	11%
Women's suits	10%
Floor covering	9%
Do-it-yourself articles	9%
Toys	8%
Sports clothing	8%
Knitwear	8%
Watches and jewellery	8%
Textiles	8%
Shoes	7%

local representative, in her office in the Shaw Center. He had met her several times before and channeled most of his communication with Herr Clausen through her office. She had also been in his factory and had talked to his brother and sister. Y.C. was aware that she had tried to collect some information about Yang Toyland's reputation from banks, suppliers and customers.

Mrs. Müller opened the meeting with some good news for Y.C. Gross-Versand had accepted the samples of Yang Toyland and now wanted to buy two of their models for next year's autumn-winter catalogue. The models selected were a four-wheel-drive jeep CXL and a Porsche 911 similar to their bestseller this year. Both products were especially designed, painted, decorated and equipped for Gross-Versand. As discussed before, Yang Toyland would not be entitled to sell these models to anybody else, even if they proved outstanding market successes.

Gross-Versand estimated it would sell 20,000 of the CXL and 120,000 of the Porsche cars either directly, or indirectly through their subsidiaries in Germany, Belgium, the Netherlands, Austria and France. Because of the distribution throughout Europe some slight changes in the outer appearance were envisaged. This could be handled easily.

Gross-Versand wanted a firm commitment from Yang Toyland for the delivery of the total volume of 140,000 pieces by 30 October next year (arrival in Germany). However, the buyer himself would place an order for only 50% of the respective quantities with a delivery date of 31 July. The rest could be ordered by Gross-Versand later and had to be shipped as specified by the buyer within a very short period, the length of it depending on the volume ordered. Prices proposed by Gross-Versand were S$23.25 for the CXL and S$16.30 for the Porsche. These prices were about 25% below those quoted for similar models in Yang Toyland's brochure. They could not be altered for the duration of the contract.

Mrs. Müller did not expect an immediate response from Y.C.. Instead she announced that Herr Clausen would pass through Singapore in two weeks and wanted to finalise the contract with Yang Toyland. She also mentioned that her role would be confined to quality control while all contract negotiations would be the responsibility of headquarters. Mrs. Müller further reminded Y.C. of the General Purchase Conditions of Gross-Versand which she had given to him some time ago (see Exhibit 4) and of the great value her company placed on long-lasting rela-

tionships with reliable suppliers. With this in mind Y.C. left the office.

Three days later Y.C. met with Paul and Rosy to discuss "Project Gross" as they had called the offer in the meantime. Y.C. brought with him a first production schedule for next year based on orders received and further orders expected. Paul had all cost statistics to hand and some brochures

---

EXHIBIT 4

GENERAL PURCHASE CONDITIONS OF GROSS-VERSAND (GERMANY)
(shortened version)

I. AWARD OF CONTRACTS
For all contracts to be awarded only standard order forms shall be applicable. Verbal orders, supplements, amendments or any other agreements regarding orders already placed shall be binding only if agreed by both parties in writing and signed on their behalf.

2. PROTECTION OF FAIR COMPETITION
Prior to the expiration of the validity period of the catalogues for which the merchandise has been ordered, such merchandise shall not be supplied either in the same or in a similar form or made to any mail-order house. Trademarked articles are excluded. Gross-Versand shall be entitled to deliver the merchandise to any enterprises with which it is associated.

3. GUARANTEE OF QUALITY
During the validity of the Gross-Versand catalogues, the merchandise ordered by Gross-Versand shall be supplied as per sample, i.e. in accordance with the description, the sample submitted to and approved by Gross-Versand as well as in the same composition of materials, shape, manufacturing, presentation and guaranteed characteristics. If for any coercive reason, the supplier can no longer supply the merchandise in accordance with the original sample, the amended supply shall be subject to a previous approval in writing by Gross-Versand. The supplier undertakes to control the merchandise prior to dispatch.

4. PRICES
The price stated in the order shall be inclusive of all packing requirements of Gross-Versand. The prices shall be binding during the validity period of the Gross-Versand catalogues for which the merchandise has been ordered.

5. PACKING AND MARKETING REQUIREMENTS
Labelling, packing and shipment of the merchandise shall at all times comply with the packing and shipment instructions of Gross-Versand.

6. DELIVERY
All deliveries are to be effected in accordance with orders placed. The date of delivery stipulated in the order is always the latest shipping date (fixed date). Should the supplier be unable to deliver within the stipulated dates, Gross-Versand shall be entitled to raise the following claims:
(a) payment of damages for non-delivery plus accrued incidental costs.
(b) to have the ordered articles manufactured by third parties. In such event, the supplier shall be liable for any additional costs incurred to Gross-Versand.
(c) payment of damages for late delivery plus accrued incidental costs if Gross-Versand has advised the supplier without delay after the expiration of the stipulated date that it insists on performance.

EXHIBIT 4 (continued)

GENERAL PURCHASE CONDITIONS OF GROSS-VERSAND (GERMANY)
(shortened version)

Gross-Versand's right of cancellation of the order shall not be affected. Any extensions of time granted by Gross-Versand are to be interpreted strictly and no further extensions of time are to be implied. They do not affect the claim for damages for late delivery. Upon receipt of goods not delivered in time no express reservation need be made with regard to the damage caused by the late delivery.

7. INSURANCE OF MERCHANDISE

The supplier shall at his sole discretion arrange insurance of the merchandise during transit and he shall only be entitled to get the costs of such an insurance repaid in case it had been arranged at the special request of Gross-Versand.

8. INVOICING

Supplier shall submit invoices to Gross-Versand in quadruplicate at the address referred to below, and each invoice shall bear the address of the consignee, in the event that the merchandise is shipped to more than one consignee the supplier shall provide Gross-Versand with separate invoices.

The assignment of claims against Gross-Versand shall be allowed only in favour of the seller's supplier.

9. PAYMENT

Payment shall be made by Gross-Versand in accordance with the terms and conditions appearing in the order. Payment shall be effected and time set for payment shall commence on receipt of merchandise and invoice only. Dispatch of a check or payment order to a bank is considered as due payment.

10. WARRANTY

Settlement of an invoice shall not imply any recognition that the goods thus paid for be free from defects, that they be in conformity with the contract or that the consignment be complete.

All quality defects and discrepancies in quantities, and measurements are covered by the supplier's warranty. The agreed warranty period will be 12 months.

The supplier is responsible under the rules of the Gerätesicherheitsgesetz (Equipment Security Act) and pursuant to the general product liability for the actual and consequential damages which are suffered by the enduser. The supplier is, upon request, obliged to produce evidence of compliance with the Gerätesicherheitsgesetz (Equipment Security Act) (i.e. attestation or certificate of testing by a testing authority) and in case of orders of prohibition under the Gerätesicherheitsgesetz (Equipment Security Act) has to take back the article irrespective of any periods of warranty.

---

of new machines which he wanted to buy and install once the contract was signed. Rosy had made some cost calculations and prepared a cash flow forecast. After seven hours of heated debate the following conclusions were reached:

- The firmly placed order of 10,000 CXLs and 60,000 Porsche cars could be fullfilled without substantial investment in additional capital equipment. To cope with the workload, overtime would not be enough. Additional staff would have to be hired—not an easy task in

Singapore. During the last two months before the dispatch of the products, no orders could be accepted in addition to those already received. Some of these they would try to reschedule by either delivering them earlier or later than requested. Bearing in mind the additional labour costs, and assuming constant prices for supplies, a profit of S$50,000 was expected.

- Any order above the 50% level would create serious capacity problems for Yang Toyland under the assumption that orders from other customers would come in and had to be sched-

EXHIBIT 4 (continued)

GENERAL PURCHASE CONDITIONS OF GROSS-VERSAND (GERMANY)

(shortened version)

If the merchandise supplied is not in conformity with the sample, with the prescriptions as to quality, packing, dispatch, marking of the material, as well as with symbol instructions for care, the supplier shall compensate Gross-Versand for any handling and administrative costs caused to Gross-Versand by control of merchandise, ascertainment of the defects, sorting out, remodeling, etc. This also applies to any inspection tests to be carried out outside the premises of Gross-Versand.

The return of defective merchandise to the supplier shall be deemed to mean notification of default, but shall not entitle the supplier to replace same. Without prejudice to any further claims, especially those resulting from damages caused to third parties, Gross-Versand shall be entitled to deduct from the supplier's next pending invoice the value of the claimed merchandise plus costs in connecting with the claim. In case such costs cannot be settled with invoices pending, then remittance of the claimed amount shall be due within ten days.

Instead of returning the defective merchandise to the supplier, Gross-Versand shall be entitled to claim a discount on the purchase price.

11. INDUSTRIAL PROPERTY RIGHTS

The supplier warrants that the offer and the sale of the goods do not infringe any rights of third parties (Copyrights, Patents, Registered Designs or Design Patents, Trademarks, Licenses, claims under the law on competition, etc) and will not violate any legal and governmental regulations. The supplier agrees to indemnify Gross-Versand as well as the enterprises associated with Gross-Versand against any claims by third parties and to make good the damage exceeding these claims and to give compensation for lost profits. The same applies, if the articles are offered and sold outside the Federal Republic of Germany, unless the supplier states on the Acknowledgement of Order that it is not permitted to offer and sell the goods abroad.

All drawings, sample designs, specifications and information supplied by Gross-Versand prepared or obtained by the supplier for and at the sole cost of Gross-Versand shall become and remain the property of Gross-Versand and shall be treated as confidential. They have to be returned to Gross-Versand after the contract has been fulfilled, and supplier is responsible not to have them misused in any way.

Supplier is not allowed to deliver merchandise bearing trademarks of Gross-Versand to any third party without written consent of Gross-Versand during winding up and after the expiration of the contract.

APPLICABLE LAW AND JURISDICTION

This contract shall be governed by and construed in accordance with the laws of the Federal Republic of Germany.

uled as they were this year. Additional machinery and equipment would be necessary, costing between S$400,000–500,000. In order to have it installed before the peak season, orders would have to be placed soon. This investment could not be financed out of the cash flow but would require a bank loan or supplier's credit since their liquidity position would be very tight during the summer months.

- Assuming a growth of their normal business of 10% p.a. and the placement of orders amounting to 15,000 CXLs and 90,000 Porsches, the investment in additional capital equipment would just make sense. Rosy reckoned that the average profit on sales should go up slightly and "Project Gross" produce a profit of about S$75,000. Should "Gross-Versand" order the full volume of 140,000 pieces and/or their business outside the mail order house grow by more than 10%, profitability would increase significantly. Should additional orders from Gross-Versand not materialise, and/or their normal business not grow as estimated, profits would quickly diminish.

Based on these calculations Rosy was not very keen on the contract with "Gross-Versand". Paul, however, was excited and saw the order as a good incentive for improving their production capability. Y.C. himself had mixed feelings. He knew that even obtaining slightly better prices from Herr Clausen would not solve the dilemma in which Yang Toyland found itself. He also knew that Herr Clausen expected a clear answer from him in less than two weeks.

DISCUSSION QUESTIONS

1. What advantages and disadvantages would you see for Yang Toyland in signing the proposed contract with Gross-Versand?
2. Consider possibilities of reducing the risk of over-investment/over-expansion.
3. What should be Y.C.'s objective in his discussion with Mr. Clausen?
4. What topics should Y.C. discuss with Mr. Clausen and in which order?

CAROLINA JAM AND JELLY

Case contributed by W. E. Patton III and the late Ronald H. King, Professors of Marketing, Appalachian State University.

INTRODUCTION

Tracy Lowe is the purchasing agent for Carolina Jam & Jelly, Inc., a large fruit processor and manufacturer of fruit jam and jelly with headquarters in Charlotte, North Carolina. Tracy is currently faced with the task of evaluating four vendors who are currently supplying Carolina Jam & Jelly with tops and lids for jelly jars. Although the firm is currently buying tops and lids from all four vendors, management has decided to reduce the number of vendors, and ideally would use only one vendor in the future.

The blanket contract for #4 jar lids will be expiring soon, and Tracy has asked the four current suppliers to submit bids. The firms were asked to submit a per-gross, FOB plant, freight-prepaid quotation for 500,000 #4 lids to be delivered during the next year. A blanket purchase order would be issued to the successful bidder, and each Carolina Jam & Jelly plant would place orders under this purchase order as lids were required during the year.

Tracy and her department, working with the other departments in the firm, have devel-

oped a rating system similar to that used in many other industries. Under this system, a vendor earns points depending on its past performance in nine different areas. These points are summed to give a score that can be used to compare vendors in overall performance and can also be used to adjust bid prices for comparison purposes. The system developed by Carolina Jam & Jelly is shown in Exhibit 1.

Each vendor would be judged along each performance dimension, points would be assigned along each dimension, and then the points would be summed for a total performance score. For example, assume that a company had a defect rate of 4 percent, delivery was typically four days late, one contact per order was required for expediting, the order routine response and technical cooperation were both satisfactory, facilities were outstanding, the financial status as indicated by a key ratio index was 95, the sales calls were helpful but irregular, and Carolina Jam & Jelly's business amounted to 30 percent of the vendor's total output. In this case the vendor would earn a total score of 1.27

R.W. Hass *Business Marketing*, 6th ed., Cincinnati: Southwestern Publishing Company, 1995. Reprinted with permission.

EXHIBIT I
CAROLINA JAM & JELLY VENDOR ANALYSIS COST RATIO RATING SYSTEM

Product Class: Component Parts: Jar Tops

Quality (defect rate)		Delivery		Expediting (number of contacts required during order cycle)	
> 5%	1.75	> 2 weeks late	+ .15	> 2 contacts	+.03
5%	1.40	1–2 weeks late	+ .07	2 contacts	+.01
4%	1.25	0–1 week late	+ .01	1 contact	.0
3%	1.10	0–1 week early	− .01	0 contacts and supplies status info	−.04
2%	1.05	1–2 weeks early	+ .02		
< 2%	1.00	> 2 weeks early	+ .05		

Response to Order Routine (i.e., order acknowledgment, invoicing, documentation)		Technical Cooperation		Facilities (capacity, dependability of equipment, technology, etc.)	
Outstanding	−.005	Outstanding	−.005	Outstanding	−.005
Satisfactory	.0	Satisfactory	.0	Satisfactory	.0
Unsatisfactory	+.01	Unsatisfactory	+.05	Unsatisfactory	+.05

Financial Status (key ratio index)		Value of Sales Calls		Our Business as a Proportion of Vendor's Total Output	
> 120	−.02	Regular, helpful, informative	−.01	> 50%	+.05
110–120	−.01	Regular only	.0	25–50%	−.01
100–109	.0	Helpful but irregular	+.005	10–25%	.0
< 100	+.02	Very infrequent	+.01	0–10%	+.01

INSTRUCTIONS: Rate each vendor on each item and sum the points. This becomes the vendor's cost ratio score. To determine an adjusted bid, multiply the cost ratio score by the amount bid.

$(1.25 + .01 + 0 + 0 + 0 − .005 + .02 + .005 − .01)$.

Note that better performance generates lower scores, reflecting the fact that good vendor performance should save money for Carolina Jam & Jelly and thus lower overall costs. Conversely, poorer vendor performance would increase costs for Carolina Jam & Jelly. The points given in each category were developed through an extensive study of the relationship between vendor performance and costs within Carolina Jam & Jelly and the magnitude of each reflects average cost and performance changes over the past four years.

The points system was also constructed so that the total score earned by each vendor could be used to adjust a vendor's bid price to reflect differences in performance-related costs. For example if vendor X bid $5 and earned a total of 1.20 points, the adjusted bid would be $5 × 1.2 or $6. Conversely, another vendor who bid $6 and earned a total point score of .90 would have an adjusted bid of $6 × .9 or $5.40 and might get the bid even though the actual raw bid was higher. The cost ratio rating system allows for the explicit recognition that the raw bid figure is not the only cost involved in a procurement action.

Tracy Lowe has just received the last of the quotations or bids from the four vendors on the bid list. Before opening the bids, Tracy quickly reviewed the previous performance of the vendors over the past year (a summary of this review is shown in Exhibit 2). After reviewing the performance summary, Tracy examined the bids from the four vendors. All bids were for 500,000 #4 lids, FOB plant, freight prepaid, and all allowed order-at-will by each plant in the Carolina system. The amounts bid were as follows:

EXHIBIT 2
INFORMATION ON CURRENT VENDORS OF #4 JAR TOPS

1. *Ajax Corporation:* Carolina Jam & Jelly's (CJJ) business accounts for 15% of Ajax output. Ajax is in good financial condition (a key ratio index of 110) and has satisfactory facilities. The quality of Ajax lids is good, with a defect rate of only 2%. They typically deliver four days before the due date, their response to order routine is satisfactory, and they typically require one expediting contact per order cycle. Their technical cooperation has been outstanding, and the sales rep calls regularly and is helpful and informative.

2. *Baker Lid Company:* CJJ's business accounts for 22% of Baker's output. Baker is in satisfactory financial condition (index = 105) and has satisfactory facilities. The quality of Baker's lids is outstanding, with a defect rate of only 1%, but their delivery is a bit slow—they usually run four days late. Their response to our order routine is satisfactory, but their expediting leaves a bit to be desired since we usually have to contact them twice for expediting during an order cycle. Their technical cooperation is satisfactory and although their sales rep calls regularly, he is not particularly helpful or informative.

3. *Charles Closure Company:* CJJ's business accounts for 26% of Charles's total output. Charles is in excellent financial condition (a ratio index of 125) and they have outstanding modern facilities. The quality of Charles's lids is not the strongest, resulting in a defect rate of 3%. Their delivery times are right on the button, usually a day early, and their expediting system is outstanding—we never have to contact them and they automatically provide us with regular status reports on shipments and delivery. Their response to our order routine and their technical cooperation are both outstanding. Their sales rep calls regularly and is helpful and informative.

4. *Dogg Top Co.:* CJJ's business accounts for only 5% of Dogg's output. Dogg is in somewhat shaky financial condition (index = 94), but their facilities are satisfactory. The defect rate of their lids is really pretty bad: 4% of them are defective. Their delivery is very slow (typically 10 days to 2 weeks late), we generally have to make three expediting calls in an order cycle, and their response to our order routine has been unsatisfactory in that they rarely acknowledge orders, only provide four copies of an invoice, etc. Their technical cooperation is limited and unsatisfactory, and their sales rep calls infrequently and is not particularly helpful or informative.

Vendor	Bid (per gross)
Ajax Corp.	$2.88
Baker Lid Co.	$2.85
Charles Closure Co.	$2.90
Dogg Top Co.	$2.04

Tracy had expected the bids to be pretty close, and she was startled by the very low bid by the Dogg Top Company. She was very glad that she had developed the vendor rating system to help her evaluate these bids.

DISCUSSION QUESTIONS

1. If Tracy must purchase all of the #4 jar lids from one vendor, which vendor should she select? Why?

2. If Tracy (and Carolina Jam & Jelly's management) decided to use two suppliers, and if Tracy thought she could negotiate with one of the firms *not* selected in question 1 above, which firm should she negotiate with and what new bid price would be required from this firm to be comparable to the one selected in question 1? Explain.

3. If Dogg Top Co. had bid $1.85 per gross instead of $2.04 (and the other three had bid as indicated earlier), what vendor should Tracy select? Why?

4. What suggestions would you make for improving Carolina Jam & Jelly's vendor rating system?

ELECTROTECH, INC.

Case contributed by Charles O'Neal, Professor of Marketing, University of Evansville.

BACKGROUND

Jim Mills and Bill Thompson have just returned from an all-day session with Bob Watson, director of procurement for one of their larger accounts. The customer, a manufacturer of major appliances, is located in central Michigan. Bob had called the meeting to discuss problems Electrotech had encountered over the past several months in meeting the customer's quality and delivery requirements.

Jim Mills is the director of marketing and Bill Thompson is the central region sales manager for Electrotech. Jean Brady, the account representative, accompanied them on the visit. She had been unable to meet with Jim and Bill as they reviewed the visit because she had immediately returned to her office to expedite replacement units for two shipments, totaling 20,000 units, that were rejected by the customer the day before due to quality problems. She was also expediting an order to this account that was three days late.

Jim had called Bill into his office to review the highlights of the customer meeting, which hadn't been a pleasant one. The relationship between the two companies had historically been a solid one. Electrotech had often been favored over their major three competitors due to their lower prices, but during the past eighteen months the relationship had deteriorated severely.

The recent meeting with Bob Watson had focused on his increasing expectations of Electrotech and other suppliers as the customer's competitive environment became more intense. He explained that his company had launched a program to become a leader in the industry with a three-pronged focus on quality, cost, and delivery. His company had initiated a total quality program committing all organizational units—product design, process engineering, material management, manufacturing, distribution, marketing, and the support units—to the program. Each unit was to cooperate fully with the other units as they worked as cross-functional teams to develop an integrated customer-oriented product development/delivery system. Key elements of this program were just-in-time (JIT) and early supplier involvement (ESI) programs. Bob Watson had expressed his concern about Electrotech's quality and delivery performance level, especially in view of the need for progressively higher quality and more rigorous delivery requirements. Bob had emphasized this as the direction of his entire industry.

THE COMPANY

Electrotech is a medium-sized producer of electrical motors with annual sales volume in the $80 million to $100 million range. While it is currently developing a line of motors for the computer industry, its primary market is the major household appliance industry—refrigerators, washers, dryers, and dishwashers. It has chosen to market its products through its own sales force, which consists of twenty field sales (account) representatives divided into three regions across the nation. The central region accounts for about 60 percent of the total volume due to the concentration of the appliance industry in the midwest.

Electrotech was formed in 1928 and has achieved steady sales and profit growth. However, profits have declined in the past couple of years due to more competitive pricing and the cost of scrapping and reprocessing a greater proportion of products because of more stringent quality demands by several of their customers. The primary emphasis in both the production and marketing of its product has been low cost-low price. It has been able to achieve relatively low costs due to its early entry in the market and the relatively steep experience curve it has enjoyed with its product. The narrow product line and its industry focus have been significant factors in holding costs at a low level. Much of its R & D investment has been aimed at keeping down manufacturing costs. As a result, it is one of the lowest cost producers in the industry.

A marketing strategy it has found effective in the past has been to bid on high-volume procurements that extend over a year or more for a single product model. This allows long production runs of a single model, thus minimizing the cost of model changeovers and the overhead costs per unit produced. These products are placed in factory inventory and shipped as requested by the customer.

THE COMPETITION

Electrotech faces a variety of competitors. There are numerous local and regional competitors that, like Electrotech, manufacture a narrow line of specialty products that are designed for one or very few industry applications. Most of the local manufacturers do not have the resources to compete for the higher-volume business at larger manufacturers. On the other hand, some of the regional producers are its toughest competitors because of their low overhead costs and proximity to their customers.

The competitors that pose the greatest threat to Electrotech are the larger, diversified, and often vertically integrated companies. These companies often produce a wide range of motors as well as complementary products and may use large quantities of their own component products. They tend to be more sophisticated in planning with customer intelligence systems and have excellent R & D facilities and manufacturing and logistics systems. These companies are also beginning to introduce JIT and ESI programs into their final equipment manufacturing operations.

THE MARKET ENVIRONMENT

The major household appliance market is a relatively stable one. Much of the demand (up to 75 percent of some mature products) consists of replacement purchases. The segment of the market of interest to Electrotech is very concentrated and also very large, as shown in Exhibit 1. Total volume of these four products is approximately 20 million units. The share of industry by manufacturer and total volume are illustrative of a typical recent year.

The major appliance industry is very mature and very competitive. While Pacific Rim producers have totally dominated the microwave oven market, their encroachment on the four major appliance markets in Exhibit 1 has been much more gradual. European-based Electrolux has become a major factor since its acquisition of White Consolidated Industries, a major producer of private-branded products.

Cost pressures stemming from stable demand and intense competition have caused the major manufacturers to move to product design and operational strategies that will result in higher-quality and lower-cost products and the additional capability of introducing new products more quickly. Significant quality and cost-responsive technologies producers are beginning to implement JIT and ESI systems.

THE JIT/ESI INDUSTRY MOVEMENT

JIT, a Japanese innovation pioneered by Toyota, was introduced into the U.S. by the automotive industry in the early 1980s. The stimulus for its adoption was the significant impact Japanese automobile producers were having on the U.S. automotive industry. Japanese cars were perceived by consumers as having substantially higher quality with prices below comparable U.S. models, and the market share held by U.S. manufactures rapidly began to erode.

JIT, broadly defined, is a business philosophy that focuses on waste elimination in all elements of an organization's systems, as well as in its organizational exchange systems. This includes waste in time, space, materials, human effort, and any activities involved in the product transformation and exchange process. The strategy resulting from the application of JIT includes a program of continuous improvement with the objective of providing perfect-quality products in exact quantities at the precise time needed by the customer, and at minimum total cost. Two additional points should be emphasized: the "customer" includes internal customers as well as the external customers; and the JIT system requires a commitment by the adopter to a total quality control process (TQC) with total people involvement (TPI).

It is obvious that JIT has a very ambitious objective and it requires a totally different mind-set than traditional operational processes. It is controlled by a market-driven "customer pull" rather than the traditional producer push. All upstream (supplier) processes are synchronized with customer demand. The potential of the JIT/TQC/TPI process is tremendous. Adopters have been able to move from quality levels measured in the traditional parts-per-hundred acceptable quality level (AQL), to measurement in parts-per-million (PPM) defective.

Surprisingly the emphasis on preventive quality measures (doing things right the first time), rather than the traditional corrective approach through inspection of the finished product with much scrap and rework, has resulted in dramatic reductions in product costs.

The ESI approach is a companion to JIT. It brings key suppliers into the product/service planning stage very early during the product concept-development phase. This allows the manufacturer to take advantage of the supplier's expertise in product design, materials selection, processing techniques, etc. The supplier becomes an extension of the producer, and partnerships are often formed. This long-term relationship fosters an atmosphere of openness and trust, which allows them to work closely together to find optimal ways of meeting the needs of the final customer.

Many industrial firms, including the major appliance industry, are beginning to realize the critical importance of their materials suppliers. Recent studies have revealed that, across all U.S.

EXHIBIT I
MAJOR APPLIANCE INDUSTRY: SELECTED PRODUCTS

Product	Manufacturer	Share	Total Volume (million units)
Refrigerators	GE	30%	6.5
	Whirlpool	25	
	WCI (Electrolux)	20	
	Admiral (Maytag)	15	
	Amana (Raytheon)	5	
Others		5	
Total		100%	
Dishwashers	GE	40%	4.0
	D&M	20	
	Whirlpool	20	
	Maytag	5	
	WCI	5	
	Hobart/Emerson	5	
	Others	5	
Total		100%	
Washers	Whirlpool	50%	6.0
	Maytag	15	
	GE	15	
	WCI	10	
	Others	10	
Total		100%	
Electric Dryers	Whirlpool	55%	3.0
	GE	15	
	Maytag	10	
	WCI	10	
	Norge (Maytag)	5	
	Others	5	
Total		100%	

manufacturing industries, externally sourced materials account for over 50 percent of the total product cost. Of course, the quality and cycle time of manufacturers are substantially influenced by external suppliers.

The JIT and ESI programs of manufacturers have caused them to become much more selective in choosing materials suppliers. As a result, they are reducing their supplier bases. These reductions frequently reach 50 percent and in some instances 80 percent to 90 percent.

The reason for the supplier reduction is two-fold: (1) to choose only those suppliers that have the capability of meeting the more rigorous demands, and (2) to reduce the number of suppliers for a single commodity (e.g., motors) to a very select few (often, only one) with which long-term partnership agreements can be negotiated.

The adoption of JIT and ESI, along with their much more demanding and precise requirements, brings additional functional representatives into the manufacturer's buying center. In addition to purchasing, which has traditionally been a major influence, significant influences often include: (1) design engineering, with a major role in working with technology capabilities in the design and development of new products; (2) materials management, with key responsibility for the inbound logistics activities, requiring materials to arrive in exact quantities and in relatively narrow time windows; (3) operations management, with their greater concern for the quality and ease (cost) of using incoming materials in the manufacturing operations; and (4) quality assurance, with a major stake in assuring that the incoming materials are "perfect" and suitable for use.

In many JIT arrangements, manufacturers are increasingly placing the responsibility for the quality of incoming materials fully on the supplier (referred to as "quality at the source"). This removes the need for incoming inspection, yet assures that incoming materials conform to the manufacturer's requirements.

ELECTROTECH'S CHALLENGE

Jim and Bill, along with Jean Brady, had been taken on a plant tour by Bob Watson during their recent visit. They were astounded by what they observed. The factory was spotless and the emphasis on quality was obvious. The aisles were clear, uncluttered by work-in-process (WIP) inventory. The only WIP inventory were very small lots being actively used at each work station.

The production facilities were arranged in U-shaped cells (referred to as group technology) with each cell producing a specific family of product models. The workers in each cell were formed into teams headed by team leaders. Each

worker and the team leader could, and often did, perform the task of each other worker. This provided much flexibility and gave each worker a sense of doing the total job.

Bob Watson took great pride in the tremendous strides his company had made in model changeover times—a very important factor given the increased number of models they were providing to customers. They had already reduced set-up times for most processes by at least 80 percent and had a goal of having all set-up times reduced to twenty minutes or less within the next year. Some of these set-up times had formerly taken from four to six hours, which had been considered a "given" by the process engineering and operations staff. The reduced set-up times allowed the company to mix models on the same production line, that is, produce a family of models that conformed to the mix desired by the customer.

Bob Watson's company was already arranging with a few major product suppliers (compressors, for instance) to produce and ship "in sequence" so that the supplier's product could be delivered directly to the point of assembly, with quality assured. This would result in major reductions in materials rehandling, transportation, storage, and inspection costs. Their plan was to gradually bring additional key components, including electric motors, into this program.

Jim and Bill grew increasingly concerned as they reflected on this visit. They were at a loss to understand why Jean Brady had not been aware of many of these customer developments. Of course, much of her time was spent calling on smaller accounts and prospects across her territory, and most of her remaining time had been spent checking, tracing, and expediting orders and shipments to try to meet her other larger accounts' more demanding requirements. She had also been on the phone frequently with Electrotech's pricing specialist to try to get more competitive price schedules. Her primary customer contacts at Bob Watson's company were Ed Field, senior buyer for electrical components, David McCray, incoming materials receiving specialist, and Betty Bevins, materials quality supervisor. Electrotech was being required to make more frequent shipments of smaller lots of motors, and the expediting problem caused by delivery delays and defective products was consuming most of Jean's attention. Jim realized that Electrotech would have to make some major changes if it was to keep Bob Watson's company as a customer. Moreover, other major customers might also be moving in the same direction. He began to see the problem as extending beyond the marketing function but he realized that his responsibility was directing marketing and sales, the primary link with customer. Another puzzling question, "What about our other major accounts?" Are they also shifting to the JIT/ESI approach? He decided that he had no time to waste if Electrotech was going to hold its position as a primary supplier to the major appliance industry.

Key questions he knew he must find answers to quickly included: "What strategy must we employ to remain an effective supplier?" "Who must become involved, and in what way?" "What is my role?"

DISCUSSION QUESTIONS

1. What strategy should Electrotech employ to remain an effective supplier to Bob Watson's company?
2. Who must become involved in Electrotech's new strategy? Who else in the company, besides marketing personnel, should be included in this strategy? Why should these others be involved?
3. What do you see as Jim Mills's role in any changing strategy?
4. What do you believe will happen in this case if Electrotech continues its present marketing strategy? Explain your answer.

MPM CORPORATION

Case contributed by Rober Haas, professor of Marketing, San Diego University..

BACKGROUND

James Dunfee is the director of marketing for the MPM Corporation, a manufacturer of electrical testing equipment. Located in central Missouri, the company had been started in the early 1960s by Milo Mapes. Mapes was an electrical engineer who had worked in the R & D departments of several large manufacturers of electrical testing equipment. He had started the business in 1962, and with his many contacts, had built a fairly successful business. By the mid-1970s, Mapes found that he did not possess the time, interest, or expertise necessary to handle both the production and marketing sides of MPM. He hired James Dunfee to manage the firm's sales and marketing activities. Mapes continued to head the engineering and production responsibil-

ities at MPM and gave Dunfee free rein in running the firm's marketing and sales programs.

James Dunfee had an excellent background in industrial marketing. In 1960, he graduated from Rensselaer Polytechnic Institute in upstate New York with a degree in electrical engineering. On graduation from college, he accepted a position in engineering sales with a large national producer of testing equipment. He performed well in that company's extensive in-house training program and then was assigned to field sales in the northern Michigan area. There, his sales performance was remarkable, and he was seen as a rising star in the company. In the mid-1970s, he met Milo Mapes at a national trade show in Chicago, and Mapes invited him to join MPM as the company's direc-

R.W. Hass *Business Marketing*, 6th ed., Cincinnati: Southwestern Publishing Company, 1995. Reprinted with permission.

tor of marketing. Mapes was so impressed with the young man that he created the position specifically for Dunfee. Dunfee was enthusiastic with the opportunity afforded him by Mapes, and he accepted Mapes's offer in April 1975.

The company's success is attributable to a small bench-testing apparatus called Testor. Although there are a number of variations of Testor, their specifications are similar, and all perform basically the same testing functions. The product possesses some advantages over those of competitors, and MPM has carved a good niche in the market. Testor is purchased by machine shops of all sizes and has a relatively horizontal demand. Sales of the product were reasonably good right from the start, although the recessions in the mid- and late 1970s did depress sales during those periods.

MPM CORPORATION'S FIELD SALES FORCE

In taking over MPM's sales force, Dunfee inherited five full-time salespeople in the field sales staff. These five people had been personally hired and trained by Mapes and covered sales territories in New England, the middle Atlantic states, the east north central states, the south Atlantic states, and the Pacific coast. These territories are shown in Exhibit 1. Back in 1980, Dunfee had seriously considered replacing some of his field salespeople with manufacturers' representatives. At that time, he had been especially concerned about sales in the south Atlantic and east north central areas and thought that replacing company salespeople with manufacturers' representatives might be more profitable. He abandoned the idea when the economy began to turn upward in the

---

EXHIBIT I
SALES TERRITORIES OF THE MPM CORPORATION

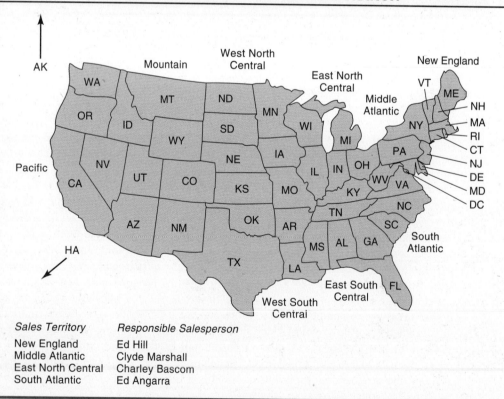

Sales Territory	Responsible Salesperson
New England	Ed Hill
Middle Atlantic	Clyde Marshall
East North Central	Charley Bascom
South Atlantic	Ed Angarra

	EXHIBIT 2		
	SALES TERRITORIES OF THE MPM CORPORATION		
Territory	Salesperson	Area	States Covered
1	Ed Hill	New England	Connecticut, Massachusetts, Maine, New Hampshire, Vermont, Rhode Island
2	Clyde Marshall	Middle Atlantic	Delaware, New Jersey, New York, Pennsylvania
3	Charley Bascom	East North Central	Illinois, Indiana, Michigan, Ohio, Wisconsin
4	Ed Angarra	South Atlantic	Florida, Georgia, Maryland, North Carolina, South Carolina, Virginia, West Virginia
5	Iris Dunn	East South Central	Alabama, Kentucky, Mississippi, Tennessee
6	Frank Hoopes	West North Central	Iowa, Kansas, Minnesota, Missouri, Nebraska, North Dakota, South Dakota
7	Kyle Whitmarsh	West South Central	Arkansas, Louisiana, Oklahoma, Texas
8	Russ Warner	North Mountain	Idaho, Montana, Nevada, Wyoming
9	Carl Meyer	South Mountain	Arizona, Colorado, New Mexico, Utah
10	Winifred Fowler	Pacific Coast	California, Oregon, Washington

early 1980s. As the company grew, however, he added more salespeople, and by early 1985, MPM had ten full-time salespeople in its field sales force. Exhibit 2 shows these salespeople, their territories, and the states covered in each.

CONSIDERATION OF MANUFACTURERS' REPRESENTATIVES

In January 1989, Dunfee again begins to consider the possible merits of switching all or some of the territories to manufacturers' representatives. He has always been a little uncomfortable about a company of MPM's size having fulltime company salespeople in territories that do not appear to justify their continued use. Dunfee knows that the marketing of Testor requires extensive personal contact, as the apparatus is fairly complicated and a considerable amount of educational selling is required. The market is characterized by nonprice competition and by buyers who place great importance on the personal contact by highly qualified salespeople and the personal touch they can provide. For this reason, Dunfee has concluded that some type of personal selling is imperative if Testor is to continue as a marketable product.

The company does some trade journal advertising and a little direct mail advertising, and it occasionally participates in regional trade shows. These efforts support and supplement the company's field sales, and Dunfee does not consider either advertising or trade show promotion as substitutes for the higher-cost personal selling efforts. He firmly believes that manufacturers' representatives, if properly selected, can provide the type of personal contact required. He is convinced that these manufacturers' representatives can be used effectively in some, if not all, of the ten territories, and he sets about investigating the possibility.

ANALYSIS OF SALES FORCE COSTS

Dunfee first analyzes direct selling costs paid by the company to its field salespeople. Each salesperson receives a fixed monthly salary plus a 5 percent commission on sales made in his or her territory. In addition, each receives monthly allowances of $1,400 for travel, lodging, meals, and entertainment purposes. Exhibit 3 shows the results of his analysis as applied to each of the company's ten sales territories.

Next, Dunfee reviews his past sales records and computes average monthly sales figures for each of his ten salespeople in their respective territories. These results are shown in Exhibit 4. For example, Ed Hill in New England averages 75 Testor sales per month, and Winifred Fowler in the Pacific coast area averages 175.

Dunfee next estimates sales for each territory by replacement manufacturers' representatives. These estimates are also shown in Exhibit 4. Based on interviews with prospective representative firms and analysis of company records, Dunfee concludes that any replacement representative probably will only sell 45 percent of what Ed Hill has been selling because the representatives either cannot or will not give undivided attention to selling Testor, as the present company salespeople are doing. Despite this shortcoming, he still thinks the move can reduce the high selling costs and result in higher profits. His investigation also reveals that an 8 percent commission is standard for manufacturers' representatives in this industry, with payment being made after MPM receives its payment from the customer. His conversations with representatives lead him to conclude that many of them are enthusiastic and willing to carry Testor. Therefore, Dunfee does not believe that finding replacement manufacturers' representatives will be a major problem in any of the ten territories.

PRICE AND COST CONSIDERATIONS

Testor currently sells for a net price of $695 FOB delivered, which means that MPM pays the freight to transport the product to the customer's job site. The freight charge currently averages $35 per unit delivered. Inasmuch as this FOB-delivered policy is reflective of common industry practice, Dunfee feels that any move to a FOB factory shipment basis will result in lost sales, as buyers probably will switch before paying the additional freight. In addition, there is relatively little price cutting in the market, and Dunfee does not feel that a price change in either direction will benefit sales or profits. He also wants to avoid competing with larger competitors on the basis of price if at all possible. MPM's total cost to manufacture Testor is $555 per unit produced.

Dunfee believes that each of the present salespeople is competent, experienced, and covers his or her territory in a conscientious manner. He does not feel that replacing any of them with other company salespersons will solve the problem of high selling costs. In addition, he does not see that much untapped potential in any of the present sales territories. He interprets these beliefs to mean that the solution to the rising sales costs does not mean replacing existing salespeople with new company salespeople; therefore, he is leaning toward their replacement with manufacturers' representatives.

THE PROBLEM

Dunfee's problem is determining whether representatives can or should be substituted for company salespeople, given the 8 percent commission rate. He is primarily concerned with

---

EXHIBIT 3
PRESENT COMPENSATION PLAN OF MPM SALESPERSONS

Territory	Salesperson	Present Monthly Salary	Present Monthly Allowances	Sales Commission Rate
1	Ed Hill	$2,795	$1,400	5%
2	Clyde Marshall	3,000	1,400	5%
3	Charley Bascom	2,400	1,400	5%
4	Ed Angarra	2,000	1,400	5%
5	Iris Dunn	2,200	1,400	5%
6	Frank Hoopes	2,395	1,400	5%
7	Kyle Whitmarsh	2,895	1,400	5%
8	Russ Warner	2,400	1,400	5%
9	Carl Meyer	2,595	1,400	5%
10	Winifred Fowler	3,000	1,400	5%

	EXHIBIT 4		
PRESENT SALES BY MPM SALESPERSONS AND ANTICIPATED SALES BY REPLACEMENT MANUFACTURERS' REPRESENTATIVES			
Territory	Area	Average Number of Monthly Sales by Present Salesperson	Percentage of Present Monthly Sales Anticipated by Replacement Manufacturers' Representatives
1	New England	75	45%
2	Middle Atlantic	125	55%
3	East North Central	72	75%
4	South Atlantic	60	45%
5	East South Central	92	60%
6	West North Central	47	45%
7	West South Central	135	75%
8	North Mountain	35	40%
9	South Mountain	65	80%
10	Pacific Coast	175	60%

increased sales profitability in the ten territories and is uncertain whether he should replace all the present salespeople with representatives, replace only some of them, or replace none of them.

Advise Mr. Dunfee, using the 8 percent commission rate.

DISCUSSION QUESTIONS

1. Dunfee finds that he must pay the representatives a 9 percent commission. How does this change affect your decision made on the basis of the 8 percent commission?

2. If Dunfee can get by with paying a 7 percent commission, how does this change affect the decision you made at an 8 percent commission?

3. How may Dunfee change the existing company salesperson compensation plan in an attempt to reduce sales costs and improve sales profitability?

4. What do you think Dunfee may be overlooking in viewing such a possible change primarily from a short-run profitability perspective?

DONALDSON COMPANY, INC.

This case was prepared by Shannon Shipp, M.J. Neeley School of Business, Texas Christian University. The U.S. Department of Education funded the preparation of this case under Grant #G00877027.

By 1985, Tom Baden, vice president of the Donaldson Company, Inc. (DCI) was convinced that the rules of competition in the industrial air and fluid filtration industry had changed. Two years earlier DCI had experienced its first loss in 50 years. While the situation improved in 1984, Baden realizes that a decision about his group's organizational structure is essential.

Baden is vice president of DCI's Original Equipment Group (OEG), whose revenues in 1984 represented over 40 percent of DCI's 1984 annual sales of $250 million. Stated simply, Baden's task is to return OEG to financial performance levels of the 1975–79 period and establish a base for long-term growth in the markets served by OEG. Baden is also responsible for reinforcing DCI's corporate image as a high-quality, high-service provider of state-of-the-art products.

THE COMPANY

History

In 1915 Frank Donaldson, Sr., the original chairman of the company, invented the first effective air cleaner for internal combustion engines. Air is a necessary ingredient for the combustion process to occur. Before his invention, engines were extremely susceptible to "dusting out," or becoming inoperative due to excessive accumulation of dust entering the engine from unfiltered air.

In subsequent years, DCI led the industry in introducing new products, such as oil-washed filters, mufflers, multistaged air cleaners, and high-tech hydraulic filters. DCI became the world's largest manufacturer of heavy-duty air cleaners and mufflers and established a worldwide reputation for technology. Facilities grew from 200 square feet of manufacturing space in 1915 to more than 3 million square feet of manufacturing and office area worldwide in 1980.

Mission

By 1984 the company had broadly defined its mission: to design, manufacture, and sell proprietary products that "separate something unwanted from something wanted." The company's product line included air cleaners, air filters, mufflers, hydraulic filters, microfiltration equipment for computers, air pollution equipment, and liquid clarifiers. These products were developed, sold, and serviced by the organizational structure appearing in Exhibit 1. According to this exhibit, DCI has a functional organizational structure, with the nine worldwide support groups responsible for product development, manufacturing, administration, finance,

and the four business groups responsible for selling and servicing products to their respective markets. The 1980 to 1984 sales of the four major business groups are listed in Exhibit 2. The fifth group listed, Microfiltration and Defense Products (MFD), was a part of the Business Development Group until 1984, when it was spun off to form a new business group.

1983–1984 Situation

In 1983 a peculiar set of external and internal causes combined to downgrade DCI's performance. Among external causes, sales of medium/heavy-duty trucks, buses, tractors and combines, construction equipment, and aftermarket replacement elements simultaneously hit five-year or all-time lows. These markets constituted the majority of sales for both the Original Equipment Group (OEG) and International. Although soft demand had been experienced in one or two of these markets before in a single year, never had all businesses declined so precipitously in the same year. Also, the strength of the dollar in 1982–84 was making DCI's customers less competitive in foreign markets. This in turn affected DCI's sales of replacement parts.

In 1984 DCI's operating results began to return to pre-1983 levels (see Exhibit 3). One reason was a success in the wet filtration area, particularly in high-stress environments. The primary reason was that sales by customers in DCI's worldwide markets, particularly heavy-duty trucks, began to return to pre-1983 levels. Because of the external causes described previously, however, DCI management thought it unlikely that sales by its customers would return to pre-1980 levels. To counter the effects of the decline in worldwide demand for DCI's products, Tom Baden concluded that OEG must address several critical internal problems.

Some of the internal problems included an inability to coordinate customer service to multinational customers, inability to provide accurate cost figures for given production quantities, and—especially for its small customers— "being difficult to buy from."

DCI found it difficult to coordinate customer service efforts for those customers with

EXHIBIT 1
DCI ORGANIZATION CHART (1983)

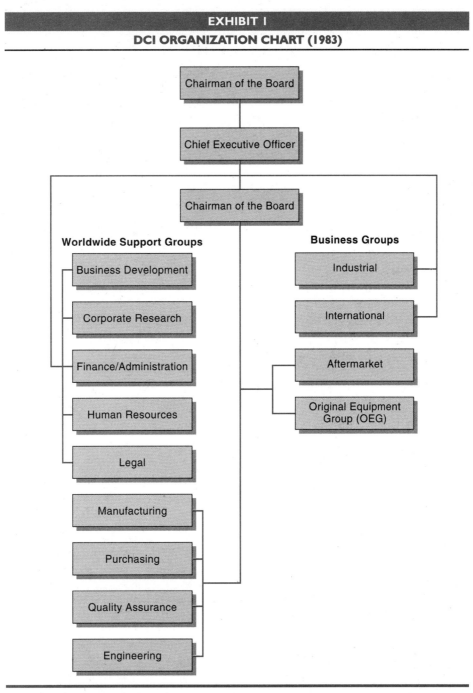

SOURCE: Internal company documents.

multiple purchasing or production facilities in different countries. Although DCI had offices in all of the countries where high sales potential existed, (e.g., in West Germany, Brazil, and Mexico) lack of coordination among the offices caused spotty customer service. For example,

EXHIBIT 2

DCI'S FOUR MAJOR BUSINESS GROUPS
(annual sales, $ millions)

	1984	1983	1982	1981	1980
Original equipment group	$102.2	$ 63.9	$101.3	$104.6	$101.6
Aftermarket	22.6	17.6	20.5	20.1	17.0
Industrial	32.2	32.0	41.3	37.0	25.0
International	71.2	68.7	81.4	87.0	69.4
MFD	26.0	21.4	17.4	15.1	11.4
Total	$254.2	$203.6	$261.9	$263.8	$234.4

SOURCE: DCI 1984 Annual Report.

EXHIBIT 3

DCI OPERATING RESULTS
($000)

	1984	1983	1982
Net sales	$254,052	$203,608	$262,018
Cost of sales	157,257	131,548	169,816
Gross earnings	96,795	72,060	92,202
Earnings (loss) before income taxes	20,238	(1,738)	12,805
Income taxes	10,546	1,800	5,572
Tax rate	52.1%	—	43.2%
Net earnings	9,692	(3,358)	7,233
Depreciation	7,694	8,320	8,518
Interest	2,670	2,076	2,345
Financial Position			
Current assets	$ 97,425	$ 81,668	$ 82,109
Current liabilities	45,022	32,796	35,574
Current ratio	2.2	2.5	2.3
Working capital	52,403	48,872	46,535
Long-term debt	19,549	21,791	18,752
Shareholder's equity	90,232	84,880	91,637
Capitalization	22.1	22.1	21.2
Return on average shareholder's equity	11.1	(4.0)	7.9
Return on average invested capital	9.0	(3.3)	6.4
Property, plant, and equipment (gross)	$118,663	$118,182	$114,465
Property, plant, and equiment (net)	55,045	59,694	63,739
Total assets	$160,613	$148,083	$151,160

SOURCE: DCI 1984 Annual Report.

customers were known to "shop" for the best prices among DCI offices. The different DCI offices were therefore competing against each other for the same business.

DCI was also unable to provide accurate cost figures for small production quantities. This hampered salespeople's efforts to quote prices that would cover DCI's costs, and yield profits. For example, setup costs in switching from producing one product to another were not factored into the costs of production runs, and hence omitted from the prices charged. Furthermore, account executives were measured primarily on sales rather than profits, thereby encouraging them to devote less attention to the costs of actually filling an order.

Although relationships with its largest customers were strong—based on its ability to work with those customers in solving problems—small customers complained to salespeople of slow response for engineering drawings and price quotes. They also complained of slow responses to questions about billing or order status. Very small customers (under $25,000 in annual sales) were not vocal with complaints about DCI because they were seldom contacted by DCI representatives.

ORIGINAL EQUIPMENT GROUP (OEG)

OEG Products and Markets

OEG constitutes the bulk of DCI's traditional businesses, such as heavy-duty trucks, and construction, mining, industrial, and agricultural equipment. It sells air and hydraulic filters, acoustical products (mufflers), and replacement elements to manufacturers and end users of heavy-duty mobile equipment in North America. OEG has not typically sold oil filters, as they are a commodity item and require much higher production runs than OEG traditionally makes. OEG is reviewing its position on producing oil filters because its customers often seek a single source for all their filter needs. About half of the annual worldwide sales of these products are in North America.

Current Organizational Structure for OEG

OEG is currently organized around the market segments it serves (see Exhibit 4). The construction, agriculture, industrial, and truck-bus market segments have their own market director and support staff that are responsible for all planning and administration as well as for maintaining good relations with the largest customers in the market. Each market group has outside salespeople who call directly on customers, as well as inside salespeople responsible for routing orders and customer service. A manager of marketing support is responsible for order-entry per-

---

EXHIBIT 4

OEG'S MARKET-BASED ORGANIZATIONAL STRUCTURE

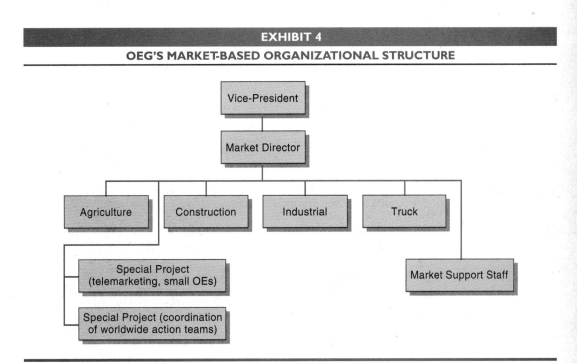

SOURCE: Internal company documents.

sonnel and clerks. There are also two special project managers in OEG. The first special project manager coordinated the efforts of the worldwide action teams responsible for gathering information on competitors and customers. The second developed a marketing program to try to understand the needs of small original equipment manufacturers (OEMs) and the feasibility of using telemarketing to reach them.

OEG's Position Within DCI

OEG has primary worldwide responsibility to serve mobile heavy-equipment OEMs. The International Group supports OEG's efforts, while the Aftermarket Group competes with OEG for the same end-users. The International Group sells OEG's products in markets outside North America. Communication between OEG and International is crucial in providing high levels of customer service for multinational customers with plants in several countries. The Aftermarket Group competes with OEG by selling mobile heavy-equipment replacement elements under the Donaldson name through fleet specialists, heavy-duty distributors, and other outlets. These replacement parts compete with similar products sold by manufacturers' dealers supplied by OEG.

Within each market segment, customers are served by size. Large accounts (more than $250,000 in annual sales) are served by market directors or salespeople assigned to that account. Mid-sized customers (between $25,000 and $250,000 in annual sales) are called upon by a salesperson responsible for that territory. Small OEMs are served, if at all, by inside salespeople or order-entry personnel in the marketing support services group.

Organization by market segment offers a number of advantages to OEG, such as (1) easy tracking of changes in demand or customer usage characteristics and (2) an organizational structure similar to that in Engineering that facilitates good communications. Organization by market segment also has some problems, such as (1) some customers straddling several markets, making it difficult to assign the costs and profits from serving that customer to a specific market, and (2) an occasional inability to coordinate the engineering support for those customers who straddled market segments because an engineer from each of two market segments might be assigned to solve the same technical problem.

ACTION TEAM REPORTS AND ANALYSES

To regain OEG's previous market position, in early 1984 Tom Baden initiated a year-long strategic analysis to study all aspects of OEG operations. Reports were prepared by action teams from DCI offices around the world. These reports were the basis of a series of meetings that included all OEG executives and were used to obtain ideas for actions to improve OEG's organizational structure and marketing policies.

Baden must reach a decision on whether the existing marketing organization structure is best able to achieve OEG's goals or whether a new structure would be better. To make that decision, four elements of the year-long strategic analysis are considered: (1) competition, (2) customers, (3) marketing-mix strategies, and (4) telemarketing and global account management as alternatives to personal selling in reaching some customers.

Major Competitors

DCI is the traditional heavy-duty mobile-equipment market leader for heavy-duty filters. Major competitors include Fleetguard, Fram, Nelson, and Mann and Hummel. Other firms, such as Wix, Baldwin, Purolator, and AC/Delco, compete in certain market segments. In general, all of the competitors are on sound financial footing. Fleetguard and Fram have very healthy parent organizations (Cummins Engine and Allied/Bendix Corporation, respectively). Mann and Hummel and Nelson are healthy from good internal financial management. Research and development costs are generally lower for these organizations than for DCI because they tend to follow DCI's technological breakthroughs. Each competitor is strong in a particular market or

---

EXHIBIT 5

SOME LARGE CURRENT OR POTENTIAL CUSTOMERS FOR OEG

North America	Europe	Japan
Ford	Daimler-Benz	Hitachi
Caterpillar	IVECO	Isuzu
Champion	Leyland	Komatsu
Clark Equipment	Lister	Kubota
Cummins	Lombardini	Mitsubishi
Detroit Diesel	MAN	Nissan

SOURCE: Internal company documents.

---

through a particular channel, and most offer a full line of air and oil filters, which enables both customers and distributors to meet their filter needs through a single source.

OEG's Customers

OEG has over 600 customers, divided into three groups: large, mid-sized, and small.

Large Accounts. OEG's large customers (more than $250,000 in annual sales), consisting of 46 original equipment manufacturer (OEM) accounts and their dealers, constitute more than 90 percent of OEG sales and more than 40 percent of DCI sales. Thirty of these customers are headquartered in the United States, eight in Europe, and eight in Japan. A partial list of these customers appears in Exhibit 5. These customers are all large, and most have sales offices and production facilities in more than one country.

The competitive environment for large OEMs is undergoing rapid change. Some large OEMs, such as Caterpillar and Ford, are experiencing reduced sales due to increasing competition from non–U.S. manufacturers. The large OEMs are coping with the reduction in sales by calling on suppliers to reduce prices. For example, Caterpillar announced a three-year program beginning in 1983 and terminating in 1985 that required its suppliers to maintain stable prices even though inflation was predicted to increase 22 percent for that period. The emphasis by large customers on cost containment is a major change from the 1970s (which emphasized

product performance) and could squeeze OEG's margins and hurt DCI's performance.

According to meetings among salespeople and account executives, OEG's largest customers have common needs for filtration equipment. At a minimum, large customers desire state-of-the-art products at the lowest possible prices for products meeting specifications. Recent demand by large customers include:

1. Just-in-time deliveries[1]
2. Long-term fixed source contracts.
3. Drop-ship arrangements to customers' dealers and/or manufacturing facilities for OE parts.
4. Worldwide availability of product.
5. The OE brand name on the product.
6. Electronic system tie-ins for improved order placement/followup and customer service and support.

These demands accompanied OEM efforts to consolidate their purchases to achieve stronger positions vis-à-vis their suppliers.

Large customers also perceive sales opportunities for replacement elements sales through their dealer networks. In North America, the large OEMs have 21,000 outlets, or original equipment dealers (OEDs), through which OEG could sell replacement elements. OEDs represent a new market opportunity for DCI. Traditionally, OEG has sold replacement elements to OEMs imprinted with the OEM's brand. Once the OEM takes title to the products, OEG expects the OEM to provide the necessary training and support to its distributors through which the products will be sold. Recently, OEDs are more actively looking for product lines to improve cash flow and profitability. Part of the impetus for the search for additional products is slow equipment sales. Service parts provide a logical line extension and source of steady cash flow for OEDs. To capitalize on the market in

---

[1]Just-in-time deliveries occur when the supplier and customer have devised a schedule to ensure the next shipment of parts or supplies is delivered when the customer is about to use the last unit from the previous shipment.

service parts, however, OEDs need extensive manufacturer support in terms of sales training, product knowledge, product literature, and merchandising, and complete lines of filters to service all makes of equipment, not just lines they represent.

Mid-Size and Small Accounts.   Mid-size ($25,000 to $250,000 in annual sales) and small (less than $25,000 in annual sales) OEMs are offered only standard products from the OEG catalog. Custom engineering is rarely provided to these customers, unless they are willing to bear its full cost.

These smaller OEMs have different needs than large OEMs. In general, they desire state-of-the-art products but are willing to wait for a large OEM to install a new product first. They also desire consistent contact with OEG salespeople to keep abreast of changing filter prices (while realizing that they do not have the volumes to command the lowest available prices) and good product quality. Some OEMs often request the DCI name on the filters used in their equipment as a marketing tool, capitalizing on DCI's reputation for high quality among end users.

Marketing-Mix Strategies

Product and Price.   DCI is known throughout the industry for its conservative management style, using strategic moves based on careful planning. OEG is no exception. OEG prefers serving selected, high-margin markets where customers are beginning to demand higher performance levels than those available from the products currently available. Pursuing these markets allows OEG to exploit its strengths of quality design and engineering, as well as allowing OEG to charge a premium price for its products. Price cutting is not a major component of OEG's market strategies.

Distribution.   Distribution of OEG's products occurs through two primary channels. The first is directly to OEMs, which purchase products for installation on new equipment. In some markets, such as heavy-duty trucks and construction equipment, more than 70 percent

of all new units shipped are factory-equipped with DCI products. OEMs depend on DCI as a reliable supplier of state-of-the-art products whose engineers design products for special applications or environmental conditions.

The second major channel is for replacement elements. These elements are often packaged and sold under the customer's name and logo and distributed through its dealer network. For example, OEG provides replacement elements for Caterpillar, International Harvester, J.I. Case, Freightliner, and Volvo, imprinted with their names and logos.

Promotion.   OEG products are promoted several ways, including advertising, direct mail, trade shows, and promotional literature. A distribution of OEG's promotional expenditures for 1984 appears in Exhibit 6. DCI encourages direct communication between OEG engineers and technicians and their customer counterparts. While this is not reflected in the promotional budget, it is an important element in OEG's communications with its customers. Other off-budget promotional expenses include sending OEG engineers to attend professional meetings and guiding customers on tours of the research and testing unit that contains some of the most modern filtration research facilities in the world.

EXHIBIT 6	
PROMOTIONAL BUDGET (1984)	
Item	Percent of Budget
Advertising	55%
Trade shows	16
Sales literature	13
Coop advertising	4
Photography	2
Public relations	2
Other sales materials	1
Advertising specialties	1
Audiovisual materials	1
Other	5
	100%

SOURCE: Internal company documents.

Selling Methods. OEG has traditionally relied on face-to-face selling to provide information to and solicit orders from customers. Two major problems exist with heavy reliance on personal selling. First, it is not cost efficient for OEG to use personal selling to reach mid-size and small customers unless a standard product already exists to fit the customer's application. As a result, service to these customers is provided primarily by local distributors or through DCI's Aftermarket Group. The lack of direct customer contact with these accounts has resulted in OEG having a low level of knowledge regarding their needs. Second, for large customers with multiple purchasing and usage sites, it is difficult to coordinate the activities of salespeople assigned to customers geographically. This problem becomes acute when the customer has purchasing or usage sites overseas, served through the International Division. This means that salespeople's activities have to be coordinated across geographic regions as well as across divisions within DCI.

Alternatives to Personal Selling

Two selling methods, telemarketing and global account management, are being considered as substitutes or supplements to the current selling method.

Telemarketing. Telemarketing involves organized, planned telephone communication between a firm and its customers. Telemarketing ranges from salespeople simply calling prospective customers to set up appointments, to complex systems with different employees responsible for different parts of selling, such as prospecting or customer service.

One special project manager explored the feasibility of telemarketing to small OEMs. The study's objective was to profile small OEMs that had purchased OEG products. These firms were questioned about their use of OEG products, needs for additional OEG support, and overall satisfaction with OEG products and services. Four hundred and sixty-one small OEMs were contacted during the month-long study, none with more than $25,000 in purchases from OEG the preceding year. Some study results appear in Exhibit 7.

Global Account Management. Global account management (GAM) is a method of assigning salespeople to accounts. Sellers use GAM when customers are large, with multiple purchase or usage points. Under a GAM system an account executive is responsible for all the communication between the customer and the seller, including (but not limited to) needs analysis, application engineering, field support, customer service, and order processing. Depending on the account size, the executive might have several subordinates provide necessary services.

EXHIBIT 7
TELEMARKETING STUDY RESULTS

	Number	Percent of Responses
Literature requests	211	46%
Satisfied customers	102	22
Not qualified as customers	58	13
Follow-up phone calls	17	4
Orders	9	2
Quotes	8	2
Terminations	5	1
Unavailable (not listed) duplicates	51	11
	461	100%

SOURCE: Internal company documents.

GAM's major advantage is communication co-ordination. Since all seller and buyer contact is monitored by the account manager, miscommunication is unlikely.

Implementing GAM would involve assigning teams to OEG's largest customers to improve support. Account teams would be composed of salespeople and applications engineers, with the number of people on the account proportional to its annual orders. Each team head, or Account Manager, would coordinate communications between all customer buying locations and OEG. Account managers would have worldwide profit and loss responsibility for their assigned customers. Sales representatives in district offices in other countries would report their customer activities to the lead account executive. Account executives are responsible for the subsidiaries of global customers in their geographic area. Account executives and sales representatives typically have multiple reporting relationships. A sample organizational chart appears in Exhibit 8. The boxes do not all represent people assigned full time to that account. For example, the account manager in Europe for Daimler-Benz would report to the sales manager in Europe. The Daimler-Benz account manager for Europe might also be a subsidiary account executive for Caterpillar in Europe, reporting to an account manager in the United States.

TOM BADEN'S DECISION

After attending the worldwide action team and OEG operations presentations, Tom Baden split OEG executives into two groups. Each group prepared a presentation explaining its vision for OEG's future corporate structure and marketing strategy.

Existing OEG Corporate Structure

One group maintained that the current organization structure (see Exhibit 4) would adequately meet the challenges posed by current external and internal problems. They believe that the 1983 problems were due to temporary forces and that the existing structure should not be changed.

Proposed New OEG Corporate Structure

Based on the results of the action team reports, the second group made several suggestions to improve OEG's performance. Two suggestions, global account management for large OEM's and telemarketing for small customers, were key features of the organizational structure proposed by the second group.

EXHIBIT 8

GLOBAL ACCOUNT MANAGEMENT: SAMPLE ORGANIZATIONAL CHART

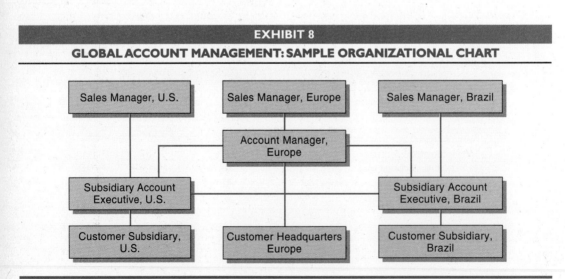

SOURCE: Internal company documents.

To incorporate these selling methods into OEG operations, the second group proposed the organization structure appearing in Exhibit 9 to replace the structure shown in Exhibit 4. The major difference is the replacement of the market groups (truck, agriculture, industrial, and construction) with the large-customer and mid-size and small-customer groups. The product/technical group is added to improve communication between engineering and marketing. Although this is a change from the current organizational structure, it is not a basis on which to accept or reject the new structure, since it could be appended to the current structure with little effort.

The suggested organizational structure would offer a number of advantages. Service to multinational customers would be coordinated under a single account manager. Current problems with lack of coordination among DCI offices could be minimized. Small OEMs would receive more attention. Although little deviation from standard products would be permitted these customers, they would be contacted more frequently under telemarketing. Service to mid-size accounts would not change.

The proposed plan has several disadvantages as well. With fewer managers at the market director level, the number of workers each must supervise would increase. For the director of large accounts, that would involve 10 to 13 account managers for 30 to 40 accounts (some managers would be responsible for more than one account). Second, the reporting relationships (see Exhibit 8) grow rather complex under a GAM structure. This can obscure good and poor performance, making it more difficult to reward outstanding performance or detect poor performance. It could also make the salesperson's job more ambiguous as orders come from several bosses. Third, new-product development would be centered around applications for specific customers. With all salespeople focusing on specific customers, no one would be charged with maintaining a perspective on the market as a whole. Without a broad perspective on changing market conditions, it would be possible to miss a trend in customer usage characteristics, which could cause OEG to fail to become a technology leader in the new market. Narrow focus on a single customer's needs might also cause the salesperson or applications engi-

---

EXHIBIT 9
ORIGINAL EQUIPMENT GROUP: PROPOSED STRUCTURE

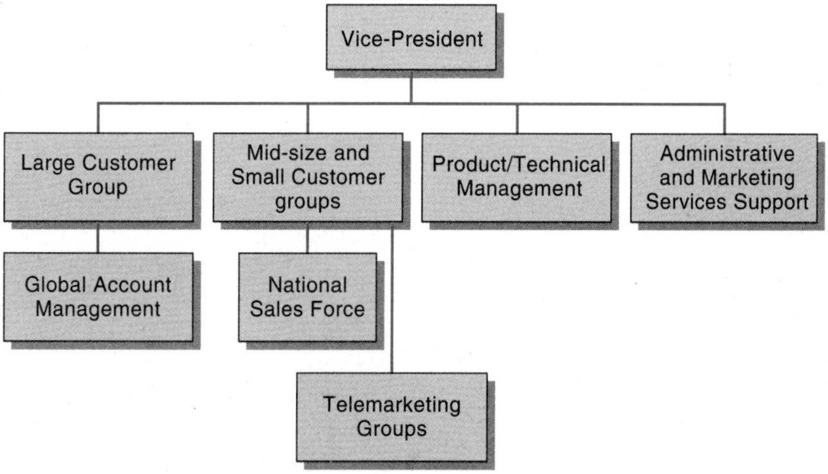

SOURCE: Internal company documents.

neer to miss similar work performed for another account, thus duplicating effort.

THE DECISION

Baden must choose one of the two organizational structures to present to corporate management. Baden is aware that any organizational change inevitably causes staff upheaval, and he wants to ensure that the OEG structure chosen will remain in place for a long time. In deciding, he also must remember that the current organizational structure has been successful for many years and that any changes must be supported by sound reasoning. To help decide, he prepares the following questions to organize his presentation on the appropriate organizational structure to top DCI management.

1. How will customers react to both plans?
2. Which plan comes closest to solving the problems OEG faced in 1983?
3. Analyze the major strengths and weaknesses of each alternative. What conclusions can be drawn from the analysis?
4. Other than the alternatives presented, what organizational structures exist to accomplish the same goals? What dangers exist in suggesting an alternative organizational structure?

MAY CHEMICALS

Case contributed by William Strahle, Associate Professor, Rider University and Dale Fox.

May Chemicals was formed in 1974. Two sales reps from the Northeast Division of Rhone-Poulenc Rorer, Ken "Kiwi" Hyde and Michael "Tex" Duffy began the company in Bristol, Pennsylvania. Initially, May was little more than an independent sales office handling part of the Rhone-Poulenc product line in the Northeast and Mid-Atlantic states.

Over the next several years, Hyde and Duffy added both salespeople and product lines. They purchased an adjoining warehouse facility when the owner retired, and began carrying an inventory of products that were occasionally hard to get because of shortages from suppliers. By 1983, May Chemicals had grown to eight sales reps who handled non competing product lines from Rhone-Poulenc Rorer, ECOLAB, ICI and Shell. Their warehousing facility had been remodeled to accommodate both drum and tank storage and had four full-time employees who had specialized EPA training to handle toxic chemical spills. Sales topped $3.8 million dollars, and Tex and Kiwi felt that it was time to bring in a sales manager who had also acquired some marketing experience in the industrial chemicals industry.

Although they interviewed more than 20 good candidates with varied backgrounds for the position, both Hyde and Duffy were impressed by what they had heard about a young product manager at Dow Chemical named Caren Conners. Ms. Conners had joined Dow in 1979 and had been promoted twice. The last was to a marketing position in Dow's New York office. She was rumored to be unhappy there as her current position had little to do with sales and her family had relocated to Yardley, Pennsylvania, with her first promotion and refused to move again. While it was obvious she was the "fast-tracked", "fair-haired girl" of Dow's Eastern Operations, Hyde and Duffy felt that they had a chance to persuade her to take the position with May Chemicals. After an informal meeting in New York, both were absolutely convinced that she was right for the job.

Ms. Conners was not interested. Period. While it was true that the commute from Yardley didn't leave her enough time with her family and she was no longer a sales manager—a position she thoroughly enjoyed—she had worked too hard to get where she was with a major manufacturer to leave for a relatively small independent distributor and the position they envisioned.

Within a week, Hyde and Duffy had "REenvisioned" the position. This time they offered her a full partnership in the firm with the title of "managing partner, sales." Duffy would become the "managing partner, marketing" as his interests had developed in that direction over the years. Hyde became "managing partner, operations," a position for which his chemical engineering degree from Rose-Hulman Institute of Technology had made him well-qualified. This time they had a deal.

By 1988, May Chemicals, Incorporated, had net revenues of $17 million·dollars and a salesforce of 22 reps. That year they acquired one of their more reliable suppliers, Harcros Chemicals. Located in neighboring Fairless Hills, Pennsylvania, Harcros manufactured a soapy acid industrial cleansing agent called "Formula 522A." Although a small, specialty chemical manufacturer, the purchase of Harcros allowed May Chemicals to become an active player in the manufacturing end of the Eastern regional market.

Formula 522A™ is a detergent-acid compound known in the trade as a soapy acid. About 60% phosphoric acid and compatible detergent by weight, it had received USDA approval for use in the food processing industry in 1982. As a non-toxic cleaning agent, it acts to clean and "revive" (brighten) stainless steel and hard-fired porcelain surfaces. In concentrated form it is also an effective oxide remover that helps prevent metal scales (rust) from entering the food processing stream. Formula 522A is sold in 55 gallon drums and can be used in solution for cleaning surfaces and equipment manually or in an immersion vat. Its most frequent use, however, is to be pumped through pipes located throughout a food processing plant. Called a "system-in-place" (SIP), this method requires delivery by tanker truck to facilities generally using a "just-in-time" (JIT) inventory method. While Harcros produced Formula 522A in drums, it lacked both the storage tanks and the resources to locate and lease tankers for delivery to SIP customers using the JIT reordering method. This put it at a tremendous disadvantage when competing with suppliers who could provide both tank and drum quantities. As May Chemicals had been in that end of the business since 1983, the purchase was synergistic to say the least.

Because ECOLAB viewed the purchase of Harcros as a conflict of interest, particularly to its 2-AMA-800 detergent/acid cleanser business, the firm terminated its distributor relationship with May Chemicals in January of 1989. Instead of declining, sales remained flat that year largely because Conners reorganized the salesforce to push the sales of Formula 522A. Eight sales reps were added and assigned primary responsibility for this product throughout the Northeast, Mid-Atlantic and Southeast sales regions. Any sales leads the other twenty-two reps uncovered were to be forwarded to the eight. Conners directed her salesforce to approach dairies, wineries, canneries and confectioneries as well as distributors. In short, *any* company that processed an edible product or sold to a company that processed an edible product became a target for the eight reps. The response to Formula 522A was beyond expectations.

By 1991 under the direction of Hyde, the Harcros Division of May Chemicals had introduced Degreasol™, a petroleum based emulsifiable solvent degreaser. Initially sold in 55 gallon drums, it was meant to "round out" sales offerings to the food processing side of the business. These facilities needed *both* EPA approved cleaning agents for their food processing streams as well as a general cleanser for other uses throughout the plant. It earned high marks from customers for quickly removing oil, grease and carbons from concrete and steel surfaces.

The marks were too high for remanufacturers to ignore. Duffy had sent test batches of Degreasol to a sample of these firms throughout May's sales regions. The results were fortuitous to say the least. They found that a 5:2 mixture of Degreasol and grain based alcohol was extremely effective in removing road asphalt from automobile bodies. With remanufacturers clamoring for the rights to develop and sell their own branded products to the retail trade, the partners agreed to supply them the Degreasol as an ingredient in tanker lot loads. While net revenues soared the following year to $93 million dollars, May Chemical's distributor side of the business lost Shell Chemicals because of a "non-competing codicil in our original contract." Unknown to the partners, Shell's Chemical Division was developing a product quite similar to Degreasol.

The "sweet sixteen", as the cleanser salesforce was now called, were already up against some pretty stiff competition. Formula 522A competed with ECOLAB's 2-AMA-800, Diversey Ltd's Diverlac™, and Castrol's Techniclean DG-3™. Degreasol competed most directly with ECOLAB's 300-ECOSOL-9 and Castrol's Tergosol™. May Chemicals could not price its cleansers on the basis of low manufacturing costs. In fact, May Chemicals had done as well as it had to this point because it was only operating on a regional basis and there were enough customers in their 17 state market area to go around. Because of the nature of the industry, her desire to "grow the business", and the supply of customers, Conners had asked her 16 person cleanser salesforce to regularly call on their *current* customers only twice a year.

This "two-a-year" restriction did *not* apply, however, to meetings whose primary purpose was to convey information about useful new applications or simply to build customer goodwill. In the chemical industry, both practices are extremely important to a firm's bottom line. So much so that Ms. Conners used meeting quotas. In order to get her reps in front of more customers, Caren encourages her salespeople to schedule at least two informal presentations a month with groups of between six and eight customers who share an

interest in an activity such as golf, or tended to have similar applications for the chemicals May manufactures or distributes. From her perspective, this would result in more complete coverage in each of their rather large territories. Whether a guest speaker was scheduled at a breakfast or luncheon meeting or the salesperson just gave a quick stand up presentation during a round of golf, the networking opportunities involved would at the very least help build goodwill between the rep and his/her customers.

By 1995 it was apparent to all three partners that to be even more competitive, Conners had to find a way to decrease selling costs by making her "sweet sixteen" more efficient. Time, after all, *is* money.

Up to this point, Conners expected her salespeople to make between six and eight calls a day. The average length of each call is about 20 minutes. However, if the customer has a question about delivery schedules or if the rep is furnishing samples for testing in the customer's quality assurance laboratory, the call can run as long as two hours. Customers and potential customers to be called are separated by their sales potential (the 1's have the highest potential and the 3's have the lowest), and by how difficult they are to see (X's are hardest to see and E's are the easiest). Caren has always liked to see her reps try and build their schedules around the times the X-1's and M-1's are available, though prospective customers are given priority because their potential is unknown. It's in the salesperson's best interest as well: "Who's more important to the company and the reps on commission, a customer who is difficult to see but who can use $100,000 a month of Formula-522A or Degreasol, or one that's easy to see but can only use $5,000 a month?"

While every customer is unique, confectionery manufacturers add a bit of complexity to the efficiency equation. Many sugar-based candy companies on the East Coast have been in business for a number of years, most before the advent of air conditioning. As a result, they rarely run afternoon shifts to take advantage of the cooler evening and early morning hours. As a general rule, then, customers who work for these firms tend to be less harried and more receptive to sales calls in the afternoons.

Both Hyde and Duffy understood the forces with which Conners had to contend. Yet from his marketing perspective, Duffy wanted Caren to ensure that the salespeople concentrated on "what they got paid for"—selling. He was sure that May's sales reps were spending too much time travelling and not enough time talking with customers and potential customers. Perhaps because he had also done the same thing, he also felt that May's reps were spending too much time reading old copies of the *Chemical Marketing Reporter* or *Purchasing* (CPI edition) while waiting for a customer to work them into his or her busy schedule. This was particularly galling since May had purchased laptop PC's for all its reps the year before to help them eliminate those deficiencies. Hyde, on the other hand, was convinced that the May reps weren't covering their territories efficiently because they weren't looking for the opportunity of arranging meetings when doing their call planning. Conners agreed with Kiwi, adding that meetings were also a relatively inexpensive way to increase customer goodwill and convert "3s" to "1s" in terms of their sales potential.

Feeling pressured, Caren decided to take a weekend in the Poconos to think about the challenges to her "sweet sixteen" sales force. While the results weren't surprising, they *were* a bit discouraging. First, like most field sales forces, May's reps should be doing a better job doing their own tour routing and call planning. The company lost money every time one of them ended up in the wrong location trying to see the wrong prospect at the wrong time. Second, like most of their counterparts in the chemical industry, a number of her salespeople had difficulty trying to schedule goodwill meetings with groups of their existing customers, preferring to waste time scheduling single appointments instead. Third, in order to help the "sweet sixteen", Conners had lobbied Hyde and Duffy to purchase fairly expensive IBM 760 CD laptops for their own use. Yet *nobody* used them, and their rea-

sons ran from being "computerphobic" and "not wanting to take the time to learn a new system" to "been doing it for years so why waste the time on an unproven gadget?" On reflection, Caren decided that she needed some help.

Ms. Conners decided to call Dr. William Strahle, managing partner of Time & Territory Management. TTM is a subsidiary of Implementation Research Associates that specializes in handling tour routing and call planning issues. Strahle suggested developing a training diskette for all the May Chemicals salespeople that could be used by each rep as they waited in a customer's office for their appointment. Interested, Conners agreed to hear Strahle out. From this point on, reader, **you** are Caren.

THE MEETING

OK Caren, let's turn on your computer. I see it's an IBM compatible. Good, now let the system boot up. Insert the diskette in the appropriately sized disk drive. Now, type **a:**[1] or the letter associated with the disk drive. Good, now type the word **mayint** and hit the enter key. This will give you the initial screen in the Tag Along Trainer. This is shown in Exhibit 1.

As you can see, Caren, the **Tag Along Trainer** consists of two major portions, the **Day Scheduler** and the **Week Scheduler**.

The **Week Scheduler** should be used to learn and reinforce priorities for matching locations with the day of the week on which they should be visited. The program reads in a database of customers and information about these customers such as their place of business, the date they were last visited, the chemicals they use, and the days and times that they are most accessible. The customers are already grouped into locations. The program allows the salesperson to decide which locations should be visited on

---

[1]Words and phrases typed by the computer that require a response from you will be underlined. Commands that you should give by typing words, letters and numbers will be typed in bold characters. The computer will know that you have finished typing the command when you hit the enter key.

EXHIBIT 1

INITIAL SCREEN

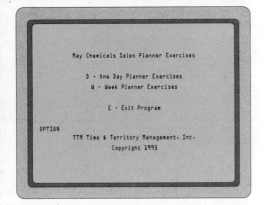

May Chemicals Sales Planner Exercises

D - One Day Planner Exercises
W - Week Planner Exercises

E - Exit Program

OPTION

TTM Time & Territory Management, Inc.
Copyright 1995

EXHIBIT 2

INITIAL WEEK SCREEN

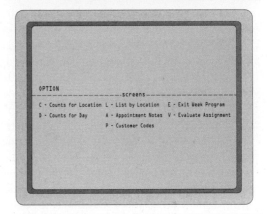

OPTION
----------------------screens--------------------
C - Counts for Location L - List by Location   E - Exit Week Program
D - Counts for Day   A - Appointment Notes   V - Evaluate Assignment
                         P - Customer Codes

which days and evaluate their decisions. The detailer will be given feedback about the decisions and suggestions about how to query the database for helpful information.

The **Day Scheduler** assumes that the decisions about which location to visit on each day have been made. May's detailers must schedule the actual appointments using the customer's accessibility, potential, date of the last visit and other information. After scheduling the customers either through one-on-one contact or meetings and scheduling their meals, they can evaluate their decisions for each day of the week, against the schedules selected by yourself and senior May sales managers.

Next your salespeople will be led through a practice walkthrough of the Week and Day Schedulers. Then we will give a description of the screens that may be accessed for information to help them make their decisions.

After choosing the letter w to enter the week program your salespeople will see a screen like the one shown in Exhibit 2.

Remember that the purpose of the Week Scheduler is to determine which location your detailers will visit each day of the week. There are seven locations and they want to assign exactly one for each day of the week, Monday through Friday. Two of the locations aren't as-

signed. Below is a brief description of the meaning of each of the options:

C   Counts for Location
Use this if you want a count of the number of customers that can meet on each day for a given location.

D   Counts for Day
Use this if you want a count of the number of customers at each location that can meet on a given day.

L   List by Location
This will give a brief listing, on one screen, of the customers, the code of their type of business, the days of the week and times they are most likely to be available.

A   Appointment Notes
These are three pages of detailed information about the customers at a particular location.

P   Customer Codes
This is a listing of the meanings of the four letter codes associated with the type of business.

E   Exit Week Program
Use this to exit the week program.

V   Evaluate Assignment
This will give you a discussion about the optimal location assignments so you can compare your assignments.

EXHIBIT 3
COUNTS FOR THE DAY

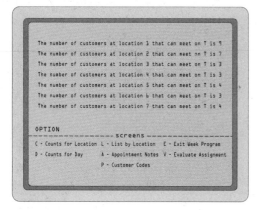

EXHIBIT 4
COUNTS FOR LOCATION 1

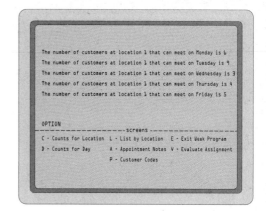

Okay Ms. Conners, now you try it on your own. Read the following text and simultaneously work through the week program. You are going to determine the location that should be visited on Tuesday. The first thing you should do is obtain counts for Tuesday.

Type **D** to get counts for the day.

Type **T** to let the program know you are interested in counts for Tuesday.

Now you should see a screen that looks like the one shown in Exhibit 3.

From this screen it is clear that location 1 is the most likely choice to visit on Tuesday since there are 9 customers that are usually available on Tuesdays. But, it is also important for the detailer to consider whether assigning location 1 to Tuesday eliminates visiting location 1 on a more appropriate day. Thus the detailer should examine the customer availability at location 1 on other days by using the C—Counts for Location option.

Type **C** to get counts for the location.

Type **1** to let the program know you want counts for location 1.

You should get the screen shown in Exhibit 4.

By examining this screen you can see that assigning location 1 to Tuesday will not eliminate any better assignments.

Finally, you should browse through the customers and see whether they are more likely to be seeing customers one-on-one or using meetings, and how long it has been since most of the customers have been visited. This can be done by choosing the

L—List by Location

and the

A—Appointment Notes

options on the screen. A listing of the three screens that are contained in the appointment notes are given on the next page. After referring to the appointment notes it is clear that the customers have not been visited for quite some time and there are a variety of times that they may be visited. The actual scheduling of the day is left for the Day Scheduler. This sort of hierarchical planning is typical in complicated operations. You are now ready to assign the other locations. Why don't you give it a try?

Finished? Good. Now let's look at the Walkthrough for the Day Scheduler. From the initial screen you should choose the **D** option to enter the Day Scheduler. Now you will get a screen that asks you which day you want to schedule, you should

EXHIBIT 5
COUNTS FOR LOCATION 1

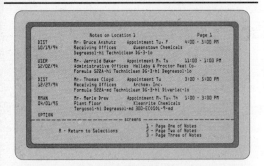

EXHIBIT 6
WALK-THROUGH SCREEN

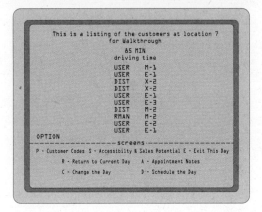

necessary due to the limited space on a screen, they will become more familiar as you work with the program. Here is a brief description of the options you can choose from the bottom of the menu.

P   Customer Codes
This gives a listing of the different customer businesses and their associated four letter codes.

S   Accessibility & Sales Potential
This gives a listing of what the accessibility & sales potential codes mean. The letters have to do with access, the numbers relate to the sales potential.

E   Exit This Day
This will allow you to exit the program for the current day.

R   Return to Current Day
This will allow you to refresh the screen with the basic information of the current day.

A   Appointment Notes
This gives a detailed listing of all the information about the customers such as the chemicals they use, and when they are most likely to be available.

C   Change the Day
This allows the detailer to change the day they are scheduling.

D   Schedule the Day
This puts the detailer into a deeper part of the program where the actual scheduling occurs. There will be a new set of options at this level.

Type **P** for Practice Walkthrough. The practice walkthrough will lead you and your sales reps through scheduling a Monday. The day scheduler uses different schedules than the Week Scheduler, but the location assignments have already been done. You should get the screen shown in Exhibit 6.

The list you and your salespeople see in the center of the screen is a short-hand form of customer information and sales and accessibility potential at location 7 for the Walkthrough to be scheduled on Monday. Although the codes are

EXHIBIT 7
DAY SCHEDULE

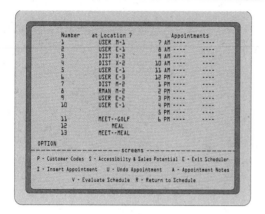

To gain some experience with the options and the meaning of the codes

Type **P** to see a listing of the abbreviations of the practice types.

Type **S** to see a listing of the accessibility and sales potential codes.

Type **A** to see a detailed listing about the customers. Make sure to examine all three pages. A print out of these screens is given on the next page. You will want to refer to it later.

Now, type **R** to return to the current day.

You and your detailers can refer to these screens at most any time. Now enter the D—Schedule the Day portion of the program.

Type **D** and you should see a different screen with a few different options. This is shown in Exhibit 7.

Although most of the options are the same as before, there are three new ones and they will be discussed below.

II **Insert Appointment**
This allows you to schedule a customer, meeting or meal from a row on the left at some time slot on the right.

U **Undo Appointment**

This allows you to remove a customer, meeting or meal from a time slot on the right and place it back in a row on the left.

V **Evaluate Schedule**
This will compare your schedule to the optimal schedule and allow you to move through a discussion of the optimal solution.

Now we will lead you through the scheduling the Walkthrough. You want to start by scheduling the customers that are harder to see and that have higher sales potential. There are two such customers at location 7

(Touloukian DIST X-2) and (Fry DIST X-2)

From looking at the appointment notes it is clear that you will be able to schedule Fry at 12 PM and that you will schedule Touloukian for 7 AM. You also will need to type the letter **R** after leaving the appointment notes to refresh the screen. Thus you need to insert (Touloukian DIST X-2) into a time slot. To do this

Type **I** and then respond to the question by typing the row **3** to identify (Touloukian DIST X-2). Then you must enter the time **7 AM** to insert the appointment into the time slot.

Type **I** and then respond to the question by typing the row **4** to identify (Fry DIST X-2). Then you must enter the time **12 PM** to insert the appointment into the time slot.

You don't actually have to type the AM or PM part of the time. If you put a customer in an inappropriate time slot you can use the undo option to move the customer back to the left side.

Of the remaining customers, the one that is most difficult to see, yet has high sales potential is the

USER M-1

From the appointment notes it is clear that you can schedule the customer at either 1 PM or 2 PM. At present it is unclear which is better, so we will schedule him earlier with the hope that the workday will be over sooner.

Type **I** and then respond to the question by typing the row **1** to identify USER M-1. Then you must enter the time **1 PM** to insert the appointment into the time slot.

You don't actually need to type the PM.

The remaining customers that are more difficult to see and of relatively high sales potential are

DIST M-2 and RMAN M-2

From the appointment notes you can tell that you have a couple different times that these can be scheduled. You should start by scheduling the DIST M-2 at 9 AM. Then you should schedule the RMAN at 1 PM since you've scheduled the DIST X-2 at noon. Unfortunately, this means you must undo the USER M-1 that you have already scheduled and move it to 2 PM.

Type **I** and then respond to the question by typing the row **7** to identify DIST M-2. Then you must enter the time **9 AM** to insert the appointment into the time slot.

To move the USER M-1

Type **U** and then respond to the question by typing the time **1 PM** to identify USER M-1. Then you must enter the row **1** to give him a temporary place to stay.

Type **I** and then respond to the question by typing the row **1** to identify USER M-1. Then you must enter the time **2 PM** to insert the appointment into the time slot.

Now the USER M-1 has been appropriately relocated. To continue

Type **I** and then respond to the question by typing the row **8** to identify RMAN M-2. Then you must enter the time **1 PM** to insert the appointment into the time slot.

Again, the AM and PM are unnecessary.

Of the remaining customers the

USER E-1

can be seen at 8 AM without conflicts.

Type **I** and then respond to the question by typing the row **5** to identify USER E-1. Then you must enter the time **8 AM** to insert the appointment into the time slot.

The

USER E-2

can be seen at 11 without interfering other appointments.

Type **I** and then respond to the question by typing the row **9** to identify USER E-2. Then you must enter the time **11 AM** to insert the appointment into the time slot.

The

USER E-3

can only be seen at 10 AM so

Type **I** and then respond to the question by typing the row **6** to identify GENP E-3. Then you must enter the time **10 AM** to insert the appointment into the time slot.

You have recently seen the USER E-1's, and considering that you have already scheduled eight customers and haven't had a meal you shouldn't schedule them. The final schedule you obtain should look like the screen shown in Exhibit 8.

Now you want to evaluate the schedule and compare it to the optimal. To do this

Type **V**

and you should see a screen that looks like the one shown in Exhibit 9.

In order to see a written discussion of the schedule you can choose **D**, choose **S** to see the scoring again, or choose **R** to return to the scheduling menu. You are now ready to schedule the other days contained in the Day Scheduler. Try it

EXHIBIT 8
FINAL SCHEDULE

```
      Number    at Location 7          Appointments
        1                         7 AM ----DIST   X-2 ----
        2         USER  E-1       8 AM ----USER   E-1 ----
        3                         9 AM ----DIST   M-2 ----
        4                        10 AM ----USER   E-3 ----
        5                        11 AM ----USER   E-2 ----
        6                        12 PM ----DIST   X-2 ----
        7                         1 PM ----RMAN   M-2 ----
        8                         2 PM ----USER   M-1 ----
        9                         3 PM ----          ----
       10         USER  E-1       4 PM ----          ----
                                  5 PM ----          ----
       11         MEET--GOLF      6 PM ----          ----
       12            MEAL
       13         MEET--MEAL
    OPTION
    ------------------- screens -------------------
    P - Customer Codes  S - Accessibilty & Sales Potential  E - Exit Scheduler
    I - Insert Appointment  U - Undo Appointment  A - Appointment Notes
              V - Evaluate Schedule   R - Return to Schedule
```

EXHIBIT 9
SCORING SCREEN

```
      The Optimal Schedule      The Schedule You Developed
      7 AM ---- USER  M-1 ----   7 AM ---- USER  M-1 ----
      8 AM ---- USER  E-1 ----   8 AM ---- USER  E-1 ----
      9 AM ---- DIST  X-2 ----   9 AM ---- DIST  X-2 ----
     10 AM ---- DIST  X-2 ----  10 AM ---- DIST  X-2 ----
     11 AM ---- USER  E-1 ----  11 AM ---- USER  E-1 ----
     12 PM ---- USER  E-3 ----  12 PM ---- USER  E-3 ----
      1 PM ---- DIST  M-2 ----   1 PM ---- DIST  M-2 ----
      2 PM ---- RMAN  M-2 ----   2 PM ---- RMAN  M-2 ----
      3 PM ---- USER  E-2 ----   3 PM ---- USER  E-2 ----
      4 PM ---- USER  E-1 ----   4 PM ---- USER  E-1 ----
      5 PM ----          ----    5 PM ----          ----
      6 PM ----          ----    6 PM ----          ----
      You are correct on 12 out of 12 appointments
    OPTION
    ------------------- screens -------------------
                 R - Return to Selections
      D - Discussion of Solution    S - Scoring and Comparison
```

MANAGING YOUR SALES RESOURCES: ORGANIZATIONAL TACTICS

10

PLANNING, RECRUITING, AND SELECTING

I'm not hiring for where I am; I'm hiring for where I'll be.

FRED BRAMANTE, JR., CEO, DADDY'S JUNKY MUSIC SHOPS, INC.

LEARNING OBJECTIVES

After reading this chapter, you should be able to answer the following questions:

- What is the planning process for selecting new salespeople?
- What are the differences between a job analysis, job qualification, and a job description?
- What methods are used to locate prospective recruits?
- What is the difference between recruiting and selecting?
- What are the basic selection tools used in the recruiting process?

In 1987 the Hudson Institute published *Workforce 2000,* a study of workplace demographic trends. The report presented a detailed picture of the customers and recruits that corporate America will be competing for in the twenty-first century. One of the most compelling statistics is that 75 percent of the population growth will emerge from three minority groups: Asians, Hispanics, and African Americans.[1] Many organizations, awakened by the report, began reevaluating their recruiting procedures to account for the growing need for a diverse salesforce. One company that immediately began looking at diversity recruiting was Prudential Insurance Company. After some internal evaluation, Prudential management began a program titled "Managing Diversity," designed to bring about a cultural change for internal hiring and for the development of new minority markets. Prudential made a commitment to attract minority and female candidates, not just because it was the right thing to do, but also because it made good business sense. The management at Prudential understood that to be successful in diversity recruiting meant a change in the cultural environment. Prudential began new, specially created developmental programs to attract and cultivate minority candidates. Managers were sent to special workshops to increase their sensitivity to diversity issues. The emphasis on diversity hiring ensures that Prudential will be better prepared for new markets as the twenty-first century approaches.[2]

Very few people would argue with the statement that the most important asset of any sales organization is its personnel. What a sales organization does regarding

EXHIBIT 10.1

THE SALESPERSON HIRING PROCESS

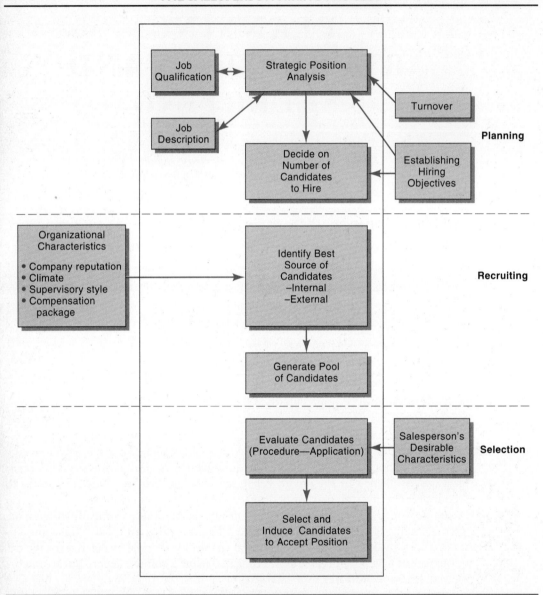

SOURCE: Based on René Y. Darmon, "Where Do the Best Sales Force Profit Producers Come From?" *Journal of Personal Selling and Sales Management,* 13(3) (Summer 1983): 17–29.

the training, mentoring, and developing of its personnel shapes its long-range success. However, the success of the organization actually begins even earlier, with the process of planning, recruiting, and selecting new sales personnel. Firms that approach the hiring process in a haphazard way—without thinking about the long-term effects—will make costly errors. The hiring process should be a carefully planned process that occurs in multiple steps.

This chapter will introduce the concept of planning, recruiting, and selecting. Most of you will go through this process more than once in your career, quite possibly as both recruiter and recruitee. The organization of this chapter is based on Exhibit 10.1, which depicts hiring as a three-stage process.[3] Stage 1 focuses on planning for the hiring process and includes examining turnover, establishing hiring objectives, creating a strategic position analysis, determining needed job qualifications, and writing a job description. Stage 2 of the hiring process focuses on recruiting. The recruiting process must identify the best source of candidates, either from internal or external sources and generate a pool of candidates. Stage 3 is selection. This stage includes evaluating candidates through a number of screening methods such as résumés, conducting interviews, testing, conducting reference and credit checks, and physicals. The screening process should lead to the selection of the best candidate and the inducement for the candidate to accept the position.

THE IMPORTANCE OF RECRUITING AND SELECTION

The hiring of new personnel is the basic foundation of the most important asset of any organization: its people. The hiring process is not a simple procedure. Considerable organizational resources go into hiring to ensure long-term success. Recruiting is an expensive process for any organization. One recruiting firm estimates costs in excess of $9,000 for filling a sales position paying $30,000 a year. Then, once the hiring occurs, an organization absorbs training expenses and territory downtime while the new hire is trained and acclimated. In some situations relocation costs are also incurred.[4] Poor selection decisions have immediate and long-term effects. By hiring an individual whose performance is mediocre at best, the organization is deprived of potential sales that an outstanding hire might have made. A mediocre hire also has higher potential of being a quicker turnover statistic which, in turn, leads to new hiring expenses. Team building and improving morale are also negatively affected by poor hiring decisions. The net result is that making bad hiring decisions decreases the overall effectiveness of the organization.

The hiring process is equally important to the recruits. Recruits are also looking for the right match between hiring organization and their career needs. Recruits who take jobs they are not really satisfied with will soon become another turnover statistic. This puts the recruits and the organization back in the recruiting and hiring process.

PLANNING

The first stage in the hiring process—planning—begins with an examination of turnover within the organization. Turnover will determine, in part, the number of necessary new hires. Organizations must also look at the long- and short-term hiring objectives of the company. Once the objectives are determined, the organization must then perform a strategic position analysis to help define and quantify the position. This analysis will help determine the needed qualifications for the position, which can then be integrated into a job description.

Turnover

People leave organizations for a variety of reasons, and management must always plan for the inevitable loss of personnel. As it relates to the salesforce, **turnover** can be defined as the average percentage of the salesforce that leaves a sales organization in a given time period. For example, if a salesforce is composed of 100 salespeople and in a given year eight quit, one is terminated, three are promoted, and two retire, then the annual turnover is 14, or 14 percent.

Turnover has become a major problem for many sales managers. Estimates have placed salesforce turnover in some industries as high as 50 percent over a 2- to 3-year period.[5] *Sales and Marketing Management* reports that a sales organization is making a passing grade on the turnover issue if its annual rate of turnover is 13.4 percent or less.[6] Unfortunately many organizations are not passing and need to look at possible methods to curb the tide of their turnover.

There are many reasons for turnover. Salespeople leave an organization to escape poor working conditions and inferior supervision, because of real or perceived low compensation, or because of dissatisfaction with the job itself. In addition, salespeople leave because they are offered a better position elsewhere, they are promoted or reassigned within the organization, or they retire. Some turnover may not be bad for the organization. Poor performers may be encouraged to leave the organization or may actually be terminated.[7]

When managers think about turnover of sales personnel, many automatically think about field personnel. However, examining turnover includes looking at all aspects of the sales organization, including telemarketing, support staff, account managers, and other strategic sales tools. For example, Bruce DaCosta, president and CEO of NetStream, says he has concerns about high turnover of tellers. High turnover in teleselling is not uncommon because many companies fail to dedicate the same effort in hiring tellers as they do to outside sales personnel. The perception that teleselling jobs are easy can lead to costly mistakes, such as damaging customer relationships.[8]

Turnover at all levels is inevitable, and it is up to management to plan and have procedures in place for replacing lost personnel. The process begins with establishing a set of hiring objectives. Box 10.1 offers some hiring tips.

Hiring Objectives

The objective of the firm is to replace leaving salespeople as quickly as possible. Traditionally, when turnover created an open territory, the sales manager immediately began searching for a replacement because an empty territory meant declining sales for the district. Hiring only when a territory becomes available is known as *just-in-time hiring*. In other words, they only hired as a territory became available. The opposite of just-in-time hiring, **stockpiling**, is defined as hiring recruits before a territory opens, with the assumption that a territory will become available in the near future. Prior to the 1990s stockpiling was common, but now

---

BOX 10.1

HIRING TIPS TO REDUCE TURNOVER

The key to successful recruiting and hiring is consistency—with a generous dollop of risk taking, flexibility, and change. That's not as contradictory as it sounds. In fact, if you keep the following tips in mind, you'll greatly increase the odds of hiring top sales talent and motivating them over the long term.

1. *Hire from other industries.* Bring in new ideas, concepts, and maybe even some new customers by hiring from outside your industry. Look for individuals who have sold a product or service into similar markets and who know the culture of that type of buyer. Product knowledge is easy to teach. Street smarts, customer contacts, and solid sales skills aren't.

2. *Don't be afraid to hire someone who doesn't fit the mold.* Don't get locked into historic profiles of sales candidates. New faces and new styles make things happen and can open doors to some tough customers. All sales forces need a blend of "missionary" types who will go out and spread the good word of your company and "hard chargers" who get the customers off their butts to either buy or move on.

3. *Hire the person, not the experience.* Managers often decide to hire from a competitor thinking that it will save time in training, that business will follow the salesperson to the new company, or that it's easier to justify hiring an experienced salesperson than a perceived long shot. My personal experience has been that unless there's a major, documentable reason why they're leaving their previous employer to come to you, find yourself another candidate.

4. *Go with your gut, but compare notes.* First impressions are the key to getting in doors in the sales profession. When you interview potential salespeople who appear to have it all together, get opinions from other people within your organization. Again, the most successful long-term relationship builders I've encountered created a strong first impression.

5. *Check references.* You're inviting trouble if you don't check references before making an offer to a new sales candidate. Driving records, police records, conflicts at previous jobs, poor sales and service records will all be revealed in a careful check of references.

6. *Listen to how they sound on the phone.* With the majority of leads being generated—and appointments being made—over the phone these days, a weak, flat, or slurred voice just won't do. Have the candidate call you both early and late in the day to get a true reading of what your customers will hear on a daily basis.

7. *Have a field trip.* Take your potential candidate on a half-day trip with one of your current sales reps to give the candidate a realistic picture of what a day in the field will be like. This serves three purposes: (1) It allows the recruit to see if he or she will like the job setting. (2) It allows the current sales rep to size up the recruit for signs of interest or disinterest. (3) It allows the current sales rep to gauge customers' first impressions.

SOURCE: Russell Riendeau, "Hiring Tips to Reduce Turnover," *Sales and Marketing Management* (November 1992): 95–96.

many organizations consider the expense of maintaining nonassigned salespeople prohibitive.

The late 1980s and the 1990s have brought about a different organizational recruiting objective. With the advent of downsizing, mergers, and cost reductions, many companies have chosen not to refill vacated positions. Territories have been redesigned and made larger to accommodate the mandate for no new hires. For example, downsized organizations such as IBM, Johnson and Johnson, and Procter & Gamble laid off salespeople and personnel in large numbers. Meanwhile, merging companies have found an excess of salespeople and have begun encouraging early retirements, as well as a policy of no new hires. Marion Labs and Merrell Dow, for example, merged to become Marion Merrell Dow, and the two salesforces became one. Management decided to freeze the hiring process while many of the "excess" positions were eliminated through termination and early retirements.

Advancements in technology (discussed in Chapter 2) has meant that many vacant positions can be replaced with other methods such as telemarketers, electronic sales offices, and independent brokers. In addition, companies have begun to flatten their organization—that is, eliminate managerial levels as well as some sales staffing positions. As a result of all of these environmental changes, the process of recruiting has taken on new objectives. Many organizations have stopped recruiting on college campuses, for example. Management has begun to reexamine traditional recruiting procedures or put them on "hold" in favor of nonactive recruiting.

Not all organizations in the 1990s have gone through these recruiting problems, and others have experienced only temporary cutbacks. Nonetheless, changes in the environment have caused most organizations to reassess their salesforce hiring objectives and, thus, make readjustments in their recruiting and selection procedures. As indicated in the opening section of this chapter, many organizations are creating selection objectives based on improving diversity within the organization.[9]

Strategic Position Analysis

A **strategic position analysis** is a systematic procedure that describes the way a sales job is performed and the skills and abilities sales personnel need to perform that job. Exhibit 10.2 provides a framework for a strategic position analysis. The analysis contains five steps: (1) determining performance measures, (2) identifying critical successes and performance dimensions of the position, (3) determining performance dimensions, (4) operationalizing and establishing human performance standards, and (5) designing assessment tools.[10]

The first step in a strategic position analysis consists of identifying the end results required of the job, as well as the critical success factors or performance measures needed to achieve the results. For example, the performance measures for a sales position might include consistently reaching quota or maintaining a profit level of 10 percent for the territory.

Step 2 is an analysis of critical successes or key activities for the job and appropriate time spent on each activity. One report determined, for example, that the appropriate division of time for national account managers is 60 percent in sales activities and 40 percent in administration.[11] Management might examine each of the two percentages in more detail to obtain precise job activities.

The next step after analyzing the position is to determine the performance dimensions needed to perform the job activities. These can include knowledge and skills such as leadership and management skills, communication and interpersonal skills, and occupational knowledge, as well as motivation and ethical considerations. Identifying the performance dimensions may not be a difficult process, but obtaining the right mix of performance dimensions can prove exacting.

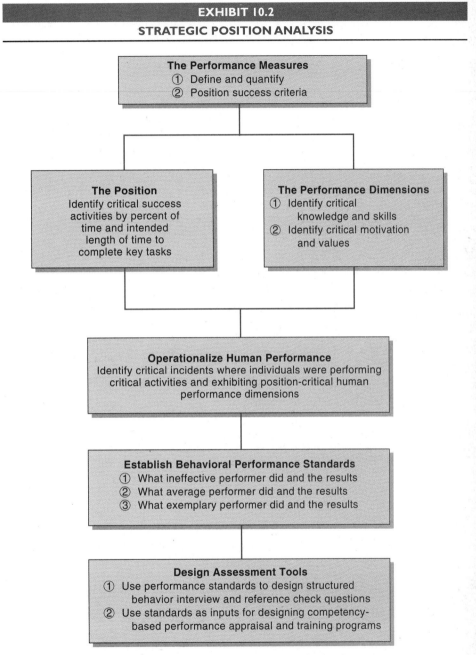

EXHIBIT 10.2
STRATEGIC POSITION ANALYSIS

The Performance Measures
① Define and quantify
② Position success criteria

The Position
Identify critical success activities by percent of time and intended length of time to complete key tasks

The Performance Dimensions
① Identify critical knowledge and skills
② Identify critical motivation and values

Operationalize Human Performance
Identify critical incidents where individuals were performing critical activities and exhibiting position-critical human performance dimensions

Establish Behavioral Performance Standards
① What ineffective performer did and the results
② What average performer did and the results
③ What exemplary performer did and the results

Design Assessment Tools
① Use performance standards to design structured behavior interview and reference check questions
② Use standards as inputs for designing competency-based performance appraisal and training programs

Source: Mark S. Van Clieaf, "In Search of Competence: Structured Behavior Interviews," *Business Horizons* (March–April 1991): 51–55.

Step 4 involves examining employee histories and identifying ineffective, average, and exemplary performers. For this step management identifies critical incidents in which individuals in each category perform a key job task and exhibit one or more of the activities on the performance dimension. The activities of individuals, how they perform, and the results of the performance are all compared and classified.

Finally, the performance standards created in the previous step become the basis for building assessment tools in the hiring of new sales personnel. Screening for exemplary recruits may then occur through résumé review and structured interviews.

Job Qualifications

Job qualifications are the aptitudes, skills, knowledge, and personality traits necessary to perform the job successfully. Determining job qualifications results from the strategic position analysis. The qualifications serve as selection criteria for hiring the best possible sales talent. As you can see in Exhibit 10.3 the qualifications for a Merck Pharmaceutical division professional representative include the specific skills, experiences, interests, and education levels required to perform a certain job. Merck's qualifications note a preference for a life sciences background, along with a variety of personality characteristics such as motivation, resilience, self-confidence, and interpersonal skills. In addition, Merck looks for strong communication skills, "a record of achievement," interest in health care, and leadership in college activities.

Certainly, the qualifications required for a sales job will vary depending on the needs of an organization. Unfortunately many recruiters search for general stereotypes when looking for new salespeople. This approach can lead to costly mistakes. A successful organization follows the strategic position analysis approach and hires based on needed performance dimensions.

EXHIBIT 10.3

JOB QUALIFICATIONS FOR MERCK HUMAN HEALTH DIVISION

MERCK HUMAN HEALTH DIVISION
MERCK & CO., INC.

PROFESSIONAL REPRESENTATIVE

Position Description. The Merck Human Health Professional Representative *manages a specific geographic territory and promotes the Company's products within that territory. Responsibilities focus on face-to-face interaction with physicians, pharmacists, and other health-care professionals to discuss advantages and limitations to our products and their use in the delivery of health care.*

The Professional Representative positions offer an extensive training program, an excellent starting salary, yearly bonus, Company car, and health and dental benefits.

QUALIFICATIONS

We consider candidates with degrees in many disciplines, but prefer those with a major or minor in life sciences, i.e. biology, chemistry, microbiology, nursing, pharmacy, etc. However, **motivation, resilience, self-confidence and interpersonal skills** are qualities we seek most. We also look for good oral and written communication skills, a record of achievement, an interest in the health-care community, work experience demonstrating increasing responsibility, and/or leadership in college activities or community service.

Job Description

A **job description** is a written document that details the characteristics, duties, and responsibilities of a job. Specific requirements should be stated along with any unusual conditions, such as extensive travel or physical requirements (e.g., moving or lifting heavy materials). Specifically, the job description should cover the following:

1. Job title
2. Title of the position's immediate supervisor
3. Job summary (general responsibilities)
4. Major job duties, such as selling activities, obligations related to customer service, market research, and administrative duties
5. Minor job duties, such as working an occasional trade show or writing reports
6. Unusual responsibilities, even if infrequent
7. The job's relation to other positions
8. The position's organizational (reporting) relationships
9. Minimum qualifications[12]

Job descriptions are designed to help applicants determine if the company and job are what they are looking for, and to determine if they have the prerequisite skills required for the job. Properly prepared job descriptions should save recruiters and applicants from wasted time by helping to eliminate applicants who are not qualified for the position. Exhibit 10.4 provides a sample job description from Merck Pharmaceuticals.

RECRUITING

In order to acquire new talent, an organization must have a first-rate recruiting program, even if there are currently no positions to fill.[13] The goal of **recruiting** is to find and attract the best pool of qualified applicants to be considered for sales positions. In today's economy it would seem that recruiting should be an easy process, since so many people are competing for so few jobs. However, thousands of large companies are not growing and thus not hiring. Many smaller companies, on the other hand, complain that they are not growing because they cannot find the right people to hire. The shrinking labor pool leaves many organizations concerned about finding good sales recruits. In the late 1970s three million baby boomers entered the job market every year. By the end of the 1980s only two million people entered the job market.[14] Thus, the labor pool has been steadily decreasing. Moreover, many potential recruits today are unwilling to work their way up the organizational chart, and others simply do not have the appropriate credentials and skills for the job.

There is no single best way to recruit, nor will any two organizations follow the same recruiting strategies. However, most sales recruiters agree that the recruiting process begins first by identifying the best source of applicants. Second, the organization must generate a pool of candidates that is large enough to allow the organization to choose the single best candidate who meets the qualifications of the organization.

EXHIBIT 10.4
MERCK PHARMACEUTICAL JOB DESCRIPTION

Positions for Which Candidates Are Sought:
Professional Representatives are responsible for promoting MHHD pharmaceutical products within specific geographic territories located throughout the United States. Accurate information is conveyed through direct consultation with physicians and other health-care professionals to determine the most appropriate use of our products where indicated.

Products:
Prescription pharmaceuticals indicated for the treatment of many conditions, including hyperlipidemia, hypertension, arthritis, glaucoma, and infectious diseases.

Location:
Approximately 2,200 territories nationwide
Corporate Headquarters: Whitehouse Station, NJ
Divisional Headquarters: West Point, PA (Suburban Philadelphia)

Educational Background:
College degree—all disciplines considered
Major or minors in life sciences desired.

Training:
Merck Human Health's Training Program is recognized as the most comprehensive and extensive in the industry. An initial three-month program includes self-paced study, lectures, case studies, videotaped presentations and instruction by physicians. Emphasis is on product knowledge, interpersonal communication skills, and territory management. Additional training continues through your career as an MHHD Professional Representative.

Compensation:
A Merck Human Health Professional Representative receives a comprehensive package which includes an excellent starting salary, annual bonus, Company car, and travel-related expenses. A Company savings plan, medical, dental and life insurance are also provided.

Honors and Awards:
Fortune magazine's "Most Admired Company" 1987 through 1993
The Wall Street Journal "One of the Top Ten Product Developers" 1990
Sales and Marketing Management magazine's "Best Sales Force," 1987, 1988, 1989, 1990, 1993
Working Mother magazine "One of the best companies for working women" 1987, 1988, 1989, 1990
Black Enterprise magazine "One of fifty of the best companies for blacks to work" 1989, 1992

For Additional Information Contact:
• Coordinator of Recruiting and Selection, WP39-244
  West Point, PA 19486 or

• Regional Recruiting Coordinator
  P.O. Box 467399
  Atlanta, GA 30346

Environmental changes in the 1990s have created some differences in the way companies recruit. *Fortune* 500 companies such as General Mills, IBM, and Xerox once had a tendency to recruit through multiple channels, relying heavily on university recruiting. Many of the best students gravitated toward large companies and at graduation might have had a job already lined up with one of the *Fortune* 500s through campus career placement offices. However, recent downsizing at many of the *Fortune* 500s has caused those companies to decrease their need for new hires.

As a result, many smaller to medium-sized companies that once could not compete with large firms in terms of recruiting are now able to attract some of the brightest and best students.

Despite changes in recruiting, there are still two primary sources of recruits: internal recruits (including lateral/upward moves, interns and co-ops, and employee referral programs) and external recruits (including other industry organizations, educational institutions, advertising, employment agencies, walk-ins, and networking).

Internal Sources

Internal recruits are found within the organization. If a firm can fill its recruiting needs internally, then two goals can be achieved: (1) positions can be filled quickly and (2) group morale can be positively influenced.[15] There are three primary sources of internal recruits. They are lateral or upward moves, interns and co-ops, and employee referral programs.

Lateral or Upward Moves.   Most firms are under pressure to hire from within whenever possible. As a result most sales managers are hired from the existing salesforce, and many new salespeople come from other positions within the organization. One study found that 84 percent of all national account managers are hired from within.[16] Personnel may periodically seek promotions in the organization or attempt to move laterally to another position within the firm. The effects of hiring from outside (especially when hiring lower levels of management) when there are competent people within can be devastating to individual and group morale.

Internal candidates come from several sources. Some of these internal candidates may have had their staffing positions or mid-level managerial jobs eliminated, thus leaving them with no job or no opportunity for promotion. In addition, many of these people were once in the field before moving to staff or sales support positions and may now desire a return to sales field. Internal recruits also come from telemarketing positions or sales support units. It should be noted, however, that telemarketers have had mixed success moving into the field. Some high-performing telemarketers may not perform as well in the field because of a different set of needed skills and aptitude. Other telemarketers have had considerable success in the field. The advantage of moving a telemarketer or someone from the sales service unit to the field is the existing knowledge level of the company, competition, and customer base.

Interns and Co-ops.   Another growing source of internal hiring is interns or co-op students who work part-time while completing an undergraduate or master's degree. **Interns** include all part-time paid or nonpaid college employees whose job has been designed to educate by providing work experience. By contrast, **co-op students** are in programs that allow them to take a semester off from their college or university to work full-time for an organization. The experience co-op students receive is much more like a full-time job because for 40 or more hours a week the students are employed.

The advantages of internship and co-op programs for the organization are numerous. First, the organization can receive free or inexpensive labor. Second, internship programs are good methods of providing needed help without committing to long-term employment. Third, and most important, the organization has the opportunity to observe the intern's or co-op's work performance to determine if the individual would make a good permanent hire.

Many of today's hires are students who proved themselves during an internship period. Indeed, the hiring of interns may be the biggest change in recruiting in the past few years. For example, Northwestern Mutual hires 1,200 new employees each year, and about 8 percent come from the annual hire of 450 internships.[17] J.C. Penney Life Insurance Company continues to hire students to sell for them part-time and then examines their performance to determine full-time status upon graduation.[18] The risk for the organization is substantially reduced because of the period of observation prior to permanent hiring.

Employee Referral Programs. A third source of internal applicants is recommendations made by individuals who currently work for the organization. **Employee referral programs** are incentive programs designed to reward existing personnel for finding and recommending applicants who are subsequently hired.

Current salespeople make good sources of referrals because they understand the needs of the job better than anyone. They are also in a position to see and hear about people who are currently in the industry and might be looking to change jobs, or high performers who might be recruitable. Some of these recruits may be existing customers, suppliers, competitors, or individuals the salesperson has met in work or nonwork situations.

External Sources

Whereas most managers are hired from within, the majority of new salespeople are hired from outside the organization. Traditionally, educational institutions and employment agencies have been the most popular sources for sales trainees. Now advertising, walk-ins, and networking referrals have gained momentum as the need for organizational cost cutting continues (see Exhibit 10.5). Regardless of the primary recruiting method used, it is important that organizations not restrict themselves to only one or two methods. Each has advantages and disadvantages, as discussed in the following sections.

Other Industry Organizations. The most logical place to look for experienced personnel is from the ranks of the competition, suppliers, and customers. All of these people have experience in the industry and should have substantial levels of contacts who can be very helpful to the hiring organization. Many people are looking for better opportunities—new challenges, higher pay, or upward mobility—which may mean a career change, such as going from a buying to a selling role.

Many companies attempt to hire sales personnel from competitors. The advantage of hiring one of the competition is the person's familiarity with the industry and customer base. In addition, the new hire probably needs minimal training. A third advantage of hiring a competitor's sales personnel is the access to a new customer base. However, there is a real danger in intentionally hiring salespeople from competitors. For example, if company A hires company B's best salesperson, then

---

EXHIBIT 10.5

CULLING THE BEST

Where Do You Find the Best Candidates?

Referrals	48%
Recruiters	31%
Competitors	10%
College placement offices	9%
Newspaper ads	9%

What Do You Look For on a Résumé?

Record of achievement	46%
Related experience	36%
Loyalty/length of previous employment	35%
Education	12%

What Factors Influence Your Final Selection?

Level of enthusiasm	31%
Professional attitude	25%
Chemistry or "fit"	23%
Experience level	21%

What Are the Most Common Mistakes You See in Hiring Sales Candidates?

"Warm body" hiring	31%
Poor interviewing techniques	21%
Not checking references	19%
Not checking previous employment	16%

NOTE: Totals may exceed 100% due to multiple responses.

SOURCE: William Keenan, Jr., "Time is Everything," *Sales and Marketing Management* (August 1993): 62.

company B may intentionally seek out company A's best salesperson and attempt to hire him or her. The result is a "hiring war" in which both sides recruit and hire the other's best personnel. The end result is that both sides eventually lose in terms of increased expenses for replacing and training the new personnel, the loss of organizational loyalty, and the potential damage to the customer base. An ethical question also arises concerning raiding competitors' personnel, and many managers are very uncomfortable about intentionally seeking to hire from a competitor, particularly if it is to gain access to new customers.

Most organizations understand, however, that salespeople occasionally move to a competitor through their own initiative. Salespeople who desire to leave their organization know that the most logical place to look for new employment is in the industry that they know, which typically means a competitor. This is just a normal consequence of doing business and is not typically considered a retaliatory offense or an ethical breach. Hiring competing salespeople who initiate the change can be risky. Such individuals have shown little loyalty to the previous company and may not be loyal to the hiring organization either. The hiring firm and its new salesperson may also be sued by the old firm if the salesperson signed a noncompeting agreement.

Many salespeople who sell supplies and equipment to the hiring organization likewise become potential candidates for hire. The advantage of this tactic is that the hiring organization has first-hand information about the skills and abilities of the individual. In addition, the supplying salesperson has thorough information about the hiring organization. A third advantage is that the firm need not be concerned about the beginnings of a hiring war because the supplier was not a competitor. The biggest disadvantage is that the supplier is not knowledgeable about the hiring organization's customer base. In addition, the hiring firm's selling process could be very different, so the supplier might have to "unlearn" sales techniques and procedures from his or her previous job.

A third source of external hires from other industry organizations is individuals from the customer base. Salespeople often have considerable experience with a buyer who is looking for a change and wants to move into a selling position. The advantage of hiring such people is that they are very knowledgeable about what customers need because they have been the customer themselves. Also the hiring organization should know something about the buyer because they have been conducting business with that individual. One disadvantage is that the hiring organization loses a valuable partner in the customer organization, especially if the new hire had been a long-term buyer. Another disadvantage is that the individual's excellent buying skills may not translate into great selling skills.

Educational Institutions.   College recruiting continues to be among the best sources for new hires. Regardless of the candidate's degree, hiring companies are looking for a number of candidate qualities including communication skills, leadership skills, detail orientation, dedication, and team-building abilities.[19]

Firm that plan to recruit in university settings need to develop a college recruiting plan, such as the seven-step process in Exhibit 10.6.[20] Craig Johnson, a regional manager for Duplex Products, Inc., has worked out arrangements where college placement centers screen candidates for him based on prearranged descriptions of hiring qualities and needs. The placement center then schedules interviews for Duplex at the university. Comdata Transportation Services used to hire new recruits from the competition. Now they have a program called "Rapid Deployment," which is designed to find high-quality candidates through college placement.[21]

Advertising.   Classified advertising is a method of recruiting that draws large numbers of potential applicants. In spite of more targeted methods, advertising can be very effective, particularly if the recruiting occurs only periodically throughout the year. The advantage of advertising is that firms may draw a number of very qualified recruits who might not otherwise have thought about interviewing with the advertising organization. However, one major disadvantage is that advertising draws a large percent of unqualified recruits who must be screened out. Another disadvantage for potential recruits is a lack of creativity in the ads. Michael Bruce, president of McFrank and Williams advertising agency, criticizes most recruiting ads because they do not create a curiosity that draws the top candidates. Compare

EXHIBIT 10.6

A MODEL OF COLLEGE RECRUITING

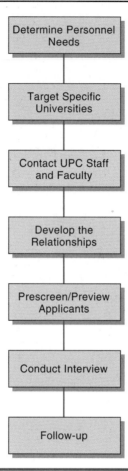

Determine Personnel Needs

Target Specific Universities

Contact UPC Staff and Faculty

Develop the Relationships

Prescreen/Preview Applicants

Conduct Interview

Follow-up

SOURCE: Jon M. Hawes, "How to Improve Your College Recruiting Program," *Journal of Personal Selling and Sales Management,* 9 (Summer 1989): 47–52.

the examples of a "typical" recruiting ad and a more "creative" recruiting advertisement in Exhibit 10.7.

Given the large number of responses, firms can expect considerable administrative time spent in screening and interviewing candidates. Abbott Laboratories once placed a large ad in a daily Dallas newspaper for open interviews beginning at 8:00 A.M. one Thursday morning. Abbott had a team of interviewers on hand to handle over 500 respondents. Interviewees who survived the initial brief screening qualified for a second round of more thorough interviews. Candidates who survived these interviews became eligible for a third round. All of these interviews occurred on the same day! Finally, the group of 500 was narrowed to six. These six were later sent to a district office for further screening. Eventually three were hired. The Abbott ex-

EXHIBIT 10.7

WHAT'S WRONG WITH YOUR RECRUITMENT ADS?

Traditional Advertisement

PHARMACEUTICAL SALES

(Chicago Area)

Pharmaceutical Sales Training opportunity in the Midwest, at expanding R.X. NESS Corp., a major international company.

Prior sales experience helpful, but not required.

Experience in pharmaceutical industry or allied areas also a plus. College graduate with 1–2 years experience and demonstrated leadership qualities or potential would be ideal.

Call today, Sunday, (800) 312-3123 or FAX your resume to (312) 987-6543.

N • E • S • S

NESS, Department 312312, 312 San Andreas St.
Chicago, IL 31271

Creative Advertisement

SALES   MIDWEST OPPORTUNITY

PHARMACEUTICAL SALES

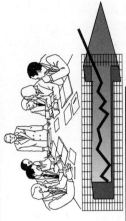

Are you articulate and persistent enough to succeed in pharmaceutical sales?

If so, you're invited to explore the challenging opportunities that R.X. NESS Corporation has to offer within the pharmaceutical industry at the Midwest Regional Headquarters.

Bring us your professionalism and competitive spirit, your sense of commitment along with your polished communication skills. We'll train you to represent NESS to our health care partners. A bachelor's degree, or equivalent, is necessary. Prior sales experience is not required, but demonstrated leadership qualities are a plus.

As you would expect, at NESS you'll receive an all-inclusive compensation package that offers immediate income, including a performance-based incentive program, and benefits, as well as future growth opportunities. For more information, call Today, Sunday, from Noon to 9 P.M. (800) 312-3123. If unable to call, please fax your resume to (312) 987-6543.

N • E • S • S

NESS, Department 312312, 312 San Andreas St.
Chicago, IL 31271

We want to keep in contact!

- Even if you are not looking for a position, send your resume and we will refer to it for future opportunities.
- If you are not from the geographical area, contact us anyway for possible national opportunities.
- If you know someone who fits this job description, do a friend a favor and refer them to us.

perience was unusual and required a large number of interview personnel for a one-day recruiting process, but the company was able to hire three very qualified people in a short period of time.

Employment Agencies.   Employment agencies charge a fee to help match a sales organization with potential sales recruits. The fee may be paid by the hiring organization or, in many cases, by the recruit. The fee typically consists of 15 to 20 percent of the new hire's first-year earnings. The benefit of using agencies is that they can reduce the time spent in recruiting for open positions and can also conduct pre-screening for the organization, thereby reducing time requirements for an organization's management.

Although employee agencies can be very helpful to the recruit and the recruiting organization, the status of their reputations has been mixed. For example, *The Wall Street Journal* obtained a confidential memo at Lee Hecht, the third largest out-placement firm in the United States, which warned its recruiters against placing laid-off employees of Baxter International with other pharmaceutical companies. Lee Hecht was attempting to protect its largest employer, Baxter, who hires many of Lee Hecht's clients, at the expense of the individuals seeking employment. Outplacement services are supposed to work in the interests of the individual seeking employment, but in many cases the client's former employer pays the bill and thus may have undue influence.[22]

Walk-ins.   Rather than seeking out potential recruits, many organizations prefer to let recruits come to them. Walk-ins include unsolicited résumés that are mailed to the organization and recruits who walk in off the street desiring an interview opportunity. From the hiring organization's perspective, the walk-in approach saves the cost of actively searching for new hires. Organizations that implement the walk-in strategy typically do not hire many people in a given year; they also rely heavily on the referral method.

From the job candidate's perspective, the walk-in approach has long odds of success for any given visit. Typically, 100 résumés have to be mailed in order to get responses from five or six organizations, and then the applicant must pass the interview process. Going to the organization in person may increase the odds of success, but it still requires a good sense of timing since the organization must have a current vacancy and be actively engaged in the hiring process.

Networking.   From the perspective of the graduating student or anyone else in today's market, probably the best method of landing a job is to have established a very strong network of contacts who can help you get your foot in the door. Recruits need a champion who will be proactive in helping to set up interviews with the proper people in an organization. It is important to know that résumés sent directly to a personnel department without someone to champion the candidate have a low probability of follow-up. Therefore it is important for students to establish a network of professors, friends of the family, past employers, and others who can help find employment opportunities. Jim Williams, managing director of the Hay Group, comments that networking can take a long time to pay off, so it is in the best interests of the college student to begin building a network in his or her sophomore year.[23] For those in graduate school, the networking process should begin immediately, building on contacts from undergraduate and prior work experience.

From the perspective of the hiring organization, an established network of friends, colleagues, faculty, and peers can provide a source of potential new recruits, particularly if the organization is looking for recent college graduates. As we discussed in Chapter 5, many network sources occur because of sales managers' associations with service organizations, community service, trade associations, churches and synagogues, university contacts (professors, staff, and administrators), and sporting or health clubs.

SELECTION

After planning for and recruiting potential new hires, the organization must then select the person it thinks is best for the job. The selection process includes two primary steps: (1) evaluating recruited candidates and (2) selecting and inducing the best candidate to join the organization. The evaluation of recruited candidates involves collecting pertinent information on a recruit's mental abilities, physical characteristics, experience, personality, and personal history. To collect that information, firms may incorporate the use of assessment centers and several selection tools including application blanks, résumés, interviews, testing, references, a credit check, and a physical examination.

Look at the steps used in the Marion Merrell Dow recruiting process shown in Exhibit 10.8. Notice the number of steps included and the different selection tools implemented. The recruiting and selection process can take an inordinate amount of time, which many students have trouble understanding. Because of the time required, employment seekers should treat the search as a full-time job and plan accordingly.

Evaluating Candidates

Evaluating candidates can be tedious and a potentially expensive process that may involve a number of people in the organization, ranging from a sales manager to the vice-president of sales. Each recruit may be interviewed by multiple people, spend a day in the field with a salesperson, and spend a day at the district office testing and interviewing. In addition, some human resource personnel may check the applicant's references, credit history, and criminal activity record, as well as administer a drug screening test. The purpose of a candidate evaluation is to collect a litany of information that will help the organization decide whether a person is the best candidate for the job. Several of the tools companies use to evaluate candidates.

Selection Tools

A hiring organization has a number of tools at its disposal to help the recruiter make a decision regarding the best possible candidate. Some of these tools include application blanks, résumés and cover letters, personal interviews, testing, reference and background checks, and physicals.

Application Blanks.   An **application blank** is designed to (1) provide information useful in making selection decisions and (2) obtain information that may be needed

EXHIBIT 10.8

MARION MERRELL DOW SELECTION PROCESS

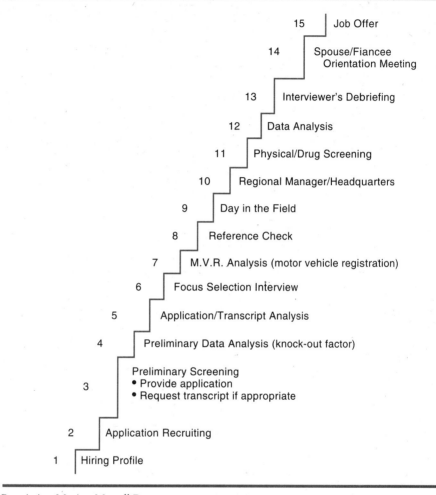

15 | Job Offer

14 | Spouse/Fiancee Orientation Meeting

13 | Interviewer's Debriefing

12 | Data Analysis

11 | Physical/Drug Screening

10 | Regional Manager/Headquarters

9 | Day in the Field

8 | Reference Check

7 | M.V.R. Analysis (motor vehicle registration)

6 | Focus Selection Interview

5 | Application/Transcript Analysis

4 | Preliminary Data Analysis (knock-out factor)

3 | Preliminary Screening
• Provide application
• Request transcript if appropriate

2 | Application Recruiting

1 | Hiring Profile

Permission Marion Merrell Dow.

during the course of an individual's employment.[24] The application blank gathers relevant written information about the candidate, including basic personal history. It also allows the hiring organization to obtain the same information on every candidate to make comparisons easier. Most application blanks are filled out in person, thus allowing the recruiting organization to judge the applicant's attention to detail, neatness, and organization. It is very important for applicants to take their time completing application blanks and to write as clearly and concisely as possible.

Long-term use of the application blank by an organization can be effective as a predictor of the success or failure of applicants. The organization can examine all of its top performers over time, looking for similar qualities or characteristics that may predict the likelihood of success in a new recruit. As a result recruiters look for these same qualities when evaluating new applicants.

Résumés and Cover Letters.   A résumé is a snapshot of a person's history and abilities. Résumés for entry-level jobs are typically one page long and summarize an individual's educational history, job experience, activities and honors, specific skills, and other information that may be targeted directly for the desired organization. Most organizations want to see a résumé prior to granting an interview.

A résumé is a good way for an organization to examine the qualifications of different individuals without actually interviewing them, and thus screen several hundred applicants down to a dozen or so. Large organizations receive thousands of unsolicited résumés every year, and most end up in the trash or a file that will never be reopened. An unsolicited mailing of your résumé to organizations will typically have little success (see Box 10.2). All résumés must be professional in appear-

---

BOX 10.2
READ THIS BEFORE SENDING YOUR RESUME

Maybe the résumé should go the way of the dinosaur. "To me, a résumé is a *deselection* device," says Dennis Lunder who, as head of marketing communications at American Greetings Corp. in Cleveland, manages about 80 people. "My method is radically different."

In six job hunts over nearly 30 years, Mr. Lunder says he sent out "thousands of résumés at a time" with little effect. Now, as a mentor in Hudson Job Search, a volunteer program in Ohio for unemployed executives, Mr. Lunder preaches this gospel.

- Treat your search as full-time work. Each weekday should be structured as a workday, with a schedule of events.
- Compile a list of the 20 companies you would most like to work for and then research them. Call the secretary of the executive who is most likely to hire you and ask for the annual report and other corporate materials.
- Keep researching. Mr. Lunder went to stores that sold American Greetings cards and products, asking the store manager: How is the service? Are you happy with American Greetings products? How can things be improved? He also received permission to accompany a sales rep for a day.
- Write a one-page personal marketing letter, selling yourself to the person who is hiring, which isn't necessarily the company's human resources executive. Explain what you have learned (including some flattering comments on the company's innovations) and how you would fit in. Enclosing a résumé is a one-way ticket to the personnel department.

- If asked for a résumé, tell them you need a week to update it. Then try to focus on aspects of your career that fit what the company is looking for.
- Try to set up a 20-minute "information meeting" with the hiring person. (Don't call it an interview.) If you get the person's voice mail, suggest a time, like 7 A.M. tomorrow.
- Tell the hiring person what you know and admire about the company, and about your skills. Have five smart questions on the company's strategy. Only at the end of the meeting suggest you are looking for work.
- Mr. Lunder advises listening to motivational tapes to keep spirits and energy high, and checking whether your target has more job cuts in its future. You wouldn't want to have to do this again.

SOURCE: Kevin Salwen, "Read This Before Sending Your Résumé," *The Wall Street Journal* (February 8, 1994): A1.

ance, but for a mailed résumé to have much chance of success it must stand apart from all of the others. For example, one student who wanted to work for a music producer sent the company her résumé, which was shaped like a phonograph record, complete with a hole in the middle. Another student was applying for a sales position for an advertising agency; his résumé resembled a selling brochure. Both students were hired, partly because of the distinctiveness of their résumés.

An emerging trend in résumés preparation and mailing is the electronic résumé. Electronic résumés are prepared on computer and sent computer to computer. They may also be a part of an applicant's home page on the Internet. It is easier and more efficient to send a résumé from computer to computer rather than mailing it. Another advantage is that hiring organizations can get instantaneous information from applicants as they need it. Electronic résumés are subject to some of the same problems as mailed résumés, however. Currently, they are somewhat unique and thus may have a greater possibility of being viewed when sent to an organization. Soon electronic résumés will be flooding hiring organizations just like their predecessors, so their uniqueness will no longer be an attraction.

Cover letters should be included with all mailed résumés. They should be addressed to a specific person and should highlight the sender's key attributes. Cover letters should conclude by asking for an interview. The student whose cover letter is discussed in Exhibit 10.9 concluded with the "Top Ten Reasons" why the company should hire her. That student was interviewed and hired, in part because of her cleverness in getting her résumé examined and an interview scheduled.

In summary, résumés are useful to organizations as a quick way to screen recruits. Recruits, in turn, should use their résumé as support during an interview and as a reminder for the organization after the interview is over.

EXHIBIT 10.9

THE CONCLUSION OF ONE COVER LETTER

One student included the following "Top 10" list at the end of her cover letter. The recruiter was impressed enough to interview the individual; eventually the student accepted a position with the organization.

Top Ten Reasons to Hire Jennifer Lewin

10. She is hardworking. She worked her way through college.
9. She has above-average intelligence. She earned a 3.67 cumulative G.P.A.
8. She is eager to learn. She called a marketing manager to learn details about the publishing industry.
7. She has initiative. She visited several campuses in order to become familiar with the major accounts.
6. She has a marketing and business background. She graduated with a business administration major and a marketing minor.
5. She has knowledge of personal sales. She took a high-level sales course in college.
4. She is highly organized.
3. She has great communication skills.
2. She enjoys working with a diverse group of people.
1. You would not want your competition to hire her.

Interviews.   An interview is the most crucial aspect of the selection process for both the candidate and the hiring organization. Both parties are judging one another and the level of professionalism of each. The interview allows a recruiter to judge the character and abilities of the individual better than other screening methods, although studies have indicated that personal interviews have not been effective in predicting future performance.[25] Nevertheless, personal interviews remain the foundation of the screening methods. Generally, candidates can expect to go through an initial interview, plus a second and possibly a third, and perhaps even a field interview before a hiring decision is made.

First Interviews.   In the first interview, which is typically brief (30 minutes), the interviewer tells the interviewee a little about the job. In turn, the interviewee has the opportunity to impress the interviewer in hopes of a second round of interviews. The first interview is designed to screen out the majority of candidates. The interviewer is looking for factors that would eliminate candidates as potential new hires or for characteristics that indicate that a person may be exactly who the organization is seeking (see Exhibit 10.10 for these positive characteristics).

First interviews vary depending on where they occur. For example, in this age of technology, Wonderlic Personnel Test, Inc., offers organizations a service in which they automate the application process. Applicants respond to a toll-free number included in an ad and receive an automated description of the client company and the job. Callers enter pertinent information and respond to a series of 15 questions. These applications are forwarded to the client company, where the top responses are identified and personal interviews are set up.[26]

A more common initial interview for college students is conducted in the job placement office of the university. The interview typically lasts 30 minutes and recruiters attempt to see as many people as possible during the day. This type of interview will be purely for screening, attempting to find three or four people to bring back for a second round of interviews, probably at a district office.

A first interview at the organizational office may be longer and more in depth, depending on how the interview is going. The recruiter may not have 15 or 20 interviews in a day, as in the university placement setting, so he or she can be more thorough and use different methods to evaluate the individual. For example, Alan Gold of the the Office Place in Anchorage, Alaska, begins with an "eyeball" text. A receptionist is assigned the duty of reporting on the candidate's behavior from the moment he or she walks in the door until the interviewer greets the candidate. The idea helps the recruiter see how the candidate behaves before the pressure on the interview begins.[27]

Interviews can take many forms. Some interviews are unstructured and informal. In **unstructured interviews** the interviewer has no set format or questions to ask. However, most first-round interviews, and many subsequent interviews, tend to be structured. **Structured interviews** are formal interviews in which a format is followed or all interviewees are asked the same set of questions. This allows a baseline to be established against which comparisons can be made of all the candidates.

Other interviewers may use a **stress interview,** in which the interviewer might be critical of some aspect of the interviewee to determine how he or she handles criticism and difficult situations. It is also very common for the interviewer to ask the interviewee to pick up a pen or pencil and sell it to the interviewer. Ken Blanchard, president of Blanchard Training and Developments, takes this approach a

EXHIBIT 10.10

HOW TO SUCCEED IN AN INTERVIEW

1. Do your homework—know something about the interviewing company.
2. Maintain the proper appearance; dress appropriately.
3. Be confident.
4. Have a 3-year, 5-year, and 10-year goal.
5. Communicate effectively (proper diction and grammar).
6. Be enthusiastic!
7. Maintain eye contact.
8. Have a firm handshake.
9. Be courteous; send a thank-you letter.
10. Keep a positive attitude.
11. Show a sense of humor (avoid silliness or defensiveness).
12. Have a good scholastic record.
13. Have some job experience (summer or part-time jobs are fine).
14. Be active on campus.
15. Have some leadership abilities.
16. Show poise and maturity.
17. Be willing to start at the bottom.
18. Be realistic.
19. Be honest and straightforward.
20. Have strong references from past employers and professors.
21. Have some social skills.
22. Be creative.
23. Be a good time manager.
24. Be punctual! (Never be late for an appointment.)
25. Indicate a strong interest in the company or industry.
26. Ask for the job.
27. Maintain high moral standards (strong sense of ethics).
28. Maintain a strong work ethic.
29. Support your community (university or city).
30. Ask questions.

step further. He provides the recruit with the description and responsibilities of the job and asks the recruit to take an hour and write an essay on what the candidate will be doing over the next three months if the person gets the job. After an hour, the candidate makes an oral presentation of his or her report. This process indicates how the candidate is able to think and react in a stressful environment, and it allows management a chance to evaluate the candidate's written and oral skills.[28]

Regardless of the technique used by the interviewer, both interviewee and interviewer need to be well prepared for an interview by thinking about some key questions (see Exhibit 10.11).

At the completion of the first round of interviewing, many organizations have the interviewer complete an evaluation form (see Exhibit 10.12 for an example). The evaluation form is then passed on to the district office to help determine who will be invited to subsequent rounds.

Subsequent Rounds.   Second rounds tend to occur in the organization's main or district office. The second round may include multiple interviews with a variety of

---

EXHIBIT 10.11
THE MACKAY SWEET SIXTEEN

"Hit the ground running" in your next interview, says Harvey Mackay, by "reading and rereading the following questions." If you're conducting the interview, use them; if you're being interviewed, be ready for them.

1. Describe your ideal job—the position you would most like to have (include title, responsibilities, who you would report to, who would report to you).
2. Describe your ideal company (size, industry, culture, location, structure).
3. Where do you want to be in your career in three to five years?
4. What do you want your next job to do for you that your last job didn't do?
5. What kinds of growth should a new job offer (promotions, training, challenges)?
6. What skills will you be able to add to your résumé while you have this job?
7. Why should a company want to hire you? (What's special about you as a candidate?)
8. What personal and professional accomplishments are you the most proud of?
9. What do you least want to be asked in an interview—what are the questions you dread the most?
10. How will you handle the tough questions?
11. What compensation, including salary and benefits, do you want to earn and can you legitimately ask for?
12. What are the most important benefits other than salary that would prompt you to go to work for a new company?
13. What tools and resources can you draw on to help you through your job transition?
14. What can you say in an interview that would really set you apart from other candidates for your ideal position?
15. What could your current employer do for you that would prevent you from looking for another job in the first place? (Have you asked?)
16. How will you know when you've become a success?

SOURCE: Harvey Mackay, *Sharkproof: Get the Job You Want, Keep the Job You Love . . . In Today's Frenzied Job Market.* Copyright 1993 by Harvey Mackay. Reprinted by permission of HarperCollins Publishers.

---

executives. Success at this stage may mean a subsequent round immediately, or at a later date for testing or discussions with other personnel. Every organization has different philosophies on how many rounds of interviews and trips the recruit should make and where these subsequent interviews should occur. It is not uncommon for some companies to require as many as five to seven rounds of interviews, although today's budget restraints have curtailed many of these multiple round interviews.

Many companies will have the last round at the national headquarters, where the offer will be determined and beginning compensation is discussed. It is important to remember that on multiple interviews any of the interviewers can determine success or failure for the applicant. You must be professional and attempt to influence *everyone* you meet in the interview process. Many companies routinely have secretaries and receptionists report how they were treated by the candidate and seek their impressions of the individual as well. Box 10.3 offers an example of a poorly handled interview.

Field Interviews.   One type of interview that many organizations have implemented is a **day in the field,** similar to ride-withs discussed in Chapter 6, in which the recruit spends a working day in the field with a sales rep from the hiring organi-

---

BOX 10.3
A BAD INTERVIEW

This is an example of a poor interview. What mistakes did the interviewee make?

Interviewer: Tell me about yourself.
Interviewee: Well, I've lived in Louisiana all my life, attended LSU for 4 years, and I'm a fun person.

Interviewer: What are your long-range and short-range goals and objectives?
Interviewee: My long-range goal is to be rich and famous. My short-range goal is to be on my own, have my own apartment and car.

Interviewer: What do you see yourself doing 5 years from now?
Interviewee: Working for a larger corporation, high pay and comfortable work hours.

Interviewer: How do you plan to achieve your career goals?
Interviewee: Through hard work during a 9-to-5 day.

Interviewer: Why should I hire you?
Interviewee: I would do a decent job.

Interviewer: How would you handle rejection?
Interviewee: I would take it as it comes.

Interviewer: Any plans for continued study?
Interviewee: No, 4 years is enough.

Interviewer: How do you work under pressure?
Interviewee: I can handle it as long as it doesn't interfere with my after-work hours.

Interviewer: What do you know about our company?
Interviewee: My uncle worked for you.

Interviewer: Do you have a geographical preference?
Interviewee: I want to live in the South; I don't like Northern weather.

Interviewer: Are you willing to travel?
Interviewee: No. I enjoy Baton Rouge and I don't enjoy living out of a suitcase.

Interviewer: What do you do in your spare time?
Interviewee: I watch television, shop, enjoy outings with my friends.

Interviewer: Do you have any questions?
Interviewee: No.

End of interview.

---

zation. This day in the field serves a number of purposes. First, it allows the recruit to determine the desirability of the job. If the recruit decides that this is not the type job he or she wants, both sides have saved future problems and expenses by ending the process at this point. In addition, the organization can learn from the salesperson how the recruit behaved and reacted during the day-long process. Recruits tend to relax in this informal setting and display more of their true personality. The day in the field has become very successful and popular with organizations, and both sides have come to appreciate this round of the interview.

Testing.   Testing is used by many organizations to help screen applicants on a number of different dimensions, depending upon the organizational goals and objectives. Testing can occur in assessment centers, in district offices, or in the office of

EXHIBIT 10.12

REGIONAL COLLEGE INTERVIEW SUMMARY REPORT

Interview Summary Report

Candidate's Name:	Date Interviewed:
Position Being Considered:	Interviewer's Name: Title:

Key Attributes: (1 = Poor; 2 = Fair; 3 = Good; 4 = Outstanding; 5 = Exceptional
Provide evidence (actual behavior, actions taken, results, etc.) to support each rated attribute.

Intellectual Ability		GPA: Science: Hrs work/wk:
Analytical Ability		
Judgment		
Leadership		
Interpersonal Skills (Persuasiveness)		
Communication Skills		
Creativity		
Team Work		

RECOMMEND FOR HIRE: YES _____ NO _____ FURTHER INTERVIEW _____

Rationale:

Relocation: Yes _____ No _____

Geographic Preference: _____ Overall Rating: _____

EXHIBIT 10.12 (continued)

REGIONAL COLLEGE INTERVIEW SUMMARY REPORT

Decisiveness		
Ethics and Values		
Results Oriented		
Problem Solving		
Flexibility		
Business Acumen		
Strategic Focus		Job Search:
Courage of Convictions		

GENERAL COMMENTS:

consulting firms that provide the testing service. The testing process typically occurs sometime after the first interview. The time requirements for taking the test or series of tests can range from one hour to a full eight-hour day.

The development of a testing procedure can be very expensive, with developing and validating the test costing tens of thousands of dollars. All tests must be validated to ensure that there is no intentional or unintentional discrimination built into the test. Outside consultants might also be used in evaluating the results of each applicant, adding to the overall cost of the process. Organizations that invest in testing procedures use them as a matter of policy. Like the application blank, testing can be used as a predictive tool by comparing scores of previous top performers with the results of those who have applied for the vacant position.

Not all firms are enamored with the testing procedure. In fact, the use of tests has declined over the past 25 years to a point where the majority of users are now only large organizations. One explanation for the decline in testing is a substantial increase in legal requirements, and thus expenses, to ensure a lack of discrimination.[29]

Tests typically evaluate candidates on five dimensions: (1) intelligence, (2) aptitude, (3) personality, (4) knowledge, and (5) interests. An organization may use multiple tests to gather information on one or more of these five dimensions.

References and Background Checks.   An applicant should have three to five references for a potential employer to check. Many firms will contact references either after the first interview or just prior to an offer. Potential employers want to know the relationship of the reference to the applicant. Past employers or professors carry more importance because they can attest to the applicant's recent work habits and abilities. References that are family friends carry less weight because of the assumption that they are biased in their judgment and, in fact, may know little about the individual's work habits. Most organizations understand that references will rarely say anything derogatory about an applicant, but checking a reference does confirm past histories and positions. Also, even though references may not say anything negative, there is a lot of information that can be gained by "reading between the lines" regarding what references are not willing to say.

Privacy laws and fear of litigation have generated an environment where many past employers say little or, in some cases, refuse to say anything about past employees as general policy. Also, many applicants are currently employed and do not want their references checked because their current employer does not know they are interviewing with other organizations.

Checking references is not a primary step in the screening process. Reference checks are usually designed to confirm already-known information about the individual. However, it is important for applicants to have a set of strong, positive references available upon request. Applicants must be sure to ask these individuals if they are willing to serve as a reference. Applicants should also let them know if there are any particular experiences they wish the reference to mention when talking with potential employers.

Background checks can include a number of other variables. PepsiCo routinely checks the applicant's driving record, credit history, and criminal history. In this age of litigation, organizations are not willing to gamble on people who have shown a history of irresponsibility or criminal behavior. Marion Merrell Dow checks driving records for people interviewing for sales positions. Its rationale is that salespeople are given company cars and any driving accident that occurs could leave Marion Merrell Dow financially responsible in litigation. If a person has a poor driving record, he or she may be a risk that is not worth taking.

There are a number of private companies who specialize in performing all forms of background searches and checks on applicants. Many people engage in **résumé inflation,** which means an overstated or highly exaggerated statement of facts. Other individuals simply lie about their credentials. These private companies search out an individual's past history, confirm previous employment, and check driving, credit, and criminal records.

Physical Examinations. Normally, the last stage of the screening process is the company physical examination. Many sales positions require physical exams because the job may involve substantial physical activities and the potential to cause stress or mental fatigue. A physical may be required to determine if there are health problems that could preclude the individual from performing the job. With the passage of the Americans With Disabilities Act, organizations cannot require a physical prior to an offer being made to the applicant. However, an employer can make an offer contingent upon a positive physical. For example, one medical supply company made an offer contingent upon the physical. The applicant took the physical and was denied the job after it was determined he had hepatitis. Fortunately for the applicant, he was treated for the illness and six months later was hired by the same medical supply firm.

Another common requirement from an increasing number of organizations is a drug screen. Studies have repeatedly indicated that the use of drugs can impede performance and can lead to accidents that may lead to litigation. A drug screen is becoming more and more common as part of the hiring process and may continue throughout employment. In fact, at Intel the drug policy states that if you don't take a required drug test within 36 hours of the job offer, you cannot be hired for that position, nor can you be considered for any other position within the organization for one year.

Pertinent Information Needed

Many sales managers state that they use their "gut instincts" when hiring salespeople and over the years have learned to "read" people. Instincts can be surprisingly efficient, but regardless of a sales manager's instincts, every good recruiter is looking for information that will indicate the applicant's probability of success and allow the recruiter to make an informed decision on the candidate.[30]

The selection process is designed to obtain information about a candidate's abilities and personal history. Specifically, the process seeks to determine the mental abilities, physical characteristics, experience levels, personality characteristics, and basic general information about recruits.

Mental Abilities. Organizations need to determine the intelligence and knowledge levels of job candidates. Several selection tools are used to determine mental abilities. First, the résumé and application blank indicate the level of education that candidates have acquired. Second, the interview helps to determine the ability of candidates to think on their feet. In addition, the testing process can also help determine if individuals have the mental skills necessary for the job.

The assessment of an individual's mental abilities can include his or her creative abilities, which can also be determined through the testing and interview process. Creativity experts make an important distinction between convergent thinking and divergent thinking. **Convergent thinking** refers to the thought process that produces a single best answer to a problem, such as that which is accomplished on a multiple choice test. **Divergent thinking,** on the other hand, refers to those thought processes that produce a variety of alternatives to a problem. Role playing and case analysis are examples of tests that produce more divergent thinking. Interestingly, many traditional forms of education emphasize convergent abilities when industry wants more divergent thinking.[31]

Physical Characteristics.   The physical examination which many organizations require is designed, in part, to determine if an individual can physically perform the job. In addition, the drug test is used by many companies to screen candidates. Last, the application blank asks for basic physical characteristics such as height, weight, and health history.

Experience Levels.   Experience is always an important attribute to consider when selecting a candidate. Obviously experience includes past work history, but it also includes skills such as language and computer proficiencies. Other experience may include leadership skills acquired as an officer in a campus organization, or communication skills acquired through education and outside activities. The application blank and résumé will describe previous job experience, but the personal interview will gather more specific details about job duties and activities, along with any experience or skills that were gained on the job.

Personality Traits.   Most sales organizations look for certain personality traits in their candidates such as enthusiasm, confidence, vivaciousness, competitiveness, a high sense of empathy, and a sense of humor. Testing procedures can be designed to examine a candidate's personality for these characteristics. The personal interview and personal references are also helpful in determining an applicant's personality traits.

Personal History.   The application blank and résumé provide basic information such as name, phone number, home address, social security number, educational degrees, interests, and hobbies. This information is primarily for permanent company records.

Selection and Inducement to Accept

Once the screening process has been completed, there are typically a small set of remaining candidates from which the recruiter must decide who will be chosen for the open position. One common solution is to hire the person who best reflects the interviewer's values. However, this cloning approach can commonly lead to organizational stagnancy. More and more organizations are looking for diversity of thought, experience, and background. Different perspectives can lead to breakthroughs for old problems.

Most hiring decisions eventually are made by using judgment models to rank order the candidates.[32] Using this approach the top candidate will be given an offer, while the second and third candidates will be put on hold until the top candidate has accepted or rejected the offer. Organizations use different philosophies as to how much time a candidate has to accept or reject the job. Ideally, the organization would like an immediate answer but normally is willing to give the candidate a week or two to reply. Organizations may offer incentives to accept the offer, such as more starting pay or a variety of perks. Much of the time given for response, as well as the willingness to negotiate pay and perks with the candidate, will depend on how badly the organization wants this individual, how many other good candidates are in waiting, the severity of need for immediate territory fulfillment, and the personality of the recruiter.

The offer typically is made orally but should be followed up with a written contract. Applicants not selected should be notified as quickly as possible. Students complain that they never hear positively or negatively from many organizations. Firms need to remember the importance of maintaining professionalism and that someday they may be conducting business with the rejected candidates. Courtesy can go a long way in maintaining a positive impression.

SUMMARY

Hiring is a function of three steps: planning, recruiting, and selection. The planning step begins with an examination of turnover. People leave organizations when they are unhappy, offered a better position internally or externally, terminated, or retired. When turnover occurs, management must establish salesforce objectives, including whether or not to replace the individual. The next step in the planning process is a strategic position analysis, which consists of determining performance measures, identifying critical successes, determining performance dimensions, establishing performance standards, and designing assessment tools.

After conducting a strategic position analysis, management must determine the job's qualifications and write a job description. The goal of recruiting is to find and attract the best qualified applicants. Recruiting begins with identifying sources of candidates. Recruits can be found internally through lateral or upward moves, interns or co-ops, and employee referral programs. However, most new hires come from outside the organization, specifically from other industry institutions such as competitors, suppliers, and customers. Educational institutions are also common sources of recruits, as are advertising and employment agencies, walk-ins, and networking.

The selection process begins with the evaluation of recruited candidates, which can include multiple interviews, testing, a day in the field, and background investigation. The selection process attempts to find information about mental and physical conditions, past experiences, personalities, and the personal history of the applicants.

The interviewing process typically includes multiple rounds of interviews which may be structured, unstructured, or stress-oriented. Another common interview technique is the day in the field, in which the applicant spends a day with one of the hiring firm's salespeople. Testing is used by many organizations and is designed to determine intelligence, aptitude, personality, knowledge, and interests. After the physical and all other screening tools have been implemented, the organization selects the best candidate.

KEY TERMS

turnover	application blank
stockpiling	unstructured interview
strategic position analysis	structured interview
job qualifications	stress interview
job description	day in the field
recruiting	résumé inflation
intern	convergent thinking
co-op student	divergent thinking
employee referral program	

DISCUSSION QUESTIONS

1. Why are planning, recruiting, and selection so important to a sales organization?
2. What is meant by salesforce turnover, and what steps must a sales manager take to replace lost sales personnel?
3. What is the difference between job analysis (strategic position analysis), job qualifications, and job descriptions?
4. What is the difference between just-in-time hiring and stockpiling?
5. What are the primary sources of recruits?
6. What information does a hiring organization seek when evaluating recruit candidates?
7. What is the difference between convergent and divergent thinking?
8. What tools does a hiring organization have at its disposal when attempting to select a new salesperson?
9. What are some different forms of interviewing?
10. What types of information about a candidate does the hiring organization need to make its decision?

PROBLEMS

1. Carline Falcone has just been promoted to a sales manager position in a small office supply company. She decides that her first priority is to hire someone for a recently vacated territory. Carline has never hired anyone before and wonders where she should start. What steps should Carline take prior to actually recruiting for the new sales position?

2. John Ingram is a senior marketing major at the University of Missouri. He wants to work for a large medical supply company located in Kansas City. His father is a doctor in the Kansas City area and has volunteered to contact someone he knows in the company. Being very independent, John is reluctant to have his father's help. He wants to land a job on his own. What would you do if you were John and why?

3. Jennifer Llewellin is a recent graduate of Millsaps College. She has decided that she wants a sales job in the publishing industry. She knows that there will be considerable competition from people with much better experience.

She wonders how to approach the cover letter and résumé to differentiate herself. What suggestions would you give her?

4. Pat Irons is a senior at the University of California, Irvine, and is beginning to interview for sales jobs. He is in the second round at PepsiCo and is pleased at how the interview has progressed. His friend James comments, "Aren't you concerned that they will find out about your DWI and the checks you bounced?" Pat replies, "Nah, they'll never find out." What selection steps might a company such as Pepsico follow? Is Pat right about Pepsico not finding out about the DWI or bounced checks?

SHORT CASE
SELECTION AND RECRUITING

INTRODUCTION

In 1993, because of a dramatic slump in sales and other financial problems, Robicheaux Manufacturing of Montreal, Canada, maker of a variety of office products (furniture, accessories, and supplies), experienced a significant layoff of personnel throughout the company. Hiring was virtually frozen for 3 years. However, an economic upswing in the office product industry has produced a substantial increase in sales. As a result, management has lifted the hiring freeze. Skilled labor has been hired by advertising in the local paper. Now it is time to look for salespeople and other staffing positions.

SCENARIO

Prior to the hiring freeze, Robicheaux had a tendency to hire new salespeople from universities in the vacated territory. The sales manager of the district would set up on-campus interviews and narrow the list to three candidates and invite them to the headquarters for second and subsequent interview rounds. Unfortunately turnover was higher than the industry average. The president and CEO of Robicheaux, Bart Simone, has told Amie LaGuarde, vice-president of sales, to rethink the recruiting process and prepare a detailed report on recruiting and selection methods.

LaGuarde begins charting the previous steps in recruiting and creates the following chart.

1. On-campus recruiting
   a. Review résumés (look for experience, activities, and grade point)
   b. Talk with the placement director and faculty
   c. Set up one or two days of 30-minute interviews
2. Subsequent interview rounds
   a. Conduct second round at district office
   b. Invite three finalists to headquarters in Baton Rouge
   c. Have each candidate talk with eight people
   d. Spend a half day on testing
   e. Take candidates to dinner and informally interview them
3. Ride-withs
   a. Have finalist(s) spend a day in the field with a salesperson
   b. Get a detailed report from salesperson
4. Check references
   a. Check all listed references
   b. Perform credit, driving check
5. Make an offer
   a. Give physical (must pass)
   b. Bring final candidate back to headquarters to discuss offer

The average time spent recruiting an individual from steps 1 to 5 was 96 days. LaGuarde hated to even estimate the cost of the process. She knew that the previous method of recruiting was not going to work for what Robicheaux needed today.

PROBLEM

LaGuarde must decrease the recruiting time, cost, and administrative commitment to selecting a new salesperson. Simone has told LaGuarde to be creative in the new recruiting and selection process.

QUESTIONS

1. What steps should LaGuarde follow in creating a new recruiting and selection process?
2. What new issues should LaGuarde consider before devising the new process?
3. What should Robicheaux's recruiters look for on a résumé and in the interview?
4. What would you recommend for the new recruiting and selection process?

INTERVIEWING ROLE PLAY

CHARACTERS

Experienced Sales Manager: Veronica Hartline or Clarence Rountree
Inexperienced Sales Manager: Jay Studdard or Julie Tonga
Good Interviewee: Alex Minyard or Aimee Breaux
Bad Interviewee: Brian Allen Lazarko or Darlene Dauer
Retiring Salesperson (optional): Mu Chin
District Manager: Richard Landry or Annella Leopold

SCENARIO

Recently EDD has had an opening in a Midwest territory owing to the retirement of Mu Chin who was with EDD for 30 years. EDD has typically let the area sales manager do introductory interviews with soon-to-be-graduates from universities that are in or near the open territory.

Richard Landry has informed two of his managers to begin recruiting at the local universities. Veronica Hartline has been a manager for 7 years and has hired over 20 sales reps in that period. She is very polished and is completely at ease interviewing. Hartline has always had the interview policy that you need to learn as much as possible about the recruit without making him or her feel uncomfortable.

Jay Studdard has just recently been promoted to sales manager and is still a little overwhelmed with the new responsibilities. He has never interviewed anyone before and has not had a chance to attend the human resources seminar that EDD holds every year to teach managers how to conduct interviews. Studdard is 27 and impressed with himself. This arrogance comes across in the interview as does some ignorance as to what cannot be asked in an interview.

SCENE 1

The first scene features Hartline and Brian Allen Lazarko, an interviewee who is totally unprepared for the interview. Hartline must suffer through an absolutely horrible interview. The bad interviewee does the worst possible interview. This interview should be very entertaining and show the class what not to do in an interview.

SCENE 2

The second scene features Hartline with Aimee Breaux, a well-prepared interviewee. The interviewee has done her homework on EDD and seems to be very professional. Breaux should try to do as good an interview as possible. (*Note:* Do not worry about being perfect in the interview. Obviously mistakes occur in every interview. The class will discuss what Breaux did well and what she could have improved on.)

SCENE 3

The third scene features Studdard, who is not well prepared for the interview, and Breaux. Studdard asks illegal questions and questions that appear to be a bit off the wall. Breaux needs to maintain her composure and do the best she can in a bad interview.

SCENE 4

The fourth scene features Hartline and Studdard. They must decide which of the two interviewees, Breaux or Lazarko, to recommend for the second step of the hiring process (the management interview). Studdard walks into Hartline's office saying, "I just finished the interview with Lazarko. A little unorthodox, but lots of enthusiasm!" The rest of the scene should be a discussion between the two managers as to whether they should recommend Lazarko or Breaux (or both, or neither) for the second stage of the hiring process. The scene should conclude with a definite recommendation (pro or con) for Breaux and Lazarko.

CHARACTER DESCRIPTIONS

Name: Richard Landry
Gender: M
Age: 54
Marital status: Married
Education: B.A., Tulane University; M.B.A., Harvard University
Title: District Manager, Eastern Region
Office location: Chicago
Reports to: V-P Sales
Employment history: Sales with competitor for 3 years; sales manager for 2 years; quit to get M.B.A.; Pharmiceaux sales manager for 5 years; district manager for 10 years
Personality: Cooperative; persevering; poised; good sense of humor; energetic
Notes: Two children, both in college; had open-heart surgery 2 years ago
Grapevine: Told to cut back stress

Name: Annella Leopold
Gender: F
Age: 41
Marital status: Married
Education: B.S., Jackson State; M.B.A., Georgetown University
Title: District Manager

Office location: Chicago
Reports to: V-P Sales
Employment history: Taught elementary school for 6 years; sales with competitor for 3 years; quit to get M.B.A.; EDD sales for 3 years; sales manager for 5 years; district manager for 2 years
Personality: Great sense of humor; down to earth; driven; well liked
Notes: Said to have photographic memory; three children, oldest at the University of California, Irvine
Grapevine: May leave for state politics.

Name: Clarence Roundtree
Gender: M
Age: 48
Martial status: Married
Education: B.S., Auburn University
Title: Sales Manager
Office location: Richmond, VA
Reports to: District Manager, New York
Employment history: A manager for 17 years; came to Pharmiceaux from a competitor
Personality: Very sensitive to the needs of his people; good sense of humor; likeable
Notes: One of the best recruiters in the country; likes recruiting college students; coaches Little League
Grapevine: May take a staff position in human resources

Name: Veronica Hartline
Gender: F
Age: 32
Marital status: Single
Education: B.A., University of Mississippi
Title: Sales Manager
Office location: Richmond, VA
Reports to: District Manager, New York
Employment history: Hired straight out of school; a manager for 5 years
Personality: Easy-going but hard working; detail oriented
Notes: Wants to mentor young females in the company; spends long hours at the office; likes movies.
Grapevine: Wants to relocate back to the deep South

Name: Julie Tonga
Gender: F
Age: 26
Marital status: Married
Education: B.B.A., State Tech
Title: Sales Manager
Office location: Columbus, OH
Reports to: District Manager, New York

Employment history: With the company for 6 years; hired originally as an intern
Personality: Intelligent; driven; little sense of humor
Notes: Career oriented; wants to be in upper management soon; not well liked by some of her peers
Grapevine: Needs some maturity

Name: Jay Studdard
Gender: M
Age: 27
Marital status: Single
Education: B.B.A., Northwest State
Title: Sales Manager
Office location: Columbus, OH
Reports to: District Manager, New York
Employment history: With the company 5 years, a manager for 6 months
Personality: Big ego; impressed with his own abilities; intelligent
Notes: Wants to be a CEO and to get there as soon as possible; loyal to himself first
Grapevine: Needs some seasoning; not sure of his managerial abilities

Name: Alex Minyard
Gender: M
Age: 22
Marital status: Single
Education: B.S. in Marketing, Stanford
Title: Student
Office location:
Employment history: Student body president; interned with a *Fortune* 500 company
Personality: Aggressive and confident; organized; high energy; good sense of humor
Notes: Highly sought after by several companies; Pharmiceaux is very interested in him
Grapevine: Potential fast-track candidate

Name: Aimee Breaux (pronounced "Bro")
Gender: F
Age: 21
Marital status: Single, engaged
Education: B.S. in Marketing, L.S.U.
Title: Recruit
Office location:
Employment history: Part-time sales experience; graduates in one month; studied in Europe one summer
Personality: Vivacious, intelligent, class leader
Notes: Daughter of a doctor; her professors ranked her as the best marketing student of the year
Grapevine: Potential fast-track candidate

Name: Darlene Dauer
Gender: F
Age: 21
Marital status: Single

Education: University of North State
Title: Student
Office location:
Employment history: No full-time work experience
Personality: Disorganized; very immature
Notes: No serious goals or plans; poor student
Grapevine: Is searching for a job to satisfy her parents

Name: Brian Allen Lazarko
Gender: M
Age: 23
Marital status: Single
Education: Cityview College
Title: Student
Office location:
Employment history: Ran a backyard lemonade stand
Personality: Disorganized; no goals; is unrealistic
Notes: Low grades; class clown; doesn't know what he wants, except high pay.
Grapevine: Probably can't pass the drug test

Name: Mu Chin
Gender: F
Age: 65
Marital status: Married
Education: B.A., National University of Singapore
Title: Senior Sales Rep
Office location: Richmond, VA
Reports to: Sales Manager, Richmond
Employment history: With Pharmiceaux since the company's beginning; is now retiring
Personality: Well-respected, "Grandfather" for the organization; hard worker
Notes: Retiring; will have honorary title
Grapevine: May be used as a part-time trainer/consultant

QUESTIONS

1. What are the characteristics of a good interviewer?
2. What are several actions the interviewer and interviewee can take to get the interview started in a positive direction?
3. How should an interviewee handle inappropriate interview questions?
4. How well did the interviewer do in learning important facts about the candidates?
5. What process did the interviewers go through in selecting a candidate for the open position?
6. What should Aimee Breaux do to ensure a high quality, positive interview?

NOTES

1. Robert J. Kelly, "Tomorrow's Labor Force," *Sales and Marketing Management* (March 1994): 34. See also James W. Loose,"New Attitudes About Minority Hiring," *Human Resources Professional,* 7(3) (May–June): 28–32.
2. Robert J. Kelly, "Toward a More Diverse Sales Force," *Sales and Marketing Management* (March 1994), 33–34.
3. Rene Y. Darmon, "Where Do the Best Sales Force Profit Producers Come From?" *Journal of Personal Selling and Sales Management,* 13(3) (Summer 1993): 17–29.
4. Jeffrey K. Sager, "How to Retain Salespeople," *Industrial Marketing Management,* 19 (1990): 155–166.
5. Edward F. Fern, Ramon A. Avila, and Dhruv Grewal, "Salesforce Turnover: Those Who Left and Those Who Stayed," *Industrial Marketing Management,* 18 (1989): 1–9.
6. William Keenan, Jr., "Time Is Everything," *Sales and Marketing Management* (August 1993): 60–63.
7. Mark W. Johnston and Charles M. Futrell, "Functional Salesforce Turnover: An Empirical Investigation Into the Positive Effects of Turnover," *Journal of Business Research* (March 1989): 141–157. See also George H. Lucas, Jr., A. Parasuraman, Robert A. Davis, and Ben M. Enis, "An Empirical Study of Salesforce Turnover," *Journal of Marketing* (July 1987): 34–59; William C. Moncrief III, Ronald Hoverstad, and George Lucas, "Survival Analysis: A New Approach to Analyzing Sales Force Retention," *Journal of Personal Selling and Sales Management* (Summer 1989): 19–30; Charles M. Futrell and A. Parasuraman, "The Relationship of Satisfaction and Performance to Salesforce Turnover," *Journal of Marketing* (Fall 1984): 33–40; and Kate Bertrand, "Is Sales Turnover Inevitable?" *Business Marketing* (November 1989): 26.
8. Lisa I. Fried, "Stop Telemarketing Turnover," *Sales and Marketing Management* (April 1994): 35.
9. Andrew Harris, "Break the Glass Ceiling for Senior Executives," *HR Focus,* 71(3) (March 1994): 1.
10. Mark S. Van Clieaf, "In Search of Competence: Structured Behavior Interviews," *Business Horizons* (March/April 1991): 51–55.
11. Thomas R. Wotruba and Stephen B. Castleberry, "Job Analysis and Hiring Practices for National Account Marketing Positions," *Journal of Personal Selling and Sales Management,* 13(3) (Summer 1993): 49-65.
12. Bristol Voss, "Six Steps to Better Hires," *Sales and Marketing Management,* (June 1993): 44–47.
13. Jack Falvey, "The Absolute Basics of Sales Force Management," *Sales and Marketing Management* (August 1990): 8–10.
14. Michael Selz, "Small Firms Say It's Tough to Fill Some Job Openings," *The Wall Street Journal* (December 19, 1993): B1.
15. Shankar Ganesan, Barton A. Weitz, and George John, "Hiring and Promotion Policies in Sales Force Management: Some Antecedents and Consequences," *Journal of Personal Selling and Sales Management,* 13(2) (Spring 1993): 15–27.
16. Thomas R. Wotruba and Stephen B. Castleberry (1993), op. cit.
17. Ginger Trumfio, "Picking the Cream of the Crop," *Sales and Marketing Management* (March 1994): 34.
18. Martin Everett, "A Higher Calling," *Sales and Marketing Management* (January 1993): 30–31.
19. Bill Kelley, "The Great Talent Search," *Sales and Marketing Management* (November 1993): 108–111. See also Dan C. Weilbaker and Nancy J. Merritt, "Attracting

Graduates to Sales Positions: The Role of Recruiter Knowledge," *Journal of Personal Selling and Sales Management,* 12(4), (Fall 1992): 49–58, and Dan C. Weilbaker and Nancy J. Merritt, (1992), op. cit.

20. Jon M. Hawes, "How to Improve Your College Recruiting Program," *Journal of Personal Selling and Sales Management,* 9 (Summer 1989): 47–52.
21. Finding Top Reps on Campus," *Sales and Marketing Management* (March 1995): 38.
22. Joann S. Lublin, "Memo Reveals Dual Allegiances of Outplacement Firm," *The Wall Street Journal* (January 27, 1995): B1.
23. Lee Smith, "Landing That First Real Job," *Fortune* (May 1994): 58–60.
24. Myron Gable, Charles Hollon, and Frank Dangello, "Increasing the Utility of the Application Blank: Relationship Between Job Application Information and Subsequent Performance and Turnover of Salespeople," *Journal of Personal Selling and Sales Management,* 12(3) (Summer 1992): 39–55.
25. John Hunter and Ronda Hunter, "Validity and Utility of Alternative Predictors of Job Performance," *Psychological Bulletin,* 96 (July 1984): 73–96.
26. "Screen Applicants by Phone," *Sales and Marketing Management* (June 1994): 41.
27. William Keenan, Jr., "Who Has the Right Stuff?" *Sales and Marketing Management* (August 1993): 28–29.
28. *Ibid.*
29. Richard Nelson, "Maybe It's Time to Take Another Look at Tests as a Selection Tool?" *Journal of Personal Selling and Sales Management,* 7 (August 1987): 33–38.
30. Robert W. Woods, "Make Hiring More of a Science, Less of an Art," *Sales and Marketing Management* (September 1991): 159–160.
31. George B. Glisson and Jon M. Hawes, "Selecting Creative People for Sales Positions," *Industrial Marketing Management,* 19 (1990): 331–337.
32. W. E. Patton, III, and Ronald H. King, "The Use of Human Judgement Models in Sales Force Selection Decisions," *Journal of Personal Selling and Sales Management,* 12(2) (Spring 1992): 1–14.

11

TRAINING THE SALESFORCE

At NCR our salespeople never stop learning.

JOHN H. PATTERSON, FOUNDER OF THE NATIONAL CASH REGISTER COMPANY

We are forced to rely on people, which is why we put so much emphasis on training.

HENRY BLOCK, CEO, H&R BLOCK

LEARNING OBJECTIVES

After reading this chapter, you should be able to answer the following questions:

- What is the need for training?
- What are typical objectives of a training program?
- What are the different types of training programs?
- What topics should be covered in a training program?
- How should an organization implement training?
- What are the differences between formal and on-the-job training (OJT)? When should an organization consider using one versus the other?

Pacific Gas and Electric (PG&E) has taken training to a new level. Its objective is to train 27,000 employees in diversity awareness in order to improve the organization's competitive advantage in productivity, customer service, employee recruitment, and employee retention. This is a task unto itself, but the biggest challenge is that PG&E is letting rank and file employees become the trainers. Employees who have indicated that they value diversity and who possess good communication skills become candidates for the diversity training certification. The certification has four phases. Phase 1 is a preliminary six-day train-the-trainer workshop in which existing skills and attitudes are determined. Phase 2 is an extensive and grueling six-day, 60-hour workshop in which the trainees become knowledgeable in diversity issues. In phase 3 the trainees become the trainers for their region and facilitate an eight-hour session. In phase 4 qualified trainees are awarded a certification as diversity awareness trainers. PG&E has made a long-term commitment to diversity training not only because it is the right thing to do, but also because it makes good business sense.[1]

This chapter will examine salesforce training; it concentrates on many new sales training issues such as diversity training, training issues in small business, and use of emerging technologies. **Sales training** can be described as the systematic attempt to identify, understand, and transfer "good selling practices" to sales personnel. Training augments the skills already possessed by sales personnel. In many cases training can also be designed to create or sharpen new skills. Regardless of its purpose, training must provide salespeople with the ability to reach acceptable effectiveness levels in less time than learning through on-the-job experiences. It is hoped that formal training will eliminate many costly errors.[2]

One national research study found five factors that positively affect salesforce performance: teamwork, training, supplier relations, hiring practices, and personality characteristics. Notice that training was the *second* most important factor.[3] Interestingly, in the same study organizational performances were ranked into five categories from lowest to highest. The study then examined the amount of money spent in each of the categories on training. The study found that there were no significant differences in organizational performance based on money spent on training! These results indicate that organizational performance is not so much a function of the *amount* of money spent on training but, rather, *how* the money is spent.

Training can be one of the most expensive processes in sales management, or it can be virtually nonexistent. Training may mean months in a classroom setting or immediate on-the-job learning. In general, students who have just graduated from college seem to prefer more formalized classroom training. Learning by performing on the job can be a very unnerving process.

EXHIBIT 11.1
SALES TRAINING PROCESS

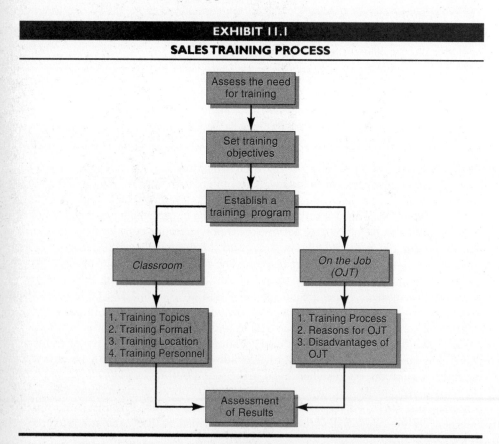

As illustrated in Exhibit 11.1, the sales training process discussed in this chapter follows a prescribed set of steps. The chapter begins by assessing the need for training. Why is so much money, time, and discussion spent on training? No two companies have the same philosophy about training, nor will they have the same needs for training. Each company must examine its own resources and determine the qualities and types of training needed for effective sales coverage.

Once a firm decides to implement a training program, it must determine and prioritize training objectives. All sales employees will not necessarily need the same levels of training. Management must determine the topics and format to be covered. In addition, management must decide upon training locations and personnel. If the company decides to forego a formal program and institute an on-the-job format, management must ensure that employees are learning appropriately. Last, every organization should make periodic assessment of the value of its training programs.

Remember, training programs are diverse, have multiple purposes, are run from different philosophical viewpoints, and will be implemented with a variety of differing methods, people, and locations.

ASSESSING THE NEEDS FOR TRAINING

Many programs fail to properly assess an individual organization's training needs. Instead, a typical scenario is for a sales executive to tell the training department, "We need some better training for our salesforce," and that becomes the charge for the training staff. In reality, however, the *needs* of the organization and the customer base should be the foundation of the training program.[4] One golden rule of assessment is that what other organizations are doing should not be the basis for what you as a company do. Organizations spend millions of dollars in copy-cat training. These programs are reactionary and not based on need. Positive results may occur, but they are probably for the short term only.[5] A good needs assessment begins with a training audit that incorporates input from numerous sources from within the organization as well as from the customer base. The audit helps the organization determine what training needs to take place.

Training Audit

A **training audit** is an analysis of the organization's resources, abilities, needs, and current directions. The audit is the critical step in determining if the organization is capable of sustaining a training program and, if so, what type. A training audit should focus on three dimensions: (1) the organization, (2) the tasks, and (3) the personnel.[6]

The **organizational assessment** is a detailed analysis of organizational structure, resources, philosophy, and leadership. The assessment concentrates on evaluating training needs and ensures that these needs are met within the existing support system and cultural environment. Management may be excited about conducting a formal training program only to find in the organizational assessment that the firm is unable to provide the resources to support the program.

The **task assessment** examines the overall sales job, as well as the individual activities performed on the job. As mentioned in Chapter 1, sales jobs differ by company and industry. The daily activities needed to perform the job may be radically different from one organization to the next. Therefore, each organization must identify its own priorities among job activities and subject areas. After identification, management must determine if these activities need to be featured in the training sessions.

The last dimension, **personnel assessment,** is an analysis of the strengths and weaknesses of the current organizational personnel. The personnel assessment is designed to determine the levels and amounts of training needed by each sales individual.

Obtaining Input

Information from several sources must be incorporated into the needs assessment, including observation, information from the salesforce, and information from the customer and supplier base. Personal selling is a complex process, and the range of important inputs to the process can be numerous and diverse. Unfortunately these inputs change over time in the dynamic and ever-evolving sales environment. Assessments conducted 5 years ago may not be accurate for the organizational salesforce today. Therefore, the information input process can be arduous and time consuming. James Hewitt, director of Lawyer's Title Insurance's training program, concurs with the need to gather data. He says, "We surveyed one hundred customers, sales managers, and sales reps to find out what everyone wanted to accomplish with the program before designing it."[7]

It is very common for organizations to routinely survey their salesforce to obtain attitudes toward the job and their ability to compete successfully with their competitors. For example, American Airlines frequently surveys its salesforce about 6 months after the completion of a new training program to determine which training topics were the most helpful and what topics they would like to have covered in the next training update. A lot of the information gathered from surveys will come by reading between the lines. In other words, the salesperson may not always directly state what problems or strengths may exist, but by "listening" closely an organization can obtain valuable information.

Types of Training and Development Programs

One aspect of the needs assessment is determining at what level the training needs to occur. Typically, when people think of training they perceive the training of new personnel, but training is a continuous process that can occur at multiple levels. It is common for salespeople and sales managers to routinely return for advanced or refresher training.

Some training is developmental in nature and differs somewhat from the more traditional forms. For the most part, training has been considered a short-term activity to help employees perform their jobs more efficiently. **Development programs,** on the other hand, give employees strengths and skills that they can capitalize on in their daily jobs. Whereas training is considered short term, development programs should serve the long-term interests of the salesperson and the organization. They build strategies for the future by broadening people and preparing them for new and higher-level opportunities within the organization, such as in upper management or product development.[8]

There are four types of training and development programs that management must consider when developing a needs assessment. They are: (1) indoctrination training, (2) refresher training, (3) salesperson development programs, and (4) executive development programs.

Indoctrination Training. **Indoctrination training** is defined as the training of new personnel in "the way" to do the job. The organization teaches the new hires the products, the organizational way to sell the products, the company history and philosophy, and teamwork. This form of training can be lengthy because a variety of topics are covered. Indoctrination training is common for *Fortune 500* companies and is the type of training that most recent college graduates perceive to be ideal. The training is thorough and intense. Organizations that are good in indoctrination training invariably see many of their best people hired away by competitors and other industries because of the thoroughness of their training on multiple levels. For example, Xerox- and IBM-trained employees are in high demand because of the rigor of each company's training program. Even the Xerox or IBM organizational-specific philosophy can be important to other companies because of the level of professionalism built into those philosophies.

Refresher Training. As the sales environment continues to evolve, salespeople must be able to adapt to the changes. This adaptation may consist of periodic **refresher training**. Most managers believe that even the most experienced reps need refresher training to keep current on new trends and changes in the product or industry, as well as to revitalize the individual. For example, in the early 1990s laptop computers became prevalent and software became more company-specific. As a result of the increasing technology, sales organizations began providing on-going refresher training to increase their representatives' job proficiency.[9]

Many companies require additional training on an annual basis, whereas others conduct refresher training only on a perceived need basis. Some refresher training is individual specific, and other training is designed for the organization's entire salesforce. One reason for refresher training is that information not repeated and reinforced continually can be forgotten.[10] There are also some organizations that use refresher training as a reward and include it as part of an annual convention in which only a few can qualify.

Exhibit 11.2 shows that organizations average 30.2 hours of refresher training a year. The training is about evenly divided between product training and selling training, and the average cost of the refresher training is $2,991 per individual per year.

Salesperson Development Programs. The purpose of salesperson development programs is to help the entire business grow and prosper. Specifically, **salesperson development programs** develop added skills, professionalism, goals, and habits for the salesperson beyond those needed for the present job. Organizations are more and more conscious about developing future managerial and staff talent from within the organization. Much of that potential talent can be found in the salesforce. In addition, because of the deletion of many mid-management roles, salespeople are being given more non-management responsibilities and support. Many salespeople who might have been promoted to sales management positions a decade ago might not be today.

EXHIBIT 11.2
TRAINING EXPERIENCED REPS

	Hours per Year of Ongoing Training	Type of Training		
		Selling Skills (%)	Product (%)	Cost
Company size				
under $5 Million	28.4	45.2%	50.9%	$2,395
$5MM–$25MM	36.5	44.9	49.4	3,919
$25MM–$100MM	28.3	42.1	51.8	2,895
$100MM–$250MM	19.0	64.0	30.0	1,525
over $250MM	31.5	36.2	51.8	3,977
Product or service				
Consumer products	30.5	44.7	51.4	2,806
Consumer services	30.8	50.1	45.6	3,039
Industrial products	30.2	39.3	52.9	3,262
Industrial services	32.0	48.7	47.0	2,966
Office products	30.0	41.3	50.5	1,962
Office services	34.6	49.5	45.0	2,733
Type of buyer				
Consumers	30.6	44.7	51.0	2,607
Distributors	29.3	45.8	45.1	3,443
Industry	29.5	46.6	49.7	3,078
Retailers	29.0	48.3	45.0	1,767
Industry				
Business services	33.1	52.4	40.6	2,529
Chemicals	18.3	56.8	44.6	4,500
Communications	45.0	50.6	45.0	4,700
Educational services	41.7	57.5	30.0	1,125
Electronics	34.4	29.4	66.0	5,483
Fabricated Metals	37.5	37.9	47.1	2,900
Health services	41.0	22.5	56.2	2,000
Hotels and other lodging places	25.3	63.8	20.0	1,400
Instruments	60.0	29.0	45.0	11,875
Insurance	31.4	46.8	42.1	4,750
Machinery	26.4	23.9	65.0	2,257
Manufacturing	18.4	43.1	61.7	1,917
Office equipment	27.5	40.0	60.0	2,000
Paper and allied products	34.5	45.0	48.3	2,300
Printing and publishing	15.7	33.3	56.1	1,510
Retail	38.8	26.4	71.4	1,220
Trucking and warehousing	0.0	100.0	0.0	2,000
Wholesale (consumer goods)	49.8	62.2	42.0	1,067
Wholesale (industrial goods)	45.3	40.0	63.1	2,494
Overall	30.2	44.7%	49.8%	$2,991

SOURCE: Dartnell Corporation, 1992.

The lack of mid-management positions means that salespeople need opportunities for further development, particularly when upward mobility is not likely. Development programs can provide salespeople with new challenges and provide the organization with creative new directions. For example, Sales Consultancy, a training consultancy company, teaches organizational salespeople how to develop a business plan for customer partners. Hewlett Packard, a Sales Consultancy client, has become a strong believer in this training designed to bring about new skills for the HP salesperson.[11]

Executive Development Programs.   Sales executives also need additional training, known as **executive development programs,** to help them expand their skills and continue an upward path. A large portion of executive development training is conducted by university business schools that offer executive M.B.A programs.[12] There are also a number of specialized managerial programs that provide executives with specific skills.

It is easier for many companies to have universities provide a higher level of training for their managers than to attempt to train in-house. For example, Tandy Corporation sends its middle managers to a two-week university training program. The training has multiple purposes. One goal of the program is to indicate to the manager that upper management views him or her as valuable enough to provide further development. Second, the training provides current information or new management methods to help the manager in daily managerial activities.

SETTING TRAINING OBJECTIVES

Once the need for training has been assessed, the next step is to determine what the objectives of the training will be. There are a number of variables that can determine what type of training an organization will choose to implement.[13] Two similar companies in the same industry may have radically different training programs because the management of each company wants to emphasize different aspects or philosophies of the job. For example, company A tends to hire salespeople straight from college, so its training tends to be heavy in indoctrination; it wants all its salespeople to be trained the same way. Company B, which sells the same product as company A, would rather hire experienced salespeople, provide them with less training, and send them out to do what has already made them successful.

Because of greater competition and higher levels of needed professionalism, small companies are increasingly establishing objectives to improve the level of training of their salesforce. They are spending more on training than in previous years. In 1992 small companies with under $5 million in sales spent $5,530 per person in training, whereas in 1990 small companies spent only $3,975 per person.[14]

Exhibit 11.3 provides information on the total cost and length of training for new hires. The average length of a training program is 3.9 months with a number of industries averaging five months or longer. Typically, the more technical the industry or product, the longer the training. One study indicated that top-performing organizations provide their salesforce with 3 to 9 months of training whereas lower-performing organizations provide less than 3 months.[15]

EXHIBIT 11.3		
TRAINING NEW HIRES (AVERAGE OF MEDIAN RANGE)		
	Training Period for New Hires (Months)	Cost
Company size		
under $5 Million	3.9	$5,530.00
$5MM–$25 MM	3.7	6,227.30
$25MM–$100MM	3.9	8,083.30
$100MM–$250MM	3.0	3,750.00
over $250MM	4.7	6,587.50
Product or service		
Consumer products	3.3	4,995.00
Consumer services	3.6	4,130.00
Industrial products	4.2	9,763.20
Industrial services	3.8	6,610.70
Office products	3.1	3,408.30
Office services	3.2	4,005.00
Type of buyer		
Consumers	3.5	4,253.60
Distributors	3.5	7,334.30
Industry	3.9	6,570.70
Retailers	3.4	4,546.20
Industry		
Business services	3.0	5,478.60
Chemicals	4.5	15,000.00
Communications	5.2	3,125.00
Educational services	3.0	3,500.00
Electronics	5.0	11,500.00
Fabricated metals	5.0	10,625.00
Health services	2.0	3,250.00
Hotels and other lodging places	3.0	5,000.00
Instruments	5.0	22,500.00
Insurance	5.6	7,083.30
Machinery	4.2	6,125.00
Manufacturing	3.3	6,125.00
Paper and allied products	2.2	6,500.00
Printing and publishing	2.7	5,566.70
Retail	4.8	2,875.00
Wholesale (consumer goods)	5.0	9,166.70
Wholesale (industrial goods)	5.9	9,333.30
Overall	**3.9**	**$6,225.60**

SOURCE: Dartnell Corporation, 1992.

ESTABLISHING A FORMALIZED TRAINING PROGRAM

Classroom training provides a sense of uniformity and consistency among the sales-force. Management knows that the salesforce will be familiar with the company philosophy, the products, the company selling approach, and whatever other factors are being emphasized during training. A formalized training program also gives

EXHIBIT 11.4

TIME OUT OF FIELD: PERCENT OF COMPANIES PROVIDING TWO OR MORE WEEKS OF TRAINING

Time Out of Field

SOURCE: "Are You Overspending on Training?" *Sales and Marketing Management* (January 1990): 59.

management some control over how it wants the job to be performed on a daily basis. Training is expensive and therefore considered an investment for increased sales and a higher level of productivity.

As can be seen in Exhibit 11.4, while classroom training plays an important role in many training programs, most firms do 2 weeks of training or less. The primary reasons against classroom training center on the cost and the use of resources (personnel).

The next few sections of this chapter examine issues associated with formalized training programs. We begin with a discussion of training topics, followed by an examination of training methods. The remaining two sections explore options on training location and discuss who should conduct the training.

TRAINING TOPICS

Every organization differs in what it highlights in its training programs. The possibilities are endless depending on resources and imagination. For ease of discussion, we divide training topics into four categories: (1) socialization, (2) selling techniques, (3) knowledge, and (4) proficiencies.

Socialization

One of the primary functions of any training program is to assimilate the new person into the sales culture of the organization. **Socialization** is defined as the process by which an individual comes to appreciate the values, abilities, expected behaviors, and social knowledge essential for assuming an organizational role, and for participating as an organizational member.[16] The goals of orientation and socialization are to make the new hire comfortable in the new environment, to provide important information about the day-to-day operations (i.e., how your paycheck is delivered), and to meet personnel.

Invariably, the socialization process includes observations and perhaps even advice about office politics. According to Dale Carnegie, **office politics** can be defined as the skill in human engineering.[17] To most people office politics is a negative concept that is summarized with words such as *manipulation, ambition, harassment, unethical,* and *brownnosing.* In reality all of these terms can be accurate, but office politics is a way of life in any organization. Most managers would agree that grasp of political savvy is a necessity for managerial success. Competence alone is no guarantee for success. A good salesperson must also be able to sell his or her ideas both publicly and behind the scenes. An understanding of the political dynamics of any organization is a necessity even if you refuse to "play the game." Box 11.1 provides some pointers for dealing with office politics.

Another form of socialization that begins in a training program and will continue throughout the individual's life with an organization is the dissemination and acquisition of information through the grapevine. The **grapevine** is any organization's informal channels of communication. The grapevine often contains rumors and gossip, but it can also be extremely accurate.

Socialization has a number of important components that can directly affect the performance of individuals. Some of these components are preconceived and others occur after arriving at the new organization. Exhibit 11.5 depicts the Feldman Organizational Socialization Model.[18] The model has three stages: anticipatory socialization, accommodation, and outcomes.

Anticipatory Socialization.   The first stage of the Feldman model, **anticipatory socialization,** is concerned with the salesperson's preconceived notions about life in the new organization. Two terms describe this perception. **Realism** reflects the degree to which the new hire has an accurate reflection of what life at the organization is like. **Congruence** is the degree to which an organization's resources and demands and that of the sales recruit are compatible. An organization will not change to meet the ideals of a new hire. Therefore, the closer to reality the new hire's concept of realism and the higher the level of congruence, the easier for the new hire to be socialized. Firms should take special care to provide new recruits with an accurate picture of the job beginning in the recruiting and selection process. Recall from Chapter 10 that Marion Merrell Dow has new recruits spend a day in the field with a salesperson to ensure that realism and congruence are more likely to be positive.

Accommodation.   The second stage of the Feldman model is **accommodation,** which is the process new hires go through as they seek to discover what the organization is really like and attempt to become a part of it. The accommodation stage has four processes that center on what happens to trainees after joining the organization.

- **Initiation to the task.** The degree to which trainees feels competent and accepted as a working partner.

BOX 11.1
OFFICE POLITICS: HOW TO PLAY THE GAME

For those times when you don't have a choice—or you're actively looking to change a political situation—

- **Focus on your job.** Work hard, demonstrate your trustworthiness, accept unpleasant tasks, assist others, and work extra hours so that you build a reserve of credit for advancing yourself and your goals later on.
- **Listen and observe.** Because the political atmosphere is subtle in most organizations, developing listening and observational skills is important. Notice who advances what ideas, who supports whom, what suggestions are made, what topics are awkward, what projects receive high priority, where informal lines of communication occur, alternate meanings to statements, seating arrangements in meetings, the pattern of workplace friendships, and the nature of alliances and animosities. Remember: The real power in organizations doesn't always reside with the visible power holders.
- **Understand the people in your organization.** In order to get along with and influence others, you must pay attention to the personality traits and organizational interests of the political players. Being a good judge of character is an ingredient of political savvy that helps you determine allies and methods of influence. For example: Who are the fence sitters? Who are the opinion leaders? Which colleagues make decisions based on tradition, evidence, cost-effectiveness, or majority sentiment? Some people are risk takers, others are cautious, others block every attempt to change.
- **Build partnerships.** Most people operate according to the principle of reciprocal favors. If someone helps, supports, or acts kindly toward you, you're likely to feel obligated to return the favor. It's rarely necessary to remind people that they owe you a favor. To make such an explicit statement is to bring the political process to an awkwardly obvious level. Also, don't overuse predictable alliances. If the work group realizes that two people always side with each other regardless of the issue, the group will discount the partnership.
- **Never overuse power.** Being blatant with power is a sure way to lose it.
- **Learn to negotiate.** Know when to make concessions and when to hold out with supervisors, subordinates, colleagues, customers, and vendors. Negotiation itself is inherently a political process, since it involves subtle attempts to influence others to gain power or achieve a goal.
- **Never alienate supervisors.** You can disagree, but not publicly. Always follow the chain of command. Find ways to make the boss look good. Say yes to most requests the boss makes of you.
- **Develop loyal and competent subordinates.** Competent subordinates make you look good. Also, you can receive essential information and perceptions from them.
- **Be patient.** Developing political awareness takes time. Build a reputation gradually, influence slowly and subtly, and acquire power incrementally. Being patient, though, doesn't mean waiting idly for things to happen. Listen quietly, observe, and unobtrusively build good relationships and alliances while cultivating competence, trust, and power.

SOURCE: Bristol Voss, "Office Politics: A Player's Guide," *Sales and Marketing Management* (October 1992): 51.

- **Initiation to the group.** The degree to which trainees feel accepted by coworkers.
- **Role definition.** Agreements that articulate the tasks that trainees are to perform.
- **Congruence of evaluation.** The similarity of evaluation between sales managers and trainees.

EXHIBIT 11.5

THE FELDMAN MODEL OF SOCIALIZATION

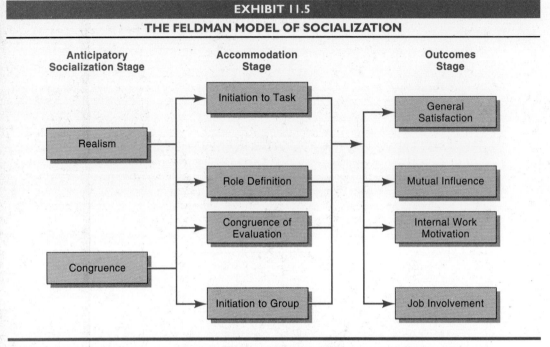

SOURCE: Alan J. Dubinsky, Roy D. Howell, Thomas N. Ingram, and Danny N. Bellenger, "Sale-force Socialization," *Journal of Marketing*, 50 (October 1986): 192–207.

The higher the trainee's levels of initiation to task, initiation to group, role definition, and congruence of evaluation, the more likely the individual will be socialized into the organization. A positive response in the accommodation stage will increase the likelihood that the trainee/new hire will assimilate rapidly into the organization.

Outcomes.   The third stage of Feldman's model focuses on outcomes of the socialization process that can further facilitate learning, participation, and performance. Based on the socialization process, new hires may feel a general satisfaction or dissatisfaction with the job, and may or may not feel that they can influence the results of doing the job. The outcome of the entire socialization process may determine the levels of motivation and commitment to the job and, ultimately, the probability of success in the job.

Sales Techniques

A second purpose of most formal training programs is to provide or enhance basic selling skills. Even if trainees have had some previous sales experience, they will typically be required to learn the hiring organization's selling philosophy. Training on sales techniques can cover a variety of subjects, with the level of emphasis depending on the organizational objectives. Most sales techniques training programs, however, cover prospecting, account management, professionalism, presentation skills, and ethics.

Prospecting.   For many salespeople, prospecting—the search for potential new customers—is the most difficult part of the selling process. Prospecting can be particularly difficult for new hires straight out of college. Training can teach new hires methods of prospecting and tips on how to reach prospects. In addition, trainees can be taught how to qualify prospects.

Account Management.   A strong trend in the 1990s has been to train salespeople on how to manage existing accounts. With the concept of relationship selling so predominant in industry, new hires need to understand how to sell to existing accounts and provide quality service as well as maintain long-term business. Every customer interaction should be considered an opportunity for understanding customer needs and providing service. For example, Bill Storer of Golf Event Management, Inc., says, "A round of golf with a customer should be looked upon as a six-hour sales call." Even if salespeople are not openly selling, they should be learning about their account's needs and building trust with the account.[19]

Professionalism.   Industry wants a high-quality professional on the sales team. Thus time emphasizing "professionalism" is spent in many training programs. As mentioned in Chapter 2, the dirty-joke-telling, back-slapping, good ol' boy system of selling is dying. Organizations want well-educated, ethical individuals who are poised and who can keep the sales call on a highly professional business level. Salespeople must become more professional in the sales and service arena.

Presentation Skills.   For over two decades industry has challenged business schools to produce students who have strong presentation skills. Many business schools are now doing just that; they are producing students who are much more comfortable making presentations. Presentation skills are an important part of training, and any training program that is emphasizing selling skills spends considerable time focused on trainee presentations. One method of developing presentation skills is through the use of cognitive scripts. A **cognitive script** is a learned mental representation describing a series of activities or events to fit a particular scenario. Scripts contain both activity content and sequence expectations. By learning cognitive scripts, new salespeople have practical experience that may influence future sales effectiveness. Certainly each sales encounter is unique, and as new salesperson gain experience, the cognitive scripts will reflect the perceptions, interpretations, and behaviors of the individual salesperson.[20] An example of a cognitive script appears in Exhibit 11.6.

Ethics.   Organizations are also demanding salespeople with high moral character and a strong sense of ethics. It seems that we are continually bombarded with news about organizations or individuals who have taken an unethical (or illegal) business approach. The results have been that organizations are incorporating ethics into their training programs, particularly through the use of role plays.

Knowledge

Training that emphasizes selling skills or disseminating knowledge tends to comprise the bulk of most training programs. The dissemination of knowledge includes infor-

EXHIBIT 11.6

INITIAL INDUSTRIAL SALES CALL SCRIPT

Actions or Behaviors

PA	Looks up and notices you
SP	Smile
	Extend greeting
	Extend handshake
	Introduce myself
	Offer business card
PA	Extends invitation to sit
SP	Sit
	State my understanding of purpose of meeting
	Ask buyer if my understanding is correct
PA	Expands purpose
SP	Ask what brought about need
PA	States cost, bid, quantity
SP	Ask how long the situation has existed
PA	Offers time frame
SP	Ask what departments are involved
PA	States departments
SP	Ask what impact has been between situations and people
PA	Is evasive
SP	Ask what prior situation was
PA	Offers history
SP	Determine problems
	Formulate action
	Restate situation
	Ask buyer what he (or she) perceives as best mode of action
PA	States his plan
SP	Agree with him
	Stress his plan as positive
	Offer him additional actions
	Suggest he contact persons involved
PA	He contacts department heads
	He arranges for two immediate meetings with them
	He notifies one person that I will contact
SP	Ask for names, titles, and telephone extensions of these people to set up meeting
	Copy down exact information
	Restate my actions with time frame
	Ask if I can be of additional assistance
	State when my actions will be completed and what results I expect
	Stand
PA/SP	Shake hands
SP	Thank him
	Say good-bye
PA	Says good-bye
	Walks you back to the reception room

NOTE: PA = purchasing agent, SP = salesperson

SOURCE: Thomas W. Leigh, "Cognitive Selling Scripts and Sales Training," *Journal of Personal Selling and Sales Management,* 7 (August 1987): 39–48.

mation about the company and its products, competition, and market and customer base. Providing this type of information is time consuming for the training organization and requires the trainees to digest a lot of information in a short period of time.

Company Knowledge.   Most large organizations begin the training process with a detailed history of the organization. It is important for trainees to become part of the organizational family, and that process begins by understanding its history and past. This type of knowledge also typically includes indoctrination into the company philosophy about the public image that the organization is pursuing. For example, EDS (the data system company founded by Ross Perot) maintains the image of a conservative, clean-cut, highly professional salesforce who wears white shirts and dark suits. Part of the EDS training is an indoctrination into the companies philosophy and mission.

Product Knowledge.   The majority of training focuses on the product base. In the pharmaceutical industry, trainees spend weeks learning some basic medical and anatomical information. The training then focuses on how the drugs they will sell work and their possible side effects, as well as the benefits and attributes of the drugs. Salespeople must be knowledgeable enough to answer doctors' questions about a product and its effects on a particular malady. Training of product knowledge can be intense if products are complicated or technical. The nightly "homework" for trainees can be mountainous; many trainees face daily exams on the material. However, the intensity of the training is justified because new hires have to be able to understand the products in order to successfully sell them.

Knowledge of Competition.   To be successful salespeople must not only be thoroughly knowledgeable about their own products but also those of the competition. An organization's products must be successfully differentiated from those of other firms. The training process includes an analysis of the strengths and weaknesses of competing products.

Knowledge of the Market and Customer Base.   The last area of knowledge training concerns the general market and the organization's specific customer base. Trainees must know something about the needs of the general customer base and the interactions of the market. Without a working knowledge of the customer base, it becomes much more difficult to establish a relationship selling approach to business. Furthermore, without a knowledge of the customer, sellers find it much more difficult to close any type of sale. For example, Unisys Corporation sent 37 district managers and 120 first-line managers to sales negotiation training sessions designed to improve their negotiation and communication skills. Unisys found that a lack of negotiation skills by its sales personnel was leading to a lack of understanding of the customer's negotiation tactics. In turn, this was leading to customer dissatisfaction with Unisys.[21]

Proficiencies

Proficiency training allows new trainees to become proficient in general skills through the use of short seminars or workshops. For example, every year W.W. Grainger, a distributor of maintenance, repair, and operating supplies, offers its

---
EXHIBIT 11.7

TOP NINE WAYS TO MANAGE TIME
---

1. Write specific goals that are challenging, but attainable, and have deadlines. Review them periodically to rework goals and adjust deadlines.
2. Begin each morning by writing a prioritized "To Do" list.
3. If there are any items other people should do, delegate them.
4. Group similar activities: one slot of time for returning calls; one for writing letters; one for updating reports.
5. Schedule time realistically, allowing for changes and interruptions.
6. Schedule both start *and* end times for meetings, and the length of discussion for each topic to be covered.
7. Keep an organized filing system; the easier it is to find information, the faster things get done.
8. If you need uninterrupted time to finish an important project, *take it.* Put a "Do Not Disturb" sign on your door.
9. Watch for time wasters and unproductive habits. Once you know what they are, you can eliminate them.

SOURCE: Ginger Trumfio, "A Minute Saved . . . ," *Sales and Marketing Management* (October 1993): 79.

salespeople up to 20 classes on topics such as consultative selling, inventory costs, probing skills, and time management. These seminars come complete with a graduation ceremony where the salespeople march to "Pomp and Circumstance."[22] These topical areas are important to management because they can increase the efficiency and productivity of the salesforce. The following topics are also currently popular: time management, impression management, creative thinking, stress management, diversity training, and global and cultural training.

Time Management.   The better able salespeople are in managing their daily allotted time, the more productive they will be. We like to think of time as endless, but in reality everyone's time is very limited. Salespeople have a 40-hour workweek plus whatever time is spent working "overtime." Because an organization cannot add a lot of extra time to the job, the next best approach is to make use of the existing time more efficient. Exhibit 11.7 provides some tips on time management from Day-Timer, Inc. maker of the Day-Timer planner system.

Impression Management.   The ways people manipulate their communications, using their voice, facial expressions, and appearance, to create a certain type of image is known as **impression management.** The most common method of communication is verbal, but communication can also be very effective through nonverbal means. In the sales world, volumes can be spoken by not speaking at all. Both sellers and buyers use impression management to convey information and images. Much of proficiency training is designed to teach salespeople how to use impression management to convey information, but the training can also center around keeping salespeople from being overly influenced by buyer impression management techniques.[23]

Creative Thinking Training.   Nearly one out of three companies now offers some type of **creative thinking training,** which stresses problem solving, creativity, and other mental skill-building exercises.[24] (See Exhibit 11.8 for ways to develop a

EXHIBIT 11.8

TWELVE WAYS TO DEVELOP A MORE CREATIVE SALES STAFF

ONE At the end of each day, ask each other, "What did you do different and better today from the way it was when you went to work in the morning?"

TWO Stop imagining all the reasons why things can't work or can't be done. Start thinking of ways to make them work and get it done. Before you abandon any idea, think of three ways to make it work.

THREE Set aside a special place and time for creative and innovative thinking each week that is separate from the normal workplace. Provide books on creative thinking, videos, educational toys and games, beanbags, modeling clay, etc. Decorate with baby pictures of your salespeople to remind them that everyone is born innocent and creative.

FOUR Post a "brainstorming" bulletin board in a central place. Write a "sales problem" to be solved on a piece of colored card and place it in the center of the board. Anyone with an idea writes it on a white piece of paper and places it under the "sales problem" card.

FIVE Have employees share "How I did it" stories at an in-house "creative selling" trade show where they could show 35mm slides, photos, etc. to help demonstrate successful selling ideas and methods. New creative teams could be formed from this occasion to help solve future problems. Encourage employees to invite their families.

SIX Assign someone to be the "creative coach" for the sales staff. The "coach" would encourage, back, and support creativeness in each salesperson. This role could be rotated every 2 or 3 months.

SEVEN Create a volunteer creative-idea committee dedicated to eliciting, debating, and implementing salespeople's ideas. Keep a record of ideas submitted by developing a "thermometer" and reward people for the quantity and quality of ideas submitted.

EIGHT Have a monthly "Idea Lottery." Give out a numbered ticket each time a salesperson provides an idea. Once a month read the ideas and draw a random number. If no one holds the winning ticket, double the prize for the next month.

NINE Let people know it's okay to fail. **All genius is inseparable from failure.** Thomas Edison said, "I failed my way to success." It took 50,000 experiments to invent the storage cell battery and after 9,000 tries at inventing the light bulb his reply to an assistant who asked why he persisted in this folly after failing 9,000 times, "I haven't failed once. I've learned 9,000 things that don't work." Ask salespeople: "What are the three biggest errors or failures you've made in the last 3 years?" If the answer is none, they haven't tried anything new.

TEN If it ain't broke, break it. Test all your assumptions about your current sales systems, processes, and methods to see if they are really necessary or if there is a better way. Sylvan Goldman, a supermarket owner, designed the shopping cart and his sales went up 40 percent. Shopping carts outnumber cars today.

ELEVEN Have an open meeting where the meeting's theme is read out loud. Invite everyone to identify a related issue for which they are willing to assume responsibility. Write each issue and sponsor on large sheets of paper and post on the wall. The next phase is the "idea marketplace." Everyone is invited to sign up for as many issues as they wish. Sponsors of each issue convene their groups to private rooms, discuss the issue, and record all ideas or suggestions.

TWELVE Encourage your salespeople to keep a conversation piece on their desks that represents their vision of selling, i.e., a crystal ball finding future markets, jumper cables for jump-starting prospects, Heinz ketchup to represent 57 new uses or markets for your goods or services, etc.

If your organization acts creative, it will become creative. There is no way of guaranteeing how far intention and action will take your company. But anyone can guarantee that with no effort there will be no action and with no action, there will be no positive results. By trying creativity, you take the first step in the right direction.

SOURCE: Michael Michalko, "That's a Bright Idea!" *Personal Selling Power* (September 1994): 60–61.

more creative salesforce.) One company that has embraced the creative training approach is Sysco, a large hotel supplier. Sysco reserves 10 percent of its 120-hour training program for creative thinking training. Sysco management says sales have increased 30 percent since the inclusion of creative thinking training.

Stress Management Thinking. **Stress management training** hopes to teach salespeople to better cope with some existing stresses and to avoid others.[25] A little stress can be healthy, but too much stress can be destructive to individuals as well as the organization. An unhealthy level of stress can lead to drug abuse and alcoholism, health problems, mental distress, and conflict at work and at home. Companies have also found that a stressful organizational environment may lead to lawsuits by employees (see Chapter 3). All of these stress-related negative results can also lead to poor performance on the job. Because of all the negative consequences of stress, more and more companies are beginning to incorporate stress reduction techniques in their training programs. Take the stress test provided in Exhibit 11.9 to determine your stress levels.

Diversity Training. Diversity training builds awareness of the differences among classes and types of people. Many sales organizations are paying consultants $10,000 per day to conduct seminars on diversity sensitivity. Harris Sussman of Workways in Cambridge, Massachusetts, argues that diversity training should increase the vitality of all aspects of the organization, but not if it is perceived as compliance training.[26] In other words, organizational personnel must believe in the need for diversity training.

Diversity training can mean many things, and it is unlikely that any one plan would prove successful for all organizations. However, there are some core components that can be taught. These are:

- The value of diversity
- The development of cultural literacy
- The incorporation of diversity in a corporate culture
- An examination of the global perspective
- Individual self-development and interpersonal effectiveness[27]

Global and Cultural Training. Many U.S.-based multinationals lack internationally experienced sales personnel. As a result, many organizations must train personnel to prepare them for international settings. These international personnel require cross-training into the culture of the assigned country. **Cross-training** is defined as a fundamental immersion into the culture of another country. Some of the training occurs in the home country; the rest must occur in the host country. Host country trainers can provide very specific information about living and doing business in the country. Much of this training involves the families of sales personnel.[28]

Sales organizations also need training in how to implement some common sales practices, but on a global level. Global Partners of Cambridge, Massachusetts, is a company that specializes in training sales personnel in how to develop global account teams and cross-cultural management. Among Global Partners' clients is Digital Equipment Corporation, which decided in 1993 that its account management strategy needed to be upgraded to consider international markets. As a result of the global training, Digital has been able to expand its market.[29]

EXHIBIT 11.9

HOW MUCH STRESS ARE YOU UNDER?

To measure the degree of stress you suffer, take the following stress test. Circle the appropriate number for each question and tally your total score.

How often do you suffer from:	Never	Hardly Ever	Sometimes	Often
1. Aches in back, head, or neck	0	1	2	3
2. Stomach aches or indigestion	0	1	2	3
3. Too many things on your mind at once	0	1	2	3
4. Feeling of fatigue	0	1	2	3
5. Chest pains	0	1	2	3
6. Less interest in physical intimacy	0	1	2	3
7. An urge to drink a lot of alcohol	0	1	2	3
8. Feelings of anxiety and being uptight	0	1	2	3
9. Difficulty falling or staying asleep	0	1	2	3
10. A feeling of depression	0	1	2	3
11. A feeling of being overwhelmed	0	1	2	3
12. An inability to think clearly	0	1	2	3

Score:

What the Numbers Mean

A score of 12 or lower indicates a low degree of personal stress reactions; between 13 and 24 reflects a moderate degree; higher than 24 indicates that you're experiencing a high degree of stress. While your score may not altogether surprise you, it would be wise to consult your physician to determine whether you have a health problem that requires medical attention, one that may be contributing both to your stress level and your ability to withstand it.

SOURCE: Sandra Lotz Fisher, "Vital Signs," *Sales and Marketing Management* (November 1992): 93.

TRAINING FORMATS

Formal classroom training can be implemented through a variety of methods, many of which are similar to what you have become used to as a student. The different types of training procedures can be categorized into four formats: (1) lecture/discussion, (2) cases and videotapes, (3) behavioral simulations, and (4) absorption training. Exhibit 11.10 shows the usage rates for some of these and other training methods.

Lecture/Discussion

Much of the information that trainees receive is provided through classroom lectures and discussions. This is particularly true for information that is knowledge-oriented. Trainers have found that new hires straight from college are most comfortable—at least initially—with a lecture format. As the program continues, the training may move away from lectures and more toward other methods.

Cases and Videotapes

Cases have been shown to be particularly effective for refresher training—that is, after trainees have organizational sales experience and some basic knowledge about the products, the market, and the competition. One of the advantages of a case for-

EXHIBIT 11.10	
USE OF TRAINING MATERIALS	
Training Method	Percent of Companies Using the Method
Training manuals	50.5%
Videotapes	46.5%
Audiotapes	25.7%
Role plays	36.6%
Case analysis	17.8%
Computer simulation	5.0%

SOURCE: Lawrence B. Chonko, John F. Tanner, Jr., and William A. Weeks, "Sales Training: Status and Needs," *Journal of Personal Selling and Sales Management,* 13(4) (Fall 1993): 81–86.

mat is that it gets trainees actively involved in the learning process. The case format also helps build skills based on problem solving and creative decision making.

Training videotapes have received mixed reviews, primarily because video is not a good medium for getting more than a few limited concepts or facts across to the audience. Video is most effective when drama or humor is used as the basic format.[30]

Behavioral Simulations

One of the best training methods is the use of behavioral simulations. **Behavioral simulations** are a variety of interactive training methods that allow trainees to learn by doing. They include role playing, computer simulations, interactive video, tele-training, and video-enhanced training. People learn better when they are involved in the education process. The key to behavioral simulation methods is that trainees actively participate in the process. Behavioral simulations became very popular with organizations as computer usage became more commonplace in the mid-1980s.

Role Plays.   **Role plays,** the oldest of the behavioral simulations, allow trainees to take on character roles and solve problems either through videotape or in a live presentation. Role plays continue to grow in popularity. They help trainers prepare trainees with specific skills by focusing on the topic of the training session.[31] If closing a sale, for example, is the training topic of the day, then the role play for that session should concentrate on closing a sale. The role plays in this book are designed to teach you how to solve problems confronted by salespeople and sales managers.

Computer Games and Simulations.   **Computer games and simulations** consist of computerized software that allows training by simulating sales scenarios. Games and simulations have three general purposes: (1) orienting and training new employees, (2) screening current or would-be managers, and (3) ongoing management training.[32] Computer simulations are a good source for providing novice and intermediate salespeople with the opportunity to expand their abilities. Learning can be enhanced and performance accelerated by repeated use of different simulations.[33] For example, Silvermine Consulting Group has created a computer-based simulation called "Maximizing Development Funds" in which salespeople make spending and other marketing decisions. Salespeople also get to see the short- and long-term results or consequences of their decisions.[34] Citicorp has developed a board game known as "The Work Ethic" to teach business ethics to its employees. Citicorp wants to teach the corporate ethical culture to employees and to encourage ethical behavior through peer pressure.[35] Harris Semiconductor created a board game to teach its sales employees basic financial information. The game takes about four hours and is played in teams as each tries to buy a fictional company. The results are a salesforce that has a better grasp of corporate financial matters.[36]

Interactive Video.   Recall from Chapter 2 that interactive video is a merger of computer, laser disc, and video technology that allows the participant to conduct trial sales presentations on computer-generated customers who then react to the decisions and approaches made by the salesperson. Current interactive video programs are complex and use artificial intelligence to determine a sequence of events in which the computer interacts with the trainee. Video recordings are played based on choices that the trainee makes, thus the trainee can practice sales calls without leaving the training center. Motorola is using an interactive video system to simulate sales calls to teach national account selling. Massachusetts Mutual Life also provides trainees with valuable sales call experience using interactive video. Pfizer has been using interactive video to simulate calls on doctors.[37] The possibilities for training using interactive video are limited only by how fast the software can be designed to provide the training interactions that the training company desires.

Teletraining.   **Teletraining** is training in one or more locations through the use of videoconferencing equipment and techniques. Training can be very expensive if all trainees must be brought to one central location. Teletraining avoids this expense. The traditional form of teletraining has been the one-way audio hookup, wherein the instructor is shown live by way of video, and the trainees have an audio link to ask questions. This format allows the trainer to be in one location and the trainees in other multiple locations. The current method of teletraining is two-way video and audio, where the instruction becomes much more personal.[38] Perhaps more important, the laptop computer is a portable training room in which salespeople can enter and learn at will. This self-administered training center may soon change the way most companies train.[39]

Corporations are also using satellite time to create their own networks, which have loosely been termed *Business TV* (BTV). Using BTV, senior executives can address sales classes in multiple locations without leaving their offices. Seventy-five percent of all BTV usage consists of training functions, but other applications of BTV include corporate communications, announcements, and company policy updates. Eastman Kodak produces weekly programming for its salespeople which is primarily training related. Texas Instruments begins every Monday morning with a BTV broadcast to its 800 salespeople around the country. As satellite availability becomes more frequent and less expensive, more and more organizations will begin using BTV for training.[40]

Self-Paced Video-Enhanced Training.   **Video-enhanced training** (VET) consists of training programs on videocassettes that are mailed to the salesforce for study. VET can be designed for initial training or be used as refresher training. Salespeople study the materials in their spare time. Once salespeople feel comfortable with the material, they call a toll-free number and provide answers to a multiple choice exam. Salespeople learn immediately whether they passed and can move to a new module or whether they have to retake the current module. VET permits organizations to continually train their sales personnel and maintain higher salesperson proficiencies than other training methods. Studies have also shown that a VET system can reduce turnover and better help the firm achieve its goals and objectives.[41]

Absorption Training

Absorption training refers to the written materials that organizations give to trainees with the expectation that the trainees will "absorb" the material on their own (typically at night after a day of training or work). Absorption materials include training and product manuals, information bulletins, and various types of internal documents. Although absorption materials can be overwhelming, trainees are typically tested on the materials and must make a passing grade. As a result, one of the keys for any form of absorption materials is that the material be very readable. Easy-to-read writing styles will increase the trainees' reading efficiency and require less discussion through the day-time formalized training program.[42]

Absorption training and other forms of training continue throughout a salesperson's career. New manuals on new products or procedures are frequently prepared, and salespeople are required to be very familiar with the new material. Exhibit 11.11 presents a table of contents from a training manual for the Riverwalk Press salesforce. Notice the variety of topics covered.

EXHIBIT 11.11
COLLEGE PUBLISHING TRAINING MANUAL

Table of Contents

Chapter 1: The College Publishing Industry
    The College Textbook Market
    The Adoption Process
    The College Bookstore

Chapter 2: Overview and History of Riverwalk Press

Chapter 3: The Riverwalk Press Sales Representative Job Description

Chapter 4: Careers in College Publishing and Advice for the Beginning Sales Representative
    Career Sales Representative
    Sales Manager
    Marketing Manager
    Developmental Editor
    Acquisitions Editor
    Editor-in-Chief

Chapter 5: Setting Up Your Office, Organizing Your Car Trunk, and Compiling Materials to Carry on Campus
    Setting Up Your Office
    Administrative Files
    Organizing Your Car Trunk
    Compiling Materials to Carry on Campus

Chapter 6:
    Completing a Territory Analysis and Itinerary
    Campus Planning

EXHIBIT 11.11 (continued)
COLLEGE PUBLISHING TRAINING MANUAL

Table of Contents

TRAINING LOCATION

The location of training can be centralized or decentralized. In a **centralized training** approach, all personnel are trained in the same location (i.e., at company headquarters or a national training center). Supporters of centralized training argue that training everyone at the same location leads to much more efficient and consistent learning. The downside to centralized training is the high level of expense for the organization. There are two primary forms of centralized training: (1) training in national training centers and (2) use of satellite centers.

In a **decentralized training** format, simultaneous training occurs at multiple locations—at a number of district offices, for example. In a decentralized format trainees are closer to their locations. Some companies have combined both a centralized and a decentralized format, with general training occurring at the corporate headquarters and then more specific training occurring at district offices. There are three basic choices of training location based on a decentralized framework: (1) local offices, (2) off-site, and (3) customer internship programs. The two centralized and three decentralized alternatives are presented in the following sections.

Training Centers

Training centers are categorized as a centralized form of training. National training centers are most frequently used for new hire and refresher training (see Box 11.2). McDonald's, for example, has an entire campus in northern Illinois that is known as McDonald's U. IBM and Xerox have long been known for their excellent training centers. Training centers take a major commitment from upper management because of the money and resources required. If the organization is large enough and large-scale training is occurring year-round, then a training center format may be justified.

Satellite Centers

Satellite centers are smaller versions of training centers. An organization may have multiple satellite centers. Rather than sending all personnel to the national headquarters, companies send their trainees to regional offices where they are trained by local staff and management. Everyone is trained the same way, but by regional rather than national personnel. Satellite centers are slightly less expensive than a national training center because district offices are used and trainees remain in their regional or district office.

Local Offices

Training at a local level is a very decentralized approach. Upper management tends to have less control over how training occurs and what methods are used. The training effectiveness is dependent on the abilities of the local manager. As a territory becomes available, a sales manager hires and trains the person in the local office. This type of training tends to be for a much shorter time frame, and much of the training is done on the job. The primary advantage of local training is the major savings in training expenses. Many organizations implementing this type of training are small and hire only a few salespeople in any given year. The effectiveness of the organization and new personnel is very dependent on the quality of the local managers. If sales management is

---

BOX 11.2

FOCUS ON TRAINING

With the growing emphasis on sales expertise as a competitive advantage, companies are beginning to see training not only as a way to pass on skills, but also as an aid to salespeople in sharpening their analytical prowess.

At Xerox Corporation's training center in Leesburg, Virginia, "The biggest change over the last 10 years is that we spend a lot more time on what the customer thinks is important," says Gary Aslin, director of Xerox Document University. That means focusing more on consultative selling techniques and ways to identify problems with systems or business processes, rather than, as Aslin terms it, "the hardware sell."

New hires at Xerox undergo 11 weeks of training, including four at the campus of Xerox Document University. The training facility—located on 109 acres, with 250 classrooms, and offering a curriculum of 180 courses—serves both Xerox sales and service employees, as well as its customers.

In the past, says Aslin, salespeople were trained to fill customer needs as they arose—for instance, for a customer who had become swamped with more paperwork, the solution might be a bigger photocopier machine. However, says Aslin, with such a prescription, "Someone might have fixed a symptom rather than a problem." Today, a salesperson is apt to take time at a customer site to analyze exactly how information is generated and then explore whether the whole system of document flow might be changed to make the process more economical and efficient for the customer.

In addition, Xerox continues providing training for salespeople throughout their careers. Henry J. Singer, General Electric's vice-president for area management and sales, also emphasizes that his company's customer-centered training has been effective for both new recruits and seasoned pros. Veteran salespeople have told him the new training material is the best they've seen—they only wish it had been available 10 years earlier.

SOURCE: W. David Gibson, "Fielding a Force of Experts," *Sales and Marketing Management* (April 1993): 90.

---

strong locally, this method of training can be effective and productive. Conversely, weaker sales managers will probably be less effective trainees.

Off-Site

The second decentralized training option is to train new hires at a non-company location. For example, some organizations hire training consultants to conduct training at the consultant's facilities. Many small companies that want a high-quality training program but are only hiring a handful of salespeople throughout the year will contract to have their personnel trained at these off-site locations. In this way, hiring and training can occur throughout the year and not at just one point in time where an organization might have a critical mass for a training class.

Customer Internship Programs

Last, one growing training trend is to teach the salesforce to think like the customer. The most efficient way to accomplish this goal is to have salespeople serve in a *customer internship program*. Triad Systems Corporation requires all new sales hires to spend a period of 2 to 3 weeks working at the customer's location. The goal is to have trainees know the way customers run their businesses. Customers get a $300 credit toward future purchases.[43]

TRAINING PERSONNEL

The last piece in establishing a training program is determining who the training personnel should be. The question of who will train is dependent to a great degree on where the training will occur. The more centralized the training, the more likely that the training team will be composed of trainers who are independent consultants or corporate staff personnel. Conversely, the more decentralized the training, the more likely the training will be led by members of management. There are advantages and disadvantages to using staff personnel, management, and independent consultants as trainers. It is important to remember that each organization has different training needs; therefore, there is no one "right" trainer for everyone.

Staff Trainers

For most companies the ideal solution to training is to have full-time personnel whose sole responsibility is training. Unfortunately, this is not always practical or possible. Full-time training staffs are expensive, so each new training class would have to be sufficiently large to warrant the expense. Most trainers begin in sales and demonstrate their abilities to teach new salespeople. Trainers are usually located in the corporate headquarters or in a separate training facility. For example, Burlington Northern Railroad maintains a separate training facility complete with classrooms, satellite capabilities, and staff offices to handle training duties for the organization.

There are a number of distinct advantages in having a full-time staff to handle training responsibilities. First, training is their complete responsibility. They can experiment with new methods of training and continue to change the process to meet evolving organizational needs. Trainers tend to be better teachers and have been recognized for their abilities to teach. The better the teacher, the more likely the information is to be conveyed to the trainees.

Another advantage is the higher probability of being able to use multiple methods for training such as role plays, computer simulations, interactive videos, and teletraining. By having the training in one location, the needed equipment for behavioral simulations is much more likely to be possible.

Last, training by staff members in a formal setting tends to reduce some of the stress and tension of beginning a new job. It allows new hires to meet their peers, better understand company procedures, and ease into the transition process.

The advantages of staff training are so significant that it would seem everyone should train using the staffing procedure. However, the primary disadvantage is the enormous cost. A second disadvantage is that the trainer is not as likely to be able to give individual instruction regarding the new territory. Moreover, if trainers have been out of the salesforce for some time, they may not be as closely attuned to the field as they once were.

Sales Management

Many organizations use members of their management team to train new personnel. These managers can range anywhere from first-line sales managers to upper-level sales managers or even marketing managers.[44] The smaller the organization, the more likely that first-line sales managers are used to perform much of the training. Usually these first-line managers will be the trainee's manager once the territory assignment is made. Learning International, a sales training organization, reports that 10 years ago 60 percent of its customers were using internal trainers; now 60 percent of the training is being led by managers.[45]

Many people feel that training will fail unless the information is continually reinforced in the workplace. As a result, the theory holds that managers are the best training personnel if the managers are well trained. To that end, the Fortune Group of Atlanta provides a series of interactive videos in a 5-day intensive seminar to facilitate manager training and thus, ultimately salesperson training. The long-run results of the video management training is better preparation for new hires.[46]

Independent Consultants

Independent consultants provide training expertise on an as-needed basis. Many training consulting firms can handle all aspects of an organization's needs. Other training consultants (such as marketing and sales professors) perform specific types of training activities. Utilizing consultants as trainers provides the organization some flexibility because the consultant can provide either specific types of training information or conduct the entire training process. The flexibility of the paid consultant is also useful as a supplement to the in-house training staff. Outside consultants are frequently brought into a formal training program to provide very specific sessions on some aspect of selling.

The primary disadvantage of consultants is their lack of knowledge about the training organization and its market, competition, and customers. They are also not as aware of the day-to-day problems of the sales environment for the organization. This lack of awareness is why many companies are more interested in consultants as supplements rather than replacements for in-house personnel.[47]

ON-THE-JOB TRAINING

Thus far this chapter has focused on types of formal training. The remainder of this chapter looks at informal training.

On-the-job training (OJT) is informal training that occurs in the field while the new hire is working. In other words, the training comes by doing. The OJT philosophy is very popular for a number of reasons and is practiced by a wide assortment of organizations and industries. The primary reason for the popularity of an OJT approach is that it is cheaper than conducting more formalized training. Estimates of the average cost for training an industrial salesperson in a more formalized setting can reach $28,000 per salesperson.[48] Many organizations question the worth of training at that price tag. For then the question becomes: Is the $28,000 an expense that may not be affordable or an investment that provides a better salesperson for the organization?

Another reason for the popularity of OJT is the prevalence of the belief that "you can't learn until you do." Sitting in a classroom can provide you with some useful information, but you are not going to learn how to sell until you get out and do it. OJT supporters concede that a lot of mistakes will be made initially, but salespeople will be productive in a much shorter time period than were they to spend up to 3 months in a classroom training format.

The Japanese are strong believers in an OJT philosophy. They put new hires in a new job, and the training occurs by making mistakes, learning from the mistakes, and moving on. Formalized training as practiced in the United States is virtually nonexistent in Japan. The Japanese system involves hands-on, trial-and-error approaches, and rotation through departments and jobs.[49]

Problems With OJT

There are a number of problems with an OJT system that may offset the cost savings. For one, the differences in training and mentoring abilities among sales managers lead to quality in training ranging from excellent to virtually nonexistent. This lack of consistency puts new hires in either an advantageous or disadvantageous position depending on their assigned sales manager's abilities.

In addition, consistency becomes a problem in that new hires are not being taught the same things. As a result, the organization may have a salesforce whose procedures, skills, and abilities are very diverse and inconsistent. If a sales manager has bad habits, these habits are passed along to the new hires under his or her influence.

Another serious problem with OJT is the lack of knowledge about the company, the people, the specifics of the product, and the organizational methods employed. Classroom training can do an excellent job of indoctrinating new hires about the company and methods. A newly OJT-trained person usually does not receive some of the basics about the company that could be received in a classroom through a formalized training program.

Combination OJT and Classroom Training

The definitions of OJT training and a more formalized training program by managers are coming closer together. The previous difference in the two centered on the "formalization" of the training. OJT typically has allowed managers to train the individuals in whatever fashion they deemed appropriate. Now, in a combination approach, more and more companies are having their new recruits spend time in the field learning *before* attending the formalized training program (see Exhibit 11.12 for percentages of companies using OJT training and other methods).

For example, Lanier Copiers sends its new hires straight into the field for 2 weeks after hiring with no training. The salespeople struggle, make blunders, and often become frustrated. However, at the end of the 2-week period they are sent to a more formalized training. The advantage of this approach is that the new hires now understand the problems of the field because they have experienced the job. The new hires also tend to view the training in a much more serious fashion. When examples are given about selling techniques, the information means much more because the trainees have probably experienced the problem during their 2-week stint in the sales world. The organization hopes that any damage done to customer relations during this 2-week period, resulting from lack of knowledge, are minimized or repaired after training.

Other companies bring in trainees for a couple of weeks to indoctrinate them into the company and train them with the products. The trainees are then sent into the field for a period of 2 weeks to a month before being brought back for more classroom

EXHIBIT 11.12

TRAINING METHODS

	Individual Instruction	Home Assignments	In-House Class	On-the-Job	External Seminars	Other
Company size						
under $5 Million	74.7%	18.4%	50.6%	82.8%	71.3%	2.3%
$5MM–$25MM	72.9	15.3	55.9	81.4	64.4	5.1
$25MM–$100MM	66.7	18.8	66.7	83.3	75.0	10.4
$100MM–$250MM	60.0	20.0	60.0	90.0	70.0	0.0
over $250MM	85.0	25.0	85.0	95.0	60.0	10.0
Product or service						
Consumer products	79.6	13.0	68.5	79.6	68.5	1.9
Consumer services	73.1	23.1	65.4	90.4	71.2	7.7
Industrial products	74.5	17.3	60.9	80.9	70.9	4.5
Industrial services	67.9	16.0	66.7	85.2	75.3	2.5
Office products	82.4	17.6	55.9	88.2	67.6	5.9
Office services	80.8	26.9	59.6	90.4	75.0	7.7
Type of buyer						
Consumer	70.1	24.7	63.6	84.4	68.8	6.5
Distributors	73.6	17.6	53.8	76.9	71.4	2.2
Industry	69.6	22.0	59.5	85.1	71.4	6.0
Retailers	69.3	20.0	56.0	81.3	69.3	5.3
Industry						
Business services	80.0	25.0	50.0	87.5	62.5	7.5
Chemicals	83.3	0.0	50.0	83.3	50.0	0.0
Communications	62.5	25.0	87.5	100.0	100.0	12.5
Educational services	60.0	40.0	60.0	80.0	40.0	0.0
Electronics	70.0	10.0	50.0	100.0	70.0	0.0
Fabricated metals	66.7	22.2	66.7	77.8	77.8	11.1
Health services	75.0	25.0	100.0	100.0	75.0	0.0
Hotels and other lodging places	50.0	0.0	66.7	66.7	83.3	0.0
Instruments	80.0	0.0	80.0	100.0	80.0	0.0
Insurance	84.6	23.1	53.8	100.0	76.9	15.4
Machinery	60.0	30.0	50.0	70.0	60.0	0.0
Manufacturing	80.0	10.0	60.0	80.0	60.0	10.0
Office equipment	75.0	0.0	75.0	100.0	50.0	0.0
Paper and allied products	100.0	33.3	50.0	83.3	66.7	0.0
Printing and publishing	85.7	21.4	57.1	92.9	92.9	0.0
Retail	87.5	12.5	62.5	62.5	75.0	0.0
Trucking and warehousing	33.3	0.0	33.3	66.7	33.3	33.3
Wholesale (consumer goods)	63.6	27.3	45.5	54.5	72.7	0.0
Wholesale (industrial goods)	84.6	30.8	61.5	92.3	76.9	15.4
Overall	72.8%	18.3%	58.9%	83.9%	69.2%	5.4%

SOURCE: Dartnell Corporation, 1992.

training. Again, like the Lanier example, the trainees have by then experienced the sales world and, as a result, the classroom sales training becomes much more effective.

ASSESSMENT OF RESULTS

The training process began with an assessment of the need for training. Likewise, the process will end with an assessment of the results. As discussed earlier in this chapter, the cost of training can be enormous, and management must continually ask whether the investment in training is worth the cost. Unfortunately the impact of training results may not be immediate. It may take years to fully determine the success of a training program.

The question asked by management remains, "How do we know the training is accomplishing our sales objectives?" The answer partially depends on the nature of the industry and the sales effort. Management can ascertain the results of the training by measuring the increase in sales, the increase in sales calls, customer satisfaction, the effectiveness of salesperson communication and service, or through a number of other variables. One serious problem with the measurement solution is that changes may have occured because of nontraining environmental factors such as the entrance of new competition, an increase in promotion, or other aspects. Therefore, the most beneficial way of determining training success is by comparing trained salespeople versus a group of untrained salespeople on the skill in question. Other methods of determining training effectiveness include observation of desired changes, questioning customers about desired changes, and obtaining impressions by those who were trained.

Assessment of training effectiveness is critical for determining whether to continue implementing training methods or to adjust the current procedures. Assessment may be the most difficult step in the training process.

SUMMARY

The first step in designing a training program is to assess the needs of the organization. A needs assessment begins with a training audit that focuses on the organization, the tasks, and the personnel. Information for the audit is obtained through observation by management, directly from the salesforce, and from customers and suppliers.

There are four types of training and development programs: indoctrination, refresher, salesperson development, and executive development. Every organization must look within to determine the objectives of training.

Training topics can be divided into four categories. The first is socialization, which is defined as assimilating new hires into the organization. The Feldman Organization Socialization Model is based on three stages: anticipatory socialization, accommodation, and outcomes. The second training topic centers around selling techniques—prospecting, account management, professionalism, presentation skills, and ethics. The third training topic is designed to increase knowledge levels of the company, product, competition, and market/customer relations. The last training topic consists of increasing proficiency levels of specific topics such as time management, stress management, and diversity training.

Training methods can be very diverse and may include case studies, lectures, videos, behavioral simulations (role playing, computer simulations, interactive video, teletraining, BTV, self-paced video-enhanced training), and absorption training.

Organizations differ on where they conduct their training. Typical locations include a national training center, training satellites (regional offices), local offices, or in other off-site locations. Trainers may be full-time staff personnel, management personnel, or outside consultants.

The alternative to formalized classroom training is on-the-job training (OJT). Many organizations feel that you can't learn until you do. OJT is much less expensive than formalized training, but it lacks the consistency of knowledge and skills that are learned in formalized training. OJT is deeply dependent on the ability of the sales manager. A more common method being implemented by many organizations is a combination of OJT and classroom training.

KEY TERMS

sales training

training audit

organizational assessment

task assessment

personnel assessment

development program

indoctrination training

refresher training

salesperson development programs

executive development programs

socialization

office politics

grapevine

anticipatory socialization

realism

congruence

accommodation

initiation to the task

initiation to the group

role definition

congruence of evaluation

cognitive scripts

impression management

creative thinking training

stress management training

cross-training

behavioral simulations

role plays

computer games and simulations

teletraining

video-enhanced training (VET)

absorption training

centralized training

decentralized training

training centers

satellite centers

on-the-job training (OJT)

DISCUSSION QUESTIONS

1. What is meant by assessing training needs?
2. What are the various types of training and development programs?
3. What are the four basic training topics, and what does each include?
4. What are some current topics that are being classified as proficiencies?
5. What are the four basic training methods, and what does each include?
6. How are behavioral simulations used in training programs?
7. What are the differences between centralized and decentralized training locations?

8. Who typically conducts the training of new recruits? Who typically conducts refresher training of existing personnel?

9. What are the differences between on-the-job training (OJT) and classroom training?

10. What are the advantages and disadvantages of OJT?

PROBLEMS

1. Madge Mason is a middle-level manager for Tandy Company. She has worked for Tandy for the past 12 years and is college educated. Madge's manager has chosen her to attend a specialized management program being offered by the local university. She will spend the next 2 weeks on campus and receive a certificate for the added management education. Madge is pleased with her selection and is eagerly awaiting being back on campus. What is this "training" experience designed to accomplish?

2. In a training program, Ginger Hamm was warned to watch the nuances of corporate politics. She tells Carlita Washington, one of her associates, that she has no intention of getting involved in office politics. Carlita thinks to herself about how naive Ginger is being. Should training programs address nonselling issues such as corporate politics? What are the effects of corporate politics on an individual?

3. After going through a 3-month training session, Khalil Ali considers how similar to school the experience has been. He tells one of his associates, "Classroom lectures, cases, role plays, computer simulations, and group discussions were all like the sales management class that I took except we were getting paid. Now, our territory assignments will depend on how we are graded on our training performance. Some things just don't change, do they?" Do you find Khalil's experiences surprising?

4. When Samantha White took a commission sales job she was concerned because there was very little formal training. Her boss told her the best way to learn was by doing. Although initially apprehensive about a lack of formal training, Samantha thinks to herself how lucky she was to have a manager who was willing to act as a mentor and teach her what she needed to be successful. What are the advantages and disadvantages of on-the-job training like Samantha's?

SHORT CASE

TRAINING

INTRODUCTION

Harbaush Electronics is a German company that makes a variety of electronic components and products. The most notable of the Harbaush products are stereo speakers and stereo component parts. Harbaush is also known for a high-quality television that is sold throughout Europe. Although the company sells very little product in the United States, it has just bought Rangermatic, Inc., a relatively small U.S. electronics producer headquartered in Dayton, Ohio. Rangermatic has a salesforce of 18 field people who sell to electronic retail outlets including the large discount houses. The Rangermatic salesforce was trained on the job by sales managers, and they have had little if any refresher training. Harbaush management is somewhat concerned about the lack of consistent training among the Rangermatic salesforce. In addition, management feels strongly that more salespeople will be needed and that over a 5-year span as many as 40 new salespeople may be hired.

SCENARIO

Harbaush has hired Joe Schmidt as sales development officer (trainer). Schmidt's responsibilities are to examine the existing abilities of both the Rangermatic salesforce and its lower sales management, and to prepare a training plan for the new hires, as well as refresher training for existing personnel if needed. The Harbaush reputation has always centered on quality with excellent service. The mandate given to Schmidt is to ensure that the Rangermatic people fit the Harbaush philosophy.

Schmidt has begun a training audit on the Rangermatic salesforce and is meeting with the salesforce in groups of four to five to talk about training needs. His initial meetings have been very positive with some members of the sales team and very disappointing with other members. One particular problem Schmidt has encountered is with three salespeople who feel that their job is to spend time selling and not on talking about training. He has been unable to schedule a meeting with these three.

PROBLEM

Schmidt must figure out what type of training to implement for Rangermatic salespeople, old and new sales managers, and the new 40 salespeople that will be hired over time. Management expects a recommendation from Schmidt about the training process and will then approve, disapprove, or modify his recommendations.

QUESTIONS

1. What training issues must Schmidt include in his recommendations?
2. What options does Schmidt have for training Rangermatic salespeople, the new hires, and sales managers?
3. Are the three salespeople who have not scheduled a meeting making a mistake? Why or why not?
4. What would your training recommendations be to management?

TRAINING ROLE PLAY

CHARACTERS

Trainee #1: Amanda Jones or Chas Browning
Trainee #2: David Smith or Maria Gonzalez
Trainer #3: Debra Joiner or Bill Nelson

SCENARIO A

Amanda Jones and David Smith are both new recruits who are currently attending EDD's 4-week training institute in New Orleans. Both are based in Dallas and will return to Dallas to receive their territory assignments upon completion of the training period.

The trainees are scheduled to fly back to their home office early Saturday morning. Bill Nelson, the executive in charge of training, calls Jones and Smith on Friday, the last day of training, to tell them that the company is holding a wine and cheese party to celebrate the conclusion of training. Jones is upset because the training schedule indicated that the training session was over Friday at 5 o'clock and she has friends and parents driving in from Baton Rouge to see her that night. She hasn't seen these friends in over 3 years. She thinks to herself that she may just have to "cut" this company function!

SCENE 1

The first scene has Nelson talking to Jones and Smith about their successful completion of the training function. He compliments them on their work during training. Nelson summarize the information from scenario A, emphasizing that this is the last day of the training period and that they have been in New Orleans for the past 4 weeks. Nelson concludes, "I realize that the party was not on the schedule, but we think the session will be beneficial and we're hoping some company executives will show." Jones asks in a somewhat sarcastic tone why the party was not on the schedule. Nelson's reply is that it was a last-minute addition. Nelson again congratulates the twosome and leaves stating, "I'll see you two at the party."

SCENE 2

This scene is a continuation of scene 1 beginning with Jones vehemently complaining about this change in schedule and how she has friends coming in from Baton Rouge. She says, "It was rude, rude, rude!" Smith tries to show her some of the advantages to attending the party, but Jones is concerned with seeing her friends. The scene ends with her planning not to attend, briefly attending, or attending the entire event.

SUMMARY

The class discussion for this role play should focus on who is right and who is wrong. Scene 2 should focus on why the party is being held and the consequences, if any, for not attending the party. Think about this! There is more to this than you might think at first glance.

SCENARIO B

Monday morning after the training program Bill Nelson has called Smith and Jones to his office. He meets with each separately to give them their territory assignments. He gives Smith his assignment and tells him to begin immediately. Nelson tells Jones she can begin only after receiving some additional training on dealing with sexual harassment. After talking with Smith, Jones feels that she is being discriminated against because she is not allowed to begin working her territory as quickly as Smith and goes in to Nelson and complains.

SCENE 1

Nelson calls Smith in first, welcomes him, and informs him that beginning Tuesday he will be covering a North Dallas territory by himself for a 2-week period and then will come back to headquarters for a week of debriefing. Smith is obviously delighted.

Nelson dismisses Smith and calls in Jones. Nelson tells her that EDD is equally impressed with her. However, Jones will be required to stay for an extra day of training. Further, for the first couple of weeks, she will have a manager ride with her in her territory. Jones, rather perturbed, asks "Why?, I spoke to Dave in the hall and you are not requiring him to attend extra training, nor is a manager going to be riding with him." Nelson explains that the company has had problems in the past with customers harassing its female reps and have in fact recently lost a rep and some accounts because of "problems." Nelson says, "We want our female reps to be prepared to handle customers who may not have enlightened attitudes about female sales representatives." Jones exclaims, "It's not fair! David isn't getting this 'extra' treatment. Make him stay too. It's blatant discrimination. I've been around, and I can take care of myself!"

SCENE 2

The second scene should be your perception of what occurs after the first scene. How would you have handled the situation if you were Nelson?

CHARACTER DESCRIPTIONS

Name: Debra Joyner
Gender: F
Age: 42
Marital status: Divorced twice
Education: B.A., Villanova
Title: Trainer
Office location: Fort Worth
Reports to: Personnel Director
Employment history: With Pharmiceaux 15 years; 10 years as a sales rep
Personality: Outgoing; friendly; a good motivator
Notes: Recently divorced; likes to travel; enjoys outdoor activities; is a good teacher
Grapevine: Burn-out from sales position led to job as a trainer

Name: Bill Nelson
Gender: M
Age: 40
Marital status: Married
Education: B.A., Indiana University
Title: Trainer
Office location: Fort Worth
Reports to: Personnel Director
Employment history: With Pharmiceaux for 12 years; 8 years as a sales rep
Personality: Outgoing; energetic; good sense of humor; motivational
Notes: Works with children's charities; athletic, likes sailing, coaches Little League; loves training
Grapevine: May have suffered from sales rep burn-out leading to this job as a trainer

Name: Amanda Jones
Gender: F
Age: 26
Marital status: Single
Education: B.A., North State Tech
Title: Sales Trainee
Office location: Dallas
Reports to: Trainer
Employment history: In retail 3 years
Personality: Uptight; self-serving and demanding; self-assured
Notes: Did well in training; does not appear to be a company person yet; likes the nightlife
Grapevine: May have an attitude problem

Name: Chas Browning
Gender: M
Age: 27
Marital status: Single
Education: B.B.A., State University
Title: Sales Trainee **Office location:** Dallas
Reports to: Trainer
Employment history: Worked in father's computer sales business
Personality: "Mr. Personality"; arrogant; rude; demanding
Notes: Did well in training; not a company person yet—not a team player; enjoys the nightlife
Grapevine: Attitude/personality may be a problem

Name: David Smith
Gender: M **Age:** 23 **Marital status:** Married
Education: B.S., South Florida
Title: Sales Trainee
Office location: To be announced
Reports to: To be announced
Employment history: Fresh out of school
Personality: Level-headed; hard working; mature; aggressive; tennis player
Notes: Recently married; company team player
Grapevine: Fast-tracker

Name: Maria Gonzales
Gender: F
Age: 24
Marital status: Single
Education: B.B.A., Northwestern
Title: Sales Trainee
Office location: To be announced
Reports to: To be announced
Employment history: Fresh out of school
Personality: Aggressive; mature; good leadership qualities
Notes: Team-player; success driven; self-starter; soccer player.
Grapevine: Fast-tracker

QUESTIONS

1. What might be the purpose(s) of a wine and cheese party at the conclusion of a training program?
2. Was the company wrong in not scheduling the party on the trainees' agenda? Should EDD have given the recruits more notice?
3. Is Jones in the wrong? Why or why not? In Scenario B, is she being discriminated against?
4. List at least three alternatives Jones has regarding the party.
5. List at least three alternatives Jones has regarding the extra training and the accompanying manager. Discuss the long-term consequences of each alternative.
6. If you were management in Scenario A, how would you have handled the party differently?

NOTES

1. Ronita B. Johnson and Julie O'Mara, "Shedding New Light on Diversity Training," *Training and Development,* 46(5) (1992): 44–52.
2. Thomas W. Leigh, "Cognitive Selling Scripts and Sales Training," *Journal of Personal Selling and Sales Management,* 7 (August 1987): 39–48.
3. Adel I. El-Ansary, "Sales Force Effectiveness Research Reveals New Insights and Reward-Penalty Patterns in Sales Force Training," *Journal of Personal Selling and Sales Management,* 13(2) (Spring 1993): 83–90.
4. S. Joe Puri, "Where Industrial Sales Training Is Weak," *Industrial Marketing Management,* 22 (1993): 101–108.
5. Jack Falvey, "Take the Mystery Out of Sales Training," *Sales and Marketing Management* (March 1993): 14–15.
6. Robert C. Erffmeyer, K. Randall Russ, and Joseph F. Hair, Jr., "Needs Assessment and Evaluation in Sales-Training Programs," *Journal of Personal Selling and Sales Management,* 11(1) (Winter 1991): 17–30.
7. Melissa Campanelli, "Can Managers Coach?" *Sales and Marketing Management* (July 1994): 59–63.
8. Harry B. Bernhard and Cynthia A. Ingols, "Six Lessons for the Corporate Classroom," *Harvard Business Review,* (September–October 1988): 40–47.
9. G. Dean Kortge, "Link Sales Training and Product Life Cycles," *Industrial Marketing Management,* 22 (1993): 239–245.
10. "Learning Through Repetition," *Sales and Marketing Management* (July 1995): 42–43.
11. Geoffrey Brewer, "Seizing the Middle Ground," *Sales and Marketing Management* (June 1994): 40.
12. Betsy Wiesendanger, "The M.B.A.: Is it Relevant in Sales?" *Sales and Marketing Management* (May 1993): 58–61, 91.
13. Earl D. Honeycutt, Jr., Vince Howe, and Thomas N. Ingram, "Shortcomings of Sales Training Programs," *Industrial Marketing Management,* 22 (1993): 117–123.
14. Dartnell Corporation (1992), p. 130.
15. Adel I. El-Ansary, op. cit.
16. M. R. Louis, "Surprise and Sense Making: What Newcomers Experience in Entering Unfamiliar Organizational Settings," *Administrative Science Quarterly,* 49 (February 1980): 24–33.
17. Bristol Voss, "Office Politics: A Player's Guide," *Sales and Marketing Management* (October 1992): 47–52.
18. D. C. Feldman, "A Contingency Theory of Socialization," *Administrative Science Quarterly,* 21 (September 1976): 433–450. See also Alan J. Dubinsky, Roy D. Howell, Thomas N. Ingram, and Danny N. Bellenger, "Salesforce Socialization," *Journal of Marketing,* 50 (October 1986): 192–207.
19. "Are Your Salespeople Just Putting Around?" *Sales and Marketing Management* (June 1994): 8.
20. Thomas W. Leigh, "Cognitive Selling Scripts and Sales Training," *Journal of Personal Selling and Sales Management,* 7 (August 1987): 39–48.
21. Andy Cohen, "Basic Training," *Sales and Marketing Management* (May 1994): 11.
22. Andy Cohen, "Practice Makes Profits," *Sales and Marketing Management* (July 1995): 24–25.
23. Ronald H. King and Martha B. Booze, "Sales Training and Impression Management," *Journal of Personal Selling and Sales Management* (August 1986): 51–60.

24. Bristol Voss, "What's the Big Idea?" *Sales and Marketing Management* (July 1991): 36–40.

25. David Strutton and James R. Lumpkin, "The Relationship Between Optimism and Coping Styles of Salespeople," *Journal of Personal Selling and Sales Management,* 13(2) (Spring 1993): 71–82. See also John F. Tanner, Jr., Mark G. Dunn, and Lawrence B. Chonko, "Vertical Exchange and Salesperson Stress," *Journal of Personal Selling and Sales Management,* 13(2) (Spring 1993): 27–36; Jerry R. Goolsby, "A Theory of Role Stress in Boundary Spanning Positions of Marketing Organizations," *Journal of the Academy of Marketing Sciences,* 20(2) (Spring 1992): 155–165; Alan J. Dubinsky, Ronald E. Michaels, Masaaki Kotabe, Chae Un Lim and Hee-Cheol Moon, "Influence of Role Stress on Industrial Salespeople's Work Outcome in the United States, Japan, and Korea," *Journal of International Business Studies,* 23(1) (Spring 1992): 77–90; and Sherry E. Sullivan and Rabi S. Bhagat, "Organizational Stress, Job Satisfaction, and Job Performance: Where Do We Go From Here?" *Journal of Management,* 18(2) (June 1992): 353–375.

26. "Is Diversity Training Worth Maintaining?" *Business and Society Review,* 89 (Spring 1994): 47–49.

27. E. K. Miller, "Diversity and Its Management: Training Managers for Cultural Competence Within the Organization," *Management Quarterly,* 35(2) (Summer 1994): 17–23. See also H. B. Karp, "Choices in Diversity Training," *Training,* 31(8) (August 1994): 73–74; Shari Caudron, "Diversity Ignites Effective Work Teams," *Personnel Journal,* 73(9) (September 1994): 54–63; Clifford Clark, "Making Diversity More Manageable," *Training and Development,* 48(9) (September 1994): 53–59; and Linda Mack Ross, "How to Have an Effective Diversity Effort," *Training and Development,* 48(6) (June 1994): 13–17.

28. Ann Tagawa, "On Trade and Cultures," *Trade and Culture* (November–December 1994): 6. See also Charles M. Vance and Eduardo S. Paderon, "An Ethical Argument for Host Country Workforce Training and Development in the Expatriate Management Assignment," *Journal of Business Ethics,* 12 (1993): 635–641.

29. Charles T. Clark, "Is Your Company Ready for Global Marketing?" *Sales and Marketing Management* (September 1994): 42. See also Cyndee Miller, "Going Overseas Requires Marketers to Learn More Than a New Language," *Marketing News,* (March 28, 1994): 8–9; and Robert C. Erffmeyer, Jamal A. Al-Khatib, Mohammed I. Al-Habib, and Joseph F. Hair, Jr., "Sales Training Practices: A Cross-National Comparison," *International Marketing Review,* 10(1) (1993): 45–59.

30. Bristol Voss, "John Cleese Gets Serious About Training," *Sales and Marketing Management* (March 1991): 68–72.

31. William C. Moncrief, "The Use of Role Playing Exercises," *Marketing Education Review* (Summer 1991): 46–55. See also William C. Moncrief and Shannon H. Shipp, "Making Role Plays More Realistic," *Marketing Education Review* (Spring 1994): 45–50; and Larry J. B. Robinson, "Role Playing as a Sales Training Tool," *Harvard Business Review* (May–June 1987): 34–35.

32. A. J. Faria and John R. Dickinson, "Simulation Gaming for Sales Management Training," *Journal of Management Development,* 13(1) (1994): 47–59.

33. Arlyn R. Rubash, Rawlie R. Sullivan, and Paul H. Herzog, "The Use of an 'Expert' to Train Salespeople," *Journal of Personal Selling and Sales Management,* 7 (August 1987): 49–55.

34. William Keenan, Jr., "Simulating Sales Success," *Sales and Marketing Management* (April 1994): 33.

35. Karin Ireland, "The Ethics Game," *Personnel Journal,* 70(3) (March 1991): 72–75.

36. Melissa Campanelli, "Board Meeting," *Sales and Marketing Management* (January 1995): 32.

37. Warren S. Martin and Ben H. Collins, "Interactive Video Technology in Sales Training: A Case Study," *Journal of Personal Selling and Sales Management,* 11(3) (Summer 1991): 61–66.

38. Randall Russ, Joseph F. Hair, Robert C. Erffmeyer, and Debbie Easterling, "Usage and Perceived Effectiveness of High-Tech Approaches to Sales Training," *Journal of Personal Selling and Sales Management* (Spring 1989): 46–54. See also Rex Spiller and Thomas J. Housel, "SMR Forum: Video Conferencing—A New Training Tool," *Sloan Management Review* (Fall 1985): 57–62.

39. Robert L. Lindstrom, "Training Hits the Road," *Sales and Marketing Management* (June 1995, Part II): 10–14.

40. Kerry J. Rottenberger, "Sales Training Enters the Space Age," *Sales and Marketing Management* (October 1990): 46–50.

41. Earl D. Honeycutt, Jr., Tom McCarty, and Vince Howe, "Sales Technology Applications: Self-Paced Video Enhanced Training: A Case Study," *Journal of Personal Selling and Sales Management,* 13(1) (Winter 1993): 73–79.

42. Peter F. Kaminski and Gary L. Clark, "The Readability of Sales Training Manuals," *Industrial Marketing Management,* 16 (1987): 179–184.

43. William Keenan, Jr., "Let Customers Train Your Salespeople," *Sales and Marketing Management* (October 1994): 41–42.

44. Earl D. Honeycutt, Jr., John B. Ford, and John F. Tanner, Jr., "Who Trains Salespeople?" *Industrial Marketing Management,* 23 (1994): 65–70.

45. Melissa Campanella, (1994), op. cit.

46. James L. Strutton, "Why Training Usually Fails; What Can Be Done About It," *Manage,* 45(3) (January 1994): 14–15. See also William Keenan, Jr., "Using Sales Managers as Trainers," *Sales and Marketing Management* (September 1994): 39–40.

47. Lawrence B. Chonko, John F. Tanner, Jr., and William A. Weeks, "Sales Training: Status and Needs," *Journal of Personal Selling and Sales Management,* 13(4) (Fall 1993): 81–86.

48. "Average Cost of Sales Training Per Salesperson," *Sales and Marketing Management* (February 1990): 23.

49. Mauicio Lorence, "Assignment USA: The Japanese Solution," *Sales and Marketing Management* (October 1992): 60–66.

12

MOTIVATING THE SALESFORCE

Motivation will almost always beat mere talent.
NORMAN R. AUGUSTINE, PRESIDENT AND CEO, MARTIN MARIETTA CORPORATION

If you aren't fired with enthusiasm, you will be fired with enthusiasm.
VINCE LOMBARDI, COACH, GREEN BAY PACKERS

LEARNING OBJECTIVES

After reading this chapter, you should be able to answer the following questions:

- What is motivation, and what is its relevance in sales management?
- What job-related factors affect motivation?
- How can motivation change as a salesperson goes through different career stages?
- What is career plateauing, and how can a manager control it?
- What are some basic content theories of motivation?

Micro-Switch, a subsidiary of Honeywell, Inc., specializing in door-opener sensors, was in big trouble. According to its CEO, Ray Alvarez, Micro-Switch was getting thoroughly beaten by international competitors, and sales were dropping rapidly. An increase in salesforce quotas was not going to solve the problem. Instead, Alvarez decided to go after customer loyalty by providing better quality and service than his competitors. To obtain that level of service, Alvarez had to motivate *everyone* in the company, not just the salesforce. He had to get "nonsales" personnel such as machine operators, sales service support, and truckers to understand the importance of the sales function. Alvarez decided that an incentive program similar to ones used with the salesforce would be a great motivator for nonsales personnel. Money, prizes, and some rather unusual games were used to motivate. For example, Micro-Switch toolmakers were involved in a mock battle on the banks of a river. As the police arrived expecting to break up a riot, Alvarez explained that the workers were throwing dummies into the river with the names of their competitors on them. These unusual motivation techniques designed to increase customer service and quality have had some extraordinary results. Micro-Switch is now the market leader in its industry, earning millions more than it did just a few years ago.[1]

Motivation is a word that is used frequently in day-to-day conversation. People use it without any real feeling for the definition, but everyone understands what is meant when someone is said to be "motivated." Anyone who has played organized

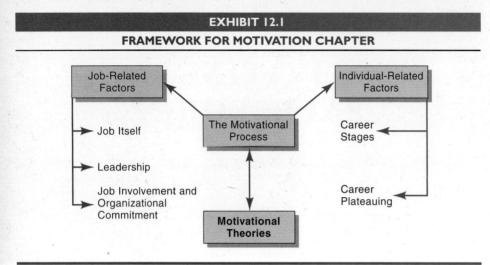

EXHIBIT 12.1

FRAMEWORK FOR MOTIVATION CHAPTER

athletics has probably had a coach who gave a motivational speech that inspired the team to a big victory. Zig Ziglar, a popular and well-known speaker, has made a successful career out of motivating people to better perform their jobs. What is motivation? What causes it? How can sales managers use motivational techniques to help the salesforce achieve maximum productivity?

This chapter will examine the concept of motivation. The framework for the presentation of the chapter is shown in Exhibit 12.1, which is based on four components: the motivational process, job-related factors of motivation, individual-related factors of motivation, and motivational theories. The chapter begins with a definition of *motivation* and a model of the motivational process. Next, job-related factors that affect the motivational process are discussed. Job involvement and organizational commitment are included in that discussion. Then individual-related factors that affect the motivational process, including the career stages of the sales individual, and the concept of career plateauing are explored. A discussion about a variety of motivational theories proposed by leading scholars will end the chapter.

WHAT IS MOTIVATION?

Motivation is the force within us that directs our behavior. Motivation is unique to every individual. In other words, a sales manager may have three seemingly similar salespeople who are motivated by different needs. Good sales managers examine each individual's needs and use those needs as the motivation for the salesperson to expend the appropriate effort on the activities required.

Motivation has three dimensions: intensity, persistence, and direction.[2] **Intensity** is the magnitude of mental and physical effort put forth by an individual toward an activity or goal. The more intense the inner drive, the more likely individuals will be to direct their effort. **Persistence** is the extension of effort *over time*. Individuals who have a high level of intensity and the persistence to expend the needed effort over some time period are typically said to be highly motivated. The third dimension is **direction,** which implies that the individual can and will choose where his or her efforts will be spent. Salespeople who are highly competitive and have a need to be the best will have a high level of intensity that will persist over time. They will attempt to determine what activities are required to reach that goal and direct their behavior accordingly. It becomes the responsibility of the sales manager to help channel the salespeople's activities to ensure the correct direction and level of work.

Traditionally, managers have attempted to persuade their salesforce to work harder using a variety of motivational techniques; that is, managers have attempted to increase the intensity or persistence of the salespeople's motivation. Although working harder is an admirable accomplishment, recent research has shown that working smarter may be more important.[3] **Working smarter** can be loosely defined as altering and improving the direction of effort. For instance, a salesperson can work smarter by being better prepared and matching the needs of the customer with the right sales presentation and service. Time spent working, in itself, should not be the indicator of high performance. The level of efficiency in the work—that is, working smarter—is more highly correlated to high performance.

Motivation can also be intrinsic or extrinsic. **Intrinsic motivation** means individuals are motivated internally by the desire to please themselves or merely by the satisfaction of performing the job. **Extrinsic motivation,** on the other hand, means that someone else must provide the motivation through some method such as pay, promotion, or recognition.

Individuals are both intrinsically and extrinsically motivated. For example, a salesperson may be heavily motivated by more and more money with very little need for internal satisfaction (more typical of commission-compensated salespeople). It is the money or extrinsic satisfaction that drives this salesperson. Another salesperson may have a strong requirement that the job be one that will provide internal satisfaction. This salesperson is more concerned about feeling content with the knowledge that he or she has done a great job. However, the same intrinsically motivated salesperson may also be motivated extrinsically with the promise of more pay for that excellent performance.

MODEL OF THE MOTIVATIONAL PROCESS

Exhibit 12.2 illustrates the motivational process. The process consists of a series of six steps:

1. Recognize need deficiency
2. Search for ways to satisfy needs
3. Establish goal-directed behavior
4. Perform
5. Provide rewards and punishments
6. Reassess needs

Although salespeople may spend different amounts of time in each step, everyone eventually passes through all six. Once through all the steps, an individual's motivation drive can change rapidly, resulting in a new start-up for the six steps. When multiple motivation processes occur at once the individual must prioritize the moti-

EXHIBIT 12.2

A BASIC MODEL OF THE MOTIVATIONAL PROCESS

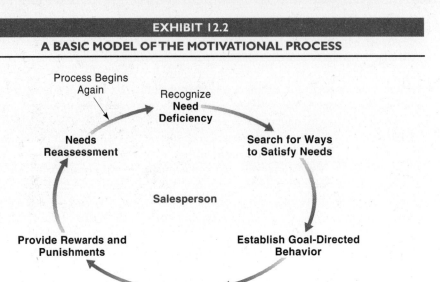

vational needs. To illustrate the motivational process let's look at Sally, a typical sales representative, as she proceeds through the model of the motivational process.

Sally is tired of driving her 6-year-old car. It needs maintenance on a regular basis, but right now Sally cannot afford a new car. She figures that she would need to save another $5,000 to provide a substantial downpayment to buy a new car and maintain a low monthly payment. Sally has now recognized *a need deficiency:* $5,000.

Sally begins *searching for ways* to raise or save the $5,000. She hears that the company has announced a bonus system for bringing in new accounts. She talks to her sales manager about the details of the bonus and decides that this is her method to raise the money and thus solve her need deficiency.

In the *goal-directed stage,* Sally decides that she is going to have to make two more calls a day in order to meet the bonus criteria. She also decides that she will do her paperwork at night rather than early in the morning. This will allow her to begin making calls a little sooner. At this point Sally is highly motivated to bring in new accounts. She is intense and persistent, and has set a direction to fulfill her needs.

After 2 months Sally has had some success in landing new accounts but she has ignored some of her regular customers, and some of the sales relationships have suffered. She has also missed some sales meetings, which has displeased her manager. Outside of work, Sally has had less time for her fiancee and tempers have flared. Her overall *performance* at work has suffered somewhat even though she has been successful at bringing in some new accounts.

The results leading to *rewards* are mixed. Sally has earned a reward consisting of some extra bonus money, but her personal relationship has suffered, as has her performance in other dimensions of the job. Her motivation to continue the extra work has lessened.

At this point Sally begins to *reassess* the need that began this motivation process. She decides that the extra work and costs are not worth the extra money she's made. Her car can last another year or two. She now has a new need deficiency—repairing the damaged relationships with her existing customers, manager, and fiancee—and the motivation circle begins again.

JOB-RELATED FACTORS

The factors that most directly affect a salesperson's motivation are job related and individually related. Job-related factors include the job itself, leadership, job involvement and organizational commitment.

The Job Itself

A key element in motivating a salesperson to work is the job itself. Management must understand how the nature of the job and the specific job activities affect the behavior of the salesperson in any sales organization. Ideally, management needs to know what part of the sales job inspires individual salespeople to dispense higher levels of smart work and allow salespeople to feel good about themselves. One method to stimulate motivation is **job enrichment,** which can best be defined as an extension of a job's depth such that the salesperson's discretion or control over the job is increased. Job enrichment may mean more responsibility in the management of the territory and greater control over day-to-day activities.

There are a number of dimensions about the job that can influence or motivate the sales individual.[4] Job motivation can be partially determined by five key ingredients: skill variety, task identity, task significance, job autonomy, and job feedback. The level of existence of each dimension and the relationships among the dimensions will determine the psychological state of the salesperson and lead to a level of motivation. Each dimension and its effect on motivation are examined in the following paragraphs.

Skill Variety.   **Skill variety** is the degree to which a job requires a variety of different activities to successfully perform the job. A sales job that requires a number of different skills is typically perceived as more meaningful than one with fewer needed skills. For example, for most sales jobs salespeople need communication, organization, problem-solving, and intellectual skills in order to be successful. The salespeople who have to employ these diverse skills may be more motivated than order takers who do not require a variety of skills.

Task Identity.   The second core dimension, **task identity,** assumes completion of the whole job. In other words, the job allows the individual to see the task or assignment begin and end. Most sales jobs are high in task identity because salespeople are responsible for prospecting the account, making the presentation, and closing the account. The higher the task identity of the job, the more highly motivated individuals may be.

Task Significance.   **Task significance** is the degree to which the job has a significant impact on the lives of others. Salespeople who feel that the job they are performing significantly affects others perceive the job as meaningful, so the work mo-

---

BOX 12.1

ARE YOU AN EFFECTIVE MOTIVATOR?

Keeping your salesforce motivated is vital to keeping them selling. How effectively do you motivate your salespeople? Answer the following questions and you be the judge.

1. What are the three most effective techniques you use for motivating your entire salesforce?
2. Do you know what motivates each person who reports to you?
3. Do you know what role compensation plays in the motivation of each salesperson?
4. Do you know what role recognition plays in the motivation of each salesperson?
5. Do you know what role "opportunity for growth" plays in the motivation of each salesperson?
6. Have you customized a motivational program for each person who reports to you?
7. What have you done in the past week with the deliberate intention of motivating a salesperson?
8. Did you praise someone today?
9. Do you show your commitment to developing each salesperson by actively (at least once a month) coaching them on skills and techniques?
10. When a salesperson seems to be feeling stressed, do you ask questions and spend time listening to the salesperson's concerns?
11. Do you ask your reps, "What can I do personally to help your sales efforts?"
12. Do you review their monthly performance with them in a timely manner?
13. Have you done anything recently to "demotivate" your salespeople? For example: failed to give recognition; embarrassed a salesperson in front of peers or clients; taken over a sales call?
14. Do you treat your salespeople with respect?
15. Do you show your salespeople trust?

SOURCE: Ginger Trumfio, "Are You an Effective Motivator?" *Sales and Marketing Management* (May 1994): 136.

---

tivation is enhanced. Salespeople may perceive their job as much more meaningful because of task significance than would employees performing a repetitive task. Workers who perform repetitive tasks may find it difficult to see a link between the task and any impact on the firm's customers. For example, an assembly-line worker who performs the same duty all day long may perceive his or her task significance as low (just a cog in the assembly procedure), whereas a salesperson for the same company may see the results of his or her independent work (sales) as greatly benefiting the company.

Job Autonomy. **Job autonomy** is the degree to which a job provides substantial freedom, independence, and discretion in meeting work responsibilities. The assembly-line job is very low in job autonomy with little independence or discretion. However, most sales positions, by their nature, are very high in job autonomy. Salespeople typically have a great deal of discretion in making decisions about how to serve their customers. In a geographically-based sales organization, for example, each individual territory is like a small profit center with the salesperson making most of the daily decisions about the account, service, scheduling, and numerous others aspects.

Job Feedback. The last core job dimension is **job feedback,** the degree to which an individual receives direct and clear information about the effectiveness and level of performance of the job. In a commission sales plan salespeople automatically receive feedback upon closing each sale when they receive the commission paycheck. In this case, the *job* rather than an individual such as a sales manager, has provided them with feedback.

In summary, there is a direct correlation between worker motivation and higher levels of the five core job dimensions. For the most part, sales jobs contain high levels of each of the core dimensions. Look at the questions in Box 12.1 to see how motivative effectiveness can be gauged.

Leadership

The job itself can motivate a person intrinsically. Leadership, however, plays a role in the extrinsic motivation of employment.[5] Recall from Chapter 6 that leadership involves the use of influence with other people through communication processes to obtain specific goals and objectives. Leadership behavior can be a great motivator if salespeople perceive their leader/manager as effective in obtaining for them desired rewards from the organization such as pay, recognition, and promotion. For a leader to be effective, subordinates need to trust the leader and feel that the leader will support the subordinates when needed.

Good leaders allow their salespeople some participation regarding choice and delivery of rewards. For example, suppose a salesperson is told by her manager that if she closes the Hanger account she will make the prestigious Top Ten Club and qualify for a trip to Hawaii. The salesperson really likes her job and is already intrinsically motivated, but she really wants to be a member of the Top Ten Club. In fact, she wants the award even more than the trip to Hawaii. Knowing this, her manager gives her a motivational boost by "dangling the ultimate prize (Top Ten Club) in front of her." The salesperson's internal competitiveness and desire to be one of the best is a strong intrinsic motivator in itself. By using good leadership skills, her manager provides additional motivation through extrinsic means.

Recent changes in sales have brought about some interesting motivational challenges for salesforce leaders. Team building, for one, has become a major salesforce strategy. In team building the leader becomes less of a power wielder and more of a team motivator.[6] Some of the motivational techniques associated with team building are a bit unusual, but they are designed to build team comraderie by group participation. Bongrain North America had its salesforce walk on hot coals. Scott Magnacca, the fire-walking consultant, says, "A few quick steps over 1,200 degree coals will result in quantum leaps in sales performance . . . cold calling is a piece of cake after this."[7] Other companies, including Digital Equipment Corporation and Metropolitan Life, are also exploring mind-over-matter exercises.

The virtual office has also created some motivational challenges for managers. One unnamed salesperson complained that the virtual office causes "a loss of the personal touch. Companies don't seem to care much anymore."[8] There is a lot of truth in what this salesperson said. Managers must find a way to reach out and motivate the salesperson who is located away from the home office. Mary Boone, vice-president of Boone Consulting, suggests that computers can be excellent motivational tools: "Electronic mail can really help a manager motivate staffers . . . It can tell them what a good job they have done or [be] a way to communicate to someone that they need to push harder."[9] Today the art of motivating a salesforce includes the ability to do so through technology.

In summary, job characteristics are more instrumental in inducing intrinsic motivation, whereas the style and methods of leadership (see Box 12.2) lead more to subordinate extrinsic motivation. The combination of intrinsic job satisfaction and extrinsic rewards can equate to a highly motivated salesforce.

Job Organizational and Involvement Commitment

Job involvement and organizational commitment is the third component in the job-related aspects of the motivational process model.

Job involvement is defined as the extent to which employees identify psychologically with their particular job. Job involvement can vary over time and can be a function of factors that can be at least partially addressed by management, such as the career plateau syndrome (discussed later in this chapter).

Organizational commitment can be defined as an employee's positive psychological identification with the organization and its goals.[10] High levels of organizational commitment by an employee implies a strong desire by that employee to remain with the company and a strong willingness to exert significant effort toward organizational goals.[11] A salesperson's motivation can partially be determined by examining his or her commitment to the sales job or to the organization itself. Employees with high levels of organizational commitment are typically motivated to go beyond traditional expectations because they are performing partially from a loyalty to the organization.

By using job involvement and organizational commitment as axis in the model shown in Exhibit 12.3, we can classify four types of sales employees, each with different motivational drives.[12] The four types are (1) institutional stars, (2) corporate citizens, (3) lone wolves, and (4) apathetics. Each type of individual is motivated by different needs based on commitment to the job or to the organization.

Institutional Stars. **Institutional stars** have high levels of both job involvement and organizational commitment and are the sales employees of choice. Institutional stars generally like their job and have a high intrinsic motivation based on loyalty to the company. These salespeople do not require a lot of motivation or management. They identify with the organization and consider their work important. These sales individuals also tend to be the high producers for the organization.

Corporate Citizens. **Corporate citizens** place little importance on the job itself. The importance of the job is linked with the association it affords the salesperson with the organization. Corporate citizens may be very loyal, but they are not highly motivated to perform their job. In all likelihood this person is mismatched as a salesperson and should be performing some other task within the organization. The corporate citizen is performing the job at adequate levels but will never be a star because the motivation is lacking in the job itself. This salesperson needs to be on salary and in an in-house sales job that requires a variety of duties that can represent the company. The salesperson's on-the-job interactions may center on affiliating with others within the company, which is a problem if the salesperson is frequently out of the office.

BOX 12.2

LOW-COST WAYS TO MOTIVATE

- A pat on the back.
- A smile.
- A simple, sincere thank you.
- A personal letter to the employee, with copies sent to your immediate supervisor and to the employee's supervisor.
- Public recognition in front of peers.
- Public recognition in front of one's boss.
- A letter of praise from a customer or vendor shared directly with the employee who delivered the service.
- A letter from a customer or vendor praising an employee, posted on the company bulletin board.
- Listening to an employee who has an idea for improving efficiency and then acting affirmatively on that suggestion.
- Arranging employee discounts from your vendors or customers.
- Allowing the employee to work on an especially exciting project that he or she would not usually work on.
- Asking employees what nonmonetary rewards they would like to have and, if possible, providing them.
- Issuing a "You Were Mentioned" certificate to employees whenever you hear something nice about them, whether from a customer, co-worker, or superior.
- Electing a high-achieving employee to a quality circle or to a companywide task force.
- Bringing in coffee and donuts after a unitwide effort.
- Providing free lunch for employees caught in the act of victory by an appointed group of companywide "catchers."
- Rotating the "company flag" or other symbol of excellence from deserving unit to deserving unit on a quarterly basis.
- Creating a small slush fund. Mete it out to managers of deserving units to do something nice for the units or for employees of particular merit.

SOURCE: Sam Deep and Lyle Sussman, *Smart Moves* (Reading, Mass.: Addison-Wesley, 1990).

Lone Wolves.   Individuals who live for the job but could care less about the organization are **lone wolves,** sometimes known as mavericks. If the organization attempts to ask too much of the lone wolf, he or she will simply quit and sell for another company. Lone wolves can be a managerial nightmare but they can produce substantial levels of sales. The motivation is based on competition, closing a sale, and collecting the resulting paycheck (typically a commission sales job). The lone wolf is monetarily driven and typically will have a high ego.

What can be done with the lone wolf/maverick employee who is a top seller but who refuses to follow the same organizational rules as everyone else? Consider the following scenario. Robert Stichman, vice-president of sales for Wyo-Ben, tells about a salesperson who was a top producer but was generally disliked by his peers. No one would work with him. He followed his own rules and was rude and crass with his peers. Stichman had several conversations with the salesperson about his work habits. The maverick salesperson would remind Stichman of the level of sales that he brought into the company. What should Stichman do with the lone wolf?

There are two schools of thought on how to handle the lone wolf. One is that an organization can afford one per district (see Box 12.3), especially because the maverick may lead the district in sales. Can managers afford to discipline and rid themselves of their top sellers? Many organizations say "no" and will tolerate the lone wolf as long as he or she is productive. Mavericks will be treated differently and probably will not follow the same rules as everyone else. Most employees understand the problems associated with this type of salesperson and tolerate the "favoritism." Is there a double standard? "Absolutely," says Richard Fruit, vice-president of sales for Diversity Water Technologies. "Talented salespeople are rare, so I'm willing to spend a lot more of my time making sure they're happy."[13]

The second line of thought on the maverick is that an organization cannot afford him or her regardless of the level of sales. Company policies are designed for reasons, and they must be followed. An organizational philosophy and commitment must be maintained. People who refuse to be a team member are not needed. Typically, this line of thought comes from large, *Fortune* 500–type organizations that have a strong professional salesforce. A smaller company might be more inclined to accept the maverick because of his or her high level of sales.

So what did Robert Stichman of Wyo-Ben do with his maverick? Stichman's solution was to terminate a top sales performer. He was damaging to the sales team and ultimately not worth the effort.[14]

Apathetics.   The final sales employee classification, **apathetic**, represents failure on the part of management, either in the recruiting process, during training, or in motivation. Apathetics simply do not care about the job or the organization and are

---

EXHIBIT 12.3

JOB INVOLVEMENT/ORGANIZATIONAL COMMITMENT SALESPERSON TYPOLOGY

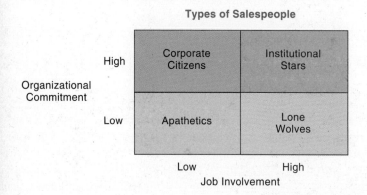

Types of Salespeople

	Low Job Involvement	High Job Involvement
High Organizational Commitment	Corporate Citizens	Institutional Stars
Low Organizational Commitment	Apathetics	Lone Wolves

SOURCE: Gary L. Blau and Kimberly B. Boal, "Conceptualizing How Job Involvement and Organizational Commitment Affect Turnover and Absenteeism," *Academy of Management Review,* 12(2) (1987): 288–300. From Thomas N. Ingram, Keun S. Lee, and George H. Lucas, Jr., "Commitment and Involvement: Assessing a Salesforce Typology," *Journal of the Academy of Marketing Science,* 19(3) (Summer 1991): 187–197.

destined to be a turnover statistic. Apathetics will contribute very little and can be a morale problem if not controlled. Their motivation level is virtually nonexistent because they are not happy and probably not sure what they should be doing.

INDIVIDUAL-RELATED FACTORS OF MOTIVATION

Although there are many aspects of the individual that may affect the level of motivation—such as aptitude, skills, job satisfaction, and personality—this section concentrates on two specific individual-related components: career stage and career plateau. Both can have substantial effects on the overall motivation of the salesperson and sales manager.

Basic marketing classes teach that products evolve through a basic product life cycle consisting of introduction, growth, maturation, and decline. As you no doubt recall, each of these product stages are accompanied by different marketing strategies. A similar process occurs with people in career stages. Several studies have indicated that salespeople go through a "career" life cycle that also consists of four stages: exploration, establishment, maintenance, and disengagement.[15] As salespeople evolve through the stages they evoke different motivations to satisfy different career needs.

One real problem for every organization comes when a salesperson begins moving into the last stage of the career life cycle and yet still has years or decades of productivity left. At this point, these salespeople may remain employed but will in all likelihood not receive increased responsibility.[16] One recent study indicates that 17.5 percent of the aggregate salesforce in the United States has reached a plateau, with the largest number being in the 40–49 age category.[17] Put another way, almost one in five salespeople have seen their careers stall. The next sections more closely examine the concepts of career stages and career plateauing.

Career Stages

Are people motivated by different rewards at different stages of their career? Do salespeople have different career and personal concerns based on career stage? The basic answer to both these questions is yes. A salesperson may be highly motivated throughout his or her career, but the desired rewards may be very different. Motivations based on career and personal concerns can differ.

There are four career stages: exploration, establishment, maintenance, and disengagement. Exhibit 12.4 summarizes the characteristics of each stage.

Exploration.   The **exploration stage** typically occurs when a salesperson is in his or her early twenties and initiates a new career. The individual is very concerned about securing the "best possible job" and beginning on the right note. Enthusiasm is high, but there is also a high degree of uncertainty about the future. Most new salespeople are not absolutely confident that they are heading in the appropriate direction. The exploration stage can last for several years and several jobs until an individual feels confident that he or she is indeed heading in the right career direction, or the stage can last a couple of years or less if an individual is fortunate enough to find the "perfect" job immediately upon graduation from college. In Europe and other parts of the world the exploration stage may be very brief because the individual has been trained and groomed since high school to move into a specific career path.

The exploration stage is about more than job direction. Once the job has been chosen, the new recruit must learn the necessary skills to perform adequately and become a contributing member of the organization. The first two years are a critical testing ground for the new salesperson and will set the tone for his or her advancement throughout the career. Just as the first 30 seconds are vital in a sales presentation or interview, so too the exploration stage is vital for setting career direction. It does not take management long to judge a salesperson's long-term abilities. On the other hand, everyone experiences some level of uncertainty in a new job. It can take 6 months or longer before people become completely comfortable with the job. With time and experience comes the ability to perform all dimensions of the new job and career.[18]

What will motivate you in the first days of your new job? Acceptance, self-development, early success, and positive recognition are typical motivators. Good managers who provide positive feedback, sufficient on-the-job training, and encouragement can go a long way helping new recruits ease into and survive the exploration stage.

Establishment.   When an individual enters the establishment stage depends to a great extent on how long it took the individual to progress through the exploration stage. Many people spend several years searching through a number of industries or different professions before trying a sales career. Others select a sales career early and thus move into the establishment stage in their mid-twenties. Regardless, the **establishment stage,** which begins as the exploration stage ends, is the time when the salesperson attempts to successfully build a career in a particular industry.

Motivation differs for people in this stage. Some people have the need to be the best and succeed rapidly, which may mean a promotion or recognition as part of the elite. This type of motivation requires much more effort than a "normal" 40-hour week. However, almost everyone expects to move up in the company or be highly financially rewarded. If these rewards are slow in arriving, the salesperson may leave the company for a competitor who promises the desired rewards. This job change does not mean a change in career and thus a new exploration stage; rather, it is a continuation of the establishment stage in which the career advances by accepting new opportunities.

In the establishment stage, the salesperson is typically working with a high level of autonomy because he or she does not need to be as closely supervised as during the exploration stage. Traditional advancement in this stage is becoming much more competitive as middle management is becoming more restricted. In addition, the stress and demands may now increase because salespeople in the establishment stage may be balancing a career and family needs as they buy new homes and expand their family with children.

The establishment stage for many is a challenging and rewarding stage because career goals remain a strong motivator and appear to be within reach. The challenges are continual but competition itself can be a strong motivator. Performance levels may be at their peak during this stage because the salesperson is now using skills acquired in the exploration stage, and is using them to produce high-quality results.

The challenge for management is to broaden the definition of needed rewards that is currently motivating the salesperson. If promotions into a sales manager position are not likely because of decreasing numbers of managerial positions and increasing competition for those positions, then management must provide substitutes. The reward expectations of the salesforce must be channeled into new directions.

Maintenance.   As salespeople approaches the late thirties or early forties they begin to reflect on their careers and lives. Many of their self-set goals may have not been met and a certain disappointment in their life status may arise. At this point the salesperson must choose between maintaining his or her current career path and making a career or life change. Many people decide to return to school to finish a degree or acquire an advanced degree such as an M.B.A. and then attempt to build on their career. Others attempt a complete career change, possibly doing something they had always dreamed of but were afraid to try. For those who continue in the same job, their motivation becomes concerned with retaining their present status, job, and performance levels.

If a redirection of career does not occur, the salespeople in the **maintenance stage** will be the foundation of the organization. Their experience is invaluable for the organization, and as a group they tend to produce the majority of the sales volume. Their motivation levels are probably changing with the realization that they are not going to move into management or possibly other staffing positions. Recognition and financial rewards become the dominant motivator, especially as their children approach college age. A salesperson who has been with the same company for many years may develop a loyalty that will allow that person to take on some additional responsibilities such as becoming a mentor for younger salespeople.

The maintenance stage of a salesperson who is content with his or her career can last up to three decades. During this time the salesperson settles into a routine and becomes a valued asset for the company. If the self-assessment of the salesperson's career and life to this point is negative, then the individual will either leave the organization or need some close supervision and counseling.

Disengagement.   At some point in their careers individuals begin to think about and plan for their retirement.[19] During the **disengagement stage**, salespeople may give greater priority to outside issues and begin withdrawing from the daily job. They may begin spending as much time on the golf course or in some other nonjob activity as they do selling. They begin to look forward to retirement. Personal time becomes much more important than at any other time in their careers. Performance during this stage is usually "acceptable," but extra time is being spent elsewhere. Much of the performance is owing to relationships with long-term customers that continue to yield sales despite a reduction in attention by the salesperson. As such, disengaging salespeople do not typically seek higher order rewards such as "managerial pats on the back," promotions, and so on. The lure of being number one on the sales chart may no longer be there. Many of these salespeople feel they no longer have to prove themselves.

EXHIBIT 12.4

CHARACTERISTICS OF DIFFERENT STAGES IN A SALESPERSON'S CAREER

	Exploration	Establishment	Maintenance	Disengagement
Career Concerns	Finding an appropriate occupational field	Successfully establishing a career in a certain occupation	Holding on to what has been achieved; reassessing career, with possible redirection	Completing one's career
Developmental Tasks	Learning the skills required to do the job well; becoming a contributing member of an organization	Using skills to produce results; adjusting to working with greater autonomy; developing creativity and innovativeness	Developing broader view of work and the organization; maintaining a high performance level	Establishing a stronger self-identity outside of work; maintaining an acceptable performance level
Personal Challenges	Establishing a good initial professional self-concept	Producing superior results on the job in order to be promoted; balancing the conflicting demands of career and family	Maintaining motivation though possible rewards have changed; facing concerns about aging and disappointment over what one has accomplished; maintaining motivation and productivity	Accepting career accomplishments; adjusting self-image
Psychosocial Needs	Support; peer acceptance; challenging position	Achievement; esteem; autonomy; competition	Reduced competitiveness; security; helping younger colleagues	Detachment from organization and organizational life

SOURCE: Adapted from William L. Cron, "Industrial Salesperson Development: A Career Stages Perspective," *Journal of Marketing* (Fall 1984): 40; and William L. Cron, Alan J. Dubinsky, and Ronald E. Michaels, "The Influence of Career Stages on Components of Salesperson Motivation," *Journal of Marketing* (January 1988): 79–92.

How does management motivate the disengaging salesperson? The challenging tough sell that motivates some younger salespeople probably ceases to be a strong motivator for older salespeople. They have been selling for years, overcoming all types of obstacles, so the sale itself may no longer be motivating. However, one theory states that the need for esteem never ceases, whether it comes from within the individual or as a form of positive feedback from peers and management. Management's task, then, is to create a form of esteem that cannot be acquired by the average salesperson. The goal is to create a group of salespeople who are considered the elite with appropriate recognition and visibility.[20]

A second premise is that at some point money ceases to motivate older sales reps. Recent evidence contradicts this premise. Many older salespeople are as motivated, or more motivated, by money than at any other point in their careers. Part of the motivation is an attempt to have enough money at retirement to be financially comfortable. The other aspect is that even if they are currently financially comfortable, money is still dominant motivator, a score-card of the success of their lives.

What happens when employees in their late forties or early fifties (i.e., still several years away from retirement) begin showing signs of disengaging and slowing down? Security can become a dominant motivator, so at times the threat of termination can motivate these salespeople back into reality. Negative motivation is not the ideal way of managing salespeople; at times, however, it may be necessary, particularly for the early disengager.

Career Plateauing

Career plateauing occurs when the job ceases to offer any opportunity for advancement or growth. Many people feel that a career plateaus when an individual is not receiving promotions up the managerial ladder. However, this is not necessarily true. If a salesperson continues to receive greater responsibility such as a larger territory, a new job title, or increasing management trust, the person is still growing on the job.

How, then, does a salesperson become plateaued? Plateauing occurs through one of three primary methods. First, the employee's performance is deficient; therefore, no added responsibilities or promotions are offered. Second, there are no further opportunities available in the organization. Third, the salesperson has a personal preference or some type of restraint that keeps him or her from accepting added responsibility. Exhibit 12.5 breaks the three categories into other subsets of reasons for plateauing.

Given that we know what causes career plateauing, the next issue is how management can prevent career plateauing or at least control the problem. The answer is different for each of the scenarios just outlined.

Performance Deficiencies.   One study suggests that there are three managerial strategies that can be used to solve the problem of career plateauing resulting from performance deficiencies. The strategies are (1) selection and training, (2) redesigning jobs for intrinsic motivation, and (3) reducing stress and burnout.[21]

Selection and Training.   Salespeople who plateau early probably should never have been hired by the company because of a poor match between job and individual skill needs. Better recruiting can go a long way in curtailing plateauing. Serious career plateauing problems can occur in organizations that do a poor job planning and managing the recruiting process (see Chapter 10).

Many new managers will eventually become plateaued because of poor preparation for managerial duties, which in turn can lead to poor managerial performance. Unfortunately, as we mentioned in Chapter 6, it is very common in the sales world for salespeople to be promoted on the basis of their current job performance and not on their suitability for management. After a few years of languishing in the job and poor performance reviews, the manager plateaus and is unable to move up or laterally. In this case, the manager possibly would not have plateaued if he or she had remained in a sales role where growth was occurring. The solution is for man-

EXHIBIT 12.5	
REASONS FOR PLATEAUING	
Reasons	Percent of Managers Citing Reason
Lack of opportunity for advancement	51.2%
Lack of advancement in the past	46.5
Not motivated	44.7
Treated unfairly by management	37.9
Bored with the job	33.8
Overworked	32.9
Earnings are already adequate	27.6
Burned out	24.1
No loyalty to the company	22.1
Poor image of the company	20.3
Unable to keep up with technology	17.6
Other	9.1

SOURCE: Robin T. Peterson, "Beyond the Plateau," *Sales and Marketing Management* (July 1993): 78–82.

agers to be promoted on managerial skills rather than successful selling (see Chapter 6 for more discussion on new managers).

Another selection and training-related solution is to do a better job of initial training or proper training and preparation for promotion. At least 50 percent of organizations rely on on-the-job training rather than formal training. As discussed in Chapter 11, the reasons for OJT are numerous and justifiable, but the lack of formal management training means that newly promoted managers must learn as they go. The lack of formal training may push a manager into a plateau position. Organizations are more likely to avoid managerial career plateauing by providing ongoing training and self-development courses.

Redesigning Jobs to Increase Intrinsic Motivation.   Much of plateauing is owing to a lack of intrinsic motivational growth. One of the reasons for the recent surge in team selling is that each salesperson is responsible for the performance of the entire team. This sense of team reliance can boost the way a salesperson feels about the contributions he or she is making toward the team and thus increase the level of intrinsic motivation toward the job itself.

The current trend of sales and marketing tasks merging, brought about by the evolving selling environment, gives salespeople more responsibility, such as budgeting, planning, and territorial market analysis. This added responsibility can also increase salespeople's intrinsic motivational levels.

A third, and perhaps the simplest, method of redesigning a job is better communication between the individual and his or her manager. The better able the two individuals can overcome the salesperson's perceived or real deficiencies, the more comfortable the salesperson will become with the job itself. In turn, intrinsic motivation may increase.

Reducing Stress and Burnout.   For some organizations rotating people through a variety of jobs—thus providing new responsibilities—can go a long way in fighting burnout.[22] However, rotating jobs is not an optimal solution for a lot of companies because of the associated training cost and administrative problems. As an alternative, a number of companies are now running stress management workshops for their employees and teaching relaxation techniques. Still others are investing in on-site workout facilities. Most companies provide counseling for employees who are experiencing high levels of stress.

Stress management can sometimes be as easy as managers doing a better job of communicating with their salespeople. For example, Maurice Levy, senior sales vice-president for Purolator Courier, found that one of his top salespeople was experiencing all the symptoms of burnout and no longer producing as she had in the past. After numerous conversations with the sales rep, Levy found that she was depressed because of negative feedback from her previous manager. Security and reassurance were important to her, so Levy worked that to his advantage. Now, she has reemerged as a leading salesperson.[23]

Increasing Growth Opportunities.   When an organization begins experiencing slow growth and opportunities for career development also begin to slow, the organization can take two important steps. First, it can start rewarding high performers with as many nonpromotion resources as possible, such as job titles, reassurance, pay raises, and increased responsibility, until the organizational growth resumes.

The second step is to eliminate the "dead wood" from the organization. Dead wood includes those who are unproductive or those who have or will soon plateau. In the early and mid-1990s much of the dead wood was eliminated as a result of mergers, downsizing, and budget cuts. The loss of the nonperforming employees should free up more resources for those salespeople the organization wants to keep and develop.

Acceptance of Growth Opportunities.   Some employees are reluctant to accept added responsibility for a variety of personal reasons. They may not understand the consequences of turning down added responsibilities, particularly if the salesperson has been offered additional responsibility on more than one occasion and has rejected the offer each time. In this case the individual becomes plateaued by his or her own choice because further promotional offers from the organization will probably cease. Better communication and information about possible long-term consequences of turning down promotions may aid the salesperson in making more informed decisions.

More and more organizations are considering **dual-career ladders,** which can give employees choices of long-term career possibilities.[24] Instead of emphasizing upward promotions in managerial roles, many organizations, knowing that managerial positions will be limited, offer a salesperson the opportunity to strive for a different career track such as a staffing position, a marketing position, a senior sales position, or management. These added opportunities, some of which may be lateral, give individuals more freedom of choice for their career.

Many people decline job advancements when the new job requires relocation to another city and working spouses are unable to move. For example, Mary, who is in Boston, has been offered a promotion that would require her to move to Nashville. Mary's husband has a job in Boston that cannot relocate him to Nashville. So Mary turns down the promotion, but this decision may move her career to a plateau. Dual spouse careers can make upward mobility very difficult if it entails a relocation.

EXHIBIT 12.6	
GETTING THEM OFF THE PLATEAU!	
Possible Solutions	Percent of Managers Who Agree
Talk with salesperson about problem	70.9%
Discuss reasons and possible solutions	69.4
Conduct motivation sessions	63.8
Manage, lead, and communicate	63.2
Cut salesperson's responsibilities	61.5
Provide new responsibilities	61.2
Assign to a new territory	57.4
Inform rep of his or her responsibilities	55.9
Provide time off	50.0
Ask to assist new reps	44.7
Use an ongoing goal assessment program	42.9
Clear the air and redefine goals	40.6
Assign to a different sales manager	32.6
Use bonus plans	30.9
Have rep come up with solutions	30.9
Provide perks after sales success	27.1
Establish recognition plans	23.8
Encourage reps to be creative	21.5
Use competent sales managers	18.8
Use training sessions	14.4
Change: new products, prospects, etc.	6.5

SOURCE: Robin T. Peterson, "Beyond the Plateau," *Sales and Marketing Management* (July 1993): 78–82.

One of the spouses may have to give up his or her position, or both spouses may keep their jobs but possibly become plateaued. The dual spouse career has become a major issue in business, and organizations are working on ways to keep both spouses happy and provide opportunities for growth even if not in the traditional sense of upward managerial promotions.

Career plateauing has become a serious problem in the 1990s. As a result organizations are having to rethink some of their motivation, recognition, and evaluation strategies. Exhibit 12.6 provides possible solutions to the career plateau problem and the percent of managers who agree with the solution.

MOTIVATIONAL THEORY

Motivation is one of the most difficult sales management concepts to comprehend because there are so many theories and approaches to understanding and applying motivation. At the broadest level, motivation theories can be divided into two general categories: content theories and process theories. Although motivational theories can be complex, it is important to understand some of their basics. Now that we have examined job-related factors and individual-related factors of motivation we need to examine how they affect basic motivational theories.

Content Theories

Content theories attempt to identify aspects that correlate motivation to individual behavior without explaining the dynamics of motivational change. For example, content theories might describe a salesperson's needs or the rewards sought. The emphasis is on individual differences. This discussion focuses on three types of content theories: need hierarchy, dual factor, and learned needs.

Need Hierarchy Theory.   The best known motivation theory was devised by Abraham Maslow and is widely cited and quoted in the marketing and sales literature (as well as in the literature of psychology, sociology, and many other disciplines).[25] Maslow's **need hierarchy theory** argues that human needs are classified into five hierarchies: physiological, safety and security, love and belongingness, self-esteem, and self-actualization. These five hierarchical classifications serve as motivators, but an individual must satisfy each level before advancing to the next.[26] In other words, a person must satisfy each level of needs before attempting to satisfy the next level of needs. The five levels and their associated sales management issues are shown in Exhibit 12.7.

Maslow's hierarchical theory has always been popular because of its simplicity: Only one level is a motivational driver at any single point in time. For example, the

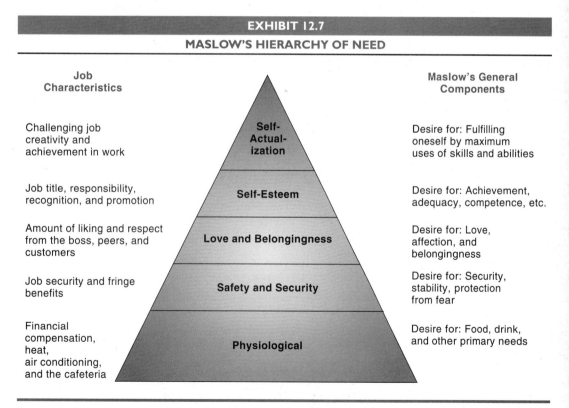

EXHIBIT 12.7

MASLOW'S HIERARCHY OF NEED

Job Characteristics

Challenging job creativity and achievement in work

Job title, responsibility, recognition, and promotion

Amount of liking and respect from the boss, peers, and customers

Job security and fringe benefits

Financial compensation, heat, air conditioning, and the cafeteria

(Pyramid levels, top to bottom: Self-Actualization, Self-Esteem, Love and Belongingness, Safety and Security, Physiological)

Maslow's General Components

Desire for: Fulfilling oneself by maximum uses of skills and abilities

Desire for: Achievement, adequacy, competence, etc.

Desire for: Love, affection, and belongingness

Desire for: Security, stability, protection from fear

Desire for: Food, drink, and other primary needs

SOURCE: Robert L. Berl, N. C. Williamson, and T. Powell, "Industrial Salesforce Motivation: A Critique and Test of Maslow's Hierarchy of Need," *Journal of Personal Selling and Sales Management* (May 1984): 33–39.

next motivation for a salesperson who has enough money for his or her basic physiological and safety needs might be to achieve social needs—love and belongingness.
Many scholars and practitioners find this theory too simplistic and faulty for a couple of reasons. First, most scholars believe that an individual has multiple motivation needs simultaneously. Second, many scholars do not believe that the needs are
hierarchical for everyone. For example, some salespeople may put self-actualization
before self-esteem needs.

Another version of the hierarchical theory has been offered by Robert Alderfer,
who argues that instead of five levels there should be only three. Alderfer's **ERG
theory** contends that the three levels consist of *existence* (physiological and safety),
relatedness (social and esteem), and *growth* (self-actualization). Perhaps more important, Alderfer maintains that an individual can move up and down the levels
without satisfying any lower level first, and that multiple levels can be motivators
simultaneously.[27]

Dual Factor Theory.   The **dual factor theory** of motivation, sometimes known as
the *Herzberg Hygiene-Motivation Theory*, proposes that there are two sets of factors that influence a salesperson's satisfaction and dissatisfaction and, thus, motivation and job performance.[28] The **hygiene factors**, or dissatisfiers, consist of those aspects that comprise the job such as pay, territories, supervision, policies, and
recognition. Herzberg argues that the hygiene factors are more important motiva-
tionally if they are absent. For example, for a salesperson who feels that his or her
pay is not sufficient, pay becomes a strong negative motivator. The best a manager
can hope for is to minimize dissatisfaction with hygiene factors. A salesperson
rarely will be totally satisfied by current pay, but a manager can minimize the salesperson's dissatisfaction by promising greater rewards if performance increases. The
hygiene factors correspond to lower levels of Maslow's and Alderfer's hierarchies
and are extrinsic in nature.

The second dimension of the dual factor theory is the **motivators,** or satisfiers,
that are held intrinsically. The motivator is the self-actualization aspect in which the
job and fulfillment become the primary focus of the salesperson.

Again, research has indicated that the dual factor theory also may be too simplistic. One 1986 study found results that were counter to the dual factor model.
The authors of the 1986 study found that pay can be a satisfier/motivator and that
work itself can be a dissatisfier/hygiene factor. The results should indicate to management that if the dual factor model is followed too closely the results may not be
as optimal as might be hoped or expected.[29]

Learned Needs Theory.   The **learned needs theory,** developed by David McClelland, suggests that salespeople strive for three dimensions: achievement, affiliation,
and power.[30] These three dimensions are not hierarchical like the previous methods
discussed. Although they can be held simultaneously, McClelland maintains that
only one of the three dimensions will be dominant at any point in time.

Some salespeople are driven by *achievement* and will be highly motivated to
succeed. These salespeople are easy to motivate from management's perspective because they are basically self-motivated. Achievement-oriented salespeople are characterized as favoring problem situations in which they can take personal responsi-

BOX 12.3
WHAT TO DO WITH A MAVERICK

The creative sales rep, as troublesome as he or she may be, can be a valuable contributor. Coming up with a solid reason for one more callback, finding a way to get hold of someone "impossible" to reach, getting the order in before the competition can even quote prices—these are what professional selling is all about, and this is where the "creative" sales pro often excels.

Take, for example, a past acquaintance of mine we'll call Henry Barker. Almost every sales unit has someone like Henry. He was his company's No. 1 salesperson. He produced more orders for mobile hospital equipment (delivery carts and trucks) than the next 10 sales reps combined. And if necessary to land an order, he'd sweet-talk the production staff into quietly customizing the ordered equipment without management ever being the wiser.

No one else (thank goodness!) could do what Henry did. He broke every rule, bent every policy and procedure, told less than the truth to all concerned, and regularly kept his sales V-P up all night worrying. He never (as far anyone knew) did anything blatantly illegal or unethical, but he never did anything strictly by the book either. His prices often differed from those in the catalogue (sometimes they were higher, sometimes lower), and he had an amazing number of bad trade show habits, including sometimes failing to show up at the booth at all. His reports were always two weeks late, and his expense filings came in once a month instead of once a week. When asked about them, Henry would respond, "Do you want paperwork or orders?"

You could never send junior salespeople out with him for "seasoning" because they might never come back, but you also knew that if you sent Henry out on what seemed like a "suicide mission," he'd always return with an order.

And with all Henry's faults, his orders somehow always managed to be delivered ahead of everyone else's in the company, and his division grew and remained profitable year after year.

Good line sales managers will recognize that their job is not to discipline mavericks like Henry Barker but rather to shield them from a system that's likely to crimp their creativity—and their productivity. On the other hand, smart sales managers should also know that they can afford only one such individual per unit.

SOURCE: Jack Falvey, "Managing the Maverick Salesperson," *Sales and Marketing Management*, (September 1990): 8–12.

bility for solutions and thus rely on their own level of effort. They are also characterized as people who strive for reachable and realistic goals. Last, while part of their motivation is self-administered, it is important that they receive feedback regarding their performance. Recognition from their manager is an important aspect for a continuation of a quality performance.

Salespeople who have a strong need to be part of a group or a "family" member in an organization are said to possess a need for *affiliation*. The strong motivator in this case is the sense of belonging. Some organizations use a salary compensation plan to develop the concept of "family" and belonging. A sense of loyalty develops toward the company and the people within the company. Individuals with a high need for affiliation will not necessarily be high producers because the drive is more social than performance based. On the other hand, if the organizational culture is high performance, then the affiliation will reflect performance and the organization as a whole may be highly productive.

Finally, some salespeople are motivated by *power*. As we discussed in Chapter 6, salespeople can achieve power by being promoted to management. Power can also be achieved by becoming the top salesperson and highly recognized as such by the rest of the salesforce. Power can be accrued through an informal process in which people (salespeople and management) recognize the individual as an informal leader.

Power and achievement can be simultaneous if achieving one can play a part in achieving the other. For example, achievement-driven people want to succeed in whatever they do. As they succeed and achieve they may also garner some power which can become a stronger motivator over time.

Process Theories

Whereas content theories attempt to identify factors that lead to behavior, **process theories** identify the elements that influence motivation and detail the processes that originate the influence. For example, a process theory might attempt to explain how different variables interact to influence motivation. Content theories are behavior based; process theories are cognitive oriented. The process theories discussed in this section are expectancy, attribution, and equity.

Expectancy Theory. Expectancy theory has probably received more attention than any other process theory since its original introduction by Vroom in 1964.[31] **Expectancy theory** is based on the judgment that job efforts will lead to performance that in turn will be rewarded with something of value to the sales individual. It is a function of three interrelated components and the linkages between each of the components: expectancies, instrumentalities, and valences, as shown in Exhibit 12.8.[32]

Expectancies are the perceived linkages between effort and resulting performance. For example, Betsy Coldwell might believe that if she increases her weekly calls from 30 to 35, her performance will increase. One of her peers might believe that increasing the number of calls is meaningless for increased performance. Their expectancies for sales calls differ.

Instrumentalities are the perceived linkage between performance and rewards. Betsy believes that if she increases her performance level based on her higher effort she will receive a high quarterly bonus.

Valence for rewards is the desirability of receiving the reward based on performance. Betsy really wants the quarterly bonus to help her save for a downpayment on a new house.

Each salesperson evaluates job tasks based on the three dimensions of expectancies, instrumentalities, and valences and decides how to disperse his or her efforts among these tasks. Salespeople will be motivated to perform the tasks that lead to a perceived higher performance which in turn leads to a desired reward. The key to this motivational theory—like most of the others—is to find the *desired* reward. If Betsy hears that the reward for top salesperson is a trip to Florida and she just returned from Florida, her valence for a return trip may be low, so she will not be motivated to increase her sales efforts.

Because this is a linkage process, management must be careful to follow through on each step. The rewards offered by management must be desired by the salesforce, and management must clearly communicate what performance level will lead to the reward. It also becomes important for management to clearly delineate what efforts might be required to lead to the desired performance.

EXHIBIT 12.8

EXPECTANCY MODEL

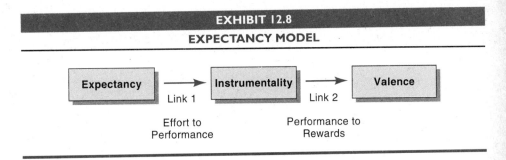

Equity Theory.   **Equity theory** states that people will compare and contrast their treatment with "relevant others." The fundamental aspect of equity theory is fairness or perceived fairness. Salespeople will compare equities with their peers.[33] For example, if a salesperson's work efforts are different from others and others are perceived as being rewarded, then the salesperson will adjust his or her work efforts to obtain similar rewards.

Equity theory assumes some level of rationality on the part of the salesperson. For example, assume Jane Kokovice and John Smithison have both recently been hired by Alcon. Jane is being paid $2,000 more than John, but Jane has an M.B.A. and John does not. Even though there is an apparent inequity, John may not perceive unfairness because Jane has an advanced degree. Moreover, if the pay discrepancy is great enough then John may be motivated to complete an M.B.A. of his own.

Inputs affecting perceived fairness may include experience levels, education, work effort, work level, and job title. Outputs may be greater pay, recognition, promotion, and status. If John Smithison feels that he is being compensated less than some of his peers, he may take one of two approaches. First, he may reduce his work effort, feeling that he is working too hard for the resulting compensation, or second, he may increase his work level, feeling that more effort could lead to a more equitable compensation.

Attribution Theory.   Attribution theory has been a dominant theoretical framework in the field of social psychology. **Attribution** pertains to the process of interpreting events by using causal explanations. For example, if someone else got a promotion that you wanted, you might attribute the promotion to favoritism by the boss. **Attribution theory** attempts to change the focus of explanation from "what if" to "why?"[34] Attributionists are interested in the relationships between behavior and the cause of the behavior.[35] The attribution process is affected by both internal and external factors. Internal attributions might include individual ability, effort, mood, and experience. External factors—those beyond the control of the individual—might include luck, the influence of others (the boss, customers, service personnel, peers), task difficulty, and unforeseen influences. Exhibit 12.9 shows the causal attribution leading to motivation expectancy.

Emotional reaction can also have an effect on salesperson motivation. After an achievement outcome of success or failure, two emotional reactions are possible. First, certain reactions occur such as happiness or sadness, contentment or disap-

EXHIBIT 12.9
CAUSAL ATTRIBUTIONS AND EXPECTANCY ESTIMATES

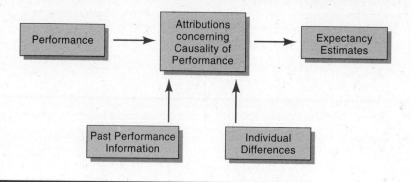

SOURCE: R. Kenneth Teas and James C. McElroy, "Causal Attributions and Expectancy Estimates: A Framework for Understanding the Dynamics of Salesforce Motivation," *Journal of Marketing*, 50 (January 1986): 75–86.

EXHIBIT 12.10
SUMMARY OF MOTIVATIONAL THEORIES

Motivation Theory	Primary Message	Key Terms
	Content Theories	
1. Need hierarchy theory—Maslow	Needs build one upon another (hierarchical)	1. Physiological needs 2. Safety and security 3. Love and belongingness 4. Self-esteem 5. Self-actualization
2. ERG theory—Aldefer	Three levels of needs, not hierarchical	1. Existence 2. Relatedness 3. Growth
3. Dual factor theory—Herzberg	Extrinsic and intrinsic motivation	1. Hygiene factors 2. Motivators
4. Learned needs theory—McClelland	Salespeople strive for three dimensions, not hierarchical	1. Achievement 2. Affiliation 3. Power
	Process Theories	
5. Expectancy theory	A linking process such that effort is linked to performance, which is linked to rewards	1. Expectancies 2. Instrumentalities 3. Valence for rewards
6. Equity theory	Assumes rationality, based on fairness	Relevant others
7. Attribution theory	Interpreting events by using causal explanations—examines "why?" not "what if?"	Attribution

pointment. Second, the salesperson might attempt to make an attribution to understand why the result occurred.[36]

Attributing an emotion to a specific cause can affect future sales scenarios. For example, suppose Jane's quota was raised 10 percent for the year and at the end of the year Jane had increased sales only 5 percent. She attributes the "failure" to an unreasonable quota adjustment and not her own abilities. She may not experience a sense of failure because she views the quota adjustments as an unreasonable managerial request. She continues to approach selling as she always has so very little has changed. Suppose, however, that she attributes the "failure" to her own abilities. She will then either increase her efforts for the next period or begin to doubt her own abilities.

Exhibit 12.10 summarizes the theories that we have just discussed. The motivational process, including job-related factors, individual-related factors, and motivational theories, can sometimes be difficult concepts but they are very important from a managerial point of view. Good managers and leaders need to understand some basics of motivation to understand how to obtain the desired results from their salesforce.

SUMMARY

Motivation is the force within us that directs our behavior. Motivation has three dimensions: intensity, persistence, and direction. It can be intrinsic or extrinsic depending on the individual. The motivational process begins with a need deficiency, which leads to a search for ways to satisfy needs. The search creates goal-directed behavior, followed by rewards based on performance, and ending with a reassessment of needs.

The motivation process is directly affected by: (1) job-related aspects, (2) individual-related aspects, and (3) motivational theories. The job-related aspects include the job itself, leadership, and job involvement and organizational commitment. Based on commitment to the organization and to the job itself, we can categorize four types of salespeople. The institutional star has a high degree of commitment to both the organization and the job. The corporate citizen has a high commitment to the organization but not to the job. The lone wolf (or maverick) has a high commitment to the job (selling) but not to the organization. The apathetic has a high commitment to neither.

Individual-related aspects are directly affected by career stages and career plateauing. The stage of your career can affect what rewards will motivate you. In the exploration stage an individual is trying to find a career and become accepted in the organization. In the establishment stage the salesperson is building a career with promotion and recognition, important motivations. The maintenance stage has the salesperson either reevaluating his or her career or attempting to maintain the current status. The last stage, disengagement, has the salesperson beginning to think about retirement and the end of his or her career with the organization.

Career plateauing occurs when an employee has a low likelihood of receiving increased responsibilities. There are a number of strategies that management can employ to control plateauing. These include controlling performance deficiencies, increasing growth opportunities, and controlling acceptance of growth opportunities.

There are a number of motivational theories; these can be categorized as either content or process theories. Content theories consist of need hierarchy theory, dual factor theory, and learned needs theory. The process theories consist of expectancy theory, attribution theory, and equity theory.

KEY TERMS

motivation	establishment stage
intensity	maintenance stage
persistence	disengagement stage
direction	career plateauing
working smarter	dual-career ladders
intrinsic motivation	content theories
extrinsic motivation	need hierarchy theory
job enrichment	ERG theory
skill variety	dual factor theory
task identity	hygiene factors
task significance	motivators
job autonomy	learned needs theory
job feedback	process theories
job involvement	expectancy theory
organizational commitment	expectancies
institutional star	instrumentalities
corporate citizen	valence for rewards
lone wolf	equity theory
apathetic	attribution
exploration stage	attribution theory

DISCUSSION QUESTIONS

1. What is motivation, and what is its relevance in sales management?
2. How do intrinsic and extrinsic motivation differ? How can a manager use these concepts to best motivate salespeople?
3. What are the six steps in the motivational process?
4. What job-related factors affect motivation?
5. What are the four different types of salespeople based on job involvement and organizational commitment? How do they differ?
6. What are the four stages of a salesperson's career? What traits differentiate the stages?
7. What is career plateauing? How can a manager keep his or her salespeople from plateauing?
8. What are the differences between need hierarchy theory and dual factor theory?

9. What are the three dimensions of the learned need theory? What is the primary difference between it and need hierarchy theory?

10. What are the three process theories, and how do they differ?

PROBLEMS

1. Simon Garstein has been on the job for 6 weeks. He is still a little uncertain about the job, but he wants to do well and get his career moving forward. He wonders how long it will take to become comfortable on the job. Do you think these early feelings of insecurity are common? Why? If they are common, what should management do about them?

2. Charlie Harris is 38 and a senior salesperson. He has been passed over for promotion into management several times, and he realizes that he will never make the management ranks. He thinks back to when he was 21 and his lofty goals for himself. Depression is setting in for Charlie even though he has been a good salesperson and is comfortable financially. What steps should management take to motivate Charlie?

3. Suzy Wong has been with American Airlines for 8 years. She has been a salesperson (sells to travel agents) for American for the past 3 years. She is not crazy about selling, but it is a good job and she loves the travel benefits. One day soon she hopes to move from sales and get into American's marketing department. Is Suzy likely to be highly motivated in her current job? What should her sales manager do to increase her motivation?

SHORT CASE

MOTIVATION

INTRODUCTION

Joannie Charleston seems to have a headache by the time she gets home every night. She is a sales manager of Xenos, Inc., and is responsible for six salespeople, three of whom are rarely a problem. It is the other three who keep giving Charleston the nightly headaches.

Xenos compensates its salesforce through a combination of salary and commission. Most Xenos people receive about 70 percent of their compensation from salary and average about $65,000 a year, but a few salespeople make as much as 50 percent of their income from commissions and can reach six figures.

SCENARIO

Charleston is talking to her husband, Carlos, and says, "I've got to find a way to motivate 'the three' to become part of the team and to quit being so self-absorbed. They're driving me crazy." She begins to summarize her people on paper and writes the following:

Name	Pros	Cons
Jay Johnson	• Top sales in district • Gets job done • Customers like him	• Not a team player • No respect for managers • Won't come to meetings
Ron O'Brien	• Been with Xenos 9 years • Hard worker, above-average salesperson • Well liked	• Moody • Sales and performance are slipping • Complainer
Julie Nelson	• Good potential • Good interactive skills • Intelligent	• Party oriented • Lazy • Poor performance

Joanie also summarized the problem for the three people:

Jay Johnson: Can't motivate him to become a part of the team. Doesn't respect me because he makes more than I do. Has a high ego and loves making money.

Ron O'Brien: According to the grapevine, he wanted a management position, but now that he's 38 he knows that won't happen. Rumor also has it that he is separated from his wife.

Julie Nelson: Julie did not make quota last year and probably will not make it this year. She simply is not working as hard as she should. Her annual evaluations have been low, but she doesn't seem to be bothered by it.

PROBLEM

Charleston must find a way to motivate these three people to do what she wants them to do. Each has a different type of problem that either must be overcome or accepted by Charleston. She wonders what to do with them. They aren't worth getting these headaches.

QUESTIONS

1. How would you characterize Jay Johnson? Can he be motivated? If so, how? If not, why not?
2. In what career life cycle stage is Ron O'Brien? What can be done to motivate him?
3. What are the realistic options for Julie Nelson? What can motivate her?
4. What chapter concepts apply to each of the three salespeople?

MOTIVATION ROLE PLAY

CHARACTERS

Sales Manager: Lyle Greenlee or Andrea Schmidt
District Manager: Manuel de la Guardia or LaDonna Mobley
Salesperson: Gerry Toll or Elle Durley

SCENARIO

Gerry Toll has been with EDD for 25 years. He is well respected by the "junior sales reps" and is well known and liked throughout the company. Over the years Toll has developed a clientele based on friendship. Many of his customers have never been called on by any EDD salesperson except Toll. He has been an excellent salesperson, winning top salesman award seven times, although not in the last 6 years. Management has noted that Toll's sales have slipped in the last 2 years, and the number of new customers that Toll has brought in has been virtually zero. More important, new market analysis has shown that Toll's territory has some untapped potential. Although it is not enough to justify creating a new territory, it is disturbing to management that Gerry is making no effort to get this business. Toll, who is 57, is making about $70,000 a year and is financially secure.

SCENE 1

The first scene features Lyle Greenlee (Toll's immediate boss) and LaDonna Mobley (the district manager) discussing the problem of Toll. This scene should bring in the basic facts of the case. The two should discuss a variety of possible alternatives commenting on the negative consequences of each alternative. The first scene ends with Greenlee stating that he will have a talk with Toll.

SCENE 2

Scene 2 opens with Toll entering Greenlee's office. After some basic small talk, Greenlee comments that Toll's performance has slipped in the last couple of years. Toll admits that he is not as gung-ho as he used to be, but he still outperforms most of the sales reps in the company. "I've been around 25 years, and I've brought this company a lot of business. I think I have the right to slow down some." Greenlee responds that there is a lot of potential that is not being developed: "EDD certainly appreciates all the hard work you've done for us, and we anticipate that you can continue to help us. However, we need this new business."

SCENE 3

Scene 3 is yours. It can continue from scene 2, or can be a completely new scene. You need to provide a workable solution to the problem. How are you successfully going to motivate Toll? The scene may feature any of the characters in any location.

CHARACTER DESCRIPTIONS

Name: Manuel De La Guardia
Gender: M
Age: 35
Marital status: Married
Education: B.B.A., University of Puerto Rico
Title: District Manager, Western Region
Office location: Los Angeles
Reports to: Regional Manager, Western Region
Employment history: Rapid promotions; started with the company at age 18 and has worked his way up
Personality: Very demanding; aggressive and autocratic; expects perfection
Notes: Youngest district manager in the last 10 years; his district has the highest profit level; handball expert
Grapevine: Probably a future V-P

Name: LaDonna Mobley
Gender: F
Age: 42
Marital status: Married
Education: B.B.A., University of Massachusetts; M.B.A., Dartmouth
Title: District Manager, Western Region
Office location: Los Angeles
Reports to: Regional Manager, Western Region
Employment history: Recruited from a major computer company where she was a national accounts salesperson; sales manager with Pharmiceaux for 5 years; district manager for 2 years
Personality: Tough; demanding; extremely competitive; very ambitious; fair
Notes: Wants her district to be on top: recently terminated a 10-year veteran for poor performance; has season tickets to the opera
Grapevine: Wants a V-P job—and maybe not with Pharmiceaux

Name: Andrea Schmidt
Gender: F
Age: 26 **Marital status:** Single
Education: B.B.A., Arizona State University
Title: Sales Manager
Office location: Phoenix
Reports to: District Manager, Los Angeles
Employment history: Sales manager for 6 months; previously a sales rep for eastern region
Personality: Aggressive; driven; good communication; highly professional
Notes: Inexperienced in management; high performer as a sales rep; youngest sales manager in company: fitness fanatic
Grapevine: Being watched closely by management because of youth

Name: Lyle Greenlee
Gender: M
Age: 28
Marital status: Single
Education: B.S., Memphis State
Title: Sales Manager
Office location: Phoenix
Reports to: District Manager, Los Angeles
Employment history: Sales manager for 1 year; previously a sales rep for southern region.
Personality: Aggressive; driven; good communication; highly professional
Notes: Athletic; inexperienced in management; received a good annual review after first year as a manager
Grapevine: Fast-tracker

Name: Elle Durley
Gender: F
Age: 57
Marital status: Widowed
Education: High school diploma; associates degree, Community Junior College
Title: Senior Sales Rep **Office location:** Phoenix
Reports to: Sales Manager, Phoenix
Employment history: 25 years with Pharmiceaux
Personality: Well-liked and respected within the company; loyal; easy-going
Notes: Brings donuts and cookies to the office every day; considers the company to be her family since her husband died
Grapevine: Content with her current position

Name: Gerry Toll
Gender: M
Age: 56
Marital status: Married
Education: Associates degree, County Community College
Title: Senior Sales
Office location: Phoenix
Reports to: Sales Manager, Phoenix
Employment history: 23 years with Pharmiceaux

Personality: Easy-going; everybody's friend; loyal to the company
Notes: Mentor for younger sales reps; hosts a backyard barbeque each spring
Grapevine: Content with current position

QUESTIONS

1. Does Toll have the right to slow down because of his age and years of service with EDD? Should we expect the same type of performance from him that we do from a 25-year-old?

2. How can management motivate salespeople?

3. List at least four alternatives for managing and motivating Toll. Discuss the long-term consequences of each alternatives.

4. Which of the alternatives in question 3 should Greenlee pursue? Defend your answer.

5. What mechanisms, if any, can Greenlee set in place to prevent this problem from occurring again?

NOTES

1. Judy Quinn, "Making Everyone a Winner," *Performance* (November 1994), 65–68.
2. Bernard Weiner, *Human Motivation* (New York: Holt, Rinehart and Winston, 1980).
3. Harish Sujan, "Smarter Versus Harder: An Exploratory Attributional Analysis of Salespeople's Motivation," *Journal of Marketing Research*, 23 (February 1986): 41–49.
4. Pradeep K. Tyagi, "Work Motivation Through the Design of Salesperson Jobs," *Journal of Personal Selling and Sales Management* (May 1985): 41–51; and G. R. Oldham, J. R. Hackman, and L. P. Stepina, "Norms for the Job Diagnostic Survey," *JSAS Catalog of Selected Documents in Psychology*, 9 (1979): 14.
5. Pradeep K. Tyagi, "Relative Importance of Key Job Dimensions and Leadership Behaviors in Motivating Salesperson Work Performance," *Journal of Marketing*, 49 (Summer 1985): 76–86.
6. Keith T. Hughes, "A Manager's Guide to the Art of Team Building," *Security Management*, 37(11) (November 1993): 20. See also Dawn M. Baskerville, "Why Business Loves Workteams," *Black Enterprise* (April 1993): 85.
7. Joseph Pereira, "Bosses Will Do Almost Anything to Light Fires Under Salespeople," *The Wall Street Journal* (April 27, 1993)
8. "Motivation: Boosting Your Bottom Line With Creative Non-sales Incentives," *Performance* (March 1995): 48.
9. Geoffrey Brewer, "Patting Them on the Back—Electronically," *Sales and Marketing Management* (February 1994): 44.
10. Gary L. Blau and Kimberly B. Boal, "Conceptualizing How Job Involvement and Organizational Commitment Affect Turnover and Absenteeism," *Academy of Management Review*, 12(2) (1987): 288–300. See also Gary L. Blau and Kimberly B. Boal, "Using Job Involvement and Organizational Commitment Interactively to Predict Turnover," *Journal of Management*, 15(1) (1989): 115–127.
11. Sanjeev Agarwal and Sridhar N. Ramaswami, "Affective Organizational Commitment of Salespeople: An Expanded Model," *Journal of Personal Selling and Sales Management*, 13(2) (Spring 1993): 49–70.
12. Thomas N. Ingram, Keun S. Lee, and George H. Lucas, Jr., "Commitment and Involvement: Assessing a Salesforce Typology," *Journal of the Academy of Marketing Sciences*, 19(3) (1991): 187–197. See also Thomas N. Ingram, Keun S. Lee, and Steven J. Skinner, "An Empirical Assessment of Salesperson Motivation, Commitment, and Job Outcomes," *Journal of Personal Selling and Sales Management*, 9 (Fall 1989): 25–33.

13. Geoffrey Brewer, "Prima Donnas . . . Trouble Makers . . . Jerks, What to Do When Your Top Performer Is a Pain in the Neck," *Sales and Marketing Management* (March 1995): 64–68.

14. *Ibid.* See also Theresa Minton-Eversole, "Managing Mavericks: The Art of Sales Management," *Training and Development*, 46(12) (December 1992): 71–72.

15. William L. Cron, "Industrial Salesperson Development: A Career Stages Perspective," *Journal of Marketing* (Fall 1984): 41–52. See also William L. Cron, Alan J. Dubinsky, and Ronald E. Michaels, "The Influence of Career Stages on Components of Salesperson Motivation," *Journal of Marketing,* 52 (January 1988): 78–92; William L. Cron and John W. Slocum, Jr., "The Influence of Career Stages on Salespeople's Job Attitudes, Work Perceptions, and Performance," *Journal of Marketing Research,* 23 (May 1986): 119–129; and Marvin Jolson, "The Salesman's Career Cycle," *Journal of Marketing,* 38 (July 1974): 39–46.

16. Daniel C. Feldman and Barton A. Weitz, "Career Plateaus in the Salesforce: Understanding and Removing Blockages to Employee Growth," *Journal of Personal Selling and Sales Management,* 7 (November 1988): 23–32.

17. Robin Peterson, "Beyond the Plateau," *Sales and Marketing Management* (July 1993): 78–82.

18. Mark W. Johnston, A. Parasuraman, Charles M. Futrell, and William C. Black, 'A Longitudinal Assessment of the Impact of Selected Organizational Influences on Salespeople's Organizational Commitment During Early Employment," *Journal of Marketing Research,* 27 (August 1990): 333–340.

19. William L. Cron, Ellen F. Jackofsky, and John W. Slocum, Jr., "Job Performance and Attitudes of Disengagement Stage Salespeople Who Are About to Retire," *Journal of Personal Selling and Sales Management,* 13(2) (Spring 1993): 1–13.

20. Thomas L. Quick, "What Makes Your Stars Want to Shine?" *Sales and Marketing Management* (April 1992): 120–121.

21. Daniel C. Feldman and Barton A. Weitz, "Career Plateaus in the Salesforce: Understanding and Removing Blockages to Employee Growth," *Journal of Personal Selling and Sales Management,* 8 (November 1988): 23–32.

22. Susan E. Jackson, Randall S. Schuler, and Richard L. Schwab, "Toward an Understanding of the Burnout Phenomenon," *Journal of Applied Psychology,* 71(4) (1986): 630–640.

23. Geoffrey Brewer, "Battling Burnout," *Sales and Marketing Management* (March 1995): 39.

24. G. W. Dalton, P. H. Thompson, and R. L. Price, "The Four Stages of Professional Careers—A New Look at Performance by Professionals," *Organizational Dynamics,* 6 (Summer 1977): 19–42.

25. Abraham H. Maslow, "A Theory of Human Motivation," *Psychological Review,* 50 (July 1943): 370–396.

26. Robert L. Berl, Nicholas C. Williamson, and Terry Powell, "Industrial Salesforce Motivation: A Critique and Test of Maslow's Hierarchy of Need," *Journal of Personal Selling and Sales Management* (May 1984): 33–40.

27. Clayton P. Alderfer, *Existence, Relatedness, and Growth* (New York: Free Press, 1972).

28. Frederick B. Herzberg, Bernard Mausner, and Barbara Snyderman, *The Motivation to Work,* 2nd edition (New York: Wiley, 1986).

29. David D. Shipley and Julia A. Kiely, "Industrial Salesforce Motivation and Herzberg's Dual Factor Theory: A UK Perspective," *Journal of Personal Selling and Sales Management* (May 1986): 9–16.

30. David C. McClelland, "Business Drive and National Achievement," *Harvard Business Review,* 40 (July–August 1962): 99–112.
31. Victor Vroom, *Work and Motivation* (New York: Wiley, 1964).
32. Orville C. Walker, Jr., Gilbert A. Churchill, Jr., and Neil M. Ford, "Motivation and Performance in Industrial Selling: Present Knowledge and Needed Research," *Journal of Marketing Research,* 14 (May 1977): 156–168. See also Kenneth R. Evans, Loren Margheim, and John L. Schlacter, "A Review of Expectancy Theory Research in Selling," *Journal of Personal Selling and Sales Management,* 2 (November 1982): 33–40.
33. J. Stacy Adams, "Toward an Understanding of Inequity," *Journal of Abnormal and Social Psychology,* 67 (November 1963): 422–436.
34. B. Weiner, *Theories of Motivation: From Mechanism to Cognition* (Chicago: Markham, 1972).
35. R. Kenneth Teas and James C. McElroy, "Causal Attributions and Expectancy Estimates: A Framework for Understanding the Dynamics of Salesforce Motivation," *Journal of Marketing,* 50 (January 1986): 75–86. See also R. M. Steers and R. T. Mowday, "Employee Turnover and Post-Decision Accommodation Processes," *Research in Organizational Behavior,* Vol. 3, L. L. Cummings and B. M. Staw (eds.) (Greenwich, Conn: JAI Press, 1981), 235–283.
36. Gordon J. Badovick, "Emotional Reactions and Salesperson Motivation: An Attributional Approach Following Inadequate Sales Performance," *Journal of the Academy of Marketing Sciences,* 18(2) (1990): 123–130. See also Gordon J. Badovick, Farrand J. Hadaway, and Peter F. Kaminski, "Attributions and Emotions: The Effects on Salesperson Motivation After Successful Versus Unsuccessful Quota Performance," *Journal of Personal Selling and Sales Management,* 12(3) (Summer 1992): 1–11.

COMPENSATION AND INCENTIVE PROGRAMS

Everyone wants a new and more equitable compensation plan provided he will then get more than he does now.

CHARLES ABOD, CFO, HUMAN SERVICE GROUP

LEARNING OBJECTIVE

After completing this chapter, you should be able to answer the following questions:

- What is the difference between financial and nonfinancial compensation?
- What aspects of a compensation plan are "at risk?"
- What are the advantages and disadvantages of a salaried compensation plan versus an at-risk compensation plan?
- What are nonfinancial methods of compensation?
- What are some current and future compensation trends?
- What are the links between motivation, evaluation, and compensation?

Executives at Texas Commerce Bank (TCB) were puzzled. Its sales of loans, annuities, and accounts to small businesses were up in some periods and down in others. Finally, the answer was determined: The TCB salesforce was performing above normal during a sales contest and slacking off when there was no contest. Kelly Cox, vice-president of sales, says, "Our salespeople just weren't as motivated when there wasn't something on the line." Cox needed a way to have the salesforce selling hard year round. The solution was to implement a Presidents Club. To be a member of the President's Club a salesperson must be among the top 10 percent of all salespeople at TCB. Each year, President's Club members receive a February trip to the Cayman Islands. Cox says, "These [incentive] programs build excitement among salespeople and help keep us consistent throughout the whole year." The results of the program have also included a 10 to 20 percent increase in sales for the bank.[1]

What do you first think of when you hear the word *compensation?* You probably answered *money.* Indeed, money is the primary component of a compensation program, but compensation also includes nonfinancial variables such as the Presidents Club implemented by TCB. The fact remains, however, that one of the first questions recent college graduates ask about a new job is, "What does it pay?" Consider the following conversation between two friends. John asks Bob, "Did you hear that Mary took a job with American Widgets?" "Yeah," replies Bob, "and did you hear what she's getting paid? Can you believe it?"

This conversation is fairly typical. Notice that the conversation centered on starting pay and not on what type of job Mary has, or what her daily activities encompass, or what her advancement opportunities are, or if it is a job that she will really enjoy. All too often a person's success quotient is measured by what he or she is being paid and not by the job itself. Compensation issues may be among the most sensitive sales management topics because money is such a driving force in much of the world culture.

However, as already noted, compensation is composed of more than pay. On average, most employees of U.S. organizations and multinational corporations, as well as most corporations in non–third world countries, receive a significant percentage of their total financial compensation in fringe benefits such as medical coverage, life insurance, and retirement benefits. In addition, salespeople often receive automobiles, trips, club memberships, and generous expense allowances that can be construed as income. This chapter will provide an overview of many of these financial and nonfinancial compensation components. It begins with a discussion of reward system management. Then, in section two, we will examine various financial reward systems, including straight salary, straight commission, and combination plans. Section three explores nonfinancial compensation such as promotions, recognition programs, benefits, perks, and contests. Section four examines other considerations in compensation management. The last section links compensation to motivation and evaluation.

REWARD SYSTEM MANAGEMENT

Reward system management involves the selection and utilization of organizational rewards to direct salespeople's behavior toward the attainment of organizational objectives. **Compensation** is defined as financial and nonfinancial methods of rewards for sales personnel. As noted on the beginning of this chapter, compensation generally includes financial rewards and nonfinancial rewards. **Financial rewards** are composed of current spendable income, deferred income, profit sharing, retirement, and various benefit packages. **Current spendable income** is the most commonly discussed aspect of financial rewards and is defined as money provided in the short term (paycheck or annual compensation) that allows salespeople to pay for goods and services. Exhibit 13.1 offers examples of current spendable income by different types of sales jobs.

Nonfinancial rewards include promotions, recognition programs, personal development, security, sales contests, expense accounts, and a sense of achievement. Some of these nonfinancial rewards can incorporate financial gain. A promotion for example, typically includes an increase in pay. A completed educational degree such as an M.B.A. might also be rewarded with a raise in pay. Sales contests and expense money both generally lead to increases in financial input, but these nonfinancial categories also typically provide individuals with much more than an added financial gain, as we will see later.

The primary purpose of an organization's reward system is to influence salespeople to achieve the objectives specified by management. A properly implemented compensation plan directly augments management coaching and leadership by giv-

EXHIBIT 13.1
TOTAL SALES COMPENSATION

Position	Current Spendable Income
Outbound Telesales Rep	$33,900
Technical Product Consultant	51,800
Sales Representative	43,100
Senior Sales Rep—Level 1	55,200
Senior Sales Rep—Level 2	71,300
Key Account Executive	68,300
National Account Executive	88,100
1st Level field sales supervisor	$72,200
2nd Level field sales supervisor	84,400
3rd Level field sales supervisor	113,100
National sales executive	127,300

SOURCE: "What Salespeople Are Paid," *Sales and Marketing Management* (February 1995): 30–32.

ing guidance and direction as to what activities management expects of the salesperson.[2] The level of rewards, the type of rewards, and the method of implementation of the rewards are important in attracting and maintaining a high-level salesforce.

The proper design, implementation, and management of the compensation program is directly correlated to the success of the salesperson and the ultimate success of the organization.

FINANCIAL REWARDS

There are only a limited number of financial compensation methods for salespeople, although a number of variations of these methods may exist. Straight salary, straight commission (possibly with a draw), salary plus bonus or other incentives, and salary plus commission are the typical financial means of compensating the salesforce. Commissions range from 0 percent (straight salary) to 100 percent (straight commission). The salary versus commission methods of compensation rely on two different schemes for controlling the salesforce. The commission form relies on incentives to align the goals of salespeople with the goals of the organization and, hopefully, motivate the salespeople to perform in the best interests of both the company and themselves. The salary version relies on supervision to monitor the activities of the salesperson and ensure that desired performance is reflective of that desired by the organization. If supervision is lowered, then incentives must be increased, and vice versa. The following sections more closely examine these types of financial plans.[3]

Straight Salary

Under a **straight salary compensation plan** a person's paycheck equals income; in other words a salesperson who is hired for $30,000 annually can expect to make that sum for the year. There are those who are paid straight salary but may receive a supplement in the form of an end-of-year bonus. For example, someone who makes $22,000 a year in straight salary and $3,000 in bonus pay is still relying on salary for 88 percent of his or her income. End-of-year bonuses are not guaranteed every year, so salary remains the predominant form of financial compensation for the salesperson.

There are a number of variables that favor the use of a straight salary compensation plan for the salesforce. These variables are (1) difficulty in assessing performance, (2) low levels of needed selling effort, (3) high levels of uncertainty and risk, and (4) high needs for relationship selling.

Difficulty in Assessing Performance. In many sales scenarios it is difficult to assess individual performance and contribution to a sale. For example, a *missionary sales person,* those salespersons who informs customers about products and promotions, does not physically take an order, thus making it difficult to pay him or her a commission. A Miles sales rep may convince a doctor to prescribe a certain drug, for example, but will not leave the doctor's office with an order in hand.

Another example of a missionary salesperson who tends to work on salary is a sales representative for a company such as Anheuser-Busch. Anheuser-Busch sales reps call on local bars, restaurants, and taverns. They explain new promotions and the advantages of the distributor and product in an attempt to build a relationship with the customer. The sales call ends without an order being taken; purchases are made later through a route driver working for the local distributor. The Anheiser-Busch reps are paid straight salary because it is difficult to assess what affected the tavern or restaurant owner's reason for purchasing. Was it the sales rep, the route driver, the new promotion campaign, or a customer request that created the sale?

Like missionary salespeople, *sales support personnel* are typically paid by straight salary because individual performance is hard to assess. Sales support personnel provide technical support, maintenance, delivery, and installation for salespeople and their customers. These individuals are frequently considered sales personnel because of their direct influence and assistance in a sale, but they are rarely paid by commission. Inside and outside order takers, telemarketers, and route drivers are usually paid by straight salary as well.

All of these sales personnel are important to the overall sales strategy of the organization, but the organization typically finds it more beneficial to pay sales support staff by salary and maintain more control over their daily activities. The nature of sales support jobs makes it difficult to determine who is really responsible for a sale. As team selling increases in popularity as a key sales strategy, it is likely that salary will become more prevalent because of the difficulty in assessing the performance contributions of each sales team member.

Low Levels of Needed Selling Effort. Salary should be inversely related to the level of selling *effort* required of the sale. In other words, if a sale is more a result of a company's reputation, advertising, and product superiority than pure sales effort, then salary should play a stronger role in the compensation package. On the other hand, if the sale requires considerable motivation and effort, incentive-based compensation is the more likely alternative. To illustrate, a salesperson working for a cereal company such as Kellogg's or General Foods is more likely to be paid by salary because the company spends considerable money advertising and promoting its products. The work of the salesperson is very important, but the selling effort and activities make a salaried approach more common.

High Levels of Uncertainty and Risk.   Salespeople who operate in an uncertain environment need the comfort of a salary. For example, as the economy turns downward a commission sales compensation plan may cause salespeople to suffer declines in income through no fault of their own. The income continuity a salary provides is a necessity when salespeople are confronted with risk or are in training, when there are seasonal fluctuations, or when product demand volatility exists.

High Needs for Relationship Selling.   If a company is trying to emphasize a relationship selling philosophy—where multiple sales calls on a customer may be the norm—it may be better advised to employ a salaried compensation plan. Salespeople who are salaried have less tendency to put undue pressure on the customer. Salaried salespeople also tend to stay with the same company longer (if the compensation plan remains competitive). In addition, a commissioned salesperson is less likely to make multiple calls on one account to procure the sales because it leads to only one commission, thus ignoring the basic philosophy of relationship selling. After all, the "ideal" scenario for commission salespeople is a commission on each successful sales call.[4]

Straight Commission

The **straight commission compensation plan** is an at-risk compensation plan in which the salesperson's income is tied directly to the amount of product sold. Commissions tend to be based on percentage of sales; if the commission rate is 10 percent and a salesperson sells $1 million worth of product, his or her income for the year would amount to $100,000. Commission rates vary by industry and company. The incentive for a commission approach is "the more you sell, the more you make." Income for commission salespeople in some industries can easily top the $100,000-a-year level.

A commission compensation approach can motivate talented salespeople and weed out poor performers. In theory a commission plan should improve customer relations because a commissioned salesperson should be more attentive to the customer to ensure that the customer buys today and in the future. Unfortunately the lure of commissions today may mean that the salesperson often overlooks the long-term organizational relationship to ensure the commission in the short term (see Box 13.1).

Two issues must be examined in conjunction with employing a commissioned salesforce. First, how is a noncontrolled outside salesforce, such as manufacturers' reps, to be compensated? Second, how can some monetary security be provided in slow sales periods? The next section examine manufacturerers' reps and the issue of draws on commission.

Manufacturers' Reps.   While many commissioned salespeople are employed by the selling company and are considered full employees of the company, a recent trend in some industries has been to move to a system of manufacturers' reps or independent agents. Recall from Chapter 8 that independent reps work on commis-

---

BOX 13.1

THERE'S NO "I" IN TEAM

How did James Preston motivate a group of highly compensated, self-motivated, top-producing salespeople to work as a team? He reduced their commission.

Preston, the vice-president of marketing and sales support of HR Strategies, Inc., a Detroit management consulting company, doesn't want the sales staff to be treated differently from other employees in terms of compensation and professional image. "We don't want heroic selling," says Preston. "So we're front-loading salaries and minimizing commissions and bonuses." The result is increased motivation owing to greater security for salespeople which, Preston feels, encourages team selling.

Although the company has grown an average of 45 percent in each of the past 5 years, Preston recognized that in order to reach the 1995 sales goal of $25 million, the company needed to be more team driven. "Team selling is what will sustain our long-term growth, stability, and profits," he says. "So we only want salespeople who are team players." Why? The company's salespeople are often teamed with people who may only spend 30 percent of their time selling. For example, each of HR Strategies's six regional offices is staffed with a business development director, who sells 100 percent of the time, and a regional office director, who may sell only 30 to 50 percent of the time. The two are often teamed up for sales calls and other projects.

So far the team selling approach is paying off: Sales grew 70 percent in the first quarter of 1995, and the company continues to set records in profits.

SOURCE: Andy Cohen, "Date With Destiny," *Sales and Marketing Management* (October 1995): 102–109.

---

sion and are not directly employed by the selling company. They are agents working for themselves or for a broker. Kraft Foods, for example, uses a system of brokers who employ independent reps. These independent reps sell Kraft products, but they also sell other competing products.

It is also possible to employ a salaried salesforce and, indirectly, a system of independent reps. Truitt Brothers', a producer and seller of canned foods, has an in-house salaried salesforce that sells to distributors who, in turn, have commissioned independent reps who sell to food wholesalers and supermarkets. The in-house salesforce sells the merits of the company's products to the distributors whose salesforce sells the products to grocers. This is not an unusual system, but it does bring about special problems in having to work with company salespeople and a system of independent reps. It combines the problems and opportunities of both systems.

Draw on Commission. A **draw** is an account from which commission-based salespeople can take a "loan" against future earnings. The ability to draw on a steady flow of money when commissions are lower than normal and pay back later when commissions are high allows the salesperson to have a relatively steady income. Draws work in two ways. The most common method is a **limited draw,** which is paid back when commissions are earned. For example, a salesperson in a slow selling period may draw $1,000 a month from the account to supplement low commissions. As the selling season arrives, the draw ceases and the account is reimbursed. The draw begins again as the next low selling season approaches.

A second type of draw is a **guaranteed draw,** which is a draw that does not have to be paid back. Guaranteed draws are most common for new salespeople who need some financial assistance until they can develop their territory.

Comparison of Straight Salary and Commission Plans

Salespeople can be salaried or commissioned. Exhibit 13.2 presents the advantages and disadvantages of implementing a salaried versus commissioned salesforce. Both methods are considered in the following paragraphs.

Straight Salary.   One common reason for implementing a straight salary approach is its simplicity. When a potential recruit wants to know what the job pays, it is easy to divulge the information because income is not dependent on commissions. In addition, it is much easier to make adjustments to salaries than it is to set up new bonuses or commission schedules. Salary is a fixed cost that can be planned for each year.

A straight salary also allows the organization to maintain better control over the salesforce. Sales jobs that require "non-face-to-face selling activities" such as attending meetings, conducting market research, and filling out paperwork may need a salaried approach to ensure that the sales reps perform these duties. Commis-

---

EXHIBIT 13.2

COMPARISON OF STRAIGHT SALARY AND STRAIGHT COMMISSION COMPENSATION

	Straight Salary[a]	Straight Commission
Appropriate Usage	• If it is difficult to assess individual performance • If a product is widely supported through promotional efforts • If there is a large *Fortune* 500–type salesforce • If there are high levels of uncertainty and risk • If there is strong desire for relationship selling	• If a product has little promotion support • If there are no physical territories • If the salesforce is highly experienced • If there is a need for strong selling effort
Advantages	• Simplicity • Better control over salesforce • Higher degree of company loyalty • Higher degree of salesperson security	• Stronger sales effort • Income directly linked to sales • Entrepreneurial spirit • Inherently fair • Savings of cost • Weeds out poor performers
Disadvantages	• Lack of financial incentives • Fosters seniority • Lower average compensation • Organizational cost	• Lack of control • Lack of loyalty • More difficult to make territorial changes • More of a "sell-at-all-costs" mentality
Common Job Usage	• Missionary sales (i.e., pharmaceuticals) • Sales support • Team sellers • Telemarketers • Route sellers • Sales trainers • Seasonal sales	• Independent reps • Insurance • Financial sales • Real estate

[a]May include some bonus.

sioned salespeople rarely want to perform any activity that is not oriented toward immediate sales because their pay depends exclusively on closing sales. The need for salesperson control has become a paramount argument by some companies in maintaining salary as the dominant method of compensation.

In addition, salaried salesforces have a tendency to be more loyal to the sales organization because money (commissions) is not the dominant reason for working for that particular company. Salaried salespeople tend to view themselves as a part of the company, whereas commissioned salespeople are more likely to view themselves as a resource that can be sold to the highest bidder. If commissioned salespeople become unhappy with management's policy, they are much more likely to quit knowing that with their skills, finding another commission selling job should not be difficult.

Salary also has the advantage of providing more security for the rep than does a commission plan. Income is stable under a salary plan. Even in bad economic times, salary levels typically do not change. A commissioned rep may have periods where income is very high and others where income is virtually nil. The security of a paycheck on a regular basis is very appealing to many salespeople.

The greatest argument against the use of straight salary is the lack of financial incentives. Many people who favor commission formats argue that as long as quota is being met, salaried salespeople will not go beyond what is required. Without a monetary incentive to push even harder, the majority of salespeople won't strive as they would if they were paid on commission. Not everyone agrees. Alfie Kohn, author and consultant, is a strong vocal critic of the commission systems. Kohn argues that commissions, bonuses, and other "bribes" lessen productivity because salespeople are more interested in the reward than the job. Kohn believes that salaried salespeople will go above what is required and deliver high performance.[5]

Commission Plans.   The greatest advantage of commission plans is the continual sales effort the company can obtain from the salesforce. Commissioned salespeople want to spend their time in front of customers and potential customers, obtaining orders and closing sales. Many sales managers argue that commissioned salespeople are concerned more with making the sale and less with performing other sales activities, such as conducting market research, attending meetings, recruiting and training new hires, and so on. Commissioned salespeople may not see the benefits of nonselling activities because such activities do not lead to income for the salesperson.

Organizations employing commissioned salespeople are generally aware that obtaining sales is the primary goal of the salesforce. Some commissioned salespeople feel that they are as much in business for themselves as they are for the company they represent. This self business philosophy is a strong incentive for those who have an entrepreneurial spirit and who want very little supervision. Commissioned salespeople tend to make more of their own decisions and determine, to a great degree, what level of income they will earn for the year. The only real limits to potential income are ability and time. Management cannot make an arbitrary earnings decision unless it revolves around a change in commission rate.

A commission system is inherently fair because it is based purely on sales performance. Seniority and other nonsales factors make little difference. Commissioned salespeople cannot complain that someone else was favored or that their evaluations and raises were unfair. Commission salespeople determine their own income.

The savings for implementing a commission salesforce system can be staggering. A company that pays on commission does not bear fixed salary expenses, and it can eliminate levels of managers who would have had responsibilities over the salesforce. Costs become flexible and rise or fall depending on the level of sales, a particularly important occurrence when times are tight and profit margins are slim. Many companies, such as Alberto Culver, have recently abandoned salaried salesforces because of the overall expense.

Salespeople already under a commission plan may be very reluctant for their company to restructure territories or make any changes in account responsibility. They do not want anything to interfere with the existing selling relationships they have developed. One complaint about commissioned sales reps is that they have a tendency to work existing accounts where the odds of a successful sale are high. Building new accounts takes time, and there is no immediate payback.

An even more serious problem with commission sales is the perception (and often reality) that commission-based salespeople sell at all cost, that they frequently ignore the marketing concept of selling the customer only products that the customer truly needs. The concept of relationship selling and marketing can sometimes be overlooked by commissioned sales reps as they seek to make the commission on an immediate sale. This type of overzealous selling is exemplified in the Sears, Roebuck and Company incident first presented in Chapter 3. In 1992 Sears received widespread national attention because sales personnel in their auto-service centers began selling products and services that were not needed in order to receive greater commissions. Sears had implemented an incentive program that unintentionally created an environment that systematically recommended unnecessary repairs. The heavy negative publicity that followed the Sears incentive mistake caused many other firms to reexamine their incentive and commission systems to ensure that the sales commission plan benefitted the company, the salesperson, and the customer.[6]

Bonuses/Incentives

A **bonus** is a one-sum supplemental payment for excellent performance. It can be paid at any point but is typically paid at the end of the fiscal year or the calendar year, or on a quarterly basis. Bonuses are not designed to be the sole method of compensation; rather, they are supplements to the primary method of financial compensation (typically salary).

Incentives are supplemental compensation programs that allow salespeople to perform some activity to earn additional income. Incentive programs can be continually running or one-time offerings. For example, Reynolds Metals has an incentive program that rewards its salespeople when they form consultative relationships with customers. Maritz Performance Company rewards its salespeople when they make improvements in identified sales deficiencies. AT&T provides incentives that reward salespeople for possessing comprehensive knowledge of AT&T's products and customer's business needs.[7] Art Halloran, vice-president of sales for Sony, says, "A good incentive program costs nothing. Unless your goals are achieved, no one gets prizes and you don't pay for them. The key to making an incentive program profitable is to set goals that are more valuable than the prizes."[8]

Bonuses and incentives are typically tied to the quota of the salesperson. They usually begin when quota is met, or may require a certain percentage above quota. Bonuses and incentives vary widely as to amounts and percentages of annual income. Some companies have a bonus or incentive program that is a token amount consisting of a few hundred dollars. A few companies allow the salesperson to earn a considerable bonus which can, on rare occasions, nearly double the salesperson's income.

Bonuses and incentives can be used by management to increase performance in specific activities. For example, Restek, makers of parts for laboratory equipment, has an incentive program in which any employee can volunteer to phone potential customers or dormant accounts. Each month 200 to 300 "extra" calls are made and in return employees receive cash. Results of the incentive program have been an increase in income for the employees. Meanwhile, Restek has grown 50 percent in the first two years of the program.[9]

Bonuses are a good method of increasing income for the salesforce and can be a very effective way to keep the levels of compensation competitive. Bonuses are also used as a recruiting tool, with the bonus being stressed as the differentiating variable among companies.

The performance bonus may be paid to an individual or to a district. For example, Procter & Gamble has a system that pays everyone in a district a bonus if the district as a whole makes quota. This keeps peer pressure on because everyone has to perform in order for anyone to receive the bonus. The advantage of this type of system is that individual salespeople in the district learn to perform as a team. The disadvantage is that outstanding salespeople might have a great year and still not receive a bonus if their peers fail to perform to expectations.

Combination Plans (Salary Plus Incentives)

Straight salary and straight commission compensation plans have their advantages and disadvantages. The limitations of these two plans have led the majority of companies to create a third option—a **salary plus incentive compensation plan**—which combines the best aspects of salary, commission, and bonus plans. The strategy is to obtain some control, a lot of incentive, and enough flexibility to motivate and reward performance.

The difficult part is creating the **compensation mix**, which is defined as the relative amounts of salary, commission, and bonus to be included in the compensation plan. The general rule of thumb is that the majority of the compensation should still come from salary to maintain control over the salesforce and to offer some regularity. Although every compensation plan is somewhat different, a reasonable compensation mix might consist of 60 percent salary, 30 percent commission, and 10 percent coming from a bonus or other incentives.

The combination plan must address the wants of the salesforce, as well as the managerial objectives. Some companies have addressed this dual need by offering **flex plans**. In this scenario the salesperson is given some liberty as to the percentage of salary and commission offered. One Canadian holding company offered four different flex plans ranging from 100 percent commission to 25 percent commission/75 percent salary. Each salesperson, in consultation with management, tailors the risk element to suit his or her particular circumstances and experience levels.

Flex plans offer a degree of security as well as the opportunity to make more money through straight commission.[10]

The most obvious disadvantage of flex plans is the increase in administrative costs. Effective and frequent communication must also occur between salespeople and managers or the flex compensation plan can be misinterpreted, leading to angry feelings and increased turnover.

Paying Managers

Sales managers commonly receive some form of incentive based on the performance of the district as a whole and/or the performance of individual salespeople. The typical level of performance is measured by the success of the district salespeople in meeting quotas. Most managers still maintain some accounts and may or may not be paid commission on these accounts. However, most managers will agree that it is important that they be paid well enough so that they are making more than the average salesperson. As previously discussed in Chapter 6, this is necessary to induce salespeople to accept management positions and to ensure their credibility with their salespeople.

Sales executives, like salespeople, are paid by a variety of methods. Executives rank pay as their number one need, and pay raises are viewed as an important form of organizational reward. Executive pay raises are given for performance, the nature of the job, effort expended, and experience and training, in that order.[11] About one-third of top executives are typically paid through a combination of salary and

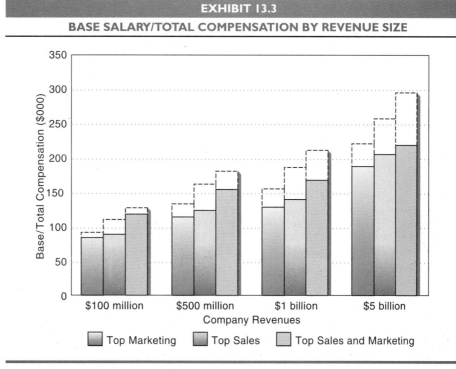

EXHIBIT 13.3

BASE SALARY/TOTAL COMPENSATION BY REVENUE SIZE

SOURCE: "Executive Compensation," *Sales and Marketing Management* (November 1992): 42.

bonus, with 25 percent of the executives paid by straight salary, about 24 percent paid by salary and commission, and the remainder paid by other alternatives.[12] If incentives are used for the executive, the average split is 59 percent salary and 41 percent incentives. Exhibit 13.3 indicates the compensation for top sales and marketing executives.

Pay can be a major motivator for executives, but not all managers are motivated by pay alone. A study of 206 sales executives found that a sense of accomplishment and personal growth were more important than pay.[13] The results of the study indicate that a complete compensation package needs to be formulated to appeal to the different needs of each executive and manager. Some of the nonfinancial rewards that factor into the total compensation package are examined in the next section.

NONFINANCIAL COMPENSATION

Everyone needs some form of financial compensation, but many people are just as motivated by nonfinancial rewards (see Exhibit 13.4). These include promotions, recognition programs, fringe benefits, expense accounts and perks, and sales contests. Remember from the opening paragraphs of this chapter that many of the rewards discussed here are termed nonfinancial when, in reality, there are money possibilities directly or indirectly involved.

Promotions

The opportunity for promotion has always been a strongly held reward preference, ranking second behind money.[14] A lot of recent college graduates and M.B.A.s enter the salesforce with the intention of moving into management as soon as possible. Traditionally, most people attempt to prove themselves in the field and then vie for the limited number of managerial openings available. There are always more deserving candidates than open positions, and management has to appease many tal-

EXHIBIT 13.4	
WHAT WORKERS WANT MOST	
Cash bonus	95%
Special training	87%
Stock options	85%
Trip	77%
Recognition at company meeting	76%
Merchandise	63%
"Pat on the back"	63%
Plaques	46%
Parking space	35%
Lunch with company president	25%

SOURCE: Christian Lovio-George, "What Motivates Best," *Sales and Marketing Management* (April 1992): 113–114, citing a Society of Incentive Travel Executives study.

ented salespeople who are not given promotions. Unfortunately, the problem of more qualified candidates than positions has only worsened because of mergers, downsizing, and elimination of many middle-management positions. There are fewer managerial positions than ever, and many salespeople are having to reassess their long-term goals.

Today, promotion does not necessarily mean moving upward into a managerial position. For many people, the sales job provides experience to obtain a job in another department such as marketing. In fact, most *Fortune* 500 companies will not hire someone directly into the marketing department without prior sales experience; they prefer those who have direct knowledge of the product, competition, customers, and market.

Although a lot of people desire promotion, they have no intention of leaving sales. As discussed in Chapter 1, several career sales paths are open to a "promoted" salesperson. The most common advancement is to a senior sales rep or some other title which implies that the individual is one of the salesforce elite. Also many salespeople aspire to be promoted to a national accounts manager position, which typically leads to more respect and more money. National accounts managers are responsible for the most profitable accounts, so only the best salespeople achieve this level.

Recognition Programs

Recognition programs are programs designed to honor individual salespeople formally or informally for excellent performance. Recognition programs are a part of virtually every kind of organization and company. A Half International survey found that 150 executives reported that "limited recognition and praise" is the number one reason for people leaving an organization.[15] A good example is the plaques you see in McDonald's or other fast food restaurants to honor employees of the month. Sales organizations also commonly feature the salesperson of the month or year. Many times the award is presented at an annual convention or in an annual newsletter. Recognition programs are numerous and can be either formal or informal.

Formal recognition programs are sponsored and heavily promoted by the company and designed to recognize excellence. Many firms in the insurance industry maintain a "Million Dollar Roundtable" award, with membership reserved for agents who achieved $1 million in sales during the previous year. In the pharmaceutical industry the "President's Golden Circle" recognizes the top 2 percent of the salesforce. Winners are treated to a title, recognition in annual newsletters, and trips to conventions in luxurious locations. Salespeople are easily motivated by formal recognition programs because most salespeople are competitive by nature. Box 13.2 gives some ideas on implementing a formal recognition program.

Formal recognition programs can be designed to recognize individual or group winners. Frequently companies recognize districts that are "most improved" or top producers in sales. Typically, companies recognize outstanding performances at conventions or national meetings where the salesperson's peers are present. To be successful, formal recognition program must include public recognition of the award winners. Normally organizations will honor outstanding employees with

---

BOX 13.2
A PRESIDENTIAL AFFAIR

An annual sales honors club can effectively motivate a salesforce to perform year-round. But if it's run haphazardly without much research, planning, and communication, then the incentive can backfire. Here are some tips to ensure a strong program.

- *Don't ignore the numbers.* When deciding the criteria for making the club, take a good look at what's needed to ensure you get a positive return.
- *Choose a lavish destination.* When planning a president's club, don't pinch pennies—salespeople will recognize it and resent it.
- *Allow winners to bring a guest.* The trip becomes even more important to salespeople when they can bring a guest at no charge. And if guests know about the trip beforehand, then they may push salespeople to perform even better.
- *Communicate the goal.* Salespeople should know exactly what they have to do to make the club. Tell them as soon as the club is announced what will be expected of them.
- *Build momentum.* Give the salesforce continuous updates about where they stand in the contest. This will keep them excited about the program throughout the year.

SOURCE: Andy Cohen, "Date With Destiny," *Sales and Marketing Management* (October 1995): 102–109.

---

some form of reward composed of money, trips, or maybe something as simple as a plaque. Plaques, though inexpensive tokens of appreciation, represent a great sense of accomplishment for most salespeople. For example, one company annually awards its top salesperson with a monetary award and takes the picture of the individual with the CEO of the company. The picture hangs in the lobby of the corporate headquarters, and a duplicate is given to the salesperson along with a nice plaque for his or her office. The value of a symbolic award represented by a plaque displayed in a public setting cannot be underestimated.

Informal recognition programs are not programmatic. Instead they are dependent on managers being good leaders, recognizing quality work by their subordinates, and providing praise for it. An encouraging word by the boss can go a long way to motivate an individual to continue to push hard. Everyone likes to be told that he or she is doing a good job and is appreciated. Informal recognition requires minimal effort, yet the results can be very positive. One manager sends memos to salespeople in recognition of superior achievements. The manager then forwards a copy of the memo to corporate headquarters. The manager's subordinates consider the manager to be the best in the company. They like and respect him, and they will do whatever he asks because they perceive him as caring about their welfare. It is the little things that separate good managers from the mediocre one, and informal recognition is a simple, but vital, differentiation.

Fringe Benefits

Fringe benefits are employment benefits in addition to wages or salary. Fringe benefits vary by company, but usually include medical benefits, retirement benefits, life insurance, stock options, and profit sharing. Fringe benefits amount to an average of $6,838 per person per year in the United States.[16]

Medical Benefits.   The core of many fringe benefit packages used to be major medical benefits. In recent years, however, this has become somewhat of a quagmire for U.S. organizations due to rapidly increasing costs. While these programs continue to be the core benefit for many firms, they are now passing on more of the cost to employees.

Retirement Plans.   Retirement plans also vary widely by company, but many companies have a matching policy such that for every dollar an employee puts into the plan, the company matches an additional dollar or perhaps two. Other companies put into a retirement fund a percentage of salary above what the employee receives. Thus, if an employee makes $30,000 annually and the company agrees to place 10 percent above salary into retirement, the employee will receive an additional $3,000 in his or her retirement fund. Retirement fund money is invested so that over a 25- to 30-year working career the employee, upon retiring, should have a steady income. Some companies require employees to remain with the company for a period of time before they become *vested*—that is, before they are allowed to receive the company's contributions to the employee's retirement fund.

Profit Sharing and Stock Options.   Profit sharing, a percentage of the organizational profits that are paid to employees, and stock options can be very attractive components of the overall compensation package. **Stock options** give employees the option of buying stock in the organization at discounted prices. Stock options are frequently offered to employees of fast-growing firms. In the early days of Microsoft and Lotus, employees were offered stock options. Early employees of Marion Labs (now Marion Merrell Dow) retired in the mid- and late-1980s as millionaires because of early profit sharing options. Stock can also become a valuable retirement benefit if the company remains strong and vibrant over time.

Other Benefits.   Fringe benefits include not only medical benefits, retirement plans, and stock options, but also paid vacations, paid holidays, sick leave, maternity leave, and family leave. Specifics for these benefits vary by company. Maternity leaves and family leaves of absence in the United States have been criticized for not being as liberal as those offered in other countries. Women in Germany, for example, may take maternity leave with pay from the time she determines she is pregnant until the child is born. After the birth, the woman can take up to 2 years off without pay and still be guaranteed that her job will be waiting for her upon her return.

Expense Accounts

Reimbursement of expenses is another major component in a compensation plan. **Expense accounts** are compensation plans that are designed to reimburse sales personnel for expenses that occur on the job. Almost all companies cover some level of expenses for employees (see Exhibit 13.5). In the past, managers periodically checked their salesperson's expense reports to determine if they were appropriate. As long as the salesperson was not abusing the expense procedure, expenses continued to be reimbursed. Rising costs and harder economic times, however, now have forced many companies to become much more strict about which expenses are covered and which are not. Today it is common for salespeople to turn in detailed ex-

EXHIBIT 13.5

SALES EXPENSES: WHAT DO COMPANIES PAY FOR?

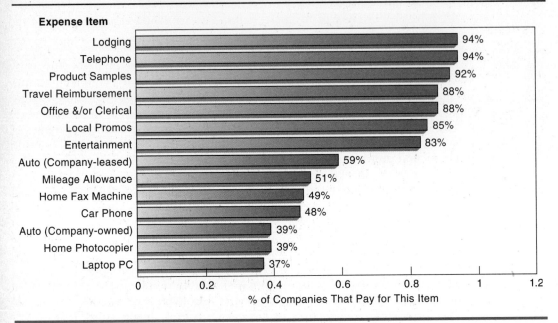

Expense Item

Expense Item	%
Lodging	94%
Telephone	94%
Product Samples	92%
Travel Reimbursement	88%
Office &/or Clerical	88%
Local Promos	85%
Entertainment	83%
Auto (Company-leased)	59%
Mileage Allowance	51%
Home Fax Machine	49%
Car Phone	48%
Auto (Company-owned)	39%
Home Photocopier	39%
Laptop PC	37%

% of Companies That Pay for This Item

SOURCE: Dartnell Corporation, 26th Survey of Sales Force Compensation, 1990.

pense reports with receipts that are closely scrutinized. (See Exhibit 13.6 for an example of an expense report.) These detailed expense reports have helped eliminate *padding,* which occurs when a salesperson overestimates expenses in order to increase (unethically) reimbursement amounts.

One common expense for salespeople is the entertaining of customers and potential customers. Entertainment expenses have tightened up considerably in the past few years, but they are still a big part of doing business on a daily basis. Typical entertainment activities include lunch, dinners, drinks (although not as widely accepted as in past years), sporting events, and leisure activities.[17] It is very common for a salesperson to take a customer to lunch to discuss business. In many cultures such as Mexico and Japan, lunch is an important aspect of building a relationship and is considered to be a social norm. Many U.S. salespeople in Mexico attempt to conduct business at the luncheon rather than getting to know the Mexican buyers and enjoying their hospitality. The ignorance of local culture may result in a loss of business for the salesperson.

In many industries it is also common to take the customer to a sporting event. Companies may have season tickets that they occasionally give or award to their sales reps. A lot of sales business occurs on golf courses. Golf is a growing worldwide sport and leisure activity. People in Japan for example, are willing to pay substantial green fees to play a round of golf. When Japanese businesspeople conduct business in the U.S. it is sometimes over a round of golf. The golf course provides a relaxed environment in which the salesperson and customer have a chance to con-

EXHIBIT 13.6

SAMPLE EXPENSE FORM

NAME			
DEPARTMENT		SOCIAL SECURITY NO.	
WORK EXT.		LOCATION:	
		PURPOSE:	

REIMBURSEMENT FORM

EXPENSE ITEM	Name of restaurant required	SUNDAY	MONDAY	TUESDAY	WEDNESDAY	THURSDAY	FRIDAY	SATURDAY	TOTALS Dollars / Cents
1. Breakfast — Cost (including tip) - attach original receipt		$	$	$	$	$	$	$	$
2. Lunch — Cost (including tip) - attach original receipt									
3. Dinner — Cost (including tip) - attach original receipt									
4. Lodging — Cost per night (including deposits) - other expenses, such as meals and telephones, parking, etc., should be reported on separate lines. Attach original itemized hotel bill.									
5. Meals/Refreshments for others — Cost (including tip and cost for self). Complete the section on back of this sheet. Attach original receipts.									
6. Air/Rail — attach original receipt (ticket). If ticket is not prepaid attach invoice or other evidence of payment.									
7. Taxi/Limousine — Cost (including tip) - attach original receipt.									
8. Mileage Reimbursement — multiply mileage by current mileage reimbursement rate (___ × ___ c = $___).									
9. Other Transportation — car rental (original itemized invoice required), tolls, etc.									
10. Telephone — If not included on itemized hotel bill, attach receipts.									
11. Registration Fee — If prepaid, evidence of attendance such as name tag, seminar agenda, etc. must be attached. If not prepaid a receipt for cost of fee must also be attached.									
12. Other — Miscellaneous expenses. Provide explanation (additional space provided on back of this sheet). Attach original receipts.									

ITEMIZE PREPAID CHARGES

DATE	AMOUNT
/ /	
/ /	
/ /	
Total PREPAID to A	

I certify that all of the above expenses were company related business.

Signature

Date Submitted

BUDGET STAMP

TOTAL	$
Less Prepaid	
A	
Less Advance	
Due	
Due Claimant	$

GENERAL INFORMATION

Reimbursement Forms should be submitted for all reimbursable expenses within 30 days after the expense has occurred.

Supporting Documentation—reimburses per receipt. Specific documents required are described in each of the lines. If the document required cannot be provided, attach an explanation and all other available supporting documents. If appropriate evidence of expenses is not attached, the Reimbursement Form will be returned to the employee.

Prepaid Items — List each prepaid item (charge appears on Employee's Account Receivable) separately in the box provided at right and transfer total to Box "A". Registration fees, hotel deposits and airline tickets are some of the most common prepaid items.

duct business. Golf has become so popular that some companies pay for their employees to take lessons. More and more women are taking golf lessons in order to be able to compete in a traditionally male setting. One female sales rep for Milliken found that her past experience as a member of a university golf team proved to be very helpful in conducting business with customers.

Perks

Perks are a special category of benefits available only to employees with some special status in the organization. There are a number of perks that can be considered part of a compensation package. They include the use of a car, office and office location, convention attendance, a country club membership, and educational opportunities. Perks can be placed into three categories: status, financial, and personal growth.

Status Perks.   Office location, job title, parking spaces, and other visible company contributions are status-oriented perks. They tend to result from a record of performance and can be considered to be very motivational. For example, office location may tell a lot about a person's status within an organization. In some corporate cultures the higher the office in a multi-storied building, the more corporate status the employee maintains. In a similar way, an office that has a window may be considered more prestigious than an interior office with no view. Not all organizations endorse providing status perks. They feel teamwork is more important than the individual, so status concepts for the individual are being eliminated.

Financial Perks.   Financial perks, are designed to add to the salesperson's compensation package. This category of perk includes the use of an automobile or membership to a country club. Of all the perks, the company car is still the most significant and remains a major component of the salesperson's compensation package. Giving a salesperson a car for daily use is equivalent to an additional $5,000 to $8,000 a year. Most companies that provide a car also pay for gasoline, insurance, and maintenance. Other companies provide a car allowance that pays salespeople a set fee for mileage on their own personal car, or a sum of money that can be contributed toward the purchase of a car of the salesperson's choice. This benefit can be a major recruiting and retention tool.[18]

Personal Growth Perks.   Perks designed to build *personal growth* include paying for additional schooling or sending salespeople to motivational or selling seminars. Some companies pay for salespeople to finish their undergraduate degree or attend an evening/weekend masters program. A company that is willing to pay for the advanced education may be adding a significant contribution to the overall compensation package.

Sales Contests

A **sales contest** is a temporary incentive program that offers monetary or nonmonetary rewards and is not a part of the regular compensation plan. Contests have multiple purposes and are typically designed to boost morale (see Exhibit 13.7). For ex-

EXHIBIT 13.7
BASICS OF SALES CONTESTS

Objectives:	• Stimulate sales
	• Increase salesforce motivation
	• Decrease inventory
	• Obtain new business
	• Increase profits
Problems:	• Hard to discontinue
	• Reduces and redirects effort elsewhere
	• If poorly designed, can devastate morale
	• Sales performance may decline after contest
	• Potential customer relations damage
	• Cheating
Planning:	• Ideal length of time: 3 months
	• Contest should revolve around a theme
	• Communication—pre, during, and post
	• Reward structure
	—merchandise, trips, cash
	—multiple winners
	—3 levels of prizes
	—40 percent should win something
	—formally recognize winners

ample, once or twice a month PCS Compleat holds a contest where a salesperson rings a large bell to signify a sale. He or she then draws the name of a nonsales employee, and they team up for the contest. The lucky person is called over the PA system to go to the sales department where either the individual or the salesperson will shoot a basketball into a hoop. A "swoosh" in three tries nets each team member money.[19]

Nonfinancial compensation is as important to managerial strategy as the financial compensation. Salespeople require different compensation packages to motivate them to excellent performance. Much of this compensation package is obtained from recognitions, perks, and other nonfinancial incentives.

OTHER CONSIDERATIONS IN COMPENSATION MANAGEMENT

Certainly sales compensation is a way to get greater sales effort and to provide appropriate pay to the salesforce. However, a sales compensation plan must be consistent with the overall organizational marketing strategy. No two businesses are alike, so compensation plans must reflect the individual needs of each organization. The plan must evolve along with the organization; compensation and performance plans may routinely change because of changing needs in the salesforce. In the pharmaceutical industry, for example, 73 percent of all companies changed their compensation plan in 1993 and expected to change it again twelve months later.[20]

There are five trends that companies should consider when designing a compensation program that will fit the changing needs of its salesforce. They are (1) compensation and customer satisfaction, (2) team selling, (3) global selling, (4) performances, and, (5) equity.

Compensation Based on Customer Satisfaction

Customer satisfaction is becoming an important base for establishing a compensation plan. For example, IBM has determined that customer satisfaction is a primary marketing strategy, so its compensation plan reflects that organizational emphasis. Thus 40 percent of the salesforce's commission is directly linked to customer satisfaction. Similarly, Indianapolis Power and Light asks its customers to rate their account reps from A to F. The results determine the reps' level of incentive pay.

Hewitt Associates, a consulting firm, estimates that 27 percent of all companies in the United States now use some measure of customer satisfaction in determining compensation. In addition, the results of Hewitt Associates' study indicate that another 23 percent of companies are exploring the adoption of some customer satisfaction measure.[21] Clearly, the trend of tying compensation to customer satisfaction should continue into the twenty-first century.

Team Compensation

The movement toward team selling, which has been discussed on several occasions, has also changed the way compensation plans are devised. Many accounts that used to be domestic are now international and require multiple sales personnel to serve them (see the next section on global compensation issue). This means several salespeople need to be compensated. The growing use of national account managers and their coordination with local field reps also requires a team pay approach. Moreover, many accounts now cut across territory lines with the district manager becoming a key player in coordinating with two or more sales reps.[22] This means that frequently a sales individual's pay is tied not only to his or her own performance but also to the performance of members of his or her team.

Traditionally, salespeople have been considered the elite of the organization, and their pay reflected this high status. Many organizations are now questioning the "eliteness" of the salesforce. Today, many companies are trying to eliminate salesforce eliteness and pay all sales personnel at the same levels. These organizations are replacing standard commission-based compensation with team-based plans that link the pay of salespeople, customer service personnel, delivery people, and managers in a team concept.

Tom Hill, vice-president for Baxter International, Inc., says, "The days of paying salespeople a straight cut of revenues are going . . . [Now] the intent is not so much to limit the amount of money they make, but to change the way they make it." Baxter uses a team commission which requires performance from everyone associated with the client.[23] Marshall Industries has also adopted a team compensation plan but for a different reason. Robert Rodin, Marshall's president and COO, stresses that the changes were not for compensation reasons but as a "quality issue aimed at aligning our compensation to support customer service." Under the old compensation program people were "too concerned with their own performance . . . Compensation was an obstacle to world-class quality."[24] Under the new system Marshall's customer is featured and employees have become more loyal to the organization and the team.

The change to team pay is not easy, but many feel that the switch is necessary because of a historical emphasis on the individual salesperson and not the organization sales team as a whole. For example, E.F. Hutton was a very well known national company whose downfall has been blamed on an elitist salesforce. E.F. Hutton's salesforce led to the bankruptcy of the firm by demanding higher levels of compensation while threatening the withholding of sales revenue. In addition, many felt that the salesforce provided misinformation to management. Management routinely gave in to salesforce demands until finally the company succumbed to the volatile stock market of the 1980s.

Technological advances have also changed the way that companies interact with customers. The process of building relationships with customers is an organizational activity, not just an individual activity. Purchasing agents in today's world can use information systems to learn about products before a sales rep calls on them. The results are that selling and service are no longer two departments; they are now a combined sales function. Procter & Gamble has realized that advertising, promotion, and service are as important as sales departments in long-term relationships with customers. Therefore, it has restructured sales compensation plans to reflect this team concept.[25]

Global Compensation Issues

Compensation plans must take into account the organization's employees in other countries, whether they are expatriates or citizens of the host country. As discussed in Chapter 4, compensating expatriates can be quite expensive. Income tax adjustments, education and housing allowances, separation allowance, and annual home leaves can increase the annual salaries of expatriates by as much as 150 percent. In addition, pay scales for the same job may vary widely from country to country.

The challenge management faces is developing an equitable, yet flexible compensation plan that works for both expatriates and domestic salesforces. Determining how to compensate the global and diverse salesforce of the twenty-first century will remain a primary challenge for management.

Performance-Based Compensation

With increases in global competitiveness, downsizing, and mergers, organizations are increasingly asking sales personnel to expand their job functions, work harder, and be more creative. As a result, seniority-oriented automatic pay raises are becoming increasingly unpopular with management; instead, pay and pay raises are being tied directly to performance. Much of this performance-based pay is being implemented in incentive pay. Monsanto, for instance, has instituted performance-based compensation in virtually every department, with the compensation linked to company track records, unit performance, sales team success, and individual achievement. Monsanto is now paying out more in compensation but, according to Monsanto management, productivity and sales have also increased.[26]

Compensation plans based on performance must be totally integrated into corporate goals and objectives. This seems like an obvious statement, but unfortunately many organizations fail to implement a compensation plan that is a direct reflection of corporate strategy. Sales compensation plans must be tailored to the specific requirements of the organization. Certainly the needs of the salesperson must be considered, but without direct inclusion of corporate strategies the plan has no chance of long-term success. Compensation has a direct influence on motivation. If the reward is automatic, then the performance result may very well be less than desired.

Equitable Compensation

Finally, compensation plans must be perceived as fair and equitable. In this age of diversity, with the heavy influx of minorities, women, and international personnel in sales organizations, management must be careful to ensure that compensation plans are equitable for everyone. Although sales executives generally believe that their sales reps' compensation is based solely on the merit of the individual and that gender discrimination is not occurring, as Exhibit 13.8 indicates, compensation between men and women is not equitable. Strides have been made in recent years to equalize compensation disparities, but overall pay still remains lower for women.[27]

Management must be cognizant of these compensation discrepancies, and policies must be in place that specifically forbid compensation discrimination. Mark H. McCormack, chair and CEO of International Management Group, a sports and entertainment rep agency, sums up his views this way:

> I don't let age affect salary decisions. If a talented and highly motivated 27 year old is outperforming people in their forties, the younger executive deserves to be paid more. I don't begrudge people their success because of their youth. I don't pay women less than men. And I don't pay a married executive more than I pay a single executive simply because he or she has a family to support or a mortgage to maintain. I like to think that our company has eliminated most of the conventional prejudices that affect employee's compensation.[28]

	EXHIBIT 13.8					
	SALESWOMEN'S PAY: MIXED RESULTS					
	Median Income		% Change 1979–1992		Female % of Male Pay	
Sales Occupation Categories	Male	Female	Male	Female	Male	Female
Sales occupation, total	$37,999	$17,924	+113%	+102%	47%	50%
Supervisors, proprietors, sales occupation, salaried	40,441	19,872	N.A.	N.A.	49	N.A.
Supervisors, proprietors, sales occupation, self-employed	24,112	7,249	+58	+7	30	45
Sales reps, financial and business services	48,289	27,327	+128	+127	57	57
Sales reps, commodities, excluding retail	44,471	26,515	+116	+119	60	59
Sales workers, retail and personal services	25,125	12,686	+78	+66	50	54

NOTES: N.A. = Not available. Based on year-round full-time workers.

SOURCE: Thayer C. Taylor, "Saleswomen's Pay Falls Short," *Sales and Marketing Management* (March 1994): 39, citing Census Bureau, Money Income of Households, Families, and Persons in the U.S.: 1992, Series P60-184.

LINKS AMONG MOTIVATION, COMPENSATION, AND EVALUATION

A large part of the compensation literature and theory focuses on what might be termed **compensation hydraulics,** which implies that compensation is nothing more than pay designed to obtain sales behavior. In other words, if you want people to sell you must pay them. This simplistic approach to pay and behavior loses the concept that compensation is an intricately complicated managerial function. Humans are complex beings and they are motivated by different rewards. Focusing on hydraulics ignores the fundamental question, "How should we pay the people responsible for working with our customers?"[29]

The compensation plan chosen for any organization will affect the type of selling in an organization, the level of service provided, the recruiting and training of new personnel, and the daily interactions between sales and other marketing and business function areas. Because of the link among compensation, motivation, and

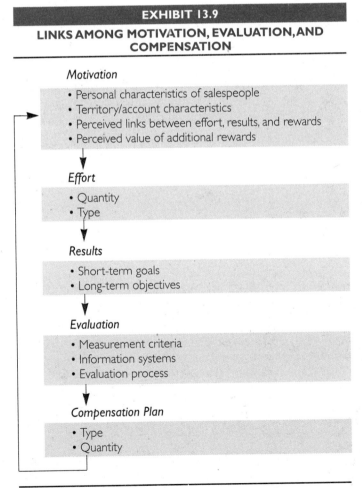

EXHIBIT 13.9

LINKS AMONG MOTIVATION, EVALUATION, AND COMPENSATION

Motivation
- Personal characteristics of salespeople
- Territory/account characteristics
- Perceived links between effort, results, and rewards
- Perceived value of additional rewards

Effort
- Quantity
- Type

Results
- Short-term goals
- Long-term objectives

Evaluation
- Measurement criteria
- Information systems
- Evaluation process

Compensation Plan
- Type
- Quantity

SOURCE: Frank Cespedes, "A Preface to Payment: Designing a Sales Compensation Plan," *Sloan Management Review* (Fall 1990): 59–69.

evaluation (see Exhibit 13.9), there are a number of issues about compensation that must be considered before a program is implemented.

Compensation has the unusual position of being a motivational tool as well as an evaluation mechanism. If used effectively, compensation should be used as a tool for achieving sales performance consistent with marketing strategy. Notice in Exhibit 13.9 that evaluation and compensation is the only two-way interaction and that compensation directly affects motivation. An ineffective compensation plan can decrease motivation and lead to less effort, poor results, and low evaluations. At that point, adjustments to the compensation plan must be assessed. Therefore, compensation should be an evolving, changing strategy that adjusts within the system. Money is the driving force in a compensation plan, but it is the compensation process that determines the long-term success of the organization.

SUMMARY

Reward system management involves the selection and utilization of organizational rewards to direct salespeople's behavior toward the attainment of organizational objectives. Compensation is composed of financial and nonfinancial rewards. Financial rewards include current spendable income, deferred income, profit sharing, retirement, and various benefits packages. Current spendable income is the most commonly discussed aspect of financial rewards and is defined as money provided in the short term. The most common forms of paying financial compensation are through straight salary, straight commission, salary and bonus, and salary and commission.

Straight salary is best used when assessing individual performance is difficult or when the sale does not require a high degree of "selling effort." Larger salesforces or high uncertainty are also reasons why a straight salary might be appropriate. Straight commission is best used when continual sales effort is a primary organizational need.

Commissions provide strong financial reward for high levels of sales performance. Commissions motivate a salesforce to stay in front of the customers selling the products of the organization. A commission system is inherently fair because the reward is based strictly on sales performance. Other forms of financially compensating a salesforce include paying a bonus or allowing a draw on commission. Also a combination approach in which the compensation mix must be determined is becoming increasingly popular.

Five trends in compensation decisions include (1) compensating salespeople based on customer salesforce, (2) paying based on team selling, (3) paying global salesforces, (4) paying based on performance, and (5) paying equitably. These trends will continue into the twenty-first century. Last, compensation is closely linked to motivation and evaluation. Compensation is much more than simply pay designed to obtained field behavior.

KEY TERMS

compensation

financial rewards

current spendable income

nonfinancial rewards

reward system management

straight salary compensation plan

straight commission compensation plan	recognition program
draw	formal recognition program
limited draw	informal recognition program
guaranteed draw	fringe benefits
bonus	stock options
incentive	expense accounts
salary plus incentive compensation plan	perks
compensation mix	sales contest
flex plans	compensation hydraulics

DISCUSSION QUESTIONS

1. What are the advantages and disadvantages of a straight salary compensation plan?
2. Why would a sales organization implement a commission plan?
3. What is meant by a compensation mix, and what aspects of a compensation plan are considered at risk?
4. What are the various methods of nonfinancial compensations?
5. What are recognition programs?
6. What are perks, and what are the three categories of perks?
7. Why are sales contests considered to be a form of compensation?
8. What are some current and future compensation trends?
9. What compensation problems have arisen because of global selling?
10. What are the links among motivation, evaluation, and compensation?

PROBLEMS

1. Brett Loughlin has just graduated from the University of Hawaii and is trying to decide between two job offers. Company A will pay him $28,000 in straight salary. Company B will pay him a base of $15,000 plus commission; the average salesperson for company B makes $38,000 a year. Brett has chosen company A, turning down the possible higher income offered by company B. Assuming the companies are similiar in other ways, why do you think he made this decision?

2. James Mejias is a salesperson on commission who is making an average of $120,000 a year. His boss, Ellen Walker, is making $65,000 in straight salary. She is having difficulty with the pay discrepancy. Ellen has complained to her boss, Ed Green, that James has told other salespeople that he will not take instruction from someone who earns less than he does. Should Ed adjust Ellen's salary, James's salary, or both?

3. Marjorie Markham has been passed over for promotion for the second time in the past 18 months. She feels she deserves the promotion to management, but her boss doesn't agree: "Too many good people and not enough promotion opportunities!" What should Marjorie do?

4. Mark Shiles, a copier salesperson, is competing in a sales contest that is nearing completion. He has an opportunity to sell an account a large copy center

that might give him enough points to be a major winner in the contest. However, the customer does not really need the copy center and Mark knows it. What would you do if you were Mark?

SHORT CASE

PAY ME NOW OR PAY FOR IT LATER

INTRODUCTION

Pruitt Cannery produces canned fruits and vegetables that are eventually sold through grocers. Pruitt has a salesforce that consists of 12 field salespeople and 5 telemarketers. The primary responsibility of the sales personnel is to sell the products to independent distributors who in turn sell multiple and competing products to the grocers. Pruitt's salesforce must convince (sell) the independent distributors to push and give preference to the Pruitt products over those of the competition.

The field salesforce is divided into large geographical territories where they call on mostly large independent distributors. The telemarketers are used to support the field people, and they also call on some of the smaller independent distributors.

SITUATION

The Pruitt salesforce has been complaining about compensation issues. Two salespeople have recently quit for other opportunities. The salesforce "grapevine" indicates that some of the independent distributors that Pruitt sells to are making six figures based on commission sales. Pruitt management believes that there may be some independent reps making that much money, but they are in the minority. Management still feels that Pruitt compensation is very competitive in the marketplace. Unfortunately, the telemarketers are also complaining because they are not paid "near" the field salesforce rates. The grumbling is becoming more vocal, and management is beginning to listen. Management has always considered Pruitt's to be a family culture and because of the small number of employees, management

has always tried to treat them well. Peter Trump, vice-president of sales, has begun looking at the entire compensation issue. He writes down the following facts:

	Salesforce	
	Field	Telemarketers
Mean Salary	$54,350	$32,500
Salary Range	$42–68,000	$31–36,000
Bonus	$3,200	none
Benefits	full	full

There has been only one promotion to management in the past 5 years because there are only two people in sales management, including Trump. Pruitt has instituted some financial and nonfinancial incentive programs in the past that were moderately successful, but none is currently being implemented. Trump knows there are a lot of alternatives and possibilities. He wonders to himself, "What am I going to do?"

PROBLEM

Trump must find a way to appease his salesforce. Because of Pruitt's "family" business culture, management wants to be fair while maintaining the salesforce's high productivity. Trump has considered going to a commission-based compensation plan but is concerned about the downside of doing so. He is also examining various other compensation alternatives.

QUESTIONS

1. What are the pros and cons of implementing a commission plan versus a salary and bonus plan?

2. How should Trump handle the telemarketers' complaint about low comparative pay?

3. What are some viable alternatives in nonfinancial compensation?

4. What solution would you implement?

COMPENSATION ROLE PLAY

CHARACTERS

Vice-President of Sales: Luis Andrade or Lois McKinney

Regional Manager Eastern District: Ty Nakamora or Sarah Fall

Recruit: Juan Garcia or Jill Benedict

SCENARIO

Juan Garcia is in the final round of interviews with EDD and has been asked to come to the home office in Fort Worth. Juan is an extremely impressive individual, and EDD had him ranked as the top graduate from Duke. He is currently in the office of Sarah Fall, the West regional manager, talking about the job. Fall has made Garcia an offer, and they begin talking about compensation. Garcia tells Fall that he has another offer and that it has a higher starting pay. Fall attempts to persuade Garcia by selling him on the entire compensation of the job and the value of working for EDD.

In the second scene, Fall is meeting with Luis Andrade, the vice-president of marketing for EDD, and tells him how they just lost signing Garcia. She also mentions that two more top salespeople have recently quit EDD to take similar positions with competitors. Fall and Andrade brainstorm about what can be done to improve morale and the compensation package. The second scene ends with Andrade telling Fall to put a task force together and solve the problem.

SCENE I

Scene 1 opens with Juan Garcia in the end of an interview with Sarah Fall. Fall tells Garcia how impressed the company is with him and that she believes he would make a nice addition to EDD. Fall offers Garcia a job and then describes the compensation package. When she finishes, Garcia expresses his appreciation but raises a problem with starting pay: "Pharmiceaux is a great company and I think there is a lot of opportunity here, but Acme Pharmaceutical has made me an offer with $3,000 more in starting pay." Fall tells Garcia that she cannot get him more pay. "Frankly, Garcia, I have offered you the top salary that we can offer. The vast majority of our new people begin at $1,500 less than what we've offered you." Garcia responds, "I appreciate your confidence in me. I need a few days to think about the offer." The scene closes with the two shaking hands.

SCENE 2

Fall is in a meeting with Andrade. The scene begins with some small talk, then Fall tells Andrade: "We lost Garcia. I really think he is making a mistake. Acme beat us on starting pay, but in the long run I really think he would have done much better with us." "We lost this one," Andrade replies, "but I think we have a very competitive starting package. We'll win the next one. I am more concerned about the fact that we just had two of our salespeople quit and go with a competitor. We need to do something to perk up our morale and improve our compensation."

The scene continues with the two discussing possible realistic changes, including an ongoing contest. The scene ends with Andrade telling Fall to put a task force together and examine the compensation issue. "Do it soon," says Andrade. "I don't want to lose anybody else."

SCENE 3

The third scene has Fall presenting her report to Andrade. Along with the report Fall offers some details of what EDD could do to improve the morale and the compensation of the salesforce.

CHARACTER DESCRIPTIONS

Name: Ty Nakamora
Gender: M
Age: 48
Marital status: Married
Education: B.B.A., University of San Diego
Title: West Regional Manager
Office location: Los Angeles
Reports to: V-P of Sales
Employment history: With Pharmiceaux for 8 years; 3 years as a regional manager; hired from a Japanese R&D company
Personality: Very professional; fair, but tough
Notes: Excellent experience; four children.
Grapevine: Seeking a CEO job, possibly with another firm

Name: Sarah Fall
Gender: F
Age: 50
Marital status: Married
Education: B.B.A., Southern Methodist University; M.B.A., Texas Christian University
Title: West Regional Manager
Office location: Los Angeles
Reports to: V-P of Sales
Employment history: With Pharmiceaux in Dallas after 3 years in nonprofit industry; worked her way through the system
Personality: Likeable; hard worker; mentors junior personnel; volunteers for a number of charities
Notes: Has been a "favored" employee because of her dedication to the company
Grapevine: In line for promotion to V-P of Sales

Name: Juan Garcia
Gender: M
Age: 25
Marital status: Single
Education: B.B.A., NC State; M.B.A., Duke University
Title: Recruit
Employment history: No full-time work experience
Personality: Ego-oriented; ambitious; intelligent; career-oriented; big tennis player
Notes: Number 1 in class; impressive résumé; numerous honors; graduated with undergrad degree in 3 years; 3 years' experience
Grapevine: Multiple offers; top management potential

Name: Jill Benedict
Gender: F
Age: 26

Marital status: divorced
Education: B.A., Furman; M.B.A., Georgia Tech
Title: Recruit
Employment history: No full-time work experience
Personality: Very professional; career-oriented; intelligent
Notes: Finished second in class; M.B.A. fully funded; recommendations are impressive; strong analytical skills
Grapevine: Multiple offers; top management potential

Name: Luis Andrade
Gender: M
Age: 52
Marital status: Married
Education: B.B.A., Texas Christian University; M.B.A., Texas Christian University
Title: V-P Sales
Office location: Fort Worth
Reports to: Henry Shannon, CEO
Employment history: Sales and middle management in food industry; hired as a regional manager for Pharmiceaux, promoted to V-P 3 years ago
Personality: Goal- and detail-oriented; solid leader; visionary
Notes: Has made sweeping changes in organization, but well-liked; rewards hard work; avid golfer
Grapevine: CEO pleased with his work

Name: Lois McKinney
Gender: F
Age: 53
Marital status: widowed
Education: B.A., Boston College; M.B.A., Dartmouth
Title: V-P Sales
Office location: Fort Worth
Reports to: Henry Shannon, CEO
Employment history: Sales in the computer industry; middle management at a pharmaceutical competitor; hired as a regional manager; promoted to V-P 5 years ago.
Personality: Detail-oriented; workaholic; perfectionist
Notes: Loves to travel when she has time; five grandchildren; gourmet chef.
Grapevine: CEO material if she can wait for Shannon to retire

QUESTIONS

1. What should a potential new recruit look for in a compensation package?
2. What are the advantages and disadvantages of running a sales contest? What are the problems that have to be overcome to run a successful contest?

3. What conditions might determine whether a company uses straight commission or straight salary?

4. List at least four realistic alternatives for the company to consider in changing its compensation package. Discuss the long-term consequences of each alternative.

5. Which of the alternatives listed in question 4 should Fall select? Defend your answer fully. What role should Andrade play in implementing the solution?

NOTES

1. Andy Cohen, "Date With Destiny," *Sales and Marketing Management* (October 1995): 102–109.
2. Lawrence B. Chonko, John F. Tanner, Jr., and William A. Weeks, "Selling and Sales Management in Action: Reward Preferences of Salespeople," *Journal of Personal Selling and Sales Management,* 12(3) (1992): 67–74.
3. George John and Barton Weitz, "Salesforce Compensation: An Empirical Investigation of Factors Related to Use of Salary Versus Incentive Compensation," *Journal of Marketing Research,* 26 (February 1989): 1–14.
4. Bill O'Connell and Lisa Bush Hankin, "If You Pay Them, They Will Come," *Sales and Marketing Management* (September 1994): 123–126.
5. William Keenan, Jr., "Breaking With Tradition," *Sales and Marketing Management* (June 1994): 94–99.
6. Gregory A. Paterson, "Distressed Shoppers, Disaffected Workers Prompt Stores to Alter Sales Commissions," *The Wall Street Journal* (July 1, 1992): B1, B6.
7. Melissa Campanelli, "Rising to the Top," *Sales and Marketing Management* (April 1994): 83–86.
8. Nancy Arnott, "You Get What You Pay For," *Sales and Marketing Management* (December 1993): 31.
9. Susan Greco, "Every Employee a Service Rep," *Inc.* (November 1993): 123.
10. Dean Walsh and Joanne Dahm, "Going Flex-Four Adjustable Comp Plans That Work," *Sales and Marketing Management* (September 1989): 16–17.
11. Charles M. Futrell and P. Rajan Varadarajan, "Marketing Executives' Perceptions of Equitable Salary Increases," *Industrial Marketing Management,* 14 (1985): 59–67.
12. William Keenan, Jr., (1993), "Naming Your Price," *Sales and Marketing Management* (April 1993): 30–31.
13. Danny N. Bellinger, James B. Wilcox, and Thomas N. Ingram, "An Examination of Reward Preferences for Sales Managers," *Journal of Personal Selling and Sales Management* (November 1984): 1–6.
14. Gilbert A. Churchill, Jr., Neil M. Ford, and Orville C. Walker, Jr., "Personal Characteristics of Salespersons and the Attractiveness of Alternative Rewards," *Journal of Business Research,* 7 (June 1979): 25–50.
15. Malia Boyd, "Motivating on a Dime," *Performance* (March 1995): 64–65.
16. *Dartnell's 27th Sales Force Compensation Survey,* (Chicago, Ill.: Dartnell Corporation, 1992), 3.
17. David W. Finn and William C. Moncrief, "Salesforce Entertainment Activities," *Industrial Marketing Management* (November 1995): 227–234.
18. "The Company Car: Still King of the Road," *Sales and Marketing Management* (October 1990): 69–73.
19. "Stoking Team Sales Spirit," *Inc.* (January 1994): 96.
20. *Total Solutions,* IMS America, 3(1) (January 1995).

21. "Labor Letter: A Special News Report on People and Their Jobs in Offices, Fields, and Factories," *The Wall Street Journal* (March 29, 1994): A1.

22. Frank V. Cespedes, Stephen X. Doyle, and Robert J. Freedman, "Teamwork for Today's Selling," *Harvard Business Review* (March–April 1989): 44–55.

23. Gilbert Fuchsbery, "Selling Isn't Everything," *The Wall Street Journal* (April 13, 1994): R8.

24. William Keenan, Jr., "Selling Without Commissions," *Sales and Marketing Management* (June 1994): 97.

25. William A. O'Connell, "Taming the Elite Salesforce," *Small Business Reports* 19(2) (February 1994): 35–43.

26. Howard Gleckman, Sandra Atchison, Tim Smart, and John A. Byrne, "Bonus Pay: Buzzword or Bonanza?" *Business Week* (November 14, 1994): 62–64.

27. Thayer C. Taylor, "Saleswomen's Pay Falls Short," *Sales and Marketing Management* (March 1994): 39.

28. Mark H. McCormack, "The Case Against Commissions," *Sales and Marketing Management* (February 1994): 47.

29. Frank V Cespedes, "A Preface to Payment: Designing a Sales Compensation Plan," *Harvard Business Review* (Fall 1990): 59–69.

EVALUATING THE SALESFORCE

How you measure the performance of your employees directly affects the way they act.

JOHN DEARDEN, PROFESSOR, HARVARD BUSINESS SCHOOL

LEARNING OBJECTIVES

After reading this chapter, you should be able to answer the following questions:

- What are the major decisions sales managers must make in evaluating salespeople?
- On what bases or criteria do managers measure performance?
- How should performance appraisal be conducted?
- How do team evaluations differ from evaluations of individuals?
- How should actual performance be compared to a standard?
- How frequently do most performance appraisals occur?
- What are the legal and ethical issues in performance appraisal?

Gordon Food Service, a food distributor in Grand Rapids, Michigan, uses laptops extensively to control and evaluate its salespeople. Salespeople download information from the firm's mainframe on each account they will call on that day. The information available on the system by account includes account contact, order status, credit terms, tax number, delivery routing, and messages about the account, such as a reminder to the salesperson to pick up a check. The system highlights any changes since the account was last accessed, such as changes in credit rating or delivery routing. As the salespeople make their calls, they keep notes of orders, special requests, changes in billing information, and other important pieces of information. At the end of the day, the sales representative updates the mainframe as to the new status of the account, and receives information on the accounts listed on the next day's call itinerary.[1] This process allows Gordon's management to access on a timely basis the number of calls made and the level of outcomes for number of sales calls made. Information on activity and outcomes are the basis for any performance evaluation system.

Evaluating salespeople by providing them with performance appraisals is one of the sales manager's most important duties. **Performance appraisal** can be defined as:

the process of evaluating the performance and qualifications of the employee in terms of the requirements of the job for which he is employed, for purposes of administration, including placement, selection for promotion, providing financial rewards, and other actions .[2]

You might think that salespeople have one of the simpler job types to evaluate. After all, a salesperson's primary responsibility is to make sales, and sales can be measured easily, right? Unfortunately, evaluating salespeople is not that simple. The process of making sales has many components. Tying rewards to performance can be difficult—especially in team situations—and managers must make many choices as to who they evaluate, how, when, and on what basis. Further, most of the selling process takes place outside the view of the sales manager. For example, it is quite difficult for field sales managers to monitor the activity of their sales reps directly. The managers must scan salesperson call reports and actual sales records to monitor salesperson activity. Last, the evaluation process should consider not only sales performance, but also issues such as whether the salesperson is responsible for developing new accounts, the level of the salesperson's product knowledge and selling skills, the level of expenses the salesperson incurs the quality of the competitive information the salesperson brings to the firm, and the level of customer satisfaction that exists among the salesperson's accounts. Given that an evaluation of performance needs to cover all these issues, you can see that the process can be complex.

Despite its complexity, a properly performed performance appraisal containing constructive suggestions for employee improvement can lead to increased motivation and performance, increased clarity in job requirements and duties, clear recommendations for career growth, and cost reductions. For example, Yellow Freight Systems, a trucking company based in Kansas, documented $20.8 million in performance improvements after installing a new performance appraisal system.[3] Improperly performed performance appraisals, however, can lead to demotivated employ-

EXHIBIT 14.1

SALES MANAGER DECISIONS IN PERFORMANCE APPRAISAL

Criteria for Measuring Performance

Conducting Performance Appraisal

Evaluating Individuals or Teams

Comparing Actual Performance to Standard

Frequency of Performance Appraisal

Legal and Ethical Issues in Performance Appraisal

ees, increased "politicking" by salespeople, increased dissatisfaction, and increased turnover.[4] In fact, there may be no single factor with more influence on salespeople's behavior than performance evaluation.

This chapter is organized around a conceptual model of the concerns that managers must address when evaluating a salesperson's performance.[5] The model, shown in Exhibit 14.1, contains the following concerns: (1) criteria for measuring performance, (2) conducting performance appraisals, (3) evaluating individuals versus teams, (4) comparing actual performance to standard, (5) frequency of performance appraisal, and (6) legal and ethical issues in performance appraisal.

CRITERIA FOR MEASURING PERFORMANCE

Sales managers can choose one of two criteria when measuring performance: outcomes or behaviors. This section provides definitions, advantages and disadvantages, and examples of each criterion.

Outcome-Based Measures

Outcome-based measures are performance criteria that measure the results of the selling process. They include measures of revenue, such as dollar sales and sales unit volume, and measures of profitability, such as net margin, sales expense, or a ratio of cost/sales.[6] A firm that uses an outcome-based measure of performance such as sales may rely on internal documentation such as purchase orders and routine management financial reports. It could also use computerized performance monitoring (CPM).

In **computerized performance monitoring (CPM)**, computers track items such as the number of calls handled, the amount of time the terminal is left idle, the number of transactions, and the number and length of phone calls. As you might imagine, there are many applications of CPM in telemarketing and an increasing number in field sales as well. For example, field salespeople who use laptops can be required to sign in as they reach a customer's location and sign out as they leave. This allows the sales manager to track salespeople's calls, the amount of time spent on a call, and the amount of time between calls.

The use of CPM is widespread and growing. In 1987, according to a federal government estimate, approximately 6 million U.S. workers had some or all of their work evaluated through CPM.[7] A more recent study of employers showed that 73 of 186 firms (approximately 39 percent) used CPM.

Behavior-Based Measures

Behavior-based measures focus on the salesperson's selling activities. They include product knowledge, presentation quality, closing ability, services performed, the number of active accounts, the number of calls made, days worked, and other measures of activities.[8]

Measuring salesperson behavior or activity is more difficult than measuring outcomes. To measure telemarketers' behavior, sales managers can listen to calls. To measure field salesperson behavior, managers can ride with salespeople and gather information from customers, other salespeople, and other managers. Sales managers use this information to complete ratings instruments. These ratings instruments include ratings forms, forced-choice scales, and behavioral observation scales.[9] To supplement the sales manager's perspective, most firms also require salespeople to provide a self-assessment of their behaviors in the field by filling out call or activity reports. Some firms also conduct customer surveys to assess salesperson behavior.

Ratings Forms.   **Ratings forms** are lists of statements or adjectives about the sales job that the sales manager uses to evaluate each salesperson. The statements might include phrases such as "organizes sample case," "plans sales calls," and "listens well." For each statement the manager can select choices such as "strongly agree," "agree," "disagree," and "strongly disagree."

Ratings forms are easy for sales managers to complete. They can cover a broad range of selling activities, provide a consistent set of activities to measure all salespeople, and, if known in advance, can help the salesperson know exactly what is expected. The disadvantages of ratings forms are that they are not very customizable, so they may not capture the full range of activities required for the job. Also some sales manager might be subject to judgment biases (which will be discussed in the next section) or do not involve the salesperson in developing individual sales and personal development goals.

Forced-Choice Scales.   **Forced-choice scales** allow sales managers to rate salespeople on a series of adjectives that describe the person's performance. An example of a forced-choice rating system appears in Exhibit 14.2. The column designated

---

EXHIBIT 14.2
FORCED CHOICE SALESPERSON RATING

Instructions:.   For each pair of adjectives, place a check in the "Most Descriptive" column by the adjective that BEST describes that salesperson.

Pair	Adjectives	Weights	Most Descriptive
1	Understanding	0	
	Thorough	3	
2	Knows the job and performs it well	2	
	Plays no favorites	0	

Instructions:.   For each pair of adjectives, place a check in the "Most Descriptive" column by the adjective that BEST describes that salesperson.

Pair	Adjectives	Weights	Least Descriptive
3	Always criticizes, never praises	−2	
	Carries out orders by "passing the buck"	0	
4	Conceited	0	
	Infantile	−2	

SOURCE: Adapted from Jan. P. Muczyk and Myron Gable, "Managing Sales Performance Through a Comprehensive Performance Appraisal System," *Journal of Personal Selling and Sales Management,* 7 (May 1987): 41–52.

"weights" would not be contained in a form sales managers would use, but it is included to show how the manager's response would be evaluated.

Developing a forced-choice instrument requires several steps. First, supervisors and managers write essays in which effective and ineffective salespeople are described. Experts from the firm's human resources department or from an outside consulting firm read the essays and generate lists of adjectives used in the essays. They assign positive weights to those that were used to describe effective salespeople and negative weights to adjectives that described ineffective salespeople. Neutral weights are assigned to adjectives that were found in descriptions of both types of salespeople.

Sales managers evaluate each salesperson by selecting one of two adjectives from each pair. For example, in the first pair of adjectives in Exhibit 14.2, sales managers must choose either "understanding" or "thorough" to describe the salesperson. As you can see, "understanding" has a neutral weight because it was found in the essays describing both effective and ineffective salespeople. Therefore, if the sales manager selects "understanding," the salesperson receives a neutral score. "Thorough," on the other hand, has a positive weight because it was found only in essays describing effective salespeople. If the sales manager describes the salesperson using "thorough," the salesperson receives a positive score. The judgmental bias is removed by not telling the managers what the weights are. Sales managers must respond to the instrument not knowing whether a given item is weighted positively, negatively, or neutral.

After rating his or her salespeople, a sales manager submits the evaluations to an expert who uses the key with the weights for each adjective to generate an overall score for each salesperson. The scores are given back to the sales manager to use in ranking the salespeople.

Behavioral Observation Scales.   **Behavior observation scales (BOS)** are based on significant incidents which describe behaviors that can either enhance or detract from performance. An example of a BOS appears in Exhibit 14.3.

BOS have several advantages over other ratings systems. First, they focus on specific behaviors that have been linked to high performance for that particular job. During the development of BOS, sales managers and salespeople are asked to identify behaviors that are most likely to enhance or detract from performance. This discussion can lead to a greater understanding between sales managers and salespeople of the important components of the job. Second, by identifying certain behaviors as being desirable or undesirable, BOS can be a much more focused development tool. Under the ratings instrument approach discussed previously, salespeople are ranked in terms of overall behavioral tendencies, such as thoroughness or follow-up. This does not tell a salesperson what specific acts demonstrate thoroughness, only that their overall performance showed thoroughness. By contrast, a properly designed BOS tells a salesperson what specific actions the company views as demonstrating thoroughness.

The disadvantages of BOS include the difficulty of relating on-the-job behavior observed by the sales manager to the BOS categories. In other words, the BOS is not easily customizable to different salespeople. There is also a concern over the amount of observation that actually takes place. For salespeople who operate independently,

---

EXHIBIT 14.3

BOS RATING

Overcoming Resistance to Change:

1. Describes the details of the change to salespeople.
    (Almost Never) 1   2   3   4   5 (Almost Always)   NA

2. Explains why the change is necessary.
    (Almost Never) 1   2   3   4   5 (Almost Always)   NA

3. Discusses how the change will affect the salesperson.
    (Almost Never) 1   2   3   4   5 (Almost Always)   NA

4. Listens to the concerns of the salespeople.
    (Almost Never) 1   2   3   4   5 (Almost Always)   NA

5. Asks salespeople for help in making the change work.
    (Almost Never) 1   2   3   4   5 (Almost Always)   NA

6. If necessary, specifies the date for a follow-up meeting to respond to the salesperson's concerns.
    (Almost Never) 1   2   3   4   5 (Almost Always)   NA

TOTAL = _____

"5" indicates that the employee engages in the specified behavior 95 to 100 percent of the time.
"4" indicates that the employee engages in the specified behavior 85 to 94 percent of the time.
"3" indicates that the employee engages in the specified behavior 75 to 84 percent of the time.
"2" indicates that the employee engages in the specified behavior 65 to 74 percent of the time.
"1" indicates that the employee engages in the specified behavior 0 to 64 percent of the time.
"NA" means not applicable. The rater circles "NA" when there has not been an opportunity to
    observe the behavior.

Scores[a]:

Below Adequate	Adequate	Good	Excellent	Superior
6–10	11–15	16–20	21–25	26–30

[a]Scores are set by management.

SOURCE: Adapted from Jan. P. Muczyk and Myron Gable, "Managing Sales Performance Through a Comprehensive Performance Appraisal System," *Journal of Personal Selling and Sales Management,* 7 (May 1987): 41–52

---

it can be quite difficult for a sales manager to perform enough observations to make the technique usable. The development of a BOS is time consuming and costly. Last, because BOS ignores outcomes the technique may be insufficient to capture all the relevant performance dimensions to create an adequate performance appraisal. Sales jobs, after all, have outcomes that can be readily identified.

Call Reports.   **Call reports** are periodic accounts prepared by salespeople of how they are spending their time. Call reports are generally organized by account. That is, a salesperson fills out a call report for each call on each client. Call reports can be invaluable to sales managers for many reasons. First, call reports give management a record of the status of each account in terms of customer information such as upcoming orders, customer satisfaction, and suggestions for improvement. As a result, they can provide accurate records for management to take over the territory in case of salesperson transfer or termination. Second, they provide an important input to the evaluation process in terms of the activities of the salesperson because they provide details of the behaviors performed during the sales call. Third, they are useful in constructing forecasts for upcoming years for firms that use the salesforce composite method for forecasting sales (see Chapter 15 for further discussion of the salesforce composite forecasting method).

Activity Reports. **Activity reports** detail unusual events that occur in the field, such as a major change in pricing by a competitor, a major change in purchasing practices by a key customer, or some other significant event.[10] Activity reports are used by manufacturers' reps instead of call reports. In the United States manufacturers' rep firms that use call reports are considered employees instead of independent contractors by the Internal Revenue Service. This distinction leads to significant negative tax implications. Yet most *principals*—the firms whose products are being represented by sales reps—desire to receive information about the status of the rep's sales efforts. As a result, rep firms must walk a fine line between giving enough information to show the principal what is happening in the field and maintaining independent contractor status.

To ensure the activity reports do not cross the line and become call reports, several guidelines should be followed. The reports should be on the stationery of the rep firm, not the principal. They should not be made periodically, but only when a significant event occurs. Finally, they should not be made for every call. This is interpreted by the IRS as providing an accounting of the rep firm's time to the principal and can endanger the independent contractor status of the rep firm.

Silent Call Monitoring Scores. **Silent call monitoring scores** consist of supervisors' ratings of employees' performance during actual calls with customers. The ratings can cover several issues, including the greeting, ascertaining customer needs, information provided, courtesy, and listening skills.

Customer Satisfaction Surveys. **Customer satisfaction surveys** are questionnaires that are mailed to customers. The scores are based on customers' responses to questions about their interaction with the rep. Customer satisfaction surveys are commonly used by automobile dealers to understand customers perceptions of the buying process.

Combining Outcome-Based and Behavior-Based Methods

In firms that use outcome-based control systems, sales managers concentrate on "objective" measures of sales success and typically spend little time monitoring salespeople and providing managerial direction. By contrast, sales managers in firms employing behavior-based control systems spend more time monitoring salespeople's activities, provide higher levels of direction and direct intervention when appropriate, and base the overall evaluation of the salesperson's performance on a

EXHIBIT 14.4	
ADVANTAGES AND DISADVANTAGES OF BEHAVIOR- AND OUTCOME-BASED CONTROL SYSTEMS	

	Outcome-Based	Behavior-Based
Advantages	• Availability of simple, objective measures of sales volume or dollars • Allows salespeople to set their own individual methods; holds them accountable for results only • Provides individual motivation; nonproducers are not paid	• Affords the manager much more control over the activities of the salesforce • Allows the manager to require actions that do not result in short-term payoffs, such as customer service • Allows the manager to eliminate inequities that can occur through the use of simple outcome measures; if sales are the basis for compensation, salespeople have little incentive to spend time developing a customer—behavior-based control allows the manager to explicitly require salespeople to develop new customers
Disadvantages	• No direction is provided to salesforce • Focuses the salesperson on activities that generate immediate payoffs • Using multiple indicators of performance to overcome the problems above can lead to complex recordkeeping and subjective judgments toward the importance of various activities	• Evaluations are complex and subjective • Manager rewards on the basis of activities the manager perceives to lead to performance—salespeople may not agree with the manager's perceptions Complex systems strain management's ability to collect and analyze the information

SOURCE: Adapted from Erin Anderson and Richard L. Oliver, "Perspectives on Behavior-Based Versus Outcome-Based Salesforce Control Systems," *Journal of Marketing*, 51 (October 1987): 76–88.

blend of what the salesperson brings to the task (experience, aptitude, product knowledge), their activities (number of new accounts, number of calls), and the quality of their selling strategies. The advantages and disadvantages of each method are listed in Exhibit 14.4.

In practice, most firms use a combination of the two control methods, although the balance is tilted toward behavior-based. An interesting pattern emerges when managers are asked to indicate whether they consider behaviors or outcomes to be more important in their evaluation of a salesperson. One study showed that behavior measures were six times as important as outcome measures in determining the sales manager's evaluation of the salesperson.[11] Another showed behaviors accounted for a larger portion of the variance in predicting sales manager's evaluations of salespeople than objective measures of sales performance.[12]

An example of combining outcome-based and behavior-based performance measures is shown in Exhibit 14.5. There the performance of a group of telemarketers is rated using CPM to measure outcomes, and silent call monitoring and customer satisfaction surveys to measure behaviors.[13]

				EXHIBIT 14.5				

INTEGRATED EVALUATION REPORT FOR TELEMARKETERS

Name	Total Contacts	Total Issues	Average Issues/ Contact	Average Contact Time (min.)	Total Minutes Score (%)	Customer Survey Score (%)	Call Monitor
Jay	500	1,122	2.24	1.7	850	55	70
Bob	225	500	2.22	3.6	810	75	80
Sandy	275	525	1.91	4.54	1,248.5	95	95
Karen	325	670	2.06	4.2	1,365	92	90
Totals	1,325	2,817			4,273.5		
Standard (per employee)	300			3.3	1,000	75	75

SOURCE: Adapted from Jay Marwaha, Monica Jenks, and John Goodman, "Performance Evaluations, Quality, and Productivity," *Journal of Quality and Participation* (September 1993): 84–89.

Exhibit 14.5 shows for each telemarketing rep the total number of contacts and issues handled, the average issues per contact, average contact time, the customer satisfaction score, and the overall rating. For example, Jay had 500 total contacts, and callers asked for help on a total of 1,122 issues. The average number of issues per call, therefore, was 2.24. Jay dealt with his 500 calls in 850 minutes, for an average of 1.7 minutes per call. His score on the customer satisfaction survey was 55 percent (out of a possible 100 percent), and his silent call monitoring score was 70 percent (out of a possible 100 percent). From the chart it can be seen that relying on quantitative measures of performance alone may give a misleading picture. Jay had the highest number of contacts and the highest number of issues handled, but worked fewer total minutes than the standard and also fell below standard on the customer satisfaction survey and the call monitoring score. Sandy, by contrast, dealt with fewer customers than the standard (275 instead of 300), but her customer survey call monitoring scores were the highest of the group. Sandy also was quite productive in terms of the total number of minutes worked.

The performance appraisals for the different reps can be constructed from Exhibit 14.5. Jay is doing a good job in terms of the number of calls handled, but his low customer satisfaction score may indicate that he is not giving customers enough time on the line. Call monitoring could determine whether Jay was cutting his customers short, and the manager could provide a series of coaching suggestions for Jay to improve his customer satisfaction ratings. Sandy, by contrast, seems to be spending a great deal of time with each customer. Her customer satisfaction and call monitoring scores show that she is very good with customers, but she is handling fewer calls than the standard. She must cut down the amount of time per call to increase the number of calls handled because she is already working almost 25 percent more minutes than the standard. Perhaps monitoring a series of calls with the objective of identifying where she is spending too much time would be useful.

CONDUCTING THE PERFORMANCE APPRAISAL

Performance appraisals can be conducted by sales managers or individual salespeople. More and more companies, however, are also offering employees the opportunity to rate their own performance. This section provides a rationale for sales managers and salespeople to conduct performance appraisals and outlines the problems with having either group conduct them.

Sales Manager Evaluation

Sales manager evaluation is the most common method of conducting performance appraisal because the supervisor is expected to have the most knowledge regarding the salesperson's performance. The sales manager is also in the best position to assess the quality of the salesperson's performance.

The primary problem sales managers have in conducting salesperson performance appraisal is the existence of bias. *Bias* occurs when sales managers inflate (give higher ratings than deserved) or deflate (give lower ratings than deserved) subordinates' performance ratings.[14] Biases in conducting performance appraisal can be conscious or unconscious.

Conscious bias can be positive or negative. *Positive conscious bias* includes the sales manager's desire to help a rookie salesperson overcome initial problems in a territory, or to help a veteran salesperson cope with problems outside the job. *Conscious negative bias* ranges from the desire to get rid of a problem employee to avoiding a confrontation with a subordinate who is not performing. The positive

	EXHIBIT 14.6	
	MOTIVES FOR BIASED RATINGS	
	Inflated Rating	Deflated Rating
Positive Motive	• Keep the employee motivated • Maximize the merit pay increase • Avoid creating a permanent record that might damage the employee's career • Reward good recent performance • Assess an employee with a personal problem • Reward good effort • Personal liking for the employee	• Scare better performance out of an employee to prevent eventual termination • Build a stronger case against an employee who is destined to be terminated
Negative Motive	• Avoid "hanging dirty laundry" in public • Make the manager look good • Avoid confrontation with the subordinate • Promote a problem employee up and out	• Punish an employee • Encourage an employee to quit • Minimize merit pay increase • Comply with an organizational edict to keep ratings low

SOURCE: Clinton Longenecker and Dean Ludwig, "Ethical Dilemmas in Performance Appraisal Revisited," *Journal of Business Ethics*, 9(12) (1990): 961–969.

and negative biases, or motives, for inflating or deflating ratings are shown in Exhibit 14.6, along with examples of each.

Inflated or deflated performance ratings can also result from *unconscious biases,* often referred to as *judgment biases,* on the part of the sales manager. Some of the more common unconscious biases include (1) ignoring regression effects, (2) underweighting base rate information, (3) the availability heuristic, (4) hindsight bias, (5) anchoring and adjustment, and (6) fundamental attribution error.[15]

Ignoring Regression Effects. **Regression effects** reflect the tendency of unusual observations to be followed by observations that are more typical of the norm. One common example of unusual observations is with new life insurance and real estate salespeople. New salespeople in these industries may have a flurry of activity from relatives and friends that results in extremely high performance in the first year. In the second year, however, many of these effects fade. The salespeople may have all of their friends and relatives as clients, so the amount of new business declines sharply. A manager who is aware of regression bias will be careful not to overreact to the occurrence of an extraordinarily good or bad quarter because it is unlikely that such performances will be repeated. Quotas might be changed for the upcoming year, but not in as extreme a fashion as may be indicated by the actual sales performance.

One way to overcome regression effects is to use *moving averages* for setting quotas (see Chapter 15 for a discussion of calculation of forecasts using moving averages). For example, rather than basing quotas on the most recent quarter or year, quotas can be set on a moving average of 4 quarters or 3 years. Unfortunately, this method does not work for rookie salespeople. For these salespeople, the manager must use experience and judgment in setting quotas for future periods because the manager does not know whether the rookie's performance is a one-time event or indicative of a steady level of performance.

Underweighting Base Rate Information. **Base rate information** is the actual distribution of outcomes being assessed. Base rate information might be the actual level of customer satisfaction expressed by all of a salesperson's customers. *Underweighting base rate information* occurs when a sales manager overlooks the average, or base rate, of customer satisfaction and concentrates instead on a particular instance that is not representative of the base. For example, if a sales manager rides with a salesperson to observe the salesperson's interaction with customers and the salesperson has productive interactions with all customers, the sales manager may believe that the salesperson always has productive encounters. This perception might persist even if the log of customer complaints shows that the salesperson's customers, by and large, are dissatisfied with the salesperson's approach. Conversely, if a sales manager is riding with a different salesperson when he or she encounters an irate customer, the sales manager may let that experience override the salesperson's good customer complaint record. Both examples show the potential problems that can arise when sales managers ignore base rate information and allow their limited personal experience to be the basis for making an evaluation.

To overcome underweighting base rate information, sales managers can conduct more frequent evaluations. They can also try to assess the salesperson's performance over longer periods of time and be required to document specific reasons why salespeople were given a certain performance rating.

Availability Heuristic.   The **availability heuristic** is a bias that occurs when managers assess subordinates based on the information that is most readily available. A *heuristic* is simply a rule of thumb used to make decisions. (See Chapter 16 for a more detailed discussion of rules and shortcuts.) Available information is that which is recent, or is so extreme that the manager immediately recalls it even if it occurred some time previously. For example, a manager who uses the availability heuristic will be more likely to recall a major sale that happened at the end of the quarter than at the beginning of the quarter. Under the availability heuristic, managers will recall information that is extremely good or extremely bad much more rapidly than information that may be more representative of the performance of the salesperson.

Managers can overcome the availability heuristic by making more frequent observations of the behavior being assessed. They can also be trained to recognize the occurrence of availability, and to make sure not to let available information overwhelm other information that may be more characteristic of the salesperson's performance.

Hindsight Bias.   **Hindsight bias** occurs when sales managers discount information received from a salesperson because they believe it would have become apparent or it would have occurred anyway. For hindsight bias to occur, the salesperson could bring information about market conditions, competitors, or customers to the attention of the sales manager. The information may help the company avert a problem such as losing an account or failing to predict a competitor's entry to the market. Hindsight bias occurs if the sales manager believes he or she would have found out the information anyway, so the contribution of the salesperson is minimized. Should hindsight bias occur repeatedly, the salesperson may stop bringing information to the sales manager because no credit is received.

Managers can be trained to overcome hindsight bias by being made aware that it exists. The training may involve asking managers to develop alternate scenarios; that is, what would have happened had the salesperson not made them aware that a potential problem existed? This encourages sales managers to give credit where it is due and increases the likelihood that the salesperson will bring items of competitive intelligence to their attention in the future.

Anchoring and Adjustment.   **Anchoring** occurs when managers rate salespeople using a scale. The anchor is the starting point on the scale from which the evaluation is made. If the firm uses a five-point Likert-type scale (1–5 scale where 1 = highly unsatisfactory, 2 = unsatisfactory, 3 = neutral, 4 = satisfactory, 5 = highly satisfactory) to rank employees, ideally a sales manager would assume that all employees start the period at the center point (3) and adjust the rating to reflect the salesperson's activity observed during the time period for which the evaluation is made. The problem arises when managers adjust inappropriately.

Assume that two new salespeople arrive at a district office. Salesperson A won the top trainee award, whereas salesperson B barely made it through training. The sales manager might use the rank in the training class as an anchor. Therefore, salesperson A might start the year with an anchor of 4, while salesperson B might start the year with an anchor of 2. Given the different starting points, for the same level of performance salesperson A would receive the highest possible ranking (5), while salesperson B would receive a neutral ranking (3). The tendency for high performers to receive consistently high ratings, even when the performance is not commensurate, is known as the *halo effect*.

The same phenomenon can occur when setting quotas. If a salesperson works extremely hard and has a very good quarter, that sales level can be used as the anchor for upcoming periods. Overachievement in the future will not be recognized because the anchor has been set at a point where overachievement is the norm.

To overcome the anchoring problem, sales managers can be trained to recognize the circumstances under which they need to adjust from the base rate. They may also be trained to set performance expectations consistently across the salesforce, rather than adjusting base rates for each individual. If each salesperson has his or her own anchor, it is very difficult to determine what "high performance" means. Suppose that the top salesperson and the bottom salesperson in the district each increase their performance by 50 percent in a given quarter. They have both achieved the same absolute percentage increase, but the top salesperson has probably exerted much more effort because he or she was starting from a higher anchor. Sales managers must be careful when making compensation decisions to take both absolute and relative performance into account.

Fundamental Attribution Error.   **Fundamental attribution error** occurs when managers view salespeople as having more control over sales outcomes than they actually do. One study identified several major factors that influence sales outcomes, including differences in economic conditions, corporate marketing support, competitive conditions, and individual salesperson's characteristics.[16] Of the factors identified in the study, only salesperson's individual characteristics were controllable by the salesperson. The rest were either under the control of the company or market factors beyond the salesperson's or the company's control. As a result, the salesperson may not be entirely responsible for outcomes that are either above or below expectations. The letter in Box 14.1 exemplifies the frustration salespeople can feel when factors affecting performance are out of their control.

Sales managers do not always take these uncontrollable events into account when assessing performance. Another study showed that sales managers ignored differences in territory difficulty when assessing salespeople's performance.[17] However, a later study showed that sales managers could use territory difficulty information to adjust performance assessments if the territory difficulty data were put in a spreadsheet format that could be readily manipulated by the sales manager.[18] Sales managers have also been shown to give salespeople they know the benefit of the doubt when faced with negative outcomes. In other words, if a salesperson has a bad month or quarter, and the sales manager knows the salesperson, he or she is likely to attribute the bad outcomes to circumstances rather than to the salesperson. If the sales manager is not familiar with the salesperson, this attribution may not be made.[19]

BOX 14.1
"THE SALES FORCE DIDN'T CREATE THE MESS AT DEC"

The following letter from a DEC salesperson appeared in *Business Week*

As a member of Digital Equipment Corp.'s sales force for the past nine years, I find it particularly offensive that we as a group continue to be blamed for the problems facing this company ("Reveille for DEC's Sleepy Sales Force," Information Processing, August 30, 1993). I have not witnessed any Digital salespeople sleeping in my office. What I do see is a group of extremely dedicated, committed, and professional individuals trying to adjust to some major organizational changes.

The sales force did not decide on the technologies, did not develop the products, or even get to design the marketing campaigns. Our senior management is out of touch with the field. How does one sell "Imagine," the current marketing theme for all our advertising? We don't need a recipe, but we need solid products for our customers to buy. And after it's sold, we need systems and people in place that let us get back in the field to sell instead of handholding every single order.

We deserve to be treated with dignity and respect. I'm disappointed that management doesn't understand the psychology of badgering the team. I was taught you can get a horse to race a lot faster with some sugar than you can by beating him with a stick.

SOURCE: Reprinted from "Readers' Report," *Business Week* (September 20, 1993): 7–10.

There are several ways to train managers to overcome fundamental attribution errors. First, managers can be encouraged to look at the salesperson's actions in the context of what is expected of the salesforce overall. For instance, if a salesperson has a bad quarter but everyone else in the firm has one also, the sales manager should not attribute the problem to the salesperson alone. Further, to avoid biasing evaluations in the favor of someone who is familiar to the sales manager, multiple raters can be used. The salesperson can be rated by the sales manager, sales managers from other territories, customers, other salespeople, and so on to get a fuller view of the salesperson's actual performance.

Whether bias is conscious or unconscious, it creates ethical and managerial problems. Performance appraisal carries two conflicting objectives. The guidelines stated in Exhibit 14.7 have been proposed to meet those two objectives.[20]

First, from the perspective of comparison across managers and across territories, performance appraisals need to be as accurate as possible. Accurate performance appraisals create an environment in which all employees compete for promotions and compensation from a common starting point. If rating inflation is common, for example, and a new sales manager tries to give accurate ratings, his or her salespeople will be rated more negatively than others in the firm. As a result, the performance appraisal system becomes less meaningful from the perspective of determining promotions or assigning raises.

The second objective for performance appraisal is to motivate salespeople and encourage them to perform at a high level. Managers often argue that they should not be brutally honest in performance appraisal as this may serve to demotivate employees and prevent them from accomplishing company goals in the future. As a result, managers often fail to provide accurate ratings.

EXHIBIT 14.7
GUIDELINES FOR ETHICAL PERFORMANCE APPRAISAL

Objective 1: Accuracy

- The firm must provide sound procedure for managers to use in performance appraisal.
- Managers must be trained to provide performance appraisals—the training should cover judgment biases and the importance of providing accurate performance appraisals.
- Top managers must demonstrate the importance of accurate performance appraisals by adhering to that standard in their own ratings.
- Performance appraisal process should be audited to ensure the data accuracy and integrity.

Objective 2: Motivation

- Managers must develop and communicate clear performance standards prior to the formal appraisal.
- Managers should provide ongoing feedback to allow subordinates to change behaviors if necessary.
- Managers should take the performance appraisal process seriously—they should plan and execute performance appraisals carefully.
- Managers who wish to deviate from the accuracy criterion should discuss the situation with their superiors in advance.

SOURCE: Adapted from Clinton O. Longenecker and Dean Ludwig, "Ethical Dilemmas in Performance Appraisal Revisited," *Journal of Business Ethics*, 9(12) (1990): 961–990

Salesperson Self-Evaluation

Salesperson self-evaluation is a form of performance appraisal wherein the employee rates his or her own performance. Most research has indicated that employees give themselves higher ratings than their supervisors do. However, given that this bias exists, using a self-evaluation can be quite helpful as part of the performance appraisal process. If a new performance appraisal instrument is being used, self-evaluation can help employees understand how managers interpret the categories. For example, when call monitoring was instituted at one firm as a means of assessing performance among telemarketers, the salespeople were allowed to tape a few of their own calls and evaluate their own performance.[21] It gave the employees a chance to see how the performance monitoring device would be used, and it gave managers and employees a chance to talk about how performance would be rated. Interestingly, in this case the salespeople were much harder on themselves than management would have been.

Another use for self-evaluation is to determine the degree of consistency between the salesperson's view of the job and the sales manager's view. If the salesperson and the sales manager agree on the performance evaluation, they have a consistent view of the behaviors and outcomes necessary to accomplish the firm's goals. If the two perceptions are quite different, the salespeople are likely to experience role ambiguity, dissatisfaction, and frustration because they are not aware of how they are being evaluated.[22] Further, the performance of the firm will suffer since the salespeople are not aware of what they must do in order to achieve the firm's goals.

EVALUATING INDIVIDUALS VERSUS TEAMS

Most performance appraisals are done on an individual basis; that is, each is aimed at assessing the performance of a single individual. For example, the ratings forms, forced-choice, and BOS approaches already discussed are based on individual performance. Although individual performance measurement is still the backbone of most firms' performance appraisal systems, the increasing use of selling teams (see Chapter 8 for a discussion of selling teams) is forcing managers to develop new measures of performance.

Teams are becoming an extremely popular means of accomplishing goals for many firms. Various types of teams are in use in nearly all the *Fortune* 1,000 companies. Nearly half of these firms are using permanent work teams for everyday business.[23] Many of these firms are experiencing problems with measuring team member performance. Problems include trying to use systems that were designed for individuals, the difficulty of distinguishing between individual and group output, the need to customize performance measures to the type of team, and the difficulty of measuring input from cross-functional team members.

To overcome these problems, sales managers can rely on a basic tool; the role result matrix. The **role-result matrix** is a specification of the roles to be played by each team member and the results that are expected from each team member and from the team as a whole. In essence it outlines the individual responsibilities necessary for the team to accomplish its overall sales goals. An example of a role-result matrix appears in Exhibit 14.8. This role-result matrix contains the people, tasks, and results expected for each member for a computer manufacturer's sales team serving a large and complex account. A sales manager can use the role-result matrix when evaluating salespeople by weighting the relative importance of individual and group performance in the appraisal process.

EXHIBIT 14.8		
ROLE-RESULT MATRIX FOR COMPUTER MANUFACTURER SALES TEAM		
	Developing New Business	Maintaining Current Business
National Account Manager	• Monitoring and bidding on new contacts • Expanding customer relationship to new buying center members	• Monitoring existing contracts • Maintaining customer relationships with existing buying center members
Application Engineer	• Identifying new product applications • Modifying existing products for new applications	• Identifying potential cost savings for existing product applications • Identifying additional applications for current products
Customer Service Representative	• Identifying customer discontent with competing products • Ensuring customer satisfaction with new products	• Maintaining delivery schedules • Resolving credit billing and return problems
Technical Support Representative	• Identifying problems with existing products that could be solved by product modification • Monitoring new product performance	• Developing database of product problems with existing product applications • Minimize customer downtime through rapid service

COMPARING ACTUAL PERFORMANCE TO STANDARD

Once the salesperson's behaviors or outcomes have been assessed by the sales manager or salesperson, the manager must compare it to a standard by ranking employees, comparing them to average, or comparing them to a norm. These three methods are illustrated in the following example. Assume that a district has six salespeople, and the manager is interested in evaluating them by the number of new accounts each has developed. The six salespeople and their number of new accounts appear in Exhibit 14.9. For the purpose of illustration, assume that the territories are equivalent in terms of difficulty and potential. In reality, of course, this would be highly unlikely.

Using the *ranking* method, the salespeople would be ranked from highest to lowest. Linda would be the top performer and David would be the lowest. *Comparison to average* would compare each salesperson's performance to the average for the group. In this case, the average number of accounts is nine ($54 \div 6 = 9$). Linda, Phil, and John would be the high performers, whereas Patricia, Mark, and David would be the low performers.

A *comparison to norm* approach evaluates salespeople by comparing their performance to the norm. As long as the salesperson had performance within the boundaries of the norm, the salesperson would be performing at an acceptable level. The boundary of the norm is determined by constructing upper and lower control limits about the means of the observations. The upper control limit is three standard deviations above the mean, while the lower control limit is three standard deviations below. In this example, the standard deviation is 3, so the upper control limit is set at 18, while the lower control limit is set at 0. Given the control limits, all the salespeople are performing at an acceptable level. The differences in performance, using this approach, result from normal variations in the process of opening new accounts. To improve performance of the office overall, sales managers should seek to increase the mean and to narrow the control limits.[24]

FREQUENCY OF PERFORMANCE MEASUREMENT

Historically, most performance reviews have taken place on an annual basis. Exhibit 14.10 shows the results of two surveys that demonstrate the pervasiveness of

EXHIBIT 14.9	
NUMBER OF NEW ACCOUNTS DEVELOPED BY SALESPERSON	
Salesperson	Number of New Accounts
Patricia	7
Linda	16
Mark	8
David	4
John	9
Phil	10
Total	54

SOURCE: Howard S. Gitlow and Shelly J. Gitlow, *The Deming Guide to Quality and Competitive Position* (Englewood Cliffs, N.J.: Prentice-Hall, 1987).

EXHIBIT 14.10		
GOAL-SETTING FREQUENCY		
	Percent of Companies	
Goal-Setting Frequency	Morris, et al. Study	Coopers and Lybrand Study
Annually	44.7	71.4
Monthly	8.7	17.1
Quarterly	18.4	11.4
Semiannually	28.2	5.0
Other	0.0	4.3

SOURCES: Michael H. Morris, Duane L. Davis, Jeffrey W. Allen, Ramon A. Avila, and Joseph Chapman, "Assessing the Relationships Among Performance Measures, Managerial Practices, and Satisfaction When Evaluating the Salesforce: A Replication and Extension," *Journal of Personal Selling and Sales Management,* 11 (Summer 1991): 25–35, based on a survey of 104 industrial and service companies located in Indiana, and Coopers and Lybrand Human Resource Advisory Group, based on a survey of 180 companies. Reported in "How Often Do You Set Sales Goals," *Sales and Marketing Management* (July 1994): 34.

the annual review. There are several advantages to annual reviews. They can be timed to coincide with the annual planning cycle, so the objectives for a salesperson can be developed based on the objectives for the business unit as a whole (see Chapter 16 for a discussion of matching business unit and salesperson goals). Annual reviews also give adequate time to observe a range of behaviors so that a base rate of performance can be identified. Finally, annual reviews are done infrequently enough so that the paperwork load on sales managers is not overwhelming.

Unfortunately, it appears that managers often fail to provide adequate annual performance appraisals. One survey showed that while 70 percent of managers at large organizations report that they review their employees' performance annually, fewer than 30 percent of the employees at the same firms report that bosses provide annual performance reviews.[25] Although the survey did not determine the cause of the discrepancy, it is clear that subordinates do not perceive they are receiving adequate performance review, even when management thinks it is providing adequate guidance. Moreover, managers may not devote sufficient time to performance appraisal. According to William Cone, a manager for Professional Development at Hughes Aircraft, "When a conflict in scheduling occurs between evaluating subordinates and hobnobbing with the boss, the appraisal session loses every time. So it goes throughout the organization, with bosses at every level spending as little time on appraisal as possible in order to have time for 'more important things.'"[26]

One possible solution to this problem may be to conduct more frequent performance appraisals, such as quarterly, monthly, or on a continuous basis.[27] More frequent performance reviews are also appropriate for several other reasons. First, when change in the industry is extremely rapid, such as in the computer industry, reviews may need to be more frequent to match market conditions. Second, if the business is experiencing severe downturn, more frequent appraisals may be appropriate because they give management more control over on programs and people. Third, more frequent reviews may be requested by top management when they perceive a need for tighter controls on salesforce behavior. Fourth, more frequent re-

EXHIBIT 14.11
OBJECTIVES AND GUIDELINES FOR PERFORMING QUARTERLY PERFORMANCE REVIEWS

Objectives	Guidelines
1. Don't let the performance reviews overwhelm the manager.	• Reduce paperwork to a minimum—only essentials should be reported. • Keep interviews between managers and employees short and to the point. • Focus interviews on coaching to counter problems that have arisen since original goals for the year were set.
2. Don't let short-term performance reviews create a short-term-results mentality.	• Put quarterly performance reviews in perspective of annual plans. • Quarterly reviews allow employees to adjust goals that are no longer appropriate or to add new goals based on environmental change.
3. Do not let annual reviews become a compilation of quarterly reviews.	• Annual reviews should focus on long-term career development.

SOURCE: Adapted from George S. Odiorne, "The Trend Toward the Quarterly Performance Review," *Business Horizons,* (July/August 1990): 38–41.

views may be appropriate when there are a significant number of new employees, because more appraisal sessions give sales managers more chances to tell employees they need to change certain behaviors before they cause a major problem. For example, after supervisors monitor a call at the GE Answer Center, the evaluation is sent instantly to the telemarketer by electronic mail.[28]

Unfortunately, frequent performance appraisals are difficult for sales managers. They increase the amount of paperwork and reduce the amount of time the managers can spend serving their own accounts. To overcome these problems, quarterly performance reviews should follow certain objectives and guidelines, such as those stated in Exhibit 14.11. These rules are aimed at improving the frequency and quality of feedback to employees while not creating an insurmountable burden for sales managers.

LEGAL AND ETHICAL ISSUES IN PERFORMANCE APPRAISAL

Managers must be aware of the legal and ethical issues in salesforce evaluation. Three important legal issues are the implications of employee testing, bias, and the use of computer performance monitoring. Performance appraisals constitute a "test" in the eyes of the law. Governmental agencies such as the Equal Employment Opportunity Commission (EEOC), Office of Federal Contract Compliance Programs, and the Supreme Court, define a "test" as any decision, formal or informal, that affects an individual's status in the organization regarding selection, promotion, demotion, transfer, pay, or admission into a training program that would affect any of the foregoing. The test does not have to be a formal annual review. It can consist of a conversation at lunch.

Companies must be careful to document performance appraisals. If an employee challenges an adverse decision, the firm is responsible for demonstrating that

---

BOX 14.2

MANAGER'S GUIDE TO PERFORMANCE APPRAISAL

1. Appraise performance as behavior: forget about personality traits.
2. Critique the work done, not the potential for work yet to be done.
3. Keep the system simple and the paperwork minimal.
4. Separate systems-oriented-toward-employee compensation from systems-oriented-to-ward-employee development—at least initially.
5. Once a system has been decided upon, apply it for several years; don't tinker with it annually.
6. Forget about applying performance appraisal to union employees once they have seniority (this has application to telemarketing sales reps who may be unionized).
7. Do not rely on formal performance appraisals alone to communicate about performance; day-to-day contacts must do the bulk of the job.
8. Review performance formally at least once a year. Write down the appraisal, but limit it to one side of an $8^{1}/_{2} \times 11$ sheet of paper.
9. Require the human resources department to audit, oversee, and spot-check the appraisals after the fact, but also stipulate that the appraisals should be kept on file for no more than 2 years.
10. Train managers to carry out their performance appraisal responsibility. Never just hand an appraisal package to managers and hope they make it all work. They won't.
11. Accept the fact that some managers will never become adept at performance appraisal. They see it as playing God—and they don't want to play.
12. Recognize that some employees couldn't care less what others think about them. A constructive appraisal requires that the participants have sufficiency, self-awareness, and insight to profit from the experience.
13. Recognize that the real experts on employees' performance are the employees and their bosses—not Freud, McGregor, Maslow, the government, or the human resources department.
14. In mature organizations, tie pay to performance appraisal.
15. Recognize that top managers who operate by the panic button, constantly shifting attention from one problem to another, cannot provide the stability required for an effective appraisal system.
16. Be sure that managers are aware of the evolving legal principles about performance appraisal and that they know how to base their evaluations and actions on defensible, objective data.

SOURCE: Adapted from Ron Zemke, "Do Performance Appraisals Change Performance?" *Training* (May 1991): 34–39.

---

the decision was not discriminatory. Given the firm's responsibility, it is not appropriate for the performance appraisal to be oral only. Written performance appraisals played key roles in two court cases in which salespeople were terminated for weak performance.[29] In the first case, a black male sued a large cereal manufacturer for racial discrimination in firing him. The firm, through written performance appraisals, was able to document that the salesperson's performance had deteriorated over time and that the salesperson had been notified of the problem and had been given sufficient time to make necessary performance improvements. Based on the written performance appraisals, the court found in favor of the cereal company.[30]

In a similar case, a salesperson sued a health and beauty aid company for age discrimination, stating that after 20 years with the company, he had been fired and replaced by a much younger sales representative. Again, the firm, through written performance appraisals, was able to prove that the salesperson's performance had deteriorated over time and, despite receiving several warnings and being given adequate time to change his behavior, performance did not improve. As a result, the court found in favor of the company.[31]

Another legal issue is that because performance appraisal constitutes a "test," it must meet all the required psychometric standards in terms of reliability and validity for the test to withstand legal challenge. The performance appraisal should also be demonstrably free of errors by sales managers, such as excessive strictness or leniency, personal bias, and ambiguous standards.[32] See Box 14.2 for a discussion of the issues managers need to know about conducting performance appraisals.

While CPM is a popular method of assessing salesperson behavior, firms must be careful of the legal and ethical consequences of using call monitoring. Call monitoring, as already discussed in Chapter 4, is regulated by state, with some states allowing monitoring with no notification to either party, some requiring notification of both parties, and others requiring notification of one party. From an ethical standpoint, careful design and use of CPM is required. One study showed that the use of CPM alone was negatively related to workers' perceptions of fairness of evaluation. As a result, CPM should not be used as a replacement for other methods of performance evaluation.

Second, CPM systems can measure everything from the number of keystrokes per second to the number of phone calls answered per hour. While many of these measures can be helpful and are relevant to workers' performance, the use of too many measures can be overwhelming to managers and workers alike. Managers may not be able to track the overwhelming amount of information, and workers may become confused as to the important aspects of their jobs.[33]

SUMMARY

Sales managers must understand and conduct proper performance appraisals of their sales people. Proper performance appraisals can lead to increased motivation, performance, cost reductions, and reduced role ambiguity. Improper performance appraisal, by contrast, can expose the firm to legal liability and result in increased turnover, demotivated employees, and increased employee dissatisfaction.

There are five major decision areas for sales managers related to performance appraisal: the criteria for measuring performance, conducting performance appraisals, evaluating individuals versus teams, comparing actual performance to standard, and the frequency of performance appraisal.

In terms of criteria on which to measure performance, sales managers have two basic choices: outcomes or behaviors. Outcomes are specific, measurable results of selling efforts, such as dollar sales and unit volume, net margins, sales expenses, or ratios of costs to sales. Behaviors are a salesperson's activities that are related to accomplishing the firm's sales objectives. Behavioral measures include product knowledge, presentation quality, closing ability, services performed, number of calls made, days worked, and other activity measures. Behavioral activities are measured via scales, including traditional rating, forced-choice rating, behavioral observation scales, call reports, and activity reports. In practice, most firms use a combination of the two methods to develop an overall performance rating for a salesperson.

Performance appraisals can be conducted by the sales manager or the salesperson. Traditionally sales managers conduct performance appraisals. In so doing, they must be careful not to demonstrate bias. Bias can be conscious or unconscious and can be either positive or negative. Unconscious bias can result from various judgment biases, including ignoring regression effects, underweighting base rate information, the availability heuristic, hindsight, anchoring and adjustment, and fundamental attribution error. Salespeople as well as customers can also conduct performance appraisals. Self-evaluation by salespeople can be an important part of the appraisal process. Comparing the evaluations of salespeople and sales managers can help salespeople understand what is important in the selling task.

While most performance appraisal is performed at the individual level, team selling is becoming more prevalent in many industries, necessitating changes in performance appraisal methods. One means of evaluating team member performance is the use of the role-result matrix. This matrix provides clarification as to the duties of each team member. The sales manager can use the role-result matrix evaluation, along with the individual evaluation, to determine an individual salesperson's performance rating.

Comparing actual performance to standard can be done by simple ranking, comparison to average, or comparison to standard. Performance is traditionally measured on an annual basis. There are strong arguments, however, for more frequent performance assessments. Quarterly or monthly performance assessments allow the salesperson to change inappropriate behavior while there is time to affect performance outcomes. Some firms have gone so far as to provide instant performance monitoring through silent monitoring of phone calls.

From a legal perspective, managers need to be aware of the status of performance appraisal as a "test" in the eyes of the EEOC, which means that the performance appraisal must be demonstrably valid and free of bias. Managers also need to be aware of the importance of adequately documenting performance appraisals.

KEY TERMS

performance appraisal	customer satisfaction surveys
outcome-based measures	regression effects
computerized performance monitoring (CPM)	base rate information
behavior-based measures	availability heuristic
ratings forms	hindsight bias
forced-choice scales	anchoring
behavioral observation scales (BOS)	fundamental attribution error
call reports	salesperson self-evaluation
activity reports	role-result matrix
silent call monitoring scores	

DISCUSSION QUESTIONS

1. What is performance appraisal? What makes salespeople so difficult to evaluate?

2. What are the two major criteria for measuring performance? Give specific examples of each criterion. Under what conditions is each criterion most appropriate?
3. Compare and contrast ratings forms, forced-choice ratings, and BOS. Which is the easiest to develop? The most difficult? Explain why.
4. What are the differences between an activity report and a call report? Why must organizations that use manufacturers' rep firms be careful about requiring the reps to fill out call reports?
5. What are the possible biases when sales managers evaluate salespeople? For one of the biases, explain how the sales manager can reduce its impact on evaluation.
6. What is the rationale for salesperson self-evaluation?
7. Discuss some of the difficulties in evaluating salespeople who operate in teams. How might a manager overcome some of these problems?
8. How can a sales manager determine whether a given level of salesperson performance is at, above, or below standard?
9. Most performance appraisals take place on an annual basis. Outline the situations under which more frequent performance appraisal is appropriate.
10. What are the legal and ethical issues firms face with the use of CPM? What other performance appraisal methods should be used in conjunction with CPM to give a more complete idea of performance?

PROBLEMS

1. PaperPlus, a paper products manufacturing company, administers annual performance reviews to all of its employees. Lisa Beach, sales manager at PaperPlus, has read in leading industry journals that it is more effective to evaluate employees on a more frequent basis. She wants to write a memo to her boss, the district manager, to explain her concerns and to recommend a new evaluation system. What suggestions should she mention in the memo to be most convincing?

2. The following chart illustrates the total number of sales calls each salesperson has completed in the month of March.

Salesperson	Total Number of Sales Calls
Shane	139
Chris	94
Daniel	122
Javier	87
Sandra	95
Joel	103
Jill	84
Total	724

As the sales manager, you must compare the performance of these salespeople. Compare their performance using (a) ranking, (b) comparison to average, and (c) comparison to standard.

3. You are a new sales manager. One day you are chatting with a colleague when the topic of salesperson evaluation arises. Your colleague, who has been a sales manager for 5 years, is upset over the amount of paperwork required to conduct performance appraisal. He says, "I don't see why the performance evaluations have to be written down anyway. I think that most salespeople would prefer having an informal luncheon in which we simply sit down and talk about their performance over the past year. Why don't you and I go to the vice-president of sales and tell him that we think the performance evaluation process should be oral, not written?" You reply, "Let me think about it," and go back to your office to consider his proposal. Write him a memo in which you outline your position on the issue of written versus oral performance evaluations.

SHORT CASE

AXXEL COMPUTER SYSTEMS

BACKGROUND

Rose Goodson is the vice-president of sales for Axxel Computer Systems, a mid-sized manufacturer of high-performance engineering workstations that are capable of handling extremely demanding graphics design packages. Axxel competes against several larger firms primarily on the basis of service after the sale. Axxel has 12 large customers that account for the bulk of its revenue. About 60 percent of the business with these customers is replacement business, while 40 percent is to new users. In selling replacement computers, the focus of the selling effort is generally price and limited training. The sales of computers to new users often requires Axxel to design applications, and new users seek far more service before and after the sale.

Goodson has instituted a national account management program to serve these 12 customers. The national account managers have overall responsibility for the large accounts, but they do not have authority over the application engineers, customer service representatives, and technical support representatives who must act in concert to provide needed levels of customer service. In essence, the national account manager, application engineers, customer service representatives, and technical support representatives must act as a team without formal recognition of the status and role each team member plays.

SITUATION

In the last 2 years, the complexity of the products Axxel sells and the level of service offered by the competition has forced Axxel to upgrade the service it provides to its customers. Axxel has found that its informal arrangement is not sufficient to deliver the needed levels of customer service. National account managers are complaining that they do not have enough control over the actions of the other informal team members. Customer service representatives resent the demands of different national account managers, all of whom think their customers should be the highest priority. Application engineers do not know how to prioritize different projects, and technical service representatives do not know how to prioritize service calls. As a result of the problems in the relationships among team members, and the consequent reduction in customer service levels, Axxel has decided to stop relying on informal arrangements between the national account managers and the other individuals responsible for providing customer service. Instead, Axxel is installing a role-result matrix approach to designing and managing teams.

PROBLEM

As the newest member of Goodson's staff, you have the only academic experience with the use of the role-result matrix. Thus Goodson has asked you to develop a role-result matrix for the national account teams. The matrix needs to give sufficient guidance to the national account managers and the other team members so that everyone is clear on his or her responsibilities. Obviously, as the

newest member of the staff, you have little awareness of the specifics of the selling process, so you may not be very specific on the details of the responsibilities. However, your matrix will provide overall guidance to the teams.

QUESTIONS

1. What is the overall purpose of the role-result matrix?
2. How can the role-result matrix be used to assess performance?
3. What are some other uses for the role-result matrix?

QUOTA ROLE PLAY

CHARACTERS

Sales Manager: Connie Hurkman or Nick Cesarone
District Manager: Lauren Calle or Timothy Fagen
Salesperson: Sally Orlando or Marvin McCormick

SCENARIO

During a semiannual meeting of EDD's sales management at the headquarters in Fort Worth, Connie Hurkman, sales manager, and Timothy Fagen, the district manager, are informally discussing a particular sales representative (Marvin McCormick) who is in Hurkman's district and seems to be having problems reaching his current quota. McCormick has been with the company for 7 years and has had favorable ratings for all but the last two years. In fact, McCormick has had superior ratings for 3 of the 7 years. McCormick did not meet quota last year, and he is not even close at this point (January; the fiscal year ends in June) of making quota. Policy states that failure to meet quota 2 years in a row can be reason for termination. Hurkman is fond of McCormick because he was one of her trainers when she entered the job 5 years previously. She must

decide what to do with McCormick because of the quota problems.

SCENE 1

The scene begins with Fagen asking about McCormick. According to recent reports Fagen has noticed that McCormick doesn't have much chance to make quota. Hurkman says, "Yeah, I know, I've seen the reports and I'm worried about McCormick. I'm not sure what the problem is. You know McCormick has really performed well in the past. I really think he is a good salesperson." The district manager replies, "He might have been good but quota was not met last year and I strongly doubt it will be met this year. His performance has steadily been going downward. Do something about it or we will have to consider termination." "Let me talk to him first," Hurkman says, "I think we can solve the problem." The scene ends.

SCENE 2

This scene is between McCormick and Hurkman and focuses on McCormick's current problem with quota.

McCormick complains about increasing competition, lack of support, stress, and personal problems. Hurkman is sympathetic but stresses the seriousness of the situation: "I think that you are a good salesperson and I don't want to lose you, but you are in trouble!"

SCENE 3

Scene 3 is yours. It may be a continuation of scene 2, or it may be an entirely new scene. The characters included are up to you. Provide a solution to the problem. Think about problems that may arise because of your solution. *Be realistic!*

CHARACTER DESCRIPTIONS

Name: Lauren B. Calle
Gender: F
Age: 48
Marital status: Divorced
Education: B.B.A., UCLA, M.B.A., University of California, Berkeley
Title: District Manager, East Region
Office location: New York
Reports to: East Region Manager
Employment history: Taught at Pepperdine for 2 years; 10 years in management with *Fortune* 500; with Pharmiceaux for 8 years
Personality: Straight by the book; believes in management from the top; very friendly
Notes: Most knowledgeable about products; photographic memory; two children in high school
Grapevine: Changes are imminent

Name: Timothy Fagen
Gender: M.B.S.
Age: 36
Marital status: Single
Education: University of Michigan; M.B.A., Emory
Title: District Manager, East Region
Office location: New York
Reports to: East Regional Manager
Employment history: Owned a management consulting firm for 5 years before selling out and coming to work for Pharmiceaux
Personality: Authoritative; competitive; frank; energetic
Notes: Finished second in the Regional Manager interview; Wants to be #1; Unforgiving of big mistakes; very fitness oriented
Grapevine: Will shape up a territory or bring in someone new

Name: Sally Orlando
Gender: F   **Age:** 35

Marital status: Single
Education: B.A. University of North State
Title: Sales Rep
Office location: Boston
Reports to: Sales Manager, Boston
Employment history: Background in marketing and public relations before coming to Pharmiceaux 9 years ago
Personality: Energetic; bubbly; somewhat dramatic
Notes: Made quota for several years; did not make quota last year
Grapevine: Personal problems with long-term boyfriend are interfering with work

Name: Marvin McCormick
Gender: M
Age: 38
Marital status: Single
Education: B.S. Mid-West Tech
Title: Sales Rep
Office location: Boston
Reports to: Sales Manager, Boston
Employment history: 4 years in advertising sales; with Pharmiceaux for 7 years
Personality: Energetic; somewhat dramatic
Notes: Sales have been slipping; seems to be moody quite often
Grapevine: Recent death of close family member

Name: Connie Hurkman
Gender: F
Age: 32
Marital status: Single
Education: B.B.A., University of Kansas
Title: Sales Manager
Office location: Boston
Reports to: District Manager, New York
Employment history: With the company for 8 years; previously worked for Baxter
Personality: Sentimental; sympathetic; warm; likeable
Notes: Occasionally crosses the line between manager and friend—too close to subordinates; open-door policy; her people really like her; loves the outdoors
Grapevine: Too trusting; not tough enough at times

Name: Nicholas "Nick" Cesarone
Gender: M
Age: 28
Marital status: Married
Education: B.S. in Biochemistry, Oregon State; M.B.A., University of Washington
Title: Sales Manager
Office location: Boston
Reports to: District Manager, New York
Employment history: Joined Pharmiceaux immediately after finishing his M.B.A. and has worked his way up from sales

Personality: Up-tight; workaholic; dominant; competitive
Notes: District finished #1 in sales; one child, age 2
Grapevine: Some of his people think he pushes too hard

QUESTIONS

1. What is the purpose of a quota system? What advantages does a quota system give management?
2. Who typically determines what quota will be set and why?
3. Should salespeople and first-level sales managers be allowed input into the quota process? What are the arguments for and against their input?
4. List at least four alternatives Hurkman could use in dealing with McCormick. Discuss the long-term consequences of each alternative.
5. Which of the alternatives in question 4 should Hurkman use to resolve the role play? Defend your answer fully.

NOTES

1. "Innovator 1991: Gordon Food Service Corporation," *Institutional Distribution* (March 1991): 82.
2. *Encyclopedia of Management,* 1992.
3. Jack Zigon, "Making Performance Appraisal Work for Teams," *Training* (June 1994): 58–63.
4. Gilbert A. Churchill, Jr., Neil M. Ford, Steve W. Hartley, and Orville C. Walker, "The Determinants of Salesperson Performance: A Meta-Analysis," *Journal of Marketing Research,* 22 (May 1985): 103–118.
5. The conceptual model of salesforce evaluation is based in part on Michael H. Morris, Duane L. Davis, Jeffrey W. Allen, Ramon A. Avila, and Joseph Chapman, "Assessing the Relationships Among Performance Measures, Managerial Practices, and Satisfaction When Evaluating the Salesforce: A Replication and Extension," *Journal of Personal Selling and Sales Management,* 11 (Summer 1991): 25–35.
6. Douglas N. Behrman and William D. Perreault, "Measuring the Performance of Industrial Salespersons," *Journal of Business Research,* 10 (September 1982): 355–370.
7. Office of Technology Assessment (OTA), *The Electronic Supervisor: New Technology, New Tensions* (Washington, D.C.: U.S. Government Printing Office, 1987).
8. The discussion of outcome-based versus behavior-based control systems is based on Erin Anderson and Richard L. Oliver, "Perspectives on Behavior-Based Versus Outcome-Based Salesforce Control Systems," *Journal of Marketing,* 51 (October 1987): 76–88.
9. The discussion of BOS and forced-choice scales ratings is based on Jan P. Muczyk and Myron Gable, "Managing Sales Performance Through a Comprehensive Performance Appraisal System," *Journal of Personal Selling and Sales Management,* 7 (May 1987): 41–52.
10. Roland Oliver, "Activity Reports," *Agency Sales Magazine* (September 1992): 25–27.
11. Ramon A. Avila, Edward F. Fern, and O. Karl Mann, "Unravelling Criteria for Assessing the Performance of Salespeople: A Causal Analysis," *Journal of Personal Selling and Sales Management,* 8 (May 1988): 45–54.
12. Scott B. Mackenzie, Philip M. Podsakoff, and Richard Fetter, "The Impact of Organizational Citizenship Behavior on Evaluations of Salesperson Performance," *Journal of Marketing,* 57 (January 1993): 70–80.
13. Using a combination of CPM, silent call monitoring, and customer satisfaction surveys to evaluate telemarketers was based on Jay Marwaha, Monica Jenks, and John Goodman, "Performance Evaluations, Quality, and Productivity," *Journal of Quality and Participation* (September 1993): 84–89.

14. Clinton O. Longenecker, D. A. Gioia, and H. P. Sims, "Behind the Mask: The Politics of Employee Appraisal," *Academy of Management Executive,* 1 (August 1987): 183–193.

15. James W. Gentry, John C. Mowen, and Lori Tasaki, "Salesperson Evaluation: A Systematic Structure for Reducing Judgmental Biases," *Journal of Personal Selling and Sales Management,* 11 (Spring 1991): 27–38.

16. Adrian B. Ryans and Charles B. Weinberg, "Territory Sales Response," *Journal of Marketing Research,* 16 (1979): 453–465.

17. John C. Mowen, Janet E. Keith, Stephen W. Brown, and Donald W. Jackson, Jr., "Utilizing Effort and Task Difficulty Information in Evaluating Salespeople," *Journal of Marketing Research,* 22 (May 1985): 185–191.

18. John C. Mowen, Keith J. Fabes, and Raymond W. LaForge, "Effects of Effort, Territory Situation, and Rater on Salesperson Evaluation," *Journal of Personal Selling and Sales Management,* 6 (May 1986): 1–8.

19. Harish Sujan, "Smarter Versus Harder: An Exploratory Attributional Analysis of Salespeople's Motivation," *Journal of Marketing Research,* 23 (February 1986): 41–49.

20. Clinton Longenecker and Dean Ludwig, "Ethical Dilemmas in Performance Appraisal Revisited," *Journal of Business Ethics,* 9 (1990): 961–969.

21. Jay Marwaha, Monica Jenks, and John Goodman (1993), op. cit.

22. Lawrence B. Chonko, Roy D. Howell, and Danny N. Bellenger, "Congruence in Sales Force Evaluations: Relation to Sales Force Perceptions of Conflict and Ambiguity," *Journal of Personal Selling and Sales Management,* 6 (May 1986): 35–48.

23. The discussion of performance appraisal in a team context is based on Zigon (1994), op. cit.

24. David W. Cravens, Raymond W. LaForge, Gregory M. Pickett, and Clifford E. Young, "Incorporating a Quality Improvement Perspective Into Measures of Salesperson Performance," *Journal of Personal Selling and Sales Management,* 13 (Winter 1993): 1–14, and Howard S. Gitlow and Paul T. Hertz, "Statistical Thinking: An Alternative to Quotas," *Singapore Marketing Review,* 2 (1987): 52–59.

25. Zigon (1994), op. cit.

26. William R. Cone, *Supervising Employees Effectively* (Reading, Mass.: Addison-Wesley, 1974).

27. The discussion of the advantages and methods of conducting quarterly performance appraisals is based on George S. Odiorne (1990), "The Trend Toward the Quarterly Performance Review," *Business Horizons* (July-August 1990): 38–41.

28. Marwaha, et al. (1993), op. cit.

29. Kathryn M. Bartol and David C. Martin, "The Legal Ramifications of Performance Appraisal: An Update," *Employee Relations Law Journal,* 17 (Autumn 1991): 257–286.

30. *Floyd v. Kellogg Sales Company,* No. 3-85, CIV 146 (D. Minn. 1988).

31. *Greely v. Clairol,* 47 Fair Empl. Prac. Cas. (BNA) 47, (D.C. Md. 1988).

32. The discussion of legal standards applying to performance appraisal is drawn from Jan P. Muczky and Myron Gable, "Managing Sales Performance Through a Comprehensive Performance Appraisal System," *Journal of Personal Selling and Sales Management,* 7 (May 1987): 41–52, and Ron Zemke, "Do Performance Appraisals Change Performance?" *Training* (May 1991): 34–39.

33. Stephen R. Hawk, "The Effects of Computerized Performance Monitoring," *Journal of Business Ethics,* 13 (December 1994): 949–957.

MOTIVATION

Case contributed by Dennis J. Moberg and David F. Caldwell, Santa Clara University.

INTRODUCTION

In this Interactive Case (and the Organizational Politics case in Part 5) you are placed in the role of a manager who is facing a problem situation. After reviewing the initial information, you must decide how to proceed. Your options range all the way from doing nothing, to collecting more information, to taking decisive action. After making your decision, you see the case unfold. If you choose to ask for more information, you get it. If you take an action, you see its consequences. Once you see the results of your first decision, you are asked to make another decision. This process of making decisions, observing their results, and making more decisions continues as you work your way through the entire problem.

Interactive Cases are not like other cases you may have used. First, they require you to develop both a solution to the problem and a procedure for implementing it. Second, they unfold over time. Instead of simply making a recommendation, you have to make a series of decisions to solve the problem. As in real life, once you make a decision or take an action, the situation changes. Third, Interactive Cases give you feedback about the decisions you make and you see what outcomes your actions produce. Unlike real-life situations, however, if your actions are not appropriate to the situation, you can reconsider your decisions.

USING INTERACTIVE CASES

All you need to complete the Interactive Cases is your book and a pen or pencil. First, you will receive a Flow Diagram from your instructor. You will use this sheet to record your decisions. You may also be asked to turn in the completed Flow Diagram to your instructor. Next, read the Case Summary which follows this Introduction. This material assigns you to a role in a fictitious organization, describes the problem you face, and introduces you to some people with whom you may have to deal in the case. At the end of this material you are asked to choose from among several alternative actions.

Each alternative is followed by a statement directing you to GO TO a decision point. For example, following alternative A might be the statement GO TO 325, and following alternative B GO TO 449. These numbers refer to decision points randomly distributed throughout the Appendix which follows the case.

As you make your choice, write the decision point number that you are referred to on your Flow Diagram. In the example above, if you decided to choose alternative A, you would write A-325 in the rectangle labeled "1st Decision." If you felt alternative B was better, you would write B-449 in the first rectangle.

Once you have chosen a decision point, turn to it in the Appendix. There you will see the results of the action you have taken and will have to decide what you will do next. Again, make your choice, write the decision point number and letter in the second rectangle on your Flow Diagram, turn to that part of the Appendix, and see the results of that decision. You continue to work your way through the case by making decisions, recording your movements on your Flow Diagram, and getting new information until you successfully solve the problem. You will know you have finished with the case when you are told the problem is solved; you will usually not fill all the rectangles on your Flow Diagram.

Occasionally, the decision you make will lead to bad outcomes. For example, you might take an action to solve one problem that creates another, worse problem. When this happens, you can reconsider your decision. When your decision is incorrect, you get information about why it was not the best option. Then you are instructed to circle your present decision point on your Flow Diagram and return to your previous decision point. Once you are back at that decision point, you will choose another alternative, mark the decision on your form, and turn to the appropriate page. Only by keeping an accurate record of all your decisions on your Flow Diagram can you move back and forth through the case.

You should not be troubled if you make a few errors as you move through the case. Applying theories to a situation is not always easy, and not every action you take will be explained by the textbook. Above all, it is important to keep in mind that experts have honest disagreements over how behavioral principles are best applied. That means your instructor may (and probably will) differ with us over which alternative is best in some situations. Therefore, as you progress through the case, if you find yourself unconvinced that an "incorrect" decision is really wrong, make a note of that and bring it up with your instructor.

THE SITUATION

You are the regional sales manager of the obstetrics division of Omega Pharmaceutical Corporation, a medium-size firm specializing in obstetric, gynecologic, and pediatric prescription drugs. You have 12 sales representatives who report to you. Each of them is responsible for a different region in the Middle Atlantic states; that is, they operate independently of one another. Sales reps call on physicians "detailing" the advantages of the firm's product line and use their personal influence to encourage them to prescribe the company's products. In addition, reps are responsible for calling on pharmaceutical wholesalers to encourage them to stock the company's products so there will be adequate supplies when retail druggists place their orders. Experience shows that if wholesaler inventories drop below 50 days in a

territory, retailer stock-outs will occur in the region. As a result, retailers will be unable to fill prescriptions with Omega's product and will substitute a competitor's product.

In reviewing the recent quarterly sales volume figures in Exhibit 1, note that five of your reps are not performing up to standard. Your boss also took notice of these five in your quarterly review with him. As he said, "You have six of the finest salespeople we have in the country. You also have the five worst. Next quarter, why don't you light a fire underneath them?"

Sales representatives are paid a straight salary plus a commission tied directly to their sales volume. The salary constitutes half of an average rep's earnings, so most reps are especially attentive to their volume figures. Promotions to sales management are infrequent, but such decisions are based on sales performance.

Turnover among reps at Omega is common. Last year 18.3 percent of Omega's reps throughout the U.S. left the firm. Presently, this is considered an acceptable turnover level. Candidates hired as reps usually have college degrees in the biological sciences and receive thorough training on the technical features of the company's total product line and on sales techniques before making their first sales call.

Several important developments have occurred in recent months. Nationwide, Omega's sales have been strong, but long-range forecasts indicate a gradual decline in the rate of growth in the obstetric line. The reason is the downturn in the birthrate coupled with the movement toward "natural childbirth." More important to your region are the economic conditions. The "softness" of the economy has forced pharmaceutical wholesalers to cut back on their inventories. Reps have had to redouble their efforts at persuading wholesalers to stock the company's products. One other development is a change in the territorial boundaries in your region. This was done to accommodate the arrival of a new rep, Lisa Dolan, to your group. Territorial boundaries are determined to allow each rep to complete a sales goal of 400 units per quarter. Factors like the birthrate, population density,

		EXHIBIT I					

QUARTERLY SALES REPORT

Sales Rep	This Quarter	Last Quarter	This Qtr. Last Yr.		This Quarter		
	Sales Volume	Volume Rank	Volume Rank	Volume Rank	Standard Vol./Birthrate in Region	% M.D.s Contacted	Days Wholesaler Supply
M. Roth	550	1	2	1	8.71	100	61
R. Smith	545	2	1	2	8.53	100	63
S. Brown	520	3	3	—	10.92	91	51
M. Sanchez	515	4	5	5	9.01	97	53
A. Bishop	510	5	4	4	8.47	89	73
S. Chapel	500	6	9	8	9.13	100	57
L. Andrews	420	7	8	10	7.88	79	60
L. Dolan	360	8	—	—	6.71	100	50
J. Crosby	330	9	6	6	13.39	61	55
J. Clemmons	320	10	7	7	8.18	73	47
W. Thomas	310	11	11	9	6.62	77	38
W. Spaulding	280	12	12	11	9.34	70	42
Standard	400					90	50

and the concentration of wholesale outlets all go into the determination of territories. At the end of each quarter, you receive a computer printout that describes your reps' quarterly sales figures like the one in Exhibit 1.

You decide to try to motivate your five lowest performing reps in descending order starting with Lisa Dolan. Lisa is a new rep who just joined Omega five months ago. She completed her B.S. in biology from State University and was very impressive in her interviews (you personally hired her). In school, she succeeded at everything she tried. She was elected senior class vice president, had a minor in marketing, and carried a fine grade point average. She worked her way through school selling hyper-allergenic cosmetics through contacts supplied to her from dermatologists (her husband is in medical school specializing in dermatology). This background gave her excellent advantages over other new sales reps. Before she began work, she completed the company three-week sales training program.

How would you open your conversation with her?

A. Ask her how well she thought she had done during the last quarter. (Go To 11)
B. Ask her if there is anything that has happened in her job that she was unprepared for. (Go To 47)
C. Point out the importance of building up wholesale inventory levels in her region. (Go To 66)
D. Offer to help her in any way you can to build up her sales. (Go To 13)
E. Ask her if she is satisfied with her present levels of sales and wholesale inventory levels. (Go To 21)

Decision Point 3

John reacts with the following: "But that's not really fair. The redistricting plan is unfair, and you know it!"

At this point how would you respond?

A. Try to persuade John that the redistricting plan is fair. Be prepared to compare his performance with Susan Brown's (such comparisons are not improper since performance records are open within the company). (Go To 72)
B. Tell John that you do not like his attitude, and that you cannot give his future employers

a good recommendation unless he improves his performance next quarter. (Go To 265)
C. Ask John what changes in redistricting that he would suggest to correct the inequity that he is experiencing. (Go To 233)
D. Tell John you will be sorry to see him go, but you understand that if he still thinks the redistricting is inequitable after your last discussion with him, perhaps this is the best thing for him to do. (Go To 60)
E. Ask John what things he likes about his present territory with the idea of trying to remind him of the positive things about his job instead of the negative things he seems to be emphasizing in his own mind. (Go To 205)

Decision Point 4

You accompany Lisa on several calls and notice several errors that she is making. First, she is not particularly friendly to receptionists and other people who could get her in to see the doctor. Second, she is too quick to leave company literature without seeing the obstetrician personally. And third, she uses powerless and overly polite language in her detailing speeches.

You give her feedback on these observations and watch her practice techniques that you give her on subsequent calls. Confident that she has benefited from your counseling, you return to your other responsibilities. In a month, you contact her again and ask for a progress report. Since it is optimistic, you decide to wait for the next quarter results. They are excellent. Her sales volume has improved to 440 units and her inventory levels to 57 days!

You correctly deduced that Lisa had a problem with abilities and skills. To recapitulate, when you originally talked with Lisa, you learned that she believed that her efforts would lead to outcomes she valued. Thus, effort was not the problem. This left "Abilities and Skills" and "Understanding of the Job" as key factors. By accompanying her on her sales calls, you were able to discover that she lacked specific skills associated with making effective sales calls to obstetricians.

Go to 71 to move on to your next motivational problem, John Crosby.

Decision Point 6

Jim says, "I really don't know. I'd miss some parts of the job like seeing some of the doctor friends I have now, and I'd really miss working with you. But I certainly don't need the job financially anymore. My dad left us a real nice inheritance, so I don't have to work to eat anymore."

How would you respond?

A. Tell Jim that you will be sorry to see him go, but that you have to have 400 units per quarter from a sales rep in his region, and you cannot afford to keep him while he decides what to do. (Go To 264)
B. Ask Jim if he needs some time off to get himself together now that his personal crisis has passed. (Go To 261)
C. Indicate to Jim that you don't want to stand in his way if he doesn't want to work anymore, but that there may be some way that you could work something out with him. (Go To 25)
D. Tell Jim that you will be personally disappointed if he gives up on his job and that you wish he would reconsider. Remind him of what he would be giving up in terms of the nonfinancial rewards the job gives him. (Go To 53)

Decision Point 7

John agrees to try harder if you promise to look into the fairness of his territory. You agree to get back to him at the end of the following quarter.

In the meantime, what would you do?

A. Get John to commit himself to calling on a specific number of M.D.s during the next quarter. (Go To 223)
B. Tell John that you are very pleased that he has agreed to improve, and encourage him to do the best he can. (Go To 236)
C. Negotiate a level of performance with John that you would consider an adequate sign John is doing all he can with the territory he has been given. (Go To 38)

Decision Point 9

You ask to accompany Jim on a sales call. He agrees and the two of you leave early the next morning. Observing him, you conclude that Jim knows the products well and is effective in detailing them. One call to a pharmaceutical wholesaler results in a hefty order. Clearly Jim's motivational problem has nothing to do with his sales abilities or job understanding.

What would you do now?

A. Ask Jim how the death of his father has changed his outlook on his work. (Go To 41)
B. Let him know you think his performance is really seriously low, and you would like to know exactly what he plans to do about it. (Go To 59)
C. Find out whether he realizes that his sales are probably suffering from the low inventory levels being held by wholesalers in his territory. (Go To 78)
D. Ask Jim if he needs some time off now that his personal crisis has passed. (Go To 261)
E. Suggest that Jim may want to attend a sales seminar sponsored by the company next month. Coincidentally, it is being conducted in the city where Jim lives. (Go To 257)
F. Ask Jim why he was only able to contact 73 percent of the doctors in his territory. (Go To 81)
G. Do nothing. It is clear to you that Jim's performance problem is caused by a factor outside of your control. (Go To 256)

Decision Point 10

With the action plan complete, you now have to decide how to implement it without regular contact with Wilson Thomas.

What would you do?

A. Keep in touch with him by phone asking for weekly progress reports. (Go To 70)
B. Schedule a return visit in one month in order to go with him on some sales calls again. (Go To 69)

Decision Point 11

"I thought I would do much better. My husband and I were counting on me making 400 units so we could make our first house payment."

"I really don't know what it is. I visited every obstetrician's office in my territory at least once. I wasn't really prepared for how difficult it is to get to see doctors. It's tough even getting in the door. And when you do, the most you have is five min-

utes. And that's a very distracted five minutes, I'll tell you. As for my relations with wholesalers, I called on each one twice during the quarter. Even though their supply is only 50 days right now, that's up from 43 when I started."

You were not aware of this improvement in inventory levels, which is fairly substantial; therefore, you congratulate her on her improvement.

Given this information, how would you motivate Lisa?

A. Transfer her to a different territory within your district known to be an easier region for sales. (Go To 214)
B. Tell her not to be discouraged since building a relationship with the doctors is often a time consuming process, and it may take a while to reach her 400-unit quota. (Go To 263)
C. Ask to accompany her on several sales calls with obstetricians. (Go To 4)
D. Ask her to attend a seminar on salesmanship offered by an industry association to develop her skills. (Go To 83)
E. Ask her how much her house payment is, and then calculate what her sales volume would have to be for her to earn a satisfactory commission. (Go To 273)
F. Indicate that unless her sales volume improves, you may be forced to take disciplinary action. (Go To 273)

Decision Point 12

Jim says, "I just am not sure. I've told you my priorities have changed. I want to spend more time with my family. I know the amount of work necessary to make my quota, and that's about all I am prepared to do."

What would you say now?

A. Tell Jim it sounds like his job with Omega isn't important enough for him to work to keep it. (Go To 6)
B. Indicate that unless he is willing to try for higher level of sales, you'll have to ask for his resignation. (Go To 264)

Decision Point 13

She thanks you for your kind offer, but she admits to not being able to determine the problem. She seems very frustrated.

At this point what would you do?

A. Ask her if her frustration stems from the low amount on her commission check. (Go To 21)
B. Indicate that her problem may be that she's not calling on pharmaceutical wholesalers. (Go To 66)
C. Ask her if there is anything that has happened in her job that she was unprepared for. (Go To 47)

Decision Point 15

You carefully review his performance record since you became his manager and detail what you've done to help him with his work. Then you ask him for a renewed commitment to do something about his "marginal" performance.

His response is markedly defensive. He blames anything and everything besides himself for his low performance. For example, he asserts that many obstetricians are more interested in the gifts and favors given to them by competing firms than the attributes of the products. He even claims that competing firms have targeted his territory as a place in which they are making most of their sales and advertising expenditures (this is impossible to verify). He then delivers a description of his sales approach that you've heard before:

"I have always believed strongly that a professional sales approach is not a pressure approach. I come on slow, building my credibility and expressing interest in the physician's individual problems with malpractice, uninformed patients, and unqualified hospital staffers. You can't be product-driven in this business; you have to be doctor-driven. What you might gain in the short run, you lose in the long haul."

While you don't disagree in principle, you are concerned that Thomas's soft-sell approach is too indirect for wholesalers. What now?

A. Accompany him on a series of sales calls. (Go To 35)
B. Confront the differences between his stated approach and the sort of approach you know works well for some of your highest performing reps. (Go To 276)
C. Tell him that you think he is being defensive. (Go To 237)
D. Tell him that this is it—that you are at the end of your rope with him. Establish your willingness to help in any way you can, but either he comes up to standard next quarter or he's through with Omega. (Go To 34)
E. Tell him his sales approach may be correct, but he can't make it work unless he improves his effort. Ask him to explain why he only was able to contact 77 percent of the doctors in his region and why his inventory figures are so low. (Go To 54)
F. Assert that you don't disagree with his personal sales technique, but you think he needs to be hard-hitting when the occasion calls for it. Schedule him for a training program known to emphasize a contingency approach to selling. Warn him that this is his last chance. (Go To 87)
G. Check to see if his job is really important to him. (Go To 74)

Decision Point 17

Jim Clemmons has worked for Omega for three and a half years, and never before has his performance been so low. You are unsure what is causing this situation. His performance figures are listed in your text.

Your meeting with Jim takes place at his home while you are on a business trip. (This is common, as most reps work out of an office in their homes; moreover, you have a friendly relationship with Jim). After a pleasant dinner, the two of you move into his office in a small bungalow behind the family residence. You ask him if he's seen the sales data. He responds: "Yes, I have, and I'm embarrassed by them. You may not know this, but my dad passed away five months ago. He'd been ill for some time, but I guess I just let things slip. I guess I'll have to put all that behind me now and build up those figures." Out of courtesy, you spend some time talking about Jim's father. Clearly Jim took the loss of his father very hard.

What would you say after the conversation turns again to his performance?

A. Ask Jim how the death of his father has changed his outlook on his work. (Go To 41)
B. Let him know you think his performance is really seriously low, and you would like to know exactly what he plans to do about it. (Go to 59)

C. Find out whether he knows that his sales are probably suffering from the low inventory levels being held by wholesalers in his region. (Go To 78)

D. Ask Jim if he needs some time off to get himself together now that his personal crisis has passed. (Go To 261)

E. Suggest that Jim may want to attend a sales seminar sponsored by the company next month (by coincidence, it is being conducted in the city where Jim lives). (Go To 257)

F. Ask to accompany Jim on a series of sales calls. (Go To 9)

G. Ask Jim why he was only able to contact 73 percent of the doctors in his area. (Go To 81)

H. Do nothing. It is clear that Jim's performance problem is caused by a factor or factors outside your control. (Go To 256)

Decision Point 19

She exclaims, "Very disappointed! My husband and I were counting on me making 400 units to make our first house payment."

How would you motivate Lisa?

A. Transfer her to a different territory within your district known to be an easier region for sales. (Go To 214)

B. Tell her not to be discouraged since building credibility with obstetricians is often a time-consuming process, and it may take a while to reach her 400-unit quota. (Go To 263)

C. Ask to accompany her on several sales calls with obstetricians. (Go To 4)

D. Ask her to attend a seminar on salesmanship offered by an industry association to hone her skills further. (Go To 83)

E. Ask her how much her house payment is, and then calculate what her sales volume would have to be for her to earn a satisfactory commission. (Go To 242)

F. Indicate that unless her sales volume improves, you may be forced to take disciplinary action. (Go To 273)

Decision Point 20

It is clear to you that Buff's goodwill could be very valuable in helping his replacement establish good relations with the doctors and wholesalers in his territory. Also, it seems to you that Buff's primary concern is in not getting immediately cut off from company benefits. You make him a proposal that would have him work with the new representative for six weeks in exchange for a continuation of his employee benefits for six months. He makes a counter proposal, and you negotiate an agreement whereby he will make calls with the new representative for three weeks and be on call to help his replacement for another three weeks. In return, you will pay him two weeks salary and continue his benefits for six months. Both personnel and your supervisor agree to his plan, and you put it in operation.

This seems like an effective solution in that Buff's replacement is likely to benefit from the goodwill that clients accord Buff. In addition, you have removed a poor performing employee with a minimum of disruption to the rest of the group. The problem presented by Buff was a difficult one. Spaulding was performing poorly because he had great incentives on nonperformance. By identifying and verifying those incentives, you were able to use those circumstances to allow Buff to make a positive contribution at the same time that you terminated him. Making an agreement such as this one represents a difficult choice.

In the six months this case covers, you have faced a variety of motivational problems. By applying the motivation theory to each individual, you have been able to diagnose and make recommendations which lead to effective solutions.

Congratulations! You have successfully completed the Motivation Interactive Case.

Decision Point 21

She exclaims, "Very disappointed! My husband and I were counting on me making 400 units to make our first house payment."

What would you say now?

A. Indicate that physician calls are important but that it is equally important for her to build up wholesale inventory levels in her region. (Go To 29)

B. Offer to help her any way you can to build her sales volume. (Go To 245)

Decision Point 22

When Buff arrives, you tell him that his plan to put off making a decision for six months is unacceptable. Also, you tell him that it appears to you that he has already decided to go with a real estate career and that under the circumstances, what he can provide Omega is not worth six months salary.

Buff responds by saying that he likes doing real estate deals and that he has been successful in them. He goes on to say that he is indeed thinking about forming a corporation and selling real estate fulltime, but he is not sure that he wants to give up the security—particularly such things as a steady paycheck and good insurance—which Omega can provide. As Buff continues to talk, it seems clearer to you that his goal is to develop his own business but that he doesn't want to leave until he has arranged some details, such as replacing the company car and getting insurance.

What dould you do now?

A. Discharge Buff and begin making plans for his replacement. (Go To 208)
B. Try to negotiate a deal with Buff in which you would keep him on in a limited capacity. (Go to 20)

Decision Point 24

"As a matter of fact, I've been giving it some thought. I view life very differently now. My priorities are my life first, my family second, and my job third. For example, I find myself more involved in my son's activities. He's been in soccer for eight years, but I never got involved. Now I'm an assistant coach. My wife's been trying to get involved in my work. She goes with me on most of the out-of-town calls I make, and as a nurse herself, she understands Omega's products. The biggest problem that I have is making calls on rural doctors. I don't like being away from home for more than two days, and that really makes certain physicians out of reach."

"If I resigned, I'd miss some parts of the job like seeing some of the doctors I know well, and I'd really miss working with you. But I certainly don't need the job anymore. My dad left us a real nice inheritance, so I don't have to work to eat anymore."

How would you respond?

A. Tell him that you will be sorry to see him go, but that you have to have 400 units per quarter from a sales rep in his region, and you cannot afford to keep him while he decides what to do. (Go To 264)
B. Ask Jim if he needs some time to get himself together now that his personal crisis has passed. (Go To 261)
C. Indicate to Jim that you don't want to stand in his way if he doesn't want to work anymore, but you aren't sure there isn't some way that you could work something out with him. (Go To 25)
D. Tell him that you will be personally disappointed if he gives up on his job and that you wish he would reconsider. Remind him of what he would be giving up in terms of the nonfinancial rewards the job gives him. (Go To 53)

Decision Point 25

The two of you begin to talk about alternatives, and it appears that if you are in agreement, he and his wife might be willing to share the territory as "co-reps." This would enable Jim to be with his son for more time while covering for the rural portions of the territory. You and Jim invite Jim's wife, Kathy, into the bungalow, and she is enthusiastic about the plan to share Jim's job.

You follow up with a call to the Director of Employee Relations (at home) to be sure that this arrangement is possible. It is, and Jim's wife is scheduled for company training. This settled, you stress the necessity of making the standard 400 units per quarter. Both Jim and Kathy agree to coordinate their work to meet that figure.

The next quarter's performance figures are better than your wildest dreams and Jim and Kathy produce 525 units! Your questioning revealed that Jim's motivational problem was the value he had for the outcomes offered by the job. Because of a personal tragedy, Jim began to question the rewards (financial and otherwise) that he was getting from his work. You determined that by problem solving with Jim, you could turn Jim's altered lifestyle into an advantage. Such successes are not always possible. However in circumstances such as this, exploring options with the employee may be useful.

Congratulations! Go To 77 to begin to deal with your next motivational challenge, Wilson Thomas.

Decision Point 26

William Spaulding has been a difficult person for you to understand ever since you joined the company. His recent sales performance figures are in your text.

"Buff," as he is called by his friends, has been with the company for eight years, and his performance has been nothing short of terrible for the last two years. What makes Spaulding's performance so hard to understand is that in so many ways, he appears a natural for this business. He has a fine educational background, is very personable, and possesses a marvelous, relaxed sense of humor. And then there is his golf. A former PGA professional, Buff is an avid golfer, a hobby he uses to entertain his clients on their days off. Buff is something of a "character" at the company. He always shows up at company functions in brightly colored golf clothes, tanned and well groomed. He asks questions articulately. What with his fashionable clothes and large home (on a golf course), you have often wondered how he maintains his lifestyle in the face of such low commissions. His persuasive, slick, sophisticated personality has bought him a great deal of time from you. In fact, you feel rather taken advantage of. He has promised improved performance on many occasions, but somehow he has never delivered. You are not proud that you have let him get away with such "subpar" performance.

How would you approach your conversation with him?

A. Ask around the company discreetly to find out more about Buff's reputation as a salesman and how he is able to maintain his lifestyle when his earnings are so low. (Go To 58)
B. Tell him that if he does not turn his performance around, you are prepared to take disciplinary action like never before. (Go To 85)
C. Ask to accompany him on several sales calls. (Go To 44)

Decision Point 27

Wilson is reluctant to put his commitments down on paper. You press him for specifics, and after making a few, it becomes clear to him that you want something quite detailed; that is, you want

him to submit a weekly schedule of planned activities on the Thursday following each week.

At that point he says: "You know, I felt you and I got to know each other this week. I began to develop an appreciation of your point of view, and I find myself respecting you more than I ever did. However, you're treating me like a five-year-old. I thought you were beginning to respect some of my sales practices, but what you're asking me to do is humiliating!"

How would you respond?

A. Review the positive feedback you have given him, and indicate that he has earned your respect on these aspects. Indicate that you don't intend humiliation, only building respect based on results. (Go To 86)
B. Tell him that you would do the same for any employee who was not performing up to expectations. Tell him that he has to earn your respect. (Go To 231)
C. Back off on your expectations a bit since you don't want to damage Wilson's self-respect. (Go To 249)

Decision Point 29

She responds as follows: "But I called on each wholesaler in my region twice during the quarter. And even though the average supply is only at 50 days right now, that's up from 43 when I started."

You were not aware of this improvement in inventory levels, which is fairly substantial; therefore, you congratulate her on her improvement. Given all this information, how would you motivate Lisa?

A. Transfer her to a different territory within your district known to be an easier region for sales. (Go To 214)
B. Tell her not to be discouraged since building credibility with obstetricians is often a time-consuming process, and it may take a while to reach her 400-unit quota. (Go To 263)
C. Ask to accompany her on several sales calls with obstetricians. (Go To 4)
D. Ask her to attend a seminar on salesmanship offered by an industry association to further hone her skills. (Go To 83)
E. Ask her how much her house payment is, and then calculate what her sales volume

would have to be for her to earn a satisfactory commission. (Go To 242)

F. Indicate that unless her sales volume improves, you may be forced to take disciplinary action. (Go To 273)

Decision Point 30

You spell out the issues for your supervisor and summarize the issues and risks as you see them. Your supervisor agrees with your analysis and says that he thinks that Buff has to go and that he will do whatever possible to back your decision. In short, your supervisor has said that he understands the situation and will support you in what you do—but he doesn't have much specific advice about how you should handle Buff and the potential problems his resignation might create. At this point what would you do?

A. Call Buff in and attempt to find out why he wants six months to make his plans about resigning. (Go To 22)

B. Discharge Buff and begin making plans for his replacement. (Go To 55)

Decision Point 32

Jim is notably nervous in responding, "I'm disturbed that I've let you down, believe me. I don't want to disappoint you, but I'm not sure what to suggest. I'll try harder if you like, but I'm hesitant to promise much more than 400 units for the time being."

How would you respond?

A. Ask Jim if he needs some time off to get himself together now that his personal crisis has passed. (Go To 261)

B. Probe whether he really wants to continue as an Omega sales rep. (Go To 6)

C. Tell Jim that you do not consider 400 units good enough. Ask him why he cannot commit to do even better. (Go To 12)

D. Do nothing. It is clear to you that Jim's performance problem is caused by a factor outside of your control. (Go To 256)

Decision Point 34

He responds: "Well, if you have your mind made up that you're going to can me, then there's nothing I can do about it."

You assure him that your mind is not made up, but you are going to have to see significant improvements in his performance. He asks you what he has to do. You respond by negotiating a standard of performance (400 units, 95 percent of doctors contacted, and wholesale inventory level of 45 days).

Halfway through the following quarter, Wilson phones you to tell you that he knows his inventory figures are not going to meet your agreed-to goal. He tells you that Omega's competitors are offering an attractive incentive plan to their reps and that he is finding it difficult to make progress.

How would you respond?

A. Tell him that you don't consider competitors' perks an acceptable excuse. Let him know that you're expecting him to live up to the terms of your agreement. (Go To 275)

B. Accompany him on a series of sales calls. (Go To 35)

C. Schedule him for a training program that involves modern sales techniques. Warn him that this is his last chance. (Go To 87)

D. Check to see if his job is really important to him. (Go To 74)

Decision Point 35

You accompany Wilson on an entire week of his sales calls. Your observations are as follows: (1) Wilson does not budget his time well. He takes a large number of breaks, and he does not push himself during the day. (2) He has an excellent reputation with older obstetricians, but the younger ones are impatient with his slow, plodding approach. (3) He has a good reputation with one of the two wholesalers in his region. The other is a very large wholesaler whose very young buyer seems to consider Wilson an old jerk.

Through the course of the week, you give Wilson repeated verbal feedback on your observations and follow this up with a written report at the end of the week. At the beginning of the week, he is quite defensive about your feedback, but by week's end you notice that he is asking you for advice and encouragement. However, when late Friday afternoon arrives, you note that Wilson is getting somewhat anxious about what you're going to do.

What would you do?

A. Ask him to prepare a series of effort and performance commitments in light of the feedback you've given him. (Go To 27)
B. Tell him that you expect him to work on the feedback you've given him. Be firm that you expect him to report next quarterly sales above 400 units or that you'll be forced to terminate him. (Go To 248)

Decision Point 38

John Crosby's performance during the next quarter improves. He calls on 86 percent of the physicians in his territory, and his sales increase to 410 units, ten greater than standard.

He calls you after the quarterly performance report appears and reminds you of your commitment to do something about the size of his territory. Since you do not want to go through a redistricting, you consult with your boss and others in the organization and find out that John could work part time with the company's market research group conducting "focus groups" of physicians in his territory. Available budgetary funds enable you to sweeten his "draw" (the salary he earns independent of his commission) for the extra responsibilities. This arrangement is a "one-shot deal," and you make that clear to John. He jumps at the offer, and his sales performance continues to be good (but not spectacular) while he works with the market research group.

Upon hearing of this situation, Susan Brown complains to you that she should have been given this special assignment; that is, she is now experiencing a perception of inequity. Luckily, however, you were careful to determine that the characteristics of the physicians in Crosby's district made them better candidates for focus groups than the physicians in other districts. Accordingly, you are able to convince Susan Brown that Crosby's special assignment was not given at her expense.

When you promised John that you would look into his assertion of inequity, you took a very serious chance. Had you done nothing, he

would have felt you had gone back on your commitment. As it was, you risked creating inequity elsewhere among your reps.

Congratulations! By bringing Crosby's perceived inequity back into line with realities, you successfully dealt with a volatile situation. You found that you had to identify a specific reference person to convince Crosby that his equity calculations were exaggerated. Additionally, you found you had to address Crosby's eroded belief that arose because of the inequity perception that his efforts would no longer matter. Go To 17 to begin your analysis of the case of Jim Clemmons, the next of your employees in need of motivation.

Decision Point 39

It is two days later and you are reading over the material Buff has given you. Looking at it, you are amazed at the extent of Buff's operation. He has involved most of his Omega clients in deals and many of their friends as well. Many of the doctors have invested with Buff for years.

The plan Buff provides for separating his real estate operations from his sales calls is unacceptable to you. In it he asks for a six-month "grace period" to "investigate" ways of reducing the overlap between his real estate deals and his sales calls. At the end of that six-month period, he says he will provide you with either a detailed plan for eliminating the "apparent conflict of interest" or his resignation. As you read over Buff's proposal, you become convinced that what he really wants to do is to set up his own real estate business but stay on your payroll for six months while he does it.

You realize that the situation you are in presents you with a number of problems. First, Buff is clearly in violation of company policies and you can't tolerate that. Second, Buff has very good relations with the doctors in his territory (both through his pleasant personality and his real estate dealings), and you don't want to create ill will on the part of the doctors toward Omega. Third, the plan that Buff has presented you was not responsive to your request, and you strongly suspect that his entire purpose was to try to buy some time before leaving. Fourth, a potential replacement for Buff is just finishing training, but you think that it would be difficult to throw that person into Buff's district without more training and help than you can provide.

What actions would you now take?

A. Lay out the entire situation for your superior and ask him for advice in dealing with Buff. (Go To 30)
B. Call Buff and attempt to find out why he wants six months to make his plans about resigning. (Go To 22)
C. Discharge Buff and begin making plans for his replacement. (Go To 208)

Decision Point 40

You meet with your boss, give him a summary of Spaulding's performance, and tell him that you have heard a rumor about him conducting personal business with his Omega clients. He informs you that there is not much you can do on the basis of rumors, but that you should do something about Buff's substandard performance.

What would you now do?

A. Ask around the company discreetly to find out more about Buff's reputation as a salesman and how he is able to maintain his lifestyle when his earnings are so low. (Go To 43)
B. Confront Buff with your hunch about his real estate deals, and ask if this is the cause of his poor performance. (Go To 251)
C. Do nothing, since it seems your feedback on his sales efforts has led him to try harder. (Go To 268)

Decision Point 41

Jim's lower lip begins to quiver as he says, "I view life very differently now. My priorities are my life first, my family second, and my job third. For example, I find myself more involved in my son's activities. He's been in soccer for eight years, but I never got involved. Now I'm an assistant coach. My wife's been trying to get involved in my work. She goes with me on most of my trips, and as a nurse herself, she understands Omega's products. The biggest problem I have is making calls on rural physicians. I don't like to be away from home for more than two

days, and that really makes certain doctors in my territory out of reach."

At this point, what would you say?

A. Acknowledge his comment but let him know that you think his performance is really low and that you would like to know exactly what he plans to do to improve it. (Go To 32)
B. Ask Jim if he needs some time off to get himself together now that his personal crisis has passed. (Go To 261)
C. Suggest that Jim may want to attend a sales seminar sponsored by the company next month. By coincidence, it is being conducted in the city where he lives. (Go To 257)
D. Probe whether he really wants to continue as an Omega sales rep. (Go To 6)

Decision Point 43

Before meeting with Spaulding, you decide to gather information discreetly about his reputation and the conflict between his low earnings and abundant lifestyle. As a result, one staff person tells you that a doctor friend of his has shown him a flyer advertising a real estate partnership put together by Buff. The staff person says that it seems that all of Buff's Omega clients are receiving these and many are investing. You now feel that you have the "iron-clad" proof necessary to confront Buff. You know you must act.

What would you do now?

A. Consult with your superior about how to handle the situation. (Go To 79)
B. Call Buff in and ask him if the rumors you have heard are true. (Go To 46)
C. Call Buff in, lay out the evidence you have and tell him he must eliminate his outside deals and improve his performance. (Go To 228)

Decision Point 44

You accompany Spaulding on several calls and you are very surprised by the results. He demonstrates a fine knowledge of the company's products, and his approach is very effective throughout all the calls. Both wholesalers and doctors seem very responsive to his efforts.

After this dazzling performance, you let him know that he did an outstanding job and ask him to explain why his performance is so low when he clearly has such aptitude for the job. He asserts that he simply has been too casual about his performance but that now he understands that he had better improve.

As you are driving back to your office, you recall something that took place in one wholesaler's office. While Buff was making a count, the wholesaler asked if you were in on any of Buff's "little deals." When you responded with an uncertain look, the wholesaler said, "You know, condos." The conversation ended there as Buff and others came into the room; however, upon reflection, the wholesaler seemed to imply that Buff was putting together real estate deals with the customers he calls on. If true, this is a direct violation of company policy. There is no clear procedure for dealing with such infringements without "iron-clad" proof.

What would you do now?

A. Ask around the company discreetly to find out more about Buff's reputation as a salesman and how he is able to maintain his lifestyle when his earnings are so low. (Go To 43)
B. Confront Buff with your hunch about his real estate deals and ask if this is the cause of his poor performance. (Go To 251)
C. Consult with your supervisor about how to deal with this situation. (Go To 40)
D. Do nothing, since it seems your feedback on his sales efforts has led him to try harder. (Go To 268)

Decision Point 46

When you call Buff in, you begin the conversation with some pleasantries. After a few minutes, you tell him that you have heard rumors about his using his job primarily to develop his real estate interests. Buff responds by talking about the problems of teamwork in any company. As he continues, you get the strong impression that he is "ducking" the issue you are trying to raise. You finally interrupt him and tell him that you have two reliable reports of his dealings and that you are asking him straight out if he is involving his Omega clients in his real estate deals. Buff seems a bit surprised by your directness, but he admits to you that the allegations are true. When you ask Buff to give you the details of his deals,

he lays out a story of real estate partnerships much broader than you thought possible. He has involved many doctors and wholesalers in a variety of partnerships. He says that his income from these deals is about the same as his salary. He also says that although some of these deals are risky, the potential payoff is great. You both know that he is in clear violation of company policy and that you must face it.

What would you do?

A. Tell Buff that you have no choice but to discharge him. (Go To 255)
B. Tell Buff that he has a choice. He can either resign or end his real estate dealings. If he doesn't resign, you expect him to deliver a plan within 48 hours for ending his real estate involvements. (Go To 39)

Decision Point 47

She responds that she wasn't prepared for the difficulty she's faced getting in to see doctors: "I'll tell you. It's tough even getting in the door. And when you do, the most you have is five minutes. And that's a very distracted five minutes, I'll tell you!"

How would you respond?

A. Ask her if she was disappointed with her commission check. (Go To 21)
B. Indicate that physician calls are important, but that is equally important for her to build up wholesale inventory levels in her region. (Go To 66)
C. Offer to help her in any way you can to build her sales volume. (Go To 245)

Decision Point 50

You meet with your supervisor, give him a summary of Spaulding's performance, and tell him that you have heard a rumor about Spaulding's conducting personal business with his Omega clients. He informs you that there is not much you can do on the basis of rumors, but that you should do something about Buff's substandard performance.

What would you do?

A. Confront Buff with the rumor about his real estate deals and ask him if this is the cause of his poor performance. (Go To 251)

B. Ask to accompany him on several sales calls, but don't mention the rumor you have heard. (Go To 82)

Decision Point 52

You express concern that John is not giving his territory a chance. With that, John responds: "Why should I? You've dealt me a low hand. Even if I did call on 100 percent of my doctors, I couldn't make my quota." At this point you challenge his observation, but he insists there is no use. What would you do now?

A. Try to persuade John that the redistricting plan is equitable. Be prepared to compare his performance with Susan Brown's (such comparisons are not a problem since performance records are open within the firm). (Go to 72)
B. Tell John that you do not like his attitude and that you will not give his new employers a good recommendation unless he improves his performance next quarter. (Go to 265)
C. Ask John what changes in redistricting he would suggest to correct the inequity he is experiencing. (Go to 233)
D. Mention to John that there may be some way to respond to his concerns, but you won't even talk about that until he demonstrates greater efforts to improve his sales. (Go to 3)
E. Tell John you will be sorry to see him go but you understand that if he still thinks the redistricting is inequitable after your last comments, perhaps it is best that he leave the company. (Go to 60)
F. Ask John what things he likes about his present territory with the idea of trying to make the positive features he mentions more salient (obvious) compared with the negatives he seems to be focusing on. (Go to 205)

Decision Point 53

Jim is persuaded by this statement. He says: "You know, I really would miss those trips with my wife. In fact, do you think the two of us could share my job?"

This is an interesting idea. It would enable Jim to be with his son for more time and at the same time provide coverage for the rural portions of the territory. You and Jim invite his wife, Kathy, into the discussion. She is enthusiastic about the idea.

You follow up with a call to the Director of Employee Relations (at home) to be sure that this arrangement is possible. It is, and Jim's wife becomes scheduled for company training. This settled, you stress the necessity of making the standard 400 units per quarter. Both Jim and Kathy agree to coordinate their work to meet that figure.

One quarter later the resulting sales figures are better than your wildest dreams. Jim and his wife produce 525 units! Your questioning revealed that Jim's motivational problem was the value he placed on the outcomes offered by Omega. Because of a personal tragedy, Jim began to question the rewards (financial and otherwise) that he was getting from his job. You determined that, by problem-solving with Jim, you could turn his altered life- style into an advantage. Nice going! Go To 77 to move on to your next motivational challenge.

Decision Point 54

When you ask Wilson to explain his low-effort figures, he is a bit taken aback by your question, but he recovers quickly.

"I always worked hard for this company. Five days a week, eight hours a day, I assure you. Do you want to look at my date-book? My territory is real spread out as you know, so I can't be expected to make 100 percent of my calls each quarter. As for my wholesale figures, I know they're low, but I called each one at least once during the quarter. I've been trying to tell you that our competitors are pulling out all the stops to take over in my territory. It's hard to beat them off with what you have given me."

How would you respond?

A. Review what you've done in the past to try and turn his performance around, and ask him to commit to do something about his "marginal performance." (Go to 15)
B. Accompany him on a series of sales calls. (Go to 35)
C. Schedule him for a training program that involves modern sales techniques. Warn him that this is his last chance. (Go to 87)

D. Check to see if his job is really important to him. (Go to 74)

E. Tell him that this is it and that you are at the end of your rope with him. Establish your willingness to help in any way you can, but either he comes up to standard next quarter or he's through with the company. (Go to 34)

Decision Point 58

Before meeting with Spaulding, you decide to gather information discreetly about his reputation and the conflict between his low earnings and opulent lifestyle. As a result, you hear a rumor from a staff person that Buff has been putting together real estate deals with many of the doctors he calls on. If these rumors are true, this is a direct violation of company policy. There is no clear procedure for dealing with such infringements, unless there is "iron-clad" proof.

What would you do now?

A. Confront Buff with the rumor about his real estate deals and ask him if this is cause of his poor performance. (Go to 251)

B. Consult with your superior about how to deal with this situation. (Go to 50)

C. Ask to accompany him on several sales calls but not mention the rumor you have heard. (Go to 82)

Decision Point 59

Jim is notably nervous in responding, "I'm disturbed that I've let you down, believe me. I don't want to disappoint you, but I'm not sure what to suggest. I'll try harder, I promise." What would you say now?

A. Nothing. Clemmons has committed himself to do better. (Go to 216)

B. Find out whether he realizes that his sales are probably suffering from the low inventory level being held by wholesalers in his region. (Go to 78)

C. Ask Jim if he needs some time off to get himself together now that his personal crisis has passed. (Go to 261)

D. Tell him you appreciate his willingness to try harder. Ask Jim how the death of his father has changed his outlook on his work. (Go to 41)

E. Press Jim for a specific performance commitment. (Go to 218)

Decision Point 60

John seems taken aback by your statement, but he thanks you for your support. You ask him how you can help him with his job search. The remainder of the meeting seems relaxed as you problem-solve various approaches John is taking to get another job. As the meeting ends, you again promise your support but indicate forcefully that the company cannot afford to keep him in his territory while he conducts his job search unless he "acts in good faith" by continuing to complete his work. You ask for his resignation effective in 30 days. In three weeks, he calls you and tells you of his new job. He also informs you that he has called 50 percent of the M.D.s in his territory (in this three-week period!).

Some people would assert that a manager should fight hard before "letting go" of an employee. In this instance, however, John Crosby was at best an average employee. In addition, he suffered from a motivational problem that was difficult for you to do anything about beyond the attempts you have already made. Luck would have it that it was relatively easy to replace him, and since John left with good feelings and a level of exit performance that was excellent, everything worked out for the best.

John suffered from a perception that his payment was inequitable. This was compounded by a belief (attributable to the perceived inequity) that effort didn't really matter. This was a difficult situation to reverse. You could have salvaged John but only at the expense of careful work and increased vigilance, and you apparently considered that not worth the effort. Go To 17 to move along to your next employee to motivate, James Clemmons.

Decision Point 66

She responds as follows: "But I called on each wholesaler twice during the quarter. And even though the average supply is only fifty days right now, that's up from forty-three when I started."

You were not aware of this improvement, which is fairly substantial. Therefore, you congratulate her for this accomplishment.

What would you say now?

A. Offer to help her in any way you can to build her sales volume. (Go to 245)
B. Try to ascertain if she is satisfied with her present level of sales. (Go to 19)

Decision Point 67

A member of the Operations Research Group explains the redistricting formula to John's satisfaction, and he indicates that he will try harder next quarter. What would you do?

A. Get John to commit himself to calling on a specific number of M.D.s during the next quarter. (Go to 223)
B. Tell John that you are very pleased that he has agreed to improve. Encourage him to do the best he can. (Go to 236)
C. Negotiate a level of performance with John that you would consider an acceptable improvement for the next quarter. (Go to 80)

Decision Point 69

You return in one month and notice some but not spectacular progress on Wilson's part. His sales calls are up, but you again have to coach him on managing his time. You note that he has altered his sales approach with the younger doctors, and you help him further refine his techniques.

The fact that you have taken over responsibility for the major wholesaler pays off. Druggist stock-outs are less frequent, and Wilson begins to see more results from his efforts. He accompanies you when you call on this troublesome wholesaler, and this serves as a model for him to copy.

In spite of these improvements, Thomas continues to be rather defensive about your criticism and he continually asks for approval in subtle ways.

With two months remaining in the quarter, you again schedule another visit to his region. This time you only stay two days, but again there is some progress. You begin to ease up a bit on the number of specific commitments you ask him to make.

At the end of the quarter, the performance figures come out and Thomas meets his quota: Sales = 400 units; M.D.s contacted = 93 percent; wholesale inventory level = 44 days.

Although Thomas will require more effort to reduce his need for your help and feedback, you have accomplished a difficult motivational assignment. Wilson Thomas is a classic plateaued performer who has developed poor work habits that he defends with excuses and closed-mindedness. In this situation, training will not suffice. He needs practice, firmness, encouragement, and frequent feedback. Your actions worked well.

Congratulations! When you are ready, Go To 26 for your last motivation problem, William Spaulding.

Decision Point 70

Wilson Thomas's phone calls are sporadic, and you are concerned that he is not living up to his commitments. What action would you take?

A. You've done enough. If he does not live up to his commitment, terminate him. (Go to 275)
B. Go on even more sales calls with him in order to refine his action plan and give him feedback. (Go to 69)

Decision Point 71

The next employee targeted for motivation is John Crosby. His performance record is shown in your text. John has worked for Omega for six years. For five of those years, his performance record was average. Six months ago, to accommodate the addition of Lisa Dolan to your staff, you had to redistrict territories. This displaced four of your sales reps including John. The redistricting was done with the use of a computerized mapping formula developed by Omega's operations staff. The formula establishes equitable territories, and birth rate is one of many factors in the program. It is an award-winning model, and one that has been used throughout the industry. When the redistricting was announced, the three other sales reps affected accepted it, but not Crosby. He asserted that the birth rate in his new territory was too low. You explained that his new territory's birth rate was actually understated because it includes a large obstetric hospital (associated with a medical school) that does not report births in an ordinary way. This did not satisfy John. Susan Brown's territory was also affected (she was also given a territory with a large hospital), yet her last quarter sales were excellent. You decide to talk with John about his low figures. You ask for his side of the story.

He responds: "My greatest fears have come to pass. You gave me too small a district. I can't be expected to come up to my 400-unit quota in that territory. It will probably come as no surprise to you that I'm actively looking for another job right now." How would you respond?

A. Indicate that you are concerned that he has not given his new territory a chance. Point out that he only contacted 61 percent of the M.D.s in his region. (Go to 52)
B. Try to persuade John that the redistricting plan is equitable. Be prepared to compare his performance with Susan Brown's (such comparisons are normal; performance records are open within the company). (Go to 72)
C. Tell John that you do not like his attitude, and that you cannot give his future employer a good recommendation unless he improves his performance next quarter. (Go to 265)
D. Ask John what changes in redistricting he would suggest to correct the inequity he is experiencing. (Go to 233)
E. Mention to John that there may be some way to respond to his concerns, but you won't even talk about that until he demonstrates greater efforts to improve his sales efforts. (Go to 3)
F. Tell John that you will be sorry to see him go but you understand that if he still thinks the redistricting is inequitable after your last discussion with him, then perhaps this is the best thing for him to do. (Go to 60)
G. Ask John what things he likes about his present territory, with the idea of reminding him of the positive features of his job compared with the negative things he seems to be emphasizing in his own mind. (Go to 205)

Decision Point 72

You try to convince John that his perception that the redistribution plan is inequitable is false. He disagrees at first, but when you describe Susan Brown's performance, he modifies his position slightly. At the same time, he persists that the redistricting is unfair. John pulls out his quarterly sales report (the same one as in your initial de-

scription of the situation). He states, "Look at Brown's standard-over-birth-rate—10.92. Now look at mine—13.39—the highest in your region. Do you still say the territories are fair?"

At this point what would you do?

A. Tell John that you do not like his attitude, and that you cannot give his future employers a good recommendation unless he improves his performance next quarter. (Go to 265)
B. Ask John what changes in redistricting he would suggest to redress the inequity he is experiencing. (Go to 33)
C. Indicate to John that you will look into the territorial question, but that you can't guarantee anything. Insist that he bring his effort up as a sign of good faith. (Go to 3)
D. Tell John that you will be sorry to see him go but you understand that if he still thinks the redistricting is inequitable after your comments to him, perhaps this is the best thing for him to do. (Go to 60)
E. Ask John what things he likes about his present territory with the idea of trying to make the positive features he mentions more salient (obvious) compared with the negatives he seems to be emphasizing in his own mind. (Go to 205)
F. Persist with your argument. Call in a member of the Operations Research Group that developed the redistricting formula to explain it to John. (Go to 67)

Decision Point 74

He responds: "What do you think? My wife and I are looking forward to retirement in four years. We've got a place down in Orlando." Now what?

A. Tell him he is dangerously close to being terminated unless he turns his performance around. Be precise about just what level of performance is necessary to keep you from taking this action. (Go to 34)
B. Ask him if he has considered an early retirement. (Go to 84)
C. Review what you've done in the past to try and turn his performance around, and ask him for a renewed commitment to do something about his "marginal" performance. (Go to 15)
D. Accompany him on a series of sales calls. (Go to 35)

E. Schedule him for a training program that involves modern sales techniques. Warn him that this is his last chance. (Go to 87)

F. Tell him that this is it; that you are at the end of your rope with him. Establish your willingness to help in any way you can, but either he comes up to standard next quarter, or he's through with Omega. (Go to 34)

Decision Point 77

Wilson Thomas has worked for Omega for 21 years, but since you arrived, his performance has been quite poor. Wilson's present sales figures are in your text.

His poor performance has been exasperating for you. For the past three years, you have "tried everything" to turn his performance around. You have sent him to company training and refresher courses. You tried skill building. However, Wilson seems to consider his old-fashioned, laid-back, soft-sell approach better than any approach he's been taught. You've tried warning him, and at one point issued him two written warnings on his performance. You stopped short of firing him only because he came up to standard nine months ago. Too often Wilson's defense is that factors outside his control are against him. He is an expert at denying personal responsibility, and will latch onto any convenient excuse to hold onto his present practices and over-inflated self-image. This time, however, you are determined to give him only one more chance.

How would you approach your conversation with him?

A. Review what you've done in the past to try and turn his performance around, and ask him for a renewed commitment to do something about his "marginal" performance. (Go to 15)

B. Accompany him on a series of sales calls. (Go to 35)

C. Schedule him for a training program that involves modern techniques. Warn him that this is his last chance. (Go to 87)

D. Check to see if his job is really important to him. (Go to 74)

E. Ask him to explain his poor figures (77 percent M.D.s contacted; 38 days inventory). (Go to 54)

F. Tell him this is it; you are at the end of your rope with him. Establish your willingness to help in any way you can, but either he comes up to standard next quarter or he's through with Omega. (Go to 34)

Decision Point 78

Jim tells you that he is aware that the wholesale inventory levels are very low. He says that he realizes that he will have to make many more calls on wholesalers if he stays on with Omega.

How would you respond?

A. Ask Jim if he needs some time off now that his personal crisis has passed. (Go to 261)

B. Ask Jim if he is considering resigning. (Go to 24)

C. Ask him why he was able to contact only 73 percent of the doctors in his territory last quarter. (Go to 81)

D. Ask Jim how the death of his father has changed his outlook on his work. (Go to 41)

Decision Point 79

You lay out the evidence that you have collected. Your supervisor agrees that you do have "iron-clad" proof that Spaulding has been using his Omega job to foster his real estate business. He says that you need to deal with Spaulding's actions buyt that you will want to make sure tht your actions don't create more difficulties with customers than necessary. Now what?

A. Call Buff in and ask him if the rumors that you have heard are true. (Go to 46)

B. Call Buff in, lay out the evidence you have, and tell him that he must eliminate his outside deals and improve his performance. (Go to 228)

Decision Point 80

John Crosby's performance during the next quarter turns around positively. He calls on 86 percent of the physicians in his territory, and his performance improves to 410 units, ten greater than the standard.

Congratulations! By bringing his perceived inequity back into line with realities, you successfully dealt with a volatile situation. You found you had to identify a specific reference person to convince Crosby that his equity calculations were faulty. Additionally, you found you had to address his problem of not believing that his efforts would pay off.

Go to 17 to begin your analysis of the motivational needs of Jim Clemmons, the next employee in a sub-par performance situation.

Decision Point 81

Jim tells you that he is embarrassed by that figure. He says that he knows he'll have to raise that figure for your sake.

How would you respond?

A. Ask Jim how the death of his father has changed his outlook on his work. (Go to 41)
B. Let him know that you think his performance is really seriously low, and you would like to know exactly what he plans to do about it. (Go to 59)
C. Find out whether he realizes that his sales are probably suffering from the low inventory levels presently being held by wholesalers in his territory. (Go to 78)
D. Ask Jim whether he needs some time off now that his personal crisis has passed. (Go to 261)
E. Suggest that Jim may want to attend a sales seminar sponsored by the company. Coincidentally, it is being conducted in the city where Jim lives. (Go to 257)
F. Ask to accompany Jim on a sales call. (Go to 9)

Decision Point 82

You accompany Spaulding on several calls, and you are very surprised by the results. He demonstrates a fine knowledge of the company's products, and his demeanor is very effective throughout the call. Both wholesalers and doctors seem very responsive to his efforts.

After this dazzling performance, you tell him that he did an outstanding job and ask him to explain why his performance is so low when he clearly has so much aptitude for his work. He tells you that he simply has been too casual about his work but he now understands that he had better improve.

About two weeks later, you receive a call from one of the doctors you visited with Buff. He tells you that Buff is a terrific sales rep and asks you to be understanding with him. You wonder whether Spaulding has asked him to call you. A few days later one of your sales reps calls you to relay some interesting information. It seems that one of this rep's obstetrician clients knows another doctor who asked whether you are "out to get" Buff Spaulding. Further, this client indicated that Spaulding and this other doctor have several real estate deals together and that the doctor is concerned that Buff may not be able to make a mortgage payment on some property if he loses his job. You now feel that you have the "iron-clad proof" necessary to confront Buff.

You know that you must act. What would you now do?

A. Consult with your boss about how to handle the situation. (Go to 79)
B. Call Buff in and ask him if the rumors you had heard are true. (Go to 46)
C. Call Buff in, lay out the evidence you have and tell him that he must eliminate his outside deals and improve his performance or resign. (Go to 228)

Decision Point 83

Lisa attends the program, and her next quarter's sales are only modestly better. Apparently this training effort was not the answer to her performance problem.

Your analysis of Lisa's motivation revealed several important things. It is clear that Lisa has a strong belief that her efforts will pay off in terms of performance since she has a history of succeeding in nearly everything she has attempted. In addition, you can be certain that Lisa believes that performance will be rewarded at Omega, since she is on an incentive pay system that relates her income directly to two indices of performance, volume, and inventory. As for Lisa's particular preference for her work outcomes, we can be sure that Lisa values the monetary outcomes of her job since she has indicated that she needs her commission check to make her first house payment. Given these factors, it is not surprising that Lisa's efforts are high (she called on 100 percent of her M.D.s, and each wholesaler twice). However, her performance is not up to expectations. In light of this assessment, think about what additional factor may account for her low performance.

Your decision to give Lisa additional training was consistent with an appraisal that she needed abilities and skills not developed in the formal training program she completed with the company. However, you know little about just what Lisa's specific training needs are at this point. Reevaluate your last decision. Circle the #83 you just wrote in your Flow Diagram, then return to the last uncircled step and try again.

Decision Point 84

Thomas indicates that he might be interested in early retirement if a satisfactory financial arrangement could be reached. You call the Director of Employee Relations and get a figure. You share that information with Wilson, and he refuses it outright. You warn him that it might be better to take the offer and remove the threat, but he is firm.

What would you do now?

A. Tell him he is dangerously close to being terminated unless he turns his performance around. Be precise about just what level of performance is necessary to keep you from taking this action. (Go to 34)
B. Review what you've done in the past to try and turn his performance around, and ask him for a renewed commitment to do something about his "marginal performance." (Go to 15)
C. Accompany him on a series of sales calls. (Go to 35)
D. Schedule him for a training program that involves modern sales techniques. Warn him that this is his last chance. (Go to 87)
E. Ask him to explain his poor figures—77 percent of doctors contacted, 38 days inventory. (Go to 54)

Decision Point 85

Your meeting with Spaulding goes better than you anticipated. He apologizes for his performance, and quickly (perhaps too quickly) agrees to a set of performance objectives that you consider reasonable. You also inform Spaulding that you will monitor his performance closely.

A few weeks later, you check Buff's log and the records from his region. Nothing seems to have changed regarding his performance. Later that day you receive a call from an obstetrician in Buff's territory. He tells you that Buff is a terrific sales rep, and asks you to be understanding with him. You wonder whether Spaulding asked him to contact you. After some independent checking you find out that this doctor is one of Spaulding's frequent golf partners. Three days later you hear from another client, this time a wholesaler, who tells you that Spaulding is one of the best reps who calls on him and that he has just decided to place a huge order that would bring his stock of Omega drugs up to 75 days. You are surprised by this call and mention it to one of your colleagues. He says that he has heard that this wholesaler "owes" Spaulding and is repaying a favor. He also told you that he doubts if the alleged order would ever be booked. He seems to be correct, as two weeks have passed and the order has not been received.

What would you now do?

A. Since his performance has not improved, begin the process of terminating Spaulding. (Go to 295)
B. Ask to accompany Spaulding on several of his sales calls. (Go to 44)
C. Ask around the company discreetly to find out more about Buff's reputation as a salesman and how he is able to maintain his lifestyle when his earnings are so low. (Go to 58)

Decision Point 86

He shrugs his shoulders and completes a rather detailed set of commitments. He balks, though, when it comes to implementing your suggestion regarding interacting with the large wholesaler with which he's had difficulty.

In light of the fact that Thomas is considered an "old jerk" and already has made a substantial series of commitments, would you assume responsibility for interacting with this wholesaler yourself for one quarter?

A. Yes. (Go to 10)
B. No. (Go to 26)

Decision Point 87

You schedule Wilson Thomas for a training program that involves sales skill building. You also warn him that this is his last chance. He attends the program, but much to your chagrin, you receive the following letter from him: "I have completed the program you scheduled me to take, and I want you to know that it was a total waste of time. Nothing covered was new, and I fail to see why a professional approach is now out of date. The trainers of the program couldn't answer that to my satisfaction."

How would you respond?

A. Review what you've done in the past to try and turn his performance around, and ask him for a renewed commitment to do something about his "marginal" performance. (Go to 15)
B. Accompany him on a series of sales calls. (Go to 35)
C. Tell him that you think he's being defensive. (Go to 237)
D. Tell him that this is it; you are at the end of your rope with him. Establish your willingness to help in any way you can, but either he comes up to standard next quarter or he's through with Omega. (Go to 34)
E. Tell him his sales approach may be correct but he can't make it work unless he improves his effort. Remind him that he only contacted 77 percent of the doctors in his territory and that his inventory figure (38 days) is very low. (Go to 54)
F. Confront the differences between his stated sales approach and the sort of approach you know works well for the highest performing reps in your region. (Go to 276)
G. Check to see if his job is really important to him. (Go to 74)

Decision Point 205

This is an excellent motivational strategy, but not in this situation. Emphasizing the positive aspects of a job is an effective approach, but only as one part of a long-range motivational strategy. In this situation, you face a short-term, emergency situation. Persuasiveness of this sort is unlikely to be enough to create a set of perceptions which would result in better performance.

Reevaluate your last decision. Circle the #205 you just wrote in your Flow Diagram, then return to the last uncircled step and try again.

Decision Point 208

In analyzing this situation, you realized that there was no alternative for Buff but discharge. His performance had been low, he consistently violated a major company policy, and you had little likelihood of changing his behavior. After discharging Buff, a new set of problems develops for you. Buff's replacement seems to have a hard time making contact with doctors, and wholesalers' inventories drop to a lower level than Buff's. Two large wholesalers tell you that they were thinking about dropping your obstetric line because "Doctors just aren't prescribing it." Your colleagues in other districts mention that there is a rumor going around among doctors that Omega was "out to get" Buff and that you summarily fired him rather than let him resign. Since Buff continues to see his old Omega clients—because of the real estate deals—you know these rumors won't die easily.

You were clearly justified in discharging Buff; however, you might like to select another way of doing so.

Reevaluate your last decision. Circle the #208 you just wrote in your Flow Diagram, then return to the last uncircled step and try again.

Decision Point 214

Lisa opposes the option of being transferred since it would separate her from her husband, who is in medical school. Moreover, this option is very unpopular with some of your other sales reps, notably John Crosby.

Your analysis of Lisa's motivational circumstances revealed several important pieces of information. First, it is clear that Lisa does believe that her efforts will produce positive results since she has a history of succeeding in nearly everything she has ever attempted. In addition, given the reward system she certainly must believe that her monetary outcomes are in direct proportion to her performance. Monetary outcomes are important to her because she is counting on her commission check to make her first house payment.

Given these factors, it is not surprising that Lisa's efforts are high (she called on 100 percent of M.D.s and each wholesaler twice). However, her performance particularly regarding her obstetrician calls is not up to expectations. In light of this assessment, think through what additional factors may account for her low performance.

Re-evaluate your last decision. Circle the #214 you just wrote in your Flow Diagram, then return to the last uncircled step and try again.

Decision Point 216

Jim's performance during the next quarter continues to be poor. His commitment to do better was not sufficient as a motivator.

Reevaluate your last decision. Circle the #216 you just wrote in your Flow Diagram, then return to the last uncircled step and try again.

Decision Point 218

Jim tells you that he will sell 425 units next quarter. However, halfway through the next quarter he phones to tell you that he won't be able to meet that goal. When you express disappointment, he tells you he has decided to resign. Establishing precise performance targets is usually an effective motivational technique. However, in this instance, it does not work. Jim is suffering from a great deal of inner conflict which you haven't dealt with.

Reevaluate your last decision. Circle the #218 you just wrote in your Flow Diagram, then return to the last uncircled step and try again.

Decision Point 223

You and John agree that he should try to call on 90 percent of the obstetricians in his territory next quarter. You follow this up with a phone call halfway through the next quarter to remind him of his commitment and to get feedback.

When the quarter is over, the record indicates that John called 90 percent of his physicians (exactly). However, his performance dropped from 330 to 315. When you call him on this performance deficiency, John asserts: "I told you the territory divisions were inequitable. Look, I called on 90 percent of the obstetricians as we agreed, but I still produced only 315

units!" This places you in an impossible situation. By increasing his effort but not his performance, he calls the entire redistricting plan into question. However, it is likely that John's calls on M.D.s were not intended to develop sales. In general, it is not prudent to establish effort goals without associated performance goals.

Reevaluate your last decision. Circle the #223 you just wrote in your Flow Diagram, then return to the last uncircled step and try again.

Decision Point 228

When Buff arrives, you lay out the evidence of his violation of policy and tell him that he could either agree to end real estate dealings with his Omega clients and improve his performance or resign. He seems taken aback by your abruptness and for the first time in your memory is at a bit of a loss for words. As you press him, he becomes defensive, first denying that his real estate interests are in any way related to his Omega responsibilities, later almost bragging about how he has signed up most of the doctors in his area to one or another of his partnerships. The meeting ends with Buff announcing that he isn't going to give up his real estate practice and if it was an "issue" with you, you could have his resignation.

The outcomes of Buff's resignation are mixed. Although you have eliminated a poor performer and someone who was in direct violation of company policy, the timing and nature of his departure cause difficulties. First, you do not have anyone to replace Buff on such short notice and the district is not covered by two months. Second, you hear from reps in other districts that doctors are saying that Omega has really been unfair to Buff. You suspect that these stories are coming from Buff and the doctors in his real estate deals, but they are affecting Omega's reputation and the reps' morale, nonetheless.

Given Buff's violation of policy, requiring him to leave Omega is appropriate and, in fact, the right thing to do. However, you might have been able to get Buff out without so many negative consequences. Therefore, reevaluate your last decision with the idea of how you might terminate Buff in a less disruptive fashion.

Reevaluate your last decision. Circle the #228 you just wrote in your Flow Diagram, then return to the last uncircled step and try again.

Decision Point 231

Wilson's statement that you are treating him like a five-year-old is an attempt to salvage his self-respect. The past week has been hard on him, and now that you are insisting that he not only digest your criticism but also act on it, his ego has become very fragile. Had your statement been more balanced and personal, it would have provided him with more motivation for turning his behavior around.

Reevaluate your last decision. Circle the #231 you just wrote in your Flow Diagram, then return to the last uncircled step and try again.

Decision Point 233

This is not advisable. Any redistricting would simply create problems with other reps. In addition, a deviation from the scheme sanctioned by the company and endorsed by others in the industry requires more than one person's lack of satisfaction with it.

Reevaluate your last decision. Circle the #233 you just wrote in your Flow Diagram, then return to the last uncircled step and try again.

Decision Point 236

You encourage John to do better, but his performance during the next quarter continues to be poor. Your conversation with John was fine except that you didn't nail down a specific performance commitment from him. In general, it is more effective to establish specific performance goals than goals that are vague such as, "Do the best you can."

Reevaluate your last decision. Circle the #236 you just wrote in your Flow Diagram, then return to the last uncircled step and try again.

Decision Point 237

You tell him he's being defensive. With that he totally clams up. Reevaluate your last decision. Circle that #237 you just wrote in your Flow Diagram, then return to the last uncircled step and try again.

Decision Point 242

You and Lisa calculate that she requires a volume of 420 units to make the house payment. With that as a salient goal, Lisa enters the next quarter with renewed vigor. However, at the end of the quarter, her volume had dipped to 340 units (from 360). Discouraged and very frustrated, Lisa resigns.

Your analysis of Lisa's motivation revealed several things. Clearly Lisa has a strong belief that her efforts will pay off in terms of performance since she has a history of succeeding in nearly everything she has attempted. You can also be certain that Lisa believes that performance will be rewarded at Omega, since she is on an incentive pay system that relates her income directly to two indices of performance, volume and inventory. As for Lisa's particular preference for her work outcomes, you know Lisa values the monetary outcomes of her job since she has indicated that she needs her commission check to make her first house payment. Given these factors, it is not surprising that Lisa's efforts are high (she called on 100 percent of her M.D.s, and each wholesaler twice). However, her performance is still low. In light of this assessment, think about what additional factor may account for her low performance.

Your approach did little more than reinforce what was already a strong belief that performance results in important outcomes. Thus, it was actually a rather redundant action that only added to Lisa's frustration level when she didn't improve.

Reevaluate your last decision. Circle the #242 you just wrote in your Flow Diagram, then return to the last uncircled step and try again.

Decision Point 245

Your conversation with Lisa is not yielding the type of information that you need to complete a motivational analysis. Reevaluate your last decision, and consider how to get information that would be helpful in identifying the correct approach to motivating Lisa.

Reevaluate your last decision. Circle the #245 you just wrote in your Flow Diagram, then return to the last uncircled step and try again.

Decision Point 248

You decide not to have him participate in the development of an action plan. Instead you are firm that he should come up to an acceptable performance level. Generally it is preferable to use participation in the development of an action plan. You could have demanded the same performance level as part of that participative process.

Reevaluate your last decision. Circle the #248 you just wrote in your Flow Diagram, then return to the last uncircled step and try again.

Decision Point 249

Just because you have bruised Thomas's ego a bit is not reason to lower your expectations.

Reevaluate your last decision. Circle the #249 you just wrote in your Flow Diagram, then return to the last uncircled step and try again.

Decision Point 251

When you talk to Buff, you lay out his record of performance and tell him that it is not at an acceptable level. As you begin to discuss possible remedies for this low performance, you mention that there is a rumor floating around that he may be involved in some real estate deals which are taking him away from his work. As soon as you say this, he asks what you are talking about and challenges you to document your charges. Buff's approach puts you on the defensive and effectively ends the discussion about his low performance. In fact, by the time he leaves, he has so thoroughly manipulated the situation that you almost feel guilty for confronting him.

Reevaluate your last decision. Circle the #251 you just wrote in your Flow Diagram, then return to the last uncircled step and try again.

Decision Point 255

Since Buff has violated company policy, you decide to terminate him. This has some negative repercussions for the district. First, you receive a substantial number of complaints from doctors and wholesalers in his district. Second, and more important, the new sales rep who replaces Buff has a difficult time establishing relationships with area doctors. Although terminating Buff may be appropriate given his poor performance, the close relationships that Buff developed had the potential to disrupt Omega's customer relationships. Under these circumstances it may be better to either work further with Buff or develop a plan for reducing the negative impact of his departure.

Given Buff's violation of policy, requiring him to leave Omega is appropriate and, in fact, the right thing to do. However, you might have been able to get Buff out without so many negative consequences. Therefore, reevaluate your last decision with the idea of how you might terminate Buff in a less disruptive fashion.

Reevaluate your last decision. Circle the #255 you just wrote in your Flow Diagram, then return to the last uncircled step and try again.

Decision Point 256

Jim's performance the next quarter continues to be poor. Inaction on your part was apparently predicated on the assumption that there was nothing you could do. However, such pessimism is premature.

Reevaluate your last decision. Circle the #256 you just wrote in your Flow Diagram, then return to the last uncircled step and try again.

Decision Point 257

Jim jumps at the chance to attend the seminar. He especially likes the convenience of being able to attend it without leaving home. Upon completion of the seminar, Jim returns to work. However, his performance continues to be marginal. Though his wholesale inventory levels improve slightly, his calls on doctors continue to be very poor (67 percent). Clearly, Jim's performance did not benefit from the training.

Reevaluate your last decision. Circle the #257 you just wrote in your Flow Diagram, then return to the last uncircled step and try again.

Decision Point 261

Jim responds as follows: "Maybe that would be a good idea. A month off would be real helpful." You work out the details and Jim starts his leave of absence immediately. When he returns to work, however, his performance continues to be poor. Apparently the time off did not enable Jim to become more motivated himself.

Reevaluate your last decision. Circle the #261 you just wrote in your Flow Diagram, then return to the last uncircled step and try again.

Decision Point 262

Deciding when you might take over some of your subordinate's work is a difficult decision. Clearly, you can't do other people's work on a regular basis or over the long term. In this situation, taking on a part of Wilson's job may be valuable. If the list of commitments you are asking from Wilson is substantial, asking him to "go it totally alone" may be overwhelming. It is important to keep the list of commitments attainable, and of all Wilson's objectives, improving his relationship with this wholesaler is perhaps unattainable. If an individual believes that goals are not reachable, there will be little motivation to work to accomplish them. Moreover, by taking over this task, you may be able to improve Omega's reputation with this firm, and use this experience as a training tool for Wilson.

You will need to develop a timetable for making Wilson responsible for this task again. However, in this situation, your temporary help may pay big dividends.

Reevaluate your last decision. Circle the #262 you just wrote in your Flow Diagram, then return to the last uncircled step and try again.

Decision Point 263

Your decision to encourage Lisa results in sales the next quarter similar to the last one. More frustrated than before, Lisa's efforts begin to wane, and she leaves the company.

When you talked to her, Lisa was at a critical point in her career. You were correct in encouraging her, because often sales of this kind lag a bit behind sales efforts and sales calls have a cumulative effect. However, she needed something more than pure encouragement.

Your analysis of Lisa's motivation revealed several important things. It is clear that Lisa has a strong belief that her efforts will pay off in terms of performance since she has a history of succeeding in nearly everything she has attempted. In addition, you can be certain that Lisa believes that performance will be rewarded

at Omega, since she is on an incentive pay system that relates her income directly to two indices of performance, volume and inventory. As for Lisa's particular preference for her work outcomes, we can be sure that Lisa values the monetary outcomes of her job since she has indicated that she needs her commission check to make her first house payment. Given these factors, it is not surprising that Lisa's efforts are high (she called on 100 percent of her M.D.s, and each wholesaler twice). However, her performance is not up to expectations. In light of this assessment, think about what additional factor may account for her low performance.

By encouraging Lisa, you may have caused her belief that effort does result in performance to weaken in the following quarter. Perhaps she concluded that a particular obstetrician call makes little real difference in determining sales volume (the "drop in the bucket" idea). Pure encouragement may have reduced the sense of urgency that she showed in your conversation with her.

Reevaluate your last decision. Circle the #263 you just wrote in your Flow Diagram, then return to the last uncircled step and try again.

Decision Point 264

Jim says he understands your position completely, and he tells you that you will have his resignation. Jim Clemmons provided you with an extremely difficult motivational problem. As a person experiencing much inner conflict, Jim was reluctant to commit to much more than average performance, and that was not good enough for you. Fundamentally, Clemmons' motivational problem is that he doesn't value the outcomes of his work very much. The rewards offered by his job are not a sufficient inducement to do more than average work. Moreover, he is obtaining valued outcomes (being with his family) for not working. Thus, his problem is compounded by positive incentives for not performing.

About the only motivational strategy that works in such situations (assuming you cannot really lower the positive incentives on non-effort) is to (1) find out the outcomes he does value and increase them or (2) change the nature of the job to conform to his present level of motivation. In contrast, your action was to insist on performance without responding specifically to what he wants from work.

Reevaluate your last decision. Circle the #264 you just wrote in your Flow Diagram, then return to the last uncircled step and try again.

Decision Point 265

He responds that he does not like your attitude either, and he walks out of the meeting. In light of this, you phone the Personnel Department to discuss your disciplinary options. Accordingly, you send John a written warning on his low performance in conjunction with company procedures, since you cannot fire him without a written warning.

Three weeks into the next quarter, you call John to check on his performance. He doesn't return your call. You call two of the wholesalers in his territory, and they indicate that they have not seen him. You send him a registered letter indicating that if he doesn't phone you, he's fired. You don't hear from him, and you fire him.

The stern posture you took resulted in John leaving under adverse circumstances. Given that he was, at best, an average performer, he was not the worst person to leave, especially since he apparently was suffering from a perceived inequity problem that is difficult to resolve. However, his exit would have been much less costly had you been less threatening and more conciliatory. In addition, your options in this case included a strategy that would have turned John's performance around.

Reevaluate your last decision. Circle the #265 you just wrote in your Flow Diagram, then return to the last uncircled step and try again.

Decision Point 268

It is four weeks later, and Buff's performance figures are lower than ever. Waiting for Spaulding to improve is not the answer.

Reevaluate your last decision. Circle the #268 you just wrote in your Flow Diagram, then return to the last uncircled step and try again.

Decision Point 273

Your analysis of Lisa's motivational circumstances revealed some important information.

First, you may conclude that Lisa has a strong belief that her efforts would pay off in terms of performance because throughout her life she succeeded in everything she attempted. In addition, it is probable that she also believes that monetary outcomes are linked to performance since much of her earnings are directly related to sales volume and inventory levels. Clearly, monetary outcomes are important to her because she is counting on her commission check to make her first house payment. It is not surprising that Lisa's efforts are high (she called on 100 percent of her M.D.s and each wholesaler twice). However, her performance, particularly regarding her obstetrician calls, is not yet satisfactory. In light of this assessment, think through what additional factors may account for her low performance. Your approach did little more than remind her of what was already a strong belief that performance is linked to outcomes. Therefore, it was actually a rather redundant action, and it added little except frustration when Lisa's performance did not improve.

Reevaluate your last decision. Circle the #273 you just wrote in your Flow Diagram, then return to the last uncircled step and try again.

Decision Point 275

He agrees to try again, but his quarterly figures continue to be poor (320 units; 83 percent of doctors contacted; 41 days inventory). You follow through on your promise and terminate him.

Wilson Thomas offered perhaps the most challenging motivational assignment any manager ever faces—the plateaued performer. There is no one remedy in cases like these, but there is one in this situation. While you might argue that Wilson Thomas is not worth salvaging as an employee, reevaluate your last decision.

Reevaluate your last decision. Circle the #275 you just wrote in your Flow Diagram, then return to the last uncircled step and try again.

Decision Point 276

You choose to debate Wilson Thomas on the type of sales approach that is most effective in selling pharmaceuticals. He reacts defensively to your comments, and comes very close to calling you a liar on several occasions.

Wilson Thomas is a very anxious and defensive person. He wants to salvage some self-respect, and your approach doesn't enable him to do that.

You are walking a tightrope with this individual. You deserve to be firm, but you also have to be somewhat acknowledging. In general, it is much easier to walk this tightrope by talking about specific behavior in specific situations than engaging in abstract debates.

Reevaluate your last decision. Circle the #276 you just wrote in your Flow Diagram, then return to the last uncircled step and try again.

D.H. HOWDEN AND CO. LIMITED: SALES DIVISION

This case was prepared by Lucie Cousineau, Dean Hillier, and Queenie Jang under the supervision of David Burgoyne for the sole purpose of providing material for class discussion at the Western Business School. Certain names and other identifying information may have been disguised to protect confidentiality. It is not intended to illustrate either effective or ineffective handling of a managerial situation.

Mr. Frank Foran (Foran) was preparing for the bi-weekly meeting with the President and Vice-Presidents of D.H. Howden and Co. Limited (Howden), a Canadian wholesale distributor of hardware products. As Vice-President of Sales, Foran would play a central role at the meeting. His proposal to change the sales force compensation plan from straight salary to straight commissions was an important item on the agenda. No one was more aware than Foran that it was he who, 18 years ago, had been instrumental in changing the sales force compensation plan from straight commission to straight salary. At this point he was convinced that his proposal made sense but he wanted to develop any needed information and to prepare himself for the hard questions he expected would be forthcoming.

THE CANADIAN HARDWARE INDUSTRY

Until the 1960's the wholesale distributor's major role was to buy merchandise in bulk and then sell smaller quantities to retail outlets. Distributors competed on price, product range, and speed of delivery. The operating costs of distributors accelerated while, at the same time, retailers started to look for ways to better serve the diversifying needs of the end users. In response, the hardware industry turned to vertical marketing systems. Distributors franchised dealers who agreed to buy from the distributor in return for assistance in merchandising, and some bookkeeping. The distributor became the "Channel Captain" organizing the flow of goods from selected manufacturers to the consumer, at the least possible cost.

In 1987, with the distributor/retailer relationship growing much closer than anyone envisioned in the 60's, vertical marketing systems were the key to success. The industry had lost 50-60% of its distributors over the last 15 years, most of whom did not have franchisees. By contrast, the three major competitors, who all had their own outlets, retained their leadership position: Canadian Tire with approximately 200 stores in Canada; Home Hardware, with 900 outlets of the same name; and Howden with 400 **PRO** Hardware franchises. Until recently, Cochrane-Dunlop with 250 Dominion Hardware stores as outlets had been another major competitor, but the company had gone into receivership in early 1987.

Although it was hard to determine the actual size of the hardware market and also difficult to delineate it because of the myriad products, Canadian Tire (1986 Gross Operating Revenues All Products, All Markets $2,326,002,000) was recognized as holding the greatest market share. The other two major players, Home Hardware and Howden ($112,075,000 1986 Gross Sales all products), were estimated to have similar shares of the Canadian hardware market. Home Hardware's total sales exceeded those of Howden, but Home Hardware sold some lines of products, such as lumber and furniture, that Howden had not sold.

The Company

Howden was founded in 1901 as a wholesaler and distributor of hardware goods. From its inception, the corporation strived to carry a well planned inventory, to be a total source of hardware to retailers, and to ship every dealer's orders the day it was received. Howden was still known throughout the trade as "The Quick Shippers".

In 1964, Howden made the decision to tie dealers closer to the company and to expand beyond Ontario. It needed to offer retailers more support and it needed to operate on a national basis to generate sufficient volume to qualify for competitive prices from manufacturers. The solution was the **PRO** Hardware network which Howden initially established in partnership with seven other provincial distributors; however by 1982, Howden held the **PRO** franchising rights exclusively in Canada. The company also acquired the Canadian rights to franchise **DO-IT-CENTERS**, outlets for building and home improvement supplies, a proven trade concept developed by one of the most progressive distributors in the U.S.

By 1987, the **PRO** Hardware chain had grown to 350 **PRO** Hardware franchises and 50 **DO-IT-CENTERS**. Howden also sold directly to 1,000 independent retailers and through buying groups, to 600 others. Currently, 58% of Howden's sales were to franchisees of **PRO** or **DO-IT-CENTERS** but the stated goal was to increase this to 80% within 5 years

RELATIONSHIP WITH FRANCHISEES

"We Think Retail" was the corporate motto. The President of Howden had summarized the corporate philosophy and the nature of the relationship with franchisees in a speech:

"Howden tries to be totally consumer and retailer oriented. In concept, we sell the retailer a profit making system, and to obtain the benefits, the retailers agree to buy their merchandise from us."

To "buy into the system", franchisees had to agree to purchase 80% of their merchandise from Howden, returnable only with Howden's approval. In return, Howden provided them, not only with nationwide advertising and promotions, but continually updated marketing and management assistance. In 1987 the following tools, systems and services were in place:

- site selection;
- store design and layout;
- basic inventory selection;
- merchandising and pricing assistance;
- computerized inventory control system;
- computerized electronic data interchange ordering system;
- monthly customer purchase analysis reports;
- the strategic profitability model: a what-if analysis tool to test impact of changes such as sales or inventory levels on profitability and ROI;
- scheduled deliveries;
- advertising and sales promotions;
- personnel training through the Creative Approach to Selling Hardware system;
- information bulletins, dealer newsletters and franchiser manuals;
- visits from company representatives.

EXHIBIT I

D.H. HOWDEN SALES DIVISION 1986/1987
Area Sales Representative Job Description Details

---

1. Achieve warehouse, Schedule A budgets.
2. Achieve targets on sales by vendor Schedule A budgets.
3. Achieve Pro, Do-it advertising requirements.
4. Achieve dealer targeted requirements on H.E.L.P. program.
5. Educate and promote area dealers on displayphone.
6. Support and execute dealer support for C.A.S.H./C.A.S.H. recap program.
7. Develop new and lost accounts for continued overall company growth.
8. Develop schedule detail selling programs with vendors as required by management.
9. Become completely knowledgeable on the firm's marketing and merchandising techniques, as outlined in the Franchise Retail Operations Manual, and familiarize area dealers where necessary.
10. Develop dealer attendance support for all Howden sponsored shows and area regional meetings.
11. Prepare and execute FAB statements for dealer face-to-face selling programs, products, advertising and on all systems and promotional events.
12. Keep dealers return goods volume within company's desired performance levels.
13. Develop necessary sales techniques to sell and execute specialty and decorative products.
14. Promote and support the acquisition of all new Franchise stores, or advise management respecting any concern over existing dealers.
15. Revise Monthly Salesmen Planning Schedules and Customer Goals and Objectives schedule each January 15/July 22nd.
16. Communicate to customers and Howden personnel on iNet messages and reduce monthly long distance telephone calls where possible.
17. Maintain harmonious employee, customer, vendor relationships.
18. May be assigned special projects or duties from time to time by regional sales manager or vice president, sales.

Howden was very selective in distributing franchising rights. An interested entrepreneur required at least 50% personal equity to be granted a franchise for which the total start up investment ranged from $150,000 to $250,000. Annual sales to recent franchise outlets varied from $1,000,000 to $2,000,000 with profits according to one industry source varying from $50,000 to $200,000. Sales to older franchise outlets were well below these levels. The initial inventory for new outlets involved $100,000 to $175,000. Mr. Foran often reminded his sales manager that "we are a wholesaler, not a banker."

SALES DIVISION: HISTORY

During the mid 1950's Howden's average sales per salesperson amounted to approximately $140,000. From Howden's perspective, this amount reflected the inefficiencies with selling on an item-by-item basis to dealers who ordered in an uncontrolled manner from a number of suppliers. Howden sales representatives at that time were largely order takers who worked mainly from dealer "want books".

The company then underwent a strategic corporate change, shifting its marketing philosophy and sales focus. New support systems were developed which were designed to be more market oriented. They aimed to increase dealers' profitability but also enhance Howden employee productivity. With respect to the sales force, the change resulted in a selling function that further emphasized the complete systems approach.

The role of the sales force in systems selling was more complex. Sales representatives were to encourage dealers to use Howden systems to maximize their profitability. This required the sales representatives to educate dealers regard-

EXHIBIT 2
D.H. HOWDEN SALES DIVISION

Regions	Managers	Number of Sales Representatives	Number of Franchise Outlets	Dec. '87 Sales Volume (Millions)
NFLD/West N.S.[a]	1	3	38	10
P.E.I./East N.S./N.B.	1	4	16	7
Central Niagara	1	3	43	12
Central Toronto	1	3	40	13
Eastern Ontario	1	3	26	10
Northern Ontario	1	4	40	18
Manitoba/Sask.	1	4	68	11
Alberta/B.C.	1	4	38	8
N.W.T./Yukon	0	1 sales agent	4	1
National Accts.	1	0	N/A	
Inside Sales	1	4	N/A	

[a]At about this time, control of D.H. Howden and Co. Ltd. was acquired by a Quebec based hardware group. The staff and accounts of D.H. Howden in Quebec were transferred and therefore are not included in this data.

ing the new systems, to detail new products and to analyze the dealers' profitability and inventory control efficiency. It also meant that the representative had to work with dealers to implement merchandising concepts and aid in dealer staff training. (See Exhibit 1.)

SALES DIVISION: POLICIES AND PROCEDURES

Foran had been with Howden for over thirty years and had played a major role in the development of the company from a small Ontario operation to a major national corporation. Foran's approach was to encourage sales growth by developing and implementing systems that increased Howden employee productivity and which also benefitted Howden dealers. Most recently Foran had been instrumental in the introduction of a state-of-the art computer support system for dealer ordering. Not only did this help dealers to better manage their inventories, it freed up sales force time to focus on systems selling.

The sales force was made up of fourteen regional sales managers and forty-four representatives largely organized by geographical regions (Exhibit 2). The primary role (80% of the time) of the regional sales manager was to sell new franchises with the remainder of their time allo-

cated to sales force coaching. Sales territories varied considerably in existing volume, potential volume, geographic size, etc. Another territorial variable was the ratio of sales to franchisees versus sales volume to other outlets which ranged from 80%–20% to 20%–80%.

In recruiting sales representatives, the company was selective and preferred individuals with previous experience in the hardware industry and/or retail business. Because of the company's emphasis on the proper fit of an individual to a job, the suitability of the candidate for the sales position was further tested by an industrial psychologist. Other major criteria used to screen for potential sales representatives included flexibility with respect to relocation and the capacity for extensive travelling.

This screening process resulted in a sales force consisting primarily of salespeople with extensive hardware industry experience and when coupled with the company's policy of promotion from within resulted in a less than 3% annual turnover rate.

Prior to the responsibility of a sales territory, sales representatives underwent an initial training period lasting from one to two years, depending on previous relevant experience. Intensive in-house training included product knowledge, pro-

EXHIBIT 3
D.H. HOWDEN SALES DIVISION

SALES COMPENSATION SUPPORT PROGRAM—EXAMPLE

1987	Base Salary	$28,000
Inflation Factor 4%		1,120
1988	Guarantee	29,120
1988	Forecasted Commissions	26,000
1988	Subsidy Required	3,120
1989	Subsidy Expected	2,080 plus inflation factor
1990	Subsidy Expected	1,039 plus inflation factor
1991	No Subsidy Program	

fessional selling skills, trade shows and extensive work with experienced sales people in the field.

Training was a continuing process at Howden and representatives received ongoing training in the area of product knowledge (old and new products) via video electronic newsletters and three national sales meetings held each year in conjunction with two company sponsored dealer trade shows.

Each representative was formally reviewed once a year by the regional sales manager who reviewed the representative's achievements of mutually agreed upon semi-annual goals and objectives, and annual sales forecast. This process was meticulously recorded for purposes of future promotability and documentation of any unsatisfactory performance. The company recognized that for staff morale, unproductive employees had to be terminated. If an individual was unable, after a suitable time, to reach mutually agreed upon performance levels, a warning was issued. Subsequent failure to meet an acceptable performance level without just cause after this initial warning, resulted in dismissal.

Since 1969 Howden had compensated its sales force using a straight base salary plan. The range in 1987 was $25,000 to $35,000 plus a benefits package. In addition each representative was reimbursed for business-related travel expenses. Regional sales managers received a base salary and also participated in a bonus program.

THE PROPOSAL

Before the planning meeting, Foran reviewed his notes of last January when he first thought of the need for change. On the left of the page, Foran had written his goals: 1. increase the productivity of the sales force, 2. lower the sales expenses, and 3. achieve a 25% increase in sales dollars over the previous year. On the right side of the page, Foran had written the changes he thought of making to attain these goals: 1. a straight commission renumeration plan based on sales volume, 2. a lump sum expense allocation to replace the existing expense reimbursement system, and 3. a dealer price reduction of 6% on Howden's price competitive products, representing 20% of the total product line.

The ultimate payback would come from increased salesforce productivity. He didn't believe the sales group would have to develop new skills. They would however have to work smarter and harder.

As Foran reviewed his notes, he recalled how commission selling had motivated him when he began his sales career with Howden nearly thirty years ago. He became the top Howden salesman despite being the youngest. He also recognized that it might be difficult for some people to initially deal with the insecurity that straight commission represented. Therefore representatives would be guaranteed that their 1988 income would, at a minimum, match their 1987 salary level. This support would continue at a declining rate until 1990 (see Exhibit 3).

EXHIBIT 4
D.H. HOWDEN SALES DIVISION

Salary and Expense Analysis—Jan–Dec/87 Selected Representatives

Sales Rep	Sales	Salary	Travel	Total Cost	Salary Plus Travel Expense to Sales Ratio
A.	$2,047,564	$28,755	$13,370	$42,125	2.06
B.	2,763,000	28,000	13,650	41,650	1.51
C.	2,575,000	27,000	13,450	40,450	1.57
D.	3,916,000	27,550	9,450	37,000	0.94
E.	3,422,000	28,660	10,000	38,660	1.13
F.	1,793,078	28,000	14,600	42,600	2.94

Salary and Expense Analysis Projected 1988 Selected Representatives

Sales Rep	Sales	Salary	Travel	Total Cost	Salary Plus Travel Expense to Sales Ratio
A.	$2,239,546	[b]$21,542	$12,000	$33,542	1.75
B.	3,210,998	30,882	10,000	40,882	1.28
C.	3,766,518	35,648	15,600	51,248	1.36
D.	5,420,394	49,450	8,000	57,450	1.06
E.	5,356,388	47,672	8,000	56,672	1.04
F.	1,793,078	[b]17,476	13,800	31,276	2.39

[a]1.0% for sales up to $4 million; 0.75% for sales between $4 million and $5 million; 0.5% for sales above $5 million.

[b]Subsidies expected $5,742 and $11,644.

THE PLANNING MEETING

Although Foran felt that most of the members on the planning committee favoured the change, he wondered how they would react to his request for $250,000 in incremental salesforce compensation that he estimated he would need for the first year of the program.

The Howden management team had always been very open with each other. Foran knew he would have to be prepared to answer questions about the potential impact of the changes on the salesforce and dealer networks. Certainly some of the salespeople wouldn't be happy with the new approach; this could create problems for the company and the dealers.

It was probable that the existing and potential volume realities in some territories would result in lower incomes for some salespeople—lower than they were now once the support program ran out (see Exhibit 4). Should this situation result in salesforce departures, empty territories could then be amalgamated into adjoining territories, increasing the potential sales base and, hence, the income base for the salespeople in those areas.

POWER & MOTION INDUSTRIAL SUPPLY, INC.

The following were actual situations experienced by the case writer during more than 15 years in business-to-business sales and sales management. The names of the firms and individuals have been disguised due to the nature of the material in this case.

It was 7:00 P.M. on Sunday evening when Hal Maybee returned to his office. He had spent the afternoon golfing with one of his customers, and he now had to decide what he was going to tell head office on Monday morning with regard to new salaries for the sales staff at his branch.

Hal had just been appointed Atlantic Region District Manager for one of Canada's largest industrial distributors. His appointment was made only two weeks before, following the sudden death of Fergie McDonald who, at 48 years old, had been in charge of the company's most profitable branch. About 70 percent of the sales in Atlantic Canada, including the four most profitable product lines, were for manufacturers that the company did not represent on a national basis. There were many manufacturers in Ontario and Quebec that served central Canada with their own sales forces, and used distributors for the east and west coasts due to the distances from their head offices and the geographical dispersion of customers in those regions. Although Power & Motion had sales agreements with over 400 North American manufacturers, only about 100 manufacturers were involved in 80 percent of the sales.

It was a complete surprise to Hal when he was promoted, and he knew there were people at the branch who expected they deserved it more. Exhibit 1 shows the performance evaluations that Fergie had completed on the six sales people just before he died. Head office had in-tended to send only five forms to Hal, but one of the secretaries mistakenly included Fergie's evaluation of Hal as well.

Nearly three weeks previously, Fergie and Hal were making some joint calls on some pulp mills in Northern New Brunswick, the territory that Fergie kept for himself, even though head office wanted him to stop selling and spend more time on sales administration. During the trip, Fergie told Hal that he was given six percent of the total sales staff salary to be divided among them for the coming year. This was the customary way of giving salary increases at the branches as it gave head office the discretion to decide the total increase in the salary expense, but it gave the district managers responsibility for allocating salary increases. Fergie was told that nationally, sales increases would average about three percent, but his branch was among the lowest paid in the company and had been the best performing branch for several years.

Hal did not want to express his opinions as he knew he and Fergie would disagree. However, he did allow Fergie to express his own thoughts on the staff. There were two salespeople that Fergie had a real problem with. He viewed Jim Stanley as his biggest problem. Jim actually had seniority at the branch. He had been hired as shipper, orderdesk salesperson, and secretary when the branch was only large enough to support one person other than Bob Laird, the first salesperson the company had in

Send correspondence to: H. F. (Herb) MacKenzie, Faculty of Business Administration, Memorial University of Newfoundland, St. John's, Newfoundland A1B 3X5, Canada; tel. (709) 737-4388; fax (709) 737-7680; e-mail hmackenz@plato.ucs.mun.ca

EXHIBIT I
EVALUATION OF SALESPERSONS

Salesperson	Evaluation Criteria	Far Worse Than Average			About Average		Far Better Than Average	
Dave Edison	Attitude	1	2	3	4	5*	6	7
	Appearance and Manner	1	2	3	4	5	6*	7
	Selling Skills	1	2	3	4	5	6*	7
	Product Knowledge	1	2	3	4*	5	6	7
	Time Management	1	2	3	4*	5	6	7
	Customer Goodwill	1	2	3	4*	5	6	7
	Expense/Budget	1	2	3	4*	5	6	7
	New Accounts Opened	1	2	3	4*	5	6	7
	Sales Calls/Quota	1	2	3	4*	5	6	7
	Sales/Quota	1	2	3	4	5*	6	7
	Sales Volume	1	2	3	4*	5	6	7
	Sales Growth	1	2	3	4	5*	6	7
	Contribution Margin	1	2	3	4	5	6*	7

Total Score: 61

Comments: Current salary $52,000. Territory is Cape Breton Island and the city of Moncton, N.B. Needs more product knowledge, but has learned a lot since hired. A bit aggressive, but he has developed some excellent new accounts through attention to detail and follow-up support.

Salesperson	Evaluation Criteria	Far Worse Than Average			About Average		Far Better Than Average	
Arne Olson	Attitude	1	2	3*	4	5	6	7
	Appearance and Manner	1	2	3*	4	5	6	7
	Selling Skills	1	2	3*	4	5	6	7
	Product Knowledge	1	2	3	4*	5	6	7
	Time Management	1	2	3*	4	5	6	7
	Customer Goodwill	1	2	3*	4	5	6	7
	Expense/Budget	1	2	3	4	5*	6	7
	New Accounts Opened	1	2	3*	4	5	6	7
	Sales Calls/Quota	1	2	3	4	5	6*	7
	Sales/Quota	1	2	3*	4	5	6	7
	Sales Volume	1	2	3	4*	5	6	7
	Sales Growth	1	2	3*	4	5	6	7
	Contribution Margin	1	2	3*	4	5	6	7

Total Score: 46

Comments: Current salary $44,500. Has been calling regularly on his existing accounts in southern New Brunswick (except Moncton). Although he has increased the number of sales calls as agreed at our last review, sales have not gone up accordingly. Some concern with product knowledge. Arne knows all of our major product lines very well, but has not shown much effort to learn about many of the new lines we have added that may become our best product lines in the future. Further concern with his contribution margin. This is the fourth year in a row that it has dropped although it is almost the same as last year.

	EXHIBIT I (continued)					

EVALUATION OF SALESPERSONS

Salesperson	Evaluation Criteria	Far Worse Than Average			About Average		Far Better Than Average	
Hal Maybee	Attitude	1	2	3	4	5*	6	7
	Appearance and Manner	1	2	3	4*	5	6	7
	Selling Skills	1	2	3	4*	5	6	7
	Product Knowledge	1	2	3	4	5*	6	7
	Time Management	1	2	3	4	5	6*	7
	Customer Goodwill	1	2	3	4	5	6*	7
	Expense/Budget	1	2	3	4*	5	6	7
	New Accounts Opened	1	2*	3	4	5	6	7
	Sales Calls/Quota	1	2	3	4*	5	6	7
	Sales/Quota	1	2	3	4	5*	6	7
	Sales Volume	1	2*	3	4	5	6	7
	Sales Growth	1	2	3*	4	5	6	7
	Contribution Margin	1	2*	3	4	5	6	7

Total Score: 52

Comments: Current salary $38,500. Although still the Office Manager, Hal has taken over Newfoundland as a territory and travels there four times a year. Hal also travels to northern New Brunswick with me occasionally due to his expert product knowledge on electric and pneumatic products which we sell to the mines and pulp mills in the two areas. Hal is very focused and successful with the big sales, but needs to develop knowledge of and interest in some of the lower sales volume, less technical products as they are generally higher margin items. Hal has a lot of respect in the office and our efficiency has improved greatly, as has the general work atmostphere within the office.

Salesperson	Evaluation Criteria	Far Worse Than Average			About Average		Far Better Than Average	
Tanya Burt	Attitude	1	2	3	4*	5	6	7
	Appearance and Manner	1	2	3	4*	5	6	7
	Selling Skills	1	2	3	4	5*	6	7
	Product Knowledge	1	2	3*	4	5	6	7
	Time Management	1	2	3	4	5*	6	7
	Customer Goodwill	1	2	3	4	5*	6	7
	Expense/Budget	1	2	3	4*	5	6	7
	New Accounts Opened	1	2	3	4	5*	6	7
	Sales Calls/Quota	1	2	3	4	5*	6*	7
	Sales/Quota	1	2	3	4	5*	6	7
	Sales Volume	1	2	3	4*	5	6	7
	Sales Growth	1	2	3	4	5*	6	7
	Contribution Margin	1	2	3	4	5*	6	7

Total Score: 59

Comments: Current salary $36,000. Very impressed with her performance. Has good knowledge of product pricing and sourcing, but needs to learn more about product applications. Tanya sells mainly maintenance and operating supplies, but she has a number of accounts that but large annual volumes as her territory is the Halifax-Dartmouth area surrounding our warehouse. Tanya is dedicated and dependable. She has opened many new accounts for us, and I predict good success for her as she continues to develop her knowledge and selling skills.

EXHIBIT I (continued)

EVALUATION OF SALESPERSONS

Salesperson	Evaluation Criteria	Far Worse Than Average			About Average		Far Better Than Average	
Jim Stanley	Attitude	1	2	3*	4	5	6	7
	Appearance and Manner	1	2	3*	4	5	6	7
	Selling Skills	1	2	3*	4	5	6	7
	Product Knowledge	1	2	3	4*	5	6	7
	Time Management	1	2*	3	4	5	6	7
	Customer Goodwill	1	2	3*	4	5	6	7
	Expense/Budget	1	2	3*	4	5	6	7
	New Accounts Opened	1	2*	3	4	5	6	7
	Sales Calls/Quota	1	2	3	4*	5	6	7
	Sales/Quota	1	2	3	4	5*	6	7
	Sales Volume	1	2	3	4*	5	6	7
	Sales Growth	1	2	3	4	5*	6	7
	Contribution Margin	1	2	3	4	5*	6	7

Total Score: 46

Comments: Current salary $42,000. Jim seems to be performing quite well, but there is concern with his behaviour. I hope that a salary increase and some direction from me will improve his performance next year. He has been making some suggestions that he might like to move back to Office Management because everyone thinks I will be promoting Hal to full-time sales and letting him take over my territory as well as Newfoundland. I really do not want Jim back in the office, and I think he should be a good salesperson. His sales and contribution margin are good, but part of his sales increase this year came from a new customer that has a manufacturing plant in his region, but actually buys from an office located in Tanya's territory. Tanya and Jim have agreed to split the credit for the sales as Tanya must do the selling, but Jim has to service the account.

Salesperson	Evaluation Criteria	Far Worse Than Average			About Average		Far Better Than Average	
Buck Thompson	Attitude	1	2	3	4*	5	6	7
	Appearance and Manner	1	2	3	4*	5	6	7
	Selling Skills	1	2	3	4	5*	6	7
	Product Knowledge	1	2	3	4	5	6*	7
	Time Management	1	2	3	4*	5	6	7
	Customer Goodwill	1	2	3	4*	5	6	7
	Expense/Budget	1	2	3*	4	5	6	7
	New Accounts Opened	1	2*	3	4	5	6	7
	Sales Calls/Quota	1	2	3*	4	5	6	7
	Sales/Quota	1	2	3	4*	5	6	7
	Sales Volume	1	2	3	4*	5	6	7
	Sales Growth	1	2	3	4*	5	6	7

Total Score: 51

Comments: Current salary $49,000. Sells in Pictou County, N.S. where we have a very established customer base and a variety of industries. Buck knows all of his customers very well as he has lived in the area all of his life. He has very good selling skills and product knowledge and has been the main reason we have done so well in his territory.

Atlantic Canada. Bob and Jim operated the branch for almost two years when Bob decided to hire Fergie as a salesperson to help develop the territory. When Bob retired, Jim thought he would get the position as District Manager as he had seniority, and he had experience with all aspects of the business including managing the office and warehouse which had grown to include seven people. He was very disappointed when head office gave the position to Fergie as he had no experience other than sales.

Within a year, Jim decided he wanted to get into sales. He was finally resigned to the fact that office management was a deadend job, and the only possibility for advancement was through sales. Now, after five years, Jim was not performing as well as he should. In fact, he hated selling and spent an increasing amount of time drinking while away from home. He hinted that he wanted to get back into the office. However, when these rumours started to spread, the staff let it be known that they did not want to work under Jim again if there were any alternatives.

Fergie was thinking about giving Jim a good salary increase. First, it might make him appreciate his job more and maybe he would put more effort into selling. Second, it would make the position more attractive than a possible return to the office as he would not want to take a tremendous salary cut.

The other problem was Arne Olsen, the other senior salesperson. As the territory developed quickly, the branch hired a secretary just after Fergie was hired. A month later, a warehouseman was hired and Jim was promoted to Office Manager. Jim immediately hired Hal Maybee as an orderdesk salesperson. Within a year, another salesperson, Arne, was hired, along with a second secretary. The branch growth slowed, but was steady from that point on. Arne was always an average salesperson. He never really had much motivation to perform, but he always did whatever he had to do so that he was never in any serious trouble as far as his job was concerned. Lately, he was starting to slip a bit, and rumour had it that he was having at least one affair. He also recently bought a Mazda Miata that he drove on weekends as he

was not allowed to drive anything but the company car through the work week.

Dave Edison was with the company for just under one year. If he had a few more years with the company, Hal knew he would have probably been the new District Manager. He came to the company from the life insurance industry, and rumour had it that he was slated for a national sales manager position within the next year as the company was rumoured to be taking on a new line of capital equipment from Europe that would be sold nationally, but would have one person at head office responsible for national sales.

Tanya Burt was also in sales for only a year. She had been hired as a secretary, but it soon became apparent that she had exceptional telephone skills. She was promoted to order desk salesperson within a year, and three years later, she requested and was given an outside sales territory. There was some concern with her product knowledge, but no concern with her attitude or sales ability. Tanya was the first and only woman to be promoted to one of the company's eighty outside sales positions.

Buck Thompson had a very solid, established territory. He needed little direction as he was doing most things very well. Fergie was a bit concerned that he was not making enough sales calls, but he certainly was performing well.

As Hal reviewed the performance evaluations, he agreed that Fergie had been very thorough and accurate in his assessment of each of the individuals. Hal wondered about the amount of salary increase he should give to each person. While he had to make this decision immediately, Hal realized there were other important decisions he would have to make soon. He recognized some of the problems Fergie had trying to decide salary increases, and these were more important for Hal as he had to get the support of the sales staff before he could hope to overcome some of these problems. He also had to start thinking about hiring another salesperson to cover Newfoundland and northern New Brunswick as head office was determined that he give up responsibility for all accounts in the region. He would, however, be allowed and encouraged to call on customers with the sales staff.

CRAVEN CHEMICALS LTD.

This case was written by Dr. T. H. Payton of the City University Business School as a basis for class discussion. It is not intended to illustrate good or bad management practice.

Early in April 1987, Richard Gibson the recently appointed sales manager of Craven Chemicals Ltd. was studying the data which had been prepared for him by his predecessor, Kenneth Craven, who had just retired after 25 years as sales manager. As his name suggests Craven is a member of the founder's family and Gibson was the first non-family member to be appointed to a senior executive position other than in the manufacturing division. He (Gibson) was very well aware that he had been appointed to bring a fresh approach and new thinking into the management of the sales force, and that not all the management team supported his appointment. He was particularly anxious, therefore, to make sure that his plans for the future were sound and that they were generally acceptable to the sales people and the Board.

Kenneth Craven was an impressive man. Tall, well-dressed and gentle mannered, he was widely respected in the industry and especially by members of the sales force. This was reflected in the stability of the thirteen man force. The average age of the team was 45 years and there had been no resignations in the past five years: in fact the only changes had been due to two retirements in the Southern region. Two others were approaching normal retirement age and there were murmurs from others about seeking early retirement. Craven firmly believed that the salesmen were best motivated by pride in what they did and the loyalty of the company to them. For this reason control and evaluation systems had not loomed large in his planning, and the two regional managers

(RMs), one Northern and one Southern, spent much of their time running the regional offices, of which there were two. However they did arrange monthly sales meetings and occasional field visits.

The company was formed 45 years ago and had enjoyed solid if not spectacular success. It produced a range of detergents, disinfectants and industrial cleaners (for example, powders for use in industrial dish-washing machines) used mainly in schools, hospitals, hotels and factories. Appendix A shows product prices and gross margins. At an early meeting with Gibson, Craven had told him that there was little to choose between products in the market and that as a result price was the most important determinant of sales. He produced no evidence to support his view. Sales and gross profit figures for the last five years are given in Exhibit 1.

Despite his views on motivation, a commission scheme had been introduced by Craven some years ago. Under the scheme each salesman (there were six in the Northern Region and five in the Southern Region) was given a total

EXHIBIT I	
SALES AND GROSS PROFIT—ALL PRODUCTS	
Total Sales (£000's)	Gross Profit (£000's)
1982	2703	1054
1983	2963	1096
1984	2605	912
1985	3028	1151
1986	3256	1204

EXHIBIT 2

SALES AND GROSS PROFIT BY REGION—1986
(£000's)

Region	Northern	Southern
No. of Salesmen	6	5
Sales Quotas	1825	1360
Sales Actual	1703	1553
Gross Profit	590	614

EXHIBIT 3

SALES EXPENSES BY REGION—1986
(£'s)

Region	Northern	Southern
Salesmen's Salaries	78,690	57,415
Commission	8,515	8,530
Salesmen's Expenses	27,218	22,350
District Office Costs	11,062	12,243
RMs Salary	17,500	15,750
RMs Expenses	6,191	5,822
Total Expenses	149,176	122,110

EXHIBIT 4

NUMBER OF ACCOUNTS BY CATEGORY AND ANNUAL CALLS PER CATEGORY

Region	Active Accounts			Annual Calls/Category		
	A	B	C	A	B	C
Northern	55	210	315	1299	3050	2120
Southern	45	180	219	1029	2619	1301

sales quota. A commission of 0.5% (i.e. half of 1%) was given on all sales up to the quota level. Sales in excess of quota earned commission of 1%. Quotas were not broken down by product. Exhibit 2 shows sales quotas and gross profit achievements for the two regions for 1986.

Gibson noted that annual sales per salesman in the Southern Region were almost 10% more than they were in the Northern Region, but at the same time selling expenses were a greater percentage of sales in the North. A detailed breakdown of expenses is given in Exhibit 3.

No estimate of the number of potential accounts was included in the data given to Gibson but the number of active accounts was shown, as was an analysis by outlet category. Accounts were classified "A" if turnover was £6000 or more per year; accounts generating annual sales of between £3000 and £5999 were classified "B"; other accounts were classified as "C" grade. Frequency of call guide lines were:

Category "A"	Every two weeks
Category "B"	Once a month
Category "C"	Every two months

EXHIBIT 5

APPENDIX A

Product	Price[a] £'s	Gross Profit £'s
A	19.50	6.20
B	18.90	7.95
C	18.50	7.00
D	20.15	6.40
E	54.50	21.25
F	29.60	9.50

[a]Price per drum/case

The number of active accounts and the total calls per account category are shown in Exhibit 4.

Besides the numerical data, Gibson was given what Craven called a pen picture of each salesman. These seemed to Gibson to be no more than a summary of personal details (age, marital status, number of dependants, health record and length of service) and Craven's subjective opinion of the personality and capabilities of each man. Gibson thought again of his plans for the future and wondered how Craven's report would help him to structure them.

PART V

MANAGING YOUR SALES RESOURCES: CORPORATE STRATEGY

FORECASTING/QUOTA

Prediction is very difficult, especially about the future.
NELS BOHR, NOBEL PRIZE–WINNING PHYSICIST

If our original plan had had a lower goal, we would have achieved less.
WILLIAM E. FOSTER, CEO, STRATUS COMPUTER INC.

LEARNING OBJECTIVES

After reading this chapter, you should be able to answer the following questions:

- What do *estimating market demand* and *sales forecasting* mean, and why are they important?
- Why is sales forecasting so important to marketing and other functional areas of the firm?
- What are sales quotas, and how can they be determined?
- What are the characteristics of quantitative and qualitative forecasting techniques?
- How can forecasters select a forecasting technique for a given problem?
- How can forecasters combine forecasts?

Ford Motor Company has made some spectacular errors in forecasting demand for two of its products, the Edsel (during the 1950s) and the Mustang (during the 1960s). With the Edsel, Ford felt it had a car that would have broad popular appeal. The estimated sales for the Edsel for its first 2 years were over 400,000 cars. Ford built production facilities and developed a dealer network to handle the forecasted level of demand. However, the actual demand for the cars was only 109,466 units for the three model years the car was available. Ford lost over $200 million (in 1957 dollars) on the Edsel, much of it directly attributable to poor forecasting.[1]

In 1964 Ford introduced the Mustang, a small, economical, but stylish sports car. Ford's estimate of sales in the first year was 75,000 units, while the actual sales were over 400,000 units in the initial 12-month period after introduction. Sales would have been higher if not for the lack of adequate production facilities to build more cars.[2] This time poor forecasting led to opportunity losses in the millions for Ford.

A similar situation to Ford's Mustang forecast was encountered more recently by Mazda during its introduction of the Miata, another small, economical sports car. Mazda underestimated demand so badly that customers were forced to place deposits on cars that would not be delivered for over 6 months. When the dealers received cars, they were able to charge a significant premium over the sticker price owing to the cars' scarcity. Mazda felt that its dealers were taking advantage of customers, with potential long-term loss of customer goodwill.[3]

Accurate forecasts are necessary for all functions of a business, so forecasting is one of the most important duties performed by sales managers. Developing accurate sales forecasts is important because many firms have experienced major problems as a result of inaccurate forecasts. Unfortunately, although forecasting may be a relatively simple task for a mature product such as corporate jets, where the market consists of a small number of new and replacement purchases by a small number of firms and individuals each year,[4] estimating demand for a new product in a new market, such as video chips, can be much more difficult. Andrew Grove, the CEO and president of Intel, the world's largest manufacturer of computer chips, has told analysts that the market for computer chips in personal computers is maturing, as the software currently available cannot use all the processing power that is now standard. As a result, Intel is now turning its focus to the applications for chips in video technology, ranging from videoconferencing to picture telephones. When analysts questioned Grove about the market potential for these products was and what effect the demand for these products would have on Intel, Grove responded, "Who are you going to ask? This is a brand-new market."[5]

The first section of this chapter discusses the importance of forecasting throughout the organization. This is followed by an explanation of different types of forecasts, which range from estimates of market potential to quotas. The next section is an overview of the quantitative and qualitative techniques used to arrive at forecasts. The chapter concludes by outlining issues involved with the selection of a forecasting technique and methods of improving forecasting accuracy.

IMPORTANCE OF FORECASTING

Forecasting is the prediction of demand or sales for upcoming periods. As shown in Exhibit 15.1, forecasting is the basis for decisions within production, finance and accounting, human resources, and sales and marketing. Some of the important decisions for which forecasting is critical include inventory control, determination of cash requirements, production schedules, and personal planning. Sales managers use demand estimates for several purposes, including determining sales territories, setting sales quotas, allocating sales resources, determining salesforce size, evaluating salespeople, and evaluating prospective accounts. Exhibit 15.1 shows how different functional areas of the firm use forecasts.

TYPES OF FORECASTS

There are five major types of forecasts: (1) market potential, (2) market forecast, (3) sales potential, (4) sales forecast, and (5) sales quotas. These types of forecasts vary on two dimensions: first, whether the forecast is for the industry as a whole, the firm, or the salesperson, and second, whether the estimate is for the best possible or the most likely results expected for a given marketing strategy. Exhibit 15.2 shows how each type of forecast ranks on the two dimensions.

It is important to note that the type of sales organization affects the development of forecasts. For instance, geographically-based salesforces develop forecasts by geographic region. Exhibit 15.3 shows the relationship among market potential, market forecast, sales potential, and sales forecast for a firm with a geographically

---

EXHIBIT 15.1

FORECASTING'S EFFECTS THROUGHOUT THE FIRM

PRODUCTION
- Helps to control finished product inventory
- Permits production to be leveled out
- Helps to stabilize employment allowing the retention of highly trained workers
- Helps schedule work to achieve optimum use of plant and equipment

PURCHASING
- Helps maintain adequate stocks of raw materials and supplies to ensure uninterrupted production
- Helps minimize overstocking and keeps warehousing and carrying costs at a minimum
- Helps purchasing to take advantage of favorable prices and discounts

TOP MANAGEMENT
- Helps guide top management policy and overall planning and control of operations
- Helps reconcile views of various functional areas as to the types and quantities of products produced

FINANCE
- Helps in estimating cash requirements
- Helps in planning long-term and short-term financing
- Helps in the development of standard costs
- Helps in the preparation of operating and capital budgets

PERSONNEL
- Helps in personnel planning
- Helps in collective bargaining

FORECASTING

PLANT EXPANSION
- Helps in making sound plant expansion decisions

ENGINEERING
- Helps in maintenance and repair scheduling

SALES & MARKETING
- Helps in establishing sales quotas for the salesforce
- Helps in the formulation of salesforce compensation plans
- Helps indicate whether or not sales territories are properly established
- Helps direct sales effort and establish sales and promotional expenses
- Helps determine the size and character of the advertising budget
- Helps direct advertising to areas where it is most needed
- Help in the development of prices that will give a reasonable level of profit
- Helps in determining which products should be further developed
- Helps schedule new product introductions

SOURCE: Adapted from Jim Cox, "Increasingly Complex Forecasting, Neglected Area of Marketing Education, Is Crucial to Firm's Success," *Marketing Educator,* 3 (Fall 1984): 2.

based salesforce. Similarly, product-based organizations develop forecasts by product, and account-based salesforces by account (see Chapter 7 for the descriptions of the different salesforce types).

Market Potential

Market potential is defined as the maximum number of sales that can occur in a given period to individuals or businesses that are willing and have the capability to

---

EXHIBIT 15.2

RELATIONSHIPS AMONG DIFFERENT TYPES OF FORECASTS

	Industry	Firm	Salesperson
Best Possible Results	Market potential	Sales potential	
Most Likely Results	Market forecast	Sales forecast	Quota

---

purchase a given product type. Market potential is a key factor in developing marketing strategy, determining allocation of resources, and in some cases, determining whether a business should stay in a given market. The personal computer industry illustrates the importance of accurately calculating market potential.[6] In 1983 and 1984, 67 new firms introduced new personal computers in the U.S. market. Most companies projected explosive growth in the purchase and use of personal computers by business, since industry forecasting services estimated that the number of personal computers used by business would rise to 28 million by the beginning of 1988. Xerox and IBM even developed their own retail distribution networks to ensure that small businesses received the necessary level of customer support. By the end of 1986, however, only 15 million units had been shipped, and it was clear that the forecast of 28 million units would not be reached. The gap between projected

---

EXHIBIT 15.3

COMPARISON OF DIFFERENT DEMAND ESTIMATES

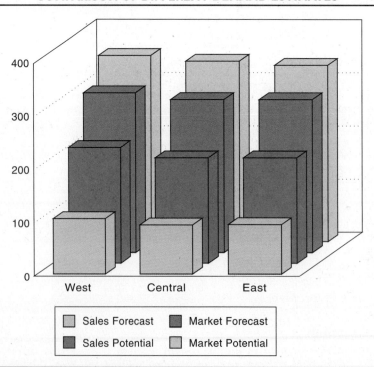

Legend: Sales Forecast, Market Forecast, Sales Potential, Market Potential

and actual sales forced many personal computer manufacturers, including Xerox, Osborne, Commodore, and Kaypro, out of business.

Businesses should follow four steps in developing market potential forecasts: (1) define the market, (2) divide total industry demand into demand by market segment, (3) look for issues that drive demand in each segment, and (4) conduct sensitivity analysis to determine which issues are most important in driving demand in each segment.[7] *Defining the market* means specifying the actual and potential users of the product in broad enough terms so that the manager can identify customers' key purchasing criteria. The purpose of this step is for firms to identify all likely possible competitors. For example, in projecting demand for overnight mail service, Federal Express must consider not only direct competitors such as other express delivery firms, but also indirect competitors such as high-quality, low-cost fax machines and teleconferences.

Dividing total industry demand into demand by market segment means understanding the different levels of demand in each market segment. For example, while the demand for soft drinks in the United States has remained fairly stable on a per capita basis for many years, the demand for certain types of soft drinks, such as bottled waters or clear drinks rather than cola-based soft drinks, has increased at a rapid rate throughout the 1980s and 1990s. If a soft drink firm that specialized in clear soft drinks, such as Clearly Canadian or Snapple, developed a forecast for its products relying on overall industry growth, it would underestimate its sales because the growth of sales in its category is higher than that for the industry as a whole.

Forecasting drivers of demand requires the forecaster to look for relationships between level of demand in a given market segment and the potential drivers of that demand. For example, in a study of laptop computers used in salesforces, it was found that laptops were used much more frequently in salesforces that encountered unique or complex selling situations, such as a salesforce for heavy capital equipment. Salesforces that handled routine and simple selling tasks, such as the Frito-Lay route salesforce, were much more likely to use dedicated, single-purpose computers designed specifically for the sales tasks they encountered.[8] As a result, laptop computer manufacturers were not likely to have much demand for their computers among route-type salesforces.

Sensitivity analysis means testing various combinations of marketing effort, such as resources devoted to the salesforce, to see which yields the highest outcome. A second type of sensitivity analysis requires a firm to consider the likelihood that another firm will develop a competing product, and takes the impact of the competing product into account when developing market potential. Let's return to the overnight delivery service example. Federal Express may need to consider the likelihood that teleconferencing and fax services may reduce the need for express delivery of certain types of documents. As a result, Federal Express may wish to focus more on small package deliveries, such as critical spare parts or small, high-cost items such as precious metals or gems, for which fax machines are not substitutes.

After developing a market potential forecast, sales managers must state the market potential in an understandable way. Statements of market potential must include five elements: (1) a description of the product, (2) the geographic region in which the sales will occur, (3) the time period during which the sales will occur, (4) a description of the consumer or business market segment, and (5) the maximum level of sales that could occur, in dollars and units (this is necessary because if demand is elastic, changing the price will have a disproportionate effect on sales).

Here is an example of a statement of market potential:

> The maximum number of futons (*product description*) that could be sold in the Chicago area (*geographic region*) during the 1996 calendar year (*time period of sales*) to college students (*consumer segment*) is 15,000 units (@ $150 a unit) for sales of $2,250,000 (*sales in units and dollars*).

Market Forecast

A **market forecast** represents the expected level of sales to a given consumer or business market segment to a given geographic area for a given commodity during a given time period. The market forecast is a subset of market potential. Look again at the futon example. Market forecast is the total expected sales of futons to college students in the Chicago area in 1996. Market forecasts are generally less than the market potential for several reasons, including (1) suppliers may not conveniently located, (2) suppliers may not offer needed services, such as delivery or easy credit terms, and (3) the styles may not be what are currently sought by the target market (college students).

Sales Potential

Whereas market potential and market forecast are estimated at the industry level, sales potential and sales forecast are estimated at the firm level. The **sales potential** is the maximum possible sales of a specific product to a given market segment in a specific geographical region by a given supplier during a given time period. For a firm to achieve sales potential, it would have to have a perfectly designed and executed marketing plan. Any factor that causes the firm's marketing plan to be less than perfect will influence what level of sales potential is achieved. For example, if quality of advertising is highly related to sales, and a firm's advertising is not as high in quality as its competitors, it will not achieve sales potential. To illustrate, when Burger King ran its "Where's Herb" ads, industry analysts said that the advertising was not as memorable or as persuasive as the McDonald's ads focusing on children using Ronald MacDonald. As a result, McDonald's came closer to reaching its sales potential than did Burger King.

Sales Forecast

The **sales forecast** is the level of sales of a specific product expected by a given suppliers to a given market segment within a given geographic area during a given time period using a given marketing plan. The sales forecast is the tool used throughout the firm for the purposes stated in Exhibit 15.1.

The sales forecast is often prepared by sales or marketing personnel. One survey of 900 small and medium-sized manufacturing firms representing a cross section of U.S. manufacturers showed that marketing and sales personnel were most frequently charged with forecasting.[9] In retailing, top management prepares forecasts most often, followed by finance, marketing, and accounting.[10]

Sales Quotas

Quotas are quantitative goals covering a specific time period assigned to salespeople and sales managers. One type of quota is for expected sales. A salesperson for a copier manufacturer may have a sales quota of $125,000 per month, with the expectation that those sales will consist of a specified number of different types of machines. A salesperson can also have a quota for expected activities. Opening a certain number of new accounts, making a certain number of calls per day, providing a certain number of training sessions to customers, and conducting training for new salespeople are all examples of activity quotas.

Quotas are an important part of the overall forecasting process. Because a sales quota represents the expected sales for a territory, and a sales forecast is the expected sales for a set of territories, there must be close correspondence between forecasts and quotas. Quotas are the primary means by which sales forecasts are translated into individual plans for action. Quotas are also used for a variety of motivational and evaluative purposes. For example, quotas provide a standard against which salespeople can measure their performance. Refer to Chapter 14 for a discussion of the use of quotas for evaluative purposes.

Quotas are one of the most widely used tools in sales management. One survey showed that 92 percent of responding manufacturing firms include either a bonus or commission in their compensation packages,[11] and that 83 percent of organizations use "reaching quota" as a basis for calculating bonuses or commissions.[12]

QUALITATIVE FORECASTING TECHNIQUES

Forecasters can use a variety of methods to develop each type of forecast. The broadest categorization of forecasting methods is qualitative versus quantitative. **Qualitative forecasting techniques** typically rely on experts' judgments rather than empirical analysis to determine the most likely level of sales. The qualitative techniques discussed in this chapter include the jury of executive opinion, the Delphi technique, salesforce composite, and survey of buying intentions. (Quantitative techniques are discussed in the next section.)

Jury of Executive (or Expert) Opinion

Jury of executive (or expert) opinion involves gathering forecasts from a variety of executives or experts in the firm. The executives providing data input for this method can be based in any of the organization's functional areas including marketing, production, and finance, as well as top management. The primary advantages of this method are that it is quick and easy to obtain, and managers who make the forecasts are in charge of allocating resources in such a way as to bring about the forecasted level of sales.

The primary disadvantage of the method is the distance of the forecasters from the market. It may be possible that some of the executives, such as those in production or finance, have very little interaction with customers. As a result, their ability to predict what customers will purchase may be suspect. On the other hand, marketing executives may be too close to the market, thereby running the risk of missing broad market changes such as changing technologies or the emergence of new competitors that may have a large impact on sales. Another disadvantage of executive opinion is that it may be difficult to break the overall sales forecast for the company into expected sales by region, product line, or territory. The overall sales forecast may be useful to the finance department in constructing the capital budget, but the lack of specificity in the forecast may make it difficult for marketing and sales managers to use.

Delphi Technique

The **Delphi technique** is a refinement of the jury of executive or expert opinion. Under the Delphi technique, each executive (expert) is asked to make an individual sales forecasts. Each forecast can be accompanied by an explanation of the factors used to derive the forecast. All forecasts are then combined and distributed anonymously to each expert. Based on the compiled forecast information, each expert is asked to make a new forecast. The new forecasts can take into account some of the issues mentioned by other experts in their initial forecast. The process may include several rounds of predictions until the forecasters converge on a solution. The process can take from a day or two to several weeks depending on other demands on experts' time. The Delphi technique avoids the problem of intimidation of one expert by another and has been shown to be quite useful in new product forecasting and forecasting in high-tech markets.[13] The primary disadvantage of the Delphi technique are the difficulty of selecting appropriate experts and the amount of experts' time the process consumes.

Salesforce Composite

The **salesforce composite** method of forecasting involves obtaining the views of salespeople, sales managers, or both as to the most likely levels of expected sales. The sales forecasts of individual salespeople or sales managers are combined to develop a sales forecast for the territory, district, region, or firm.[14] It is one of the most familiar methods to sales managers and is used by between 62 percent and 71 percent of firms on a regular basis.[15] It is most commonly used for short- and medium-term forecasting and is seldom used to forecast beyond a 2-year period.[16]

The salesforce composite method offers several advantages to its users. First, it relies on the judgment of those closest to the customers. Second, it is simple to aggregate to develop forecasts by product, territory, district, or region. Finally, it is likely to foster confidence in salespeople when it is used to develop quotas. Salesforce composite forecasting also has disadvantages, however. Individuals can be overly pessimistic, particularly when the forecast is used to develop quotas. Lower forecasts lead to lower quotas, which are easier for the salesperson to reach. Individuals can also be overly optimistic, especially when predicting the sales of a new product. Because of these potential biases, salesforce composites can be less accurate than quantitative approaches. To improve the accuracy of sales composites forecasts, sales managers can follow the five steps discussed in Box 15.1.[17]

If the salespeople work in teams, team-based forecasting can be used. **Team-based forecasting** is an average of all the team members' individual forecasts. Although this technique is no more accurate than nonteam forecasting, team members may express much higher levels of satisfaction with team forecasting because of their participation in the forecasting process.[18]

BOX 15.1
FIVE STEPS FOR IMPROVING THE ACCURACY OF SALES COMPOSITE FORECASTS

1. *Providing salespeople more information.* This includes giving salespeople information about major changes in the competitive environment that might affect their customers, helping salespeople maintain records to monitor customers' past purchasing behavior, providing feedback to salespeople on the accuracy of past sales forecasts, and encouraging salespeople to ascertain customers' expectations for future purchases.

2. *Provide salespeople with enough time to do a good forecast.* This includes giving salespeople adequate time to prepare a thoughtful forecast, encouraging salespeople to allocate their time according to customer size (i.e., spend more time on forecasting large customers' needs and less time on forecasting the needs of small customers), providing a standardized format for salespeople to follow in developing and submitting a forecast, and adding the forecasting task to salespeoples' job descriptions so that the importance of developing sales forecasts is underscored.

3. *Provide incentives for accuracy.* Incentives for accurate forecasting begin with formally recording each salesperson's forecast and holding him or her responsible for its accuracy. Salespeople with accurate forecasts can be given bonuses. Managers should also make sure that salespeople understand the importance of accurate forecasts to the firm. To ensure accurate forecasts, firms can improve forecasting procedures. Improvement can be in the form of requiring salespeople to justify their forecasts and in requiring salespeople to provide forecasts that reflect pessimistic, most likely, and optimistic scenarios. Managers should also be careful about awarding bonuses on the basis of percent over quota. This may cause salespeople to make artificially low forecasts. Last, sales managers should allow salespeople to revise forecasts if a major sales opportunity arises or if a major sales opportunity is lost. This helps avoid end-of-the-period surprises and maintains open lines of communication between salespeople and sales managers.

4. *Make formal adjustments to the salesperson's forecast.* This should occur when a salesperson consistently makes forecasts that are above or below actual sales. Managers can monitor past forecasts, determine whether patterns of overestimating or underestimating sales exist, and adjust the salesperson's forecast accordingly. This must be done carefully, however, because it could cause salespeople not to take the process seriously if they know their sales forecasts are likely to be revised anyway.

5. *Change the organization.* Make sure that there are no organizational policies that lead to overestimation or underestimation of demand. For example, if customers' orders are filled in order of size, with larger customers getting their orders first and smaller customers last, salespeople might be tempted to overestimate their customers' overall purchases to improve the speed at which their orders are filled. Managers also need to make sure that salespeople receive sufficient training on various forecasting techniques to be able to make accurate forecasts, as well as understand the impact of inaccurate forecasts on the rest of the organization.

SOURCE: Paul A. Herbig, John Milewicz, and James E. Golden, "The Do's and Don'ts of Sales Forecasting," *Industrial Marketing Management*, 22 (1993): 49–57.

Survey of Buying Intentions

The **survey of buying intentions** is a method whereby sellers ask their customers what level of purchases they expect to make over a certain time period, such as the next quarter or year. Some customers are much more willing than others to provide information and much more likely to provide accurate answers. For example, a supplier of a part used in manufacturing cars may be able to develop a sales forecast based on the forecast of the car company on the sales expected for that car in the upcoming year. Assume that Ford is forecasting sales of 40,000 Crown Victorias for the upcoming year and that its record of sales forecasts is extremely accurate. If your firm is the only supplier of a special type of headlight used only with that car, your sales forecast of 80,000 units for the year (assuming that Ford did not have any headlights in inventory already and that each car uses two headlights) should be accurate.

Another example of a situation where the survey of buying intentions would be a good forecasting method is in the case of a supplier that has a long-term supply agreement with a customer. If a customer's long-term supply agreement commits it to take a certain number of your firm's product each year, the sales forecast for that customer is based on the stated figures in the contract. If the long-term supply agreement allows the customer to adjust the amount purchased up or down based on prevailing business conditions (as many of the agreements do), a survey of the customer's buying intentions can allow the seller to adjust the sales forecast to reflect the customer's expected purchases for the time period.

Some consumer goods manufacturers seek information directly from consumers to predict sales. Certain organizations, such as the Conference Board (a nonprofit business research firm), collect information periodically from consumers on their confidence in the economy, which is translated into likelihood to purchase based on previously observed relationships. Unfortunately, this method is extremely general. For example, if you were the sales manager for kitchen appliances for Whirlpool, a measure of consumer confidence might give you a general idea of the number of large appliances that would be sold in the near future, but you would not get much assistance in determining the mix of models that would be sold. As a result, the forecast may be useful for financial purposes (capital budgeting, etc.), but it would not be helpful for production purposes. It would also not be of use to the salesforce when helping customers determine the appropriate mix of Whirlpool products to carry in their stores.

QUANTITATIVE FORECASTING TECHNIQUES

Instead of relying on experts' opinions as with qualitative techniques, **quantitative forecasting techniques** rely on some form of mathematical analysis of historical data to derive a forecast. The quantitative forecasting methods discussed in the following section include (1) time series models, (2) correlation/regression methods, and (3) market factor indices.

Time Series Models

Time series models are a family of methods that make forecasts based on past patterns of data. In other words, if you are interested in forecasting sales for future periods, time series models require you to collect information about sales in prior periods as input to the forecast. Time series models are most effective when the market is relatively stable. If new products or competitors enter the market, the underlying time series may alter radically. Actions taken by the firm are also not taken into account. Thus, if an advertising campaign "wears out," the same amount of money may be spent on advertising, yet the return is less. In addition, prices may be altered, customers may be offered quantity discounts, new distribution outlets may be identified, and new uses may be found for existing products. Any of these conditions may cause the underlying time series to shift dramatically, thereby reducing the ability of time series models to forecast effectively.

All time series models look for patterns in the past data. The four components of the past data that are of interest in time series analysis are (1) trend, (2) seasonality, (3) cyclicality, and (4) irregularity. *Trend* is the underlying movement in the time series. For example, the trend for many basic commodities, such as flour, steel, sugar, and lumber, follows population growth closely. If population growth is increasing at a steady 1 percent per year, the trend in flour consumption will be an increase of approximately 1 percent per year also. Trend can move up or down depending on product development efforts, consumer tastes, changes in technology, broad economic trends, and other fundamental issues in the market for the product.

Seasonality is the extent to which the time series varies consistently within the period of one year. For example, retail sales in the United States are highly seasonal, with a sales bulge occurring in December corresponding to the Christmas gift-giving season. Sales of many consumer products, ranging from swimsuits to fireworks to winter coats, are highly seasonal as well.

Cyclicality is change that occurs over a period exceeding one year. Certain changes in the economy, such as significant interest rate changes, tend to occur over periods of greater than one year. Cyclical industries include automobiles, housing, and furniture. Customers are likely to finance their purchases of these items, so demand is influenced by fluctuations in interest rates. Car purchases, for example, tend to go up when interest rates decrease and go down when interest rates increase.

Finally, *irregularity* is change in sales pattern that occurs randomly. For example, in 1993 floods in the midwestern part of the United States cut rail lines and disrupted rail service for weeks. Trains were rerouted and cargos were shipped, where possible, by alternate means of transportation. As a result of the floods, the railroads lost significant sales revenues. This occurrence was random in that it was impossible to predict. Yet random influences such as this one can clearly have major effects on sales.

The more common time series models include trend projections, decomposition, moving averages, exponential smoothing, and autoregressive moving averages. The primary differences among these time series models arise in the methods by which they assign weights to trend, seasonality, cyclicality, and irregular influences.

Trend Projection.   **Trend projection** is a set of simple time series forecasting techniques which assume that past sales levels and rates of change in sales levels will remain the same in future periods. These technique are best suited for markets in which very little change occurs.

The simplest trend projection is known as the *"naive" method.* Under this approach, the sales for a future period are forecasted as the value of sales for the previous period. In other words, sales for next month are forecasted to be the same as sales for this month. This approach ignores the irregular component, assumes that seasonality and cyclicality do not exist, and assumes that the trend is flat. The naive method trend projection formula is as follows:

$$\text{Sales}_t = \text{sales}_{t-1}$$

where sales_t = sales for this period
                sales_{t-1} = sales for last period

A slightly more complex form of trend projection accounts for the influence of the trend component in the time series. Using this method, forecasters are required to calculate the rate of change of sales in prior periods. One simple way to calculate the rate of change in sales is by dividing the most recent period by the period immediately preceding it. The following formula shows how to adjust the naive method to account for a change in rate of sales levels.

$$\text{Sales}_t = \text{sales}_{t-1} \times \frac{\text{sales}_{t-1}}{\text{sales}_{t-2}}$$

where sales_t = sales for this period
                sales_{t-1} = sales for last period
                sales_{t-2} = sales for two periods ago

Assume that a firm is interested in predicting sales for March. It had sales in January of $150,000 and in February of $175,000. Substituting the values in the formula yields the following equation:

$$\text{March sales} = 175,000 \times \frac{175,000}{150,000}$$

$$= \$204,167$$

The advantages of trend projection include ease of use, need for only a limited number of data points, and low cost. The disadvantages are failure to consider seasonal and cyclical influences and overresponsiveness to irregular influences.

Decomposition.   **Decomposition** is a time series technique that takes seasonality into account. Performing decomposition requires three steps: (1) calculating seasonal index numbers, (2) making the sales forecast, and (3) adjusting the forecast for seasonality.

Step 1: Calculate Seasonal Index Numbers.   *Seasonal index numbers* are calculated by determining the average sales for the specific time period (such as quarters, months, or weeks) across at least three preceding years and dividing those averages by the overall average sales. For example, the seasonal index number for the first quarter for the data shown in Exhibit 15.4 can be calculated as follows:

1. Calculate the mean sales for the first quarter using 1994–1996 data (average sales for quarter 1 across 1994–1996 = 163).
2. Determine the mean sales for all 12 quarters (average quarterly sales across 1994–1996 = 207.25).
3. Divide the mean sales for the first quarter by the overall mean for all quarters to determine the seasonal index number (163 ÷ 207.25 = .786).

| | | | | | EXHIBIT 15.4 | | | |

DECOMPOSITION FORECASTING DATA

Annual Sales (in thousands of units)

Quarter	1994	1995	1996	3-Year Average	Average Sales for all Quarters	Seasonal Index (col. 5 ÷ col. 6)	1997 Forecast	1997 Seasonally Adjusted Forecast
1	148	168	173	163	207.25	.786	247	194
2	180	185	205	190	207.25	.917	247	226
3	164	190	210	188	207.25	.907	247	224
4	245	300	322	288	207.25	1.394	247	344
Total Sales	737	840	910				988	988

Step 2: Make the Sales Forecast.   Using the formula for trend and substituting data from Exhibit 15.4 yields:

$$1997 \text{ sales (forecasted)} = 1996 \text{ sales} \times \frac{1996 \text{ sales}}{1995 \text{ sales}}$$

$$= 910 \times \frac{910}{840}$$

$$= 986 \text{ units}$$

Therefore, our sales forecast for next year is 986 units. If sales are equal in each quarter, we expect to sell 246.5 units (986 ÷ 4) per quarter. In the example we rounded up to 247 units since it is not possible to sell a half-unit.

Step 3: Adjust the Forecast for Seasonality.   To adjust the quarterly forecasts for seasonality, multiply the quarterly sales forecast by the seasonal index for that quarter. The seasonal index for the first quarter from Exhibit 15.4 is .786. Therefore, the sales forecast for the first quarter will be 246.5 × .786 = 193.75, or 194 units. Sales forecasts for other quarters can be calculated using the same process.

The primary advantage of decomposition is that it allows for explicit recognition of the importance of seasonal influences. As a result, it is often used by firms with a heavy seasonal variation in sales, such as retail stores. The primary concern in adjusting for seasonality is the interaction between the number of years of data in the model and the sensitivity of the model. As additional years of data are obtained, the earliest year of data can be dropped and the most recent year added to the table. The more years of data, the less responsive the index numbers are to short-term changes. The fewer the years of data, the more responsive the index numbers are, but the more likely they are to be affected by the irregular component.

Moving Average.   A **moving average** is a technique by which forecasters estimate sales based on an average of previous time periods. Moving averages are simple to calculate. Exhibit 15.5 shows data for 16 quarters of sales for a retail record store. The four-quarter moving average is calculated by adding the actual sales from previous four quarters and dividing by four. The eight-quarter moving average is calculated by adding the actual sales from the previous eight quarters and dividing by eight. To derive the forecast for the first quarter of 1995 using the four-quarter moving average, add the actual sales from previous four quarters (148 + 180 + 164 + 245 = 737) and divide by 4. The result (shown in Exhibit 15.5) is 184.25. The eight-quarter moving average is calculated the same way, except using eight quarters of data instead of four.

Moving averages reduce the influence of the irregular component by reducing the reliance on a single data point. It can also account for the influence of seasonality if, as is the case with the four-quarter moving average, the average includes all the periods in a season. The eight-quarter moving average can reduce the likelihood of cyclical influences that occur over a 2-year period. The advantage of this technique is that by accounting for irregular, seasonal, and cyclical influences, it "smooths out" variability in estimates, thereby simplifying production schedules and cash requirements. The major disadvantages of the technique are that if the sales pattern exhibits a heavy seasonal variation, it will systematically overestimate sales during the "off" season and underestimate sales during the busy season. Also, if a firm desires the use of an eight-quarter or twelve-quarter moving average, data availability and data consistency may cause problems.

Exponential Smoothing.   **Exponential smoothing** is the name for a series of techniques similar to moving averages, except with exponential smoothing the forecaster is allowed to vary the weights assigned to past data points. Exponential smoothing techniques vary in terms of how they address trend, seasonality, cyclicality, and irregular influences. *Simple exponential smoothing* accounts for only irregular and trend influences. It takes the following form:

$$F_t = (\alpha \times X_{t-1}) + [(1 - \alpha) \times F_{t-1}]$$

where F_t = the forecast for the current time period
   α = the smoothing constant
   X_{t-1} = the actual sales for the previous time period
   F_{t-1} = the forecasted sales for the previous period

The data in Exhibit 15.5 can be used to develop a forecast using exponential smoothing. Suppose that at the end of quarter 1, 1995, the manager is interested in forecasting sales for quarter 2, 1995. Substituting values from Exhibit 15.5, and using $\alpha = .80$, $X_{t-1} = 154$, and $F_{t-1} = 184.25$ (using the four-quarter moving average forecast). Therefore:

$$F_t = (.80 \times 154) + [(1 - .80) \times 184.25]$$

$$= 160.05, \text{ or } 160,050 \text{ units}$$

α is set by the forecaster and can range from 0 to 1. The closer α is to 1, the greater the emphasis placed on the most recent sales information. If $\alpha = 1$, the formula simply becomes:

$$F_t = X_{t-1}$$

EXHIBIT 15.5

MOVING AVERAGE DATA OF RETAIL RECORD STORE SALES

| | | | Sales Forecasts | |
| | | Actual Sales | Four-Quarter | Eight-Quarter |
Year	Quarter	(in thousands of units)	Moving Average	Moving Average
1993	1	150		
	2	173		
	3	162		
	4	242		
1994	1	148	181.75	
	2	180	181.25	
	3	164	183	
	4	245	183.5	
1995	1	154	184.25	183
	2	179	185.75	183.5
	3	169	185.5	184.25
	4	255	186.75	185.125
1996	1	157	189.25	186.75
	2	186	190	187.875
	3	171	191.75	188.625
	4	250	192.25	189.5

Therefore, the forecast for the current time period is simply the actual sales for the previous time period. As α approaches 0, the forecast places less and less emphasis on the most recent sales information. As a result, the forecast becomes less a function of recent events and more a function of past sales history.

Forecasters should set α based on the characteristics of the data. If there are a significant number of random events, a low smoothing constant should be used. This minimizes the effect of the irregular component. Low smoothing constants make the forecast less susceptible to rapid, transient market fluctuations, but may make it miss important changes in the underlying pattern of demand. If there are few random events, a high smoothing constant can be selected. This may make the forecast very responsive to recent market changes, but overresponsive to irregular influences.

The major advantage of exponential smoothing is that it requires fewer observations than the moving averages method. It also requires the forecaster to estimate only the value of α to perform the analysis. The disadvantages of exponential smoothing are the potential difficulties in setting α if the forecaster is not an experienced user, and the overreaction of the model to irregular influences if α is close to 1.

Autoregressive Moving Averages. **Autoregressive moving averages** is the most sophisticated form of time series analysis. It uses a different procedure than the preceding methods in identifying the proper number of past observations to be included in the analysis, and the weights that should be attached to those observations. The basis on which the parameters are selected is to minimize the difference between the actual value and the forecast value for any time period. This method is extremely flexible but has little empirical support to favor its selection over simpler time series methods.

Correlation/Regression Models

The underlying principle of correlation/regression approaches is quite different from that of time series. In time series models, sales history is expected to provide sufficient information to predict future sales, but that doesn't always work. To overcome this problem, some firms use correlation/regression approaches instead of time series.

Correlation Models.   With **correlation models,** managers seek variables that correlate with, or relate to, sales. Correlations may be direct or inverse. For example, temperature is directly related to sales of Coca-Cola. Hotter areas of the United States and the rest of the world tend to have higher per capita consumption of Coke than cooler areas. If Coca-Cola were to try to predict sales in a new country, it might look at mean annual or monthly temperature as a guide to the expected level of per capita sales. By contrast, temperature is inversely correlated with sales of swimming suits. The colder an area is, the less likely consumers are to have a large selection of swimwear in their closets.

Managers may also look at variables that relate to the competitive marketplace. Drug manufacturers might use the number of new drugs introduced by competitors as a measure of the degree of competition in their markets. If a high number of new products is being introduced, competition may be high, and the firm may expect sales to be lower than during periods when fewer products are being introduced. A retail firm trying to predict sales may monitor store openings by competitors. If a competing firm announces it is building a number of new stores in your main target area, there may be some effect on sales.

Regression Models.   Regression models are another form of correlational technique. **Regression models** try to predict a dependent variable (typically sales) with one or more independent variables thought to have a relationship with sales. The independent variables may be developed through correlation analysis or based on previously observed relationships. **Simple regression models** have only one independent variable. For example, a diaper manufacturer might use the birth rate to determine the number of diapers to be sold in a given market. **Multiple regression models** have multiple independent variables. Lydia Pinkham, a tonic manufacturer, has used a multiple regression equation model with five independent variables to explain 94 percent of the variance in sales over a period of five decades.[19]

Regression can also be used to calculate sales quotas. The dependent variable is sales, and the independent variables can be related to the environment, the organization, or the salesperson.[20] For example, a quota forecast can be developed using the level of competition in a given territory (environment), the extent of advertising support the firm will provide in that territory (organization), and the experience level of the salesperson. By combining these variables or others the firm feels appropriate, a forecast can be developed for each salesperson. A set of variables that might be included in developing quotas using a regression approach can be seen in

Exhibit 15.6. The first three statements could be used to develop the environmental variables used in a regression equation. The other statements could be used in developing variables representing the organization or the salesperson.

There are several types of regression models. One of the most popular forms is **multiple linear regression,** which assumes that the relationship between the combination of independent variables and the dependent variable is linear. An example of multiple linear regression model is:

$$Y = a + b_1x_1 + b_2x_2 + e$$

where:
- Y = sales forecast (the dependent variable)
- a = the point at which the forecast crosses the vertical axis (y-intercept)
- b_1 = the weight (β) for the independent variable x_1
- x_1 = the first independent variable
- b_2 = the weight (β) for the independent variable x_2
- x_2 = the second independent variable
- e = error

Several widely available programs, such as Lotus 1-2-3, Excel, SPSS, and SAS, have detailed routines and instructions for running multiple linear regression models on PCs and mainframes. These techniques and their associated statistics are explained in detail in those manuals and in statistics textbooks that cover multivariate methods.

Regression models must be carefully developed. They are subject to several problems that can significantly affect their ability to forecast sales accurately. Those problems include spurious relationships, multicollinearity, autocorrelation, and the inclusion of too many independent variables. *Spurious relationships* arise when there is no apparent reason for the relationship between the independent variable and the dependent variable. For example, there is no reason to expect phases of the moon to be correlated with sales of dog food. If the two variables were found to be correlated empirically, however, some might be tempted to include phases of the moon in a forecasting model. This temptation should be resisted.

Multicollinearity arises when the independent variables are highly correlated among themselves. For example, in predicting retail sales for a given market, population and total disposable income in the market area might be highly related to sales. However, these variables are also probably highly correlated with each other. As a result, the forecaster should use a single variable, such as per capita income, in constructing the model. Forecasters can also use other techniques for collapsing the number of independent variables if it is shown that they are highly correlated among themselves.

While multicollinearity does not affect the overall ability of the equation to predict sales, it does affect one important use of regression.[21] Suppose a multiple regression equation has three variables. The sales manager is interested in how a change in one of the variables might affect the sales forecast. If multicollinearity exists, the manager cannot assess the impact of changing the level of a single variable. Multicollinearity makes the beta weights unstable.

EXHIBIT 15.6			
IMPORTANT ELEMENTS IN ASSIGNING QUOTAS FOR SALES PROFESSIONALS			
Statement	Mean[a,b]	Standard Deviation	Rank
Concentration of businesses within the sales rep's territory is important in determining the amount of quota	1.82	0.64	1
The geographical size of territory is important in determining the amount of quota	1.95	0.86	2
Growth of businesses within the sales rep's territory is important in determining the amount of quota	2.11	0.83	3
Commitment by the sales manager to assisting the sales rep is important in determining the amount of quota	2.23	1.07	4
Complexity of products sold is important in determining the amount of quota	2.50	1.12	5
The sales rep's past sales performance is important in determining the amount of quota	2.54	1.10	6
Extent of product line is important in determining the amount of quota	2.59	0.88	7
The financial support (e.g., compensation) a firm provides sales reps is important in assigning quota	2.76	0.99	8
The relationship of a firm's product line is important in determining the amount of quota	2.82	1.02	9
The amount of clerical support given to a sales rep is important in determining the amount of quota	3.13	1.09	10

[a] The rating scale and weights used to rate the importance of each statement were: 1 = strongly agree; 2 = agree; 3 = neutral; 4 = disagree; and 5 = strongly disagree.

[b] The responses numbered 186.

SOURCE: David J. Good and Robert W. Stone, "Attitudes and Applications of Quotas by Sales Executives and Sales Managers," *Journal of Personal Selling and Sales Management,* 11 (Summer 1991): 57–60.

Autocorrelation in regression equations occurs when the observations on the independent variable are correlated. This most commonly occurs when time is treated as an independent variable. Although a technical discussion of autocorrelation is beyond the scope of this text, it is enough to say that it can be detected through the calculation of the Durbin-Watson statistic. If autocorrelation exists, the forecaster can eliminate the variable or use another method of regression, called generalized least squares (GLS), which overcomes the problems.

The final problem with the use of regression models is the identification of the appropriate number of independent variables in the regression equation. The forecaster needs to be careful in constructing the regression equation to use only *the number of independent variables* which are absolutely necessary. The temptation is to use more independent variables because, as the number of variables increases, the amount of variance explained in the dependent variable also increases. Unfortunately this occurs even if there is no relationship between the independent and the dependent variables. The problem with using too many independent variables is that the greater the number of independent variables that are used, the greater the number of observations that are necessary to develop the equation. Several rules of thumb exist, with estimates of the needed number of observations per independent variable ranging from five to ten. While these rules of thumb are common, there are more sophisticated approaches for determining the correct number of observations per independent variable that use the level of forecast error the sales manager is willing to accept.[22]

Market Factor Indices

A third type of quantitative forecasting technique is market factor indices. Perhaps the most common market factor index is the **Buying Power Index (BPI)**. The BPI is a proprietary system developed by *Sales and Marketing Management,* a widely read magazine in the field of sales management. The BPI is used to predict sales for specific geographic regions for manufacturers and distributors of retail goods, such as clothing, food, autos, and other consumer items. Besides its use in forecasting sales of consumer items, BPI can also be used to set sales quotas.

The rationale underlying the BPI is that retail sales for a company are based on three components: demographic, economic, and distribution. The demographic component is defined in terms of age. BPI has five categories of age: under 18, 18–24, 25–34, 35–49, and 50 and over. The economic component is defined in terms of household incomes. BPI has four categories of household income: $10,000–19,999; $20,000–34,999; $35,000–49,999; and $50,000 and over. The distribution component is defined in terms of the sales through a particular store type. BPI has six categories of store type: food, eating and drinking places, general merchandise, automotive, drug, and furniture/furnishings/appliances.

Using the BPI to forecast sales requires the manager to follow five steps. The following paragraphs outline the steps for a manager seeking to sell high-quality men's shirts in the Lansing–East Lansing, Michigan, market area.

Step 1: The manager must identify the market area, the age of the product's potential customers, the household income of the target market, and the stores through which the product will be distributed. In this example, the market area is Lansing–East Lansing, which encompasses three counties (Clinton, Eaton, and Ingham) and two cities (Lansing and East Lansing [LEL]). The age of the market for high-quality men's shirts is predicted to be 25–49. The household income for purchases of these shirts is over $35,000 because these shirts are expensive. The distribution of the product will be through general merchandise stores (including department stores and discount stores).

Step 2: Using the information from step 1, the manager determines the values that will be used in the BPI forecasting equation.

- The value for the demographic variable:

$$X\% = \frac{\text{LEL population between 25–49}}{\text{U.S. population between 25–49}}$$

$$= \frac{191,099}{100,947,500}$$

$$= 0.00189$$

- The value for the economic variable:

$$Y\% = \frac{\text{LEL households with incomes over } \$35,000}{\text{U.S. households with incomes over } \$35,000}$$

$$= \frac{92,856}{50,951,500}$$

$$= 0.00182$$

- The value for the distribution variable:

$$Z\% = \frac{\text{LEL general merchandise sales}}{\text{U.S. general merchandise sales}}$$

$$= \frac{959,418}{285,351,264}$$

$$= 0.00336$$

Step 3: Once the values for the demographic, economic, and distribution variables have been established, the manager must decide how much weight to place on each component. Assume in this case that the economic variable is the most important predictor of sales, the distribution variable second in importance, and the demographic variable is last. The manager places a value of .5 on the economic variable, .3 on the distribution variable, and .2 on the demographic variable (although the manager could have chosen whatever values for the three variables that would be appropriate). Please note that the sum of the weights must equal 1.0. Using the weights assigned by the manager yields the following forecasting equation:

$$BPI = .2X\% + .5Y\% + .3Z\%$$

Substituting the values for the variables for LEL yields the following forecast:

$$BPI = .2(0.00189) + .5(0.00182) + .3(0.00336)$$

$$= 0.002296$$

To use BPI for forecasting purposes, forecast the company's total expected sales for the upcoming time period (assume sales of $100 million across the United States for the next year). Multiplying the BPI by the firm's expected sales (0.002296 × 100,000,000) generates a forecast for sales in Lansing–East Lansing for the upcoming year of $229,600.

To calculate a sales quota using the BPI approach, the forecaster starts with an estimate of sales in the territory. For the firm selling men's shirts in LEL, the expected sales next year are $229,600. Therefore, management could set quota at

$229,600. However, management could also take into account last year's sales. If last year's sales were $300,000, management has a choice of setting quota at the BPI suggested level or higher. If the manager investigated and found that this territory's sales were consistently above the BPI suggested level, the BPI formula could be changed or additional information could be sought as to why the territory was performing so well. If the sales were significantly lower, management could set the quota higher to spur additional effort. Unfortunately, the causes of low sales can often be long term, and short-term fixes may not be possible. Therefore, setting an unrealistically high quota, even if it is justified using BPI, may be counterproductive.

The BPI approach to setting sales quotas takes into account the environment but not necessarily the characteristics of the organization or those of the salesperson. It has the advantage, however, of being simple to calculate.

ISSUES IN SELECTING A FORECASTING TECHNIQUE

We have covered a variety of qualitative and quantitative methods in the chapter, all of which have their advantages and disadvantages. One of the toughest choices facing a forecaster is which technique to use. In selecting a forecasting technique, managers must keep several things in mind. First, there is no single best technique for forecasting. Although several studies have shown that quantitative techniques provide more accurate forecasts than qualitative methods, other studies have shown that qualitative methods may be superior for short-range predictions or when managers have a great deal of experience in forecasting.[23] As a result, managers should not assume that quantitative forecasting techniques are always superior to qualitative methods simply because they involve mathematical models.

Second, many firms have found that combining forecasts developed using different methods leads to more accurate results.[24] As a result, rather than trying to find the perfect method, firms might be better served by constructing multiple forecasts using a variety of methods. The empirical evidence favors a combination of sales forecasts whenever possible. It is best to combine several forecasts based on different techniques or information. In other words, it is best to combine two very different techniques, such as salesforce composite forecasts and exponential smoothing, rather than similar techniques.[25]

How should the forecasts be combined? Different forecasts can be combined using simple arithmetic means. There have been some studies on weighting different forecasts, but there is no overwhelming evidence to favor any particular weighting method. Another finding is that the biggest gains in accuracy come about when a small number of forecasts (two to four) are combined. As the number of forecasts combined increases, the accuracy continues to improve, but at a lower rate. Therefore, the forecaster needn't try to develop dozens of forecasts. A small number of forecasts is sufficient.

Third, the wide availability of personal computer–based forecasting packages has made the use of sophisticated forecasting techniques by relative novices fairly accessible. The accessibility of these packages makes it less necessary for sales managers to learn the computations involved in a given procedure. However, it makes the choice of technique more difficult. If a personal computer can generate forecasts using 25 different techniques, the sales manager is faced with the choice of which ones to use. To make a rational choice, the manager must know enough about the assumptions underlying each technique, and its strengths and weaknesses.

Exhibit 15.7 shows the results from a study of 900 small and medium-sized manufacturing firms in the United States. The table shows the relative use of different quantitative techniques by those firms. One important observation is the low number of users of more esoteric forecasting techniques, such as autoregressive moving averages and time series decomposition. The respondents to the study suggested several problems that limit the use of quantitative forecasting techniques. These problems include the following: (1) complex forecasting techniques perform no better than simple ones; (2) lengthy, complex methods such as regression, econometric models, and time series take too much time and money; (3) there is confusion as to which forecasting model or models is most appropriate in a given situation; and (4) forecasting is usually a part-time job; the forecaster has other job responsibilities. As a result, it is difficult for anyone to develop significant expertise in forecasting when there are other duties to attend.

Regardless of problems in developing forecasts, managers must make a choice of a particular method or combination of methods to perform a sales forecast. To make that choice, sales managers must rank the forecasting techniques using certain criteria, including time horizon, technical sophistication, cost, data availability, variability and consistency of data, amount of detail necessary, turning points, accuracy, and the ability to capture levels of risk or variability.[26] Each criterion is discussed in the following paragraphs.

Time Horizon

Forecasting techniques vary in their ability to handle forecasts of different lengths of time. For example, the naive method is a very short-term technique, whereas sales-force composite may be useful for intermediate-term forecasts, such as 1 or 2 years, and the Delphi technique is designed to aid managers in forecasting several years in the future. In general, however, the longer the time horizon (i.e., the farther into the future you are trying to predict), the lower the accuracy of any forecasting technique. This makes logical as well as statistical sense. It is much easier to predict what will happen tomorrow than what will happen in 5 years.

Technical Sophistication

Several of these models, especially the quantitative ones, require a high level of technical sophistication to be used correctly. As mentioned earlier, the availability of forecasting packages for personal computers has reduced managers' need to have a great deal of computation skill in calculating forecasts using different techniques. However, the choice of which technique to use does require a clear understanding of the underlying assumptions and the strengths and weaknesses of each technique.

Cost

There are two types of costs to consider when preparing forecasts: development and execution. *Development costs* are those associated with collecting the data, entering it in the system, and modifying software to prepare the desired forecast. *Execution costs* are those associated with choosing a technique, generating a forecast using that

---

EXHIBIT 15.7

RELATIVE APPLICATION OF FORECASTING TECHNIQUES

Degree of Use in %

	Never (1)	Hardly Ever (2)	Sometimes (3)	Frequently (4)	Very Frequently (5)	Mean[a]
Regression analysis	65.1	4.7	18.6	9.3	2.3	1.79
Exponential smoothing	74.4	7.1	16.3	0.0	2.3	1.49
Classical decomposition time series	90.7	4.7	0.0	2.3	2.3	1.21
Moving average	39.6	7.0	30.2	11.6	11.6	2.49
Autoregressive moving averages	97.7	2.3	0.0	0.0	0.0	1.02
Trend analysis	27.9	4.7	27.9	30.2	9.3	2.88
Seasonal and cyclical indexes	39.5	4.7	25.6	18.6	11.6	2.88
Leading indicators	46.5	4.7	30.2	9.3	9.3	2.30
Econometric models	67.4	7.0	11.6	9.3	4.7	1.76

[a]Mean of numbers at the top of the table.

SOURCE: Ronald L. Coccari, "How Quantitative Business Techniques Are Being Used," *Business Horizons* (July/August 1989): 70–74.

technique, and putting it in a form that is useful to management. In general, costs are at their highest level during the introduction of a forecasting system or method. As the preparation of the forecast becomes routine, costs generally decline. Costs are also typically greater for quantitative techniques than for qualitative techniques.

Data Availability

Data availability refers to the existence of necessary data to calculate the forecast. Especially for new products, data may simply not be available for forecasting purposes using quantitative techniques. In these cases, qualitative techniques may be the only option available to the manager. The data may also not be available in the form needed for the forecast. For instance, if a firm is trying to forecast sales by model, and sales data are organized only by product type, the level of specificity required to make the forecast may simply not exist.

Variability and Consistency of Data

Data must be consistent over time to allow for accurate forecasts. Firms can experience problems with data consistency when using outside sources and internal sources of data. For example, based on the 1990 census, the U.S. government changed its definition of several Metropolitan Statistical Areas (MSAs),[27] a measurement used to organize federal data. Certain MSAs were merged, and others were split. If a firm was using population by MSA as an input to a forecast, the underlying data would be inconsistent over time owing to the changing nature of the MSAs.

Amount of Detail Necessary

Different types of forecasts may be needed for different levels of detail. For example, top management may be more concerned with overall sales levels, whereas functional-area managers will find more detailed forecasts of greater use. Top management may also be concerned with forecasts with long time horizons, which typically have less detail than short-term forecasts.

Turning Points

Turning points indicate fundamental changes in the underlying patterns of demand. Turning points may occur because of rapid changes in consumer preferences that make current product offerings less desirable, or because of the introduction of new technology. Rapid changes in consumer preferences occur with fad products. For example, troll dolls were very popular during the 1970s, but the fad ran out. During the early 1990s, troll dolls became popular again, perhaps because the 1994 Winter Olympics in Norway where trolls are part of the region's folklore. Certain companies, such as Coleco Industries, base their sales on the fad items with dramatic turning points. One of Coleco's products, Cabbage Patch kids, was so popular that the dolls were impossible to find for several Christmases, but demand has now decreased to the point that they are widely available at discount prices.

Introduction of new technology can also have a notable effect on the demand for existing products. For example, as newer, faster computer chips are introduced, they make older chips obsolete, thereby reducing demand for older chips. Predicting turning points, therefore, is particularly important for producers in industries with high rates of technological change.[28] These producers will want to use sales forecasting methods that rely heavily on the most recent periods of sales. Examples of these methods include exponential smoothing and the Delphi technique.

Accuracy

Accuracy generally refers to the gap between actual and predicted sales. Techniques with lower gaps are more accurate. One commonly used method to calculate the accuracy of a forecast is a statistic called **MAPE (mean absolute percentage error)**. MAPE looks at all discrepancies between the values that were forecast and the values that were actually achieved. The formula for calculating MAPE is:

$$\text{MAPE} = \frac{\sum_{j=1}^{n} \frac{|\text{FORECAST} - \text{ACTUAL}|}{\text{ACTUAL}}}{n}$$

It seems obvious that the most accurate forecast would be the one that managers preferred. Hence, the task of selecting a forecasting technique should be to calculate the MAPE for each method and select the one with the highest MAPE. However, this is not always possible. First, the data may not be available for calculation of MAPE. If a product is new or has just entered a new market, sales figures will not be available. Second, although accuracy is important, it is not the only issue in selecting a forecasting method. Managers may be willing to sacrifice accuracy for forecasts that can accurately predict turning points. Managers may also find that certain types of accuracy are more valuable than others.[29] MAPE does not distinguish between errors because the forecast is too high or errors because the forecast is too low. In other words, if actual sales were 100 units, MAPE would be exactly the same whether the forecast was 90 or 110.

Assume, however, that a firm manufactures a nonperishable product. It finds that underestimating demand causes a failure in filling customer orders, which leads customers to seek alternate suppliers. Overestimating demand, on the other hand, leads to a buildup of inventory. However, since the inventory is nonperishable, the firm does not incur significant inventory-carrying costs. As a result, if the firm were given a choice between a highly accurate forecasting method that underestimates in some months or a less accurate method that never underestimates, it would probably accept the less accurate sales forecasting method. Alternate forecasting methods must be evaluated based on the use to which they will be put, rather than on a single criterion, such as MAPE.

Ability to Capture Levels of Risk or Variability

It is important to provide managers with not only the best guess as to the levels of sales expected under a given forecasting technique, but also the range of expected values. This can be done rather easily using salesforce composite by asking salespeople to provide pessimistic, most likely, and optimistic sales levels. In quantitative methods, the calculation of pessimistic and optimistic ranges can be done using previous data. If previous data do not exist, it is quite difficult to develop a range using quantitative methods.

SUMMARY

Sales forecasting is the basis for decisions in a wide range of areas within the firm. It is used within marketing, finance, production, accounting, and human resources for decisions ranging from setting sales quotas to setting production schedules to capital budgeting. Given the wide usage of forecasts throughout the firm, the importance of timely and accurate forecasts is unquestionable. In recent years the advent of personal computers has eased much of the computation burden in preparing forecasts. However, the proliferation of forecasting aids has increased managers' need to understand the pros and cons of various techniques so they can understand when a certain method can or should be used and when another should not.

The types of forecasts that are prepared include market potential, market forecasts, sales potential, sales forecast, and sales quota. These forecasts differ by whether they are prepared for the industry, firm, or salesperson, and whether they represent the highest possible sales or the expected sales. Different forecasts are prepared for different levels of management and for different purposes. Market potential may be useful for top management to decide whether to enter a certain market, whereas sales forecasts may be important for production scheduling.

Forecast techniques can be broadly characterized as either qualitative or quantitative. Qualitative techniques include jury of executive opinion, Delphi technique, salesforce composite, and survey of buying intentions. These techniques all involve some form of expert judgment in deriving the sales forecast. Quantitative techniques include various time series methods, such as trend projections, decomposition, moving averages, exponential smoothing, autoregressive moving averages, correlation/regression methods, and market factors. Most of these techniques are available on a wide range of PC software; therefore, the hardest issue facing many forecasters is deciding which technique to use.

Selecting a forecasting technique can be done on several grounds, including time horizon, technical sophistication, cost, data availability, variability and consistency of data, amount of detail necessary, turning points, accuracy, and ability to capture levels of risk or variability. Each technique varies in terms of how it meets these issues. The forecaster has to determine which issue is most important to the manager using the forecast because a technique that might be good at indicating turning points might be less accurate than a technique that is quite accurate but not able to predict turning points. Spending a tremendous amount of time selecting the perfect forecasting technique is probably not worth the effort because studies show that the most accurate forecasts come from averaging multiple forecasts, preferably those using different data or different methods.

KEY TERMS

forecasting	time series models
market potential	trend projection
market forecast	decomposition
sales potential	moving average
sales forecast	exponential smoothing
quotas	autoregressive moving averages
qualitative forecasting techniques	correlation models
jury of executive (or expert) opinion	regression models
Delphi technique	simple regression models
salesforce composite	multiple regression models
team-based forecasting	multiple linear regression
survey of buying intentions	Buying Power Index (BPI)
quantitative forecasting techniques	mean absolute percentage error (MAPE)

DISCUSSION QUESTIONS

1. What types of decisions are influenced by estimating market demand and sales forecasting?
2. What are the five major types of forecasts? How do they differ?
3. Why would a sales manager utilize a market potential forecast? What are the four steps in developing a market potential forecast?
4. What are sales quotas, and why are they important? How are sales quotas determined?
5. What is the difference between qualitative and quantitative techniques of forecasting?
6. What are the four qualitative techniques discussed in this chapter? What are the advantages and disadvantages of each technique?
7. What are the three quantitative techniques discussed in this chapter? What are the advantages and disadvantages of each technique?

8. When selecting a forecasting method, what broad issues should a sales manager keep in mind?
9. How can forecasters combine forecasts?
10. Using which criteria can managers rank the forecasting methods?

PROBLEMS

1. Katrina Bettendorf is the director of marketing for Elko, a medium-sized firm that manufactures and distributes products in the electrical industry. Katrina has come to you, a marketing consultant, for help. Katrina is considering becoming a distributor for a product manufactured by Myenko, a firm in Slovenia. Katrina thinks that Myenko's product will help round out her product line. Before agreeing to distribute the product, however, she wants a study of the market potential of the product to ensure Elko can make money by distributing it. What issues should you consider in developing a market potential for Myenko's product for Elko?

2. Eldridge Smalley works as a sales manager for a small firm that has traditionally divided the expected annual sales into 12 equal monthly parts for production purposes. Eldridge notices that his firm experiences high levels of inventory in some months and runs out of critical products in other months. Eldridge's salespeople often lose sales because they are unable to fill orders. When Eldridge asks the vice-president of marketing about changing the forecasting system, the vice-president puts Eldridge in charge of a task force to evaluate different forecasting techniques and make recommendations for change. What techniques should Eldridge consider? How can Eldridge choose among the forecasting techniques that exist?

3. Philip Larson, a newly promoted sales manager, is discussing his firm's approach to setting quotas with Angie Washington, an experienced sales manager. Philip says, "I know we have used BPI to set quotas for many years, but I think a salesperson's experience also has a lot to do with sales in a territory." Angie agrees, but says, "I'm not sure if other methods for setting quotas exist." What other methods for setting quotas could Philip suggest to Angie? What are their advantages and disadvantages? If the salesperson's experience has an influence on sales in a given territory, what method for setting quotas would be best?

SHORT CASE

MAXWELL'S

BACKGROUND

Roger Lipscomb is the sales manager of Maxwell's, a small chain of retail furniture stores in the southeast United States. As part of his job for the last 3 years, Lipscomb has prepared a chainwide sales forecast using the trend projection method. Each year he calculated the rate of growth in sales from 2 years ago to 1 year ago and multiplied that by the most recent year's sales to determine next year's sales.

SITUATION

Last year the weakness of the trend projection approach to forecasting became apparent. In the aftermath of a hurricane, sales for several stores increased dramatically (but temporarily) as consumers purchased furniture to replace what was destroyed by the storm. When the demand abated, the sales for the stores also declined. Unfortunately the trend projection method for sales forecasting was not able to distinguish between the temporary increase in sales owing to the hurricane and an underlying change in the trend for furniture sales, and the sales forecast for this year was much greater than actual sales. As a result, Maxwell's had too much inventory and was forced to have a giant inventory clearance sale that significantly cut into operating margins.

Maxwell's. One of your tasks is to help Lipscomb develop the sales forecast. You have 4 years of sales data:

Year	Quarter	Actual Sales (in thousands of dollars)
1995	1	$3,150
	2	4,275
	3	4,005
	4	5,807
1996	1	$3,260
	2	3,880
	3	4,466
	4	6,105
1997	1	$3,394
	2	3,772
	3	7,756
	4	8,743
1998	1	$3,447
	2	4,006
	3	4,552
	4	6,230

PROBLEM

Lipscomb is now in charge of developing a forecast for 1999. He is concerned, however, that he will make another error like last year. You are a new graduate who has recently come to work as a management trainee at

QUESTIONS

1. Given the data available to you, what forecasting techniques could be used?
2. What forecasting technique(s) should be used? Why?
3. Using the technique(s) you selected, calculate a forecast for first quarter 1999.

FORECASTING ROLE PLAY

CHARACTERS

Sales Manager: Rebecca Goldberg or Howard Sierra
Sales Rep: Vinnie Canseca or Nancy Chee
District Manager: LaDonna Mobley or Manuel de la Guardia

SCENARIO

Pharmiceaux forecasts sales using a salesforce composite approach. Salespeople forecast sales for their territories taking into account current sales, likely competitive actions, and Pharmiceaux's likely product introductions and promotion and price changes on existing products. Salespeople discuss their forecasts with their sales managers and make any adjustments jointly. After this adjustment, salesperson forecasts become the basis for their sales quotas. Sales forecasts are combined on each successive level until they reach regional sales management. At that time the sales forecasts for the field sales group are combined with those from other groups, such as the medical equipment group and telemarketing, to develop the sales forecast for the company as a whole for the upcoming year.

SCENE 1

The sales manager for San Francisco, Rebecca Goldberg, is talking to one of her salespeople, Vinnie Canseca, about his latest forecast. Goldberg says, "Vinnie, I've noticed that in the last 2 years, your forecasts have been significantly below what you have actually sold. In fact, last year your sales exceeded your forecast by 30 percent! While I am delighted that your sales have exceeded forecast, I am getting a little heat from regional management about the poor forecast. It seems that underforecasting is a companywide problem."

Canseca replies, "Underforecasting is a problem? It seems to me that exceeding forecast would be a reason for everybody to dance in the streets. Instead, however, here I am trying to justify my forecast. If management needs a really accurate forecast, let them hire someone to do it. I'm not a forecaster! I need to be out in the field selling."

"Calm down," returns Goldberg, "no one is saying that you have to be a statistician. However, these forecasts have to improve. Management is not just being picky—the rest of the company depends on these forecasts being accurate."

Canseca says, "I really can't afford to be accurate. Since my bonus is based on percent of quota achieved, an accurate forecast is against my interest."

"I know," Goldberg acknowledges. "I'll see what I can do. At the same time, you need to work on the accuracy of the forecast."

SCENE 2

Goldberg discusses the situation with her district manager, LaDonna Mobley. Goldberg says, "LaDonna, I know that we need to improve the accuracy of our forecasts but our salespeople see it as an attempt by management to reduce their bonus. They also don't understand what they are supposed to do to improve the accuracy of their forecasts. I'm not sure what to tell them."

At this point, Mobley and Goldberg address alternatives to the issues raised by Canseca. Their discussion should address helping the salespeople become better able to prepare a forecast, the use of forecasts in the quota-setting process, and the importance of forecasting for the company as a whole. The meeting ends with Mobley saying that she will work on the issues and meet with Goldberg next week.

SCENE 3

Mobley meets with Goldberg and presents the new forecasting procedures. Goldberg says that she will see to it that the procedure is implemented for the following year.

SCENE 4 (2 years later)

Goldberg is meeting with Canseca about his latest forecast. Goldberg says, "Vinnie, I have noticed that since our meeting two years ago that your forecasting has . . ." At this point it is up to your to determine how the conversation ends.

CHARACTER DESCRIPTIONS

Name: Rebecca Goldberg
Gender: F
Age: 34
Marital status: Married
Education: B.B.A., Lehigh University
Title: Sales Manager
Office location: San Francisco
Reports to: District Sales Manager, Los Angeles
Employment history: Hired as a manager from a competitor
Personality: Sensitive to employees; company profit takes priority; fair; wants to be liked and respected
Notes: District has always been profitable; spends a lot of time "putting out fires"; chess player
Grapevine: Very loyal to the company

Name: Howard Sierra
Gender: M
Age: 37
Marital status: Married
Education: B.A., Murray State University
Title: Sales Manager
Office location: San Francisco
Reports to: District Sales Manager, Los Angeles
Employment history: Salesperson for 4 years; manager for 6 years; previously worked for a competitor

Personality: Sensitive to employees; company profit takes priority; fair; wants to be liked and respected

Notes: District has always been profitable; spends a lot of time "putting out fires"; owns a Harley

Grapevine: Very loyal to the company

Name: Vinnie Canseca
Gender: M
Age: 43
Marital status: Married
Education: B.S., Ball State University
Title: Sales Rep
Office location: Oakland
Reports to: Sales Manager, San Francisco
Employment history: 10 years with Pharmiceaux; same territory for 7 years
Personality: Strong customer advocate; among top 5 salespeople in Pharmiceaux for last 5 years; needs little supervision; baseball fanatic
Notes: Likely to produce for a long time
Grapevine: Needs work on interpersonal skills

Name: Nancy Chee
Gender: F
Age: 43
Marital status: Widowed
Education: B.B.A., Oklahoma State University
Title: Sales Rep
Office Location: Oakland
Reports to: Sales Manager, San Francisco
Employment history: 10 years with Pharmiceaux; same territory for 7 years
Personality: Goal- and task-oriented; very competitive; competent; dependable; very personable
Notes: Among the top 3 salespeople in Pharmiceaux for last 5 years; needs little supervision; strong customer advocate; Native American advocate
Grapevine: Likely to produce for a long time

Name: LaDonna Mobley
Gender: F
Age: 42
Marital status: Married
Education: B.B.A., University of Massachusetts; M.B.A., Dartmouth.

Title: District Manager
Office location: Los Angeles
Reports to: West Regional Manager
Employment history: Recruited from a major computer company where she was a national accounts salesperson; sales manager with Pharmiceaux for 5 years
Personality: Tough; demanding; extremely competitive; very ambitious; fair
Notes: Wants her district to be on top; recently terminated a 10-year veteran for poor performance; has season tickets to the opera
Grapevine: Wants a V-P job and maybe not with Pharmiceaux.

Name: Manuel de la Guardia
Gender: M
Age: 35
Marital status: Married
Education: B.B.A., University of Puerto Rico
Title: District Manager
Office location: Los Angeles
Reports to: West Regional Manager
Employment history: Rapid promotions; started with the company at age 18 and has worked his way up
Personality: Very demanding; aggressive; and autocratic; expects perfection
Notes: Youngest district manager in the last 10 years; his district has the highest profit level; handball expert
Grapevine: Probably a future V-P

QUESTIONS

1. What difficulties do sales managers and reps face when developing sales forecasts?
2. How do motivational issues influence the choice of forecasting methods?
3. List at least four realistic alternatives in this case. What are the long-term consequences of each alternative?
4. Which of the alternatives in question 3 should Goldberg select? Defend your answer fully.

NOTES

1. Robert F. Hartley, *Marketing Mistakes*, 4th ed. (New York: Wiley, 1989).
2. *Ibid.*
3. Rebecca Fannin, "Mazda's Sporting Chance," *Marketing and Media Decisions*, 24 (October 1989): 24–30.

4. Thomas V. Bonoma, "Major Industrial Sales: Who Really Does the Buying?" *Harvard Business Review,* 60 (May–June 1984): 111–119.

5. David Kirkpatrick, "Intel Goes for Broke," *Fortune,* 129 (May 16, 1994): 62.

6. R. William Barnett, "Four Steps to Forecast Total Market Demand," *Harvard Business Review* (July–August 1988): 28–37.

7. *Ibid.*

8. Jane M. Mackay, Charles W. Lamb, Jr., and William C. Moncrief III, "The Diffusion of Laptop Computers Among Industrial Salesforces," *Journal of Microcomputer Systems Management,* 3(4) (1991): 10–21.

9. Ronald L. Coccari, "How Quantitative Business Techniques Are Being Used," *Business Horizons* (July/August 1989): 70–74.

10. Robin T. Peterson, "Forecasting Practices in Retail Industry," *Journal of Business Forecasting,* 12(1) (1993): 11–14.

11. "1989 Survey of Selling Costs," *Sales and Marketing Management,* 14(3) (1989): 5–62.

12. Charles A. Peck, *Compensating Field Sales Representatives,* Report No. 828 (New York: The Conference Board, 1982).

13. Ken Goldfisher, "Modified Delphi: A Concept for New Product Forecasting," *Journal of Business Forecasting,* 11(4) (1992–93): 10–11.

14. James E. Cox, Jr., "Approaches for Improving Salespersons' Forecasts," *Industrial Marketing Management,* 18(4) (November 1989): 307–311.

15. Douglas J. Dalrymple, "Sales Forecasting Practices," *International Journal of Forecasting,* 3 (1987): 379–391.

16. John T. Mentzer and James E. Cox, Jr., "Familiarity, Application, and Performance of Sales Forecasting Techniques," *Journal of Forecasting,* 3 (January–March 1984): 27–36.

17. Cox (1989), op. cit., and Robin T. Peterson, "Improving Sales Force Composite: Forecasting by Using Scripts," *Journal of Business Forecasting,* 12 (Fall 1993): 10–14.

18. Kenneth B. Kahn and John T. Mentzer, "The Impact of Team-Based Forecasting," *Journal of Business Forecasting,* 13 (Summer 1994): 18–21.

19. Kristin S. Palda, *The Measurement of Cumulative Advertising Effects,* (Englewood Cliffs, N.J.: Prentice-Hall, 1964), 67–68.

20. The classification of independent variables discussed here—environment, organization, and salesperson—were suggested by Adrian B. Ryans and Charles B. Weinberg, "Territory Sales Response Models: Stability Over Time," *Journal of Marketing Research,* 24 (May 1987): 229–233.

21. Charlotte H. Mason and William D. Perreault, "Collinearity, Power, and Interpretation of Multiple Regression Analysis," *Journal of Marketing Research,* 28 (August 1991): 268–280.

22. Sande Milton, "A Simple Size Formula for Multiple Regression Studies,"*Public Opinion Quarterly,* 50 (Spring 1986): 112–118.

23. Papers showing the superiority of quantitative methods include Robin M. Hogarth and Spyros Makridakis, "Forecasting and Planning: An Evaluation," *Management Science,* 27 (February 1981): 115–138; E. Mahmoud, "Accuracy in Forecasting," *Journal of Forecasting,* 2 (1984): 139–159; and Spyros Makridakis and Michele Hibon, "Accuracy of Forecasting: An Empirical Investigation," *Journal of the Royal Statistical Society,* 142(2) (1979): 97–145. Papers showing the superiority of qualitative methods include J. Scott Armstrong, "Relative Accuracy of Judgmental and Extrapolative Methods in Forecasting Annual Earnings," *Journal of Forecasting,* 2 (1983): 437–447, and Mark M. Moriarty and Arthur J. Adams, "Management

Judgment Forecasts, Composite Forecasting Models, and Conditional Efficiency," *Journal of Marketing Research*, 21 (August 1984): 239–250. There are several reasons for the differences in findings, including different time horizons, different levels of expertise among forecasters, and different means used to evaluate the quality of the forecasts.

24. See, for example, Mark M. Moriarty, "Boundary Value Models for the Combination of Forecasts," *Journal of Marketing Research*, 27 (November 1990): 402–417; Spyros Makridakis and Robert L. Winkler, "Averages of Forecasts: Some Empirical Results," *Management Science*, 29 (September 1983): 987–996; and Benito E. Flores and Edna M. White, "A Framework for the Combination of Forecasts," *Journal of the Academy of Marketing Science*, 16 (Fall 1988): 95–103.

25. The discussion of issues related to combination of forecasts is based on Flores and White, *ibid.*, and J. Holton Wilson and Deborah Allison-Koerber, "Combining Subjective and Objective Forecasts Improve Results," *Journal of Business Forecasting*, 11(Fall 1992): 3–8.

26. These characteristics are based on David M. Georgoff and Robert G. Murdick, "Manager's Guide to Forecasting," *Harvard Business Review*, (January–February 1986): 110–120.

27. "A User's Guide to the Survey of Buying Power," *Sales and Marketing Management*, 145(10) (August 30, 1993): A6.

28. John A. Norton and Frank M. Bass, "A Diffusion Theory Model of Adoption and Substitution for Successive Generations of High-Technology Products," *Management Science*, 33(9) (1987): 1069–1086.

29. This example is based on David J. Wright, "Decision Support Oriented Forecasting Methods," *Journal of the Academy of Marketing Science*, 16 (Fall 1988): 71–78.

SALES STRATEGY: PLANNING AND IMPLEMENTATION

If you don't know where you are going, you will probably end up somewhere else.

YOGI BERRA, FORMER NEW YORK YANKEE BASEBALL PLAYER AND MANAGER

LEARNING OBJECTIVES

After reading this chapter, you should be able to answer the following questions:

- Why is sales strategy important in marketing planning?
- What is the role of sales marketing in each step in the marketing planning process?
- What is the relationship between the orientation of the firm and its sales management practices?
- How can a sales manager develop a sales strategy that is consistent with the goals of the firm or the business unit?
- How should a sales manager implement a sales strategy at the business unit level?

The Saturn car company has made its sales strategy a cornerstone of its identity. In its ads Saturn tells customers that its salespeople will treat them fairly and that Saturn will not use "hard-sell" tactics. Whereas pricing is a traditional source of contention between car buyers and car salespeople, Saturn clearly marks nonnegotiable prices on all cars. As a result, rather than quarreling over price with customers, Saturn salespeople act as counselors in the car purchase. The Saturn salesforce and selling approach is closely identified to the reputation of Saturn in customers' minds.

Another company that has made sales a cornerstone of its strategy is Mackay Envelope. Mackay Envelope distributes envelopes and other paper products. Because there are numerous companies that distribute similar or identical products, competition in the industry is intense and based primarily on price. Mackay Envelope uses sales strategy as the primary means to compete with larger firms at lower costs. It uses its salesforce as the primary means to develop long-lasting relationships with its customers. Sales is so important at Mackay that when Harvey Mackay, CEO, was asked how many salespeople he employed, he answered, "Three hundred and fifty. "When asked how many total employees he had, he answered, "Three hundred and fifty."[1]

It is important to understand the role of sales strategy within the overall strategic marketing process. That process begins with determining corporate strategy. **Corporate strategy** can be defined as deciding what mix of businesses should comprise the firm. If a pharmaceutical company is deciding whether to purchase a small biotechnology firm to acquire a new product or patent, it is making a corporate-level strategic decision. **Business unit strategy** is a subset of corporate strategy. It refers to actually running the mix of businesses. Assume that the pharmaceutical firm just mentioned decided to purchase the small biotech firm and installed its own management team. If the new management decides to change the marketing strategy for the newly acquired biotechnology firm's drugs, it would be making a business-unit level strategic decision.

Sales strategy is a subset of business unit strategy. Sales strategy delineates the objectives of the firm's or business unit's selling efforts, the means the firm intends to use to achieve these objectives, and the means by which the selling efforts will be monitored and evaluated.[2] Sales strategy supports elements of the promotion mix (sales promotion, advertising, and public relations) and elements of the marketing mix (price, product, and place) in order to accomplish the business unit's and the corporation's goals. In our example of the small biotech firm sales strategy would involve decisions regarding how the salesforce would be used to accomplish the overall communication and sales goals of the firm, and how it would relate to pricing, product, and distribution decisions.

This chapter will address several important issues about sales strategy. It begins with a discussion about the importance of sales strategy. Then the process of developing a sales strategy is detailed. Sales managers must develop sales strategy in the context of the firm's corporate and business unit goals. As a result, the discussion of the overall process of marketing planning also shows how sales planning is integrated throughout the overall planning process. The next section discusses sales strategy implementation. The sales manager can devise the most clever sales strategy, but if it is implemented poorly, the plan will not yield positive results. Finally common problems in sales strategy implementation are considered, and several methods for overcoming these problems are described.

IMPORTANCE OF SALES STRATEGY?

The importance of sales strategy to a firm depends on the relative importance of sales in the promotional mix and the difficulty of coordinating the various components of the selling mix. In Exhibit 16.1, the relative importance of sales versus advertising are stated for a variety of environmental circumstances. This chart shows that the characteristics of the product, the message, and the market all have a bearing on the circumstances under which personal selling—and hence sales management—becomes more strategically important to the firm. In situations where personal selling is more important than advertising, sales strategy is more critical to accomplishing the firm's goals than advertising or other elements of the promotional mix. For example, most industrial firms rely much more heavily on personal selling than advertising to communicate with customers. As a result, sales strategy for most industrial firms is more important to the firm's overall success, warrants a larger budget, and receives more attention than advertising.

EXHIBIT 16.1		
RELATIVE APPROPRIATENESS OF PERSONAL SELLING AND ADVERTISING		
		Personal Selling is More Appropriate When:	Advertising Is More Appropriate When:
Product Characteristics	Complexity	High	Low
	Difficulty in use	High	Low
	Product offering	Many services bundled with product	Simple
Message Characteristics	Selling approach	Must adapt to each customer	Same for each customer
	Message repetition	Unimportant	Important
Market Characteristics	Geographic dispersion	Narrow	Wide
	Customers	Few, large	Many, small
	Long-term relationship between buyer and seller	Important	Unimportant
	Purchase quantity	Large	Small

One of the major issues throughout this text has been the need for today's sales managers to coordinate the efforts of many elements of the selling approach, including telemarketing, national account management, electronic data interchange, manufacturers' reps, and the field salesforce, in order to achieve the firm's sales objectives.

Sales strategy plays a fundamental role in coordinating the different elements of the selling approach because it gives the managers of these different areas the opportunity to formally coordinate their efforts through the development of a common plan to serve a given group of customers. For example, the telemarketing manager and the field salesforce manager may have joint responsibility for a given group of customers. To ensure that their efforts are coordinated, they may develop a joint plan to serve those customers.

DEVELOPING SALES STRATEGY

Developing sales strategy consists of three stages: planning, implementation, and control. A conceptual model of those three stages, along with their associated key questions and a marketing planning process, is shown in Exhibit 16.2.

Sales strategy begins with a plan—that is, some consciously intended course of action.[3] In most large organizations, sales plans are a component of the firms' formal written marketing plans. The marketing plan is "a written document containing the guidelines for the business center's marketing programs and allocations over the planning period."[4]

Written sales plans can be prepared by customer, market, geographic region, or product, depending on how the plan will be used. For example, most national account salespeople develop plans for their accounts. These plans generally include a specification of the seller's current position, a statement of the intended goals for

EXHIBIT 16.2

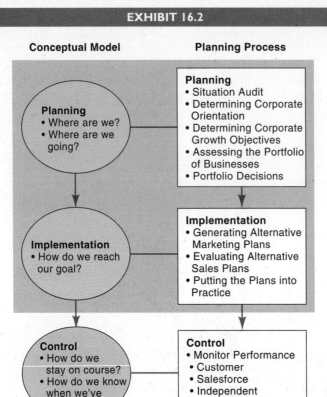

Conceptual Model

Planning Process

the upcoming year, and a description of how the salesperson or national account team intends to accomplish those goals. Account plans perform several functions. First, they act as a means of orchestrating the seller's efforts toward the buyer. They also establish clear objectives toward each buyer. Clear statements of objectives at the beginning of a sales period allow sales management to determine at the end of the sales period the extent to which the objectives were met. This allows sales managers to construct quotas that can be used for evaluative purposes.

In developing sales strategy, managers must not only plan but also implement the plan and control the selling effort. Marketing implementation answers "how" questions.[5] If the marketing plan states that the salesforce should increase the number of distributors of its products by 30 percent, marketing implementation is concerned with the question of specifically how that growth in number of distributors is to be achieved. Some firms include implementation issues in their marketing plans; others do not. All firms, however, must concern themselves with implementation issues because success in the marketplace depends on knowing what to do (the correct strategy) as well as how to do it (the appropriate implementation).

The third stage in sales strategy is control, which will be addressed in Chapter 17. Control consists of monitoring the progress toward achieving the objectives of the marketing plan. If poor progress is observed, good control systems quickly detect the existence of a problem and diagnose why the problem is occurring. By diagnosing the cause of the problem, management can take quick corrective action.

Marketing planning is an important task for marketing executives. Over 90 percent of marketing executives engage in formal planning.[6] The executives average approximately 45 days per year in planning activities. Although developing sales strategy may seem simple conceptually, in reality it is quite time-consuming and difficult. Information may be difficult to obtain, major competitors' moves may be hard to predict, the likely end-user response to marketing programs may not be easy to predict, and given marketing programs, while well thought out, may be difficult to implement.

One of the most important sources of information for marketing planning is the salesforce. The salesforce provides important information about customers and competitors for use in the planning process. Therefore, sales management is involved not only in planning their own activities, but also in providing information to other managers to help in the overall planning process. The next section describes the marketing planning process and places sales planning in that context.

THE ROLE OF SALES PLANNING IN MARKETING PLANNING

The marketing planning process outlined in Exhibit 16.2 shows the following steps in planning: situation audit, determining corporate orientation, determining corporate and business unit objectives, determining corporate growth opportunities, assessing the portfolio of businesses, and portfolio decisions.[7] All the steps in marketing planning are discussed in detail in the following sections, along with their associated sales planning issues.

Situation Audit

The initial step in marketing planning is the **situation audit,** which is the determination of the firm's or business unit's current competitive position. The situation audit consists of four components: product-market analysis, product positioning, product opportunity analysis, and corporate and industry analysis.

Product-market analysis assesses the current position and anticipated changes in sales and share by product by market. It typically involves gathering actual current sales and profit data for all products in a market. **Product positioning** assesses how each segment served views the product and compares it to the competition. Product positioning involves formal or informal marketing research to assess customers' views of the product. **Product opportunity analysis** seeks to identify segments where the current product line is vulnerable, and to detect opportunities in new segments or among customers in existing segments for the firm to increase its sales. **Corporate and industry analysis** is intended to identify the firm's place within the industry. It involves gathering information on how the firm compares to its competitors in terms of technology, management strengths and weaknesses, marketing capabilities, and financial resources. Corporate and industry analysis relies on information from several sources, including customers, competitors, and internal sources.

To gather information on customers and competitors, many firms use electronic bibliographic searches or clipping services that allow the firm to monitor any mention of their customers or competitors in the press. As already mentioned, another important method of gathering information is through the salesforce. Box 16.1 contains a panel discussion relating to the importance of the salesforce in gathering competitive information.

Sales managers must be careful to encourage salespeople to employ ethical methods when gathering information about competitors. Methods such as sifting through competitors' garbage or tapping competitors' phones are not only highly unethical, they are illegal in many states as well.[8] Exhibit 16.3 shows a more formal process whereby firms can collect competitive information using a customer-based approach. For each major customer, firms must define their competitors, identify on what basis customers select suppliers, evaluate the importance of the supplier selection criteria and analyze competitor performance on each criterion, and assess their salesforce's strengths and weaknesses.

Determining Corporate Orientation

The firm's orientation—specified as marketing, selling, or quality—is an important factor in developing sales strategy because it is a pervasive influence on all the actions taken by managers in the firm.

Marketing-Oriented Firms. **Marketing-oriented firms** are organized according to the marketing concept. The **marketing concept** consists of several related issues: (1) finding customer wants; (2) organizing the firm to meet those wants, and (3) meeting customer wants while meeting organizational objectives, such as profit, market share, growth, and ethical considerations.

Marketing-oriented firms are externally focused and are likely to concentrate on developing long-term relationships with their customers. This occurs naturally from the firm's recognition that customers direct the activities and behavior of the firm. Ford Motor Company is a good example of a firm that has become marketing oriented.[9] From 1978 to 1980 Ford's share of the U.S. automobile market declined from 23.5 percent to 17.2 percent owing to a weak product line. Starting in 1980 Ford began an intensive effort to involve customers with the design of new cars. Ford annually surveys 2.5 million customers to discuss quality issues and customer needs. This intensive effort at involving customers in new product development efforts has yielded a very attractive product line. In 1993 four of the top ten selling cars in the United States were Ford products, with the largest selling car being the Ford Taurus. In 1990 Ford's chairman of the board, Donald Peterson, succinctly summed up the importance of being marketing oriented by saying, "If we aren't customer-driven, our cars won't be either."[10]

From a sales management perspective, marketing-oriented firms are likely to be relationship oriented rather than transaction oriented. Being marketing oriented affects salespeople's attitudes. One study found that the salespeople in firms that were highly marketing-oriented had a greater orientation toward solving customer prob-

BOX 16.1

USING THE SALESFORCE TO GATHER COMPETITIVE INFORMATION

(The following is a discussion on using the salesforce to gather competitive information by a panel of sales managers)

Question:. **Is competitor intelligence important to your sales and marketing efforts?**

Answer:. **It most certainly is, say panelists. In a unanimous voice, respondents stress that knowing about a competitor's products and services is essential to improving marketing strategies, gaining a better understanding of their own products, and keeping abreast of their industry's newest developments.**

Jim Groves, executive vice-president of Lil Drug Store Products in Iowa, sums it up best when he says that obtaining competitor intelligence will not only help you determine your market's direction but might also quite possibly signal the need for a change within your own company. Good competition, he notes, will always provide new opportunities.

WHAT'S THE SCOOP?

When we asked our panelists what type of information they try to obtain, pricing, quality, and service were the most frequently cited areas.

"I try to find out who and what type of salespeople [the competition has] on staff," remarks Kenneth Hayes, general manager for Biggam Enterprises in California. "We also look to see how large their facility is, who their suppliers and manufacturers are, and what innovative approaches they're focusing on."

"We're more concerned with our competitors' numbers," says Cynthia Meade, marketing specialist for M&T Harshaw in Ohio. "We go right for their sales volume and profit margins."

Others, like Joel W. Barrett, sales and marketing manager for Florida-based Unlimited Processing, say they seek out the weaknesses in their competitor's products to help them promote their own product's position.

HOW TO GET IT

As for how they go about gathering this information, our panelists employ a number of methods. While many claim that their own customers are their best sources, others resort to prospects, suppliers—and even the competitors themselves.

"In addition to our own contacts," reports Pasquale Fucale, retail account manager for Symbol Technologies in New York, "we rely on value-added resellers, trade shows, and calling the company directly to request information."

"We gather most of our information through trade journals and newsletters," notes Joel Barrett, "although some information is acquired through actual product evaluations."

"We talk to competing salespeople and third-party associates to gather our facts," says Mike Calderaro, eastern regional sales manager for Web Service Co., Inc., in Maryland. "We also read the 'trades' and pick up the competition's literature when we can."

One panelist, Jack O'Reilly, divisional sales manger for Massachusetts-based Allied Int'l, reports that he tracks any customers who haven't purchased his product in over 90 days and he calls them himself. "The way I see it," he says, "simple communication works best."

However, some of our panelists are aware of the disadvantages posed by such easy access to vital information. As Gordon Hansen, vice-president of distributor sales for Monarch Tile in Alabama, puts it: "We usually obtain our info by visiting our competitors' customers. It never ceases to amaze me how open they are. I only hope our customers aren't so open."

Cynthia Meade concurs: "Since our industry doesn't use exclusive reps, a competitor's distributor can, and often does, do business with other competitors. While they can be a valuable source of information for us, it unfortunately works both ways."

BOX 16.1 (continued)

USING THE SALESFORCE TO GATHER COMPETITIVE INFORMATION

IS IT PART OF THEIR JOB?

When asked if gathering competitor intelligence is one of a salesperson's responsibilities, panelists are again united in their opinions.

"Although it's not a responsibility by definition," says Pasquale Fucale, "all salespeople should try to obtain information and filter it to corporate, so it can be transmitted to the field."

"We must always be aware of the competition's pricing strategies and product mix," adds Kenneth Hayes. "Most times it's better to know who the individual salesperson is rather than the company or industry he represents."

"Our salespeople are responsible for gathering as much information as possible from their customers—providing it doesn't jeopardize their relationship with them," notes Cynthia Meade.

"They're the proverbial eyes and ears of the company," concludes Mike Calderaro. "Keeping an eye on the competition is tantamount to surveying the periphery to protect yourself in battle."

USING THE INFORMATION

Panelists differ in their approach to making use of the information that's gathered. While some will take full advantage of the competition's weaknesses by incorporating them into their marketing efforts, others are more subtle.

"We cover all the bases that are logical and affordable," says Bob Siler, vice chairman for Sales Force Companies in Illinois. "We can then analyze the information and try to identify a competitive opening."

"I suggest attaching a list of competitors' weak points right to the account forms," says Kenneth Hayes. "You can then redirect part of your product line to fill the hole and crowd the competition out."

Those who don't officially incorporate this type of information into their selling strategy say they rely on their individual salespeople to use their discretion in utilizing such information.

"Facts picked up about the competition are used as an internal database for sales reps only," declares Jack McDade, sales manager for 3M Company in New Jersey. "We stress that it's not to be given as evidence of our product's advantages."

"We don't directly bring it into our marketing efforts," concurs Mike Calderaro, "but we might drop a casual comment to confirm what we've heard."

WHERE TO DRAW THE LINE

Although many of our panelists report that they haven't experienced any repercussions from putting competitor information to use, practically all see the potential for a disastrous situation if honesty and tact aren't observed.

"One can never underestimate the relationship between a competitor and a prospect or existing account," warns Kenneth Hayes. "It's always the largest unknown part of the fundamental strategy equation."

"Creating a situation that could backfire is the primary reason we don't incorporate the information into our sales efforts," says Mike Calderaro. "Although it's important for us to know what the competition is doing, it's not important for us to tell our customers what they're doing."

"Here's where the importance of verification comes in," states Gordon Hansen. "You must be certain your information is accurate and not based on rumor. If you're good at gathering intelligence, you should be able to separate the truth from the rumors."

SOURCE: Kerry Rottenberger, "Is Competitor Intelligence Important to Your Sales and Marketing Efforts?" *Sales and Marketing Management*, 143(11) (September 1991): 24–25.

EXHIBIT 16.3

FRAMEWORK FOR CUSTOMER-BASED COMPETITIVE ANALYSIS

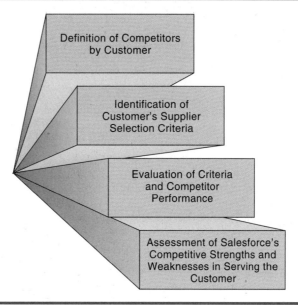

Definition of Competitors
by Customer

Identification of
Customer's Supplier
Selection Criteria

Evaluation of Criteria
and Competitor
Performance

Assessment of Salesforce's
Competitive Strengths and
Weaknesses in Serving the
Customer

lems, had reduced role conflict and ambiguity, and expressed greater job satisfaction and commitment to the firm.[11]

The firms most likely to profit from a marketing orientation are those that provide a differentiated product. For firms in commodity businesses, the positive effect of a marketing orientation is only noted among businesses that are above the median in marketing orientation.[12]

Selling-Oriented Firms.   **Selling-oriented firms** are focused on delivering a certain group of goods and services rather than meeting customer needs. Selling-oriented firms are internally focused. Their major concern is selling what they can make rather than making what they can sell.

Sales management practices in selling-oriented firms differ from those in marketing-oriented firms. Selling-oriented firms tend to be transaction oriented. Their goal is to maximize sales volume, not customer satisfaction. As a result, salespeople are encouraged to maximize sales volume not customer satisfaction. Compensation tends to be on the basis of sales volume and does not typically include a measure of customer satisfaction.

Quality-Oriented Firms.   **Quality-oriented firms** focus on providing high-quality products and services to external and internal customers.[13] *External customers* are companies or individuals who buy the firm's products, whereas *internal customers* are members of the firm who depend on output from other employees. For example, if a sales manager wants to purchase laptop computers for her sales reps, she

---

EXHIBIT 16.4

MOTOROLA'S VISION FOR QUALITY

Dedication to quality is a way of life at our company, so much so that it goes far beyond rhetorical slogans. Our ongoing program of continued improvement reaches out for change, refinement, and even revolution in our pursuit of quality excellence. It is the objective of Motorola, Inc. to produce and provide products and services of the highest quality. In its activities, Motorola will pursue goals aimed at the achievement of quality excellence. These results will be derived from the dedicated efforts of each employee in conjunction with supportive participation from management at all levels of the corporation.

SOURCE: Richard M. Hodgetts, "Quality Lessons From America's Baldridge Winners," *Business Horizons*, 37 (July/August 1994): 74–79.

---

would probably submit a purchase requisition to the firm's purchasing department. In this case, the sales manager is the purchasing department's internal customer. The purchasing department has to meet the needs of the sales manager in terms of cost, delivery, training, and whatever else the sales manager deems important.

Implementing a quality orientation requires companies to perform several tasks, including developing a vision of quality, involving top management, focusing on customer needs, setting quality objectives, training employees to use quality tools, empowering employees, adjusting reward and recognition systems, and making a commitment for continuous improvements in quality. One example of a firm that has adopted a quality orientation is Motorola, a large manufacturer of electronics. As shown in Exhibit 16.4, Motorola has developed a vision for quality for the entire company, including its salesforce.

There are at least two important reasons for firms to adopt a quality orientation. First, firms can save significant amounts of money by implementing a quality perspective. Xerox has dealt with numerous sales management issues from a quality perspective, including time spent by sales and service personnel on work other than customer calls and sales management turnover. These issues, and several others, account for $43 million in savings the first year they were explicitly identified and treated.[14]

Second, customers are demanding that their suppliers improve quality. As discussed in Chapter 8, many large firms require suppliers to have quality programs in place before being considered for a place on the approved supplier list. Noel Pooler, the CEO of Pooler Industries, which makes products for the automobile industry, says that many of his customers have adopted total quality management (TQM): "It doesn't just change how those folks do business. It changes how everybody who deals with them does business. They're attempting to reduce the number of suppliers that they have—they want long-term contracts, fewer and fewer suppliers, and better and better quality."[15] Pooler says that increasing quality of delivered parts is only the tip of the iceberg. Pooler's customers expect quality in all phases of Pooler's products and services—including how it handles deliveries, how rapidly it responds to requests to change specifications, and how quickly and politely the phones are answered.

Determining Corporate Growth Opportunities

After performing the situation audit and identifying the firm's orientation, the next step in the marketing planning process is to *determine corporate growth opportuni-*

EXHIBIT 16.5
CORPORATE GROWTH PREFERENCES

	Direction of Growth	
Source of New Products	Current Markets	New Markets
Internal Development	Timoptic XE, a once-a-day formulation of Timoptic, a Merck drug for glaucoma patients that currently requires multiple applications daily Trusopt, a drug that acts as a supplement to or replacement for patients currently taking Timoptic	Pepcid AC, an over-the-counter formulation of a prescription drug that treats gastro-intestinal problems
Acquisition	Cozaar, developed in collaboration with DuPont/Merck, is a once-daily therapy for the treatment of high blood pressure; Merck already has Vasotec, the leading drug world-wide for the treatment of high blood pressure	Fosamax, a drug that treats postmenopausal osteoporosis (licensed from Istituto Gentili in Italy) MedCo, a drug wholesaler, whose acquisition allows Merck to provide drugs to emerging markets such as HMOs and PPOs

SOURCE: Merck Annual Report (1994).

ties. Firms must always seek new opportunities for growth because old businesses become less attractive as they experience increasing competition, as changing technology, changing consumer tastes, and shifting legal and political realities. Firms can grow through two basic means: by increasing their sales to their current customers or by finding new markets. To find the products necessary to achieve either growth goal, they can develop new products internally or acquire the products externally. These growth choices are shown in Exhibit 16.5 for the Merck Company, a large manufacturer of pharmaceuticals.

The choice of which growth opportunity to pursue has a significant influence on sales management. For Merck to be successful in each cell of Exhibit 16.5, it must perform appropriate sales management procedures. For example, to be successful in operating Medco, Merck must combine its salesforce and systems with Medco's (Merck's acquisition of Medco was discussed in Chapter 8). To continue to remain competitive in selling new drugs, such as Timoptic XE, to existing markets, Merck must train its salesforce in the new products and focus on becoming more productive. To increase its sales to new customers, Merck must provide its salesforce with information on new products, such as Pepcid AC or Fosamax, and with information on the needs of the new markets.

Assessing the Portfolio of Businesses

The **portfolio of businesses** is the mix of business units that comprise the firm. Assessing the portfolio of businesses involves the comparison of different business units on common criteria, such as market share, market growth rates, business attractiveness, and business strength. Comparing business units on these criteria allows top management to understand the competitive positions of all businesses owned by the firm. By understanding the competitive position of each business, top management can make portfolio decisions, which are discussed in the next stage.

One of the most common procedures to compare different business units is to use a portfolio matrix. The first such matrix was developed by the Boston Consulting Group (BCG). The **BCG matrix** compares strategic business units (SBUs) on two dimensions: market growth rate and relative market share. Market growth rate (MGR) shows the rate of growth over two time periods. It is defined as:

$$\text{MGR} = \frac{S_1 - S_0}{S_0}$$

where S_1 = total industry sales during time period $t + 1$
S_0 = total industry sales during time period t

Relative market share (RMS) shows the market share of the business compared to that of its largest competitor. It is calculated by the following formula:

$$\text{RMS} = \frac{\text{SBU market share}}{\text{leading competitor's market share}}$$

The reason for using relative rather than absolute market share is that it corrects for interindustry differences in industry concentration.

Exhibit 16.6 shows a BCG matrix for a firm composed of eight SBUs. Each SBU is represented by a circle. The areas of the circles represent the SBUs' relative sizes, expressed as annual sales in dollars (or the appropriate currency). Grouping the SBUs into the four categories in the matrix is somewhat arbitrary. There are no hard-and-fast rules for establishing the cut-off points between high and low market growth rate, and high and low relative market share. However, the general rule of thumb is that businesses in markets with a growth rate in excess of 10 percent per year are classified as "high-growth," whereas a relative market share of greater than 1.0 is viewed as a "high" relative share. In Exhibit 16.6, business 4 has a MGR of 19, and a RMS = 1.5, so it is classified in the high MGR, high RMS category.

Another widely used matrix is shown in Exhibit 16.7. This matrix, known as the **directional policy matrix (DPM)**, also has two axes but is divided into nine cells instead of four. The advantage of the DPM over BCG is that each axis (business sector prospects and company's competitive strengths) consists of several components. For example, in BCG the vertical axis is market growth rate, whereas in DPM the vertical axis is business sector prospects. Business sector prospects includes market growth rate, but it also takes into account issues such as the level of competition and the rate of technological change. As a result, the vertical axis of DPM is more broadly based and hence more representative of the actual market conditions in which the businesses must compete.

Although both matrices are widely used, each suffers from numerous flaws. These flaws range from difficulty in identifying the relative market to questions of how the factors within the DPM should be weighted.[16] One of the most vexing problems is that planners have found that using different models yields different

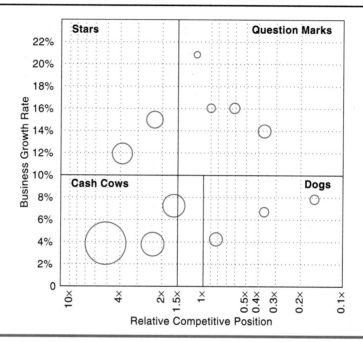

EXHIBIT 16.6

THE BCG GROWTH-SHARE MATRIX

SOURCE: B. Hedley, "Strategy and the Business Portfolio," *Long Range Planning,* (February 1977): 9–15.

classifications of the same set of SBUs.[17] For example, planners using one model may classify an SBU as a strong business worthy of additional investment, but another planner using a different model may classify the same business as being in a weak position and ripe for selling off. Despite these problems, however, many firms continue to use models similar to these because they are useful tools in classifying a number of businesses.

Making Portfolio Decisions

Once the SBUs have been grouped into categories using BCG or DPM, two major decisions must be made. First, the firm must decide whether to retain or delete each business unit. Unattractive business units [those in the low-growth (MGR)/low relative market share position (RMS)] may be deleted. Second, for the remaining businesses, the decision must be made as to the appropriate market share objective.

Probably the best known categories of market share objectives are build, hold, or harvest.[18] *Build* means to increase market share, *hold* means to maintain market position, and *harvest* means to gradually reduce investment to maintain profits. SBUs in the high MGR/high RMS quadrant in the BCG matrix are assigned a "build" objective, SBUs in the high MGR/low RMS are assigned the "build" or "harvest" objective, based on the firm's overall cash position, and SBUs in the low MGR/high RMS quad-

EXHIBIT 16.7
THE DIRECTIONAL POLICY MATRIX

		Business Sector Prospects		
		Unattractive	Average	Attractive
Company's Competitive Capabilities	Low	Divest	Phased withdrawal Custodial	Double or quit
	Med	Phased withdraw	Custodial Growth	Try harder
	High	Cash generation	Growth Leader	Leader

SOURCE: S. J. Q. Robinson, R. E. Hichen, and D. P. Wade, "The Directional Policy Matrix—Tool for Strategic Planning," *Long Range Planning,* 11 (June 1994): 8–15.

rant are assigned a "hold" or "harvest" objective, depending on the costs of maintaining market position and the firm's need for cash for other SBUs.[19]

It is important for top management to take an active role in comparing SBUs and assigning market share objectives. Business unit managers have been shown to systematically overestimate the business sector prospects and the strength of the business unit.[20] As a result, if resources are allocated according to the SBU manager's assessment of the SBU's MGR and RMS, misallocations could occur.

SALES STRATEGY IMPLEMENTATION

Implementing strategy involves generation and evaluation of alternative marketing plans, as well as selection and implementation of a plan. The following paragraphs discuss this for marketing planning as a whole, and place sales implementation in that context.

Generating Alternative Marketing Plans

After the strategic objectives have been identified for each business unit, the process of developing sales strategy for each unit can get underway. One set of suggested sales strategies appears in Exhibit 16.8. The sales strategies link the objectives of the salesforce, the primary sales tasks, and the recommended compensation system to the business unit objectives derived previously. They also link the suggested sales strategies directly to the business unit objectives derived in the previous step. For example, the "build market share" objective developed previously is linked with the primary sales objectives of building sales volume and securing distribution outlets, the primary sales tasks of calling on prospective and new accounts, and the recommended compensation of salary plus incentive.

This approach has one major weakness, however. It does not discuss from a customer standpoint how the market share objectives are to be obtained. For example, while the recommendation for build is to increase sales and share, the model does not describe where the sales will come from to support the market share objec-

	EXHIBIT 16.8		
MARKET SHARE OBJECTIVES AND SALESFORCE STRATEGY			
Market Share Objective	Primary Sales Objective	Primary Sales Tasks	Recommended Compensation System
Build	Build sales volume; secure distribution outlets	Call on prospective and new accounts; produce high presale service levels; provide product/market feedback	Salary plus incentive
Hold	Maintain sales volume; consolidate market position through concentration on targeted segments; secure additional outlets	Call on targeted current accounts; increase service levels to current accounts	Salary plus commission or bonus
Harvest	Reduce selling costs; target profitable accounts	Call on and service most profitable accounts only and eliminate unprofitable accounts; reduce service levels; reduce inventory	Salary plus possible bonus
Divest/Liquidate	Minimize selling costs; clear out inventory	Dump inventory; eliminate service	Salary

SOURCE: William Strahle and Rosann L. Spiro, "Linking Market Share Objectives to Salesforce Objectives, Activities, and Compensation Policies," *Journal of Personal Selling and Sales Management,* 6 (August 1986): 11–18.

tives. Sales managers can approach this problem of deriving the necessary level of sales by assigning a specific objective, such as retain, increase, convert, or attract, to specific groups of customers. For example, assume that a business unit's sales come from two major market segments. If the business unit's share objective is to hold, and one of the target market segments begins to show a sales decline, the other must show a sales gain in order to maintain the current share position in the market. As a result, for the second target market, the business unit's manager must increase its sales to existing customers in the second target market, convert customers who use competing products, or attract new users to the product. Exhibit 16.9 describes the four customer objectives: retain, increase, convert, and attract. It also shows under what circumstances each objective is appropriate and describes which sales appeals should be used with each objective.

Evaluating Alternate Sales Plans

After generating several possible choices for sales plans, managers must choose which sales plan is most likely to achieve the stated strategic goals. Managers have several decision methods to help them choose among the plans. These decision methods, arranged in a pyramid in Exhibit 16.10, include intuition, rules and short-cuts, importance weighting, and value analysis.

	EXHIBIT 16.9	
	CUSTOMER OBJECTIVES AND SALES APPEALS	
Competitive Objective	**Where Appropriate**	**Sales Appeals**
Retain	Seller has high share of business	Develop joint projects, regular calls, joint training sessions, joint promotional efforts, systems integration, long-term supply agreements
Increase	Seller's share is below that desired	Look for profitable new applications; develop custom applications
Convert	Seller must switch buyer from competition	Demonstrate technical superiority; consider free trial; show success in similar applications; do life cycle costing study
Attract	Seller has identified a new set of potential users	Solve application problems; develop new distribution channels; develop new selling approaches tailored to customer needs

SOURCE: Adapted from John O'Shaughnessy, *Competitive Marketing: A Strategic Approach* (Boston: Unwin Hyman, 1988).

Intuition.   Making decisions by **intuition,** also known as seat-of-the-pants decision making or gut feel, is when the sales manager makes a quick judgment based on immediately available facts and experience. For example, a manager might decide that a certain plan should be selected because it matches the characteristics of a successful plan for another product. The manager does not conduct elaborate analysis, so this method is fast, and the data requirements are limited.

Intuitive decision making is quite common. It reflects the sales manager's judgment and experience and in many situations can yield satisfactory decisions without requiring additional analysis. It is particularly useful in fast-moving industries,

	EXHIBIT 16.10
	PYRAMID OF DECISION APPROACHES

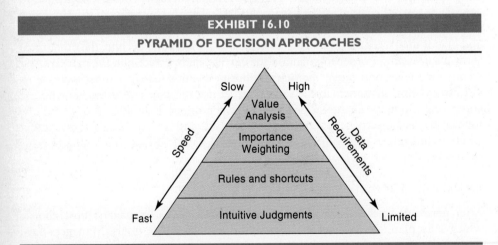

SOURCE: Paul Schoemaker and J. Edward Russo, "A Pyramid of Decision Approaches," *California Management Review,* 36 (Fall 1993): 9–31.

where the speed of change may preclude more leisurely analysis and decision making. Ed McCracken, the CEO of Silicon Graphics, a $1.5 billion, rapidly growing firm in the computer industry, says, "You have to do all your homework, but then you have to go with your intuition without letting your mind get in the way."[21]

Despite its widespread use, there are at least four problems with intuitive decision making. First, it is inconsistent. Although there has been little research on intuitive decision making among sales managers, studies have shown that highly trained professionals are inconsistent in their judgments across time. In one study radiologists were presented with a set of 96 X-rays and asked to evaluate the likelihood of a malignancy in each case. A week later they were presented with the same 96 X-rays in different order. Their decisions were inconsistent in 23 percent of the cases. Given that inconsistency occurred despite the radiologists' high levels of training, and awareness that they would be retested, it is not hard to imagine that sales managers' decisions would be at least equally inconsistent when using intuitive decision making to select a sales strategy.

Another problem with the intuition approach is that it reduces the reliance on other, perhaps more appropriate, decision-making methods. Because intuition is fast and works some of the time, managers may come to rely on it even when additional data should be gathered.

A third problem of intuitive approaches is that the decision can be distorted by primacy-recency. *Primacy-recency effects* occur when the decision is affected by the order in which data are received. Primacy-recency effects essentially overemphasize or underemphasize certain pieces of information, thereby potentially leading to suboptimal decisions. One well-known primacy effect occurs in the interviewing process. If an applicant makes a good first impression (a primacy effect), that impression influences all further judgments about the applicant by the manager. Recency effects occur when a manager gives greater weight to recent information when making a decision. For example, if a sales manager bases his annual evaluation of a salesperson on that person's most recent quarter's efforts, the evaluation would be the result of the recency effect.

A fourth problem of intuitive decision making is that it is quite difficult for a manager to train and develop intuition in others. Because the decisions are often made almost subconsciously, the manager may find it difficult to show a subordinate the components of the decision. As a result, intuitive decision making harms the ability of the manager to coach and train subordinates.

Rules and Shortcuts.   A second type of decision making is already based on **rules and shortcuts.** Rules and shortcuts, also known as heuristics (as discussed in Chapter 14) require managers to rely on rules of thumb from personal experience or those based on industry or company standards. Rules and shortcuts are fast and simple to apply, and can be widely applicable. Some rules that have been observed in sales situations, along with the problems that can occur when applying them, are shown in Exhibit 16.11.

The major advantages of rules are that they greatly speed up and simplify routine decision making, and they free decision makers from having to make the same decisions over and over. The major disadvantage of rules is that they are inflexible.

	EXHIBIT 16.11	
	SALES MANAGEMENT RULES OF THUMB	
Issue	**Rule**	**Potential Problems**
Bank lending	Never make a business loan to a sole proprietor who wears a black cowboy hat or drives a new sports car	Doesn't relate to business criteria for making the loan
Allocation of sales effort	Only pursue a prospect in the computer industry if (1) the money to purchase the system has been approved, (2) our product offers a unique benefit, (3) our firm is a qualified vendor, and (4) the order will be placed in the next 6 months	Doesn't allow the salesperson to develop relationships with customers that may not bear fruition for several years
Number of sales calls	Salespeople must make at least eight calls per day	Fails to take into account the different amounts of time salespeople may take for different types of calls—a routine call for reordering takes less time than a call to a new customer
Salesforce sizing	Split territories when the number of customers exceeds 250 or when the sales potential exceeds $5 million	Doesn't take into account the mix of customers—if 250 customers are small, the firm may not be able to justify the expense of an additional salesperson
Overseas expansion	Only expand into countries where the seller can own its distribution outlets	Fails to consider the demands such a policy makes on management—managing subsidiaries overseas is more difficult than managing at home

SOURCE: These rules come from a variety of sources, including the authors' participation in executive development programs, consulting with firms in several industries, and Paul Schoemaker and J. Edward Russo, "A Pyramid of Decision Approaches," *California Management Review,* 36(1) (1993): 9–31.

If a firm has the rule that it will use only face-to-face selling, it will continue using this selling method even if the environment changes. Relevant environmental changes may include pressure on margins from competitors which make face-to-face selling too expensive, or large customers who need additional services that cannot be provided with face-to-face selling. Having the rule of always using face-to-face selling ignores the existence of other selling methods, such as catalogs and telemarketing. Rules also allow competitors to guess what the firm will do next. If a firm has the rule of always using face-to-face selling and a competitor recognizes that a portion of the market is underserved by personal selling, the competitor may seize market share by using another selling method, such as telemarketing, to serve a segment of the market. The competitor would be able to do this knowing that the other firm would probably not use telemarketing.

Importance Weighting.   **Importance weighting** requires a manager to explicitly compare different alternatives on several attributes. *Alternatives* are different possible courses of action, and *attributes* are characteristics, such as cost or customer service levels, attached to the alternatives. Managers use judgment or experience to attach weights to each attribute. A score for each alternative is obtained by multiplying the weight of the attribute by the alternative's score on that attribute. The alternative with the best score is selected for implementation. By varying the weights attached to different attributes, the sales manager can conduct "what-if" analyses. *What-if analyses* allow the manager to determine the effect of varying the importance of different attributes on the decision.

GTE faced a decision during the mid- to late-1980s which can be represented in an importance weighting decision matrix. GTE had a telemarketing salesforce organized by activity. One telemarketing group handled service initiation, another handled service problems, and another credit and billing. Although the high level of specialization was very efficient from GTE's standpoint, customers with multiple questions were often frustrated by the necessity of talking with several different salespeople. The firm began to consider the use of a single point of contact for the customer. There were, of course obvious advantages in terms of customer service, but there were also major cost and training considerations for the firm.

An importance rating approach to resolving the decision facing GTE is shown in Exhibit 16.12, which contains the alternatives—highly specialized (HS) vs. single point of contact (SPOC)—and the attributes—customer service, training implications, competition and compensation. Each alternative is scored on each attribute. Although the firm did not use this exact matrix, it is a fairly accurate representation of the decision process that actually occurred. Based on the results of the analysis, GTE went to a modified SPOC approach.

There are several advantages of the importance weighting system: (1) it requires managers to state the alternatives and attributes explicitly; (2) the weights allow managers to vary the importance of different attributes, (3) the model can be used for training and development purposes, and (4) the model can be used for future decisions. The

EXHIBIT 16.12
IMPORTANCE RATING EXAMPLE

Importance Weights	0.5	0.2	0.1	0.2
	Customer Service	Training Implications	Competition	Compensation
Highly specialized (HS)	Customers will have to be routed to the person who can answer specific questions	Lower cost—each salesperson can be trained to perform a specific task	Will meet or lag	Can be tailored to the specific task
SPOC	Each representative can handle any incoming call —no switching necessary	Training will be long and expensive—each new hire must be trained to handle any question that might arise	Will meet or beat	Must develop a more complicated scheme that will capture multiple dimensions of performance for each salesperson
Winner:	SPOC	HS	SPOC	HS

Decision: SPOC wins on 60 percent of criteria; therefore, select SPOC.

last advantage is extremely important. If the model is based on all the available expert opinion, it can actually be used to substitute for expert opinion in future decision situations. This is a process known as *bootstrapping*.[22] Models that are used to replace human decision makers provide consistent results, are not affected by the order in which information is presented, and are not bothered by distractions, fatigue, or boredom.

Several PC software packages allow managers to develop their own importance weighting decision models. One dedicated importance weighting package, Decision Pad®, is designed to automate the process of building and calculating importance weighting decision matrices. It allows managers to construct matrices of alternatives and attributes, and rate each alternative on each attribute. The rating system used for the alternatives can be numerical or verbal. Decision Pad® converts verbal rating systems to numerical information and determines the best alternative. It also allows managers to run "what-ifs" to determine the sensitivity of the model to slight changes in the attribute weights. Spreadsheet packages can also be used to construct decision matrices, although they must be customized to generate appropriate reports and they cannot handle verbal rating systems (such as high, medium, and low).

The advantage of using a software package is that it allows managers to run many models by computer in the time it would take to run only one by hand. It also allows easy recalculation of the model upon changing attribute importance weights. Moreover, managers can retain the models to use in the future or modify the existing model by adding alternatives or attributes.

Value Analysis.   **Value analysis** is a refinement of the importance weighting technique. To develop a value analysis, the modeler links the specific attributes in the model to the values of various levels of decision makers in the firm. Computationally, value analysis involves adjustment of the attribute weights by a procedure that incorporates the underlying goals and objectives of the top executives. The goal of value analysis is to identify overriding themes or objectives that can be used to help adjust the weights to reflect not only the preferences of the manager developing the model but also the preferences of other levels of management as well.

Value analysis offers several advantages over the importance weighting model described previously. First, it determines a goal hierarchy from the perspective of top management which is used to adjust the attribute weights. Second, it addresses the issue that values of the alternatives may have declining marginal utility. Unless the underlying characteristics of the market are well understood, it is not possible to predict the consequence of increasing marketing expenditures. In a situation where marketing expenditures have declining marginal utility, increasing marketing spending will lead to less-than-proportional increases in sales. For example, one alternative plan might call for deploying 100 salespeople, while a second plan calls for deploying 200 salespeople. Is the second plan likely to yield twice the sales of the first? The answer depends on the level of unmet needs that exist in the market. If the first alternative can serve 70 percent of the market, and adding 100 more salespeople only increases the served market to 85 percent, it is highly unlikely that doubling the number of salespeople will double sales. The benefit of value analysis is that it explicitly adjusts the value of each alternative to account for declining marginal utility.

The major disadvantage of value analysis is that it is by far the most time-consuming and costly of the decision-making models presented here. As a result, its use should probably be reserved for the most critical decisions, where the amounts of money at stake are large and the risks arc high.

Putting the Plan Into Practice

Putting the plan into practice involves the daily decisions made by managers in accomplishing the objectives stated in the plan. Issues in putting the plan into practice are often overlooked when developing strategic plans. Effective implementation must occur at several levels of the firm: functions, programs, systems, and policy directives. Managers have the following tools to implement their strategies: interacting, allocating, and organizing.[23] Examples of implementation decisions at each level requiring the use of these skills are shown in Exhibit 16.13. A definition of each implementation level and some of the problems that frequently occur at that level are described in the following paragraphs.

EXHIBIT 16.13

EFFECTIVE IMPLEMENTATION SKILLS BY LEVEL OF THE FIRM

		Skills		
		Interacting	Allocating	Organizing
Structure	Functions	How can telemarketers and face-to-face sales people serving the same account be encouraged to plan the account jointly?	How is salesforce territory allocation best done by a printing company?	How should the account planning process be organized in a national account sales organization?
	Programs	How can sales and marketing effectively collaborate on a new national account program?	How should the prospects be selected for demonstration rides in a corporate jet?	How should a salesforce be reorganized to emphasize a marketing shift from products utilizing old technology to those utilizing newer technology?
	Systems	How should ownership of a competitive pricing intelligence system be divided between sales and marketing in an ethical drug company?	How should a firm allocate access to its ordering systems to allow customers to track orders?	How should customer service engineers be redeployed to avoid hardware-software "by-passing" in a computer graphics manufacturer?
	Policies	How should a recall of a defective building component be managed by a major steel producer in order to minimize the impact on long-term customer relationships?	How should dollars and service resources be allocated to service key accounts by segment and country for a computer-aided design manufacturer?	How can a sales organization be restructured to reflect management's shift toward being relationship oriented rather than transaction oriented in dealing with customers?

SOURCE: Adapted from Thomas V. Bonoma and Victoria L. Crittendon, "Managing Marketing Implementation," *Sloan Management Review,* 28 (Winter 1988); 7–14.

Functions.   Marketing **functions** are the issues related to the point of contact between the customer and the firm. Such concerns as salesforce management, distribution, consumer and trade promotions, and the like are considered to be functional-level issues. Functional-level issues are a major concern to management throughout the firm. The most well-conceived sales or marketing plan will not succeed without sound execution of functional-level issues.

There are three major problems with implementing plans at the functional level. First, policies developed at one level may not translate well into action at the functional level. For instance, top management at one firm decided to reduce prices overall rather than relying on programmatic discounting. By reducing the number of discount plans it offered, the company hoped to simplify its pricing structure and make prices more uniform. One unexpected consequence was that sales slipped. Buyers in this particular industry were historically measured by the amount of discount they were able to negotiate. When prices were reduced overall, buyers were not able to negotiate discounts as high as those to which they were accustomed. Therefore, the buyers sought alternate suppliers who offered higher discounts, even though the final price was the same.

Second, firms may develop contradictory structures. That is, the organizational structure within the firm is such that it is difficult for different members of the firm to coordinate their efforts. This is particularly true for companies that pursue international markets. One firm developed a sales organization in the United States that consisted of a geographically based field salesforce. To expand overseas, however, it used a different independent rep firm for each country. Although this allowed the firm to enter many markets at minimal cost, it was extremely difficult to coordinate the efforts of the different distributors with those of the salesforce in the United States. This became particularly apparent when a customer had operations in several countries. Coordination of pricing, service levels, and even product offerings was difficult with so many different salesforces involved.

A third problem with implementation at the functional level is that firms split their marketing efforts across all areas, rather than focusing on doing a few things very well. Frito-Lay illustrates a company that focuses on doing a few things very well. It concentrates its marketing efforts in distribution and sales. It has made daily service to customers its major focus. Over 99 percent of all Frito-Lay customers are called upon each day by route salespeople. Frito-Lay's sales strategy is focused on the planning and implementation activities the firm must conduct to support its daily service to customers. By contrast, firms that split their energy and attention across many different areas will experience global mediocrity.

Program.   A marketing **program** is a combination of marketing and nonmarketing activities that must be performed in order to achieve a business objective. For example, to successfully introduce the Mazda Miata, Mazda had to coordinate the efforts of production, marketing, and design and development. One interesting example of the coordination that was necessary involved the sound the engine would make. Mazda's marketing team wanted the Miata's engine to remind customers of a traditional sports car. To ensure this characteristic sound, Mazda engineers tuned the exhaust a certain way and monitored engine sound during the production process.

The major problems that occur in marketing programs relate to internal or external inconsistency. *Internal inconsistency* occurs when the elements of the program do not match. For example, if a firm introduces a new product at a price higher than what is currently prevailing in the market (premium pricing) but compensates the salesforce purely on quantity sold, the elements of the marketing program are inconsistent. To maintain a premium pricing approach, salespeople should be compensated on the profitability of their sales, not solely on quantity. If the salesforce is asked to sell a premium-priced good with compensation based on quantity sold, the salesforce will quite possibly either refuse to put much effort into selling the product or try to get management to give it the ability to negotiate price with customers. Of course, if management gives salespeople the right to negotiate price, the salespeople will reduce the price of the item, thereby negating the premium pricing approach that management is trying to follow.

External inconsistency occurs when the program does not match the environment or when the program does not match company strategy. The failure of a program to match the environment could occur if management tried to develop a national account program when the characteristics of the market did not support that selling approach. National account management is an appropriate selling method in a market where the majority of sales come from a small number of customers. However, if most customers are small, there is little justification for the development of a national account program. Trying to develop an NAM program for a company serving a market composed entirely of small customers would be an example of developing a program that is inconsistent with the external environment.

Marketing programs can also fail to match company strategy. Monsanto recognized the pitfalls of trying to enter a market when the marketing program required for product success failed to match its strategy. Monsanto's strategy in the chemicals market was to sell bulk chemicals to large industrial customers. Therefore, its sales efforts were concentrated in industrial markets, where the order sizes were large. When Monsanto developed the first low-sudsing laundry detergent, the marketing program necessary to be successful was inconsistent with the company's strategy. Monsanto did not have a salesforce in place to sell the product in retail channels, nor did it have expertise in promoting to consumer markets. As a result, Monsanto licensed the detergent to consumer products manufacturers, where the marketing programs necessary to make the product a success were consistent with those companies' strategies.

Systems.   **Systems** are operations within the firm that enhance or hamper marketing implementation. For example, if a firm uses telemarketing customer representatives to solicit orders, the firm needs to have a system in place to track customers' purchasing patterns. This system allows the firm to call customers that represent the highest potential for sales. A firm that also uses outside sales representatives to call on the same customers needs a system that can merge the sales history of each customer by either telemarketing or face-to-face selling methods, thereby allowing decisions to be made regarding the allocation of selling effort to each customer based on its total purchases.

Systems can be a pervasive impediment to implementing sales programs. One example is when a firm switches to an NAM program. To ensure that the services offered under the program are justified by the total profitability of the account, it is necessary for sales management to have a system whereby revenue and costs by customer can be tracked. What often happens, however, is that sales reports are organized by plant, region, or product. It is not feasible to develop customer profitability from those reports because the costs to serve the customer are not clearly identified. This problem is widespread. One author who had made an intensive study of marketing implementation said, "Few executives have any idea of profitability by segment. Rarer still are good numbers on profitability by product, and only once have I seen a system that allowed profitability to be computed by individual account."[24] The same author also commented, "In all but a handful of companies I studied, the financial accounting and sales accounting systems can only be called perverse in failing to meet marketing's requests."[25]

Lack of solid accounting data can also be an impediment to establishing a quality orientation. Management at Xerox found that accounting systems failed to capture about 70 percent of the costs of poor quality. The solution to the lack of accounting data was to separate quality measures from standard accounting data, and to use "roughly right" data instead of waiting until the accounting data were pristine.[26]

Policies.   Marketing **policies** represent management's overall theme for its marketing programs. These themes can be simply stated. For example, 3M, a St. Paul, Minnesota–based manufacturer, has a marketing theme of encouraging a high level of new product development. New product development is vital to 3M's continued survival and growth. The company feels so strongly about its theme that 3M's corporate mission statement includes a goal that 25 percent of the company's sales in any given year will result from products introduced in the preceding 5 years. This clear statement and commitment of the firm's theme clarifies the tasks that managers at all levels of the firm must undertake. For example, sales managers must encourage salespeople to keep abreast of technological changes in their markets so they can act as information resources for customers and to ensure they are capable of interacting with customers on prevailing technology.

The major problem with marketing policies is that the external environment can change, rendering the policies inappropriate. If the policy in a firm is to pursue niche markets with high-cost/high-profit items, marketing functions, programs, and systems should be geared to accomplishing that goal. Hewlett Packard, a Palo Alto, California–based high-technology company, is a clear example of a firm that has pursued niche markets. In one market, however, this approach was not appropriate. Computer printers, a lucrative market that H-P dominated, was attracting attention from other manufacturers.[27] If H-P competed in its traditional fashion, it would adopt a marketing program that would focus on continuing to maintain technological leadership and serving markets that would pay a premium price for leading-edge products. Over time, however, this program would lead to erosion in market share as competitors entered the market with lower-priced products.

Therefore, H-P's printer business adopted a different marketing policy. It aggressively sought to maintain market share by cutting manufacturing costs, reducing prices, and introducing improved new versions. H-P's traditional marketing policy was so strong, however, and the new policy was so revolutionary, that it was necessary to physically remove H-P's printer business team to Boise, Idaho, to ensure the business could continue "breaking the rules."

Required Managerial Skills for Implementation

After deciding on a plan and ensuring that the marketing functions, programs, systems, and policies are consistent, the final piece is a manager who can ensure that all the necessary activities are carried out. Some of the important responsibilities of sales managers include interaction, allocation, and organization, which are discussed in the following paragraphs. Two other important skills, monitoring and control, are discussed in Chapter 17.

Interaction.   The job of the sales manager often involves *interacting* with others in the organization to perform tasks. This job is complicated because the sales manager must often influence those over whom he or she has no direct control. For example, while national account managers are usually given total account responsibility, they are often not given direct control over some of the individuals in the organization whose efforts are vital to satisfactory customer service. If the national account manager does not have direct control over the support people, such as telemarketers, who provide routine service to the account, there is little the manager can do to force the telemarketers to provide desired customer service levels. Instead, the manager must influence the support staff to ensure that they realize the importance of serving the customer. One way of doing this is to develop personal relationships with the support staff to ensure they understand the importance of their efforts in providing the needed service levels. In essence, the manager must sell his or her priorities within the organization.

Allocation.   Sales managers are often involved in *allocating* time, people, and money. Because people, money, and time are always scarce resources, good managers must allocate them where they are likely to have the greatest impact. For example, sales managers must allocate enough money to serve existing customers, but they must also continue to prospect for new customers. After all, existing customers can experience business problems themselves or find alternate suppliers, which would reduce purchases. If a sales manager fails to allocate resources for searching for new customers, sales over time will decline.

Organization.   *Organizing* consists of managers' attempts to develop networks of contacts in the organization or to make formal organizational adjustments to achieve sales objectives. For example, one large firm organized its salesforce by market and customer size. Large customers were served by a salesforce specialized by market. All small customers, however, regardless of market, were served by a single salesforce. The sales manager for the division that served small customers was responsible for developing plans for each customer and submitting those plans to the relevant market sales manager. The sales manager for the small customer division found a structural impediment to coordinating sales planning: each market used a different planning document, and the salespeople for the small customers had to develop plans following different guidelines depending on the market into which the customer fell. To streamline the planning process for small customers, the manager suggested that all small customer plans follow a common procedure, which would eliminate the need for salespeople to be familiar with each market's planning procedures. The change was necessary to reduce the amount of time salespeople spent in planning. The proposal was an attempt to make an organizational adjustment that would increase salespeople's selling time, thereby freeing them to accomplish their sales objectives.

SUMMARY

Sales strategy is a critical element in marketing strategy for many firms, particularly those in which personal selling is the most important promotional method or those where multiple selling methods are to be coordinated. The first step in developing a sales strategy is sales planning. Sales planning is a subset of overall marketing planning. Sales management is strongly affected by decisions made in the overall marketing planning process; sales managers are major contributors to that process. The planning effort is divided into two phases: planning and implementation.

The planning phase consists of five sections: conducting a situation audit, determining corporate orientation, determining corporate growth objectives, assessing the portfolio of businesses, and making portfolio decisions. Sales plays a very important role in gathering the information to be used in auditing the situation. Salespeople are often used as primary sources of information about the competition, customers, technology, and other important parts of the competitive environment. Sales is strongly affected by corporate orientation. Marketing- and quality-oriented firms take a longer view of customer relationships than do selling-oriented firms. Determining corporate growth objectives has an important effect on sales management—to the extent that growth involves pursuing new markets and new customers, sales management practices may have to change. Setting business unit objectives is probably among the most important influences on the development of a sales strategy. Business unit objectives have pervasive influences on several sales management issues, including compensation, sales objectives, and sales tasks.

Implementation of sales objectives requires generation of alternative plans, evaluation of alternative plans, and selection and implementation of a plan. Alternative plans for reaching sales objectives include determining the proper mix of which customers to retain, increase sales to, attract, or convert. Sales managers can evaluate plans several ways—through intuition, rules and shortcuts, importance weighting, and value analysis. The importance of implementation cannot be overlooked in the overall marketing planning process; a large number of plans fail because of poor implementation. Effective implementation must occur at several levels of the firm: functions, programs, systems, and policy directives. Managers must use their interacting, allocating, and organizing skills to ensure that proper implementation occurs at each level.

KEY TERMS

corporate strategy	product positioning
business unit strategy	product opportunity analysis
sales strategy	corporate and industry analysis
situation audit	marketing-oriented firms
product-market analysis	marketing concept

selling-oriented firms

quality-oriented firms

portfolio of businesses

Boston Consulting Group (BCG) matrix

directional policy matrix (DPM)

intuition

rules and shortcuts

importance weighting

value analysis

functions

program

systems

policies

DISCUSSION QUESTIONS

1. How is sales strategy different from corporate strategy? Why is sales strategy important to a firm?
2. What are the stages in developing sales strategy? What are the key questions associated with each stage?
3. What is involved in a situation audit? Why is it important to conduct?
4. How are the three corporate orientations unique? In what situations would you choose each particular orientation?
5. Why would a company choose to seek new opportunities for growth? What growth strategies are available to a firm?
6. What tools are available to assess a business portfolio? How are the tools unique?
7. What is involved in implementing strategy?
8. What decision methods are available to managers when evaluating alternate sales plans? What are the advantages and disadvantages of each method?
9. At which levels of the firm must implementation of the marketing plan occur? What issues are unique to each level?
10. What are the essential qualities of a sales manager? Why is each quality important to successfully implementing marketing plans?

PROBLEMS

1. Rafael Martinez, a business unit manager at a large manufacturer of automotive parts and accessories, is faced with some pressing questions on sales-force strategy. For years Rafael's business unit has been the growth leader of all the business units in the firm. Recently, however, the growth of his unit has been slowing. Although the business unit's market share remains high, there has been increasing competition, especially in terms of price. As a result, the attractiveness of the market has been decreasing. In the review of his strategic plan for next year, top management suggested that Rafael consider ways to adjust his unit for a hold, rather than a build, strategy. Since approximately 25 percent of his unit's discretionary funds are spent on the sales-force, he has decided to start his adjustments with changes to the salesforce. As Rafael's sales manager, what suggestions might you have for changing the salesforce to reflect the new competitive arena in which your business unit now competes?

2. In a recent meeting between top management and the sales managers of a software development company, the CEO discussed several instances where top management was unaware of important market developments until too late. As a result, customers were dissatisfied and the competition was able to make inroads on important customers. The CEO told the sales managers that this was at least partially their fault—that salespeople were an important source of information on competitive developments and that they had not been providing critical information about market trends to top managers fast enough. He said that the firm had conducted a little experiment to test this. Ten pieces of information about market trends and customer needs had been planted in the field with key customers. Only one of these pieces of information had ever appeared in a salesperson's monthly report. The CEO has challenged the sales management team to improve its gathering and dissemination of important market information. The vice-president of sales has appointed you to head a team to make whatever changes are necessary. What sorts of changes should you consider?

3. You have been asked to consult with a small family-owned firm that specializes in providing custom software solutions to members of the trucking industry. The software is used in warehouse management, shipment tracking, billing, and bidding. The company has come to you for help in developing its promotional budget. In the past, most of its promotional budget has gone to advertising. You think, however, that the firm should spend the majority of its promotional budget on personal selling. Why?

SHORT CASE
EXPEDIM

BACKGROUND

Yvette Moses is the vice-president of sales for Expedim, a rapidly growing software company that sells a variety of accounting software packages to large commercial users. Since the inception of the company, the salesforce has been employed geographically, with salespeople responsible for selling all of the firm's products to all customers in a given geographic area. The sales reps must be well versed in all packages to serve their territories adequately.

SITUATION

In the last 2 years, Expedim has dramatically increased the rate of new product introductions. In the last year alone, Expedim has added five major new products and made significant upgrades to three others.

Although Expedim must continue to upgrade its product line to remain competitive in its industry, the rapid pace of new product introduction has had several negative consequences. Sales reps are finding it more and more difficult to keep up with the rate of change in the company's product line. Training sessions are becoming longer and longer, taking more time away from the salespeople's coverage of their territories. Customers have begun to complain that they are not receiving adequate support from their sales representative because the reps lack specific industry and product knowledge.

		Criteria		
		Cost	Responsiveness to Customer Needs	Meeting the Competition
	Criteria importance	.2	.5	.3
Alternatives[a]	Product	3	3	5
	Industry	4	4	3

[a]The alternatives were assigned weights from 1 to 5 for each criterion, with 5 being best.

PROBLEM

Given the problems with customers and the salesforce, Moses is considering changing the way her salesforce is deployed. To overcome the problems of having generalist salespeople when the customers want specialists, she is considering switching to a product specialist sales organization. However, she also knows that the needs of customers vary tremendously by industry, since accounting practices vary by industry. Therefore, she is also considering redeploying the salesforce by industry. To help make the decision, she has constructed the following matrix. She has listed her two deployment options (product vs. industry) and her criteria (cost, responsiveness to customer needs, and meeting the competition). She has also filled out her best estimate of how each alternative ranks on each criterion.

QUESTIONS

1. Which alternative should Moses select?
2. If the weights of the criteria were changed so that cost became .5, responsiveness to customers became .3, and meeting competitors became .2, would Moses's decision in question 1 change?
3. Should Moses consider any other criteria in making her decision? How could those be incorporated in her model?

NOTES

1. Harvey Mackay, *Swim With the Sharks Without Being Eaten Alive* (New York: Ballantine Books, 1988), 181.
2. John O'Shaughnessy, *Competitive Marketing: A Strategic Approach* (Boston: Unwin Hyman, 1988).
3. Henry Mintzberg, "The Strategy Concept I: Five Ps for Strategy," *California Management Review*, 31(1) (1987): 11–24.
4. Donald R. Lehmann and Russell S. Winer, *Analysis for Marketing Planning* (Plano, Tex.: Business Publications, Inc., 1988), 2.
5. Thomas V. Bonoma and Victoria L. Crittendon, "Managing Marketing Implementation," *Sloan Management Review*, 28 (Winter 1988): 7–14.
6. James M. Hurlbert, Donald R. Lehmann, and Scott Hoenig, "Practices and Impacts of Marketing Planning," working paper, Columbia University Graduate School of Business, 1987.
7. The planning process used is based on several sources, including Edward F. Walsh, "A Primer for Planning," *Sales and Marketing Management* (November 1990): 75–78; Roger A. Kerin, Vijay Mahajan, and P. Rajan Varadarajan, *Contemporary Perspectives on Strategic Market Planning* (Boston: Allyn and Bacon, 1990); and O'Shaughnessy, (1988), op. cit.
8. John H. Hallaq and Kirk Steinhorst, "Business Intelligence Methods—How Ethical?" *Journal of Business Ethics*, 13 (October 1994): 787–794.
9. See "King Customer," *Business Week* (March 12, 1990): 90, for a description of how Ford and other firms are trying to become more customer- (and marketing-) oriented.

10. *Ibid.*

11. Judy A. Siguaw, Gene Brown, and Robert E. Widing II, "The Influence of the Market Orientation of the Firm on Sales Force Behavior and Attitudes," *Journal of Marketing Research,* 31 (February 1994): 106–116.

12. John C. Narver and Stanley F. Slater, "The Effect of a Market Orientation on Business Profitability," *Journal of Marketing,* 54 (October 1990): 20–35.

13. The discussion of TQM is drawn from Michael Barrier, "Small Firms Put Quality First," *Nation's Business,* 80 (May 1992): 22–32; Richard M. Hodgetts, "Quality Lessons From America's Baldridge Winners," *Business Horizons,* 37(4) (July/August 1994): 74–79; and Philip Crosby, *Quality Is Free* (New York: McGraw-Hill, 1979).

14. Lawrence P. Carr, "Applying Cost of Quality to a Service Business," *Sloan Management Review,* 33 (Summer 1992): 72–78.

15. Barrier (1992), op. cit., 22.

16. Robin Wensley, "Strategic Marketing: Betas, Boxes, or Basics?" *Journal of Marketing,* 45 (Summer 1981): 173–182.

17. Yoram Wind, Vijay Mahajan, and Donald Swire, "An Empirical Comparison of Standardized Portfolio Models," *Journal of Marketing,* 47 (Spring 1983): 89–99.

18. T. D. Herbert and H. Deresky, "Generic Strategies: An Empirical Investigation of Typology Validity and Strategy Content," *Strategy Management Journal* (8)2 (March–April 1987): 135–147.

19. Laurence P. Feldman and Albert L. Page, "Harvesting: The Misunderstood Market Exit Strategy," *Journal of Business Strategy* (5)4 (Spring 1985): 79–85.

20. Marian C. Burke, "Strategic Choice and Marketing Managers: An Examination of Business Level Marketing Objectives," *Journal of Marketing Research* (21)4 (November 1984): 345–359.

21. Stratford Sherman, "Leaders Learn to Heed the Voice Within," *Fortune* (August 22, 1994): 93.

22. Bootstrapping is discussed in many texts and articles on decision making. One useful introductory article is C. Camerer, "General Conditions for the Success of Bootstrapping Models," *Organizational Behavior and Human Performance,* 27 (1981): 411–422.

23. The discussion of implementation is drawn from Thomas V. Bonoma, "Making Your Marketing Strategy Work," *Harvard Business Review,* 62 (March–April 1984): 69–76; Thomas V. Bonoma, "Marketing Subversives," *Harvard Business Review,* 64 (November/December 1986): 113–118; and Thomas V. Bonoma and Victoria L. Crittendon, "Managing Marketing Implementation," *Sloan Management Review,* 28 (Winter 1988): 7–14.

24. Bonoma (1984), op. cit., 74.

25. Bonoma (1984), op. cit., 74.

26. Carr (1992), op. cit.

27. Stephen Kreider Yoder, "How H-P Used Tactics of the Japanese to Beat Them at Their Game," *The Wall Street Journal* (September 8, 1994): A1.

SALES STRATEGY: CONTROLLING

The budget is our guide. It tells us what we're supposed to do for the year. We couldn't get along without it.

JIM BELL, PLANT MANAGER, INTERNATIONAL STEEL PRODUCTS

LEARNING OBJECTIVES

After reading this chapter, you should be able to answer the following questions:

- What is the role of control in the strategic marketing/sales management process?
- How do firms allocate resources across different selling methods using marketing effort analysis?
- How do firms uncover reasons behind failure to meet sales objectives?
- How can firms use DPA and CDM as methods of controlling distributors?
- Why is it necessary for sellers to exert control over their customers, and how can they do so?
- How can firms use sales budgets to control the salesforce?
- What methods can firms use to set the sales budget?
- How can firms use sales and marketing audits as comprehensive means of control?

GTE, one of the largest telecommunications firms in the world, uses telemarketing sales representatives to sell long-distance service in its Consumer Markets group in Dallas, Texas. Management maintains tight controls over the length of time the sales reps speak to customers. Controlling the length of calls is also emphasized in sales training. The tight controls over length of calls is needed because GTE estimates that as the average call increases in length by as little as ten seconds, 80 new sales representatives must be hired. GTE monitors the length of calls to control costs and to plan for the number of workers to be present on a given shift.

Conceptually, control is the part of strategic marketing/sales management where firms try to answer the questions, "How do we stay on course?" and "How do we know when we've arrived?" That is, once a strategic direction has been determined and a plan of action has been carried out, how can the success of the plan be monitored? Control fits into the overall strategic marketing/sales management process after planning and implementation, as shown in Exhibit 17.1.

Even if a firm has devised a brilliant plan and developed a great implementation schedule, sales efforts can still fail if management does not put in place the appropriate sales controls. **Sales controls** are means by which management sets standards,

EXHIBIT 17.1

STRATEGIC MARKETING MODEL

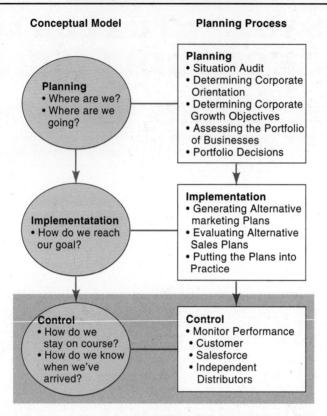

obtains information on the extent to which the standards are met, and takes corrective action if needed.

Firms must develop sales controls at multiple levels of the distribution channel, including: salesforce, independent distributors, and customers. First, firms must control the high cost of maintaining a salesforce. For IBM, through the early 1990's, the salesforce had accounted for up to 37 percent of the cost of the typical product. Through careful management, that cost has been reduced to 30 percent. The industry average, however, is still lower, so IBM must continue to monitor and control salesforce expenditures if it wishes to remain competitive. Second, firms that use independent distributors must put controls in place to ensure that customers are being served properly. If controls are in place, management will know when problems arise before serious damage to customer relationships takes place. Third, firms must also control customers. If a seller identifies a group of national accounts, it is important to monitor the accounts' purchases and profitability to justify the level of resources devoted to customer service. If those accounts continue to grow, the firm may wish to devote more resources to building or maintaining these customer relationships. If the national accounts are not profitable, the seller may wish to modify the program or concentrate only on the largest accounts.

This chapter will address two fundamental issues of sales control: what should be controlled and how it should be controlled. What should be controlled includes the selling approach, independent distributors, customers, and the salesforce. Control procedures include sales budgets, marketing and sales audits, and analyses of customers, selling approaches, distributors, and the salesforce.

CONTROLLING THE SELLING APPROACH

One of the fundamental issues in control is allocation of resources. For example, how should a firm allocate resources among personal selling, advertising, sales promotion, and public relations? How should a firm allocate resources among selling methods such as telemarketing, face-to-face sales, or national account management? In either case, if results are not what were expected, how can the firm identify the source of the discrepancy? Two methods of analysis are used to answer these questions: marketing effort analysis and variance decomposition analysis.

Marketing Effort Analysis

In **marketing effort analysis,** the relative effectiveness of promotional methods or selling methods is compared directly in terms of sales response per amount of resource. This method allows a firm to identify those promotional methods or selling methods that will yield the highest level of sales or service per dollars spent. From the marketing effort analysis, the proper level of resources to allocate to advertising, personal selling, sales promotion, and public relations can be determined. Marketing effort analysis, therefore, is done as a precursor to setting the sales budget. If a firm determines that its promotional resources can be better spent using a promotional method other than direct sales, less money will be allocated to the sales budget.

One firm, AAA Small Auto World, has used marketing effort analysis to double sales in 7 years while reducing its marketing budget by 40 percent.[1] Ron Sturgeon, CEO of AAA, uses marketing effort analysis to determine what proportion of his promotions budget should be spent on telemarketing, direct mail, and advertising. As the head of a small firm (1993 revenues of $8 million), Sturgeon needs to ensure that he is getting the most revenue per marketing dollar spent.

AAA sells primarily by phone to customers responding to direct mail or advertising. By 1991 AAA's database had grown to 350,000 names, and the cost of sending a single direct mail piece to all 350,000 names was over $100,000. Given that a single mailing constituted a significant proportion of AAA's marketing budget, Sturgeon had to be sure that the money was best spent in direct mail as opposed to advertising or outbound telemarketing. He analyzed sales by state, type of customer, amount of the sale, and source of the lead (ad or direct mail) on a monthly basis. He also analyzed the number of leads by state. To estimate the efficiency of advertising versus direct mail, he compared costs and sales for each method. This comparison is shown in Exhibit 17.2. We can conclude from the analysis that direct mail was more efficient than advertising, which argues for devoting more revenues to direct mail. The same approach can be used to compare direct mail to personal selling,

EXHIBIT 17.2
MARKETING EFFORT ANALYSIS

SELLING METHOD EFFICIENCY

Determining the efficiency of a given selling method required the calculation of costs and total sales in the region.

Direct Mail.

1. *Costs:* The initial mailing was 2,000 pieces. Mailing costs were $.30 per piece for a total of $600.
2. *Region Sales:* Sales were $8,000.
3. *Efficiency:* To determine the efficiency of direct mail, divide the total sales per region by the costs. The efficiency of the direct mail selling method is $600 ÷ $8,000 = .075. For each dollar in revenue generated through direct mail, the firm had to spend $.075.

Advertising.

1. *Costs:* Insertion costs = $1,000. Unique "800" numbers were provided for each ad so that the source of the response could be tracked.
2. *Region Sales:* $10,000.
3. *Efficiency:* To determine the efficiency of advertising, divide the total sales per region by the costs. The efficiency of advertising was $1,000 ÷ $10,000 = .10. To generate a dollar of revenue using advertising, the firm had to spend $.10.

CONCLUSION

Direct mail is more efficient than advertising.

---

telemarketing to personal selling, or any other combination of selling methods or promotional methods a firm is considering.

Sturgeon also used marketing effort analysis to allocate resources that had already been committed to a certain selling method. If a monthly report showed that 60 direct mail responses from Utah yielded only one sale, and the 40 direct mail responses from Arizona yielded four sales, Sturgeon would reallocate direct mail resources from Utah to Arizona.

A more comprehensive analysis would compare territories on dollar sales, average sales per order, and number of orders. Exhibit 17.3 shows such an analysis for three territories: Utah, Arizona, and Oklahoma. Depending on the objectives of the company, a manager could reallocate resources based on three different decision rules: highest total sales, highest sales per order, and highest number of orders. If the objective is to maximize sales, the manager should reallocate resources to Arizona. If the objective is to maximize efficiency—that is, have the highest ratio of sales per order—new resources should be allocated to Utah. If the objective is to maximize the number of customers served, new resources should be allocated to Oklahoma.

EXHIBIT 17.3			
MARKETING EFFORT ANALYSIS: REALLOCATION OF SELLING RESOURCES:			
	Utah	Arizona	Oklahoma
Dollar sales	$10,000	$18,000	$12,000
Number of orders	25	100	120
Average sales per order	$400	$180	$100

Variance Decomposition Analysis

Variance decomposition analysis is similar to the decomposition forecasting methods discussed in Chapter 15; its purpose is to break down the discrepancy between planned and actual results into their constituent parts.[2] The constituent parts identify the source of the problem and point toward solutions. Variance decomposition analysis is used to answer the third question posed at the beginning of this section: If the results are not what were expected, how can the firm identify the source of discrepancy from the plan?

An example of a variance decomposition analysis is shown in Exhibit 17.4. The first table shows a planned and actual income statement for a product. The second

EXHIBIT 17.4A			
VARIANCE DECOMPOSITION ANALYSIS			

Line	Operating Results for a New Industrial Product		
	Planned	Actual	Variance
Revenues			
Sales (units)	20,000	23,000	+3000
Price per unit	$10	$9.00	−$1.00
Revenues	$200,000	$207,000	+$7000
Total market (units)	50,000	100,000	+50,000
Market share	40%	23%	−17%
Costs			
Variable costs per unit	$3.50	$4.00	−$.50
Contribution			
Per unit ($)	$6.50	$5.00	−$1.50
Total	$130,000	$115,000	−$15,000

SOURCE: Adapted from James M. Hulbert and Norman E. Toy, "Strategic Framework for Marketing Control," *Journal of Marketing*, 40 (April 1977): 12–20.

EXHIBIT 17.4B
VARIANCE DECOMPOSITION ANALYSIS

Market volume variance = (actual total market units − planned total market units)
$\qquad$ × (planned market share) × (planned contribution per unit)
$\qquad$ = (100,000 − 50,000) × (.40) × ($6.5)
$\qquad$ = $130,000

Company share variance = (actual market share − planned market share)
$\qquad$ × (actual total market in units) × (planned contribution per unit)
$\qquad$ = (.23 − .40) × (100,000) × ($6.50)
$\qquad$ = −$110,500

Contribution variance = (actual contribution per unit − planned contribution per unit) × (actual sales in units)
$\qquad$ = ($5.00 − $6.5) × (23,000)
$\qquad$ = −$34,500

Total variance = market volume variance + company share variance + contribution variance
$\qquad$ = ($130,000 − $110,500) − $34,500
$\qquad$ = −$15,000

table shows the formulas for which the sources of the variances are identified. *Variances* are simply the differences between what was anticipated and what actually occurred. There are three types of variances: market volume variance, company share variance, and contribution variance.

Market volume variance is the extent to which the market size differs from what was anticipated. It shows the contribution the firm would have received had the estimate been accurate. **Company share variance** shows the financial consequences of overestimating or underestimating the company's market share. The **contribution variance** shows the effect any deviation from the expected contribution margin had on total contribution dollars. The **total variance** is the sum of all the variances.

The total variance in Exhibit 17.4 is −$15,000, but note that the analysis does not point out specific problems; rather, it shows areas where problems have occurred. It is up to management to identify the specific source of problems. Here are a few problem areas and their associated questions for further management analysis:

- The market forecast was only half of actual. What was the source of our forecasting error? Are our forecasting methods appropriate?
- Our share of the market is well below estimate. Who has the rest of the share? Is our competitive intelligence accurate?
- Contribution variance is negative. This can be caused by lower prices than anticipated or higher costs than anticipated. In this case, both events occurred—prices were lower and costs were higher than anticipated. Is the market more price sensitive than we had supposed? Can we reduce costs by increasing volume?

CONTROLLING DISTRIBUTORS

Another important control issue in sales is the determination of which distributors are making the most important contribution to the firm's overall selling effort. Distributors can be wholesalers who purchase products for resale or manufacturers' reps who simply act as agents for the manufacturer. Other examples of distributors and agents can be found in Chapter 8. Firms must evaluate distributors' performance to ensure that their sales objectives are being met. The evaluation must provide management with the information necessary to determine which distributors should be retained and which should be dropped. For those that are being retained, the firm must determine what training efforts or other programs are most appropriate for each distributor.

Two methods for making decisions regarding distributors are distributor portfolio analysis (DPA) and the channel dependence matrix (CDM).[3] These two methods are complementary. They allow firms to classify their distributors for the purpose of retention or termination and to determine their position in different channels, respectively.

Distributor Portfolio Analysis

Distributor portfolio analysis (DPA) is a technique that allows firms to assess their distributors and make retention/termination decisions and resource allocation deci-

EXHIBIT 17.5

DISTRIBUTOR PORTFOLIO ANALYSIS

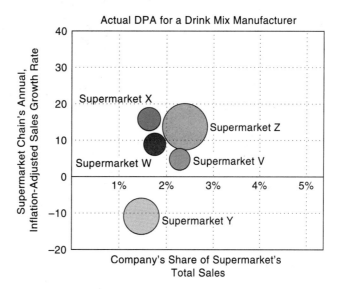

SOURCE: Adapted from Peter R. Dickson, "Distributor Portfolio Analysis and the Channel Dependence Matrix: New Techniques for Understanding and Managing the Channel," *Journal of Marketing*, 47 (Summer 1983): 35–44.

sions for those it chooses to retain. As you can see in the sample DPA for a soft drink manufacturer in Exhibit 17.5, a DPA plots distributors on two axes. The vertical axis measures the distributor's rate of sales growth after adjusting for inflation. This dimension indicates the extent to which the distributor is maintaining, increasing, or decreasing its share of the market. The horizontal axis assesses the manufacturer's share of the distributor's sales of that particular product line. A high share of a distributor's sales indicates that the manufacturer is a key supplier. Lower share indicates that the manufacturer is less important as a supplier.

Distributors are represented by circles. The area of each circle is proportional to the manufacturer's sales of the product being analyzed to that of the distributor. In this DPA, supermarkets W, X, V, and Z are growing, while Y has negative growth. Of the growing supermarkets, the soft drink manufacturer has the largest share of the sale from supermarkets' V and Z. Supermarket Z is the largest, which is reflected by the size of the circle representing it.

A DPA can be extremely useful to a seller. It aids in determining which distributors represent important outlets. It also shows which distributors are experiencing increasing or decreasing market share. This information can be essential when deciding which distributors to retain. If a distributor who is a major customer for the seller becomes less competitive, the seller will inevitably begin to see erosion in market share and quality of customer service to the end user. Before that occurs, the seller needs to cultivate another distributor to take over the business from the dis-

---

EXHIBIT 17.6

DISTRIBUTOR PORTFOLIO ANALYSIS

		Company's Share of Distributor's Product Line	
		Low	High
Distributor's Inflation-Adjusted Growth Rate	High	Offensive investment	Defensive retrenchment
	Low	Abandonment strategy	Strategic retreat

SOURCE: Peter R. Dickson, "Distributor Portfolio Analysis and the Channel Dependence Matrix: New Techniques for Understanding and Managing the Channel," *Journal of Marketing*, 47 (Summer 1983): 35–44.

---

tributor who is becoming less competitive. Exhibit 17.6 shows the four strategies sellers can use with distributors that are experiencing increasing or decreasing market share and that represent high or low share of the seller's products: (1) offensive investment, (2) defensive entrenchment, (3) strategic retreat, and (4) abandonment.

Offensive Investment.   The **offensive investment strategy** is used when the distributor is growing rapidly but the seller's product line represents a relatively small proportion of the distributor's total sales in that product area. This strategy should be used with supermarket X in Exhibit 17.5. Sellers should seek to increase their share of the distributors' total sales of that product category because these distributors represent attractive growth opportunities within the market. Other suppliers already have significant positions with these distributors, however, so the seller has to pursue growth aggressively. This might entail development of unique product offerings, special training programs, special discounts, or some other approach that would increase the seller's share of the distributors' sales of that product.

Defensive Entrenchment.   **Defensive entrenchment strategy** is appropriate with a distributor that is growing and that already has a substantial relationship with the seller. This strategy would be appropriate for supermarket Z in Exhibit 17.5. The manufacturer must keep a close watch on the distributor to ensure that no competitor tries to convert the distributor away from the seller's product line. The key here is to maintain market share by finding ways to increase the strength of the relationship between the distributor and the seller. However, this must be done while conserving costs. The reason for conserving costs is that this relationship is a source of resources for developing new relationships and converting distributors who are currently carrying competitors' products. As a result, if all revenues from the distributor are spent in maintaining the relationship, the seller will not have resources to pursue new distributors in new markets or to replace distributors that are not performing well in existing markets.

Strategic Retreat.   **Strategic retreat strategy** is pursued with distributors that have low growth rates and whose sales in a product line are composed of the seller's products. This strategy might be appropriate for supermarket V in Exhibit 17.5. The reason for the retreat is that the distributor is losing its competitive position in the marketplace. If the seller continues to rely on this distributor to serve a given market, the seller's position in that market will also be at risk. Therefore, the seller must either find a means to help the distributor to become more competitive or begin to look for a new distributor that can take over the market.

Abandonment. **Abandonment strategy** is appropriate when the distributor is a weak competitor and when the seller's product line comprises only a small percentage of the distributor's total sales of that product category. This strategy appears appropriate for supermarket Y in Exhibit 17.5. This is a bad position for the seller. The distributor does not have a strong market position, and the seller does not have much leverage over the distributor because the seller's product line is only a small proportion of the distributor's sales in that product category. The best move for the seller here is to try to find a replacement distributor as quickly as possible.

Channel Dependence Matrix

Another technique for controlling channels, the **channel dependence matrix (CDM),** depicts the market share of different sellers and distributors to show which sellers and which distributors have power in which channels. *Power* is assessed according to the extent to which one firm relies on another. For example, if a seller depends on one distributor to represent its products, that distributor has power over the seller because the seller does not have an alternate route to market. Conversely, if a distributor carries only one seller's products in a given product area, that distributor is dependent on the seller. Therefore, the seller has power over that distributor.

A sample CDM representing the share relationships among five distributors and four sellers is shown in Exhibit 17.7. The numbers in the cells are market shares. The row and column totals are the seller's and the distributor's market shares, respectively.

The CDM can be used in several ways to complement DPA. First, the sellers' and distributors' market shares show the extent to which the market is concentrated. Market concentration is important because if a few sellers account for disproportionate market share, they can exert power over the distributors. Conversely, to the extent that market share is concentrated among a few distributors, distributors can exert power over the sellers. In either case, the firm(s) with power can direct the behavior of other channel members.

Second, the CDM allows sellers to assess the likely impact of increasing or decreasing resources devoted to certain distributors. It also allows sellers to determine how a competitor will react to their attempts to change the level of share through a certain distributor. Assume that seller 3 in Exhibit 17.7 is looking for the best distributor through which to increase market share. Seller 3 sells through distributors' A, D, and E. It would make little sense to try to grow by increasing share through distributor E because distributor E represents only 10 percent of the total market. Even if seller 3 could double its sales through distributor E, it would realize a share increase of only 5 points. Also, since seller 4 sells only through distributors A and E, and distributor E accounts for half of seller 4's sales, seller 4 would probably react strongly to any attempt by seller 3 to increase its sales through distributor E. If seller 3 wants to increase sales, it might want to use distributor D. Distributor D has higher market share than distributor E, and its sales are evenly split among sellers 1,

EXHIBIT 17.7
CHANNEL DEPENDENCE MATRIX

	Distributor					
Seller	A	B	C	D	E	Total
1	5	10	20	10	0	45
2	5	0	10	10	0	25
3	5	0	0	10	5	20
4	5	0	0	0	5	10
Total	20	10	30	30	10	100

SOURCE: Adapted from Peter R. Dickson, "Distributor Portfolio Analysis and the Channel Dependence Matrix: New Techniques for Understanding and Managing the Channel," *Journal of Marketing,* 47 (Summer 1983): 35–44.

2, and 3. Sellers 1 and 2 have alternate routes to market in that they both sell through other distributors. As a result, seller 3 might be able to siphon off sales from sellers 1 and 2 without exciting strong competitive responses. Increasing its sales by 50 percent through distributor D would be the same as doubling its sales through distributor E.

Using DPA and CDM together allows a firm to determine its position relative to others in the channel and to determine the likely result of any effort to influence other channel members. If, for example, the soft drink manufacturer in Exhibit 17.5 wanted to increase its sales to rapidly growing distributors, it would focus on supermarkets V and Z. They are growing rapidly, and the manufacturer constitutes a large share of their sales. Supermarkets W and X, while rapidly growing, are not as dependent on the manufacturer for their products. Therefore, W and X would probably be less likely than V and Z to act in accordance with the manufacturer's wishes.

CONTROLLING CUSTOMERS

Firms control customers through periodic analysis and monitoring. To ensure their sales justify the expense of the selling approach that is used to serve them, firms must carefully analyze customers. For example, if a firm serves a customer through national account management, it is important to organize financial data by account so that the firm can determine account profitability. These reports must include not only revenue information but cost information as well.[4] One approach to key (or national) account analysis involves developing reports that show the total net sales, discounts, gross profit, trade promotion expenses, salesforce costs, distribution costs, and trading profit.[5] This allows the seller to determine the profitability of each account.

Another technique for analyzing customers is shown in Exhibit 17.8. This technique allows the seller to compare its customers in terms of two dimensions: (1) total purchases in a given product category and (2) percentage of purchases accounted for by the seller's product line. Like CDM and DPA, the value of this analysis is that it categorizes buyers as to the direction of power between the buyers and the seller.

The primary use of this technique is to give the seller an idea of the appropriate strategy for customers in each quadrant.

For buyers in the upper left-hand quadrant, where the seller has a low share of the customer's high total purchases, the seller has a significant opportunity. The seller should investigate the cause of the failure to attain higher sales and make appropriate adjustments. The primary selling task becomes converting the buyer away from existing competing suppliers.

For buyers in the upper right-hand quadrant, where the seller has a high share of a large customer's purchases, the seller should continue to make product improvements so as to forestall competitive encroachment. The appropriate selling task is maintaining the customer relationship.

For buyers in the lower left-hand quadrant, the seller has a low share, but the buyer's total purchases are also low. As a result, the opportunity available to the seller, even if significant selling efforts were made, are limited. In this case the seller should not put significant additional resources into securing the rest of the buyer's business.

In the lower right-hand quadrant, the buyer purchases a large proportion of its requirements from the seller. However, its total purchases are relatively small. The seller should seek to maintain the business, but extraordinary efforts to increase business are inappropriate because the level of purchases is already high.

One of the important reasons for performing customer analysis is to determine whether the level of selling resources devoted to a particular customer is cost-justified. Another is to ensure that the seller avoids becoming controlled by the customer. Some firms have become so close to their customers that they are substituting what is good for their customers in place of their own corporate goals. This is fine in principle, but customers merge, go out of business, switch to alternate technologies, and switch suppliers. By building the entire firm around existing customers, the firm runs a serious risk if the customer base changes. To avoid becoming customer-controlled, sellers should take steps to ensure that they stay abreast of market trends and maintain sufficient organizational flexibility so that if the customer base does change, they are not caught flat-footed.[6] These steps include maintaining an active environmental scanning system, monitoring changes in the industry or technology that might foreshadow changes in the customer base, and putting someone in charge of making sure environmental monitoring actually takes place. As stated in Chapter 16, active environmental scanning is an important responsibility of the salesforce.

EXHIBIT 17.8		
CUSTOMER ANALYSIS		

		Seller's Share of Customer's Purchases	
		Low	High
Customer's Total Purchases	High	High opportunity for seller; try to convert customer	Aggressively maintain; look for new applications; develop closer relationships
	Low	Maintain	Maintain

CONTROLLING THE SALESFORCE

The **sales budget** is the statement of revenues and costs that are expected for a given time period. Sales budgets are among the most important control devices available to sales managers. Sales budgets allow managers to monitor whether sales costs are consistent or appropriate for the level of expected sales. This section covers several important issues regarding sales budgeting; the importance of sales budgeting, the components of the sales budget, the means of setting budgets, and the extent to which budgets are set from the bottom up or the top down, what level of flexibility should exist, and what level of detail should be provided.

Importance of Sales Budgets

Firms need sales budgets for a variety of reasons, including planning, coordination, control, and evaluation.

Planning.   Budgeting is an integral part of the overall planning process. "Good budgets are part of good planning," says Jack Wilner, president of Wilner and Associates in North Carolina and former training director for Blue Bell/Wrangler.[7] Budgets can be used as part of the planning process during the evaluation of alternative phases of strategy implementation, discussed in Chapter 16. If managers have several different alternatives, the cost of each alternative can be calculated and compared directly. The widespread availability of spreadsheet software allows managers to perform "what-if" analyses quickly and easily when constructing sales budgets. Heublein, Inc., a large manufacturer and distributor of beverages and spirits, has reduced the amount of time necessary to create and calculate a budget to about 2 hours using spreadsheet software.[8] It is important to recognize, however, that the process of calculating a budget takes much less time than negotiating the amounts and deciding which manager will be responsible for which costs.

Coordination.   Budgets allow coordination across the organization and among different selling approaches. As discussed in Chapter 15, the sales forecast is used to develop sales revenue estimates. These estimates are used by departments ranging from human resources to finance to develop everything from human resources planning models to capital budgets (budgets for the purchase of plant and equipment) and cash flow analyses (used to determine if the firm needs to borrow cash to meet financial needs). The sales revenue estimate is also used by production to develop manufacturing and shipping schedules that will ensure needed levels of inventory to meet customer service standards.

Within the marketing function, sales budgets are used to indicate the level of emphasis the firm or business unit wishes to place on sales as opposed to other means of communicating with customers. The sales budget should be considered in light of the budget for public relations, advertising, and sales promotions to ensure the appropriate resources are allocated to each element of the promotion mix.

Within the sales area, sales budgets are used to coordinate efforts between different selling approaches. There are trade-offs, for example, between the number of field salespeople, the use of independent distributors, the number of telemarketing representatives, and the number of national account representatives. The trade-offs between the use of a field salesforce and independent representatives were discussed in detail in Chapter 8. Since different selling methods vary in costs and are capable of providing different levels of customer service to different customer types, the costs of the various combinations must be calculated and compared. This process of *costing out* various combinations involves the construction of possible sales budgets for each combination.

Control. Sales budgets are used to constrain the level of expenditures. Without a budget, sales managers have no guides as to the expected amount of money they can spend to generate a given level of sales. In short, the budget serves as a guide for spending. Without this guide, a manager might spend 70 percent of his or her resources during the first 50 percent of the budget time period. As a result, the manager would run out of money before the end of the budget period. The budget also allows sales managers to track the source of profitability problems. If profitability for a product or a department is down, the manager can look to the budget to see if the cause is inadequate revenue or excess expenses. The cause is quite important because inadequate revenues lead to one set of solutions, whereas excess expenses lead to another.

Evaluation. The final use of budgets is to evaluate management performance. Managers are often compensated on the extent to which they meet budget. In essence, the sales budget provides a benchmark for performance. Managers are typically thought to be good performers if they can achieve the budgeted levels of sales while not exceeding the budgeted sales expenses.

Categories of a Sales Budget

The sales budget contains two major categories: revenue and expenses. **Sales revenue** is the total income expected in the period for which the budget is developed. It is typically derived from the sales forecast (for a review of methods to derive sales forecasts, see Chapter 15.) Sales forecasts can be in dollars or units. If it is in dollars, the number can be transferred from the forecast to the budget. If the sales forecast is in units, revenue can be obtained by multiplying the number of units to be sold by the estimated average price per unit.

Sales expenses are the specific dollar expenditures on selling and sales management that are required to generate the forecasted revenues. Sales expenses can be a large percentage of expected sales revenues. IBM, for example, finds that selling expenses account for approximately 30 percent of revenue from sales. This leaves 70 percent of total sales revenue to cover all other corporate expenses, including the cost of goods sold, all indirect expenses (such as general administration and indirect labor and material costs), and profits. Given that sales expenses can consume such a large part of a firm's revenues, it is important for top management to know how the money is spent and to ensure that the firm allocates selling resources in accordance with the marketing plan.

Sales expenses may include (but are not limited to) the following line items: salesforce compensation (salaries, bonuses, commissions); travel and entertainment expenses (includes lodging, meals, and travel); salaries and expenses of sales support staff (order trackers, customer service reps, sales trainers, and billing specialists); selling aids (catalogs, brochures, price lists, samples, and promotional materials); trade show expenses (booth rentals, hospitality expenses); training expenses (training materials and travel costs); customer training seminars; and sales administration (sales manager salaries, clerical and staff salaries). Salaries, bonuses, and commissions are typically the largest portion of the sales budget, generally followed by travel and entertainment (T&E).

Sales managers assign different priorities to different categories of the sales budget. Speaking as members of an expert panel for *Sales and Marketing Management*, Robert Weiss, sales manager for American Paging in Minneapolis, and Fred Riddell, southwest regional manager for Teledyne Post in Texas, say that their top priority for the sales budget is salesperson compensation. Low-priority items, according to Jack Wilner of Wilner and Associates, are sales meetings. Sales meetings are not as important as in the past because they can be conducted by phone or teleconferencing.[9] The same panelists, when asked where they would allocate excess funds, mentioned salesforce automation and salesforce training as high-priority items.

Setting Sales Budgets

Given that sales budgets play an important role in planning, control, coordination, and evaluation, determining the sales budget level is an important responsibility for sales managers. Several methods are available for managers to use in constructing sales budgets.[10] These methods include all-you-can-afford, percentage of sales, industry parity, objective-and-task, zero-base budgeting, and return on investment. Each of these methods has strengths and weaknesses. Often, sales managers use a combination of approaches to triangulate on the most appropriate sales budget level. The following paragraphs examine the development of a sales budget using each of these method.

All-You-Can-Afford.   **All-you-can-afford budgeting** is a simple method whereby the sales budget consists of funds left over after all other operations have been budgeted. This approach, simple and easy to determine, has a number of significant flaws. First, it does not take into account the marginal utility of funds spent on sales. If the sales budget is inadequate, direct selling efforts might be insufficient to meet the needs of customers. The level of postsale service might also be inadequate to ensure repeat business. On the other hand, if the sales budget is excessive, money is being spent on sales that could be spent better elsewhere. All in all, owing to the serious flaws in its use, the all-you-can-afford method should be avoided if at all possible.

Percentage Of Sales.   **Percentage of sales budgeting** is a method whereby the sales budget is set as a percent of the sales projected for the coming period. For example, if sales are projected to be $2 million for the coming period, and the firm sets its sales budget at 15 percent of sales, the sales budget will be $300,000.

Percentage of sales is probably the most popular method of setting the sales budget. It is quick, simple, and easy to calculate and understand. If the percentage base remains the same from time period to time period, it also makes the manager's job of "selling" the budget to higher levels of management quite simple.

Unfortunately, percentage of sales also suffers from serious flaws. Conceptually, the percent of sales reverses the relationship between sales and selling effort. Using this budget approach, sales budget (selling effort) is set as a function of sales. In reality, sales is a function of selling effort, not the other way around. The percent of sales method also fails to take into account possible changes in the competitive environment—including changes in technology or changes in the customer base—or the objectives of the selling effort. If technology becomes more complex or customers begin to demand higher levels of service, the percent of sales that should be devoted to selling effort should increase. Yet the percentage of sales method relies on historical cost of sales ratios. The historical trend, by definition, lags in taking into account the most recent developments in the market. Therefore, setting the budget using historical trends fails to provide the level of resources that are necessary to obtain sales in the current market environment. If the budget is set using historical cost of sales ratios in such a market, sales levels will erode, thereby reducing the sales budget even more over time. Lower sales budgets will lead to even less customer satisfaction, which will lead to even lower sales, and so on.

The objectives of the selling effort might also change, necessitating a change in the sales budget. If a firm has traditionally used a face-to-face field salesforce and switches to a combination of telemarketing and face-to-face, the old ratios no longer apply. Similarly if a new market is identified, the sales budget might need to be temporarily increased to penetrate the new market. If the sales budget is not increased, it may not be possible to provide salespeople with adequate compensation to encourage them to pursue the new market.

Industry Parity.   **Industry parity budgeting** is a type of percentage of sales in which the firm sets its sales budget using industry averages. Industry averages for 19 industries are shown in Exhibit 17.9. Averages are provided for salesforce compensation, salesforce travel and entertainment expense, total salesforce expenses, and total selling expenses. These averages provide a benchmark for developing sales budgets for firms in the industry.

Like percentage of sales, industry parity also suffers from several flaws, including availability, timeliness, competitor omniscience, and fostering of selling mediocrity. Firms may have difficulty finding industry data, particularly if the industry is new or changing rapidly. Firms must also realize that the data may not be timely. Firms that use data from the 1994 *Sales and Marketing Management* survey are actually using data collected in 1993 based on 1992 sales budgets. If major market changes have occurred during that time span, the usability of the data may be suspect. Using industry parity also assumes competitor omniscience. In other words, for firms to rely on industry parity to set their budgets, they must assume that their competitors know what they are doing. If they do not, or if the competitors' own sales efforts are mediocre, the firm may be condemning itself to sales mediocrity as well.

Last, the use of industry parity precludes building a distinctive competency by using the salesforce. If a firm sets its budget based on the average amount budgeted by competing firms, the firm is setting its budget based on the performance of all competing firms, regardless of whether their selling efforts are good, bad, or mediocre. It is very difficult for a firm to build a distinctive competency using selling effort if budget is merely based on the average selling effort of other firms. This flaw

EXHIBIT 17.9

SALESFORCE BUDGET RATIOS BY INDUSTRY

Industry	Salesforce Compensation	Salesforce Travel and Entertainment Expenses	Total Salesforce Expenses	Total Selling Expenses
Consumer Goods				
Durable goods	1.8	0.7	2.5	6.3
Ethical drugs, surgical items	3.4	1.6	5.0	6.9
Food	1.4	0.5	1.9	2.7
Major household items	1.8	0.6	2.5	5.8
Consumer goods average	2.1	0.8	2.9	5.4
Industrial Goods				
Automotive parts	2.2	0.7	2.9	2.1
Building materials	1.2	0.3	1.5	2.4
Chemicals	1.6	0.5	2.1	3.1
Computers	1.5	0.4	1.9	2.9
Containers	0.4	0.2	0.6	1.1
Electrical equipment	1.5	0.5	2.0	5.4
Electronics	2.2	1.6	3.8	4.2
Fabricated metals (heavy)	1.5	0.5	2.0	1.9
Fabricated metals (light)	2.0	0.7	2.7	6.4
Fabrics and apparel	2.1	0.7	2.8	4.5
Iron and steel	0.8	0.3	1.1	1.8
Machinery (heavy)	2.1	0.8	2.9	5.8
Machinery (light)	1.3	1.2	2.5	8.5
Office equipment	8.2	1.2	9.4	10.4
Printing	5.5	1.1	6.6	7.0
Industrial goods average	2.3	0.7	3.0	4.5

SOURCE: "Sales Force Selling Expenses as a Percentage of Sales," *Sales and Marketing Management* (February 17, 1986): 56.

leads to an important question: What are the objectives the firm is trying to achieve with its selling efforts? If the firm is trying to use selling effort as a basis for developing a distinctive competence, it should develop a sales budget that allocates resources based on the specific objectives for the selling effort. That is the basis for the next sales budgeting approach: objective and task.

Objective-and-Task.   The **objective-and-task budgeting** method does not look at historical trends, as do the percentage of sales and industry parity approaches. Rather, it requires managers to state specific objectives, identify the tasks necessary to accomplish these objectives, and determine the budget required to perform the tasks. Exhibit 17.10 shows a simplified objective-and-task budgeting process. In this example, the manager is using two selling methods—telemarketing and field sales—to determine the needed budget to meet the sales objectives. The primary advantage of the objective-and-task budgeting approach is that it considers the firm's selling goals. The budget is derived based on a link between tasks performed and the selling objectives of the firm.

	EXHIBIT 17.10			
	OBJECTIVE-AND-TASK SALES BUDGET APPROACH			
Task	Telemarketing Calls	Telemarketing Costs ($25/Call)	Field Sales Calls	Field Sales Costs ($225/Call)
Objective 1: Sell $20 million of current product to existing customers				
Routine reorders	10,000	$250,000	100	$22,500
Billing issues	1,000	$25,000	100	$25,000
Order tracking	1,000	$25,000	100	$25,000
Routine service	1,000	$25,000	50	$12,500
Look for new applications of existing products	100	$2,500	250	$56,250
Total	13,000	$327,500	600	$141,250
Objective 2: Sell $5 million of current product to new customers				
Prospecting	5,000	$125,000	250	$56,250
Preparing requests for bids	1,000	$25,000	100	$22,500
Sending promotional materials	1,000	$25,000	0	0
Closing sales	100	$2,500	500	$112,500
Training users	0	0	250	$56,250
Training distributor personnel	0	0	100	$22,500
Total	7,100	$177,500	1,200	$270,000

Flaws of the objective-and-task method include the difficulty of determining the relationship between the task and the objective, as well as the difficulty of determining the value of accomplishing a given objective. If a firm does not have experience at the relationship between the task and the objective for a given selling method in a given market, the budgeted amounts could be incorrect. For example, a firm that enters a new market under the assumption that the average number of sales calls to close a sale is four but finds that it actually takes five has underestimated the number of sales calls by 25 percent. Accordingly, if the salesforce is paid on salary, the number of salespeople has been underestimated by 25 percent; therefore, the compensation budget line has been underestimated by 25 percent as well.

Determining the value of reaching a certain objective can be difficult. Assume, for example, that a firm sets an objective that 40 percent of the potential market be aware of its products. The salesforce makes the required number of calls to achieve a 40 percent market awareness of their products, but only 10 percent of those customers buy. The firm's market share, therefore, is 4 percent (40% × 10%). The question now facing management is whether there was a link between the 40 percent awareness and the 10 percent purchase rate. Would the 4 percent share have occurred with 30 percent or 20 percent awareness? Unless the firm has established clear links between objectives and outcomes, it may be difficult to show the profitability of the task of making customers aware of the product.

Zero-Base Budget.   **Zero-base budgeting (ZBB)** is a process that disregards historical patterns and previous budgets. Each period starts with a budget of zero, and sales managers are required to justify all amounts in terms of specific objectives or programs that are to be offered in the coming budget period. One of the most vocal supporters of ZBB was Jimmy Carter, former president of the United States. His argument for ZBB was as follows:

> In contrast to the traditional budgeting approach of incrementing the new on the old, zero-base budgeting demands a total rejustification of everything from zero. It means chopping up the organization into individual functions and analyzing each annually, regardless of whether it is 50 years old or a brand-new proposal for a future program. The budget is broken into units called decision packages, prepared by managers at each level. These packages cover every existing or proposed activity of each department. They include analyses of purpose, costs, measures of performance and benefits, alternative courses of actions, and consequences of disapproval.[11]

Although the concept of ZBB is appealing from the standpoint that all spending must be justified before any money is allocated, in practice this method can be extremely cumbersome. Managers spend their time developing budgets and presentations to higher management to justify their budget amounts. Developing the budget becomes an extremely time-consuming task. As a result, few firms use this method, although sales managers with government contracts may encounter it.

Return on Investment.   The **return on investment (ROI) budgeting** method treats expenditures on developing customer relationships as long-term investments. As a long-term investment, sales expenditures should compete with other long-term investment options for funds. The ROI budgeting method addresses a problem common to all methods discussed so far: the matching of revenue to expense. Sales expenditures often have a carryover effect. That is, sales expenditures incurred today may not generate revenue until some point in the future. In industries where purchase cycle times are long, such as supercomputers and machine tools, sales expenditures today may not yield sales revenue until 3 to 5 years in the future. All the budgeting approaches so far, however, have assumed that sales expenditures for the current period result in sales revenues for the current period. No carryover effects are assumed.

Using the ROI method requires the manager to calculate **return on assets managed (ROAM)**, which consists of two ratios: sales/investment and profit/sales (in dollars).[12] Sales/investment shows how efficiently the assets (investment) are used. *Investment* can consist of additional equipment, training, inventory, or any other assets that are required to implement the alternative. The higher the sales/investment ratio, the more efficient the use of the assets. Profit/sales shows the profitability per dollar of sales. Higher ratios show higher profits being earned per sales dollar. ROAM is the product of sales/investment and profit/sales. Therefore, comparing alternate courses of action on ROAM allows for the simultaneous consideration of efficiency and profitability when making decisions.

ROAM offers sales managers the ability to make decisions, such as choices among alternatives in opening new sales offices and the use of different combinations of selling methods. Exhibit 17.11 shows a ROAM analysis comparing the profitability of three proposed new office locations. In Exhibit 17.11, ROAM is the final row. The alternative with the highest ROAM is Tulsa. In order to determine

EXHIBIT 17.11			
ROAM COMPARING POTENTIAL SALES OFFICES			
Projected	Tulsa	New Orleans	Memphis
Sales	$200,000	$300,000	$240,000
Cost of goods sold	$100,000	$150,000	$120,000
Gross margin	$100,000	$150,000	$120,000
Selling costs[a]	$50,000	$80,000	$50,000
Profit	$50,000	$70,000	$60,000
Accounts receivable	$25,000	$55,000	$50,000
Inventories	$35,000	$35,000	$50,000
Total investment	$60,000	$90,000	$100,000
Sales/investment	3.3	3.3	2.4
Profit/sales	25%	23%	30%
ROAM[b]	83%	78%	70%

[a]Assume no other costs.

[b]ROAM = (profit/sales) × (sales/investment)

Decision Rule:. Select the option with the highest ROAM, in this case, Tulsa.

which offices should be opened, the firm would compare ROAM of the offices with ROAM of other proposed projects. Depending on the minimum acceptable level of ROAM and the total resources available to the firm, one, two, or three offices could be opened.

Combination. Some firms use a combination of budgeting approaches. Rich Connell, sales director for SmithKline Beecham Clinical Laboratories in Michigan, uses a combination of percentage of sales and objective-and-task to set his sales budget. To develop a budget for the upcoming year, Connell adds a 6 to 8 percent increase over the current level of expenses to cover increases in insurance, salaries, and materials. Then he takes into account any new products or major new projects the division is planning. Last, he puts in an unallocated amount to take into account add-on programs and expansions.[13] The combination approach allows Connell to take advantage of the ease of percentage of sales, with the flexibility and stronger logic of objective-and-task.

Top-Down Versus Bottom-Up Budgeting

There are two basic approaches to setting sales budgets: top-down or bottom-up. In the **top-down budgeting** approach, top management determines budget levels, and sales management is charged with developing a budget that will meet sales objectives while staying within the overall budget parameters. American Paging in Minneapolis follows the top-down approach. Senior corporate managers meet for an entire week to determine the overall sales budget. Sales managers are then responsible for allocating the sales budget into specific activities to accomplish sales objectives.[14] Conversely, in the **bottom-up budgeting** approach sales managers are charged with determining the specific budget requirements to accomplish given sales objectives.

Both approaches to setting sales budgets have advantages. The top-down approach allows top management to set overall budget levels based on the firm's financial position. It also allows top management to recognize explicitly the relationship between corporate objectives and budget levels. The bottom-up approach, by contrast, allows sales managers—who are closer to the customer—to specify the resources they need to accomplish their sales objectives. Another advantage of the bottom-up approach is that managers are more likely to accept and feel responsible for a budget that they had a hand in developing. In practice, many firms combine the two approaches. They solicit needed budgets from sales managers, and top management sets budgets based on requests from all managers.[15]

Budget Flexibility

Flexibility is necessary in sales budgeting. Environmental circumstances change over the budget period, necessitating changes in overall levels of sales budgets or reallocations of funds within the budget. Firms that do not allow flexibility force managers to be less than realistic in preparing budgets. As a result, the managers may be tempted to underestimate revenues and overestimate expenses to give themselves flexibility in reaching sales revenue and profitability goals.

Budget flexibility does not mean that sales managers should be able to change budgets at will, however, because such freedom will reduces the incentive to keep a close eye on expenses and may allow managers to hide problems until they become major. Rather, budget flexibility is necessary to cope with new responsibilities or market changes that occur during the budget period.

Sales budget flexibility can be achieved through several means. For one, sales managers can develop *multiple budgets,* based on optimistic, pessimistic, and most likely market conditions. This is cumbersome, however, and can lead to confusion as to which budget applies. Another method is to prepare rolling budgets. *Rolling budgets* adjust the expected revenues and expenses periodically over the course of the budget period. Suppose a company budgets on an annual basis. In this case, sales managers prepare rolling budgets by breaking the budget into shorter periods, such as monthly or quarterly. If the managers prepare quarterly rolling budgets, they can assess the extent to which the sales budget is being met on a quarter-by-quarter basis. If expenses are higher than anticipated in a given quarter, management is alerted to the existence of a possible problem, such as inefficient use of selling resources or market changes that are rendering the allocation of budget resources inappropriate. Without a rolling budget, the existence of a problem might not be detected until the following budget cycle. By pinpointing the problem early, steps can be taken to reduce or increase selling expenses, as the case required, to put the firm back on track.

Level of Detail

The level of detail is the extent to which budgets are made specific. Highly detailed budgets specify how all resources will be spent; less-detailed budgets give little information as to how the resources will be spent. Each type of budget has advantages and disadvantages. Detailed budgets allow top management to monitor expenses closely, whereas less detailed budgets provide little information to top management.

Detailed budgets, however, give the operating manager very little flexibility in real-locating resources if necessary. Detailed budgets also increase the time sales managers and sales representatives must spend on budgeting.

The level of detail depends on several issues. First, the total level of selling expenses has an effect—higher levels of selling expenses probably necessitate higher levels of detail in budgeting. Higher levels of detail are also diagnostic in that they offer management greater insight as to potential sources of problems if expenses are too high or sales revenue does not reach targeted levels.

Potential Problems in Budgeting

There are several potential problems with developing sales budgets. The problems include poor forecasts, overreliance on historical trends, and politicization of the budget process.

Poor Forecasts. The quality of the budget depends on the quality of the sales forecast. If the sales revenue forecast is significantly different from actual market, the budget will be in error. Forecasts that are too high or too low can be problematic, as described in Chapter 15. If forecasts are too high, the firm will budget sales expenses to cover the high level of expected sales. When the sales do not materialize, the firm must radically reduce the budget. This can be quite difficult if many expenses are fixed. For example, if a firm uses salaries to compensate its salespeople, the only way to significantly reduce salesforce compensation is to fire salespeople. This has obvious negative consequences for the current period. It also has negative consequences for future periods, because the firm will have to make higher than expected training and recruiting expenditures to replace those salespeople. Conversely, forecasts that are too low will result in an insufficient sales budget to meet customer demand. This creates a window for competitors to enter the market and establish a position with customers who are not receiving the level of service they need.

Overreliance on Historical Trends. Using budget approaches that rely on historical averages, such as percentage of sales and competitive parity, can lead to serious problems in the event that the characteristics of the market change significantly. Yet the ease of the historical budget average approaches can lull managers into continuing their use even when the market has changed, with potentially disastrous results.

The use of historic budget averages also precludes the development of new ways to communicate with the market. For example, if the firm has a field salesforce and develops its budget using percentage of sales, it will not have sufficient resources to initiate a national accounts program. Conversely, a firm that uses percentage of sales will not be encouraged to use selling methods that reduce selling costs, such as telemarketing. The use of historical trends for these firms can become a formidable obstacle to changing business practices.

Politicization. A third major problem that can arise during the budgeting process is politics. That is, it is possible for the budget to be assigned based on management's commitment to a project or the persuasive power of a particular manager, rather than on the merits of the product. Politics becomes a problem when the level of detail demanded is great and management places a great deal of value on meeting

---

BOX 17.1

SALESFORCE AUDIT QUIZ

Instructions: *Answer each question with "Yes" or "No." Keep track of your responses.*

1. Our salespeople have more sales leads than they are able to handle.
2. Our sales organization uses both field and telephone salespeople.
3. We have a specific sales process and our salespeople understand and use it.
4. Our salespeople are trained in sales presentation methods and tools and use them.
5. We have a formal sales training program in place to develop product and industry knowledge, as well as selling skills.
6. We have a formal program for reporting sales activity.
7. Our salespeople know how they are being measured in areas other than revenue.
8. Our sales manager conducts regular in-field coaching sessions on an individual basis with salespeople.
9. We have a formal program in place to develop our salespeople's skills.
10. Our sales compensation plan promotes the proper product mix and rewards high performance and penalizes low performance.
11. We regularly communicate product and industry update information to our salespeople.
12. Our salespeople provide regular product and industry feedback in writing.
13. Our product is being represented in the best possible manner by our salespeople.
14. Our salespeople report on sales that we lost and why.
15. Our salespeople have a program to contact accounts that should be buying but are not.
16. We all know which accounts should be buying but are not.
17. Our company has a formal performance improvement program to prescribe help and set minimum acceptable levels of sales performance.
18. Our salespeople are satisfied with their territories.
19. Our sales organization maintains the best use of its time.
20. Our sales organization uses computers and contact management software.

Scoring: The more "Yes" answers, the better
18–20 "Yes" answers—Outstanding selling effort
16–17 "Yes" answers—Strong selling effort—could be selectively improved
14–15 "Yes" answers—Good selling effort—some improvement needed
13 and below—Mediocre to poor selling effort—need serious analysis of correct selling practices

---

the budget in performance appraisal and compensation. In those cases, the sales manager is almost forced to build some slack into the budget to cover emergencies. Building such slack into the budget, however, reduces the credence top management can place on the budget and renders the budget-making process one of trying to "slip something over" on top management rather than providing an accurate picture of the resources necessary to accomplish the sales objectives.[16]

SALES AND MARKETING AUDITS

Marketing effort analysis, distributor portfolio analysis, channel dependence matrix, customer analysis, and sales budgets are important techniques for control, but they address only specific areas or issues and there are few specific links among them. A more comprehensive approach to controlling the sales effort is to perform a sales audit. **Sales audits** are comprehensive reviews of the firm's selling effort that allow the firm to identify underlying problems in the selling approach and salesforce, improve effectiveness and profitability, and ensure that customer needs are being met. A sample sales audit is shown in Box 17.1. In this sales audit, sales managers score themselves in terms of how well they meet certain goals. This audit could also be used by top management or by an outside auditor to ensure that the salesforce is operating at maximum effectiveness and efficiency.

EXHIBIT 17.12

COMPONENTS OF A MARKETING AUDIT

1. Macro-environment
   a. Economic-demographic
   b. Technology
   c. Political-legal
   d. Social-cultural
2. Task environment
   a. Markets
   b. Customers
   c. Competitors
   d. Distributors and dealers
   e. Suppliers
   f. Facilitators (transportation, advertising, public relations suppliers)
3. Marketing strategy
   a. Marketing objectives
   b. Strategy
4. Marketing organization
   a. Formal structure
   b. Functional efficiency
   c. Interface efficiency (interunit coordination)
5. Marketing systems
   a. Marketing information systems
   b. Marketing planning systems
   c. Marketing control systems
   d. New product development systems
6. Marketing productivity audit
   a. Profitability analysis
   b. Cost-effectiveness analysis
7. Marketing function audit
   a. Products
   b. Price
   c. Distribution
   d. Salesforce
   e. Advertising, promotion, publicity

SOURCE: Adapted from Philip Kotler, William Gregor, and William Rogers, "The Marketing Audit Comes of Age," *Sloan Management Review,* 18 (Winter 1977): 25–43.

Sales audits can be performed by themselves or as a part of a marketing audit (sales are audited under the marketing function category of the marketing audit). **Marketing audits** are:

> comprehensive, systematic, independent and periodic examinations of a company's—or business unit's—marketing environment, objectives, strategies, and activities with a view of determining problem areas and opportunities and recommending a plan of action to improve the company's marketing performance.[17]

Marketing audits go deeper than the annual marketing plan. They provide a thorough and objective review of the entire marketing function. The elements of a marketing audit are described in Exhibit 17.12. Many of the elements of the marketing audit, including technology, political-legal, social-cultural, customers, distribution and dealers, issues of marketing strategy, marketing systems, marketing productivity, and marketing functions have major implications for sales management.

SUMMARY

Salesforce control is a critical part of the marketing/sales management process. Outstanding planning and implementation are important, but control is essential for a firm to meet its sales objectives. The main purpose of this chapter is to explain, from the point of view of the sales manager, what needs to be controlled and how it can be controlled. What needs to be controlled are the firm's selling methods, distributors, customers, and salesforce.

Firms must analyze their selling methods to see whether they are using the most efficient means possible to reach their customers. Selling methods are analyzed using marketing effort analysis. Marketing effort analysis allows the firm to calculate directly the comparative performance of alternative selling methods. Variance decomposition analysis can also be used. This technique allows firms to understand the source of problems in the selling effort—whether it is forecasting, lack of sales coverage, aggressive discounting, or some other problem that keeps the firm from reaching its sales and profitability objectives.

Firms can analyze—and gain control over—their distributors using distributor portfolio analysis (DPA) and the channel dependence matrix (CDM). DPA ranks distributors on the basis of their growth rate and the percent of purchases they make in a given product category from the supplier conducting the analysis. Sellers use DPA to determine which distributors should be kept and which should be terminated based on the classifications. CDM is a method for showing the market shares of all distributors and sellers in a given market. CDM, when used in tandem with DPA, allows sellers to determine how competitors and distributors will respond to its attempts at increasing market share.

Controlling customers is important for at least two reasons. First, certain selling methods, such as national account management, assume that a particular level of profit can be achieved from a customer, thereby justifying the higher expense of service. Customer analysis shows which customers justify more expensive selling methods and higher levels of customer service. Customer analysis also shows firms when they are becoming customer-controlled. This happens when a firm begins to rely too much on its existing customers. Because customers merge, go out of business, change technologies, and change suppliers, sellers must be sure to continually assess the needs of not only their existing customers, but potential new customers as well.

Firms must also control the salesforce, especially if the salesforce constitutes a significant proportion of the promotion budget. Sales budgets are used to plan, coordinate, control, and evaluate the salesforce. There are several methods of constructing sales budgets, including all-you-can-afford, percentage of sales, industry parity, objective-and-task, zero-base budgeting, and return on investment. Each method has its strengths and weaknesses. The construction of sales budgets whether top-down, bottom-up, or a combination of both—must allow for the flexibility and level of detail needed by the firm. Problems for sales budgeting include poor forecasts, overreliance on historical trends, and politicization.

The most comprehensive forms of control available to sales and marketing managers are sales and marketing audits. These audits allow sales managers to determine the overall effectiveness and efficiency of the salesforce and point out potential problem areas.

KEY TERMS

sales controls	sales revenue
marketing effort analysis	sales expenses
variance decomposition analysis	all-you-can-afford budgeting
market volume variance	percentage of sales budgeting
company share variance	industry parity budgeting
contribution variance	objective-and-task budgeting
total variance	zero-based budgeting (ZBB)
distributor portfolio analysis (DPA)	return on investment (ROI) budgeting
offensive investment strategy	return on assets managed (ROAM)
defensive entrenchment strategy	top-down budgeting
strategic retreat strategy	bottom-up budgeting
abandonment strategy	sales audits
channel dependence matrix (CDM)	marketing audits
sales budget	

DISCUSSION QUESTIONS

1. What are sales controls? What is the role of control in the strategic marketing process?
2. How can marketing effort analysis be used to allocate marketing resources?
3. When would a company utilize variance decomposition analysis?
4. What tools are available for management to evaluate distributors' performance? How do the techniques complement each other?
5. What four strategies are presented in a DPA? In what situations would each strategy be appropriate?
6. Why is it important for a firm to perform a customer analysis? How can it be done?

7. What is a sales budget? Why do firms need sales budgets?
8. What methods can a firm use to set sales budgets?
9. What are the potential problems with developing sales budgets? How can the potential for the problems be minimized?
10. How can firms use sales and marketing audits as comprehensive means of control?

PROBLEMS

1. Robert Halton, the owner and sales manager for a small record distributor, has a difficult problem. He sells hard-to-find imports and out-of-print albums to retail record stores. He uses several selling methods to generate sales for his firm, including telemarketing, field sales, direct mail, and direct-response ads in trade magazines. Robert has a limited sales budget and must get the maximum return for each dollar spent. How can he analyze his sales to understand which selling method is the most profitable?

2. Janeen Gruen, a regional sales manager for a small specialty electronics firm, uses manufacturers' reps to sell one product line. Janeen's boss, the vice-president of sales, wants a report that shows clearly and logically which distributors are performing well. From the report, he will decide which firms will be kept and which will be terminated. For those that are kept, he will allocate extra training and cooperative promotional dollars. How can Janeen rank her different rep firms to generate such a report for her boss?

3. Shirley Burch, a regional sales manager with a large lumber products manufacturer, has a problem with sales budgeting. The traditional method of determining the current year's sales budget has been to add to last year's budget an amount to corner inflation. If last year's budget was $1,000,000, and inflation was 5 percent, this year's sales budget would be $1,050,000. However, the industry is changing radically. The selling methods prevalent to the industry are different from what Shirley used in the past, and the customers are demanding higher levels of customer service. How should Shirley derive future sales budgets?

SHORT CASE
MASLOW INSURANCE

BACKGROUND

The Maslow Insurance Company, a highly profitable, rapidly growing firm that specializes in providing printing services, is considering opening several new sales offices in different cities. The cities vary in terms of size, potential sales, costs, and investment required to enter the market.

SITUATION

The vice-president of sales, Nelson Lambert, has been given the assignment of prioritizing three cities in terms of which Maslow should enter first. In the past Lambert has selected cities based on gut feel, without much analysis. However, that method is unsatisfactory given the level of investment now required to enter cities. In addition, the board of directors wants to have a more sophisticated model to rely on in case Lambert is promoted or retires. As a result, Lambert must use a more formal type of analysis.

You are a recent graduate of a major university who is doing freelance consulting work in sales management. After Lambert meets you at a networking luncheon in your city, he asks you to help him create a model that will prioritize the cities he has been given as possible sites for new offices. You collect from Lambert the information shown in the following table.

COMPARATIVE INFORMATION ON POTENTIAL SALES OFFICE SITES

Projected	Madison, WI	Oklahoma City, OK	Sacramento, CA
Sales	$1,200,000	$800,000	$1,550,000
Cost of goods sold	$600,000	$400,000	$775,000
Gross margin	$600,000	$400,000	$775,000
Selling costs	$150,000	$80,000	$250,000
Profit	$450,000	$320,000	$525,000
Accounts receivable	$125,000	$73,000	$200,000
Inventories	$230,000	$150,000	$375,000
Total investment	$355,000	$223,000	$575,000

PROBLEM

You must now decide how to prioritize the cities Maslow is considering. This means you must perform the analysis and interpret the results. If you do a convincing job, you may be asked to perform additional jobs in the future. If your analysis is not convincing, it could harm your fledgling career as a consultant.

QUESTIONS

1. What method would you use to prioritize the cities?
2. Which cities (or city) would you suggest as the highest priority for Maslow to enter?
3. Specify the decision rule you used to answer question 2. What other decision rules could you use?

NOTES

1. Phaedra Hise, "The Do-It-Yourself Marketing-Effort Analysis," *Inc.,* 16 (June 1994): 81–83.
2. The discussion of variance decomposition analysis is based on James M. Hulbert and Norman E. Toy, "Strategic Framework for Marketing Control," *Journal of Marketing,* 40 (April 1977): 12–20
3. Peter Dickson, "Distributor Portfolio Analysis and the Channel Dependence Matrix: New Techniques for Understanding and Managing the Channel," *Journal of Marketing,* 47 (Summer 1983): 35–44.
4. Thomas Bonoma, "Making Your Marketing Strategy Work," *Harvard Business Review,* 62 (March/April 1984): 69–76.
5. Dieter J. Pommerening, "Brand Marketing: Fresh Thinking Needed," *Marketing Trends: An International Review* (Northbrook, Ill: A.C. Nielsen Company, 1979), 7–9.
6. Richard N. Cardozo, Shannon H. Shipp, and Kenneth J. Roering, "Proactive Strategic Partnerships: A New Business Markets Strategy," *Journal of Business and Industrial Marketing,* 7 (Winter 1992): 51–63.
7. "How Do You Balance Your Sales Budget?," *Sales and Marketing Management* (1992): 24–25.
8. "Creating Budgets is a Snap at Heublein," *Sales and Marketing Management* (January 1987): 76–77.
9. *Sales and Marketing Management* (1992), op. cit.
10. Douglas J. Dalrymple and Hans B. Thorelli, "Sales Force Budgeting," *Business Horizons,* 27 (July/August 1984): 31–36.

11. *Nation's Business* (1977).
12. J. S. Schiff and Michael Schiff, "New Sales Management Tool: ROAM," *Harvard Business Review*, 45 (July/August 1967): 59–66.
13. *Sales and Marketing Management* (1992), op. cit.
14. *Sales and Marketing Management* (1992), op. cit.
15. Nigel Piercy, "The Marketing Budgeting Process: Marketing Management Implications," *Journal of Marketing*, 51 (October 1987): 45–59.
16. *Sales and Marketing Management* (1992), op. cit.
17. Philip Kotler, William Gregor, William Rogers, "The Marketing Audit Comes of Age," *Sloan Management Review*, 18 (Winter 1977): 27.

ORGANIZATIONAL POLITICS

Case contributed by Dennis J. Moberg and David F. Caldwell, Santa Clara University.

THE SITUATION

You are the Sales Manager of the Automation Systems Group of the Fluid Products Division of the Blake-Emerson Corporation, a Fortune 500 conglomerate. The Fluid Products Division manufactures and sells pumps, valves, cylinders, and compressors for industrial use. Emerson Billingsworth is the Director of the Fluid Products Division, and Bill Banquet, your boss, reports to him as Marketing Manager. An organization chart appears in Exhibit 1.

Banquet has five subordinates including you. Each of the others is responsible for a different product line: pneumatics, hydraulics, microproducts (miniature valves and cylinders), and delivery systems (pumps, tubing, storage vessels, etc.). Your product line is the most diverse, for you sell automation systems (i.e., integrated clusters of valves and cylinders used with tools in automated machinery). Such systems are used in packaging, customized fabrication, and robotics.

You have eight sales engineers reporting to you. Each is responsible for different sets of industrial applications, and each travels 50 percent of the time. They are a close-knit group, and your relationship with them is extraordinarily good considering that you have been with the corporation and in your position for only eight months. Your predecessor left the firm in what some describe as a messy situation arising from a difference of opinion with Bill Banquet's predecessor. Banquet himself has only been Marketing Manager for two months having formerly served as Sales Manager of the Delivery Systems Group.

EXHIBIT I
ORGANIZATION CHART

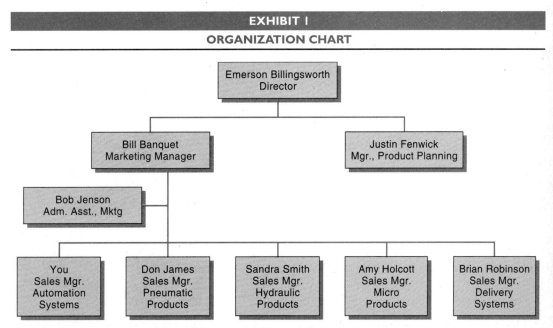

Your relationship with Banquet seems fine, although he lacks the sense of humor on which you pride yourself. He is very bright and is clearly cautious about making waves until he has established himself in his position.

The performance of the Fluid Products Division has been very poor for the last 18 months. This has resulted in layoffs in most parts of the organization dealing with hydraulic and pneumatic products. The staff organization was surprisingly spared these cuts. In Product Planning, for example, no layoffs have yet occurred. Indeed, this department has had increasing influence due to its central role in cost control during these hard times. This unit was known to be a favorite of top division management. Fortunately, your sales organization was relatively unscathed by the cuts. Only one sales engineer was laid off, and that was a year before you became Sales Manager. The reason your department has fared so well is that the demand for automation systems maintained acceptable levels throughout the downturn.

Two days ago a bombshell memo appeared in your morning mail. A copy appears in Exhibit 2.

You are very concerned about the effects of this new policy on your group. Your product line is the most diverse among all those in the division, and sales are the most uneven. Thus, the new policy places extraordinary pressure on your subordinates to plan in the face of almost incalculable uncertainties. You know with certainty that if you enforce this policy, there will be many instances of overages and underages. This will surely discourage efforts to develop new accounts unless these new customers have product needs that are easy to estimate.

In general, how would you approach this situation?

A. Diplomatically oppose the new policy as it applies to your unique circumstances. Petition for an exemption. (Go To 205)
B. Gather information about what this policy means to your peers, your boss, and the staff unit involved (Product Planning). (Go To 34)
C. Instruct your subordinates what to do about this new policy. (Go To 208)

APPENDIX: DECISION POINTS

Decision Point 3

Your opening question to Bill Banquet results in the following answer: "When I first heard of the new policy, I really tried putting the damper on it. But Fenwick had a lot of influence with Billingsworth. With the upcoming cuts in Product Planning, he had no choice. Somebody had to take on the planning responsibility Product Planning used to have, and I sure didn't want Manufacturing to call the shots.

"Now we're under a microscope. If we can show that we can plan well, we'll be able to keep production schedules responsive to the market. My concern is that if we resist this thing, or water it down, the pressure on inventory costs will mean more stock-outs when we really need product."

At this point what would you do?

A. Deliver your proposal as planned. (Go to 254)
B. Center the discussion on the alternatives of shorter planning periods and training for the sales engineers. (Go To 27)
C. Abandon your efforts to find relief from the policy and, after telling your people what Banquet just said, ask them to live with the policy. (Go To 251)

Decision Point 4

You have an opportunity to chat with three of your peers (Amy Holcott is out of town). All of them expressed irritability with the new policy, but none seemed put out enough to fight it. Don James' (Sales Manager—Pneumatic Products) opinion was typical:

"I don't know if my people are good enough planners for us to make our estimates within the 20% window. I suspect that they are, but there's no telling. Right now, with the market so sour, most of our business is repeat business. My hunch is that simply keeping our esti-

---

EXHIBIT 2

MEMORANDUM

To: Sales Managers, Fluid Products Division
From: Emerson Billingsworth, Director
Re: New Policy

As you know, the economic performance of our division has suffered at the hands of the worst recession that has hit our industry in recent memory. A central factor that has contributed to our poor performance is our lack of control of inventory costs. At the recommendation of Justin Fenwick, and after careful consultation with several managers, I have decided to put in place a new policy. Add the following to your policy manual:

> "To facilitate production planning and to get inventory costs under control, all sales engineers must specify their monthly expected sales in all product categories. Any actual sales over the expected figure by 20 percent or more must be back-ordered if a stock-out is experienced. Any sales under the expected figure by 20 percent will require a negative adjustment against the unit's reported sales volume goals in direct proportion to the additional carrying costs that accrue."

I ask your cooperation in complying with this new policy. Mr. Fenwick's people have developed forms that should simplify reporting our monthly sales estimates. Those for next month should be submitted by the 15th to his office.

---

mates to the high side of historical figures should suffice. That's what I am telling my people to do. They're sure not going to like the extra paperwork, that I can assure you. But most of my sales engineers are still jittery about being laid off, so it shouldn't be too hard a sell."

What would you do now?

A. Speak with Bill Banquet (your boss) about his "reading" of the new policy. (Go To 36)
B. Phone a friend of yours who works as a financial analyst at the corporate level (Blake-Emerson, the parent company) for his perspective on how to respond to this policy change. (Go To 10)
C. Call your predecessor (now with another firm) for his perspective on how to handle this situation. (Go To 202)
D. Wait and bring this issue up at a weekly staff meeting of the sales managers (chaired by Bill Banquet). (Go To 248)
E. Diplomatically oppose the new policy as it applies to your unique circumstances. Petition for an exemption. (Go To 18)
F. Instruct your subordinates what to do about the new policy. (Go To 19)

Decision Point 6

Sterling Cartwright is a man of about 40 who has been with the company for only three weeks. You ask him about Banquet's opinion of the way the new policy is working. He responds: "Bill is concerned. He really is. He doesn't like the way it puts the burden on you. Just the other day he met with Mr. Billingsworth about it."

You ask him what Banquet is doing about this situation. "Bill has a plan, and I'm sure it will work in time, but with the cuts in product planning, things are a bit uncertain. I'm sure you can expect something in the next few months."

What would you do now? (Bill Banquet is out of town.)

A. Go see Mildred Barnes of the Product Planning Department. (Go To 40)
B. Meet privately with Brian Robinson to work out a strategy for addressing this policy problem. (Go To 24)
C. Phone William Barstow, your friend at the corporate headquarters. (Go To 28)
D. Instruct your subordinates about what to do now. (Go To 251)

Decision Point 10

You have known William Barstow for years. You attended the same university together. When you tell him of the policy directive, he gives you some interesting information:

"I haven't heard anything about the policy, but I can tell you that the Fluid Products Division is getting a lot of heat to get its costs under control. The word is that Billingsworth's argument that his division has strong profit potential is no longer credible until he can produce the numbers. The division is now under considerable pressure not to cut its line personnel, but rather its staff. One view from these lofty heights is that the axe is due to fall soon on just about every staff unit in the Division."

If true, this would mean that Justin Fenwick's group is in for some cuts, but your group should not be affected.

What would you do now?

A. Speak with Bill Banquet (your boss) about his "reading" of the new policy. (Go To 29)
B. Call your predecessor (now with another firm) for his perspective on how to handle this situation. (Go To 202)
C. Wait and bring this issue up at a weekly staff meeting of the sales managers (chaired by Bill Banquet). (Go To 248)
D. Diplomatically oppose the new policy as it applies to your unique circumstances. Petition for an exemption. (Go To 18)
E. Instruct your subordinates what to do about the new policy. (Go To 19)

Decision Point 11

There are several ways for you to diplomatically oppose this new policy. Which option would you choose?

A. Ask Bill Banquet to use his influence to earn an exemption from this policy requirement in light of your group's special circumstances. (Go To 59)
B. Go directly to Justin Fenwick and petition him for an exemption from this policy requirement. (Go To 235)
C. Send a memo to Emerson Billingsworth (the announcement came from him, so it is proper) detailing in explicit form your case

for an exemption from this new policy. (Go To 243)

Decision Point 12

Will Barstow has much to say, "Well, by now you've heard about the personnel cuts in Product Planning. My hunch is that these are the last cuts. This quarter's earnings are up, and it now appears that we are about as lean as we can be.

"I've checked with some of my contacts. It's clear that your policy problem is not without precedent in the corporation. Two other divisions in Atlanta and Trenton have their salespeople estimate product demand as part of the planning effort. Marketing managers there gave their salespeople extensive training in statistical estimation procedures. Each has access to a computer terminal so they can report deviations from the plan in real time."

As you hang up the phone, Mildred Barnes of the Product Planning Department appears in the doorway of your office. Mildred Barnes and you have established a pleasant relationship during the past month. Through mutual and harmless teasing, you have built a rapport that both of you relish. When you ask her views of the policy, she has much to say.

"You know why the policy was created, don't you? Well, Billingsworth was facing significant pressure from corporate headquarters to cut staff personnel. Justin (Fenwick) had been successful in protecting us until then. But when the axe fell, we could no longer do all the product planning for manufacturing. You know we had been analyzing sales trends and setting manufacturing requirements accordingly. Well, the new policy was followed by a 22 percent cut in our staff. Jack Collins was the last of these cuts, and he left just last week. I was really lucky to survive this purge, believe me . . .

"Your group and Robinson's are the most hard-hit. But that's not really surprising. When we were doing the product forecasting, your two units were always the hardest to predict. Don't quote me, but you are getting screwed in all this.

"If you ask me, product scheduling is going toward shorter time frames. Now we are asking for projections one month ahead. In the next few months with the computer models we are playing with, we should be able to shorten that to two weeks."

Later in the conversation she says, ". . . If your people are having a rough time, there is one thing I could do—training. I've been teaching planning methods at a junior college where I live. I'd be more than willing to work with your salespeople to give them tools to use in figuring their product requirements."

What would you do now?

A. Talk to your peers about their experiences with the new policy. (Go To 55)
B. Instruct your subordinates about what to do now. (Go To 251)

Decision Point 13

You have known William Barstow for years. You attended the same university together. When you tell him of the policy directive, he gives you some interesting information:

"I haven't heard anything about the policy, but I can tell you that the Fluid Products Division is getting a lot of heat to get its costs under control. The word is that Billingsworth's argument that his division has strong profit potential is no longer credible until he can produce the numbers. The division is now under considerable pressure not to cut its line personnel, but rather its staff. One view from these lofty heights is that the axe is due to fall soon on just about every staff unit in the Division."

If true, this would mean that Justin Fenwick's group is in for some cuts, but your group should not be affected.

What would you do now?

A. Call your predecessor (now with another firm) for his perspective on how to handle this situation. (Go To 202)
B. Wait and bring this issue up at a weekly staff meeting of the sales managers (chaired by Bill Banquet). (Go To 248)
C. Diplomatically oppose the new policy as it applies to your unique circumstances. Petition for an exemption. (Go To 11)
D. Instruct your subordinates what to do about the new policy. (Go To 41)

Decision Point 14

You have an opportunity to chat with three of your peers (Amy Holcott is out of town). All of them expressed irritability with the new policy, but none seemed put out enough to fight it. Don James' (Sales Manager—Pneumatic Products) opinion was typical:

"I don't know if my people are good enough planners for us to make our estimates within the 20% window. I suspect that they are, but there's no telling. Right now, with the market so sour, most of our business is repeat business. My hunch is that simply keeping our estimates to the high side of historical figures should suffice, at least that's what I am telling my people to do. They're sure not going to like the extra paperwork, that I can assure you. But most of my sales engineers are still jittery about being laid off, so it shouldn't be too bad."

What would you do now?

A. Call your predecessor (now with another firm) for his perspective on how to handle this situation. (Go To 202)
B. Wait and bring this issue up at a weekly staff meeting of the sales managers (chaired by Bill Banquet). (Go To 248)
C. Diplomatically oppose the new policy as it applies to your unique circumstances. Petition for an exemption. (Go To 11)
D. Instruct your subordinates what to do about the new policy. (Go To 41)

Decision Point 15

Bill Banquet is out of town. This gives you time to gather other information. The following information sources are available to you.

Which would you choose first?

A. Your peers. (Go To 22)
B. Mildred Barnes of the Product Planning Department. (Go To 38)
C. Sterling Cartwright (Bill Banquet's new administrative assistant). (Go To 30)
D. William Barstow, your friend at the corporate headquarters. (Go To 44)

Decision Point 16

Mildred Barnes and you have established a pleasant relationship during the past month.

Through mutual and harmless teasing, you have built a rapport that both of you relish. You ask her views on the new policy.

"You know why the policy was created, don't you? Well, Billingsworth was facing significant pressure from corporate headquarters to cut staff personnel. Justin (Fenwick) had been successful in protecting us until then. When the axe fell, it was obvious that we could no longer do all the product planning for manufacturing. You know, we had been analyzing sales trends and setting manufacturing requirements accordingly. Well, the new policy was followed by a 22% cut in our staff. Jack Collins was the last of these cuts, and he left just last week. I was really lucky to survive this purge, believe me . . .

"Your group and Robinson's are the most hard-hit. But that's not really surprising. When we were doing the product forecasting, your two units were always the hardest to predict. Don't quote me, but you are getting screwed in all this.

"If you ask me, product scheduling is going toward shorter time frames. Now we are asking for projections one month ahead. In the next few months with our new computer models, we can probably shorten that to two weeks."

Later in the conversation she says, "If your people are having a rough time, there is one thing I could do—training. I've been teaching planning methods at a junior college where I live, and I'd be more than willing to work with your salespeople to give them tools to use in figuring their product requirements."

As you are leaving Mildred's office, her secretary slips you a note that William Barstow, your friend in the corporate office is trying to reach you by phone. You ask to use a phone in a deserted office and phone him. He tells you that he wanted to get back to you with the latest gossip:

"Well, by now you've heard about the personnel cuts in Product Planning. My hunch that personnel cuts are now a thing of past is a conviction. This quarter's earnings are up, and it now appears that we are about as lean as we can be.

"I've checked with some of my contacts. It's clear that your policy problem is not without precedent in the corporation. Two other divisions in Atlanta and Trenton have their salespeople estimate product demand as part of the planning effort. Marketing managers there gave their sales people extensive training in statistical estimation procedures. Each has access to a computer terminal so they can report deviations from the plan in real time."

What would you do now?

A. Since Bill Banquet is out of town, talk to Sterling Cartwright (his new administrative assistant). (Go To 52)
B. Meet privately with Brian Robinson to work out a strategy for addressing this policy problem. (Go To 46)
C. Instruct your subordinates about what to do now. (Go To 251)

Decision Point 17

Sterling Cartwright is a man of about 40 who has been with the company for only three weeks. You ask him about Banquet's opinion of the way the new policy is working. He responds: "Bill is concerned. He really is. He doesn't like the way it puts the burden on you. Just the other day he met with Mr. Billingsworth about it."

You ask him what Banquet is doing about this situation. "Bill has a plan, and I'm sure it will work in time, but with the cuts in product planning, things are a bit uncertain. I'm sure you can expect something in the next few months."

What would you do now? (Bill Banquet is out of town.)

A. Meet with your peers to learn about their experience with the new policy. (Go To 55)
B. Instruct your subordinates about what to do now. (Go To 251)

Decision Point 18

In deciding to act before consulting your boss, you are risking taking action that your boss would disagree with. This policy seems to have negative effects on your unit, so there is good reason to oppose it. However, the policy came from a level above your boss, so you do not want to oppose it without getting your boss' guidance. To remedy this situation, read the results of a discussion with Bill Banquet that appear below and then decide what to do.

Your meeting with Bill Banquet was unexpectedly short. Bill confessed to being distracted by Bob Jenson's resignation. Jenson was his administrative assistant. Jenson was known to be looking for another position, but the timing of his decision seemed to have taken Banquet by surprise.

You: "Did you see the memo about the new product planning policy?"

Bill: "Yes, I've seen it. I wasn't consulted on it in advance, but I was told that it was coming. I know the sales people are not going to like it."

You: "Not only that, but I doubt if my people can be expected to estimate their product needs within the 20% window. You know that our situation is different from the other groups."

Bill: "I know; I know. Listen, I've got to go. I've got to get over to Human Resources to sign the authorization forms to replace Jenson before my flight to Toledo. Look, do the best you can with the policy. I'll see you in a week."

What would you do now?

A. If you have not done so yet, phone a friend of yours who works as a financial analyst at the corporate level (Blake-Emerson—the parent company) for his perspective on how to respond to this policy change. (Go To 13)
B. If you have not done so yet, call your predecessor (now with another firm) for his perspective on how to handle this situation. (Go To 202)
C. Wait and bring this issue up at a weekly staff meeting of the sales managers (chaired by Bill Banquet). (Go To 248)
D. Diplomatically oppose the new policy as it applies to your unique circumstances. Petition for an exemption. (Go To 11)
E. Instruct your subordinates what to do about the new policy. (Go To 41)

Decision Point 19

In deciding to act before consulting your boss, you are risking taking action that your boss

would disagree with. This policy seems to have negative effects on your unit, so there is good reason to oppose it. However, the policy came from a level above your boss, so you do not want to oppose it without getting your boss' guidance. To remedy this situation, read the results of a discussion with Bill Banquet that appear below and then decide to do.

Your meeting with Bill Banquet was unexpectedly short. Bill confessed to being distracted by Bob Jenson's resignation that morning. Jenson was his administrative assistant. Jenson was known to be looking for another position, but the timing of his decision seemed to have taken Banquet by surprise.

You: "Did you see the memo about the new product planning policy?"

Bill: "Yes, I've seen it. I wasn't consulted on it in advance, but I was told that it was coming. I know the sales people are not going to like it."

You: "Not only that, but I doubt if my people can be expected to estimate their product needs within the 20% window. You know that our situation is different from the other groups."

Bill: "I know; I know. Listen, I've got to go. I've got to get over to Human Resources to sign the authorization forms to replace Jenson before my flight to Toledo. Look, do the best you can with the policy. I'll see you in a week."

What would you do now?

A. If you have not done so yet, phone a friend of yours who works as a financial analyst at the corporate level (Blake-Emerson—the parent company) for his perspective on how to respond to this policy change. (Go To 13)
B. If you have not done so yet, call your predecessor (now with another firm) for his perspective on how to handle this situation. (Go To 202)
C. Wait and bring this issue up at a weekly staff meeting of the sales managers (chaired by Bill Banquet). (Go To 248)
D. Diplomatically oppose the new policy as it applies to your unique circumstances. Petition for an exemption. (Go To 11)

E. Instruct your subordinates what to do about the new policy. (Go To 41)

Decision Point 20

You have an opportunity to chat with three of your peers (Amy Holcott is out of town). All of them expressed irritability with the new policy, but none seemed put out enough to fight it. Don James' (Sales Manager—Pneumatic Products) opinion was typical:

"I don't know if my people are good enough planners for us to make our estimates within the 20% window. I suspect that they are, but there's no telling. Right now, with the market so sour, most of our business is repeat business. My hunch is that simply keeping our estimates to the high side of historical figures should suffice, at least that's what I am telling my people to do. They're sure not going to like the extra paperwork, that I can assure you. But most of my sales engineers are still jittery about being laid off, so it shouldn't be too bad."

What would you do now?

A. Speak with Bill Banquet (your boss) about his "reading" of the new policy. (Go To 29)
B. Call your predecessor (now with another firm) for his perspective on how to handle this situation. (Go To 202)
C. Wait and bring this issue up at a weekly staff meeting of the sales managers (chaired by Bill Banquet). (Go To 248)
D. Diplomatically oppose the new policy as it applies to your unique circumstances. Petition for an exemption. (Go To 18)
E. Instruct your subordinates what to do about the new policy. (Go To 19)

Decision Point 21

You have a chance to "buttonhole" several of the other sales managers. Their comments follow:

Sandra Smith (Sales Mgr—Hydraulic Products): "I'll tell you one thing. My sales engineers certainly don't like the extra paperwork, but we've been able to do pretty well making the 20% window. In fact (she winks), it feels good moving from #4 to #2! All kidding aside, I think it's good that we now require our salespeople to

plan their product needs. After all, the personnel people are always harping that we should prepare them for moving into the managerial ranks."

Brian Robinson (Sales Mgr—Delivery Systems): "All that sounds fine and good, but the fact remains that the policy penalizes those of us who have uncertain demand or complex lines. No, this thing is stupid. The strategic plan for this year identifies my line as vitally important, and then they turn around and discourage our development of new accounts because one can never plan them systematically. I've talked to Banquet about this and he agrees, but he hasn't done anything about it!"

Don James (Sales Mgr—Pneumatic Products): "My sales engineers have had a helluva time getting their numbers right. Even with our standard lines, they consistently overestimated their needs. I suspect that they will get better and that the product will be available. It's creating hell with our volume, I'll tell you."

What would you do now? (Bill Banquet is out of town.)

A. Talk with Sterling Cartwright, Bill Banquet's new administrative assistant. (Go To 52)
B. Meet privately with Brian Robinson to work out a strategy for addressing this policy problem. (Go To 46)
C. Instruct your subordinates about what to do now. (Go To 251)

Decision Point 22

You have a chance to "buttonhole" several of the other sales managers. Their comments follow:

Sandra Smith (Sales Mgr—Hydraulic Products): "I'll tell you one thing. My sales engineers certainly don't like the extra paperwork, but we've been able to do pretty well making the 20% window. In fact (she winks), it feels good moving from #4 to #2! All kidding aside, I think it's good that we now require our salespeople to plan their product needs. After all, the personnel people are always harping that we should prepare them for moving into the managerial ranks."

Brian Robinson (Sales Mgr—Delivery Systems): "All that sounds fine and good, but the fact remains that the policy penalizes those of us who have uncertain demand or complex lines. No, this thing is stupid. The strategic plan for this year identifies my line as vitally important, and then they turn around and discourage our development of new accounts because one can never plan them systematically. I've talked to Banquet about this and he agrees, but he hasn't done anything about it!"

Don James (Sales Mgr—Pneumatic Products): "My sales engineers have had a helluva time getting their numbers right. Even with our standard lines, they consistently overestimated their needs. I suspect that they will get better and that the product will be available. It's creating hell with our volume, I'll tell you."

What would you do now? (Bill Banquet is out of town.)

A. Go see Mildred Barnes of the Product Planning Department. (Go To 16)
B. Since Bill Banquet is out of town, talk with Sterling Cartwright (his new administrative assistant). (Go To 6)
C. Phone William Barstow, your friend at the corporate headquarters. (Go To 47)
D. Meet privately with Brian Robinson to work out a strategy for addressing this policy problem. (Go To 24)
E. Instruct your subordinates about what to do now. (Go To 251)

Decision Point 24

You meet privately with Brian Robinson to discuss how you might approach the policy problem together. You agree that your first step should be information gathering. Robinson agrees to talk with Sterling Cartwright if you will contact Mildred Barnes and William Barstow. You first contact Mildred Barnes. Mildred Barnes and you have established a pleasant relationship during the past month. Through mutual and harmless teasing you have built a rapport that both of you relish. When you ask her opinions about the new policy, she replies:

"You know why the policy was created, don't you? Well, Billingsworth was facing significant pressure from corporate headquarters to cut staff personnel. Justin (Fenwick) had been

successful in protecting us until then. When the axe fell, we could no longer do all the product planning for manufacturing like we had been doing. You know, we had been analyzing sales trends and setting manufacturing requirements accordingly. Well, the new policy was followed by a 22% cut in our staff. Jack Collins was the last of these cuts, and he left just last week. I was really lucky to survive this purge, believe me . . .

"Your group and Robinson's are the most hard-hit. But that's not really surprising. When we were doing the product forecasting, your two units were always the hardest to predict. Don't quote me, but you are getting screwed in all this. If you ask me, product scheduling is headed toward shorter time frames. Now we are asking for projections one month ahead. In the next few months with our new computer models, we can shorten that to two weeks."

Later in the conversation she says, "If your people are having a rough time, there is one thing I could do—training. I've been teaching planning methods at a junior college where I live. I'd be more than willing to work with your salespeople to give them tools to use in figuring their product requitements."

You next contact William Barstow. He says:

"Well, by now you've heard about the personnel cuts in Product Planning. My hunch that personnel cuts are now a thing of past is a conviction. This quarter's earnings are up, and it now appears that we are about as lean as we can be.

"I've checked with some of my contacts. It's clear that your policy problem is not without precedent in the corporation. Two other divisions in Atlanta and Trenton have their salespeople estimate product demand as part of the planning effort. Marketing managers there gave their sales people extensive training on statistical estimation procedures. Each has access to a computer terminal so they can report deviations from the plan in real time."

When you meet Brian Robinson again, he characterizes his conversation with Cartwright as totally worthless: "The guy's a spineless lackey who will never express an independent thought. He just wants to protect his boss, that's all. He's a jerk."

From these inputs, it seems that you two have three major alternatives: (1) lobby for an exemption for strategically important units (your unit and Robinson's are strategically important), (2) lobby for planning period reduction from one month to one or two weeks, or (3) lobby for training for your sales engineers. You both agree that alternative (1) is the most preferred, (2) is the second best, and (3) is the worst. You now have to decide how to go forward with your proposals for policy modifications. Which would you do?

A. Once he returns, propose alternative (1) to Banquet , being prepared to settle for alternatives (2) or (3) if he does not think it feasible. (Go To 254)
B. Same as A above except begin by asking Banquet his assessment of how well the policy is working. (Go To 3)

Decision Point 26

You have a chance to "buttonhole" several of the other sales managers. Their comments follow:

Sandra Smith (Sales Mgr—Hydraulic Products): "I'll tell you one thing. My sales engineers certainly don't like the extra paperwork, but we've done pretty well making the 20% window. In fact (she winks), it feels good moving from #4 to #2! All kidding aside, I think it's good that we now require our salespeople to plan their product needs. After all, the personnel people are always harping that we should prepare them for moving into the managerial ranks."

Brian Robinson (Sales Mgr—Delivery Systems): "All that sounds fine and good, but the fact remains that the policy penalizes those of us who have uncertain demand or complex lines. No, this thing is stupid. The strategic plan for this year identifies my line as vitally important, and then they turn around and discourage our development of new accounts because one can never plan them systematically. I've talked to Banquet about this and he agrees, but he hasn't done anything about it!"

Don James (Sales Mgr—Pneumatic Products): "My sales engineers have had a helluva time getting their numbers right. Even with our standard lines, they consistently overestimated their needs. I suspect that they will get better and that the product will be available. It's creating hell with our volume, I'll tell you."

What would you do now? (Bill Banquet is out of town.)

A. Go see Mildred Barnes of the Product Planning Department. (Go To 40)
B. Phone William Barstow, your friend at the corporate headquarters. (Go To 28)
C. Meet privately with Brian Robinson to work out a strategy for addressing this policy problem. (Go To 24)
D. Instruct your subordinates about what to do now. (Go To 251)

Decision Point 27

You present your proposal, and it goes well. Banquet agrees to lobby with Fenwick and Billingsworth to explore the possibility of shorter time frames for certain products, especially those that are strategically important. This proposal is appealing to both parties. It is a practice used in other divisions of the corporation, and it allows Fenwick to argue effectively for restoring some of his staff cuts. Banquet also agrees to free up $2,500 from his discretionary budget for training to cover the time it requires to take your case to Billingsworth and Fenwick.

Both actions bear fruit. Two months later the policy is modified to suit your unit's needs, and all but one product plan falls within the 20% window. No customers are lost due to the inventory underage contingency.

In order to successfully oppose the new policy, you had to develop a coalition and build a rational case for modifying the policy. This was possible only because you were able to collect information before expressing your opposition publicly and irrevocably. Congratulations! You have just completed the Organizational Politics Interactive Case.

Decision Point 28

Will Barstow has much to say, "Well, by now you've heard about the personnel cuts in Product Planning. My hunch is that these are the last cuts. This quarter's earnings are up, and it now appears that we are about as lean as we can be.

"I've checked with some of my contacts. It's clear that your policy problem is not without precedent in the corporation. Two other divisions in Atlanta and Trenton have their salespeople estimate product demand as part of the planning effort. Marketing managers there gave their salespeople extensive training in statistical estimation procedures. Each has access to a computer terminal so they can report deviations from the plan in real time."

As you hang up the phone, Mildred Barnes of the Product Planning Department appears in the doorway of your office. Mildred Barnes and you have established a pleasant relationship during the past month. Through mutual and harmless teasing, you have built a rapport that both of you relish. When you ask her views of the policy, she has much to say.

"You know why the policy was created, don't you? Well, Billingsworth was facing significant pressure from corporate to cut staff personnel. Justin (Fenwick) had been successful in protecting us until then. When the axe fell, we could no longer do all the product planning for manufacturing. You know we had been analyzing sales trends and setting manufacturing requirements accordingly. Well, the new policy was followed by a 22% cut in our staff. Jack Collins was the last of these cuts, and he left just last week. I was really lucky to survive this purge, believe me . . .

"Your group and Robinson's are the most hard-hit. But that's not really surprising. When we were doing the product forecasting, your two units were always the hardest to predict. Don't quote me, but you are getting screwed in all this.

"If you ask me, product scheduling is going toward shorter time frames. Now we are asking for projections one month ahead. In the next few months with our new computer models, we can shorten that to two weeks."

Later in the conversation she says, ". . . If your people are having a rough time, there is

one thing I could do—training. I've been teaching planning methods at a junior college where I live. I'd be more than willing to work with your salespeople to give them tools to use in figuring their product requirements."

What would you do now?

A. Meet privately with Brian Robinson to work out a strategy for how to address this policy problem. (Go To 46)
B. Instruct your subordinates about what to do now. (Go To 251)

Decision Point 29

Your meeting with Bill Banquet was unexpectedly short. Bill confessed to being distracted by the resignation that morning of Bob Jenson, his administrative assistant. Jenson was known to be looking for another position, but the timing of his decision seemed to have taken Banquet by surprise.

You: "Did you see the memo about the new product planning policy?"
Bill: "Yes, I've seen it. I wasn't consulted on it in advance, but I was told that it was coming. I know the sales people are not going to like it."
You: "Not only that, but I doubt if my people can be expected to estimate their product needs within the 20% window. You know that our situation is different from the other groups."
Bill: "I know; I know. Listen, I've got to go. I've got to get over to Human Resources to sign the authorization forms to replace Jenson before my flight to Toledo. Look, do the best you can with the policy. I'll see you in a week."

What would you do now?

A. Call your predecessor (now with another firm) for his perspective on how to handle this situation. (Go To 202)
B. Wait and bring this issue up at a weekly staff meeting of the sales managers (chaired by Bill Banquet). (Go To 248)
C. Diplomatically oppose the new policy as it applies to your unique circumstances. Petition for an exemption. (Go To 11)

D. Instruct your subordinates what to do about the new policy. (Go To 41)

Decision Point 30

Sterling Cartwright is a man of about 40 who has been with the company for only three weeks. You ask him about Banquet's opinion of the way the new policy is working. He responds: "Bill is concerned. He really is. He doesn't like the way it puts the burden on you. Just the other day he met with Mr. Billingsworth about it."

You ask him what Banquet is doing about this situation. "Bill has a plan, and I'm sure it will work in time, but with the cuts in product planning, things are a bit uncertain. I'm sure you can expect something in the next few months."

What would you do now? (Bill Banquet is out of town.)

A. Talk to your peers about their experience with the new policy (Go To 26).
B. Go see Mildred Barnes of the Product Planning Department. (Go To 57)
C. Phone William Barstow, your friend at the corporate headquarters.(Go To 12)
D. Instruct your subordinates about what to do now. (Go To 251)

Decision Point 31

In deciding to act before consulting your peers, you now lack adequate information about the potential force that might be mobilized in opposition to this policy. Accordingly, your last decision was not correct. To remedy this situation, the results of a discussion with your peers are shown below.

You have an opportunity to chat with three of your peers (Amy Holcott is out of town). All of them expressed irritability with the new policy, but none seemed put out enough to fight it. Don James' (Sales Manager—Pneumatic Products) opinion was typical:

"I don't know if my people are good enough planners for us to make our estimates within the 20% window. I suspect that they are, but there's no telling. Right now, with the market so sour, most of our business is repeat business. My hunch is that simply keeping our estimates to the high side of historical figures

should suffice, at least that's what I am telling my people to do. They're sure not going to like the extra paperwork, that I can assure you. But most of my sales engineers are still jittery about being laid off, so it shouldn't be too bad."

What would you do now?

A. If you have not done so yet, phone a friend of yours who works as a financial analyst at the corporate level (Blake-Emerson—the parent company) for his perspective on how to respond to this policy change. (Go To 13)
B. If you have not done so yet, call your predecessor (now with another firm) for his perspective on how to handle this situation. (Go To 202)
C. Wait and bring this issue up at a weekly staff meeting of the sales managers (chaired by Bill Banquet). (Go To 248)
D. Diplomatically oppose the new policy as it applies to your unique circumstances. Petition for an exemption. (Go To 11)
E. Instruct your subordinates what to do about the new policy. (Go To 41)

Decision Point 32

You have known William Barstow for years. You attended the same university together. When you tell him of the policy directive, he gives you some interesting information:

"I haven't heard anything about the policy, but I can tell you that the Fluid Products Division is getting a lot of heat to get its costs under control. The word is that Billingsworth's argument that his division has strong profit potential is no longer credible until he can produce the numbers. The division is now under considerable pressure not to cut its line personnel, but rather its staff. One view from these lofty heights is that the axe is due to fall soon on just about every staff unit in the Division."

If true, this would mean that Justin Fenwick's group is in for some cuts, but your group should not be affected.

What would you do now?

A. Talk with your peers (the other sales managers who report to Bill Banquet) to gauge their reaction to the new policy. (Go To 14)

B. Call your predecessor (now with another firm) for his perspective on how to handle this situation. (Go To 202)
C. Wait and bring this issue up at a weekly staff meeting of the sales managers (chaired by Bill Banquet). (Go To 248)
D. Diplomatically oppose the new policy as it applies to your unique circumstances. Petition for an exemption. (Go To 50)
E. Instruct your subordinates what to do about the new policy. (Go To 31)

Decision Point 33

You decided to act before consulting either your boss or your peers. This was incorrect. First, in deciding to act before consulting your peers, you now lack adequate information about the potential force that might be mobilized in opposing this policy. To remedy this situation, the results of a discussion with your peers is shown below.

You have an opportunity to chat with three of your peers (Amy Holcott is out of town). All of them expressed irritability with the new policy, but none seemed put out enough to fight it. Don James' (Sales Manager—Pneumatic Products) opinion was typical:

"I don't know if my people are good enough planners for us to make our estimates within the 20% window. I suspect that they are, but there's no telling. Right now, with the market so sour, most of our business is repeat business. My hunch is that simply keeping our estimates to the high side of historical figures should suffice, at least that's what I am telling my people to do. They're sure not going to like the extra paperwork, that I can assure you. But most of my sales engineers are still jittery about being laid off, so it shouldn't be too bad."

Your second error was choosing to act before consulting your boss. In doing so, you were running the risk of implementing a policy that he may want to oppose or to implement in a way that is beneficial to the goals of the sales force. To remedy this situation, read the results of a discussion with Bill Banquet shown below.

Your meeting with Bill Banquet was unexpectedly short. Bill confessed being distracted by the resignation that morning of Bob Jenson, his administrative assistant. Jenson was known to be looking for another position, but the timing of his decision seemed to have taken Banquet by surprise.

You: "Did you see the memo about the new product planning policy?"
Bill: "Yes, I've seen it. I wasn't consulted on it in advance, but I was told that it was coming. I know the salespeople are not going to like it."
You: "Not only that, but I doubt if my people can be expected to estimate their product needs within the 20% window. You know that our situation is different from the other groups."
Bill: "I know; I know. Listen, I've got to go. I've got to get over to Human Resources to sign the authorization forms to replace Jenson before my flight to Toledo. Look, do the best you can with the policy. I'll see you in a week."

What would you do now?

A. If you have not done so yet, phone a friend of yours who works as a financial analyst at the corporate level (Blake-Emerson, the parent company) for his perspective on how to respond to this policy change. (Go To 13)
B. If you have not done so yet, call your predecessor (now with another firm) for his perspective on how to handle this situation. (Go To 202)
C. Wait and bring this issue up at a weekly staff meeting of the sales managers (chaired by Bill Banquet). (Go To 248)
D. Diplomatically oppose the new policy as it applies to your unique circumstances. Petition for an exemption. (Go To 11)
E. Instruct your subordinates what to do about the new policy. (Go To 41)

Decision Point 34

The following information sources are available to you. Which would you choose first?

A. Talk with your peers (the other sales managers who report to Bill Banquet) to gauge their reaction to the new policy. (Go To 4)

B. Speak with Bill Banquet (your boss) about his "reading" of the new policy. (Go To 58)

C. Phone a friend of yours who works as a financial analyst at the corporate level (Blake-Emerson, the parent company) for his perspective on how to respond to this policy change. (Go To 56)

D. Call your predecessor (now with another firm) for his perspective on how to handle this situation. (Go To 202)

E. Wait and bring the issue up at a weekly staff meeting of the sales managers (chaired by Bill Banquet). (Go To 248)

Decision Point 36

Your meeting with Bill Banquet was unexpectedly short. Bill confessed being distracted by the resignation that morning of Bob Jenson, his administrative assistant. Jenson was known to be looking for another position, but the timing of his decision seemed to have taken Banquet by surprise.

> You: "Did you see the memo about the new product planning policy?"
>
> Bill: "Yes, I've seen it. I wasn't consulted on it in advance, but I was told that it was coming. I know the sales people are not going to like it."
>
> You: "Not only that, but I doubt if my people can be expected to estimate their product needs within the 20% window. You know that our situation is different from the other groups."
>
> Bill: "I know; I know. Listen, I've got to go. I've got to get over to Human Resources to sign the authorization forms to replace Jenson before my flight to Toledo. Look, do the best you can with the policy. I'll see you in a week."

What would you do now?

A. Phone a friend of yours who works as a financial analyst at the corporate level (Blake-Emerson, the parent company) for his perspective on how to respond to this policy change. (Go To 13)

B. Call your predecessor (now with another firm) for his perspective on how to handle this situation. (Go To 202)

C. Wait and bring this issue up at a weekly staff meeting of the sales managers (chaired by Bill Banquet). (Go To 248)

D. Diplomatically oppose the new policy as it applies to your unique circumstances. Petition for an exemption. (Go To 11)

E. Instruct your subordinates what to do about the new policy. (Go To 41)

Decision Point 37

You have a chance to "buttonhole" several of the other sales managers. Their comments follow:

Sandra Smith (Sales Mgr—Hydraulic Products): "I'll tell you one thing. My sales engineers certainly don't like the extra paperwork, but we've done pretty well making the 20% window. In fact (she winks), it feels good moving from #4 to #2! All kidding aside, I think it's good that we now require our salespeople to plan their product needs. After all, the personnel people are always harping that we should prepare them for moving into the managerial ranks."

Brian Robinson (Sales Mgr—Delivery Systems): "All that sounds fine and good, but the fact remains that the policy penalizes those of us who have uncertain demand or complex lines. No, this thing is stupid. The strategic plan for this year identifies my line as vitally important, and then they turn around and discourage our development of new accounts because one can never plan them systematically. I've talked to Banquet about this and he agrees, but he hasn't done anything about it!"

Don James (Sales Mgr—Pneumatic Products): "My sales engineers have had a helluva time getting their numbers right. Even with our standard lines, they consistently overestimated their needs. I suspect that they will get better and that the product will be available. It's creating hell with our volume, I'll tell you."

What would you do now? (Bill Banquet is out of town.)

A. Since Bill Banquet is out of town, talk with Sterling Cartwright, (his new administrative assistant). (Go To 52)

B. Meet privately with Brian Robinson to work out a strategy for addressing this policy problem. (Go To 46)

C. Instruct your subordinates about what to do now. (Go To 251)

Decision Point 38

Mildred Barnes and you have established a pleasant relationship during the past month. Through mutual and harmless teasing you have built a rapport that both of you relish. You ask her views on the new policy.

"You know why the policy was created, don't you? Well, Billingsworth was facing significant pressure from corporate headquarters to cut staff personnel. Justin (Fenwick) had been successful in protecting us until then. When the axe fell, we could not keep doing all the product planning for manufacturing. You know, we had been analyzing sales trends and setting manufacturing requirements accordingly. Well, the new policy was followed by a 22% cut in our staff. Jack Collins was the last of these cuts, and he left just last week. I was really lucky to survive this purge, believe me . . .

"Your group and Robinson's are the most hard-hit. But that's not really surprising. When we were doing the product forecasting, your two units were always the hardest to predict. Don't quote me, but you are getting screwed in all this.

"If you ask me, where product scheduling is going is toward shorter time frames. Now we are asking for projections one month ahead. In the next few months with our new computer models, we can shorten that to two weeks."

Later in the conversation she says, "If your people are having a rough time, there is one thing I could do—training. I've been teaching planning methods at a junior college where I live. I'd be more than willing to work with your salespeople to give them tools to use in figuring their product requirements."

As you are leaving Mildred's office, her secretary slips you a note that William Barstow, your friend in the corporate office is trying to reach you by phone. You ask to use a phone in a deserted office and phone him. He tells you that he wanted to get back to you with the latest gossip:

"Well, by now you've heard about the personnel cuts in Product Planning. My hunch that personnel cuts are now a thing of past is a conviction. This quarter's earnings are up, and it now appears that we are about as lean as can be.

Atlanta and Trenton have their salespeople estimate product demand as part of the planning effort. Marketing managers there gave their sales people extensive training in statistical estimation procedures. Each has access to a computer terminal so they can report deviations from the plan in real time."

What would you do now?

A. Since Bill Banquet is out of town, talk with Sterling Cartwright (his new administrative assistant). (Go To 17)
B. Talk with your peers about their experience with the new policy. (Go To 37)
C. Instruct your subordinates about what to do now. (Go To 251)

Decision Point 39

You decided to act before consulting either your boss or your peers. This was incorrect. First of all, in deciding to act before consulting your peers, you now lack adequate information about the potential force that might be mobilized in opposition to this policy. To remedy this situation, the results of a discussion with your peers is shown below.

You have an opportunity to chat with three of your peers (Amy Holcott is out of town). All of them expressed irritability with the new policy, but none seemed put out enough to fight it. Don James' (Sales Manager—Pneumatic Products) opinion was typical:

"I don't know if my people are good enough planners for us to make our estimates within the 20% window. I suspect that they are, but there's no telling. Right now, with the market so sour, most of our business is repeat business. My hunch is that simply keeping our estimates to the high side of historical figures should suffice, at least that's what I am telling my people to do. They're sure not going to like the extra paperwork, that I can assure you. But most of my sales engineers are still jittery about being laid off, so it shouldn't be too bad."

Your second error was choosing to act before consulting your boss. In doing so, you were running the risk of implementing a policy that he may want to oppose or to implement in a way that is beneficial to the goals of the sales force. To remedy this situation, read the results of a discussion with Bill Banquet shown below.

Your meeting with Bill Banquet was unexpectedly short. Bill confessed being distracted by the resignation that morning of Bob Jenson, his administrative assistant. Jenson was known to be looking for another position, but the timing of his decision seemed to have taken Banquet by surprise.

You: "Did you see the memo about the new product planning policy?"
Bill: "Yes, I've seen it. I wasn't consulted on it in advance, but I was told that it was coming. I know the salespeople are not going to like it."
You: "Not only that, but I doubt if my people can be expected to estimate their product needs within the 20% window. You know that our situation is different from the other groups."
Bill: "I know; I know. Listen, I've got to go. I've got to get over to Human Resources to sign the authorization forms to replace Jenson before my flight to Toledo. Look, do the best you can with the policy. I'll see you in a week."

What would you do now?

A. If you have not done so yet, phone a friend of yours who works as a financial analyst at the corporate level (Blake-Emerson, the parent company) for his perspective on how to respond to this policy change. (Go To 13)
B. If you have not done so yet, call your predecessor (now with another firm) for his perspective on how to handle this situation. (Go To 202)
C. Wait and bring this issue up at a weekly staff meeting of the sales managers (chaired by Bill Banquet). (Go To 248)
D. Diplomatically oppose the new policy as it applies to your unique circumstances. Petition for an exemption. (Go To 11)
E. Instruct your subordinates what to do about the new policy. (Go To 41)

Decision Point 40

Mildred Barnes and you have established a pleasant relationship during the past month. Through mutual and harmless teasing, you have built a rapport that both of you relish. You ask her views on the new policy.

"You know why the policy was created, don't you? Well, Billingsworth was facing significant pressure from corporate headquarters to cut staff personnel. Justin (Fenwick) had been successful in protecting us until then. When the axe fell we could no longer do all the product planning for manufacturing. You know, we had been analyzing sales trends and setting manufacturing requirements accordingly. Well, the new policy was followed by a 22% cut in our staff. Jack Collins was the last of these cuts, and he left just last week. I was really lucky to survive this purge, believe me . . .

"Your group and Robinson's are the most hard-hit. But that's not really surprising. When we were doing the product forecasting, your two units were always the hardest to predict. Don't quote me, but you are getting screwed in all this.

"If you ask me, where product scheduling is going is toward shorter time frames. Now we are asking for projections one month ahead. In the next few months with our new computer models, we can shorten that to two weeks."

Later in the conversation she says, "If your people are having a rough time, there is one thing I could do—training. I've been teaching planning methods at a junior college where I live. I'd be more than willing to work with your salespeople to give them tools to use in figuring their product requirements."

As you are leaving Mildred's office, her secretary slips you a note that William Barstow, your friend in the corporate office is trying to reach you by phone. You ask to use a phone in a deserted office and phone him. He tells you that he wanted to get back to you with the latest gossip:

"Well, by now you've heard about the personnel cuts in Product Planning. My hunch that personnel cuts are now a thing of past is a conviction. This quarter's earnings are up, and it now appears that we are about as lean as we can be.

"I've checked with some of my contacts. It's clear that your policy problem is not without precedent in the corporation. Two other divisions in Atlanta and Trenton have their salespeople estimate product demand as part of the planning effort. Marketing managers there gave their sales people extensive training in statistical estimation procedures. Each has access to a computer terminal so they can report deviations from the plan in real time."

What would you do now?

A. Meet privately with Brian Robinson to work out a strategy for addressing this policy problem. (Go To 46)
B. Instruct your subordinates about what to do now. (Go To 251)

Decision Point 41

There are several ways for you to instruct your subordinates to respond to this new policy. Which option would you choose?

A. Tell your subordinates to ignore the policy directive and the product planning forms for the time being until you have a chance to appeal for an exemption. (Go To 223)
B. Instruct your subordinates to comply with the new policy. When they resist, be prepared to defend the need for better product planning but assure them that you are working to bring the new policy into line with your group's special circumstances. (Go To 225)
C. Ask for your group's advice as to how to implement this new policy requirement. Be prepared to justify the logic behind the policy should the group advocate resistance. (Go To 45)
D. Instruct your subordinates to comply with the new policy but to report to you any significant deviations from the monthly product plan as they arise. By reporting these deviations to Justin Fenwick as addenda to each plan, you will have grounds to argue against penalties imposed against your group for inaccurate estimates. (Go To 209)

Decision Point 42

Your meeting with Bill Banquet was unexpectedly short. Bill confessed being distracted by the resignation that morning of Bob Jenson, his administrative assistant. Jenson was known to be looking for another position, but the timing of his decision seemed to have taken Banquet by surprise.

You: "Did you see the memo about the new product planning policy?"

Bill: "Yes, I've seen it. I wasn't consulted on it in advance, but I was told that it was coming. I know the sales people are not going to like it."

You: "Not only that, but I doubt if my people can be expected to estimate their product needs within the 20% window. You know that our situation is different from the other groups."

Bill: "I know; I know. Listen, I've got to go. I've got to get over to Human Resources to sign the authorization forms to replace Jenson before my flight to Toledo. Look, do the best you can with the policy. I'll see you in a week."

What would you do now?

A. Talk with your peers (the other sales managers who report to Bill Banquet) to gauge their reactions to the new policy edict. (Go To 14)
B. Call your predecessor (now with another firm) for his perspective on how to handle this situation. (Go To 202)
C. Wait and bring this issue up at a weekly staff meeting of the sales managers (chaired by Bill Banquet). (Go To 248)
D. Diplomatically oppose the new policy as it applies to your unique circumstances. Petition for an exemption. (Go To 50)
E. Instruct your subordinates what to do about the new policy (Go To 31).

Decision Point 44

Will Barstow has much to say, "Well, by now you've heard about the personnel cuts in Product Planning. My hunch is that these are the last cuts. This quarter's earnings are up, and it now appears that we are about as lean as we can be.

"I've checked with some of my contacts. It's clear that your policy problem is not without precedent in the corporation. Two other divisions in Atlanta and Trenton have their salespeople estimate product demand as part of the planning effort. Marketing managers there gave their salespeople extensive training in statistical estimation procedures. Each has access to a computer terminal so they can report deviations from the plan in real time."

As you hang up the phone, Mildred Barnes of the Product Planning Department appears in the doorway of your office. Mildred Barnes and you have established a pleasant relationship during the past month. Through mutual and harmless teasing, you have built a rapport that both of you relish. When you ask her views of the policy, she has much to say.

"You know why the policy was created, don't you? Well, Billingsworth was facing significant pressure from corporate to cut staff personnel. Justin (Fenwick) had been successful in protecting us until then. When the axe fell, we could no longer do all the product planning for manufacturing. You know we had been analyzing sales trends and setting manufacturing requirements accordingly. Well, the new policy was followed by a 22% cut in our staff. Jack Collins was the last of these cuts, and he left just last week. I was really lucky to survive this purge, believe me . . .

"Your group and Robinson's are the most hard-hit. But that's not really surprising. When we were doing the product forecasting, your two units were always the hardest to predict. Don't quote me, but you are getting screwed in all this.

"If you ask me, product scheduling is going toward shorter time frames. Now we are asking for projections one month ahead. In the next few months with our new computer models, we can shorten that to two weeks."

Later in the conversation she says, ". . . If your people are having a rough time, there is one thing I could do—training. I've been teaching planning methods at a junior college where I live. I'd be more than willing to work with your

salespeople to give them tools to use in figuring their product requirements."

What would you do now?

A. Talk to your peers about their experience with the new policy. (Go To 21)
B. Since Bill Banquet is out of town, talk with Sterling Cartwright (his new administrative assistant). (Go To 17)
C. Instruct your subordinates about what to do now. (Go To 251)

Decision Point 45

You directed your subordinates to comply with the new policy for the time being. However, you asked them for their advice about how to implement the policy. The resulting discussion is rocky, but it does develop the group sentiment that they are in it together and they should make the best of it.

Since the new policy came from a level above your boss, talking with your boss before taking action was critical. In addition, by talking with other people within the company, you have learned some information that would have helped you in planning how to approach the situation.

Two months later the effects of the new policy have had an opportunity to be felt, and felt they were. Your unit failed to make the 20% planning window on 30% of the products sold. As a result, four orders are delayed, two of which are cancelled by customers due to the delay. Additionally, fifteen parts are over-ordered leading to a decrease by 17% of the reported sales volume credited to your unit. This results in your unit falling from the number two position in sales volume to the number three position.

Your sales engineers complain bitterly about the new policy, especially when their estimates over- or undershoot actual product requirements. Accounting for penalties, all but one of your sales engineers failed to meet their volume goals, and all expressed concern that their merit pay would be adversely affected.

Because of your heavy travel schedule during the month, you have had little opportunity to interact with your boss, your peers, or with others outside your immediate sphere of responsibility. The sole exception is Mildred Barnes, an analyst in the Product Planning Department. Barnes reports directly to Justin Fenwick and is the analyst responsible for translating your unit's product plans into production schedules.

At this point, what would you do?

A. Tell your boss your concerns to elicit his help in moderating the policy. (Go To 15)
B. Gather information about how others in the organization view this policy now that it has been in place for two months. (Go To 53)
C. Instruct your subordinates about what to do now. (Go To 251)

Decision Point 46

After discussing strategy with Robinson in some detail, you consider three major alternative actions:

1. Lobby for an exemption for strategically important units (your unit and Robinson's are considered strategically important).
2. Lobby to reduce the planning period from one month to one or two weeks.
3. Lobby for training for your sales engineers.

You both agree that alternative (1) is the most preferred, (2) is the second best, and (3) is the worst. You now have to decide how to go forward with your proposals for policy modifications. Which would you do?

A. When he is back from his trip, propose alternative (1) to Bill Banquet being prepared to settle for alternative (2) or (3) if he does not think it feasible. (Go To 254)
B. Same as A above except begin by asking Banquet his assessment of how well the policy is working. (Go To 3)

Decision Point 47

Will Barstow has much to say, "Well, by now you've heard about the personnel cuts in Product Planning. My hunch is that these are the last cuts. This quarter's earnings are up, and it now appears that we are about as lean as we can be.

"I've checked with some of my contacts. It's clear that your policy problem is not without

precedent in the corporation. Two other divisions in Atlanta and Trenton have their salespeople estimate product demand as part of the planning effort. Marketing managers there gave their salespeople extensive training in statistical estimation procedures. Each has access to a computer terminal so they can report deviations from the plan in real time."

As you hang up the phone, Mildred Barnes of the Product Planning Department appears in the doorway of your office. Mildred Barnes and you have established a pleasant relationship during the past month. Through mutual and harmless teasing, you have built a rapport that both of you relish. When you ask her views of the policy, she has much to say.

"You know why the policy was created, don't you? Well, Billingsworth was facing significant pressure from corporate headquarters to cut staff personnel. Justin (Fenwick) had been successful in protecting us until then. When the axe fell, we could no longer do all the product planning for manufacturing. You know we had been analyzing sales trends and setting manufacturing requirements accordingly. Well, the new policy was followed by a 22% cut in our staff. Jack Collins was the last of these cuts, and he left just last week. I was really lucky to survive this purge, believe me . . .

"Your group and Robinson's are the most hard-hit. But that's not really surprising. When we were doing the product forecasting, your two units were always the hardest to predict. Don't quote me, but you are getting screwed in all this.

"If you ask me, product scheduling is going toward shorter time frames. Now we are asking for projections one month ahead. In the next few months with our new computer models, we can shorten that to two weeks."

Later in the conversation she says, ". . . If your people are having a rough time, there is one thing I could do—training. I've been teaching planning methods at a junior college where I live. I'd be more than willing to work with your salespeople to give them tools to use in figuring their product requirements."

What would you do now?

A. Since Bill Banquet is out of town, talk with Sterling Cartwright (his new administrative assistant). (Go To 52)
B. Meet privately with Brian Robinson to work out a strategy for how to address this policy problem. (Go To 46)
C. Instruct your subordinates about what to do now. (Go To 251)

Decision Point 49

You have an opportunity to chat with three of your peers (Amy Holcott is out of town). All of them expressed irritability with the new policy, but none seemed put out enough to fight it. Don James' (Sales Manager—Pneumatic Products) opinion was typical:

"I don't know if my people are good enough planners for us to make our estimates within the 20% window. I suspect that they are, but there's no telling. Right now, with the market so sour, most of our business is repeat business. My hunch is that simply keeping our estimates to the high side of historical figures should suffice, at least that's what I am telling my people to do. They're sure not going to like the extra paperwork, that I can assure you. But most of my sales engineers are still jittery about being laid off, so it shouldn't be too bad."

What would you do now?

A. Phone a friend of yours who works as a financial analyst at the corporate level (Blake-Emerson—the parent company) for his perspective on how to respond to this policy change. (Go To 13)
B. Call your predecessor (now with another firm) for his perspective on how to handle this situation. (Go To 202)
C. Wait and bring this issue up at a weekly staff meeting of the sales managers (chaired by Bill Banquet). (Go To 248)
D. Diplomatically oppose the new policy as it applies to your unique circumstances. Petition for an exemption. (Go To 11)
E. Instruct your subordinates what to do about the new policy. (Go To 41)

Decision Point 50

In deciding to act before consulting your peers, you now lack adequate information about the potential force that might be mobilized in opposition to this policy. Accordingly, your last decision was not correct. To remedy this situation, the results of a discussion with your peers are shown below.

You have an opportunity to chat with three of your peers (Amy Holcott is out of town). All of them expressed irritability with the new policy, but none seemed put out enough to fight it. Don James' (Sales Manager—Pneumatic Products) opinion was typical:

"I don't know if my people are good enough planners for us to make our estimates within the 20% window. I suspect that they are, but there's no telling. Right now, with the market so sour, most of our business is repeat business. My hunch is that simply keeping our estimates to the high side of historical figures should suffice, at least that's what I am telling my people to do. They're sure not going to like the extra paperwork, that I can assure you. But most of my sales engineers are still jittery about being laid off, so it shouldn't be too bad."

What would you do now?

A. If you have not done so yet, phone a friend of yours who works as a financial analyst at the corporate level (Blake-Emerson—the parent company) for his perspective on how to respond to this policy change. (Go To 13)
B. If you have not done so yet, call your predecessor (now with another firm) for his perspective on how to handle this situation. (Go To 202)
C. Wait and bring this issue up at a weekly staff meeting of the sales managers (chaired by Bill Banquet). (Go To 248)
D. Diplomatically oppose the new policy as it applies to your unique circumstances. Petition for an exemption. (Go To 11)
E. Instruct your subordinates what to do about the new policy. (Go To 41)

Decision Point 52

Sterling Cartwright is a man of about 40 who has been with the company for only three weeks. You ask him about Banquet's opinion of the way the new policy is working. He responds: "Bill is concerned. He really is. He doesn't like the way it puts the burden on you. Just the other day he met with Mr. Billingsworth about it."

You ask him what Banquet is doing about this situation. "Bill has a plan, and I'm sure it will work in time, but with the cuts in product planning, things are a bit uncertain. I'm sure you can expect something in the next few months."

What would you do now? (Bill Banquet is out of town.)

A. Meet privately with Brian Robinson to work out a strategy for how to address this policy problem. (Go To 46)
B. Instruct your subordinates about what to do now. (Go To 251)

Decision Point 53

The following information sources are available to you. Which would you choose?

A. Your peers. (Go To 22)
B. Mildred Barnes of the Product Planning Department. (Go To 38)
C. Since Bill Banquet is out of town, Sterling Cartwright (his new administrative assistant). (Go To 30)
D. William Barstow, your friend at the corporate headquarters. (Go To 44)

Decision Point 55

You have a chance to "buttonhole" several of the other sales managers. Their comments follow:

Sandra Smith (Sales Mgr—Hydraulic Products): "I'll tell you one thing. My sales engineers certainly don't like the extra paperwork, but we've made the 20% window. In fact (she winks), it feels good moving from #4 to #2! All kidding aside, I think it's good that we now require our salespeople to plan their product needs. After all, the personnel people are always harping that we should prepare them for moving into the managerial ranks."

Brian Robinson (Sales Mgr—Delivery Systems): "All that sounds fine and good, but the fact remains that the policy penalizes those of us who have uncertain demand or complex lines. No, this thing is stupid. The strategic plan for this year identifies my line as vitally important, and then they turn around and discourage our development of new accounts because one can never plan them systematically. I've talked to

Banquet about this and he agrees, but he hasn't done anything about it!"

Don James (Sales Mgr—Pneumatic Products): "My sales engineers have had a helluva time getting their numbers right. Even with our standard lines, they consistently overestimated their needs. I suspect that they will get better and that the product will be available. It's creating hell with our volume, I'll tell you."

What would you do now? (Bill Banquet is out of town.)

A. Meet privately with Brian Robinson to work out a strategy for addressing this policy problem. (Go To 46)
B. Instruct your subordinates about what to do now. (Go To 251)

Decision Point 56

You have known William Barstow for years. You attended the same university together. When you tell him of the policy directive, he gives you some interesting information:

"I haven't heard anything about the policy, but I can tell you that the Fluid Products Division is getting a lot of heat to get its costs under control. The word is that Billingsworth's argument that his division has strong profit potential is no longer credible until he can produce the numbers. The division is now under considerable pressure not to cut its line personnel, but rather its staff. One view from these lofty heights is that the axe is due to fall soon on just about every staff unit in the Division."

If true, this would mean that Justin Fenwick's group is in for some cuts, but your group should not be affected.

What would you do now?

A. Talk with your peers (the other sales managers who report to Bill Banquet) to gauge their reaction to the new policy edict. (Go To 20)
B. Speak with Bill Banquet (your boss) about his "reading" on the new policy. (Go To 42)
C. Call your predecessor (now with another firm) for his perspective on how to handle this situation. (Go To 202)
D. Wait and bring this issue up at a weekly staff meeting of the sales managers (chaired by Bill Banquet). (Go To 248)

E. Diplomatically oppose the new policy as it applies to your unique circumstances. Petition for an exemption. (Go To 34)

F. Instruct your subordinates what to do about the new policy. (Go To 33)

Decision Point 57

Mildred Barnes and you have established a pleasant relationship during the past month. Through mutual and harmless teasing, you have built a rapport that both of you relish. You ask her views on the new policy.

"You know why the policy was created, don't you? Well, Billingsworth was facing significant pressure from corporate headquarters to cut staff personnel. Justin (Fenwick) had been successful in protecting us until then. When the axe fell, we could no longer do all the product planning for manufacturing. You know, we had been analyzing sales trends and setting manufacturing requirements accordingly. Well, the new policy was followed by a 22% cut in our staff. Jack Collins was the last of these cuts, and he left just last week. I was really lucky to survive this purge, believe me . . .

"Your group and Robinson's are the most hard-hit. But that's not really surprising. When we were doing the product forecasting, your two units were always the hardest to predict. Don't quote me, but you are getting screwed in all this.

"If you ask me, where product scheduling is going is toward shorter time frames. Now we are asking for projections one month ahead. In the next few months with our new computer models, we can shorten that to two weeks."

Later in the conversation she says, "If your people are having a rough time, there is one thing I could do—training. I've been teaching planning methods at a junior college where I live. I'd be more than willing to work with your salespeople to give them tools to use in figuring their product requirements."

As you are leaving Mildred's office, her secretary slips you a note that William Barstow, your friend in the corporate office is trying to reach you by phone. You ask to use a phone in a deserted office and phone him. He tells you

that he wanted to get back to you with the latest gossip:

"Well, by now you've heard about the personnel cuts in Product Planning. My hunch that personnel cuts are now a thing of past is a conviction. This quarter's earnings are up, and it now appears that we are about as lean as we can be.

"I've checked with some of my contacts. It's clear that your policy problem is not without precedent in the corporation. Two other divisions in Atlanta and Trenton have their salespeople estimate product demand as part of the planning effort. Marketing managers there gave their sales people extensive training in statistical estimation procedures. Each has access to a computer terminal so they can report deviations from the plan in real time."

What would you do now?

A. Talk to your peers about their experiences with the new policy. (Go To 55)

B. Instruct your subordinates about what to do now. (Go To 251)

Decision Point 58

Your meeting with Bill Banquet was unexpectedly short. Bill confessed being distracted by the resignation that morning of Bob Jenson, his administrative assistant. Jenson was known to be looking for another position, but the timing of his decision seemed to have taken Banquet by surprise.

You: "Did you see the memo about the new product planning policy?"

Bill: "Yes, I've seen it. I wasn't consulted on it in advance, but I was told that it was coming. I know the sales people are not going to like it."

You: "Not only that, but I doubt if my people can be expected to estimate their product needs within the 20% window. You know that our situation is different from the other groups."

Bill: "I know; I know. Listen, I've got to go. I've got to get over to Human Resources to sign the authorization forms to replace Jenson before my flight to Toledo. Look, do the best you can with the policy. I'll see you in a week."

What would you do now?

A. Talk with your peers (the other sales managers who report to Bill Banquet) to gauge their reactions to the new policy. (Go To 49)
B. Phone a friend of yours who works as a financial analyst at the corporate level (Blake-Emerson, the parent company) for his perspective on how to respond to this policy change. (Go To 32)
C. Call your predecessor (now with another firm) for his perspective on how to handle this situation. (Go To 202)
D. Wait and bring this issue up at a weekly staff meeting of the sales managers (chaired by Bill Banquet). (Go To 248)
E. Diplomatically oppose the new policy as it applies to your unique circumstances. Petition for an exemption. (Go To 50)
F. Instruct your subordinates what to do about the new policy. (Go To 31)

Decision Point 59

You ask Bill Banquet to use his influence to earn an exemption for aeronaut. He responds as follows:

"I understand that you may have difficulties abiding by this policy. However, it's not at all clear to me that you can't make it work."

You respond with facts that your sales group uses a more complex array of products and experiences a more uncertain demand than Banquet's other units. Further, you indicate the morale problems that will be created if your unit is adversely penalized due to the unique nature of the business it does. He then asks you for your recommendation, and you propose an exemption. He reacts:

"Well, we'll have to see about that. I understand your concerns, but we have to be very sure before we propose anything that far-reaching."

How would you respond to this?

A. Say that you will direct your subordinates to comply with the policy for the time being, and that you will keep him up to date on

how successful your people are at estimating their product requirements. (Go To 41)
B. Ask Bill what exactly it is that he wants you to do. (Go To 207)
C. Go to Emerson Billingsworth and petition your case there. (Go To 243)

Decision Point 202

Sam Blakestone was manager of the Automation Systems Group for five years, and he was with the Division for seven. Now with a competing firm, Sam jumps at the chance to express his opinion when you phone him.

"It sounds like Fenwick finally got his way. He's been trying to get the monkey off his back for years. He's no professional, I'll tell you that! He's probably been getting heat for inventory costs, so he invents a policy to put the heat elsewhere. Typical, real typical. You are just lucky he's planning to retire in one year!"

Unfortunately, this is not the type of information that you can really act upon. The opinions of a former employee are not really relevant here. While you were not in error for talking with Blakestone, re-evaluate your last decision. Re-evaluate your last decision. Circle the #202 you just wrote in your Flow Diagram, then return to the last uncircled step and try again.

Decision Point 205

No matter how diplomatic you are, this course of action is entirely too premature. You work for a person who has been in his job for a short time, and you have found him to be cautious. Declaring yourself opposed to this policy change now would lead to uncertain results at best. You need more information before committing yourself (even if it is a commitment to comply).

When policies like this are announced, especially policies that require 100% compliance to be effective and that were not arrived at democratically, those responsible are likely to be in a defensive posture. That is, those who have publicly committed themselves are unlikely to reverse their position even when the force of logic is compelling. Clearly, you should gather more information before deciding how best to respond to this situation.

Re-evaluate your last decision. Circle the #205 you just wrote in your Flow Diagram, then return to the last uncircled step and try again.

Decision Point 207

By pressing Bill Banquet for a decision, you are implicitly handing complete control of the situation over to him. You have given him the rationale for an exemption. However, he has signaled you indirectly that he is unprepared for anything as bold as what you have proposed (an all-out exemption).

Re-evaluate your last decision. Circle the #207 you just wrote in your Flow Diagram, then return to the last uncircled step and try again.

Decision Point 208

How do you know if compliance to this policy is necessary? Obviously it affects your unit in a negative way. Yet, you have not gauged others' reactions to it. Deciding to comply presumes that no one but Emerson Billingsworth has any influence over policy. Further, if you plan to tell your subordinates to partially comply with this policy, how do you know this will work without first finding out what others are going to do? Clearly, you should first gather more information before deciding what to do. Blind obedience or precipitous reaction is rarely as effective as an informed, deliberate move.

Re-evaluate your last decision. Circle the #208 you just wrote in your Flow Diagram, then return to the last uncircled step and try again.

Decision Point 209

The first time you send Fenwick a memo detailing expected deviations, he sends you back the following memo:[(See top of next column)]

As well intentioned as your action might have been, it certainly back-fired. Re-evaluate your last decision.

Circle the #209 you just wrote in your Flow Diagram, then return to the last uncircled step and try again.

Memorandum

TO: YOU
FR: JUSTIN FENWICK
RE: PRODUCT PLANNING

I received your recent memo detailing expected deviations from this month's product plan. I hope you appreciate that production planning is a highly complex endeavor. With our shrinking staff, we simply cannot integrate these deviations into this month's plan. Accordingly, there is no need for you to send us these data. Presumably, they will be useful for your own purposes.

I certainly hope you did not send us these unrequested figures as a sign of unwillingness to fully cooperate with the new policy. As you no doubt appreciate, Mr. Billingsworth expects total cooperation with the policy. Anything short of that and we cannot guarantee product availability. I know I can count on you to make this new system a success.

cc: E. Billingsworth; B. Banquet

Decision Point 223

You instruct your subordinates to ignore the policy. Two days after the planning reports are due you receive a call from Justin Fenwick's secretary. He says that unless you submit them at once, you cannot expect adequate supplies of product to meet sales. You are now left with no option but to comply. Now, however, you have been identified as uncooperative and resistant to change, and this label reduces your ability to mount a campaign for an exemption.

Re-evaluate your last decision. Circle the #223 you just wrote in your Flow Diagram, then return to the last uncircled step and try again.

Decision Point 225

The group responds very negatively to the new policy. They grouse at having to process more paperwork and express pessimism at trying to forecast their needs with the required accuracy. Their first month's estimates are very uneven. Some of your people spend a great deal of effort on their plans and some approach it in entirely too cavalier a fashion. The estimates are accordingly among the least accurate in the Marketing Department. While you expected miscalculations, you did not expect this.

Re-evaluate your last decision. Circle the #225 you just wrote in your Flow Diagram, then return to the last uncircled step and try again.

Decision Point 235

Your meeting with Justin Fenwick is strained, and Fenwick responds to your petition defensively, re-explaining the logic of the policy and attempting to persuade you to go along. He is unyielding even when you outline your reservations.

Several days after your meeting, you hear through the grapevine that as far as the Product Planning Group is concerned, you are a troublemaker.

Re-evaluate your last decision. Circle the #235 you just wrote in your Flow Diagram, then return to the last uncircled step and try again.

Decision Point 243

Approaching Emerson Billingsworth at this point produces disastrous consequences. He informs your boss of your action and takes no action to relieve your unit of responsibility to complete the product planning task.

Re-evaluate your last decision. Circle the #243 you just wrote in your Flow Diagram, then return to the last uncircled step and try again.

Decision Point 248

Bill Banquet returns from Toledo and promptly calls a regular staff meeting. You bring up the policy at the meeting, and this opens up a gripe session that causes Bill Banquet to wince. Forced to make a public declaration, he throws his weight behind the policy. He says that managers should try the new system for a while to see if it will bring down inventory costs without jeopardizing sales. When pressed for how long this trial period would be, Banquet says, "three months."

The problem with this action is that you have chosen a forum for information gathering that (1) is outside your control, and (2) forces your boss into making commitments he may not be prepared to make. The results speak for themselves. Bill Banquet's hand was forced, and now you face the certainty of three months of compliance. You might have been able to do better for your unit. You have also created a situation where your boss has had to appear weak in the face of this edict.

Re-evaluate your last decision. Circle the #248 you just wrote in your Flow Diagram, then return to the last uncircled step and try again.

Decision Point 251

It is premature for you to give your subordinates directions as to how to proceed. You simply do not know at this point whether some sort of modification more favorable to your unit can be worked out.

Re-evaluate your last decision. Circle the #251 you just wrote in your Flow Diagram, then return to the last uncircled step and try again.

Decision Point 254

Banquet listens carefully to your proposal, but reacts negatively to your first alternative (an exemption). When you try to emphasize the other alternatives as a fall back position, he keeps reintroducing the infeasibility of an exemption. Even when you agree that an exemption would be out of the question, Banquet seems to hold onto the view that the other alternatives would be perceived by "the powers that be" as a sign that the original policy was ill-conceived.

Your negotiation posture has caused your alternatives to be seen as versions of the same overall action—resistance. Clearly you need a different negotiation strategy with Bill Banquet.

Re-evaluate your last decision. Circle the #254 you just wrote in your Flow Diagram, then return to the last uncircled step and try again.

KRIX FILTERS CANADA INC.

This case was prepared by David Burgoyne for the sole purpose of providing material for class discussion at the Western Business School. Certain names and other identifying information have been disguised to protect confidentiality. It is not intended to illustrate either effective or ineffective handling of a managerial situation.

Frank Grant, Vice-President of Marketing for KRIX Filters Canada Inc. (KRIX) based in Cambridge, Ontario (located some 50 km. west of Toronto), had just finished reading a consultants' report which, among other things, indicated that the KRIX 1991 line fill of 85 percent (range 75 percent–94 percent by month) of branded oil, fuel and air filters was below the automotive parts aftermarket industry standard of 90-95 percent, and was deteriorating. Of particular concern to Grant was an inclusion in the executive summary written by the consultants that "forecasting by Marketing must be improved". In the consultants' view about 1/3 of the line fill problems on high volume items were directly attributable to poor forecasting. Within the new few weeks, the consultants would meet with the Canadian Management team, and would then forward their report to Head Office in Chicago. Grant needed to prepare for this meeting and for the inevitable questions from Headquarters' people. (See Exhibit 1 for an organizational chart of KRIX International and KRIX CANADA.)

LINE FILL ISSUES

For some time, Grant, himself, had also been concerned about the line fill problem within the KRIX distribution system which included: Private Labels, Warehouse Distributors, Other Retailers, Industrial Suppliers, and other categories. (See Exhibit 2 for details of the distribution system.) Of particular concern were the Warehouse Distributors, who represented over 60 percent of total company sales of $50,000,000. All Canadian Original Equipment Manufacturers of significance, were handled directly by the U.S. operation. Private Label sales to automotive chains, oil companies, and the aftermarket divisions of automobile manufacturers, presented relatively few line fill problems. These accounts tended to order with longer lead times, took delivery of significant quantities at one time, and limited their product line coverage to the big sellers. They suffered somewhat from line fill problems when they ordered KRIX branded products, although they ordered them with reasonably long lead times.

The line fill measurement was rigorous. Only complete satisfaction of the customer's order counted. If an order involved 20 Stock Keeping Units (S.K.U.s) from the just over 2,000 branded product S.K.U.s were shipped *exactly* as ordered in one shipment, that was 80 percent line fill. If 800 units of a particular S.K.U. were ordered and 750 were shipped, that was *not* a line fill. If some items couldn't be shipped on a Monday by transport with the main order, but were shipped on Tuesday the next day by courier, that was *not* a line fill.

EXHIBIT I

ORGANIZATION CHART

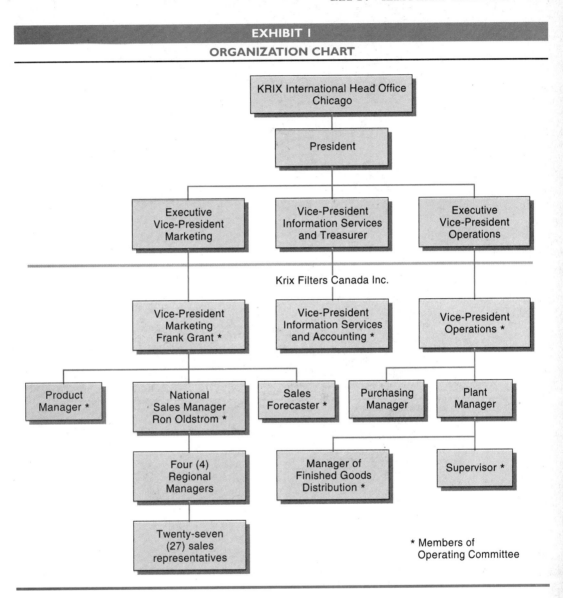

Krix Filters Canada Inc.

* Members of Operating Committee

Shipments to KRIX accounts were made from depots located in Edmonton, Alberta; in Cambridge, Ontario; and in Montreal, Quebec. The line fill rate didn't vary significantly from depot to depot, although, at any given time the problem S.K.U.s at one depot could be different from those at other depots. All depots operated on a first in-first out customer order basis. They did not have information on items in-transit to them. Product allocation to depots was determined by the Manager of Finished Goods Distribution. The decision on shipments to depots included a safety stock level, shipping time, and a product movement prediction calculation. A moving average that used the latest four months S.K.U. movements weighted 80 percent and the

EXHIBIT 2
DISTRIBUTION SYSTEM OUTLINE

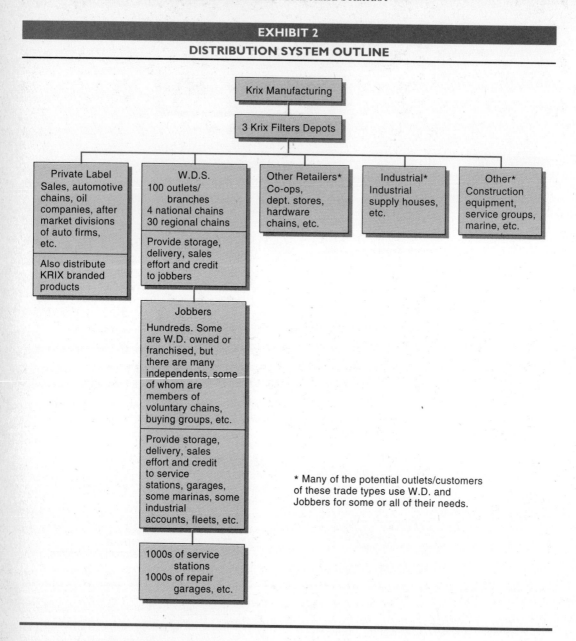

* Many of the potential outlets/customers of these trade types use W.D. and Jobbers for some or all of their needs.

comparable two months of the previous year weighted 20 percent. For example, a 1992 May decision would involve January, February, March, April of 1992 and May, June of 1991. These calculations were by S.K.U. per depot. No depot was considered more important than an-

other when product allocation decisions were involved.

THE CONSULTANTS' CONCERNS

For their analytical purposes, the consultants had separated the product line into five categories: A (50 percent of unit sales), B (25 percent of unit sales), C and D (20 percent of unit volume), and E (5 percent of unit volume) categories. These definitions didn't fit those used by the Marketing Department, but that was not of concern to Grant since the fill rate for the consultants' A category was only 84 percent, with the other categories ranging from 80 percent to 83 percent. Many of the lower volume S.K.U.s were for industrial purposes (engines used in factories, construction, mines, logging operations, etc.) or for cars and trucks that were older, limited editions, or special imports, etc. Many of these low volume S.K.U.s were purchased as completely manufactured products from sister plants in the U.S. and could be obtained on short notice. In some cases, the Cambridge plant manufactured such S.K.U.s and supplied the U.S. operations.

The consultants also referred to the very weak "overall forecast accuracy" by Marketing. The measurement used was a ratio of the actual monthly demand (actual orders received) by S.K.U. to the monthly forecast by S.K.U. This information was reported monthly on one of the Production Department reports. If demand was 50 and the forecast was 50, that was 100 percent accuracy. If demand was 25 and the forecast was 50, that was 50 percent accuracy. If demand was 100 and the forecast was 50, that was 50 percent accuracy. The annualized monthly "overall forecast accuracy" was 58 percent for the A and B categories, declining to 12 percent for the E division.

DISTRIBUTION SYSTEM CHANGES

Historically, fill rate had not been a major company or industry issue. However, the recession of the 1990s, coupled with an ever expanding number of makes and models of vehicles and vehicle parts, had recently created significant inventory issues throughout the system. The impossibility of stocking a basic coverage of parts and accessories for service stations and garages, combined with their reduced profits and cash flow, resulted in these and other retailers putting more pressure on their supplying jobbers. An all-too-common viewpoint of service station and garage operators was: "We keep a very basic stock of some standard items, but we usually put the customer's car up on the hoist, figure out what is needed and then call the jobber: if they can't supply quickly we call another jobber." As a result, a busy service station/garage would receive 10 to 15 deliveries per day from jobbers and auto dealerships. Jobbers were also suffering financially. This problem, combined with their limited space, resulted in their ordering smaller quantities of more items each day from their supplying Warehouse Distributors. They usually ordered by 7 p.m. for delivery by 10 a.m. or earlier the next day. In turn, Warehouse Distributors ordered smaller quantities more often from manufacturers.

In Grant's view, the "good old days" of a distribution pipeline that was content to be overly full with inventory were gone forever. Customers holding less inventory and demanding quicker delivery would be a continuing reality. KRIX, which had been working with considerable success with its suppliers to tighten up its sourcing, had made a number of production line changes that enhanced flexibility. Most S.K.U.s could be manufactured in three to five days. There was no question, however, that KRIX and other manufacturers were going to bear the brunt of the change. One indicator of the demands on KRIX was that, during the previous month, KRIX had issued double the number of invoices when compared to three years previously, and they were spread about evenly over the whole month in spite of credit terms that were net 30, two percent 10 days.

The increased service demands throughout the system were *not* accompanied by any apparent willingness to pay higher prices. A popular auto filter, the KPI, had a suggested retail of $24.90, a suggested dealer of $19.03, a jobber net of $13.32 and a Warehouse Distributor net of $10.00. If anything, price pressure at all levels appeared to be increasing. A bright spot, however, was one Volkswagen dealer in a major centre in Ontario who was experimenting with a

$1.00 delivery charge to service station/garages for parts delivery.

THE FORECASTING PROCESS

Grant decided to "walk through" the Marketing Department's forecasting process to prepare himself for the forthcoming meetings.

The four Regional Managers submitted their forecasts of sales for their respective territories for each of the following *two* months on the 20th of each month. They stated their estimates as a percentage of their month's sales quota which had been established as part of the prior fall's planning process. If the sales quota for February for a region was $500,000 and the Regional Manager determined that the forecasted figure should be $450,000, that would be a forecast of 90 percent of quota. To assist them in their calculations, they had their salespeoples' inputs (eight to 12 per Regional Manager), their own interactions with major accounts, and their sales reports from Cambridge which were sent to them on the 5th of each month. These sales reports showed sales by S.K.U. by account for the month and year to-date, with prior year comparisons. Principal accountabilities and bonus program details for Regional Managers are included as Exhibit 3.

EXHIBIT 3
REGIONAL MANAGERS

PRINCIPAL ACCOUNTABILITIES (*Source: Position description from Human Resources*)

1. Maintain a sound, progressive distribution system, that will ensure fulfillment of the sales plan, through effective delivery of marketing and selling programs, excellent customer service, and strong personal contact with key customers.
2. Recommend and administer pricing and selling policies, to maintain and improve the Company's competitive position in the marketplace.
3. Select, assign and develop sales staff in the Region, to support the Division's sales and marketing goals.
4. Increase sales volume, by recommending and implementing sales programs.
5. Increase market penetration and broaden customer base, by identifying potential new opportunities, and by recommending and implementing programs to sell to them.
6. Recommend sales budgets and control expenses within approved budgets, to achieve lowest possible selling costs, consistent with assigned sales objectives.
7. Recommend advertising and promotion programs to maintain and increase sales volumes, and to deliver approved programs to customers.
8. Ensure that the Company's sales program and policies are carried out in the Region, by communicating them to all Regional sales personnel, and by monitoring to verify implementation.
9. Keep current on all activities by the competition, reporting any changes to Head Office for possible action to be taken.

BONUS PROGRAM
(Value—up to 20% of base salary)

1. A maximum of 50% of the bonus potential is earned upon 100% achievement of the regional sales quota.* Bonus starts at 90% of quota graduated up to 100%.
2. A maximum of 25% of the bonus potential is earned upon 100% achievement of the national sales plan.* Bonus starts at 90% of plan graduated up to 100%.
3. A maximum of 15% of the bonus potential is earned if the regional travel budget is met.
4. A maximum of 10% of the bonus potential will be determined by the needs of the various regions and may vary from year to year.

---

*The sum of the four regional sales quotas exceeded the national sales plan by about 5 percent.

EXHIBIT 4
MONTHLY SALES PROJECTIONS VS ACTUALS

MEMORANDUM

To: Regional Managers, Frank Grant
From: Ron Oldstrom
Re: Monthly Sales Projections vs Actuals

I am certain that you have received and reviewed your copy of my March operations report by now. There is one point that I feel we must focus particular attention upon, as it directly impacts on our overall customer satisfaction level. That point is *our* monthly projection of estimated dollar sales. Following is the year-to-date summary report showing your project dollar sales versus the actual sales result for each month and the resulting weighted total.

Monthly Sales Projection vs Actual Sales

	Jan. Proj. % of Plan	Actual % of Proj.	Feb. Proj. % of Plan	Actual % of Proj.	Mar. Proj. % of Plan	Actual % of Proj.	Y-T-D Proj. % of Plan	Y-T-D Actual % of Proj.
Regions								
1	100.4	83.9	96.1	78.5	101.4	84.7	98.2	81.8
2	100.0	75.9	99.7	82.5	106.5	80.7	99.4	79.7
3	101.8	80.1	100.1	84.8	96.3	90.0	100.2	85.0
4	100.0	96.0	86.3	70.1	100.0	82.4	95.8	82.8
Cdn.	100.6	84.2	95.2	79.0	100.9	84.3	98.4	82.5

The Canadian number is utilized as the *basis* for our forecast in combination with historical demand and planned promotions to ultimately arrive at a quantity by model projection for each model number in each of our lines.

We all realize full well that no one can precisely forecast dollar sales each month. However, being as close as possible is most important.

- Over forecasting results in over stocking and *usually* in the wrong mix. This results in very large inventories of the slow moving numbers putting resulting in decreased customer service, etc.

- Under forecasting results in a constant scramble at all levels—salesforce, distribution, production, purchasing, production distribution, salesforce, etc. Results in very unhappy customers and employees.

I would ask you to please be certain the numbers that you provide me are indeed *your best estimates.* You may want to initially set a personal objective to be within + or −15% of actuals with your estimates.

The National Sales Manager, Ron Oldstrom, combined the inputs from the four Regional Managers, adjusted the total somewhat (usually by less then three percent), and forwarded these totals to the Sales Forecaster. From this information, the Sales Forecaster prepared a summary report of the monthly forecasts and sales by region, and sent copies to Oldstrom and

Grant. Oldstrom then prepared a memo for the Regional Salesmanagers, presenting only the data on their regions, accompanied by his comments. (See Exhibit 4 for a sample memo.)

Each month, the Sales Forecaster ran updated projected volumes by S.K.U. for each of the next 12 months. These estimates were formulated from the 12 months actual sales by S.K.U. for the prior year, combined with an averaging adjustment based on the latest three months sales. There were manual overrides by the Forecaster based upon inputs from the Product Manager (forthcoming or historical promotional activities, price changes, etc.) and judgments by the Forecaster relating to such things as new or deleted products for which the historical data approach was not appropriate. From all this information, a projected total sales volume in dollars was calculated.

To facilitate integration among production, physical distribution and sales/marketing in Canada, a committee of key people known as the Operating Committee had been established five years previously. Although everyone worked in the same building in Cambridge, they reported through and to different executives at Cambridge and Head Office. This committee met monthly to discuss the agenda items, such as current production schedule problems (problems requiring trade-offs on what S.K.U.s could be run), and short-run future problems (vacation shutdown for two weeks in July; plant shut-downs for two or three days next week because total finished inventory was about to exceed the limit imposed by the finance group at headquarters, etc.). Plant shutdowns, not surprisingly, created problems with the fill rate dropping to 74 percent in the two months following the two-week vacation shut-down. A major agenda item each month was dealing with the differences between the volume projections provided the Sales Forecaster and by the National Sales Manager. Historical demand, sales and forecasts for selected higher volume S.K.U.s are shown in Exhibit 5.

THE DECISION

Grant knew the Canadian Vice-President of Operations would also be reviewing his areas of responsibility. The consultants' report, in addition to indicating serious flaws in forecasting by the Marketing Department, also indicated that Productions needed to improve its scheduling approaches and processes. He wondered if a meeting to address joint issues might be of value.

EXHIBIT 5

HISTORICAL DEMAND, SALES AND FORECASTS FOR SELECTED HIGHER VOLUME S.K.U.S

Part #A31

Month	1989 Sales	1990 Sales	1990 Demand	1990 Forecasts	1991 Sales	1991 Demand	1991 Forecasts	1992 Sales
Jan	6680	7072	7278	7742	5738	7118	14000	6198
Feb	17335	13652	21897	11000	14106	12978	14000	10158
Mar	13221	13312	5281	11000	8784	11297	7000	7378
Apr	13598	10483	10801	15000	12233	9661	10000	9100
May	12474	6226	5793	13000	6168	6091	8000	0
Jun	8350	7424	11392	10000	14077	15137	13000	0
Jly	8935	8555	5710	13000	5224	4780	5600	0
Aug	9354	6712	6340	10000	9254	9624	7000	0
Sep	10821	8402	10484	16000	5314	7570	10000	0
Oct	10907	12001	10875	9800	11662	8501	11000	0
Nov	12480	9342	8688	10000	5883	6721	8700	0
Dec	5674	3980	3569	6000	9845	11263	5000	0

EXHIBIT 5 (continued)

HISTORICAL DEMAND, SALES AND FORECASTS FOR SELECTED HIGHER VOLUME S.K.U.S

Part #A8

Month	1989 Sales	1990 Sales	1990 Demand	1990 Forecasts	1991 Sales	1991 Demand	1991 Forecasts	1992 Sales
Jan	12433	11047	11212	15279	10565	12586	20000	10550
Feb	24198	20246	29406	20000	22661	20892	20000	16074
Mar	15817	15683	8559	20000	14422	18375	14000	12695
Apr	16452	17571	16571	21000	18257	14822	15000	14410
May	18891	11419	11444	18200	10595	9861	12000	0
Jun	14618	12971	19830	12000	18444	20765	19000	0
Jly	14838	13315	8939	16000	9029	7777	9000	0
Aug	13294	11734	11372	14000	17384	17860	10000	0
Sep	19561	13490	15609	22000	9190	11744	15000	0
Oct	14297	19179	17912	15000	16239	12527	18000	0
Nov	18046	15417	14665	17000	11289	12298	15000	0
Dec	10980	7329	6453	8000	14816	17224	7200	0

Part #416

Month	1989 Sales	1990 Sales	1990 Demand	1990 Forecasts	1991 Sales	1991 Demand	1991 Forecasts	1992 Sales
Jan	2773	3760	4023	3681	4670	5439	6000	3801
Feb	6772	6530	9134	7000	8508	7880	8400	7357
Mar	6912	4911	3724	5000	5483	6387	4000	6221
Apr	6390	7855	9605	6500	7776	7824	9176	6570
May	5332	5996	3028	5600	4669	3962	5700	0
Jun	4758	4122	5170	5500	8139	9840	7000	0
Jly	5272	3287	3282	5400	5648	4560	3000	0
Aug	5292	4634	5302	5800	6399	6680	5500	0
Sep	8115	5679	6996	9000	3428	4144	7300	0
Oct	5547	9128	8552	6000	8351	6786	8600	0
Nov	5566	6026	5551	5300	4689	5298	5600	0
Dec	3786	3829	2483	3000	6281	6305	731	0

Part #A78

Month	1989 Sales	1990 Sales	1990 Demand	1990 Forecasts	1991 Sales	1991 Demand	1991 Forecasts	1992 Sales
Jan	3934	5556	5564	4254	5098	6135	9000	5945
Feb	11693	9757	13070	10000	11084	10155	10000	8974
Mar	10227	9028	7241	9000	6862	8028	7300	9200
Apr	7828	10973	11337	9000	11412	11985	8000	8455
May	9641	8265	6530	9000	3869	6046	6525	0
Jun	7319	6043	7033	7000	14510	12993	10000	0
Jly	8770	6043	5619	10000	7699	6395	5500	0
Aug	9446	7747	7455	9000	9078	10261	7500	0
Sep	11616	9779	10253	13000	6561	6767	10200	0
Oct	8460	11263	13242	9000	12180	10459	13200	0
Nov	9068	9159	7271	8000	7874	8663	7300	0
Dec	5596	6629	5271	5000	10142	10000	6000	0

	EXHIBIT 5 (continued)						

HISTORICAL DEMAND, SALES AND FORECASTS FOR SELECTED HIGHER VOLUME S.K.U.S

Part #291

Month	1989 Sales	1990 Sales	1990 Demand	1990 Forecasts	1991 Sales	1991 Demand	1991 Forecasts	1992 Sales
Jan	1778	898	851	1920	1219	1255	1500	964
Feb	1387	2595	3221	1200	2051	2009	2500	1318
Mar	1885	1889	1256	2200	1791	2183	1300	1806
Apr	3650	2701	3200	3010	2327	2005	2000	1884
May	2028	1492	1282	1800	871	841	1600	0
Jun	1409	1270	1732	1700	1812	2068	2000	0
Jly	1633	1602	1314	1700	1227	976	1300	0
Aug	1822	1026	1094	1800	1253	1522	1000	0
Sep	2430	2097	2138	3000	1085	1046	2100	0
Oct	2097	2643	2774	2509	2389	2268	2700	0
Nov	2958	1740	1644	2400	1453	1452	1600	0
Dec	1505	1262	1070	1100	1656	1710	1200	0

Part #153

Month	1989 Sales	1990 Sales	1990 Demand	1990 Forecasts	1991 Sales	1991 Demand	1991 Forecasts	1992 Sales
Jan	3288	1616	1258	2639	1250	1348	700	543
Feb	1475	3066	4344	1400	2685	2738	2800	1555
Mar	2928	2572	1378	3000	1904	2615	1317	1599
Apr	3626	4016	4153	4168	2119	1262	2300	1736
May	2736	1182	1045	2300	939	1055	1300	0
Jun	2473	863	1676	1700	2608	2698	1700	0
Jly	1609	1746	1216	2000	985	788	1100	0
Aug	1879	955	1028	1500	1006	1645	1100	0
Sep	1639	1539	1821	4000	1595	1214	1800	0
Oct	2604	2432	2366	2320	1873	1656	2498	0
Nov	3298	1927	1772	3000	1434	1533	1800	0
Dec	1411	1083	1122	1658	1596	1617	1150	0

Part #623

Month	1989 Sales	1990 Sales	1990 Demand	1990 Forecasts	1991 Sales	1991 Demand	1991 Forecasts	1992 Sales
Jan	3757	2116	2163	4542	3026	3194	4000	2455
Feb	2754	5993	8599	2700	6644	6494	7800	3937
Mar	5821	4750	2673	5800	4697	5999	3000	4331
Apr	8596	8138	7869	8617	5245	3886	6000	5854
May	6129	3559	3322	5800	2651	3111	4100	0
Jun	3788	2851	4535	5000	6269	6932	5000	0
Jly	4737	4983	3847	5000	3733	2991	3700	0
Aug	4203	3224	3392	4500	4101	5876	3700	0
Sep	6440	5340	5700	7800	5150	5906	5500	0
Oct	6186	5909	6448	6466	6255	5549	6500	0
Nov	6402	5600	4864	6500	3633	3876	5000	0
Dec	3602	2955	2804	2500	3952	3803	3000	0

EXHIBIT 5
HISTORICAL DEMAND, SALES AND FORECASTS FOR SELECTED HIGHER VOLUME S.K.U.S

Part #535

Month	1989 Sales	1990 Sales	1990 Demand	1990 Forecasts	1991 Sales	1991 Demand	1991 Forecasts	1992 Sales
Jan	5750	3001	3130	3314	4192	4870	7000	5095
Feb	7789	7332	10046	6000	7173	6502	8400	6567
Mar	4952	6289	4000	4000	5287	5959	4100	5945
Apr	3666	6517	8719	4600	7655	7056	7000	6755
May	4981	5312	3029	5300	3728	3935	4000	0
Jun	5267	4735	5658	4900	6510	6823	5450	0
Jly	3731	3957	3531	4500	5030	5635	3600	0
Aug	6400	4512	5122	6000	9694	9115	4800	0
Sep	6261	5439	7088	8000	3751	5161	7000	0
Oct	6384	10240	8531	6000	9549	7971	8600	0
Nov	6426	5093	4559	6035	5927	6141	5000	0
Dec	3699	3695	3110	3200	6573	7105	3700	0

Part #061

Month	1989 Sales	1990 Sales	1990 Demand	1990 Forecasts	1991 Sales	1991 Demand	1991 Forecasts	1992 Sales
Jan	3183	1191	1155	2377	1141	1261	2500	1288
Feb	2044	3024	4643	1500	2660	2577	3000	1784
Mar	3339	2578	1197	3400	2234	3045	1300	1948
Apr	4200	3631	3557	4635	3053	2569	2400	2689
May	3145	1273	1195	2500	1457	1271	1700	0
Jun	1893	1460	2578	1800	2703	3053	2300	0
Jly	1990	2339	1569	2100	1573	1109	1500	0
Aug	2445	1468	1617	2000	1067	1694	1600	0
Sep	2531	2051	2282	3500	1939	1533	2200	0
Oct	3332	2891	3037	2960	2423	2289	2900	0
Nov	3431	2271	2012	3400	1503	1661	2000	0
Dec	2072	1390	1309	1600	1823	2093	1300	0

Part #746

Month	1989 Sales	1990 Sales	1990 Demand	1990 Forecasts	1991 Sales	1991 Demand	1991 Forecasts	1992 Sales
Jan	2510	1668	1421	1627	1658	1680	1400	2199
Feb	1404	1569	3700	1706	2803	2770	2600	2454
Mar	2139	4213	2068	2300	2616	2771	1860	2545
Apr	2387	3135	3199	3222	2988	2946	2600	3194
May	3297	1203	1145	2200	1120	1089	1400	0
Jun	1677	1406	1581	2000	2605	3520	1900	0
Jly	1680	1645	1526	2100	2462	1782	1400	0
Aug	2329	1359	1563	2000	2102	2383	2000	0
Sep	1721	2317	2264	3200	1748	1475	2300	0
Oct	2385	2707	2863	2500	3119	2625	2900	0
Nov	2608	2173	1982	1900	2461	2488	2100	0
Dec	1890	1360	1071	2141	1303	2195	1500	0

PARKE-DAVIS PROFESSIONAL HEALTH GROUP

This case was prepared by Professor Adrian B. Ryans as a basis for class discussion rather than to illustrate either effective or ineffective handling of an administrative situation.

In May 1984 Mr. Marvin Skripitsky, the Marketing Director of the Parke-Davis Professional Health Group, was in the process of preparing the 1985 Strategic Plan recommendations for his group. A formal presentation of his recommendations was to be made to Mr. Robert Serenbetz, the President of Warner-Lambert Canada, at the end of May. As Mr. Skripitsky reviewed the Group's situation, he was convinced that the most pressing problem facing the Group was the lack of detailing capacity in the sales force. The Professional Health Group was planning to introduce a number of new products over the next three years and there appeared to be insufficient sales force time available to adequately present new and existing products (i.e., to "detail" the products) to the medical community. He viewed this inability to properly promote the Group's pharmaceutical products as the major barrier to meeting the Group's growth objectives. Mr. Skripitsky knew that he, in consultation with Mr. Malcolm Seath the General Manager of the Health Care Division and Mr. Gerry Gibson the Group's Director of Sales, would have to make specific recommendations for dealing with the detailing capacity problem at the presentation to Mr. Serenbetz.

COMPANY

Parke-Davis was the pharmaceutical affiliate of Warner-Lambert, a major U.S.-based multinational. With worldwide sales of over $3.1 billion (U.S.) Warner-Lambert manufactured a wide range of pharmaceutical, personal care and other products including such well-known brands as Listerine, Chiclets and Schick. Parke-Davis had been founded in Detroit, Michigan in 1866, and the company began operations in Canada in 1887 making it the second pharmaceutical company to operate in Canada. Over the years Parke-Davis had pioneered many significant health care products including the first anti-diptheric serum in 1893, Dilantin for the control of epilepsy in 1938, Benadryl the first antihistamine in North America in 1946, and in 1949 Chloromycetin the first wide spectrum antibiotic to be discovered. Parke-Davis was acquired by Warner-Lambert in 1970. In 1979 Parke-Davis and Warner-Chilcott, the original pharmaceutical division of Warner-Lambert, were merged into one division to become the pharmaceutical component of Warner-Lambert Canada Inc. In 1983 Parke-Davis was merged with Warner Lambert's Personal Products business unit to form a new Health Care Division. In 1984 the Health Care Division was projected to have sales of $87 million with Parke-Davis accounting for $62 million of these sales.

The mission of the Health Care Division was to be a Canadian leader in developing and providing pharmaceutical and personal care products for health and well being while achieving steady growth in sales and profits. In the five year strategic planning period beginning in 1985 the division was targeting for annual sales growth 4% above the level of inflation to achieve sales of approximately $133 million by 1989. Management of the health care division believed that this objective was attainable, since the division enjoyed a number of major strengths, including a planned stream of major new products during the planning period, a broadly based product line that was not dependent on one or two major products or product categories, and a strong clinical trial and registration capability to expedite the approval of new pharmaceuticals and new claims for existing products. In addition, Parke-Davis had a strong image in the minds of consumers, pharmacists, doctors and government. Most image studies placed Parke-Davis within the top five firms on almost every image criterion. This strong corporate image was useful in gaining access to doctors and the drug trade, and was helpful in developing and maintaining a consumer franchise for smaller non-prescription brands that could not support direct consumer advertising. While the broadly-based product line was a strength in many respects, it also represented a weakness in that it made it difficult for the sales force to find the time to adequately detail all the products to the doctors. In addition, many physicians no longer viewed Parke-Davis as an innovator, since the product line was relatively old. A successful introduction of the planned new products was expected to correct this.

In Canada, the Health Care Division was comprised of two major groups: the Consumer Health Group and the Professional Health Group. Because both Warner-Chilcott and Parke-Davis had several big proprietary and OTC pharmaceuticals in 1979, the merger resulted in the Consumer Health Group becoming the largest supplier of self-medication products in Canada including such well known brands as Benylin, Agarol, Sinutab and Gelusil.[1] These products were sold under the Parke-Davis name. The Consumer Health Group also marketed a wide range of personal care products, including Listerine, Bromo, Softsoap, Showermate, Schick, Topol and Lensrins, that were distributed through drug stores and other convenient retail outlets. In addition to its extensive line of prescription ethical pharmaceuticals the Professional Health Group was responsible for promoting selected Consumer Health Group brands, such as Benylin, a major brand of cough syrup, to physicians. The General Manager of the Health Care Division was Mr. Malcolm Seath.

Professional Health Group

The 1984 sales of the Professional Health Group were forecasted to be $33 million and the Group had an objective of increasing sales to over $50 million by 1989. Direct cost of goods sold and freight typically amounted to about 25% of selling price. During this period the Professional Health Group hoped to increase its market share in ethical (prescription) pharmaceuticals from 1.8% to 2.2%. The Professional Health Group was headed by the Marketing Director, Mr. Marvin Skripitsky. Reporting to the Marketing Director were two group product managers and the Director of Sales, Mr. Gerry Gibson. A simplified organization chart for the Group is shown in Exhibit 1. By 1984 the sales force consisted of 56 Medical Representatives, 4 Medical Information Associates, 8 District Managers and 3 Regional Managers.

The Professional Health Group was responsible for the 24 products or product groups shown in Exhibit 2. The Professional Health Group planned to add fifteen additional products to the product line over the next three years with these products having potential sales of over $25 million by 1989.

---

[1]Pharmaceutical products were usually divided into ethical and proprietary categories depending on how they were marketed by the manufacturer. Ethical products were marketed directly to the medical profession, whereas proprietary products were promoted directly to the consumer. Ethical products were commonly divided into two further categories: prescription pharmaceuticals and over-the-counter (OTC) pharmaceuticals. As the name implies prescription pharmaceuticals were available only on a prescription written by a physician. OTC pharmaceuticals could be purchased by the consumer without a prescription.

EXHIBIT I

PARKE-DAVIS PROFESSIONAL HEALTH GROUP, PARTIAL ORGANIZATION CHART OF THE HEALTH CARE DIVISION

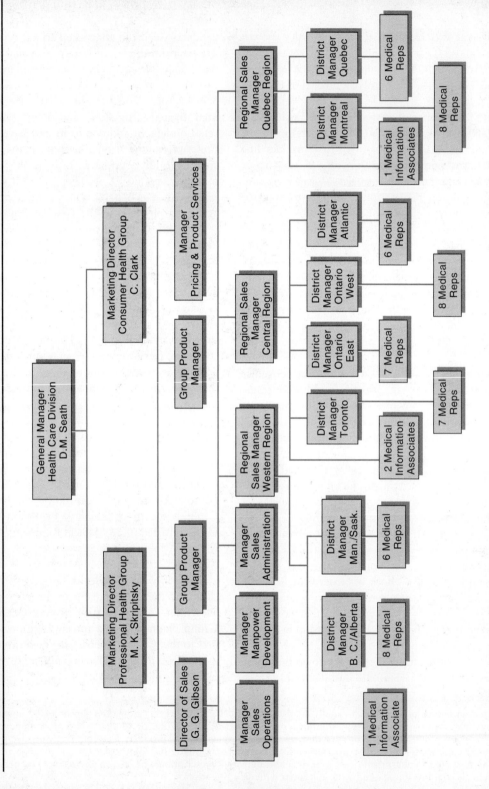

EXHIBIT 2		
PARKE-DAVIS PROFESSIONAL HEALTH GROUP		
Parke-Davis Products		
Anticonvulsants	Eryc	Ponstan
Prescription hemorrhoidals (Anusol)	Hose	Tucks
Amsa	Lopid	Tedral
Benadryl	Mylanta	Thrombostat
Choledyl	Nardil	Pyridium
Chloro/Vira-A	Nicrostat	Mandelamine
Colymycin	Oral contraceptives	Beben
Elase	Peritrate	Vanquin

INDUSTRY ENVIRONMENT

Management of the Health Care Division saw both threats and opportunities in the external environment. Health care costs were expected to continue to increase faster than the economy as a whole due to technological developments and an aging population. Although management felt that pharmaceuticals were the most cost effective part of the health care system, they believed that pharmaceuticals would continue to attract the attention of politicians and others responsible for controlling health care costs. Some provinces had adopted "formularies" in an attempt to control pharmaceutical costs. In these cases the provincial government would only pay for pharmaceuticals listed in the formulary for people who were receiving government assistance in paying for pharmaceuticals. In addition management believed that the increasing complexity of the the health care system would force politicians to give more power to bureaucrats who would be perceived as "unbiased". In this environment access to key politicians and bureaucrats would be the key.

Insurance companies, which paid at least some drug bills for 70% of Canadians, were expected to become increasingly important. Historically they had been passive participants in the health care system paying whatever pharmacists charged for whatever pharmaceuticals were prescribed by doctors. Some were now attempting to restrict the choice of pharmaceuticals for which they would provide full reimbursement and in some cases they were attempting to force mandatory substitution of generic drugs.

On the more positive side there was a growing feeling in the industry that the Federal Government might change Canada's compulsory licensing laws to encourage more innovation in pharmaceuticals in Canada and to encourage more pharmaceutical firms to conduct more of their research in Canada. The compulsory licensing law in Canada required the patent-holding manufacturer to license patented products to other manufacturers.

Parke-Davis executives continued to believe that the keys to growth in the pharmaceutical industry in Canada would be the development of innovative new products and strong marketing of these products.

MARKET FOR PHARMACEUTICAL PRODUCTS IN CANADA

The total market for ethical and proprietary pharmaceutical products in Canada was more than $2.5 billion with 17% of these sales being made to hospitals. The medical community in Canada was comprised of about 43,000 doctors and over 1,000 hospitals. There were also almost 5,000 retail pharmacies in Canada.

Competition

The overall pharmaceutical industry in Canada was highly competitive with the largest company, American Home Products, having less than 8% market share of the combined ethical and proprietary pharmaceutical market sold through hospitals and drug stores. An additional 14 companies had market shares greater than 2%. The various divisions of Warner-Lambert had a combined market share of over 3%. Most of these companies were broad line pharmaceutical companies. Competition in the industry seemed to be increasing with the recent entry of major non-pharmaceutical companies through the acquisition of small pharmaceutical companies. Both Proctor and Gamble and Dow Chemical had entered the market using this mechanism in the early 1980s.

In total by the end of 1983 there were 55 pharmaceutical companies with sales forces operating in Canada. The number of medical representatives employed by these companies are shown in Exhibit 3. Some of the major competitors operated under more than one name and corporate structure. American Home Products operated under the Wyeth, Ayerst and Whitehall names. Johnson and Johnson sold its products under the Ortho, Johnson and Johnson, McNeil and Janssen names. Several companies, including both American Home Products and Johnson and Johnson, had more than one sales force. Merck Frosst, the company with the largest number of medical representatives in Canada had three different sales forces operating under different names with almost 140 representatives at the end of 1983. When a company had more than one sales force, they usually operated under the names of different divisions (often the names of predecessor companies). Thus Johnson and Johnson had two sales forces operating under the McNeil and Ortho names. Earlier in 1984, one relatively small pharmaceutical company, Boehringer-Ingelheim, had added a second sales force. The two sales forces were using the same name and the calling cards of the salespersons simply indicated that they were specialists in particular therapeutic classes. It was too early to measure the acceptance of this approach by the medical community. The large number of sales forces meant that the competition for a doctor's time was intense—Mr. Gibson estimated that some doctors could have as many as 40 to 50 medical representatives trying to see them in a given two month period.

EXHIBIT 3
PARKE-DAVIS PROFESSIONAL HEALTH GROUP

Number of Medical Representatives Employed by Competitors in Canada

Size of Sales Force[a]	Number of Companies
0–10	3
11–20	4
21–30	9
31–40	4
41–50	15
51–60	13
61–70	6
71 or greater	1
Total number of sales forces	55

[a]Excludes managers and OTC representatives.

All the major brand name manufacturers of pharmaceuticals faced competition from generic manufacturers.

The Selling of Ethical Pharmaceuticals in Canada

Medical representatives (over 25,000 of them in North America alone) played a key role in the selling of ethical pharmaceuticals. Often called "detail men" (although they were increasingly women) for the details they provide doctors and pharmacists about pharmaceuticals, they played a key role in trying to convince doctors to prescribe their company's pharmaceuticals to the doctor's patients. Many market research studies concluded that doctors relied very heavily on medical representatives for information on prescribing pharmaceuticals. Some authorities suggested that the success of a new pharmaceutical could depend almost as much on the effectiveness of the medical representatives promoting the new product as on the product itself. The medical profession was faced with the difficult problem of keeping up with the flood of new pharmaceuticals that were continually becoming available. While the pharmaceuticals in major therapeutic product classes such as those designed to treat heart disease shared many similarities the differences could be critical to the patients using the pharmaceutical. Detail men played a crucial role in providing the kind of information that would help a doctor decide whether a particular pharmaceutical was appropriate for a particular patient's condition. Many doctors, particularly harried general practitioners with a diverse practice, found it difficult to keep up with all the literature on the products that they might use in their practice, and they appreciated the information a detail man could provide. A well-trained detail man could provide the doctor with information on the chemical composition of the pharmaceutical, its possible side effects, and how it would interact with other medicines a patient might be taking. From the pharmaceutical company's point of view detail men provided a valuable feedback channel sometimes alerting the company to side effects that might not have been noticed before. Detail men also frequently organized symposia for groups of doctors often bringing in outside medical authorities to help bring doctors up to date on current medical practice and pharmaceuticals. Major pharmaceutical companies regularly had their representatives set up displays in major hospitals in their territories. These displays of products and literature were staffed by the representative

and many doctors dropped by after their morning rounds in the hospital or at the end of the working day.

One of the toughest jobs many detail men faced was getting past the receptionist or the nurse in a doctor's office, particularly when the office was crowded and the doctor was behind schedule. Increasingly doctors were establishing rules that they would only see one medical representative a day. Parke-Davis representatives tried to make appointments with the doctor ahead of time, when this was possible. Even when the medical representative got into the doctor's office the doctor might keep the representative waiting and might be interrupted by a nurse or a telephone call during their conversation. The representative typically only had 5 to 10 minutes to make his presentation. During the presentation he might place primary emphasis on one or two products with brief reminders about one or two others. The pharmaceuticals presented to a particular doctor depended on the nature of the doctor's speciality and practice. Doctors frequently asked questions about products or might have questions about the appropriateness of particular products in a given situation.

EXHIBIT 4
PARKE-DAVIS PROFESSIONAL HEALTH GROUP
Coverage of Physicians and Retail Pharmacies by Parke-Davis Sales Force by Province

	British Columbia	Alberta	Saskatchewan	Manitoba	Ontario	Quebec	Atlantic Provinces	Total Canada
Physicians								
Total Physicians[a]	5,180	3,310	1,410	1,870	15,900	12,470	3,340	43,480
Covered by Parke-Davis	1,750	1,400	700	700	6,300	4,550	1,750	17,500
% Covered by Parke-Davis	33.8	42.3	49.7	37.4	39.6	36.5	52.4	40.2
Retail Pharmacies								
Total Retail Pharmacies	593	559	229	285	1,648	1,079	502	4,965
Covered by Parke-Davis	400	320	160	160	1,440	1,040	400	4,000
% Covered by Parke-Davis	67.5	57.5	53.5	56.1	87.4	96.4	79.7	80.6

[a]This includes all physicians registered in a province. Not all physicians registered in a province were active in a medical practice. For example, some were retired or employed in teaching, research or administrative positions.

Parke-Davis sales representatives were expected to make 5-6 calls per day on doctors, about two calls per day on retail pharmacies and perhaps one call every two days on a hospital. As did many other major pharmaceutical companies Parke-Davis divided each year into six two month sales cycles. A major planning issue was the decision as to which one or two products should get primary emphasis in each of these sales cycles for each medical specialty. Each medical representative attempted to call on all the doctors, retail pharmacies and hospitals targeted by Parke-Davis at least once during each sales cycle. By 1984 Parke-Davis was targeting its sales force at some 18,000 doctors out of the 43,000 in Canada, and at over 80% of the retail pharmacies. The approximate Parke-Davis coverage of physicians and retail pharmacies by province is shown in Exhibit 4.

THE PROFESSIONAL HEALTH GROUP SALES FORCE

Organization

The field sales force of 60 persons was divided into two groups: the 56 Medical Representatives and 4 Medical Information Associates (MIAs). The Medical Representatives were organized into 8 geographical districts, each headed by a District Manager, and had responsibility for detailing the full Professional Health Group product line to the medical community in their geographical territories.

In 1983 top management of the Professional Health Group had become very concerned about the ability of the Medical Representatives to detail their large existing product line, and at the same time introduce the large number of sophisticated new products that were planned in the future. The introduction of a sophisticated new pharmaceutical often required that the medical representative focus on key specialists and other potential opinion leaders. Since the Medical Representatives had largely been trying to maintain sales of existing products rather than introduce new ones over the preceding three or four years, they often were not actively working these key specialists. To overcome this problem management decided to add a small number of more sophisticated representatives with stronger medical and pharmacological training, and very strong communication skills. These representatives would specialize in launching new products and would do the initial follow-up with doctors after the launch of the product. Given their strong educational background and the fact that at any point in time they would be focusing on a very small number of new products, it would be possible to provide them with more in-depth knowledge about each new product than could be given to the Medical Representatives.

The company began to add the MIAs in 1983. They were also given geographical territories, but these territories were obviously much larger than those of the Medical Representatives, since 4 of them had to cover the whole of Canada. The four MIAs reported directly to the Regional Managers. Two were assigned to the Central Region and one each to the Quebec and Western Regions.

Recruiting and Selection

In selecting new representatives the Professional Health Group sought individuals with a strong background in one of the health sciences. Most recent recruits had Bachelors degrees in Science, Nursing or Pharmacy. Some were recruited directly out of university, but many had worked in the health care industry before joining Parke-Davis. One recent recruit was a Registered Nurse with several years of nursing experience in a hospital. Another was a pharmacist in his early 30s, who had become bored with the routine of dispensing pharmaceuticals and the long hours associated with operating a retail pharmacy.

Training

After joining Parke-Davis each Medical Representative attended two two-week training programs in Toronto. This training included material on Parke-Davis, and intensive training on biology and pharmacology, product information on the Parke-Davis product line and some basic selling skills training. Between the sessions the representative was in his or her territory under the close supervision of the district manager. Training was a continuing process in any pharmaceutical company with each representative receiving training in new products as they were introduced. When a major new product was introduced it was common to provide the representatives with programmed learning materials, followed by an intensive two day training meeting in Toronto. Many salesperson were also continually trying to update their skills by reading textbooks and a variety of other medical and pharmacological information made available to them by their companies. About every two years all medical representatives come to Toronto for an intensive "refresher" sales training course.

Compensation

Parke-Davis compensated its representatives using a base salary plus bonus compensation plan. In 1984 base salaries for representatives varied from $21,000 for a new sales trainee with no experience to $36,000 for a senior sales representative. In addition each representative was eligible for a regional bonus of up to 15% of base salary and an individual merit bonus of up to 10% of base salary. Thus a high-performing medical representative could earn as much as $45,000 plus fringe benefits and the use of a company automobile.

The regional bonus was based on the region's success in meeting sales objectives. For the purpose of calculating the regional bonus the product line was divided into A, B, and C brands. "A" brands were those that in the opinion of management were the most profitable and had the greatest potential for future growth. "B" brands included high volume brands with less potential for growth, but whose sales should be maintained. "C" brands included all other brands, which were not typically actively promoted. Management established objectives for each of the three groups of brands for each of the three regions and performance against these objectives was measured. Approximately 55% of the bonus was applied to the achievement of

the A objective, 30% to the achievement of the B objective, and 15% to the achievement of the C objective. If a region met exactly 100% of its objectives for each group of brands each member of the regional team would receive a bonus of 10.5% of base salary. If 102% or more of the objective for each group was met, the full 15% bonus was awarded. Management did not believe it was feasible to do this monitoring at lower than a region level due to the difficulty of establishing exactly which representative or even district was responsible for a given sale. It was not uncommon for a prescription to be written by a doctor in one city, for the prescription to be filled at a retail pharmacy in another city, and for that pharmacy to have its drugs shipped from a warehouse in a different province.

The individual bonus was based on the district manager's judgment of the individual's contribution relative to others in the region. In order to make this judgment the district manager reviewed territory sales data, call activity and other activities, such as the number of symposia organized by the representative and the number of physicians who attended these symposia. The individual bonus decisions had to be reviewed and approved by the responsible regional manager and Mr. Gibson. District managers were in a good position to make this subjective judgment since they spent at least one day every month in the field with each of the representatives they supervised.

Performance Appraisal

Each representative was formally reviewed once a year by his or her manager. In this performance appraisal the district manager carefully reviewed the representative's achievements since the last review and any areas of concern. Particular attention was paid to the employee's skills in managing the work and in dealing with other people. The manager also focused on the individual's promotability and training and development needs. Each performance appraisal was reviewed by the regional manager and Mr. Gibson.

Motivation

A sales meeting was held once during each of the six sales cycles during the year. These meetings played an important role in the training and motivation of the sales force. Frequently these meetings would be held at the district level, but occasionally regional or national meetings would be held, particularly when a major new program or product was about to be launched.

THE DETAILING CAPACITY PROBLEM

In the strategic planning process for the Parke-Davis Professional Health Group in May 1984, Mr. Seath, Mr. Skripitsky and Mr. Gibson viewed the Professional Health Group's lack of detailing capacity as its most pressing problem. The Group had launched Eryc, a major new antibiotic, in December 1983 with a first year sales objective of $600,000. While the MIA sales force had played a major role in the pre-launch and launch activities for the product and was actively involved in the follow-up, the Medical Representatives would have to support it aggressively in their detailing calls for the next eighteen months or so, if it was to achieve its market potential. In May 1984, Lopid, a major new cardiovascular pharmaceutical, was introduced with a first year sales objective of almost $500,000. Again, the MIAs were playing a major role in the introduction. With three more new products slated for introduction in 1985, seven more in 1986, and at least five more in 1987, the detailing capacity problem was critical.

The magnitude of the problem was evident to Mr. Skripitsky and Mr. Gibson as they looked at the tentative 1985 Medical Promotion Schedule for the year beginning January 1, 1985 shown in Exhibit 5. Eryc and Lopid, the two new products, would require much of the available primary detailing time. In the case of General Practitioners (GPs) six of the twelve available spots were taken up by the two new products, with an additional two of the twelve spots taken up by Choledyl SA, another relatively new product introduced early in 1983. Increasingly the inclusion of new products meant that important "bread and butter" products, many with good growth potential, would have to be dropped from active sale force promotion.

One brand that would fall in this category was Anusol HC, a pharmaceutically elegant prescription hemorrhoidal preparation, that was targeted at general practitioners, family physicians and surgeons. With projected 1984 sales of $3.1 million, a market share of almost 50% in a market with a real growth rate of over 5%, and a manufacturing contribution margin of over 60% it was a major contributor to Parke-Davis' sales and profits. In 1984 total advertising and promotional spending on the product was expected to be over $500,000 with about 40% of this for samples. A breakdown of the actual advertising and promotion budget for 1984 and the planned budget for 1985 are shown in Exhibit 6. A projected 34% increase in the budget to support a 10% increase in sales was a partial response to the decreased availability of detailing time for the brand.

Alternatives Under Consideration

As the management team of the Professional Health Group grappled with the problem of insufficient personal medical detailing time it was apparent that there were several options open to them. The major options open to them were:

1. *Expand utilization of the MIAs to provide pre-launch, launch and the entire post-launch responsibility for new products for key specialists.* This option would insure that the new products would be very effectively detailed to the key potential prescribing specialists for a particular new product. The major disadvantage of this option was that the MIAs would be of little assistance in detailing the new products to general practitioners.
2. *Increase the size of the regular sales force.* This would allow the geographical territories to be smaller permitting Parke-Davis to reach more doctors. However management felt it was unlikely to increase the detailing time a salesperson could spend with key doctors for the Parke-Davis product line, since doctors would be unlikely to be willing to talk to the medical representative more

EXHIBIT 5

PARKE-DAVIS PROFESSIONAL HEALTH GROUP

Planned 1985 Medical Promotion Schedule Two-Month Sales Promotion Cycle

		1	2	3	4	5	6
General Practitioners (GPs)	Primary	Lopid Benylin	Eryc Choledyl SA	Lopid Benadryl	Choledyl SA Lopid	Lopid Ponstan	Eryc Mylanta
	Reminder	Eryc Mylanta	Mylanta Anusol/Tucks	Ponstan Mylanta	Eryc Ponstan	Eryc Mylanta	Anusol/T Benylin
Surgeons	Primary	Mylanta Thrombostat	Anusol/Tucks	Mylanta Thrombostat	Mylanta	Thrombostat	Anusol/T
	Reminder	Hose	Hose	Anusol/Tucks Hose	Hose	Mylanta Hose	Mylanta Hose
Pediatricians	Primary	Benylin Choledyl Liquid	Benylin Choledyl Liquid	Benadryl Colymycin	Benadryl Vanquin	Choledyl Liquid Benylin	Benylin Choledyl Liquid
Obstetrics/ Gynecology (OB/GYNs)	Primary	Ponstan	Ponstan Mylanta	Ponstan	Ponstan	Mylanta Thrombostat	OC's Ponstan
	Reminder	Mylanta Tucks OC's	Tucks	Tucks OC's	OC's Tucks	Mylanta Tucks	Mylanta Hose
Internal Medicine	Primary	Lopid	Lopid Nitrostat IV Eryc	Lopid Eryc	Lopid Nitrostat IV Eryc	Lopid Nitrostat IV	Lopid Eryc
	Reminder	Mylanta Eryc	Mylanta	Mylanta Benadryl	Mylanta	Mylanta Eryc	Mylanta Benylin
Hospital Staff		Thrombostat Chloromycetin Mylanta	Nitrostat IV Benadryl Elase	Thrombostat Benadryl Mylanta	Nitrostat IV Elase	Thrombostat Chloromycetin Mylanta	Nitro IV Elase
Misc. Samples		Ponstan Hose	Hose Benylin	Hose Colymycin Eryc Anusol/Tucks	Benadryl Hose	Benadryl Hose Benylin	Ponstan Hose

EXHIBIT 6

PARKE-DAVIS PROFESSIONAL HEALTH GROUP

Advertising and Promotion Budget for Prescription Anusol in 1984 and 1985 (Planned)

	1984 (Estimated) (in $000)	1985 (Planned) (in $000)	Percentage change from 1984 to 1985
Promotion			
"Loss of Revenue"[a]	221	242	10
Medical Promotion	8	10	25
Mailing of samples	15	15	0
Samples (cost of goods)	224	307	37
Total	468	574	23
Advertising			
Print	78	150	92
Print Production	0	12	—
Agency Fees	24	26	8
Audits and Surveys	6	7	17
Total	108	195	81
Total Advertising and Promotion Budget	574	769	34
% of Sales	18	22	

[a]"Loss of revenue" was the estimated cost of price discounts and free-goods (buy 11 and get 1 free) that would be offered to the retail drug trade.

than once during each two month sales cycle. Thus the representative's capacity to detail more products to any one physician would not be enhanced.

3. *Develop a second medical sales force for the Professional Health Group.* The existing product line could be split between the two sales forces, perhaps with one sales force specializing in the cardiovascular and pulmonary products and the other sales force specializing in the anti-infective and anti-inflammatory products. If the few miscellaneous products in the Parke-Davis product line were also assigned to the second sales force, the two sales forces would have similar dollar volumes. Of the 15 new products planned for the 1985-87 period six would be in the first group of products and nine in the second group of products. With this option many physicians, drug stores and hospitals would be detailed by two Parke-Davis medical representatives, thus doubling the number of products that could be detailed in any two-month sales cycle. However management was unsure how the medical profession would react to this strategy—would doctors agree to

see two different Parke-Davis representatives during a given two month sales cycle, or would they only see one in each sales cycle? Management were also unsure how competition might react to this strategy. While some other competitors did have more than one sales force, with the exception of the recent move by Boehringer-Ingelheim these different sales forces operated under different names—often the names of predecessor companies.

4. *Make no changes in the sales force, but make adjustments elsewhere to reflect the detailing capacity problem.* Some managers felt it would be possible to revamp the detailing schedule to maximize the number of products on promotion. Substantial increases in the advertising and promotion support to brands might also reduce the need for detailing time on some of the products. To handle the large number of anticipated new product introductions, these introductions could be delayed to provide a minimum four to six months interval between the introduction of new brands. The detailing load could also be reduced by licensing the new products with low sales potential to other pharmaceutical manufacturers.

EXHIBIT 7

PARKE-DAVIS PROFESSIONAL HEALTH GROUP, PROPOSED SALES ORGANIZATION WITH TWO SALES FORCES

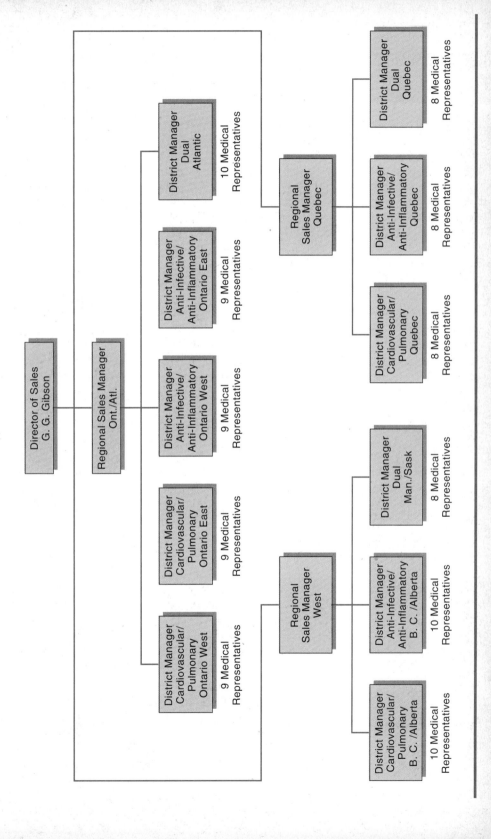

The Second Sales Force Option

By far the most radical of the four options under consideration was the addition of the second sales force. It was viewed to be quite risky and if the decision to proceed with it was made there were several major implementation issues that would need to be addressed.

In "fleshing out" the two sales force option for discussion purposes, Mr. Skripitsky and Mr. Gibson thought that they would require 49 representatives for each sales force organized as shown in Exhibit 7. Where feasible district managers would be responsible for medical representatives from only one of the sales forces, although in the more geographically dispersed areas like Manitoba/Saskatchewan, rural Quebec and the Atlantic Provinces, the district managers would have medical representatives from both sales forces reporting to them. Mr. Skripitsky and Mr. Gibson envisioned the continuance of the MIA sales force with five representatives assigned to it. The MIAs would support both sales forces as needed. The 1985 incremental cost of adding salespersons, managers and support staff and facilities was estimated to average about $57,000 per person in the field, that is $2.4 million for the 42 incremental persons that would be required to staff the two sales forces.

Sales force costs were expected to rise about 7% per year during the rest of the 1980s.

If a second sales force was added the number of detailing slots available would be increased from 24 (four slots in each of the six sales cycles) to 48. In a preliminary look at the potential impact of this doubling of slots management thought that the 1985 Medical Promotion Schedule for general practitioners might be modified as shown in Exhibit 8. This would allow several more products to be detailed, some of them at high frequencies. In consultation with the product managers for the various products involved Mr. Skripitsky and Mr. Gibson estimated that under the two sales force options sales might be $1.3 million higher in 1985 than they would be with the continuance of current policies. Incremental sales of $4.6 million, $5.6 million, $7.9 million and $9.5 million were expected in 1986, 1987, 1988, and 1989 respectively. The sources of these incremental sales are shown in Exhibit 9.

If the decision was made to add a second sales force there were several major implementation issues that needed to be addressed. A major concern was the naming of the two sales forces. Two major options had been proposed. Some managers thought that both sales forces should

---

EXHIBIT 8
PARKE-DAVIS PROFESSIONAL HEALTH GROUP

1985 Product Exposure to General Practitioners (GPs) without and with Second Sales Force (Frequency on Detail Schedule)

Product	Current Plan	Plan with Second Sales Force	Change
Lopid	4	5	1
Benylin	2	4	2
Eryc	5	4	(1)
Mylanta	5	6	1
Choledyl	2	4	2
Anusol/Tucks	2	5	3
Benadryl	1	2	1
Ponstan	3	3	—
Hose	—	3	3
Oral Contraceptives	—	6	6
Colymycin OTC	—	1	1
Procan	—	5	5
	24	48	24

EXHIBIT 9					
PARKE-DAVIS PROFESSIONAL HEALTH GROUP					
Estimated Impact of Second Sales Force on Sales (in Thousands of Dollars)					
	1985	1986	1987	1988	1989
Incremental Sales from Existing Ethical Products	615	1,215	1,680	2,440	3,040
Incremental Sales from Consumer Health Group Products[a]	300	350	400	450	500
Incremental Sales from New Products	400	3,000	3,500	5,000	6,000
Total Incremental Sales	1,315	4,565	5,580	7,890	9,540

[a]Consumer Health Group products sold under the Parke-Davis brand, e.g. Benylin and Gelusil.

operate clearly under the Parke-Davis name with one sales force being called the Cardiovascular/Pulmonary Sales Group and the other the Anti-Infective/Anti-Inflammatory Sales Group. Others thought that the Parke-Davis name should be used but that the salespersons be represented as coming from two separate divisions. Suggestions for the division names included Research Laboratories Division of Parke-Davis, the Scientific Laboratories Division of Parke-Davis, and the Warner Laboratories Division of Parke-Davis. The chosen name would appear on the representative's calling card. Another issue was whether all medical representatives should be trained on the full Parke-Davis product line, or just on the part of the product line sold by their sales force. As more new products were introduced training on the full product line would probably require that the sales training program be lengthened. Perhaps the major implementation issue was how to introduce the idea of two Parke-Davis sales forces to the doctor and his or her receptionist/nurse. A negative reaction on their part could jeopardize the whole two sales force plan. A continuing problem would be the need for the two sales representatives serving a particular geographical area to coordinate their activities so that they didn't end up calling on the same doctors at about the same time.

Mr. Gibson also wondered how the sales force would react if a second sales force were to be introduced. He could imagine some salespersons being concerned that an additional salesperson in their territory would make it more difficult for them to see their doctors and to gain as frequent access to hospitals. Many would be concerned about how any changes would affect their compensation and would want assurance that they wouldn't be expected to generate the same absolute dollar increases in sales on a reduced business base.

Possible Test

If the decision was made to add a second sales force, Mr. Skripitsky and Mr. Gibson wondered if they should first test the concept in one part of Canada, prior to introducing it nationally. If they proposed a test, they would have to recommend how it should be conducted, where it should be conducted, and how long it should last. The choice of a test area would not be an easy one. Every province or region of the country had significant drawbacks. British Columbia was geographically large and the Vancouver area had a very high ratio of physicians to people. Alberta had the advantages of being a relatively isolated market with little government intervention and having the Parke-Davis Western Region office in Edmonton. The latter would facilitate monitoring of any test. On the negative side it was a market in which Parke-Davis did extremely well and might not be representative from that point of view. The Alberta economy was also depressed in 1984. Both Saskatchewan and Manitoba were isolated markets, but both provincial governments had very restrictive formularies making them unrepresentative of the rest of Canada. Ontario's major disadvantage was its size. With over 36% of Canada's population, it seemed too large for a test market. If only part of the province was used, monitoring the results of the test would be extremely difficult and expensive given the potential spillover effects of marketing activity in one part of the province into other areas. Quebec was also large and was a market where Parke-Davis was having some problems in early 1984. In addition, while the company had the capability to train French-speaking representatives, the burden of training people for the test would fall heavily on the shoulders of one individual. The Atlantic Provinces were viewed as being somewhat unique in Canada from a pharmaceutical marketing prospective, and Mr. Skripitsky and Mr. Gibson did not feel that any results obtained there would necessarily be projectable to the rest of the country.

THE SITUATION IN MAY 1984

As Mr. Skripitsky sat down in late May to decide what sales force recommendations should be included in the five year plan he knew that he would have to deal with a number of key issues that Mr. Seath was likely to bring up. Mr. Skripitsky felt that Mr. Seath would have major concerns about the two sales forces option. One of his concerns would be the large, continuing, fixed costs that would be associated with a second sales force. Warner-Lambert considered itself a very "people-oriented" company, and there would be no question of dismissing members of the second sales force, if it did not work out. The investment of resources in a new salesperson was also considerable.

Mr. Skripitsky felt the company's investment in a new salesperson could add up to $50,000 in the first two years the representative was with the company. Mr. Seath would want to be convinced that any additions to the sales force head count would be fully warranted and that the additions were meeting a permanent need not a temporary one. While Mr. Skripitsky expected that the fifteen new products would be introduced, there was always the possibility that some of the introductions might have to be delayed or cancelled, if unforseen problems, such as a failure to get regulatory approval for a product, occurred. Mr. Seath would also want Mr. Skripitsky's assurance that the older products would in fact respond to more detailing time.

Mr. Skripitsky also knew that a key element of Mr. Seath's strategy for the Health Care Division was the continuing establishment of the Parke-Davis name as a highly respected brand name in the medical community. Mr. Seath would need to be convinced that the addition of a second sales force would not lead to any dilution of the Parke-Davis name.

Before presenting his recommendations Mr. Skripitsky knew he'd have to develop a detailed set of recommendations for whichever option he chose. If he decided on the two sales forces option, he would have to have specific recommendations on its size, timing, the naming of the sales forces, whether or not to test market the concept, and a host of implementation issues. He realized he had a lot of work to do within the next week to prepare his recommendations.

BAY CITY STEAM FITTINGS, INC.

Case contributed by Ronald H. King and W. E. Patton III, Professors of Marketing, Appalachian State University.

THE BEGINNING

Bay City Steam Fittings, Inc., of Bay City, Michigan, was founded by Jerry Ball in the spring of 1970. Jerry had previously been a sales engineer with Toledo Forging Company but had left that firm when his father died, leaving him a sizeable inheritance. Jerry had then taken a year to develop and patent a new type of thermostatic steam trap that would have broad application in a variety of types of industrial steam systems. With his own funds and a small loan from a group of investors, Jerry was able to lease a small casting, forging, machining, and assembly facility in his home town of Bay City, Michigan, and was ready to begin production of his newly patented steam trap by April of 1970.

Prior to starting production, Jerry had visited with key people at the larger manufacturing facilities with extensive steam systems and with utility companies in the Great Lakes region. The engineers and purchasing people at these firms were quite receptive, and by April, ten of these firms had given Jerry orders for a sufficient number of traps for Jerry to begin production. Once production began, Jerry began to call on major industrial distributors in the region, and six of these agreed to stock the Bay City trap. By the end of 1970, Jerry had secured enough business so that he could project a break-even year for 1971.

The year 1971 turned out to be better than break-even. The Bay City steam trap found a strong acceptance in the marketplace and positive word-of-mouth about Bay City's quality, durability, and dependability spread quickly. Several of the buyers suggested that Jerry add a line of strainers and relief valves, and Jerry began manufacturing and selling these in late 1971. By mid-1972, Bay City had outgrown its original facilities, and in early 1973 Bay City Steam Fittings moved into a larger plant in the new industrial park outside of Bay City.

EARLY GROWTH

As the production facilities expanded, Jerry Ball found that it was becoming impossible for him to maintain contact with customers and oversee the operation of the entire firm, so in March 1973 Jerry hired Arlen Frost as a sales rep. Arlen had a degree in business from the University of Michigan, had served in Viet Nam, and had a year of experience on the road selling for a major industrial distributor. Arlen began to rapidly expand the number of major distributors carrying Bay City's steam fittings throughout the

midwest, while Jerry added a few more major end user accounts (the large manufacturing firms and utility companies).

Each man negotiated prices individually with buyers, and the prices and other terms-of-sale conditions varied from buyer to buyer. This allowed Bay City to meet any competition and adjust quickly to a changing, growing market, but by 1975 the number of customers had grown so large that pricing problems began to emerge. It was becoming difficult to keep up with who paid what for which fittings, and some of the distributors began to get together and discover that some paid more than others without apparent justification. After several complaints, Arlen suggested to Jerry that they establish a more formal, stable pricing policy.

The policy that Jerry and Arlen developed was quite simple. Bay City established a list price for each unit in Bay City's product line that was slightly higher than the price a mid-sized end user might be expected to pay. Distributors were then offered a discount of 25 percent from the list price, but prices to the larger end user accounts would continue to be based on Jerry's negotiations with those buyers. All purchases would be shipped FOB origin, freight prepaid and added. As part of the pricing package, Bay City developed a list of its large key end user accounts and notified the distributors that these would be "house accounts" for Bay City and thus off-limits to the distributors.

This pricing package seemed to clear up what little conflict had existed with the distributors, and soon Arlen had established distribution through industrial distributors in most of the major markets in the midwest. By 1977, Bay City had added additional lines of steam valves and the list of individual stock keeping units (SKUs) expanded to over fifty. Arlen and Jerry had also decided that Bay City needed another sales rep to keep up with the demand, so they hired Bill Jennings who took over sales in the eastern and southern parts of the midwest. By the end of 1977, Jennings had expanded sales so that Bay City was now selling to industrial dis-

From R. W. Haas *Business Marketing*, 6th ed., Cincinnati: Southwestern Publishing Company, 1995. Reprinted with permission.

tributors as far east as Pittsburgh and as far south as Louisville, Kentucky. Arlen took on the title of sales manager but continued to maintain responsibility for sales in the upper midwest and Great Lakes region.

MAJOR EXPANSION

In early 1978, Arlen and Jerry attended an industrial trade show in New York and met Saul Cohen, an established manufacturers' representative who handled a full line of steam fittings in the northeastern part of the country. Saul showed some interest in taking Bay City on as a principal because of Jerry's patented steam trap and because of Bay City's growing reputation as a major vendor of quality steam fittings. Arlen and Jerry were impressed by Saul's enthusiasm, and after checking him out carefully through friends in the industry, Arlen sat down with Saul and hammered out an agency agreement.

Saul Cohen would have responsibility for representing Bay City to industrial distributors and end users in eastern New York, eastern Pennsylvania, and all of New England. List prices, discounts and shipping terms would be the same as for all of Bay City's customers: Distributors would get a 25 percent discount from list, prices to major end users would be negotiated with Arlen's approval, and all shipments, would be FOB origin, freight prepaid and added. Saul would be paid a 10 percent commission on all sales and would agree to adhere to Bay City's pricing schedule and territorial limitations. The impact of the agreement was immediate and impressive: By the end of 1979, sales of Bay City's fittings through Saul Cohen amounted to over $750,000.

Although the additional volume generated by Cohen was substantial, this volume was nearly matched when Arlen hired another company sales rep, Hugh Long, in 1980. Despite the strong recession in 1980, Bay City continued to grow in sales volume by expanding slowly into new territories. By the end of 1982, Arlen Frost was handling the distributors along the Chicago-Cleveland axis and the Michigan peninsula, while Bill

Jennings took over the northern midwest and Hugh Long assumed responsibility for the "frontier"—the southern part of the midwest. Long developed strong sales to several industrial distributors in Kentucky and Virginia, and even established a "beachhead" across the Mississippi River by setting up an industrial distributor in St. Louis.

In 1983, the economy began a strong recovery, and Bay City's sales volume grew sharply. Bay City added several new lines of Ys, nipples, pumps, and retrofit kits and became established as a major vendor for a full line of steam fittings. The company moved into newer, larger facilities in Bay City to handle the new product lines. At the same time, sales manager Arlen Frost began to study the possibility of expanding the company's sales force to keep up with the increasing demand.

Three factors had caused Arlen to consider this expansion. First, there appeared to be a strong potential for growth in the "frontier"—Kentucky, Virginia, and even Tennessee and North Carolina were becoming very attractive markets. Second, Saul Cohen was not keeping up with the growing market in New England—Cohen's sales volume had not grown substantially since 1980. Finally, there was a strong indication that Bay City was stretching its sales force too thin—it was becoming difficult to call on all of the growing number of smaller and middle-sized industrial distributors who were now expressing interest in Bay City fittings.

RESTRUCTURING FOR THE 1980S

Arlen spent nearly three months studying the situation, visiting industrial distributors, talking to his own sales reps, and even consulting with Saul Cohen and other independent manufacturers' representatives. By September 1983, Arlen had realized that the problem was more than a sales force problem but was also a channels of distribution and pricing problem. After considering several alternatives, Arlen developed the proposal outlined in Exhibit 1, and he presented the proposal to Jerry Ball in early October. A key element of this

EXHIBIT 1

PROPOSED BAY CITY FITTINGS SALES, DISTRIBUTION, AND PRICING POLICY, OCTOBER 1983

1. Bay City Fittings will sell direct to major key end user accounts to major industrial distributors, as identified in a list to be developed by Bay City and updated quarterly. The end users on the list will be called "key accounts" and the major industrial distributors will be called "Class A dealers."

2. The Class A dealers will have responsibility for stocking a full line of Bay City fittings at appropriate stocking levels, and will sell to smaller distributors (to be called "Class B dealers") in their markets as well as to non-key account end users in their markets. Bay City agrees to avoid selling to Class B dealers or non-key account end users in the market of Class A dealers. Areas of market responsibility for each Class A dealer will be established by Bay City Fittings in consultation with the Class A dealer involved, and the Class A dealers will agree to market Bay City fittings aggressively to customers in their respective areas of market responsibility.

3. Class B dealers will have no stocking of market responsibilities but will develop appropriate relationships with Class A dealers to ensure adequate responsibilities in the market.

4. Independent manufacturers' representatives will no longer be utilized. The agreement with Saul Cohen will not be renewed for 1984.

5. The Bay City sales force will be responsible for calling on all key accounts and Class A dealers. The sales force will have six sales representatives. One of these will be designated as a key account rep and will have responsibility for selling to all major end user accounts designated as key accounts and developing new prospects to become key accounts. The other five representatives will sell to Class A dealers and will be assigned to territories that will cover the area east of the Mississippi River and as far south as Tennessee and North Carolina. The sales force will expand as market conditions demand. Total sales force expenses are expected to be within 4 percent to 5 percent of sales.

6. A new pricing policy will go into force that recognizes: (1) the new tole of Class A dealers, (2) that there can be a considerable difference in volume of purchases among these dealers, and (3) that Class A dealers should be encouraged to generate larger volumes and to order in larger quantities where possible.

7. The new pricing policy will be as follows:

   a. Bay City Fittings will establish and publish an appropriate list price for each SKU in the product line. The list prices will be established to represent a price that would be appropriate for most end users to expect to pay and would be competitive in the end user marketplace.

   b. A trade discount structure of 20/10 will be adopted. Class B dealers would be entitled to a 20 percent discount from list. Class A dealers would get an additional 10 percent discount from list. For example, SKU 4267109 lists for $100. Class B dealers would pay $80 for this item ($100 − $20 = $80). Class A dealers would pay $72 for the item ($80 − $8 = $72). Thus, Class A dealers would earn a 10 percent margin on items sold to Class B dealers. They would earn a 28 percent margin on items sold as list to end users.

   c. Prices to key accounts will continue to be on an individually negotiated or bid basis.

   d. Cumulative quantity discounts will be offered to customers whose purchases for a given calendar year exceed certain levels. The discount level achieved will apply to total calendar year sales and only the highest level achieved applies. The quantity discount for the calendar year will be paid in the form of a rebate to be paid by the end of January of the following year. Calendar year purchase requirements and discount level are as follows:

EXHIBIT 1 (continued)	

PROPOSED BAY CITY FITTINGS SALES, DISTRIBUTION, AND PRICING POLICY, OCTOBER 1983

Calendar Year Purchase Requirement (if purchases exceed this amount)	Discount Level (The buyer will receive a rebate of this percentage of total sales)
$100,000	1%
$200,000	2%
$300,000	3%
$400,000	4%
$500,000 and up	5%

Thus, a Class A dealer who purchases $250,000 in a year would receive a rebate check of $5,000 in January of the following year. This rebate plan is quite forward-looking in that only 40 percent of Bay City's current accounts would qualify for the 1 percent level or above, and only 5 percent would currently qualify for the 2 percent level. The above structure allows for growth in volume in the future.

e. With the exception of shipments with a net invoice value of over $30,000 per shipment, all shipments will continue to be shipped FOB origin, freight prepaid and added. Orders with a net invoice value of over $30,000 will be shipped FOB destination, freight prepaid. It is hoped that his policy will encourage larger orders and shipments and thus save Bay City the handling and billing costs associated with small orders.

f. Payment terms are net thirty with a 1-1/2 percent service charge per month on past-due balances. Terms are COD for accounts sixty days of more past due.

8. Bay City's lawyer will develop a contract reflecting the above terms for execution with the Class A dealers. The contract will be for an indefinite term with provisions for cancellation by either party with thirty days' notice. The contract would stipulate that list prices, discount levels, and other terms of sale could be modified by Bay City Fittings with ten days' notice.

---

proposal was the classification of distributors as Class A and Class B dealers as defined in Exhibit 1. After being assured that Bay City's current distributors would be happy with the new structure, Jerry enthusiastically endorsed the proposal and told Arlen to put the plan into effect—under his new title: Arlen Frost, vice president for sales.

By the end of 1984, Arlen had implemented the plan. The industrial distributors were generally enthusiastic and agreed to the terms of the proposal with only minor disagreements with Class A dealers over definitions of market areas and what constituted appropriate stocking levels. The dealers were impressed with Bay City's sense of fair play and cooperation, and particularly liked Bay City's promise to refrain from selling direct to their potential customers.

While getting the dealers signed up was time consuming, Arlen found that the toughest part of

the implementation was expanding the sales force. Good reps were hard to find and hire, the compensation plan had to be revised, and there were some squabbles over territory assignment. Bill Jennings became the key account sales rep and Hugh Long became a "frontier" specialist with responsibility for southern Indiana, southern Illinois, Kentucky, Tennessee, Virginia, and North Carolina. The four new reps were assigned territories in the western midwest, Great Lakes region, New England, and central Atlantic.

The plan worked well and provided for orderly expansion. A solid network of industrial distributors was developed throughout Bay City's coverage area, even down through Tennessee and North Carolina. By the end of 1987, Bay City was selling to approximately 120 Class A dealers and to forty key accounts. The Class A dealers served nearly 1,800 Class B dealers and 6,000 end user accounts. Class B dealers, in turn, were serving over 50,000 small end user accounts, from Maine to Memphis. Bay City was generating sales volume of nearly $16 million, with 90 percent of sales going to Class A dealers and 10 percent to end users. The business seemed quite stable, growing in a controlled manner and generating a solid bottom line profit.

LOOKING SOUTH

By mid-1988 Arlen Frost was beginning to tire of stability. He had been accustomed to the fast growth of the 1970s and early 1980s, and he missed the excitement of new ventures. About this time, Arlen read several articles about the boom in the Sun Belt, and particularly about the growth in manufacturing in the south. "If there is that much growth in manufacturing," he thought, "that must mean more and bigger factories, which means more steam pipes and systems, and more demand for steam traps, valves, and fittings." Arlen decided to investigate.

Arlen flew to Nashville where he met Hugh Long, and the two of them headed south. Their first stop was a major industrial distributor who served the thriving area of Huntsville, Alabama. The owner of the firm was willing to spend over an hour with Arlen and Hugh, describing his business and the industry in north Alabama in detail. Arlen and Hugh quickly realized that the industrial distributors in north Alabama were similar to the Class A and Class B dealers in Bay City's current coverage area, with one large exception. The Class A dealers tended to buy many of their lines from industrial wholesalers rather than directly from the manufacturer.

The Huntsville distributor explained that he purchased about 85 percent of his MRO items from Jackson Supply Company, a large industrial "superdistributor" in Atlanta. The distributor explained that Jackson provided quicker and better service than most manufacturers could at virtually the same price that the manufacturer would charge. The distributor pointed out that Atlanta was a lot closer than most industrial manufacturers (who tended to be located in the north), both geographically and culturally. It was clear that the Huntsville distributor was very pleased with his relationship with Jackson, and the loyalty would be difficult to shake. The distributor did indicate, however, that he would be very interested in stocking Bay City items if he could buy them through Jackson Supply.

THE GEORGIA CONNECTION

Arlen and Hugh encountered the Jackson Supply Company again in Birmingham. The industrial distributor they visited there was actually owned by Jackson Supply Company and was physically housed in Jackson Supply's large regional warehouse in southern Birmingham. The manager of the Birmingham operation gave Arlen and Hugh a tour of the facilities, explaining that Jackson operated similar warehouse/sales branch facilities in Columbia, South Carolina, and Jacksonville, Florida, in addition to a huge facility just outside Atlanta, Georgia. All of the facilities utilized state-of-the-art materials handling equipment, inventory control systems, and order processing systems, and the firm owned its own fleet of trucks for delivery throughout the southeast.

After the visit with the Jackson distributor in Birmingham, Arlen sent Hugh back to Nashville and then flew to Atlanta. He was able to set up an appointment with Jackson Supply's steam parts buyer for the next afternoon and he planned the meeting to be one of information gathering rather than a sales call. The Jackson Supply buyer was quite helpful in answering Arlen's questions and even provided him with a professionally prepared vendor's information kit, which contained a complete financial report, a description of the firm's distributor network, details on sales volume by product type, and other such information.

Arlen was amazed. He had never heard of the firm, and yet it generated sales of over $200 million per year (including nearly $5 million in steam system items) in the coverage area of Alabama, Mississippi, Georgia, South Carolina, and Florida. Jackson Supply had developed a network of Class A dealers and end users that was similar in structure to that of Bay City's, with the exception that Jackson actually owned or held part interest in ten of the Class A dealers in the south, including those housed at Jackson's warehouses. The thing that most impressed Arlen, however, was the high degree of professionalism of everyone he had met—they were all enthusiastic go-getters who seemed to be on top of everything. Near the end of the visit, the steam parts buyer brought Arlen into the office of Emmett Jackson, the founder and CEO of Jackson Supply. Arlen was introduced to the CEO and his son, Emmett, Jr. (who had just received his MBA from the University of Georgia), and found them both to be bright, energetic, and very friendly people. Arlen was quite surprised when the senior Jackson said that he was familiar with Bay City fittings and had been impressed with their reputation for quality and durability. He would certainly be open to a proposal from Bay City, since there had been a few problems with their current vendor of steam traps and fittings. The CEO suggested that Arlen and the steam parts buyer see if they could come up with something.

They could "come up with something," and they did in a surprisingly short time. The tentative agreement reached was quite similar to the agreement Bay City had reached with its Class A dealers to the north, with the exception of the inclusion of a new level of trade discount for Jackson Supply. Jackson Supply would agree to aggressively market Bay City's product lines to Class A dealers and end users throughout Jackson Supply's coverage area and agreed to stock the full line of Bay City items in appropriate quantities in all of its warehouses. Furthermore, Jackson Supply guaranteed to purchase a minimum of $2 million (net) in Bay City items per calendar year.

In return, Bay City would agree not to sell directly to Class A or Class B dealers or to end users (other than those identified as key accounts) in Jackson's market area. After some negotiation, a trade discount structure of 20/10/10 was agreed on, with the discounts to be applied to Bay City's standard published list prices. Under this plan, Jackson would pay $64.80 for an item that listed for $100, and would be expected to resell it to Class A dealers for $72. Bay City and Jackson also would agree to the quantity discount and shipping terms implemented by Bay City in 1984, with the additional agreement that Jackson could request shipment direct to its regional warehouses or "captive" Class A dealers, if desired.

Prior to signing any formal agreement, Arlen presented the proposed new distribution and pricing structure to Jerry Ball for approval (see Exhibit 2). Jerry was a bit concerned at giving control of such a large area of the south to an independent wholesale distributor and giving up an additional 10 percent in margin to Jackson in the discount structure. Arlen pointed out that the discount structure was similar to that offered by Jackson's other vendors, and furthermore, Jackson had such a stranglehold on the south that it would be difficult to penetrate the deep south without using them. Finally, Arlen pointed out that they would not have to expand Bay City's sales force with the attendant costs and headaches, and that using Jackson Supply would greatly simplify shipping and reduce the amount of inventory Bay City would normally have to carry to facilitate such an expansion.

Jerry finally gave his blessing to the agreement, and a formal contract with Jackson Supply was signed in October 1988. The contract was for an indefinite term, cancelable by either party with thirty days' notice, but the parties also agreed to review the terms of the contract annually to determine if any revisions were needed. Bay City shipped its first truckload of fittings to Jackson in November, and by the end of December 1988 the Jackson warehouses were fully stocked with the full line of Bay City Fittings steam system parts.

CLOSING THE 1980S ON THE UPSWING

By far the biggest year in Bay City Fittings' history was 1989. Sales in its traditional coverage area (the midwest, northeast, and south through Tennessee and North Carolina) were almost $18 million despite an economy that was beginning to show some signs of softness. The brightest spot in the firm's performance for 1989, however, was the volume generated by Jackson Supply in the deep south. Jackson had purchased just over $3 million in Bay City merchandise over the course of the year, with increases in vol-

EXHIBIT 2
NEW CHANNEL AND PRICING STRUCTURE: 1989

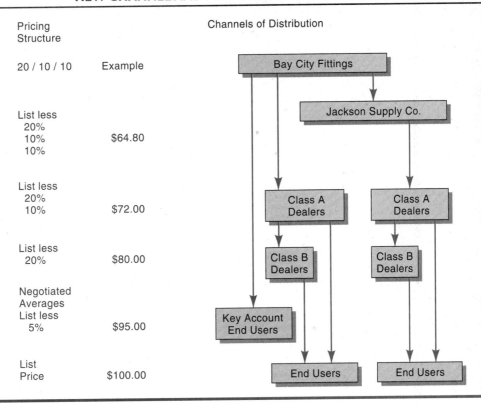

Pricing Structure		Channels of Distribution
20 / 10 / 10	Example	
List less 20% 10% 10%	$64.80	
List less 20% 10%	$72.00	
List less 20%	$80.00	
Negotiated Averages List less 5%	$95.00	
List Price	$100.00	

ume each month. Bay City was now generating total sales of $21 million, with almost 15 percent of that coming from Jackson Supply.

The people at Jackson Supply were also quite pleased with the venture with Bay City. Although the sales of Bay City merchandise amounted to less than 2 percent of Jackson's volume, the quality of the products and the dependability of Bay City's deliveries had made the venture virtually trouble-free. Jackson had been so satisfied that they had included the Bay City items in one of their quarterly direct mail pieces and featured the Bay City thermostatic steam trap on the cover of the semiannual Jackson catalog published in June.

At Emmett Jackson's invitation, Jerry Ball and Arlen Frost flew to Atlanta in early January 1990 to review the previous year and to plan for the future. The meeting at Jackson headquarters was most pleasant for everyone since everyone seemed to be happy with 1989's performance, all were optimistic about 1990, and it appeared that no adjustments in the contract were needed for the next year. The meeting ended with a presentation by Emmett Jackson, Jr. (the CEO's son), who had been named Jackson Supply's Vice President for Marketing in late 1989.

Emmett, Jr. (called "Stoney" by his dad, a truncation of Emmett, Jr.'s nickname—Stonewall) presented a well-developed, professionally prepared view of the year ahead for Jackson Supply and its vendors. He pointed out that the economy throughout the nation would be flat at best for 1990, but the chance for a recession was minimal until 1991 at the earliest. He made a strong case, however, for the fact that any growth in sales volume for an industrial supplies marketer would have to be the result of aggressive marketing rather than economic growth. Any dollars in growth would have to come either from expansion into new markets or from competitors.

Stoney Jackson gave few specifics for Jackson's plans for 1990, but he closed the meeting with a spirited claim that Jackson Supply could he counted on to mount an extremely aggressive sales and marketing plan for 1990, and he could promise that sales of Bay City items through Jackson would increase by 25 percent in 1990. Despite the fact that they had snickered a bit at Emmett, Jr.'s nickname, Jerry and Arlen were very impressed and returned to Bay City with a very positive feeling about 1990.

JACKSON'S ATTACK

The positive feeling did not last long. In March 1990, Arlen received a frantic call from Hugh Long in Nashville. At first Arlen thought Hugh was drunk—he was babbling about an "invasion" and "double cross" and used a large amount of profanity. Arlen finally calmed Hugh and as Hugh began to explain what he was calling about, Arlen began to understand why Hugh was so upset.

It seems that Hugh had just discovered that Jackson Supply had recently purchased controlling interest in the two largest Class A dealers in Tennessee and North Carolina—the Nashville dealer and the Raleigh dealer. Furthermore the manager of the Nashville dealer had told Hugh that Jackson Supply was planning on expanding into Tennessee, North Carolina, and even into Tidewater, Virginia, by mid-year, and planned on establishing a regional warehouse in at least one of the states.

Arlen could hardly believe what he was hearing and wanted to check things out on his own. He first called Jackson Supply in Atlanta, but both Jacksons were out of town. Arlen then flew to Nashville and visited the Class A dealer there to verify Hugh's story. It turned out to be correct and was only the tip of the iceberg. Arlen called on three Class A dealers in middle Tennessee and all three apologetically told Arlen the same story: a sales rep from Jackson Supply had called on them and had offered their full lines (including Bay City Fittings) at com-

petitive prices and with free delivery on any size order.

The dealers pointed out that their orders from Bay City were always too small to get the freight paid by Bay City, and Jackson Supply could not only provide free delivery, they could actually deliver more quickly since they ran their own trucks up from Birmingham. Finally, the dealers pointed out that they could vastly simplify their ordering by buying a wide variety of merchandise from one source rather than from many different vendors. They were fond of Hugh and Arlen, but all three dealers said they planned to buy their lines of steam system parts from Jackson Supply rather than direct from Bay City, and they suspected most other Class A dealers and some of the major end users would do likewise.

Arlen kept his laptop computer busy on the flight back to Atlanta. The Class A dealers' decisions to buy from Jackson Supply were built on sound economics, and certainly the business would be profitable for Jackson Supply. Everything was very rational, but there was a very large problem for Bay City—they stood to lose as many as twenty Class A dealers and five key accounts to Jackson Supply. By Arlen's calculations, the lost sales volume to these accounts could amount to nearly $3 million annually, half of Hugh Long's total sales!

THE STONEWALL AND RETREAT

Arlen reported to Jerry immediately upon his return to Bay City, and Jerry's response was an explosive "They can't do that! That wasn't part of our agreement! That's our territory!" He picked up the phone, called Jackson Supply, and reached Stoney Jackson. Jerry pointed out in no uncertain terms that he didn't like Jackson straying out of the deep south and "bootlegging" in Tennessee and North Carolina, and he wanted Jackson to retreat.

Stoney responded that he could certainly understand Jerry's initial response to Jackson's move north, but this was part of Jackson's aggressive marketing and expansion plans that he had mentioned back in January. Furthermore, he was expanding all of Jackson Supply's business into new territories, not just the Bay City lines, and Bay City was a fairly small portion of Jackson's volume. Stoney suggested that if Jerry really strongly objected to Jackson Supply selling the Bay City items in Tennessee and North Carolina, they could simply cancel the contract with Jackson—the whole contract. Jackson Supply would find another vendor to take Bay City's place in Jackson's catalogs throughout the deep south.

Jerry took a deep breath. Jackson Supply's business could well exceed $4 million in 1990, and it was business that Bay City might not be able to pick up through any other channel of distribution. Before Jerry could speak, Stoney said, "Jerry, don't worry. Think about this. You will still be selling Bay City steam parts in Tennessee, North Carolina, or wherever we sell them; we'll just be doing the hard work. Sure, your sales rep in Nashville may not sell a Bay City steam trap—but you will be selling it to us instead. You are still getting the business without having the burden. And I'll promise you a ton of business—we'll sell more of your merchandise than your sales force ever could."

Jerry recognized that Jackson was not going to back down, and he feared losing the Jackson account altogether, so he ended the conversation by telling Stoney that while he did not like what was happening, he hoped that everything would turn out well for both parties if they continued to work together. When he hung up the phone, Jerry turned to Arlen and shook his head, "We'll just have to adjust to it," he said.

Adjusting wasn't easy. Arlen was faced with the problem of completely restructuring the sales force to cope with the loss of direct sales in Tennessee and North Carolina. Neither of the possible ways of doing it was pleasant: Arlen could either keep all of the current reps and reassign them to new, smaller territories, or he could lay off a rep and reassign the remainder to newly structured territories. He was sure that the business would continue to grow somehow, so he decided to keep all of the reps and reassign them. None of the reps was happy with the reassignment, and all of them grumbled about lower earnings, changed customers, and anything else they could think of.

By August, it was clear that Jackson's move north was having an impact, but the impact was not exactly what Jerry and Arlen had expected it to be. Arlen prepared a set of sales and margin figures showing Bay City's performance for 1989, the projections Bay City had made in early 1990 prior to Jackson's change in tactics, and a set of projections for 1990 based on actual performance through July (see Exhibit 3).

Jerry scanned the figures, but his eyes moved quickly to the "bottom line" figures—the contribution margin figure in this instance. He was not at all pleased with what he saw. "We're going to be way under projection—and even under last year! What gives?" he asked, looking at Arlen.

Arlen pointed out first of all that unit volume (as measured by sales at list) was holding up to 1989 figures but was well under the original projections. Jackson Supply was moving more merchandise than originally projected, but the original projections had not taken Jackson's move north into account. The problem appeared to be that Bay City's lost sales in Tennessee and Kentucky were not being made up by Jackson Supply. Arlen had originally thought that the flat economy might have caused a decrease in sales volume, but a check of shipments to Bay City's current Class A dealers and key accounts indicated that their purchases were within two percentage points of the original 1990 projections. The problem, then, appeared to be in the south.

Jerry Ball called Stoney Jackson to discuss the matter, but Stoney was aggressively defensive. He blustered that business was tough to get—anyone who read the Wall Street Journal knew that. Furthermore, Stoney said that he couldn't believe Jerry was calling to complain. "Look at your own numbers," Stoney said, "We're going to buy twice as much from you this year than last. Look, if you don't want our business, say so and I'll get another vendor. In the meantime, we have some aggressive marketing plans for the last quarter and I'll ensure that they include Bay City steam parts as a prominent feature. We'll move some brass for you."

EXHIBIT 3

BAY CITY FITTINGS SALES AND PROFIT FIGURES: ACTUAL 1989 AND 1990 PROJECTIONS

1989 Actual Performance by Customer Type and Total (figures in $000)

	To Class A Dealers	To Key Accounts	To Jackson Supply	Total
Volume at list price	$22,501	$2,001	$4,816	$29,318
Sales	16,201	1,900	3,121	21,222
Gross margin	4,950	900	713	6,563
Less volume rebate	(243)	(10)	(156)	(409)
Free freight exp.	(104)	(7)	(36)	(147)
Contribution margin	4,603	884	521	6,008

1990 Initial Projections[a] by Customer Type and Total (figures in $000)

	To Class A Dealers	To Key Accounts	To Jackson Supply	Total
Volume at list price	$23,611	$2,105	$6,173	$31,889
Sales	17,000	2,000	4,000	23,000
Gross margin	5,194	947	914	7,055
Less volume rebate	(225)	(10)	(200)	(465)
Free freight exp.	(105)	(8)	(40)	(153)
Contribution margin	4,834	929	674	6,437

[a]Projections made in January prior to Jackson Supply's move north.

1990 Revised Projections[a] by Customer Type and Total (figures in $000)

	To Class A Dealers	To Key Accounts	To Jackson Supply	Total
Volume at list price	$18,631	$1,814	$9,418	$29,862
Sales	13,414	1,723	6,103	21,240
Gross margin	4,099	816	1,394	6,309
Less volume rebate	(201)	(9)	(305)	(515)
Free freight exp.	(92)	(6)	(55)	(153)
Contribution margin	3,806	802	1,034	5,641

[a]Revised, based on actual 1990 performance through July 1990.

Again, Jerry could find no argument to present to Stoney that would not risk losing the Jackson Supply account. After the call, he called in his top executives and presented Arlen's figures to them. He asked them to take measures to cut costs to try to make up for the potential loss of nearly $800,000 in contribution margin from the original projections even if it meant laying off people. "A fine thing," Jerry thought, "I try to expand my business and end up having to lay people off."

JACKSON'S FLANKING MANEUVER

Bay City Fitting's problems with Jackson Supply were just beginning. In mid-October 1990, Arlen received another hysterical call from Hugh Long, who was now the Bay City sales rep for Kentucky, Virginia, West Virginia, and Maryland. Hugh had just received a royal chewing out by the owner of a large Class A account in Louisville. The owner waved an eight-page direct mail flyer in Hugh's face and shouted that he just couldn't continue to do business with

Bay City unless Hugh did something about what was going on.

Hugh had grabbed the direct mail piece out of the owner's hands and was horrified at what he saw. On the cover was a picture of Bay City's best-selling line—the patented thermostatic steam trap—with a headline underneath that screamed "30% off of List Price on America's Finest!" The copy offered a 30 percent discount from list price on any Bay City steam parts, and even gave three examples showing the list price and the discount price. There was also an 800 number to call and a promise of next-day shipment out of Nashville or Richmond, FOB origin, freight prepaid and added. The remainder of the minicatalog included another page with a complete listing of Bay City Fittings product lines with list prices and discount prices along with six pages of illustrations and listings for the lines of a dozen or so other major manufacturers with a similar cut-price offering. The mailer was from Jackson Supply Company, and it had been sent to every Class A dealer, every Class B dealer, and even to small and middle-sized end users throughout Hugh's territory.

The Louisville dealer told Hugh that Jackson was also calling potential accounts on the phone offering the "direct marketing" service, quicker delivery, as well as the discount prices. The tactic had obviously been effective, since most of the Louisville dealer's Class B accounts in southern Kentucky had made at least one purchase from Jackson. The Class B dealers had offered to continue to buy from Louisville if Louisville could meet Jackson Supply's price, but the Louisville dealer pointed out that under the 20/10 discount structure he did not even get a full 30 percent discount from Bay City. In fact, the Class A dealer in Louisville could now actually buy an item from Jackson Supply for less than he could buy it direct from Bay City Fittings—the only problem was that he couldn't sell it at a profit.

Arlen told Hugh to settle down, that he'd check into what was going on and come up with something. After hanging up, Arlen rushed to Jerry Ball's office to give him the news. His mind was spinning as he tried to understand what was happening, what it could mean to Bay City Fittings, and what could be done about it.

Jerry greeted Arlen at the office door with a stunned look on his face. He had just gotten angry phone calls from Class A dealers in Richmond, Baltimore, and Norfolk, and a particularly nasty call from a major key account in Washington, D.C., had really rattled him. Every one of the calls was about Jackson Supply's new telemarketing/direct mail campaign. The Class A dealers were upset at being undercut by an outside "bootlegger" who could sell Bay City merchandise to their customers for less than they paid Bay City for the items. The major key account was upset because he felt Bay City had been overcharging him and he would henceforth buy from Jackson Supply who not only would sell for less but would also give quicker delivery.

"How can they do that?" exclaimed Jerry. "I think I know why they're doing it, but how can they do it?"

Arlen responded with an example, using the pricing structure of the steam trap Jackson had featured on the front page of the mailer. The steam trap listed for $500 and would be sold for that figure to most end user accounts (except key accounts, who might pay as little as $450 in a negotiated deal). Under the current trade discount structure, Class B dealers bought the trap from Class A dealers for $400 ($500 less 20 percent). Class A dealers, in turn, bought the traps from Bay City for $360 ($400 less 10 percent).

In the case of traps sold through Jackson Supply, Jackson received an additional 10 percent trade discount, so that Jackson Supply paid only $324 for the traps purchased from Bay City. Furthermore, Jackson Supply also earned the full 5 percent quantity rebate (something few of Bay City's other accounts could do) and always ordered in sufficient quantities to earn the freight-paid shipping. Thus, a Bay City steam trap that listed for $500 would cost Jackson Supply only $307.80, delivered to Nashville, or Richmond—or wherever Jackson Supply had a major warehouse facility. Jackson could sell the trap for list less 30 percent (or $350) and still earn a gross margin of $42.20 per trap, which translated to a margin of about 12 percent of sales.

Jackson Supply could indeed undercut even Bay City itself and still earn a reasonable margin. Direct mail and telemarketing costs could be spread over several product lines so the marginal cost for any given line would be negligible. Furthermore, Jackson's warehouse facilities in Nashville and Richmond were much closer to customers in the direct marketing target area than was Bay City's facility in Michigan, so Jackson could deliver more quickly and at lower freight cost.

Jerry and Arlen agreed that although Jackson's direct marketing approach made economic sense to Jackson Supply—and to the Class B dealers and end users in the target area who would probably now buy from Jackson—the approach would cause a complete disruption to Bay City's dealer network in the area. It would be quite likely that Bay City would lose at least twenty-five Class A dealers in the area, and Class A dealers averaged buying $135,000 per year in Bay City items. And the danger existed that Jackson might even penetrate even further north. It became obvious that Bay City had to put a stop to Jackson Supply's latest tactic.

A FAILING DEFENSE

Once again Jerry Ball found himself talking to Stoney Jackson about Jackson Supply's invasion of Bay City's market area. Jerry demanded that Jackson stop this bootlegging and return to selling Bay City's steam parts in the part of the country they had originally agreed on. Furthermore, Jerry demanded that Jackson Supply immediately stop the price cutting and adhere to the discount structure they had agreed on.

Stoney was silent for a moment and then responded icily: "Jerry, I buy merchandise from Bay City and I take title to it. I can sell it wherever I wish, to whomever I wish, at whatever price I wish. Don't you forget that. The only way you can stop me is to not sell me the merchandise in the first place, and for a variety of reasons, I don't think you'll stop selling to me."

Before Jerry could respond, Stoney continued, "Jerry, you've got to change with the times. Telemarketing and direct mail are the modern, cost-effective way of reaching large numbers of smaller customers, and this direct marketing approach will continue to be a part of our aggressive marketing plan if this trial run in Kentucky, Tennessee, and the coast works as well as it looks like it will. In fact, we're hoping to give it a try in Arkansas, Louisiana, and Missouri after the first of the year. And remember, every Bay City fitting we sell, we buy from you—you aren't losing any volume, and if we expand west, you'll gain right along with us. Give it some thought after you've settled down, and let me know what you want to do." And Stoney hung up.

Jerry slumped in his chair. How in the world had he gotten into this mess? A simple agreement with some hospitable southern gentlemen had turned into a nightmare. What seemed like an easy, painless way of expanding into the south through Jackson Supply had turned into a situation in which many of Bay City's customers were very angry, Jackson Supply could well control half of Bay City's volume by 1991, and there seemed to be nothing Bay City could do to get control.

RETREAT, SURRENDER, OR COUNTER-ATTACK?

Jerry looked up and stared at Arlen across the desk. "Arlen," he said, you're the one who got us into this mess. If you hadn't cooked up that deal with Jackson, this would never have happened. You got us into it—you get us out! I want you to develop a set of alternatives for us to consider, and I want your recommended course of action. And, I want it tomorrow. Get on it *now!*"

DISCUSSION QUESTIONS

1. Exactly what is Bay City's problem? What caused the problem to develop? What could Bay City have done to avoid the problem in the first place?
2. What should Bay City do now? What alternatives should Arlen develop? Which should he recommend? Why?

FAIRCHILD LUBRICANTS, INC.

Case contributed by Robert W. Haas, professor of Marketing, San Diego State University.

BACKGROUND

Fairchild Lubricants, Inc., located in Racine, Wisconsin, is a nationally known supplier of cleaning and lubricant products and equipment. The company has for sixty years produced and marketed a broad line of products that includes tank degreasers, strippers, lubricants, and hand-care products. Its customers are primarily industrial and transportation users of these types of industrial products. Fairchild has never served the household market and has no intention now of entering that market.

Sales in 1991 are $25 million, with 75 percent of sales being made by company field sales representatives. The remaining 25 percent of sales are made through industrial distributors. The company recently completed a two-year study that revealed that Fairchild's freight and personal selling costs were rising far out of proportion to all other company costs. Based on this study, company management has decided to expand sales through distributors in an attempt to lower both freight and selling costs. Therefore, a number of company field sales representatives will be replaced by distributors.

The termination of field sales representatives and their replacement with industrial distributors is somewhat bothersome to company management, but the step is seen as a necessary move. In addition to lowering freight and sales costs, it is estimated that distributors can help attract customers that the sales reps have been unable to reach. Management estimates that distributors can expand the industrial and transportation sales potential to ten times that of last year's sales. The company feels this potential can be realized if sales through distributors are increased from the present 25 percent of sales to 50 per-

cent. Product lines average approximately 25 percent gross profit margins, and Fairchild products appear to be widely accepted in the marketplace. The company is well established and has a sound reputation that has been built up over the years. Management believes that these traits will attract good distributors and that a network of distributors will not be difficult to develop.

THE PROBLEM

Mac Ghormley is the national sales manager of Fairchild Lubricants. His office is located in the company headquarters building in Racine. Ghormley has been in charge of Fairchild's field sales representatives for the past nine years and is seen by top management as the most logical member of management to supervise the potential distributor network. He will have the responsibility of establishing a total distributor network as well as screening and selecting individual distributors and then managing the network. Ghormley has mixed emotions about the added responsibility. On one hand, he has worked with the field sales representatives long enough to know many of them personally. Replacing some of these people with distributors will be difficult and stressful. On the other hand, he has also seen the rising sales and transportation costs and knows something has to be done. He sees the replacement of some field sales representatives with distributors as a necessity if these costs are to be controlled effectively.

The first sales territory Ghormley wants to address is the Pacific northwest (Oregon and Washington). Since he has been sales manager, this territory has been a thorn in his side and a disappointment. Ghormley feels that the company sales representative covering this territory,

From R. W. Haas *Business Marketing*, 6th ed., Cincinnati: Southwestern Publishing Company, 1995. Reprinted with permission.

Mitch Greenwood, has not been doing an acceptable job. Although Greenwood has always met sales quotas, he is difficult to manage and sometimes quite unwilling to take orders from Ghormley. Greenwood is also overbearing and abrasive, and Ghormley has never personally liked the man. Thus, he sees the company's decision to move to distributors as an opportunity to get rid of Greenwood once and for all. He selects the Pacific northwest territory as a test case for replacing field representatives with distributors. He does not, however, intend to notify Greenwood of his dismissal until he has found a suitable distributor to cover the area. Once that task is accomplished, Ghormley plans to terminate Greenwood's employment with Fairchild Lubricants. His problem is finding a distributor to replace Mitch Greenwood.

DETERMINING DISTRIBUTOR SELECTION CRITERIA

One of the first tasks Ghormley undertakes is to determine the criteria to be used in the distributor selection process. He knows that distributors may be selected based on any number of factors, but he also knows that any selection process cannot use every conceivable factor that may be involved. Therefore, he decides on five criteria to be used in evaluating and selecting prospective distributors. These are (1) sales capabilities—the size and experience of a distributor's field and inside sales force; (2) interest—the level of interest expressed by a distributor's management in carrying Fairchild products; (3) product line compatibility—the compatibility of a distributor's present product lines with Fairchild products; (4) service capabilities—the distributor's service facilities and experience of its service personnel to handle Fairchild products; and (5) warehousing and delivery capabilities—the size of the distributor's warehouse, inventory levels, number of branch sites, and transportation abilities. After considerable thought, Ghormley is convinced that these five factors are the most important. He will use these criteria in selecting among prospective distributors.

Ghormley acknowledges that these five criteria are not equal in importance and should not

EXHIBIT I	
WEIGHTING OF CRITERIA FOR PROSPECTIVE DISTRIBUTORS	
Rating Criterion	Relative Weight in the Selection Process
Sales capabilities	35%
Product line compatibility	25%
Service capabilities	15%
Warehousing and delivery capabilities	15%
Interest in carrying Fairchild products	10%

be weighted the same in any selection process. Since the distributors are to replace existing company field sales representatives, he believes strongly that any prospective distributor must be able to provide outstanding sales coverage. At the same time, he believes that the product lines of a prospective distributor must complement and help sell Fairchild products. He is also concerned that any prospective distributor be able to provide adequate service to Fairchild customers and possess ample warehouse space and equipment. Finally, he believes the interest level expressed by the distributor's management in carrying Fairchild's products should be considered. Based on these feelings, Ghormley weights these five criteria as shown in Exhibit 1.

Ghormley feels this weighting scheme adequately represents his objectives in replacing company field sales representatives with industrial distributors. He plans to evaluate all prospective distributors on the basis of these five criteria and then select the single distributor for each territory that best meets his criteria. He intends to test this selection process on the Pacific northwest territory.

DETERMINING POSSIBLE DISTRIBUTORS

At this point, Ghormley faces the task of finding potential distributors for the Pacific northwest territory. Knowing that in the past, Fairchild's products have been purchased by many types of industrial and transportation users, Ghormley decides that general line distributors make the most logical prospects. Thus, he rules out spe-

	EXHIBIT 2		
	PROSPECTIVE DISTRIBUTORS FOR PACIFIC NORTHWEST TERRITORY		
Distributor	Main Office Location	Number of Branches	Branch Locations
Pacific Distributing Company	Seattle, WA	2	Portland, OR Everett, WA
Northwest Distributors, Inc.	Tacoma, WA	0	N/A
Ames & Hobart Company	Seattle, WA	1	Spokane, WA
Devon Distributing Company	Tacoma, WA	2	Portland, OR Seattle, WA
Shasta Distributors, Inc.	Portland, OR	2	Seattle, WA Spokane, WA

cialist distributors from further consideration. Using the Directory of Industrial Distributors, Ghormley finds twenty-one general line distributors that can possibly carry Fairchild products in the Pacific northwest. By careful analysis of information provided in the directory, Ghormley is able to determine that many of these distributors are not acceptable. In his estimation, some are simply too small to cover the territory. Others appear to lack sufficient numbers of salespeople. Still others do not possess sufficient warehouse space to retain Ghormley's interest. After this screening, Ghormley is left with five distributors that he believes can adequately cover the territory for Fairchild if they had the interest to do so. He realizes now that he cannot judge these five distributors without visiting them personally for a more detailed investigation of their facilities, personnel, and interest level. The five distributors are shown in Exhibit 2.

GHORMLEY MAKES A TRIP TO THE PACIFIC NORTHWEST TERRITORY

Ghormley decides to fly to the Pacific northwest and spend a week with the prospective distributor candidates. Since only five prospects are involved, he believes he can spend approximately one day with each and come away with a reasonably good assessment of their respective strengths and weaknesses. From information in the Directory of Industrial Distributors Ghormley obtains the names of the general managers and their phone numbers. He then calls each of them, introduces himself, and explains his rea-

son for calling. He explains to each manager that Fairchild is considering his or her company for an exclusive distributorship in Oregon and Washington and states that he would like to visit, talk to personnel, and tour the facilities. All five general managers are aware of the Fairchild line, and all five express an interest in at least talking to Ghormley. After some scheduling difficulties are ironed out, he is able to find a week in which all five general managers are available. Appointments are made by phone, and Ghormley makes his travel plans. He will fly first to Seattle, visiting the Pacific Distributing Company on the first day. Remaining in Seattle on the second day, he will see the Ames & Hobart Company. On the morning of the third day, he will rent a car and drive to Tacoma to spend a day each with Northwest Distributors and Devon Distributing Company. On the evening of the fourth day, he plans to fly to Portland, and spend the final day with Shasta Distributors. He will then return to Racine.

Typically, his visits take place as follows. He first meets with the respective distributor's general manager and management team. They discuss topics such as the distributor's interest in carrying Fairchild products, suppliers of other products in the distributor's line, territories covered, inventory levels, methods of payment, and other factors. He then interviews the distributor's sales manager, and later the service manager. When possible, he talks to field sales personnel. The interviews usually end with a tour of both warehouse and service facilities. The days are full, and

Ghormley is convinced he knows each distributor's total operation much better than before. He is pleased with the reception at every distributor and is gratified to hear that all five general managers think highly of the Fairchild line. All five also appear to be impressed by the fact that he is visiting them personally. His trip convinces him of two things. First, it appears that industrial distributors are interested and can be used to replace some field sales representatives. Second, any selection process must include such personal visits.

GHORMLEY DRAWS HIS IMPRESSIONS OF THE VISITED DISTRIBUTORS

On his return to Racine, Ghormley reviews his notes and summarizes his impressions of each of the five distributors based on his observations and other materials he has brought back. He attempts to focus these impressions principally on the five selection criteria he has chosen. He realizes, however, that other points may creep in. He summarizes his impressions as follows.

Pacific Distributing Company

Main office in Seattle, with branch offices in Portland, Oregon, and Everett, Washington. Seattle warehouse has 15,000 square feet of space, and Portland and Everett warehouses have 10,000 square feet of space each. Inventory records in all three warehouses are totally computerized, and combined average monthly inventory in all three warehouses is $500,000. The company has eight outside field salespeople and five inside salespeople working out of the three offices. Salespeople appear to be very experienced, and there has been very little sales turnover in the past five years. Interviews with field salespeople leave the impression that they are aggressive, competent, and fairly satisfied. They have no real dissatisfactions with the company's compensation plan. Fairchild products fit in well with the existing product lines, although some product lines are good and others are not. Service personnel appear competent, and service equipment is modern and in good shape. Service space is quite limited in all three sites. The general manager expresses real interest in handling Fairchild products and seems fairly willing to

follow Fairchild policies and directions. No problems with inventory level requirements as long as they are "reasonable."

Northwest Distributors, Inc.

Only one office in Tacoma and one warehouse of 10,000 square feet at that location. Inventory records are not totally computerized as yet, and average monthly inventory is estimated at $250,000. Company has three outside salespeople and three inside salespeople, all working out of the Tacoma office. Sales turnover has been a problem. Interviewed salespeople seem aggressive but also appear to lack experience. Product line is "average," but the company does have a gap that Fairchild products can easily fill. Service staff is small, and there is a relatively small service area. Service equipment is not the most modern, and some appears run down. General manager seems only moderately interested. He appears to have some other options and seems more interested in them than in Fairchild. He also balks at some of Fairchild's inventory level requirements.

Ames & Hobart Company

Main office is in Seattle with one branch in Spokane. Each location has a 10,000 square foot warehouse and a totally computerized inventory system. Average monthly inventory is valued at $400,000. There are two outside salespersons and two inside salespersons working out of each office. There has been some turnover in the past, but interviewed salespeople appear experienced. Compensation plan is about average. Product line is uneven, with some excellent lines and some rather poor lines. However, Fairchild products appear to fit well into the total line. Service staff, equipment, and space are about average. Distributor seems interested in carrying Fairchild products, but it also insists on carrying competitive products as well. General manager expresses some concerns regarding Fairchild's inventory level requirements.

Devon Distributing Company

Main office is in Tacoma with two offices in Seattle and Portland. In Tacoma, there is 18,000 square feet of warehouse space, and 10,000 square feet in both the Seattle and Portland branch locations. Inventory system is totally computerized throughout the three locations, and average monthly inventory in all three is about $480,000. Working out of the three locations are ten outside salespeople and three inside salespeople. Salespeople have been with the company a long time, and turnover has been very low. Interviewed salespeople appear very experienced, dedicated, and well prepared. All are satisfied with the company's compensation plan. Good products in their existing line, and Fairchild products provide a very good fit with other lines. Fairchild would be replacing a competitor's line that has not done well for Devon. Service staff appears good, but equipment not the most modern, and service area space is only average. General manager likes our products and will carry our lines, but he insists on carrying competitive lines if occasion presents itself. He also wants a consignment deal for carrying our inventory.

Shasta Distributors, Inc.

Main office is in Portland with branch locations in Seattle and Spokane. There are 16,000 square feet of warehouse space at main office, 12,000 square feet in Spokane, and 9,000 square feet in

Seattle. Company has a totally computerized inventory system integrated throughout the three offices, and combined average monthly inventory is about $495,000. In the three locations, there are six outside salespeople and four inside salespeople. Salespeople appear competent, experienced, and dedicated, but they have many gripes about the company's compensation plan. There is a good fit between Fairchild products and distributor's present line. Our products complement many others in their present line. Their line includes a number of good lines but also a couple of weak ones. Good modern service facilities with ample space at all three locations. Interviewed service personnel appear very experienced and competent, and other suppliers recommend their service capabilities. The interest level is there, and general manager likes Fairchild's reputation, but he indicates that he will probably ignore our directions if they are not in his company's best interests. He also expresses some concerns about our inventory level requirements.

To help determine an overall or composite rating of each of the prospective distributors, Ghormley develops the rating form shown in Exhibit 3. He wants to transcribe his impressions and notes onto a rating form for each dis-

---

EXHIBIT 3
DISTRIBUTOR RATING FORM

Distributor: _____

Rating Criteria	Rating Scale
1. Sales capabilities—size and experience of field and inside sales force sales force	1 2 3 4 5 Low High
2. Interest—level of interest of distributor in carrying the manufacturer's products	1 2 3 4 5 Low High
3. Product line compatibility—compatibility of distributor's present product line with the manufacturer's products	1 2 3 4 5 Low High
4. Service capabilities—service facilities and experience of service personnel to handle the manufacturer's products	1 2 3 4 5 Low High
5. Warehousing and delivery capabilities—size of warehouse, inventory levels, and transportation abilities	1 2 3 4 5 Low High

Additional Comments:

tributor, so that he may better summarize his evaluations. He also believes that by completing such a rating form for each distributor, he can facilitate his decision to select one of the five to cover exclusively the Pacific northwest territory of Oregon and Washington.

Recommend to Ghormley which one of the five distributors he should appoint to cover this territory.

DISCUSSION QUESTIONS

1. If Ghormley decides to use a selective rather than an exclusive distributor system in Oregon and Washington and wants three distributors to cover the territory, which three do you recommend?

2. Assume Ghormley changes his mind and now perceives service as the most important criterion in selecting distributors. He reweights the criteria as follows: sales capabilities, 25 percent; interest level, 10 percent; product line compatibility, 25 percent; service capabilities, 35 percent; and warehousing and delivery capabilities, 5 percent. Now, which distributor do you recommend to cover the territory if Ghormley still wants an exclusive distributorship arrangement?

3. If none of the five selected distributors will agree to carry the Fairchild line in the Pacific Northwest territory, what do you think Ghormley should do?

Glossary

Abandonment strategy. A strategy a seller can use with a distributor when the distributor is a weak competitor and the seller's product line only comprises a small percentage of the distributor's total sales of that product category; in this case, the seller must to try to find a replacement distributor as quickly as possible. *17*

Absorption training. The written materials that the organization gives to a trainee with the expectation that the trainee will "absorb" the material on his or her own; include training and product manuals, information bulletins, and various types of internal documents. *11*

Accommodation. The process a new hire goes through as he or she seeks to discover what the organization is really like and attempts to become a part of the organization; the second stage of the Feldman model. *11*

Activity/function-based salesforce. A type of field sales force organization in which the salesforce is organized by sales function, such as prospecting, qualifying, presentation, closing, customer service, or routine orders. *8*

Activity reports. Detail unusual events that occur in the field, such as a major change in pricing by a competitor, a major change in purchasing practices by a key customer, or some other significant event; used to measure behavior-based performance. *14*

Administrative law. Law that is created by regulations. *2*

Adversarial model of purchasing. This traditional purchasing model relies on three major components: (1) the buyer maintains a large number of suppliers who can be pitted against one another in a bid for any business; (2) the buyer is careful to allocate purchases among all suppliers in order to keep sellers in a state of tension; and (3) the buyer uses only short-term contracts to be able to shift from one supplier to another as market conditions dictate. *7*

Aftermarketing. A strategic program designed to maintain the business of existing customers; changes the focus from competing for and completing a sale to beginning and maintaining a relationship. *5*

Age Discrimination in Employment Act (1967). Extends Title VII of the Civil Rights Act (1964) to include individuals 40 years of age and older. *3*

All-you-can-afford budgeting. A simple budgeting method whereby the sales budget consists of funds left over after all other operations have been budgeted. *17*

American With Disabilities Act (ADA) (1990). Extends Title VII of the Civil Rights Act (1964) and the Vocation Rehabilitation Act (1973) to include disabled workers in the private sector. Under this legislation, disabled workers who are otherwise capable of performing the essential functions of a job cannot be discriminated against because of their disability; in addition, companies are responsible for making reasonable accommodations in the workplace for the disabled worker. *3*

Anchoring. Occurs when managers rate salespeople using a scale; the anchor is the starting point on the scale from which the evaluation is made. *14*

Anticipating socialization. Concerned with the salesperson's preconceived notions about life in the new organization. The first stage of the Feldman model. *11*

Antitrust. Whenever firms engage in anticompetitive business practices, such as dividing up markets to reduce competition or colluding to set prices. *3*

Apathetic. A sales employee who does not care about the job or the organization and is destined to be a turnover statistic; represents failure on the part of management, either in the recruiting process, during training, or in motivation. *12*

Application blank. A selection tool designed to

(1) provide information useful in making selection decisions and (2) obtain information that may be needed during the course of the individual's employment. *10*

Approach. The strategies and tactics employed by salespeople when gaining an audience and establishing rapport with prospects. The third step in the selling process. *5*

Approved vendor list. A roster of products, services, and sellers that have been qualified by the purchasing firm. *7*

Asterisk bills. Legislation that requires publishers of telephone directories or firms that sell prospect lists to include asterisks by the names of consumers or firms that do not wish to be solicited by telephone. *3*

Attribution. Pertains to the process of interpreting events by using causal explanations. *12*

Attribution theory. Attempts to change the focus of explanation from "what if" to "why"; focuses on the relationships between behavior and the cause of the behavior. *12*

Autoregressive moving averages. The most sophisticated form of time series (quantitative) forecasting; selects values for the trend, seasonal, cyclical, and irregular parameters that minimize the difference between actual and forecast values for any time period. *15*

Availability heuristic. Occurs when managers assess subordinates based on the information that is most readily available; a type of performance judgment bias. *14*

Base rate information. The actual distribution of performance outcomes being assessed; underweighting base rate information is a type of performance judgment bias. *14*

Behavior-based measures. A set of performance criteria which focuses on the salesperson's selling activities, including product knowledge, presentation quality, closing ability, services performed, the number of active accounts, the number of calls made, and days worked. *14*

Behavioral observation scales (BOS). A performance evaluation method that is based on significant incidents describing behaviors that can either enhance or detract from performance. *14*

Behavioral simulations. A variety of interactive training methods, including role playing, computer simulations, interactive video, teletraining, and video-enhanced training, that allow the trainee to learn by doing. *11*

Bird dog. An individual who is paid to provide a referral; may be a source inside or outside the company. *5*

Bonus. A one-sum supplemental payment for excellent performance, typically paid at the end of the fiscal year or calendar year, or on a quarterly basis. *13*

Boston Consulting Group (BCG) Matrix. A type of portfolio matrix that compares strategic business units (SBUs) on two dimensions: market growth rate and relative market share. *16*

Bottom-up budgeting. A basic approach to setting sales budgets whereby sales managers are charged with determining the specific budget requirements to accomplish given sales objectives. *17*

Boundary spanner. The person in the middle; specifically, the dual role of the sales manager, who is a part of both the salesforce world and the management world. *6*

Breakdown method. The simplest means of determining a salesforce size; calculated by dividing the forecasted sales by the average expected sales per salesperson. *9*

Broker. An independent agent whose main function is to bring together buyers and sellers for the purpose of making a sale. *8*

Business unit strategy. Running the mix of businesses in a firm; a subset of *corporate strategy*. *16*

Buyer. The specific individual (or individuals) responsible for purchasing for the buying company. *2*

Buying center. Anyone in an organization who directly or indirectly influences the purchase decision-making process. *2*

Buying Power Index (BPI). A type of quantitative forecasting technique; a proprietary system developed by *Sales and Marketing Management* which is used to predict sales and set sales quotas for specific geographic regions for manufacturers and distributors of retail goods. *15*

Call agenda. An outline of the purpose of the sales call and what the salesperson hopes to present on this particular sales call. *5*

Call reports. Periodic accounts prepared by salespeople of how they are spending their time, which can be used by sales managers, as important input into the evaluating salespeople because they provide details of the behaviors performed during the sales call. *14*

Career plateauing.   Occurs when the job ceases to offer any opportunity for growth or advancement. *12*

Caveat Emptor. Latin for "Let the buyer beware." *2*

Centralized training.   Training that occurs in one location, such as company headquarters or a national training center. *11*

Channel dependence matrix (CDM).   A matrix that depicts the market share of different sellers and distributors to show which sellers and which distributors have power in which channels. *17*

Civil Rights Act (1964).   A sweeping piece of antidiscrimination legislation that covers all firms with more than 15 employees engaged in interstate commerce. Specifically, the act makes it unlawful for an employer to discriminate on the basis of race, color, religions, gender or national origin with respect to (1) classified advertising; (2) testing for the purpose of hiring or promotion; (3) hiring or terminating employees; (4) pay, job classification, or job assignment; (5) transfers and promotions; (6) use of company facilities; (7) fringe benefits; (8) pensions; (9) training; (10) disability leave and pay; and (11) any other terms and conditions of employment. *3*

Clayton Act (1914).   Clarifies the Sherman Act, particularly as it pertains to exclusive dealing. It is a violation of the Clayton Act when the intent or effect of the exclusive dealing arrangement is to create a monopoly or to substantially reduce competition. See also *exclusive dealing. 3*

Closing.   The successful completion of the sales presentation culminating in the acceptance of a product or service order. The sixth stage in the selling process. *5*

Code of ethics.   A statement that "embodies the collective conscience of a profession and is testimony to the group's recognition of its moral dimension." *3*

Coercive power.   The ability to sanction subordinates for lack of compliance. *6*

Cognitive dissonance.   A feeling of uneasiness or regret about a purchase or decision. *5*

Cognitive script.   A learned mental representation describing a series of activities or events to fit a particular scenario. *11*

Cold canvassing.   Synonymous with door-to-door selling. *5*

Combination role.   The hybrid role assigned to telemarketing in which telemarketing acts in a support role with the organization's large customers and in a primary role with the small customers. *8*

Commercial agents.   Firms that solicit orders for a manufacturer but do not take title to the goods. *4*

Commission merchant.   An agent primarily used to sell agricultural commodities from farmers who do not wish to sell their own output and who do not belong to a producers' cooperative. *8*

Common law.   Law created by different levels of the courts. *2*

Company share variance.   Shows the financial sequence of overestimating or underestimating the company's marked share. *17*

Compensation.   Financial and nonfinancial methods of rewards for sales personnel. *13*

Compensation hydraulics.   Implies that compensation is nothing more than pay designed to obtain sales behavior. *13*

Compensation mix.   The relative amounts of salary, commission, and bonus to be included in the compensation plan. *13*

Computer games and simulations.   Computerized software that allows training by simulating sales scenarios. *11*

Computerized performance monitoring (CPM).   A method of obtaining outcome-based measures of performance in which computers track items such as number of calls handled, the amount of time the terminal is left idle, the number of transactions, and the number and length of phone calls. *14*

Congruence.   The degree to which an organization's resources and demands and that of the sales recruit are compatible. *11*

Congruence of evaluation.   The similarity of evaluation between the sales manager and the trainee; the fourth process in the accommodation stage of the Feldman model. *11*

Consultative selling.   Establishing the end user's particular needs with regard not only to price but also to applications, urgency of service, quality of products, and other factors important to the customer. *5*

Content theories.   Attempt to identify aspects that correlate motivation to individual behavior without explaining the dynamics of motivational change. *12*

Contribution variance.   Shows the effect any deviation from the expected contribution margin had on total contribution dollars. *17*

Control unit.   The smallest geographic area used to build sales territories; can be states, counties, trading areas, metropolitan statistical areas (MSAs), or ZIP codes. *9*

Convergent thinking.   The thought processes that produce a single best answer to a problem, such as that which is accomplished on a multiple choice test. *10*

Cooling-off periods.   A period of time during which customers who purchase an item in their home have a certain period of time (usually 72 hours) to change their minds. *3*

Co-op students.   Students who take a semester off from their college or university to work full time for an organization. *10*

Cooperative model of purchasing.   This contemporary model of purchasing focuses less on price and more on joint buyer-seller efforts to achieve common goals; characterized by the use of a limited number of suppliers and long-term agreements between the parties. *7*

Corporate and industry analysis.   Intended to identify the firm's place within the industry; the fourth and final step in a situation audit. *16*

Corporate citizen.   A sales employee who places little importance on the job itself and high levels of importance on the association the job gives the sales employee with the organization. *12*

Corporate strategy.   Decides what mix of businesses should comprise the firm. *16*

Correlation models.   A set of quantitative forecasting techniques with which managers can seek variables that correlate with, or relate to, sales; may be direct or inverse. *15*

Counseling.   The ability of the organization to provide professional help for employees' personal problems. *6*

Countertrade.   A modern-day barter system wherein international partners agree to help one another in the selling or developing of their respective products and needs. *5*

Creative thinking training.   A type of training that emphasizes problem solving, creativity, and other mental skill-building exercises. *11*

Crook.   A category of managers who know that taking a certain action is morally wrong, but take it anyway using the justification of personal gain or temporary organizational gain. *3*

Cross-function selling.   A method of selling wherein the salesperson teams up with experts in various departments to provide higher-level service to the customer at all levels. *1*

Cross-training.   A type of training that prepares personnel to reside in international settings; a fundamental immersion into the culture of another country. *11*

Cultural universals.   The unique aspects of a particular society such as etiquette and manners, courtships, socialization, gestures, status, customs, values, and materialism. *5*

Culture.   "A learned, shared, compelling, interrelated set of symbols whose meanings provide a set of orientations for members of a society." *4*

Curbstone conference.   An in-person observation and critique by the manager following a joint call on one of the salesperson's customers in which the sales manager needs to ask, "How was the relationship with the customer advanced?" *6*

Current spendable income.   Money provided in the short term (paycheck or annual compensation) that allows salespeople to pay for goods and services. *13*

Customer orientation.   An organizational philosophy that places the customer as the primary focus of the business strategy. *1*

Customer satisfaction surveys.   Questionnaires mailed to customers; scores are based on customers' responses to a series of questions about their interaction with their representative; used to measure behavior-based performance. *14*

Day in the field.   An interview type in which the recruit spends a working day in the field with a sales rep from the hiring organization. *10*

Dealers.   Independent firms that represent a variety of manufacturers. *8*

Decentralized training.   Training that occurs at multiple locations, such as district offices. *11*

Decider.   A member of the buying center who has the power to actually make the product and vendor decision. *7*

Decision models.   Consist of one or more response functions that relate selling effort to sales response. *9*

Decomposition.   A time series (quantitative) forecasting technique that takes seasonality into account and involves performing three steps: (1) calculating seasonal index numbers, (2) making the sales forecast, and (3) adjusting the forecast for seasonality. *15*

Defensive entrenchment strategy.   A strategy a

seller can use with a distributor when the distributor is growing and already has a substantial relationship with the seller; in this case, the seller must keep a close watch on the distributor to ensure that no competitor tries to convert the distributor away from the seller's product line and maintain market share by finding ways to increase the strength of the relationship with the distributor. *17*

Delphi technique. A qualitative forecasting technique that involves combining and revising executives' (or experts') individual sales forecasts, each of which is accompanied by an explanation of the factors used to derive the forecast. *15*

Derived demand. A type of demand that depends on the anticipated demand for a product by the manufacturer's customers. In this case, products are purchased to be used in the production of other products that will eventually be resold. *7*

Determination of need. In purchasing, forming a general description of the product or service that would address the purchaser's problem. *7*

Development program. A type of training that gives existing employees strengths and skills that they can capitalize on in their daily jobs. *11*

Diagnostic skills. The ability to recognize a problem, develop alternatives, and formulate a solution. *6*

Direct investment. The investing firm owns 100 percent of its foreign subsidiaries. *4*

Direction. The ability and will to choose where a person's efforts will be spent. *12*

Directional policy matrix (DPM). A type of portfolio matrix that compares strategic business units (SBUs) on several components. *16*

Discrete transaction. A single transaction based on no previous relationship and assuming no future relationship. *5*

Disengagement stage. The fourth and final stage in one's sales career in which one begins to give greater priority to outside issues and to withdraw from the daily job. *12*

Distributor portfolio analysis (DPA). A technique that allows firms to assess their distributors and make retention/termination decisions and resource allocation decision for those it chooses to retain. *17*

Divergent thinking. The thought processes that produce a variety of alternative to a problem, such as that which is accomplished with role plays and case analyses. *10*

Dominator. A manager who believes that people

must be pushed and prodded to do their work; has power and uses it to gain compliance. *6*

Downsizing. Reducing personnel. Also known as *rightsizing*. *1*

Draw. An account from which commission-based salespeople can take a "loan" against future earnings. *13*

Drummer. The slick-talking, disreputable peddler in nineteenth century United States immortalized in movies as selling elixir from the back of his wagon. *2*

Dual-career ladder. The opportunity to choose from more than one long-term career possibilities within an organization, some of which may be lateral. *12*

Dual factor theory. Proposes that there are two sets of factors that influence a salesperson's satisfaction/dissatisfaction and thus motivation and job performance: hygiene factors and motivators; also known as the Hertzberg Hygiene-Motivation Theory. *12*

Dyadic relationship. The one-on-one relationship that has traditionally existed between buyers and sellers. *5*

Electronic data interchange (EDI). The electronic exchange of information between business partners in a structured format. *8*

Electronic mail (e-mail). A method of communication that allows a salesperson to stay in contact with the customer base through an on-line computer network interface such as the Internet. *2*

Electronic sales office. The process of taking orders from the customer's computer to the seller's computer; primarily for simple reorder and rebuy situations. Human interaction does not take place until the product is actually picked up and delivered. *2*

E-mail protocols. Rules as to how the e-mail system can be used within the organization. *2*

Empirically based decision models. A type of decision model that relies on gathering data on several factors (e.g., customer's previous response to different levels of selling effort, previous levels of competition, and the customer's buying patterns) to generate sales response functions. *9*

Employee referral programs. Incentive programs designed to reward existing personnel for finding and recommending applicants who are subsequently hired. *10*

Employment at will. A doctrine which states that

either the employer or the employee can end the relationship at any time for virtually any reason. *3*

Empowerment. The process of involving the salesforce in their work through the concept of inclusion. *6*

Equity theory. States that salespeople will compare and contrast their treatment with "relevant others"; the fundamental aspect of this theory is fairness or perceived fairness. *12*

ERG theory. Contends that human needs are classified into three levels: (1) existence, (2) relatedness, and (3) growth; an individual can move up and down the levels without satisfying any lower level first; multiple levels can be motivators simultaneously. Also known as *Alderfer's ERG theory. 12*

Establishment stage. The second stage in one's professional career in which one attempts to successfully build a career in a particular industry. *12*

Exclusive dealing. Occurs when the seller agrees to sell to a buyer only if the buyer agrees not to purchase the same items from any other seller. *3*

Executive development programs. Designed to help sales executives expand their skills and continue an upward path. *11*

Expatriates. Home-country nationals on assignment in the host country. *4*

Expectancies. The perceived linkages between effort and resulting performance. *12*

Expectancy theory. A theory of motivation based on the judgment that job efforts will lead to performance that in turn will be rewarded and with the assumption that the rewards have value to the sales individual. *12*

Expense account. A sum of money that is reimbursed to the employee for job-related expenses such as travel, meals, and customer entertainment. *13*

Expert power. A type of power based on the manager's specialized or perceived specialized knowledge and skills. *6*

Exploration stage. The first stage in one's professional career, usually in one's early twenties, in which one initiates a new career and is very concerned about securing the "best possible job" and beginning on the right note. *12*

Exponential smoothing. A type of time series (qualitative) forecasting that allows the forecaster to vary the weights assigned to past data points. *15*

Export Administration Act (1979). Forbids U.S. firms from selling computer technology that could be used in developing weapons to certain countries. *3*

Exporting. Shipping from manufacturing or distribution facilities in one country to customers in another; one of the most frequently used methods of entering foreign markets. *4*

External problem recognition. Occurs when a consultant, salesperson, or other source outside the purchasing organization identifies or highlights a problem that exists in the organization. *7*

Extrinsic motivation. Motivation provided through some external method such as pay, promotion, or recognition. *12*

Field salesforce. Sales representatives who work primarily with customers in person, although they may also use the telephone or rely on computer links to expedite orders and customer service. *8*

Financial rewards. Composed of *current spendable income,* deferred income, profit sharing, retirement, and various benefits packages. *13*

Flex plan. A form of financial compensation plan in which the salesperson is given some liberty as to percentage of salary and commission offered. *13*

Fluctuating demand. A characteristic of demand in industrial markets. The differences between high and low levels of demand are more pronounced in industrial markets than in consumer markets. *7*

Follow-up. Occurs after a sale has been completed and is designed to ensure that customers remain happy with their purchase decision and the relationship that has been developed throughout the selling process. The seventh stage in the selling process. *5*

Forced-choice scales. A performance evaluation method whereby sales managers rate salespeople on a series of adjectives that describe the person's performance. *14*

Forecasting. The prediction of demand or sales for upcoming periods. *15*

Foreign Corrupt Practices Act (1976, amended 1988). Restricts the giving of bribes by U.S. companies to foreign nationals to obtain contracts. *3*

Foreign direct investment (FDI). The book value (total cost less depreciation) of the investment in a country by firms headquartered in another. *4*

Formal recognition program.   A type of recognition program that is sponsored and heavily promoted by the company and designed to recognize excellence. *13*

Fraud.   Committed when a seller knowingly misrepresents material facts on which buyers rely which cause damage; considered a crime under the Uniform Commercial Code. *3*

Fringe benefits.   An employment benefit given in addition to one's wages or salary. *13*

FTC Act (1914).   Created the Federal Trade Commission, charged with enforcing laws pertaining to unfair methods of competition and issue regulations relating to competition. *3*

Functions.   The issues related to the point of contact between the customer and the firm, including salesforce management, distribution, and consumer and trade promotions. *16*

Fundamental attribution error.   Occurs when managers view salespeople as having more control over sales outcomes than they actually do; a type of performance judgment bias. *14*

Gatekeeper.   An individual who, by design or by chance, controls the communication flow among members of the buying center and between the buying center and the sellers. *5*

General Agreement on Tariffs and Trade (GATT).   An agreement that governs trade among over 90 countries; offers its members a chance to negotiate trade differences and has the goal of reducing trade barriers around the world. *4*

Geographic-information systems (GIS) software.   Software that contains maps of specific regions and allows the user to input additional relevant information, such as customer characteristics, to help managers overcome problems in designing sales territories. *9*

Geographically-based salesforce.   A type of field salesforce organization in which a salesperson calls on all current and prospective accounts in a given geographic territory. *8*

Globetrotters.   Managers who are trained to think in global, not domestic, terms. *4*

Good Samaritan.   A category of managers who generally arrive at moral and just decisions based on careful analysis of relevant moral principles. *3*

Government purchasers.   Include all federal, state, county, and city government units. *7*

Grapevine.   Any organization's informal channels of communication; often contains rumors and gossip, but it can also be extremely accurate. *11*

Green marketing.   Laws and/or corporate responsibilities that are designed to protect the global environment. *2*

Green River ordinances.   Local ordinances that require nonresident door-to-door salespeople to pay a fee, put up a bond (in many cases), and obtain a city license; referred to as such because the first legislation was passed in Green River, Wyoming, in 1933. *3*

Growth effect.   States that the existence of reduced trade barriers within a regional market should increase overall trade opportunities. Increased trade opportunities, in turn, offer increased sales opportunities to all firms within the regional market. *4*

Guaranteed draw.   A *draw* that does not have to be paid back. *13*

High-context cultures.   Cultures in which the message is communicated as much by the background and relationships between the communicators as by the actual content of the message. *4*

Hindsight bias.   Occurs when sales managers discount information received from a salesperson because they believe it would have become apparent or occurred anyway; a type of performance judgment bias. *14*

Horizontal price fixing.   A *per se* violation of the Sherman Act; occurs when competitors at the same level collude to set a price for a certain commodity. *3*

House account.   Large customers in a salesperson's territory for which he or she does not receive compensation. A seller might designate a customer as a house account if the level of service required to maintain the account exceeds that which can be provided by the salesperson. *3*

Humanist.   A type of manager who believes that the human element is an organization's most prized possession; treats subordinates with respect and warmth. *6*

Hybrid salesforce.   A type of field salesforce organization in which the salesforce is organized with two or more organizational types (i.e., geography, product, market/account, or activity/function). *8*

Hygiene factors.   Factors that comprise the job, such as pay, territories, supervision, policies, and recognition, that influence a salesperson's satisfaction/dissatisfaction and thus motivation and job performance according to the *dual factor theory;* also known as *dissatisfiers.* 12

Importance weighting.   A type of decision making that requires a manager to explicitly compare different alternatives on several attributes. 16

Impression management.   The ways people manipulate their communications using their voice, facial expressions, and appearance. 11

Incentive.   A supplemental compensation program that allows the salesperson to perform some activity to earn additional income. 13

Incremental method.   A means of determining salesforce size; compares the marginal revenue from adding one salesperson to the marginal cost of adding that salesperson. 9

Independent distributors.   Local firms with an in-depth knowledge of the market that purchase products from manufacturers (i.e., take title to the goods) and resell them. 4

Independent sales organizations.   Sales organizations composed of individuals who are not employees of the seller. 8

Indoctrination training.   The training of new personnel in "the way" to do the job; teaches the products, organizational way to sell the products, company history and philosophy, and teamwork. 11

Industrial buyers.   Buyers who purchase goods or services for resale or for use in making products for resale. 7

Industry parity budgeting.   A type of percentage of sales budgeting in which the firm sets its sales budget using industry averages. 17

Inelastic demand.   A type of demand wherein an increase or decrease in the price of the product will not have a material effect on the number of products purchased. 7

Influencer.   A member of the buying center whose expertise will influence other buying center members' decisions. 7

Informal recognition program.   A type of recognition program that is not programmatic, but rather dependent on managers being good leaders, recognizing quality work by their subordinates, and providing praise for it. 13

Information Superhighway.   An information and communication channel. A loosely configured,

rapidly growing network of 25,000 corporate, institutional, educational, and research computer systems around the world. 2

Initiation to the group.   The degree to which the trainee feels accepted by co-workers; the second process in the accommodation stage of the Feldman model. 11

Initiation to the task.   The degree to which the trainee feels competent and accepted as a working partner; the first process in the accommodation stage of the Feldman model. 11

Initiator.   A member of the buying center who recognizes that a problem can be solved by the purchase of a product or service. 7

Institutional star.   A sales employee who has high levels of both organizational commitment and job involvement; the sales employee of choice. 12

Institutions.   For-profit and not-for-profit service organizations such as hospitals, universities, churches, labor unions, and foundations that purchase goods for their own use. 7

Instrumentalities.   The perceived linkages between performance and rewards. 12

Intensity.   The magnitude of mental and physical effort put forth on an activity or goal; a dimension of motivation. 12

Interactive video.   A merger of computer, laser disc, and video technology that allows the participant to conduct trial sales presentations on computer-generated customers, who then react to the decisions and approaches made by the salesperson. 2

Intern.   Any part-time paid or nonpaid college employee where the purpose of the job is to educate individuals by providing work experience. 10

Internal problem recognition.   Occurs when a member of the purchasing organization finds a problem that exists in the organization. 7

Intrinsic motivation.   Motivation that comes internally from the desire to please oneself or from the satisfaction of performing a job. 12

Intuition.   Making a quick judgment on immediately available facts and experience; also known as seat-of-the-pants decision making or gut feel. 16

ISO 9000.   European Union certification standards for a wide range of products which are rapidly becoming a requirement for doing business in Europe; necessitates certification of the vendor by a third party. 7

Job autonomy. The degree to which a job provides substantial freedom, independence, and discretion in meeting work responsibilities *12*

Job description. A written document that details the characteristics, duties, and responsibilities of a job. *10*

Job enrichment. An extension of a job's depth such that the salesperson's discretion or control over the job is increased. *12*

Job feedback. The degree to which the individual receives direct and clear information about the effectiveness and level of performance of the job. *12*

Job involvement. The extent to which employees identify psychologically with their particular job. *12*

Job qualifications. The aptitudes, skills, knowledge, and personality traits necessary to perform a particular job successfully. *10*

Joint demand. A type of demand which occurs when two or more commodities are purchased and used together in a finished product. In this case, items that are used together can be combined by the seller to increase the amount of purchases by a given customer. *7*

Joint venture. Two or more companies share stock ownership of a new entity.

Judgment-based decision models. A type of decision models that derives the sales response functions by having salespeople or sales managers estimate the likely customer response to given levels of selling effort or numbers of sales calls. *9*

Jury of executive (or expert) opinion. A qualitative forecasting technique that involves gathering forecasts from a variety of executives or experts in the firm. *15*

Just-in-time (JIT). The delivery or exchange of the precise amount of needed product with a minimum of waste in the exchange. *5, 7*

Leader. A type of manager who believes that it is his or her job to get the best out of the salesforce and to provide outstanding results. *6*

Leadership. Involves the use of influence with other people through communications processes to obtain specific goals and objectives; going beyond basic management and getting the best out of people and the organization. *6*

Learned needs theory. Suggests that salespeople strive for three dimensions: (1) achievement, (2) affiliation, and (3) power; these dimensions are not hierarchical and can be held simultaneously, although one will be dominant at any point in time. *12*

Learning organization. An organization which focuses on continual learning rather than controlling. *6*

Legitimate power. A type of power based on a manager's hierarchical position in the organization. *6*

Licensing. Occurs when one firm allows another to use its patents, trademarks, technology, or something else of value. *4*

Limited draw. A *draw* that is paid back when commissions are earned. *13*

Local hires. Host-country nationals who are hired by the foreign firm. *4*

Lone wolf. A sales employee who lives for the job but could care less about the organization; also known as a *maverick*. *12*

Low-context cultures. Cultures in which the message is communicated primarily by the content of the message. *4*

Maintenance stage. The third stage in one's professional career, usually in one's late thirties or early forties, when one begins to reflect on one's career and life and decides whether to continue on the current career path or make a life change. *12*

Management. Involves rationally analyzing situations, setting goals, and then organizing, coordinating, and directing employees to achieve those goals. *6*

Management by walking around (MBWA). A management style that ensures a manager is continually talking with his or her salespeople and other publics; includes more days in the field with salespeople, more spontaneous visits with customers, visits to the buyer's corporate headquarters, and a close monitoring of reports and salesperson inputs. *6*

Manufacturers' representatives. Independent firms that represent two or more complementary lines of merchandise. *8*

Market/account-based salesforce. A type of field salesforce organization in which the salesforce is organized by the type of customer market it serves. *8*

Market forecast. The level of sales expected by a given set of suppliers to a given geographic area for a given commodity during a given time period. *15*

Market potential. The maximum number of sales that can occur in a given period to individuals or businesses that are willing and have the capacity to purchase a given product type. *15*

Market volume variance. The extent to which the market size is different from what was anticipated. *17*

Marketing. The process of planning and executing the conception, pricing, promotion, and distribution of ideas, goods, and services to create exchanges that satisfy individual and organizational objectives. *1*

Marketing audit. A comprehensive, systematic, independent and periodic examinations of a company's—or business unit's—marketing environment, objectives, strategies, and activities with a view of determining problem areas and opportunities and recommending a plan of action to improve the company's marketing performance. *17*

Marketing concept. Consists of (1) finding customer wants, (2) organizing the firm to meet the wants, and 3) meeting customer wants while meeting organizational objectives, such as profit, market share, growth, and ethical considerations. *16*

Marketing effort analysis. A comparison of the relative effectiveness of promotional methods or selling methods in terms of their sales response per amount of resources; allows the firm to identify which promotional methods or selling methods will yield the highest level of sales or service per dollars spent. *17*

Marketing-oriented firm. Organized according to the *marketing concept. 16*

Mean absolute percentage error (MAPE). A method of calculating the accuracy of a forecast; MAPE looks at all discrepancies between the values that were forecast and the values that were actually achieved. *15*

Mentoring. A formal or informal program in which sales executives take junior sales employees under their wing and make a concerted effort to help them develop and learn the job and organizational system. Also called *coaching. 6*

Mobile-oriented selling. Advances in technology allowing the salesperson to have all the necessities of a physical office in a nonoffice setting. *2*

Motivation. The force within us that directs our behavior; delineated by three dimensions: intensity, persistence, and direction. *12*

Motivators. The self-actualization aspect of one's motivation in which the job and fulfillment become the primary focus of the salesperson, according to the *dual factor theory;* also known as *satisfiers. 12*

Moving average. A type of time series (quantitative) forecasting technique by which forecasters estimate sales based on an average of previous time periods. *15*

Multimedia. A broad category that encompasses applications far beyond the simple text and graphics limitations of traditional computing systems and allows access to wider spectrums of technology including full-motion video, high-fidelity audio, graphic animation, still photographs, and other developing techniques. *2*

Multiple-factor models. A method of classifying customers; involves using multiple factors (e.g., sales potential, customer service required, or type of business) simultaneously to determine how many calls should be devoted to a given group of customers. *9*

Multiple linear regression. A type of regression (quantitative) model which assumes that the relationship between the combination of independent variables and the dependent variable is linear. *15*

Multiple regression models. A type of quantitative forecasting technique in which multiple independent variables have a relationship with sales. *15*

National account management (NAM). A team approach to selling to a firm's largest customers; usually combines a national accounts manager with other members of the selling organization (such as engineers, trainers, and service technicians) as needed. *8*

Need hierarchy theory. Argues that human needs are classified into five hierarchies: (1) physiological, (2) safety and security, (3) love and belongingness, (4) self-esteem, and (5) self-actualization; an individual must satisfy each level before advancing to the next level. Also known as *Maslow's hierarchy of needs. 12*

Needs analysis. A type of analysis which dictates that the seller spend time in the customer environment examining the needs and wants of the customer. *2*

Negotiation. A decision-making process through which a buyer and seller establish the terms of a purchase agreement. *7*

Networking. The method of using friends, business contacts, co-workers, and acquaintances as a means of meeting new people who could become potential customers. *5*

Nonfinancial rewards. Include promotions,

recognition programs, personal development, security, sales contests, expense accounts, and a sense of achievement. *13*

Objection. A customer question or hesitancy about the product or company. Encountering objections is the fifth step in the selling process. *5*

Objective-and-task budgeting. A budgeting method that requires the manager to state specific objectives, identify the tasks necessary to accomplish those objectives, and determine the budget required to perform the tasks. *17*

Offensive investment strategy. A strategy a seller can use with a distributor when the distributor is growing rapidly but the seller's product line represents a relatively small proportion of the distributor's total sales in that product area; in this case, the seller should seek to increase its share of the distributor's total sales of that product category because these distributors represent attractive growth opportunities within the market. *17*

Office politics. The skill in human engineering. *11*

On-the-job training (OJT). Informal training that occurs in the field while the new hire is working; training by doing. *11*

Order routine. Includes methods by which orders are made, placed, traced, and inspected.

Organizational assessment. The portion of the training audit that analyzes the organizational structure, resources, philosophy, and leadership; concentrates on evaluating training needs of the organization and ensures that these needs are met within the existing support system and cultural environment. *11*

Organizational buying. The purchase of goods by firms for use in making other goods or for eventual resale to other firms, such as distributors or retailers. Also known as *purchasing*. *7*

Organizational commitment. An employee's positive psychological identification with the organization and its goals. *12*

Outcome-based measures. A set of performance criteria that measures the results of the selling process, including measures of revenue such as dollar sales and sales unit volume, and profitability such as net margin, sales expense, or a ratio of cost/sales. *14*

Part-time employees. Those who work less than the traditional 40-hour week. *8*

Per se **violations.** Practices including allocating markets, price fixing, boycotting certain resellers, and tying contracts. If an organization is found guilty of these practices, no defense of justification is allowed. See also *Sherman Act*. *3*

Percentage-of-sales budgeting. A budgeting method whereby the sales budget is set as a percent of the sales projected for the coming period. *17*

Performance appraisal. "The process of evaluating the performance and qualifications of the employee in terms of the requirements of the job for which he is employed, for purposes of administration, including placement, selection for promotion, providing financial rewards, and other actions which require differential treatment among members of a group as distinguished from actions affecting all members equally." *14*

Perks. A special category of benefits available only to employees with some special status in the organization. *13*

Persistence. The extension of effort over time. *12*

Personal selling. Personal communication between the seller and the buyer for the purpose of determining and satisfying customer needs. *1*

Personnel assessment. The portion of the training audit that analyzes the strengths and weaknesses of the current organizational personnel; designed to determine the levels and amounts of training needed by each sales individual. *11*

Pipeline manager. A type of manager who conveys decisions from above to those below but adds no value to the process; does not like to make decisions and delays them for as long as possible. *6*

Policies. Represent management's overall theme for its marketing programs. *16*

Portfolio models. A type of multiple-factor model that classifies customers on two dimensions: opportunity and competitive strength. *9*

Portfolio of businesses. The mix of business units that comprise the firm. *16*

Power. A position of controlling influence over others. *6*

Preapproach. The preparation one does before walking into a customer's office; this includes doing research about the customer organization, knowing the buyer, talking with the gatekeeper, regrouping, and reading the office. The second step in the selling process. *5*

Preference effect. Occurs when businesses located within a regional market are favored by others within the regional market, resulting in the potential exclusion of businesses outside the regional market. *4*

Pregnancy Discrimination Act (1978). Amended Title VII of the Civil Rights Act (1964) to include discrimination based on pregnancy, childbirth, or associated mental conditions. *3*

Price discrimination. Occurs when a firm offers two competing companies the same product amount at different prices. *2*

Price fixing. A *per se* violation of the Sherman Act. See also *horizontal price fixing* and *vertical price fixing. 3*

Primary role. The role assigned to telemarketing when a firm uses telemarketing representatives instead of a field salesforce. *8*

Problem recognition. In purchasing, the identification of the problem that the product or service is intended to remedy. *7*

Process theories. Identify the elements that influence motivation and detail the processes that originate the influence. *12*

Producers. Individuals or organizations that purchase goods and services for the purpose of using them to generate sales and profits. *7*

Product-based salesforce. A type of field salesforce organization in which the salesforce is specialized according to product line. *8*

Product-market analysis. Assesses the current position of the firm or business unit and anticipated changes in sales and share by product by market; the first step in a situation audit. *16*

Product opportunity analysis. Seeks to identify segments where the current product line is vulnerable, and to detect opportunities in new segments or among customers in existing segments for the firm to increase its sales; the third step in a situation audit. *16*

Product positioning. Assesses how each segment served views the product and values it compared to the competition; the second step in a situation audit. *16*

Product specifications. Exact statements of required characteristics of products and services that may be purchased to fulfill an organizational need; typically include quantity, desired quality levels, timeliness requirements, and other issues related to the characteristics of the specific product or service. Also known as *specs. 7*

Program. A combination of marketing and nonmarketing activities that must be performed in order to achieve a business objective. *16*

Prospect. A potential customer who may have a need for a product; this definition relies on factual information on the potential customer, not merely the feelings, prejudices, or hope of the salesperson. *5*

Prospecting. The search for potential new customers. The first step in the selling process. *5*

Pseudo objection. A negotiation tool in which the buyer objects as a stalling approach or in an effort to improve his or her negotiation position by not immediately showing a desire or need for the product. *5*

Puffery. Occurs when a salesperson overstates a product's performance. *3*

Purchaser. A member of the buying center who is responsible for contacting the supplier, negotiating the terms of sale, and actually consummating the sale. *7*

Purchasing. The purchase of goods by firms for use in making other goods or for eventual resale to other firms, such as distributors or retailers. Also known as *organizational buying. 7*

Qualified. A potential customer is qualified when the following three conditions are satisfied: (1) they must have a need or want that can be satisfied by the purchase of the product; (2) they must have the financial means to purchase the product along with the authority to make a purchase decision; and (3) they must be receptive to a sales contact by the selling organization. *5*

Qualitative forecasting techniques. Those which rely on experts' judgments to determine the most likely level of sales. *15*

Quality-oriented firms. Focus on providing high-quality products and services to external and internal customers. *16*

Quantitative forecasting techniques. Those which rely on some form of mathematical analysis of historical data to derive a forecast. *15*

Quota. A quantitative goal, covering a specific time period, assigned to salespeople and sales managers. *15*

Ratings forms. Lists of statements or adjectives about the sales job that the sales manager uses to evaluate each salesperson. *14*

Rationalizer. A category of managers who recognize that certain decisions have ethical consequences, but look for ways to justify the solution that yields the highest economic payoff, regardless of its ethicality. *3*

Realism.   The degree to which a new hire has an accurate reflection of what life at the organization is like. *11*

Recognition program.   Designed to honor individual salespeople formally or informally for excellent performance. *13*

Recruiting.   Finding and attracting the best pool of qualified applicants to be considered for sales positions. *10*

Referent power.   A type of power based on a manager's sense of friendship and respect with subordinates. *6*

Referral.   A prospect that is provided to the salesperson by someone else. *5*

Refresher training.   Training that keeps even the most experienced reps current on new trends and/or changes in the product or industry, or simply revitalizes the individual. *11*

Regional markets.   Geographic areas with common sets of regulations and economic policies. *4*

Regression effects.   Reflect the tendency of unusual observations to be followed by observations that are more typical of the norm; ignoring regression effects is a type of performance judgment bias. *14*

Regression models.   A set of quantitative forecasting techniques that try to predict a dependent variable (typically sales) with one or more independent variables thought to have a relationship with sales. *15*

Relational exchange.   A type of exchange that assumes a relationship is ongoing over time; the most common exchange in the existing business-to-business selling environment. *5*

Relationship selling.   The process whereby a sales organization builds long-term alliances with both prospective and current customers so that seller and buyer work toward a common set of specified goals. *2*

Request for proposal (RFP).   Formal documentation that contains product specifications, especially in government procurement and many purchasing departments of large organizations. *7*

Resale price maintenance.   Another term for *horizontal price fixing*. *3*

Reseller.   A wholesaler or a retailer or some type of agent/broker that buys finished goods in bulk and resells them. *1, 7*

Responsible commercial success.   Reaping profits while at the same time making the world a better place to live. *1*

Résumé inflation.   Overstating or highly exaggerating one's qualifications on a résumé. *10*

Retailing.   All activities directly related to the sale of goods and services to the ultimate consumer for personal, nonbusiness use or consumption. *1*

Return on assets managed (ROAM).   A product of two ratios: sales/investment and profit/sales (in dollars); offers sales managers the ability to make decisions such as choices among alternatives in opening new sales offices and which combination of selling methods to use. *17*

Return on investment (ROI) budgeting.   A budgeting method that treats expenditures on developing customer relationships as long-term investments. Managers develop ROI budgets by calculating sales/investment and profits/sales for any intended expenditure, such as sales training, opening new sales offices, or sales incentives. *17*

Reward power.   A type of power based on a manager's ability to reward subordinates for performance. *6*

Reward system management.   The selection and utilization of organizational rewards to direct salespeople's behavior toward the attainment of organizational objectives. *13*

Ride-with.   The amount of time a sales manager spends in the field with his or her salespeople. *6*

Rightsizing.   Reducing personnel. Also known as *downsizing*. *1*

Risk diversification.   Occurs when a company tries to spread its risk over a large number of markets. *4*

Robinson-Patman Act (1936).   Enacted to clarify some of the language in the second section of the Clayton Act, which referred to price discrimination. *3*

Role definition.   Agreements that articulate the tasks that the trainee is to perform; the third process in the accommodation stage of the Feldman model. *11*

Role plays.   The oldest of the behavioral simulations; allows trainees to take on character roles and solve problems either through videotape or in a live presentation. *11*

Role-result matrix.   A specification of the roles to be played by each sales team member and the results that are expected from each team member and from the team as a whole; an outline of the individual responsibilities necessary for the team to accomplish its overall sales goals. *14*

Rules and shortcuts. A type of decision making that requires managers to rely on rules of thumb (heuristics) from personal experience or those based on industry or company standards. *16*

Salary plus incentive compensation plan. A combination compensation plan that combines the best aspects of salary, commission, and bonus plans. The goal is to combine control, incentive, and enough flexibility to motivate and reward performance. *13*

Sales audit. A comprehensive review of the firm's selling effort which allows the firm to identify underlying problems in the selling approach and salesforce, improve effectiveness and profitability, and ensure that customer needs are being met. *17*

Sales budget. The statement of revenues and costs that are expected for a given time period; allows managers to monitor whether sales costs are consistent or appropriate for the level of expected sales. *17*

Sales contest. A temporary salesperson incentive program that offers monetary or nonmonetary rewards and is not a part of the regular compensation plan. *13*

Sales controls. The means by which management sets standards, obtains information on the extent to which the standards are met, and takes corrective action if needed. *17*

Sales environment. Those forces over which a sales organization has no control. These uncontrollable variables include customers, competitors, technology, social-demographic forces, economic forces, and legal and political forces. *2*

Sales expenses. The specific dollar expenditures on selling and sales management that are required to generate the forecasted revenues. *17*

Sales forecast. The level of expected sales by a given firm from a given market segment within a given geographic area during a given time period using a given marketing plan. *15*

Sales management. The administration and direction of those people who are engaged in personal selling or who provide direct support to the salesforce. *1*

Sales organization. The organizational structure through which sales strategy is implemented. *8*

Sales potential. The maximum possible sales for a specified product to a given market segment by a given supplier during a given period of time. *15*

Sales presentation. The phase of a sales call in which the object is to convince the prospect or customer that the seller's product and product attributes can satisfy the customer's needs better than can those of the competition. The fourth step in the selling process. *5*

Sales proposal. A written document that specifies why the buyer should buy from the selling company. *5*

Sales revenue. The total income expected in the period for which the budget is developed; typically derived from the sales forecast. *17*

Sales strategy. Delineates the objectives of the firm's or business unit's selling efforts, the means the firm intends to use to achieve these objectives, and the means by which the selling efforts will be monitored and evaluated; a subset of *business unit strategy*. *16*

Sales team. A group of people, representing the seller, who are assigned to accomplish specific types of transactions. *8*

Sales training. The systematic attempt to identify, understand, and transfer "good selling practices" to sales personnel; provides the salesperson with the ability to reach acceptable effectiveness levels in less time than learning through on-the-job experiences. *11*

Salesforce composite. A qualitative forecasting technique that involves obtaining and combining the views of salespeople, sales managers, or both as to the most likely levels of expected sales. *15*

Salesforce deployment. The collective process of classifying customers, determining salesforce size, and designing sales territories. *9*

Salesperson development programs. Designed to develop added skills, professionalism, goals, and habits for the salesperson beyond those needed for the present job. *11*

Salesperson self-evaluation. A form of performance appraisal wherein the employee rates his or her own performance. *14*

Satellite center. A smaller, regionalized version of a *training center*. *11*

Seekers. A category of managers who want to do the right thing, but who do not have the tools to make the appropriate decisions or to recognize that a given situation has ethical overtones. *3*

Selling agent. An independent rep given contractual authority to sell the entire output of his or her principals. *8*

Selling center. Anyone in an organization who is active in the selling process to a given set of customers or potential customers. *2*

Selling mix. The combination of field selling, telemarketing, national account management, team selling, independent reps, part-time salesforces, and electronic selling to create an overall selling strategy. *1*

Selling-oriented firms. Focus on delivering a certain group of goods and services rather than meeting customers needs. *16*

Services. Activities or benefits provided to consumers. Four unique characteristics distinguish services from goods: intangibility, inseparability, heterogeneity, and perishability. *1*

Set-asides. Governmental and public works contracts that are reserved for small firms or firms owned by women or minorities. *7*

Sexual harassment. Exists when unwelcome sexual advances, requests for sexual favors, and physical contact of a sexual nature occur in the workplace and if (1) submission to such treatment is made a condition of employment, (2) employment decisions are based on the individual's submission or rejection of such treatment, or (3) such conduct has the purpose of unreasonably interfering with an individual's work performance or creates a hostile work environment. *3*

Sherman Act (1890). The first major piece of federal antitrust legislation. Regulates several business practices that reduce competition, including agreements by competitors to allocate markets, price fixing, boycotting certain resellers, and tying contracts. See also *per se violations*. *3*

Silent call monitoring scores. An instrument used to measure telemarketers' behavior-based performance; supervisors' ratings of an employee's performance during actual calls with customers can cover several issues, including the greeting, ascertaining customer needs, information provided, courtesy, and listening skills. *14*

Simple regression models. A type of quantitative forecasting technique in which only one independent variable has a relationship with sales. *15*

Single-factor models. The most basic way of classifying customers involves using a single factor (e.g., sales potential, customer service required, or type of business): a customer classification on the

factor will determine how many sales calls will be made. *9*

Situation audit. The determination of the firm's or business unit's current competitive position; consists of four components: (1) product-market analysis, (2) product positioning, (3) product opportunity analysis, and (4) corporate and industry analysis. *16*

Skill variety. The degree to which a job requires a variety of different activities to successfully fulfill the job work load. *12*

Snowballing. Much like a chain letter, a snowball begins by asking a customer for two or more names of people who might be interested in a product. Those names are contacted and after a sales presentation is made, the new prospect is asked for two or more names until a prospect list develops. *5*

Socialization. The process by which an individual comes to appreciate the values, abilities, expected behaviors, and social knowledge essential for assuming an organizational role, and for participating as an organizational member. *11*

Standard Industrial Classification (SIC) Codes. Data derived from Census of Business figures that classifies all organizations into similar categories and subcategories. *1*

Statutory law. Law created by federal, state, and local governments. *2*

Stock option. A type of fringe benefit in which the employee is offered an opportunity to purchase stock in the organization at a discounted price. *13*

Stockpiling. The practicing of hiring recruits before a territory opens, with the assumption that a territory will become available in the near future. *10*

Straight commission compensation plan. An at-risk compensation plan in which the salesperson's income is tied directly to the amount of product sold; tends to be based on percentage of sales. *13*

Straight salary compensation plan. Compensation that comes solely from one's paycheck. *13*

Strategic position analysis. A systematic procedure that describes the way a sales job is performed and the skills and abilities sales personnel need to perform a sales job; contains five steps: (1) determining performance measures, (2) identifying critical successes and performance dimensions of the position, (3) determining performance dimensions, (4) operationalizing and establishing human performance standards, and (5) designing assessment tools. *10*

Strategic retreat strategy. A strategy a seller can use with a distributor when the distributor has low growth rates in product lines that are composed of the seller's products; in this case, the seller must either find a means to help the distributor become more competitive or begin to look for a new distributor that can take over the market. *17*

Stress interview. An interview in which the interviewer might be critical of some aspect of the interviewee to determine how he or she handles criticism and difficult situations. *10*

Stress management. A type of training that hopes to teach the salesperson to better cope with some existing stresses and to avoid others. *11*

Structured interview. A formal interview in which a format is followed or all interviewees are asked the same set of questions. *10*

Supervision. The day-to-day control of the salesforce under routine operating conditions; a single function of the manager's job. *6*

Supporting role. The role assigned to telemarketing when a field salesforce is required to deliver a high level of face-to-face customer contact. *8*

Survey of buying intentions. A qualitative forecasting technique whereby sellers ask their customers what level of purchases they expect to make over a certain time period. *15*

Suspect. A person or organization that may become a customer prospect based on the personal reflections or perceptions (feelings, prejudices, or hopes) of the salesperson. *5*

Systems. Operations within the firm that enhance or hamper marketing implementation. *16*

Task assessment. Portion of the training audit that examines the overall sales job, as well as the individual activities performed on the job. *11*

Task identity. Completion of the whole job; seeing a task or assignment begin and end. *12*

Task significance. The degree to which the job has a significant impact on the lives of others. *12*

Team-based forecasting. A qualitative forecasting technique that involves averaging all team members' individual forecasts into one. *15*

Telemarketing. A systematic and continuous program of communicating with customers and prospects via telephone and/or other person-to-person electronic media. *2*

Teleprospecting. Qualifying new organizational customers through telephone surveys. *5*

Teletraining. Training in one or more locations through the use of videoconferencing equipment and techniques. *11*

Territory. A group of customers and prospects that is the responsibility of a single salesperson. *9*

Third-country nationals (TCNs). Employees who are transferred from one host country to another, but who are citizens of neither the host country nor the home country of the firm. *4*

Time series models. A family of quantitative forecasting techniques that make forecasts based on past patterns of data. *15*

Top-down budgeting. A basic approach to setting sales budgets whereby top management determines budget levels and sales management is charged with developing a budget that will meet sales objectives while staying within the overall budget parameters. *17*

Tortious interference with business relationships. An act committed by a salesperson which interferes with a competitor's right to do business; prohibited under the Uniform Commercial Code. *3*

Total variance. The sum of the market volume, company share, and contribution variances. *17*

Training audit. An analysis of the organization's resources, abilities, needs, and current directions; focuses on three dimensions: (1) the organization, (2) the tasks, and (3) the personnel. *11*

Training center. A centralized training location such as a national training center where all of an organization's new hire and refresher training occurs. *11*

Transaction terms. The specifics of the sale and delivery; include price, quantity, quality standards, discounts, rebates, and payment terms. *7*

Treaty of Rome (1957). A treaty governing commercial transactions in Western Europe. It, along with its amendments, includes many of the same regulations found in the United States. *3*

Trend projection. A set of simple time series (quantitative) forecasting techniques which assume that past sales levels and rates of change in sales levels will remain the same in future periods. *15*

Trial close. An early closure attempt in a sales call that helps salespeople determine the status of the presentation and what information or objection they need to concentrate on. *5*

Turnover. As it relates to the salesforce, the average percentage of the salesforce that leaves the sales organization in a given time period. *10*

Two-way global marketing. Relationships and markets that are built globally as well as domestically. *1*

Tying agreements. A *per se* violation of the Sherman Act; occurs when the seller requires the buyer to purchase not only the item the buyer wishes to purchase, but also another product as a condition of sale of the initial product. *3*

Uniform Commercial Code (UCC). Consists of a body of statutes, or regulations, defined by legislators. Adopted by 49 states (Louisiana is the exception) in the 1960s as a means of establishing uniform rules across the United States for commercial transactions. *3*

Unsolicited orders. Orders which come from buyers in countries where no organized effort to generate sales has taken place. *4*

Unstructured interview. An informal interview in which the interviewer has no set format or questions that he or she will ask. *10*

User. A member of the buying center who actually uses the product or service purchased. *7*

Valence for rewards. The desirability of receiving the reward based on performance. *12*

Value-added reseller (VAR). Retailers or other channel personnel who can provide more service for the ultimate customer than the manufacturer is able to deliver. *2*

Value analysis. A refinement of the importance weighting (decision-making) technique wherein the modeler links the specific attributes in the model to the values of various levels of decision makers in the firm. *16*

Variance decomposition analysis. Used to answer the question, "If the results are not what were expected, how can the firm identify the source of discrepancy from the plan?"; breaks down the discrepancy into its constituent parts. *17*

Vertical dyad linkage (VDL) model. Argues that the sales manager spans or links two levels and that the organization is only as strong as its weakest link; an extension of the boundary spanner concept. *6*

Vertical price fixing. A *per se* violation of the Sherman Act; occurs when a manufacturer refuses to sell to a distributor or a retailer unless the buyer agrees to charge a minimum price for the commodity. *3*

Video conferencing. Allows people in separate geographic locations to see each other and work together over phone lines. *2*

Video-enhanced training (VET). Training programs on videocassettes that are mailed to salesforces for study. *11*

Virtual office. An office that consists of the salesperson's portable computer and other technological tools, whether they reside in a home office or are portable. Dependent on the establishment of "anytime, anywhere" communication links between the salesperson and a district office and sales reps having access to high-quality information. *2*

Vocational Rehabilitation Act (1973). Extends Title VII of the Civil Rights Act (1964) protection to the disabled who are employed by federal, state, and local governments, their agencies, and certain federal contractors. *3*

Voice mail. A telephone answering device that allows a caller to leave a detailed message for a salesperson, who can then retrieve the message from the voice mail system while away from the office. *2*

Warranties. Promises by sellers that the product is fit for use in a certain way. *3*

Whistleblowers. Employees who detect company wrongdoing and make their charges public or go over the heads of their immediate supervisors. *3*

Work load method. A means of determining salesforce size; sets salesforce size on the basis of the required level of selling effort needed to reach a sales goal. *9*

Working smarter. Altering and improving the direction of one's effort. *12*

Wrongful dismissal. Occurs when an employer shows bad faith or is malicious in dismissing an employee. *3*

Yankee peddler. A name for the respectable traveling merchant who sold his goods from his wagons in the late 1700s to mid-1800s in the United States. *2*

Zero-base budgeting. A budgeting process wherein each period starts with a budget of zero and sales managers are required to justify all amounts in terms of specific objectives or programs that are to be offered in the coming budget period. *17*

CREDITS

Exhibit 1.7: From Michael J. Swensen, et al., "The Appeal of Personal Selling as a Career: A Decade Later" from *Journal of Personal Selling and Sales Management*, Vol. 13, No. 1, Winter 1993, p. 53. Reprinted by permission of the publisher; **Exhibit 1.9:** "How Salespeople Spend Their Time" adapted from *Sales & Marketing Management*, January 1990. Reprinted by permission of Bill Communications, Inc., NY; **Exhibit 1.10:** Adapted from William Moncrief, "Ten Key Activities of Industrial Salespeople" in *Industrial Marketing Management*, Vol. 15, pp.309–317. Copyright © 1986 by Elsevier Science Inc. Reprinted with permission of the publisher. **Box 1.1:** From "Should Salespeople be Certified?" excerpted from *Sales & Marketing Management*, September 1992, p. 37. Reprinted by permission of Bill Communications, Inc., NY; **Box 1.2:** From "Sales Trends for 2000" from *Sales & Marketing Management*, December 1994, p. 9. Reprinted by permission of Bill Communications, Inc., NY; **Exhibit 2.1:** Adapted from Ronald Fullerton, "How Modern is Modern Marketing? Marketing's Evolution and the Myth of the 'Production Era'" from *Journal of Marketing*, Vol. 52, January 1988, pp. 108–125. Reprinted by permission of American Marketing Association; **Exhibit 2.3:** From Castleberry and Sheperd, "Effective Interpersonal Listening and Personal Selling" from *Journal of Personal Selling and Sales Management*, Vol. 13, No. 1, Winter 1993, pp. 35–49. Reprinted by permission of the publisher; **Exhibit 2.4:** From "Women in Sales: Percentage by Industry" from *Sales & Marketing Management*, 1990. Reprinted by permission of Bill Communications, Inc., NY; **Exhibit 2.7:** From Ross Weiland, "The Message is the Medium" from *Performance*, Sept. 1995, p. 37. Reprinted by permission of Performance, September 1995; **Exhibit 2.8:** "Calling the Hotlines: What We Found." Reprinted by permission of *The Wall Street Journal*, © 1994 Dow Jones & Company, Inc. All Rights Reserved Worldwide; **Box 2.1:** From Tony Seideman, "Way Cool!" from *Sales & Marketing Management*, January 1990. Reprinted by permission of Bill Communications, Inc., NY; **Box 2.2:** From Melissa Campanelli, "No More Dark Age Hotels" from *Sales & Marketing Management*, Part 2, June 1995. Reprinted by permission of Bill Communications, Inc., NY; **Box 2.3:** From Ginger Trumfio, "Getting Value from Voice Mail" from *Sales & Marketing Management*, May 1994. Reprinted by permission of Bill Communications, Inc., NY; **Exhibit 3.1:** From Reidenbach & Robin, "A Conceptual Model of Corporate Moral Development" from *Journal of Business Ethics*, Vol. 10, 1991, pp. 273–284. Reprinted by permission of Kluwer Academic Publishers; **Exhibit 3.1:** From D. Harrington, "What Corporate America is Teaching About Ethics" from *Academy of Management Executive*, Vol. 5, No. 1, 1991, pp. 21–30. Reprinted by permission of Academy of Management, NY; **Exhibit 3.2:** Adapted from Robin T. Peterson, "Sales Representatives' Perceptions of the Legality of Various Activities" from *Journal of Personal Selling and Sales Management*, Vol. 14, Spring 1994, p. 69. Reprinted by permission of the publisher; **Exhibit 3.5:** From Karl Boedecker, et al., "An Overview of Salesperson Statements That Can Create Legal Obligations for the Firm" from *Journal of Marketing*, January 1991, p. 72. Reprinted by permission of American Marketing Association; **Exhibit 3.6:** From Karl Boedecker, et al., "Legal Dimensions of Salespersons' Statements: A Review and Managerial Suggestions" from *Journal of Marketing*, Vol. 55, January 1991, p. 76. Reprinted by permission of American Marketing Association; **Exhibit 3.7:** From Robert J. McHatton, "Legal and Ethical Rules in Telemarketing" from *Total Telemarketing*, Copyright © 1988, p. 215. Reprinted with permission of John Wiley & Sons, Inc; **Exhibit 3.8:** Excerpt from Swift & Denton, "Teaching About Sexual Harassment Issues: A Sales Management Approach" from *Marketing Education Review*, Fall 1994, p. 37. Reprinted by permission of C & C Press,

1996; **Exhibit 3.12:** From Hyman, Skipper & Tansey, "General Ethical Checklist" in "Ethical Codes Are Not Enough" from *Business Horizons*, Vol. 33, March/April 1990, p. 17. Copyright © 1990 by the Foundation for the School of Business at Indiana University. Reprinted by permission; **Box 3.1:** Excerpt from Ruth Marcus, "Minnesota Defense Contractor Fined for Bribing Two Niger Officials" from *The Washington Post*, May 3, 1989, F1. Copyright © 1989 The Washington Post. Reprinted with permission; **Exhibit 4.1:** Excerpt from Secil Tuncalp, "US Needs More Marketing in Saudi Arabian Market" from *Marketing News*, June 19, 1987, p. 10. Reprinted by permission from Marketing News, published by the American Marketing Association; **Exhibit 4.5:** From Sue Shellenbarger, "Spouses Must Pass Test Before Global Transfers." Reprinted by permission of *The Wall Street Journal*, © 1991 Dow Jones & Company, Inc. All Rights Reserved Worldwide; **Exhibit 4.5:** Adapted from Rob Norton, "Strategies for the New Export Boom" from *Fortune*, August 22, 1994, p. 132. Table compiled by Therese Eiben. © 1994 Time Inc. Reprinted by permission. All rights reserved; **Exhibit 4.5:** Adapted from "Europe Sans Horaires." © 1988 The Economist Newspaper Group, Inc. Reprinted with permission. Further reproduction prohibited; **Exhibit 4.8:** Adaption from Luqmani, Quraeshi & Delene, "Marketing in Islamic Countries: A Viewpoint" in *MSU Business Topics*, Summer 1980, pp. 20–21. Reprinted with permission of the Broad College of Business, Michigan State University. **Exhibit 4.9:** From Thomas F. O'Boyle, "Little Benefit to Careers Seen in Foreign Stints." Reprinted by permission of *The Wall Street Journal*, © 1989 Dow Jones & Company, Inc. All Rights Reserved Worldwide; **Exhibit 4.10:** From Black & Gregson, "Serving Two Masters: Managing the Dual Allegiance of Expatriate Employees" in *Sloan Management Review*, Summer 1992, pp. 62, 69, 70. Reprinted by permission of Sloan Management Review Association (MIT Sloan School of Management). All rights reserved; **Box 4.1:** From Cindy Kano, "Matsushita Shows How to Go Global" from *Fortune*, July 11, 1994, pp. 159–166. © 1994 Time Inc. All rights reserved; **Exhibit 5.3:** Adapted from Jolson & Wotruba, "Selling and Sales Management in Action: Prospecting: A New Look at this Old Challenge" from *Journal of Personal Selling and Sales Management*, Vol. 12, No. 4, pp. 59–66. Reprinted by permission of the publisher; **Exhibit 5.3:** Adapted from Weld Royal, "It's No Wonder We Need the Baldrige" from *Sales & Marketing Management*, August 1994. Reprinted by permission of Bill Communications, Inc., NY; **Exhibit 5.5:** Adapted from William Moncrief & Shannon Shipp, "Presentation Approaches" from *Marketing Education Review*, Vol. 4, No. 1, Spring 1996, pp. 45–50. Reprinted by permission of C & C Press, 1996; **Exhibit 5.7:** Adapted from Robin T. Peterson, "How Do You Answer Objections?" from *The American Salesman*, February 1993, pp. 9–11. Reprinted by permission of © National Research Bureau, PO Box 1, Burlington, Iowa 52601–0001; **Box 5.1:** From Ginger Trumfio, "Panning for Gold" from *Sales & Marketing Management*, December 1993. Reprinted by permission of Bill Communications, Inc., NY; **Box 5.2:** From Ginger Trumfio, "I Knew That" from *Sales & Marketing Management*, February 1994. Reprinted by permission of Bill Communications, Inc., NY; **Exhibit 6.1:** Adapted from Pradeep K. Tyagi, "Relative Importance of Key Job Dimensions and Leadership Behaviors in Motivating Salesperson Work Performance" from *Journal of Marketing*, Vol. 49, Spring 1985, pp. 76–86. Reprinted by permission of American Marketing Association; **Exhibit 6.2:** Adapted from Stephen Castleberry and John Tanner, Jr., "The Manager Salesperson Relationship: An Exploratory Examination of the Vertical Dyad Linkage Model" from *Journal of Personal Selling and Sales Management*, Vol. 6, No. 3, November 1986, pp. 29–38. Reprinted by permission of the publisher; **Exhibit 6.3** From "Daily Activities of the Sales Manager Compared to the Sales Person" appearing as "How Salespeople Spend Their

ORGANIZATION INDEX

NAME INDEX

SUBJECT INDEX